A COMPANION
TO ANCIENT HISTO.

BLACKWELL COMPANIONS TO THE ANCIENT WORLD

This series provides sophisticated and authoritative overviews of periods of ancient history, genres of classical literature, and the most important themes in ancient culture. Each volume comprises approximately twenty-five and forty concise essays written by individual scholars within their area of specialization. The essays are written in a clear, provocative, and lively manner, designed for an international audience of scholars, students, and general readers.

ANCIENT HISTORY

Published

A Companion to the Roman Army
Edited by Paul Erdkamp

A Companion to the Roman Republic
Edited by Nathan Rosenstein and Robert Morstein-Marx

A Companion to the Roman Empire
Edited by David S. Potter

A Companion to the Classical Greek World
Edited by Konrad H. Kinzl

A Companion to the Ancient Near East
Edited by Daniel C. Snell

A Companion to the Hellenistic World
Edited by Andrew Erskine

A Companion to Late Antiquity
Edited by Philip Rousseau

A Companion to Ancient History
Edited by Andrew Erskine

A Companion to Archaic Greece
Edited by Kurt A. Raaflaub and Hans van Wees

A Companion to Julius Caesar
Edited by Miriam Griffin

A Companion to Byzantium
Edited by Liz James

A Companion to Ancient Egypt
Edited by Alan B. Lloyd

A Companion to Ancient Macedonia
Edited by Joseph Roisman and Ian Worthington

A Companion to the Punic Wars
Edited by Dexter Hoyos

A Companion to Augustine
Edited by Mark Vessey

A Companion to Marcus Aurelius
Edited by Marcel van Ackeren

A Companion to Ancient Greek Government
Edited by Hans Beck

LITERATURE AND CULTURE

Published

A Companion to Classical Receptions
Edited by Lorna Hardwick and Christopher Stray

A Companion to Greek and Roman Historiography
Edited by John Marincola

A Companion to Catullus
Edited by Marilyn B. Skinner

A Companion to Roman Religion
Edited by Jörg Rüpke

A Companion to Greek Religion
Edited by Daniel Ogden

A Companion to the Classical Tradition
Edited by Craig W. Kallendorf

A Companion to Roman Rhetoric
Edited by William Dominik and Jon Hall

A Companion to Greek Rhetoric
Edited by Ian Worthington

A Companion to Ancient Epic
Edited by John Miles Foley

A Companion to Greek Tragedy
Edited by Justina Gregory

A Companion to Latin Literature
Edited by Stephen Harrison

A Companion to Greek and Roman Political Thought
Edited by Ryan K. Balot

A Companion to Ovid
Edited by Peter E. Knox

A Companion to the Ancient Greek Language
Edited by Egbert Bakker

A Companion to Hellenistic Literature
Edited by Martine Cuypers and James J. Clauss

A Companion to Vergil's *Aeneid* and its Tradition
Edited by Joseph Farrell and Michael C. J. Putnam

A Companion to Horace
Edited by Gregson Davis

A Companion to Families in the Greek and Roman Worlds
Edited by Beryl Rawson

A Companion to Greek Mythology
Edited by Ken Dowden and Niall Livingstone

A Companion to the Latin Language
Edited by James Clackson

A Companion to Tacitus
Edited by Victoria Emma Pagán

A Companion to Women in the Ancient World
Edited by Sharon L. James and Sheila Dillon

A Companion to Sophocles
Edited by Kirk Ormand

A Companion to the Archaeology of the Ancient Near East
Edited by Daniel Potts

A Companion to Roman Love Elegy
Edited by Barbara K. Gold

A Companion to Greek Art
Edited by Tyler Jo Smith and Dimitris Plantzos

A Companion to Persius and Juvenal
Edited by Susanna Braund and Josiah Osgood

A COMPANION TO ANCIENT HISTORY

Edited by

Andrew Erskine

WILEY-BLACKWELL

A John Wiley & Sons, Ltd., Publication

This paperback edition first published 2013
© 2013 Blackwell Publishing Ltd

Edition history: (hardback, 2009)

Blackwell Publishing was acquired by John Wiley & Sons in February 2007. Blackwell's publishing program has been merged with Wiley's global Scientific, Technical, and Medical business to form Wiley-Blackwell.

Registered Office
John Wiley & Sons Ltd, The Atrium, Southern Gate, Chichester, West Sussex, PO19 8SQ, UK

Editorial Offices
350 Main Street, Malden, MA 02148-5020, USA
9600 Garsington Road, Oxford, OX4 2DQ, UK
The Atrium, Southern Gate, Chichester, West Sussex, PO19 8SQ, UK

For details of our global editorial offices, for customer services, and for information about how to apply for permission to reuse the copyright material in this book please see our website at www.wiley.com/wiley-blackwell.

The right of Andrew Erskine to be identified as the author of the editorial material in this work has been asserted in accordance with the UK Copyright, Designs and Patents Act 1988.

Library of Congress Cataloging-in-Publication Data

A companion to ancient history / edited by Andrew Erskine.
    p. cm. – (Blackwell companions to the ancient world)
  Includes bibliographical references and index.
  ISBN 978-1-4051-3150-6 (hardcover : alk. paper) 978-1-1184-5136-6 (pbk. : alk. paper)
  1. History, Ancient. I. Erskine, Andrew.
  D57.C66 2009
  930–dc22

                                                                                      2008046753

A catalogue record for this book is available from the British Library.

Cover image: A Capriccio View of Rome by Giovanni Paolo Panini (1692–1765). © Christie's Images/Corbis

Cover design by Workhaus

Set in 10/12.5 pt Galliard by Toppan Best-set Premedia Limited

1   2013

In Memory of
Peter Derow
and
George Forrest

Contents

Figures

Maps

Notes on Contributors

Peter Fibiger Bang is an Associate Professor at the University of Copenhagen. His interests range from the comparative history of the Roman empire to ancient economic history and the reception of classical antiquity in European culture. Publications include *The Roman Bazaar* (2008).

Hans Beck is John MacNaughton Professor of Classics at McGill University in Montreal. He has published widely on both the Roman republic and the history of Greek federalism. Books include *Polis und Koinon* (1997) and, on the republican nobility, *Karriere und Hierarchie* (2005). He is also co-editor of *Brill's New Jacoby*.

Gideon Bohak is an Associate Professor at Tel Aviv University, working on Jewish literature and culture in the Greco-Roman world, on ethnic stereotypes in ancient literature, and on Jewish magic. His most recent book is *Ancient Jewish Magic: A History* (2008).

Alan K. Bowman is Camden Professor of Ancient History and Fellow of Brasenose College Oxford. His main research interests are the social and economic history of the Roman empire, Papyrology, and Greco-Roman Egypt. Publications include *Egypt after the Pharoahs* (1990²), *Life and Letters on the Roman Frontier* (2003²).

Maria Brosius is Reader in Ancient History at the University of Newcastle. She is the author of *The Persians: an introduction* (2006) and editor of *Ancient Archives and Archival Traditions* (2003).

Christer Bruun is Professor in the Department of Classics, University of Toronto. Among his research interests are Roman topography, and the government and social history of Rome and Ostia. His publications include *The Water Supply of Ancient Rome* (1991) and as editor *The Roman Middle Republic* (2000).

John Curran is Senior Lecturer in Ancient History at The Queen's University of Belfast. He is the author of *Pagan City and Christian Capital: Rome in the Fourth*

Century (2000), as well as of articles on the Christianization of Rome, the relationship between the Jews and Rome, and the testimony of Flavius Josephus.

James Davidson is Reader in Ancient History at the University of Warwick. He works on ancient Greek cultural and social history. He is the author of *Courtesans and Fishcakes* (1997), and *The Greeks and Greek Love* (2007), and contributes to the *London Review of Books* and the *Times Literary Supplement*.

John Davies FBA was Rathbone Professor of Ancient History and Classical Archaeology at Liverpool University. His books include *Athenian Propertied Families 600–300 BC* (1971), *Wealth and the power of wealth in classical Athens* (1981), *Democracy and classical Greece* (1993²). His recent work has concentrated on the Hellenistic period and economic history.

Peter Derow was Hody Fellow and Tutor in Ancient History, Wadham College. His research focused on Hellenistic history and epigraphy and Roman republican history – with a particular interest in Polybius. In addition to many articles he was (with R. S. Bagnall) the author of *The Hellenistic Period: Historical Sources in Translation* (2004).

Carol Dougherty is Professor of Classical Studies at Wellesley College. Her research interests focus on Greek literary and cultural history. She is the author most recently of *The Raft of Odysseus* and a volume on Prometheus. She is currently working on representations of the city in classical Athens.

Stephen Dyson is Park Professor of Classics at the State University of New York, Buffalo. His books include *Community and Society in Roman Italy* (1992), *The Roman Countryside* (2003), and *In Pursuit of Ancient Pasts* (2006).

Andrew Erskine is Professor of Ancient History at the University of Edinburgh. A specialist in Hellenistic history, he is the author of *Troy between Greece and Rome: Local Tradition and Imperial Power* (2001) and *The Hellenistic Stoa: Political Thought and Action* (1990).

Andy Fear is Lecturer in Classics at the University of Manchester. His research interests are in Roman and Visigothic Spain, early Christianity and theories of Universal History. He is the author of *Rome and Baetica: Urbanization in Southern Spain c.50 BC–AD 150* (1996).

Andrea Giardina is a Professor at the Istituto Italiano di Scienza Umane. His principal research interests are the social, administrative and political history of the Roman world and the fortunes of antiquity in the contemporary world. Recent publications include *Cassiodoro politico* (2006) and (with A. Vauchez) *Rome, l'idée et le mythe. Du Moyen Âge à nos jours* (2000).

Mary Harlow is Senior Lecturer in Roman History at the University of Birmingham. Her research interests include Roman life course, family history in classical and late antique periods, and dress and identity.

Thomas Harrison is Rathbone Professor of Ancient History and Classical Archaeology at the University of Liverpool. His publications include *Divinity and History:*

The Religion of Herodotus (2000); *The Emptiness of Asia: Aeschylus' Persians and the History of the Fifth Century* (2000).

Edward Herring is Head of the School of Languages, Literatures and Cultures at the National University of Ireland, Galway. His principal research interest concerns the relations between the Greek, Roman, and native populations of South Italy. Publications include *Explaining Change in the Matt-Painted Pottery of Southern Italy* (1998).

R. Bruce Hitchner is Professor and Chair of the Department of Classics, Tufts University, and Chair of the Dayton Peace Accords Project. He was formerly editor-in-chief of the *American Journal of Archaeology*.

Mark Humphries is Professor of Ancient History at Swansea University. He has published various books and articles on ancient religions and late antiquity, most recently *Early Christianity* (2006). He is one of the general editors of the series *Translated Texts for Historians* (Liverpool University Press).

Helen King is Professor of the History of Classical Medicine at the University of Reading. Her publications on the history of medicine, especially gynaecology, cover both the ancient world and its reception, most recently *Midwifery, Obstetrics and the Rise of Gynaecology: Users of a sixteenth-century compendium* (2007).

Jason König is Senior Lecturer in Greek and Classical Studies at the University of St. Andrews. His research interests focus broadly on the Greek literature and culture of the Roman empire. His publications include *Athletics and Literature in the Roman Empire* (2005).

Andrew Lintott is now retired, after teaching first Classics, then Ancient History, successively at King's College, London, Aberdeen University, and Worcester College, Oxford. His many publications include *Violence in Republican Rome, Judicial Reform and Land Reform in the Roman Republic,* and most recently *Cicero as Evidence: a Historian's Companion.*

Lloyd Llewellyn-Jones lectures in Ancient History in the School of History, Classics and Archaeology at the University of Edinburgh. He is the author of *Aphrodite's Tortoise: the veiled woman of ancient Greece*. His interests include ancient dress and gender, Achaemenid Persia, Ptolemaic Egypt, ancient court societies, and the reception of antiquity in popular culture.

Kathryn Lomas is Senior Research Fellow at the Institute of Archaeology, University College London. She is the author of *Rome and the Western Greeks* and *Roman Italy, 338 BC–AD 200*, and has published numerous articles on Roman Italy, urbanism and colonization in the Greek and Roman world, and on ethnic and cultural identity.

John Marincola is Leon Golden Professor of Classics at Florida State University. He is the author of *Authority and Tradition in Ancient Historiography* (1997), *Greek Historians* (2001), and (with M. A. Flower) *Herodotus: Histories IX* (2002). He is currently at work on a book on Hellenistic historiography.

Rosamond McKitterick is Professor of Medieval History and Fellow of Sidney Sussex College, Cambridge. Her principal research interests are in the politics, religion and culture of Europe in the eighth and ninth centuries. Recent publications include *Charlemagne: the formation of a European identity* (2008) and *Perceptions of the past in the early middle ages* (2006).

Neil McLynn is Fellow in Later Roman History, Corpus Christi College, Oxford. He previously taught in the Faculty of Law, Keio University, Japan. His research interests revolve mostly around the intricacies of religious politics in late antiquity. His publications include *Ambrose of Milan: Church and Court in an Imperial Capital* (1994).

Andrew Meadows is Deputy Director of the American Numismatic Society in New York. He has edited the Royal Numismatic Society's *Coin Hoards,* and three volumes in the *Sylloge Nummorum Graecorum* series, and is currently completing a study of the monetary history of Karia in the Hellenistic period.

Elizabeth A. Meyer is Associate Professor of History at the University of Virginia. Her interests include the social and cultural history of ancient Greece and Rome, epigraphy, Roman Law, and ancient legal culture. She is the author of *Legitimacy and Law:* Tabulae *in Roman Belief and Practice* (2004) and the forthcoming *Metics and the Athenian* Phialai-*Inscriptions.*

Paul Millett is Senior Lecturer in the Classical Faculty, Cambridge University, and Fellow in Classics at Downing College. His recent publications include articles on the trial of Socrates and Aristotle on slavery, and a book, *Theophrastus and His World.*

Neville Morley is Professor of Ancient Economic History and Historical Theory at the University of Bristol. His books include *Theories, Models and Concepts in Ancient History* (2004), *Trade in Classical Antiquity* (2007) and *Antiquity and Modernity* (2008).

Robert Morstein-Marx is Professor of Classics at the University of California, Santa Barbara. His research currently focuses on the ideological and communicative dimensions of late republican politics. Publications include *Mass Oratory and Political Power in the Late Roman Republic* (2004), and (as co-editor) *A Companion to the Roman Republic* (2007).

Lisa Nevett is Associate Professor of Greek Archaeology at the University of Michigan. Her research focuses on using the material remains of Greek and Roman domestic life as a source for social history. Her publications include *House and Society in the Ancient Greek World* (1999).

J. A. North taught Ancient History at UCL, 1963 to 2003. He was Head of the History Department in the 1990s, and is now Emeritus Professor. His research has mostly concerned the religious history of the Romans and of their empire, including *Religions of Rome,* with Mary Beard and Simon Price.

David Noy is the author of *Foreigners at Rome* (2000), several volumes of Jewish inscriptions, and a number of papers on Roman death and burial practices. He is currently working on a study of Roman deathbeds. He teaches Classics for Lampeter and the Open University.

Josiah Ober holds the Constantine Mitsotakis Chair in the School of Humanities and Sciences, Stanford University. His books include *Fortress Attica* (1985), *Mass and Elite in Democratic Athens* (1989), *The Athenian Revolution* (1996), *Political Dissent in Democratic Athens* (1998), *Athenian Legacies* (2005) and *Democracy and Knowledge* (2008).

Tim Parkin is Professor of Ancient History, University of Manchester. His research focuses on the ancient family and the life course. Publications include *Demography and Roman Society* (1992) and *Old Age in the Roman World* (2003).

David Potter is Arthur F. Thurnau Professor of Greek and Latin at the University of Michigan. His recent books include *The Roman Empire at Bay* (2004), *Emperors of Rome* (2007) and *Ancient Rome: a new history* (2009).

Josephine Crawley Quinn is Fellow and Tutor in Ancient History at Worcester College, Oxford. Her current research is on imperialism, trade and culture in Hellenistic North Africa.

John Ray is Herbert Thompson Professor of Egyptology in the University of Cambridge. His research centers on the demotic texts from Hellenistic Egypt, and on the history of the Egyptian language.

Louis Rawlings is a Lecturer in Ancient History at Cardiff University. His research interests include Italian, Greek, Punic, and Gallic warfare. He is the author of *The Ancient Greeks at War* (2007), and is co-editor (with H. Bowden) of *Herakles and Hercules: Exploring a Graeco-Roman Divinity* (2005).

Amy Richlin is Professor of Classics at the University of California, Los Angeles. She works on the history of sexuality, Roman humor, women's history, and feminist theory. Her most recent books are *Rome and the Mysterious Orient* (2005) and *Marcus Aurelius in Love* (2007).

Tracey Rihll is a Senior Lecturer in Ancient History at Swansea University. She has been studying ancient science and technology for about twenty years. Her publications include *Greek Science* (1999) and *The Catapult: a history* (2007).

Gregory Rowe is Associate Professor in the Department of Greek and Roman Studies at the University of Victoria, Canada. He is the author of *Princes and Political Cultures: The New Tiberian Senatorial Decrees* (2002).

Robert Sallares (University of Manchester) is the author of *The Ecology of the Ancient Greek World* (1991), *Malaria and Rome: a History of Malaria in Ancient Italy* (2002) and numerous articles in the fields of ancient history, medical history and biomolecular archaeology.

Walter Scheidel is Dickason Professor in the Humanities and Professor of Classics at Stanford University. His research focuses on ancient social and economic history, premodern historical demography, and comparative and transdisciplinary world history. His publications include *Measuring Sex, Age and Death in the Roman empire* (1996) and *Death on the Nile: Disease and the Demography of Roman Egypt* (2001).

Catherine Steel is Professor of Classics at the University of Glasgow. Her research interests include late republican history and Cicero's writings, particularly his speeches. Recent publications include *Reading Cicero: genre and performance in late Republican Rome* (2005) and *Roman Oratory* (2006).

Peter Thonemann is Forrest-Derow Fellow and Tutor in Ancient History at Wadham College, Oxford. He is currently writing a book on the historical geography of the Maeander valley.

Kathryn Welch is a Senior Lecturer in Classics and Ancient History at the University of Sydney. She researches in Roman History with a special interest in the transition from republic to empire. She is currently completing a monograph entitled *Magnus Pius: Sextus Pompeius and the Transformation of the Roman Republic.*

Tim Whitmarsh is E. P. Warren Praelector in Classics, Corpus Christi College, Oxford. He works primarily on Greek literature of the Roman period, particularly in relation to literary and cultural theory. His books include *Greek literature and the Roman empire* (2001), *Ancient Greek literature* (2004).

John Wilkins is Professor of Greek Culture at the University of Exeter. Books on food include *Food in Antiquity* (ed. with D. Harvey and M. Dobson, 1995) and *Food in the Ancient World* (with Shaun Hill, 2006). He is currently editing Galen's nutritional treatise, *On the Powers of Foods.*

Robert Witcher is Lecturer in Classical Archaeology at Durham University, UK. His research uses archaeological field survey to explore the socio-economic organization of ancient Italy. Ongoing collaborative research includes the British School at Rome's Tiber valley project and a study of Hadrian's Wall and its landscape.

Constanze Witt is a Lecturer in archaeology in the Department of Classics at the University of Texas at Austin. Her current research interests lie in the art and archaeology of Iron Age Europe, in Hellenistic urbanization and in anthropological theory.

Preface

When Al Bertrand asked me to edit this *Companion to Ancient History*, I hesitated. It seemed rather a large task. Now that I have finished it, I realize that I was naive – it was a far larger task than I had initially imagined. One of the things that has made it manageable has been the enthusiasm and goodwill of the contributors, and to them all I am especially grateful.

Sadly, one of the contributors to this volume, Peter Derow, died not long after completing his piece on what Ancient History meant to him. Peter was not only my doctoral supervisor but a good friend. This volume is dedicated to his memory and that of his own tutor, George Forrest, both of whom through their teaching of Ancient History inspired many, a number of whom are contributors to this book.

This *Companion* may have been a substantial undertaking, but it has been fun to do, and I have learnt a lot from reading through all the contributions. It aims to provide a series of accessible introductions to key topics in the study of Ancient History: forms of evidence, problems and approaches, and major themes in current research. Rather than offering definitive overviews, however, these are intended to reflect the vitality and excitement of scholarship at the front line. The potential subject matter is vast, so a certain selectivity has been necessary. While the focus is on the history of Greece and Rome, I have also been concerned that these are not viewed in isolation but are seen in the broader context.

Staff at Blackwell have all been enormously helpful, in particular Al Bertrand, whose great contribution to Classics in general is evident from Blackwell's growing list of Classics and Ancient History books. Kyle Hall kindly translated the section by Andrea Giardina which appears in Chapter One. My own chapter is well away from my usual territory, and I must thank Robert Anderson for generously taking a look at it with the eyes of a historian of the nineteenth century. This book has moved round the Celtic fringe, begun at the National University of Ireland Galway and completed at the University of Edinburgh; I am grateful to colleagues at both institutions for their help.

Most of all I am indebted to my wife Michelle, not only for all her support and encouragement, but also for her knack of asking the right question.

Andrew Erskine, Edinburgh

Note on paperback edition: A number of errors are corrected in this paperback edition, many thanks to the careful reading of Yan Shaoxiang of Capital Normal University Beijing. Otherwise the text is little changed apart from supplements to John Davies' chapter on ancient economies and to Christer Bruun's chapter on Rome.

Abbreviations, Reference Works

For fuller information on papyrological publications, see Oates et al. 2001 (http://scriptorium.lib.duke.edu/papyrus/texts/clist.html).

AE	*L'Année épigraphique*
AHR	*American Historical Review*
AJA	*American Journal of Archaeology*
AJAH	*American Journal of Ancient History*
AJHG	*American Journal of Human Genetics*
AJP	*American Journal of Philology*
ANET	Pritchard, J. B. (ed.), *Ancient Near Eastern Texts Relating to the Old Testament*, Princeton 1955[2]
AnPhil	*L'Année philologique*
ANRW	*Aufstieg und Niedergang der römischen Welt*. Berlin. 1972–
AR	*Archaeological Reports*
ASNP	*Annali della Scuola Normale Superiore di Pisa, Classe di Lettere e Filosofia*
Austin	Austin, M. M. *The Hellenistic world from Alexander to the Roman conquest: a selection of ancient sources in translation*. Cambridge. 1st edn 1981; 2nd edn 2006; this volume uses the numbering of the 1st edn
BA	Beazley Archive (http://www.beazley.ox.ac.uk)
BD	Bagnall, R. S. and Derow, P. S. *The Hellenistic Period: Historical Sources in Translation*. 2004. Oxford
BE	*Bulletin épigraphique*, published in *Revue des études grecques*
BGU	*Aegyptische Urkunden aus den Staatlichen Museen zu Berlin, Griechische Urkunden*. Berlin. 1895–
Burstein	Burstein, S. M. *The Hellenistic Age from the battle of Ipsos to the death of Kleopatra VII*. Translated Documents of Greece and Rome 3. Cambridge. 1985

CAH²	*Cambridge Ancient History.* 2nd edn. Cambridge. 1961–
CAH³	*Cambridge Ancient History.* 3rd edn. Cambridge. 1970–
CIJ	Frey, J. B. *Corpus Inscriptionum Iudaicarum.* Rome 1936–52
CIL	*Corpus Inscriptionum Latinarum.* 1863–
CP	*Classical Philology*
CPJ	Tcherikover, V. and Fuks, A. *Corpus Papyrorum Judaicarum.* Cambridge, Mass. 1957–64
CQ	*Classical Quarterly*
FGrH	Jacoby, F. *Die Fragmente der griechischen Historiker.* 1923–
FIRA	Riccobono, S. et al. *Fontes Iuris Romani Anteiustiniani.* 3 vols. Florence. 1943–68
Fornara	Fornara, C. W. *Archaic Times to the End of the Peloponnesian War.* Translated Documents of Greece and Rome 1. 2nd edn. Cambridge. 1983
GRBS	*Greek, Roman and Byzantine Studies*
Harding	Harding, P. *From the end of the Peloponnesian War to the battle of Ipsus.* Translated Documents of Greece and Rome 2. Cambridge. 1985
HSCP	*Harvard Studies in Classical Philology*
IG	*Inscriptiones Graecae.* 1873–
IGRR	Cagnat, R. *Inscriptiones Graecae ad res Romanas pertinentes.* Paris, 1906–27
IK	*Inschriften griechischer Städte aus Kleinasien.* Bonn. 1972–
ILLRP	Degrassi, A. *Inscriptiones Latinae Liberae Rei Republicae.* Florence. 1963 (vol. 2). 1965 (vol. 12)
ILS	Dessau, H. *Inscriptiones Latinae Selectae.* Berlin. 1892–1916
ISE	Moretti, L. *Iscrizioni storiche ellenistiche.* Florence. 1967–76
JEA	*Journal of Egyptian Archaeology*
JHS	*Journal of Hellenic Studies*
JRA	*Journal of Roman Archaeology*
JRS	*Journal of Roman Studies*
LIMC	Ackermann, H. C. and Gisler, J.-R. (eds), *Lexicon iconographicum mythologiae classicae.* Zurich. 1981–99
ML	Meiggs, R. and Lewis, D. *A Selection of Greek Historical Inscriptions to the End of the Fifth Century* BC. Rev. edn. Oxford. 1988
OCD³	Hornblower, S. and Spawforth, A. *The Oxford Classical Dictionary.* 3rd edn. Oxford. 1996
OGIS	Dittenberger, W. *Orientis Graeci Inscriptiones Selectae.* Leipzig, 1903–5
P.Berl.Leihg	*Berliner Leihgabe griechischer Papyri*
P.Giss.	Eger, O. et al. *Griechische Papyri im Museum des oberhessischen Geschichtsvereins zu Giessen.* Leipzig-Berlin 1910–12
P.Oxy	*The Oxyrhynchus Papyri.* London. 1898–
P.Ryl.	*Catalogue of the Greek and Latin Papyri in the John Rylands Library, Manchester*
PBSR	*Papers of the British School at Rome*

PCG	Kassel, R., and Austin, C., *Poetae Comici Graeci*. Berlin, 1983–
PCPS	*Proceedings of the Cambridge Philological Society*
PMG	Page, D. L. *Poeticae Melici Graeci*, Oxford, 1962
RE	Pauly, A., Wissowa, G. and Kroll, W. *Realencyclopädie des classischen Altertumswissenschaft*. 1893–
REA	*Revue des études anciennes*
RIB	*Roman Inscriptions of Britain*, Oxford 1965–
RIG	*Recueil des inscriptions gauloises*, 4 vols, 1985–2002
RIL	Chabot, J.-B., *Recueil des inscriptions libyques*. Paris 1940–41
ROL	Warmington, E. H. *Remains of Old Latin*. 4 vols. Loeb Classical Library
RS	Crawford, M. (ed.). *Roman Statutes*. 2 vols. London. 1996
SEG	*Supplementum Epigraphicum Graecum*. 1923–
Sel.Pap.	Hunt, A. S., Edgar, C. C. and Page, D. L. *Select Papyri*, 4 vols, Loeb Classical Library, Cambridge, Mass. 1950
SIG³	Dittenberger, W. *Sylloge Inscriptionum Graecarum*. 3rd edn. Leipzig. 1915–24
Tab.Vindol.	*Tabulae Vindolandenses* I–III = Bowman and Thomas 1983, 1994, and 2003
TAPA	*Transactions and Proceedings of the American Philological Association*
Tod	Tod, M. N. *Greek Historical Inscriptions*. 2 vols. Oxford. 1946–48
ZPE	*Zeitschrift für Papyrologie und Epigraphik*

Abbreviations and Glossary, Ancient Authors

Acts	Acts of the Apostles
Ael.	Aelian, Latin writer, c. AD 165/70–230/35
NA	*De natura animalium* (*On the nature of animals*)
Aesch.	Aeschylus, Athenian tragedian, first half fifth century BC
Ag.	*Agamemnon*
Pers	*Persae* (*The Persians*)
Aeschin.	Aeschines, Athenian orator, fourth century BC
Alexis	Alexis, comic playwright, fourth–third century BC, fragments in *PCG*
Amm. Marc.	Ammianus Marcellinus, Latin historian, c. AD 330–395
Anth. Pal.	*Anthologia Palatina* (*Palatine Anthology*)
App.	Appian, Greek historian, second century AD
BC	*Bella civilia* (*Civil Wars*)
Hisp.	*Spanish Wars* (*Iberike*)
Mith.	*Mithridatic Wars*
Apul.	Apuleius of Madaura, Latin prose writer, second century AD
Met.	*Metamorphoses,* or *The Golden Ass*
Arist.	Aristotle, Greek philosopher, 384–322 BC
Eth. Nic.	*Nicomachean Ethics*
Mete	*Meteorologica*
Pol.	*Politics*
Rhet.	*Rhetoric*
[Arist.] *Ath. Pol.*	*Athenaion politeia* (*Constitution of the Athenians*), for which see Rhodes 1981
Oec.	*Oeconomica*
Aristoph.	Aristophanes, Athenian comic playwright, fifth century BC
Ach.	*Acharnenses* (*Acharnians*)
Av.	*Aves* (*Birds*)

Eq.	*Equites* (*Knights*)
Pax	*Pax* (*Peace*)
Plut.	*Plutus* (*Wealth*)
Ran.	*Ranae* (*Frogs*)
Vesp.	*Vespae* (*Wasps*)
Arr.	Arrian, Greek historian, c. AD 86–160
Anab.	*Anabasis*
Tact.	*Tactica*
Athen.	Athenaeus, c. AD 200, *The Deipnosophists*, learned conversation at dinner
August.	Augustine of Hippo, bishop and writer, AD 354–430
De civ. D	*De civitate Dei* (*City of God*)
Conf.	*Confessions*
Ep.	*Epistulae* (*Letters*)
Caes.	Julius Caesar (C. Iulius Caesar), 100–44 BC
BAf	*Bellum Africum*
BC	*Bellum Civile*
BG	*Bellum Gallicum*
Cato	Cato the Elder, M. Porcius Cato, Roman politician and writer, 234–149 BC
Agric.	*De agricultura* (*On Agriculture*)
Celsus *Med.*	A. Cornelius Celsus, first century AD, *De medicina*
Cic.	M. Tullius Cicero, Roman politician and writer, 106–43 BC
Ad Brut.	*Epistulae ad Brutum* (*Letters to Brutus*)
Arch.	*Pro Archia*
Att.	*Epistulae ad Atticum* (*Letters to Atticus*)
Balb	*Pro Balbo*
Cat.	*In Catilinam*
Clu.	*Pro Cluentio*
Deiot.	*Pro rege Deiotaro*
Div.	*De divinatione* (*On Divination*)
Dom.	*De domo sua*
Fam.	*Epistulae ad familiares* (*Letters to Friends*)
Leg.	*De legibus* (*On Laws*)
Nat. D.	*De natura deorum* (*On the Nature of the Gods*)
Off.	*De officiis* (*On Duties*)
Q. Fr.	*Epistulae ad Quintum Fratrem* (*Letters to his brother Quintus*)
Tusc.	*Tusculan Disputations*
1 Clement	First Letter of Clement to the Corinthians, in Loeb Classical Library, *Apostolic Fathers*, vol. 1
Columella	Columella, first century AD, *De re rustica*, an agricultural manual
Cod. Iust.	*Codex Iustinianus*
Cod. Theod.	*Codex Theodosianus* or *Theodosian Code* (edition: T. Mommsen and P. Meyer, 1905; translation: C. Pharr, 1952)

1 Cor.	The First Letter of Paul to the Corinthians, New Testament
Dem.	Demosthenes, Athenian orator, 384–322 BC
Deut.	Deuteronomy, Old Testament
Dig.	*Digesta*, legal text, 6th C. AD (edition: T. Mommsen [1905]; translation: A. Watson)
Dio	Cassius Dio, Greek historian of Rome, c.164 to after AD 229
Dio Chrys.	Dio Chrysostom, Greek orator and philosopher, mid-first century to early second century AD
Diod.	Diodorus Siculus (Diodoros of Sicily), author of a world history, first century BC
D.L.	Diogenes Laertius, probably early third century AD, *Lives of the Philosophers*
D.H. *Ant. Rom.*	Dionysius of Halicarnassus, first century BC, *Roman Antiquities*
Eur.	Euripides, Athenian tragedian, c.480s to 407/406 BC
Euseb.	Eusebius of Caesarea, bishop and scholar, c. AD 260–339
Chron.	*Chronica*
Dem. Evang.	*Demonstratio Evangelica*
HE.	*Historia ecclesiastica*
Praep. Evang	*Praeparatio evangelica* (*Preparation for the Gospel*)
VC	*Vita Constantini* (*Life of Constantine*)
Eutrop.	Eutropius, historian, 4th C. AD, *Breviarum ab urbe condita*
Flor.	L. Annaeus Florus, Latin historian, second century AD, *Epitome of Seven Hundred Years' Worth of Wars*
Frontin.	Sex. Iulius Frontinus, first century AD
Aq.	*De aquaeductibus urbis Romae* (*On Aqueducts*)
Fronto *Aur.*	M. Cornelius Fronto, orator, second century AD, *Letters to Marcus Aurelius*
Gai. *Inst.*	Gaius, *Institutiones*
Gal.	Galen, Greek medical writer, second century AD
Prog.	*On Prognosis*
Comp. Med. Loc.	*De compositione medicamentorum secundum locos*
Galat.	The Letter of Paul to the Galatians, New Testament
Gell.	Aulus Gellius, Roman miscellanist, second century AD, *Noctes Atticae* (*Attic Nights*)
Hdt.	Herodotus of Halicarnassus, Greek historian, fifth century BC
Herodian	Herodian, Greek historian, third century AD, *History of the empire from the time of Marcus*
Hes.	Hesiod, Greek poet, probably c.700 BC
Theog.	*Theogony*
Works	*Works and Days*
Hesych.	Hesychius of Alexandria, author of lexicon, c.fifth century AD
Hom.	Homer
Il.	*Iliad*
Od.	*Odyssey*

Hor.	Horace, Latin poet, 65–8 BC
Isoc.	Isocrates, Athenian orator, 436–338 BC
Phil.	*Philippus*
Panath.	*Panathenaicus*
Paneg.	*Panegyricus*
Jos.	Josephus, Jewish historian, first century AD
AJ	*Antiquitates Judaicae*
BJ	*Bellum Judaicum* (*The Jewish War*)
Just.	Justin, *Epitome*, of the *Historiae Philippicae* of Pompeius Trogus
Juv.	Juvenal, probably early second century AD, *Satires*
Lactant. *De mort.*	*Lactantius*, Christian writer, c.240 to c. AD 320, *De mortibus persecutorum* (*On the Deaths of the Persecutors*)
Lib. *Or.*	Libanius, Greek rhetorician, fourth century AD, *Orations*
Livy	Livy, probably 59 BC to AD 17; history of Rome cited as "Livy"
Per.	*Periochae*
Lucan	Lucan, Latin poet, AD 39–65, *De bello civili*
Lucian	Lucian of Samosata, Greek writer, second century AD
Dom.	*de Domo* (*The Hall*)
Hist. conscr.	*Quomodo historia conscribenda sit* (*How to Write History*)
Luct.	*De luctu*
Peregr.	*De morte Peregrini*
Lucil.	Lucilius, Roman satirist, second century BC, fragments edited by F. Marx, 1904–5, for translation *ROL 3*
Lucr.	Lucretius, Epicurean Latin poet, first century BC, *De rerum natura* (*On the Nature of Things*)
Lysias	Lysias, Attic orator, mid-fifth century to c.380 BC
Macc.	Maccabees
Macrob. *Sat.*	Macrobius, late empire, *Saturnalia*
Mart.	Martial, Latin poet, first century AD
Menander	Menander, Athenian playwright, late 4th to early third century BC
Nep.	Cornelius Nepos, Latin biographer, first century BC, author of *De viris illustribus* (*On Famous Men*)
Origen,	Origen, Christian writer, c. AD 185–254
C. Cels.	*Contra Celsum* (*Against Celsus*)
Comm. Matt.	*Commentary on Matthew*
Ovid *Met.*	Ovid, Latin poet, 43 BC to AD 17, *Metamorphoses*
Paus.	Pausanias, Greek traveler and writer, second century AD, *Description of Greece*
Petron. *Sat.*	Petronius, Roman prose writer, first century AD, *Satyricon*
Philet.	Philetaerus, comic playwright, fourth century BC, fragments in *PCG*

Philo	Philo, Jewish writer, early first century AD
In Flacc.	*In Flaccum*
Philostr.	Philostratus, Greek sophist and writer, third century AD
Her.	*Heroikos* (*Heroic Discourse*)
VS	*Vitae Sophistarum* (*Lives of the Sophists*)
Phot.	Photius, bishop and scholar, ninth century AD
Bib.	*Bibliotheca*
Lex.	*Lexicon*
Pind.	Pindar, Boiotian poet, late sixth to mid-fifth century BC
Ol	*Olympian Odes*
Pl.	Plato, Athenian philosopher, c.429–347 BC
Grg.	*Gorgias*
Phdr.	*Phaedrus*
Prt.	*Protogoras*
Rep.	*Republic*
Symp.	*Symposium*
Tht.	*Theaetetus*
Plaut.	Plautus, Latin comic playwright, late third to early second century BC
Cist.	*Cistellaria*
Rud.	*Rudens* (*The Rope*)
Pliny, *HN*	Pliny the Elder, AD 23/24–79, *Naturalis historia* (*Natural History*)
Pliny, *Ep.*	Pliny the Younger, Roman politician, c.61 to c. AD 112, *Letters*
Plut.	Plutarch, Greek biographer and philosopher, mid-first to second century AD
Ages.	*Agesilaus*
Alc.	*Alcibiades*
Alex.	*Alexander*
Ant.	*Antony*
Caes.	*Caesar*
Cam.	*Camillus*
Cato mai	*Cato maior* (*Cato the Elder*)
Cic.	*Cicero*
Crass.	*Crassus*
Dem.	*Demosthenes*
Lyc.	*Lycurgus*
Marc.	*Marcellus*
Mar.	*Marius*
Mor.	*Moralia*
Pel.	*Pelopidas*
Pyrrh.	*Pyrrhus*
Sert.	*Sertorius*

Sol.	*Solon*
TG	*Tiberius Gracchus*
Them.	*Themistocles*
Polyb.	Polybius, Greek historian, c.200 to c.118 BC
Procop.	Procopius, Greek historian, sixth century AD
Aed.	*De aedificiis* (*On Buildings*)
Prop.	Propertius, Latin poet, first century BC
Romans	Letter of Paul to the Romans
Quint.	Quintilian, Roman rhetorician, first century AD
Inst.	*Institutio oratoria* (*Orator's Education*)
Sall.	Sallust, C. Sallustius Crispus, probably 86–35 BC, Latin historian
Iug.	*Bellum Iugurthinum* (*The Jugurthine War*)
Cat.	*Bellum Catilinae*
Sen.	Seneca the Elder, Latin rhetorical writer, c.50 BC to c. AD 40
Con.	*Controversiae*
Sen.	Seneca the Younger, Roman politician, philosopher and tragedian, first century AD
Ep.	*Letters*
Serv. *Aen.*	Servius, fourth century AD, commentary on Vergil's *Aeneid*
SHA	Scriptores Historiae Augustae, anonymous collection of imperial biographies, fourth or fifth century AD
Tyr. Trig.	*Tyranni Triginta*
Sil. *Pun.*	Silius Italicus, c. AD 26–102, Latin poet, *Punica*
Socrates *HE.*	Socrates Scholasticus, *Historia Ecclesiastica*
Soph	Sophocles, Athenian tragedian, 490s to 406 BC
Aj.	*Ajax*
Ant.	*Antigone*
Trach	*Trachiniae*
Soz. *HE.*	Sozomen, *Historia Ecclesiastica*
Strabo	Strabo, c.64 BC to after AD 20, *Geography*
Suet.	Suetonius, Latin biographer, c.70 to c. AD 130
Aug.	*Divus Augustus*
Calig.	*Gaius Caligula*
Claud.	*Divus Claudius*
Tib.	*Tiberius*
Vesp.	*Divus Vespasianus*
Tac.	Tacitus, Latin historian, c.56 to after c. AD 118
Agr.	*Agricola*
Ann.	*Annals*
Hist.	*Histories*
Theocr. *Id.*	Theocritus, Greek poet, third century BC, *Idylls*
Theod. *HE*	*Theodoret*, bishop, c. AD 393–466, *Historia Ecclesiastica*
Theophr.	Theophrastus, Greek philosopher, late 370s to early 280s BC
Hist. pl.	*Historia plantarum*

1 Thessalonians	First Letter of Paul to the Thessalonians, New Testament
Thuc.	Thucydides, Athenian historian, fifth century BC
Titus	Letter of Paul to Titus, New Testament
Val. Max.	Valerius Maximus, Latin writer, first century AD
Varro, *RR*	M. Terentius Varro, Roman scholar, first century BC, *De re rustica*, an agricultural manual
Veg.	Flavius Vegetius Renatus, Latin military, probably late fourth century AD, *De re militari*
Vell. Pat.	Velleius Paterculus, early imperial, *Historiae Romanae*
Verg.	Vergil or Virgil, Latin poet, 70–19 BC
Aen.	*Aeneid*
Ecl.	*Eclogues*
Georg.	*Georgics*
Vitr.	Vitruvius, late first century BC, *De architectura*
Xen.	Xenophon, Athenian writer, c.430 to mid-fourth century BC
Anab.	*Anabasis*
Cyr.	*Cyropaedia*
Hell.	*Hellenica*
LP	*Lakedaimonion Politeia* (*Constitution of the Lacedaimonians*)
Mem.	*Memorabilia*
Oik	*Oikonomikos* or *Oeconomicus* (*On the Management of the Household*)
Symp.	*Symposium*
[Xen.] *Ath. Pol.*	*Athenaion Politeia* or *Constitution of Athens*, included among the works of Xenophon; author often referred to as the "Old Oligarch"

Timeline

This is intended as a very selective guide to put the material in the following chapters in some form of chronological context. Dates are often approximate, particularly those before the sixth century BC. Not all Roman emperors are included, especially after the third century AD.

BC

2700–2150	Old Kingdom, Egypt; building of Great Pyramid
c.2500	Stonehenge built
2350–2150	The empire of Akkad, Mesopotamia
2112–2004	The Third Dynasty of Ur, Mesopotamia
2050–1650	Middle Kingdom, Egypt
1650–1200	Hittite empire
1550–1050	New Kingdom, Egypt
1450	Collapse of Minoan civilization on Crete
1200	Destruction of the Mycenaean palaces
1100–700	Phoenician colonization across the Mediterranean
814	Traditional date for foundation of Carthage (archaeological evidence later)
c.800	Introduction of the alphabet to Greece
776	Traditional date for the foundation of the Olympic Games
753	Traditional date for the foundation of Rome
750–580	Greek colonization in the Mediterranean and Black Sea
745–727	Emergence of Assyrian empire under Tiglath-pileser III
c.700	Homer's *Iliad* and *Odyssey*
700–500	Etruscan ascendancy in Italy
612	Fall of Nineveh to Babylonians and Medes, ending the Assyrian empire

604–562	Nebuchadnezzar II, king of Babylon
c.600	Invention of coinage in Asia Minor
594	Solon's legislation in Athens
550–530	Rise of Persian empire under Cyrus
525	Egypt becomes part of Persian empire
c.546–10	Peisistratid tyranny in Athens
509	First year of the Roman republic after the expulsion of the kings
508	Reforms of Kleisthenes at Athens
499	Ionian revolt begins
494	First plebeian secession at Rome; beginning of the tribunate
490	First Persian War; Battle of Marathon
480–79	Second Persian War; battles of Thermopylae, Artemisium and Salamis (480); battles of Plataea and Mykale (479)
480	Carthaginians invade Sicily; defeated by Gelon of Syracuse at Himera
478	Foundation of Delian League and beginning of the Athenian empire
472	Aeschylus's *Persians* performed; 5th century sees first performance of the plays of Athenian tragedians Aeschylus, Sophocles, and Euripides
462	Democratic reforms of Ephialtes in Athens
451–49	Decemvirate and publication of the Twelve Tables at Rome, followed by secession of the Plebs in Rome
440s/430s	Perikles leading politician in Athens
447	Building of Parthenon begins in Athens
431–04	The Peloponnesian War (431–421 Archidamian War; 415–413 Athenian expedition to Sicily; Ionian War), ending with fall of Athens
399	Death of Socrates
390 (or 387)	Gauls (Celts) capture Rome
371	Battle of Leuktra: Thebans defeat Spartans
367	Consulship at Rome opened to plebeians
359–336	Rise of Macedon under Philip II
341–338	Rome's conquest of Latium
336–323	Reign of Alexander and Macedonian conquest of Persian empire; battles of Granicus (334), Issos (333), Gaugamela (331)
331	Foundation of Alexandria in Egypt
326–304	Rome fights Second Samnite War
323–270s	Wars of the Successors and the establishment of the Hellenistic Kingdoms
298–290	Rome fights Third Samnite War
287	End of "Conflict of Orders" at Rome

280–275	Pyrrhus comes to the aid of Tarentum against Rome; campaigns in Italy and Sicily.
280–279	Gauls (Celts) invade Macedon and Greece
c.270	Romans complete conquest of Italian peninsula
264–241	First Punic War, at the end of which Sicily becomes the first Roman province
240–237	Carthage's Mercenaries War, following defeat in First Punic War
218–202	Second Punic War
216	Battle of Cannae: Hannibal defeats the Romans
200–168	Rome's Wars in the East against Macedon and Seleukids
168	Battle of Pydna brings an end to kingdom of Macedon
c.166–164	Maccabean Revolt against Antiochos IV in Judaea
146	Rome sacks Carthage and Corinth; creation of provinces of Africa and Macedon
133	Tribunate of Tiberius Gracchus; death of Attalos III of Pergamon; beginnings of Roman province of Asia
123–122	Tribunate of Gaius Gracchus
107–100	C. Marius consul six times; wins victories against Jugurtha and the Cimbri and Teutones
91–87	Social War between Rome and its allies; Roman citizenship given to all Italians
82–81	Sulla dictator in Rome (becomes consul in 80, retires in 79)
73–71	Slave revolt of Spartacus in Italy
67–62	Pompey campaigns against pirates, defeats Mithridates and reorganizes the East
63	Consulship of Cicero; conspiracy of Catiline
58–50	Caesar conquers Gaul
55 and 54	Caesar's expeditions to Britain
49	Caesar crosses Rubicon and civil war begins
47–44	Dictatorship of Caesar
44–31	Intermittent Roman civil wars following assassination of Caesar
43	Murder of Cicero
31	Battle of Actium; Octavian defeats Antony and Cleopatra
27	Octavian takes the name Augustus
19	Death of Vergil
16 BC–AD 6	Danube provinces added to Roman empire
AD	
9	Arminius wipes out three Roman legions under Varus in the Teutoburg Forest in Germany
14	Death of Augustus
14–69	Julio-Claudian dynasty
14–37	Tiberius emperor
30	Death of Christ

37–41	Gaius Caligula emperor, murdered
41–54	Claudius emperor, rumored to have been murdered
43	Claudius's invasion of Britain
54–68	Nero emperor
60–61	Revolt of Boudicca in Britain
64	The Great Fire of Rome; Nero's persecution of Christians
66–70	Revolt in Judaea
69	Year of the four emperors following fall of Nero
69–96	Flavian dynasty
69–79	Vespasian emperor
79–81	Titus emperor
79	Eruption of Mt Vesuvius and burial of Pompeii and Herculaneum
80	Inauguration of the Colosseum
81–96	Domitian emperor, murdered, followed briefly by Nerva
98–117	Trajan emperor; campaigns against Dacians and Parthians
117–138	Hadrian emperor
122–126	Building of Hadrian's Wall
132–135	Bar Kokhba revolt in Judaea
138–161	Antoninus Pius emperor
161–180	Marcus Aurelius emperor (until 169 with Lucius Verus)
162–166	Roman campaigns against Parthia
166–168	German tribes invade across the Danube
180–192	Commodus emperor, murdered
193–194	Civil war
193–211	Septimius Severus emperor (from 198 with Caracalla)
211–17	Caracalla emperor, murdered, followed briefly by Macrinus
212	Antonine Constitution gives Roman citizenship to all free men and women in the Roman empire
218–222	Elagabalus emperor, murdered
222–235	Alexander Severus emperor, murdered
224–40	Ardashir (Artaxerxes) I establishes Sassanian empire in East
235–84	"Third-Century Crisis"
240–72	Shapur (Sapor) I, Sassanian ruler
284–305	Diocletian and (from 293) the Tetrarchy
303–311	Diocletian and Galerius's Persecution of the Christians
306–337	Constantine emperor
312	Battle of Milvian Bridge: Constantine defeats Maxentius
325	Council of Nicaea (Christian)
330	Dedication of new city of Constantinople (first planned in 324)
363	Death of the emperor Julian while campaigning against Sassanians
374–397	Ambrose Bishop of Milan
378	Battle of Adrianople: Valens dies in battle against the Goths
379–395	Theodosius I emperor

410	Sack of Rome by Alaric and the Goths; Britain abandoned
429	Vandals invade Africa
430	Death of Augustine
438	Theodosian code
450s–470s	End of the Roman empire in the West
474–491	Zeno emperor
493–526	Ostrogothic king Theodoric rules Italy
491–518	Anastasius emperor
527–65	Justinian emperor

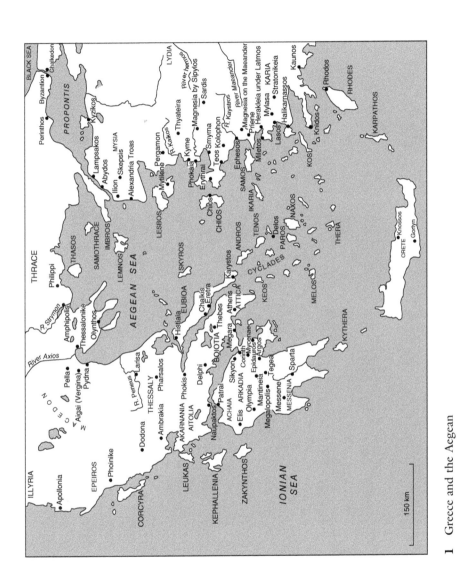

1   Greece and the Aegean

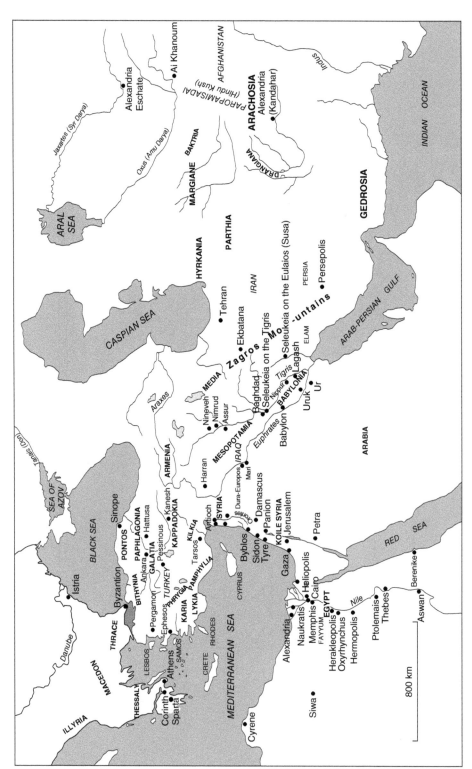

2 Egypt and the Near East

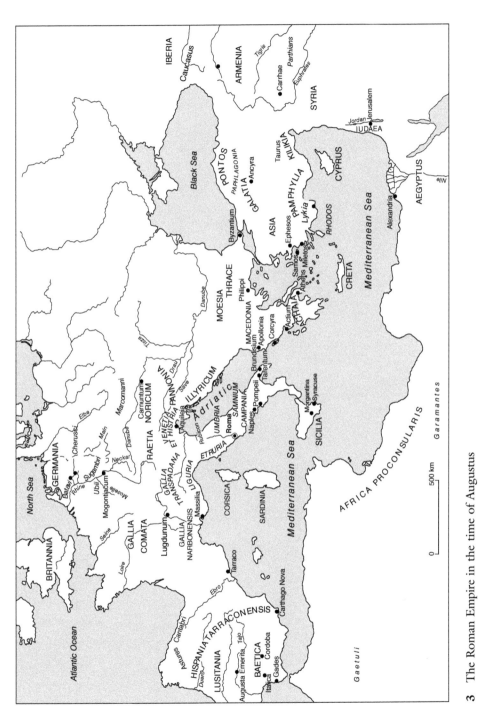

3 The Roman Empire in the time of Augustus

CHAPTER ONE

Personal Perspectives

The worlds of Ancient Greece and Rome may be long ago, but ancient history itself is an ongoing process, discovering, interpreting and reinterpreting the past. In the study of ancient history the present is never far away. The chapters in this *Companion* show ancient historians and their colleagues at work, but by way of introduction I have asked several scholars to reflect on their experience of ancient history and what it means for them.

Why I Study Ancient History, and Why I Suppose it Matters

Josiah Ober, Professor of Classics and Political Science, Stanford University

I have always been fascinated by politics – not parties or elections, but the play of power, legitimacy, and justice. Politics, in this extended sense, is at once a practical issue, an interpretative problem, and a moral concern: understanding any given political system or regime requires describing how it actually works, explaining why it works that way, and offering defensible reasons for why it ought to be otherwise (if in fact it ought). When I was young, I found I had a simple intuitive sense of how power worked in small groups, and discovered that it was possible to make some sense of social behavior by a rough-and-ready calculus of costs, benefits, and ideological legitimacy. Yet I lacked anything like a satisfactory vocabulary for parsing my intuitions about interpersonal politics. I could not begin to answer the descriptive, analytical, and normative questions that I might have asked had I been able to frame them in the first place.

When I arrived at university, more or less by accident, in 1971 I sought out courses that I imagined might help to me to make sense of my intuitions: sociology, anthropology, and so on. But only history held my dilettante's attention. The ancient world – and especially the world of the classical Greek *poleis* – seemed to offer the raw materials for understanding politics. Not surprisingly, reading Thucydides was a revelation. I realized, as have so many others, that Thucydides' narrative of the events of the Peloponnesian war was the product of a profoundly powerful intelligence working at the descriptive and analytical sides of the power and legitimacy equation. Thucydides showed me that it was possible to conjoin the study of internal (intra-*polis*) and external (foreign policy) power relations; to ground political choice in a plausible conception of human nature; that relations between social classes were inherently political; and that thinking about power outside history made no sense. It was only later that I realized Thucydides also had much to say about morally defensible norms of interpersonal behavior and the possibility for justice in what appears to be an anarchic world of inter-state relations.

So I was hooked. Yet when doing my graduate training in the late 1970s I knew enough to see that I would not be able to work out my own Thucydidean explanation, or for that matter to do original work on Thucydides, until I knew a lot more about the concrete realities of Greek history. So I spent a long time studying Greek warfare. By the mid-1980s I felt ready to take on bigger political questions, including (over the next two decades) political sociology, ideology and discourse, revolution, expertise and dissent, social identity, moral authority, and collective action. Each of these emerged clearly in the context of democratic Athens, and so Athens became my case study: a model political system whose changes and continuities over two centuries allowed me to explore diverse aspects of the set of political issues that remained my abiding concern.

When I moved to Princeton in 1990, I saw more clearly than ever that the academic field of classical studies was a perfect environment for the work that interested me, because it demands no sharp distinction between various aspects of history (military, economic, social, cultural, intellectual), or between history, literature, and philosophy. Those undeterred by the disapproval of the few who feel that ancient history must *only* be pursued for its own sake are free to bring in contemporary work on sociology, anthropology, psychology, political theory, and so on. Although this was not always so, the field (publishers of scholarly books and journals, readers, many reviewers) is now remarkably liberal in its acceptance of methodological experimentation. This liberalism rightly carries a requirement that innovators manifest a respect for evidence, reasonable clarity in expression, and honesty in laying out premises and framing arguments. Ancient history is currently a very good field for someone who plans to devote a life to the study of politics and political change.

Ancient history matters to me because it seems to offer insight into questions that ought to matter to anyone living in a complex society, and especially to every citizen in a democracy. These questions have inseparable descriptive, analytical, and normative aspects: historians cannot avoid bringing together the question of *what happened*, with *why it happened*, and *how what happened ought to be evaluated*. That evaluation inevitably means moral judgment of some kind. Historians are necessarily concerned with description. But there is limited value in *describing* the past accurately without being able to *explain* it. And there is little value in explaining something without the capacity to judge its value. The difference between history and moral philosophy is, perhaps, that the historian is likely to see limited value in moral judgments that require historical outcomes no human community has ever, or ever could provide.

Capacities and trade-offs really matter. For a student of democracy, for example, it matters whether democracy is capable of generating its values through participatory practice: Can liberty as absence of domination be sustained by liberty as right of entry? Can equality of opportunity support fair distribution? Will dignity as recognition support the integrity of the individual or the minority community? It matters whether or not social justice is achievable at a cost low enough that democratic communities can compete with undemocratic rivals. It matters if democratic institutions and civic education can sustain democratic discourse and culture while promoting economic growth. Deciding if politics (like medicine) demands a highly specialized expertise, or if political craftsmanship can be attained by ordinary men and women, matters a lot. Those kinds of questions can only be answered by linking political description with analysis and moral reasoning, and by assessing historical processes of change and continuity over time.

It is, I think, easy to get politics badly wrong by approaching the question of politics too narrowly or ahistorically. Basic errors include severing the issue of power from that of legitimacy and legitimacy from justice; ignoring class distinction by imagining politics as an intra-elite game; focusing too narrowly on discourse, or critique, or beliefs; or institutions, or decision-process, or personalities; or chance, or environmental factors, or technological change; or social structure, or agency; or change, or stability. Ancient history offers special benefits to the student of politics seeking to avoid the errors encouraged by narrowness and ahistoricism because it is at once expansive and limited: Its sweep is huge in respect to time and space, but its scale, in terms of relevant facts that can be securely established, is small when compared with modernity. Achieving the level of expertise necessary to bring the manifold aspects of politics into play, even over a lifetime of scholarly activity, is impossible if there is too much to know – which is one reason the study of modernity is so fragmented by discipline. By contrast, antiquity allows me to dream of a sort of "unified political field theory," in which power, legitimacy, and justice could be grasped as a whole.

Achieving that dream may prove impossible. Yet even approaching it represents progress in understanding how communities impede or sustain human lives that go well. So, at the end of the day, my reason for thinking ancient history is worth doing is ethical. Any historian who denies that the fundamental ethical question of "what it is for a human life to go well" lies within the realm of *historia* must answer to the Father of History. Herodotus may have got the facts wrong in his tale of Solon's reply to Croesus's query about who had lived the happiest life. Yet Herodotus's clear conviction that ethics, politics, and history belong together is, I should say, dead right.

Why Ancient History?

Peter Derow, formerly Hody Fellow and Tutor in Ancient History, Wadham College, Oxford

I think there is one very particular reason, and that is its relevance, by which I mean the way in which the study of ancient history can (and should) contribute to our understanding of the world around us and enhance our awareness of much that is going on in it. I think in the first instance, of course, of Polybius, who wrote of the expansion of Roman dominion in the Mediterranean world, of what was effectively the establishment of a single power in a world where before there had been a number of centers of power. He was aware of the importance of this process, which was the theme of his work:

> Is there any human being so low-minded or lazy as not to want to understand how, and being overcome by what sort of state in the space of not even 53 years, almost the whole world fell under a single dominion, that of the Romans – something which is not found to have happened before – and is anyone so little disposed to spectacles or to learning as to consider anything more important than this knowledge? (1.1.5–6)

He did not stop there. Concerned as he was with the elucidation of this process, he reckoned that the elucidation of its effects, on both ruled and rulers, was at least as important:

> ...and to the aforementioned actions one must add both an account of the policy of those in control – what it was after this and how they exercised their universal control, and also an account of the number and variety of the responses and opinions of the rest to and about the rulers. And beyond this one must also tell of the inclinations and pursuits which prevailed and took hold among the individual peoples in their private lives and in their public affairs, for it is evident that it will be clear from these things to those now living whether the dominion of the Romans is turning out to be something to be shunned or, rather, to be embraced, and to those of future generations whether their rule should be judged to have been worthy of praise and emulation or deserving of censure. (3.4.6–7)

The relevance of what was going on in Polybius's world to what is going on in that of today is inescapable, and there is, I think, no doubt that other analogous processes have unfolded in the course of human history. The important thing is always to ask about them, "How and why?" Explanation requires understanding, and it is explanation that Polybius defined as the primary task of the historian. Explanation, and the pursuit of the understanding on which it must be based, should be the aim of all of us. This dual undertaking is certainly what doing ancient history is all about. And doing ancient history is all about evidence. The range of evidence – literary, documentary, archaeological, and more – is wide. The quantity is substantial, but it is not, of course, limitless. For some areas of inquiry it is relatively, sometimes decidedly, limited, and this can have the advantage of making ancient history particularly accessible. And the nature of the evidence is another advantage. Whether one is dealing with an historian, a document or a material artifact, one is always dealing with a form of human utterance, a representation, and these utterances, these representations are always in need of interpretation and of all kinds of contextualization before they can be knitted into the story the ancient historian wants to tell. The ancient historian must accordingly develop self-awareness and the capacity for self-contextualization. If Plato was right to say that it is improper for a human being to live a life which is unexamined, and if one may extend the purview of his remark from the confines of the individual life to include concern for the world in which that life is lived, then the study of ancient history is available as a most appropriate form of human endeavor.

Polybius and his world are profoundly relevant to the world of today, but it will have become clear that the real relevance of ancient history is to be found in the fact that it is about people and the breadth of human experience. It is an aspect of this, to my mind an absolutely crucial one, to which Thucydides attributed the importance of his work:

> But as many as wish to see with clarity the things which have happened, and the similar and analogous things which are going, according to the human condition, to happen sometime again – it will be enough for them to judge this work to be useful. (1.22.4)

History does not repeat itself, but people are people, and ancient history involves the study, within a chronological microcosm, of people's responses to circumstances, both political (at local and global levels) and other. It is a deeply humane kind of study, and, given the nature and range both of the evidence it uses and of the intellectual engagement and activity it requires, it is also fun.

A Roman Historian Reflects

Andrea Giardina, Professor, Istituto Italiano di Scienze Umane

Fortunately, no cultured person today deigns to find in ancient Rome a simple mirror of reality. We can recognize, of course, that this mistaken perception of resemblance did not always have negative consequences: it has sustained intellectual curiosity, stimulated research, and favored the preservation of documents and monuments. Even in the political realm, it has at times provided authority and even some good ideas to both medieval and modern proponents of reform and change. All of this is indisputable. We must recognize, however, that much more often, the Roman mirror, in addition to dissolving into a sea of rhetoric and worthless bibliography, has fuelled passions of conquest, imperialistic tendencies and tyrannies.

In truth, the mirror fantasy today has an unconscious echo in the rhetoric of roots. In Europe this has recently provoked lively debates with reference to the text of the European Constitution. There has been much discussion about adjectives (Christian roots or Judeo-Christian roots, etc.) without consideration of the fact that the noun is much more venomous than all of its possible modifiers. The idea of the root is, in fact, a racist metaphor, and it will remain such, notwithstanding the good intentions and candor of those who use it: "Race is likened to a tree; it does not change. The roots of the race are always the same. There are the branches of the tree, there is the foliage. And this is all." (George Mosse). Even if we succeeded in confining its resonance to a purely humanistic domain, we would end by establishing its danger: constructing a hierarchy of historic objects, separating the green limbs from the dry, removing creative value from failed or spent experiences: this in fact suggests a sort of historiographic eugenics. But everyone should recognize that the past does not acquire greater value only if it is capable of demonstrating traces of our lifeblood.

The most suggestive remedy was the attribution to our ancestors of a certain exotic or foreign character. When the Jacobins put on the clothes of Brutus and posed as imitators of the ancient defenders of the republics and of liberty, the "ideologue" Volney responded with a brilliant taunt: "I am always struck by the analogy that I detect daily between the savages of North America and the ancient peoples, so highly lauded, of Greece and Italy." Today, after psychoanalysis and anthropology have taught us the advantages of detached vision, we are particularly aware of the cultural influences in the exotic perspective (obviously with the condition that we do not fall into exoticism). Still, this does not succeed in satisfying us completely. Nothing can explain this dissatisfaction better than the Latin language. When we read *religio, respublica, familia, imperium, libertas,* and so many other fundamental terms of the society, institutions and politics of Rome, we read words that reoccur almost identically in the principal languages of Europe and the Western world. That vocabulary, so similar to ours, truly seems to encapsulate our "roots," and it transmits to us at first glance a reassuring sense of identity. But if, just as archaeologists working in the soil, we proceed to the substrata of these words, we immediately become aware of the successive and numerous changes that have occurred over the centuries and we perceive that at the base of this excavation we are in a world that has strong elements of foreignness. The *religio* of the Romans is not exactly the *religion* of the English, the *religion* of the French, the *Religion* of the Germans, the *religione* of the Italians, and the *religión* of the Spanish, and the same can be said for many other essential terms. The appeal of the relationship with the Romans is in this diversity both oscillating and dramatic: discovering the alien in the similar is a beautiful adventure of both intelligence and sensibility.

Moderns have often looked for, and sometimes found, in the ancient world a lost harmony: harmony of form, of comportment, of poetry, of stories and of scenery. This research has looked more at the Greek world, the cradle of classicism, than the Roman world. In the case of Rome, it has concentrated on civic virtues: for centuries the readers of Livy and Plutarch have learned to recognize in the Romans (up to the crisis of the republic) the most authentic cultivators of discipline, capable of examples of extreme self-denial for the benefit of their country and the collective interest. Today all this provokes little enthusiasm, even if the old theme, already ancient, of "the virtue of the Romans" would merit serious sociological attention and would be useful as a way of explaining, at least in part, the success of Rome. The more fascinating element in Roman history is, however, a harmony of another kind, one which appears to us retrospectively, if we isolate a series of contradictions arranged in equilibrium, of contrasting yet at the same time complementary colors which embody the principal aspects of Rome from the highest levels of the empire to the microcosm of the family.

Rome was in fact a "foreign" city, a city that took its origins from a lost and prestigious world, the city of Troy destroyed by the Greeks, and did not have at its core the idea of consanguinity: in the rich ideological repertoire of domination and

Roman 'diplomacy' the concept of lineage was in fact the most ephemeral and marginal. But this sense of being foreign associated itself, quite naturally, with an extraordinarily broad extension of the right of citizenship that could not be found in equal measure in any other ancient (and perhaps even modern) empire. Rome had a very deep sense of its own honor and an ostentatious perception of its own superiority, but declared with pride that it had as ancestors men who were bastards, ethnically promiscuous, socially dangerous (the myth of Romulus's asylum) or even downright servile in origin. Rome ably exploited slaves and punished them with chilling penalties, but simple will on the part of their owner could transform them almost into citizens (and their children would eventually be citizens). Not being a democracy, and not cultivating the principle of direct participation, Rome could entrust to single citizens, by means of manumission, the reproduction – partial yet significant – of the civic body. The *potestas* of the *paterfamilias* was immense and potentially terrifying, but the Roman family was an open organism, and adoption was perceived as an imitation of nature.

At various levels, then, a characteristic polarity repeated itself between dominance and flexibility, between a rigid and invariable sense of command and elasticity, between rigor and openness. For the scholar, the exploration of this universe, composite and coherent at the same time, is a true challenge, because at the point of contact of each of these contradictions he or she sees the great history of Rome taking shape and its evolutionary processes developing in often surprising ways.

A View from Japan

Neil McLynn, University Lecturer and Fellow in Later Roman History, Corpus Christi College, Oxford, formerly of the Faculty of Law, Keio University, Japan

Sixteen years of doing my ancient history in Japan have given a distinctive accent to those persistently nagging questions, what I think I might be doing, and why. For even if the answers remain much the same (do we not all continue our wrestling because we have somehow been allowed to?), the questions sound quite different in an environment without even the vestigial framework of a Greco-Latin educational tradition. In Japan, to ask students and colleagues why *they* do what they do (and what they think it is) is not quite to throw questions into the mirror.

Why, then, do they do it? The relatively few captivated in early youth attest the various channels through which the ancient Mediterranean laps the shores of modern Japan. Childhood reading accounts for some. Plutarch's *Lives* are much translated, with an improving adaptation designed specifically for the young, while the stirring vision of Rome presented in Nanami Shiono's phenomenally successful popularizing treatments has left its imprint on all age groups. A thesis will one day be written, meanwhile, on the *manga* sub-genre that broods on the decline and fall of archaized, and safely occidentalized, empires; the theme seems peculiarly resonant here, and those who succumb duly proceed to their Gibbon (another much-translated text).

But those who study the subject at university in Japan have survived high school World History, the formidable barrier of names and dates from which university entrance examinations are constructed. Candidates even for a Law faculty, for example, might have to identify Pompey and Hadrian, as conquerors of Jerusalem, from a list also including Caesar, Nero, Trajan, and Caracalla, in a test that demands similar precision concerning Portuguese Malacca and Spanish Manila, or Lumumba and Nkrumah. No wonder, then, that many undergraduates cherish an instinctive, and understandable, aversion to all things historical, while others insist stubbornly, but forgivably, that history *is* their cherished Gradgrindian list and nothing more. But then one meets the happy few capable of putting their feats of memorization to creative use, who have made their accumulated store of facts a playground for their historical imagination; and such meetings, for me at least, raise vexing questions about the propaedeutics appropriate for a discipline such as ours.

Only at university level does the subject emerge in its own right, perched at the end of the sprawling archipelago of "Western History." Its workings seem haphazard and, to the foreigner, strikingly personalized. Few institutions can afford the luxury of specialized sub-departments, and even there most students are entangled gradually, through their optional courses and special subjects, in a process which can last into postgraduate studies. A thesis originally aimed at the French Revolution, for example, might end up in Late Antique Gaul. Such conversions are generally attributed to professorial apothegms rather than to the student's own sense of direction, for this is a culture which takes discipleship seriously. And the physiognomy of Japanese ancient history today bears the imprint of its genealogy. Such themes as Athenian Democracy and Roman Slavery found powerful resonance in the immediate post-war period, helping to generate a critical mass of researchers. Still today, dry specialists will come alive when they discuss their academic pedigrees – the real debt felt to one's teachers' teachers clearly serves to inspire.

For the Western ancient historian washed up on these shores, perhaps the most delightful stimulus is the license to teach so much that is *not* ancient history. It is strangely liberating to spend the bulk of the teaching week leaping from Safavid Iran to Shakespearian Comedy, from the Cold War to Angevin Hungary. And in making these leaps one constantly feels the benefit of a training in Herodotus and Thucydides, and of a continuing engagement with the politics of Cappadocian Christianity; which is (perhaps) merely to sum up one principal message from this assemblage of contributions, that ours is a discipline which to an unusual degree serves as a springboard rather than a straitjacket.

The Relevance of Ancient History: an Australian Perspective
sidere mens eadem mutato?

Kathryn Welch, Senior Lecturer, Department of Classics and Ancient History, University of Sydney

According to the Board of Studies statistics in my home state of New South Wales, almost one in three students does history in the final year of school. Of that cohort, however, more students select ancient history than modern – and in ever increasing numbers. They go on to study it at university too. Whether the trend away from studying the more recent past is a good thing might be questioned, but it is worth considering why ancient history is so popular in modern Australia.

It cannot be explained only by the cultural ties Australia shares with Europe, which, while strong, have mutated under the influence of a multicultural social experience, especially in urban centers. Instead, as with Neil McLynn's Japanese students, many from diverse ethnic backgrounds have embraced ancient history with no less passion than their Anglo-Irish classmates. I like to think that they are drawn instinctively to the humanity articulated by Peter Derow. But why specifically *ancient* history? Partly, perhaps, because it offers a medium, at once alien and familiar, through which to explore all kinds of historical questions. The broadly based New South Wales school syllabus covers Egypt, Greece, Rome and the "Near East." The narrative histories and material remains of all these areas have a wide appeal. But there is more. Ancient history puts us in touch with the serious debates of the past and the different ways in which antiquity (and not just classical antiquity) has been reinvented by later generations. In our study of ancient history we meet many other histories, the Renaissance, the Enlightenment, the American and French Revolutions, Napoleon and his use of Roman and Egyptian models of imperialism, institutions such as the Fabian Society and the Spartacists, and the whole development of Western (and some non-Western) democracies. And this is just a sample! The ancient past has provided diverse cultures with a conceptual framework for articulating their present, and each layer has added an ingredient to our study. We are the cultural heirs of Machiavelli as much as we are of his hero Livy.

This dialogue with the past is infinitely portable. It arrived in Australia very soon after European settlement began in 1788. According to Edwin Judge, who wrote the supplementary entry on classical studies in Australia and New Zealand for *Der Neue Pauly*, at least two types of people taught classics in early Australia. One group represented members of the establishment who felt extreme separation anxiety from the elite British education system, hence the motto, accompanied by a crest which combines that of Oxford and Cambridge, of Sydney University quoted above: "The constellations have changed but the mind (mentality?) remains the same." The second was made up of revolutionary Romantics who wanted to (or were forced to) escape to the freer intellectual environment of "The Colonies." Both types can still be found teaching ancient history in Australian schools and universities. The tension between conservatism and revolution is not always comfortable, but it is part of who we are and has the beneficial effect of making us think about why we do what we do instead of taking our relevance for granted.

Ancient history is a sociable subject. As well as constantly debating with the past, with other published scholars and sometimes even with the authorities, its adherents love to debate historical questions with each other in both formal and informal settings, one of which is often the local hostelry. Sometimes the partisan nature of such conversations can be disturbing when one thinks about the distance between us and, say, the rights and wrongs of the assassination of Julius Caesar or whether the establishment of the principate was a "good thing" or not. The passion of the debate reflects our ability to empathize. Because of the huge distance between us and our fragmentary evidence, our conclusions are contestable, and so the debate can keep going.

We cannot change the past: we can only challenge and interpret its narratives. And we have to accept what we find rather than what we think we want to find. We can observe that thousands of years ago people could be as silly and as passionate as ourselves – and often smarter (something I realized the first time I read Thucydides!). The study of ancient history insists upon a long-term view of human endeavor and human problems. This is a humbling thing and we should approach it with an open mind and in the knowledge that it will end up being a lot more complex than we thought. What we can and should do is to analyze and explain the past from new perspectives and with our own questions. This is what will always separate history from mere antiquarianism.

Although ancient history has sometimes been appropriated by both respectable and less-respectable interest groups, no one really owns it, or, at least, not all of it. It belongs to everyone who has access to the evidence upon which it is based. This raises the question of the relationship between ancient history and the classics. Jerry Toner recently expressed the view that Roman historians should cut their losses and escape from moribund classics to the nearest convenient history department. In some ways it is easy to see what he means. Yet the ancient historian should be at home in either setting and welcomed in both. In its Greek and Roman guises, it shares a common area of study with classics, but its discipline and methodologies lie with history. Let's be realistic. The relationship between all history and language should be symbiotic. University professionals cannot operate without the languages in which their texts were written. But neither should they restrict their horizons to the relatively narrow temporal and cultural worlds of the "Classical." Moreover, ancient history, along with lively expositions of ancient literature, has the ability to make people from amazingly different backgrounds fall in love with a translated foreign world and even to encourage a few to discover language skills they never knew they wanted. Because of this drawing power, new classicists as well as new ancient historians can emerge from among the ranks of previously monoglottal enthusiasts. When all who approach the ancient world from different disciplinary perspectives treat each other as equal allies in the same enterprise, ancient historians should have no need to escape.

I leave the final words to my undergraduate students whom I questioned about the relevance of ancient history to them. Overwhelmingly they stated that ancient history helped them to understand their own world. One spoke of "the most complex and enthralling narratives of all time," another of its interconnection with directly neighboring fields. Perhaps the most honest stated that it helped him win at Trivia. But that just suggests that ancient history is as firmly entrenched in popular culture as it is in the New South Wales school curriculum. It is part of the fabric of who we are and where we are.

PART I

Evidence

CHAPTER TWO

Historiography

John Marincola

1 The Writing of History in Antiquity

Despite the vast contributions made by archaeology, epigraphy, and numismatics, the bulk of our knowledge of the ancient world comes from the narratives of ancient historians. Our ability to write the story of any particular time and place in antiquity depends in large part on whether some ancient historian has already done so. Thus it is extremely important for those who study the ancient world to understand the conventions and approaches of ancient historians.

Even though the tradition of history-writing from Herodotus in the fifth century BC to Ammianus in the fourth century AD shows a range of different purposes and presumes a variety of different audiences, there is still a certain uniformity visible in the tradition, as later practitioners of the genre imitated and tried to surpass the earlier models that were acknowledged as definitive (Marincola 1997). Ancient historiography, with few exceptions, was the product of an elite writing for an elite, and this resulted in several characteristic features: the prominence of individuals, whether they were the generals of Athens, the kings of the Hellenistic world, or the magistrates and emperors of Rome; a focus on the activities of the governing class, whether that be waging war or running the state at home; an ongoing concern with the apportionment of praise and blame, with an examination and evaluation of the individual active in history; and a tendency to portray the lower classes (when they were portrayed at all) in dismissive or contemptuous terms (Fornara 1983b: 91–141). Most of these characteristics can be found already in Homer's *Iliad*, which indirectly, through Herodotus and Thucydides, became the model for much of ancient historiography, both Greek and Roman (Strasburger 1972).

After the fifth century BC, no era of antiquity lacked historians. Contemporary history, inaugurated by Thucydides, seems to have been preferred by the ancients (D. H. *Ant. Rom.* 1.4.1; Livy *praef.* 4) and its practitioners included Xenophon, Polybius, Sallust (in the *Catiline* and *Histories*), Tacitus (in the *Histories*) and

Ammianus. Even those historians known for their non-contemporary history –
Diodorus, Livy, and Dio – wrote histories that began in the dim past but extended
to their own day. The contemporary historian had the benefit not only of having
lived through the events but also of being able to interview other participants and
eyewitnesses. Non-contemporary history, by contrast, was often difficult to disen-
tangle, and one was inevitably thrown back to earlier writers of varying reliability.
But in some eras, when repressive regimes made the writing of contemporary history
dangerous, non-contemporary history seemed an attractive alternative (T. Luce 1989:
25–7), not least because one might use it to critique indirectly the present age's evils
(cf. Tac. *Ann.* 4.33.4; Quint. 9.2.66–71).

Writers of ancient histories were not professionals in the modern sense; in
many cases they were politicians and generals who turned to history in their retirement (forced or otherwise). That does not mean that they necessarily wrote history
to make the record more favorable to themselves (*pace* Syme 1958b), but it does
mean that their histories had a far more intimate connection to the world of action
than their modern counterparts do. The desire of the Greek and Roman elite
for acknowledgment and renown also meant that public men cared a great deal
about the record left of themselves: as "the witness to the ages" (Cic. *De oratore*
2.36), history could enshrine a man in glory for ever or condemn him to eternal
ignominy. Men, therefore, cared greatly about how history – their own or others' –
portrayed them.

Our knowledge of the theoretical presuppositions underlying the writing of history
is based on the occasional passages (often polemical) to be found in the ancient historians themselves. Many writers composed independent "theoretical" works on the
topic, but we have no way of knowing whether the three that have come down
to us – Dionysius of Halicarnassus's *On Thucydides*, Plutarch's *On the Malice of
Herodotus*, and Lucian's *How to Write History* – are in any way characteristic. Dionysius's treatise is a classic example of stylistic criticism: he faults Thucydides for his
difficult language, and his "inartistic" arrangement, judgments that are not surprising
given the tremendous importance accorded literary merit in all branches of writing
in antiquity: no less than other genres, history was thought to require the appropriate
language (Avenarius 1956: 55–70). Plutarch, by contrast, takes Herodotus to task
for composing an account of the Persian Wars that portrayed the Greek city-states
as quarrelsome and disunited, whereas he ought to have focused on the glorious
nature of the Greek victory over Persia. Here we see the interest in the proper interpretation of events, and the common ancient point of view that history's business is
with glorious deeds rather than shameful ones (Marincola, forthcoming). Lucian's
work is in some ways the most promising. It begins with a satirical punch against
adulatory historians of Lucius Verus's Parthian War (it was written in AD 166: C.
Jones 1986: 60), then turns to offering rules for the proper writing of history. Alas,
it is more of a mixed bag than one might have hoped for, since the prescriptions
break little new ground, deal almost exclusively with the "ideal" historian (D. Potter
1999a: 134–35), and mostly repeat the platitudes of earlier writers on historiography
(Avenarius 1956 for a wealth of parallels).

2   The Debate over the Nature of History

How the ancients wrote history is an important question, and the nature of that
enterprise has been debated vigorously over the past thirty years or so (see Further
Reading). Much of the debate revolves around the relationship between form and
content, more specifically the extent to which rhetoric and rhetorical training affected
the content of ancient histories. That ancient historiography was a rhetorical genre
cannot be denied, although the consequences of this have been evaluated in very
different ways. Some scholars believe that one can discount much of the rhetorical
adornment found in ancient histories and recover a core of solid fact, while others
counter that rhetoric is not like the icing one can slice off a cake (to use the image
of Moles 1993: 114), but rather part of the very fabric of the work, and thus form
and content cannot easily be separated.

The former view often requires the modern historian to engage in a process of
rationalization not entirely different from that practiced by the ancients. It presup-
poses, to put it crudely, that there is no smoke without fire, and that traditions,
however modified or adorned, are usually based on some factual content. That is a
view with a respectable ancient pedigree (see e.g. Isoc. *Panath.* 149–50), but it presumes that traditions are reliable and nothing is ever invented out of whole cloth –
possibly, very dangerous presumptions.

On the other hand, those who deny to the ancient historians a concern with fact
argue that the "truth" they pursued was a rhetorical truth based on probability rather
than actuality. Yet such a viewpoint must overlook both the distinction often made
by the ancients between oratory and history (D. Potter 1999a: 137–38) and the great
number of remarks made by historians and other ancient writers in which they seem
quite concerned with finding out what really happened, rather than simply settling
for a story that satisfied the demands of probability (Avenarius 1956: 76–79).

Part of the problem lies in the ambiguity of the Greek term *heuresis* and its Latin
equivalent *inventio*, words that mean both "discovery" and "invention." It has been
argued that the rhetorical education of the ancients meant that they did not consciously see themselves as *inventing* material when they did not know it so much as
discovering it, i.e. using the techniques that their rhetorical training had given them.
It is not difficult to see that this must have been the case very often when historians
inserted speeches into their histories, simply because exact recollection was impossible
(Walbank 1965); but was it also operative in the realm of deeds and of characters'
motivations and goals? If so, the concept of "what they must have said" could easily
bleed into "what they must have done." Modern scholars who propose such a model
thus rescue ancient historians from the charge of lying, but at the cost of calling all
or much of the content of their work into question.

We are not close to any definitive answers on these topics, and scholars will continue to debate them. Rather than summarizing all of the issues at stake, therefore,
I propose to look at one topic in particular – that of the ancient historians' interest
in and understanding of historical change.

3 Change and "Unhistorical Thinking"

Perhaps the most serious claim brought against ancient historians is the charge of "unhistorical thinking," which suggests an inability to imagine the past except as being very much like the present. The charge is an old one, but has recently been made in a more sophisticated way by T. P. Wiseman:

> The historians of Greece and Rome did *not* "put their authorities to the question." They did not have the questions to put, because they were incapable of the "historical imagination" needed for the historian to relive for himself, as Collingwood put it, the states of mind into which he inquires. (Wiseman 1979a: 42)

Wiseman points out that Livy or Dionysius of Halicarnassus tell of a regal and early republican Rome scarcely different from the city of their own day. One could add many other examples, including even Thucydides' portrait of early Greece in his "Archaeology" (1.2–19), where the historian delineates a Greece concerned with all the same matters – power, compulsion, naval strength, material surplus – as in Thucydides' own day: Agamemnon is simply Athens writ small.

While earlier scholars ascribed the failure of the ancients to their conception of time (background in Momigliano 1966; Starr 1966; V. Hunter 1982), Wiseman saw the culprit as the rhetorical way of thinking, that reliance on *heuresis* and *inventio* just mentioned. Having satisfied themselves that a story fulfilled the requirements of probability, ancient historians did not seek to investigate further. Now while much of Wiseman's analysis is sound, I think that the reasons for this "unhistorical thinking" (if such it is) are more complex than simply the influence of rhetoric. Rhetoric is, after all, only a tool of expression, an indication of something deeper in a society's educative values. Moreover, it cannot be denied that the ancient historians, beginning with Herodotus, recognized that change was essential to history – indeed in some sense change *was* history – so they were not unaware that past times were different from their own. Since the topic, then, is extremely important both for our understanding of what ancient historians thought they were doing and for an evaluation of their actual narratives, I will use the rest of this essay to explore it further.

There are, broadly speaking, three kinds of change that are of interest to ancient historians. First, the historians shared with other thinkers an interest in the development of society from early times to their own day. Thucydides' "Archaeology" (1.2–19), the first treatment of this theme in historiography, narrates the rise of Greece from its poor and powerless beginnings to the standards of wealth and surplus of his own day. Polybius takes an even larger view, treating the development of humankind from its savage beginnings to civilized states and societies (6.2–10), even attempting to integrate this with his discussion of political change (see below). Diodorus, writing a "universal" history in the first century BC, gives the fullest historiographic treatment of the rise of mankind (1.8), and he reflects the intense interest in the subject that had developed in the Hellenistic world (Spoerri 1959). In all these cases, however, the treatment of this particular type of change is ancillary to the historians' main narrative, since their interest is focused on what humans do when they have reached the "civilized" stage of their development.

The second type of change with which the ancient historians concerned themselves was constitutional change. This interest was ubiquitous in ancient historiography, and it is found in Herodotus (1.65–66; 3.80–83; 5.66–78), Thucydides (8.63.3–72), Xenophon (*Hell.* 2.3.1–4.43), Sallust (*Cat.* 6.1–13.5), Tacitus (*Ann.* 1.1.1, 1.9.1–10.7), Dio (52.1–40) and others. It reaches a kind of theoretical peak in Polybius's notion of the *anacyclosis* (6.4.7–9.14), a cycle whereby states are said to go through a certain progression involving the three ideal forms of government (monarchy, aristocracy, and democracy) and their debased offspring (respectively: tyranny, oligarchy, and ochlocracy). As Polybius tells it, men begin in a state of barbarism. The first stage is the rise of a primitive monarch ruling a rude people. He then becomes a true king, but his descendants live luxuriously and wantonly, and this causes the best men to overthrow the monarchy and establish an aristocracy. The descendants of these aristocrats, in turn, likewise fall into depravity, at which point the people rise up and establish a democracy. Over time the people in their turn become corrupted and descend into such savagery that their only hope is a monarch. And thus the circle is completed. A modified form of this circle is hinted at in the preface of Tacitus's *Annals* (1.1.1), whereby the Romans originally were ruled by kings, then by an oligarchy, and then again by a king (the emperor). The important point, however, is that even without cyclical notions, the ancient historians devoted a great deal of energy to treating constitutional changes in their histories.

A third interest of the ancient historians was in rise and fall, both on the grand scale (a nation's advancement and decline) as well as on the small (an individual's reversal of fortune). Herodotus makes reversals of fortune a main reason for his investigations (1.5.2), and rise and fall continue to play an important role in histories thereafter, finding consistent expression in Polybius (29.21, quoting Demetrios of Phaleron's *On Fortune*), Livy (*praef.* 9), and Tacitus (*Hist.* 1.2–3). On the grand scale this could be seen in the development of the notion of the "succession" of empires, whereby one great empire eventually gave way to the next: Aemilius Sura, a contemporary of Polybius, created a sequence of empires that ran Assyrians – Medes – Persians – Macedonians – Romans (Vell. Pat. 1.6.6; cf. Polyb. 1.2.2–6).

On the individual scale, this interest in rise and fall focused on the reversals of fortune of great men, either brought low by chance or fate, or (less commonly) dealt some great blow from which they rise again. Indeed, Polybius thought that one of his history's most important purposes was to teach individuals how to bear reversals of fortune nobly, by recognizing that great men have often dealt with disasters in their own lives (1.1.2).

This interest in rise and fall sometimes revealed itself in a concern with moral decline. The destructive and long-lasting civil wars of the late republic engendered in the Romans in particular an obsession with explaining how their city, which had risen to such prominence by defeating one foreign foe after another, could then, although mistress of the Mediterranean, turn on itself and destroy itself from within as brother fought brother (Earl 1961: 41–59; Jal 1963: *passim*, esp. 360–488). Both Sallust (*Cat.* 10.1) and Livy (*praef.* 9; 39.6.7), writing in this time of revolution, sought answers to the question, and if their explanations – the decline of morality ushered in by the very benefits of empire, with the concomitant loss of any considerable rival that could keep Rome in a state of readiness – might strike us as inadequate, the important point is that they recognized the change, and discussed and debated the origins and causes of it (Lintott 1972).

4   The Present and the Past

Even from these few examples, it is clear that ancient historians had an interest in historical change, and in the difference between past and present. But these interests were, we might say, narrowly defined. The reasons for this and for the general attitude of ancient historians towards the past are, I believe, at least five, some of which were pragmatic, others more indicative of *mentalités*, but all of them interlocking in complex ways. (Naturally, my list is not meant to be exhaustive.)

Let us begin with some of the pragmatic reasons, which, though obvious, are not thereby less important. First, the pace of change in the ancient world was glacial. In antiquity agricultural and daily life for the majority of peoples were much the same over a thousand years, and the ordinary rhythms of nature were the most common and the most insistent indicators of change. Technical innovation, though always present, occurred slowly (K. Greene 2000), such that the span of one or even two or three human generations was insufficient to perceive any kind of long-term alteration – and in any case, as we said, change was slow. So far as we can tell, no event in antiquity matched the world-altering effect of, say, the Industrial Revolution or even of the French Revolution, not to mention the intellectual and moral upheavals brought in their train.

A second reason is that the ancients lacked or discounted many of the tools that modern scholarship values, particularly archaeology, comparative studies, and the systematic examination of archives. Interestingly enough, they had *versions* of all of these. There was a great interest, if not in digging, then certainly in monuments, which were used by both antiquarians and narrative historians. But the employment of monuments was always ad hoc, focused on the single monument which had attached to it, usually, a tradition that could be recounted to "explain" the origin and purpose of the monument (Wiseman 1986; E. Rawson 1990). The tradition was not questioned, and by itself seemed to take the place of any type of independent inquiry about the monument, or, more importantly, about the monument's place in a larger system.

The ancients had "comparative" material as well: they looked at other societies, and in many cases made inquiries about them. Yet here several obstacles stood in the way of the use of this kind of comparative material. First, as is well known, what they often saw when they looked at other societies was themselves, and simple binary oppositions took the place of more complex or nuanced examinations. Here, I think, the initial impulse by Herodotus towards seeing other peoples in a more open and expansive way (though he, of course, is no stranger to binary oppositions) was abruptly arrested by Thucydides, who had a strong sense of the universality of human motivation and action (1.22.4; 3.82.2, 3.84.2). But it is more than that, of course. Ethnographical inquiry did not lead to greater appreciation of the complexity of change because the studies tended to be "timeless," that is, they portrayed their subjects as always having had such customs and practices, rather than as developed over time and in relation to or reaction against external or internal stimuli (Trüdinger 1918; Müller 1972; valuable overview in Rives 1999a: 11–21). And finally, and perhaps most importantly of all, Greeks and Romans – not all of them, of course, but many – approached ethnography with a sense of their own superiority, such that it could hardly be said that they were engaged in a dispassionate or neutral examination. Even when they took the opposite position – placing themselves as inferior to a foreign people, as Tacitus seems to do in the *Germania* – the portrait that arose was equally a timeless and idealized construction (R. Martin 1981: 49–58).

As to documents, ancient historians seem never to have used these in the ongoing way that modern scholars since the eighteenth century have – that is, as a reliable underlying basis for an historical account. There were several reasons for this: first, documentary evidence was not systematically kept and was not easy to use in any regular way (Sickinger 1999; Bucher 1987); second, historians always preferred to inquire of eyewitnesses and participants (Lucian, *Hist. conscr.* 47); third, the focus on great individuals and great battles – on a great *story*, in short – meant that documents would have little importance in the fashioning of such a narrative; and finally, the ancients did not see documents as dispassionate witnesses, but as just another form of testimony that might or might not be reliable (Momigliano 1950; Marincola 1997: 103–5; but cf. D. Potter 1999a: 81–90).

A third factor in the ancient approach to the past was tradition, especially the belief in traditional values (Momigliano 1972). Although the value system of antiquity was far from uniform, it is nevertheless remarkable how much continuity existed: for example, much of what Plutarch thinks makes up good character and just behavior was not so very different from what Plato thought five hundred years earlier; and both Greek and Roman writers a thousand years after Homer can still appeal to his authority and his view of human life. This kind of consistency, together with the very slow pace of actual change in people's lives, led to an assumption (and it must be emphasized that it was by no means an illogical assumption) that the past was *not* in fact very different from the present. We mentioned above the belief of historians that they could figure things out about the past from their rhetorical training in probability. But this was not a *cause* so much as a *result* of their own experience of the past and of human nature. They maintained a fairly persistent belief in consistency of character, both individual and collective (Champion 2004: 30–63, 173–203). The tradition of the Athenian funeral speech, with its assumption of an unchanging Athenian character from the very origins of Athens to the present day, was merely one manifestation of the tendency to see people in a timeless way: fifth- and fourth-century Athenians were no different in essence from their ancestors centuries before (Loraux 1986). And it was from such beliefs as these that the ancient historian felt assured when ascribing motives and explanations.

Moreover, the past provided the most highly valued *exempla* for the present. Although notions such as "the ancestral constitution" (*patrios politeia*) or "the ways of our ancestors" (*mos maiorum*) might be a rallying cry for certain kinds of narrow and manipulative political interest, these concepts were also revered deeply and often seen as the source and inspiration for the present (Finley 1971; Linke and Stemmler 2000). Tradition and a traditional way of thinking meant that historians were constantly on the lookout for what joined them to the past, not for what separated them from it.

Fourth – and here we come to historiography itself – the genre of history in antiquity was also "traditional." Its early practitioners, Herodotus and Thucydides, served as models for all who came thereafter, and although there were indeed many innovators throughout the long history of classical historiography, change was, as in real life, on the small scale, never on the grand. The presence of polemic in ancient historiography must not blind us to the fact that historians did not seek so much to strike out in a bold and innovative direction as to present themselves, by various incremental means, as "improved" versions of their honored forerunners (Marincola 1997: *passim*).

They did this not least in the way that they composed their works. If a man chose to write up non-contemporary history, his method of doing so was to consult what earlier writers had written before him. These, rather than archival documents, were the basis of his account. When Pliny the Younger is trying to decide whether to write contemporary or non-contemporary history, he notes of the latter that "the research has already been done, but comparing accounts is burdensome" (*parata inquisitio sed onerosa collatio*, *Ep.* 5.8.12). Thus the historian's "improvement" of the tradition consisted not in a wholesale re-evaluation of what his predecessors had done nor in a fundamentally new and independent analysis of the events of the past. Rather, he sifted through the tradition and sought to improve it by adding new material gathered from other sources, by correcting a few of the errors of his predecessors, by trying to eliminate the biases of those earlier writers, by removing greater or lesser improbabilities, or by investing the deeds with a finer or more up-to-date style – or indeed any combination of these (Marincola 1997: 95–117). History, as the ancients saw it, was the telling of the story of the past, not the solving of historical problems (see Quint. 10.1.31). Here, then, we must be clear: when Wiseman says that ancient historians did not put their authorities to the question, he means this, of course, in a very specific (and modern) way. But they did in fact put them to the question; it was just that the questions they asked were not the ones we would.

A word here about bias. Ancient writers had the keenest eye for partiality, and they consistently oppose "truth" not to "falsehood" (as we might expect) but to "partiality" or "bias" (Woodman 1988: 71–74, 79–83; T. Luce 1989). Now given that the people who wrote history were often men of public affairs, it was not surprising perhaps that readers would have an eye out for how historical characters treated themselves and their opponents. Yet at the same time, the ancients speak only occasionally and very briefly about the difficulty of finding out what actually happened in the past. Thucydides' remarks on the faulty memory and prejudice of his informants (1.22.3), or Cassius Dio's observations on the difficulty of acquiring information under the empire (53.19) are the exception; more commonly, Thucydides' "difficulty" of discovering what actually happened became in the later tradition the "effort" required for writing history in its form as a literary work (cf. Isoc. *Paneg.* 13; Diod.

1.4.1; Sall. *Cat.* 3.2). The matter is difficult to explain, but two points should be noted. First, since bias usually revealed itself in the invention of things that did not happen or the suppression of those that did (cf. Cic. *De oratore* 2.62), a charge of partiality did reflect on the historian's inquiry and on his attitude towards the facts (so Marincola 1997: 160–62). Second, ancient writers may discount the difficulty of finding out what actually happened because of their beliefs in the consistency of people's characters or in assumptions of universality in human nature. In other words, given a few established actions, they may have felt it was an easy matter to then connect the points in such a way as to make a cohesive narrative (cf. Walbank 1993 on Polybius, although the observations there could be extended to all ancient historians).

However that may be, it remains the case that for non-contemporary history the historian based himself on tradition, nor could he do otherwise, since the rejection of the tradition *tout court* would have called into question not only what might be known about the past but also the ethical framework within which both private and personal morality was formed. In other words, because ancient historiography was so closely connected with a people's identity and its reinforcement, the doubt over whether one's ancestors really did this or that could lead ultimately to a questioning of what it meant to be an Athenian or a Spartan or a Roman.

Finally, historiography in antiquity was a genre with pretensions to usefulness. Nearly every Greek and Roman historian asserts that his work will be useful and that the reader will learn from his work (Avenarius 1956: 22–26 collects many of them). That by itself was not determinative of anything: what *was* important was the kind of learning that history offered, and this involved predictability and the correction of one's own life. In this kind of learning, the thing to be learned could only be apprehended if it was similar to something else or partook of a pattern (Shrimpton 1997: 114–15); indeed, its similarity to past events was in large part the guarantee of its truth (Gentili and Cerra 1975: 19–45).

Patterning in ancient historiography arose because history needs to turn disparate facts into a meaningful whole. If history is just "one damn thing after another" it cannot offer much beyond individual and unrelated incidents, and it certainly cannot afford instruction. Thus a desire for pattern: Herodotus, for example, has each of his four Persian kings move to the edges of the earth, where a rugged people repulse them: Cyrus against the Massagetae (1.204–14), Cambyses against the Ethiopians (3.17–25), Darius against the Scythians (4.89–144), and Xerxes against the Greeks (Books 7–9 *passim*). This produces a recognizable pattern (Immerwahr 1966), but at the cost of discarding certain inconvenient facts, such as Cambyses' actual achievements in Egypt (Gammie 1986) or Darius's limited but successful conquests in the Black Sea area (Gardiner-Garden 1987; Georges 1987).

At the same time, historians were not reluctant to borrow (either consciously or unconsciously) time-established motifs from their predecessors. Thucydides, it has been argued, modeled his extended narrative of the Athenian attempt to conquer Sicily in Books 6 and 7 on the pattern of Herodotus's account of the Persians' assault on the Greeks (Rood 1999). The historian might also interpret characters in the light of his predecessors' portraits of similar figures: Sallust's Catiline is a model for both

Livy's Hannibal (J. Clauss 1997: 169–82; on the larger phenomenon, Miles 1995: 75–109) and Tacitus's Sejanus (Martin and Woodman 1989: 84–85). This ahistorical treatment was facilitated by history's claim to teach moral values, and teach them in a timeless way.

The modern academic and professionalized study of history has divorced the genre from this sort of learning, and has thereby been able to examine societies far different from the historian's own, without the sense that these societies either had anything to teach or contributed in any way to the identity of the examining society. Moreover, modern academics pursuing history do not generally believe that their research will have universal or near-universal application. The ancients, by contrast, did, and they made it a cornerstone of their historiography. The desire to write something that would have continued applicability, either political or moral, determined what they focused on and how they formed their interest.

5   Conclusion

What all of these interlocking aspects led to was a history and a society where continuity and consistency – of character, of disposition, of action, of viewpoint – was of primary importance. In this respect historiography merely reflected the values of society; it did not direct them and it certainly did not challenge them. It is not so much that the ancients were guilty of "unhistorical thinking" as that their focus from the start was on different things from ours, and their appreciation of change, while always present, revealed itself in a narrow band of interest: rise and fall of empires, changes of fortunes of individuals and countries, and the constant and insistent dichotomy of whether one ruled or was ruled. There were deep-seated reasons – political, social, moral, and even literary – why this was so, and why the ancients could not accept, and possibly would not have understood, the notion that the past was a foreign country.

FURTHER READING

The debate over the nature of ancient historiography is spread over many publications, but representative positions can be found in the following (to limit ourselves to English-language publications): Wiseman 1979a; Brunt 1980a; Fornara 1983b; Cornell 1986; Woodman 1988; Moles 1993; see also D. Potter 1999a: 121–38 (with very useful treatment of the background and interesting modern comparanda); and, from a different perspective, C. Pelling 2000: 61–81, 112–22. The essays in Marincola 2007 provide numerous viewpoints and approaches to Greek and Roman historiography

For some valuable observations on change in classical historiography, see Momigliano 1972. Discussions of Polybius's *anacyclosis* are legion, and are inevitably drawn into Polybius's notion of the "mixed constitution": see von Fritz 1954; Walbank 1957; Walbank 1972: 137–46; Podes 1991. On the rise and fall of states, de Romilly 1977 is illuminating.

CHAPTER THREE

Epigraphical Cultures of the Classical Mediterranean: Greek, Latin, and Beyond

Gregory Rowe

1 Introduction

The practice of inscribing and displaying texts on durable surfaces, or epigraphy, is characteristically Greek. Take, for example, a stele, or inscribed pillar, discovered a decade ago at Kaunos in Karia, Asia Minor (340s–330s BC; Blümel et al. 1998). The stele was found in the Kaunian stoa, among other stelai and statue-bases inscribed in Greek. And the document inscribed on the stele is typically Greek: a "proxeny" decree, recognizing two Athenians and their descendents as representatives and benefactors of the Kaunian people. But the document is not only Greek. It is also inscribed in Karian, the indigenous language of Kaunos. The text on the stele represents one of the few documents in Karian from Karia itself – most are from Egypt, where the Pharaohs employed Karian mercenaries – and the only public document in Karian. It even served to confirm the decipherment of the Karian script, which combines the Greek alphabet with some twenty additional characters whose values were unknown.

The decree from Kaunos reflects the interaction of two epigraphical cultures, one minor and regional, the other major and pan-Mediterranean. So the decree prompts a series of questions. What were the epigraphical cultures of the classical world? What peoples, or language-groups, inscribed texts on durable surfaces for display? How did different language-groups use inscriptions? How did different epigraphical cultures affect each other? In particular, how were minor epigraphical cultures like the Karian affected by Greek and Latin epigraphy? This chapter answers these questions by surveying the epigraphical cultures of the classical Mediterranean, c.800 BC to AD 300. It treats first Greek epigraphy and its relationship to the Greek city, then Latin epigraphy and its diffusion in the Roman empire, and lastly regional epigraphies and the influence of Greek and Latin. Its running theme is the way Greek and Latin continuously stimulated new epigraphical cultures.

2   The Alphabet and Greek Public Epigraphy

Classical Greek epigraphy was born with the invention of the alphabet. The alphabet was essentially distinct from the principal earlier Greek writing system, Linear B. Linear B was used not for display, but for palace archives; it was employed by a narrow range of writers and readers; and it ceased to be used some five centuries before alphabetic writing appeared. Where and when the alphabet emerged are disputed. Recent theories suggest that the alphabet was invented on Cyprus (Woodard 1997), perhaps as early as the tenth century BC (Brixhe 2004a); but the earliest known Greek alphabetic writing comes from eighth-century BC Italy. How the alphabet was invented is however clear: Greeks interpreted the unvoiced Phoenician letters ʿaleph, he, and ʿayin as the vowels *alpha* (a), *epsilon* (e), and *omicron* (o), and the semi-vocalic Phoenician letters *yodh* and *waw* as the vowels *iota* (i) and *upsilon* (u; later). In this way, Greeks created the first fully phonetic writing system, potentially capable of representing any language.

From the first, Greeks employed alphabetic epigraphy for a range of uses. They engraved epitaphs, the commonest type of inscription in all epigraphical cultures. An early Greek epitaph from Thera, carved into a large volcanic slab, commemorates Rheksanor, Arkhagetas, and Prokles, names meaning "he who breaks enemy lines," "first leader," and "far-renowned" (650–550 BC; *IG* 12.3.762). (Note that, because Greek names had meanings, their interpretation can be uncertain. Is *arkhagetas* (first leader) a name – or a noun qualifying Rheksanor or Prokles, and therefore the first public title recorded in Greek epigraphy?) Greeks used the alphabet for graffiti – graffiti which also seems to have had readers. Again on Thera, one writer carved into unquarried rock, "Phedipidas mounted. Timagoras and Eupheres and I mounted . . . Enpedokles engraved these (letters) and was made to dance, by Apollo!", and a second writer scratched "*pornos*" (meaning "male willing to be penetrated during anal intercourse") beside one of the names (end of eighth century BC; *IG* 12.3.536). The second writer had read what the first had written; so the earliest Greek epigraphy had readers as well as writers. Greeks used epigraphy to express their religious identities and beliefs. In what now seems to be the earliest Greek writing, from a graveyard in Gabii, Italy, an inscribed vase from a woman's grave reads εὔοιν – arguably a Bacchic greeting, welcoming the deceased woman as an initiate (c.770 BC; Peruzzi 1992). And Greeks used alphabetic epigraphy to transmit their culture and mythology. A verse-inscription on a drinking cup from the Euboean colony at Pithekoussai (Ischia), Italy, reads, "I am Nestor's cup, good to drink from. Whenever someone drinks from this cup, immediately the pleasure of beautifully crowned Aphrodite will seize him." The verses are written right to left, as in Phoenician, and they allude to the story in the *Iliad* or an Iliadic song of a cup that only Nestor could lift (*Nestor's*

Cup: 750–700 BC; ML 1; cf. Hom. *Il.* 11.632–37). In this way, Greeks introduced the Homeric heroes into the cultures of Italy, where they would reappear as founders of cities, like Aeneas.

In the seventh century BC, Greeks began using inscriptions for collective, or communal, expressions. Through this public epigraphy, we can trace the evolution of the Greek *polis* and its institutions. Cretan cities used epigraphy to display their laws. The oldest Cretan law – and the oldest Greek public inscription – is the earliest of eight laws inscribed on the wall of the Temple of Apollo Delphinios at Dreros. The law prohibits officials' succeeding themselves in office, and contains the first epigraphical attestation of the word *polis* (650–600 BC; ML 2). We learn that the Dreran *polis* comprised magistrates, popular assembly, and council (*kosmos, damioi*, and "the twenty of the *polis*"), the tripartite structure that would become universal in the Mediterranean. At pan-Hellenic sanctuaries, cities forged treaties under divine sanction and posted them on bronze plaques at the gods' temples. (Greeks normally favored marble for inscriptions, and seem to have reserved bronze for treaties.) An early treaty from Olympia, between Elis and Heraia, distinguishes between the private, public, and collective capacities of individuals (525–500 BC; ML 17): "If anyone harms this writing, whether private citizen or official or community (*wetas, telesta*, or *damos*), he shall be liable for the sacred penalty written here." By the end of the sixth century BC, the Athenian *boule* (council) and people were publishing their decrees in marble on the Acropolis. The oldest-known Athenian decree is inscribed in vertical lines running down a tapering stele; the letters of each line are aligned with those of the following line, as on a grid, in the style called *stoichedon* (in rank and file) that came to characterize Athenian public documents. The decree, which is no longer complete, lays down terms for Athenian *klerouchs* (settlers) on Salamis (*IG* 1³.1; ML 14): *klerouchs* must pay taxes and serve Athens militarily, lease land only to kinsmen (?), provide arms worth 30 drachmae, and submit themselves to an archon. As it happens, these terms embody all three spheres of what Aristotle would identify as the citizen's rights and responsibilities with respect to the *polis*: military, financial, and deliberative (archons were chosen by lot from an elected list).

In fifth-century BC Athens Greek inscriptions became a primary political tool. Athens used inscriptions to proclaim its wealth and power, and listed the 'allied' cities, one-sixtieth of whose tribute was offered to the Goddess Athena, on a massive 3.66-meter stele on the Acropolis – the temple records now known as the first of the Athenian Tribute Lists (454/453–440/439 BC; ML 39). Athens also used inscriptions to govern its empire and impose its institutions. Thus, the Athenian Standards Decree, requiring allies to use Athenian coins, weights, and measures, was diffused by Athenian heralds, engraved by local Athenian governors, and displayed in the agora of each city (ML 45). Copies of the Athenian Standards Decree in fact survive from seven different allied cities, Syme, Kos, Siphnos, Smyrna, Odessa, Hamaxitos, and Aphytis, where a second fragment has recently emerged (Hatzopoulos 2000–2003).

From the fourth century BC on, other Greek cities followed suit, and inscribed long, retrospective documents that expressed their place in history and in the

Hellenistic and Roman worlds. Using backward-looking inscriptions to secure future political ends went back to the aftermath of the Persian Wars, when cities and individuals inscribed claims about their contributions to the Greek cause in order to secure their place in the postwar world. These were cities like Corinth, which boasted on an inscription at Salamis, "O friend! In the well-watered city of Corinth we once lived. But we now lie in Ajax's island of Salamis. Here we captured Phoenician ships and Persian, and we saved holy Greece from the Medes" (early fifth century BC; ML 24). They were individuals like the Spartan general Pausanias, who added to Apollo's thank-offering at Delphi – a golden tripod atop a six-meter column listing the Greek cities that had fought the war – the epigram, "Leader of the Greeks when he destroyed the army of the Medes, Pausanias dedicated this memorial to Phoebus" – an epigram which Pausanias's fellow Spartans promptly erased (cf. ML 27). At times, historical inscriptions were anodyne epigraphic expressions of local pride. At Paros, birthplace of Archilochos, the local shrine to the poet was adorned with five inscribed stelai (264/263 BC; Chaniotis 1988: 23–34, 57–68; cf. Clay 2004): one (the *Parian Marble*) relating the history of Greece "from Kekrops, the first king of Athens," down to the present; two relating Archilochos's biography, "dating his deeds according to each Parian archon," and quoting from his poetry; and two explaining the foundation of Archilochos's cult – how the young Archilochos had encountered the Muses while bringing a cow to market, lost the cow, but received a lyre. Other times, real or forged historical documents were produced to create precedents for present policies. Doubtless, third-century BC Troezen wished to remind Athens of past friendship when it inscribed a document purporting to be the fifth-century Athenian Decree of Themistokles on the eve of the Battle of Salamis (ML 23). The supposed Athenian decree set out measures for preparing the Athenian fleet and for sending Athenian evacuees abroad, namely, to Troezen. The text of the Decree of Themistokles can only be as reliable as any posterior historical source, but the inscription is an incontrovertible part of third-century Troezenian history. In the Hellenistic and Roman worlds, retrospective inscriptions became matters of political necessity. Hellenistic kings and Roman emperors ruled cities by means of letters, much as Athens had ruled by means of the Athenian Standards Decree. Cities were expected to publish royal letters, along with civic decrees confirming their terms. And cities did so, because there was no other way to advertise any honors and protect any privileges they had received. One example among thousands comes from Pergamon during the final years of Attalid rule (142–135 BC; Welles, *RC* 65–67). On a marble stele, Pergamenes inscribed three royal letters and a civic decree dating from the previous seven years and pertaining to one Athenaios of Kyzikos and the civic priesthoods he had received from the Attalids. The third royal letter describes how Queen Stratonike had introduced a "new ancestral" god to Pergamon and "given orders about the sacrifices and processions and mysteries which are to be held for the god." "In order, therefore, that the honors of the god and the grants made to Athenaios may remain inviolable and unchanged for ever, we decided that the ordinances written by us be entered in your sacred laws." In their subsequent decree, Pergamenes could only amend the city's laws according to the queen's orders and declare the laws sovereign for ever.

3   The Diffusion of Latin Epigraphy

It used to be thought that the Latin alphabet was derived from the Greek alphabet by way of Etruscan; it is now thought that the Latin alphabet was derived from the Greek directly. The point of transmission was the Bacchic community at Gabii, in whose graveyard the earliest specimen of Greek writing was found (section 2 above). From the same graveyard also comes the earliest known Latin writing, another Bacchic greeting to a female initiate inscribed on a vessel (650–550 BC; Peruzzi 1992): "*saluetod tita*," "protected from harm, be well." Certainly, early Latin epigraphy was profoundly influenced by Greek. On a thin bronze plate from Lanuvium, once affixed to a votive object, the Latin dedication reads: "to Castor and Pollux, young men" (550–500 BC; *ILLRP* 2.1271a). The word for "young men," "*qurois*," is Greek (*kouros*) and declined in the Greek fashion; the word might be described as a loan-word from Greek in a Latin text – or as a Greek word in a bilingual text. Yet, with Etruscan and other Italic languages like Oscan and Umbrian, early Latin shared a distinctly Italian epigraphical culture, a culture consisting mainly of epitaphs and ex-votos, but also including several significant sacred laws. The earliest Latin sacred law is the *Lapis Niger* from the Roman Forum. Inscribed in vertical lines on four sides of a square pillar, the *Lapis Niger* prohibits yoked animals from fouling a precinct. It also contains the word *rex* ("*recei*") – a witness either to the Etruscan kings of Rome, or, if the inscription is later, to a priest named after the kings. More importantly, the *Lapis Niger* provides a strong argument that the language of archaic Rome was Latin, not Etruscan (*Lapis Niger*: c.500 BC; *ILLRP* 3).

Latin epigraphy came into its own from about 200 BC, the same time Latin literature as we know it was born and Rome became the leading power in the Mediterranean. In the western Mediterranean, Latin epigraphy was distinguished by its wide diffusion. Several factors contributed to this diffusion. One was self-promotion by Roman officials. Like the Roman state itself, Latin epigraphy provided a stage on which individual Romans could be seen performing deeds and demonstrating virtues. The earliest Latin epitaph, for L. Cornelius Scipio Barbatus (*cos.* 298 BC), was composed posthumously c.200 BC and inscribed two centuries later. It shows Scipio Barbatus performing Homeric deeds (sacking cities, taking hostages) and demonstrating Homeric virtues (bravery, wisdom, beauty) in the un-Homeric context of Roman elective office (c.200 BC; *ILLRP* 309): "Lucius Cornelius Scipio Barbatus, son of Gnaeus, a brave and wise man, whose beauty was most equal to his courage, who was consul, censor, aedile among you. He seized Tarausia, Cisauna in Samnium. He subdues all Lucania, and he leads away hostages!" This proud Latin epigraphy was first brought outside Italy by L. Aemilius Paullus (*cos.* 182 BC). On a bronze tablet from Spain, Paullus inscribed a decree freeing a group of loyal Spanish slaves "provided that the Roman people and the senate so wish" (191–89 BC; *ILLRP* 514). (Or did he? Such inscriptions were normally set up by those whom they benefited; so the first Latin inscription from outside Italy may have been the work of Spanish ex-slaves.) At Delphi, Paullus also set up the first Latin inscription in the Greek world (*ILLRP* 323). Taking over a monumental equestrian statue from his defeated adversary in the

Battle of Pydna (168 BC), Paullus inscribed on the base: "Lucius Aemilius, son of Lucius, commander, seized (this) from King Perseus and the Macedonians."

Another factor contributing to the diffusion of Latin epigraphy was the Roman state's active promulgation of its laws and decrees. The oldest inscribed Roman senatorial decree, outlawing Bacchic rites like those once performed at Gabii, was to be read aloud in municipal assemblies for three eight-day periods, inscribed in bronze, and displayed where it could be most easily read in each Italian town (*SC de Bacchanalibus*: 186 BC; *ILLRP* 511). The surviving copy of the decree, on a bronze plaque with nail-holes where it was affixed to a wall, is marked "in the Teuranus territory" and was found near the village of Tiriolo in Bruttium, southern Italy. At the end of the second century BC, with the Gracchi, publication of Roman statutes became an explicit part of a populist program. The seemingly forbidding legalese of Roman statutes – their abbreviations, their chains of apparently synonymous clauses – was a recognized way of conferring authority and solemnity (Meyer 2004). In any case, actual literacy and readership levels are less important than the fact that the Roman state presumed that its subjects had universal access to literacy. With Augustus and the Principate, the diffusion of Latin inscriptions increased sharply, and the Roman state began to produce marble inscriptions as well as bronze. The Roman senate's honors for the dead prince Germanicus, for instance, were promulgated in Rome, in colonies and municipalities in Italy and abroad, and in the most frequented places of the provinces; copies of the honors have emerged in marble from Rome and in bronze from Etruria and southern Spain (*Tabb. Siarensis* and *Hebana*; Crawford 1996: no. 37). The senate also decreed inscribed arches for Germanicus in Rome, Syria, and Germany, and eulogies by Tiberius and the younger Drusus are inscribed in bronze at locations of their choosing. The senate's words about Tiberius's eulogy exemplify the paternalism underlying Roman public epigraphy: the eulogy would be "handed down in eternal remembrance . . . because the senate judged that it would be useful to the youth of the next generation and of posterity."

Latin public epigraphy, unlike Greek, was never confined to cities and sanctuaries. Diplomas were carried wherever Roman veterans traveled. Milestones stood wherever Roman roads ran. Surviving diplomas are copies of the original bronzes that hung on the Capitol in Rome. Nearly always the copies are themselves bronze, on plaques a little larger than a paperback book which were sandwiched together and sealed to provide inner and outer copies of the text. Diplomas were used by veterans to prove their status and secure privileges, much as posted inscriptions were used by cities. Milestones were round pillars six Roman feet high recording distances and the date of their erection. Their banality is illustrated by a milestone on the road from Tacape to Capsa in North Africa (AD 14–15; *ILS* 151). While their legionary brothers on the Rhine and Danube were in open revolt, the Legion II Augusta greeted the new emperor Tiberius by laying a road, erecting a milestone, and dating the milestone to the first or second year of the reign of "Tiberius Caesar Augustus, holding the tribunician power for the 16th time." Lastly, Latin epigraphy was widely diffused because, for Rome's subjects, putting up Latin inscriptions was part of becoming Roman. Their fellow Celtiberians having just been conquered, the newly formed senate of Contrebia in the Ebro valley of Spain used Roman law to settle a local dispute and inscribed its decision on a bronze plaque, in flawless Latin: the Contrebians adopted Latin epigraphic practice alongside Roman law and the Latin language (*Tab. Contrebiensis*: 89 BC; Richardson 1983). At about the same time, the citizens of Heraclea in Lucania gave themselves an inscribed municipal code by simply copying chunks of Roman statutes out on a reused bronze plaque, without even changing the name in the text from Rome to Heraclea (*Tab. Heracleensis*: Riccobono *FIRA* 1.13). Even when the Roman state designed a text for dissemination, subjects were left to acquire the text and inscribe it. Thus only twenty years after Vespasian had granted municipal status to the towns of Spain, did the citizens of Irni in Baetica acquire and inscribe their copy of the Flavian Municipal Law, leaving us the longest Latin inscription known from the classical world (*Lex Irnitana*: AD 91; González 1986). We possess six of the original ten tablets, each inscribed in three columns; the original inscription would have been more than nine meters wide and the text some 1,500 lines long.

In the East, Latin and Greek epigraphy merged to form a hybrid Greco-Latin epigraphic culture. Much of Roman state epigraphy in the East was in the Greek language; it included senatorial decrees and magistrates' letters (Sherk 1969), statutes (cf. the *Lex de provinciis praetoriis*, with variant Greek translations from Knidos and Delphi: Crawford 1996: no. 12), and administrative laws (Neronian customs law from Ephesos: AD 62; Cottier et al. 2008). In the case of the most famous Latin inscription of all, the *Res Gestae* of Augustus, the badly damaged Latin text has to be reconstructed on the basis of better-surviving Greek translations. The *Res Gestae* was originally inscribed in Latin on bronze pillars flanking the entrance to Augustus's Mausoleum in Rome, but it survives only in Latin copies and Greek translations from three communities in Galatia, Asia Minor. The bilingual *Res Gestae* is one example of the bilingual epigraphy that emerged in Roman colonies in the East, eastern cities with large Roman populations, and western cities with large Greek populations. Everywhere, Greek absorbed Latin loan-words, especially military terms. Even Greek syntax came to be marked by Latinisms. At first, Latin dedications had followed Greek syntax, with the honorand's name in the accusative case, as in a second-century BC dedication from the Italici on Sicily to L. Cornelius Scipio (193 BC; *ILLRP* 320): "*Italicei L. Cornelium Scipionem honoris caussa*." By the first century BC, Greek dedications were following Latin syntax, with the honorand's name in the dative case, as in a bilingual dedication to C. Salluius Naso from two Phrygian peoples found at Lake Nemora in Italy (73 BC; *ILLRP* 372): "*C. Salluio C. f. Nasoni*; Γ[αί]ω<ι> Σαλλυίωι Γαίου υἱῶι Νάσωνι." The Latin dative became normal in Greek epigraphy, especially in dedications to the emperor, where, however, it retained the connotation that the honorand was divine.

4   Greek, Latin, and Regional Epigraphy

From the seventh century BC on, Greek spawned a number of regional alphabetic epigraphical cultures in both Anatolia and Italy. In Anatolia, the different language groups could also draw on indigenous epigraphical traditions. Phrygians, who spoke a language close to Greek, and whose culture filled the vacuum in central Anatolia left by the collapse of second-millennium Hittite civilization, were the first to adopt the Greek alphabet. In the sixth and fifth centuries, the Phrygians were followed by speakers of languages deriving from second-millennium Luwian: Karian, Lykian, and Lydian. The inscriptions of these peoples were mostly funerary. When they wished to compose longer, public texts, they could look to Hittite and Luwian models, but they now added Greek translations. Thus, the longest surviving Phrygian inscription combines indigenous and Greek epigraphical cultures (*Vezirhan stele:* late fifth to early fourth century BC; Brixhe 2004b: 42–67). The *Vezirhan stele* is topped with reliefs of the Phrygian goddess the Great Mother, a hunting scene, and a banqueting scene. Below the reliefs, the original Phrygian dedication and a Greek summary are inscribed. Kallias (a Greek name), son of Abiktos (a Phrygian name), dedicated a sanctuary to the Great Mother. Kallias hoped that whoever harmed the sanctuary would be deprived of life and progeny, and he wished happiness to those who came and read his inscription. Similarly, the longest Lykian text and the longest Aramaic text of the Persian period are both found on a trilingual Lykian-Greek-Aramaic stele from Xanthos (357 BC; Metzger et al. 1979). The Lykian original begins with a list of local officials appointed by the local satrap before giving the text of a Xanthian decree moved by the satrap – a documentary form with neo-Hittite precedents.

Italy lacked indigenous epigraphical traditions. But Etruscans, adopting the Greek alphabet in the seventh century BC, soon developed an important epigraphical culture – with more than 13,000 inscriptions, the largest of the classical world after Greek and Latin, dwarfing Latin in archaic Italy. The Etruscan adoption of the Greek alphabet has left a particularly vivid witness (700–650 BC; Jeffery and Johnston 1990: 236–39, pl. 98). Across the top frame of an ivory writing tablet from a child's grave in Marsiliana d'Albegna, northern Etruria, a model Greek alphabet has been incised; on the writing surface below, the alphabet would have been copied by the child. The model was Greek, but the copy would be Etruscan, and would discard several Greek letters that Etruscan never employed. Other Etruscan abecedaria attest to a similarly conscious adoption of the Greek writing system throughout Etruria. In principle, Etruscans might have taken their script directly from Phoenicians, since there is a bilingual Etruscan-Phoenician dedication on gold leaves from Pyrgi, the port of Etruscan Caere (c.500 BC; Morandi 1982). But the Pyrgi gold leaves represent the only Phoenician writing known from Italy. The gold leaves are more important for confirming, at a date precisely contemporaneous with the *Lapis Niger* from Rome, that Etruscans did have a figure they called king (*mlk* in Phoenician), though he seems to have served only a three-year term. Etruscan epigraphy consists mostly of epitaphs and stereotyped dedications. The handful of longer Etruscan texts are difficult to decipher, but seem to be sacred laws. The most recent of these is a transfer of (sacred?) land between two parties inscribed on the front and back of a bronze tablet from second-century Cortona (*Tab. Cortonensis*; c.200 BC; Agostiniani and Nicosia 2000).

Other peoples in Italy also adopted the Greek alphabet directly. We have seen new evidence from Gabii that Latin speakers did so. In southern Italy, the Messapii used Greek characters to produce a series of gravestones, and the first text of the Oenotri in their own language is now receiving scholarly attention (fifth–sixth century BC; Lazzarini and Poccetti 2001). In central Italy, however, speakers of the Italic languages other than Latin adopted the Greek alphabet via Etruscan. They used the alphabet to create epigraphical cultures that were comparable to Latin in extent and included public as well as private inscriptions. Thus the Samnites, whose language was Oscan, set down the order of sacrifices to be performed in a sanctuary to Ceres on two sides of a bronze tablet (*Agnone Tablet:* c.250 BC; Del Tutto Palma 1996). And the Umbrians used both sides of seven bronze tablets to record the acts of the Atiedian Brothers, a public priesthood, over several generations – at 400 lines, the longest bronze inscription from classical Italy (*Tabb. Iguvinae:* late second to early first century BC; Prosdocimi 1984). Two points must be emphasized about these Italian epigraphical cultures. The first is that they were interrelated. One indication of this is the physical similarity of their inscriptions. The Etruscan *Tabula Cortonensis*, the Oscan *Agnone Tablet*, and the Umbrian *Tabulae Iguvinae* are all bronze tablets, with handles, that were inscribed on both sides. Presumably these are to be associated with Roman *tabulae ansatae*, tablets with handles. This epigraphical tradition seems to have been foreign to the Greek world. The other point that needs to be emphasized about Italian epigraphical cultures is that they all withstood Rome and the Latin language – for a time. Thus the Oscan *Agnone Tablet* seems to date from the period just after the Samnites were defeated by Rome. The first half of the Umbrian *Tabulae Iguvinae* is written right to left in the Etruscan-derived Umbrian alphabet, and the second half left to right in Latin characters, without noticeable change of content. And the Latin text on one side of the *Tabula Bantina* seems to predate the Oscan text on the other (*Tab. Bantina*; Latin: late second century BC; M. Crawford 1996: no. 7; Oscan: early first century BC; no. 13). However, with the growth of Greek and Roman power came epigraphical standardization, and the first generation of regional alphabetic epigraphical cultures disappeared. Greek cities adopted a uniform script between 450 and 350 BC and a uniform dialect (*koine*) in the centuries following; and the regional epigraphies of Anatolia all disappeared in the early Hellenistic period. Etruscan and Italic epigraphy other than Latin disappeared after the Social War and the unification of Italy under Roman rule (91–89 BC).

Yet at all times during the classical period there were Mediterranean epigraphical cultures other than Greek and Latin. Particularly under Roman rule, regional epigraphical cultures flourished anew. For one, Semitic-language epigraphies had a continuous history throughout the period. And these Semitic epigraphical cultures continued to develop in company with Greek and Latin. In North Africa and elsewhere in the western Mediterranean, Punic (Carthaginian, down to 146 BC), neo-Punic (after 146 BC), and Berber (or Libyan: a Semitic language in neo-Punic characters) all appear in bilingual inscriptions alongside Greek and Latin. Egyptian hieroglyphics continued to be inscribed until the fourth century AD; hieroglyphics were joined by Egyptian demotic, a cursive hieroglyphic that became an epigraphical language under the Ptolemies (an example is the trilingual hieroglyphic-demotic-Greek *Rosetta Stone*). Later, in the Christian period, the Egyptian language would come to be written in Greek characters (Coptic). In the Near East, Hebrew, Jewish Aramaic, and the Nabataean, Palmyrene, and Edessan (Syriac) dialects of Aramaic all appear in bilingual inscriptions with Greek and sometimes Latin. The most striking example of the cohabitation of Semitic and Greek epigraphy is the bilingual public epigraphy of Palmyra in Roman Syria. The Palmyrene-Greek epigraphy includes a monumental tariff from the reign of Hadrian covering, it has been shown, not international, but local trade (AD 137; Matthews 1984). A slighter but no less telling example of ongoing regional epigraphy in the Roman period comes from Anatolia, where a second generation of inscribed indigenous languages using Greek letters appeared. These Anatolian languages included Sidetic, Pisidian, and, after a hiatus of eight centuries, neo-Phrygian. All were limited to private uses. Neo-Phrygian, for example, was used only for imprecations at the end of Greek-language epitaphs, such as, "(Greek:) Aristoxenos, for his own father-in-law Adymetos, son of Thalameidas; (neo-Phrygian:) let whoever harms this grave be punished" (AD 250–300; Brixhe and Waelkens 1981). But the survival of the language, and its reappearance in Greek characters in a Greek epigraphic context, have a lot to tell us about the culture and society of the Greco-Roman Mediterranean. Two of the most arresting cases of emergent regional epigraphical expression come from the Celtic world. One is from first-century BC Spain and the region of Contrebia – from the same time and place as the *Tabula Contrebiensis*, the Latin inscription in which a newly formed local senate settled a dispute by applying Roman law (section 3 above). From the same excavations has now come a monumental bronze tablet inscribed in Celtiberian, a Celtic language written in Iberian characters, themselves a combination of Greek and Phoenician (*Botorrita* 3: early first century BC; Beltrán et al. 1996). While the inscription is not fully deciphered, its overall appearance – four neat columns containing some 300 personal names – eloquently testifies to the influence of Latin epigraphy. The Celtiberians simultaneously embraced the Latin language and Roman institutions and employed alphabetic epigraphy to express their own language and culture. The same can be said of the second-century AD Celtic calendar from Coligny in France (fig. 3.1: second century AD; Olmsted 1992). The surviving 73 fragments of the calendar were originally part of a single 148 × 90 cm bronze tablet, presenting, in 16 columns, the 62-month Celtic lunisolar cycle, with peg-holes to keep track of the date. The language of the calendar is Celtic, the letters and numerals are Latin. Thus Latin writing and Latin epigraphy enabled Celts to preserve and display their month names, festivals, and mathematical and astronomical knowledge.

5 Conclusion

During the Christian period, Greek and Latin epigraphy continued, and new regional scripts and epigraphical cultures emerged (Coptic, Germanic, Armenian). But the primary function of these new scripts was the diffusion of the Bible; their epigraphic use was secondary. The years 800 BC to AD 300 had marked a distinct era in the history of epigraphy, in which Greeks devised the alphabet and produced a public epigraphy, Romans spread Latin epigraphy, and others took up the Greek and Latin scripts and epigraphical practices to create their own epigraphical cultures across the Mediterranean. In light of the mutual influences, it may be better to speak of a single,

3.1 Portion of the Celtic calendar from Coligny, France (first or second century AD). This 148 × 90 cm bronze inscription sets out a five-year perpetual calendar of sixty-four months (5 × 12 lunar months of 29 or 30 days + 2 intercalary months before the first and third years), with peg-holes for marking the date. In the portion shown here, M is an abbreviation of MID, "month," EQVOS and SAMON are names of months, and ANMAT and MAT mean "unlawful" and "lawful for public business." Below, the days of the month are listed in two sets of fifteen, and ritual observances are indicated for most days. ATENOVX means "renewal" and marks the beginning of the second phase of the lunar cycle. The Coligny calendar shows how Celts used Roman letters, numerals, and epigraphical practices to express their language, calendar, and astronomical knowledge. (Photo: Christian Thioc, Musée Gallo-Romain de Lyon, France)

manifold epigraphical culture during the classical period: a culture dominated by Greek and Latin, but one in which indigenous languages, like Karian, could always be read.

FURTHER READING

The epigraphist's indispensable companion is the *Guide de l'épigraphiste* (Bérard et al. 2000), a selective bibliography of ancient and medieval epigraphy now approaching some 3,000 items. The *Guide* catalogs publications of Greek inscriptions down to the fall of Constantinople and Latin inscriptions down to the Merovingian period, and includes a section on "Epigraphies périphériques," on which this chapter is based. The *Guide* also lists collections of documents by theme, monographs, reference-books, and works of leading epigraphists. An annual *Supplément* appears each June, and is available in pdf format at: www.antiquite.ens.fr/txt/dsa-publications-guidepigraphiste-fr.htm

For ancient languages see Woodard 2004 and, on bilingualism, Adams et al. 2002 and Adams 2003; for scripts see also Daniels and Bright 1996. The best introduction to ancient epigraphy is Millar 1983. For Greek epigraphy see also "epigraphy, Greek" in *OCD*[3] (Pleket) and the classic Robert 1961 (now available in Robert 2007). An excellent introduction to Latin epigraphy, particularly the journey from monument to edited text, is provided at the website of the upcoming supplement volume to *CIL* XIII (Germany): www.geschichte.uni-osnabrueck.de/ausstell/ausstell.html

For Latin see also "epigraphy, Latin" in *OCD*[3] (Reynolds) and Bodel 2001, which also treats Greek epigraphy. For Anatolian epigraphy see Neumann 1993; for Etruscan see "*Étrusque (Langue)*" in Leclant 2005 (Briquel); for Italic see "Italy, languages of" in *OCD*[3] (Penney).

One way to begin reading inscriptions in the original languages is with a manual that sets out complete texts. For Greek see Guarducci 1967–78 (4 vols.); cf. Guarducci 1987 (1 vol.; both in Italian). For Latin (and Greek relating to Roman history), Lassère 2005 now seems to replace the excellent Cagnat 1914 (both in French); very handy is Schumacher 1988 (in German); in English, Gordon 1983.

Another way to begin reading inscriptions is with an anthology that provides translations as well as original texts. For Greek see Pouilloux 1960 and Institut Fernand-Courby 1971 (in French); in English, one might try Rhodes and Osborne 2003 (fourth century BC). For Aramaic, Porten and Yardeni 1986; for Syriac, Drijvers and Healey 1998.

Manuals without texts include, for Greek, the wonderful McLean 2002 (Hellenistic and Roman periods); see also Woodhead 1959. Invaluable ancillaries to work on Greek public inscriptions are Rhodes and Lewis 1997 and Hansen et al. 2004.

There are also excellent anthologies offering only translations. In English, note Bagnall and Derow 2004 (Hellenistic Greece); Crawford and Whitehead 1983 (archaic and classical Greece), Austin 2006 (Hellenistic Greece; volumes in this series for republican and imperial Rome forthcoming); and the *Translated Documents of Greece and Rome* series: Fornara 1983 (archaic and classical Greece), Harding 1985 (fourth century BC Greece), Burstein 1985 (Hellenistic Greece), and Sherk 1984 (Roman East to Augustus) and 1988 (imperial Rome).

After the manuals and anthologies, one should read the classic annotated selections of inscriptions. For Greek there are Dittenberger, *Sylloge inscriptionum graecarum*[3] (*Syll*[3] or *SIG*[3]) and Dittenberger, *Orientis graeci inscriptiones selectae* (*OGIS*); see also Meiggs and Lewis 1988 (ML or *GHI*: archaic and classical). For Latin there are Degrassi, *Inscriptiones latinae liberae rei publicae* (*ILLRP*, republican) and Dessau, *Inscriptiones latinae selectae* (*ILS*). All have notes in Latin.

For an idea of the physical aspect of inscriptions, one might start with Hooker 1990 (hieroglyphics, Greek, Etruscan). For Greek inscriptions see Guarducci 1967–78. Images of dated Attic inscriptions can be found at the website of the Center for Epigraphical and Paleographical Studies (Ohio State University): http://omega.cohums.ohio-state.edu/epigraphy. For Latin see Gordon 1958–65 and Degrassi 1965. Images of Latin inscriptions can also be found at the website for *CIL* II (Spain): www2.uah.es/imagines_cilii. For the carving of Latin inscriptions, Susini 1983 is not to be missed.

The person doing in-depth epigraphical research will eventually want to consult the (rather unwieldy) standard corpora of inscriptions, organized by region. The basic collections of Greek inscriptions are, for the mainland and islands, *Inscriptiones graecae* (*IG*), and, for Asia Minor, *Tituli Asiae Minoris* (*TAM*), *Monumenta Asiae Minoris Antiqua* (*MAMA*), and *Inschriften griechischer Städte aus Kleinasien* (*IK*). The present survey is restricted to the Mediterranean world; for Greek inscriptions from east of the Euphrates see Canali De Rossi 2004. For Latin there is the *Corpus inscriptionum latinarum* (*CIL*); see also *Inscriptiones Italiae* (*InscrIt* or *InscrItal*), *Supplementa Italica* (*SupplIt*) (Italy), and *Roman Inscriptions of Britain* (*RIB*). For Semitic languages see the *Corpus inscriptionum semiticarum* (*CIS*). For Celtic and other languages from the West besides Latin see Untermann 1975– (Spain) and Duval 1985 (Gaul). For Etruscan there is the *Corpus inscriptionum etruscarum* (*CIE*). For a refreshing exception to linguistic parochialism note the *Inscriptions of Israel/Palestine* project, which will publish texts in Hebrew, Aramaic, Greek, Latin, and other languages: www.stg.brown.edu/projects/Inscriptions (still in its infancy).

More convenient than the bound corpora are searchable electronic databases, which now incorporate most Greek and Latin inscriptions. For Greek see the website of the Packard Humanities Institute, http://epigraphy.packhum.org/inscriptions (replacing the earlier CD-ROM #7), with inscriptions from corpora, thematic collections, monographs, and even journals. For Latin, the *Epigraphische Datenbank* Heidelberg (www.uni-heidelberg.de/institute/sonst/adw/edh) aims to give up-to-date texts and full bibliography for all Latin inscriptions; it dovetails with the *Electronic Archive of Greek and Latin Epigraphy* (*Eagle*), which comprises the *Epigraphic Database Roma*, www.edr-edr.it/index_it.html and, for Christian Rome, the *Epigraphic Database Bari*, www.edb.uniba.it

These databases are searchable by find-spot, material, individual word, name, date, and publication, but they take some getting used to. It is also important to note that in most cases the electronic editions of texts do not yet supersede printed ones.

Books still have their uses. For example, to find epigraphical instances of a particular Greek word, it is still best to start with the indexes to *SIG*[3] (mainland) and to *BE* (see Bérard et al. 2000 no. 1147; esp. Asia Minor). For other epigraphical research tools see Bérard et al. 2000 §8.

A standard format for digitally encoding inscriptions called *EpiDoc* has been proposed: http://epidoc.sourceforge.net

The best advertisement for *EpiDoc* is the electronic second edition of Charlotte RouECH's *Aphrodisias in Late Antiquity: The Late Roman and Byzantine Inscriptions*, http://insaph.kcl.ac.uk/ala2004, a model of economical and intuitive presentation.

Web portals to the world of epigraphy include the heavily annotated *Fonti epigrafiche* (Bologna), www.rassegna.unibo.it/epigrafi.html, and the well-organized *Épigraphie* (Louvain), http://bcs.fltr.ucl.ac.be/Epi.html

In English, see the websites of the American Society of Greek and Latin Epigraphy, http://asgle.classics.unc.edu/links.html, and the Centre for the Study of Ancient Documents (Oxford), www.csad.ox.ac.uk/index.html

New discoveries and new editions of old texts are surveyed in several annual publications. For Greek see the *Bulletin épigraphique,* published in the *Revue des études grecques* (*BE* or *Bull. ép*: extensive quotations), and *Supplementum epigraphicum graecum* (*SEG*: full texts of documents outside corpora). To keep track of new editions of Greek inscriptions see *Claros: Concordance of Greek inscriptions,* a by-product of the *Diccionario Griego-Español,* www.dge.filol.csic.es/claros/cnc/2cnc.htm

For texts relevant to Roman history see *L'Année épigraphique* (*AE*); also the quinquennial survey in the *Journal of Roman Studies* (most recently in vol. 97, 2007). For epigraphical bibliography see the newly expanded 'Epigraphie' section of *L'Année philologique* (*AnPhil*) and the annual supplements to Bérard et al. 2000 mentioned above.

Lastly, to get an idea of what can be done with inscriptions, it is instructive to read exemplary publications of single inscriptions: for Greek see Wörrle 1988; for Latin see Eck et al. 1996. It is also instructive to read historical essays and monographs that make masterly use of epigraphic evidence: for Hellenistic Greece see Habicht 1997 and Ma 1999; for Rome see Eck 1995– and 1996 and Ando 2000. For methodological considerations see Millar 1983 and Robert 1939, 1952, and 1961, and everything else by Louis Robert (see now Robert 2007; cf. Robert 1969–90). For a portrait of the modern epigraphist at work in the field see Ma 2000.

CHAPTER FOUR

Papyrology

Alan K. Bowman

1 Material, Methods, and Approaches

The contribution made by Egypt to the history of the Mediterranean world during the millennium from 332 BC to AD 642 when it was dominated by Greek and Roman institutions and culture was so immensely rich, diverse and important that it may seem banal to emphasize the fact that one of its major services was to provide a large part of that world with its supply of basic writing-material: the papyrus plant grew abundantly in the Nile delta, and sheets for writing were manufactured from its fibers in a process described in some detail by Pliny the Elder (*HN* 13.74–82, cf. Lewis 1974: 34–69). The use of papyri for writing was, of course, traditional in Egypt long before the conquest by Alexander the Great. Numerous papyri written in Egyptian hieratic and demotic survive, and the latter continued, albeit in dwindling quantities, well into the Roman period. Texts in Coptic appear from the fourth century AD onwards, and thousands of documents in Arabic have survived from the early Islamic period (Van Minnen 2007). The present survey focuses firmly on the Greek and Latin papyri from Egypt and elsewhere and on similar kinds of texts written on other media, with which papyrologists are concerned, principally ostraka (potsherds), wooden writing-tablets and parchment (that is, 'papyrus' as defined by Bagnall 1995: 9–10). It attempts to describe the character of the papyrological evidence and the discipline of papyrology, and to assess the contribution they make to our understanding of the history and culture of the Mediterranean in the Hellenistic, Roman and Byzantine periods.

The discipline of papyrology is, relatively speaking, a newcomer to the field of classical ancient history (Montevecchi 1973–88, Turner 1980, Van Minnen 1993 and 2007). The existence of significant quantities of papyri from antiquity first became known in Europe through the discovery of 800 carbonized rolls from Herculaneum in 1752, and the first edition of a documentary Greek papyrus from Egypt, the Charta Borgiana, appeared in 1787, a list of men assigned to the dyke-corvée in the Fayyum (Schow 1787). But it was not until the 1860s, with the appearance of several important literary rolls, that the potential of this source of written material from Egypt began to be more fully appreciated. The acquisition of Greek papyri in significant quantities, both by excavation and by legitimate purchase on the antiquities market, began in the 1880s, as a result of which European and North American institutions, museums, learned societies, and universities (as well as wealthy individuals) began to accumulate important collections (Turner 1980: 25–41, A. Martin 2007). Major examples of such collections are those in Berlin, Vienna, Oxford, London, Florence, and Ann Arbor (http://lhpc.arts.kuleuven.ac.be/index.html).

The first half of the 1890s saw the earliest major publications of Greek documentary papyri (*P.Petrie* I, *P.Lond.* I, *BGU* I). The more or less unrestricted flow of papyri from Egypt continued unabated until the Second World War, but in the wake of Nasser's revolution much stricter controls were imposed, excavation was more carefully monitored, and the sale and export of papyri from Egypt became illegal (though not completely eradicated). But major new discoveries of papyri and ostraka in Egypt have continued and are available for study, and in addition there has been a steady and increasing accretion of similar texts, in smaller quantities, from places outside Egypt (see below).

The corpus of published Greek and Latin papyri, ostraka, and related texts now numbers approximately 60,000, of which about 7,500 are literary (Van Minnen, 2007, plus my own estimates of non-Egyptian documents). They are unevenly spread in time and place. Within Egypt, Alexandria and the Nile Delta are almost completely absent from the record, since the damp conditions there are not conducive to the survival of papyri. Given its cultural and administrative importance, the almost total absence of Alexandria is particularly regrettable. The surviving copy of its city-laws (*P.Hal.* 1) was found elsewhere, at Apollonopolis Magna (Edfu). The most important group of papyri originating in Alexandria was found at Herakleopolis (Abusir el Meleq, *BGU* IV 1050–61, 1098–1209, Bowman 2001, Brashear 1996, Schubart 1913), and the major find from the Delta is the carbonized papyri from Thmuis (some published as *P.Thmuis*). Most heavily represented are the Fayyum villages and the larger towns of Middle Egypt, such as Oxyrhynchus and Hermopolis, and Upper Egypt, where the area around Thebes is a particularly rich source of ostraka. The Oases and sites in the eastern desert have also made more of a showing recently, notably in the form of papyri and ostraka from Berenike (*O.Berenike* I–II), ostraka from the Roman quarries at Mons Claudianus (*O.Claud.* I–III), and papyri from Kellis in the Dakleh Oasis (*P.Kellis*). Apart from the dry physical conditions, there is no reason to suppose that the uneven spread is attributable to anything other than chance and the vagaries of archaeological investigation. Similarly in the chronological distribution, the graph shows a high level in the third century BC, a reduction in the second and first centuries, some increase in the first century AD, a sharp growth in the second and third centuries, some fall in the fourth, and a sharp decline in the fifth before it picks up again in the sixth. These trends do not reflect fluctuations in the incidence of documentation, but rather the location and composition of the deposits in which papyri were found, either in clandestine foraging or controlled archaeological investigations (Habermann 1998; for locations in Egypt, Map 2).

Outside Egypt, the picture is much more random and sporadic, but it is of great importance that similar kinds of texts have been found in widely scattered locations, tending to indicate that if Egypt is remarkable for the rate of survival of documents, it may be less untypical than was once thought in its habits of literacy and documentation (Cotton et al. 1995). Virtually all the non-Egyptian texts come from the Roman or late Roman/Byzantine period. The third-century archives of the military unit stationed at Dura-Europos on the Euphrates (*P.Dura*) have been known since the 1920s, and the Tablettes Albertini from Vandal Africa were also published several decades ago (Courtois et al. 1952). Very important collections of documents relating to the Roman army have accrued more recently: the first-century papyri from Herod's fortress at Masada (*P.Masada*), third-century ostraka from Bu-Djem in Libya (*O. Bu-Djem*), writing-tablets from Vindonissa in Switzerland (Speidel 1996) and from Vindolanda and Carlisle in northern Britain (fig. 4.1; *Tab.Vindol.* I–III; Tomlin 1998 = *Tab.Luguv.*). To these may be added three remarkable groups of papyri, the second-century archive of Babatha and related texts from the Dead Sea Caves in Judaea (*P.Yadin*, Cotton 1995), the papyri from Mesopotamia (*P.Euphrates*, third century), and the carbonized rolls from Petra (*P.Petra* I, sixth century). These documents can in no way rival the quantity of detailed information we can derive from Egyptian

4.1 Letter from Martius to Victor, c.180 AD, with address on right-hand fragment, from Vindolanda, *Tab. Vind.* III.670. (by permission of the British Museum and the Centre for the Study of Ancient Documents, University of Oxford)

texts, but they offer pinpricks of intense illumination for areas hitherto completely unrepresented in the documentary record.

In papyrological scholarship as in epigraphy, there are those whose principal activity consists of editing texts, very often texts of different genres (literary, documentary, theological), there are "applied papyrologists" who both edit texts and deploy them in broader synthesizing studies of Greek and Latin literature, or Ptolemaic, Roman, and Byzantine history, and there are those who simply comment. All types of activity are vital, but the provision of reliable and usable texts is the first and most basic requirement of papyrological scholarship (Turner 1973, 1980, Pestman 1990, Youtie 1974). Editing texts demands specialized skills and some knowledge of a wide range of sub-disciplines in classical scholarship. Of all the skills needed by an editor, the hardest to acquire and the one which undoubtedly requires some natural propensity is the paleographical, particularly in the case of cursive documentary texts where the scripts are generally much harder than the majuscule hands in which literary papyri are more often written. The mental processes involved in deciphering and transcribing papyri have never been better characterized than by the late H. C. Youtie (1973a: 26–27):

> In the face of such discouragements [sc. the poor physical state of the papyrus], in whatever combination they may occur, the transcriber repeatedly finds that his most strenuous efforts to obtain a reading are frustrated. His only hope lies in supplementing his knowledge of handwriting with as full an understanding as he can get of the scribe's purpose in writing the text. He tries to take account of the text as a communication, as a message, as a linguistic pattern of meaning. He forms a concept of the writer's intention and uses this to aid him in transcription. As his decipherment progresses, the amount of text that he has available for judging the writer's intention increases, and as this increases he may be forced to revise his idea of the meaning or direction of the entire text, and as the meaning changes for him, he may revise his reading of portions of the text which he had previously thought to be well read. And so he constantly oscillates between the written text and his mental picture of its meaning, altering his view of one or both as his expanding knowledge of them seems to make necessary. Only when they at last cover each other is he able to feel that he has solved his problem. The tension between the script and its content is then relaxed: the two have become one.

Beyond that, it is essential to appreciate what has gone into editing a text, and to use published editions *critically* and with sensitivity to the original which the edition represents. An editor's restorations must always be accepted with caution; readings and interpretations, especially those alleging some extraordinary or unique contribution to knowledge, have to be carefully scrutinized if possible against the original or a facsimile in the original edition or elsewhere (now helped by the increasing availability of on-line images): it is not unusual to find that in a first edition of a text ink traces have been overlooked, fragments misplaced, or restorations suggested which are too long for the lacuna.

From the outset, the aids to scholarly use and research in papyrology were generally effective and well organized, partly because the total corpus is far smaller and coherent than is the case with inscriptions (see, for example, Mitteis-Wilcken 1912).

Volumes of edited texts are often a miscellany, reflecting the nature of acquisition by the institution which owns the papyri, but the principal *instrumenta studiorum* were initiated early in the history of papyrology. Valuable lexica (Preisigke 1925–, Daris 1968), name-lists (Preisigke 1922, Foraboschi 1967), geographical gazetteers (Calderini 1935–2003), collections of scattered editions (Preisigke 1915–), and catalogs of corrections to edited texts (Preisigke-Bilabel 1922–) have long been, and continue to be, produced. The potential of many of the most exciting developments in Information Technology has been well appreciated and exploited by papyrologists in the past twenty years. This has led to the appearance of searchable on-line corpora and databases of various kinds, including some which present electronic texts with their full apparatus of critical signs and other conventions, as well as catalogs of high-quality digital images (see the websites and abbreviations listed at the end of this chapter). The latter, in conjunction with gazetteers of different collections and data-bases of texts by genre (LDAB, LHPC, GPBC), are particularly important because they now offer the opportunity to reconstruct the original context of groups of texts which were effectively dismembered by the often haphazard and capricious methods of acquisition in the late nineteenth and early twentieth centuries (Vandorpe 1994, A. Martin 2007). So too is the development of computer-based techniques of image enhancement for damaged, faded, abraded or carbonized texts, where multi-spectral imaging and other methods offer significant promise of improvement in visibility and reading of texts written in carbon ink, as well as incised documents. Such techniques are sometimes credited with miraculous epiphanies of hitherto invisible texts, but in practice improvements are more often gradual and incremental than dramatic and revelatory (Bowman-Deegan 1997, Bowman-Brady 2005, Bowman-Tomlin 2005). We can look forward not only to improving our understanding of published texts, but also to the continuing publication of the tens of thousands of unread texts in university and museum collections.

2   The Impact of the Papyri

The range, quantity and depth of information that has emerged from this heteroge-neous mass of material has had an enormous impact on the study of the classical world, so significant that Mommsen suggested that the twentieth century should be dubbed "the century of papyrology" (Van Minnen 1993). There is virtually no aspect of Greco-Roman history and culture that has remained untouched or unenhanced by the evidence of papyri and related texts. It is particularly important to emphasize that even the knowledge accrued from the papyri found in Egypt does not simply bear on the parochial affairs of the Ptolemaic kingdom or the Roman/Byzantine province of Egypt, although admittedly much of the historically valuable detail in the documents – administrative, social and economic – is specific to Egypt. Egypt was at all times after the conquest by Alexander part of a wider Greco-Roman universe. It is not difficult to highlight information in the papyri which bears on the wider politi-cal history of the Hellenistic and Roman worlds, and it gains added value when we can actually link the document and the information to a local context. The instability of the Ptolemaic dynasty in the struggle with the Seleukid Antiochos IV is vividly emphasized by Greek and demotic texts from the archive of Hor (Ray 1976). A letter of 130 BC records that "Paos [general of Ptolemy VIII] is sailing up . . . with abundant forces to subdue the mobs at Hermonthis and deal with them as rebels" (*Sel.Pap.* I.101). The internal strife under Ptolemy VIII, which amounted to civil war, announced a termination in the form of indulgences and benefactions granted in an Amnesty Decree of 118 BC, a copy of which was found among the papers of Menches, the village scribe of Kerkeosiris in the south-west Fayyum (*C.Ord.Ptol.* 53). A few years later preparations were made in the village of Tebtunis for the visit of a Roman senator, Lucius Memmius, "Let him be received with special magnificence, and take care that at the proper spots the guest-chambers be prepared . . . and that the gifts mentioned below be presented to him . . . and that the furniture for the guest-chamber, the tidbits for Petesouchos and the crocodiles, the conveniences for viewing the Labyrinth, and the offering and sacrifices be provided" (*Sel.Pap.* II.416). At the end of the Ptolemaic period, when Egypt was, despite the best efforts of Cleopatra, subject to the will of Rome and her powerful generals, we apparently find the queen granting land, financial benefits and tax concessions to a leading Roman, perhaps an associate of Mark Antony called Canidius. But questions remain about this tantalizing text: the Roman name is hard to read – is it really Canidius or some other Roman? At the end there is a single-word subscription γνεσθωι (let it be done) by a second hand – is this really Cleopatra's autograph? (Van Minnen 2000, 2001, 2003, Zimmerman 2002).

After the battle of Actium and the fall of Alexandria, Egypt was placed more firmly in the Roman dominion, as a province, and it continues to yield treasures which illuminate the history of the wider empire. Without the chance survival of a scrap of papyrus, now in Cologne, we would have no record of the words which the emperor Augustus spoke in Rome in 12 BC as a funeral oration for M. Agrippa, his friend, right-hand man, and son-in-law (*P.Köln* I.10). Nor would we have evidence for the precise terms in which the *Constitutio Antoniniana* was couched, the edict by which Caracalla conferred Roman citizenship on most inhabitants of the empire; in this latter case what survives is a damaged text which left a significant problem to be illuminated, if perhaps not definitively solved, by the discovery of a bronze tablet in North Africa (*P.Giss.* 40.ii, Sherwin-White 1973, Lintott, CITIZENSHIP, section 5). The extravagant words and demonstrations which greeted the arrival in Alexandria of Tiberius's adopted son Germanicus in AD 19 are vividly recorded in the *procès-verbal* of the assembly, and on the other side of that papyrus is an account of the proceedings of an Alexandrian embassy received by the emperor Augustus in Rome, sitting with his advisory council of relatives and leading senators (*P.Oxy.* XXV.2435). That papyrus was found at Oxyrhynchus, and another of the same provenance records an Alexandrian embassy seeking out the emperor Augustus in Gaul (*P.Oxy.* XLII.3020). One might wonder in whose possession these texts were, and why, in a town about 300 kilometers south of Alexandria. In the case of the famous letter of the emperor Claudius to the Alexandrians, responding to embassies on matters relating to cult of himself and to the strife between the Greek and Jewish communities, we are in a position to answer this question, for we know that the copy of the letter was made by a person called Nemesion, a tax collector in the Fayyum village of Philadelphia in the 40s AD (*CPJ* 153, A. Hanson 1990). Alexandria was, of course, very important, but the wider importance to would-be emperors of Egypt's resources is emphasized by papyri which reflect Vespasian's control in AD 69/70 (*P.Fuad* 8, Henrichs 1968) and that of the unsuccessful usurper Avidius Cassius, who challenged Marcus Aurelius in AD 175, the latter probably from the papers of one of the ambassadors who went to Alexandria to acclaim the new emperor (*P.Oxy.* LXVII.4592, Bowman 1970). This emphasizes the fact that, in the context of the transmission of knowledge and information, the papyri can show in ways that no other source does the involvement and the interest of "ordinary people" in high politics.

Even with this wealth of information, we sometimes lament the fact that there is not enough of it concentrated in one time and place to yield a vivid picture of social and economic life such as that of Montaillou in medieval France (Le Roy Ladurie 1980). From another perspective, however, the evidence of the papyri does give us a real sense of the character of communities of various different kinds. On one level, we can describe some of the key features of the larger towns and the villages of Egypt. Greek and demotic papyri give us a vivid picture of the community of *choachytai* (undertakers) in Ptolemaic Memphis, a huge city which best illustrates the interactions between the new Greek dominance and the traditional Egyptian religion (Thompson 1988). As for the physical aspects, for the early second century AD we have detailed evidence for the water supply of the city of Arsinoe, capital of the Fayyum, (Habermann 2000) and we know that by the early third century it boasted a temple of Jupiter Capitolinus, adorned with a colossal statue of the emperor Caracalla (*BGU* II.362). By this time many of the major towns of Egypt (some of them with populations in excess of 30,000) were conspicuously striving to achieve their version of Greek civic life and institutions in the context of Roman patterns of local government: councils, magistrates, *gerousia*, Capitoline Games, public pensions for athletes, a public *grammatikos* (Bowman 2000, *P.Coll.Youtie* 66). It is the papyrological evidence which allows us to see that at Hermopolis in the 260s there was an extensive program of repairs to public buildings, financed by a special levy on the inhabitants of the town (Van Minnen 2002). In the early fourth century at the center of Oxyrhynchus a visitor would have seen, among other things, four stoas, a doctor's surgery, the schoolmaster's residence, temples of Fortune, of Achilles, of Hadrian, a record office, market, proclamation hall, a public bath, and an imperial palace. All this we know from one of the most recently published papyri, a report to the *logistes* (*curator civitatis*) from AD 315/6 which tells us that the buildings were being looked after and surveyed for purposes of repair and refurbishment (*P.Oxy.* LXIV.4441). A few years later, we have the earliest evidence for the recognition of Sunday as the Lord's day, as Christianity emerged into official toleration, and the townscape shows more two church buildings (*P.Oxy.* LIV.3759.38, *P.Oxy.* I.43 verso, Bowman 2007). From that same town a few decades earlier we have evidence of a corn-dole available to 4,000 of its male citizens, interesting not only *per se* but for the opportunity it offers for comparison with the Roman model (*P.Oxy.* XL).

Because so many of the papyri, archives, and individual texts relate to the affairs of individuals, they afford a unique opportunity to view the lives of the elite and more "ordinary" people in the context of the institutions, political, social, economic, and religious, which governed them over a huge span of time and space. The individual voice can always be found, whether of the woman complaining about an accident in the baths which left her scalded (*Sel.Pap.* II.269), the husband advising his wife to expose a new-born infant if it is a girl (*Sel.Pap.* I.105), the student reproaching his father (*Sel.Pap.* I.133), the trader who has been beaten by the military (*Tab Vindol.* II.344); sometimes, but rarely, the more intimate details of personal relationships (*Sel.Pap.* I.125 cf. Parsons 1980, Bagnall-Cribiore 2005). As for the smaller villages, rural settlements where the flood, the crops, and the taxes were matters of perennial concern, in a few cases we can glimpse them, if not continuously, at least in snapshots over several centuries: Philadelphia in the Fayyum from the Zenon archive of the third century BC (Rostovtzeff 1922, Orrieux 1983) through the archive of Nemesion the tax collector in the reign of Claudius (A. Hanson 1979, 1984) and the register of land owned by villagers and Alexandrians in the early third century (*P.Yale* III.137). If we want to see how people organize and document their livelihood, on a small and a large scale, we can compare agrarian estate management in great detail over almost a millennium, from Zenon in the third century BC (Rostovtzeff 1922, Orrieux 1983) through Appianus in the third century AD (Rathbone 1991) and the grandee Apion family at Oxyrhynchus in the sixth, with significant similarities and significant differences (Banaji 2001, Mazza 2001).

Our sense of the pervasiveness of Greek culture in many places, but especially in Oxyrhynchus, is reinforced by the extraordinary discoveries of literary papyri, mostly Greek, but some Latin too, which bear witness to the existence of a highly cultivated readership: "Make and send me copies of books 6 and 7 of Hypsicrates' *Characters in Comedy*. For Harpocration says they are among Polion's books . . . he also has epitomes of Thersagoras's work on the myths of tragedy" (*P.Oxy.* XVIII.2192, Turner 1979). It is essential to remember that the owners of such books were spread across a wide spectrum of location and activity. Even in the agricultural villages there is remarkable evidence for the existence of a bookseller (*P.Petaus* 30), and a tax collector apparently familiar with the works of Callimachus who owned Greek literary papyri, including one of Menander (Van Minnen 1994). The preponderance of Greek papyri, literary and documentary, makes it all to easy to assume that this was a thoroughly homogeneous Greek or Greco-Roman milieu. Against that, it should be emphasized that in addition to the evidence for the survival of indigenous religious traditions well into late antiquity, the persevering Egyptian linguistic and cultural patterns remain visible in demotic texts and in the emergence of Coptic, as well as other non-written material culture; and they are also implied in a slightly different and interesting way in the form of a Greek readership for Egyptian history and literature (for example a romance involving a person called Amenophis, *P.Oxy.* XLII.3011), as well as translations of originally Egyptian texts such as the Law-Code of Hermopolis West (*P.Oxy.* XLVI.3285), and the apocalyptic Oracle of the Potter (*P.Oxy.* XXII.2332).

The world revealed by the papyrological evidence is far from being sealed within Egypt's borders. Not a few of the papyri found in Egypt give evidence for connections and networks stretching far afield. Persons based in Egypt record their activities in other parts of the Roman East, the estate manager Zenon in the Levant on behalf of his employer Apollonios the finance minister (*dioiketes*) of Ptolemy II Philadelphos (*P.Cair.Zen.* 59012), Theophanes the fourth-century *scholasticus* (advocate) in Syria (*P.Ryl.* IV.616–42). A few papyri give us a glimpse of transactions implying international commercial networks, slave sales at Rhodes, Aurelia Tripolis in Phoenicia, and Bostra (*P.Oxy.* L.3593–4 [238–44], XLII.3053 [252], 3054 [?265]), immensely valuable cargoes of luxury goods from India (Rathbone 2001). Furthermore, light is cast on communities and institutions of a rather different kind from the Egyptian towns and villages. Two in particular attract attention. The recently augmented corpus of evidence for the Roman army stretches from the quarries of the eastern desert to Vindolanda in northern Britain, inviting comparison of types of documentation, integration of the military into the local community, linguistic influences and revealing links across the empire, such as a letter found at Vindolanda written by a local equestrian officer who later in his career achieved the prefecture of Egypt (*Tab. Vindol.* III.611). Second, the evidence for Jewish communities which warns us against assuming too great a degree of homogeneity. Particularly notable in this respect are the Ptolemaic papyri which reveal the existence of a Jewish *politeuma* (corporate community) at Herakleopolis in the second century BC (*P.Polit.Jud.*) and the documents of the early second century AD from the Dead Sea Caves. The Archive of Babatha and other smaller groups of papyri, Greek and Aramaic (*P.Yadin*, Cotton 1995) cast unique light on the relationship between Roman, Greek and Jewish law and institutions in the new province of Arabia, showing the ways in which provincialization brought local law and procedures of documentation into the framework of the Roman legal and governmental system.

It is the evidence of the papyri, particularly from Egypt, which has supplied us with the best evidence for the organization of government and society in the Mediterranean world under Greek, Roman and Byzantine rule. Although there is a debt to the long scribal tradition in dynastic Egypt, we should not underestimate the extent to which the early Ptolemies deliberately set out to create a functioning bureaucratic system in Greek, diminishing (without destroying) the role of demotic documents, a process which was to culminate early in the Roman period (Thompson 1992a, 1992b, Lewis 1993). The tendency to view Egypt as quite exceptional in the context of the classical Mediterranean is now less prevalent than it was a generation ago, and is further weakened by every find of similar material from areas outside Egypt. The Alexandrian author Philo described the administration of Roman Egypt as "intricate and diversified, hardly grasped even by those who have made a business of studying them from their earliest years" (*In Flacc.* 3). This is confirmed by edicts of governors, one ordering registration of all property and mortgages, another instructing all *nomikoi* to send copies of their reports to the Library of Hadrian, one of the record offices in Alexandria, and, finally, a much longer and more explicit text painting a grim picture of the state of disorganization which needed to be rectified in the record office of the capital of the Arsinoite Nome in the late first and early second century AD (*P.Oxy.* II.237, *P.Fam.Teb.* 15). This emphasizes the continuing preoccupation with the proper maintenance of the records, some of which will undoubtedly have been available in the archives of the provincial governor (Haensch

1997). Another is the attention to detail in the local record offices of towns and villages throughout the country, and the fact that these were part of a hierarchical structure in which copies of local records had to be supplied to the appropriate central office in Alexandria. We can get a good sense of the great quantity of such archival material in a far smaller place, the village of Tebtunis in the Arsinoite Nome for which we have abstracts of contracts deposited in the registry (*grapheion*) during three years of the reign of the emperor Claudius between AD 41 and 47. These records show the care with which contracts were summarized and catalogued, and yield, by a simple calculation, the mean volume of such contracts (most in Greek but some few in demotic Egyptian): 58 per month for the periods represented, involving, at a rough estimate, at least 20–25 percent of the adult population of the village who documented their business in writing even if not all these individuals wrote or could have written their own contracts (*P.Mich.* II.121, 123, V.238 cf. Toepel 1973).

A fundamental aspect which underpins this is the prevalence and organization of literate education and writing practices in Greek and Latin in this world, in Egypt and beyond. Here the evidence is far from answering all the questions, but a start can be made with the evidence of literary texts and their distribution, the nature of school exercises and the analysis of paleographical and other literate habits which, on a very superficial judgment, display a remarkable similarity across time and space (Clarysse 1983, Van Minnen 1998, Cribiore 1996, 2001, T. Morgan 1998). Some aspects of the uses of writing material have attracted a lot of scholarly attention, for example the roll and the codex (Blanchard 1989, Turner 1978, Roberts and Skeat 1983); others, such as the layout and orthography of private letters, less so. This subject area is only one of those which offer challenges and possibilities for the next generation and beyond (Bagnall 1995). We might look forward also, for instance, to a greater understanding of the achievement of the ancient economy and standards of living in quantifiable terms, of the cultural interaction between the Egyptian and the Greek traditions, of the factors which determined the ways in which Christianity developed from the third century onwards, or the contribution which papyri make to our understanding the development of the Greek language in non-literary contexts. Whatever answers may emerge to questions on these topics, of one thing we can be sure. The capacity of papyri to surprise us is far from exhausted.

FURTHER READING

The standard account of the role of papyrus, including manufacture and technology, is Lewis 1974. The most comprehensive handbook on papyrology is Montevecchi 1973 (with Supplement 1988), including lists of texts classified by type, but note also the forthcoming handbook by Bagnall. Turner 1980 covers all aspects of the subject in a readable and accessible manner. The history of papyrology and the prospects for future research are discussed by Van Minnen (1993; 2007). For those interested in the techniques and technicalities of editing papyri, it is best to begin with Pestman 1990, followed by the more detailed discussions by Turner 1973 and Youtie 1973a, 1973b and 1974. This would be enhanced by consultation of a good and readily available collection of facsimiles, Turner 1987. Further detail on the Oxyrhynchus papyri can be found in Turner 1979 and Bowman, Coles et al. 2007. Bagnall 1995 offers a selective but very illuminating account of the ways in which documentary papyri can be used as the basis for historical studies, and Rowlandson 1998 is an excellent collection of a wide range of documentary texts in translation with introductions and commentaries. Bagnall 1993 is a detailed historical study of Egypt from the late third to the mid-fifth century. A broader overview, from Alexander to the Arab conquest, based largely on the evidence of papyri, is offered by Bowman 1996. Those interested in placing the papyri of the Greco-Roman period in their geographical and archaeological context should begin with Bagnall and Rathbone 2004. For an introduction to Vindolanda, Bowman 2003.

Abbreviations used for editions of papyri, including those cited in this chapter, may be found in the *Checklist of Editions of Greek and Latin Papyri, Ostraca and Tablets* (Oates et al. 2001): http://scriptorium.lib.duke.edu/papyrus/texts/clist.html

Electronic Resources:
APIS (Advanced Papyrological Information Service):
   www.columbia.edu/dlc/apis
Archives Photographiques Internationales de Papyrologie, København:
   www.igl.ku.dk/~bulow/aipdescr.html
Bibliographie Papyrologique (G. Nachtergael, A. Martin):
   www.ulb.ac.be/philo/cpeg/bp.htm
Catalogue des papyrus littéraires grecs et latins (Mertens-Pack3):
   http://promethee.philo.ulg.ac.be/cedopal/index.htm
Centre for the Study of Ancient Documents:
   www.csad.ox.ac.uk
Duke Data Bank of Documentary Papyri (DDBDP):
   http://scriptorium.lib.duke.edu/papyrus/texts/DDBDP.html
Gazetteer of Papyri in British Collections (GPBC):
   http://gpbc.csad.ox.ac.uk
Leuven Database of Ancient Books (LDAB):
   http://ldab.arts.kuleuven.ac.be
Leuven Homepage of Papyrus Archives and Collections (LHPC):
   http://lhpc.arts.kuleuven.ac.be/index.html
Oxyrhynchus Papyri:
   www.papyrology.ox.ac.uk
Prosopographia Ptolemaica (W. Clarysse, H. Hauben, L. Mooren, K. Vandorpe):
   http://prosptol.arts.kuleuven.ac.be
Recording, Processing and Archiving Carbonized Papyri (Helsinki University of Technology, Laboratory of Information Processing Science):
   www.cs.hut.fi/papyrus
Vindolanda Tablets Online:
   http://vindolanda.csad.ox.ac.uk
Wörterlisten aus den Registern von Publikationen griechischer und lateinischer dokumentarischer Papyri und Ostraka (D. Hagedorn):
   www.iaw.uni-heidelberg.de/hps/pap/WL/WL.html

CHAPTER FIVE

Numismatics

A. R. Meadows

1 Introduction

Why should numismatics be entitled to an entry of its own in a Companion to Ancient History, when other categories of ancient archaeological evidence such as seals, which are artistically similar, or potsherds, which survive in greater numbers, are not? The answer, of course, lies in the multidimensional capabilities of ancient coins as historical sources. In different ways different coinages have much to tell us about the social, economic and political history, as well as the basic chronology, of the ancient world. This latent evidentiary power resides in the basic nature of coinage in general, and ancient coinage in particular, and it will be as well to start with some definitions which make clear these natures.

Numismatics, narrowly defined, is the study of ancient coins. The modern European words for the discipline, almost all cognate, derive from the Greek word for coin, *nomisma*, which in turn seems to be derived from the word for a man-made law or convention, *nomos*. Herein lies one of the principal reasons for the usefulness of coinage to the ancient historian. Unlike, say, vases or curse tablets, coins are the product of, and, at the beginning of their lives at least, functioned within, a regulated system. Ancient coinage was on the whole the product of an official body – a city-state, an empire or a kingdom – and thus to a certain extent reflects an official policy. In this sense it is analogous in origin to official inscriptions such as laws and decrees. From certain features of coinage, therefore, we may infer certain facts about official policies and actions. At the same time, once coinage is in circulation, it circulates and potentially becomes divorced from its point of origin. In this context coinage can be used to deduce certain patterns of behavior in the spheres of private social and economic history. Again, to take an analogy from the world of epigraphy, coins may serve as evidence for behavior at the personal level in the same way as funerary inscriptions or private dedications. At a broader level, the patterns of movement of coinage, with due care and attention to methodology, can be used to infer larger-scale patterns of social and economic behavior. As do pots, so coins travel and offer the possibility of tracking movements of goods and people. Unlike pots, and most other ancient artifacts, coins tell us explicitly through their designs and legends where they originated. Often they can tell us quite precisely when they were made too.

These, then, are some of the possibilities afforded by numismatic study. In practice, the opportunities offered by Greek and Roman coinages, and thus far taken by numismatists and by historians, vary considerably according to the precise nature both of the coinages concerned and of the numismatic and archaeological methods that have been applied to them. Some further definition will be necessary.

Roman numismatics is perhaps the easiest to define. It is concerned with the study of the coins produced by the Roman state. These began in the late fourth century BC and continued through the republican period fairly straightforwardly. Coins were on the whole official issues of the Roman state, that became, if they were not originally, the responsibility of a group of monetary magistrates. In the last years of the republic, issues were produced by various rival imperators and renegades, which might not strictly be termed state coinage. They were nevertheless recognizably Roman in conception and behavior. Under the empire the tradition of the republic continued, with some modification of denominations, until the third century AD. The principal mint of the imperial coinage remained Rome, with occasional use of subsidiary mints in Gaul or Spain. To a certain extent the central administration also became involved in the monetary affairs of the provinces in this period. During the third quarter of the third century AD a wholesale monetary reform of the empire by the emperors Valerian and Gallienus marked the end of local coinages and devolved the production of the common imperial coinage to a number of provincial mints in the West and East.

Greek numismatics is concerned with a far more amorphous body of material. As traditionally defined it is concerned with all the coinages of the ancient world with the exception of the Roman coinage described above and the pre-Roman Iron Age coinages of northern Europe. In practice this assigns to the field of Greek numismatics the coinages produced from Spain in the west to India and Afghanistan in the east, from the Black Sea coast of Ukraine in the north, to Arabia and Africa in the south, and from the beginnings of coinage in Asia Minor in the late seventh century BC through the end of civic coinage in the East in the third century AD. This is clearly a massive body of material, of widely differing natures. It encompasses the beginning of the phenomenon of coinage and its spread to the city-states of Greece in the late sixth and fifth centuries BC, the adoption of coinage by larger imperial powers such as Persia and Carthage, the spread of royal coinage under Alexander and his successors, as well as the use of coinages by numerous non-Greek peoples around the Mediterranean and in the Near East.

A third area of numismatics falls squarely between the Greek and Roman coinages described above. Traditionally the coinages concerned have been termed "Greek Imperial" coinages, and their study has been subsumed within the field of Greek numismatics. More recently, and particularly as the result of the publication of a standard reference work in the field, the term "Roman Provincial Coinage" has come into more common usage (see Further Reading). Essentially this is the coinage produced within the Roman empire by non-Roman authorities. During the late first

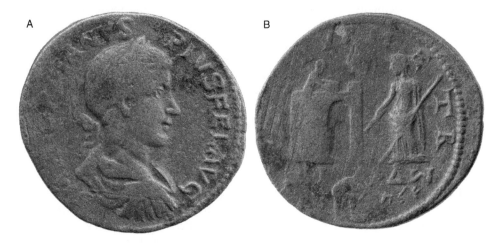

5.1 Bronze coin of Tyre in Phoenicia, struck in the reign of Gordian III (AD 238–244). Twice actual size. This issue of the Roman colony of Tyre features a bust of the reigning emperor Gordian on the obverse, with a legend describing him in Latin (the usual language for coins of Roman colonies in the East). On the reverse is depicted the scene of Dido founding Carthage. The scene was perhaps picked by the local coin designers for its Roman resonance, but, unusually, supplementary legends beneath the design describe the standing figure, in both Greek and Phoenician, as Dido and Elissar, suggesting that this design was also the product of more local sensibilities. See Howgego 2005: 14. (Copyright Trustees of the British Museum)

century BC and early first AD such coinage was issued from Spain to Syria. The Western provincial coinages petered out during this period, however, and by the end of the first century AD the provincial coinage was largely a phenomenon of the cities of the Greek East. On the whole the provincial issues were civic issues, produced, like earlier coinages, in the name of cities. However, they resemble the coinage of the mint of Rome, in that they frequently portrayed the ruling emperor or members of his family on one side of the coin.

Each of these three areas of ancient numismatics has been subject to different developments and incorporation into broader historical discourse, but before examining these, it is necessary briefly to describe the nature of the ancient coin. On the one hand the coin is one of the more familiar-looking artifacts to survive from the ancient world. We still use coins today, and it is all too easy to fall into the trap of applying modern assumptions about the function and nature of coinage to the ancient phenomenon. In fact ancient coinage is fundamentally different from modern coinage in a number of ways, and this ought to have a profound effect on the ways that we use it as a historical source.

Ancient coinage was hand made, in two senses. First the actual process of striking the coins was carried out by hand. A coin was produced by placing a blank piece of metal on a die set within an anvil, or similar anchoring device. This is known to numismatists as the "obverse die." A second die (the "reverse die") was then placed on top of the blank and hit forcefully with a hammer. The result was a flat, roundish piece of metal with, potentially, designs on both sides. The second hand-crafted element of coin production was the engraving of the designs that appeared on ancient coins. Unlike modern coin dies, which are all mechanically copied from a single master engraving, each ancient die was individually engraved and thus different from every other. These two elements of hand-production produce an interesting mixture of results. On the one hand, there is an individuality of design of dies which allows us to trace the products of an ancient mint in a way that is impossible for modern coins. On the other, hand striking, although not nearly so fast as modern machine production, allows for the production of thousands of identical or closely similar objects within a very short space of time. Coins in this sense are one of the very rare examples from the premodern world of mass production.

The substance of ancient coinage was also profoundly different. In origin, coinage was a monetary instrument of intrinsic value. The earliest coins, produced in Asia Minor from the mid-seventh to mid-sixth centuries BC were made of carefully controlled amounts of electrum, the alloy of gold and silver. Subsequently, most probably under the influence of the prevailing monetary tradition of the Near East, coinage was throughout the latter part of the sixth century through to the first century AD largely produced in high-quality silver, with gold being produced when circumstances of supply or demand particularly prompted it. The intrinsic value of these precious-metal coins often made it possible for them to circulate over wide areas, and beyond the borders of the political authorities that had produced them. Nevertheless, there were constraining factors. The novelty of coinage, in contrast to the earlier Near Eastern practice of making payments with weighed amounts of silver bullion, lay both in the carefully regulated weights (denominations) at which coins were produced, which added facility of use, and in the designs that were struck on them, which provided clear statement of origin, and thus guaranteed their metal quality (value). While both developments added convenience and functionality, they also served potentially to constrain monetary behavior. The localized system of weight standards of the ancient world and according to which ancient coins were denominated could fragment as well as unify monetary behavior. Similarly a mark of guarantee could only function where it was recognized. This was particularly the case when the phenomenon of bronze coinage arose in the latter part of the fifth century BC. Such coinages were, on the whole, produced as fiduciary instruments, whose value lay not so much in their metal content, which was far less tightly controlled than in the precious metal coinage, but in the guaranteed system in which they circulated. Such fiduciary coinages depended for their value essentially on the confidence of the recipients of the coin in their ability to reuse it later.

There exist, then, basic tensions within the nature of ancient coinage between hand-making and mass production, between the inherent value of its substance and the man-made constraints placed upon this – the intrinsic and fiduciary elements of coinage – that present different possibilities for the historian at different periods and in different places. It is well also for the historian to bear in mind the simplest difference of all between ancient and modern coinage. To the twenty-first-century user coinage is the lowest value of all monetary instruments. In the ancient context coinage is a high-value medium. A gold coin may represent a month's wages or more, a silver one a day's or a week's pay. In Britain of the first century AD there was no coin small enough, not even in bronze, to pay for a pint of beer.

Given the alien nature of ancient coinage to the modern eye, and its lack of suitability for many of the functions to which it is put today, even the simple question of the motivation for its production by ancient states requires sustained historical inquiry. There has been a tendency in recent years to regard the production of ancient coinage as essentially expenditure driven (e.g. M. Crawford 1970), but cases can be made for more sophisticated motivations of profit or ideology in some cases (Howgego 1990; T. Martin 1996).

2   Greek Numismatics

Greek numismatics, as has been noted, is a vast discipline. A substantial part of the effort of its practitioners has been devoted simply to its taxonomy. Faced with more than a thousand issuing authorities and a thousand years of production, the process of organizing the numismatic material of the Greek world by place and date of production has been an immense task, and the work continues. Over the years, numerous attempts have been made to provide grand corpora of Greek coinage, beginning with J. H. Eckhel's *Doctrina Numorum Veterum* (Eckhel 1792–98). Two attempts to provide complete descriptions of Greek coinage in multiple volumes were aborted early in the twentieth century, leaving B. V. Head's *Historia Numorum* (Head 1911) as the only modern overview of Greek coinage. In the early days of the discipline efforts to attribute coins to mints and to date them were based largely on antiquarian scholarship and aesthetic perception, both applied to the designs and legends that appeared on coins. Advances in attribution from the nineteenth century onwards came largely in the form of the observations of travelers of the coins they were shown or acquired in particular locales. The rise of scientific excavation over a similar period has also allowed considerable advance in attribution. By the same token, the principle that bronze coinages at least tend not to travel far from point of production has brought to archaeologists the ability to identify ancient sites on the basis of coins found there. Cataloguing of coins has thus helped in the cataloguing of sites. During the late nineteenth and early twentieth centuries the appreciation of the value of hoard evidence also led to advances in the dating of material, independent of subjective criteria of stylistic development. Hoards, or groups of coins deposited together in antiquity, allow by the collocation of different coinages within a single context the establishment of relative chronologies between different mints. Where coins appear in a hoard in different states of wear (usage) they can also suggest chronological sequences within homogeneous bodies of material.

Corpora and hoard studies aside, two other activities have become fundamental to the study of Greek coinage. The existence of collections of Greek coins, both public and private, has stimulated the production of the *catalogue raisonée*. Where the collection is sufficiently extensive and publication correspondingly full, such catalogs take on the form of reference works, and have developed into quasi-corpora. The largest and most influential example has been the *British Museum Catalogue*, begun in 1873 and now in 30 volumes. Since the 1930s, however, the tendency has been to move away from such textually detailed catalogs with limited illustrations towards a textually sparer but fully illustrated presentation of collections in the form of the *Sylloge Nummorum Graecorum* series. The impetus for this faster publication came from the invention of the die-study, which in turn became possible with the widespread use of photographic reproduction a generation earlier. The die-study exploits the hand-made nature of Greek coin-dies to construct a complete picture of a particular mint's production. The assembly of a large body of material from a mint allows the identification of individual dies used to strike the coinage. Because there is a disparity in life between anvil or obverse dies, which last longer, and punch or reverse dies, which break more quickly, it is possible to reproduce sequences of dies used. This, in combination with hoard and other objective dating criteria, allows a reconstruction of both the sequence of production at a mint, and also a reasonably precise chronology. However, this method of study of ancient coins is extremely labor intensive, and the results of what can be a purely numismatic exercise are often not well integrated into broader historical pictures.

The combination of numismatic methodologies and the nature of Greek coinage have offered a number of possibilities to ancient historians. Of particular interest in recent years has been the relationship between the development of early coinage in Greek lands and the relationship between this new economic mode and concurrent social upheaval (e.g. Seaford 2004; Kurke 1999a). The mass production of a monetary medium against the perceived background of a society with socially embedded concepts of wealth and status offers fruitful ground for socio-economic speculation. The establishment in recent years of firmer chronologies for the earliest Greek coinage has helped to clarify the problems here, if not yet the solutions. Debate continues, and should do, on the speed with which the Classical Greek state developed a market economy. Constraints of volume of coinage, rate of production, value of individual coins and extent of money supply, which must all be understood from numismatic material and method, are fundamental to such inquiry, and remain to be utilized fully.

The place of coinage within political constructs of empires, kingdoms and autonomous states is also a fertile area for debate. Modernistic assumptions of the symbolic importance and potential of coinage as a symbol of autonomy, for example, have recently come under attack (e.g. T. Martin 1985; Meadows 2001). An obvious flashpoint for such discussion is the Athenian Standards Decree, and its apparent attempt to curtail minting activity in the Athenian empire (e.g. Figueira 1998). But the question has also been the subject of discussion in the context of Alexander's

5.2 Silver tetradrachm of Artaxerxes III, King of Persia, minted in Egypt, c.343 BC. Twice actual size. The silver coinage of Athens achieved such popularity in the markets of the eastern Mediterranean during the early fourth century BC that even the king of Persia imitated the designs, to make his coinage acceptable, it is often suggested, to mercenaries. This specimen has the head of Athena and Owl design familiar from Athenian coins, but the legend, written in demotic Egyptian, reads "Artaxerxes Pharaoh. Life Prosperity Wealth." These are Greek coins produced by a Persian king, legible only to Egyptians. (Copyright Trustees of the British Museum)

empire, the kingdoms of the Successors and the Roman domination of Greece. Proper understanding of the nature of ancient coinage and the monetary behavior of ancient states, both derived from numismatic study, have formed the focus of a pendulum swing against imported notions of the nature of coinage based on modern analogy.

It should not require explicit statement that the study of coinage has an important role to play in the study of the ancient economy, but this fact has been denied by some economic historians (e.g. Finley 1999). Theoretical questions of the nature of the ancient economy aside, numismatics in the form of the die-study has obvious potential for the quantification of at least one aspect of the ancient economy: official state coin production. By comparing the numbers of dies used by different cities at different periods it is possible to compare the monetary outputs of different cities and of royal mints (for surveys see de Callataÿ 1997 and 2003). The conversion of these numbers of dies into actual numbers of coins produced remains a matter of controversy among numismatists (see de Callataÿ 1995), but more work remains to be done at least in identifying probable ranges of output.

In addition to the chronological significance noted above, hoard evidence also offers the possibility of discussing the circulation patterns of ancient coinage. In practice, however, we are not often well enough informed about find-spots of hoards, which are often illegally excavated. Moreover, the quantity of evidence available for

Greek hoards (collected in Thompson et al. 1973 and supplemented in the periodical *Coin Hoards*), given the geographical and chronological extent that is covered, is still not sufficient for the reconstruction of significant patterns.

The same may be said of the publication of Greek coins from scientifically excavated sites and the interpretation of the patterns that might emerge. There are still too few publications over too broad an area for meaningful analysis to have taken place. In recording and interpretation of both hoards and site-finds, Roman numismatics has had the opportunity for considerably more work and methodological advance.

3 Roman Numismatics

As with Greek numismatics, a considerable amount of Roman numismatic scholarship has been devoted to the taxonomy of the coinage. The difference for the Roman world lies in the ease with which its coinage may, for the most part, be categorized. The imperial period is rendered relatively straightforward by the appearance of the coinage and the legends (inscriptions) that appear on it. Generally, the head or bust of the emperor or a family member appears on the obverse, making attribution to reigns straightforward. The addition of a legend naming the emperor often has appended an element of official titulature such as years of consulship or tribunician power that enable highly precise dates to be assigned to the coins. As a result there now exist two well-established reference works for this coinage which serve as firm foundations for the identification and interpretation of all new material that appears. The first of these is the well-illustrated *British Museum Catalogue*, completed down to the reign of Balbinus and Pupienus. The second is the massive type corpus, *Roman Imperial Coinage*, which now runs in ten volumes from Augustus to Romulus Augustulus. A certain level of complexity is introduced by the reform of the coinage in the 250s and 260s AD which radically altered the structure of the coinage. In place of the central mint at Rome, aided by one or two sporadic, subsidiary mints, the production of coinage was devolved to a series of mints spread throughout the provinces of the empire. For half a century the number and locations of these varied, until under Diocletian a network extended from London, Trier, Lyon, Ticinum, Rome, and Carthage in the West, via Siscia, Sirmium and Thessalonica in the Balkans, to Thracian Heraclea, Cyzicus, Nicomedia, Antioch and Alexandria in the East. The coinage of the Roman republican period is also well served by a standard reference work, *Roman Republican Coinage*. In its later phases the coinage of the republic is susceptible to a similar sort of organization as the imperial period, since the names of the Imperators responsible for the coins often appear on them, and the chronology of the period is well understood. In earlier periods, Roman numismatic method is more akin to that of the Greek world, with hoard evidence playing a prominent role in the organization of material. Only limited use of the die-study has been made, however.

Three facets of Roman coinage in particular have been exploited by historians and archaeologists of the Roman world. First there is the internal development of the coinage. Roman coinage in its earliest form was essentially a Greek phenomenon: a precious metal coinage, principally in silver, with occasional supplementary gold issues, accompanied at times, and from the reign of Augustus more systematically, by bronze coinage. From the reign of Nero (AD 54–68) onwards, however, the silver coinage began a long slide into debasement in a way that Greek coinages never had. This decrease in the quality of silver coinage seems to be linked both to a general rise in the numbers of coins in circulation in the empire and to a gradual increase in prices. By the 260s the notionally silver coinage of the empire had virtually no silver in it, and prices seem to have been running at around three times the levels of the early first century AD. Against the background of the collapse of the silver coinage can be set the fluctuating fortunes of the gold coinage. The picture is one of an observably large coinage in the first and second centuries AD becoming debased in the third century before being reformed and returned to a high-quality coinage under Aurelian (AD 270–275). From these patterns of metal content and their comparisons with literary and documentary evidence can be written, at least to some extent, the broad monetary history of the empire.

A more local picture has been the focus of an important strand of archaeological interpretation, particularly for the well-studied province of Britain (Reece 2002 and 2003). Here, a large body of published hoard material, as well as a significant number of site-finds, allows a relatively detailed picture of coin circulation and monetary behavior to be built up. Hoards have a considerable amount to tell us (Abdy 2002). Their contents supplement the picture offered by the nature of the coinage itself for the nature of the Roman monetary system. Where chemical analysis can reveal the official policy of debasement of the coinage, hoards provide the evidence for the effect of this on monetary behavior. Patterns of deposition of hoards, at a variety of periods, and not just in Roman Britain, may often attest to period of crisis or fears of personal safety. Individual finds of coins may be no less indicative of historical patterns. By building up a broad picture of coin-finds from different categories of site, such as urban, rural, military settlements, it is possible to compare social and economic behavior across categories, but also within categories of site, and between different periods. Much work remains to be done here, more elsewhere in the Roman empire and more still for other periods such as Iron Age northern Europe or the Greek East.

Finally there is the design of coinage, which can be deployed as historical evidence at different levels. Of incidental interest are the portraits that begin to appear on Greek and Roman coins during the Hellenistic period. Often these provide the only portrayal of major historical figures to survive from their own lifetimes (J. Toynbee 1978). On Greek coins this began after the death of Alexander the Great, on Roman with Julius Caesar. Unlike the Greek cities, the Romans also decorated their coinage with buildings and monuments. These representations often have something to tell us about the architectural and civic history of Rome and the empire. It is in such superficial contexts of illustration that coinage is often deployed in modern historical works. But, at different times in its development, Roman coinage presents different appearances, and different paradigms of design (e.g. Meadows and Williams 2001). The nature of these paradigms, whether they draw upon concepts of Romanness, family history or political ideologies, can also be fertile ground for the political and social historian of republic and empire.

4 Roman Provincial Numismatics

Roman provincial numismatics is still a comparatively young discipline. Thanks to the regular appearance on provincial coins of the portrait and name of the reigning emperor, much of the material is relatively straightforward to categorize chronologically. The appearance on the reverse of the issuing authority's name and, often, a locally relevant design makes the process of attributing the coins to regions, cities and kings relatively easy, too. However, the broad geographical sweep of the provincial coinages, as well as the large number of issuing authorities, has until recently stifled attempts to organize and categorize the phenomenon as a whole. The advent of the *Roman Provincial Coinage* series is revolutionizing this field. The early volumes serve to highlight the fundamental difference between the Western part of the empire, where provincial coinages had entirely disappeared by the death of Tiberius (AD 14–37), and the East, where provincial issues flourished throughout the late first century AD, reaching a high point in the Antonine and Severan periods, finally coming to an end in the reign of Tacitus (AD 275–76).

The insights offered by this vast body of material to the historian are considerable. At the highest level, the differing fortunes of coinage in the West and East serve to highlight fundamental differences in the monetary behavior of different parts of the empire (Burnett 2005). Differing explanations for the demise of the Western issues have been advanced according to the desire of the proponent to see local markets and issuers reacting to Roman economic superiority on the one hand, or a *dirigiste* central Roman state suppressing local economic autonomy on the other. Whichever end of the spectrum is preferred for the West, the circumstances in the East were undeniably different. The civic coinage of the East was almost entirely a low-value bronze affair, well adapted for exchange at the local level, but a far cry from the high-value silver coinages of earlier periods. The existence of these coinages opens up major avenues for the interpretation of the economies of the Roman East. At the same time, the physical appearance of these coinages, a hybrid of imperial iconography on the one hand and local civic pride on the other, encapsulates the tension between Roman center and local periphery in the most graphic and easily comprehensible form. A plethora of approaches to self-representation emerges on the reverse, in marked contrast to the uniformity of the obverse designs (Howgego et al. 2005). Technical numismatic study of the provincial coinage has revealed some evidence in the form of shared obverse dies for a level of coordination across civic mints (Kraft 1972; Johnston 1983). This fact, along with clear intervention on the part of the Roman state, such as in the maintenance of the closed-currency status of Egypt, or the production of local silver coinages with Latin legends in Asia, raises important questions about the extent of Roman control of the money supply in the East, no less than in the West.

5 The Future

From the foregoing, it will be clear that ancient numismatics presents a variety of challenges and opportunities for future study. For Rome itself, the major organization of material has taken place, and future work must consist largely of determining patterns and density of monetary circulation and penetration. The provincial coinages of the Roman empire are gradually being assimilated in a similar system of corpora. The volumes of *Roman Provincial Coinage* that exist already provide a wealth of opportunities for surveying the social, political, and economic variegation of the cities of the empire. In the Greek world, by contrast, much work of basic organization and study remains to be done. In this the creation of digital resources will be the next major step in preparing this fertile ground for historical use.

FURTHER READING

The only complete guide to ancient Greek coinage is Head 1911. A multi-volume third edition is now under way, the first part of which has been published: Rutter et al. 2001. Greek coin hoards are collected in Thompson, Mørkholm and Kraay, 1973, supplemented since by the periodical *Coin Hoards* (London, nine volumes thus far). The *British Museum Catalogue* (30 vols, London 1873–1991) remains an important reference work, but is inevitably dated. Of the numerous *Sylloge Numorum Graecorum* (*SNG*) series, the only one to publish an entire collection is that devoted to the Royal Danish collection: *SNG Copenhagen* (43 vols, Copenhagen, 1942–79). Slowly, collections are beginning to appear on the World Wide Web. The only *SNG* series so far to be digitized is that devoted to UK collections: www.sylloge-nummorum-graecorum.org. Useful summaries of the outputs of Greek mints, based on die-studies thus far completed, are provided in de Callataÿ 1997 and 2003. A fine guide to the broad possibilities of ancient coinage for the ancient historian exists in Howgego 1995. Reliable narrative accounts of the development of Greek coinage can be found in Kraay 1976, Mørkholm 1991, and Carradice and Price 1988. Some approaches to thinking about Greek coinage as a historical source are presented in Meadows and Shipton 2001.

The two basic reference works for Roman republican coinage are M. Crawford 1969 and 1974. For the imperial coinage the basic references are the six volumes of the *British Museum Catalogue* (London, 1923–62) and the ten volumes of *Roman Imperial Coinage* (London, 1923–94). Hoards of the imperial period have not been subject to systematic collection as a whole. For Britain there exists an inventory of finds to 1992 in Robertson 2000, and 12 volumes in the series of *Coin Hoards from Roman Britain* (London, 1979–2002). For the rest of the empire, *Coin Hoards* I–VII contain surveys of hoards reported during the period 1975–1985. For narrative accounts of the development of Roman coinage, reliable accounts can be found in M. Crawford 1985, Carson 1990 and Burnett 1987. On the use and value of Roman coin hoards there is a good guide in Abdy 2002. A good introduction to an archaeological approach to coin finds can be found in Reece 2003. For the potential of the republican material to inform social and political history see Meadows and Williams 2001.

Greek imperial or Roman provincial coinage is now blessed with a corpus project: *Roman Provincial Coinage*. Two volumes have so far appeared: Burnett, Amandry and Ripollès 1992 and Amandry, Carradice and Burnett 1999. An excellent survey of the potential of the provincial material for historical research is provided by Howgego et al. 2005. A useful narrative account of the phenomenon can be found in Butcher 1988.

Summaries of numismatic research are regularly published in New York by the American Numismatic Society in the periodical *Numismatic Literature*. The *Survey of Numismatic Research* is published regularly by the International Numismatic Commission. Articles are now arranged by period and geographical area.

CHAPTER SIX

Archaeology and Ancient History

Stephen L. Dyson

1 From the Renaissance to the Nineteenth Century

Archaeology and ancient history have been bound together in a tight, complex, and not overly satisfactory relationship since the Renaissance. The archaeologist depends on the ancient historian to provide chronological order and historical context to his/her material. The ancient historian relies on the archaeologist to enhance our sense of the physical world of antiquity and expand the corpus of material, preferably with written components that will deepen our understanding of the past.

By the end of the Renaissance the monasteries and libraries had been combed and the bulk of the Greek and Roman manuscripts recovered and published. Classical scholars and especially historians began to realize that it was only through the investigation of the material world that their corpus of information would be significantly expanded. The ancient historians established a tripartite mission for the archaeologist that continues to operate down to the present day. Classical archaeologists were to produce inscriptions that would expand the body of written materials available for study. They were to expand the topographical information provided by the ancient geographers and help create fuller and more accurate maps of the ancient world and better plans and reconstructions of the major sites. Finally they were to enrich the body of material culture from architecture through sculpture to minor arts like vases and bronzes that would not only inspire contemporary artists but also inform the cultural historian.

Archaeology took another turn in the seventeen and eighteenth centuries with the rise of the antiquarian. They often lacked the broad vision of the humanist, but had a more factual and scientific approach to the study of the past. Sometimes dismissed as overly concerned with minutiae, the antiquarians did lay the foundations for more rigorous scholarship in such combined historical and archaeological fields as numismatics. They also represented a greater geographical range in their interests in antiquity. The humanists centered their activities in Italy. Antiquarians were located throughout Europe, and they played an important role in integrating prehistory, classical and national history in countries like France, Germany, and England.

The goals of ancient history changed during the nineteenth century, and with that the relationship to archaeology. The ancient historians were pioneers in the new critical history that rigorously analyzed sources and attempted to separate fact and fiction in the study of Greek and Roman texts. As the nineteenth century progressed, the study of history in general became more empirical, and with those developments ancient historians faced new dilemmas. Their own research had challenged the historical validity of many of the canonical writers such as Homer and Livy. However, an ancient historian could not compensate for the limitations of the major works by emulating contemporary historians like the German Leopold Ranke and expanding the body of information on antiquity through archival research. Greek and Roman archives, if they ever existed, had long since been destroyed. As the historical discipline demanded an ever more precise reconstruction of the past, the ancient historians could not deliver. The only significant expansion of information had to come from archaeology.

Epigraphy came in the nineteenth century to form an important link between archaeology and ancient history. Scholars like Bartolomeo Borghesi, August Boeckh and Theodor Mommsen realized the importance of the historical evidence contained in inscriptions, and set out developing a scientific system for their collection, analysis, and publication. Since many of the Latin inscriptions first studied in Italy and Western Europe were already in collections or publicly accessible, the role of the archaeologist was initially limited. Different was the Hellenic world of Greece and Asia Minor, where systematic investigations only began in the nineteenth century. The archaeological pioneers there had the three-fold task of finding and charting sites, relating them to ancient geography, and recording and publishing the large number of Greek language inscriptions they found.

Hellenic archaeology in the early nineteenth century was largely shaped by the work of the great topographers like the Englishman William Leake. They described the remains at often little-known sites, attempted to ascertain their ancient identity, and published the texts of inscriptions that they had discovered during in their explorations. They were generally well-read classicists, intrepid explorers, and skilled observers. Their agenda was shaped to a great degree by the surviving ancient geographical writers, such as Strabo, who lived in the Augustan period, and the Greek Pausanias of the second century AD. Far less studied in the schools and universities than the histories of Herodotus or Thucydides, those ancient geographical guidebooks became the key links between the worlds of the historian and the archaeologist.

The scholarly agenda did not change markedly when the archaeologist turned from geographical investigation and epigraphical collection to actual excavation. The Germans set the pattern when they started excavations at Olympia in 1875. It was a site of great historical and cultural importance to Greek civilization, undisturbed by post-classical development. Pausanias provided a detailed description of Olympia in the second century AD that shaped and guided the archaeological program. The stress was on the uncovering and reconstruction of the great public monuments. The excavations produced inscriptions for the epigrapher, architecture and sculpture for the art historian, and some visual "realia" for the text-based ancient historian. Other major digs of the late nineteenth and early twentieth centuries at places like Delos, Delphi, Corinth, Ephesos, Miletos, and Samothrace followed a similar course. In spite of many exciting finds and new insights into the classical past provided by these excavations, the ancient historical hierarchy still remained in place, one based on the ongoing premise that the discipline should first focus on political history, with cultural, social, and economic history following behind. First the canonical ancient texts must be mastered, then the inscriptions and secondary texts, and finally the physical remains.

Archaeology did become central to ancient historical studies for those time periods and geographical areas, where the information provided by the textual sources was limited or the validity of canonical texts had been seriously challenged. Archaeology was called upon here to validate Homer's description of the Trojan War or Livy's account of early Rome, since the veracity of those authors had been challenged by the "higher critical" methodologies of the philologists and ancient historians. Schliemann excavated at Hissarlik to find Homer's Troy, while Giacomo Boni discovered Romulus's Rome in the Forum.

2   The Twentieth Century

The period after the First World War saw major methodological changes and debates in most areas of post-classical historiography. The growing influence of Marxism fostered research in economic and social history. The foundation of the *Annales* group led by young French scholars like Marc Bloch (1886–1944) stimulated a whole range of social and cultural research based on fields like Marxist economics, historical geography, and social anthropology. Such research carried scholars back into the middle ages, a period still rich in documentary sources, but stopped there.

Ancient historians lacked the rich and diverse written documentation available in monastic registers and town archives that medieval and post-medieval scholars possessed. However, the problems were deeper and more fundamental. Ancient history was increasingly concentrated in classics programs where philological mastery received first and at times exclusive priority. The *Totalwissenschaft* of the nineteenth-century Germans was replaced by Oxford "Greats"-style programs, where the detailed study of chronologically limited time periods in Greek and Roman history based on a few elite texts dominated. The goals were still empirical and positivistic, driven by the hope that mercilessly analyzed Greek and Latin texts would provide all necessary detail on the Peloponnesian War or the reign of Augustus. Contacts with other branches of historical studies diminished.

Classical archaeology continued to pursue a relatively unchanged agenda still focused on major excavations at sites of great "historical" significance. Two interwar major excavations that encapsulated that agenda were those of Mussolini in central Rome and of the Americans in the Athenian Agora. The first, focused on the recovery of Augustan Rome, were driven by propaganda and were poor in technical quality (for context, Erskine, ANCIENT HISTORY AND NATIONAL IDENTITY, section 2). The second was mainly concerned with the Golden Age of democratic Athens, and was for its time a leader in archaeological methodology. Its discoveries, especially topographical and epigraphical, were rapidly incorporated into historical research on ancient Greece. In contrast, one of the most important Roman historical works of the 1930s, and one shaped by consciousness of the fascist experience, Ronald Syme's 1939 *The Roman Revolution* made little use of evidence from the fascist excavations. The potential for such material for understanding Augustan ideology and propaganda would only be fully appreciated two generations later with the publication of Paul Zanker's 1988 *The Power of Images in the Age of Augustus*.

The ancient historian who best appreciated the potential of archaeological material for reconstructing ancient social and economic history was the Russian exile Michael Rostovtzeff (1870–1952). He received a solid classical education in pre-Soviet Russia, where appreciation for the earlier nineteenth-century integration of philology, ancient history, and archaeology seems to have survived more than in the West. He was early drawn to such archaeologically based historical problems as the interrelation between Greek colonists and the indigenous population such as the Scythians who lived along the shores of the Black Sea. The archaeologically rich world of Pompeii also attracted him. He realized that a new ancient social and economic history could only be written by a full use of all the written and material sources, and not just a few elite texts. He published Hellenistic economic archives written on papyri that were recovered from the Egyptian desert and organized the 1930s American excavations at the multicultural Roman frontier post of Dura Europos in Syria. Both his 1926 *Social and Economic History of the Roman Empire* and his 1941 *Social and Economic History of the Hellenistic World* employed numerous illustrations of archaeological objects with full captions that explained their significance to the historian. Unfortunately, while Rostovtzeff prepared many graduate students for the profession, he did not found a school that attempted to bridge the domains of material culture and written texts. The study of ancient history went on into the 1950s and 1960s as though Rostovtzeff had never lived.

Classical archaeology, and especially American classical archaeology, enjoyed a brilliant period in the generation after the Second World War as abundant funding allowed an increased number of large excavations, and new field opportunities opened up in Italy and Turkey. Excavation techniques improved, and the uses of scientific applications in areas like dating and material analysis enhanced the ability of the archaeologists to extract information from the objects they were excavating. However, the scholarly agendas remained largely unchanged. The focus of this new generation continued on major sites and public monuments. The aim of archaeology was still to provide inscriptions, affirm rather specific historical facts, and provide a scenic background for an ancient history still largely written from a narrow range of literary sources.

This limited appreciation of the wider potential of archaeological evidence was even manifest in subfields like the study of Roman provinces, where scholars had long depended on archaeology for most of their base information. Ancient historians like Francis Haverfield (1860–1919) did try to use archaeology to reconstruct such socio-economic developments as rural Romanization in Britain. Robin Collingwood (1889–1943), who was both a philosopher of history and Haverfield's successor as the leading figure in Romano-British archaeology, advocated the potential of meticulous field archaeology for getting an insight into the thought processes of past humans in non-literate society.

Collingwood's approach has had some impact on recent archaeological theory, but neither his legacy nor that of Haverfield produced much sophisticated integration of archaeology and ancient history. Most of the use of the archaeological evidence in the study of Roman Britain continued for long to center on event history, associating burnt levels at sites with Boudicca's destruction of Romano-British cities or ordering the construction and occupation phases on Hadrian's Wall. Not until recently have archaeologists and ancient historians appreciated the potential of archaeology for writing the social and economic history of areas where written sources were few.

Classical archaeology was until the 1960s not significantly more conservative than most other branches of archaeology, and technically generally superior. However, beginning in the 1960s, anthropological archaeology was convulsed by a range of theoretical and methodological debates. These so-called "new" or "processual" archaeologists had diverse theoretical and professional agendas, but proclaimed as their general aim the transformation of archaeology into a discipline more in tune with contemporary social science. At the same time a similar application of new social sciences approaches were transforming many areas of historical studies outside Greek and Roman antiquity. In the Anglophone world the writing of post-classical history was reshaped by the application of various perspectives and methodologies derived from the social sciences, Marxism, the varied *longue durée* approaches best represented by the articles that appeared in the French historical journal of *Annales*, and finally the diverse manifestations of post-modernism and post-colonial studies. Classical archaeology largely ignored those developments, while the writing of Greek and Roman history still reflected the elite text centrality and chronological limits of the Oxbridge and Ivy League ancient historical curricula.

Ironically it was the persecution of Marxists in the United States during the McCarthy era in the early 1950s that laid the foundations for a significant revival of interest in social and economic history among classicists, and a new, more creative linking of classical history and archaeology. The American Marxist ancient historian Moses Finley was forced into exile in Britain. Finley (1912–86) found a home at Cambridge University and proceeded to establish a school of ancient studies that emphasized social and economic history. Finley himself had little of Michael Rostovtzeff's openness toward archaeological evidence, and was at times highly skeptical about the ways in which the discipline could help the ancient historian. However, some of his followers realized that they could not reconstruct the histories of the non-elite classes in Greek and Roman society if they did not move beyond the literary texts and come to grips with the archaeological data. The question was how to get that information from a very conservative archaeological community and convey it to an equally conservative ancient historical community.

Two fields of research advocated by Finley, the reconstruction of the classical countryside and the structure of the ancient economy, gradually demonstrated the potential of archaeological-historical collaboration. Greece and Rome were at the core rural societies, but the ancient writers had little interest in the countryside. Aphorism, prejudice, and unfounded generalization dominated their narratives about rural life. For a few societies like Hellenistic and Roman Egypt the papyri provided the land-holding and production data that modern rural historians required. However, Egypt was always a very peculiar, exceptional case study in a diverse ancient rural world. The small number of rural inscriptions provided limited insight into the social and economic structures of the Greco-Roman countryside. The archaeologists had generally only studied elite sites like Roman villas, and there had focused on the recovery of mosaics, wall painting, and sculpture, with little attention paid to production facilities. Key moments in classical rural history, like the supposed decline of the small farmers in Roman Italy during the late second century BC that led to the failed land reforms of Tiberius and Gaius Gracchus, were often analyzed from strong ideological positions, but with evidence derived largely from elite literary sources. Such approaches would be regarded with skepticism in any other area of rural historical studies.

However, archaeologists were in a position to provide much more diverse data on the nature of ancient rural society. Since the Second World War field workers had been conducting rural surveys that discovered and mapped a great range of sites and collected surface materials that facilitated at least a partial reconstruction of rural occupation patterns over long periods of time. The British had pioneered this approach in the area of ancient Veii north of Rome, and those data were gradually and often grudgingly incorporated into the debate on the Gracchan crisis. Such archaeological investigations did have their limitations. Different areas had different site surface visibility, and sampling strategies had to be continuously refined. The dating of occupation phases at Greek and Roman rural sites depends heavily on the dating of ceramics, some of which had long use histories. Still survey provides real information on thousands of settlements in the actual countryside, and allowed for the creation of a rural history not based mainly on the musings or polemics of some urban Greek or Roman. Moreover, the expansion of survey archaeology in both the Greek and the Roman world has provided much evidence on regional variation and diachronic change, something almost impossible from the written sources that derive from a very limited number of urban centers and from restricted time periods. This new rural archaeology has also stimulated the more precise and complete excavation of a range of rural sites from elite dwellings to humble farmsteads, excavations that stress economic and environmental reconstruction as well as the recovery of objects of art. An increasingly sophisticated archaeology of the countryside is indeed laying the foundations for an understanding of the complexity and diversity of classical rural history.

The classical economy is another area where the use of archaeological information is vital for any sophisticated reconstruction of historical development. Until recently it had been little employed. The ancient writers were little interested in economic life, and even if they had been, they lacked informational tools like statistics that would have allowed them to move beyond opinionated remarks to something approaching true economic history. Rostovtzeff realized the potential of material culture for understanding the ancient economy, but could employ it in only an anecdotal and illustrative manner. Finley had less confidence in the potential of archaeology. He wrote an extremely influential book, *The Ancient Economy* (1st edn 1973, 3rd edn 1999) with a minimum use of the archaeological record. Indeed, he and some of his followers marginalized the use of the archaeological evidence in part by arguing for a relatively primitive ancient economy with limited consumer activity. Such reconstructions restricted the role of complicated economic processes in ancient society and marginalized the relevance of such consumer goods as ceramics, which are the staples of the archaeologist (on economic history, see Morley, ECONOMIC AND SOCIAL HISTORY).

Archaeologists have meanwhile provided much evidence for the complexity of the ancient, and especially the Roman, economy. While ancient economic theory may have been simplistic and the instruments of economic activity like book-keeping primitive, those engaged especially in the Hellenistic and Roman economies produced and shipped large quantities of durable goods to supply a complicated demand for consumer products that reached most levels of their societies. Research by underwater archaeologists since the Second World War has located thousands of shipwrecks in the Mediterranean dating from the Bronze Age to the middle ages. Analyses of their cargoes, and especially of the amphorae, the shipping containers of antiquity, have allowed the reconstruction of complex "source to market" trading patterns. The study of major Roman ceramic industries like the red-glazed potteries of Italy, Gaul, and North Africa again show the existence of a Roman imperial-period production-consumption economy unparalleled until the eighteenth century.

3   Future Directions

All of this demonstrates that the future of ancient historical-archaeological research lies in the study of social and economic historical processes rather than in the reconstruction of particular historical events. Archaeology can occasionally be brought to bear to solve a specific historical problem. A recent example from military history has been the identification of the site in Germany where in AD 9 the Roman general Varus was defeated by the German leader Arminius. However, this use of archaeology for detailed historical reconstruction will always remain an exception. Few other ancient battle sites have yielded, or are likely to yield, the quantity of military artifacts that were found in Germany. Generally the identification of even major ancient battle-grounds is very difficult, as the long and futile search for the battlefield of Cannae in South Italy demonstrates. Destruction levels are abundant at archaeological sites, but seldom can they be precisely associated with major events. Roman historians and archaeologists have in the abundant and precisely dated Roman coinage one of the most temporally sensitive instruments available to scholars of material culture, but seldom can it provide the "to the year" dates that event-oriented ancient historians require. Little destruction debris can be associated with the sack of Rome by the Goths in AD 410, and even less with the Gallic sack in 390 BC.

In contrast, the new approaches to archaeology can supply vital help to the ancient historian in reconstructing the economic and social processes that shaped the foundations of ancient society. Significantly it is survey-oriented archaeologists who have advocated the application of the *Annales* approaches to the study of antiquity. It is especially important for understanding the worlds of the peasants and humble dwellers in small towns and villages, who formed the productive base of Greek and Roman society. Such non-elite groups are seldom, or at best scornfully, mentioned in the literary sources. Archaeologists can recover their house plans and reconstruct how their settlements and fields distributed themselves over the land. They can determine what they purchased and what they ate. From their bones they can recover information on age and health. Moreover, the potential of archaeology for a fuller recovery of the past increases, while the problems with the texts are being increasingly highlighted. Few new literary works will be recovered. Contemporary literary and cultural criticism of ancient writers has increasingly stressed the degree to which ideology and personal agendas shaped their presentation of the past. In contrast, not only is our archaeological data pool increasing, but it is being analyzed with ever increasing methodological sophistication. While all approaches provide important mirrors to the past, a truly modern ancient history can only ignore archaeology to its peril.

FURTHER READING

There is no general study of the long and complex historical relationship between ancient history and classical archaeology. Indeed there is no good, modern study of the history of ancient history available in English. The history of classical archaeology has been better served. Three useful works are Barbanera 1998, Dyson 2006, and Gran-Aymerich 1998. Haverfield and Collingwood can best be approached through Freeman 2007 and Hingley 2000. For Collingwood and the "archaeology of mind," as well as the recent theoretical debates in archaeology, Hodder 1991. Both Rostovtzeff and Finley lack major studies. Arnaldo Momigliano's essay on Rostovtzeff in his *Studies in Modern Scholarship* (1994) provides the best brief overview of that important classical scholar. Some of Finley's attitudes toward archaeology can be seen in his *The Use and Abuse of History* (1975). A good introduction to the use of survey archaeology in Italy is Timothy Potter's *The Changing Landscape of South Etruria* (1979). K. Greene 1986 provides good insights into the use of archaeology in reconstructing the Roman economy. Martin Millett's *The Romanization of Britain* (1990) is a good exercise in the employment of archaeological data to ask more general questions about the development of a Roman province. A useful set of essays on the potential of the *Annales* approach for understanding classical antiquity is Bintliff 1991. P. Wells 2003 provides a good study of the archaeology of the battle between Arminius and Varus.

CHAPTER SEVEN

Oratory

Catherine Steel

1 Introduction

Some of the most striking vignettes in ancient history concern the figure of the orator addressing his fellow-citizens. Demosthenes urging the Athenians to resist Philip; Tiberius Gracchus lynched by a band of senators as he addressed a gathering of Romans on the Capitol; Cicero driving Catiline from Rome by the sheer force of his speaking in the Senate. Public speaking was at the heart of political life in both democratic Athens and republican Rome; and even in states with less democratic forms of government, oratory was often an important skill for members of the elite to possess, to persuade their peers and to demonstrate their cultural awareness. The surviving texts of Greek and Roman oratory are one of the supreme literary monuments of antiquity; they are also texts which historians rely on in answering a wide variety of questions. Yet the nature of oratory imposes considerable constraints on the conclusions one can legitimately draw from it.

Ancient theorists of public speaking divided oratory into three categories, depending upon the context of speaking. Forensic oratory is oratory delivered in the law-courts, either in prosecution or in defense; deliberative oratory deals with determining courses of action, such as speeches given to the Athenian or Roman popular assemblies or in the Senate; epideictic oratory involves the praise or blame of an individual. Oratory, then, while being possible in any political system, becomes a particularly important skill in states whose constitution contains a democratic element, and where, in turn, the ability to persuade large groups of people contributes to political power.

So important was public speech to political activity in democratic communities that a whole science of speaking – rhetoric – developed in the fifth-century Greek world. The essential claim made by rhetoric is that speaking well is a skill which can be taught: natural talent is not irrelevant, but an individual's innate capacity can be improved by systematic training and practice. Furthermore, the techniques of effective speaking are morally neutral: that is, they can be applied to bad arguments as well as to good ones. These two characteristics made rhetoric an object of profound suspicion to many ancient thinkers, among whom Plato is the most prominent: his attack on rhetoric, and corresponding elevation of philosophy, dominates both *Phaedrus* and *Gorgias*.

Rhetoric is not central to modern education, and the term itself, in everyday speech, tends to be used in a hostile or derogatory fashion. But for historians who use ancient oratory, rhetoric is an important concept because it helps us to deal with one of the chief difficulties of using evidence from oratory: its systematic distortion of the events it describes and analyzes. An orator seeks the best possible presentation of his case, and not balance, fairness, or accuracy – unless such qualities will assist him in securing his aim in speaking, whatever that may be.

2   Oratory and the Courts

At some point during the 350s or 340s BC, an Athenian called Ariston brought a private prosecution for assault against a fellow-citizen of his called Konon. Athenian legal practice demanded that plaintiffs in such cases speak on their own behalf, and Ariston turned for assistance to a logographer, i.e. a professional speech-writer, in this case the orator Demosthenes. Ariston's speech survives in the corpus of Demonsthenes' works, as speech 54, but there is no explicit statement within the text itself to link the work with Demosthenes: it consists only of Ariston's first person exposition of his case.

Ariston claims that he had been assaulted during an evening stroll through Athens by Konon, along with his son Ktesias and the (unnamed) son of Andromenes, who kicked him, verbally abused him, and stole his cloak; his injuries were so severe that he almost died. This assault was connected with the ill-feeling which developed between Ariston and Konon's sons when they had all been in the army together some years earlier, and, on the evening in question, had been preceded by an encounter between Ariston and a drunken Ktesias. Ariston also produced witness testimony and depositions: about what had happened in the army, from the men who carried Ariston to the baths and then to a friend's house, from the doctor who attended him and from those who visited him when injured, as well as about Konon's conduct at the earlier arbitration stage. However, the evidence itself was not preserved.

Ariston seems to have a good case: he can demonstrate that his assailants had a grudge against him, and that he was badly hurt. But there are some indications that what happened may not be as simple as the story which he tells. The most telling point is that Ariston may not have had any witnesses to the attack itself. He claims towards the end of the speech (32) that his witnesses testified "that they saw me beaten by Konon and stripped of my cloak and the victim of *hubris* in respect of the other things I suffered"; but the force of this paraphrase is undermined by the tense usage on other occasions in the speech where Ariston refers to this evidence, which suggests that these witnesses arrived only after the fight was over. If Ariston *did* have a witness to the attack itself, it is certainly curious that he does not make more emphatic use of his testimony. Furthermore, there was sworn testimony, produced by the other side, that Konon had *not* participated in the attack (31) but had come across his son Ktesias and Ariston fighting; and Ariston works hard to demolish the credibility of this evidence on the grounds that it comes from Konon's drinking pals.

Another argument which Ariston claims Konon was going to use is that both Ktesias and Ariston are members of drinking clubs, and that what happened was simply the result of a drunken encounter (13–23). Ariston turns this into a further argument against Konon, inasmuch as his lack of concern about this kind of assault is a demonstration of his brutal nature and distance from the norms of behavior which Ariston and his audience of jurors share. But it is easy enough, if one steps away from Ariston's perspective, to see the case which Konon might have constructed. He was not personally part of the assault; his sons and Ariston had a history of mutual ill feeling; they came across one another while both drunk, and there was a scuffle; no one was seriously hurt; boys will be boys.

To consider Konon's case is not necessarily to conclude that Konon was innocent: and the fact that Ariston does not have a witness to his assault, but speaks as though he does, is not in itself evidence that he was not attacked by Konon in the way that he alleges. But the exercise does reveal that Ariston's case is not perhaps as strong as an initial reading suggests. The apparent strength, indeed, depends as much on the way Demosthenes constructs the speech as on the facts of the case, and above all on the characterization he applies to both Ariston and Konon throughout the speech. Ariston is made to seem like a respectable young man, reluctant to engage in legal action until provoked beyond bearing and the victim of unprovoked hostility from Konon and his family: "without ever offering a shred of solid evidence to his own good character Ariston emerges as an excellent young man" (Carey and Reid 1985: 74). Konon, by contrast, is brutal and untrustworthy, contemptuous of normal decent behavior, a member of a sworn association whose members are willing to perjure themselves – accusations (at 38–40 in particular) for which Ariston produces no evidence beyond his own statement. If his audience accepts this relentless and consistent polarization it will be much more likely that they will believe an interpretation of events in which Ariston is the victim and Konon the aggressor. Aristotle, who was writing and teaching on rhetoric at around the same time that Demosthenes and the other Athenian orators were producing forensic speeches for their clients, divided the material of rhetoric into three parts: *ethos*, which concerns characterization; *pathos*, which deals with the arousal of the listener's emotions; and *logos*, which covers evidence and rational arguments (Arist. *Rhet.* 1356a1–4). *Ethos* and *pathos* offer the skillful orator, or speech-writer, enormous scope to generate material which is favorable to his client and which creates an atmosphere in which his audience is likely to be favorable to the arguments drawn from the facts of the case. An excellent way to counter the insidious effects of character and emotion would be to read the opposite side's case. Quintilian, a Roman theorist of oratory writing in the first century AD, counsels precisely this when explaining how to make the best use of studying speeches: "The most useful steps are to get to know the cases which the speeches you have taken up deal with and, whenever possible, to read the speeches given on both sides . . . even if they seem not to be well matched, it is nevertheless good to get hold of them so as to understand the nature of the case" (Quint. 10.1.22–23).

Quintilian's suggestion is phrased in such a way to indicate that even for him it was often not possible: the consequence in part of patterns of recording speeches in writing, an issue to which I return below. Our position is even worse because of the additional losses in subsequent transmission; indeed, only two matched pairs of speeches survive, both involving clashes between Demosthenes and Aeschines. In reading deliberative oratory, too, we do not have the opportunity of putting opposing cases side by side; indeed, some locations of speaking, such as the public meeting at Rome, did not always involve the presentation of opposing points of view. Nevertheless, the subject matter of much deliberative oratory is more liable to external check. We have no other evidence about Konon's behavior than what Ariston tells us; but we can sometimes speculate in a more informed manner about what ancient politicians tell us.

3   Oratory and Politics

In 66 BC Gnaeus Pompeius (Pompey), already known as *Magnus* (the Great), was proposed, in a law put forward by the tribune Manilius, as supreme commander in the war against Mithridates. The proposal had widespread support, and among those who spoke in its favor was Cicero, at that time praetor, and ambitious for the consulship. His speech *On the command of Gnaeus Pompeius* is notable for its clear structure and for the elaborate praise of Pompey which dominates it: the whole offers a very convincing justification for the law. But there are grounds for being skeptical about what Cicero says, as two examples will demonstrate.

One way in which Cicero demonstrates Pompey's suitability for this appointment is by appealing to his past record, and particularly to his campaign against the pirates the previous summer. Cicero emphasizes Pompey's speed and his comprehensiveness: the entire Mediterranean has been cleared of piracy through his actions in the course of a single season (31–35), and he speaks as though the problem has been solved once and for all. And yet other evidence indicates that piracy did not cease to be a problem in the years after Pompey's command: indeed, in 59 BC, Cicero himself had to explain why there were still pirates in the Mediterranean, in the course of defending Flaccus, who was facing prosecution for extortion while governor of Asia: one of the charges was of extorting money to pay for a fleet (*On behalf of Flaccus* 29). Cicero greatly exaggerates the scale and scope of what Pompey achieved (de Souza 1999: 149–78).

Another point at which Cicero embellishes Pompey is in his description of Pompey's early career, which he does three times during the course of the speech: providing evidence of both his knowledge and his skill as a commander and of the beneficial effects of previous constitutional innovations which were made in Pompey's case. Cicero draws attention to Pompey's youth, his unbroken run of success in military matters, and the range of enemies which he has faced: these are all topics likely to appeal to his audience of Roman citizens. However, it would be misleading to use Cicero's evidence here as the basis for an account of Pompey's early career, and the bias lies not only in the hyperbole of Cicero's praise – Pompey's talents alone, for example, are greater than those of all other generals put together (29) – but also in a number of omissions and misleading descriptions which serve to conceal certain aspects of what Pompey has done which might not appeal so much to his audience. In discussing Pompey's military knowledge, Cicero implies that he moved without break from serving in the army of his father (Pompeius Strabo, who was consul in 89 BC) to command of his own forces (28). Cicero's use of the word *imperator* to describe Pompey's position at this time is a sleight-of-hand, since his raising of an army was illegal, and only retrospectively approved by Sulla. And he also obscures the period of four years which intervenes between the two periods of military service, during which time Pompey was, like many Romans, accommodating himself to Cinna's regime.

When Cicero moves to Pompey's warfare from the time of Sulla's dictatorship onward, he emphasizes the geographical scope of his activity: Italy, Sicily, Africa, Gaul and Spain have all witnessed Pompey's courage and his defeat of the enemies of Rome. As soon, however, as one reflects on the circumstances, it becomes obvious that these campaigns were all part of the civil war between Sulla and his opponents which carried on in parts of the Roman empire outside Italy for some years after Sulla's capture of Rome, and indeed his death. Pompey fought against Roman forces in Sicily, in North Africa and finally in Spain, and had been responsible for the execution of a number of the opposing Roman commanders at the conclusion of hostilities. Cicero substantially improves the appeal of the narrative of Pompey's early activities by removing the ugly details of civil war from it. He also turns Pompey into a solitary figure who achieves his successes on his own (28). This, too, is a statement which could be challenged. In Spain, in the campaign against Sertorius, Pompey joined Metellus Pius; in the slave war in Italy, he arrived only when Crassus had substantially concluded the fighting; and during the recent campaign against the pirates, he found himself in dispute with the governor of Crete, who regarded the defeat of those pirates with a land base in Crete as his achievement. So far from being a lone hero, Pompey might seem to some to be someone whose career has been marked by episodes of unhappy collaboration.

Cicero's oratory offers his audiences an improved version of Pompey. It is far from being fictional, but it provides an interpretation of what Pompey has done, backed up by Cicero's own authority as a speaker, which is as favorable as possible. It is necessary to approach the factual content of ancient oratory with sustained skepticism. The questions to be asked, above all, are in what way does this piece of evidence support the speaker's case, and would his audience have access to material which could disprove it. If, as is very often the case, the answers to those questions are, respectively, "to a very great extent" and "no," then one cannot place much confidence in the material the orator presents. Ancient orators were trained to make the best possible case; and doing this in the face of contrary evidence was a source of pride. Cicero, for example, is said to have boasted of having thoroughly confused the jury at the trial of Cluentius, who was being prosecuted for murder (Quint. 2.17.21).

These observations about the unreliability of the evidence provided by ancient oratory would still be true even if what we were dealing with, when reading ancient oratory, were impartial transcriptions of the actual words spoken. However, that is not the case; and considering the ways in which speeches survived in written form offers a further set of concerns about their use as historical evidence. The difficulty in relation to oratory arises not only because of the processes of transmission during the post-antique period until the invention of printing; the initial transfer from speech to writing is also far from straightforward. Greek and Roman orators almost always delivered their speeches from memory: the capacity to speak fluently and at length from memory was one of the five canonical skills of the orator, and highly elaborate methods of memory training were part of what young men acquired when they trained to be orators. Written texts were not therefore an essential part of speaking in public, and almost all of the surviving texts of speeches are the result of conscious decisions, usually on the part of the orator himself, to write down what he had said and make this version available to others. In the case of Athenian forensic oratory, the creation of texts is a consequence of the absence of advocacy: since plaintiff and defendant spoke on their own behalf, professional help could most easily be transferred by means of a written text. This, indeed, can be regarded as the product for which payment was made: after all, no logographer could guarantee his client's success. But deliberative oratory in the Greek world, and oratory generally at Rome, did not automatically make the transition to written form. Those speeches which were written down were the product of conscious decisions that they were worth disseminating and thereafter being preserved.

4   Writing and Reading Speeches

This aspect of oratory raises two further questions. One, how accurate are ancient speeches as guides to what was actually said? And two, why did orators choose to prepare and disseminate written texts?

The accuracy of written versions has been much discussed. Ancient historians generally settle for a guarded trust in the accuracy of written versions, relying primarily on two arguments: ancient memory techniques were good enough to enable reasonably accurate transcriptions; and the overlap between the audiences of the spoken and written versions must have acted as a check on wholesale fabrication. In certain instances, these assumptions must be wrong: for example, Roman legal procedure in criminal cases could not have included speeches of precisely the form that Cicero's take, because of scheduled adjournments and the inclusion of witness evidence. Indeed, some of Cicero's speeches include the headings where evidence would have been presented, which he has left out of the version disseminated. Similarly, surviving texts of Athenian forensic oratory include headings where spoken and written evidence was produced. At these points, there is a tension between the demands of oral performance and the conventions of a written genre. Quintilian acknowledges the existence of differing standards in evaluating spoken and written speeches at Rome, even though he argues that the same standards can and should be applied to both types (12.10.49–57). Ancient orators were conscious that those reading their speeches, as opposed to hearing them, would be highly educated in exactly those techniques of rhetoric which the speeches relied on; and would have the opportunity to study a speech closely.

In general, then, we must allow for an orator's tidying up of a speech in preparation for written dissemination and for its offering the very best words that its author could produce, given the opportunity to reflect at leisure. Moreover, a written text cannot convey the extra-textual elements in oratorical performance; yet delivery, comprising gesture and voice, was one of the five fundamental divisions of oratorical technique, and regarded by many practitioners as the most important of these. A story about Demosthenes is often repeated: when asked what the most important aspect of speaking was, he gave the answer "Delivery," and said that delivery was also the second and third most important thing. And a text does not include the audience's original response. Written speeches thus offer the pretence of being an accurate record of the words said, to the extent of removing everything but the orator's words; and yet in the absence of what other people said on the same occasion, and the audience's response to what it heard, a written speech is missing crucial elements which would have helped its readers to assess its impact. In particular, speeches do not give any indication of the outcome, i.e. the eventual verdict for a forensic speech, or the vote for a deliberative one. In many cases, that evidence is now lost, and with it an important means of assessing the situation dealt with in the speech. We would be in a somewhat stronger position to assess Ariston's case, for example, if we knew how the jury responded to his speech. And we should not assume that ancient readers had better access to this kind of information than we do. Asconius's set of notes on five of Cicero's speeches, written about a century later, show that he thought it valuable to include the verdicts. Writing concentrates even further the single, dominant viewpoint of the orator which prevails while he speaks.

These observations apply to all written speeches. There are a number of occasions where the illusion generated by a written speech requires even greater scrutiny: occasions where no speech was actually delivered. Demosthenes may never have given *Against Meidias*, and two of Cicero's most famous speeches, the *Verrines* and the *Second Philippic*, certainly come into this category; of similar interest is the text of the speech *On behalf of Milo*, which almost certainly bears little relationship to what Cicero may have said at the trial. It is worth considering the circumstances of each case, which throw some light on the reasons why an orator might write up a speech.

Cicero was denied his opportunity to complete his prosecution of Verres in 70 BC by the defendant's decision to go into exile during the adjournment between the first and second hearing of the case. By disseminating the five parts of the second hearing, as though he had in fact delivered them, Cicero was able, through his display of all the material he had gathered in Sicily, to demonstrate his diligence and his brilliance. A further motive may have been the desire to show conclusively that Verres was guilty and thereby negate any unpopularity Cicero himself might have acquired through the fact of prosecution and the benefits he personally obtained by so doing. He could not use the excuse of being at the start of his career to justify undertaking a prosecution, and since Verres was a praetor and thus senior to Cicero, he probably acquired Verres' status at the conclusion of the trial. The non-delivery of the *Second Philippic* has a different cause: fear. Given Marcus Antonius's military dominance in Rome by the autumn of 44 BC, Cicero was unwilling to respond to Antonius's attack on him in the Senate on September 19th in person. Writing gave him a safer means of response, and he did not speak again in the Senate until after Antonius had left Rome. In both these cases, writing allowed Cicero to reach an audience on occasions when it was not possible for him actually to speak. It is evidence of the authority which Cicero believed he possessed as an orator, and which inhered to the occasions of public speech, whether forensic or deliberative, that he maintained in every respect the conventions of a written speech on these occasions where he did not, in fact, speak.

The circumstances relating to the speech *On behalf of Milo* are different: Cicero did give a defense speech at Milo's trial on charges arising from the murder of Clodius in 52 BC, but what we know of the speech's transmission suggests that the version we have is substantially altered from what Cicero may have actually said. It is unusual among Cicero's forensic speeches in recording a case where Cicero's client lost: normally, defeats did not make the transition to written form. One could argue that the political circumstances of the time, and in particular Cicero's own deep hostility to Clodius, might have led to Cicero's wanting a permanent record of the case; but there is also some evidence to suggest that Cicero's own performance at the trial was not very effective, and that an unauthorized version of what he said was taken down and circulated immediately afterwards. The speech we have could therefore mark an attempt to replace a text which records a poor performance by one which displays Cicero as a competent speaker; and, if so, this strategy has been largely successful, inasmuch as the *On behalf of Milo* is regarded as one of Cicero's finest speeches, and nothing has survived of the other version.

These three cases support an expectation that what we read is a polished-up version: orators' reputations are at stake in writing, and writing provides a chance of bolstering and maintaining reputations. Some orators never had any written versions disseminated, precisely because they feared the continuing existence of their speeches could do them harm. Marcus Antonius – the grandfather of the triumvir – was afraid that writing down his speeches would leave him vulnerable to charges of self-contradiction (Cic. *Clu.* 140). Cicero was forced into denial when an attack on a rival entered the public domain: he asked Atticus to try to spread the word that the speech was a forgery (Cic. *Att.* 3.12.2). The motives of those who did disseminate can be analyzed under three headings: persuasion, reputation, and education.

Persuasion relates particularly to deliberative oratory, if the circumstances to which the speech is contributing may continue, and is less applicable to forensic cases, which conclude at the close of the trial. So, for example, the struggle against Marcus Antonius in 44–43 BC was spread over months, and over an extended geographical range: by sending out copies of the speeches he had delivered, Cicero was able to give a demonstration to commanders distant from Rome of the strength of the senatorial position. However, this is a relatively unusual situation: in most cases, including deliberative ones, directly influencing opinion was not needed once the vote had been taken. But dissemination could always be a means of promoting an orator's reputation: either for simple competence as a speaker, or as a demonstration of an orator's adherence to particular views which might increase his popularity. For Lysias, for example, a non-citizen working as a logographer in Athens, circulation of the written text of one of his speeches would act primarily as an advertisement of his skills and thereby a means to secure clients. For orators who were politically active, however, the implications could be wider. By the time Cicero spread the written version of his speech *On the command of Gnaeus Pompeius* the vote had already been taken and the command bestowed. But Cicero's public support of Pompey was still potentially of value to him in helping him to secure the support of those who favored Pompey in the coming election for the consulship. As for the final possibility, education, Cicero claims that aspiring orators read his works, and theoretical writers on oratory such as Quintilian draw many of their examples from actual speeches. Becoming a model for subsequent generations was a pleasing achievement; but there is little evidence that ancient orators were primarily altruistic in their dissemination practices. The pedagogical value of speeches was a happy side-effect.

5   Conclusion

Consideration of how and why speeches get written down can also lead to identifying some of the more interesting and promising questions to ask of oratory. Much of the discussion in this chapter has been pessimistic about the use of oratory by historians, stressing the extent to which the factual content of oratory is distorted by the need to be persuasive. But oratory can nevertheless be a productive genre for ancient historians to explore. Given the importance of oratory to political careers in both Athens and Rome, surviving speeches are a valuable indicator of an individual's position and alliances at various points in his career; with the further factor that we can normally be confident that what we are reading is something that an orator positively wanted an audience to read. The processes of selection become an advantage when one approaches oratory as a corpus relating to a particular individual.

Oratory, too, is an extraordinarily rich source for social history. It can be informative about habits. We know more, for example, about the use of domestic space in fourth century Athens, from Lysias's *On the murder of Eratosthenes*, and about baths as a location for socializing in the late republic, thanks to Cicero's *On behalf of Caelius*, than we might otherwise do: both orators are drawing on shared and accepted behaviors in order to sketch a background for what they claim happened on a specific occasion. Forensic oratory tells us a great deal about how the law operated and was conceptualized; passages of invective indicate what qualities were admired and what behaviors could be presented as disgraceful at different periods. As an index of a variety of broader themes in ancient social and political history, then, oratory has a substantial contribution to make. What it is much less good at indicating, however, is what happened at a particular time and place; and if we are to make good use of oratory, we need to begin with attitude of profound mistrust of what orators tell us.

FURTHER READING

Good starting points on ancient oratory include G. Kennedy 1994's history of classical rhetoric, M. Edwards 1994 on Attic orators and M. Clarke 1996 on Rome. On the role of popular oratory in political decision-making, see Ober 1989b and Yunis 1996 for Athens, while Millar 1998, Mouritsen 2001 and Morstein-Marx 2004 treat Rome. There is a commentary on Demosthenes' speech for Ariston in Carey and Reid 1985, and a translation in Bers 2003. Issues relating to the written records of spoken oratory are addressed in J. Trevett 1996 and Powell and Paterson 2004: 1–57. The problems of publication in relation to Roman oratory are covered in very much greater detail in Humbert 1925 and Stroh 1975. On orators' gestures, see Aldrete 1999. S. Butler 2002 discusses Cicero's use of writing; on the trial of Milo and Cicero's speeches *On behalf of Milo*, see A. Stone 1980 and C. Steel 2005: 116–131.

CHAPTER EIGHT

Ancient History Through Ancient Literature

Tim Whitmarsh

1 Introduction

There are many good reasons why literature should be central to the practice of ancient history. Texts provide a huge bulk of ancient evidence, all but inexhaustible to the individual reader. What is more, much of this material can be read pretty much complete, in good-quality modern editions that have the additional benefit of being electronically searchable. A good range of translations, commentaries, and other interpretative media are available. Dates and contexts can often be determined with relative precision.

These are not benefits to be taken lightly. Anyone who has ever worked on the material remains of antiquity – papyri, inscriptions, artifacts, coins, sites, architecture – may well look enviously upon the lot of literary scholars. Material culture is liable to be damaged by time, and problems of context loom large: even if a precise record exists of where a given item was discovered, serious questions still arise as to how it got there. Does a coin found in an unidentified building make it a treasury? Or was it dropped there by accident? How do we know whether an inscription was located in a given place by the original commissioner, or by a medieval farmer in need of a plinth for his pig trough? Such issues do not arise in the same way for literary texts. It would of course be instructive to know more than we do about the circumstances of production, performance and circulation of individual works, but the meaning of literary texts is not conditioned by their material form and context to the same extent.

There are, however, many other equally good reasons for historians to treat literary texts with suspicion. Because education was a select privilege in antiquity, the vast majority of our literary texts represent the outlook of elite males alone. Literature always embodies a set of values: it constructs an imaginary world (even if, as in historiography, that world is based upon reality) where certain character types predominate, and particular actions have particular consequences. To accept literary texts as guides to historical reality usually involves subscribing to these core values. There was, for sure, a time when many scholars of ancient history could subscribe, minor adjustments notwithstanding, to most of the (elite, male) values: and so Thucydides' and Plato's view of classical Athens' decline into mob rule, for example, might be accepted as broadly accurate. Those days are gone; narrative history is now held in deep suspicion, precisely because we are so aware that narratives are partial and self-invested.

Nevertheless, because of the sheer weighting of our evidence, dealing with literary texts is an inevitability. What is more, historians, I shall argue, stand to gain much from engaging with the issues of interpretation raised by literary texts – just as, conversely, it behooves literary students to locate their texts in a historical landscape. The stand-off between "literary" readings of texts, focusing upon aesthetic and formal aspects (allusion, narratology, and so forth), and "historicism" (emphasizing points of contact with a text's contemporary world) is unproductive. In conclusion to this chapter, I shall point to what I hope to be a more constructive form of historicism.

2   Transmission

The most fundamental problem raised by ancient literature is that of establishing the text. What were the original words composed by the author? This is an area where we never have the luxury of confidence. Much ancient literature, particularly poetry (but also prose oratory, and perhaps even some history) was designed for oral performance, and may have been substantially altered (and/or the variants "normalized") when transcribed into written form. These issues are most keenly felt in relation to the earliest Greek epics (Homer, Hesiod, and the cycle), but in fact the same problems arise throughout the ancient world. Can we really be sure that the *Verrine* orations, for example, reflect the words Cicero delivered in court? Or that the *Aeneid* as we have it is the same text that may have thrilled Maecenas in private recitations? Many Greek tragedies are probably patchworks of original words and actors' interpolations – but the extent of this phenomenon is highly debated.

At one level, it pays to have a relaxed attitude towards this kind of imponderable: we still have, in each case, (approximately) contemporary testimony, in a form designed to complement the original. So long as we remain aware of the nature of the text that we have – that, for example, the *Verrines* are Cicero's self-promoting literary publication rather than a *verbatim* court transcript – then the problem is relatively minor (on Cicero, cf. Steel, ORATORY). Romantic conceptions of authorship have lost their grip: it is no longer the spontaneous outpourings of the originating genius that are sought so much as evidence for cultural machinery at work.

The problems, however, run deeper than this. Ancient society had no means of mechanical reproduction: each copy of a text had to be produced laboriously by hand, which made variation an ever-present possibility, even if the same scribe was copying. As a result, our sources for ancient texts tend to conflict with each other. We have two principal sources for ancient literature: manuscripts and papyri (the biggest exception is an anomaly, the corpus of epigrams that survive in massive numbers on stone inscriptions). Manuscripts raise two major issues, aside from that of actually reading crabby medieval handwriting. The first is that the tradition is unrepresentative of the range of ancient literature. What survives of Greek literature reflects the taste of Byzantine and to a lesser extent Baghdadi religious-scholastic communities, to whose labors we owe the fact that anything at all survived the gulf between late antiquity and the Renaissance. Latin was read more widely (throughout western Europe), but again choices were made about what to copy and what not. It is for this reason that we have literally thousands of late-antique Christian texts, filling hundreds of volumes of Migne's awesome *Patrologia Latina* and *Patrologia Graeca*, but only seven complete plays each by Aeschylus and Sophocles. Some of the greatest ancient authors have survived by the slenderest of threads: Catullus was transmitted in a single manuscript, while Sappho and Menander were only minimally represented until the papyrus dump at Oxyrhynchus began to be excavated in the late nineteenth century (see Bowman, PAPYROLOGY).

The other issue presented by manuscripts is, evidently, that they represent texts that have been copied and recopied numerous times. The possibilities for error are massive. A glance at the foot of any Teubner or Oxford Classical Text of an author for whom multiple copies survive will demonstrate quickly just how many variations can be introduced. Nor is the fame of a particular text proof against this kind of corruption (as paleographers style it). Corruption was just as likely to result from the macho attempts of ancient experts to attempt to "remedy" a canonical text as from the ignorance of a scribe. The textual tradition of Herodotus, for example, shows signs of attempts to rationalize his distinctive Ionic dialect. The Homeric poems became a playground for editors from the early third century onwards: one well-known wag, Timon of Phlius, advised the poet Aratus to use old copies of Homer, not those now "corrected" (D.L. 9.113).

For this reason, ancient papyri are not necessarily a surer guide to the original reading. Of course, these texts were written at an earlier stage in the transmission, and hence *a priori* were less open to corruption. But while papyri sometimes do offer new readings, they can also be highly eccentric. For the novelist Achilles Tatius, for example, the one papyrus covering the problematic beginning of book 2 offers a different order for the episodes from that in the manuscript tradition – different, and much less satisfactory too. Add to this that the texts are always fragmentary, and that the sample is highly limited (almost all are from one locale, viz. the area around Oxyrhynchus in Egypt), and we can quickly see that papyri are more likely to add to our problems than solve them finally.

These issues often have little real impact upon our understanding of historical narrative – but they can affect them substantially. In his seventh book, Herodotus tells us of Kadmos's capture of the town of Zankle (later Messene): some manuscripts tell us that he captured it "from" the Samians, some say "with" (7.164.1). Also significant is the episode in book 6, where he defends the Athenian Alcmeonids against accusations of complicity with the Persians. A passage (6.122) omitted from many of the manuscripts fills out the defence with a digression on Callias, who exalted freedom to the extent that he let his daughters choose their own husbands (!). This passage is widely condemned as un-Herodotean ("probably a note of some reader": How and Wells 1912: 115), but has proven attractive to scholars of gender, who have often taken it as authentic.

The texts that we read in modern editions may well be closer, on balance, to the original than those of 100 years ago, but they are still products of decisions based upon the editor's own (personal, culturally circumscribed decisions, ideological) ideas about the ancient author's likely intentions.

3   Lost in Translation?

These problems are redoubled when we consider the difficulty of using a translated text. Let us take a brief example. In book 2 of Homer's *Iliad*, Thersites publicly attacks Agamemnon's policy (2.211–42). The Homeric text says nothing about Thersites' social class: one might conclude from his fearsome ugliness and his attacks on "the lords" that he was of lower station, but in fact the later tradition places him on an equal demographic footing (this is how he appears in Quintus of Smyrna, for example). If we consider the three best-known translations of Homer, however, we see strikingly different practice. Richmond Lattimore's rendition of the passage avoids all mention of class; on the other hand, E. V. Rieu (". . . never at a loss for some vulgar quip . . .") and Robert Fagles (". . . insubordinate . . .") clearly imply a differentiation of rank. In such cases, translation slopes visibly into interpretation.

Modern translations form part of the reception history of an ancient text. They perform a double function: on the one hand, they keep literature alive, by furnishing it with the idioms and resonances that will appeal to a modern culture; on the other hand, they inevitably introduce a certain distance from the ancient language itself. Let us consider, for example, the Latin word *virtus*. An obvious translation would be "virtue"; and indeed *virtus* is used, like its English derivative, primarily in contexts suggesting individual moral excellence. But *virtus* is formed from *vir* (man): Roman culture exploits the links between ethical quality and manliness in a way that modern English simply does not. For example, a number of Roman moralists toy with the concept of the *virtutes* of women, a paradox that is completely dissipated in English translation (Langlands 2006, e.g. 51, 182, 186).

Ancient ethical vocabulary, indeed, poses particular problems. Greek is notably rich in untranslatable abstractions, which only make sense within their own specific cultural framework: examples include *sophrosune* (broadly self-control), *aidos* (shame, or reverence), *hubris* (interpersonal aggression). Political language is also difficult. Many terms (e.g. *basileus, polis, consul*) are often left untranslated, so as to avoid the misleading associations that English equivalents (e.g. feudal lord, city, prime minister) might suggest. From one perspective, however, avoiding translation does not avoid the problems associated with it; rather, it simply avoids dealing with the question of what these institutions actually were, while concealing that avoidance under a mask of authenticity. Let us note finally that there is a class of words that are impossible to translate because we simply do not know what they mean. Items of food, plants, animals and fish often pose significant problems. It is at times like this (when, for example, we are trying to make sense of Theophrastus's *On the causes of plants* or Athenaeus's *Sophists at supper*) that we are reminded of just how much we do not know about the ancient world.

The problems raised by translation are emblematic of the wider interpretative issues presented by ancient texts. Even those fortunate enough to possess the language skills to read complex literary works in the original are still faced with the need to *make sense* of a text that belongs to a very different culture. For example, the Greek biographer Plutarch (second century AD) comments that Cicero was worried by what he saw as Julius Caesar's tyrannical intentions: "On the other hand, when I see him arranging his hair so ornately, and that hair being scratched by his one finger, I cannot believe that this man could conceive of such an evil as to overthrow the Roman state" (*Caes.* 4.9). What is the significance of the finger-scratching action? Plutarch's lack of explanation suggests that this gesture would have been readily identifiable not only to Romans in the first century BC but also to Greek readers of his own age, some 150 years later. Its meaning is lost on us, however: it looks from the context as though it is seen as a sign of effeminacy, but we have no real way of knowing.

4   The Meaning of the Text

Caesar's itchy scalp is perhaps an extreme case, but it is nevertheless a good indication of a general principle: ancient texts need to be translated – not just linguistically, but also culturally – in order to be made sense of. Nor is this phenomenon limited to tiny individual features of a text. Quite the contrary: as a rule, it is the biggest questions that provoke the biggest controversies. For example, arguably the central question of modern literary scholarship on the ancient world relates to Vergil's *Aeneid*: is this an unequivocally pro-Augustan text (a view argued for most forcefully in recent years by Galinsky, e.g. 1994 and 1996)? Or does its periodic emphasis upon the sufferings of innocents suggest doubts over the ideology of empire (as, notably, claimed by Lyne 1987 and Thomas 2001)? The questions crystallize around the closing scene, where Aeneas succumbs to anger (*furor*) on the sight of the dead Pallas's belt around Turnus, and runs his enemy through. Does this show uncompromising, righteous vengeance? Or the failure of Aeneas's rational control over his emotions?

Such issues can, once again, be seen as an extension of the problems raised by cultural "translation." What kind of Vergil do we want? And, relatedly, what kind of Augustus do we want? Do we want to see Rome's most important poet as the ready apostle of an all-powerful *princeps*, whose influence pervaded every aspect of contemporary culture? Or do we want an *Aeneid* too rich and complex to be reduced to political dogma? There can, surely, be no final way of resolving this dilemma. The answer is determined by the interpretative tools we choose: whether, to put it simply, we emphasize the systemic nature of the Augustan political world or the subtleties of Vergilian text.

One way to cut through the Gordian knot is to concede all possibility of reaching a final interpretation. For "reception theorists" (i.e. students of the subsequent "reception" of a work), the quest for the original meaning of a text is misguided (Martindale 1992 and 1993; Fowler 1997). All that we can analyze are attempts to interpret it; our attempts then contribute to the ever increasing proliferation of meanings of that text, each (more or less) with its own validity. Thus Duncan Kennedy, for example, argues that works of the Augustan period cannot be definitively labeled pro- or anti-Augustan: the "degree to which a voice is heard as conflicting or supportive is a function of the audience's – or critic's – ideology, a function, therefore, of *reception*" (Kennedy 1992: 41).

From this vantage, there is no such thing as reading "in the original": all we can ever hope to do is to translate (using the term broadly) ancient texts into modern cultural reference systems. I shall return to the interpretation of the *Aeneid* presently; for now, let us stick to the matter of reception. As will be quickly grasped, this represents an extreme challenge to the historicist reading of texts; indeed, in a sense, it is an apocalyptic challenge to history itself, which threatens to collapse into a series of ever-disappearing instants.

Like all forms of skepticism, reception theory is difficult to combat on its own terms (although there are theoretical weaknesses in the way that it has been presented: Whitmarsh 2006). It is possible, however, to take a less fundamentalist form of reception as complementary to historicism. Studying cultural constructions of interpretation, both in the modern West and further afield, exposes us to aspects of ancient texts that may otherwise concealed from us. Thus for example whereas modern scholarship on Greek tragedy tends primarily to emphasize the political context of Athenian democracy, West African versions explore issues of ritual (Budelmann 2004) and modern Arabic versions determinist theology (Chorfi 2006). Each tradition – the secular West, the West African tradition with its own ritual theater, liberal Islam – stakes its own claim to being the true inheritor of this privileged cultural form. Reception can point up the blind spots in intellectual traditions, and at the same time offer a salutary reminder that all things will pass.

Reception theory is at one level undeniably right: there are few unshakeable truths in the interpretation of ancient texts, beyond the banal. And even if we could conceive of an absolute truth, that truth could not be expressed in a language innocent of modern cultural priorities. Where a historicist might disagree with reception theorists, however, is in relation to the consequences. Does this mean that historicist reading is a hopeless quest? Surely not. There are few certainties in life in general (except for those with a totalized faith in religion or science), but that does prevent us from speaking or acting. Civilized living means struggling to make sense of the world, even as we are confronted with the limitations and provisionalities of that sense-making process. For ancient historians, the process is similar. If we want the fullest picture of ancient societies, we cannot ignore the call to interpret literary texts, even if we know that no interpretation will last for ever. The best response to the challenge of reception theory is perhaps to build pluralism into our accounts of ancient interpretative communities. All texts no doubt "meant" in different ways to different people: rather than seeing them as contain unitary, fixed meanings, we should consider the likely range of possible responses in a given historical context.

5   Interpretative Pluralism and Literary "Resistance"

It is no surprise that debates over interpretative pluralism are most vigorous in connection with literature's relation to politics. No question in classical historicism generates quite so much heat as that of literature's ability (or not) to stand outside the structures of power. Once again, the case of the *Aeneid* is instructive. It matters fundamentally how we tell the story of Vergil's relationship to Augustus, as cultural lackey (Speer to his Hitler) or critic (Solzhenitsyn to his Stalin). At stake here is not just the question of whether we can (or cannot) rescue Vergil as a good liberal humanist, but also (as we shall see in my final section, below) that of disciplinary hierarchies in the modern academy.

There is little by way of direct oppositionalism in extant ancient literature. The major exception is classical Athens, where there was an anti-democratic tradition: this is represented in surviving literature most crudely by the so-called "Old Oligarch" (an anonymous *Constitution of Athens* once attributed to Xenophon), but in fact much of our surviving prose literature ("literature" in the strict sense, as opposed to rhetoric) from the period is written by elitists hostile to mob rule: Thucydides, Plato, Isocrates, Xenophon. The supercilious contempt of a literate elite towards the ignorance of the masses, however, hardly counts as radical counter-ideology. When scholars speak of literary resistance, they are usually thinking of opponents of autocracy, particularly in imperial Rome.

There are few traces of explicit criticism of Rome or her emperors. We hear whispers of anti-Roman historians at the time of Augustus. Dionysius of Halicarnassus writes that some of his fellow-Greeks believe that Rome owes her dominion to chance (*Ant. Rom.* 1.4.2); Livy tells us that some "trivial" Greeks claimed that Alexander would have conquered the Romans (9.18.6–7; Morello 2002). Perhaps the notorious Metrodoros and Timagenes were behind these claims (e.g. Bowersock 1965: 109–10). The historian Tacitus, of whom more will be said below, has a curious (but hardly straightforward) fascination with republicanism – but never directly advocates the overthrow of the imperial order and a return to the old days of senatorial control. Individual emperors or governors might be excoriated for their moral failures (sometimes vigorously, but invariably after their deaths: for example, by Tacitus, Epictetus, or the anonymous *Acts of the Alexandrians*), but the political system itself is never challenged in extant (pagan) literature.

Are we, then, entitled to look for implicit criticism? The most promising place to start is with "figured speech" (*logos eskhematismenos*), a rhetorical device that allows the speaker to condense two messages into one, to deliver what one Greek writer calls "both-sidedness" (*to epamphoteron*: Philostr. *VS* 542–43; Ahl 1984). Figured speech was, it seems, particularly used before those in power – and, as one source tells us, considered particularly vexatious by them (pseudo-Longinus *On the sublime* 17.1). Taking their cue from this ancient theory, some critics have argued that texts that engage with power should be interpreted as designed to appeal to at least two different interpretative communities: the potentate and his adherents, who might wish to be praised, and others more skeptical, who might wish to tease out subtexts that contradict the dominant "script." This mode of scholarship most commonly considers the productions of imperial Rome (see especially Ahl 1984; Bartsch 1994; Newlands 2002), but variants can also be found in relation to e.g. Pindar's praise poems (Kurke 1991).

The problem – a problem of which none of the scholars above is unaware – is the implausibility, indeed crudity, of a model that imagines an emperor (for example) naively preening himself at the poet's words while others snigger, unbeknownst to him, at the secret meaning. Not all emperors were quite that dumb. There are, however, more credible ways of present the pluralist model. Powerful men are not always hostile to criticism. In the early years of the reign of Trajan (AD 97–117), the Greek philosophical orator Dio Chrysostom delivered (or at least claimed to have delivered) a series of orations to the emperor, orations that contain much advice for his moral improvement (Dio Chrys. 1–4; Moles 1990; Whitmarsh 2001: 186–216). In this case, the emperor would presumably have tolerated that he received instruction from a minor provincial because it bolstered his image as a civilized ruler, in contrast to his reviled predecessor-but-one Domitian.

More immediately surprising than Trajan's complaisance is that of Ptolemy Philadelphos, ruler of Alexandria in the early third century BC, whose marriage to his sister Arsinoe seems to have been the butt of crude jokes. The poet Sotades wrote a risqué couplet: "that is not a holy hole into which you coax your cock" (fragment 1). Late sources tells us that he was punished for this kind of insinuation, either by imprisonment (pseudo-Plutarch, *On the education of children* 11a) or by being drowned at sea in a leaden jar (Athen. 621a). This looks, however, like myth making; and, in fact, Ptolemy seems to have been remarkably willing to accept criticism, in certain contexts. A certain Timagenes, meanwhile, is said to have mispronounced a line of Euripides: *tende Mousan* (this muse) became *tend' emousan* (this vomiting woman) (Plut., *Sympotic questions* 634e; Athen. 616c). This kind of ribald mockery seems to have been tolerated within the culture of the symposium, where poets enjoyed a greater license (Cameron 1995: 98–99).

We should not, then, automatically assume that ancient societies were Stalinist in their eradication of all views running counter to dominant state ideology. Greeks and Romans alike promoted the idea of "free speech" (*parrhesia*, *libertas*), of the individual's right – and, as the concept developed beyond democratic Athens, duty – to speak what she or (more commonly) he felt was right as the situation developed. An ability to tolerate criticism, conversely, was seen as an index of good kingship. In Lucian's satirical account of the philosopher Proteus Peregrinos, for example, the anti-imperial rants of the eponymous anti-hero are gently ignored by Antoninus Pius, "whom he knew to be a most mild and humane man" (*Peregr.* 18).

There does exist, however, evidence for that kind of intolerance, particularly in the works of Tacitus. Writing under Trajan, whom he praises for lifting the repression (*Agr.* 3.1; *Hist.* 1.1.4), the Roman historian recurs repeatedly to the theme of the danger of addressing certain themes under the first-century emperors: "When Thrasea Paetus was praised by Rusticus Arulenus and Helvidius Priscus by Herennius Senecio, it was a capital offence, and fury pursued not only the authors, but even their books too" (*Agr.* 2.1). Elsewhere, Tacitus offers the memorable story of Cremutius Cordus, whose books were (he tells us) burned under Tiberius when he praised Caesar's assassins Brutus and Cassius (*Ann.* 4.35–36).

Although Tacitus's characterization of pre-Trajanic Rome as repressive is of course designed to buttress the presentation of Trajanic Rome as liberated, claims like these are unlikely to be inventions: after all, emperors were rarely sluggish in silencing their enemies. The written word is a powerful tool: records of the past help shape the future, as Romans (who were obsessive chroniclers) were all too aware. It is no surprise to find powerful figures attempting to monopolize the composition of history.

Ancient authors needed to tread very carefully. Our best evidence for literary repression comes for imperial Rome, but we can find examples elsewhere too. In fifth-century Athens, for example, dramatists were liable to penalties if they over-stepped the mark. Herodotus famously reports of Phrynichos's play *The capture of Miletos* (describing a recent military disaster) that "the audience burst into tears, then fined him 1,000 drachmas for reminding them of matters close to home" (6.21.2). Alexander the Great is said to have killed one of his courtiers, Kleitos, after he deliv-ered a set-piece oration with a critical undertow at a symposium (Plut. *Alex.* 51; a similar speech by Kallisthenes at 53 marks the beginning of the latter's fall from grace). No acknowledgement of sympotic license in these cases. What we do not know, however, is how frequently or consistently such repression was applied, nor how far it extended. These are difficult questions; it is no doubt prudent to avoid absolutism.

My central point here, however, is about modern strategies of interpretation. We can find evidence both for tolerance of criticism and for brutal, "Stalinist" repression of literature. Historical context alone can never guide us towards a single, final "meaning" for a text that contains ambiguities. The undeniable likelihood that there would have been contemporary readers who took Vergil's *Aeneid* as an unquestioning glorification of Augustan ideals does not rule out the possibility (very likely, in my view) that there would have been those who would have been troubled by its moral opacities. A true historicist reading, I suggest, would accommodate the full latitude of possible responses.

6 Literature and Historicism

I have argued over the course of this chapter that studying ancient history through ancient literature brings to the fore the issue of interpretation. There are, indeed, at least three layers of interpretation involved: the editorial judgment as to the constitu-tion of the text, the response to the translational challenge of an alien cultural artifact, and the search for the "meaning" of (often) a complex text. As I have stressed throughout, these issues need not discourage historians from using texts, but they do mean that we need historical models that are capacious enough to accommodate the possibility of semantic pluralism.

Reception theorists are right to emphasize that the meaning of a work lies not in the author's original blueprint (which we can never access anyhow), but in the range of ways that it was received. We never have the same depth of evidence for controversies over the interpretation of texts in the ancient world as we do in the modern. This does not mean that such controversies did not exist. Occasionally a historian will tell us of such a case (as with Tacitus's account of Cremutius Cordus, alluded to above: *Ann.* 4.35–6). The *scholia* (or ancient commentaries) on texts like the *Aeneid* and the *Iliad* offer ample testimony for a vigorous debating culture, albeit invariably evidence from a later period. In general, however, we are required to do the work of imaginative reconstruction of original reception contexts ourselves, to create our own maps of possible readings. This, I submit, is the proper task of literary historicism.

For much of the last twenty years or so, historicism and literary studies have been antagonists. Historicists have accused literary students of privileging an elite perspective, of idealist aestheticism, of prissiness in the face of the nasty realities of ancient society. The other camp has pointed the finger at naive or partial readings of texts, which simply pass over aspects that do not fit the particular view of society being promoted. We can quickly see that the kinds of debates discussed in the previous section are thinly veiled allegories for the disciplinary warfare of the modern academy: "historicists" tend to read texts as products of a larger system, while "literary" types tend to value instead the autonomy of the individual creation. This is, as an earlier generation might have said, a quarrel between lumpers and splitters. Neither approach, however, is *per se* satisfactory. Literary texts are cultural products, no more or less than material artifacts; but they are also (often) designed to generate multiple interpretations, and for that reason they cannot be reduced to the status of epiphenomena of a cultural system.

FURTHER READING

A number of good general surveys of Greek and Latin literature exist. The Cambridge Histories, Kenney 1982, and Easterling and Knox 1985, are rather dated now, especially on non-canonical literature, but still useful especially for cultural context (there are some excellent discussions of e.g. book production in the ancient world). Good coverage and up-to-date discussion can be found in Taplin 2000 and Rutherford 2004. Saïd and Trédé 1999 and Whitmarsh 2004 focus upon Greek literature; Morton Braund 2002 and S. Harrison 2005 on Latin. For specific discussion of the problems faced by ancient historians in using literature, see (for Greek texts) C. Pelling 1997 and 2000, and (for Roman) D. Potter 1999a. For general introductions to literary-critical methodologies in relation to ancient literature, see T. Schmitz 2002 (in German); also Whitmarsh 2004 specifically upon the Greek material, Conte 1994 and Habinek 1998 on the Latin. Good general introductions to literary theory also exist: see in particular Culler 1975 and 1997. Reception is now a massive field. For theoretical approaches, see esp. Martindale 1992, Fowler 1997, Hardwick 2003, Martindale and Thomas 2006. Lorna Hardwick's work (see also Hardwick 2000, which focuses upon translations) has been particularly important in widening reception studies beyond elite European males; see also Goff 2005. The perils of translation are discussed by the contributors to Lianeri and Zajko 2008. On manuscript traditions, Reynolds and Wilson 1991 is fascinating and indispensable.

PART II

Problems and Approaches

CHAPTER NINE

Ancient History Today

J. A. North

1 Public Perceptions

Ancient history today is never far from the public's attention. Television dramas and documentaries succeed one another furiously and are circulated round the world. Epic films from the 60s, such as *Spartacus* and *Ben Hur*, are revived with loving regularity, and the genre itself has had a recent revival with some spectacular successes, not least *Gladiator* and *Troy*. New novels on the classical world are also regularly published, ranging from serious struggles with the nature of ancient experience to pot-boiling whodunnits; even *The Da Vinci Code*, that most astonishing of recent publishing success stories, takes its readers into the world of antiquity, among many other times. Meanwhile, an interest in ancient sites and in museums of antiquities is a great driver of tourism in Greece, Italy, Turkey, Egypt, the Holy Land, and many other parts of the Roman empire and beyond. Mediterranean holidays are typically perceived as mixtures of sunshine and self-indulgence with some element at least of cultural self-improvement, mostly through visiting the local antiquities. It is a case of rest and ruins.

Even to the casual observer of these facts, it ought to seem that ancient history as a topic of interest stands at a high level in this first decade of the new century; it might, therefore, seem a reasonable assumption that this popular interest should continue to support a healthy level of activity in the teaching of the subject and in research on it. This optimistic view may well prove to be true, but, as we shall see, there are problems as well as advantages that should be taken seriously by anyone concerned to see the subject thrive in the long term. Ancient historians themselves do not always seem as happy with the public interest as they might be expected to be; and it is true that much of it focuses on particular themes – the moral degeneration of the Roman empire and its emperors, for instance – that they would not themselves have chosen. Their efforts to steer the interest do, admittedly, only have erratic success: they find a role and some profit in offering technical advice to films and television programs, but are frequently unhappy with the extent to which they are taken seriously or their advice followed.

Whatever the misgivings, there can be no doubt that the extent of interest offers an opportunity to ancient historians that should not be wasted. Throughout the second half of the twentieth century the subject has shown considerable vigor and creativity. Student numbers in many countries have increased, in some cases dramatically so. Courses have multiplied and become far more sophisticated. The expectation, widely held in the 1960s, that universities would progressively cut back their provision for all aspects of teaching about the ancient world, has so far only been fulfilled in a limited number of cases, though the situation in Germany has recently become worrying; meanwhile, the rate of publication by scholars working in universities in many parts of Europe and in the USA has risen rather than fallen; and ancient history jobs are vigorously competed for. On the basis of such general indicators, it would not be difficult to argue that the subject is as well placed for long-term survival as any other branch of Arts, Humanities or Social Sciences. It is true that occasionally a prominent politician or industrialist can be heard on air putting forward a degree in Ancient History as the ultimate example of a useless education, as compared to Civil Engineering or Business Administration; but it is clear that potential students are not much impressed by such harangues, and that democratic governments will continue, rightly, to be hesitant about directing young people into "economically useful" courses, as opposed to offering incentives to those economically minded enough to be diverted.

All the same, the twentieth century has to be seen as a period of the major retreat of ancient history from the shared knowledge of educated people. A century ago, Greek myths, the New Testament and the Roman poets formed a stock of information and text to which literature, political speech and even everyday conversation could confidently refer. Such allusions may still be used today, but they need explanation, if not apology; at the same time, any knowledge of Greek and Latin has become a rarity, valued perhaps in some quarters, but in no sense part of the basic education expected by society. So, the student today comes to university without the skills and knowledge that might once have been automatically available to him or her. University courses have of course been adjusting to these new expectations throughout the second half of the twentieth century, and with great success; but where these adjustments will eventually lead the subject is not yet so clear.

2   Boundaries of the Subject

At the same time, the boundaries of the subject, and perhaps even more its preoccupations, have changed quite dramatically over the course of the twentieth century. How far that has involved a change in its basic character is somewhat more debatable. First, the boundaries: there is no doubt that the study of Greek and Roman history originated from the study of texts: first, literary texts of the great Greek and Roman authors, and especially the historians; then epigraphic and papyrus texts, as they became available in increasing numbers by the later decades of the nineteenth century. It is hardly surprising if concentration was mostly on the great periods of literary and artistic production, the "Golden Ages" of Athens and Rome, since these were the periods also for which the major historians (Herodotus, Thucydides, Livy and Tacitus) and other literary sources (such as Cicero and Plutarch) have survived, where the historiography of other periods has not. This tradition did not, of course, prevent discussion of other periods – the early history of Rome, for instance, or, after the work of Droysen, the Hellenistic period – but it did mean that both teaching and research privileged what were then seen as the periods and places of unique achievement.

This resulted in both strengths and weaknesses: it fostered a method of teaching that placed great emphasis on the student's direct use of the "primary" sources, and this has continued to be an appealing feature of how the subject is taught, even if "primary" in this context really means modern texts derived by generations of scholarly effort from manuscripts, preserved often in a poor state and copied and recopied over centuries. On the other hand it has also fostered an empirical approach to all questions and reluctance to deal either with issues of theory or with the historiography of the subject. Boundaries were also to some extent fixed by disciplinary divisions: ancient historians tended not to regard either the history of the Jews or the history of the rise of Christianity as properly part of their subject. Few, perhaps as a result, devoted their time to the period after the second century AD, when the development of Christianity becomes an inescapable theme.

Controversial issues are attached to both the beginning and the ending of what we now mean by "ancient history." Conventionally the date of 776 BC (allegedly the first Olympic Games) provides a possible starting-point for the period, and that may well include the date at which Homer wrote – if there was a Homer and if he did write; but it is agreed that the epics must have had a long history before the eighth century and that Greek had long been spoken at least in parts of what later became the Greek world. To look wider, we also have written documents in enormous quantities from earlier civilizations in Egypt, and in several Near and Middle Eastern regions, particularly Mesopotamia; the earliest of these documents date from two thousand years before Homer, and the great empires of the East continue to co-exist, or sometimes conflict, with Greeks and Romans throughout the centuries of their dominance in the West. These early written records form a vital part of our evidence about the ancient world, without which our picture of it must be grossly distorted; but they tend to be treated as if the history of the early Near East were no part of the story and had little or no influence on all that followed.

The issue of how much the Greeks had inherited from earlier civilizations caused bitter controversy in the last years of the twentieth century, when Martin Bernal in the first volume of *Black Athena* argued that nineteenth-century scholarship had methodically excluded from consideration influences that had been fully recognized in earlier centuries, in what he regarded as a racially motivated attempt to promote the Greeks as the originators of modern Western civilization. His thesis and his methods of argument have both been strongly resisted, but it can hardly be denied that the relationship of Greek culture to those of their predecessors is now firmly on the agenda for future study. In the meantime, the achievements of the Greeks are still popularly honored as the single origin of all modern culture, as they were for instance in the preamble to the – now abandoned – constitution of the European Union. Professors of Greek continue to write books that claim, quite reasonably, that fifth-century Athenian culture has continued to have profound effects on later European civilization, while totally ignoring the influence of pre-Greek and non-Greek cultures on the development of Greek civilization itself, except as a "mirror" in which Greek identity was defined. The debate illustrates vividly how essential it is to maintain continuity of study from the earliest recorded history onwards. But this is an ideal rarely achieved.

Meanwhile, a very different debate has concerned the end of ancient history. In the first place, there has been a substantial increase in interest in the period from the third century onwards, and a major revision of ideas about the character and achievements of late antique culture. This has had various consequences: it has placed cultural and religious history at the center of debate in this period; it has sought to establish that the period was one of economic success and high artistic endeavor, rather than of decline; it has led to a reassessment of the governance of the empire and diminished the alleged difference between early and late imperial systems; it has also extended the range of debate beyond the fourth/fifth centuries, where it has traditionally ended. Peter Brown, who (building on the achievements particularly of A. H. M Jones) has played a formative role in all this revisionist research, famously argued for the term "Late Antiquity," putting the terminal date forward beyond the fifth and sixth centuries. How widely this suggestion is being followed, particularly outside English-language scholarship, is not yet clear, but there is every reason to think that ancient historians by dint of concentrating far more on the fourth and fifth centuries are increasingly becoming involved with the history of Judaism and of Christianity, which itself implies taking some view of the pagan religion, which, though increasingly marginalized from the fourth century onwards, is now being recognized as a major force through the earlier centuries of the empire.

If these chronological changes are the most obvious indicators of expansion, they are not the only ones, and may not be the most significant in the longer run. Perhaps more important is the ancient historian's relation with the parallel world of antiquity revealed by archaeology. The boundary between history and archaeology is never clearly defined, but it runs through all large questions. Archaeology reveals to us those aspects of Greco-Roman societies that the texts largely miss, such as art and architecture, or that are below the dignity required by the texts we have, such as the life of the poor; but it also reveals the lives of the pre-Greco-Roman or non-Greco-Roman peoples with whom the Greeks and Romans constantly interacted. So, the historian working on the rise of Roman power in Italy has to be far more concerned with the archaeology of the different areas than with the later, and in some ways prejudiced, accounts of the Romans themselves and exactly so with the historian of the Greek cities of Asia Minor or of Sicily or many other areas. Increasingly this dialogue of disciplines must provide the material with which both historians and archaeologists (if they can be meaningfully distinguished at all) have to work.

3   Some Pioneers

If it is true that the boundaries of the subject have indeed expanded, we should be able to identify some of the key pioneers of the twentieth century who pushed the boundaries outwards. Four men, none of them still living today, had an unquestionably profound influence on the debates of their successors and will clearly continue to do so in the future. They are also remarkable in that their work has been extensively read and used outside the circle of those who take a professional interest in the history of the ancient world as such. The four would be M. I. Rostovtzeff, A. D. Momigliano, M. I. Finley and J.-P. Vernant. Rostovtzeff, born in Tsarist Russia in 1870, and living in exile from the Revolution onwards, wrote ambitious social and economic histories of the Hellenistic world and of the Roman empire, proving by his example that these were possible enterprises and that such histories could be based on many different types of evidence, including the evidence of archaeology. Momigliano, born in Piedmont in 1908, and also exiled from his homeland – but in his case as a result of the Second World War – showed, again by example, that it was possible to combine the study of the ancient sources with the successive understandings of those sources by generations of scholars from antiquity until the twentieth century; each of these forerunners of the discipline had to be placed in his context just as much as the historians of antiquity. Finley, born in the USA, but living in Europe as a result of the anti-communist persecutions of the 1950s, revived and redirected fundamental debates about the nature of the ancient economy, and so placed a whole swath of issues in front of a new generation of economic historians. Vernant, a French resistance leader in the Second World War, transformed established ideas just as profoundly by showing how Greek myth, religion, and rationality could all be understood in relation to the social and political evolution of the early Greek city.

The lives of all four, as of so many others, were deeply marked by the conflicts of the twentieth century, and their thought informed by the battle of ideologies through which all their contemporaries lived. Two of the four (Finley and Vernant) were at least in the early part of their careers committed Marxists; it could be said of all four of them that they engaged with the issues raised by the application of Marx's ideas to the ancient world. Rostovtzeff, in particular, while being in principle hostile to Marxism and all that it had brought about, produced theories of the overall direction of ancient society that bear a remarkably Marxist stamp. Momigliano was far from being a Marxist at any stage of his life, but he did have a very clear understanding of how important the dialogue with Marxist ideas continued to be. What all four of these men shared was an extraordinary capacity to build on predecessors' work – whether it was Marx, Weber, Mommsen or Meyer – while seeing how to extend the scope of ancient history irrespective of old boundaries, whether chronological, disciplinary, or conceptual.

4   Changing Directions

Whether as a result of the activities of these powerful figures or not, there seems to have been an unmistakable change in recent years in the driving agenda of ancient history. There has been a relative decline in such traditional preoccupations as political, constitutional, and diplomatic history, but also in more recently developed areas, once quite dominant, such as the history of the ancient economy; these are not of course being totally neglected, but the balance has shifted unmistakably towards the study of gender, of religion, of ethnicity and identity, and, currently, of the emotions. It might be said to be a shift away from the history of states and groups and towards the experience of the individual, or at least of the individual in relation to the group.

The place of religion in the study of the Greco-Roman world is a fair indicator of the direction of change in question. In the first half of the twentieth century it was commonly treated as a marginal area of life, of interest only to those with eccentric, even antiquarian tastes. Survey volumes included it, but normally as a separate chapter, frequently the last one. It was assumed to have little influence on the activities of the city's elites, and none at all on political life. The effect of this set of assumptions was to create, at least for key periods such as fourth-century Athens or late republican Rome, a secular world, highly sympathetic at least to those looking in the context of their own time for the progressive decline in the influence of religion, which they expected as the inevitable consequence of the Enlightenment. The second half of the twentieth century saw arguments put forward that this vision of a world free of religion was based on a highly selective reading of the evidence about the ancient world and on a failure to grasp how profoundly the religious life of pagan societies differed from the models that modern scholars had sought, almost unthinkingly, to impose on it. The result has been to open up areas of debate that once seemed arid and unprofitable to re-examination. But it is hardly a coincidence that the same period of the twentieth century has seen the resurgence of religious commitment and conflict in many parts of the world, while the expectation that religion would disappear in a more rational, secular world has receded as a result.

It might be tempting to connect the shift with the collapse of Marxism, on the basis that both advocates and opponents of Marxism focused on issues of political, economic, and social evolution and that this great debate gave a sense of direction to historical research on all periods, which has now evaporated. All history has to be rethought in the light of 1989. At the same time, some areas that fifty years ago seemed straightforward and inspiring points of contact between ancient and modern political experience have become far more problematic: for instance, Greek democracy and even the Roman republic were once viewed as inspiring models of how power could be effectively disseminated to wider sections of the community. Athenian direct democracy was even proposed for practical use, if not so much in the government of modern states, then at least of factories and universities. Today, although the idea of direct democracy is again a talking-point, we tend to see ancient systems as flawed examples of effective democratic practice, and concentrate rather on the means by which women, non-citizens and slaves were excluded from any share in power than on the remarkable fact that peasant farmers were ever given power and that their power was sustained over considerable periods of time. Once again, modern concerns can be seen as having a direct influence on the themes of debate.

The fact is, however, that while Marxism certainly, as we have seen, influenced the work of individual ancient historians and had a marked effect on the study of slavery and slave-revolts, especially in Communist Europe, it never became a dominant model or the focal point of conflict in the study of ancient history, in the way it did in so many other periods and subjects. Partly, this is undoubtedly due to the bad fit between class-based evolutionary models and the character of ancient social structures, especially ancient slavery; partly, to the conservative tendencies of many ancient historians, not least in the period after the Second World War. However that may be, it is hard to argue that the shift in agenda was caused by the collapse of a theory that was never well established in the first place.

One very remarkable aspect of what has happened during the last twenty-five years is that the trends affecting ancient history seem now to reflect those in other historical periods of European and American History in a way that was surely not the case in the first half of the twentieth century. One extreme example would be economic history, which became a major issue in ancient history for some years in the 1970s, when modern economic history was also at its height, with the introduction of separate economic history departments in many universities; the 1980s and 1990s have seen a gradual decline of interest in ancient economic history, just as the subject declined (at least temporarily) for modern periods as well. Much the same could be said of political history. At the same time, new themes of interest have arisen across all periods – women's history, the history of the human body, the history of emotion. Sometimes, these ideas can be traced back to the work of particular thinkers who are widely read, widely reviewed and have influence over the historiography of all periods – Claude Lévi-Strauss or Michel Foucault. But it is reasonable to detect not just interdisciplinary influence but mutual contact between the study of different historical periods.

5   Structural Factors

Whatever the explanation for the convergence discussed in the last section, it does not seem to result from any change in the organization of the subject. Ancient historians virtually never have the opportunity to form a university department on their own. There are two normal structures in Britain and the USA: in one, ancient history is part of History; in the other, it is part of Classics. This second model is predominant and becoming ever more so. Its undoubted strength is that it associates closely those working on all aspects of the Greco-Roman world, historians, philologists, literary or textual critics, philosophers and archaeologists, all of whom have much to profit from close association. Its limitations are, first, that it divides the practitioners of all these specializations from those who share their own discipline; secondly, that it tends to exclude aspects of the study of the ancient world that do not concern the activities of Greeks or Romans, most obviously the history of the ancient world before the first millennium, but also the cultures of the peoples living outside the boundaries of the Roman empire. The recently developing emphasis on reception studies, however valuable in itself, must exaggerate these tendencies, since it is concerned mostly with those aspects of the ancient world that have been celebrated through the centuries and far less with those that depend heavily on recent discoveries and decipherments. It provides yet another reason for excluding the historical study of the early civilizations.

Whatever the merits and demerits of these two structures, or of a single department covering all aspects of the study of the ancient world, it is quite clear that the institutional separation between historians of antiquity and those of later periods has increased rather than diminished, and hence that the convergence of themes cannot be explained by such organizational factors. In fact, looking to continental Europe, since there are various different traditions in different countries, sometimes associating ancient history with archaeology, sometimes with philology, sometimes associating all branches of the ancient world together, it would be impossible to make the same analysis of the trend, but the trend seems to be widespread all the same.

Whether the trend is altogether a healthy one is a subject of some concern. It has certainly led to much research on topics that were previously ignored or only covered in antiquarian dictionaries, and it has forced the rethinking of important areas of ancient life where ideas were fixed or scarcely detectable at all. It is continuing exactly the tradition of widening boundaries that has been so characteristic of the subject in the last century. So, for instance, the concept of identity has provided a starting point for rethinking the character of ancient societies and people's sense of themselves within those societies; on this theme, work of great importance has been produced in recent years, even though "identity" itself, some would argue, is a slippery conception to exploit. There may be an element of fashion in the choice of research topics, but that is not in itself necessarily a disadvantage; it has the effect of playing a searchlight across a particular topic, so that seminars in many universities simultaneously work on the same topic. The disadvantage is that more traditional research areas have become less appealing: the core understanding of any period must surely rest, as it always has in the past, on evolving ideas about the politics, economy, and society of a given region; new results need to be integrated into wider narratives and the narratives themselves rethought in the light of the new research context. Otherwise there is a risk of a gulf developing between out-of-date general histories and the radical revisions of specific topics.

6 Problems and Opportunities

It must be obvious that serious problems arise from the very success of the ancient historians of the twentieth century in redefining and extending their discipline. The subject depends heavily on high skill in ancient languages; but schools in almost all countries are less and less likely to offer the two classical languages, except where teachers and pupils are willing to give up their own time to extra classes.

For most of the many other ancient languages (Sumerian, Akkadian, Egyptian of several periods, Persian, Aramaic, Syriac, and so on) the situation has of course always been that they are normally available only at the undergraduate, or even postgraduate, stage. It is not, however, only ancient languages that are needed: work of importance is written in many modern languages, and it is not possible to conduct research without some reading ability in at least half a dozen.

Linguistic skills, however essential, are still only the starting-point: there are other tools as well that are just as much needed. In many areas of work, and in any attempt to write general history, understanding archaeology is as important as knowing languages. It is, of course, still possible to find topics of work where written materials provide the only evidence to be studied; but even then the context of discovery and the use made of written materials raise archaeological issues that may be crucial to the argument. Meanwhile for many questions, essential to the writing of history, where the evidence would once have been seen as primarily linguistic, modern scientific techniques are providing material that will give us hard data on such subjects as diet, health, expectation of life, climate and agricultural methods. The need to control such results will give a major advantage to the ancient historian who has archaeological training and practical experience. Archaeologists sometimes maintain that they can pursue their discipline without recourse to written texts; ancient historians cannot be allowed the converse luxury. They have to go wherever their problem leads them.

The expanding boundaries of the subject raise practical problems. The more ambitious the program that ancient historians, who are all too few in number, are seeking to maintain, the more difficult it becomes for the new recruit to meet the requirements of the subject. What once seemed to be a simple affair of reading a limited number of texts and using little but "common sense" to interpret them has become more complex, more theoretically demanding and more interdisciplinary. Ideal postgraduates, in addition to their languages and archaeological experience, will also have a wide knowledge of modern history, a good deal of philosophy, anthropology, sociology, and political theory; they will also be very much at home in the application of modern critical theory to the interpretation of ancient texts. Without all these skills, they will be sent vulnerable into the conference-chamber.

If initiation into the discipline is one problem, the relationship of ancient history to its various parent departments is certainly another. The intellectual ambition of the subject, as it is now understood, does not fit readily into a department of Classics. Nor is it desirable to split away the archaeologists who work on the classical period from those who precede and follow them in a department of Archaeology. My ideal (I admit not shared with many) would see history departments everywhere accepting the need to cover all periods from the early Near Eastern civilizations onwards as an essential part of their discipline; there would then, of course, have to be collaboration at all levels, but especially research level, with colleagues in archaeology, philosophy and language and literature departments. Of course, there can be many different ways of achieving effective collaborations; but issues of disciplinary organization can easily have repercussions on the possibilities of research activity and on the distribution of research funding. If ancient history is in the end isolated and not taken seriously by historians of other periods as part of their discipline, that can only weaken it in the longer run.

It is not easy to strike a balance between these hesitations about the future of an important intellectual enterprise and the undoubted strength of the tradition of study that supports it. In fact, there are very good reasons to be optimistic, to think that, as it has in the recent past, so the subject will overcome the current round of obstacles. Extremely able young ancient historians have continued to choose this as their field and are now working in many different parts of the world, sometimes with limited local support, but sometimes as part of a strong culture of debate and cooperation. Their choice is the best guarantee that the great vitality shown in recent decades is not an ephemeral episode, but a phase in the ongoing development of a natural and fundamental human concern with the remote past and with its continuing effects on our life today. It is most important to emphasize that the problems discussed are all the direct consequence of the vitality and innovativeness of the subject in the recent past. Long may it so continue.

CHAPTER TEN

Political History

Robert Morstein-Marx

1 The Changing Character of Political History

Political history has traditionally been understood as the study of states of the past (institutions, constitutions, and laws) and the events that involved them either as agents, such as wars, or as the field of action, such as elections. History itself was given a distinctly political form by its original creators in the late fifth century BC. Herodotus and Thucydides chose as their subject the great wars that convulsed the Greek world in the fifth century (Hdt. *Proemium*, Thuc. 1.1–12) and invited comparison in their magnitude to the Trojan War, the great foundational event of the Hellenic consciousness. In that broad sense they may be seen as continuing in the tradition of Homeric Epic, with evident consequences for the style of the histories that they produced. Words – in the form of direct, "quoted" speech, as in Homer – were tested against deeds in the great crucible of "war, where men win fame" (e.g. Hom. *Il.* 4.225). Great wars remained the typical subject matter for history even with the development of "universal history" in the Hellenistic age (cf. Polybius) and *Annales* in Rome. The Roman tradition was heavily influenced by the sub-genre of Greek "local history" or "foundations" (*ktiseis;* cf. Cato the Elder's *Origines*), but service to the *res publica*, especially in its wars, remained the major criterion for what was worthy of *memoria* and thus of *historia*. At the relatively basic level on which most readers probably did and do appreciate it, ancient historiography was a kind of manual of political leadership, whose greatest test was in war.

To judge from television documentaries and popular books, this characterization remains prevalent in the culture today, despite the fact that it has been largely repudiated by modern professional historians. In the late twentieth century "political history" (which it was now called in order to distinguish it from a rapidly proliferating menu of histories – economic, social, intellectual, cultural, gender, to cite only a few broad categories) was pushed from the center of the discipline at large to its margins. In an age in which the rise of the social sciences and social theory had shown ways to trace power and historical agency much more widely than among the actions of "great men," this was an understandable reaction to the narrowness of the now well-worn paths – military, diplomatic, legal, and constitutional – that traditional political history had taken. But after the heyday of social history in the 1960s and 1970s impelled by the brief intellectual hegemony of Marxism, and the subsequent "cultural turn" taken in the 1980s and 1990s, we have now come full circle to the realization that virtually everything is political – if "the political" be understood in a much broader sense than was usual in the past. If the negotiation and distribution of power and authority in society form the essence of the political, then politics permeates society much more widely than the traditional subjects of political history. A wide range of cultural practices, from child rearing, schooling, and policing of gender-roles through media consumption, religious and civic rituals, the construction of physical monuments, and even historical "memory" itself, can be seen to shape individuals' political consciousness, including their very assumptions about what is politically possible or impossible, desirable or undesirable – and what they can do about it. Political history, then, can be greatly broadened and reconceived as an examination not only of the products and individual agents of actions directly involving states but also, and equally, of how, by a variety of overt, but more often latent or disguised, social processes, "political subjects" and "subjectivities" are constructed within a distinct "political culture" (on which see further section 3 below) that gives a *meaning* to political practices. In this new form, political history is back in fashion within the broader discipline as a whole (S. Pedersen 2002).

True, in Greek and Roman studies political history was never routed from the field as it was in the larger historical discipline. Sir Moses Finley (1912–86) and his "Cambridge School" of social-scientific historians critical of the "antiquarian" methods of ancient (political) historians certainly offered a salutary challenge to the conservative, classicizing bias of much modern work in ancient history; but this was not a direct attack on political history as such. Undeniably, there are serious evidentiary reasons too for the relatively conservative tendency of ancient political history. In our source material, narrative accounts of the deeds of "great men" predominate, typically supplemented by public monuments such as inscriptions, law-codes, or coins, which in sum tend to encourage a rather traditional sort of historiography. Historians of ancient Greece and Rome simply do not have the archival records on which most reputable social and economic history is based, nor do our texts, most of which are elaborate literary products, often offer the directly observed and copious circumstantial detail needed to trace convincingly the "self-spun webs of significance" (Max Weber) that are the focus of contemporary cultural history in the style of the anthropologist Clifford Geertz. But on the other hand it is the very paucity of our evidence relative to other periods that must be a spur to innovation; the extremely limited, and barely increasing, quantity of source material, and its relatively narrow purview, *force* us to turn to new interpretative strategies, since the old ones, fundamental as they remain as basic tools of the discipline, have largely exhausted their creative force – their ability to move the field *as a whole* forward by producing valuable new insights into a very old body of knowledge. The unusual preponderance of literary evidence for Greek and Roman history may even be a strength now rather than an embarrassment: literature is a particularly useful source for investigating larger cultural questions, and the interests of literary classicists and ancient historians (and art historians) have notably converged in mutually beneficial dialogues about central moments in ancient political history such as the fifth-century Athenian democracy (Boedeker and Raaflaub 1998, Morris and Raaflaub 1998; on tragedy and "democratic culture," cf. Goldhill 2000 and Rhodes 2003b) or the transition to the Principate and the "Age of Augustus" (Galinsky 2005 will lead back to earlier milestones in the discussion). It would be quite hard today to draw a neat line between Greek or Roman political history and studies of ancient collective memory, rhetoric, historiography, gender, the body – even much work on the political aspects of poetry, drama, or the novel. Such broadening of the scope of ancient political history is all to the good, multiplying the available perspectives upon historical phenomena, encouraging fruitful connections between historians and literary scholars, renewing and refreshing our field, and perhaps thereby bringing ancient history back to the forefront of the wider historical discipline.

2 Historicizing Historiography

"All that we now regard as ancient was once new": so protests the emperor Claudius (or rather, Tacitus's rhetorically much improved Claudius) against unreflective adherence to time-honored practices without recognizing at a deeper level the underlying continuity of adaptation and change (Tac. *Ann.* 11.24.7). Claudius/Tacitus might equally have been talking about historiography, since for historians, as for Roman senators, certain *exempla* or models from the past have a powerful normative effect.

Take for example Sir Ronald Syme (1903–89). Even today Roman historians in the Anglophone tradition find it difficult to free themselves entirely from the powerful magnetism exerted by his classic work, *The Roman Revolution*, published in 1939. This enormously influential book may well have shaped our basic conceptions of "how it really was" in the final days of the republic and the Augustan era more than the original source material; written in a clipped, abrupt idiom reminiscent of Tacitus's *Annals*, it sometimes even *sounds* like the original source material. Yet on closer examination, *The Roman Revolution* proves to be distinctively shaped by the intellectual and political currents of the early twentieth century. Syme is well known to have envisioned Octavian's rise to power through the lens of contemporary politics, which had seen in recent years the rise of Hitler, Stalin and Mussolini. Less obvious, his famous assertion that "In all ages, whatever the form and name of government, be it monarchy, republic, or democracy, an oligarchy lurks behind the façade" (Syme 1939: 7) certainly bears more than a passing resemblance to the early-twentieth-century sociologist Robert Michels' claim that the demands of societal organization reduce all forms of government to oligarchy (the famous "iron law of oligarchy": Michels 1915), and in general to the "elitist" political theories of the First World War and the inter-war years elaborated by Gaetano Mosca, Vilfredo Pareto, and Joseph Schumpeter. Methodologically the most distinctive feature of his work, the use of the prosopographical method (see further below) to undermine traditional historiographical dichotomies such as "optimate" vs. *popularis* or Caesarian vs. republican, echoes the then-radical revisionism of the great British historian Lewis Namier (1888–1960). Namier had broken down the party-political framework in which the political landscape of eighteenth-century Britain had long been interpreted (Whigs vs. Tories) and interpreted it instead as structured by the flow of benefits from "court" and "country," and determined chiefly by the pursuit of narrow personal interest (Namier 1957, first published 1929). Tacitus's master trope contrasting a public "façade" or "screen" with the underlying, "real" workings of power was obviously congenial to the prosopographical approach and lent a powerful air of ancient authenticity to this kind of analysis; but it is not as if in using it Syme was simply "letting the sources speak for themselves" (compare Cicero), nor is this interpretative framework self-evidently correct and free of any need for theoretical justification. A typical objection brought against both Namier and Syme, for instance, is that they suppress the ideological content of politics; Tacitus, for his part, and Syme following him, arguably discounts the "performative" aspects of politics, for which "hypocrisy," in the Greek, etymological sense of "acting," is probably always a central feature, if also always a problematic one. In short, there is nothing "commonsensical" about Ronald Syme's compelling vision of the late republic and early principate. It is a brilliant, and in its day powerfully revisionist interpretation, drawing upon intellectual currents both inside and outside the historical discipline of its time, which presumably enjoyed no privileged insight into historical truth unavailable to other eras, such as even our own. If Syme's method and historiographical principles *do* now seem no more than "common sense," it is worth recalling Tacitus's Claudius and considering that today's "common sense" is frequently yesterday's radical revisionism.

Each year, the urban praetor in Rome posted an edict laying out the formal procedures he would follow in applying the civil law; since these were broadly speaking the same in a gradually accretive process, one praetor's edict substantially reproduced his predecessor's in a manner Cicero called *tra(ns)laticium* (from *transfero*), whence comes our (rare) word "tralatician." I would like to suggest that, like the Praetor's Edict, the political historian's roster of methods and approaches is tralatician, in that new ways of conducting historical research do not annul the proved, older ones, but pose new questions and challenges which established methods will still be needed to resolve. The historical "culture wars" are based on a false dichotomy between traditional and new approaches whose dividing-line is always inexorably sliding toward the present: "all that we now regard as ancient was once new."

3   From Historical Positivism to Political Culture

A necessarily brief consideration of certain crucial moments in modern political historiography of the ancient world will reinforce the point. For clarity and cohesion, I focus on a circumscribed segment of ancient political history; I have chosen the study of the Roman republic because this sub-discipline is the one whose historiography is best known to me. However, it should be possible to recognize identical or similar issues and developments in other areas of ancient history. Of the various approaches

I consider, prosopography has had the least impact upon Greek history – but this seems only to be the result of the relative paucity of useful biographical information for a large number of minor characters even in the better-known periods (classical and Hellenistic Athens).

Historical positivism is an approach to historical research defined by a focus upon independently verifiable fact, stripped of all (or as much as possible) subjective "taint," and typically attended by the conviction, based on this reverence for facticity, that historical interpretation is something that somehow "emerges" from the facts themselves after they have been thus properly verified. This approach to historical evidence and the modern techniques of source-criticism that were associated with it were explored by the ground-breaking Roman historian Barthold Georg Niebuhr (1776–1831) and the founder-figure of modern European historiography, Leopold von Ranke (1795–1886), inspired by the model of classical philologists seeking to reconstruct the authentic readings of a lost archetype from the surviving witnesses to the text (i.e. manuscripts) of varying authority. This strong link between historical positivism and philology has remained an enduring nineteenth-century legacy in ancient-historical scholarship.

Source-criticism, or *Quellenkritik*, set historical research on a firm basis, stripping away the patina of legend that surrounds so much of ancient history (for example, the traditional narrative of early Rome), laying bare the tortuous lines of transmission by which contemporary knowledge of ancient events reached often much later writers, and sending historians forth on a hunt for inscriptions and other ostensibly more reliable, contemporary documentation of the distant past. Yet by the dawn of the twentieth century source-criticism had run its course as a central project in ancient political history. We are still in the process of shedding one discredited feature of the method: the often highly speculative attempt to track down the ultimate sources of information we find in relatively late extant accounts such as Livy, Diodorus, or Plutarch. Too frequently this became a sort of game in which "nuggets" of factual information were somewhat arbitrarily parceled out to authors of lost works, resulting in little if any gain in historical understanding, while the real possibility that a later author might have shaped his narrative according to his own literary and historical judgment tended to be dismissed as an inconvenient complication for the larger project of building stemmas of transmission. More profoundly, the philological-positivist approach encouraged a merely descriptive and rather jejune version of history, for at the level of verifiable facts there is little one can do but point to them; any interpretative move takes the interpreter into that nebulous world of progressively greater unverifiability that the positivist has implicitly forsworn. We can, for instance, analyze in great detail – thanks to a uniquely rich array of source material – the moves and counter-moves of Caesar and Pompey (and Cato and Curio) in the run-up to the civil war of 49–45 BC; yet if we understand our mission as historians to reflect upon the *causes* of that war and indeed of the end of the Roman republic, we soon find ourselves forced to choose between staying at the level of factual verifiability and venturing into discussion of the ability of the republic's institutions to govern an empire, of the consequences of agrarian discontent and possible changes in military recruitment, or of the erosion of traditional self-regulating norms of elite behavior (to give just three popular candidates) – all of which reach beyond what the positivist can actually prove in a manner fully consistent with his or her principles.

Yet, though positivism cannot be the leading principle of historical reconstruction, it is also perfectly true that much of its theoretical underpinning and its associated methods remain indispensable. History as it has come to be conceived within our culture cannot dispense with the conception of relatively objective fact, though facts should be seen as the provisional products of reasoned discourse, not metaphysical entities "out there" waiting to be discovered. History, *qua* history, will remain rooted in facts, and when we are establishing facts, positivist methods of source-criticism – duly chastened, to be sure, by a contemporary recognition of the literary and rhetorical character of ancient historiography (Woodman 1988) – remain an essential part of our Standard Operating Procedure.

In a comparable fashion the juristic-constitutional approach to ancient history yielded important results that every ancient historian must make use of, but it is no longer a driving force in the field. This tradition is best exemplified by the towering figure of Theodor Mommsen (1817–1903), whose achievement and overall impact not merely on Roman history but on the field of ancient history generally remain unparalleled. Recipient of the Nobel Prize for Literature in 1902 (beating Leo Tolstoy!) for his great *Römische Geschichte* (*Roman History*) written half a century before, Mommsen's most lasting legacies were, however, the comprehensive collection of Latin inscriptions (the *Corpus inscriptionum Latinarum*, or *CIL*, from 1863), whose scores of volumes are still being supplemented by international teams of epigraphic scholars, and the great compendium of Roman constitutional law, *Römisches Staatsrecht* (first published from 1871), whose five volumes are never very far from the Roman historian's hand. In a great age of constitution making, and strongly influenced by the conception that a people expresses its true spirit through its laws, Mommsen, whose academic training had been in jurisprudence, laid forth the fundamental principles of the unwritten Roman constitution on the basis of a minute analysis of the scattered references in our sources to the actual functioning of governmental institutions. Mommsen had, in a sense, retroactively given Rome that great gift of the modern age: a written constitution.

One hundred thirty-five years after its original publication, *Römisches Staatsrecht* remains the standard reference work on Roman constitutional law and practice, superseded in details but not as a whole. Indeed, as a project it hardly *can* be superseded, since few, if any, modern scholars would accept that the Roman *res publica* ever was such a static, coherent and well-defined system of rules and norms as Mommsen made it in this work. Indirectly, this great work of ex-post-facto systematization has tended to encourage some Roman historians to treat Roman constitutional conceptions and norms, whose application was frequently fought over in highly partisan political struggles, as if they were clear-cut legal standards on the basis of which a definitive answer was and therefore now is possible. An example is the unending debate sparked by Mommsen himself over the legality of Caesar's position at the outbreak of the civil war in 50–49 – the so-called *Rechtsfrage*. Well over a century after Mommsen's opening salvo, most would probably agree that this was a misfire: not only are the legal details that might resolve the question apparently unavailable to us, but more important, the legal position seems to have been fundamentally ambiguous. Even if Caesar's command had run its formal term, which remains uncertain, it had not been transferred by the Senate to a successor; and the "Law of the Ten Tribunes" of 52 could easily be interpreted as recognizing his right to hold on to his command (within reasonable limits, which were, however, disputable) until he stood for his second consulship *in absentia*. Moreover, the legal question is not anyway treated by our sources as the real issue in the coming of the civil war. Similarly, the Mommsenian tradition of interpreting Augustus's consolidation of his position chiefly from a legal-constitutional perspective has been generally discredited. (See, however, Linderski 1990.) But while the limitations and conceptual flaws of Mommsen's modern artifice of the "Roman constitution" and the legalistic approach it inspired ultimately became conspicuous, the *Staatsrecht* remains indispensable as a reference work for every Roman historian, and its occasional correction and supplementation by contemporary scholars remain valuable services to the field.

In the English-speaking countries at least, the legal-constitutional tradition of ancient history was overturned above all by Ronald Syme's exceptionally illuminating use of prosopography, especially in his masterpieces, *The Roman Revolution* (1939) and *Tacitus* (1958a). As I have noted above, the method itself did not emerge from thin air. In *The Roman Revolution*, indeed, he explicitly acknowledges in his Preface (Syme 1939: viii) not Lewis Namier (whom he apparently had not read: Stone 1971: 52) but the great German prosopographer Friedrich Münzer (born 1868), whose articles on Roman persons appeared in the volumes of Pauly and Wissowa's *Real-Encyclopädie der klassischen Altertumswissenschaft* from 1897 until well after his death at Theresienstadt concentration camp in 1942. (These 716 articles remain the fundamental prosopographical source for Roman republican historians, supplemented but not superseded by T. R. S. Broughton's *Magistrates of the Roman Republic*.) However, it was Syme (and here, in the area of reception at least, Namier's precedent must have been important) who showed how the prosopographical method could cast new and revealing light upon the old narratives of ancient history.

Prosopography (literarily, "descriptions of characters in a drama," [= *prosopa*]) in ancient political history may be understood as the study of the "minor characters" of history, those figures who make brief and sporadic appearances in the literary sources that provide our dominant narratives, or are indeed totally overlooked by them and revealed only by the often-random preservation of ancient inscriptions or other documentary evidence. The method typically involves painstaking analysis and organization of scattered facts and anecdotes preserved in our literary and inscriptional evidence to reveal the outline of a political career and perhaps a sense of the personality of such characters, which might then be used to establish their relationships to other minor and major figures in history and to the events and larger historical movements of their time. Like the positivist-philological and juristic approaches, the prosopographic approach implies a certain style of history. It tends to focus our attention on the strategies of both major and minor figures to expand their personal influence over networks of kinship and "friendship," typically through the exchange of personal favors and services (*beneficia* and *officia*) within a broad relationship of formal or informal patronage. The result, in the hands of a Ronald Syme, can be history of the first order: a richly textured account revealing the interests and aims of a wide circle of historical agents, not just the "great men" of history, but also the minor figures whose support was essential for their success, and yielding meaningful socio-political patterns such as the rise of *tota Italia* under Augustus and of the Transpadane and Transalpine Gauls in the early Principate.

The prosopographical method has often served as a valuable corrective to the close, telescopic focus of our major narrative sources on the leading agents of the historical drama. Full recognition of the fact that no leader can succeed without committed followers, who will have their own agendas not necessarily identical with that of a figurehead, has helped us to appreciate properly the constraints upon Julius Caesar's actions even in civil war: could a Marcus Aemilius Lepidus or a Marcus Antonius, with their noble pedigrees, really have wanted to set a *de facto* king (*rex*) over themselves (Bruhns 1978)? Loose generalizations form a perfect target for this kind of detailed research, for instance those regarding the adherence of the nobility to the Pompeian cause in 50 BC or the resistance of "the Senate" to Tiberius Gracchus in 133 BC. Prosopography has also been well used to challenge influential "master narratives" in our ancient sources. In his great study of *The Last Generation of the Roman Republic* (1974), Erich Gruen effectively used the prosopographical method to undermine the traditional narrative of "The Fall of the Roman Republic," arguing that right through the 60s and 50s BC the abiding continuities of Roman political life – mutual cultivation of patrons, clients and "friends" – were more notable than any symptoms of discontinuity and "crisis," which had long received the greatest emphasis.

Yet the prosopographical approach too has its limitations (Hölkeskamp 2001a). One is the conjectural nature of much prosopographic argument, not merely in the reconstruction of familial and personal ties but above all in the large conclusions one draws from them: the Gracchan bloodletting and Caesarian civil war alone offer all the proof necessary to show that connections of kin and friendship in no way precluded even extreme forms of political opposition (Brunt 1988: esp. 443–502). A deeper problem lies with the focus on narrow maneuver and concrete personal interest that generally attends political history written from a prosopographical standpoint. While most of us would be willing to grant that these are indeed perennially significant determinants of human action, it is surely reductive to insist (and it certainly could not be claimed to be empirically proved) that these are the *only* or *the most* important factors. One could indeed plausibly argue that, particularly in the face of great events in which important principles are in play, people have a perverse way of *not* pursuing their narrow self-interest. (Was it really in Cicero's narrow self-interest to launch a crusade against Antony in 44–43 BC? Was it really in Cassius's and Brutus's narrow self-interest to assassinate Julius Caesar?) Of course, even with the best of evidence we can never be very sure about motivation; but where we are unusually well informed, as we are for instance about Cicero's anguished self-interrogation on which course to choose for himself as all Italy was consumed by the "madness" of war in 50–49 BC, the assumption that cherished political and moral ideals had no real traction upon actual decision making in a time of crisis looks particularly dubious (Brunt 1986). The tendency among English-speaking Roman historians to neglect political ideology after Syme's memorable debunking of Ciceronian oratory as mere "political catchwords" (Syme 1939: 149–61) ultimately landed us in what John North memorably called "the Frozen Waste Theory" of Roman politics (North 1990), according to which (one might say rather crudely) what most of us recognize as politics – competing interests and visions of the public good, and how they might be realized – was largely overlooked in Roman political history, and along with it much of its power and interest. Simultaneously – and not coincidentally – the patron-client model, which is peculiarly congenial to prosopography, no longer enjoys the favor it once did as a global explanation of political action (Morstein-Marx 2004: 6).

None of this is to say that prosopography can, or should, ever be neglected. As is the case with the positivist-philological and juristic approaches, prosopography constitutes a powerful method of making the raw evidence speak to us in historically relevant ways. But like those other approaches, prosopography is bound by certain limitations that become more salient the more exclusively it is emphasized over all other ways of interpreting our evidence.

Current trends are less easy to characterize, and especially to evaluate, for the simple reason that reception is the only concrete test of value in historiography, and even historians do not possess a crystal ball. The intellectual ferment of the last third of the twentieth century has laid before the historian a veritable smorgasbord of eye-catching theories, each of which seems to grow out of at least one powerful truth – all too often suppressing others in the process. This is not the place to attempt an intellectual history of the late twentieth century and our emergence into the new millennium, which in any case would lie beyond my capacity. But a few brief comments may help to characterize contemporary developments in ancient political history in broad terms.

From a large perspective the most notable change in the way ancient political history is researched and written over the last decades of the twentieth century and the dawn of the twenty-first has been its opening toward theoretical frameworks and methodological techniques drawn from related disciplines, especially anthropology, sociology, and political science, but also literary studies (which has itself been strongly historicized) and social philosophy. The dominance of the traditional form of narrative historiography has been heavily shaken, partly in reaction to the often-conservative political assumptions of "great man" history, but perhaps more importantly by the relatively broad acceptance of the once-heretical claim that history can never meet the very high epistemological standards that have traditionally been ascribed to it, and therefore that historical narrative is a form of writing that is closer to literary fiction than the positivist historians who originally shaped the modern discipline would have acknowledged. One result – lamented by some "defenders of History" but probably accepted or even greeted by most – is that much political history now being written looks more like literary, sociological, or anthropological scholarship, even political theory (e.g. Ober 2005), than it does Mommsen's *Römische Geschichte* or Syme's *Roman Revolution*. There are many distinct and sometimes divergent external sources of these interdisciplinary currents: Pierre Bourdieu, Michel Foucault, Clifford Geertz, Jürgen Habermas, and Hayden White are among the names that recur especially frequently and must now be familiar to the young scholar.

However, one could venture a general characterization of the central current project in ancient political history as a study of "political culture," that is, of politics interpreted as a *system of signification* or meaning in which historical agents are situated and operate.

Political culture embraces such fundamental questions such as where and how the boundary is drawn between the political and the apolitical, how actively or passively "political subjects" relate themselves to what is culturally construed as the political, and how social values and the distinct ideologies that map out the possibilities for political action are transmitted, policed, and contested. It therefore offers an explanation for the differing ways in which comparable political systems actually operate in practice, or the slightly paradoxical ways in which a given political system functions in practice. For example, on the face of things the Roman republic would seem to have highly democratic institutions: direct popular election of virtually all officials, legislation strictly by direct popular vote, the tribunician office with its powerful veto, backed by sacrosanctity, legislative power, and a mandate to pursue the popular interest. Yet it would be difficult to characterize the Roman republic as a democracy (Millar 1998 and 2002) without a great deal of qualification; and although social and institutional reasons must be given their due (e.g. patronage and the relatively unrepresentative structure of the voting assemblies), much of the explanation is likely to come from peculiarities of political culture (Hölkeskamp 2000). For it is this that to a great extent shapes conscious agents' *use* of their institutions: when to cast a veto and when to withdraw it, for instance; or how much deference to give, when voting, to the opinions of the leaders of the state (*principes civitatis*). Indeed, the very construction of this elevated category of top senators is an aspect of political culture.

As my example of the debate over the character of the Roman republic shows, political culture not only prompts a new agenda but can also advance our understanding of older problems in political history. Another, narrower example may reinforce the point. When Julius Caesar harangued his soldiers before crossing the Rubicon he stressed the offence committed by his enemies against his "honor," or more correctly "worth" (*dignitas, BC* 1.7.7) as a central justification of his decision to resort to arms against those who controlled the Senate in Rome. Modern scholars have tended to regard this as evidence either of an almost psychotic megalomania or as an utterly shameless pretext. But neither attempt to dismiss Caesar's claim can explain why his soldiers would have responded to it with enthusiasm. The student of political culture would ask precisely how such a shockingly (to our mind) egotistical demand can be understood within the framework of republican concepts such as *dignitas* and *honor* and seek to give an account of its apparent rhetorical power. (At Pharsalus, the centurion Crastinus is said to have begun the Caesarian charge by calling upon his men to recover Caesar's *dignitas* and their own freedom, Caes. *BC* 3.91 – a notable collocation!) This might, in turn, plausibly complicate our picture of the issues in play during the coming of the civil war (for Caesar's men may no longer be seen as rebels against "the republic"), and lead to fruitful pondering of the deeper implications of a conception of individual meritorious service and public honor that is so pronounced, and so outweighed Rome's quite minimalist conception of equality (cognitive, moral, and political).

The student of political culture will, however, be less interested in shifting perspectives upon the traditional narrative of events and individual decision making than in the ways in which political subjects were constituted through a great variety of cultural practices, including, for example, formerly neglected areas such as public speech, memorialization, and political rituals, to name just three areas that have recently proved particularly fruitful in the study of Roman republican political culture. These three kinds of practice can all be profitably analyzed as communicative systems of signification through which central political values and norms were "dramatized" in public performance, recreated and reinforced, each in their own ways contributing to the remarkably durable dominance of the republican ruling elite, whose social and political power cannot be reduced to the merely coercive. In a predominantly oral political culture like Rome's, the power to articulate the arguments by which collective action was requested and justified gave senators an extraordinarily privileged ideological position in the negotiation of interests in the Forum (Morstein-Marx 2004). Likewise, inasmuch as memory establishes identity, senators' (and the Senate's) exclusive rights over public memorialization, both in physical form (monuments) and verbal (speeches), can be viewed as a vitally important further source of ideological hegemony (Hölkeskamp 2006). And the great civic events such as elections, censuses, triumphs, and other processions (funeral and circus), along with the often-spectacular religious rites celebrated in the city, can be fruitfully interpreted as "political rituals" whose function is to confirm civic identity or "naturalize" sociopolitical hierarchies (or both) through performance, and perhaps often to dramatize the interdependence of the political elite and the mass of Roman citizens (Jehne 2006: 20–22). It seems increasingly plausible as a result of work such as this to explain the remarkable durability of the republican political system – which functioned successfully, after all, for nearly half a millennium – as a product not so much of social mechanisms such as patronage as of the successful creation and reproduction of cultural meaning through symbolic means.

Some hard-nosed historians will feel queasy at what may seem to be the infinite malleability of the analysis of ancient political culture. Having moved beyond the positivist foundations of our field, and lacking the surveys and field data that can bring a sense of empirical verifiability to works of sociology or anthropology, we are sometimes hard put to distinguish what is verifiable (and, as important, what is at least potentially *falsifiable*) from what is merely an attractive "reading" of a text or phenomenon. What, a skeptic might ask, is left of history if its empirical foundations are thus eroded? (The response might be that they were not so stable to begin with.) A more cogent criticism of the thrust of much work in "political culture" is perhaps that it adopts a questionable "functionalist" sociological emphasis, and accordingly exaggerates tendencies toward societal cohesion and solidarity rather than the sites where concord is challenged and meaning contested from differing social and subject-positions (Faulks 2000: 107–25). This is a fair criticism, but perhaps should be seen more as a stimulus to a future, more nuanced exploration of political culture, including its areas of contradiction and social tension, than a decisive condemnation of the entire approach.

Finally, it is no doubt true that political culture is very march a mark of the age: it too therefore can be readily "historicized." The concept itself was arguably born of "whiggish" complacency in the post-Second World War years, and used to enshrine English and American democracy as the consummation of an ideal which other, more "primitive" forms of democratic culture have failed to achieve (so, arguably, the classic study by Almond and Verba 1963). The attempts, with varying success, to spread Western-style democracy after the fall of the Iron Curtain in 1989 and after the 2003 US-led invasion of Iraq have given renewed impetus to the idea of political culture, as did also the brutal atrocities perpetrated on European soil during the break-up of Yugoslavia and the recent and ongoing debates over the integration of Muslims into Europe and the European Union. Like it or not, these *are* among the most salient problems of political history in our age, and they will inevitably shape the kind of political history *we* write.

4   A Tralatician Historiography

We are all still, as the need arises, philological positivists, Mommsenian jurists, and prosopographers. But new forms of inquiry and ways of interrogating the evidence are *added* to the old ones, with new points of emphasis drawn from the intellectual history of the age, in a constantly enriched synthesis. Nothing of real value is ever entirely abandoned; as has occurred in the case of Marxism, an immensely powerful intellectual stimulus for much of the twentieth century, those features that have proved most illuminating will eventually be folded into the mainstream of historical research and the less useful parts quietly jettisoned. Wrong turns there will be, and they will be exposed as such in due course – but by the generations who follow us, not by the self-appointed "gatekeepers" or "defenders of History" in our own.

FURTHER READING

E. Clark 2004 offers a valuable survey of modern historiographic theory from an ancient historian's perspective; Morley 2004, an accessible and thoughtful introduction to "theory" in ancient history. L. Stone 1971 remains an excellent account of prosopography, including its intellectual origins, successes and failings, from the wider disciplinary perspective. Suny 2002 helpfully analyses the "cultural turn" in the historical discipline (see also Cannadine 2002); as it happens, for some historians we are already "beyond the cultural turn" (Bonnell and Hunt 1999). On political culture, the concise encyclopedia entries by Aronoff 2001 and A. Brown 2004 give a good orientation; Faulks 2000: 107–25 offers illuminating criticism of the sociological concept. Jehne 2006 is an excellent, recent historiographical survey of modern and contemporary work in Roman republican political history. On the Greek side, Rhodes 2003a traces a line of development in the study of Athenian democracy analogous to the one sketched here, though he criticizes much recent scholarship as insufficiently respectful of the distinctness of the past. Those interested in the political-culture approach in Greek history will also learn from the Hansen-Ober debate over the relative importance of institutions and ideology in sustaining Athenian democracy (Hansen 1989, Ober 1989a); cf. also Boedeker and Raaflaub 1998, Morris and Raaflaub 1998. Finley 1983, though now a bit dated, remains a powerful stimulus to thinking about Greek and Roman politics, above all because of its comparative consideration of both. For the view of the outbreak of the Roman civil war of 49–45 adumbrated above, see now Morstein-Marx (forthcoming.)

CHAPTER ELEVEN

Economic and Social History

Neville Morley

1 Introduction

Non-specialists often regard economic and social history as "history with the politics left out" – the left-overs after the significant events of classical antiquity like the Peloponnesian War, Alexander's conquests and the struggle for mastery in Rome have been considered. The label encompasses a vast range of apparently miscellaneous subjects – agriculture, trade, health and disease, family life, patronage and friendship, to highlight just the most prominent – providing the background against which the activities of political and military leaders were played out. Studying such topics may increase our store of information, offering a wealth of period detail and an impression of "everyday life," but it does not affect our basic understanding of events. Ancient economic and social history is merely a supplement to mainstream history, for those who like that sort of thing, not an alternative approach that offers a radically different account.

The majority of historians who actually practice economic and social history would offer a very different account of the importance of their subject. First, economic and social structures are not merely background, but the indispensable basis for political and military activity. In order to understand ancient history in the conventional sense, we need to understand how ancient society produced a surplus of food and other resources that could be devoted to inessential activities like politics and war, and how this surplus was mobilized. Rome's military adventures depended on the interaction of agricultural production, the demography of the peasant family (supplying surplus young men for the army: Rosenstein 2004) and relationships between the political elite and the masses on whom their power ultimately depended. Everything commonly associated with "classical civilization," including the leisure that enabled elite authors to describe and analyze it, depended on the unacknowledged work of millions of peasants, slaves, and other workers.

Secondly, this "background" was not unchanging – though change tended to take place over decades, or even centuries. We can for some purposes generalize about "ancient" agriculture, slavery or family structures, since there were significant conti-nuities throughout classical antiquity, but there were also significant developments: the abolition of debt-bondage in Athens, so that henceforth only foreign barbarians were enslaved, or the mass influx of slaves into Italy in the later republic and the development of the slave-based, market-oriented villa. This last example emphasizes that such changes could affect or even bring about events in the world of politics and war; the history of the Roman civil wars and the fall of the republic cannot be understood apart from the history of the Roman peasant class and its grievances (see e.g. Hopkins 1978b). Economic and social change set the limits within which indi-viduals had to operate, and it created forces to which they were forced to react, without ever fully comprehending them.

Finally, but no less importantly, economic and social history seeks to redress the balance between the history of the elite, who produced the vast majority of written sources and so have shaped our understanding of antiquity, and the vast, silent, exploited numbers of the rest of the population. We focus on politics, war, and high culture because those were the main interests of the elite, and we study them in a particular way because that is how the elite saw them. Politics and war would surely have looked quite different from the perspective of the ordinary citizen, the slave or the resident foreigner, the conscript, his parents, or his wife; and then there are the aspects of ancient society on which the sources have little to say, like family life, work, health, death, the world of the marketplace and the small farm. In many cases, given the state of the evidence, the historian's conclusion can only be that we cannot be certain; but it is better to have some idea what we do not know about antiquity rather than to accept the elite account as if it was complete and wholly reliable.

2   Social Science, History, and Classical Studies

In the course of the last two centuries, economic and social approaches to under-standing society have drifted apart and become more specialized, divided institution-ally between economics and sociology (not to mention anthropology). An approximate distinction is that economic history focuses on the means of obtaining necessary resources and overcoming scarcity, on the processes of consumption, production, and distribution. Social history focuses on the organization of human relationships; on the structures, both natural (families, up to a point) and artificial (clubs, associations), both formal and informal, within which people interact. Both approaches have to take into account the broader ecological context, which determines the distribution and availability of scarce resources and the population dynamics that in turn shape family and social structures. Both also overlap frequently with one another; social relationships can be the key determinant of access to resources and the organization of labor, while economic position and power can have a direct effect on social stand-ing. Historians may follow different social science disciplines in regarding certain processes as primary – interpreting economic behavior in social terms, or vice versa – or take a more holistic view of their complex interaction.

Analytical approaches to the study of ancient economy and society, as opposed to compilations of exotic trivia about "ancient life," are relatively recent developments. The origins of the "social sciences" lie in the eighteenth century, in particular with figures like David Hume and Adam Smith and the emerging discipline of "political economy." Many of these writers made extensive use of ancient examples and evidence in developing their theories, but their interest was not reciprocated by ancient historians, who continued to see their subject in the terms set down by ancient historiographers. This tendency was simply accelerated by nineteenth-century historians' idolization of Thucydides and the consequent narrowing of the scope of history to politics and war, while mainstream economic thought became increasingly uninterested in historical questions. Alternative, more historical, approaches to understanding the economy, such as Karl Marx's theories, were likewise ignored by ancient historians; so too the new ways of studying present and past societies offered by proto-sociologists and proto-anthropologists like Auguste Comte, Max Weber and Emile Durkheim, again despite the importance of classical antiquity for them as an example of a complex, non-modern society.

The twentieth century did at last see greater interest in the economic and social dimension, both in mainstream historical studies – above all through the influence of the French *Annales* school – and in ancient history, with the works of historians like M. I. Rostovtzeff, Tenney Frank, A. H. M. Jones and M. I. Finley. It is possible to identify three major themes in the subject over this period, which continue to resonate in contemporary debates. The first is the changing nature of the evidence, above all the expansion of archaeological data; Rostovtzeff's work is renowned, and still well worth reading, for its use of material evidence to support his interpretation of antiquity, but it also marks the beginning of a debate about the relative value of material and literary sources. Second, there is the dispute about whether it is appropriate to describe antiquity in modern terms, whether in Rostovtzeff's fairly casual deployment of words like "bourgeoisie" and "capitalism" or the explicit adoption of the terminology and assumptions of neo-classical economic theory. Thirdly, there is the closely related and sometimes inextricably intertwined argument about the actual nature of antiquity, often characterized as "primitivism" versus "modernism."

Many nineteenth-century economists had been struck by the realization that, economically, their own society was both significantly different from and greatly superior to classical antiquity (see Morley 1998). Ancient historians, on the other hand, were more often struck by the sophistication and apparent "modernity" of Greece and Rome, especially in comparison to other historical societies. The differences between ancient and modern were seen as quantitative rather than qualitative – a matter of the volume of trade and industry, rather than the nature of the activity – and the key research question became why this sophisticated society had not "taken off" into full modernity. Others, from Marx to Weber to Finley, insisted instead on the absolute distinction between the two, with the rise of capitalism and the industrial revolution marking a fundamental break in historical development. For such writers, antiquity was manifestly not modern: predominantly agrarian, dominated not by the production-ethic of modern capitalism but by a consumption ethic; marked by the absence of an integrated market system, economic rationality, double-entry bookkeeping and everything else that had made possible the economic transformation of early modern Europe; in short, primitive, or at any rate underdeveloped.

3   Evidence and Interpretation

It may seem astonishing that such completely different views of antiquity could have arisen, let alone that they should continue to dominate the debate. The explanation lies above all in the nature of the ancient evidence. It is, as ever, only a limited and unrepresentative sample of what once existed, favoring certain sorts of materials and the products of the elite rather than the masses. One of its most striking features, compared with the evidence for political or military history, is the absence of any ancient discussions of their own practices. Quite simply, the Greeks and Romans did not conceptualize "the economy" or discuss "economic activity" in abstract terms (Finley 1999). This has been interpreted by the "primitivists" as a clear indication of the undeveloped nature of the ancient economy – if the economy had been important, surely a philosopher like Aristotle would have engaged with it – but in any case it has the consequence that we cannot ever discuss ancient economic history in the Greeks' and Romans' own terms; our frameworks for interpreting it can only be drawn from elsewhere, whether from our own experiences or from the study of other premodern societies. The choice of an appropriate comparison, to help us make sense of the fragmentary surviving evidence, depends on our prior assumptions about what sort of society we are dealing with.

This problem can be illustrated by considering the ways that historians have responded to gaps in the evidence. Many of the kinds of evidence on which more modern economic studies are based simply do not exist: no extensive business archives, no state tax records or customs accounts. Is absence of evidence actually evidence of absence, then, or simply an accident of survival – and if the Greeks did indeed lack proper accounting techniques, is this necessarily a sign of economic primitivism? Where examples of estate records or customs receipts do exist, above all papyrus documents from the Egyptian desert, does this mean that such practices were widespread although few records survive, or are they chance survivals of rare and atypical activities? Do we take at face value the assertion, in Roman upper-class writings, that no respectable member of the elite would ever get involved in trade, or do we point to comparative examples from early modern Europe that such a rule could be flouted and that aristocrats would conceal the true origins of their wealth?

Archaeological evidence can be just as problematic. Tens of thousands of wine amphorae from Italy have been recovered from French rivers, presumably only a sample of the original total (Tchernia 1983). Clear evidence of large-scale trade, one might think – except that goods can be moved through many different mechanisms, most of them entirely outside any market system, and the amphorae themselves cannot indicate whether they were sold, exchanged as gifts or transported by the state to supply the army. The significance even of such substantial finds depends on the historian's prior beliefs about the context in which the evidence should be interpreted: a predominantly agrarian society in which trade was only a thin "veneer" on a subsistence economy, or a world of large-scale international trade, markets and sophisticated economic institutions?

4 Concepts and Terminology

One of the fiercest debates in the social sciences is about the choice of concepts to describe premodern societies; above all, in the choice between what are termed "actors' categories" and "observers' categories." On the one hand, it is argued, to understand properly how a society worked, we need to try to see it through the eyes of those who experienced it directly, rather than imposing our own foreign and anachronistic terms on it; this is the approach known as *Verstehen* (the German word "to understand," here implying "to understand from within") developed by the philosopher and historian Wilhelm Dilthey and widely followed within anthropology (P. Burke 2005). On the other hand, sociologists of a different theoretical orientation argue, actors' categories can only ever be limited and subjective, and frequently incoherent; to gain a proper understanding, we need to analyze society in terms of more general social categories which will enable us to compare different societies and see how they actually work, rather than just how their inhabitants believe they are supposed to work.

These issues can be illustrated by considering the social structure of Rome in the late republic, as presented by Cicero in his fourth speech against Catiline in 63 BC. "All men are here, of every order, of all origins and indeed of all ages," he declared to the Senate, and listed the different groups: the *equites* (the wealthy Romans from whom the Senate drew its members); the tribunes of the treasury and the clerks; the mass of the *ingenui* (free-born citizens), "even the poorest"; the *liberti*, former slaves "who, having gained the benefit of citizenship by their own virtue, truly judge this to be their native land"; and even the slaves (*Cat.* 4.14–16). Cicero recognized that Roman society consisted of different groups whose interests did not necessarily coincide; the force of his argument is that Catiline is so dangerous that he has united everyone against him.

This sort of account – which is echoed in other sources – is frequently taken as the basis for descriptions of "Roman society." We can safely assume that it reflects the way that Cicero and his fellow senators viewed the world – though in other writings Cicero offered slightly different versions, for example emphasizing distinctions between richer and poorer citizens, *assidui* and *proletarii* – and this "actors' perspective" is an important part of understanding Roman social history. The question is whether it is sufficient. Cicero's list comprises different kinds of groups, some defined by wealth, some by legal status, some by political rights, some by birth; elsewhere he includes occupation, place of origin and moral virtue as further means of dividing Romans into groups. There is, on the other hand, no mention of gender or race as principles of social organization, although modern scholars would emphasize at least the first of these. Cicero does not indicate which of these distinctions is most significant in ordering society, or, given that many individuals would have fallen into several categories, which ones were most important for a Roman's sense of his own social identity. Finally, the account is self-serving, intended to rally the support of "all Romans" for Cicero's policy and to present Catiline's followers as outcasts from society. The "actors' perspective," subjective, partial and sometimes contradictory, tells us what society looks like from the vantage point of those at its pinnacle, seen through the lens of their prejudices and assumptions; it does not offer an objective picture of social structure.

For that, historians have often turned to modern sociological concepts. One important issue here is that there is no universal system for interpreting social structure, but a number of competing theories, each of which represents society differently and raises different questions. One approach is that of the "status group," developed by Max Weber. Society is made up of a number of such groups, which are defined by indicators such as birth, occupation, way of life, and shared cultural practices; these groups are arranged in a hierarchy, and membership of a group determines one's level of access to political power and other resources as well as shaping social behavior. This can clearly be seen in republican Rome, where "new men" like Cicero who aspired to join the established elite had to adopt wholesale the attitudes and customs of that elite, and where political rivals constantly sought to show how their opponents' behavior was unworthy of their status; to be "slavish" in any respect was a devastating indictment. Considering such a status society, the crucial issue for historians is to explore how far the groups were closed and how far social mobility was possible; this involves consideration both of the actors' perspective (Rome had a long-established hereditary elite which only rarely accepted new blood) and of the likely reality (the elite did not breed fast enough to replace itself, and so always depended on absorbing new members: Hopkins 1983).

In the absence of direct evidence, it is impossible to say whether the elite obsession with status was echoed in other groups. According to Cicero, manual labor, crafts and petty trade were "slavish" and so degrading (*Off.* 1.151); the fact that potters signed their work and merchants recorded their trading activities on their tombstones suggest that elite attitudes were not universally accepted. However, the main objection to the idea of status groups is not that they did not exist or did not affect individuals' behavior, but that they were less important than other sorts of social groups. In particular, status divisions are seen to be secondary to class divisions. Following the ideas sketched out by Marx, society is understood in terms of different classes, defined by their position within the organization of production. Wealthy owners of land and other capital, free peasants with small plots of their own land, free laborers who needed to rent land or to hire themselves out to make a living, and different sorts of slaves, all had different roles and different levels of access to resources and power – slaves, tenants and smallholders were all exploited, but in quite different ways. Whereas status groups might coexist quite peacefully, classes exist in an antagonistic relationship, as the interests of one can be served only at the expense of another: what's good for landlords is rarely good for their tenants. The historian's prime task, then, is to study the forms of exploitation, the social conflict that this produced, and the way that this shaped the course of events. Classical Athens was the great exception to the ancient norm, as the masses seized power and put limits on the power of the rich (Wood 1988); in Rome, however, the changing balance of power in the struggle between the classes of landowners, peasants and slaves has been seen as the primary cause of upheaval in the late republic (de Ste. Croix 1981).

Two obvious objections to the use of "class" as a means of analyzing ancient society are first that it is overtly political – something which Marxist historians never deny – and second that it is anachronistic to apply it to a premodern society. Describing Athens or Rome in terms of "observers' categories," it is argued, presents ancient society as more modern than it really was, creating a false and misleading impression; it is no different, even if it is rather more systematic, from Rostovtzeff's habit of describing certain groups in the cities of the Hellenistic East as "bourgeoisie." The problem is that there is no truly neutral, non-anachronistic terminology which we could use instead; even if we use the ancients' own terms, we have to translate them and understand them in terms of our own experiences and knowledge. The decision as to whether the Roman word *ordo* should be translated as rank, order, class or station – or, if it is simply italicized and left untranslated, how it is explained to the reader – depends on assumptions both about the workings of society in general and about the nature of Roman society. Modern concepts are more precise: they make it easier to compare ancient society with other premodern societies, and they highlight the difficult issues involved in choosing the right words to describe antiquity, where more "everyday" language might conceal the fact that there is a problem.

5   Models and Theories

Certainly no one in Athens or Rome thought of themselves as members of a class or a status group; historians making use of these terms tend to argue that such groups have an objective existence, regardless of whether their members realize it, and that it is necessary to look beyond the surface appearance of society to understand what is "really" going on. This is the claim of all social-scientific theories, that they reveal underlying structures and processes, on the basis of a general understanding of the ways that societies and economies work. The reason why many historians, especially those working in more traditional fields like political history, are frequently suspicious of the use of "theory" in ancient history is precisely because it is felt to be too general, disregarding the specifics of the evidence and its ancient context (Morley 2004).

All historians, even the most apparently untheoretical, make use of generalizations: in their use of concepts like "emperor," "democracy," or "city," and in the assumptions about "human nature" that underpin their interpretations of, for example, why the Spartans and Athenians fought one another or why Constantine converted to Christianity. Social-scientific history is distinguished in the first place by its aim, namely to study individual institutions or events as a means of drawing more general conclusions about the antiquity (and even, perhaps, about other human societies), rather than as an end in itself (cf. Morris 2002). Secondly, it tends to be explicit about the way that it makes use of generalizations: identifying them and their origins, offering arguments to justify their use, and discussing whether and how far they do illuminate classical antiquity. It offers a particular sort of knowledge about the past; sometimes lacking the sort of vivid detail and eye for the particular that "brings the past to life," but claiming to provide an understanding of *why* things were as they were, rather than just a description of them.

A classic example is the study of the ancient city. It is widely agreed that classical civilization was "urban," despite the fact that the vast majority of the population lived in the countryside; not only were Greece and Rome highly urbanized, but the city was the center of political, social, cultural, and intellectual life. Cities are the place of origin of much of our evidence for antiquity; the question is what we should seek to do with this mass of information. With the exception of Athens and Rome – Pompeii is of course archaeologically rich, but there are very few literary sources – we lack the evidence to write a proper history of any individual city, and it is arguable how much it would tell us even if we could (Finley 1981a). Historians have tended instead to generalize about "the ancient city," and to draw on all the available material to discuss and analyze the nature of "ancient urbanism" – the basic structures of demography, society, economics and food supply, the cultural idea of the city, and so forth. Individual cities are understood in terms of this more general framework of knowledge and ideas.

This immediately raises the question of the appropriate level of generalization; does it make more sense to talk of "the Greek city" and "the Roman city" than to subsume them under a broader category? Conversely, are there useful things that can be said about "the premodern city" that might help in interpreting the ancient evidence? Within a single society, individual cities differ from one another in important ways; at the same time, one can argue that the concentration of a number of people into a relatively small space, along with the concentration of wealth and power, creates conditions that are common to cities of all sizes and all historical periods. Too narrow and specific a focus may make the study less useful; too broad a generalization – for example, the idea, drawn largely from studies of modern American cities, that "city air is liberating" and that urbanism automatically promotes social mobility – may be either implausible or unhelpfully vague, or both.

One approach to the study of ancient urbanism which illustrates both its advantages and potential problems is the "consumer city" model, developed by M. I. Finley (1981a) on the basis of work by earlier historians and sociologists like Weber. Finley's interest was in defining the essential characteristics of the ancient city compared with those of other periods, above all the late medieval city. Following Weber's methodology, he devised the "ideal type" of the "consumer city": a model, a mental construct, so to speak an idealized version of a particular sort of city (contrasted with the model of the "producer city") which could then be compared with historical reality. The aim of such a model is to simplify a complex reality, to identify the basic characteristics shared by all ancient cities; it does not imply that all ancient cities will exactly match the model. For Finley, what distinguished the ancient city from its medieval counterpart was its relationship with the surrounding countryside: it was primarily a collector of rents and taxes rather than a center of manufacture engaged in trade with rural producers; it was primarily a political rather than an economic institution, and this explained why ancient cities, in contrast to medieval ones, did not have a dynamic role in promoting economic growth and development. This was an important refinement of the much broader theory, found in many general accounts of urbanism, that cities will always have a dynamic effect on the economies of their hinterlands (cf. Morley 1996).

There are plenty of grounds on which the "consumer city" model could be attacked. It draws attention away from the significant differences between cities in different periods of classical antiquity and it can focus too much on what the ancient city was not, rather than saying anything positive about what it was like. The contrast between the ancient and the medieval city can be overdone – they had a great deal in common, compared with modern industrial cities – and the argument conceals a leap of logic: the fact that the ancient and medieval cities had different relationships with the countryside, and the fact that the medieval economy developed (eventually) into industrialized capitalism while antiquity did not, are not necessarily connected. However, what most historians sought to argue in response to Finley was that the ancient city was not a consumer, identifying examples of urban textile production, milling complexes, market activity, and so forth. This misses the point; models cannot be proved or disproved in this way, since they don't claim to be images of reality but simplified, abstracted versions of it. They can only be judged more or less persuasive and useful; historians today discuss the consumer city less frequently than before, not because it has been shown to be wrong but because conceptualizing ancient cities in this way is no longer felt to generate interesting research questions (cf. Parkins 1997).

The same can be said of all kinds of general theories and concepts. Economic theory, the subject of so much controversy in ancient economic history, offers a drastically simplified model of reality; it highlights the interaction of certain key variables – supply and demand, at the simplest level – by ignoring, for the purposes of the model, all the other variables (individual irrationality, imperfect information, the costs of transactions, and so forth). The theory does not tell you how things are, let alone how they must be, even in the modern world; it offers one way of understanding what is going on. It is perfectly possible to describe the ancient world in terms of economic theory, without thereby making it modern, in the same way that we can call Athens a "city" without assuming that it was like London. The question is always whether this is plausible – whether the generalization is too broad, or the number of simplifying assumptions required simply too great – and whether it then offers a persuasive, productive interpretation of the available evidence.

6   Structures and Events

Economic and social history can sometimes seem static, focused on the description and analysis of structures that lasted more or less unchanged for decades or centuries. Ancient peasant farming practices changed remarkably little in a thousand years, Roman merchants relied on the same form of maritime loan as the fourth-century Athenians, and changes in the system of client-patron relations in Rome took place over a century or more; in general, this is an ideal topic for those with a poor memory for exact dates.

However, although it developed in explicit opposition to traditional event-focused political and military history, economic and social history is not uninterested in change; but it focuses on what it regards as the real causes of events. One of the clearest expositions of this approach was put forward by the French historian Fernand Braudel, who characterized the different speeds of historical time through an oceanic metaphor (1980; cf. P. Burke 1990). At the surface there are many waves and much activity, but these are driven largely by the tides and deeper currents; just so, the "history of events" catches our attention – it is, after all, history at the human scale, focused on individuals – but what really determines the development of a society is change at the level of social and economic structures, shaping and constraining the freedom of action of individuals and establishing the limits of what is possible. We can narrate the establishment of the Athenian democracy or the fall of the Roman republic in terms of the actions and choices of a few aristocrats, but to understand these events properly we have to see how they were shaped and propelled by deeper changes and developments, taking place over decades or centuries, of which the actors were only vaguely aware. Below this level is the "long term," the deep ocean currents of the almost changeless environment, which has shaped and set limits on social and economic structures – as, for example, ancient agricultural practices were influenced by the particular conditions of the Mediterranean.

Social and economic historians focus on changes in the medium and long term, in the belief that these are more significant for understanding the development of the ancient world than short-term events. They then tend to display preferences for economic explanations over social ones, or vice versa. Ultimately, however, the task is interdisciplinary and integrative; to show how different structures and processes interact, and to show how the different levels of historical time influence one another. The key question is always to understand the nature and dynamics of change, and to identify the best intellectual tools for this purpose. As ancient historians have, over the last decade or so, become frustrated with the limitations of the old primitivist-modernizer debate, so they have started to draw on ideas from a wider range of disciplines to illuminate antiquity: for example, from ecology, demography and other material sciences, which provide a deeper understanding of the physical and biological contexts of historical developments; from anthropology and sociology, offering more detailed and subtle readings of the ways that economic and social behavior is embedded in culture; and from new developments in economic theory, such as the New Institutional Economics, that offer a more sophisticated interpretation of the relationship between "the economy" and the rest of society. Each approach, of course, presents itself as the best way of making sense of the past; ancient economic and social history will continue to be a subject of fierce debate for the foreseeable future.

FURTHER READING

The best introduction to key topics in ancient economic and social history is Garnsey and Saller 1987; although it focuses on Rome, many of the issues discussed are equally relevant to Greece. Austin and Vidal-Naquet 1977 has less discussion but an excellent selection of ancient evidence. Scheidel, Morris, and Saller 2007 is now the indispensable reference volume for the economic history of antiquity. The "classics" of the subject, Rostozvtzeff 1941 and 1957 (2nd edn) and Finley 1999 (3rd edn), remain well worth reading. The papers collected in Scheidel and von Reden 2002, especially those by Cartledge and Andreau, offer a useful overview of the modernizer-primitivist debate and the contribution of Finley. K. Greene 1986 provides a clear survey of the archaeological evidence and its uses. Morley 1998 discusses the way that early economists discussed the ancient economy. Examples of new approaches to the subject can be found in recent collections of articles like Cartledge et al. 2002 and Manning and Morris 2005, and in books like Horden and Purcell 2000 and Morley 2007. See also Davies, ANCIENT ECONOMIES, with further reading there.

On social history and social theory, P. Burke 2005 offers an excellent general introduction. Morley 2004 discusses both the theoretical aspects of using models, theories, and modern terminology, and a range of examples including "class" and "status." Further reading on this topic includes de Ste. Croix 1981, Beard and Crawford 1985 and Nicolet 1980. For the "consumer city" model, Finley 1981a, Hopkins 1978a and Morley 1996. Hopkins 1978b and 1983 remain classics of sociologically informed and theoretically sophisticated ancient social history.

CHAPTER TWELVE

Ethnicity and Culture

Edward Herring

1 Background to the Study of Ancient Identities

This chapter is concerned with identity and how it was perceived in the ancient world. The principal issue can be simplified down to whether blood (kinship) relationships or a shared cultural background (such as a common language, material culture, belief system, cultural practices) were what united ancient socio-political groups. Thus, the issue is in some sense related to the nature/nurture debate of the modern social sciences and, perhaps more pertinently, the *nomos/physis* divide in Greek philosophy. Scholars on each side of the debate are, of course, well aware that both ethnicity (blood) and culture (a shared heritage) played a part in the construction of ancient identities.

It is a well-rehearsed truism that scholars frame their interpretations of the past in terms of the preoccupations of the present. It is hardly coincidental that interest in identity has blossomed over the past two decades. The same period has witnessed the collapse of the Eastern Bloc and the re-emergence of nationalism from the Baltic to the Balkans, ethnic cleansing in Rwanda and elsewhere, concerns about globalization and the desire to promote local diversity and identity, and the emergence of a militant brand of Islam that privileges a religious identity over the nation-state entities familiar to and favored by the West.

While a preoccupation with identity and especially cultural identity may be in vogue in post-modern and post-colonial scholarship, interest in the origins of groups is by no means new. Leaving aside the interest among ancient writers (e.g. Herodotus and Cato the Elder, to name but two), modern scholarship once took a keen interest in such matters. Darwinian-type evolutionary theories, when applied to matters of race and the origins of peoples, were the stuff of respectable scholarship in the late nineteenth and early twentieth century. This applies not just to studies of the past but also to the social sciences, including ethnography and physical anthropology (Trigger 1989: 113–47). The more extreme versions of this type of scholarship (e.g.

the work of Gustaf Kossina) gave a veneer of intellectual integrity to the racial policies of German fascism, and were wholly discredited when the horrors of the Holocaust were revealed. The study of the origins and characteristics of ancient races was consigned to the dustbin of scholarship. Physical anthropology now maintains that there is no way to recognize racial types in individual skeletons, though comparisons across a broad sample of a population may allow identifications to be posited with varying degrees of certainty. With the advent of research into ancient DNA, the issue of true ancestry is back on the academic agenda, though issues of race are mostly avoided. At the moment, the difficulty of recovering ancient DNA makes the sample sizes from ancient populations quite small, but we may assume that the datasets will grow over time. Recent studies on the origins of Ashkenazi Jews are just one example of where this kind of research might go in future (Behar et al. 2006).

After the Second World War the study of ethnicity was either put aside or safely sanitized by the recognition, by virtue of ethnographic analogy, that kinship relationships could be highly, if not entirely, fictional. Antiquity usefully provided plentiful examples of this. Much of the kinship diplomacy of the Greek world is based on mythological genealogies, often tenuously constructed by means of erudite and arcane scholarship. The focus on the cultural aspects of group identity similarly served to insulate the study of the past from the taboo of race. Nevertheless, the study of identity was largely downplayed until political events in the modern world brought the topic back into fashion. The new scholarship on identity could feel safe in that it was concerned not with race but with how ancient groups perceived themselves (and others) and how they were perceived by others. Such scholarship might well cast light on ancient and scholarly attitudes to race and racism (cf. Bernal 1987 and its numerous critiques, e.g. Lefkowitz and Rogers 1996), but was not concerned with race itself.

Thus, the emphasis shifted away from who people really were (and where they came from) to who they thought they were (i.e. the "construction" of identity). Group identity can be predominantly about the shared factors that united people. This is sometimes referred to as "aggregative identity." Equally important is what excludes an individual from membership of the group and how one group recognizes another. Groups often define themselves in relation to, and especially in contrast with, others. This is referred to as "contrastive" or "oppositional identity"; a familiar example of this from classical antiquity would be the contrast between Greeks and "Barbarians." In the language of post-colonial scholarship this is a matter of "othering" the outsider (i.e. emphasizing what is different, deviant and dangerous about the outsider). Again, the onus can be on ethnic differences or divergence from cultural norms or some mixture of the two. The contrast can be extreme – that the "other" is the polar opposite of the group – and is often pejorative, focusing on the dangerous and decadent. At the same time, that which is different, especially if it is decadent and a little dangerous, can also be attractive. This too has a negative undercurrent, with the "other" being characterized as seductive and corrupting. Many of these ideas can be seen in Western attitudes to the East (Said 1978).

These kinds of attitudes affect how a group sees itself and how it depicts other groups in writing and the visual arts, but can also influence how groups interact.

When studying identity we must be aware of the crucial difference between a perspective from within the group itself (an emic viewpoint) and that from without (an etic perspective).

Another factor that warrants consideration when looking at identity concerns our sources of evidence. We need to consider in what context people discuss or stress their identity. Passing references to how a group sees itself may be largely coincidental, but explicit discussions of identity are unlikely to be so. The motives for explicit expression of identity may vary (for example, group identity may be perceived to be under threat, or the informant may be seeking to flatter the reader), but as a conscious choice the evidence it provides cannot be taken at face value, and must be evaluated in context.

Physical manifestations of identity in the visual arts and material culture are even more problematic. The difficulty is this: changes in material culture need not necessarily be connected with group identity. Consistent patterning in physical evidence (e.g. in terms of artifact styles, settlement types, burial customs) allows the identification of "archaeological cultures" (Trigger 1989: 148–206). This is a meaningful way to structure the evidence for non-literate societies; when there are written sources we can hope for some evidence of a self-ascribed identity to survive. There is no *a priori* reason to assume that "archaeological cultures" correlate with socio-political or ethnic groupings; they are effectively modern constructs. Moreover, group identity need not be manifested physically or may have been marked in ways that leave little archaeological trace; costume is one very obvious possible example. Equally, variability in material culture need not be connected with group identity. Indeed, there is a lively theoretical debate on the meaning of stylistic variability (e.g. the papers in Conkey and Hastorf 1990). To take a crude example, in AD 384 the use of ivory diptychs was restricted to those of consular rank by imperial edict (*Cod. Theod.* 15.19.1). Thus ivory diptychs are a marker of social status, not ethnicity.

To discuss ethnicity in the archaeological record, the interpreter must first evaluate whether the physical evidence or representation is a manifestation of group identity; it might mark some other element in personal identity (such as gender or status). Secondly, even if it is a manifestation of group identity, one must consider whether it is a conscious expression or simply a by-product of subscribing to cultural norms (e.g. is a Roman depicted wearing a toga making an explicit reference to his citizenship or simply wearing the normal garb of a citizen?); this roughly equates to Wiessner's (1990) concepts of "emblemic" and "assertive" style. Some scholars see these problems as insurmountable and eschew the use of physical evidence in this area (cf. J. Hall 2002: 24, who feels archaeological evidence for ethnicity must be informed by text). Others, including the present author, disagree while stressing the importance of context as the key to identifying conscious choice in the physical manifestation of group identity (e.g. Herring 1995).

The aim of this introduction has been to outline something of the background to and issues surrounding the study of identity in antiquity. There were a great many peoples living in and around the Mediterranean in antiquity, including Egyptians, Phoenicians, Etruscans, to list but a few well-known examples. We shall focus on the

Greeks and the Romans while referring to some of the others groups with whom they had direct contact.

2 Identity in the Greek World

In ancient Greece group identity operated at a number of levels. Despite extreme political fragmentation, there was a sense of a common Hellenic identity. The Hellenes were divided into four major subgroups: the Achaeans, Aeolians, Dorians and Ionians. Each *polis* would consider itself to belong to one of these sub-groups.

One of the most quoted passages of Herodotus (8.144) deals explicitly with the shared Greek identity. He puts the words into the mouths of the Athenians in response to the envoys of Sparta, who have expressed concern that Athens might go over to the Persians. Having rejected the Persian overtures (delivered by Alexander of Macedon), the Athenians rebuke the Spartans for their lack of confidence in the Athenian character. The Athenian explanation for their resolute refusal to join the Persians consists of two main thrusts. The first, the requirement to avenge the burning of the temples, is purely Athenocentric and need not concern us here (save aside to note its primacy). The second concerns the common bond among Greeks. For Herodotus's Athenians this consists of common blood, language, shrines, ritual practices, and a broadly common way of life – matters which are both "aggregative" and implicitly "oppositional." Thus, Herodotus has an appeal to both kinship (ethnicity) and culture (language, religious practices, common customs), though scholars who support the idea that blood was the most significant factor would draw attention to the fact that it is first on the list. It is a remarkable passage that deserves the attention it has received, but it needs to be put in context. It is designed to be a rational explanation for Athenian steadfastness in the face of the seductive calls of *Realpolitik*. These are exactly the sorts of arguments that would have been used. They are a rhetorically effective appeal to unity. Within the historical context of the time, the speech makes perfect sense; whether such an event ever took place is debated, but if it did, the kind of arguments expressed by Herodotus may well have been voiced. In the context of Herodotus's narrative, with its subtext of Greek unity and freedom, it is a manifesto for panhellenism. Jonathan Hall (2002: 190) goes further to suggest that Herodotus's intention was to extend the definition of Greek identity to include cultural factors as well as blood.

It is worth considering each of the factors that Herodotus emphasizes in turn. The idea of shared kinship was very much based around an elaborate system of mythological genealogies that allowed the local heroes and leading families in an area to be tied to a wider, shared, but by no means unified corpus of stories. This was clearly a fiction, but it served its purposes of legitimizing local authority and providing a mechanism for explaining and developing between-group connections (kinship-diplomacy).

The commonality of language is interesting, given that there was no uniform version of Greek until the development of *koine* – a form of Greek developed in the third century BC from the Attic and Ionic dialects that became the *lingua franca* of the Hellenistic world (see Morpurgo Davis 1987 for an excellent discussion of the issues surrounding the dialects of Greek). Over the wide area covered by the Greek *diaspora* there were four principal dialects (Ionic, Attic, Western Greek and Aeolic), each with local variants. The degree of mutual intelligibility between these may not have been as great, in all instances, as the popular concept of the word dialect implies. There was, however, an awareness and familiarity with different forms of Greek due to the language used in literature. This would have made the different Greek dialects familiar in a way that "Barbarian" tongues would not have been to many. Nevertheless, the unifying factor identified by Herodotus is curiously divided. Language is often seen as a key element in group identity, yet in reality languages often spread beyond socio-political boundaries (as in ancient Greece), while some states can have several languages of equal status (cf. the case of modern Switzerland).

Religious shrines and practices may be taken together. There were shrines that were common to all Greeks and many that welcomed "Barbarians" too. The most celebrated was perhaps the Delphic oracle, which was consulted by Greeks and foreigners alike. The majority of temples and sanctuaries had a decidedly local character, belonging to and being frequented by the people of a single *polis*. Shrines of wider significance were either in locations that were conducive to trade or grew up in locations where they could not be dominated by any one state (such as Delphi and Olympia). It is, however, also the case that there was a generic similarity between the form sanctuaries and their associated buildings took across the Greek world. An Ionian temple would have seemed familiar to a western Greek in a way that "Barbarian" religious sites and structures may not have. Certainly the Greeks had a common pantheon, but this fact disguises a high degree of localization. The ways in which individual gods were honored, the particular attributes that were privileged, the festivals and stories commemorated tended to be *polis*-specific. Thus, all Greeks recognized Athena as a goddess but the Panathenaic Festival was distinctly Athenian. Here again the story is one of a level of general similarity nuanced by a high degree of local particularity. The gods might be absolutes but the ways in which they were worshipped was a matter for local custom (*nomos*).

The final factor, a common way of life, is an appeal to culture *par excellence*. It is Herodotus's last, and perhaps least significant, bond that unites the Greeks. It is the hardest to define and may well have been the "fuzziest" in the minds of ancient readers. Certainly there would have been broad similarities of culture across the Greek world, but some of these could also extend beyond the margins into areas that were not Greek, particularly in Asia Minor. In general, ancient Greece was characterized by cultural particularism. Many of the attributes that we see as characteristic of ancient Greece either were in their original form products of a specific place (e.g. Athenian drama) or could spread beyond the confines of Greece (e.g. vase-painting). Nowadays the Parthenon is claimed by the Greek state as an icon of national identity. By contrast, in antiquity it was symbolic of the culture of one particular *polis*, which was often in conflict with other Greek states. When Aeschines (2.105) suggested that the Theban general Epaminondas wanted to transfer the Propylaia to the Kadmeia, he was hardly seeing the Acropolis monuments as universal symbols of Greece: the orator was seeking to inflame Athenian pride.

The commonalities (save aside myth, religion, ritual practice, and language which have already been addressed) of culture would have resided in matters like the shared appreciation of the Homeric epics and the values espoused within them, and general attitudes to freedom, foreigners, and the relative position of men and women in society; but in these latter cases there was a great deal of local variability.

The passage under discussion makes much of the factors that unite Greeks because of the context in which it is presented (as part of a reassurance to their Spartan allies that the Athenians were not tempted by Persian overtures). However, panhellenism was not the norm, certainly not in the fifth century. The group identity that was paramount in the minds of the Classical Greeks was the sense of belonging to a particular *polis* (for the archetypal ancient expression of this, see Perikles' funeral oration as presented by Thucydides, 2.35–46). This is not to say that the people did not have a sense of certain overarching identities, like being a Hellene or a Dorian, but that *polis* identity always came first. A Spartan would have felt no conflict of loyalty if his *polis* waged war on fellow Dorians, as it often did, let alone fellow Greeks. To the Classical Greeks anyone who was not a member of one's own *polis* was a foreigner (*xenos*), be they Greek or "Barbarian." Greeks from other states were just as excluded from political participation as "Barbarians" were.

The relationship between the *polis* and identity is something of a "chicken and egg" conundrum. A sense of common identity would certainly help larger socio-political groups cohere, which would have been essential to *polis* formation. Yet one cannot have a *polis* identity without a *polis*. Some scholars consider the "colonial experience" to be crucial to *polis* formation (though the Copenhagen *Polis* Project would see colonization as accelerating the emergence of the fully fledged *polis* rather than giving birth to the whole concept; e.g. Hansen 2003: 281). The idea runs that as individuals from diverse origins came together to form new communities in close proximity to alien, and potentially hostile, indigenous populations, so they began to look for things to unite them, such as common shrines and festivals, and the fiction of a shared heritage. Many early colonies, in fact, seem to have been very mixed enterprises, not only involving settlers from numerous Greek places but also local peoples and settlers from other Mediterranean cultures (cf. Pithekoussai, on the island of Ischia, shows evidence for a mixed Greek, Phoenician, and Italian population, but acquired a Euboean-derived identity; Buchner and Ridgway 1993). Not all scholars agree that ethnicity was particularly significant in defining relations between populations in colonial situations, however (cf. Purcell 2005a). Back in mainland Greece, *poleis* must have formed as smaller groups came together. They too needed things to bind the population that individuals could subscribe to (or "internalize"). Shared cults and kinship groups satisfied this need. The concept of blood relationships is easily understood. A sense of loyalty to one's relations is an effective force for social cohesion because it seems natural; the extended family is a meaningful social unit in many societies. Many small-scale societies are predicated on the assumption of shared descent from a founding ancestor who established the community's customs; the blood relationships and lines of decent may be largely fictive, but the members of the group accept them. The Greek *poleis*, as new communities, had to create a heritage for themselves. To do so, they used the same basic building blocks of ancestry from a heroic or semi-mythical founder. To put it simply, people found it easier to unite with others to whom they believed themselves (or could pretend to be) related. Once the *polis* was established, local customs and shared experience added layers of cultural attributes to reinforce this identity.

Over time loyalty to, and identification with, the *polis* became paramount. Membership of a *polis* was fixed and inherited, usually down the male line (Lintott, CITIZENSHIP, on the concept of citizenship in the Greek and Roman worlds). It was not easy to acquire citizenship if you were not entitled to it as a birthright. This, combined with the various "kinship" groupings that existed within the *polis*, served to reinforce the fiction of blood relationship. The granting of citizenship to outsiders (or groups of outsiders) was relatively uncommon. Thus, citizenship was a closed system.

While citizenship was mostly closed to outsiders, this does not necessarily mean that individuals or states were hostile to them. In terms of state attitudes there was a range of responses. At one end of the spectrum was Sparta, which was famously closed to, and suspicious of, outsiders. Up at the other end were places with strong trading traditions, like Corinth. Athens had a large population of resident aliens (*metics*), Greek and non-Greek, who participated in city life but had no political stake in the state. Individual responses also varied. In the Archaic period many aristocrats married women from similar families from *poleis* other than their own; this did not affect the citizenship rights of their offspring, as only the male line mattered. The tyrants enthusiastically embraced this custom, using it to forge alliances with powerful men in other communities (cf. the story of Kleisthenes of Sikyon's contest for the hand of his daughter, Agariste: Hdt. 6.126–30). Presumably this would have strengthened the sense of a panhellenic identity, but to some extent it was also dependent on it. The aristocrats of different communities claimed descent from the heroes of Greek mythology. By examining the relationship between the heroes in myth, elaborate genealogies could be established for people and populations. This was an important strand in Greek identity. Crucially it was based on the notion of kinship, but was reinforced culturally in the arenas of inter-elite competition, such as the panhellenic games.

To many modern analysts, the Persian Wars were a watershed in the development of Greek identity, particularly in terms of attitudes to non-Greeks (or "Barbarians"). The argument runs that prior to the Persian invasions Greeks had a belief in shared identity that was very much tied to the system of mythic genealogies mentioned above. Thus, Greek identity was, at that stage, primarily aggregative. They viewed "Barbarians" as different (i.e. outside that system), but not necessarily in an unfavorable light. The Persian Wars changed all that. Greek identity became increasingly defined in terms of difference from (and superiority to) the "Barbarian," especially the Easterner. This new contrastive identity condemned the "other" as decadent, sacrilegious, and subservient – everything the Greeks were (in their own eyes) not. To be Greek was to be civilized; to be non-Greek was to be the opposite. An additional factor was what each state had done in the Persian campaigns. Thus, the character of relations was changed not only between East and West but also among Greek *poleis*; the stain of Medizing was hard to remove, as Thebes famously discovered.

Attitudes towards the "Barbarian" were a factor in the increased interest in panhellenism in the fourth century, but it was Alexander's conquest of the East that ushered in the next significant changes. The Hellenistic kingdoms brought Greeks into contact with "Barbarians" in greater numbers than ever before. Stereotypes could have been challenged by this, but in many respects the cultural bonds of Greekness were reinforced, not least by the development of *koine* Greek. The dominant position of Greek culture meant that "Barbarians" began to assimilate. Acculturation is seldom a one-way street, and over time Greek culture was changed by exposure to local traditions; the mixing of cultures in colonial situations is often discussed in terms of "hybridization" or "creolization" or "middle ground" theory (e.g. Malkin 1998 and 2001). Contact and acculturation blurred the distinction between Greeks and "Barbarians," but by no means obliterated it. Indeed, being Greek was perhaps now more important than ever.

An additional factor in this period was the rise of Rome. Initially, the Romans could be seen as just another "Barbarian" race from the West. As their significance grew so they had to be accommodated into the Greek worldview. Not only was a Greek myth of their origins established (ignoring local traditions), but their importance was recognized by the fact that they were tied to an established figure from mythology, albeit a Trojan, rather than some barely sketched eponymous founder. Nevertheless, the Romans were not Greeks, but "Barbarians." Equivocation grew alongside Rome's power in the East. Some writers made Rome a special case, being neither Greek nor "Barbarian" but something else again (cf. Browning 2002: 262). With the Roman conquest of Greece in the second century BC the lines began to blur further. Greek pride made it easier to see the Romans as "us" rather than "them." Rome's great fascination with Greek culture, so memorably summed up by Horace (*Epistles* 2.1.156–57), made this fiction easier to maintain. The ultimate ancient formulation of the notion that the Romans were really "long-lost" Greeks is in Dionysius of Halicarnassus's *Roman Antiquities*. The relationship between Greek and Roman identity became more complex as Roman citizenship was extended to Greece and beyond. Greeks could now be Romans, but never lost a sense of pride in their local heritage. This was not incompatible with the flexibility of Roman notions of identity, which accommodated local pride as long as it was subservient to that in Rome (cf. Cic. *Leg.* 2.2.5). Ironically, in late antiquity the Eastern empire, which spoke Greek, prided itself on being Roman. As the Western empire collapsed, those in the East saw themselves as the last bastions of civilization: the term Roman now being synonymous with the concept. The word "Hellene" had, as Browning notes (2002: 268), become associated with paganism, due to this usage in the New Testament.

3   Identity in the Roman World

If Greek identity can be seen as a complex interplay of ethnic and cultural elements with kinship always being a prominent, if not the most significant, factor, Roman identity seems different and evidently culturally, or rather politically defined. What mattered in the Roman world was citizenship. This could be inherited, but crucially it could also be acquired – theoretically by anyone: a factor recognized even in antiquity as contributing to the success of Roman imperialism. The myth of Romulus's grant of asylum (Livy 1.8.5–6) was the ancient sanction for Roman openness. In reality, of course, Rome was not always so open, especially during its early history (Lintott, CITIZENSHIP). Even in terms of myth, Rome's position was not as clear-cut as it seems on first inspection. By accepting the Greek foundation myth and grafting it onto their own, Rome was able to insert itself into the system of kinship diplomacy that operated in the Greek world (Erskine 2001: 162–97). This system, however, was predicated on the assumption of blood relationships, and was thus exclusive.

Nevertheless, by the end of the first millennium BC, what mattered was citizenship. Rome was flexible enough to allow local pride to be retained and even celebrated as long as it was complementary to Rome. The notion of pride in both local and Roman identity had existed in Italy for some considerable time. We see it in Ennius's reference to his "two hearts" (cited in Gell. 17.17.1) and the passage of Cicero mentioned previously. Once extended across the empire, it helped make the provinces governable and ultimately Roman in identity. Provincial elites had something to aspire to – the chance to become citizens and later participants in the central system of authority. Their success could then become a matter of local pride. These factors gave individuals and communities a strong motivation to assimilate. Greg Woolf (1998) persuasively argues that provincial elites did not just assimilate the external signs of Roman culture, as a cynical display of conformity to the new regime, but rather internalized (or consciously subscribed to) a Roman identity. This process of what has traditionally been called "Romanization" could be quite rapid, as Woolf demonstrates for Gaul. Local customs were not forgotten, but they were changed and redefined in the Roman context. They could be embraced or ignored by the imperial state provided they did not profoundly contradict Roman norms. Through this open system Rome could incorporate Greeks, Celts, and all manner of others. All could feel equally Roman without abrogating their specific local heritages. The differences that mattered were between citizen and non-citizen within the empire and being under Roman rule or beyond it.

The Romans appropriated the Greek notion of the "Barbarian" but changed its meaning. The "Barbarian" lived beyond Rome's rule at the extreme edges of the world. This way Roman identity came to be seen as synonymous with civilization. Beyond the boundaries of the empire lay wild, dangerous places populated by "Barbarian" savages. Thus, Roman conquest was civilizing – not the last time that civilization would be invoked as a justification for imperialism. These imperialist and culturally supremacist notions sat comfortably with ancient views on geography and its impact on human behavior and society. At the edges of the world, where the environment and climate were untamed and harsh, lived savage men shaped by that world. Such peoples needed to be either conquered and brought into the civilized world or shut out from it by strongly defended borders.

In late antiquity there were further changes. The important differences ceased to be between citizen and non-citizen once Caracalla extended the right to virtually all free people with the "Antonine Constitution" (c. AD 212). The boundary between free and slave was permeable, especially in imperial times as manumission became a commonplace. Later on, this division became even less important as a new and fundamental distinction arose – that between Christian and pagan. This new dichotomy appropriated many of the ideas and assumptions that had underpinned the "othering" of the "Barbarian." The word pagan (*paganus*) played on the stereotypes of the city dweller as civilized and the rural population as uncouth and backward. The Roman attitude to "barbarianism" could be largely retained as beyond the borders of the empire lay the non-Christian world.

Thus, if we compare the Roman and Greek worlds, we can see how in the former a political concept of identity became increasingly significant. This was coupled to a set of cultural values but ethnic factors were downplayed. By contrast, in the Greek world, while there was a keen sense of a political identity, it was constructed in terms of ethnic (and cultural) factors. *Polis* affiliation existed within the framework of a larger, though less important, panhellenic identity, again constructed in ethnic and cultural terms. By contrast, in the Roman world, the most important level of identity was also that which operated at the largest scale – citizenship. Other factors making up a person's identity, including ethnicity and local heritage, were still important but could be subsumed by *Romanitas*.

4   Closing Remarks

Identity in the ancient world is a productive, if contentious, field of study. A few key points deserve reiteration. First of all, identity in antiquity (as in the modern world) was not a given, established for the individual at birth, though biological facts like race and sex fed into it, but a "construction." Identity is both constructed for the individual, by the values of the culture in which he or she is reared and lives, and by the individual who defines himself or herself in relation to society's norms. Societies create customs, traditions, and myths to bolster and legitimize a sense of belonging; individuals can subscribe to such values in a more or less self-conscious way. Moreover, identity is a flexible construction. It can change over time, as can the ways in which it is manifested and the customs which underpin it.

In the above remarks the role of the individual is being stressed. Scholars of antiquity often blithely talk about Greeks (or better Athenians, Spartans, etc.) or Romans without properly considering the huge numbers of sophisticated individual human beings, with their own interests and attitudes, that such terms mask; the present chapter is guilty of the same fault. Societies are made up of individuals, who each have distinct identities. A sense of common belonging to a state is normally part of that identity; and states promote these elements of commonality among the population. Adherence to a state is only one factor in an individual's identity, however. Others include some or all of the following: age, biological sex, social gender (which may not coincide exactly with biological sex), occupation, political affiliations, race, religious beliefs, sexual orientation, social status, and wealth. These and other cross-cutting factors affect how individuals see themselves and how society views the individuals. Thus, future studies of identity in the ancient world need to be more sensitive to the differences between individuals and interest groups and to the ways identity, and how it is constructed and manifested, changed over time.

FURTHER READING

Hutchinson and Smith 1996 is a valuable introduction to the theoretical debate on ethnicity. Said 1978 remains essential on Western perceptions of the East. A good starting point for the Greek world is to be found in the essays contained in T. Harrison 2002b, including those of Browning and Morpugo Davies cited above. Cartledge 2002a explores Greek identity through a series of binary oppositions. The essays in Malkin 2001 also focus on what it was to be Greek. The works of Edith Hall (1989) and her unrelated namesake Jonathan Hall (1997) and (2002) cannot be ignored. The seminal examination of origin myths is Bickerman 1952. Generally work on the Roman world has focused on "Romanization" of the provinces. Woolf 1998, looking at Gaul, is an excellent study, while M. Millett 1990, which took Britain as its subject, pioneered seeing the conquered as active in the change in their cultural identity. Dench 2005 examines Rome's treatment and integration of conquered peoples. Hingley 2005 uses approaches from culture studies to examine how Roman identity functioned throughout the empire. The papers in Keay and Terrenato 2001 critique the whole notion of "Romanization." Two recent collections in the *JRA* Supplementary Series are also worthy of mention for their discussion of interplay between Roman and other identities: van Dommelen and Terrenato 2007 and Roth and Keller 2007. For late antiquity see the essays in Mitchell and Greatrex 2000. For the problems in using material culture evidence, S. Jones 1997.

CHAPTER THIRTEEN

Population and Demography

Walter Scheidel

1 The Challenge of Demography

Demography, the study of the size, structure and development of human populations, is finally beginning to receive more attention among ancient historians (Scheidel 2001b). Yet we still have a long way to go, not only in establishing even the most basic features of ancient populations but even more so in applying this information to our interpretations of all aspects of the Greco-Roman world. Concerned with birth, death, and migration, and desperate to measure, model, and quantify, populations studies may seem both forbiddingly technical and safely remote from the humanistic interests and skills of most students of antiquity. Moreover, usable evidence is scarce, and generally requires comparative and interdisciplinary approaches to make any sense at all. At the same time, however, we must bear in mind that demography is much more than just numbers, and relevant to much of what we seek to know and understand about the distant past. In premodern societies, population size was the best indicator of economic performance; the distribution of people between town and country was instrumental in the creation of collective identity, and may reflect the scale of division of labor and commerce; human mobility mediated information flows and culture change; mortality and morbidity were principal determinants of well-being, and determined fertility (and thus gender relations), investment in human capital, and economic productivity, and more generally shaped people's hopes and fears. The same is true of marriage customs and household structure. Classical civilization was the product of a thoroughly alien environment of frequent pregnancy and sudden death. Along with technological progress and scientific discovery, it was demographic change that separated the modern world from the more distant past. Archaic patterns of marriage, reproduction, and death seemed as natural and immutable then as they are exotic to us, and we cannot hope to approach ancient history without a solid understanding of what these conditions were and how they permeated life. This is the true challenge of demography. All I can do here is provide a short road map of recent progress, abiding problems, the principal areas of controversy, and the broader historical implications of ancient population studies.

2 Death and Disease

Thanks to modern advances in public health, medicine, and nutrition, mean life expectancy at birth today exceeds 80 years in Japan and reaches the high 60s for the world as a whole. These conditions represent a dramatic break even from the fairly recent past: averages of less than 30 years still prevailed in parts of eighteenth-century France, nineteenth-century Spain and Russia, and early twentieth-century India and China. This leaves no doubt that ancient societies must have experienced similarly low levels of life expectancy. Precision is beyond our reach: modern estimates are guided by the fact that at levels below 20 years, even very fertile populations would have found it difficult to survive, and that comparative evidence rules out levels of well above 30 years for the ancient world overall. Considerable variation may have occurred within this range, from particularly high mortality in large unhealthy cities and malarious lowlands to significantly better odds of survival in sparsely settled and salubrious areas, especially at higher altitudes. Empirical data are rare and of uneven quality. Several hundred census returns from Roman Egypt from the first three centuries AD that have survived on papyrus and list the members of individual households with their ages and family ties provide the best demographic evidence for classical antiquity. The aggregate age distribution of the recorded population is consistent with a mean life expectancy at birth of between 20 and 30 years (Bagnall and Frier 1994: 75–110 with Scheidel 2001a: 118–80). Human skeletal remains have been unearthed in large numbers but are of limited value for demographic analysis: despite ongoing progress (e.g. Hoppa and Vaupel 2002), it remains difficult to determine the precise age of adult bones, and, more seriously, we cannot tell whether the age structure of cemetery populations matched that of actual living groups or was distorted by burial customs or migration. Owing to selective funerary commemoration governed by age and gender, the tens of thousands of ages at death recorded on Roman tombstones do not permit us to infer levels of life expectancy (Parkin 1992: 5–58; Scheidel 2001c). Differential mortality is almost impossible to trace: all we know is that Roman emperors who died of natural causes and other elite groups seem to have experienced a mean life expectancy at birth in the high 20s, which suggests that the rich and powerful could not expect to live significantly – if at all – longer than the general population (Scheidel 1999). The health hazards of urban residence may have been to blame.

Faced with such inadequate sources, ancient historians have increasingly embraced model life tables to arrive at a better idea of the probable age structure of ancient populations (e.g. Hopkins 1966; Hansen 1985; Parkin 1992; Frier 2000). Models for high-mortality environments are derived through algorithmic extrapolation from known historical population structures (Coale and Demeny 1983; see fig. 13.1). Unfortunately, this method requires reliable base data that are only available for relatively recent populations that had already overcome pernicious diseases such as

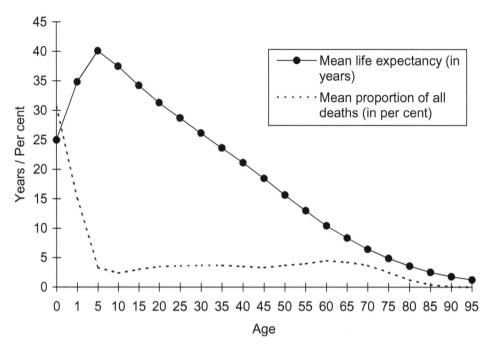

13.1 Mean life expectancy at age x (0, 1, 5, etc.) and mean proportion of all deaths occurring between ages x and $x + n$ (0–1, 1–5, 5–10, etc.) in a model population with a mean life expectancy at birth of 25 years. (Source: Coale and Demeny 1983: 43 [Model West Level 3 Females])

endemic smallpox or plague, malaria, and tuberculosis that used to wreak havoc in earlier periods of history and distorted age structures in unpredictable ways (Scheidel 2001c). Growing awareness of this problem has encouraged attempts to create high-mortality models that accommodate such factors and might offer a more realistic approximation of ancient conditions (Woods 2007). Even so, we will always have to allow for wide margins of uncertainty. For all these reasons, it seems unlikely that our knowledge of ancient mortality will ever progress much beyond the most basic features: that infant mortality (i.e. in the first year of life) was very high, perhaps around 30 percent; that maybe half of all people died before they were old enough to bear or father children; that death was as much a phenomenon of childhood as of old age; and that ancient populations were therefore necessarily very young, similar (albeit for different reasons) to those of developing countries today.

At the same time, two areas in particular hold considerable promise: the study of the causes of mortality, and our understanding of its broader historical implications. Ancient demography and medical history, usually two separate fields, have finally begun to merge. Dates of death recorded in epitaphs allow us to reconstruct the seasonal distribution of mortality which is indicative of the underlying causes of death, especially infectious diseases which tend to be seasonal in character: this approach has produced new insights into the disease environments of ancient Rome, Italy, North Africa, and Egypt (Shaw 1996; Scheidel 2001a: 1–117 and 2003a). Moreover, rich literary evidence for the prevalence of malaria and its effects in Italy from antiquity to the recent past has made it possible to account for demographic variation in the peninsula (Sallares 2002). DNA recovered from ancient skeletons increasingly provides direct evidence of ancient pathogens: recent findings include the discovery of malignant tertian malaria (*P. falciparum*) in a late Roman child cemetery in Italy (Sallares et al. 2004), and the identification of typhoid fever in an Athenian mass grave that has been linked to the plague of 430 BC famously described by Thucydides (2.47–55; Papagrigorakis et al. 2006). Epidemiological computer simulations have been marshaled to model the likely demographic impact of the so-called "Antonine Plague" that spread through the Roman world in the late second century AD (Zelener 2003), and scientific knowledge can also be brought to bear on the plague pandemic of the sixth century AD (Sallares 2007) or the gradual dissemination of leprosy. Further progress will depend on the extent of transdisciplinary collaboration between ancient historians and scientists.

More traditionally minded historians will want to focus on the manifold consequences of high and unpredictable mortality: the destabilization of families, the ubiquity of widows and orphans, disincentives to investment in education, the disruption of trust networks that sustain commerce, and more generally the social and cultural responses to pervasive risk and frequent loss, including religious beliefs. For these purposes, even rough models of ancient mortality proffer a useful approximation of demographic conditions, and comparative source material from the more recent past – shaped by similar experiences – is abundant, yet still largely neglected by students of antiquity. Ancient social, economic, and cultural history can only gain from an enhanced appreciation of how pervasively mortality regimes shaped all aspects of people's lives.

3   Reproduction and Fertility Control

High mortality logically implies high fertility. For instance, a mean life expectancy at birth of 25 years compels – on average – every woman surviving to menopause to give birth to approximately five children to maintain existing population size. The corresponding rate was higher still for married women: one reconstruction posits a lifetime mean of 8.4 births for continuously married women in Roman Egypt (Frier 2000: 801). While allowing for short-term variation, the balance of births and deaths must have been fairly stable in the long run: even a seemingly moderate net shortfall of one birth per woman (of, say, four instead of five) would have halved a given population within three generations, whereas a net surplus of one birth per woman would have doubled it, neither of which was at all likely to happen. At the same time, even high fertility was mediated by an array of reproductive strategies. While the modern concept of family planning (defined as the deliberate cessation of reproduction contingent on the number or sex of existing offspring) cannot be transposed to early societies, various mechanisms of fertility control were available and employed to varying degrees. Historically, female age at first marriage and the overall incidence of female marriage, as well as remarriage, used to be crucial determinants of fertility levels. Means of control within marriage include birth-spacing through lactational amenorrhea (i.e. temporary infertility induced by breastfeeding) or abstinence, chemical contraception, and more invasive forms of intervention such as abortion, exposure, "benign neglect," and outright infanticide.

While changes in marriage age or frequency may well have been important, we are unable to observe them in the record. By contrast, fertility control within marriage is at least dimly perceptible: the Egyptian census returns show multi-year intervals between births that must have been determined by cultural practices (Frier 1994). Some of the contraceptives and abortifacients discussed in ancient literature may indeed have been effective (Riddle 1992, 1997), yet we cannot tell whether married couples would have resorted to such hazardous means or would even have wished to have fewer children in the first place. For the most part, ancient concerns about deliberately low fertility are best understood as moralizing rhetoric (Scheidel 2001b: 37–44): there is no sign that ancient populations shrank out of sync with available resources. Comparative evidence suggests that elites may have been most likely to curtail family size in order to preserve their estates and attendant status (Caldwell 2004). Roman emperors can be shown to have reproduced at replacement level, but the representative value of this sample remains unclear (Scheidel 1999). At the other end of the social spectrum, the reproductive performance of slaves is largely unknown (Scheidel 2005). Exposure, while reducing family size, did not always depress overall reproductivity since some babies were picked up and raised as slaves (Boswell 1990b: 53–179): the scale of this practice is obscure but may have been considerable (W. Harris 1994). Overall, the potential of postnatal intervention to ease population pressure is a big unknown for ancient historians (cf. Scheidel 2007a).

Sex selection is a related problem. Even today, femicidal practices are known to create imbalanced sex ratios (most notably in parts of South and East Asia), and anthropological evidence for this custom is not uncommon: some scholars have used records of male-biased sex ratios to argue that something similar may have happened in the ancient world, especially among the Greeks (S. Pomeroy 1983; Brulé 1992). However, we cannot normally tell if such imbalances reflect actual femicide or merely discriminatory underreporting. Moreover, if femicide did indeed occur, it may have aimed to offset male excess mortality in violent conflict, analogous to strategies observed in some tribal cultures (Scheidel forthcoming). In the end, postnatal intervention for the purposes of fertility control or sex selection *may* conceivably have been an important determinant of social relations and even economic development, but is almost impossible to investigate. This serves as a powerful reminder that demography mattered even when we cannot hope to find out how.

4   Marriage, Families, and Households

Moving beyond impressionist accounts derived from literary sources, demographic study of the ancient family now focuses on quantifiable features such as marriage age and household structure. In general, and in keeping with later Mediterranean practice, early marriage for women and late marriage for men appears to have been common among Greeks and Romans. Like other elites in history, Roman aristocrats entered unions at unusually young ages, in the early to mid-teens for women and the late teens for men (Lelis et al. 2003: 103–25). Non-elite customs can only be assessed indirectly, by measuring shifts in commemorative patterns in epitaphs: thus, the age at which spouses replaced parents as commemorators for young adults is taken to reflect the age of first marriage. This method implies a substantial gap between a mean female marriage age of around age 20 and male marriage around age 30 in the Western half of the empire (Shaw 1987; Saller 1994: 25–41). However, as the available evidence is largely limited to urban environments and the first few centuries AD, we are left wondering about marriage practice in the countryside – where men may have married earlier (as they did in late medieval Tuscany, for example) – and about conditions in republican Italy. The latter is particularly vexing because our understanding of the social impact of Roman mass conscription of young men critically depends on the average age of first marriage (Rosenstein 2004): if recruits had already acquired spouses and children, their absence might have been more disruptive than in the event of delayed marriage. As it is, the current model of late male marriage papers over big gaps in our knowledge but is simply the best we have got (Scheidel 2007b). By comparison, the Roman Egyptian census returns indicate slightly less delay, with first marriage in the late teens for women and from the early twenties onward for men (Bagnall and Frier 1994: 111–18).

The same census documents allow us to determine the mix of nuclear and complex households in that province: well over half of all recorded individuals belonged to extended-family or multi-couple households (Bagnall and Frier 1994: 57–74). While the Greek evidence is meager, Roman conditions are once again inferred from funerary epigraphy: since most deceased free civilians were commemorated by members of the nuclear family (spouses or children), single-couple households are thought to have been common (Saller and Shaw 1984). Urban bias, however, raises the possibility that rural households may have been more complex, as they were in Roman Egypt. Complex households are likewise known from other Eastern provinces of the Roman empire (D. Martin 1996; Sadurska and Bounni 1994). Household composition matters because it is associated with the degree of autonomy of married couples – who may strike out on their own ("neolocality") or remain embedded in extended families – as well as economic performance. Extended families provide better safeguards against risk but are also conducive to higher fertility that may lower living standards, whereas neolocality would make it harder for widows and orphans to cope.

These broader consequences of ancient marriage and household patterns have gradually begun to attract attention among historians (see fig. 13.2). The later men married, the more likely their wives were to be widowed and their children to grow up fatherless (Krause 1994–95). In Roman society, paternal mortality severely constricted the actual scope of *patria potestas*, a father's (fairly) absolute authority over his household (Saller 1994: 114–32). Divorce, generally easier to come by than in

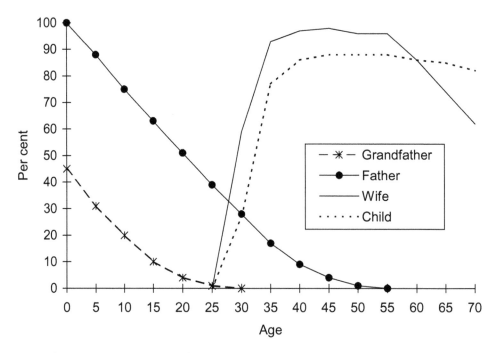

13.2 Approximate proportion of Roman men at age *x* with at least one living relative in a given category. (Source: Saller 1994: 52)

the recent past, would have added further to the instability of families. All in all, we end up with a picture that has much in common with modern conditions of fluidity and hybrid reconfiguration: step-parenting and adoption of relatives were common, creating complex arrangements that can only be documented for elite circles (K. Bradley 1991: 125–76) but would likely have occurred across all classes. Stereotypical ideologies of patriarchy were hard to reconcile with demographic realities.

Meanwhile, what is arguably the single most striking feature of Greco-Roman marriage has failed to raise any curiosity at all – the fact that Greeks (after Homer's heroes) and Romans were strictly (serially) monogamous regardless of their socio-economic status, just like modern Westerners but unlike most other early civilizations. While our own experience might tempt us to take this for granted, we must ask how this principle came to be so firmly established even among (customarily polygynous) elites – the egalitarian ethos of the city-state is a plausible candidate –, how it coexisted with de facto polygyny facilitated by sexual congress with chattel slaves (Scheidel 2009), and how it became entrenched in Christian doctrine that survived the fall of the Roman state and ensured its survival and spread in later European (and subsequently world) history. In this strangely neglected area, ancient history has a vital contribution to make to our understanding of the global evolution of marriage.

5   Population Number

Questions of size have long occupied center stage in the study of ancient population, reaching back at least as far as David Hume in the eighteenth century (Hume [1752] 1998). Following a shift in focus from size to structure in the 1980s and 1990s, controversies over population number are now experiencing a comeback and force us to reconsider our most fundamental assumptions about the character of ancient societies. Studies of particular locales or groups can take us only so far, increasingly for want of anything new to say: this is certainly true of the perennial favorites, the debates about the size of the number of residents of classical Attica and the imperial metropolis of Rome. The key question for Athens is whether, when and to what extent its population outstripped local food production and relied on maritime grain imports (Garnsey 1998: 183–200), an issue that is of more than antiquarian interest since it shapes our understanding of the driving forces behind political and military developments. By contrast, Rome's utter dependence on imported food has never been in doubt: here, the main problem is how to reconcile the huge population size implied by the recorded number of recipients of the grain dole with the limited extent of residential areas within the city boundaries: a grand total of up to a million would imply extremely high – though perhaps not impossible – settlement density (Lo Cascio 1997; Storey 1997). Much depends on the question of whether the *suburbium* was demographically integrated into the urban core (Witcher 2005). Attempts to gauge the numerical size of social groups face even more formidable obstacles: thus, questions about the number of slaves in Attica or in Roman Italy, to name just two of the most prominent examples, are ultimately unanswerable, and can only be addressed on the basis of probabilistic modeling of demand for labor that puts some constraints on otherwise completely free-floating guesses (Scheidel 2005). Similar problems bedevil the demographic study of religious groups such as Jews or early Christians in the Roman empire (Wasserstein 1996; Hopkins 1998).

In any case, all these debates are dwarfed in importance by more general questions about the gross population of the core regions of the ancient Mediterranean world. A new comprehensive survey of all the evidence for the size of Greek *poleis* has prompted a higher estimate of the total number of all Greeks (Hansen 2006a): we may now have to reckon with some 7 to 9 million people, albeit including assimilated indigenes, resident aliens, and slaves. Indeed, on some readings, parts of classical Greece such as Boiotia or Aigina were more densely settled than in any subsequent period prior to the twentieth century. These observations raise profound questions about the scale of Greek population growth between the nadir of the Early Iron Age around 1000 BC and the classical period 500 years later (Scheidel 2003b), about the relative demographic strength of the Greeks and their competitors (although the population size of the Persian empire, for instance, is also unclear: cf. Aperghis 2004: 35–58), and most importantly about economic performance. If the Greeks of the archaic and classical periods grew to be very numerous and even added to natural growth by importing lots of slaves but nevertheless experienced substantial improvements in living standards (Morris 2004), their economies must have been unusually strong by premodern standards, which makes it necessary to revisit long-standing debates about the nature of "the ancient economy" (Finley 1999; Manning and Morris 2005).

Roman population size is an even greater conundrum. While the number of Roman citizens – and hence the population of Italy as a whole – may seem unusually well documented, thanks to a series of surviving census tallies stretching from the early republic into the first century AD, on closer inspection these records create more problems than they solve. These counts, traditionally thought to have been confined to adult men, rise gently in the second century BC but jump tenfold between 114 and 28 BC (roughly from 400,000 to 4 million) before returning to much slower growth to 5 million in AD 14 and 6 million in AD 47. As this cannot possibly be read as a straightforward demographic progression, we have to choose between two ways of making sense of these figures. What we might call the "low count" assumes that the republican figures are broadly correct and the later ones are so much higher because of an undocumented switch to the registration of all men, women and children of citizen status, and allows us to read the apparent tenfold increase as a tripling or at best quadrupling of the citizenry caused by the enfranchisement of the Italian allies and residents of northern Italy and the beginning spread of citizenship to the provinces (Beloch 1886; Brunt 1971; Scheidel 2004). Conversely, the "high count" is based on the belief that coverage remained unchanged but holds that republican counts were increasingly defective and thus exaggerated the apparent scale of the first-century BC increase. In this scenario, 4 to 6 million adult male citizens (or even more allowing for some undercount), most of them located in Italy proper translate to a final Italian population of anywhere from 15 to 20 million, including women, children, aliens and slaves (Frank 1930; Lo Cascio 1994; Morley 2001; Lo Cascio and Malanima 2005; Kron 2005b), and, therefore, a regional population density not encountered again until the nineteenth century.

Unfortunately, both interpretations raise logical problems (Scheidel 2008a). Hence, the "low count" requires very high levels of popular military mobilization in the republican period (Lo Cascio 2001), very high levels of urbanization and metropolitan primacy, and high levels of mobility (Scheidel 2004), and suggests that Roman population numbers fell short of those of the high middle ages (Kron 2005b). The "high count," on the other hand, renders Roman Italy exceptionally densely populated by premodern standards, calls for a massive demographic collapse at the end of this period, and leaves us wondering why Romans imported millions of slaves at a time of rapid indigenous population growth when they already faced conflict over access to land and underemployment – and why these conflicts ceased in the Principate even as population would at least initially have continued to grow. Perhaps most crucially, it likewise raises questions about the size of the empire's population as a whole: while the "low count" envisions some 60 to 70 million imperial subjects (comparable to the contemporaneous and similarly sized Han empire in China), with one-tenth of them located in Italy itself, the "high count" must assume either that the imperial heartland was massively overpopulated relative to its provinces or that the entire empire was much more populous than commonly assumed, presumably in excess of 100 million (Scheidel 2004). It does not help that independent consideration of provincial population size is largely unfeasible outside Egypt, and fails to yield unequivocal results even for that province (Scheidel 2001a: 181–250). If the ancient Greek experience is anything to go by, a "super-sized" empire is by no means impossible: in fact, it is widely accepted that the Asian and African parts of the empire did not re-attain Roman population densities until the nineteenth century (Frier 2000: 814). The key question is whether the same was true of Italy as well, and how other parts of the Mediterranean measured up. However, this problem would be mitigated by the latest suggestion (Hin 2008) that the Roman census figures originally referred to household heads rather than all adult men and from 28 BC onwards, in addition to these household heads they also included the orphans and widows who had previously been counted but excluded from the official tallies: this approach yields an "intermediate" scenario (with an eventual Italian population of perhaps closer to 10–12 million) that is less burdened by unpalatable implications than the "low" and "high" counts, and merits careful consideration.

In the end, just as for the Greek *poleis*, if we could be certain about population size, we would be better able to compare economic performance in antiquity to conditions in the medieval and early modern periods. Archaeological data may hold the key to this issue: while field surveys can cast some light on patterns of land use in different periods, physical indices of well-being, such as body height and dietary regimes, may reflect the extent of population pressure. In this sphere, despite an abundance of published local field work, major synthetic analyses are only beginning to appear (Koepke and Baten 2005; Kron 2005a; Jongman 2007; Pelgrom forthcoming). These questions will continue to occupy ancient historians for some time to come, all the more so as they are of fundamental importance for our understanding of classical civilization: how good were very different kinds of ancient states – Greek city-states on the one hand, the Roman mega-empire on the other – at fostering economic development, how many people could these economies support, and in what style?

6   Distribution and Mobility

The urban-rural split of ancient populations is a closely related issue. More than most premodern societies, the Greco-Roman world was dominated by cities. Moving away from old debates about the economic character of ancient cities (revolving around the concepts of the "consumer" and "producer" city: e.g. Whittaker 1995; Erdkamp 2001), demographic research needs to concentrate on the degree of urbanization and its social and political consequences. While urbanization is usually regarded as an indicator of economic development, we often cannot tell whether urban residence was linked to non-agrarian occupations: if many farmers lived in urban settlements, a high level of urbanization might create a misleading impression of economic progress. Thus, if it is true that perhaps half of all Greeks in the classical period lived in (mostly very small) towns (Hansen 2006a), this would tell us a lot about the foundations of civic identity but little about division of labor or agricultural productivity.

The contrast between Greece and Roman Italy on the one hand and Roman Egypt on the other is particularly telling: most of the 1,000-odd *polis* centers of the classical Greek world or the more than 400 towns of Roman Italy must necessarily have been small and somewhat agrarian in character, whereas the 50 or so cities of Roman Egypt coexisted with numerous and sometimes massive villages that in Greece or Italy might well have been classified as urban communities (Tacoma 2006: 37–68). Ancient urbanization defies straightforward categorization and hinders cross-regional comparisons even within the same timeframe, let alone with later periods. Greco-Roman urbanism often needs to be studied on its own terms.

Even more than other branches of ancient demography, the study of population movements suffers greatly from the paucity of quantifiable evidence. Qualitative impressions (e.g. Horden and Purcell 2000: 377–91) simply will not do, and parametric models of putatively plausible flow volumes push us onto thin ice: my attempts to quantify Greek colonization (Scheidel 2003b), migration from and within Roman Italy (Scheidel 2004), and the Roman slave trade (Scheidel 2005) give an idea of what can and cannot be expected from this conjectural approach. Luckily, an entirely new source of information has been opened up by the study of the genetic properties of current populations that allow us to infer earlier migration patterns. Earlier studies of blood group gene frequencies already produced tantalizing results, for instance regarding the extent to which ancient Greek immigrants came to demographically dominate Sicily and southern Italy (Cavalli-Sforza et al. 1994: 277–80). Research on mitochondrial DNA and the Y-chromosome are now the principal means of mapping migratory trajectories, although the ancient Mediterranean has only begun to be covered by this kind of work (e.g. Semino et al. 2004; Belle et al. 2006). Other methods add to the scientific armory, such as stable isotope analysis that helps establish where interred individuals had been raised – and thus indicates migration when the isotope signatures associated with their place of origin differ significantly from those of their place of burial: for example, it has been shown that many individuals buried in the Isola Sacra necropolis near the ports of imperial Rome had moved there from other regions (Schwarcz 2002: 194). Science stands to make a major contribution to our understanding of ancient population movements.

7 Outlook

Beginning in the 1960s, but primarily since the 1980s, ancient population history has been revolutionized by the adoption of the concepts, methods, and questions of the historical demography of the more recent past. This has helped us integrate ancient demography into the wider field of population studies and draw on demographic insights to reshape our vision of the ancient world. Further progress will result from more synthetic studies of archaeological remains and the application of scientific techniques from anthropometry to genetics. Our ultimate goal is a better appreciation of the "demographic regimes" of the ancient past, that is the culturally and ecologically specific configuration of demographic factors that governed people's lives, and of how they changed over time. This would make it easier to merge demography with social, economic, cultural and environmental history, and bring us a step closer to a truly integrative "total history" of the ancient world. Unfortunately, this goal may never be achieved: much of what we would need to know about ancient demography will for ever remain out of reach, even as comparative history teaches us how much it would matter in principle. This may seem frustrating, but it also means that demography will keep ancient historians on their toes – and that is a good thing.

FURTHER READING

There is currently no single handbook in English that covers all the bases: Scheidel, *The Demography of the Greco-Roman World* (Cambridge, forthcoming) aims to fill this gap. Corvisier and Suder 2000 give a brief general overview in French, while Parkin 1992 and Frier 2000 offer more sophisticated accounts of Roman demography. Scheidel 2001b provides a detailed critical review of existing scholarship. For comprehensive bibliographies, see Suder 1988 and Corvisier and Suder 1996. Bagnall and Frier 1994, a path-breaking analysis of the demographic regime of Roman Egypt, should be read together with the partial reinterpretation in Scheidel 2001a. Scheidel 2001c explores the pitfalls of ancient mortality history, while Sallares 2002 and Scheidel 2001a: ch. 1 and 2003a seek to reconstruct the relationship between disease and death in different parts of the Roman empire. Sallares 1991 is an exceptionally rich interdisciplinary study of the ecological context of Greek population history. Frier 1994 provides a fundamental discussion of ancient fertility regimes, and Eyben 1980/1 collects evidence on fertility control. The history of the Greek family and household has most recently been summarized by S. Pomeroy 1997. On the Roman side, the key works are Saller and Shaw 1984, arguing for the nuclear character of the Roman household, and Saller 1994, an analysis of Roman family structure and household dynamics. Lacey 1968 and Dixon 1992 offer more general accounts of ancient family life (cf. also Harlow and Parkin, THE FAMILY), Treggiari 1991 focuses on Roman marriage, and Gardner and Wiedemann 1991 collect relevant sources in translation. Hansen 1985 is still the best discussion of Athenian population number, while Hansen 2006a presents a new reconstruction of the overall number of Greeks and the scale of urbanization. Brunt 1971 is the standard work on Roman citizen numbers. Lo Cascio 1994, 1999, Scheidel 2004, 2008a, and Kron 2005b give a flavor of the controversy about Roman population size. Conjectural attempts to quantify mobility can be found in Scheidel 2003b, 2004, 2005. Scheidel 2007 considers the relationship between demography and the ancient economy.

CHAPTER FOURTEEN

Writing Women into History

Amy Richlin

1 Why a History of Women?

A noted Roman historian, when approached in the early 1970s by a group of women students requesting a course in women's history, is said to have replied, "Why not dogs' history?" That women, like dogs, are somehow outside history, doing nothing that could make a mark on the historical record, may perhaps, thirty years later, not seem so evident. Like men, women do things; we might think of "things done" as "facts" – what *facta* means in Latin. As E. H. Carr suggests (1961: 10–11), no fact begins as historical; facts acquire historicity by being pulled into the historical canon by historians. As for the question of whether, or how nearly, we can know any fact – the crux of postmodern theory in history – that is beside the point here. If all we can know is discourse – things written and made, records – the question is, can we turn our attention to discourse that concerns women? The desire to do so has depended on a change in the group here denoted by "we."

The story of women's history is then, to begin with, the story of historians of women. What made writing women's history desirable, hence possible? Some women have always been noticed; even Carr, who largely ignores women, finds room for Cleopatra. What might be called "queens' history" has a niche in the history of elite men, along with the exemplary women (Artemisia, Lucretia, Beruria, Mary) handed down to the Renaissance from antiquity. But only with the rising of the women, in the two waves of modern feminism, have women as a class been written into the historical record.

Jane Austen famously quipped, through the innocent mouth of Catherine Morland,

> I read [history] a little as a duty, but it tells me nothing that does not either vex or weary me. The quarrels of popes and kings, with wars or pestilences, in every page; the men all so good for nothing, and hardly any women at all – it is very tiresome: and yet I often think it odd that it should be so dull, for a great deal of it must be invention. (*Northanger Abbey*, chap. 14)

Part of this passage indeed stands as the epigraph to Carr's *What Is History?*; he leaves out everything before the last "I," choosing to focus on the invention and not the skew. Virginia Woolf, in *A Room of One's Own* (1929), points out the constraints of family life and economics that kept most women out of the public record and from writing themselves. The second wave of feminism, springing out of the New Left in the late 1960s, soon took notice that half humankind is female and argued that a true history of the human world would reflect that fact; an early history of women in Europe was titled *Becoming Visible* (Bridenthal and Koonz 1977). The Berkshire Conference, a first-wave project that brought together women historians in the 1920s, was reinvented as a conference of women's historians, starting in 1975 (J. Scott 2002: 1). From the beginning, these projects included attention to women in the ancient Mediterranean.

This movement was partly enabled by developments in the field of history itself, as the *Annales* school turned historians' attention to "history from below," and Marxist historians wrote of the laboring classes (S. Clark 1985; G. Turner 1990: 38–77). "Women in antiquity" became a recognized subfield of classics in the 1980s, as has been charted by Barbara McManus (1997). The publication of Sarah Pomeroy's textbook *Goddesses, Whores, Wives, and Slaves* in 1975 can be taken as an important starting point. However, although Pomeroy, as a papyrologist, paid substantial attention to social history in this book, the field at first was dominated by attention to women in literary texts – to representations of women, or to stereotypes of women, rather than to actual women of whom we have direct evidence. The nature of classical training meant that most scholars in the field began from the "reading list" – the literary texts canonized by the set list for graduate qualifying exams; scholars trained in history departments were swimming against this tide.

This early start in literature, however, perhaps allowed historians of ancient women to confront at an early period the question of what can be direct about evidence, never mind evidence removed from us by two thousand years and more. We suffer from a dearth of first-person texts – diaries, letters, memoirs – and must view most accounts of women with suspicion, most literary characters as, to some degree, stereotypes. Still, by 1985, at a famous session of the Women's Classical Caucus at the annual meeting of the American Philological Association, panelists who advocated reclaiming ancient poets (in this case, Ovid) as proto-feminists were confronted by women historians who argued that the proper occupation for feminists in classics was "counting the steps to the fountain house," not reading poetry at all. In other words, except for our few instances of texts by women, we should be working on recovering the realities of everyday existence for the majority of ancient women (Culham 1990, with responses in the same issue of *Helios*). This project impelled historians of ancient women into the study of papyri, inscriptions, and material culture, though none of these in fact yields direct access to anything; yet, arguably, they get closer than any literary text can do. But we still need contemporary texts – histories, laws, ethnographies – to provide context.

The problems of writing women's history partake of the general problem of the sources extant from antiquity: the texts are overwhelmingly written by elite males. Thus the question of women's history has the same problems as all non-elite history, though elite women are somewhat more visible in the sources than are non-elite women. We always face a "lamp-post problem," as in the old joke where the man is looking for his keys under the lamp-post because it's dark in the alley where he lost them. Likewise, particularly for women's history, it is not always the classical periods that provide the most evidence, so that historians of women in antiquity have called for a shift in our attention to the most promising periods, particularly late antiquity (Hallett 1993). The historian Joan Kelly asked whether women had a Renaissance (i.e. did this rising tide float all boats?); we might ask similar questions about Greek and Roman women (Culham 1997). And we need not only an expanded timeline but an expanded definition of "the ancient world," which obviously was not made up just of Greek and Roman pagan cultures.

2   Retrieving Women From Male-Authored Texts

The nature of the evidence has dictated that writing women into ancient history still often depends on wringing what can be wrung from texts written by elite males. This project, then, still deals largely with ideology, moving from literature into the linked cultural areas of philosophy, law, religion, and medicine, areas which produced masses of theory within antiquity itself. Study of this material cannot tell us what ancient women really thought or did, but can give a sense of what they had to put up with.

Scholars of Greek culture have worked from the 1970s on issues in which all four of these areas overlap. Page duBois (1982, 1988), Giulia Sissa (1990), and Nicole Loraux (1993) applied the insights of French structuralism and Freudian psychoanalysis to arrive at an understanding of Athenian concepts of the female. Their work has in turn been closely linked with that of scholars working on representations of women in Athenian drama (Rabinowitz 1993; Zeitlin 1984). Roman historians have tended to view literature as remote from reality, as in Marilyn Skinner's classic demonstration of the different versions of Clodia Metelli in Catullus's poetry, Cicero's speeches, and Cicero's letters (1983). Historians writing in antiquity, as Sandra Joshel has argued (1993, 1997), use women to think with; their accounts cannot be taken as transparent or veridical. Indeed, the female body stands for concepts of purity and pollution in a wide range of ancient cultures (Eilberg-Schwartz and Doniger 1995); Kathy Gaca (2003) shows how moralists Greek, Roman, Jewish, and Christian used men's sexual intercourse with women as a key index of right behavior.

Law provides a seemingly simpler avenue of approach. Basic compendia of Greek (Just 1989), Roman (Gardner 1986, Evans Grubbs 2002), and rabbinic (Wegner 1988) law affecting women lay out what the rules were, and more specialized studies have worked out the implications for e.g. Greek women's participation in the economy (Schaps 1979) or Roman prostitution (McGinn 1998) or marriage (Treggiari 1991). But, as always, law gives mainly an index of cultural preoccupations and fears, although corresponding efforts in social control can sometimes be documented. At the intersection of law and rhetoric, studies of published versions of ancient courtroom speeches in both Athens (D. Cohen 1991a; V. Hunter 1994) and Rome (M. Skinner 1983) have canonized Lysias *On the Murder of Eratosthenes* (a case of adultery and revenge), pseudo-Demosthenes *Against Neaira* (a case of fraud brought against a woman prostituted from her childhood), and Cicero *Pro Caelio* (an *ad feminam* attack on Clodia Metelli). These texts show what forces could be brought to bear on individual women.

Studies of religion look at women's agency in worship as well as at the feminine divine and regulation of women by religious codes (on which S. Cohen 2005). Scholars have not only examined canonical texts (Meyers et al. 2000, Hebrew Bible and New Testament; Boyarin 1993, Satlow 1995, rabbinic Judaism), but have also expanded the canon to deal with texts rich in material related to women (Foley 1999, the Homeric Hymn to Demeter; K. King 1988, Gnostic Christian texts). Other scholars have searched both texts and evidence from papyri and inscriptions to find women as active participants in religious cult, as in Susan Guettel Cole's survey of regional sanctuaries throughout the Greek world (2004); Mary Beard's anthropological analysis of the Vestal Virgins (1980, 1995a); Karen Jo Torjesen on women priests in the early Church (1993); Rebecca Krawiec on the women of the monasteries in the Egyptian desert in the fourth century AD (2002). This field has particularly attracted scholars who look at women across the whole ancient Mediterranean, notably Ross Kraemer (1992, 2004; cf. also K. King 1997, a collection which examines women and goddess worship in world religion).

Studies of medicine have again tended to deal with the construction of women by the texts, or what Helen King calls "Hippocrates' woman" (H. King 1998; cf. Dean-Jones 1994). What would it have meant for women that doctors believed the womb was prone to wandering around the body, or that women in particular should be treated with medicines made of dung, or that a cat's liver tied to your ankle made a good contraceptive? Some have looked in the medical texts for attestations of women practitioners; the elder Pliny includes in his *Natural History* many traces of women's own medical beliefs and practices (Richlin 1997b).

The powerful women who have always been visible to history have continued to receive a share of scholarly attention, although the closer we look, the more they vanish into the haze of gossip and propaganda that cloaked them. A cross-cultural comparison of stereotypes of women in power (Garlick et al. 1992) suggests that similar mechanisms indeed beset all such women; Madeleine Henry's study of Aspasia, Perikles' famous partner, is titled *Prisoner of History* (1995). Yet there are local differences; Judith Hallett argues (1989) that the elite male writers of Roman texts view their female kin as both "same" and "other," crediting them at times with virtues almost male. Where rhetorical education was the key to male advancement, the extent to which women did gain an education clearly matters (cf. S. Pomeroy 1977 on women in Hellenistic Greece and Egypt; Hemelrijk 1999 on Roman women). Some did, to some degree.

One area of ancient history writing has been firmly co-ed from the start of its current incarnation: family history perforce includes female kin. Studies of the Greek family (even the pre-second-wave Lacey 1968) and the Roman family (B. Rawson 1986, 2003) deal with women of all ages, from babyhood upwards; in particular,

Mark Golden has studied childhood in classical Greece (1990), Suzanne Dixon has argued for a strict Roman mother, actively involved in her children's upbringing (1988), and Judith Hallett has argued for the high value placed on the father/daughter bond in Roman culture (1984).

Similarly, the history of sexuality (see Davidson, EROS: LOVE AND SEXUALITY) has managed to devote at least some attention to women, though studies of male–female erotics are relatively rare (but see Gaca 2003; overview in M. Skinner 2005). Sources are plentiful from all periods, including lowly evidence like graffiti and the archaeology of brothels (McGinn 2004). Sex between women is only thinly attested, the subject seemingly being of little interest to ancient male writers; Bernadette Brooten (1996), in a study of attitudes towards female homoeroticism in the early Church, as a preamble provides the fullest account of the pre-Christian sources, including astrology, magic spells, and a horrific chapter on medical writings.

Once we attempt to leave the upper classes and find out about slaves, or even ordinary working women, we have to turn to a different kind of source material. Although texts can provide a sense of how male writers saw female slaves in comparison with citizen women – weighing the pros and cons of each as sexual partner (Xen. *Oik.* 10.13; Ovid *Amores* 2.7–8), depicting St Augustine's mother's alcohol-related troubles with her household staff (*Conf.* 9.8.18, cf. P. Clark 1998) – they cannot tell us how slave women's lives felt to them. For this, we must turn to inscriptions, as in Sandra Joshel's general study of work and identity for slaves and freed slaves in the city of Rome in the early empire (1992), or in Susan Treggiari's long series of essays on working women (e.g. 1976). These carvings on stone might be viewed as female-authored, although they do not indicate who dictated the wording to the mason. Similarly, Natalie Boymel Kampen sees the subject position of Ostia market women expressed in the commemorative relief sculptures that show them selling everything from cabbages to snails (1982). They or their kin at least had enough money to buy a decorated tombstone, and sometimes the stones state *d. s. p.* (*de sua pecunia*, from her own money); such workaday art also shows women engaged in the medical profession or just sitting and having their hair done, thereby also recording the work of the hairdressers who stood around them. The incidental objectification of slave women by their owners is entirely typical of ancient cultures, where citizen women at times explicitly defined themselves in terms of their superiority to slave women (Richlin 1997a).

3   Female-Authored Texts

How enviable are the sources available for modern history, from the earliest periods on up: autograph letters, diaries, even published books, and, since the nineteenth century, photographs, films, and sound recordings. In comparison, the women of antiquity are close to lost. But not altogether; most famously, of course, the poetry of Sappho attests to a woman's ability to leave a literary mark (see essays collected in E. Greene 1996). It should be noted that Sappho is not the only extant woman writer from antiquity – far from it; Jane Snyder (1989) provides a reliable guide to ancient women authors, not only poets but philosophers, letter writers, travel writers. The Hellenistic epigrammatist Nossis should be considered along with any reading of Sappho (M. Skinner 1989).

However, the mere fact of the disappearance of so much that women wrote must make us wonder about the cultures that found what they had to say so dispensable. Some was destroyed by early Christians, it is true; Tatian, for example, remarks on how the members of his community – particularly women – strive to rid themselves of "licentiousness," such as Sappho's works (Gaca 2003: 237–38). But it was Cicero's freed slave Tiro, or whoever collected Cicero's letters, who passed over the letters of Cicero's wife Terentia, his beloved daughter Tullia, and his friend Caerellia, along with, in all probability, his correspondence with Clodia Metelli. Whatever the Christians did with Sappho, and granted the letters of Jerome remain while the replies from his numerous female correspondents do not, we still have many more pages of writing by Christian women than from all of the previous millennium. The poet Proba, the travel writer Egeria, and, venturing into the middle ages, the tenth-century nun Hrotsvitha, with her plays modeled on the language of Terence – all suggest what has been lost from the earlier period. This is a major lamp-post issue: if we want to know about ancient women, we'd do better if we looked late rather than early (G. Clark 1993; Holum 1982).

4   Letters and Documents

In fact, though, if we want to read ordinary women's letters from antiquity, it is not impossible. They may not be written in full by the women's own hands – people usually employed scribes – but the letters are sometimes signed by women, or incorporate postscripts written by women. And we have these precious ephemeral texts from far-flung parts of the ancient world, from the Roman frontier fort of Vindolanda on Hadrian's Wall (Bowman 2003) to the deserts of Egypt, which are probably the single largest source of knowledge about the everyday lives of real ancient women. Jane Rowlandson's sourcebook gathers papyrus letters together with all kinds of documents and material evidence (1998). Roger Bagnall and Raffaella Cribiore collect all the letters known to have been written by women, including a number of family archives, starting in 300 BC in Greek and Demotic Egyptian and continuing through the appearance of letters in Coptic up to the eighth century AD (2005). Lamp-post strategy: Bagnall and Cribiore use family archives from late medieval England as a basis for comparison (2005: 25–32), exploring these more complete family dossiers to get an idea of what a full picture could look like. This collection stands as a reminder of what a truly polyglot, multicultural world the ancient Mediterranean was. Ruled by Rome for much of the period covered, these writers communicated in Greek and Egyptian with Latin trimmings, often bearing double or hybrid names to suit their context. Although it is hard to know much about rural areas in antiquity, we can be sure that cities shared widely in this feature of Egyptian life, and that we should never imagine "Greek women" or "Roman women" as homogeneous entities (on papyrology, Bowman, PAPYROLOGY).

5   Geographical Range

Early on, the study of women in antiquity did bring together scholars who worked on the entire ancient Mediterranean. One early collection (Cameron and Kuhrt 1983) covered the ancient Near East and Greece but not Rome. Over time, the disciplinary self-definitions of classics have taken over, so that study of "Greek" and "Roman" women dominates syllabi and constitutes the bulk of work in the field (but see Kampen 1996). Meanwhile, work on women in the early Christian Church and on women in ancient Judaism has continued, mostly done by historians of religion and usually showing a familiarity with pagan culture; classicists do not usually reciprocate.

The drive to recognize cultures as polychrome rather than monochrome seems likely, however, to produce a change in this trend. Egypt maintains its hold on the imagination of students and scholars, and accessible overviews are increasingly available (see Robins 1993 for pharaonic Egypt; Montserrat 1996 for the Ptolemies onward). It is to be hoped that the next thirty years will see the normal definition of the ancient Mediterranean broaden out to include not only Egypt and Judaea but Syria, Palmyra, Armenia, Persia, North Africa. Few at this point have the skills needed to cope with so many languages, histories, traditions, but this we must change.

6   Basic Achievements and a Question for the Future

The most solid achievements of the study of women in antiquity remain two basic sourcebooks produced early on: *Women's Lives in Greece and Rome*, edited by Mary Lefkowitz and Maureen Fant (1992, 1st edn 1982) and *Women's Religions in the Greco-Roman World*, edited by Ross Kraemer (2004, a revision of Kraemer 1988). The potential of these massive collections of sources has yet to be fully exploited, and many classicists remain unfamiliar with their contents. Yet undergraduates trained in ancient women's history all know how Neaira is attacked for having been a child prostitute (Lefkowitz and Fant 1992: 73–82), and how the younger Pliny brags about his wife behind her curtain listening agog to him as he recites (Lefkowitz and Fant 1992: 184–88), and how the story is told of the brave Thecla, risking her life in the arena where she is threatened by ravenous seals (Kraemer 2004: 297–307). The fundamental misogyny of Aristotle's philosophy is a familiar fact to anyone who has studied Lefkowitz and Fant (1992: 38–41); also his will, in which he provides for the marriage of his daughter (unnamed, since she is respectable) and leaves money, slaves, and real estate to his concubine Herpyllis (1992: 59–61). As so many have argued for such a long time now, the world looks different when you look at all the people, not just half of them.

The question is, will students thirty years from now still be taking courses called "Women in Antiquity"? The mainstreaming (if any) of the study of gender in general courses on ancient civilization seems unlikely to preserve a full picture of women's history (see Blundell 2005 on current conditions in Britain); compare the page count of this chapter plus any accounts of women in the rest of the book with the book's total page count. Check the index for women's names; look in the bibliography for Ruby and Raffaella, Phyllis and Page, Sue, Susan, Suzanne, Bella and Beryl, Gillian and Giulia and Gay, Claudia, Patricia, and Pauline, Averil, Amélie, Emily, and Amy, Ellen and Helen, Elaine and Helene, Karen and Carol and Jane and Joan, Barbara, Bernadette, Kathy, and Cecelia, Sarah and Natalie, Judith and Marilyn, Froma and Renate, Lesley and Toni and Ross, Madeleine and Virginia, Sandra and Sheila, Nancy and Ann, Nicole and Wendy, Mary and Mary-Kay and Maureen. If the second wave of feminism goes the way of the first, and we are in for another regression, another return to domesticity, will it all be lost again? This we must work to prevent.

FURTHER READING

A good place to start would be Fantham et al. 1994; this lavishly illustrated textbook provides a sound introduction to Greek and Roman women's history, including sections on Hellenistic Egypt and the Etruscans. Similarly helpful is Meyers et al. 2000, subtitled "A dictionary of named and unnamed women in the Hebrew Bible, the Apocryphal/Deuterocanonical Books, and the New Testament"; a user-friendly appendix explains what all these sources are. The field's flagship website is Diotima (www.stoa.org/diotima) which includes bibliography, short essays, syllabi, links to dozens of sites for images, and more. Indispensable to the student are two sourcebooks: Kraemer 2004 covers all aspects of religion, Greek, Roman, Jewish, and Christian, from goddess theology to records of worshipers' donations; Lefkowitz and Fant 1992 deals mostly with pagan culture. High points in Kraemer include the *Acts of Thecla* (heroic deeds of a cross-dressing Christian convert), *Thunder: Perfect Mind* (Gnostic Christian revelation text), and *Joseph and Aseneth* (a Jewish novel). Lovers of Greek tragedy should see Blondell et al. 1999. For a focus on Egypt from the time of the Ptolemies on, two more sourcebooks are highly recommended: Rowlandson 1998 covers a wide range of documentary and material evidence; Bagnall and Cribiore 2005 cover all extant letters by women from 300 BC to AD 800. The latter is also available, in expanded form, as an e-book (www.historyebook.org).

On special subjects: Schaps 1979 on Greek law actually gets outside Athens and surveys all of mainland Greece and the islands; Cole 2004 does the same for Greek religion. Satlow 1995 explains the rabbis' cryptic legal opinions and sets them in the context of contemporary Greek, Roman, and Christian parallels. Snyder 1989 is a must for those interested in ancient women writers. The easiest way to get at the elusive lives of ancient slave women is through the essays in Joshel and Murnaghan 1998. On women's homoeroticism, see above all Brooten 1996; M. Skinner 2005 provides a general overview of Greek and Roman sexuality from Homer onwards, while Montserrat 1996 deals with Greco-Roman Egypt. A more challenging read, Gaca 2003 is the best single work on attitudes towards sexuality in ancient philosophy. Kampen 1996 includes numerous essays on visual representations of women. For background on the study of women in antiquity and on feminism in classics, see McManus 1997, which has extensive statistical appendices. Rabinowitz and Richlin 1993 provides an introduction to various areas of feminist theory that have major applications in classics. For your Latin class, there is now an intermediate reader titled *The Worlds of Roman Women* (Raia et al. 2005).

CHAPTER FIFTEEN

Interpreting Myth

Carol Dougherty

"History is probably our myth."

Michel de Certeau, *The Writing of History*

The great ancient historian Sir Moses Finley opened his essay on "Myth, Memory, and History" with Aristotle's famous distinction between poetry and history in the *Poetics*:

> Poetry is more philosophic and of graver import than history, since its statements are of the nature of universals, whereas those of history are singulars. By a universal statement I mean one as to what such or such a kind of man will probably or necessarily say or do – which is the aim of poetry, though it affixes proper names to the characters; by a singular statement, one as to what, say, Alkibiades did or had done to him. (*Poetics* 1451b5–11; trans. I. Bywater)

Finley points out that Aristotle is not questioning the historicity of epic poetry here in the way that we sometimes do, but rather he is concerned with the bigger, more general question of the truth about life. And so, the debate is really one between history and myth, for long before anyone invented history, myth was what helped the Greeks make sense of their past, and without myth the first Greek historians could never have begun their work (Finley 1975: 11–13).

For Herodotus of Halicarnassus, known as the Father of History, myths, legends, and other chronicles of the past provided the necessary access to former times and enabled him to accomplish his twofold goal of preserving events of the past and investigating the causes of the Persian Wars. In his *Histories*, arguably the first Western historical text, Herodotus willingly embraced a wide range of stories about the peoples and places of the past – some, like that of the Indian gold-digging ants (3.102–5), are so outrageous as to defy credulity, others, such as his analysis of political institutions (e.g. 3.80–82) or descriptions of battle tactics (e.g. 7.201–33,

Thermopylae), conform to more conventional notions of what belongs in a historical narrative. In fact, Herodotus welcomed myth and other fantastical elements into the scope of historical analysis a bit too generously in the eyes of some, prompting another, somewhat less flattering sobriquet, the Father of Lies.

His very near contemporary, Thucydides, however, adopted a very different attitude toward the role of myth in history, dismissing myths and other fanciful tales of the past as inimical to the job of the serious historian. In the opening book of his history of the Peloponnesian War, Thucydides elaborates his preference for contemporary history by dismissing the works of poets and other chroniclers of the past who sacrifice truth to pleasure. The passage of time leads to an inevitable distortion of events, Thucydides claims, transforming and transporting them ultimately into the realm of myth and rendering them unfit for historical analysis. As Peter Green observes in his introduction to Herodotus's *Histories*, the verb Thucydides uses to capture the tension between history and myth is *eknikan* (to fight completely). As Green translates the passage, "most of the events of the past, through the lapse of time, have fought their way, past credence, into the country of myth" (Green 1987:1). Far from seeing myth as a useful source of information about past events, Thucydides represents its potential contribution as hostile – a kind of military threat to the historical truth – and he is anxious to stake out his own territory far from the dangerous country of myth.

The groundbreaking, genre-making historical works of Herodotus and Thucydides thus attempt to situate themselves with respect to myth – but each with rather different results. Herodotus welcomes myth and other kinds of narratives about the past equally into his historical vision, while Thucydides distinguishes himself from his predecessor in large part by choosing to reject the pleasurable aspects of myth. And we might take these two ancient Greek historians and their works as emblematic of what have come to be competing, and occasionally antagonistic, approaches to doing ancient history. Either way, however, it is clear that what to do with myth is a question that has challenged historians from the very beginning, and in this essay I want to clear some middle ground between these two extreme positions. Ancient historians should include myth within their analysis, but to do so productively, they need to understand just what it is that myth has to say. The term history, of course, is today commonly understood to refer to two things: what actually happened in the past, and representations of what happened, and I should make clear at this point that I am interested in the second sense of the term, with the historical narrative. First I will elaborate briefly some of the assumptions and pitfalls of the "Herodotean" and "Thucydidean" approaches to writing history before turning to Roland Barthes to articulate a third way of accommodating myth within the historical narrative.

1 History Without Myth

According to Aristotle it is the business of history to focus on the particular, the specifics – "what Alkibiades did or had done to him" – and this distinction is often held as definitive. Myth concerns itself with the imagination, pleasure, and caters to its audience while history deals with the facts. This focus on the positivist empirical nature of the historical endeavor was perhaps most powerfully expressed in the nineteenth century by Leopold von Ranke's formulation of the historian's task as "simply to show how it really was" (*wie es eigentlich gewesen*) (cited in Tosh 2002: 7). The natural extension of this historiographical position is to reject myth (among other things) entirely, as Thucydides did, setting up a false set of oppositions that links historical analysis with facts and truth and opposes it to the lies, deception, and unreliability of myth. As Lucian puts it in his essay *How to Write History*, the historian must sacrifice pleasure to usefulness and truth. As with the athlete for whom good looks should be merely an incidental feature, "So it is with history – if she were to make the mistake of dealing in pleasure as well she would attract a host of lovers, but as long as she keeps only what is hers alone in all its fullness – I mean the publication of the truth – she will give little thought to beauty" (*How to Write History*, 9; trans. K. Kilburn).

While this complete and total rejection of myth in favor of factual accounts of "how things really were" may work for writers of contemporary history (such as Thucydides), it creates particularly difficult problems for ancient historians, especially those working on periods (e.g. pre-classical Greece) for which myth serves as the only narrative source. It would be impossible, for example, to have much to say about the archaic Greek world if we had to reject all the mythic narratives found in the works of Homer, early Greek poetry, and the work of Herodotus.

2   Myth as History

It is due in large part, no doubt, to this complete absence of non-mythic narrative sources for the pre-classical period, that other ancient historians have taken a more inclusive "Herodotean" approach and welcomed myth within the scope of historical analysis, recognizing the fundamental similarities between the two kinds of narratives. Both, after all, enact a dialogue between the past and the present. Each is fundamentally concerned not just with representing what happened in the past, but also with asking "Why?"

For the historian interested in learning about the origins of Athens or the causes of the Trojan War, then, the poems of Homer and the plays of Euripides offer a wealth of tempting stories full of nuggets of historical truth amid their fanciful plots and mythical characters. But, as Herodotus already knew, the historian needs a critical apparatus to evaluate the credibility or historicity of these mythic sources. His term *historia* (from which we get our word history) comes from the verb *historein* (to make an inquiry or investigation, to adjudicate disputes), and Herodotus brings this investigative focus to, among other things, the stories that he collects from around the world in his history of the Persian War. While myth and history certainly do overlap, their narrative goals and discursive strategies, as will be seen below, are not completely identical, and to read myth literally, as if it were history, can lead the historian seriously astray. The Homeric poems tell a story that is quite compatible with what the archaeological and linguistic evidence can tell us about a conflict between Greeks and

Trojans at the end of the second millennium BC, but that doesn't mean that a Trojan named Paris really made off with Menelaos's wife. It is the willingness to read myth as if it were telling us "what really happened," to take just one example, that is at the heart of much of the shortcomings (on both sides) between classicists and Afrocentrists over the *Black Athena* issue.

3   Myth and History

Both of these approaches are founded upon overly simplistic assumptions about the relationship between myth and history. The Thucydidean impulse to set up myth and history as mutually exclusive rules out a great deal of valuable historical information, while the temptation to which practitioners of the Herodotean approach are susceptible, to read myths as if they were indistinguishable from historical narratives, fails to acknowledge their differences. While historical content can be absorbed into the traditional form of the myth, that process is never transparent or straightforward, informed instead by cultural elements and generic constraints. Instead, as Carlo Brillante points out in his essay on myth and history, the relationships between myth and history are far from simple: "their reciprocal limits do not appear clearly definable, but rather from time to time changeable and complicated" (Brillante 1990: 117). And so while much can be (and has been) said about the similarities and differences between myth and history, for the rest of this essay I want to focus on the nature of their relationship with each other.

Rather than pit myth against history (or vice versa), the French theorist Roland Barthes has suggested the following way to think about their mutual indebtedness:

> What the world supplies to myth is an historical reality, defined, even if this goes back quite a while, by the way in which men have produced or used it; and what myth gives in return is a *natural* image of this reality. (Barthes 1972: 142)

What Barthes has done here is to articulate the ways in which myth and history work together, and his formulation can give us real insight into how myth works, revealing the kinds of historical information it can (and cannot) provide. Barthes explains that myth pulls this off as a kind of magic trick – when successful, myth has "turned reality inside out, it has emptied it of history and has filled it with nature" (142). In this respect, the naturalizing force of myth is ideological, rooted in cultural and political strategies of self-expression and legitimation. Mythic narratives are stories that a culture tells itself to make sense of its world to itself and others, and as part of this process, they often forge strong relationships between the past and the present. Myth, thus, itself is a social product and properly included within the historical project.

In particular, insofar as myth naturalizes reality, it can offer a wealth of material to the ancient historian who is particularly short on contemporary sources – a way to get back to the "historical reality" that has been lost to us. But, to do this right, we must remember that myth is always embedded within a cultural text – a literary, artistic text or ritual activity – whose own generic rules and interests will inevitably condition and influence its form and inflection. Second, myth is the product of a culture, not a single author; it is composite and multiple in origin.

Above all we need to realize, as Barthes emphasized, that the *raison d'être* of myth is to make a specific historical context seem natural – the only way things could possibly be – whether it be Athenian democratic institutions, patriarchal family structure, or a Greek colonial presence in Sicily. Myth is not concerned with an accurate description of what really happened. Instead, as Barthes explains, "myth has the task of giving an historical intention a natural justification and making contingency appear eternal" (Barthes 1972: 142). And so, if myth naturalizes rather than reflects historical reality, what strategies must the ancient historian bring to bear upon myth to read it productively as a historical source? How does a historian interpret myth? To begin to get a sense of what myth can and cannot tell us, I want to conclude with a brief look at two different examples of the intersection of myth and history in ancient Greece – the first, the familiar Athenian myth of autochthony, and the second, perhaps less familiar, the colonial traditions of Syracuse.

4   The Myth of Athenian Autochthony

On vase paintings, in political rhetoric, and on the tragic stage, Athenians of the fifth and fourth centuries BC boasted that they were the indigenous occupants of their land, descended from snake kings, literally born from the earth, in a word – autochthonous. Non-Athenians, boasts Praxithea in a fragment from Euripides' lost play *Erechtheus*, have migrated from one land to another, but Athenians are born autochthonous: "Some cities are divided as if by throws of the dice, while others are imported from other cities. Whoever moves from one city to another is like a peg badly fixed on wood; in name he is a citizen, but not in his actions" (Eur. *Erechtheus* fr. 50.5–13 Austin). Perhaps the best expression of these autochthonous origins can be found in the myth of the birth of Erichthonios: Hephaistos caught an unwilling Athena in an amorous embrace; as the virgin goddess, patron deity of Athens, fled in disgust, Hephaistos ejaculated onto her leg. Athena wiped off the seed with some wool and threw it on the ground. From the Athenian ground, thus, emerged baby Erichthonios, his name derived from *eris* (wool) and *chthonos* (ground), literally born from the earth together with a myth that brilliantly joins the city's patron deity to the native tradition of earthborn kings.

This myth of Athenian autochthony was a powerful one, and yet, as Vincent Rosivach has shown, Athenians were not continuous occupants of Attica, nor did they think they were. He shows that the myth of Athenian autochthony first appears in the middle of the fifth century BC and helps express political and ideological beliefs related to Athenian democracy (Rosivach 1987). Since all citizens are born equally from the earth, all have equal access to political power, and Athenian public discourse linked democracy explicitly to autochthony. In addition, since autochthony traced the genealogy of its citizens back to the earth itself, instead of to the four Ionian tribes that had earlier restricted political access to a limited aristocracy, Athens' autochthonous myth helped distance the city from Ionia even though Athenian–

Ionian connections remained strong, the two cultures bound together by common dialect, ritual, and ancestry.

So what do we do with this Athenian myth of autochthony? Do we completely reject it? Exclude it from our historical inquiry because it does not tell the truth? No, but we need to recognize what it is telling us. In Barthes' terms the myth of autochthony naturalizes a historical reality – a fifth-century one, not that of the city's origins. The myth does not tell us how the city originated, but rather what it thinks to be important at the time of its telling – that all Athenians have equal access to political power. The myth also celebrates the homogeneity of the Athenian citizen body by contrast with those cities with mixed populations. When Euripides' Praxithea celebrates Athens' autochthony, she includes a parallel critique of other cities whose colonial origins or traditions of immigration created a citizen body comprised of random assemblies of poorly assimilated strangers, leaving the city prone to tyranny or civil war.

In other words, once we welcome the mythic into the scope of historical analysis it can tell us a lot, provided we learn how to read it. The first step is to recognize that it is not just about the facts, and so checking their accuracy misses the point. Instead, it is all about how these "facts" are arranged, and so we need to think about and decode their discursive strategies, their modes of representation. In Athenian public discourse the myth of autochthony, embodied by baby Erichthonios, draws upon a set of metaphorical images to legitimate current political practice: mother earth gives birth to all Athenian citizens equally; they are all brothers. The language of familial relations helps naturalize a radical political institution in the most basic terms – the relationship of city to citizen has been recast as that of mother to son.

In this respect, as Hayden White has argued so effectively, historians must approach myth a bit more like literary scholars would, and recognize its culturally significant plot structures and metaphors (White 1973; 1978; 1987). We need the historical context to read myth, but the opposite is true as well. To get a better idea of how this works, let's turn to three different narratives of the colonial foundation of Syracuse. The archaic Greek colonial movement is a good test case for reading myth and history together because of the lack of contemporary written accounts, together with the prominence and continued popularity of colonial myths in literary contexts long after the colonies themselves had been settled.

5   The Foundation of Syracuse

Plutarch tells us that the archaic Greek colony of Syracuse was founded by the Bacchiad noble, Archias of Corinth. A Corinthian named Melissos had a very handsome and modest son named Aktaion. This Aktaion had many lovers, among them Archias, a descendant of the Herakleidai and an extremely wealthy and powerful man. When Aktaion rejected the amorous advances of Archias, Archias, together with a drunken crowd of friends and servants, stormed his house and attempted to take him away by force. Aktaion's friends and family resisted, and in the end (like his mythic namesake) the young man was pulled to pieces and killed. Archias and his gang ran away and Melissos carried his son's body into the Corinthian marketplace and demanded reparations for his son's death. When he was refused, he went to the temple of Poseidon at Isthmia and, heaping blame upon the Bacchiads, hurled himself to his death, bringing drought and plague upon the city. The Corinthians consulted the god at Delphi about relief and were told that Aktaion's death must be expiated. When Archias learned this news, he vowed not to return to Corinth, and instead sailed to Sicily where he founded the colony of Syracuse. (Plut. *Mor.* 772e–3b)

Pausanias, on the other hand, tells a slightly different tale. He, too, says that Archias consulted Delphic Apollo, but without giving any reason why. He then includes the text of the oracle that he received: "A certain Ortygia lies in the misty sea, above Thrinacia, where the mouth of the Alpheus gushes forth, having been mingled with the streams of fair-flowing Arethusa" (Paus. 5.7.3). Pausanias mentions Archias's founding of Syracuse as part of the legend that explains why the Alpheus river, which originates in Greek Arcadia, passes through the sea and mixes its waters with a spring in Syracuse. Alpheus was a huntsman who fell in love with a huntress Arethusa, but she, not wanting to marry, fled and crossed the sea to an island opposite Syracuse called Ortygia. There she turned into a local water-spring, and Alpheus changed into an Arcadian river for love. Pausanias concludes by explaining that he believes that the Greek river does, in fact, pass through the sea to mingle its waters in the waters of the Syracusan spring.

The fifth-century Athenian historian Thucydides, finally, offers a much simpler and more straightforward narrative: "Archias, one of the Herakleidai from Corinth, founded Syracuse, having first expelled the Sikels from the island where the inner city now is – though it is no longer surrounded by water" (Thuc. 6.3.2). After reading all three versions, one might be tempted first to reject stories of murder or love in favor of Thucydides' simple and straightforward account: the Corinthians came, expelled the natives, and settled their new city. Thucydides' version might also appear more persuasive on chronological grounds, although the three-hundred-year gap between Thucydides' work and the founding of Syracuse (734 BC) hardly makes his a contemporary account, and scholars have come to acknowledge the value of antiquarian texts such as those of Plutarch and Pausanias for recording and preserving authentic nuggets of earlier material. Moreover, if we take a closer look at the plot elements that structure the mythical versions of Plutarch and Pausanias, we will see some important points of convergence with Thucydides' account.

Plutarch's tale of a murderer who goes to Delphic Apollo to be purified and who is then sent to found a new city in Sicily combines two narrative patterns familiar from Greek literature. First, the murderer sent into exile is a story that goes back to the Homeric poems: Tlepolemos killed his uncle and fled Argos (*Il.* 2.661–69); Patroklos killed a young boy in anger over a game of knuckle-bones and fled with his father to the house of Peleus (*Il.* 23.84–90); Theoklymenos fled home after killing a relative and sought purification and sanctuary from Telemachos (*Od.* 15.272–78). This theme is perhaps most powerfully enacted on the Athenian stage in Aeschylus's *Oresteia* – a set of plays that (among other things) looks to the myth of Orestes' family to legitimate a shift from exile to trial by jury as a way to address homicide.

This narrative pattern continues to influence the ways that Greeks think about how to deal with murder. The murderer's exile is conceptualized as a kind of purification – a ritual expulsion of the dangerous element – and the purification of murderers becomes an important function of Apollo's sanctuary at Delphi. It is at this point – at Delphi – that the homicide/purification narrative converges with another one whereby a civic crisis prompts the consultation of the Delphic oracle, often resulting in Apollo's sponsorship of colonial enterprises. In both cases, Apollo's oracular response articulates a resolution to the crisis.

Once we recognize these powerful narrative patterns at work in structuring Plutarch's account of the foundation of Syracuse, we can begin to read the mythic elements more productively. Colonial expeditions were often initiated in response to some kind of domestic crisis (drought, political unrest, extreme poverty) and offered relief at home as well as new opportunities abroad. Furthermore, we recognize the purificatory function of Delphic Apollo here as well. As we can see from Thucydides' account, the Corinthians forcibly expelled native Sikels from the territory that they eventually settled, a detail that is often overlooked in histories of the colonial movement precisely because it is not elaborated in any conventional historical narrative. And yet, the plot structure and metaphors of Plutarch's narrative (and others like it) suggest that this violence was very much a part of the colonial experience, and offer a context for addressing it. The theme of murder first acknowledges the violent nature of a colonial expedition, and then expiates that violence by representing colonial conquest as the movement from crisis to resolution, from murder to purification. So while it may not be true that Archias killed a fellow Corinthian named Aktaion, the Corinthian colonists certainly did kill, or at least forcibly evict, Sikels as part of their colonial conquest. What the myth does is naturalize the violence inherent in the colonial project, violence against the former occupants of the land, by redescribing it within a familiar framework of murder and purification. In the end, the myth legitimates Greek presence on Syracusan soil (and the corresponding absence of Sikels) rather than describing how they got there.

Let's turn now to Pausanias's account of the foundation of Syracuse. Embedded in the oracular response given to Archias describing the geographical site of the new colony is yet another story of the colony's foundation – one that tells the story of colonial foundation as the tale of the attempted rape of the nymph Arethusa by the river god Alpheus. Marriage, another familiar cultural metaphor and narrative pattern in Greek literature, structures the colonial story in significant ways, offering a more positive model for addressing the inevitable confrontation between Greeks and native populations that forms part of the colonial process.

Many mythic tales recall the founding of a colony as the rape and/or marriage of an indigenous young girl by a Greek god. Perhaps the best known – the rape and subsequent marriage of the Libyan Cyrene by Apollo – appears in Pindar's Ninth Pythian Ode as a representation of the Spartan settlement of Cyrene in terms of fertility and abundance. While, as in the murder metaphor, the attempted rape of Arethusa or Cyrene acknowledges the violence to native lands and peoples, the civilizing and unifying ideology of marriage, suggested here by the image of two separate streams mingling together, comes to represent the relationship between the Greek settlers and native inhabitants in positive terms – a civilized Greek city where once there was just wilderness.

Here, Ortygia, the colonial site, is identified as the place where the Greek river Alpheus and the local spring Arethusa join, their waters mingled together. Thus marriage and colonial themes merge: the Greek river's transoceanic travel from the Peloponnese to Sicily prefigures the colonists' own westward movement from Corinth; erotic conquest symbolizes a new political foundation, and the intermingling of the two streams becomes an emblem for positive Greek and native interaction.

And so, as Barthes has argued, we can begin to see how the mythic nature of these colonial narratives "naturalizes" a specific historical reality – one that we find recorded in Thucydides without any of the trappings of myth, demystified, with all the power issues made explicit. The Corinthians expelled the native Sikels from the land and settled there in their place, and reading all three versions together provides the fullest picture of this event. Since myth is often embedded in literary texts, the historian eager to embrace myth must learn to appreciate the discursive strategies that organize historical facts into narratives. The Greeks filtered the historical experience of founding new colonies overseas through their pre-existing mythical system of Delphic Apollo and his powers of purification. New experiences of cross-cultural violence and contact are interpreted through familiar patterns of purification and marriage. Similarly, the Athenian autochthony myth draws upon the language of family to tell a story of Athens' origins that legitimates a fifth-century political ideology.

6   From Aristotle to Barthes

Barthes' formulation of the symbiotic relationship of myth and history suggests a productive way for ancient historians to think about the role of myth in the historical endeavor. Rather than conceptualizing them as mutually exclusive categories, he shows how myth and history, each with its own discursive qualities and narrative goals, work together to help cultures learn about and legitimate their past. Moreover, his observations about the naturalizing force of myth take us full circle, back to the Aristotle passage with which we began. For both Aristotle and Barthes recognize that while history aims to tells us the particulars about "what really happened" (e.g. what Alkibiades did and had done to him), the universalizing voice of poetry (or myth), its ability to turn a particular historical reality "inside out," aims at something very different, and should not be overlooked. What Barthes adds to Aristotle's formulation is his valuable insight into the powerful relationship between these two kinds of discourses about the past. His thoughtful articulation of the ideological function of myth, its power to naturalize historical reality, provides the key to a productive historical analysis of myth. Failing to appreciate the underlying narrative patterns and cultural metaphors that structure these narratives can lead a historian either to take the narrative at face value, that is to miss the naturalizing force of myth, or to reject it all together. Both are big mistakes. Instead, the historian needs to bring the tools of literary and narrative analysis to bear upon these mythic narratives to read them productively as legitimate historical sources.

FURTHER READING

Good general treatments of myth and mythology include Csapo 2005, the introduction to R. Martin 2003, Detienne 1986, Lincoln 1999, Barthes 1972. For the literary and artistic sources for classical myth, see the *Lexicon iconographicum mythologiae classicae* (*LIMC*) and Gantz 1993. For a helpful treatment of Roman myth, see Bremmer and Horsfall 1987. For a discussion of the ideological function of myth, Eagleton 1991. On the relationship between myth and history, see Finley 1975 and Brillante 1990. Excellent examples of scholars whose work offers productive historical readings of myth include Connor 1987, Vidal-Naquet 1986 and Vernant 1980. More recently, see Malkin 1994, Dougherty 2001, and on the Roman side, the essays collected in Braund and Gill 2003 and Wiseman 1995 which explores the Remus myth; for the overlap between Greece and Rome see Erskine 2001 on the Trojan myth. For further discussions of the nature of history as a discipline, see Carr 2001, G. Elton 2002, Tosh 2002, de Certeau 1988, H. White 1973, 1978, 1987. For further reading on the controversial use of the classical tradition by Afrocentrists (often referred to as the Black Athena controversy), see M. Bernal, *Black Athena: the Afroasiatic Roots of Classical Civilization*, (1987; 1991) as well as the numerous responses to this work: e.g. the essays collected in Lefkowitz and Rogers 1996. For further discussion of the Athenian autochthony myth, see Rosivach 1987. To read more about the interaction of myth and history in the traditions of the archaic Greek colonial movement, Dougherty 1993.

CHAPTER SIXTEEN

Environmental History

Robert Sallares

1 Introduction

Ecology, the study of the natural environment of living organisms, is a modern concept. The word, which is derived etymologically from the ancient Greek word *oikos* (household), was coined in German (Ökologie) by Häckel, a disciple of Charles Darwin, in 1866. Nevertheless, even in antiquity there were instances of an interest in what are now regarded as ecological problems. Such problems were mainly discussed not by historians, whose interests were biased towards political history, but by philosophers. For example, Plato (*Critias* 111c) maintained that deforestation had occurred in Attica, and in so doing made the first contribution to the most enduring theme of Mediterranean environmental history (section 4 below). Aristotle (*Mete.* 352a6–18) attempted to explain the shift in the balance of power in the Argolid in Greece from Mycenae in the Bronze Age to Argos in the Iron Age in terms of changes in the hydrology of the region. He suggested that Mycenae became too dry for agriculture, while the area around Argos became less marshy, implying that environmental changes altered the agricultural potential of the hinterlands of these city-states, and so their carrying capacity for human populations. The expansion of the ancient Greek world following the conquests of Alexander the Great made the Greeks aware of a range of new environments in the Near East, Egypt, and as far away as India. This helped Theophrastus to realize that different regions had different communities of plants, leading to the foundation of the subject of plant biogeography.

Modern historiography has mainly followed the bias towards political history of historians in antiquity. Nevertheless a few scholars did take an interest in the ecology of the ancient world from the early years of the twentieth century onwards. The most notable of these scholars were Ellsworth Huntington, who studied such problems as the burial of Olympia following catastrophic floods in late antiquity (Huntington 1910), and the role of climatic change and soil exhaustion in the fall of the Roman empire; Ellen Churchill Semple, who wrote a book (1932) and numerous articles about various aspects of the geography of the ancient Mediterranean world; and M. Cary, who wrote a well known introduction to the geographic background of ancient history (1949). The writings of Fernand Braudel introduced a new focus on the explanatory value of the Mediterranean as a historical concept (1972, first published 1949). From the 1960s onward Claudio Vita-Finzi (1969) emphasized the importance of physical changes in the river valleys and coastal plains of the lands around the Mediterranean. In fact it is now clear that the topography of large parts of the coastal regions around the Mediterranean has changed very substantially over the last 3,000 years, and this helps to explain, for example, the difficulty that modern scholars have had in understanding the topography of the plain of Troy as described by Homer. Over the last thirty years or so, however, the environmental history of the ancient world has been the subject of increasing scholarly attention, which is reflected in the range of material covered in this chapter.

2   Physical Geography

The Mediterranean Sea is the world's largest inland sea, about 3,800 kilometers long. It requires a constant influx of water from the Atlantic Ocean since evaporation is much greater than the inflow from rivers. Most parts of the Mediterranean coast have a very narrow continental shelf, reducing the size of offshore fishing grounds. The Mediterranean is rather poor in fish. However, the sea has always been extremely important for inter-regional contact because of the proximity of mountain ranges to much of the Mediterranean coastline, and also for access to the numerous islands in the sea. The lands around the Mediterranean are frequently mountainous or hilly, the result of intense tectonic uplift caused by the movement of the African and Eurasian plates towards each other, at about two centimeters per year. Mediterranean geology is mainly based on limestone, which is easily eroded by catastrophic floods and rainstorms, creating very uneven topographies. Large, flat plains are rare in Mediterranean lands. Many rivers descend from the uplands towards the sea. The Nile is the only major river whose water supply originates almost entirely outside the vicinity of the Mediterranean basin. Other rivers are fed by Mediterranean winter rainfall. Many watercourses dry up during the summer, as do many coastal wetlands. Mediterranean countries display great ecological contrasts over very short distances. The lands around the Mediterranean have a high level of biodiversity, although population sizes of plants and animals are frequently very small as a result of poor habitats.

3   The Mediterranean Climate

The Mediterranean climate is characterized by a seasonal pattern of mild, wet winters and hot, dry summers. The summer drought favors annual rather than perennial vegetation. It also means that fire is an important agent of natural selection on vegetation communities. Bioclimatic indicators such as the distribution of the olive tree are sometimes used to provide alternative definitions of Mediterranean-climate regions (Blondel and Aronson 1999: 13–18). The distribution of the olive tree, which is killed by severe frost but requires temperatures to drop to a certain level to initiate flowering the following year, defines the Mediterranean winter. The total volume of winter rainfall can support evergreen trees, but is too low for deciduous trees (Sallares 1991: 307).

Dendrochronological evidence from the Parthenon in Athens shows patterns of climatic variability in the fifth century BC similar to the modern pattern. Evidence from ancient authors confirms that the climate of Greece was basically the same in the fourth century BC as it is today. Theophrastus wrote that date-palm trees planted in Greece could grow there but not set fruit, indicating that mean summer temperatures in the southern Aegean c.300 BC were very similar to recent values (Eginitis 1908 on Theophr. *Hist. pl.* 3.3.5). Rainfall exhibits extreme seasonal and interannual variability. This frequently created shortfalls in agricultural production in the past, with runs of several successive good or bad harvests (Garnsey 1988). In classical Greece there were periods of food shortages probably caused by drought c.360 and c.330 BC, but Theophrastus recorded heavy rainfall which raised Lake Kopais in Boiotia to an unusually high level in the years before the battle of Chaeronea in 338 BC (Sallares 1991: 390–5). However, documentary sources do not provide the statistical data required to investigate possible long-term climatic trends.

The pattern of hot dry summers and cool wet winters has only existed since about c.3000 BC. Evidence from pollen cores shows that annual Mediterranean rainfall was higher and more evenly distributed in the Neolithic period, permitting deciduous lime and oak trees to flourish in areas dominated by drought-resistant evergreen vegetation today (Vernet 1997). Many important Mediterranean plants (e.g. the vine) are dormant in winter and grow in the hot, dry summer, when it would be better to grow in winter instead, when more water is available. As a result irrigation in the summer is very important for Mediterranean agriculture today. The degree to which artificial irrigation was practiced in antiquity is an important question. The emphasis of the Roman agronomists on wheat and barley cultivation, crops of semi-arid drylands, and their lack of attention to rice, a much more productive way of exploiting coastal Mediterranean plains, suggests that irrigation was not important in the Mediterranean in antiquity (Sallares 1991: 22–4).

There were also periodic climatic cycles lasting for centuries or longer, caused by variations in annual-mean solar radiation. In the Levant, for instance, warm and dry periods alternated with cold and humid periods. The Iron Age was cold and humid, the Persian period dry, the Hellenistic period cold and humid, the Roman period warm, while the Byzantine period was yet again cold and humid (Issar and Zohar 2007). Cold and humid conditions signified more rainfall, which benefited cereal production and favored population growth. A decline in solar radiation leading to colder and more humid conditions c.850 BC may well have been the critical factor behind the simultaneous development of Iron Age cultures around the Mediterranean, which is otherwise hard to explain (Speranza et al. 2002).

Research on periodic advances and retreats of the Alpine glaciers during the Holocene indicates that most of the time of the Roman empire (c.100–400 AD) was a warm period (Röthlisberger 1986). Other types of climatological evidence yield similar conclusions. For example, analysis of atmospheric mercury deposition (a process influenced by temperature) in a peat bog in Galicia in north-western Spain suggests that the Roman Warm Period at its peak was about 2°C warmer than the present and was more prolonged than the Medieval Warm Period (Martínez-Cortizas et al. 1999). The reality of the Roman Warm Period can be corroborated by proxy data, for example the spread of viticulture into Roman Britain, as illustrated by recent archaeological finds in the Nene Valley in Northamptonshire (Brown et al. 2001). Olive presses and olive wood have been found near the Roman city of Sagalassos in south-western Anatolia in areas where it is too cold for the olive tree to survive today, suggesting that average temperatures might have been 2–3°C higher than today (Waelkens et al. 1999). The economic effects of climate change were complex. The warmer conditions of the Roman empire permitted the geographical extension of olive and vine cultivation and favored arable farming in northern Europe, but probably adversely affected it in some semi-arid areas such as the Near East. Whether climatic trends can be correlated with and played a causal role in human population fluctuations is a very important question for ancient history. Just to give one more example, favorable climatic conditions probably facilitated the spread of olive cultivation and human populations in Syria in late antiquity (Hirschfeld 2004).

4 The Natural Environment

In addition to regular climatic cycles, the Mediterranean environment was also a world of sudden catastrophes throughout antiquity (Horden and Purcell 2000: 298–341), all the way from the Santorini volcanic eruption in the late seventeenth century BC to the complex of catastrophes at the end of antiquity in the middle of the sixth century AD – the extremely cold years following the dust-veil event of AD 536 (Arjava 2005), the plague of Justinian from AD 541 onwards (Sallares 2007), and the tsunami that struck Phoenicia in AD 551 (Elias et al. 2007). There were earthquakes, tidal waves, dust storms, disease epidemics, swarms of locusts, devastating floods, and volcanic eruptions. Mt Vesuvius played a prominent role in the Roman period, destroying Pompeii and Herculaneum in AD 79. The eruptions of Mt Etna, an important source of carbon dioxide and sulphur dioxide, in Sicily (44–42 BC) probably had a significant short-term impact on the climate (Stothers and Rampino 1983).

Tectonic activity caused numerous earthquakes, for example at Helike on the Corinthian Gulf in 373 BC, Pompeii in AD 62, and Olympia in AD 426 (Huntington 1910). Earthquakes caused substantial short-term damage to the urban economy of affected towns; whether they also affected agriculture in the countryside is unclear. Dust storms arrived in southern Europe from the Sahara, and also had local origins in soil erosion, as in the case of the dust storms which buried the city of Stobi in Macedonia in late antiquity. Swarms of locusts were one type of calamity which hit the countryside harder than the towns. Livy mentions a devastating locust onslaught on North Africa in 125 BC, for example. Early modern accounts of locust swarms suggest that they would have had a severe short-term impact on agriculture in antiquity (Sallares 2002: 183; Livy *Per.* 60).

Floods were the type of catastrophe which had the most substantial long-term impact by permanently altering the landscape. The Tiber river experienced a long series of severe floods in the past which deposited sediments in the valleys between the hills of Rome (Aldrete 2007). Strata in the Roman Forum dating to the time of the Roman empire are several meters above archaic levels and six to seven meters below the current ground level. The construction of the *Cloaca Maxima* shows that ancient Rome had drainage problems from the beginning of its history. High rainfall in mountains around the Mediterranean frequently resulted in deluges, causing erosion in the uplands and interior, while the eroded sediments were redeposited in deltas like those of the Po and Tiber in Italy, the Achelous in Greece, and the Ebro in Spain. The silt brought down by the Nile is responsible for the fertility of Egypt. In the case of the Tiber the existing delta has only developed since about AD 1500, but in antiquity large lagoons that existed on either side of the river near Ostia were being filled in (Bellotti et al. 1995). Such developments created new economic opportunities in the shape of extremely fertile agricultural land, but the expansion of easily flooded coastal plains which could turn into marshes facilitated the spread of malaria around the coastal regions of Italy during the Roman period. The recent remarkable finds of buried Roman ships at Pisa illustrate the importance of catastrophic floods in modifying many coastal regions of the Mediterranean in Roman times, a phenomenon also observed in the Rhône delta in southern France, for example (Benvenuti et al. 2006; Lippi et al. 2007).

The question of the causes of soil erosion leads us to the problem of deforestation, the most controversial issue in Mediterranean environmental history. Many historians have believed that extensive deforestation occurred in the Mediterranean in antiquity, leaving a denuded landscape. Undoubtedly by the late republic the city of Rome, for example, had huge requirements for building work, heating houses and baths, industrial activities and many other purposes, which could not be met locally (Meiggs 1982: 218–59). These requirements were mainly met by floating timber down the Tiber to Rome. Wood was also important for metal smelting, for example silver ores in Attica and Spain, copper in Cyprus, iron from Elba near Populonia in Tuscany, and for shipbuilding.

Despite the importance of the timber industry in antiquity, the "ruined landscape theory" of Mediterranean deforestation has attracted criticism (Grove and Rackham 2001 *contra* Hughes 1994 and 2005). There is a great diversity of opinion about this controversial issue among scientists who are specialists in Mediterranean ecology (e.g. Blondel and Aronson 1999: 201–6 *contra* Grove and Rackham 2001). Similarly, those historians who do believe in large-scale deforestation have differences of opinion regarding its chronology. One study concluded that there has indeed been extensive deforestation in five mountain zones of the Mediterranean world (McNeill 1992). However the conclusion was reached that it occurred principally in the early modern period, not in classical antiquity.

The view that little has changed is based on the observation that many regions of Mediterranean countries with low annual rainfall, a limestone-based geology that does not retain water, and a summer drought could never have supported significant forests. This theory maintains that savannah-style vegetation, with scattered trees in open country but no closed forest canopy (like the Spanish *dehesas*), is characteristic of many Mediterranean areas now as in the past, and little or nothing has changed over the last three thousand years; little deforestation has occurred and it is not responsible for soil erosion. Erosion is interpreted as predominantly gully erosion of badlands caused by deluges, for example in Basilicata in southern Italy, producing the alluvial deposits of Metapontum on the coast (Abbott and Valastro 1995). Where soil erosion from cultivated land has occurred it is attributed principally to plowing, not to deforestation.

The history of erosion is tied to the problem of the Younger Fill (originally described by Vita-Finzi 1969), a heterogeneous mix of depositional episodes that occurred at different times in different areas; some are definitely classical in date, for example those at Metapontum mentioned above, or on the coasts of western Anatolia (Kayan 1999); others date to late antiquity or the early medieval period, for instance the burial of Olympia in Greece (Huntington 1910), while yet others are only a few hundred years old (Grove and Rackham 2001: 291–4). Some of these episodes can be associated with human activity, while for others cyclical changes in the climate offer a more convincing explanation.

The critical point to emerge from the whole debate is that it is impossible to generalize about the Mediterranean as a whole. The human impact varied from area to area. Consequently the Mediterranean countries as a whole cannot be described either as an unchanged or as a ruined landscape. The theory that little has changed in the last few thousand years is reasonably convincing for some of the most arid parts of the Mediterranean, such as south-eastern Greece. However, even in southern Attica there is archaeological evidence for farming in the fourth century BC on limestone ground which has virtually no soil cover today (Lohmann 1994). The question of environmental degradation cannot be considered independently of the question of human population pressure on the landscape. Some of the details of the theory of no change seem to be self-defeating. For example, the importance of anthropogenic erosion is minimized, but it is then acknowledged that soil erosion can be caused by plowing arable land to grow rain-fed, autumn-sown cereals, leading to criticism of the cultivation in southern Italy of durum wheat, the type of wheat best suited to the local environment. What are large human populations supposed to have eaten in the past if they had not been allowed to grow cereals, to avoid soil erosion? (Grove and Rackham 2001: 89, 265 and 270).

By focusing on Mediterranean Europe, Grove and Rackham excluded North Africa from their consideration of the problem of "desertification," but it is surely in the vicinity of the Sahara (in an area where megafauna such as lions and elephants existed until Roman times) that this problem was and is most acute. Literary sources suggest that some parts of North Africa had plenty of trees, while others did not (Contrast Caes. *BC* 2.37 with *BAf* 20). Computer modeling of the climate about two thousand years ago to study the effects of the presence of substantial vegetation in such areas on the climate suggests that there was more rainfall in Armenia, Spain, North Africa, and Egypt than there is today (Reale and Dirmeyer 2000; Reale and Shukla 2000).

These conclusions help to make sense of Ptolemy's weather diary, written in Alexandria during the second century AD, which describes a weather pattern with rain in every month except August and thunder throughout the summer (G. W. Murray 1935: 19–20). This helps to explain the agricultural prosperity of North Africa in antiquity, as well as the prosperity of southern Spain during the Roman period. The rise and fall of the kingdom of the Garamantes in North Africa has been linked to rainfall fluctuations.

Leaving aside marginal areas such as those bordering deserts, the greatest degree of human impact on the natural environment in antiquity is most likely to have occurred in the immediate vicinity of the largest human population centers, but such areas are actually rarely considered in detail in the debates between ecologists. It has been argued that the rate of soil erosion in Latium increased *ten times* in the second century BC (Judson 1968). This trend is surely associated with the increase in settlement numbers in south Etruria revealed by archaeological field surveys, linked to intensive agriculture and market gardening to feed the population of the city of Rome, which was increasing rapidly at the time (T. Potter 1979). Environmental degradation would then have spread away from large settlements along communication lines such as river valleys and roads. It has been suggested that the major Mediterranean river valleys were once generally forested, since perennial rivers compensated for the shortage of summer rainfall, but are now largely deforested, with a few exceptions, such as the River Strymon in northern Greece (Blondel and Aronson 1999: 122).

Livy described the Ciminian Forest north of Rome c.300 BC as if it was the Amazon jungle (Livy 9.36). His account is sometimes regarded as exaggerated, but in the opinion of Italian specialists in environmental studies little of the ancient beech forest in the area of the Monti Cimini remains today (Pratesi and Tassi 1977: 49 *contra* Grove and Rackham 2001: 172). A series of detailed local studies do support the idea of substantial human impact on the natural environment in many areas in classical antiquity. In the Biferno valley in the Molise region of eastern Italy a field survey revealed a massive expansion of rural settlements from the fourth century BC to the first century AD accompanying extensive erosion and sediment deposition (Barker and Hunt 1995). Similarly, in the hinterland of Metapontum in southern Italy ten meters of sediment was deposited during the period c.600 to c.300 BC, when this Greek colony was flourishing. The affected areas quickly became marshy, a development which accelerated the spread of malaria in this region and subsequently led to the decline of the human population (Henneberg et al. 1992).

A balanced interpretation of the problem of environmental degradation in antiquity is that it is difficult to generalize; there were different outcomes in different areas. In many areas the vegetation cover was probably much the same as it is today. For example palynology yields this conclusion in the vicinity of the Lago di Pergusa in central Sicily (Sadori and Narcisi 2001). In other areas there was a substantial degree of deforestation in the past. For instance the Roman boundary stones which enclose the famous cedar forest on Mt Lebanon include considerable areas where there are hardly any trees today, although the question arises of whether this already became the case in antiquity or whether deforestation only happened later (Mikesell

1969). In the lower Rhône valley in France the scarcity of tree pollen indicates that this area was largely deforested in the classical period (Andrieu-Ponel et al. 2000). Of course there are other areas where forests have spread, either naturally or through human planting, since antiquity. Pollen cores document the gradual spread of Aleppo pine (*Pinus halepensis*), which is now common in Attica for example. It has increased in frequency because it is a good colonizer of cleared terrain, since its seeds germinate readily after forest fires.

The effects of human pressure on the environment in classical antiquity took other forms besides deforestation. It is easy to think of pollution as a modern problem, but it has been demonstrated that there were considerable increases in the concentration of lead and copper in ice strata in the Greenland ice cap (Hong et al. 1994 and 1996), in peat bogs in Switzerland (Shotyk et al. 1998) and Spain (Martínez-Cortizas et al. 1999), and in lake sediments in Sweden from about 600 BC onwards (Renberg et al. 1994), by-products of the great increase in the scale of mining in classical antiquity. The Laurion silver mines of Attica, which paid for the Athenian navy constructed by Themistokles, and so for the Athenian empire, were also the first major source of anthropogenic pollution in world history. Mining for other metals, such as mercury, also made a contribution to atmospheric pollution. Thus cinnabar mining increased from the fifth century BC onwards at Almadén in Galicia in Spain, as shown by paleoenvironmental data (Martínez-Cortizas et al. 1999).

The Mediterranean Sea, since it is almost entirely landlocked and surrounded by large human populations, is one of the most heavily polluted seas on earth today. However, such problems are not unique to the modern epoch. Seneca clearly described the high level of atmospheric pollution in the city of Rome, which is not surprising in view of the extensive burning of wood for fuel that was mentioned earlier (Capasso 2000; Nutton 2000). Pollution is important not only for environmental history and for human health; it is also a key indicator of the scale of "industrial" activity in antiquity (see also Pyatt et al. 2002 for another approach to this problem). Although the metal deposition data do not tell us anything about productivity, they do demonstrate that the scale of mining activity in the period c.500 BC to c. AD 500 was substantially greater than anything seen before or for a long time afterwards. This supports the theory that substantial economic growth (at least in terms of total production levels) occurred during the time of the Roman empire.

5 Health and Disease

In order to explain the glories of Greco-Roman civilization it would be easy to assume that ancient populations must have been extremely healthy. However, such an assumption would be false. There is a considerable volume of evidence that many ancient populations suffered from a substantial disease burden. It is safe to assume that diarrheal diseases were a major cause of high infant mortality, and consequently of low life expectancy at birth, in ancient populations. Celsus recorded that dysentery mainly affected infants and children up to the age of 10 (Celsus, *Med.* 2.8.30). Older age groups also suffered from a heavy disease burden. Nearly a fifth of the skeletons of the people who were killed trying to flee Herculaneum during the eruption of Mt Vesuvius in AD 79 have symptoms of brucellosis, a disease contracted by consumption of infected animal products, particularly milk from goats (Capasso 1999). This indicates that much of the food and drink consumed by the Romans was not sterile. It also indicates the scale of the problem; nearly 20 percent of the adult population of one of the most well known Roman towns was afflicted by just one out of the numerous infectious diseases that were active in antiquity.

Herculaneum was certainly not unique. Similar findings have emerged from research on the human biology of the skeletal remains from the Greek colony of Metapontum in southern Italy. A number of skeletons display probable traces of thalassemia, a human genetic disease which confers some resistance to malaria. As the physical environment of the territory of Metapontum became steadily more marshy, providing more breeding sites for the mosquito vectors of malaria, malaria probably played a major role in the decline of the population of Metapontum during the Hellenistic period (Henneberg et al. 1992).

The books of *Epidemics* in the Hippocratic corpus show that numerous infectious diseases of varying degrees of severity were present in the small city-states of northern Greece during the fifth and fourth centuries BC; for example it is possible to recognize an epidemic of mumps on Thasos, while there are many references to more deadly diseases (Grmek 1989). Among the respiratory diseases tuberculosis was particularly feared. It had a high mortality rate. The various types of human malaria were well known in northern Greece. The Hippocratic texts describe other dangerous infectious diseases that are less well known today, such as relapsing fever. As far as health and disease were concerned, the lands around the Mediterranean were part of the tropical world in antiquity.

Malaria did not occur everywhere for two reasons. Firstly, it is a temperature dependent disease. Consequently the most dangerous species of human malaria, *Plasmodium falciparum*, was confined to Mediterranean-climate regions and was only active during the summer and autumn, although other less virulent types of malaria also occurred in northern Europe in antiquity. Secondly, it requires the presence of certain types of mosquito as a vector; not all species of mosquito can transmit malaria to humans, and mosquito breeding sites do not occur everywhere. Nevertheless, malaria was common in some areas in antiquity, such as western central Italy around Rome, as well as large parts of southern Italy, Sicily, Sardinia, North Africa, and the eastern Mediterranean lands. A malaria epidemic in late antiquity has been identified using ancient DNA at a late Roman archaeological site in Umbria in central Italy (Sallares et al. 2004). Where malaria occurred in antiquity, in the long run it was the single most important component of the pathocoenosis (Sallares 2005), or ecological community of pathogens, not only because of its own direct effects on mortality and morbidity but also because of its synergistic interactions with other diseases, especially respiratory and intestinal diseases. This combination drastically reduced both life expectancy at birth and adult life expectancy in areas where malaria was endemic. Its effects were so severe that malaria had a direct influence on human settlement patterns, encouraging people to live in hilltop settlements, since mosquitoes as weak fliers are generally confined to low-lying areas. The seven hills of Rome are the best example of this phenomenon (Sallares 2002).

Besides its purely demographic effects, malaria had considerable effects on the agricultural economy because repeated chronic infections have a debilitating effect on farm workers, particularly at harvest time. The economic divide observed in recent times between highly developed northern Italy and underdeveloped southern Italy commenced in antiquity with the spread of falciparum malaria from North Africa to southern Italy. Since malaria requires the presence of certain types of mosquitoes, it is likely that the spread of malaria northwards in the western Mediterranean in the first millennium BC required the prior spread of these mosquitoes, presumably on board ships, an unintended side-effect of the increase in trade by sea in classical times as indicated by the increasing number of shipwrecks. Malaria was probably already common in Greece and the Near East before its spread to central Italy (Sallares 2004).

Galen regarded *P. falciparum* malaria as particularly common in the city of Rome in his own time in the second century AD, but he was also well aware that different diseases were common in different cities (Galen 7.435K; Gourevitch 2001). His view was undoubtedly correct; we have already seen the examples of malaria in Rome, brucellosis in Herculaneum, tuberculosis in the cities of northern Greece; leprosy in Alexandria, according to Galen, is another example. Leprosy is the best example of the spread of a new disease in classical times (Grmek 1989: 152–76). Galen's perception implies that there was a diversity of urban mortality patterns in the ancient world. In general, cities were less healthy than the countryside in the past, as Celsus was aware (Mudry 2007), although malaria can produce extremely high mortality rates in small rural communities (Sallares 2002: 151–67).

In addition to the endemic diseases mentioned so far, there were acute infectious epidemic diseases, which were often density dependent. These diseases were favored by increasing urbanization in the classical world. The texts in the Hippocratic corpus provide evidence for the presence of numerous diseases in classical Greece, but really major epidemics were rare in Greece in the fifth and fourth centuries BC. Only the so-called "plague of Athens" in 430–426 BC described by Thucydides (2.47–54), in which about a third of the population of Athens perished, stands out. The pathogen responsible for that calamity was certainly not bubonic plague; numerous identifications have been proposed, of which typhus and smallpox remain the most plausible. However, Livy, following the annalistic tradition, does record a series of epidemics in the city of Rome as it grew during the republic. In general not enough detail is given to be able to even attempt a retrospective diagnosis, but it is clear that epidemics became more frequent in Rome as it eclipsed the cities of classical Greece in terms of size.

Nevertheless it is not until the time of the Roman empire that epidemics appeared which affected virtually the whole of the then known world. The appearance of pandemics was a side-effect of the general increase in inter-regional trade and movements of people in classical times. The first pandemic was the so-called "Antonine plague," which raged for about twenty years in the second half of the second century AD. The causative agent responsible for the "Antonine plague" is widely agreed to have been smallpox (Rijkels 2005: 22–76). Owing to the fragmentary nature of the sources it is difficult to trace its effects in detail (Duncan-Jones 1996), but later parallels make it plausible that the "Antonine plague" might have killed about a third of the population, at least in some areas. In the middle of the third century AD there was another major epidemic, the "plague of Cyprian," whose cause cannot be definitely identified (Rijkels 2005: 77–130). True plague (*Yersinia pestis*) did not become an important human disease until the time of the plague of Justinian in the sixth century AD. However the foundations for the early medieval explosion of true plague were laid during the time of the Roman empire by the silent spread of its rodent host, the black rat (*Rattus rattus*), which is now gradually being revealed by archaeology, yet another ecological consequence of increased inter-regional contact in classical antiquity (Sallares 2007).

FURTHER READING

In recent years the study of the environmental history of the ancient world has attracted a considerable amount of attention and has been the focus of a series of important books. Sallares 1991 is a wide-ranging study of the ecology of the Greek world; Hughes 1994 examines the impact of Greek and Roman civilization upon their environment; the Mediterranean has been the subject of a number of recent studies, notably Horden and Purcell 2000, Grove and Rackham 2001 and Hughes 2005, see also Hitchner, THE MEDITERRANEAN AND THE HISTORY OF ANTIQUITY. The history of malaria in Italy is explored in Sallares 2002, while Grmek 1989 draws attention to the effects of micro-organisms on human populations in antiquity, yet another area of debate.

PART III

People and Places

CHAPTER SEVENTEEN

The Near East

Maria Brosius

1 Introduction

The ancient Near East describes a geographical region which includes Mesopotamia, the Levant, and at least the northern part of the Arab peninsula, as well as Anatolia and Iran. Egypt may also be added to these regions, though due to its distinct language, society, and culture it is often treated as a separate entity. The Near East is defined by natural boundaries – seas, rivers, mountain ranges, and deserts – which determine the accessibility of its regions: the Black Sea and the Caspian Sea, the Euphrates river in the west, the Syr Darya (mod. Jaxartes) in the north-east, and the Indus in the east, as well as the mountain ranges of the Caucasus, the Zagros, and in its most eastern extent, the Paropamisadai (mod. Hindu Kush), as well as the Dasht-e Kavir, the Dasht-e Lut and the Gedrosian deserts in east and south-east Iran. Among these regions Mesopotamia, the land between the Euphrates and the Tigris rivers, witnessed the birth of ancient civilizations. The fertile lands of southern Mesopotamia allowed for a surplus agriculture (producing barley, emmer, wheat, and millet), while the northern plains permitted animal husbandry and horse breeding. The urbanization of Mesopotamia, the establishment of international trade, the creation of writing, and the birth of literature mark such a revolutionary change in human history that Mesopotamia became rightly known as "the cradle of civilization" (for Near East see Map 1).

While European travelers to the Orient are attested as early as the fifteenth and sixteenth centuries, modern interest in the ancient Near East awoke in earnest in the late eighteenth and early nineteenth centuries. One of the driving factors was the desire to find the famed cities of the East which were mentioned in the Bible, especially places like Nineveh, Babylon, and Susa. The discovery of ancient Mesopotamia is owed to two figures in particular, Austen Henry Layard and Paul Emile Botta. Layard excavated the sites of Kalhu (mod. Nimrud) and Nineveh (1845–55), and Botta Sargon's city Dur-Sharrukin (mod. Khorsabad) (1843–54), discovering reliefs of the palace walls and copying down inscriptions written in cuneiform (Larsen 1996). The decipherment of this script had only become possible after Henry C. Rawlinson, a British officer stationed at Kermanshah in north-west Iran, had copied the monumental trilingual inscription of the Persian king Darius I (522–486 BC) at Mt Bisitun, written in Elamite, Babylonian and Old Persian. It allowed Rawlinson and, independently from him, Georg Friedrich Grotefend, to decipher cuneiform (cf. Wiesehöfer 2002: 223–45). Now, tens of thousands of cuneiform documents, including literary and religious texts, as well as legal, administrative, and economic documents, which had been preserved over millennia because they were written on clay, and then sun-dried or baked, could be studied by Assyriologists, scholars of Near Eastern languages written in cuneiform scripts. In contrast, it took several more decades before Near Eastern archaeology was established as a scientific discipline. Research in both fields requires specialized knowledge in the different languages and dialects, geographical areas, and periods of history, and therefore often depends on scholarly collaboration. General difficulties are posed by the fact that the tablets from the numerous sites are dispersed in museums and private collections worldwide or are unprovenanced due to illicit excavations, while political events of the twentieth century and the relative instability of the modern Middle East make it difficult to carry out continuous and systematic excavation of archaeological sites.

2   Near Eastern Society and History

The historical account of the ancient Near East begins with the fourth millennium BC, though evidence for human habitation is attested as early as 10,000 BC, when different peoples lived in small settlements, adhering to an agricultural lifestyle (Nissen 1988; Pollock 1999; *CAH*³ I). But in contrast to the preceding millennia, the fourth millennium witnessed two decisive changes in the existing societies – the foundation of large settlements and the appearance of writing (Van de Mieroop 1999; Liverani 1993; Nissen et al. 1993; Schmandt-Besserat 1992). With the creation of the city-states of Mesopotamia, ancient Near Eastern societies reached a new height in the history of mankind: these were self-governed and economically self-sufficient cities with a hierarchical social structure, an extensive administration, and a rich and complex religious and cultural community. Within the advanced stage of self-government we observe the appearance of concepts of (divine) kingship, and the ruler's role as guardian of his city who endeavors to enhance the city's splendor by initiating building programs and increasing his subjects' prosperity by improving agricultural production through the construction of irrigation channels and underground canals, as well as encouraging international trade and commerce. The latter led to the construction of trade routes which connected Mesopotamia with Anatolia and western Asia Minor, with Egypt and Arabia, as well as India (cf. *CAH*³ I: 131–33; Kuhrt 1995: 20).

Though the societies of Mesopotamia and the Near East were diverse, and developed continuously over the next centuries and millennia into increasingly complex social groups and classes, we principally find a hierarchical society with the king as the center of political power. The king ruled with the divine sanctioning of the god or gods, under whose protection his city stood. Unlike Egyptian pharaohs, who by their very office were divine beings, Near Eastern kings did not necessarily regard themselves as gods. The king was surrounded by an extensive court which included members of his immediate family – the king's mother, the royal wives, his sons and daughters, as well as concubines, and members of the aristocracy, who served as high officials and courtiers. Though linked to the king and the palace, the priesthood of the city temples constituted a further important group within that society. Temples, and the sacred enclosures within which they stood, were the dominating feature of Near Eastern cities, often erected on high, raised platforms. These ziggurats housed the cult statues of the gods, and it was the responsibility of the high priest, the king, and the priesthood, to observe religious festivals and to perform religious rituals in the presence of the populace. Like the palaces, the temples conducted their own administration and economy, and it is not surprising, therefore, that much of the scribal tradition centers on both these institutions. A further level of society was made up by the citizenry, who included landowners, farmers, and peasants, as well as craftsmen, artisans, merchants, and traders. Prisoners of war and slaves were among the unfree population.

The Near East was inhabited by many different peoples speaking a variety of languages and dialects. In Mesopotamia two main languages can be identified: Sumerian, which was spoken in the south, and Akkadian, a Semitic language, which was used in the northern region. The earliest people attested in the written sources were the Sumerians. The initial view that they had migrated to the area from the East around the fourth millennium BC has now made way to the idea that they most likely had inhabited that region for centuries, if not millennia (Bottéro 2001: chap. 1). With the appearance of the Sumerians, the history of Near Eastern civilizations begins a decisive new phase, characterized by the formation of large cities and states. The simultaneous invention of writing was a revolutionary achievement which transformed this society. Sumerian is neither a Semitic nor an Indo-European language. It is written in cuneiform script, using a reed stylus on clay, though other writing media, such as writing boards, were also used. While the earliest documents support the idea that writing grew out of the need for economic record keeping, including receipts and accounts (cf. Schmandt-Besserat 1992; Nissen 1993), it quickly became a fundamental tool to commit religious and literary texts to written form. Our oldest literary texts originate in Sumerian society, though they are best preserved in Old Babylonian copies. The most important of these texts is the Epic of Gilgamesh, the story of the eponymous hero of Uruk, whose actions are driven by his fear of death, and whose quest for immortality leads him on a journey in which he experiences the full scope of human emotions – friendship, loss, upheaval, and, finally, acceptance and contentment. In another literary text, the Story of the Flood, in which the gods sent a deluge to punish man, we recognize the immediate antecedent of the biblical story of Noah and the Flood (for the texts, A. George 1999).

Among the cities of southern Mesopotamia Uruk defines the change from settlement to city most strikingly. At the end of the fourth millennium BC it was the largest city of the region, covering c.100 ha, compared to other cities such as Ur, Lagash,

and Nippur, which covered between 15 and 50 ha.; by c.2800 BC Uruk covered an
area of c.494 ha. (Van de Mieroop 1999: 37). The prerequisites which allow a large
group of people to live in such a formation determine that such a society is highly
advanced, able to secure the food supply for a sizeable community, and to allow a
division of labor in which work could be specialized and professions developed. The
emerging economy needed skillful and professional managing, requiring a highly
organized administrative system, in which scribes, accountants, and administrators
were employed within the city's public and private spheres, serving in temple and
palace archives, as well as in the archives of private businessmen.

3   The Empire of Akkad (2350–2150 BC) and the Third Dynasty of Ur (2112–2004 BC)

Strife for more land caused rivalries among the different cities of Mesopotamia, and
eventually led to the dominance of one king, Lugalzagesi of Umma, who, some time
after 2400 BC, was able to take control of the most important cities of southern
Mesopotamia, including Ur, Uruk, and Lagash, thus beginning a process of centralized political rule which eventually led to the establishment of the first empire of the
dynasty of Akkad:

> When Enlil [the god], king of all lands, gave to Lugalzagesi the kingship of the nation,
> directed all the eyes of the land (obediently) toward him, put all the lands at his feet,
> and from the east to the west made them subject to him: then, from the Lower Sea,
> (along) the Tigris and the Euphrates to the Upper Sea, he (Enlil) put their routes in
> good order for him. From east to west Enlil permitted him no [riv]al; under him the
> lands rested contentedly, the people made merry, and the suzerainty of Sumer and rulers
> of other lands conceded sovereignty to him at Uruk.
>   Then (also) under him, Uruk spent its time rejoicing; Ur, like a bull, raised high its
> head; Larsa, the beloved city of Utu, made merry, Umma, the beloved city of Shara
> lifted its huge horns; the region of Zabala cried out like a ewe reunited(?) with its lamb;
> and Kidingir raised high its neck. (after J. Cooper 1986: 94 no. 7.1)

The actual dynasty was founded by Sargon I (2340–2284), who, in commemoration
of his achievements, built a new city, Akkad (*or* Agade), which became the seat of
royal power. Sargon thus set a precedent which many of the kings of Assyria, Babylon,
and other Near Eastern kingdoms, including Persia, came to emulate: the foundation
of a new city as a core element in the expression of kingship. It has not yet been
possible to locate Sargon's city, but it is thought to be near the confluence of the
Tigris and Diyala rivers (Kuhrt 1995: 44; cf. Van de Mieroop 2004: 60). Sargon
took control of Babylonia after defeating Lugalzagesi in battle, and was able to extend
his power as far as Mari in the north and Elam in the east:

> Sargon the king of Akkad, the [. . .] of Innana, king of Kish, anointed of Anu, [king]
> of lands, governor of Enlil, conquered the city of Uruk and destroyed its walls. He

challenged (the man of) Uruk in battle and took Lugalzagesi, the king of Uruk, prisoner in the course of the battle; he led him in a wooden collar to the gate of Enlil.

Sargon, king of Akkad, challenged (the man of) Ur in a battle and defeated the city and destroyed its walls. He defeated (the town of) E-Nin-kimara and destroyed its walls and destroyed its land from Lagash to the sea. He washed his weapons in the sea. He challenged Umma in a battle [and he defeated the city and destroyed its walls].

To Sargon, king of lands, Enlil gave no rival; Enlil gave him the Upper Sea and the Lower Sea. From the Lower Sea, citizens of Akkad held the government. Mari and Elam were subject to Sargon, king of lands. Sargon, king of lands, restored Kish and made (its fugitive inhabitants re)occupy the city. (after Kuhrt 1995: 49)

Previously independent city rulers now became governors under Sargon's kingship. The change of political rule had an effect on the way government was conducted centrally in order to take account of the large dimension of the new empire. As a result, Akkadian became the dominant administrative language, though Sumerian remained part of the scribal education and continued to be used to write literary and religious texts. As the increasing corpus of cuneiform tablets indicates, writing became much more extensive.

The concept of empire was further anchored by Sargon's grandson Naram-Sin (2260–2223), when he consolidated the empire of Akkad by appointing members of the royal family to cultic offices in the cities and by installing them as governors (Kuhrt 1995: 50). Kingship became more pronounced, when Naram-Sin called himself "king of the four quarters (of the universe)," and even proclaimed himself to be a living god:

Naram-Sin, the mighty king of Akkad: when the four corners of the world opposed him with hostility, he remained victorious in nine battles because of the love of Ishtar and even took the kings who had campaigned against him prisoner. Because he succeeded when heavily pressed in maintaining his city in strength, his city implored Ishtar of Eanna, Enlil of Nippur, Dagan of Tuttul, Ninhursanga of Kesh, Enki of Eridu, Sin of Ur, Shamah of Sippar, Nergal of Kutha to have him as the god of their city Akkad and they built him a temple in the midst of Akkad. (Farber 1983)

However, the fundamental problem was the control of such a vast area at central level, and it provoked internal strife from the cities which reclaimed their independence. When, in addition to the instability caused internally, external pressures were placed upon the first empire by invading peoples, the empire of Akkad was unable to survive much beyond the reign of Naram-Sin's successor, Shar-kali-sharri (2175–2150). The end of the dynasty of Akkad allowed the creation of a new state at Ur, known as Ur III (2112–2004), founded by Ur-Nammu. He appears to have established himself in the city after having served there as governor under its ruler Utuhegal. Ur-Nammu defeated the king of Lagash and forced other city kings to accept his sovereignty. As "king of Sumer and Akkad" he claimed power over all of Babylonia. His reign led to a revival of Sumerian language and literature. In Ur itself Ur-Nammu built a vast ziggurat (Roaf 1990), and instituted the first known law-code:

> Then did Ur-Nammu, the mighty warrior, king of Ur, king of Sumer and Akkad, by the might of Nanna, lord of the city, and in accordance with the word of Utu, establish equity in the land (and) banish malediction, violence and strife. By granting immunity in Akkad to the maritime trade from the seafarers' overseer, to the herdsman from the "oxen trader," the "sheep taker," and the "donkey taker," he set Sumer and Akkad free. (*ANET* II: 31–4, lines 104–24)

With the reigns of the last two kings of this dynasty, Shu-Sin and Ibbi-Sin, the state of Ur III came to an end. One of the reasons for this may have been internal problems, as the state had become unable to secure the grain supply for its population, possibly due to bad harvests, but it has also been suggested that it may have been caused by the refusal of some provinces to pay taxes (cf. Van de Mieroop 2004: 77). External threats added to the instability of the state. From northern Syria a semi-nomadic people, the Amorites, carried out attacks on the region, and Elamite troops attacked from the east. When Elam itself was seized by the rulers of Shimashki (northeast Khuzestan) (cf. Potts 1999: chap. 5), they advanced to Babylonia. The last ruler of Ur III, Ibbi-Sin, was taken prisoner and deported to Susa.

4   The Near Eastern Kingdoms in the Second Millennium BC

In the period following the fall of Ur III, cities such as Mari, Isin, Larsa, and Babylon established themselves as powerful states which competed for political dominance. The kings of Isin were able to create a new dynasty which lasted from 2017 to 1794, when they were threatened by the Amorite king Rim-Sin of Larsa (1822–1763). However, Rim-Sin's own rule soon came to an end when Larsa was conquered by Hammurabi of Babylon (1792–1750). Hammurabi expanded his empire further when he defeated the city of Eshunna in 1766, and conquered Elam and Mari, which fell in 1761. Mari had already been a powerful state in the third millennium (c.2600–2300), but flourished especially in the early second millennium BC, evidenced in the extensive archives recovered from the site. Excavations have revealed a large palace complex set around several courtyards and temples with extraordinarily well preserved structures and wall paintings (for current research see *Mari. Annales des Recherches Interdisciplinaires*).

One of the most famous documents of the ancient Near East is the law-code of Hammurabi, inscribed on a stele which also bears an image of the ruler standing before the sun-god Shamash. The stele was found in Susa, where it had been taken by the Elamite king Shutruk-Nahhunte; it is now in the Louvre Museum. Scholarly debate is divided over the question whether this text is indeed a law-code or an "example of royal self-praise," the "account of the king at the end of his reign to the gods of his achievements" (Kuhrt 1995: 112. For the text, *ANET* I: 138–67). The c.300 "laws," or rather legal statements made here advise on a number of legal issues for daily life, but they do not constitute a complete cover of legal issues.

Meanwhile small states had emerged throughout the Near East from Anatolia to Iran. Their creation was most likely fostered by international trade, and is evidenced in the numerous administrative documents from Assur. A network of trade routes had been established linking Anatolia with Mesopotamia. Assyrian bronze production was dependent on the import of tin which was brought from the Iranian plateau, while Babylonia delivered textiles. One of the most important corpora of documents for this period comes from the archives of Assyrian traders at Kanesh (mod. Kültepe) in central Anatolia, who established a trading colony here called *karum*. Around 20,000 cuneiform tablets have been found on the site to date, most of them belonging to Assyrian traders. The documents include private letters as well as administrative texts recording the life and business of this Assyrian trading community. The traders journeyed between Assur and Kanesh in donkey caravans loaded with tin and wool textiles which were sold or exchanged in Anatolia, either directly or indirectly. The commodity taken back to Assur was precious metal, gold or silver. The records, which cover a period of two generations, ended abruptly when Kanesh, for reasons we do not know, was destroyed in 1830 BC (cf. Veenhof 1972).

Under Hammurabi's successors Babylonian influence in the region gradually decreased due to new ascending powers, such as the kingdom of Hana, which covered an area similar to that of Mari, and the loss of the Gulf trade. The decisive political blow came with the attack of the Hittite king Mursili I in 1595, when Babylon was sacked. The Hittite kingdom had been founded by Hattusili I (1650–1620), who built his capital Hattusa (mod. Bogazköy) in central Anatolia. The Hittites were an Indo-European people who had settled in the region during the third millennium BC. Hattusili first extended his power in Anatolia and was soon able to enter northern Syria. He suffered a temporary setback when he was attacked by the Hurrians, but he was able to continue to exert his control over northern Syria. His successor Mursili I (1620–1590) advanced as far as Aleppo, which was sacked, and raided Babylon in 1595. Following the attack of Babylon, a people called the Kassites stepped into this power vacuum and established a new dynasty in the city, thus bringing the Old Babylonian period to an end. The origins of the Kassites remain obscure. A mountain tribe, the Kassites were neither Indo-Europeans nor a Semitic people. Thus, they were not only linguistically distinct from the Babylonians, but also followed different cultural practices. Evolving as a strong political state, Kassite Babylonia was increasingly regarded as a serious contender for Assyria in the battle for political dominance. Its power lasted for over 400 years, from c.1595 to 1155, when the Kassites finally succumbed to Assyrian and Elamite attacks.

Hittite power itself was soon to be threatened by the Hurrians, who founded the state of Mitanni, occupying roughly the area of northern Syria and parts of southern Anatolia. The origin of the Hurrians is much debated; they seem to have been different groups of people who, however, shared a common language. Consisting probably of several smaller states, the Hurrians were united into one political entity by the end of the sixteenth century BC. The capital of the new state of Mitanni was the city of Washshuganni, which has not yet been found (cf. Bryce 2005: 138 and n.57). Their military power was largely characterized by warriors fighting on chariots, the so-called *maryannu*. Mitanni competed with Egypt for control of the Levant, but eventually both sides entered an alliance. Internal strife weakened the state, though, creating a situation which allowed the Hittite king Shuppiluliuma (1370–1330) to reduce Mitanni to a vassal state. The Assyrian king Adad-nirari (1305–1274) finally incorporated Mitanni into Assyria. The state of Hatti thrived for a short period of time but was threatened by the Gasga, a people who inhabited the Pontic Alps, whose raids into Hatti territory eventually forced the Hittite king Muwatalli II (c.1295–1272) to abandon the capital, Hattusa. Hittite control over the Levant continued to be contested by Egypt. After a successful Syrian campaign in 1275 in which Ramesses II reasserted Egyptian control there, he prepared to lead his army against the Hittites. The battle of Kadesh, a border city on the Orontes, was fought in 1274. According to Ramesses' accounts, the battle ended in an overwhelming victory for him, yet his subsequent withdrawal from the region forces us to regard his claim with suspicion. In addition, a reference in an inscription of Muwattalli's brother Hattusili indicates that the Hittites, too, claimed victory in the battle:

> Because my brother Muwattalli campaigned against the king of Egypt and the king of Amurru, when he defeated the kings of Egypt and Amurru, he went back to Aba. When Muwattalli my brother defeated Aba, he (. . .) went back to Hatti, but he left me in Aba. (*Keilschrifturkunden aus Boghazköi*, Berlin XXI: 17; Beal 1992: 307)

Most likely, the battle had ended in a stalemate. For a brief period Hittite control was re-established under Muwatalli's successors, but the state came under external threat from Assyria under Takulti-Ninurta I (1243–1207), and uprisings of western vassals. The end of the Hittite kingdom around 1200, however, was due to the collapse of the civilizations of the eastern Mediterranean following an immense natural catastrophe and a series of raids led by the so-called "Sea-peoples" (Drews 1993).

5   The Neo-Assyrian, Neo-Elamite, and Neo-Babylonian Empires (1180–539 BC)

Assyria had politically benefited from the weakness of the state of Mitanni since the mid-fourteenth century and the reign of King Assur-uballit (1365–1330 or 1353–18). Assur-uballit had successfully managed to assert his power, and even attempted to create a political alliance with Babylonia by offering his daughter Muballitat-Sherua in marriage to the Kassite king Burnaburiash. But their son was killed after his accession to the throne, forcing the now aged Assur-uballit to lead a campaign against Babylonia. Attempts to put Assyria back on the political map also become visible in Assur-uballit's attempt at establishing international relations. Two of his letters were found among the correspondence of Amenophis IV of Egypt. In one of these, Assur-uballit made a barely disguised demand for Egyptian gold:

> I send as your greeting-gift a beautiful royal chariot, out[fitt]ed for me, and 2 white horses, also [out]fitted for me, 1 chariot not outfitted, and 1 seal of genuine lapis lazuli. Is such a present that of a Great King? Gold in your country is dirt; one simply gathers it up. Why are you so sparing of it? I am engaged in building a new palace. Send me as much gold as is needed for its adornment. When Ashur-nadin-ahhe, my ancestor, wrote to Egypt, 20 talents of gold were sent to him. [W]hen the king of Hanigalbat (Hatti)

[wr]ote to your father in Egy[pt], [h]e sent 20 talents of gold to him. [Now], I am the [equal] of the king of Hani[galba]t, but you sent me [. . .] of gold, and it is not enough [f]or the pay of my messengers on the journey to and back. If your purpose is graciously one of friendship, send me much gold. (transl. Moran 1992: no. 16, ll. 9–33)

Adad-nirari strengthened Assyria's position even further by recovering Babylonian territory in the Diyala region and conquering the Mitanni state. By replacing the king of Mitanni with an Assyrian official (Akk. *sukkallu rabû*), and appointing Assyrian governors in the cities of upper Mesopotamia under Shalmaneser I (1274–1245/1263–1234), Assyrian power was consolidated. Military campaigns of his successors ensured that Assyria's control extended as far north as Lake Van and as far west as the Mediterranean. The relationship with Babylon remained hostile, and with Tiglath-pileser I's attempts to regain border territory, Assyria went to war against Babylon. Assyria faced a further threat from Aramaean tribes who invaded from the west, causing the destruction of harvests and the desertion of villages. By 1050 the Middle Assyrian empire had come to an end.

Only in the ninth century, beginning with the reign of Ashurnasirpal II (883–859), was Assyria able to reassert its power. The king was able to exact control over smaller states and to demand tribute from them, and thus gradually extended his political sphere of influence. He even built a new royal city, Kalhu (mod. Nimrud). Between the mid-eighth and mid-seventh centuries Neo-Assyrian power reached its zenith, with Tiglath-pileser III (744–727) succeeding in taking control of Babylon. Consolidation of the Neo-Assyrian empire is tangible in the wealth of archival documents, legal, and administrative texts, and royal inscriptions.

The state which now came into political view was Elam, the region east of the River Tigris and roughly identical with modern Khuzestan. Elam appears in Mesopotamian sources as early as the third millennium BC, but its history is difficult to establish. At that time contact with Mesopotamian cities was both hostile and peaceful. By the Late Ur III period the rulers of Shimashki in western Iran gained political control over Elam and only ceded power with the rise of the *sukkalmahs*, the "Grand Regents" of Elam, under whose rule Elam's influence extended throughout western Asia. By the late twentieth century BC Elam had power over Larsa, and entered alliances with other city-states, including Mari, which traded Elamite tin with Syria and Palestine. With Hammurabi's reign, Elam's political power in this region was curbed. During the Middle Elamite period (c.1500–1100) different dynasties ruled in Elam; their kings were known in Near Eastern sources as "kings of Susa and Anshan," marking the two capitals west and east of the Zagros mountains as equal royal cities. Now Elamite came to replace Akkadian as the official written language. Like Akkadian, Elamite was written in cuneiform script, but it is unrelated to Akkadian or any other Semitic or Indo-European language. Under the kings Tepti-ahar and Untash-Napirisha the cities Haft-Tepe and Al-Untash-Napirisha (mod. Choga Zanbil) were founded. In the twelfth century BC the Elamite king Shutruk-Nahhunte was able to expel the Kassites, and he even invaded Babylonia. His son Kudur-Nahhunte continued his father's campaigns against Babylon and carried off the statues of Babylonian gods, including that of the city-god Marduk. The latter was triumphantly returned after the Babylonian king Nebuchadnezzar (1126–1105) defeated the Elamite king Hutelutush-Inshushinak (1120–1100) in battle, and for several centuries Elam seems to have all but disappeared from the political landscape.

Most of the reign of the Assyrian king Sargon II (721–705) – a name that undoubtedly harked back to the founder of the first empire of Akkad – was spent campaigning, confronting the Babylonians, but he was defeated by the forces of Babylonia's ally Elam at Der in 720. Yet towards the end of his reign Sargon finally succeeded in re-establishing his control over Babylon. But by then Assyria was threatened by a northern power, Urartu, a kingdom centered upon the area around Lake Van, which was extending its power in central Anatolia and northern Iran, and by the Phrygian king Mita of Mushki, in whom we recognize King Midas of Gordion mentioned in Greek sources. Sargon was killed in 705 in a battle against a people called Kimmerians who were located in Anatolia. Assyrian campaigns against Egypt determined the foreign policy of his successors. In 701 Sennaherib confronted the Egyptian army, and in 671 Esarhaddon took Memphis and Thebes was attacked by Ashurbanipal. When Elam fostered rebellions in Babylonia, supporting Ashurbanipal's brother, the Assyrian king led campaigns against Babylon, which was destroyed in 648, and Elam, culminating in the destruction of Susa:

> I tore out the raging bull(-figures), the attachments of the gates; the temples of Elam I destroyed so that they ceased to exist. I counted their gods and goddesses as powerless ghosts. Into their hidden groves, into which no stranger goes, whose bounds he does not enter, my battle troops penetrated, beheld its hidden (place), burnt it with fire. The burial places of their early (and) later kings, who had not feared Ashur and Ishtar, my lords, (and) who had made my royal predecessors tremble, I devastated, I destroyed (and) let them see the sun; their bones I removed from Assyria. I laid restlessness on their spirits. Food offerings (to the dead) and water libations I denied them. For the distance of the month (and) 25 days, I devastated the region of Elam. Salt and cress I sowed over them. (Kuhrt 1995: 500)

Assyria's fortune in Babylonia changed with the accession of Nabopolassar, who, by 616, began to lead attacks on Assyrian territory, assisted by a new political power, the Medes, an Iranian people who inhabited parts of north-west Iran. Nabopolassar took several Assyrian cities and eventually seized control of Assyria proper. After repeated campaigns, his son Nebuchadnezzar II (604–562) finally expelled the Egyptians from the Levant.

6   The Persian Empire (559–330 BC)

During the reign of Nebuchadnezzar II Babylonia revived and its cities were rebuilt. Babylon itself expanded to an enormous city covering 850 ha. But Babylon's political power was not to last long. In 555 a usurper acceded to the throne called Nabonidus (555–539). In contrast to Nebuchadnezzar's care for Babylon and the temple of Marduk, Nabonidus favored the moon-god Sin whose sanctuary was located in Harran, a preference which brought him little sympathy with the Babylonians. His reign ended when Nabonidus had to succumb to the Persians, who, under the reign of Cyrus II (559–530), had conquered the lands of Media and Urartu and even brought the kingdom of Lydia under their control in the 540s. Cyrus took Babylon in 539 BC after having seized the cities of Opis and Sippar. Accounts vary as to whether this was a peaceful surrender or involved a battle outside the city gates. According to Cyrus's own account, recorded in the famous Cyrus-Cylinder found in Babylon and now in the British Museum, Cyrus took the city with the blessing of the god Marduk:

> He (Marduk) commanded him (Cyrus) to go to Babylon, and let him take the road to Babylon. Like a friend and companion he walked by his side, while his extensive troops, whose number was immeasurable like the water of a river, marched at his side, with their weapons fastened. Without battle and fighting he led him enter Babylon. He saved his (Marduk's) city Babylon from its oppression; he handed over to him Nabonidus, the king who did not revere him. (Cyrus-Cylinder lines 15–17; for full text, Brosius 2000)

Babylonia became a satrapy of the new Persian empire, leaving intact its legal and economic administration, and its religious and social customs. With the foundation of the first Persian empire, known as the Achaemenid empire (559–330 BC), the entire world of the ancient Near East, from Egypt to India, came under the control of one single power. The Persians integrated the past kingdoms into a vast world empire which was to last for about 230 years, ending with its conquest by Alexander III of Macedon.

While the Macedonian conquest of Achaemenid Persia undoubtedly signifies a marked change in the development of the history of the ancient Near East, a political, historical, and cultural continuity can nevertheless be traced here, albeit to a varying extent. Vestiges of Near Eastern cultures remain tangible throughout the Seleukid and the Parthian periods. Perhaps a more decisive political chasm occurred with the fall of the last Persian power, the Sasanians (AD 224–651), and the Arab conquest of the Near East in the mid-seventh century AD. The Sasanians, rivals of Rome, claimed heritage to the lands west of the Euphrates river which had been the recognized border between the two empires since the Parthian period. After more than four centuries of Sasanian rule, which witnessed frequent wars, first with Rome, and then with Byzantium, and had left both empires politically and militarily exhausted, Sasanid Persia, as well as the Roman Near East, succumbed to invasions of Arab tribes. With them they brought a new, monotheistic religion and a new form of writing which they imposed upon the conquered peoples. Five thousand years of ancient Near Eastern history thus finally came to an end.

FURTHER READING

Kuhrt 1995 is fundamental reading for anyone studying the ancient Near East, offering clear and precise outlines of historical events, supported with extensive quotations from Near Eastern sources, while highlighting the problems involved in the reading and interpreting of the material, as well as guiding the reader to key issues of scholarly debate. Van de Mieroop 2004 gives a concise account of the main political events. Further introductions include Liverani 1988, 1993, 1998, Nissen 1988, Pollock 1999, Postgate 1992, and the contributions in volumes I–IV of the *Cambridge Ancient History* (3rd edn) and Snell 2005. Reference works include Sasson 1995, Meyers 1997, Roaf 1990.

Specific peoples and areas are discussed by Potts 1999 (Elam), Bryce 2005 (Hittites), Wilhelm 1989 (Hurrians), Wiesehöfer 2002, Brosius 2006 (Persians), Lipiński 2000 (Aramaeans). Aspects of Near Eastern society are the subject of various studies: on the Mesopotamian city, Van de Mieroop 1999; on the use and origins of writing, Nissen et al. 1993, Schmandt-Besserat 1992, Glassner 2003; on religion, Bottéro 1998; on society in general, Bottéro 2001. For a vivid account of the archaeological rediscovery of the ancient Near East Larsen 1996 is highly recommended.

Source material can be found Pritchard 1955's collection of Ancient Near Eastern Texts (= *ANET*), also Grayson 1975a, 1975b, and Luckenbill 1926–27 (Assyria and Babylonian), Lecoq 1997 and Brosius 2000 (Persian texts), Schmitt 1991 (Darius, Bisitun Inscription).

CHAPTER EIGHTEEN

Egypt under the Pharaohs

John Ray

1   Setting the Scene

Egypt is in many ways unique within the study of the ancient world. Much of its surface area is desert, where rainfall is minimal, and this has preserved countless objects which would have perished in a different climate. Wooden ships, furniture, and children's toys survive, often intact, and there is no need to reconstruct such things from two-dimensional art or our imagination. In addition, stone was plentiful, and whole temple complexes still stand which in other regions would have been made out of mud brick or other less permanent materials. Temples and tombs are the major source of monumental inscriptions, and this is the basis for much of our information about the official side of ancient Egypt. However, this brings dangers with it, and there is no doubt that our picture of how that society functioned is biased as a result. Most towns and cities, for example, were situated in the floodplain close to the Nile, and consequently our knowledge of these is limited. The popular image of the Egyptians as obsessed with death and arcane rituals is part of this bias: there is some truth in the conception, but it is also something of a caricature, which can get in the way of a better understanding. Anyone familiar with Egyptian literature will know that here was a culture with a pronounced sense of humor, and one which valued the life that was vouchsafed to it. Morbid they were not.

The situation is helped to a considerable extent by the survival of texts on papyrus. Papyrus as a medium is vulnerable to dampness, fire, and the actions of insects, but the dry sands of Egypt have enabled many texts to survive which would have perished elsewhere. The same is true of ostraka (inscribed potsherds or flakes of limestone), which tend to contain ephemeral or less formal texts. It is possible for an Egyptologist to excavate an inscription with his own hand, and to become the first person for millennia to know what it says. A letter may be found sealed, in which case the student who works on it will perhaps be the first person to read it, since the intended recipient never did. Sometimes the name of a scribe will be unknown, but his inky thumbprint will still be there on the potsherd which he used to record his thoughts. Here too the circumstances of where most texts are found can determine the nature of the information they contain. Funerary guides to the underworld, for example, exist in many copies, and it would be tempting to trade a few of them in for something which more closely reflects a modern view of history. However, we are not in a position to impose on the ancients our own sense of what is important, and we must be content with the way the past chooses to reveal itself.

One of the advantages of Egyptian texts is that they are not subject to the process of transmission which we find in other societies. In much of the ancient world, texts would be copied and recopied, since they had a limited life. A work which contained ideas which were thought unacceptable or out of fashion would simply cease to be reproduced. In effect a process of censorship is at work, whether conscious or unconscious. In Egypt much the same process applied, but discarded or marginal texts can still come down to us. It is no accident that many of the most subversive or heretical texts from early Christianity are the product of the Egyptian deserts. Egypt can preserve for us voices which in most other societies would have fallen silent long ago.

The Egyptian language has the longest history so far attested, stretching from around 3100 BC until the disappearance of texts in Coptic, its medieval descendant, around the time of the Crusades. The linguistic aspect of this long history deserves to be better known. Almost all periods are well represented in our sources, with the exception of short interludes where political anarchy or social upheaval affected the production of texts or their survival. Administrative texts are commonly attested, as are most of the familiar genres of literature, with the exception of epic poetry, which made its appearance in Egypt at a late date, apparently under the influence of Greek models. The biggest gap in our knowledge is technical. Temple libraries, for example, certainly existed, but none have been found before the end of the Hellenistic or the beginning of the Roman period. Nevertheless, a handful of medical papyri are known, and these at least give a glimpse of the wealth of expertise which there must have been. The same is true of mathematics and topography. Similarly, the sources for reconstructing the legal system are patchy, and often reflect the interests of the party that is doing the narrating rather than the underlying principles of justice. In spite of this, what remains is considerable, and the story of excavation in Egypt is far from over. It is good to think that new discoveries may still overturn our knowledge.

In spite of the vicissitudes of time, climate and the chances of survival, the sources which have come down to us are extremely numerous, even if many of them are fragmentary or elliptical in their content. The following short summary can be nothing but highly selective, although I have tried to make the selection representative. The quotations from Egyptian texts are the author's own translations.

2   The Old Kingdom (c.2700–2150 BC)

Egyptian prehistory is less spectacular than many of its counterparts elsewhere, but what emerges from this long period of preparation is unique (Bard in I. Shaw 2000: 61–88). Instead of the competing cities which are the norm for most early societies,

Egypt came up with the world's first unified state. This centers on the figure of the king (the term Pharaoh, which originally referred to the royal palace, was later transferred to the monarch himself. In the first half of Egypt's long history the term is often used, although strictly speaking this is an anachronism). The king united divine and human authority within himself, and was thought to merge with the god Osiris upon his death. Unification under the divinity of the Pharaoh was the ideal to which Egypt always aspired, even in periods where central authority had broken down, and the princes who succeeded in reunifying the country at the beginning of the Middle and New Kingdoms were given almost legendary honor. The concept of a single focus for authority is a remarkable feat of abstract thinking, one that is paralleled in other Pharaonic achievements, such as the creation of a streamlined calendar which was no longer shackled to the phases of the moon, and the adoption of a strictly decimal numbering system.

The Old Kingdom is often referred to as the Pyramid Age, after its most conspicuous monuments. These have attracted fascination, and fantasy, since the days of the ancient Egyptians themselves, and the literature on this subject alone is considerable, though of greatly varying quality (Lehner 1997 and Verner 2001 are clear and authoritative). Pyramids may be seen as the stone equivalent of the abstract thinking which produced the unified state in the first place, since each one is unique, yet is also the latest in a sequence which was meant to recreate itself for eternity. From the point of view of the literary historian, the value of the pyramids increases as they progress, since from the end of the Fifth Dynasty (c.2375 BC) the inner walls of the pyramid chambers begin to be inscribed with a series of religious compositions. These are known, correctly but unimaginatively, as the Pyramid Texts (Faulkner 1969). These recensions represent the oldest connected body of literature in the world, and some of the individual spells, or chapters, may well go back into prehistory. The value of these texts to the political historian is limited, but their importance to the history of religion can scarcely be exaggerated.

Inscriptions in private tombs are needed to supplement this picture, and the earliest autobiographical inscriptions are found even in the Third Dynasty (c.2650 BC). Most of these sources are collected in Roccati 1982. Among them is the account of the extremely versatile Weni, whose career embraced the roles of judge, confidential advisor, canal digger and organizer of a military expedition to the region of Mt Carmel in Palestine (Lichtheim I 1973: 18–23). Then there is the explorer and desert ranger Harkhuf, who went on a series of expeditions into the southern Sudan, on one occasion bringing back with him a dancing pygmy. His copy of the letter that he received from the young king Pepi II, with its mixture of officialese struggling with childish over-excitement, is one of the most vivid documents to have survived from the ancient world (Lichtheim I 1973: 23–27). There is also the less-known, but delightful letter sent by King Isesi to his vizier Rashepses (Roccati 1982: 78–79), part of which runs as follows:

> My majesty was more happy at seeing your letter than anything else, because you know how to say what my majesty loves, and what you say is more pleasing to me than anything . . . Rashepses, I speak of you a million times, saying "a man who is loved of his

lord, favored of his lord, one who is in the heart of his lord, and charged with his secrets."
Truly I know that Re [the sun god] loves me, because he gave me you. As Isesi lives
for ever, tell me any wish whatever in a letter from you, now, this very day, and my
majesty will grant it there and then.

Official documents from the Old Kingdom are scarce, but a small corpus of royal
decrees has survived, and these are collected in Goedicke 1967. However, the principal source of our knowledge must be the archives from the funerary temple attached
to the pyramid of the Fifth Dynasty king Neferirkare, which are known as the Abusir
papyri (Posener-Kriéger 1976; extracts in Roccati 1982: 277–87). These are essentially inventories and duty rosters, kept by the outgoing teams of priests as they
handed over their monthly duties to their incoming replacements. There are also lists
of deliveries from the various estates which supplied the cult of the dead king. Even
the measurements of the cracks and blemishes on dishes and ritual vases were
recorded meticulously, since these utensils were the property of the dead king, who
was now among his fellow gods. More papyri from Abusir are now known, and the
site is still being excavated (Verner 2001: 265–321).

3   The Middle Kingdom (c.2050–1650 BC)

The Old Kingdom came to an end for reasons that are still obscure, although there
are several references in the sources to food shortages. These may have been either
the symptom or the cause of the political anarchy which has earned this interlude the
name of the First Intermediate Period. During this period two power centers competed for dominance – Herakleopolis in Middle Egypt and Thebes further south.
Thebes, a small town which had been quite obscure during the Old Kingdom,
emerged victorious from this conflict.

The Middle Kingdom imitates the Old Kingdom in many respects, but it never
forgot that things could go wrong and that regimes could falter. Spiritually and culturally, a chillier wind is now blowing. There is a certain resemblance with a civilization which also referred to itself as a Middle Kingdom, namely China. The visual art
of the period is some of the finest that Egypt ever produced, and it is a favorite with
connoisseurs because of its elegance combined with austerity. But the hand of the
state weighs heavier than it did in the Old Kingdom, and there are no more letters
like the one Isesi wrote to Rashepses. The careworn faces of the monarchs of the
Twelfth Dynasty are deliberately recorded by sculptors, to emphasize the weight of
responsibility which accompanies authority. The kings are still buried in pyramids,
but the interiors of these are complex, with blind alleys and hidden entrances designed
in vain to foil robbers. The town of Thebes was too provincial a place to remain as
the seat of government. However, the capital of the Old Kingdom, Memphis, is no
longer favored, and a new capital was constructed some 50 kilometers to the south,
on a virgin site. It is as if the old regime could not be trusted. One of the most
characteristic compositions of the period is a discourse from the first king of the
Twelfth Dynasty, Amenemhat I, who has died following an assassination attempt,

giving his political testimony to his son and heir, Sesostris (Parkinson 1997: 203–11). It is a text about survival, from someone who has not survived.

The potential instability of politics was the reason why the new dynasty resorted to the practice of co-regencies. This was begun by the same Amenemhat I, who for the last decade of his reign shared the throne with his son Sesostris I, with the latter concentrating on foreign affairs and military expeditions while his father applied himself to domestic policy and constructing his architectural legacy. The pattern was repeated throughout the dynasty, and was one of the reasons for its successful longevity (Simpson 1963; Murnane 1977).

The Middle Kingdom was recognized as a classic age by the Egyptians themselves. The phase of the language which was in use at this time became canonical, in a way that the language of the Old Kingdom never did. Middle Egyptian, as this stage is called, was still in use for formal inscriptions down to the Roman period, and the hieroglyphic register of the Rosetta Stone, which dates from 196 BC, is composed in Middle Egyptian. A principal reason for this veneration of Middle Egyptian is the quality of the texts which were produced in it. It is no coincidence that many of the greatest works of Egyptian literature make their appearance during the Twelfth Dynasty: the point is that the regime itself was involved with the creation of that literature. Eloquence and persuasion were a major tool for gaining hearts and minds, and literature which emphasized the qualities of the dynasty and its concern for the well-being of its subjects was deliberately fostered (this theme and its implications are incomparably explored in Posener 1957). The Old Kingdom, after all, was thought to have failed because it lacked empathy and persuasion, though one wonders what the vizier Rashepses would have thought of this generalization. Similarly, King Pepi II of the Old Kingdom (the one who wrote the letter about the dancing pygmy) could later be portrayed as having a nocturnal affair with one of his generals, while the builder of the Great Pyramid is characterized in another tale as an arbitrary tyrant who foreshadows Herod the Great when he hears that future kings are about to be born (Parkinson 1991: 54–56 and 1997: 102–27). The implication was that the previous regime had come to grief through moral deficiency. This was a mistake which its Theban successor had no intention of repeating.

The somber tone of some Middle-Kingdom literature is well captured in a remarkable dialogue between a man and his own soul, which is often known by its German byname, the *Lebensmüde*. The theme is about the futility of life, and the man contemplates suicide. The soul seeks to restrain him, with a variety of arguments, including a parable about a mother and her children who come to grief by a pool. The soul observes that life of a sort must be better than no life at all:

> I do not mourn for the mother, even though she has no way out of the West [the next world] to live on earth another time, but I think about her children, broken in the egg, who looked upon the face of the Crocodile [death] before they had lived.

The psychological content, and the imagery, of this remarkable work should earn it a place among modern audiences (Parkinson 1997: 151–65).

The Tale of Sinuhe is recognized as one of the most powerful works of this period. It resembles a short novella rather than a conventional tale, and it was admired, among others, by Rudyard Kipling. Sinuhe is a courtier who overhears a conspiracy against the crown prince, Sesostris I, while on an expedition against the Libyans. Fear of being implicated leads him into flight, and he finds himself among the Bedouin of Palestine. Eventually he finds a promised land, where he settles and raises a family. His life among the Asiatics is a success, and the portrayal of his foreign hosts is sympathetic. But he needs to be reconciled with his home and his king, and to be buried where he began. The tale is about fragmentation, and the necessity of being made whole again. It also makes the point that an alien life is possible, perhaps pleasurable, but it is not a complete one. Only Pharaoh can grant that (Parkinson 1997: 21–53).

A text found inscribed on coffins in the early part of the Middle Kingdom can stand as the epitome of one of the period's main themes, the question of moral responsibility:

> Words spoken by Him whose names are hidden. The Lord of the Universe says in the presence of those who still the tempest, at the time when the conclave sets sail, "Proceed in peace. I shall recall to you four good deeds that my heart devised when I was in the coils of the serpent, in order to overcome evil. I did four deeds within the portals of the horizon. I made the four winds, that every man might breathe, wherever he may be. That is one deed. I made the great inundation, that the bereft might share in it like the great. That is one deed. I made every man like his fellow; I did not command them to do evil, but it was their own hearts which overthrew what I devised. That is one deed. I made their hearts cease from ignoring the West, so that offerings might be made to the gods of the provinces. That too is one deed. I created the gods from my sweat, and men are the tears of my eye . . ."

This preoccupation with human worth surfaces in other works. In the Teaching for King Merikare, a king who is a source of expert advice about how to rule is also great enough to admit that offences had happened during his reign. The fact that this narrator is located safely in the past is important, because a ruling king would not have been free to confess in this way (Parkinson 1997: 211–34). A similar theme emerges from the Story of the Eloquent Peasant, in which the eponymous peasant suffers injustice at the hands of an unscrupulous official, but eventually, and after long examples of the eloquence that he possesses, gains the justice he has been denied (Parkinson 1997: 54–88).

The Middle Kingdom did not last for ever, as its founders had no doubt intended, but it is in many ways the classic age of ancient Egypt, and one to which later ages deferred and wished to return.

4   The New Kingdom (c.1550–1050 BC)

The New Kingdom is regularly referred to as Egypt's imperial age. It is debatable whether the term "empire" can be imported uncritically into the second millennium

BC, but the term has its uses all the same. The Egyptians of the Eighteenth Dynasty staged major campaigns into the Sudan and western Asia, exacted tribute, claimed the right to replace rulers with others of their own choosing, and, in the case of the Sudan, introduced colonies and state-of-the-art agriculture (W. Adams 1977; Kemp 1978). Several of the New Kingdom temple sites in the latter country are the equals of many in Egypt. In the Near East Egyptian aims were to control the coast and its ports, but Egyptian armies twice crossed the Euphrates in Syria to overawe the power of Mitanni, which lay beyond.

The impetus for this aggression came from the fact that Egypt had fallen under the control of a Near Eastern people known conventionally as the Hyksos. These were eventually driven from the country, again by princes from the city of Thebes, but the memory of this episode left its mark upon Egyptian strategy. The culmination of Egyptian military success came with the battle of Megiddo (c.1450 BC), won by Pharaoh Tuthmosis III against a formidable Syrian coalition. This is the first battle in history which can be reconstructed (Cline 2000: 15–24). The enemy, Mitanni, was later to fall victim to the Hittites, who were to prove far less amenable. Some of northern Syria was lost to the Hittites, and the two powers eventually met at Qadesh on the river Orontes (c.1275 BC), where the young and boastful Ramesses II came near to losing the day until he was saved by last-minute reinforcements from the coast (Murnane 1990).

One of the most striking personalities from the ancient world is Hatshepsut, kinswoman of Tuthmosis III who effectively seized the throne from him and held it for 22 years. On her obelisks at Karnak, the seat of the Theban god Amun who was the patron of empire, she records how the creator god made her privy to his secrets before the creation of the universe itself. Modesty was not an affectation to which Hatshepsut felt the need to succumb:

> Those who shall see my monument in future years, and shall speak of what I have done, beware lest you say, "I know not, I know not how this has been done, fashioning a mountain of gold like something self-created" . . . Nor shall he who hears this say it was a boast, but rather, "How like her this is, how worthy of her father."

In the eyes of history, Hatshepsut describes herself as "the fine gold of kings," and the very language of inscriptions was altered to reflect her gender (Bryan in I. Shaw 2000: 237–43; Ray 2001: 40–59).

The cult of Amun of Thebes attracted envy as well as adulation, and its older rival, the sun worship centered on Heliopolis, staged an increasing comeback. There are clear signs of this in the reign of Tuthmosis IV and his son Amenophis III (c.1390–1352 BC). This culminated in the remarkable reign of Akhenaten, in which the worship of Amun was first marginalized and then proscribed. Akhenaten's introduction of a sole creator god has been the subject of libraries of research since the 1880s, and this shows no signs of abating (bibliography in G. Martin 1991; comparative study by Montserrat 2000 and many others, including a good summary by van Dijk in I. Shaw 2000: 272–94). This religious revolution was mirrored in literature and art, and may have left traces in the Hebrew Psalm 104 (Lichtheim 1973–80 II:

96–100; Rodd 2001). A unique find from the new capital is the diplomatic archives, written in Babylonian cuneiform by the various rulers of cities which were loyal to Egypt, who were coming under attack for this loyalty (Moran 1992).

The revolution of Akhenaten was short lived, and the following two dynasties, the Nineteenth and Twentieth, are normally known as the Ramesside period (c.1295–1069 BC). For some reason, the bulk of papyri from the New Kingdom, both documentary and literary, date to this period. Egypt, like other Near Eastern states, needed to train scribes for its bureaucracy, and several collections of exercises survive showing pupils going through stages of their education and being corrected or reprimanded by teachers (Caminos 1954; Johnson 1994). One of the many distractions which pupils may have encountered is the existence of erotic and romantic poetry. Examples of this poetry, which was collected in ways that resemble a song cycle, are known, and the influence on the Biblical Song of Songs has often been noted (Fox 1985).

Literary tales abound from this period, many of which contain elements which surface in the folklore of other cultures, ancient and modern (Lichtheim 1973–80 II: 197–230). The influence of Syria and the Levant is noticeable, both in the geographical settings of many of the tales and in loanwords, which entered New Kingdom Egyptian in considerable quantities (Hoch 1994). The masterpiece of this collection is the Voyage of Wenamun, a text which begins like a documentary report on a mission to fetch cedar wood from Lebanon, but which rapidly turns into a set of maritime adventures which would not be out of place in Homer's *Odyssey* (Lichtheim 1973–80 II: 224–30). Here is the atmospheric way in which the hero first meets the ruler of Byblos:

> He took me up, while the [statue of] the god was resting in its tent by the shore of the sea. I found the ruler sitting in his upper room, with his back turned to a window, and the waves of the great Syrian sea were beating behind his head.

Then there is the reply of the same ruler to a monologue about civilization which Wenamun has given him as a substitute for ready cash (his own having been stolen):

> Amun thunders in the sky, but only when he has placed the storm god there beside him. And Amun created all the lands of the earth, but only after he had created the land of Egypt, where you came from the other day. And culture came from there to end up in the place where I am, and wisdom likewise. So why these pointless journeyings you are busy with?

Wenamun is a masterpiece of irony, suspenseful timing, and keen sense of place.

Official documents are more common from the New Kingdom than in previous periods. Tomb records are fuller, including legal texts such as the inscription of Mose (Gaballa 1977) and a series of didactic texts covering questions such as the ethics of political conduct (most recently Hagen 2005). The walls of colossal temples needed to be covered with inscriptions, although these are of varying degrees of historical value. A remarkable document from near the end of the New Kingdom is the Great

Papyrus Harris, which lists the achievements of Ramesses III and outlines the turbulent history which preceded him (Grandet 1994).

Probably the most informative site from ancient Egypt is the workman's village of Deir el Medineh, on the west bank at Thebes. This has yielded not only houses and furniture, but an entire archive covering work diaries, economic transactions, complaints about corruption, an account of a series of strikes and the official response to them, letters, literary tales, and a list of Pharaohs, unfortunately fragmentary, with the precise lengths of their reigns. A list of a rival workman's extramarital affairs survives, drawn up as part of a petition to the authorities. Work on this wealth of documents still continues (Černý 1973; McDowell 1990; Meskell 2002, and Janssen 1975).

5   The Late Period (664–330 BC)

In the Late Period the nature of our sources changes, and in some ways for the better. The usual sources of hieroglyphic inscriptions still exist, but they are supplemented by a large number of papyri and ostraka written in demotic, a shorthand form of the earlier hieratic script. The range of demotic texts is considerable (Depauw 1997), and there are many still awaiting publication in museums or as a result of excavation. Demotic originated in the Delta, but it spread south into Upper Egypt in the sixth century, and this is the part of the country where most texts survive. In addition, Greek sources start to appear, notably the detailed description found in Herodotus Book II (A. Lloyd 1975–88). Herodotus's account is so valuable that it is a matter of regret that nothing like it exists from earlier periods. Here, Egypt is being seen through the eyes of an intelligent outsider. Documentary and literary texts in Greek begin in the early fourth century, and increase sharply following the conquest by Alexander the Great in 332 BC. The account by the historian Manetho, which survives only in later summaries, is the basis of modern work on dynastic history, and for the Late Period it enables us to produce an absolute chronology where in earlier dynasties approximations are still needed (Waddell 1940).

The Late Period is often singled out as the time when mass immigration into Egypt altered the character of the country. It is true that inscriptions and papyri written in most of the languages of the Aegean and the Near East are found in later Egypt, but the New Kingdom is now recognized to have had a similar attraction to economic migrants, and the same may be true of earlier periods as well.

The principal dynasty of the period is the Twenty-sixth, founded by Psammetichus I in the years after 664 BC, following a long period of domination by the Napatans from the Sudan (Welsby 1996). The dynasty faced major powers on its northeastern frontier, first the Assyrians and later the Neo-Babylonians, and its foreign policy oscillated between defensive consolidation and sudden offensive campaigns inspired by changes of rulers. In 570 Pharaoh Apries was deposed in favor of Amasis, and a remarkable stele describes the events following this upheaval, including an opportunistic raid by the Babylonians (Leahy 1988; Lloyd in I. Shaw 2000: 369–94).

In 525 Egypt was incorporated into the Achaemenid empire. This brought technical improvements in agriculture, and also the use of Aramaic as a *lingua franca* (Grelot 1972), but the later decades of Persian rule were restless, leading to liberation in 404 (Ray 1987). One of the most informative texts of this or any period is the petition of Petiese (*P.Ryl.* IX), which is a rambling account of a feud over temple revenues which had lasted for generations and ruined a small town (Ray 2001: 101–12). It contains some cynical advice given to the narrator's ancestor:

> "There is nothing to be gained in going to the house of judgment. Your opponent in the case is richer than you. If there were a hundred pieces of silver in your hand, he would still defeat you." So they persuaded Petiese not to go to the house of judgment.

It also records the sort of distinctly provincial incident which other sources would rather we did not know:

> On the 13 Mekhir [10 June 512 BC], the festival of Shu, every one who was in Teudjoy was drinking beer, and the warders who were guarding us drank beer and fell asleep. Then Djebastefankh [the disgraced temple president] absconded. The warders awoke, but could not find him, and the warders who were guarding us also absconded.

The fourth century BC was haunted by the prospect that the Achaemenids would reinvade, and several attempts to do this needed to be repulsed. This is the period of the Demotic Chronicle, a historical survey which interprets oracles about kingship, and which connects a ruler's piety with the length of his reign (Johnson 1974). The quality put into comparatively mundane inscriptions can be gauged from the magnificently produced customs decree from Naukratis (text in Lichtheim 1973–80 III: 86–89; a submerged duplicate has now been excavated under the sea near Alexandria). A raid on the Phoenician coast in 361 led to the deposition of the ruler Teos and his replacement by his nephew Nectanebo II. There survives part of the autobiography of a doctor who accompanied the expedition, only to find himself falsely denounced by means of a forged letter (von Kaenel 1980). Nectanebo II was the last purely native Pharaoh, who was forced to flee the country in 343, but found a posthumous role in folklore as the tutor of Alexander, and even his father (Ray 2001: 117–29; for the last short-lived Persian reconquest in 343, see fig. 5.2).

The more detailed sources which survive from the Late Period allow us greater insight into the political structure of ancient Egypt. Pharaohs can be sidelined or deposed (a fact which we may suspect earlier but can rarely if ever document), and dynasties turn out to vary in their character. Dynasty XXIX (399–380) is revealed as a series of competing freedom fighters, with a perpetual eye on the threat from Persia, while the succeeding Dynasty XXX appears more as a military junta, keeping itself assiduously in power. God-kings the last Pharaohs may still have been, but their human frailties are more exposed to the gaze of the historian than their earlier counterparts.

FURTHER READING

The literature on ancient Egypt is seemingly limitless. For the history, a good up-to-date introduction is I. Shaw 2000. There is also the elegant general history in Grimal 1992. Drioton and Vandier 1962 contains detailed bibliographies which are still useful. Individual chapters in the second edition of the *Cambridge Ancient History* are also helpful, although the earlier ones are showing their age. A Blackwell *Companion to Ancient Egypt*, edited by Alan Lloyd, is forthcoming.

The topology and cultural background are the subject of Kees 1961 and Baines and Malek 2000. Egyptian prehistory, an area in which noticeable progress has recently been made, is the theme of Midant-Reynes 2000. The archaeological background to Egyptian civilization can be studied to advantage in Kemp 1989. The society which emerged at the beginning of the dynastic period is the subject of Wilkinson 1999. A sophisticated introduction to the problems of Egyptian history can be found in Trigger et al. 1983. Short biographies of some individual Egyptians are contained in Ray 2001. A good survey of the social make-up of ancient Egypt is Donadoni 1997. There is no self-contained history of the Old Kingdom, but one of the best contributions to the subject can be found in Roccati 1982. The Middle Kingdom is well served by Parkinson 1997 and Quirke 1991, and there is still much to be gained from Winlock 1947. The study by Posener 1957 remains one of the classics of Egyptology. One of the most stimulating recent works on Egyptian literature is Quirke 2004. For the New Kingdom there are the studies by Redford 1967 and Vandersleyen 1995, while military history is well summarized in Murnane 1990. The texts from the Amarna period are collected in Murnane 1995, while the most stimulating study of Akhenaten himself is probably Montserrat 2000. The Amarna letters from the various states of the Near East are translated with a full commentary in Moran 1992. One of the best studies of Egyptian imperialism is still Kemp 1978. The community at Deir el Medineh is the subject of McDowell 1990 and Meskell 2002. The indispensable introduction to the economic history of the period is Janssen 1975. The standard treatment of the later New Kingdom (also known as the Third Intermediate Period) is Kitchen 1995. Herodotus's account of Egypt is best studied with the aid of A. Lloyd 1975–88, and the Late Period is also the subject of James 1991 and A. Lloyd 1994. The Persian occupation is described in Ray 1987. The chronological survey by Kienitz 1953 is still valuable. For the Ptolemaic period, which is not covered in the present chapter, there is the excellent introduction by D. Thompson 2003, as well as Lloyd in I. Shaw 2000: 395–421. The Roman and Byzantine periods are impressively described in Bowman 1996. The conference volume Johnson 1992 is extremely useful for the later periods as a whole. Plutarch's account of Egyptian religion is discussed in Griffiths 1970, a book which is close to being an encyclopedia of the subject. Burkert 2004 is a remarkable study of the transmission of ideas in the ancient world, which reminds us that Egypt should not be taken in isolation. Ancient Egyptian medicine is explained in detail by Nunn 1996, and the most recent treatment of their mathematics is Imhausen 2003. The material culture is superbly outlined, by one of the best writers the subject has produced, in Hayes 1953–59. For Egyptian art, the comprehensive article by Bianchi et al. 1996 is invaluable. Nubia, an area of great importance to Egyptology, is the subject of Adams 1977 and Welsby 1996.

Anthologies of literature can be found in Lichtheim 1973–80 and Parkinson 1991 and 1997. Wisdom (or didactic) literature, a genre taken seriously throughout the ancient Near East, is the subject of Shupak 1993. The most authoritative treatment of ancient Egypt as a whole is the multi-volume *Lexikon der Ägyptologie* (Helck et al., 1975–92), although in such an all-embracing work the standard of individual entries is bound to vary. The same applies to Redford 2001, although this is more accessible. A more concise treatment can be found in Shaw and Nicholson 1995. A useful introduction to the Egyptian language can be found in Allen 2000, while the scope of the surviving Egyptian documentation is the subject of Sauneron et al. 1972. P. Wilson 2003 is a stimulating short guide to the hieroglyphic script, and Parkinson 1999 is a well-researched account of the Rosetta Stone and its decipherment. A view of the present state of research in Egyptology can be gained from Hawass 2002, which publishes the papers from an international conference held in Cairo at the turn of the millennium.

CHAPTER NINETEEN

The Jews

Gideon Bohak

1 A Question of Perspective

How do ancient Jews fit into the wider patterns of ancient history? The answer to this question depends on the perspective one adopts. On the one hand, one could describe the Jews as yet another minor oriental ethnic group, more significant perhaps than the Nabateans or Palmyreans, but certainly not as important or visible as the Egyptians, the Persians, or the Phoenicians. Unlike these nations, the Jews are totally absent from the pages of archaic and "classical" (fifth-century) Greek literature, and were first noticed by Greek writers around the time of Alexander's conquest of the East. Even in later periods, they never were deemed worthy of the extensive historical, geographical, ethnographical, or mythographical attention accorded their more powerful and exotic neighbors, and even the small independent kingdom they established for a short period from the mid-second century BC apparently failed to attract much outside attention. Like all other people around the Mediterranean, they too were conquered by the Romans, and although they staged two or three major revolts they never became registered in the Roman psyche as a real threat to Roman power, on a par with the Carthaginians and Germans, or even the Egyptians. Moreover, unlike some Greek-writing Orientals, who made at least some contributions to Greek literary life, Jews hardly figure in the annals of Greek literature, even though they produced numerous Greek-language texts. Even in the pages of the more technical, scientific, or philosophical literature, Jews hardly make an appearance, and this in spite of the numerous (real and imagined) oriental contributions to Greek and Roman geography, medicine, philosophy, astronomy, or astrology; only in late-antique Greek magical texts are Jewish elements more easily discernible. And when it comes to figurative art, architecture, or music, the Jewish contribution to ancient culture is simply non-existent. Even Jewish religion, which we see as entirely different from that of all other ethnic groups in the Greco-Roman world (monotheism as against polytheism) was not seen as such in antiquity, and mostly failed to arouse a great deal of interest.

Seen from this perspective, the Jews hardly merit a chapter of their own in a companion to ancient history.

But one could also adopt a very different perspective, and insist that in spite of their small numbers and provincial location, the Jews are a very special case in ancient history. First and foremost, one could note that while the Greeks were busy molding bronze statues and writing brilliant speeches, just as the Babylonians and Egyptians charted the heavenly orbits of stars and constellations and the Romans were conquering the world and imposing law and order, the Jews gave birth, almost incidentally, to a social and religious movement that conquered the Roman empire from within and entirely transformed European and world history (cf. Curran, THE EMERGENCE OF CHRISTIANITY). One could also argue that whereas the Nabateans and Palmyreans vanished long ago from the annals of history, the Jews are still with us, and that while the Egyptians and Phoenicians have changed both their language and their religion, and are now Arabic-speaking Muslims and Christians, and while the Greeks and the Romans still retain their ancient scripts and a shadow of a reflection of their ancient languages, but not their ancient religions or much of their ancient cultures, one can easily trace a tortuous but unbroken line of linguistic, religious, and cultural continuity from the Jews of antiquity to their modern heirs. Finally, and at the very least, one may note that the Jews are one of the better-documented nations of antiquity, and that in addition to what others said about them we know a great deal about what many Jews actually thought and wrote, as many of these writings were preserved through Christian and Jewish channels of textual transmission, while many others have been found by modern archaeologists. Thus, the Jews provide ancient historians with what is perhaps the best-documented example of the impact of Greco-Roman history and culture on one, albeit not necessarily typical, ethnic group. It is for these reasons that the present chapter will seek to provide both an outline of Jewish history and culture in the Greco-Roman world and an assessment of its wider significance – for ancient history, and for its modern viewers.

2   The Jews from Cyrus to Muhammad: a Very Brief Political History

Reading the historical accounts and myths penned by some ancient Jews, one becomes convinced that their finest hour had come and gone in the very distant past, when their god, the creator of the universe, changed many of the laws of nature on their behalf while leading them out of Egypt and into the promised land, and granting them his divine law on the way (see esp. Exodus 3–24). And it was only a few centuries later, under David and Solomon, that they acquired their greatest empire (see, e.g. 1 Kings 3:1; 5:1–14, etc.; 2 Chronicles 8–9, etc.). But this was long ago, and it had been mostly downhill ever since, the decline culminating in the Babylonian destruction of Jerusalem in 586 BC, the extirpation of the Davidic royal line, and the exile of much of the Jewish nobility, and numerous other Jews, to Babylon (2 Kings 25). From this time onwards, Jewish political history would depend not so much on what the Jews themselves did, but on what happened in the wider historical arena, and in such distant cities as Babylon, Susa, Pella, Rome and Medina.

The first major shift came with Cyrus's spectacular destruction of the Babylonian empire in 539 BC, and his dramatic reversal of older Babylonian policies. Those Jews who were exiled to the East were now allowed to return to Judaea, and some of them indeed seized the opportunity to do so; they also were granted permission to rebuild their temple in the same place it had once stood, and to reinstate their priestly caste (Ezra 1–3; 6:3–5; 2 Chronicles 36:22–23). For the next 200 years, the Jews paid their taxes to the Persian rulers and governed their internal affairs by means of their native priesthood, headed by a line of high priests. Then came Alexander the Great, whose lightning conquest of the East and untimely death ushered a long period of political instability, with the Jews' own homeland becoming one of the favorite battlegrounds between the Ptolemies, based in Alexandria, and the Antioch-based Seleukids. Throughout the third century Judaea remained under Ptolemaic rule, in spite of major Seleukid incursions, but in 200 BC Antiochos III the Great beat Ptolemy V at Panion, and the Jews of Judaea acquired a new master (Jos. *AJ* 12.129–46). As we shall see below, it is from about this period that the amount of evidence for the Jews' own views of things begins to rise exponentially, perhaps because for the first time these views became hotly contested among the Jews themselves. For the time being, we may note how, one generation later, Antiochos IV invaded Egypt and lay siege to Alexandria. Repelled by the threats of Roman envoys, he returned home and vented his anger on the Jews of Jerusalem (Daniel 11:30–31), who soon responded with open revolt (167 BC). Within another generation the Jews, led by the five sons of a provincial priest (the Maccabees, or Hasmonaeans), managed to establish their political independence (143/142 BC), which soon acquired many of the trappings of a minor Hellenistic kingdom, including territorial expansion, kingship, the minting of coins, and fierce dynastic warfare which reached its height in the mid-60s BC, and much facilitated the conquest of Jerusalem by Pompey in 63 BC (Jos. *BJ* 1.36–158; *AJ* 12.246–14.79). Judaea was now governed by Roman clients, first by Hasmonaean dynasts, then by King Herod, whose long reign (37–4 BC) was characterized by frantic building activities (including rebuilding the Jerusalem temple itself), economic development (including the construction of a new port-city, Caesarea Maritima), and endless struggles within the royal court, during which Herod eliminated most of his family members and potential rivals (Jos. *BJ* 1.282–673; *AJ* 14.381–17.199). Upon his death, he was replaced by one of his sons, Archelaos, but the Romans soon annexed Judaea and subjected it to direct Roman rule (AD 6). This ushered a period of ever-growing religious and social tensions – between the Jews and their non-Jewish neighbors, between Jews and Romans, and among the Jews themselves – which exploded in the great revolt of AD 66 (Jos. *BJ* 2.284–486). Successful at first, especially because the Romans had their own troubles to worry about (the year 69 saw four different emperors!), the revolt soon climaxed in the inevitable Roman victory and the complete destruction of Jerusalem and its temple (Jos. *BJ* 6.68–442, cf. fig. 28.1). Two generations later, another major revolt, led by the Messianic pretender Simon bar Kokhba, culminated in another major defeat (AD 135), bringing an end to the Jewish uprisings and ushering a long period of peace and prosperity for the Jews of Palestine (with few Jews now in Judaea proper). But with the Christianization of the empire, the growing Christian presence in Palestine, and, finally, the Muslim conquest, the Jewish population of Palestine suffered a blow from which it would not recover until the Zionist revolution.

In addition to the Jews of Judaea, any history of the Jews in antiquity must take into account the growing Jewish diaspora, which for many centuries existed side-by-side with the Jewish communities in the Jews' ancestral homeland. Going back perhaps to the Babylonian period, and certainly to the Persian and early Hellenistic periods, the Jewish communities in Alexandria, Egypt, Rome, Mesopotamia, and elsewhere saw extensive growth and prosperity throughout much of antiquity (Barclay 1996). Unfortunately, a history of these Jewish communities – with the possible exception of the Jews of Egypt – cannot be written, as the evidence for each of these communities often is quite scanty. In several cases, we hear of Jewish struggles for civic rights or civic equality with their non-Jewish neighbors, and we also hear of a Jewish revolt in AD 115–117, which seems to have been centered in Egypt and to have caused much damage to Jews and Egyptians alike (Mélèze Modrzejewski 1995). From the fourth or fifth century AD, the Jewish diaspora communities also had to contend with a growing Christian pressure, and with an increasingly hostile imperial legislation, both laying the foundations for the pariah status of the Jewish people in the Christian middle ages (Linder 1987; Millar 1992 and 2004). Yet what is perhaps most striking about the Jewish diaspora is the ability, and even the desire, of many Jews to retain their unique ethnic and religious identity even in faraway lands.

Many of the Jews who left Palestine – as war-captives and slaves or of their own free will – probably assimilated into the non-Jewish society within which they settled so that their descendants were no longer Jewish. But some Jews apparently insisted upon, and sometimes even succeeded in, transmitting their Jewish identity to their children, and this at a time when there were no external pressures that served to isolate the Jews from non-Jewish society and force them to huddle together. Thus, whereas forced and voluntary migrations were a constant feature of the ancient world, the development of elaborate mechanisms which enabled the migrants to retain their separate identity after they gave up their ancestral homeland and even their ancestral language, was far from common (Bohak 2002b). It is for this reason that the Jewish diaspora gradually evolved into a loose network of local Jewish communities, a structure quite unparalleled by those created by other migrants in the Hellenistic or Roman periods.

3   The Jews from Ezra to the Talmud: a Cultural and Religious History

Looking at the Jews of Judaea in the Persian period, we find a small ethnic group which hardly was noticed by any of its near or distant neighbors, but which already shows some signs of its future uniqueness. First and foremost, we must note the existence in Jewish hands of a body of ancient texts which was slowly coalescing into what we now know as the Hebrew Bible, and which provided its readers and users with an ethnic history, a body of religious and secular law, an endless string of prophetic exhortations to piety and justice, and an assorted range of poetic and literary masterpieces. No other people in antiquity possessed such a corpus of texts which were sacred, binding upon the entire nation, and universally accessible. Moreover, unlike all other ancient peoples, who had many gods and temples, the Jews insisted that there was only one God and that he should – in theory at least – have only one temple. These two features assured the Jews a strong sense of ethnic and religious identity and a high degree of social cohesiveness, invisible but potent forces which would help shape their future history (Bohak 1999).

The first major test came with the arrival of Greek kings, and Greek culture, after Alexander. This spelled a period of "Hellenization" – namely, the extensive exposure to at least some aspects of Greek culture, a culture with its own sense of superiority and with much to show for it. As a case in point, we may note the descriptions, written by supporters of the victorious Hasmonaeans, of how Jerusalem of the 170s AD saw the building of a Greek gymnasium with the Jewish priests leaving their temple duties and flocking to watch the competitions (1 Macc. 1:14; cf. 2 Macc. 4:9, 12–15). And yet, while the Hasmonaeans presented their own struggle as aimed not only against the Seleukid empire but also against the abominable Jewish "Hellenizers," the same Hasmonaeans soon adopted many elements of the Greek culture which flourished all around them. The issue, for them as for the Jews of subsequent generations, was not whether Jews should "Hellenize" or not, but whether one could adopt some features of Hellenistic culture while avoiding others, and whether one could "Judaize" the adopted elements by adapting them into cultural frameworks which were, or could be conceived as, intrinsically "Jewish" (Levine 1998). Looking at Hasmonaean coins, for example, we see how the rulers of the independent Jewish kingdom readily adopted the standard Hellenistic practice of minting coins – not doing so would have been like trying to keep a whole country disconnected from the Internet in the early twenty-first century – but also set their own limits on the images these coins might carry. Human figures clearly were out of the question – in spite of the all too human temptation of any king to see his face in his subjects' wallets – and animal figures were equally offensive, while plants, such as a palm tree or a lily, were deemed entirely acceptable. These specifically Jewish sensitivities stemmed from a strict interpretation of the Second Commandment (Exodus 20:4–6 = Deut. 5:8–10: "You shall make for yourself no idol or any image . . ."), which generated a great aversion to all types of iconography (Meshorer 1997).

But the encounter with "Hellenism," important as it surely was, was only one force shaping the development of Jewish culture at the time. Another, and no less important, was the desire, of at least some Jews, to abide by the ancestral laws spelled out in their holy books (what the rabbis would call *halakha*, the Hebrew equivalent of the Greek *agôgê*, a people's way of life and modes of conduct), and the difficulty of doing so. Most of all, it was the different views of what exactly should go on in and around their one and only temple which brought division among the Jews, and this division grew exponentially once the Jews, under the Hasmonaeans, were fully in charge of the Jerusalem Temple and priesthood. This, and the Hasmonaean need to legitimize their own rule – including their control of the high priesthood, to which they were not originally entitled – and to compromise with reality (e.g. by conducting wars even on Sabbath days, or hiring "pagan" mercenaries, like all other Hellenistic rulers) or change it (e.g. by forcing some of the non-Jews in their newly acquired territories to convert to the Jewish laws), soon led to ideological–religious divisions and to civil war. As Josephus, our main source for the period, would have it, there arose at about this time three Jewish "sects," or schools – Sadducees, Pharisees, and Essenes – which differed greatly on issues of faith and ideology (Jos. *BJ* 2.119–166; *AJ* 18.11–22). Judging from the Dead Sea Scrolls, which probably were written by the Essenes or a sub-sect thereof, issues of religious behavior, and especially those centered on the calendar and the temple cult, loomed large in the mind of some of these sectarians (A. Baumgarten 1997). Moreover, even as the temple was still standing, synagogues were beginning to emerge in different communities – first in the diaspora, then in Palestine itself, and even in Jerusalem – in which Jews could gather on the Sabbath, read their holy books and worship their God without any resort to a temple sacrifice (Levine 2000). These new modes of worship, which were based in part on non-Jewish models but infused much specifically Jewish content into them, were to have a major impact not only on the future of post-temple Judaism, but on that of Christianity (and, later, Islam) as well.

Looking at the many products of the Jewish cultural activity of the Second Temple period (from 540 BC to AD 70 or 135) which have come down to us, we may note both some glaring lacunae and some areas of prodigious productivity. On the one hand, we may note that plastic art, for example, clearly was abhorred by most Jews at the time, as may be judged not only from Josephus's reports of the Jews who were willing to die rather than see any image in Jerusalem (e.g. *AJ* 17.149–63), but also from the above-mentioned Hasmonaean coins or the imageless mosaics excavated in some of the richest neighborhoods of pre-destruction Jerusalem (Avigad 1983). On the other hand, we may examine the long list of texts written by Jews at the time – in Hebrew, Aramaic, and Greek – and admire the wide range of genres and interests they display. Here we find wisdom literature, apocalyptic visions, historical writings, philosophical diatribes, poetry of different types and varied qualities, novelistic tales, biblical exegesis and the retellings of biblical stories, *halakhic* discussions, and many other types of written texts (but not, for example, works of science), a sure testimony of the enormous vitality of the Jewish scribal, literary and religious tradition at the time (Nickelsburg 1981; Collins 1983; Charlesworth 1983–85; Vermes 2004). The Jews' logocentric productivity may also be discerned in such enormous undertakings as the translation of the Hebrew Bible and related texts into Greek – first the Pentateuch (in the third century BC), then many other books (in the second and first centuries BC, and perhaps even later) – by far the largest translation project ever attempted in pre-Christian antiquity. We may also note that much of this religious and cultural activity had strong sociological implications, be it in the unifying effect of the Greek translation of the Bible, around which Greek-speaking Jews could structure their own brand of Judaism, or in the deleterious effect of Jewish apocalyptic speculations, which were a major factor in the outbreak of the calamitous Jewish revolts. And it was in the context of Jewish eschatological calculations and messianic expectations that a new, and originally minor, Jewish group broke away from the bonds of Jewish *halakha*, began missionizing among non-Jews, and established a new religion that would soon transform world history as a whole.

The destruction of Jerusalem and its temple, and the subsequent failure of Bar Kokhba's revolt two generations later, brought about some major changes in the development of Jewish culture. With apocalypticism and Messianism no longer in vogue, and debates about how to run the temple no longer relevant, the rabbis – who were the intellectual descendants of the Pharisees, and the group best equipped to survive in a world without the Jewish temple and its elaborate cultic mechanisms – developed a new agenda for Jewish religion and culture. It too was based on *halakha*, but tended to offer new interpretations of the biblical laws, and even replacements thereof, embedded in a new *halakhic* code, the Mishnah. And it offered a value system which prized the study and teaching of Torah more than any other activity, and thus discouraged many of the literary activities so favored by earlier generations of Jews. On the other hand, it proved far more lenient, for example, in its attitude to plastic art, even developing such ideas as the possibility of "nullifying" an "idolatrous" statue and turning it into a non-religious, and quite inoffensive, statue (Mishnah, *Avoda Zara* 4.4–6). The rabbis could even speculate, quite anachronistically, about the coins supposedly minted by such Jewish ancestors as Abraham and Joshua, including coins with human and animal figures upon them, in marked contrast with the coins actually minted by Jews during the Hasmonaean period or the two revolts (Bohak 2002a). It is with this in mind that we may examine the spectacular floor mosaics of late antique synagogues, so different from the mosaics of pre-destruction Jerusalem and so exuberant in their iconography. The synagogue mosaics, with such images as Helios on his chariot at the center of the zodiac circle, have been interpreted by some scholars as evidence of their Jewish owners' lack of interest in what the rabbis had to say (Schwartz 2002), but in fact are not far removed from what we find in rabbinic literature itself. Moreover, when in one synagogue mosaic (at Sepphoris, in the Lower Galilee) we find not Helios, but a solar disc riding his chariot at the center of the zodiac circle (Z. Weiss 2005), we know that for some late-antique Jews Helios was an acceptable symbol in their holiest religious structure, while others thought that human figures, and even the zodiac, were quite acceptable, but the "pagan" sun-god was beyond the pale (fig. 19.1). The question of which images were permitted and which were not clearly did not receive a uniform answer in all the Jewish communities of late antiquity, and even in rabbinic literature we find more than one attitude towards figurative art and its religious implications (J. Baumgarten 1999). But while the question of how much influence the rabbis had on late antique Jewish society is likely to remain a matter of some debate (a debate which is greatly shaped by the current turmoil within the Jewish world, and the search for religious, ethnic, or cultural axes upon which to reconstruct a modern Jewish identity), there is little doubt that they gave birth to that form of Judaism which reigned supreme in the Jewish world up to the late eighteenth century, and is still considered binding by many Jews today.

19.1 The zodiac circle, with a solar disc riding in Helios's chariot. The inscriptions in Hebrew identify the months, zodiac signs, and seasons, and those in Greek identify the seasons and commemorate the mosaic's donors. From a late-antique synagogue in Sepphoris, in the Lower Galilee. (Courtesy of the Sepphoris Expedition, the Hebrew University of Jerusalem. Photo: G. Laron)

4 Jews and Non-Jews: Jewish and Non-Jewish Perspectives

Looking at the contacts between Jews and non-Jews in antiquity, we find the same asymmetry which tends to characterize the relations of small elitist groups with their surrounding society. From the Jewish perspective, the idea (so elaborately developed in the Hebrew Bible) that the Jews were God's chosen people meant that all the "Gentiles" (a Jewish term, borrowed by Christianity and therefore well known to modern readers) were basically the same, and characterized especially by not having any covenantal relations with God, and not even recognizing his supremacy over their "idols." With such a self-centered perspective so deeply ingrained into the Jewish psyche, it hardly is surprising that ancient Jews showed little interest in the different ethnic or religious groups among whom they lived. They did, of course, develop detailed discourses of what contacts one might or might not have with non-Jews – guidelines which differed greatly from one Jewish group to the next and from one period to another – and they also developed mechanisms for the conversion of non-Jews into Jews, either by force (in the Hasmonaean period) or voluntarily (S. Cohen 1999). Beyond this, however, they showed little interest in the "Gentile" world, and no penchant for geography, ethnography, or the study of foreign religions (see e.g. S. Stern 1994).

While the Jews were quite convinced of their own uniqueness and importance – the rabbis, for example, had no doubt that the entire world and the whole of humanity were created only so that the Jews could study their Torah – from the Greek and Roman perspectives things looked quite different. Although the Greeks had their own "us"/"not us" dichotomy, they did display quite an interest in "barbarians" (that is, non-Greeks) from a relatively early date in their cultural development, with special emphasis on the highly developed nations to their east. From this perspective, however, it was especially the Persians, the Egyptians, and the Phoenicians who loomed large as ancient nations with numerous cultural achievements and equally numerous vile ethnic characteristics. The Jews came to be noticed by Greek observers only from the mid-fourth century BC onwards, and even then they received relatively little attention (M. Stern 1976–84). Their land was there for all to visit, but Egypt, or the cities of Asia Minor, had far more attractions to offer to the curious tourist. Their sacred writings, and numerous other Jewish texts, were available in Greek for all to read, but few non-Jews bothered to make the effort, and those who did apparently were not impressed by what they found there (only from the late second century AD, and in response to the Christian challenge, did "pagan" intellectuals begin to read the Bible). And while the existence of an extensive Jewish diaspora made the encounter between Jews and non-Jews a daily affair in many parts of the ancient world, it seems that Jews were deemed to have little to offer to the aristocrats and intellectuals who wrote much of Greek and Latin literature. Even what we might see as the Jews' most conspicuous characteristic – their monotheism – was mostly lost on their non-Jewish observers. From the perspective of the "polytheists" – who did not even know that this is what they were (the word was coined by Philo Judaeus in the first century AD, and was popularized only by the Church Fathers) – the fact that the Jews believed in only one god and refused to worship all the others was, at best, a sign of their obstinate nature; as far as the Greeks could tell, such insistence was not even unique to the Jews (see e.g. Hdt. 4.94). Thus, one could speculate over the identity of the Jewish god, known in Greek as Iaô, and argue whether this was the Jews' special name for Zeus, for Ouranos, or maybe even for Dionysos (Bohak 2000). One could also wonder why the Jews insisted that no images should be made of this god, but even here there was nothing unique, for aniconic cults were far from unusual in antiquity. The Jews' own convictions notwithstanding, few non-Jews in antiquity found them worthy of special attention, and even when these non-Jews told good or bad things about the Jews, both types of discourse paled in comparison with what they had to say about some of the Jews' closest, and much more prominent, neighbors (Isaac 2004).

5   Begging to Differ: the Mechanics of Ethnic Survival

Perhaps the most interesting question to be asked in a survey of the Jews' place in ancient history is how the Jews managed to retain their ancestral cultural and ethnic identity in the millennium separating Alexander the Great from the Muslim conquests, a timeframe which saw most ancient ethnic groups either vanish off the face of the earth or entirely transformed. To fully understand the import of this question, we may note that whereas in the middle ages there was much external pressure on the Jewish communities of medieval Christendom and Islam – in the form of anti-Semitism, ghettoization, special identity markers, and numerous social restrictions – throughout antiquity there were very few such pressures, and the road was wide open for those Jews who wanted to mingle in non-Jewish society and give up their ancestral commitments and ethnic identity to do so. Moreover, the road was wide open for the entire Jewish people to adopt new ways of life, new modes of thought, and new religious beliefs, as they repeatedly did. It is the ability of many generations of Jews to undergo substantial historical and cultural changes without being entirely transformed into oblivion which makes ancient Jewish history so worthy of a closer look.

To see how the Jews managed to survive, we may examine both the cultural and the social mechanisms which enabled, or facilitated, this process. It must be stressed, however, that ancient Jews did not set out to beat some world record of ethnic survival; their own assumption was that they must adhere to God's commandments until he sends his redeemer to change history for ever; had they known that two thousand years later their descendants would still be around with the redeemer nowhere in sight, they would have been quite shocked and extremely displeased. But it is a habit of teleological religious systems, as of all other ideological movements which influence people's behaviors through the conceptual frameworks they provide and the promises they make, to achieve great things they never aimed for while failing to fulfill their most basic promises, and Judaism – ancient or modern – is no exception. Long-term ethnic survival, at a time when other ethnic groups gradually vanished into oblivion, certainly was an unintended by-product of the actions taken by many individual Jews over the centuries in their efforts to abide by what they interpreted as their ancestral religious duties, and in the hope of gaining collective and individual salvation.

Among the many mechanisms which abetted the Jews' survival, we may note especially the presence of the Hebrew Bible, and of its Greek translation(s), as providing those Jews who wanted it with an axis around which to build their lives. The interpretation of the biblical laws was a much contested affair throughout ancient Jewish history, but while the meaning of specific biblical injunctions varied greatly over time (witness the changing interpretations of the Second Commandment), the very commitment to these laws, and the debates about their meanings, often encouraged the creation of Jewish "sects," but also enabled many Jews to develop new ways of being Jewish and passing their Judaism to their descendants. We may also note that the Jews' ancestral writings provided them not only with blueprints for life, but also with a map of their own history, distinct from that of all the peoples around them, and that the Jewish synagogues, which clearly served as the places where Jews could read their ancient texts together – in the original, or in a Greek translation – and pray together, were a major facilitator of inner-Jewish social cohesion.

As a second factor, we may stress the Jews' belief in a single god, and the conviction of quite a few Jews that the gods worshiped all around them were nothing but useless "idols," as a major factor contributing to setting the Jews apart from their neighbors and preventing their gradual assimilation into their "pagan" environment. It was especially the notion of a wide gulf separating those who had a covenant with God from those who did not that repeatedly enabled ancient Jews to borrow from their non-Jewish neighbors those cultural elements which they found useful or appealing, censor out those which they found offensive, and embed those they were borrowing in a new, and specifically Jewish, cultural framework. Finally, we must note that while the rise of Christianity, and then Islam, spelled the ruin of all other religions of antiquity, Judaism survived – in part because both Christians and Muslims refused to forcibly convert the Jews as they did the "pagans," in part because the Jews had ready-made answers to the challenges raised by two religions which were quite like their own in so many ways.

While noting the Jews' survival and analyzing its causes, we should not forget the price they paid for this unintended success. The thousand years between Alexander and Muhammad apparently saw no major growth, and perhaps even much decline, in the number of Jews in the world, a sure result of the unwillingness of many Jews to remain loyal to the ancestral covenant and avoid assimilation into the majority culture (one must stress, however, that we lack reliable data on the size of the Jewish population in antiquity – see McGing 2002). The same period also saw only one major Jewish contribution to world history, which happened to be the one they disliked the most, and the fulfillment of none of the promises they found in their sacred books. And while in the time of Alexander they were mostly living on their own land, recollecting their glorious past and hopeful of a glorious future, the Muslim conquest found them dispersed in many lands but never really at home, still recollecting their glorious past but facing a very uncertain future. Always begging to differ, and always convinced of their own superiority, Jews learned to suffer the consequences, and while in antiquity their haughty exclusivity was mostly ignored by their non-Jewish neighbors, in Christian and Muslim environments it often earned them the ire of their intolerant hosts, who were convinced that it was to them that God revealed his truest revelation, which superseded his revelation to the Jews. Survive the Jews certainly did, but theirs was a very precarious existence.

6   Conclusion

As noted throughout the present chapter, it is far from easy to fit ancient Jews into the wider patterns of ancient history. A narrow synchronic perspective might lead to the conclusion that the Jews were quite insignificant in the Greco-Roman world, while a diachronic perspective might make us overemphasize their significance as the odd men out in every empire in which they lived. In either case, however, we must marvel at the manners by which so many ancient Jewish texts have come down to us, and learn to utilize this evidence not only in the study of ancient Jews, but of ancient history as a whole. The Jews may not be the most typical ethnic group in the Greco-Roman world, but it often is the less typical examples which teach us most about the contours and significance of long stretches of human history.

FURTHER READING

All the major textual sources pertaining to the study of ancient Jews – Josephus, Philo, the Hebrew Bible and the New Testament, the Apocrypha and Pseudepigrapha, the Dead Sea Scrolls, and rabbinic literature – are readily available in English translations. As for contemporary scholarship, the study of ancient Jews is booming, and there is a bewildering assortment of English-language surveys of different aspects of ancient Jewish history and culture. Newcomers to Jewish studies would benefit from consulting Goodman 2002 for a broad overview of this vibrant field. Among the many surveys of Jewish history in the Second Temple period, Schürer 1973–87 is the most authoritative, but also the least accessible to the non-specialist, who would be better served by Schiffman 1991 or Schäfer 1995. Those in search of a good overview of Jewish religion and culture at the time will find much in Sanders 1992, Grabbe 2000, S. Cohen 2006 and Goodman 2007. The period from the destruction of the Jerusalem temple to the Muslim conquest is far less covered, partly because it is of less interest to Christian scholars in search of the "historical context" of early Christianity, partly because rabbinic literature – which is our main source for the study of this period – is much less amenable to historical inquiries. For a useful survey of rabbinic literature, see Stemberger 1996. For a broad survey of rabbinic thought, Urbach 1975 remains fundamental. The Jewish encounter with Hellenism is well covered by Levine 1998 (but for rabbinic Hellenism Lieberman 1942 and 1950 remain essential), and everything written by Greek and Roman authors about ancient Jews is found in M. Stern 1976–84. For more optimistic accounts of Jewish/non-Jewish relations, see Feldman 1993 and Gruen 2002.

CHAPTER TWENTY

The Greeks

Thomas Harrison

1 Being Greek

What is it about the Greeks – their culture and their history – that is distinct? This simple question, needless to say, can be approached in any number of ways and yields almost any number of answers. It could be approached, for example, through an analysis of the Greeks' own views of what it was to be Greek, of their identity – or of others' views of *them*. Alternatively one could examine what the Greeks have meant to subsequent generations, in particular to the modern world, and how modern versions of the Greeks have merged ancient reality and modern experience (how the debate on the Athenian empire, say, is informed by modern debates on the "balance sheet" of the British empire, or how new discussions of Hellenistic history reflect a focus on modern multiculturalism). Finally, one could attempt to examine the Greeks dispassionately in comparative perspective, and to ask again what characteristics in their culture, self-definition or history may distinguish them usefully from others. Of course, no dispassionate claims are possible: we cannot perhaps *avoid* – at least without conveying an unduly pallid picture – creating a mythology of Greek uniqueness, or fail to invoke (no matter in how nuanced a form) some version of the "Greek miracle." In the case of each of these approaches, we need to acknowledge the existence of (even if we cannot here describe) myriad different perspectives, ancient and modern. In what follows, all these approaches will be adopted, at least passingly; the chronological focus will be mainly on the classical period, though with nods both forward and back.

Greekness, like any other form of identity, is inherently unstable. The most famous statement of what it is to be Greek – the Athenians' statement in Herodotus's *Histories* of their reasons for not going over to the Persian side – may appear to be clear-cut evidence for a list of criteria for Greek identity:

> You [Spartans] should have known that there isn't enough gold on earth, or any land of such outstanding beauty and fertility, that we would accept it in return for

collaborating with the enemy and enslaving Greece. Even if we were inclined to do so, there are plenty of important obstacles in the way. First and foremost, there is the burning and destruction of the statues and homes of our gods; rather than entering into a treaty with the perpetrator of these deeds, we are duty bound to do our utmost to avenge them. Then again, there is the fact that we are all Greeks – one race speaking one language, with temples to the gods and religious rites in common, and with a common way of life. It would not be good for Athens to betray all this shared heritage. (Hdt. 8.144, tr. R. Waterfield)

The context of the passage undercuts the Athenians' "patriotic" fervor, however. Not only must we acknowledge the rhetorical purpose of the passage (Herring, ETHNICITY AND CULTURE, section 2), but also that – only shortly afterwards – Spartan dilatoriness provokes the Athenians to do precisely what they swore they would never do: contemplate, if not consummate, a reluctant alliance with the Persians (9.6). Even if the Greeks do eventually muster themselves to defeat the Persian invasion of Greece, moreover, Herodotus's account scarcely presents a united Greek front. Certainly there is a contrast between the free fighters of the Greeks and the Persians' subjects working unwillingly for a tyrannical master (esp. those Greeks in the King's service). But, as Thucydides also realized (Thuc. 1.69.5), Greek victory was in large part the result of Persian mistakes (and their refusal to resort to underhand tactics such as bribery: T. Harrison 2002a: 569 on Hdt. 9.2). The fleeting unity that results in the Greek victory at Salamis is the result, on the other hand, of Greek deceit: Themistokles' encouragement to the King to block his allies' route of escape from the straits at Salamis (8.75.2–3).

Even if, then, we agree with the approximate modern consensus that a sense of common Greekness was finally forged by the experience of the Persian wars, Herodotus's *statement* of this common feeling coincides with the fragmentation of this common Greekness. (Arguably such statements of common identity are characteristically made when that identity is most under threat, just as flag waving today might be interpreted as "protesting too much".) This is true in two senses, both of the Greek world of his *Histories* and of his own day. Herodotus's account was written half a century after the Persian wars under the shadow of the conflict of Athens and Sparta, a rivalry whose origins he chooses to highlight throughout his work (Fornara 1971, Moles 1996, Stadter 1996). The fifth century BC also saw the extensive appropriation (or indeed construction) of "Greek" values by the Athenians – so that any version of what holds them together would inevitably have been subject to contestation (Mills 1997, T. Harrison 2000a: 58–65).

Each of the aspects of Herodotus's statement of Greek identity also deserves our scrutiny. First, his definition of Greekness in terms of common blood (or descent) is far from unproblematic. This statement might be put together with others in fifth-century texts to suggest a "genetic" distinction between Greeks and non-Greeks (or "barbarians" as they were often termed), for example the statements in Euripidean tragedy that to be a barbarian is a matter of birth (*genos*, but see Saïd 1984, E. Hall 1989) or the "environmental determinism" of the Hippocratic *Airs Waters Places* (but see Thomas 2000 chap. 3). It should be stressed at the outset that we need to draw a firm distinction between imagined kinship or "subjective ethnicity" on the one hand, and reality or "objective ethnicity" on the other. The *Airs, Waters, Places* aside, moreover, the Greek world presents little evidence of scientific or pseudo-scientific theorizing on biological differences, and scarce evidence at best for a focus on color (Snowden 1983; cf. Isaac 2004).

Once you start the game of tracing ancestors, things also quickly get very complicated. If one were to take at face value Greek myths of origins, one would suppose that Greek culture was to a significant extent an amalgam of foreign influences. One need not subscribe to the literalist readings of such myths by Martin Bernal in his *Black Athena* to take seriously such myths as myths (E. Hall 1996 on Bernal and myth). Heroic ancestries mark out the identities of individual aristocratic families, of clans (or phratries, lit. brotherhoods) or of particular cities or peoples within the Greek world (J. Hall 1997). The boundaries between Greek and non-Greek are notably fluid. Just as foreign peoples are ascribed conveniently named ancestors (Perses, the father of Perseus – the ancestor of the Persians, for example), suggesting a form of appropriation of the foreign land in question, conversely some Greek cities have non-Greek ancestors (so, for example, Kadmos and Danaos – founders of Thebes and Argos respectively). The even more creative articulation of kinship relations between cities in the Hellenistic world, most famously the Trojan origins of the city of Rome, stretches any conception of distinct Greek and other identities even further (Erskine 2001, C. Jones 1999). The articulation of distinct "intra-Hellenic" identities is frequently also competitive. The Greeks are made up of more than one *ethnos* (so, the Aeolians, Dorians, Ionians), each with a related dialect. In the context of the Athenians' fifth-century empire, the Athenians' Ionian ancestry not only connected them to many of their imperial subjects (arguably providing a fig-leaf of justification) but also distinguished them from their Peloponnesian rivals (Thuc. 1.95). The Athenians' claim of authochthony (i.e. that they were indigenous, or that they were born from the earth of Attica) implies the opposite of their fellow-Greeks, indeed that the Athenians were in a significant sense – one borne out by their other characteristics – more Greek than others (Mills 1997: chap. 2). The situation is further muddled by the (distinctly confused and confusing) Greek idea of the pre-Greek inhabitants of Greece, the Pelasgians (Sourvinou-Inwood 2003).

Similar difficulties affect Herodotus's (and the Greeks') distinction of Greekness in terms of language. The Greeks spoke and wrote in a number of dialects: Doric, Ionic, Attic, Aeolic. The distinction between a dialect and a language has been seen in modern scholarship (and in modern experience, most recently in the development of distinct languages in former Yugoslavia) to be a largely arbitrary one, contingent on broader political factors (Morpurgo Davies 1987); a dialect, moreover, is generally recognized to be a dialect *of a language* and yet – though the abstract notion of a single Greek language existed in Greek thought (not least reflected at Hdt. 8.144) – until the development of the Hellenistic *Koinê* or common language, no such language existed.

When we turn to the *Greek* differentiation of Greek from non-Greek language there are further complications. Foreign languages, or at least foreign speech, are often characterized in terms that implicitly contrast them with what is Greek and good: as incomprehensible (Thuc. 3.94.5), verbose and lacking in content (Simonides 653 *PMG*, or the Phrygian in Eur. *Orestes;* cf. Pind. *Ol.* 2.86f., Anacreon 403 *PMG*, Simonides 600 *PMG*), resembling a variety of birds and other animals (Aesch. *Ag.* 1050–52, Hdt. 4.183, Soph. *Trach.* 1060, *Ant.* 1002, Eur. *Bacchae* 1034–35, Aristoph. *Av.* 199–200, *Ran.* 679–82, *Pax* 681), as being anonymous (i.e. having no personal names, Hdt 4.184), somehow innately unfree (Soph. *Trach.* 62–63), or as being indistinct from one another but constituting a single barbarian language (Soph. *Aj.* 1262–63; cf. terms *barbaristi*, Aristoph. fr. 81 *PCG*, *barbarikos*, Xen. *Anab.* 1.8.1, "the *phone* of the barbarians," Pl. *Tht.* 163b). But, as ever, these stark polarities crumble on closer examination. It is on the grounds, presumably, of incomprehensibility that Greek dialects can be termed barbarian (Pl. *Prt.* 341c) or that a man can be said to have lapsed into "sub-barbarian speech" (Pl. *Lysis* 223a, the translation of Halliwell 1990: 70). The notion that language or manner of speech reflects natural characteristics can be seen at a local as well as "national" level, for example in the idea that freedom of speech (*parrhesia*) is innate to Athenians (Eur. *Ion* 670–75; cf. Eur. *Hippolytus* 421–3, Hdt. 6.138). The idea of a single barbarian language in opposition to Greek coincides with a more common cliché of barbarians as an untidy horde made up of countless different peoples and languages (Hom. *Il.* 2.803–4, 4.436–38, Aesch. *Pers.* 399–407, Polyb. 1.67.3, 23.13). Some Greek writers, moreover, recognized that the language one spoke was a matter of *nomos* rather than *physis*, nurture rather than nature: if a Greek infant were to be deposited in Persia he would speak Persian (and vice versa), according to the author of the *Dissoi Logoi*. In a significant passage (that will be discussed further below) Herodotus shows himself aware that the Egyptians displayed a linguistic ethnocentrism very similar to the Greeks, calling "barbarians" all who spoke a language different from their own (Hdt. 2.158).

Herodotus's distinction of Greek and foreign religion is interesting, firstly, because that is not what it is. The emphasis is on common shrines and common cults; there is no distinct notion of Greek as opposed to foreign "religion" (Gould 1994). Nor indeed is there a clear distinction of Greek and foreign gods. Herodotus and other Greek authors conceived of the gods (with some exceptions: those associated with barbaric rituals tend to be termed local, e.g. Hdt 4.93–94) as universal, bearing different names and having different cult features with different peoples (Parker 1996, Rudhardt 1992). In Herodotus's own account, the origins of many of the gods (or of their names – there are different interpretations of what is meant by the "name of a god") can be traced back to different foreign countries: some gods were native to the pre-Greek inhabitants of Greece, the Pelasgians; Poseidon on the other hand came from Libya, and a large number of other gods from Egypt. It is unlikely that this understanding would often, or ever, have revealed itself in cult observance of foreign deities (unless they had been formally integrated into the cult system of one's own city), so we should not get too excited about this possible evidence of tolerance in religion (T. Harrison 2000b: chap. 8). Just because you should not actually mock foreign cults (Hdt. 3.38) does not mean you should be any less firmly or exclusively devoted to your own cults. At the same time, however, any notion of a firm boundary in religious terms between what is Greek and what is not cannot really be sustained. Greek cult is pre-eminently articulated at local (i.e. *polis*) level (Sourvinou-Inwood 1990). There were shrines, such as Delphi or Olympia, which were common to all Greek *poleis* (and in the case of Delphi also to non-Greeks). Clearly also there is a level at which Athena, say, is Athena regardless of her cult epithet or the cult that she received in any locality. Nevertheless Greek particularism in this area is extraordinarily resilient; one often gets the impression that a "local manifestation" of a divinity is almost a distinct divinity. When sixth-century Greeks were allowed to settle at the Egyptian trading-post of Naukratis, it is characteristic that – while other cities founded a shrine, the Hellenion, in common – the Aiginetans, Samians, and Milesians founded their own temples, of Zeus, Hera and Apollo respectively (Hdt. 2.178).

By the time that we reach Herodotus's (or Herodotus's Athenians') final criterion of Greekness, it is clear that any firm definition will elude us: a "common way of life" (or customs of the same sort) is a kind of catch-all for all the other things that Greeks have in common ("aggregative identity," in the modern term) and which non-Greeks, or barbarians, incidentally do not share. Though Herodotus gives no details in this context, we might (on the basis of other passages of his *Histories* and other authors) think, for example, of the Greeks' freedom (by contrast with non-Greeks' submission to tyranny), their manliness (as opposed to the effeminacy of eastern Barbarians), and so on, all aspects that have been well emphasized in the modern literature on the Greek "othering" of Barbarians (esp. E. Hall 1989, T. Harrison 2002b).

2 Greeks and Foreigners

Greek representations of foreign peoples tend to emphasize the polarities between themselves and others, but it is important to emphasize that there are a number of overlapping models for understanding the relationship of Greek and foreign identities which cannot always be reconciled into a single consistent pattern. Alongside the neat polarities of the Nile and Danube rivers and the way Greek and Egyptian customs mirror each other (Hdt. 2.33–35), Greece (or particular localities: Ionia or Athens) can be represented in terms of climate as the center of the whole inhabited earth (Hdt. 1.142, Xen. *Poroi* 1.6); the further one goes north or south, the more extreme and inhospitable the conditions. As we have seen in the context of the names of the gods, there is also a powerful model of diffusion at work: everything must have had its origin somewhere, someone must have been the first inventor of any custom, and so one can trace the route by which pederasty, say, was acquired by the Persians or Poseidon by the Greeks. The tag of being open to foreign customs – applied typically to two imperial peoples, the Persians and Athenians – is at least ambivalent in the weight given to it ([Xen]. *Ath. Pol.* 2.8, Thuc. 2.38, Hdt. 1.135). At the same time, in some cases we can suspect a sneaky sense of cultural superiority beneath the pattern of diffusion: it is at least a happy accident that in Herodotus's own day the Greeks possess the names of more gods even than the Egyptians. Here and in a few other instances we can also see rare glimpses of a developmental schema at work, the idea for example that barbarians represent an earlier stage of development (see esp. Thuc. 1.6; cf. Hdt. 1.56–58 on Pelasgians).

All these models for the explanation of difference can also collapse and reveal that they are underpinned by universal (Greek?) rules. Accounts of the different sacrificial or divinatory customs of x or y people all take for granted common assumptions: that sacrifice or divination are conceived of in fundamentally similar ways. Darius's famous demonstration of the diametrically opposed customs for the disposal of the dead of Greeks and Indians – often represented as a soft statement of cultural relativism – in fact illustrates a universal principle (Hdt. 3.38; cf. 7.136): that custom is king of all, and that anyone who dares mock another's custom is mad (as the bad end of the Persian king Cambyses then demonstrates). Similarly, if the Scythian climate is the reverse of all other countries, with rain and thunder so rare in winter that they are counted as marvels when they occur (Hdt. 4.28), the underlying explanatory framework – that reversals of what can normally be expected in a particular location count as marvels, *terata* – is a universal one that can be applied to any context.

At the same time, as has been much emphasized in recent scholarship, polarities between Greeks and others can also be undermined and problematized. A number of authors blur the lines between Greek and barbarian – this can be seen, for example, in Euripides' questioning of whether Greek behavior is in fact barbaric (Said 1984), or Herodotus's insinuation that the Athenians have taken on the imperial mantle of the Persians (Moles 1996). Foreign peoples can be characterized as providing a tidy analogue to Greek experience: so, for example, the Scythians are figured in their nomadism as foreshadowing the Athenian evacuation of Attica in the Persian Wars (Hartog 1988), the Persian expedition to Greece as a parallel to the Athenian expedition to Sicily (Rood 1999). Surprising questions are also asked about the nature of identity itself, over what are the crucial markers of identity, for example, or whether a people can determine their own identity at all: so, for example, Herodotus's account of two communities on the border of Egypt and Libya, determined (because of their desire to eat beef) to be Libyans, but who are told in forthright terms that they have no say in the matter (Hdt. 2.18; cf. 2.30). Herodotus's report of Egyptian linguistic ethnocentrism (2.158), while it may also be accurate (cf. the Greek graffiti at Abu Simbel: ML 6), might be interpreted as undermining Greek ethnocentrism, as showing a degree of sophisticated, self-conscious concern over the kinds of distinctions between Greeks and barbarians found elsewhere in his work. Like the "justification" for racism that other peoples are racist too, at another level it could also enable and "justify" Greek ethnocentrism (Redfield 1985).

At this point, it is perhaps necessary to throw some cold water over this kaleidoscopic analysis of Greek perceptions of their own identity *vis-à-vis* others. We need first to understand how perceptions of what divides the Greeks and others culturally change over time. If the opposition Greek–barbarian was only really brought into sharp focus in the aftermath or at the time of the Persian wars, it also took on a very different significance over time: the fourth century sees both Xenophon's elevation of the barbarian Persian Cyrus into a model of just kingship (albeit Cyrus was a high point from which the Persian monarchy declined steeply) and Isocrates' rousing of Panhellenic feeling for a crusade of vengeance for the Persian wars. The Hellenistic period, with its creation of Greek elites in the successor kingdoms of Egypt and the Near East reconfigured the boundaries of "Greek" identity yet further. To describe the character of Greek identity then by assigning places in a seemingly timeless hierarchy to the various criteria for identity ultimately appears as an artificial, even a sterile, exercise. Though, despite the evidence we have seen, Greeks did not theorize or agonize over their identity as we do, it is perhaps no less true of them than of us that it is the character of their *confusion* over who they were that distinguished them rather than any shopping list of distinct characteristics that they liked to see as their own.

3   Greeks and the Greek World

It is also crucial to see the various articulations of Greek identity in the context of "actual" historical conditions. It is crucial in particular to examine issues of identity in the context of the political fragmentation and the wide geographical scattering of what we may call loosely the "Greek world." This world encompassed much more than the modern European state of Greece: the cities of the Black Sea, of the Ionian coast, Libya, southern Italy (or Magna Graecia) and Sicily, as well as Cyprus. A recent attempt to calculate the number of Greeks living at any time in the classical period suggests that as many as 40 percent of the 7.5 million estimated lived outside what we would suppose to be the Greek "mainland" (Hansen 2006b). It was not only in "colonial" Greece – the applicability of the term "colony" to the Greek context has been challenged (Osborne 1998) – that Greeks lived cheek-by-jowl with non-Greeks. Non-Greeks were omnipresent in the heart of Greek cities such as Athens – if not as metics (resident foreigners, a category that includes other Greeks), then as slaves. The contribution of slaves – some of them, presumably, well assimilated in some sense to "Greek" society – was not confined to domestic service, mining, agriculture and other characteristic slave occupations. Slaves could be bankers or estate managers, they acted as an embryonic police force for Athens, and even took part – albeit unheralded – in the most emblematic victories of the Persian wars (P. Hunt 1998). Evidence of the borrowing or adaptation of artifacts from Persia suggests that – in parallel to the "othering" of Eastern peoples (contrast M. Miller 1997: 1) – such artifacts could become the emblems of an elite self-fashioning within the Greek world. This appropriation of Eastern artifacts is just one aspect of a confident curiosity towards the outside world, but one which was at the same time very clearly bounded – both by the Greeks' overwhelming monolingualism and by the powerful tendency to fit experiences into preconceived molds, to travel to discover what they already knew.

   Until the Hellenistic period and the formation of the Aitolian and Achaean leagues, moves towards federalism, still less anything resembling "Greek unity," were rare, and usually veils for the domination of one partner (Perlman 1976, Walbank 1951): so, for example, the fourth-century League of Corinth was a mechanism for Macedonian control, and the so-called "Delian League" of the fifth century for Athenian dominance over the Aegean. Though modern focus tends to be on the Greeks' (or usually just the Athenians') invention of democracy (cf. Fleming 2004),

Greek cities manifested a whole range of forms of government, from democracies with more or less limited franchises to more or less constitutionally bounded monarchies or tyrannies (Brock and Hodkinson 2000, Walbank 1984). Since innovation was often masked, even imagined, in terms of a return to an ancestral and therefore authoritative constitution, it is likely that we even underestimate in some instances the vibrancy of Greek political culture. Greek identity is likely to have been configured very differently depending on the particular political context. This is a point brought into even sharper relief over the larger geographical distances of the Hellenistic period. How are we to understand assertions of Greek culture at Ai Khanum, at the furthest end of the far-flung Seleukid empire in what is now Afghanistan, or dreams of Arcadian landscapes, such as Theocritus's *Idylls* generated in Ptolemaic Alexandria?

Against the background of this multiple fragmentation of the Greek world, and given that Greek identity was formed in such a substantially different context (notably in the absence of the nation-state, racial theory, or modern communications) the articulation of such a clear common identity by the Greeks might be thought remarkable. It is tempting to imagine that such a common identity was forged *in despite of* the Greeks' powerful particularism – as if Greekness could only be measured on a single scale. The example of the panhellenic festivals, however, suggests that the development of a common identity took place *in equal step* to that of local identities. Competitiveness whether between or within cities is arguably one of the Greeks' most sharply distinct cultural features. The circulation of coins, with legends operating as shorthand symbols of the city in question, suggests the existence of a common medium for the negotiation of distinct identities (Rutter 2000, J. Skinner forthcoming). The experience of being a Greek in the furthest extreme of the "diaspora," for example the Black Sea region, may not only, as has been argued, have focused their mind on political organization in a way that fed back to the mainland, but also have sharpened their sense of common belonging by contrast to their non-Greek neighbors (cf. Erskine 2005).

4 Our Greeks

Finally, though we should not desist from the pursuit of the historical Greeks, it is to a significant extent true that the Greeks are what we ourselves – and previous generations of scholars and students – have made of them, and that just as previous generations' versions of the Greeks may look bizarrely and transparently of their age to us, so ours will do likewise to future generations of ancient historians.

For us, as for previous generations, Greek identity is formed by analogy to the nation state, so that (at least since the nineteenth century) "fringe" regions of the Greek world, such as southern Italy, Sicily or the Black Sea, too easily drop from our attention. Analogy with the Cold War, together with the attraction of a simple binary plot derived from Thucydides, arguably encouraged a disproportionate concentration on the rivalry of Athens and Sparta and their respective power blocks (though it is worth remembering that this also forms a significant subplot of Herodotus's version of archaic Greek history). It is no coincidence that the emphasis on ethnic identity (and its fragmentation) and on the construction of the Other has largely arisen since the breakdown of Cold War certainties and the identification/creation of other external threats (cf. Herring, ETHNICITY AND CULTURE, section 1). The emphasis in the latter half of the twentieth century on excavating women's lives was, in some cases explicitly, linked to contemporary feminist movements (cf. Richlin, WRITING WOMEN INTO HISTORY); recent work on the "oriental" seclusion of Greek women or on the constructed nature of gender and sexuality again reflects modern concerns (Llewellyn-Jones 2003, Golden and Toohey 2004).

The Greeks have also been – and arguably indeed continue to be – exemplary in any number of areas: in providing privileged models for art, architecture and literature (or more recently for sexual liberation), or as an archetype of a superior rationality of which "we" are inheritors. Increasingly there has been a discomfort about any such essentialist claims, and the "Greek miracle" has instead become articulated in more specific or nuanced terms: of the unique experience of the face-to-face community (so a common emphasis on the questioning nature of Greek tragedy), the quality of the literature that Greek society gave rise to, or by emphasizing the Greeks' *having been seen* to be exemplary, the importance of the classical tradition, without ever quite seeming to identify with those claims of exemplariness ourselves. Needless to say, like the custom of one British national newspaper of publishing salacious "royal stories" only in so far as they are media stories, this is to have one's cake and eat it. We do not know how to sell the Greeks.

FURTHER READING

For a single-volume introduction to Greek history and society (representing the Greek world as "an astonishing culture but no Utopia"), see Morris and Powell 2006; excellent introductions to the different periods of Greek history can be found in series published by Blackwell (J. M. Hall on the archaic period, P. J. Rhodes on classical, Errington on Hellenistic), Fontana (Murray, J. K. Davies, and Walbank respectively on archaic, classical and Hellenistic history) and Routledge (Osborne on archaic history, Shipley on Hellenistic). A compelling (and condensed) account of Greek political and social organization can be found in Hansen 2006b. Note also the substantial collections of essays, Kinzl 2006 (Classical Greece) and Erskine 2003 (Hellenistic).

For the theme of Greek identity (by contrast to foreigners) see the important work of Edith Hall 1989 on Greek tragedy or Jonathan Hall's *Hellenicity. Between Ethnicity and Culture* (2002); for a selection of recent work, see T. Harrison 2002b. The collection of O. Murray and S. Price, *The Greek City* (1990), contains stimulating discussions of a number of aspects of Greek society.

CHAPTER TWENTY-ONE

Asia Minor

Peter Thonemann

1 This Side of the River Halys

"Croesus was Lydian by descent, the son of Alyattes, and lord of the peoples on this side of the river Halys." So begins the main narrative of the *Histories* of Herodotus, native of Halikarnassos on the Aegean coast. Looking east across the vast expanse of Achaemenid Asia, Herodotus saw the river Halys, the ancient limit of Croesus's kingdom, as the geographical marker which divided the lands to the east into "Upper" and "Lower" Asia. "The Halys," he writes, "was once the boundary between the empires of the Medes and the Lydians . . . this river cuts off almost all of Lower Asia, from the sea facing Cyprus to the Euxine ocean, and forms a kind of isthmus for the whole peninsula" (1.72).

Herodotus's conception of Asia Minor ("Lower Asia"), as a peninsula connected to the main Asiatic land-mass by a narrow isthmus, is geographically questionable to say the least. But the idea of a "Halys frontier," an imaginary line running from the gulf of Issos in the south to Sinope in the north, was a durable one. The lands west of this line, roughly corresponding to the western half of modern Turkey, were regularly conceived by both Greeks and Romans as a separate (and separable) part of the greater Asiatic land-mass. In the 340s BC, Isocrates urged Philip II of Macedon, if he could not conquer the whole of Asia, at least "to tear off a vast stretch of land and occupy Asia, to use the current phrase, 'from Kilikia to Sinope' " (Isoc. *Phil.* 120). It was not until 1923 that Greece finally gave up her ancient claim to "our own piece of the East."

The Asia Minor peninsula, the land west of the Halys river, is dominated by two great mountain ranges, the Pontic Alps to the north, and the Tauros to the south. In the south, the Tauros mountain-chain runs from Karia and Lykia in the west, far into Armenia in the east. The south coast of Asia Minor is correspondingly rough and inaccessible from the land. At only two points does the mountain draw back from the shore to produce broad and fertile coastal plains: in Pamphylia, around the

4 Asia Minor

modern harbor-city of Antalya (ancient Attaleia), and in eastern or "smooth" Kilikia (Casabonne 2004: 31–36). Between these two low-lying plains rises the most formidable stretch of the Tauros range, ancient Isauria and "rough" Kilikia. The fastnesses of Isauria were never truly integrated into either the Hellenistic kingdoms or the Roman empire: "for their district, though in the midst of lands belonging to the Romans, is encircled by a rare manner of defense, like a frontier fortification; it is protected not by men, but by the landscape" (SHA *Tyr. Trig.* 26.6; Lenski 1999). The Tauros barrier effectively cuts off Asia Minor from the rest of the ancient Near East, Mesopotamia, and the Levant. In the third century BC, the Seleukid monarchs, looking north-west from the heart of their kingdom in central Mesopotamia, conceptualized their territorial possessions in Asia Minor as those "on the far side of the Tauros" (Ma 1999: 123–30; Giovannini 1982).

In the north, the great ridge of the Pontic Alps marks an even sharper ecological boundary. Routes across the mountains were few. East of Sinope, only a single major road connected central Anatolia with the Black Sea littoral, following the lower reaches of the Iris river between Amaseia (Amasya) and Amisos (Samsun). It was the wealth of the mountains, above all in metals and timber, which supported the prosperous trading cities of coastal Bithynia, Paphlagonia, and Pontos (Robert 1980: 1–150). The region of Kytoros in coastal Paphlagonia was famous for its boxwood (Verg., *Georg.* 2.437), and the hinterland of Sinope provided timber especially suitable for shipbuilding (Bryer and Winfield 1985: 1–16; Marek 2003: 160–73).

Between these two mountain ranges stretch the vast, monotonous plains of Galatia, Lykaonia, and Kappodokia (Mitchell 1993: I. 143–47). The western part of the Anatolian plateau was known in antiquity as the *Axylon*, the "treeless country." In the absence of wood, building materials and fuel have to be sought elsewhere: houses are built of *kerpiç*, dried bricks of clay and straw, and today, as in antiquity, the visitor to smaller villages in summer is greeted with the tart smell of drying animal dung (*tezek*), which serves as the main combustible fuel in winter (Robert 1980: 257–307; Robert 1990: 19–38). The economy of the steppe depended on large-scale stock rearing. Galatian and Paphlagonian fullers and traders in coarse wool were a common sight in late-antique Constantinople and Odessos (*BE* 1962: 214; *BE* 1966: 99), and a lavish sarcophagus from Ikonion declares itself to be the tomb of a *gausaparios*, a maker of woolen frieze (*AE* 2003: 1720).

To the west, between the Galatian steppe and the Aegean valleys, lie the rolling highlands of Phrygia, eastern Lydia and Mysia. The Anatolian mid-west was a land of villages, with a mixed economy of agriculture and animal husbandry. Thanks to an extraordinary abundance of epigraphical evidence, mostly of the Roman imperial period, we are probably better informed about rural life in the Phrygian highlands than for any other part of the ancient world (Mitchell 1993: I. 143–97; II. 122–50). Perhaps the most remarkable single body of material consists of several hundred small stone dedications to Zeus Alsenos and Zeus Petarenos from a peasants' sanctuary near Amorion in central Phrygia. Here, in the vicinity of the great marble quarries at Dokimeion, small marble off-cuts were unusually cheap and easily available. These tiny *stelae*, dating to the late second century AD, were dedicated by marginally literate shepherds and oxherds, people who usually leave no trace in the historical record. Many of the votives carry images of the shepherds themselves and their wives, sometimes of entire families, clad in thick sheepskin capes of the kind still worn in the Anatolian highlands (Drew-Bear et al. 1999).

The westernmost part of the peninsula is defined by the valleys of four great rivers, running down from the Phrygian hills into the Aegean sea: the Maeander, Cayster, Hermos, and Kaïkos. These alluvial valleys, the heartland of the Lydian kingdom of Croesus, were the richest part of Asia Minor, densely populated and blessed with a pleasant and equable climate. To quote Menekrates, a farmer of the middle Hermos valley near Sardis: "I had the good fortune to place my livelihood in my crops, and I loved to break up the clods of earth for the grain-bearing shoots; nor did my hands rest from their labor, until the day's warmth departed from the sun's setting rays; and with the joy of Demeter, I took delight in guiding the plough" (Merkelbach and Stauber 1998: 484–85). By contrast, the Aegean coast itself, ancient Ionia, is relatively poor in natural resources. The delta-plains of the west-Asiatic rivers, although potentially highly fertile, were in their natural state marshy and insalubrious; some time in the Hellenistic period, the entire city of Myus had to be abandoned when its harbor degenerated into a malarial swamp (Mackil 2004: 494–97). The prosperity of many of the coastal cities – Miletos, Ephesos, Smyrna – was based not so much on their natural resources as on their geographical position. With the great river-valleys at their back, face to the ocean, these were the gateways which connected the deep Anatolian peninsula to the wider Mediterranean world.

2 Hellenism and the Development of the Cities

In the Anatolian Iron Age – the period between the fall of the Hittite kingdom in the twelfth century BC and the fourth century conquests of Alexander – the Asia Minor peninsula was home to a bewildering variety of peoples, distinct from one another in language and culture. "In time, almost all the people on this side of the river Halys had been conquered, and with the exception of the Kilikians and Lykians, Croesus held all the others under his sway. They are the following: Lydians, Phrygians, Mysians, Mariandynoi, Chalybes, Paphlagonians, Thynian and Bithynian Thracians, Karians, Ionians, Dorians, Aeolians, and Pamphylians" (Hdt. 1.28). The dominant population-groups of the west and south-west, Lydians, Lykians, and Karians, seem on the basis of their linguistic affiliations to be descendants of the Luwian Bronze Age population of western Anatolia (Melchert 2003; Benda-Weber 2005: 15–34); the most important of the peoples of central and northern Asia Minor, the Phrygians, probably arrived in Anatolia only in the late second millennium BC (Brixhe 1997). Greek settlement in Asia Minor was still largely confined to the Aegean seaboard, as it had been since the first Mycenaean colonists settled permanently at Miletos in the fourteenth century BC (Niemeier and Niemeier 1997). In the eighth and seventh centuries, Ionian colonization had extended this narrow fringe northwards along the shores of the Propontis and the Black Sea, but a fringe it remained; not a single Greek settlement in Asia Minor before the mid-third century BC lay out of sight of the sea.

Greek influence in south-western Asia Minor increased steadily in the fifth and fourth centuries BC. In Karia, the satrapal dynasty of the Hekatomnids (c.392–326 BC) engaged in a deliberate program of Hellenization, rapidly transforming the urban fabric of coastal and inland Karia beyond recognition (fig. 21.1; Hornblower 1980); by the late fourth century, even isolated inland communities such as Amyzon on Mt Latmos were at least as Greek as they were Karian (Robert and Robert 1983: 97–118). In Lykia, by contrast, Greek culture seems to have developed largely as an affectation of the native ruling class. The ostentatious Hellenism of the Lykian elite is well illustrated by the Nereid monument from Xanthos in the British Museum (c.380 BC), the visual counterpart of the wordy and execrable Greek verse in which the dynasts of Xanthos celebrated their various military exploits (Rhodes and Osborne 2003: no. 13); what we lack is any sign of the sort of profound linguistic, institutional and architectural transformation which was under way in Karia at the time.

When Alexander crossed to Asia Minor in 334 BC, the greater part of inland Anatolia was still largely untouched by Greek influence. Neither Alexander nor his immediate successors showed any inclination to change this. Beyond the Greek

21.1   Alinda in Karia. Part of the fourth-century Hekatomnid fortifications (McNicoll 1997: 26–31). (Photo: author)

coastal strip, vast tracts of land, along with their indigenous populations, were parceled out as the private estates of royal "friends" and relatives (Chandezon 2003); but the sort of intense Greco-Macedonian immigration and urbanization which characterized early Hellenistic Syria, Mesopotamia, or Baktria is here entirely absent.

Circumstances were soon to force a change in royal policy. In the winter of 278/277 BC, a vast confederation of Celtic tribes, migrating south-eastwards from their traditional homelands in the upper Danube region, crossed the Hellespont into northern Asia Minor. The ultimate cause of this migration remains unknown, but it is clear that the Galatians were aiming to lay down permanent roots in new territory, by force if necessary (Darbyshire et al. 2000). After a profitable decade ravaging the fertile lowlands of western Asia Minor, the Galatians finally settled on the fringe of the Anatolian plateau north-west of Ankara, a thinly populated region henceforth known as Galatia (Mitchell 1993: I. 13–58). Raiding bands continued to cause trouble in western Asia Minor down to the mid-second century BC, a convenience for the Attalid dynasty of Pergamon, successors to the Seleukids in western Asia Minor, who could thereby periodically claim to be the champions of Hellenism in the East against the barbarian, much as the Athenians had done in the fifth century and Alexander in the fourth (Strobel 1994).

The Seleukid king Antiochos I claimed the credit for driving the Galatians from the western part of the peninsula in the early 260s BC. It seems to have been as a consequence of the Galatian invasion that Antiochos I and his successor Antiochos II established an ambitious chain of forts and military colonies in inland Asia Minor along the "Southern Highway," the main strategic and commercial land route linking the Aegean to the Anatolian hinterland (Magie 1950: 40). It was these new Seleukid settlements, although founded for practical rather than cultural purposes, which served as the avatars of Hellenism in inland Anatolia (G. Cohen 1995: 15–71).

A glimpse into the life of the Anatolian countryside at the time of Antiochos's Galatian war, shortly before the beginning of this process of urbanization, is provided by a remarkable inscription from southern Phrygia, dated to January 267 BC, set up by the inhabitants of two otherwise unknown villages, Neoteichos and Kiddioukome:

> In the reign of Antiochos and Seleukos, in the 45th year [of the Seleukid era], in the month Peritios, when Helenos was overseer of the district. It was resolved by the Neo-teicheitai and the Kiddiokomitai, in full assembly: since Banabelos, manager of the estates of Achaios, and Lachares son of Papos, financial administrator of the estates of Achaios, have shown themselves to be the villages' benefactors in all things, and have given assistance both publicly and privately to each individual during the Galatian war, and when many of them were taken hostage by the Galatians, they reported this to Achaios, and ransomed them; (it was resolved to) praise them and write up their benefaction on a stone stele and place it in the sanctuary of Zeus in Babakome and in the sanctuary of Apollo in Kiddoukome; to grant a seat of honor at the public festivals to them and their descendants in perpetuity, and also to sacrifice an ox every year in the temple of Zeus to Achaios, master of the district and savior, and two rams to our benefactors Lachares and Banabelos, and also three sheep in the sanctuary of Apollo in Kiddioukome, so that others too may know that the Neoteicheitai and the Kiddiokomitai know how to repay honors to those from whom they have benefited. (Wörrle 1975)

The inscription was discovered near the site of the later Seleukid colony of Laodikeia on the Lykos, founded by Antiochos II in the early 250s BC. Before this date, this part of the Southern Highway "corridor" appears to have formed part of the private estate of a Seleukid dignitary by the name of Achaios (Strabo 13.4.2). Achaios himself is a shadowy figure in this text; the individuals with whom the local villagers had regular dealings were his estate-managers, Banabelos and Lachares. These officials are honored for their assistance during the Galatian war, in which the Celts had taken hostage a number of the local peasantry. What is most remarkable about this text is the distance which the villagers of this part of the Phrygian coun-tryside have traveled towards Hellenism, even *before* the first major phase of Seleukid urbanization in this region. The villages have an assembly (*ekklesia*), a procedure for honoring benefactors, public festivals and Hellenic or Hellenizing cults – not to mention the wherewithal to set up a long honorific inscription in perfectly fluent *koine* Greek.

It is unlikely that the Hellenization of inland Asia Minor was a deliberate act of royal policy. The case of Pisidia is revealing. This mountainous district in the western Tauros, difficult of access and warlike by reputation, was more or less untouched by Seleukid military colonization: it is significant that the most important Seleukid city foundation in the region was known as Antioch *by* Pisidia, not *in* Pisidia (as Alexandria was Alexandria *by* Egypt). Nevertheless, in the course of the Hellenistic period the native cities of central and southern Pisidia underwent a total transformation in their language, political system, and public architecture. At the city of Sagalassos, unmistakably "barbarian" at the time of Alexander's conquest (Arr. *Anab*. 1.28), extensive olive cultivation began in the fourth or early third century BC; it is very tempting to see this agricultural change as reflecting the city's aspirations to "Greekness," since Greek gymnastic culture required a regular supply of olive oil (Mitchell 2005: 92–93). By the mid-first century BC, Sagalassos was equipped with an elegant marble *bouleuterion* (council house), of exactly the same design and proportions as that constructed at the Ionian city of Priene a century earlier (Waelkens 2002: 313–21). Pisidia appears to have undergone a process of "auto-Hellenization," a wholesale aspirational adoption of Greco-Macedonian cultural artifacts, comparable to that seen in Karia and Lykia in the fifth and fourth centuries BC.

The Hellenization of the Anatolian interior in the three centuries after Alexander's conquest was uneven and largely undirected. In south and south-western Asia Minor, the region most exposed to contacts with the wider Mediterranean world, the acculturation of Karia, Lykia, and Pisidia continued along lines familiar from the fifth and fourth centuries. The inland regions most directly touched by the Macedonian presence, such as the military corridor between Kilikia and the lower Maeander valley, underwent a more rapid transformation, here assisted by the presence of large numbers of Greek-speaking military settlers. But the greater part of inland Anatolia – rural Lydia, Phrygia, Mysia, Lykaonia, and Galatia – remained profoundly unaffected by Macedonian rule. An inscription from the territory of Anazarbos in eastern Kilikia, dating to 110 AD, illustrates the point. "In the year 129, in the month Dystros, the throne was dedicated to the God Kronos by the association of Athenodoros son of Wanawarbasis, grandson of Ereus and Aroeraknas: Julius son of Artabanas, Athenodoros son of Megistanos, Wambaissasis son of Tarkondimotos, Motadas son of Wanawarbasis, Julius son of Liabeitis, Phandedis son of Liwasis, Antonius son of Ginatis, Antonius son of Antonius, also called Koulis, Julius son of Tarkondimotos" (Ehling et al. 2004: 244). The name Athenodoros aside, the personal names are all either native Kilikian or Roman. To all appearances, rural Kilikia had missed out on the process of Hellenization altogether; the first foreign cultural influence to impose itself firmly on the Kilikian countryside was that of the Roman empire.

3 Civic Life and Civic Identity under the Roman Empire

The explosion of public building in the cities of Asia Minor in the first and, above all, the second centuries AD is visible almost anywhere you look. The tourist industry of modern Turkey has reason to be grateful to the Romanized civic elites of the early and high empire, who spared no expense in the attempt to make their cities look and feel as Roman as possible. However, the dazzling urban façade of the cities ought to be understood as only one element in a wider pattern of elite self-representation. Along with flashy marble piles of sometimes questionable usefulness, the local equestrian and senatorial class were expected to fund the establishment of lavish festivals (Rogers 1991), the minting of civic bronze coinages (P. Weiss 2005), and straightforward handouts of grain or cash; in return, the cities voted them brash honorific statues (R. Smith 1998), often paid for by the benefactor himself. That these various items of elite expenditure were all regarded as parts of a single process is suggested by a famous inscription of the early second century BC, in which the great benefactor C. Julius Demosthenes of Oinoanda in northern Lykia describes his benefactions to the city as follows:

> Since I have loved my dearest homeland since earliest youth, and have not only maintained but thoroughly surpassed the generosity of my ancestors towards it, in the annual subsidies which I made to ensure fair prices in the market and in providing a boundless supply of [. . .] to the magistrates, and since I have constructed a food market with three stoas facing it, two with one and one with two storeys, and have spent more than 15,000 denarii on this and the purchase of houses which were removed to make way for this building, and since I wish additionally to leave behind for my homeland, in like manner with these buildings, a permanent capital fund, I publicly promise the foundation of a theatrical festival to be called the Demostheneia, which will be celebrated after three-year intervals just as the other quadrennial festivals are celebrated. (Wörrle 1988; Mitchell 1990, with English translation)

For Demosthenes, the construction of a market hall and stoas and the establishment of a capital fund to pay for a quadrennial festival evidently came to more or less the same thing: both were part of making one's native "city" worthy of the name.

The growing pains of urbanization are well illustrated by the development of the city of Aizanoi in north-west Phrygia in the first two centuries AD (Rheidt 1999). Aizanoi lay on one of the major trade routes across western Anatolia, running northeast from Sardis towards Kotiaion and Dorylaion in northern Phrygia. It also boasted proximity to a major Phrygian cult center, the cave of Meter Steunenos, in a rocky outcrop some distance from the center of the pre-Roman settlement of Aizanoi. No pre-Roman monumental architecture is known, and Hellenistic Aizanoi seems to have been little more than a busy roadside village. Two stages of urbanization at Aizanoi can be discerned (fig. 21.2). The first century AD saw a feverish program of public building, beginning with a temple of Artemis and the emperors, probably constructed under Claudius, on the east bank of the Penkalas river, and culminating with the great temple of Zeus on the west bank (Fig 21.3), with a grid plan orientated around it. This period saw a violent break with Aizanoi's Phrygian past; the town's physical fabric was transformed beyond all recognition, and the civic space was articulated entirely around new, Roman (or at least heavily Romanized) cults.

In the latter half of the second century, however, things get more complicated. The central part of the city was laid out on a new grid-plan on a different axis,

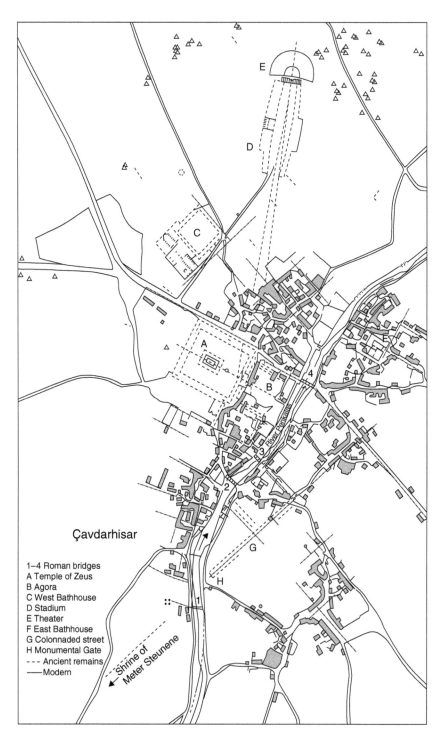

21.2 The urban center of Aizanoi and the modern village of Çavdarhisar. Note the two different axes around which the Roman city was laid out: that of the temple of Zeus (A) and the eastern bathhouse (F), and that of the colonnaded street (G) and the western bathhouse (C). Adapted from Rheidt 1997: 486. (By permission of K. Rheidt)

21.3 The temple of Zeus at Aizanoi. (Photo: author)

orientated around a great processional way on the east bank of the Penkalas, pointing directly towards the cave of Meter Steunene, two and a half kilometers south-west of the city. This second phase of Aizanoi's development under Roman rule seems to be driven by a desire to reintegrate the old indigenous cult of Meter Steunene into the religious identity and physical structure of the city. The tension between the two aspects of the cultural identity of Aizanoi, Phrygian, and Greco-Roman, was graphically represented on Aizanetic bronze coins of the late second century AD, depicting the birth of Zeus, the patron deity of Roman Aizanoi, to Rhea, identified with the Phrygian Meter Steunene (Robert 1987: 241–70).

This change in the cultural orientation of Aizanoi needs to be put in the context of a more general shift in the self-perception of the cities of Asia Minor in the second century AD. Roman policy towards the Greek cities of the Eastern empire might have been designed to exacerbate the inferiority complex of the modern cities of Asia Minor *vis-à-vis* their senior counterparts in mainland Greece. The doling out of favors and privileges to one city or another was all too often determined on the basis of antiquity (*archaiotes*) and sound – that is to say, Hellenic – ancestry (*eugeneia*) (Tac. *Ann.* 4.55). The establishment at Hadrianic Athens of a religious confederation of *bona fide* Greek cities, the Panhellenion, was the culmination of this process (C. Jones 1996; Spawforth 1999). Wealthy and ambitious Asiatic cities such as Aizanoi, all too obviously physical creations of the *pax Romana*, were at a serious disadvantage. In the intensively competitive civic culture which characterized the high Roman imperial period in Asia Minor (Robert 1977), convincing Hellenic origins were imperative to stand out from one's neighbors; creative misinterpretation of local history and mythology was the best way forward (Strubbe 1984–86).

Eumeneia in southern Phrygia and Philadelpheia in south-eastern Lydia were Attalid royal foundations of the 160s BC, named after the brothers Eumenes II and Attalos II Philadelphos ("brother-lover") respectively. A history dating back no further than the second century BC was a serious disadvantage – the city of Ptolemais-Barke in Libya had been disqualified from full membership of the Panhellenion precisely because of her Macedonian dynastic name – and both cities developed alternative foundation myths. According to Euripides, the wooden statue of the Tauric Artemis, stolen from the Taurians by Orestes and Iphigeneia, had been carried to Attica and dedicated at Halai, where it was still worshipped under the name Artemis Tauropolos. The Philadelphians knew better. The siblings had brought the statue to Lydia, not Athens, where it survived to be worshipped under the cult name of Artemis Anaïtis, patron deity of the city of Philadelpheia. The city's name was taken as confirmation of this: Philadelpheia was the "city of sibling love," that is to say, the love between Orestes and his sister Iphigeneia. The city's foundation was thereby backdated to the generation after the Trojan wars, making it one of the oldest cities in Asia (Burrell 2005; Nollé 2005b: 73–83). The Eumeneians, even more ambitiously, claimed to have been founded by Hyllos, son of the Argive Herakles, who was "happy to stay" (*eu menein*) at Eumeneia during the exile of the Herakleidai from the Peloponnese (P. Weiss 2000). These convoluted mythological origins can seem faintly risible. But the Roman authorities took them seriously enough, and practical benefits accrued. In the 120s AD, the Eumeneians' Achaean ancestry was the foundation of a successful bid for membership of the Panhellenion; soon after, Philadelpheia gained the valuable status of an independent assize center, and was briefly made one of the peninsula's *metropoleis* (mother cities) in the reign of Elagabalus. Quite apart from local prestige, these titles made a real difference to the city's legal position and tax status (*Dig.* 27.6.2).

In the mid-third century, the bishop Pionios thunderously denounced the vanities of the citizens of Smyrna, who "plume themselves on the beauty of Smyrna," and boast of being the native city of the poet Homer (Robert 1994: 1–9). The rise of the Church obviously required the cities to rethink their collective past. In the mid-320s AD, the town of Orkistos in Phrygia appealed to the emperor Constantine to be restored to the status of a city after a period of subordination to the neighboring city of Nakoleia. Antiquity and mythological origins seem simply not to have come into question; instead, city status was granted on the basis of the town's favorable position, the size of its population, the existence of a curial class, and the fact that "as a kind of crown on all these things, the inhabitants are all said to be followers of the most sacred religion (i.e. Christianity)" (Chastagnol 1981). However, the transforming power of the Church ought not to be overstated. Christian Tarsos's claims to fame in the late fifth century AD have a familiar ring to them: "a city priding itself on its beauty and size . . . and what is most important and glorious of all, the fact of being the native city of the most great and holy apostle Paul" (Miracles of St Thecla, *Mir.* 29). There is little here which would have shocked the pagans of third-century Smyrna.

Tarsos, of course, was fortunate in being able to make symbolic capital out of a direct connection with the Apostolic age. Others found the negotiation more difficult. In the late fifth century, the Isaurian imperial dynasty, natives of a notoriously barbarous part of Asia Minor, found it convenient to claim that the Isaurian race were the descendants of the prophet Esau (Photius, *Bibl.* 79); the citizens of Apameia *Kibotos* (the Chest) in Phrygia were reduced to claiming that the *kibotos* (also Ark) of Noah had come to rest on a nearby hill (Lightfoot 2008). At any rate, it is clear that the rise of the Church did little to dent the basic collective values of the Greco-Roman city in Asia Minor, even if it was now Esau rather than Rhea to whom they looked.

4   The Triumph of the Anatolian Village

The dramatic cultural and architectural achievements of the cities can trick us into regarding Greco-Roman Anatolia as a basically urban society. This is to fall into a trap deliberately set for us by the civic elites themselves. Asia Minor always remained a land of villages. This has recently been underlined by the extraordinary Tübingen survey of the city and territory of Kyaneai, a small *polis* in the barren Yavu highlands of central Lykia. Kyaneai has no direct access to the sea; its territory (c.136 km²) possesses no natural water sources, and its soil is relatively poor. In the Roman imperial period, the urban center of Kyaneai was home to no more than around 1,000 inhabitants. The remainder of the population was equally distributed between three smaller kinds of rural habitat: seven larger villages (*demoi, peripolia*) of 100–300 inhabitants each, around 50 smaller hamlets, of perhaps 30 inhabitants each, and around 250 isolated farmhouses. The total population of city and territory in the Roman imperial period is estimated at 6,200. For comparison, the population of this region in 1985 stood at a mere 1,640 inhabitants, a startling indication of the intensity of land-use and density of rural settlement in antiquity. The crucial point here is the relative demographic insignificance of the urban center of Kyaneai. Kyaneai may have been the political, religious and cultural center of its territory, but only a small minority of its citizens ever actually lived there. (Kolb and Thomsen 2004)

The urban culture of Greco-Roman Asia Minor was a fragile thing, highly vulnerable to changes in the pattern of elite behavior. The decisive change seems to have occurred – although chronology and causation remain controversial – between the fifth and seventh centuries AD. The key example here is the city of Sagalassos in Pisidia, where the establishment of a firm chronology for the dominant local pottery type (Sagalassos red slip ware) permits a much tighter diachronic analysis of changes in settlement and population than is possible anywhere else in inland Anatolia. Here it seems clear that the fourth and fifth centuries were a period of relative prosperity. Large building projects continue, with the inevitable shift in elite priorities, neatly exemplified by the construction in the fifth century AD of a lavish cathedral on the

site of the former council house. Real urban decline sets in after 500 AD. Large public
and private buildings were broken up into workshops and poor housing, and the
population of the urban center of Sagalassos dropped rapidly. The city seems to have
been totally abandoned in the mid-seventh century (Waelkens et al. 2006). Even
those cities of western Asia Minor which survived the sixth-century crisis seem to
have done so on a greatly reduced scale; Ephesos, Sardis, Aphrodisias, and Hierapolis
all show the effects of drastic urban impoverishment in the course of the sixth century
(Whittow 2001; for Aphrodisias, Ratté 2001).

However, the fortunes of the Sagalassian countryside seem to have been wholly
unaffected by the collapse of the urban center. From the mid-fifth century onwards,
the isolated farms (*monagriai*) which had characterized the high imperial period are
abandoned, to the benefit of a growing number of large and relatively prosperous
villages on Sagalassian territory. Certain kinds of specialized services previously
restricted to the urban center, such as ceramic production and metallurgy, start to
be provided by the larger settlements. What we appear to be seeing at Sagalassos is
a collective crisis of confidence in urban life, leading to a process of ruralization and
increasing village self-sufficiency.

The changing world of late antique Asia Minor, with the abandonment of the
cities by the old urban elite, and the revival of the Anatolian countryside, is wonder-
fully evoked by the sixth-century Life of St Nicholas of Sion. The great plague reached
the Lykian city of Myra in AD 541/2. The misery of the urban population was com-
pounded when the farmers of the outlying villages refused to bring grain, flour, wine,
or wood into the city. St Nicholas, the wealthy abbot of the monastery of Sion in
the mountains north-west of Myra, was accused by the civic authorities of keeping
the farmers away from the city, probably with some justification. Meanwhile, Nicholas
embarked on a tour of rural shrines and oratories in the Lykian mountains, beginning
in the village of Traglassos, "where he slaughtered a pair of oxen, and called together
all the people; and there was feasting, and great joy" (Sevcenko and Sevcenko 1984:
82–85). The rural feasts held at the saint's own expense recall the great public banquets laid on by the urban elites of the cities of Asia Minor in the Hellenistic and
Roman imperial periods (Robert 1955, 199–200). But by the sixth century, the old
civic nobility, men like St Nicholas, had withdrawn to the countryside, leaving the
cities to fare for themselves. The urban civilization of the Hellenistic and Roman
imperial periods, never more than a temporary and superficial interruption to the
deep history of village life in Asia Minor, was all too clearly at an end.

FURTHER READING

The starting point for any study of Asia Minor in the Roman and Late Roman periods is
Stephen Mitchell's magnificent *Anatolia: Land, Men, and Gods in Asia Minor* (Mitchell 1993).
Particularly remarkable are his studies of village life in Asia Minor (I. 143–97; II. 122–50).
There is no general work of comparable quality for earlier periods. For the Achaemenid period,
excellent monographs exist on Achaemenid Kilikia (Casabonne 2004) and the Hekatomnid
dynasty of Karia (Hornblower 1980); for the Hellenistic period, Ma 1999 (Seleukids) is fun-

damental. The inspirational work of Louis Robert, the last of the great Anatolian travelers, underlies most scholarship of value on ancient Asia Minor. Robert 1987 is a good starting point.

Among regional studies, Marek 2003 (Bithynia and Pontos) is highly recommended, and not just for its mouth-watering photography of North Anatolian landscapes. Robert and Robert 1954 is an ambitious attempt to write the total history of an isolated plateau in eastern Karia, primarily from epigraphical and numismatic sources. Monographs on individual cities are mostly dull; two sparkling exceptions are Rogers 1991 (Ephesos) and Mitchell 1995 (Kremna). A sense of the robust health of urban archaeology in Asia Minor can be gained from Parrish 2001 and, above all, Radt 2006. This has not yet been matched by serious study of landscape, rural society and environment; for some heroic and imaginative attempts to redress the balance, see R. Matthews 1998. Anyone who doubts the importance of field-mice in Anatolian history may have cause to think again after reading Nollé 2005a.

CHAPTER TWENTY-TWO

Rome

Christer Bruun

1 Introduction: Inhabiting Rome

For many centuries Rome was the largest city in the Western world, but no one knows how many people lived there. The figure of one million is nothing but the most frequently cited modern estimate. There are many more or less ingenious attempts at using what hard data have survived from antiquity (such as the number of *domus* and residential *insulae*, aqueducts, or grain recipients; cf. Lo Cascio 1997; Coarelli 1997b), but no certainty. Comparisons with modern megacities based on residents per square area are hardly decisive, even though they can give us an idea of the magnitude of the figures we should be considering (Stambaugh 1988: 90), because the geographical concept of "Rome" is vague. A mistake, still sometimes encountered, is to take ancient Rome as the area of some 1,370 ha inside the Aurelian Wall built in the 270s AD. The ancient city stretched far beyond those walls, and the Romans themselves defined the city as *continentia aedificia* (*Dig.* 50.16.139), "as far as the built-up area stretches" (Champlin 1982; Frézouls 1987). On the other hand, conspicuous gardens (*horti*) occupied much space and could not be used for habitation, although they were important for various social activities (Cima and La Rocca 1995).

It could well be that the population was in fact less numerous (Witcher 2005). Scholars working in the field of demography point to the high mortality rates in all cities before the recent advances in health and hygiene, and apply this insight to Rome (Sallares 2002; Jongman 2003; Scheidel 2003a). Such considerations may lead one to doubt whether a population of one million could be sustained for any amount of time. Others hold that the conspicuous achievements of the Romans in organizing urban infrastructure, such as water supply and sewers (on the latter Panciera 2000) will have created more favorable conditions than anywhere else before recent times. During the high empire the government was undoubtedly aware that a rich supply of running water in Rome created a more salubrious atmosphere (Frontin. *Aq.* 88.3; see further on population, Scheidel, POPULATION AND DEMOGRAPHY, section 5).

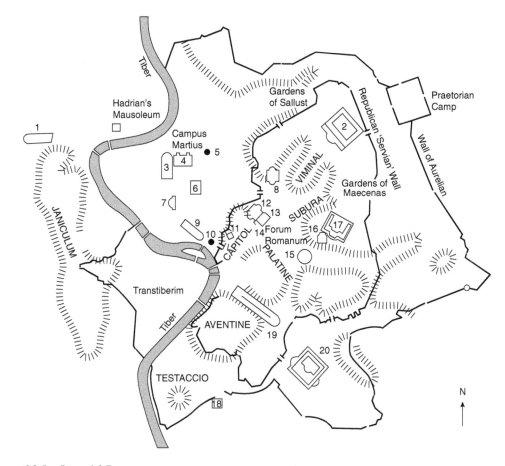

22.1 Imperial Rome
1. Circus of Gaius (Caligula) and Nero
2. Baths of Diocletian
3. Stadium of Domitian
4. Baths of Nero
5. Column of Marcus Aurelius
6. Baths of Agrippa
7. Theater of Pompey
8. Baths of Constantine
9. Circus Flaminius
10. Theater of Marcellus
11. Temple of Jupiter Optimus Maximus
12. Forum of Trajan
13. Forum of Augustus
14. Forum of Caesar
15. Flavian Amphitheater (Colosseum)
16. Baths of Titus
17. Baths of Trajan
18. Pyramid of Cestius
19. Circus Maximus
20. Baths of Caracalla

If anything, we can be certain that conditions in Rome changed over some twelve centuries of classical history. The history of the city of Rome is in itself a topic worthy of a monograph, but practically no such works exists (Kolb 2002 is a rare exception; cf. Giardina 2000). This is understandable; the scholar who attempts to cover the period from Rome's legendary foundation in 753 BC to, say, AD 410 when for the first time a late-antique invader (the Visigoth Alaric) conquered and plundered the city faces a daunting task. The sources are, as always in the study of classical antiquity, mainly of three types: literary, epigraphical, and archaeological. Each kind contributes in its own way, and the scholar needs to master them all.

2   The Evidence

The city of Rome, as the center of the world and the symbol of Roman civilization, plays a role in much of what was written by authors living in that civilization (as emphasized by literary scholars such as C. Edwards 1996, W. Jaeger 1997; cf. Stambaugh 1988: 61–66; for source collections see Dudley 1967, Neumeister 1993, and above all Lugli 1952–60). Of particular interest to historians are contemporary literary sources that specifically refer to life in the city of Rome and to the physical setting itself. They range from frequent references in Cicero's letters or Propertius's description of the temple of Apollo on the Palatine (Prop. 2.21) to Juvenal's Third Satire (Braund 1996) and Martial's epigrams (Rodriguez Almeida 2003). The literary sources further include passages by historians such as Tacitus's lamentation at the destruction of the Capitol in AD 69 (*Hist.* 3.70–74, cf. 3.72.1 "the saddest and foulest crime ever perpetrated on the Roman state") or Ammianus Marcellinus's account of the events during the imperial visit of Constantius II to the city in 357 (Amm. Marc. 16.13–18).

The earliest surviving contemporary mention of Rome is to be found in Greek texts from the late fifth century. Somewhat later, Aristotle's writings show awareness of the famous attack on Rome by a band of Gauls in 387 BC (Plut. *Cam.* 22.3). That episode is much elaborated in the historian Livy's account (5.32.5–49.7), but Livy, whose romantic national history of Rome has ideological affinities with the Western films directed by John Ford, is not a trustworthy source for the earlier centuries of Roman history. As is well known, Livy's canonical list of Rome's kings in Book 1 takes the city's history back to 753, but the only thing one can claim with absolute certainty for the regal period 753–510 is that Rome was not ruled by a series of seven kings, regardless of what Livy tells us. The government was surely monarchical ("tyrannical") in the beginning, as elsewhere in the Mediterranean, but there can be no certainty about the number of rulers nor about most of the names.

Not everyone agrees, and in fact references to the Roman kings as historical figures appear more frequently today than fifty years ago in serious scholarship. A common denominator in such works, which sometimes are marshaled under the slogan "The Great Rome of the Tarquinian dynasty," is their strong reliance on recent excavations that have reached very early layers in the city's archaeological record (Cristofani 1990; Carandini and Cappelli 2000). Discoveries such as those of the foundations of the temple of Jupiter Optimus Maximus on the Capitol (Mura Sommella 2000), the early date (before 500 BC) and impressive size of which seem to confirm Livy's account of the Tarquinian dynasty, has shown that Rome was indeed a rich and powerful city at a much earlier stage than skeptics (cf. Gjerstad 1953–63) used to think. Blind faith in Livy and the rest of the historical tradition can, however, also lead seriously astray (Wiseman 2000 on Carandini 1997; cf. Carandini 2004).

There have been three major periods of archaeological discoveries in Rome since the city became the capital of modern Italy in 1870. The decades after that moment saw furious construction all over the city, and while much was brought to light, far too little was properly recorded (well illustrated by Lanciani 1988). A similar frenzy centered on the very heart of ancient Rome during Mussolini's urbanistic revolution of the area between the Colosseum and the Piazza Venezia in the 1930s; again proper documentation of the findings was deficient (Muñoz 1932, and Erskine, ANCIENT HISTORY AND NATIONAL IDENTITY, for the context). A new period began in the late 1970s, when a revitalized archaeological administration under A. La Regina authorized a large number of excavations and studies with the objective both of making new discoveries and of preserving the existing structures (La Regina 1999). As an aid to future scholarship on the city of Rome and its physical structures, and as the legacy of a particularly creative generation of Rome scholars, the six-volume *Lexicon Topographicum Urbis Romae* was published in 1993–2000 (*LTUR*). The work contains numerous contributions by Filippo Coarelli, the recognized current master of Roman topography, whose work combines the history of art, epigraphy, Roman politics, and social history in an often unparalleled, yet not unchallenged, way.

3   Building a City

The archaeological record in combination with literary sources permits us to describe various aspects of the urban expansion of Rome, especially during the imperial period, which has left far more traces in the existing monuments. No complete history of Rome's urban development is possible, as too many aspects are unknown. For the republic, scholars are often restricted to tracing the history of certain types of conspicuous buildings, such as temples (A. Ziolkowski 1992) or the city wall (Säflund 1932). Rome's growth was a combination of private and communal or government initiative. The influence of powerful individuals and families on the city's development can be seen for instance in how they erected buildings that immortalized their name along the route that the triumphal procession took through the city to the temple of Jupiter on the Capitol (Pietilä-Castrén 1987). Among communal measures was the establishment of the *pomerium*, the sacred boundary of Rome, which could be enlarged on certain occasions and constituted a separation between the domestic and foreign spheres as well as a limit to the power of Rome's generals. In other regards there was little planning and republican Rome largely grew in an organic way. In the early Principate, there seems to have been a certain need to explain away the lack of regular structure in the urban fabric, which made Rome look inferior to Greek cities founded on hippodamic grids (Livy 5.55.2–5).

22.2 The Colosseum, begun by the emperor Vespasian and dedicated by his successor Titus in AD 80. (Photo: A. Erskine)

During the empire, attempts at urbanistic renewal were made, thanks to the huge resources that the emperors had at their disposal. The political topography of Rome underwent great changes from Augustus onward (Haselberger 2007). A series of *fora* were built in the center of Rome by a succession of emperors, each an ensemble of open space and public buildings of various kinds and intended to glorify its author and gratify the citizenry (see Packer 1997, 2001, 2003, and La Rocca 2004 on the most splendid, the Forum of Trajan and Spannagel 1999 on the Forum of Augustus, although in both cases there is an ongoing discussion due to new archaeological discoveries). The traditional venues for political decision making, the Forum Romanum and the adjacent *comitium*, largely lost their function (Purcell 1995), while the nearby Curia continued to host the meetings of the senate which now mostly took place in the shadow of the emperor. The Palatine hill which loomed over the Forum Romanum and looked across at the Capitolium, Rome's religious center, was appropriated by successive imperial dynasties starting with Augustus (Royo 1999 for the first century AD).

Even though the senate continued to formally authorize the erection of certain public buildings during the Principate (mainly temples and, typically enough, honorary arches for the rulers), the emperors practically monopolized public building in the capital. The first two centuries AD demonstrate the truth of a famous saying of Juvenal, that the emperor ruled through his use of "bread and circus games" (*panem et circenses*, Juv. 10.81). Grain distribution was organized in the Porticus Minucia probably built under Claudius (Rickman 1980; Bruun 1989), and the number of arenas grew when the Colosseum (fig. 22.2), the circus of Domitian and other venues were added to the Circus Maximus (which may have held more spectators than any permanent structure ever built; Humphrey 1986: 126). A third concern for the imperial government was the water supply of Rome, which, although it is not mentioned by Juvenal, played an equally important role. By 125 BC Rome had four aqueducts, and after a hiatus during the late republic, a period apparently not conducive to the kind of costly long-term investment that the construction of an aqueduct represented, the emperors greatly increased the water supply by adding at least six new aqueducts (Bruun 1991; Aicher 1995). A large portion of the water was used outside the context of private households, and in particular the imperial *thermae* consumed great quantities. The urban impact of the largest imperial baths (those of Trajan, Caracalla, and Diocletian) was considerable, simply because of their sheer size (c.320 × 320 m in the case of the Baths of Caracalla), but also because of the thousands of visitors they accommodated daily, and the social and cultural events that took place in them (as well as in other baths) (DeLaine 1997).

4 Social Relations

To claim, as Juvenal did, that the emperors resorted to "bribing" the common people in Rome through spectacles and provisions might seem like rather primitive sociology or a paternalistic distortion of the realities of power in ancient Rome. Yet there are many factors to consider when analyzing the social relations in imperial Rome. Already by the late republic Rome had grown beyond what could strictly speaking be called a "face-to-face" society. The republican city was peculiar, however, from our modern point of view, in that it had no police force (Nippel 1995), and the upper classes and the magistrates had to deal directly with members of the common people. The situation occasionally turned ugly for those in power and leading senators might see their authority severely challenged (Cic. *Att.* 4.3: Cicero attacked by followers of P. Clodius). Starting with the first emperor, Augustus, changes were made that aimed at strengthening the ruling power, and an imperial guard (the praetorian cohorts) was quartered in Rome together with the paramilitary urban cohorts and the fire brigade (the *vigiles*), in all a force of some 20,000 men. Nevertheless we read about episodes such as the emperor Claudius being pelted with breadcrumbs and abused by the common people in the Forum when Rome suffered from an interruption in the food supply (Suet. *Claud.* 18.2). The "structural importance" of the emperor in the Roman world was that of being a "super-*patronus*," the person to whom everyone in distress could turn and from whom one could always expect relief (Millar 1977). The emperor could ill afford to disappoint those who depended on him, and this was nowhere more true than in his own capital Rome, where any sign of disaffection would immediately be observed and might inspire ambitious challengers for the imperial purple. So it was also precisely in the realm of the amphitheater and the *circus* that a special relation between the emperor and the people developed; here the great anonymous mass was able to deliver with impunity loud and outspoken criticism of the ruler, while the emperor through his actions and behavior (which included being present, visibly enjoying the spectacle) hoped to see his authority reinforced by the acclamation of the crowd (Yavetz 1969; Wiedemann 1992: 165–83; Coleman 1993).

How such spontaneous expressions of "popular will" in reality originated, and what, for instance, the role of agents working either for or against the government were, we have no means of investigating. What we can observe are certain measures taken by the emperors for the purpose of organizing the common people and further-ing imperial loyalty in their ranks. Again first steps were taken by the great innovator Augustus, during whose reign the city was divided into *vici* (districts). The districts were headed by local community leaders, *magistri vici*, who were intended to repre-sent government at the grassroots level. Dedications to the emperor by joint deputa-tions of *magistri vici* are recorded in inscriptions (as in *CIL* VI 975); this must have been a regular ceremony (Wallace-Hadrill 2003b; Lott 2004).

Making Rome "a city that worked" was another aim of the first emperor. Even though the republican government apparatus was intended for a city-state (and the gravest deficiencies were felt in Rome's provincial administration), there was clearly an administrative deficit by the late republic, for Rome had outgrown the capacity of its civic organs. Augustus initiated several administrative reforms and founded new offices for senators and Roman knights during his long reign (Suet. *Aug.* 37; Eck 1986). Now the most prominent senator in Rome, besides the holders of the ever more ceremonial consulship, was the Urban Prefect who commanded the urban cohorts. Supervising the improvement of the infrastructure became the task of urban curators, some in charge of the aqueducts, others concerned with regulating the course of the Tiber, whose inclination to flood especially the Campus Martius district was a constant threat. At the same time the river needed to hold enough water to permit navigation down to the harbor of Ostia-Portus and upstream into the Sabine country and Umbria, which provided Rome with firewood, timber, brick, and other products. Still other curators oversaw public spaces, upon which various interests exerted a constant pressure, and the repair of certain public buildings. Some officials, who like the urban curators were chosen by the emperor, were responsible for the organization of the grain dole and the upkeep of the city streets (Bruun 2006).

The creation of new offices was determined both by practical concerns and by con-siderations of status and the dignity of the senatorial order; some of the new senatorial functions were to a certain degree ceremonial. It is significant that two crucial offices, that of *praefectus praetorio* (Commander of the Guard), which was collegial, held by two men simultaneously, and that of *praefectus annonae* (the man in charge of procur-ing corn for Rome, and later oil as well) were reserved for Roman knights. These were professional officers and administrators, innocent of senatorial pride, who had risen by their own merit and had proved their loyalty to the imperial government.

5   Capital of the World

The emperor Augustus is known to have boasted that he found a city of brick and left behind a city of marble (Suet. *Aug.* 28.5). It is true that the use of marble, both white Italian Carrara stone and imported colored varieties, grew enormously during the Principate (Maischberger 1997; Pensabene 1997), but the brick industry grew even more. Imperial Rome was mostly built of bricks, and this applies in particular to the high-rise buildings, commonly but wrongly called *insulae* (islands) by modern scholars, that were built in order to accommodate the growing population. While few remaining buildings in Rome can give an idea of what this meant for the cityscape (Packer 1968–69; Priester 2002), some quarters in the harbor town of Ostia provide a more evocative milieu (Packer 1971). The brick industry that provided most of the raw material for Rome's urban transformation grew to very large proportions, and represents an important topic in the study of the ancient economy, not least because of the heavy involvement of the senatorial elite (Bruun 2005, incompletely treated in Scheidel et al. 2007: 561–2).

Brick or marble, Rome of the imperial period was a marvel of the world. It was merely the fact that the ancient lists of the (Seven) Wonders of the World had been drawn up before Rome reached the height of its development that prevented Rome or some of its buildings – for instance the aqueducts, the Pantheon, Trajan's Column, or the Baths of Caracalla – from having a decisive impact on that list. The most recent among the canonical buildings in the list of Wonders, the light tower of Alexandria, dated to before 246 BC (Clayton and Price 1988). Classical literature of the imperial period is indeed full of admiration for Rome. The speech in praise of the city delivered and published in Greek by the intellectual Aelius Aristides c. AD 144 is the most famous example (*Oration* 26: *To Rome*). Other equally complimentary if shorter passages (such as Strabo 5.3.8, Pliny, *HN* 36.101–23, Frontin. *Aq.*, *passim*, and Claudian, *On the Consulship of Stilicho* 3.65–70, 130–37) reflected and contributed to Rome's reputation. When to this is added the impact of centuries of political dominance and, from late antiquity onwards, the renewed importance of Rome as the seat of the successor of St Peter, it is easy to explain how "Rome" could assume the character of an abstract concept, and how, in later times, other imperial capitals laid claim to being the "Second Rome" (Constantinople), or even the "Third" (Moscow) (Catalano and Siniscalco 1983–86).

Rome, however, did not achieve legendary status only because of its marble temples and senatorial luxury. Rome was also the origin of some of the most powerful social movements in Western history. The tribune of the people Tiberius Gracchus, the archetype of all agrarian reformers, was murdered on the Capitol in 133 BC; his brother Gaius Gracchus, promoter of an even larger program of social reform, was hunted down and killed ten years later. Less than two centuries later, another popular movement, driven perhaps more by ideological than by economic motives, namely the Christians, contributed to the fame of pagan Rome, this time all in the negative (*Book of Revelation*). The first organized persecution of the Christians seems to have taken place in AD 64 after the great fire of Rome. The emperor Nero blamed the fire on the Christians, while possibly having promoted it himself (Tac. *Ann.* 15.38–44, cf. Curran, THE EMERGENCE OF CHRISTIANITY, section 6). In modern scholarship there is, however, a growing sense that Christian fanatics, steeped in confused apocalyptic beliefs, may in fact have been the instigators (Baudy 1991). If so, Rome could also sport the worst case of terrorism ever recorded.

From the late republic onwards Rome was truly the capital of the world. Its predominance was above all of political and financial nature, but this soon had consequences also in the cultural and intellectual spheres. The influx of Hellenistic culture also had a significant impact on the city itself. Statues and other works of art from the eastern Mediterranean decorated the city. Pliny the Elder provides an impressive list of statues taken from abroad (*HN* 36.27–29, 33–39), and the residents of Rome were, for instance, able to admire at least fifteen statues of Lysippos exhibited in various public places in Rome (Moreno 1981). The statues and other works of art in the modern museums of Rome provide bountiful evidence for the riches that once decorated public places and aristocratic abodes in the city. Under Augustus, a fascination with Egyptian objects and art gripped Rome after the annexation of that country, as exemplified by the Pyramid of Cestius (Vout 2003). The three canonical Greek architectural orders were ubiquitous, and skillful architects from the East were fundamental for the building programs of the emperors, the most famous among them Apollodoros of Damascus (Scagliarini Corlaità 1993; J. C. Anderson 2003), whose vision and talent can still be admired in Trajan's Forum.

The power and wealth in Rome attracted intellectuals and artists from all over the world, as has been the case in more recent times with London, New York, and other leading cities. The arrival in Rome of Aelius Aristides from the East in the mid-second century AD is a case in point, but already in 155 BC the heads of three philosophical schools in Athens came to Rome on official business. They used their stay in Rome to give public lectures, which gave a boost to the intellectual development of the city already in progress (Gell. 6.14.8–10; Plut. *Cato mai.* 22). One might claim that the Hellenistic civilizatory mission on which they had embarked was completed almost three hundred years later, when the emperor Hadrian instituted a new fashion in Rome by donning a philosopher's beard as a mark of his philhellenic cultural preferences. What might look like a predetermined case of cultural progress was nevertheless a multifaceted process that included Roman resistance and adaptation, and continues to fascinate scholars and to trigger debate (Wallace-Hadrill 2008).

Rome was full of bearded characters, however, long before Hadrian changed the fashion among the upper classes. In ancient iconography the full beard was characteristic not only of philosophers, but also of ancient Romans (the bronze head of "Brutus" in the Capitoline Museum, for example) and of barbarians. If in earlier times grisly trophies and conquered weapons decorating public and private buildings bore witness to the victorious battles of Rome's legions (Plut. *Marc.* 21), during the empire the conquest of the world was celebrated in a more civilized way through art and architecture in the capital. The erection of triumphal arches began in the 190s BC or even earlier (De Maria 1988; L. Richardson 1992: 22), while the representation of conquered barbarians, bearded, wretched and clad in trousers, was a common way of reminding the people in Rome that they were the masters of the world (Levi 1952; Schneider 1986).

Some monuments were less militaristic in tone. The temple of the Deified Hadrian was decorated with a series of splendid reliefs of young women representing the provinces of the empire. Here the many parts of the empire appear not in the guise of *provinciae captae*, subjugated territories, but as *provinciae fideles*, loyal partners of Rome, correctly reflecting the increasing importance of provincials in Rome (Sapelli 1999; Claridge 2010: 223–26 differently on the location of the reliefs).

Immigration had always been a factor in Rome. According to the foundation legend, Romulus made Rome a refuge for the wretched and outcast from all over Italy. The Claudii, a powerful clan from the neighboring Sabine country, are said to have moved to Rome in the early republic (Livy 2.16.4–5). We are on safer historical ground when dealing with republican legislation that tried to stem the influx of people with Latin rights (i.e. less than full Roman citizenship) to Rome. The capital clearly exerted a strong pull on communities in Italy, and the trend intensified and involved the whole Mediterranean when the *pax Romana* improved communications during the Principate (Noy 2000; Ricci 2005, 2006). It is tempting to imagine that the ethnic composition of imperial Rome must have resembled modern multi-cultural megacities such as Toronto, London, or New York. The Roman author Juvenal complained about the Syrian river Orontes pouring into the Tiber (3.62). He was, unfortunately, neither a demographer nor a statistician, but a satirist with an axe to grind.

Rome was a melting pot also for religious beliefs. The traditional cults and temples often remained strong but faced competition from new creeds brought by newcomers who manifested their cults with ceremonies and buildings (Le Glay 1987; Lampe 1989; Beard et al. 1998: I. 167–210, 245–312; S. Price 1996).

Many came to Rome against their own free will. The import of slaves must have been considerable, and currently a hot topic in Roman history is the attempt to evaluate the number of slaves in Rome and Italy, in absolute and relative numbers (de Ligt and Northwood 2008). The demographic approach is a welcome addition to the tools of the ancient historian, but the lack of hard data makes it impossible to say anything beyond that in Rome's heyday there were very many slaves in the city, perhaps around 300,000 (Scheidel 2005: 67) and per capita surely more than anywhere else (see further on demography, Scheidel, POPULATION AND DEMOGRAPHY).

Earlier attempts to study the impact of slavery on Rome's population have focused on individual data, namely on the people mentioned in tombstones and other inscriptions from the city. Greek names (*cognomina*) are far more common than Latin ones, and scholars used to take this as proof that "Orientals" had overrun the Latin element in Rome, thereby ultimately causing the ruin of the empire (Frank 1916). A modern study of the Greek names has shown that they do not necessarily indicate the bearer's ethnic origin, but that they were indeed very commonly given to slaves (Solin 1971). Yet it would be wrong to use this insight to conclude that the city was populated predominantly by slaves. The surviving inscriptions do not faithfully reflect the demographics of ancient Rome. It has been argued that the portion of the population to which we find at least some reference in ancient inscriptions is in the range 0.5–1.5 percent (Huttunen 1974; Duncan-Jones 1978), but it may well be much lower still (Eck 1989: 87). Secondly, the erection of tombstones depended on cultural practices and financial means, and it seems clear that a disproportionate number of freed slaves invested in lavish funerary monuments that showed off their social advancement and preserved their memory to the present day (for tombs, see Noy, DEATH, section 3). Finally, it is unlikely that a stigma was attached to Greek names in every social context in the multicultural microcosmos that was Rome, and there is evidence that a Greek cognomen could be given to a child born of free citizens (Taylor 1961: 126). All these factors warn against exaggerating the dominance of slaves and freed slaves in Rome.

We are similarly at the mercy of the skewed and incomplete epigraphic evidence when it comes to investigating how the ancient Romans earned their living. Inscriptions provide an astonishing variety of professional designations, which seems to indicate that Rome was quite advanced as far as concerns the specialization of its artisans and tradespeople (Treggiari 1980). Yet we lack information on the proportion of free citizens and slaves among the laborers who built Rome, and have no clear picture yet of how public works were organized (Brunt 1980b; Bruun 2006).

As always, the elite are better documented in our sources. This is true especially for the senators, as well as for members of the equestrian order and the leading imperial freedmen. We can assume that most, if not all, of the 600 senators (300 until c.80 BC) had lavish residences in Rome. From the reign of Trajan onwards an imperial edict indeed required every senator to have a home in the capital. That regulation, on the other hand, also indicates that owning a *domus* in Rome was no longer self-evident, surely because of the rising number of senators hailing from the provinces. In recent times, the social as well as political function of the senatorial *domus* has received major attention (Saller 1994; Guilhembet 2001; von Hesberg 2005; cf. Wallace-Hadrill 2003b on housing in general). The topic is well illustrated by the fierce battle around the house of Cicero in the 50s BC. The tribune Clodius secured official permission to tear down Cicero's *domus*, after which he erected a shrine to *Libertas* (Freedom) on the site. Cicero's exertions at redeeming the site and rebuilding his residence are famous (Cic. *Dom.*). During the Principate, senatorial *domus* still had a semi-official function, and the site of these aristocratic palaces can sometimes be identified due to a concentration of statue bases and dedicatory inscriptions in honor of the senator, which were erected in the areas open to visitors. Other attempts at writing the social topography of Rome by identifying the site of senatorial *domus* on the basis of stamps on water conduits are, on the contrary, fraught with problems (Bruun 2000, 2003; Panciera 2003).

The foundation of Constantinople as a new imperial capital in AD 330 significantly reduced the importance of Rome, but already for some time the emperors had preferred to set up their courts in other cities closer to the focal points of military and political events. The population undoubtedly shrank, but the senatorial elite largely remained faithful to the city, even though many may have moved their residences to suburban areas. The scathing condemnation by Ammianus Marcellinus of the superficiality of the late-antique aristocracy and the people of Rome is famous (14.6). Yet his attack did nothing to reduce the fame of the Eternal City (Graf 1882–83), firmly established during the preceding millennium. In fact victorious Christianity introduced new ideological and political trends in Rome, and the changes that the city underwent in late antiquity have for some time been the focus of much debate and creative scholarship (Pietri 1976; Brent 1995; W. Harris 1999; Curran 2000; Pergola 2003, for the later history of Rome, see McKitterick, IMPACT OF ANTIQUITY, section 3).

FURTHER READING

Politics, government and social unrest in Rome:
Today the city of Rome plays a larger role in Roman history than before; contributions such as Purcell 1994, 1996, and 2000 in the new *Cambridge Ancient History* have no predecessors in the first edition from the 1930s (cf. Horsfall 2003). The emphasis is due to the overwhelming importance of the events in the capital. During the republic, the senate, the magistrates, and the people's assemblies shaped the policy of Rome, while during the empire, the imperial court was mostly stationed in the city. Scholars have come to realize the importance of the physical setting in which various social forces interacted, as is shown by works such as Wiseman 1979b, Millar 1998, J. Patterson 2000, Mouritsen 2001, Hölkeskamp 2001b, and Morstein-Marx 2004. Some works analyze popular movements much denigrated in the ancient sources (Benner 1987; Vanderbroeck 1987; Tatum 1999 on P. Clodius). For the imperial period (cf. *La Rome impériale*; Lo Cascio 2000) the sources are equally hostile to grassroots movements, but Rome provides a series of events that continue to garner attention, such as hunger revolts (Virlouvet 1985), conflicts between soldiers and civilians (Whittaker 1964), the changing moods of the people in relation to the imperial power and the rulers' attempt at dominating popular unrest (Flaig 1992, Sünskes-Thompson 1993), and not least the conflicts among religious groups, including clashes among Christians.

Topography:
The buildings of ancient Rome, the architecture and urban structure of the city have received serious attention since the 1400s. Older archaeological discoveries are recorded in Lanciani 1989–2002. The identification of ancient buildings known from literary sources is often hotly contested, and new excavations and the study of previous discoveries continuously generate new interpretations (Leone et al. 2007). Central areas of debate include the Campus Martius (Coarelli 1997a) and the Forum Romanum with the Via Sacra (Coarelli 1983–85; La Regina 1999; Ziolkowski 2004); cf. L. Richardson 1992; Claridge 1998; Steinby 1993–2000. Ancient maps of Rome are of special interest (Rodriguez-Almeida 2002; Najbjerg and Trimble 2004).

Topography, Triumphs, the Tiber (2012):
A new topographical dictionary is in the making, covering the suburban area outside the Aurelianic city wall: A. La Regina et al., *Lexicon Topographicum Urbis Romae. Suburbium* (2001–, 5 vols. so far). Among general archaeological-historical guides to Rome's still visible monuments, pride of place goes to the second edition of Claridge 1998, while F. Coarelli, *Rome and Environs: An Archaeological Guide* (2007) is more useful on the historical layers; J. Patterson, *JRS* 100 (2010), 210–32 surveys recent scholarship. Rome under Augustus is discussed in Haselberger 2007, while L. Haselberger and J. Humphrey (eds.), *Imaging Ancient Rome* (2006) focuses on digital reconstructions. See also the extensive entries under 'Rome, city of' in the R. Bagnall et al., *The Encyclopedia of Ancient History* (2012). Much attention has recently been devoted to the Roman triumph and the procession's route through the city, see K.-J. Hölkeskamp, *Reconstructing the Roman Republic* (2010) 57–60, I. Östenberg, *Historia* 59 (2010) 303–20. For the recurring floods of the Tiber note Aldrete 2007; more generally on the river and its importance for Rome, J. Le Gall, *Il Tevere fiume di Roma nell'antichità* (2005). Transport amphorae brought up on the Tiber from Ostia, once discarded, formed the hill known as Monte Testaccio, a unique depository of information on Rome's economy, see Rodriguez Almeida 1984 and recent work by J. Remesal Rodríguez. In general on supplying Rome, see E. Papi (ed.) *Supplying Rome and the Empire* (2007).

CHAPTER TWENTY-THREE

Italy Beyond Rome

Kathryn Lomas

1 Approaching Italy

The history of ancient Italy is frequently examined primarily in terms of Roman conquest and expansion, but the Romans were only one of many different peoples and communities. Ancient Italy was not an ethnic or political unit, but a region of extreme diversity. It contained many different ethnic and cultural groups, each with its own language, culture, economies, and forms of social and political organization, and with a rich history independent of that of Rome (fig. 23.1). Ancient writers name – among others – the Etruscans, Umbrians, Campanians, Messapians, Picenes, Lucanians, Bruttians, Veneti, Raeti, and Samnites, as well as the Celts who settled in parts of northern Italy and the Greeks who colonized the south coast, and many other smaller ethnic/cultural groups or sub-groups whose culture and location remain archaeologically badly attested. Inevitably, the rise of Rome posed important questions for other Italian peoples, and the strategies which they used both to integrate with and to resist the influence of Rome are an essential element in their history from the fourth century BC onwards. Both before and during the period of Roman conquest, however, Italy outside Rome shows a varied and fascinating pattern of social and cultural development. Inevitably, a single chapter cannot discuss these individual cultures in detail, but will aim instead to give an overview of the main ethnic/cultural groups and the major socio-political developments in Italy from the sixth to first centuries BC, although due to constraints of space it will focus mainly on the period before the Roman conquest.

Perhaps an obvious – but by no means trivial – starting point is the geographical diversity of Italy, which had a major bearing on some important social and political developments. The coastal plain along the Tyrrhenian coast was inhabited by a number of ancient groups – Etruscans, Latins, and Campanians, especially, but also a number of smaller and less-well-attested groups such as the Volsci, Hernici, Aurunci and others – who developed forms of state based on the city-state from a relatively

23.1   The peoples of Italy

early date (as early as the seventh century BC in many cases), as did parts of north-east and south-east Italy. The fertile plains of Campania, Latium, and southern Etruria were rich and densely populated areas, characterized by a density of urban settlement which was virtually unequalled in western Europe until the eighteenth century. The Adriatic coast also shows a similar pattern, although it was less-heavily urbanized. Unlike Greece, where the natural boundaries of the territory of each city-state tended to be fairly clear, even in regions of fairly dense urban settlement, Italy was topographically divided only by the Apennines. In the lower-lying regions, there were large areas where there were no clear natural boundaries, creating a built-in potential for territorial conflict and inter-state wrangling, despite their fertile territory and natural resources.

In contrast, the Apennines and other upland areas of Italy maintained a loosely federal political organization and pattern of smaller non-urban settlements – a form of organization which is well adapted to a terrain which could support only small concentrations of population in any one place (Salmon 1965: 64–77). On the Adriatic coast, there seems to have been a much more varied pattern, with the development of urbanization during the sixth to fourth centuries in south-east Italy and in the Veneto, but a society based on chiefdoms predominating in Picenum until the period of Roman conquest (Naso 2000). One factor which Italian communities seem to have in common, however, is the development of a strong sense of local culture and identity which remained important until well after the Roman conquest, and in many regions this was linked to the emergence of complex forms of state organization (whether urban or not). The extent to which each particular people or region was conscious of an identity as a specific ethnic group is much harder to determine (see section 2 below and Herring, ETHNICITY AND CULTURE). However, it seems clear that whatever the level of common language and culture within a region, the primary form of identity was that of the state. Some level of inter-state cooperation and organization into loose federations certainly existed, and there is some evidence for the emergence of more general ethnic identities, but these remain relatively weak. The concept of a national identity and of the emergence of political units above and beyond the level of the city-state, or federal equivalent, was largely absent in ancient Italy, even after the Roman conquest imposed a level of integration in the form of Roman domination.

One key issue is that the cultural and ethnic map of Italy was not static. Major changes took place, which have been variously characterized as processes of invasion, migration, or acculturation (Pallottino 1991: 2–55). Probably the best-known example is the ongoing debate over the origins of the Etruscans, whose material culture indicates continuity with the preceding period, modified by intense exposure to a new range of cultural influences from the eastern Mediterranean in the eighth century BC, but whose language is very distinct from anything else spoken in Italy (Barker and Rasmussen 1998: 53–58; Bonfante and Bonfante 2002: 49–57; Ridgway 1986: 634–46). Currently, scholarship leans towards the idea that the Etruscans were indeed an indigenous people, but the language problem remains unresolved, and ancient sources support both indigenous Italian origin and migration from Lydia (D.H. *Ant. Rom.* 1.30, Hdt. 1.93–96, Strabo 5.2.2–4).

By the late fifth century, there was a rapid expansion of the Oscan-speaking peoples of the central Apennines, which affected much of central and southern Italy. At the same time, the Etruscans, some of whom had migrated into parts of Campania during the sixth century, disappeared from this region. The indigenous populations were to a large extent subsumed into a general Oscanized culture, and much of southern Italy, and in particular the upland regions, was dominated by groups of Oscan origin – Lucanians and Bruttians in Calabria, Campani in Campania, Samnites in the central Apennine heartland, and Vestini, Hirpini, Marrucini, Paeligni, and Frentani in the northern Apennines and along the Adriatic coast (Pallottino 1991: 99–105). However, it is again unclear what processes lay behind these changes. Ancient sources (Livy 4.37, Diod. 12.31.1, 12.76.4) speak of invasion and violent takeover, but it seems much more likely that it was at least in part the result of large-scale migration and cultural changes linked to this (Dench 1997). The impact on the regions affected varies. Almost all adopt the Oscan language, and aristocrats with Oscan names are dominant, while material culture, such as the objects found in burials, and the depictions of the population in visual arts such as painted pottery or frescoes found in some tombs, shows a high degree of Samnite influence (Frederiksen 1984: 135–57; Pedley 1990: 99–108). Despite this common Oscan strand of language and culture, the areas affected soon developed their own cultural and ethnic identities. The Campani and some of the Lucani, who inhabited regions which were already substantially urbanized, retained urban forms of organization, while groups such as the Bruttians who lived in more upland areas lived in smaller and more dispersed settlements (Pontrandolfo Greco 1982: 127–66). Equally, the more southerly Oscan-speaking groups had intensive contact with the Greek colonies along the south coast of Italy, and their culture became markedly more Hellenized than that of the Oscan speakers of the Apennines and central Italy, marked by the adoption of elements of Greek culture such as Greek-style coinage, Greek pottery and material goods, and the use of the Greek alphabet.

Two other areas of Italy which illustrate this fluidity of culture and ethnicity are northern Italy – the Po valley and beyond – and the coast of southern Italy. In the south, Greek migrants begin to arrive in significant numbers by the eighth century BC, settling initially in communities of mixed population such as that at Pithekoussai (mod. Ischia), but eventually forming large and dynamic city-states, which included some of the most prominent cities of the Greek world. Communities such as Sybaris and Tarentum became bywords in antiquity for their wealth and sophistication. In the north, the Veneti of north-east Italy begin to develop a dynamic urban culture from the seventh to sixth centuries, and were open to a wide variety of economic and cultural influences from the Greek world, the rest of Italy, and from continental Europe. In particular, they had close contacts (and probably conflicts) with the Celts who migrated in parts of Lombardy and Picenum in growing numbers from the late fifth century (Witt, THE "CELTS"). As with many migration processes, the ancient sources focus on the aggressive elements of this process, describing it in terms of invasion and conquest, but the archaeological evidence shows a much more complex and nuanced picture of gradual migration, settlement, and cultural interaction, as well as periodic violent incursions.

The Roman conquest and the post-conquest processes of cultural change introduced important new developments, but it was not a linear process of Romanization and did not involve wholesale disappearance of local cultures and identities (Lomas 1996; G. Bradley 1997; Herring and Lomas 2000: 1–19). As Roman power began to expand, complex systems for controlling conquered areas and mediating relations with other states evolved piecemeal, with the result that Italy became a mosaic of territory directly annexed or colonized by Rome, areas in which the indigenous population had received Roman citizenship, and large areas which were only loosely linked to Rome by treaty. Most communities, apart from those which were colonies or were granted citizenship, were in theory independent, although Roman control could be (and was) exercised in some circumstances. Even after 90–89 BC, when

Roman citizenship was extended to the whole of Italy, communities were expected to remain locally self-governing. As a result, Roman Italy, although now a politically unified entity, had a high level of cultural diversity and strong regional identities which coexisted with central control and Roman influence.

2   Sources and Perspectives

One important factor which affects our understanding of the non-Roman peoples of Italy is the range of sources and evidence for these peoples and the various questions which can be asked of them. Our evidence is very rich, comprising a vast and ever-growing quantity of archaeological evidence, visual depictions of non-Roman peoples, inscriptions, in some cases coinage, and often the testimony of Greek and Roman authors. However, this very diversity of evidence poses problems for the study of ethnic and cultural identity, and it must be handled carefully.

The evidence of Greek and Roman writers is notoriously problematic because it presents a view of non-Roman Italy drawn from a largely external perspective, and sometimes a politically and culturally hostile one. It is also frequently written long after the events it describes. Even when broadly contemporary, it can show a vast amount of cultural misunderstanding. The fourth-century Greek historian Theompompos (Athen. 12.517 d–f), for instance, famously described Etruscan society in lurid terms, as a culture in which women attended banquets along with men, were permitted to drink wine, and pursued a luxurious, immoral, and decadent lifestyle. There is some corroboration from other sources for the basic facts of female social integration, the importance of banqueting, and the wealth of the elite in the society of fourth-century Etruria (Barker and Rasmussen 1998: 86–87, 99–111). Tomb paintings and other visual arts from the region contain lively depictions of such scenes. However, the spin placed on them – that they indicate widespread immorality, particularly by women – tells us far more about the social anxieties of the fourth-century Greek male than the social behavior of the Etruscans.

Perhaps a more pressing problem in terms of this chapter is that Greek and Roman writers have a view of the social and political organization of Italy which is distinctly at odds with our archaeological evidence. Trying to compile a geography of Italy from ancient sources results in a confusing picture of ethnic groups whose names are disputed and whose whereabouts are vague. More fundamentally, they almost all refer to non-Roman Italy, with the possible exception of the Etruscans, in terms of ethnic units ruled by chieftains or kings. The inhabitants of Umbria, for instance are referred to mostly by their collective name "Umbri," or "Ombrikoi" (Hdt. 4.49, Strabo 5.4.10–11, Pliny *HN*. 3.50, 3.115; G. Bradley 2000: 19–23), for example, while various regions of south-east Italy are described as inhabited by Daunians, Peucetians, Messapi, Sallentini, or Iapygians, each of which is ascribed a foundation myth involving descent from a Greek hero, and they are described as being tribal societies ruled by kings (Hdt. 7.170, Strabo 6.3.4, 6.3.9, Pliny *HN* 3.104, Paus. 10.13.10, Thuc. 7.33, Just. 12.2.5). The problem arises when we compare this evidence with that generated by the peoples in question. In both of these regions, archaeological evidence suggests that the basic form of organization was some form of city-state which evolved during the sixth to fourth centuries, each of which had its own distinctive identity while sharing certain basic cultural features such as language, religious rituals, and material culture (G. Bradley 1997; Herring 2000; Lomas 2000). Even more to the point, the few written documents produced by these societies themselves emphasize the importance of the individual state rather than the wider ethnic group. In Umbria, many inscriptions are set up in the name of particular states or communities, but there are no references to a collective ethnic identity until a much later date, possibly as late as the first century BC (G. Bradley 1997; 2000: 23–28), while in Puglia there is little written evidence for a self-defined identity as Daunians, Peucetians, etc.

In attempting to reach an understanding of the non-Roman peoples of Italy, we therefore have to constantly tread a path between those forms of evidence – archaeological, epigraphic or numismatic – which is generated from within the societies concerned, and the testimony of ancient literature, which may contain valuable information but is inevitably presenting the views of the Greeks and Romans, filtered through their own preconceptions, about the societies they describe. Methodologically, any attempt to equate archaeological cultures with the ethnic labels recorded by ancient historians is almost impossible.

3   Urbanization and Settlement

The primary form of settlement and social organization in many areas of Italy was the city-state. From the seventh century BC onwards, many Latin communities, including Rome, start to develop a distinctive urban identity, as do settlements in Etruria and Campania. By the sixth century BC, all of these regions have flourishing urban centers, with a high degree of social and economic complexity, monumental public buildings and a rich material culture (Barker and Rasmussen 1998; Holloway 1994; Cornell 1995: 96–118). South-east Italy also starts to develop towards an urbanized society in the sixth century. Settlements grow rapidly in size and complexity, and by the fourth century, many can also be described as cities (Lomas 1993; Herring 2000). However, the form of city which develops is in many cases very different from that of the Greeks and to some extent, the Romans.

In most parts of Italy, the beginnings of urbanization are marked by an increase in the number of inhabited sites in a particular region, and also a growth in the size and complexity of the larger settlements. These in many cases go on to develop into urban centers, controlling the surrounding territory and its population. Many of them adopted a formal use of space which is very different from that of the Greco-Roman city which forms a single cohesive area of habitation in which all major functions of civic life take place. Areas of housing were often arranged in small groups, sometimes with an associated burial plot, separated by a small distance from the next group, but within an overall city boundary. These may represent family enclaves with the city. Religious sanctuaries were arranged in various ways. In some communities, they were used to reinforce subdivision of the city. Veii, in Etruria, for instance, had a temple for each of the main enclaves of population within the boundary (Torelli 1982: 15–22; Barker and Rasmussen 1998: 219–27). Elsewhere, they were placed outside the city, to delimit that boundary, or on the edges of territory controlled by the city. Este, in the Veneto, for instance, had a complex ritual geography with five sanctuaries placed around the edge of the city, each dedicated to a different deity and with distinctive votive offerings (Balista et al. 2002). The extent to which these religious centers involved monumental temples of the type familiar from Greece varied. In Etruria, Campania, and Latium, monumental temples with distinctive decorations of painted terracotta were constructed, while in some other regions cult centers – particularly in their early phases – consisted of open enclosures containing altars but relatively few permanent stone structures. The sanctuaries of the Veneto seem to have been of this type, despite their rich deposits of votive offerings and obvious importance to the community (Balista et al. 2002). Those of south-east Italy were located in natural features such as caves, or were open enclosures containing tall columns, which may or may not have been the focus of cult activity or been used for the display of sacred objects (Lamboley 1996: 361–66). Many cities also developed important cemeteries, usually located on the edges of cities, for the burial of their more important dead. The best known and most spectacular are those of the Etruscan cities, which included painted tombs buried under large earth mounds, and dominated the approaches to many cities (Barker and Rasmussen 1998: 232–61).

By the end of the fourth century BC, many communities underwent major changes in both their socio-political organization and their physical structures. There was a greater degree of nucleation of cities which had previously had a rather dispersed use of space, and there was a much greater emphasis on formal urban layout and monumentalization of buildings. Many communities adopted a more regular street pattern, with a central area for public business analogous to the forum at Rome or the agora of a Greek city. Statistics for the construction of large public buildings in Italy during the fourth to first centuries BC (Jouffroy 1986; Lomas 1997) demonstrate that significant amounts of money were being invested in such projects. Temples and city fortifications were the most frequent building types, but there was an increasing trend towards construction of buildings connected with civic government in the third century and towards the addition of buildings to the forum, providing more formalized settings for the business of ruling the city. In the second and first centuries, particularly in Campania and other areas of central Italy, there was a shift towards buildings used for various forms of civic entertainment. Many communities acquired their first stone theaters at this date, and also baths. In general, this trend towards the development of what we might see as a more Greco-Roman concept of urban life takes place in parallel with the expansion of Roman power and culture, and also increased contacts with the Greek world, but it should not be seen just as a manifestation of Romanization or of Hellenization. Rather, it represents an Italy-wide shift which crosses regional and cultural boundaries.

In Apennine Italy, by contrast, the indigenous form of state organization is non-urban. The Samnites, for instance, maintained a separation between settlements and the focus of various forms of communal or state activity. The population lived in villages or on farms dispersed throughout their territory (Livy 9.13.7), but each locality (*pagus*) had a hill fort for defensive purposes, and a religious sanctuary, which acted as a focus not just for sacrifices and festivals, but also for markets, law hearings and assemblies of the local people (Salmon 1965: 78–81; Dench 1995). These seem to have chosen magistrates to govern them in much the same way as a city, and to have been banded together into larger political units, each known as a *touto*. These in turn seem to have formed a federation, known to modern historians as the Samnite League, which had the power of declaring peace and war (Salmon 1965: 78–81, 95–101). A number of larger and more elaborate sanctuaries probably served as the meeting points of the *touto* and a particularly large and imposing example at Pietrabbondante has been identified as a possible headquarters of the Samnite League (Coarelli and La Regina 1984: 230–57). It would be untrue, however, to regard Apennine Italy as either entirely non-urbanized or as more backward in its culture and organization than other regions. Recent research suggests that some sites, such as Larinum, started urbanizing as early as the fourth century BC, and certainly before the Roman conquest (J. Lloyd 1995). Even areas such as central Samnium, Sabine territory, and Picenum, which in some cases did not urbanize until the first century BC, should not be regarded as primitive. It is clear from the evidence of inscriptions, coin legends, and the physical remains of the sanctuaries that communities in these regions had a strong state identity and effective forms of organization which were well adapted to a highland area.

4 Social and Political Organization

Although each of the peoples of Italy had its own cultural traditions, there are strong similarities between them in the ways in which society was organized. During the seventh to fourth centuries BC, one common feature shared by all of them was that they were highly stratified societies, dominated by a wealthy elite. During the seventh century, in particular, grave goods deposited in the richest burials in many areas become significantly richer, signaling the emergence of a much more dominant aristocracy. The so-called princely tombs of central Italy, in particular, give some insight into this stratum of society. These are found throughout Campania, Etruria and Latium, and also in Picenum – including tombs at Caere, Praeneste, Cumae, and many other sites – and contained large quantities of fine pottery, metal vessels and ornaments, armour, weapons, and other personal possessions (Barker and Rasmussen 1998:116–36; Ridgway 1986: 653–67). Many of the grave goods were of precious metals or bronze, and they included many items imported from Greece or the Near East (Rathje 1979). Apart from the obvious wealth and status indicated by these tombs, the similarities of the grave goods buried in them also demonstrate that this was a very international elite, which could access the same range of exotic imports, and exchange prestige goods between families, across state and ethnic boundaries.

Our evidence for the aristocratic domination of society at this period is not confined to the burials of the super rich. In many areas of Etruria, but especially at Caere, large family tombs predominate, with multiple tomb chambers containing several depositions as well as elaborate carved or painted decoration and grave goods (Barker and Rasmussen 1998: 120–25. These probably indicate a strong emphasis on the primacy of the aristocratic kinship group, symbolized by the maintenance of a lavish communal tomb. Elsewhere, we find variations on a similar theme. In the Veneto, burials in the Casa di Ricovero cemetery at Este were grouped into what appears to be family groups, often clustered around the richest tomb, and demarcated from neighboring groups by stone boundary markers (Balista and Ruta Serafini 1992). In southern Italy, we have examples of frescoed chamber tombs from some sites, and many examples of wealthy burials (Pedley 1990: 99–108; Lamboley 1996: 366–73, 389–91; Pontrandolfo Greco 1982). The visual arts also reinforce this view of society. Frescoed tombs in Etruria depict richly dressed aristocrats hunting, dancing, banqueting and engaged in athletic contests. Contemporary engraved bronzes from northern Italy depict a similar society, with aristocrats – denoted by specific marks of rank – presiding over processions of armed men, sometimes leading captives, and presiding over feasts (Kastelic 1966).

Towards the end of the fifth century BC, the extreme social hierarchization found in archaic Italy gives way to a different social structure – still dominated by an elite but a larger and less socially and economically restricted one, with a greater emphasis on the nuclear family than on the wider kinship group. In many areas of Italy, tombs change from large multi-deposition chamber tombs to individual or family tombs, which contained substantial but less lavish grave goods. At Orvieto, for instance, the fourth-century necropolis is structured around individual chamber tombs of roughly equal size, arranged in terrace-like streets, each of which has a single chamber and a single family name inscribed over the doorway (Barker and Rasmussen 1998: 232–38). This is not to suggest that society was not still highly stratified. Inscriptions show that most positions of power and influence in many communities were monopolized by the same families for generations. A very high proportion of both Etruscan and Latin inscriptions from Volterra are set up to commemorate the Caecina family, which seems to have dominated the city from the seventh century to the early empire (Hohti 1975) and Arretium is said to have been dominated by a single family, the Cilnii (Livy 10.3.2, 10.5.13). Elsewhere in Italy, we find very much the same pattern of domination of social and political power by relatively small elites. Whether these were formally structured into demarcated orders, as at Rome, is impossible to say. A possible status term, "*ekupetaris*," is found in inscriptions in the Veneto and has led to a lively debate about whether it represents the existence of a defined elite class corresponding to the equestrian order at Rome (Marinetti 2003), but given the uncertainties about the actual meaning of the word it is not possible to build too much on this. What we can say with some degree of certainty is that the society of ancient Italy was dominated by powerful elite families which maintained widespread social networks based on intermarriage, guest-friendships and similar relations with their peers, both within their own communities and across state and ethnic boundaries, and also extensive networks of clientship with lower social groups.

Relatively little is known about the political organization of Italian communities, and what we do know comes mainly from Greek and Roman sources. However, by the fourth century most seem to have developed some form of elective annual magistracy analogous to the consulship in Rome, and many may also have had some form of deliberative assembly similar to the senate. Livy describes Campanian cities in the third century as each being governed by elected magistrates (Livy 23.2.1–7.2), something which is confirmed by inscriptions (Vetter 1953), and the same seems to have been true of the non-urbanized states of Samnium (Salmon 1965; Poccetti 1977, nos 14 and 175 [trans. in Lomas 1996, nos 284 and 286]). Etruscan cities are variously described as being ruled by magistrates or kings, with kingship apparently giving way to elected leadership by the late fifth century (Livy 5.16.3, DH *Ant. Rom.* 3.61, Bonfante and Bonfante 2002: 66–68; Barker and Rasmussen 1998: 87–91). Umbrian inscriptions (G. Bradley 2000: 100–102, 178–83) make reference to the activities of the *marones*, and also to the office of *uhtur*, all of whom seem to have been elected magistrates. Relations between cities are more difficult to pin down. The possible federal nature of statehood in Apennine Italy has been described above, but we also have references (DH *Ant. Rom.* 3.61, 4.49; Livy 4.24–25, 5.18) to leagues or federations of cities in Latium, Etruria, and Campania. It is, therefore, possible that there may have been loose inter-state networks, but without further evidence it is difficult to be sure how these might have been structured or how they worked.

5 Italian Economies

Like most of the ancient world, the economy of Italy was primarily agrarian. Communities were, on the Weberian model of premodern states, consumer cities, living off the produce of their own territories and directing any economic surplus into the development of the urban center or, in Apennine Italy, the religious sanctuaries which fulfilled similar functions (on the Weberian model of the consumer city, see Whittaker 1995; Capogrosso Colognesi 1995). Most of lowland Italy produced a standard range of Mediterranean crops and products such as cereals, wine, olive oil, and fruit, although the emphasis varied from region to region, and much of it was consumed locally or traded within a small area. Upland Italy, where arable land was in more limited supply, relied more heavily on the rearing of livestock, and especially sheep (Barker 1995; Frayn 1984). The organization of agriculture and landholdings varied tremendously from area to area. Some cities had territories with dense patterns of small farms, indicating farming in small units by people living on the land (for two contrasting case-studies – Veii and Capena – see T. Potter 1979 and Barker and Rasmussen 1998: 174–5, 183–200). In other areas, landholdings may have been larger and resources concentrated in fewer hands. From the fourth century onwards, and in particular after a cheap supply of slave labor became available in the second century, there was a tendency towards the development of larger estates and villas, which in some regions led to greater agricultural specialization, although this was by no means universal (A. Toynbee 1965; Brunt 1971; Hopkins 1978b; Dyson 1992). Some areas of Campania, notably the *ager Falernus*, developed as wine-producing areas from the end of the third century, and Puglia was noted for its olive oil (Arthur 1991: 62–79; Désy 1993). Even within the villa economies which developed during the second century, however, mixed production was the norm, and small subsistence farms coexisted with these large units.

Craft production was organized on a small scale, concentrated in small workshops, although in some cases production may have taken place in the home. Weaving and textile production was a major part of the economy in some areas, such as Puglia, and the large quantities of terracotta loom-weights which are found in many different contexts attest to this (Lamboley 1996: 397–409). The involvement of women in spinning and weaving may have resulted in textile production being located mainly in domestic contexts. Other crafts, such as metalwork and pottery production, were workshop based or possibly, in some cases, undertaken by itinerant craftsmen. The small scale of the production units did not, however, mean that trade and craft production was negligible. By the third century, circulation of certain types of pottery – especially black gloss wares such as Campana pottery – was widespread (Morel 1989). Prestige objects gained wide circulation, either as the result of trade or of social forms of exchange such as dowries or gift-exchange between members of the elite. Many areas of Italy were also involved with long-distance trade with other areas of the Mediterranean, especially the Greek world, and imports from the eastern Mediterranean were significant parts of the culture and economy of Italy throughout this period.

6   The Arrival of Rome

One result of the multicultural nature of Italy was that processes of cultural exchange and acculturation between regions were frequent throughout the period in question. Cultural interactions between Etruscans and various areas outside in which they settled are an important element in the cultures of Campania, Latium, and northern Italy (Camporeale 2001), and the impact of Oscan language and culture on large areas of southern and central Italy is discussed above. In addition, large areas of Italy were also exposed to Greek culture, particularly in the archaic period and the second century BC. Finally, from the fourth century (and even earlier in some regions) the Roman conquest brought all of Italy into close contact with Roman culture.

However, the processes of cultural change and exchange were highly complex, affecting different sections of society and different areas of Italy in different ways. Adoption of elements of Greek culture, such as the alphabet, which was used to write indigenous languages throughout southern Italy and Sicily, Greek-style coinage, or Greek imported objects, did not necessarily indicate adoption of Greek values, and in many cases these cultural borrowings were used to express local identities. Equally, the increasing adoption of Roman culture was not a one-way process of Romanization or the top-down imposition of a cultural package of Roman features. It was a process of cultural dialogue between Roman and other Italian cultures. Features such as the use of Latin, Roman dress, nomenclature and other symbols of Roman citizenship, Roman architecture, urban layout, burial customs, etc. were adopted by local communities but frequently adapted by them (Terrenato 1997). For instance, non-Roman languages – an important marker of cultural identity – disappear in favor of

Latin by the late first century BC, but local variations in the type and format of inscriptions remain. The "Romanizing" adoption of Latin did not mean the loss of local tradition and identity, but the development of different ways of expressing this (Häussler 2002). The gradual emergence of a unified culture in Italy by the first century AD was not a process of imposition of a monolithic Roman culture, but a more interactive process of cultural convergence in which local traditions remained important, although often expressed within a Roman idiom or by Roman symbols, and in which Roman culture itself underwent many changes.

FURTHER READING

Useful introductions to ancient Italy, both before and after the Roman conquest, are: David 1996, Pallottino 1991 and Salmon 1982. A selection of ancient sources in translation can be found in Lomas 1996. Studies of many individual regions and peoples can be found in the essays in Bradley, Isayev and Riva 2007. Studies of specific regions and peoples include: Barker and Rasmussen 1998, Spivey and Stoddart 1990, Torelli 2001 (Etruscans), G. Bradley 2000 (Umbria), Dench 1995 (Apennines), Frederiksen 1984 (Campania), W. Harris 1971 (Etruria and Umbria), Lomas 1993 (Greeks), Salmon 1967 (Samnites), Cornell 1995, C. Smith 1996 (Early Rome and Latium), J. Williams 2001 (Celts). In addition to regionally specific works, there are also a number of collections of papers which provide a selection of more detailed studies: Barker and Lloyd 1991 and Herring and Lomas 2000. Finally, the contentious question of Romanization and the processes of culture change are addressed in the following: Barrett 1997, Hingley 2005, Keay and Terrenato 2001, Mattingly 2002, Witcher 2000, Woolf 1992.

CHAPTER TWENTY-FOUR

North Africa

Josephine Crawley Quinn

1 Introduction

Pomponius Mela, a popular travel writer of the 40s AD, tells us that in Cyrenaica there is a spring "they call the Fountain of the Sun," which "boils in the middle of the night, and then, gradually cooling down, at dawn becomes cold; then, as the sun rises, it promptly gets colder until at midday it is solid ice . . ." (1.39).

For Mela, Africa was full of such strangeness and paradox, and little known beyond the coast. He takes his reader on a sailing trip, or *periplus*, along the Mediterranean shore ("our sea") from west to east as far as Egypt, describing the coastal towns and landscape, but seeing beyond them in only the haziest way, and reporting much in the interior as uncertain or open to doubt (1.25–40; cf. 3.100–107 for the Atlantic coast of North Africa). Mela then gives an account of the peoples of the region, written in a continuous ethnographic present that emphasizes their inactivity and primitive state (1.41–48). He works in from the inhabitants of the coast, who are relatively similar to "us" other than in language and religious affiliation, through the pastoral peoples of the interior who do not have cities, laws, beds, or tables, to the inhabitants of the desert without names, dreams, or voices. Finally we reach the monsters of the deep interior, including the Blemyes "who lack heads; their face is on their chest" and the Goat-Pans whose form "is celebrated in their name." Mela relies largely on Herodotus and sources of similar antiquity for his ethnographic information, which adds to the sense of ahistoricism and exoticism in his account. The Roman reader is distanced and separated from Africa in time as well as space (cf. B. Shaw 1982 on the Mediterranean ideology of nomadism).

But this is odd: North Africa was by then well known to Romans, after centuries of war with Carthage, decades of colonial activity and military occupation in the coastal region, and several famous expeditions into the interior in the time of Augustus. It may have suited Mela's immediate purposes to portray Africa as distant, peripheral, and increasingly strange – not least as a way of justifying the narrow limits of Roman territorial control there to his readers (Mattingly 2003: 9) – but it is also the inevitable result of his interpretative framework, common among ancient authors, working out from "our sea" and "our customs" to the increasingly other beyond.

This Romanocentric approach still guided the construction of colonialist models of ancient North Africa almost two millennia later: T. R. S. Broughton's 1929 account of "the general social development" of the region consists for the most part of a long quotation from Mela's ethnography describing the people of Africa from the inhabitants of the coastal cities to the "roving nomads" without homes (the completely implausible section on monsters is tacitly suppressed), followed by the comforting remark that "it was Rome's task to organize, administer, and colonize the sea regions" (Broughton 1929: 10–12).

New paradigms of interpretation in ancient history now offer alternatives to periphery-periphery models. Rather than focusing on or from one city, many historians are looking to broader geographical contexts of interpretation, of which one of the most popular has been the Mediterranean. There has also been a turn to more complex conceptual frameworks, such as globalization (Hingley 2005) and most recently network theory, which analyzes society in terms of complex and dynamic interconnected systems with fluctuating nodes rather than fixed central points (Malkin 2003). The internet provides a striking example of such a network, illustrating too the way in which developments in historical interpretation are always of their time, depending heavily on contemporary scholarly and political concerns in a postcolonial era (Morris 2003). This is no criticism: models have to make sense of the time they are written in as well as the time they are written about. But can these new approaches make good sense of ancient North Africa?

In the now classic elaboration of the "Mediterraneanism" model, *The Corrupting Sea*, Peregrine Horden and Nicholas Purcell define the Mediterranean as characterized by an unusual amount of topographical and environmental fragmentation into "micro-regions" alongside an unusual level of communication, or connectivity, between those micro-regions; within this ideal model, relative levels of connectivity and fragmentation of course vary according to time and place (Horden and Purcell 2000; cf. Hitchner, THE MEDITERRANEAN AND THE HISTORY OF ANTIQUITY). This thesis has prompted Brent Shaw to make a case for North Africa as "characterized by a peculiar insularity" (B. Shaw 2003: 93). For him, "[t]he northern fringe of the African continent . . . is isolated, locked between the world's largest inland sea . . . on the one side and the world's largest desert on the other." (95). Within this North African island, Shaw vividly evokes three distinct micro-regions created by plate tectonics and cut off from each other and from the wider Mediterranean world: Cyrenaica in north-eastern Libya, the Maghrib proper, and the Maghrib Al-Aqsa, or modern Morocco. For him, this ecological fragmentation at multiple levels and the subsequent lack of regular and consistent contact with the rest of the Mediterranean means that socio-economic development in North Africa is out of step with the rest of the Mediterranean world, but that when Africans do adopt new economic and cultural practices from elsewhere change is often fast, dramatic and strikingly localized.

Shaw investigates these themes primarily in the prehistoric and Roman periods; in this chapter I want to explore the nature of connectivity with and within the region

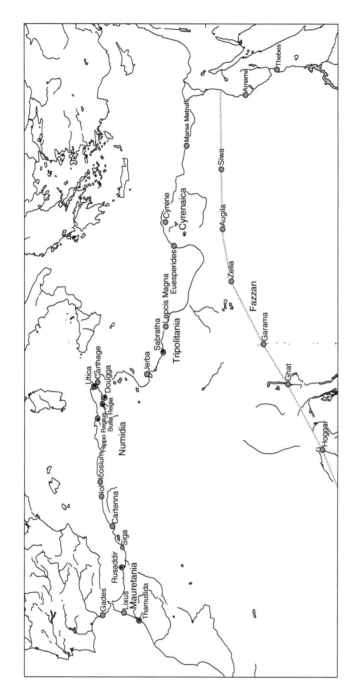

5　North Africa, showing caravan route discussed in Liverani 2000b

between these eras. Recent research on North Africa in different historical periods has highlighted the extent to which the Mediterranean and the Sahara can operate as bridges as well as barriers, as contact and exchange zones, places of work, habitation and transit (e.g. Mansouri 2000 on the Mediterranean, Keenan 2005 on the Sahara; cf. Côte 2002 and Abulafia 2005 on the Sahara as another Mediterranean). At the same time, the latest archaeological work in the region is revealing new evidence for economic and cultural interaction between North African regions and other peoples beyond the sea and desert from ever earlier periods. What follows will be a brief and impressionistic map of developments in three rather different areas in the first millennium BC, focusing on the links between peoples and places rather than the boundaries around and between them. Despite Mela's picture, the Punic colonies of the coast, the Garamantian settlements in the desert and the inland Numidian kingdoms all participated in major "international" networks of trade, diplomacy, imperialism and culture, and they illustrate the fluctuations and variety to be found in such networks.

2   Connections Across the Sea

I will start with the coastal strip of the Maghrib, settled in the early first millennium BC by Phoenician immigrants who came in the West to be called *Poeni*, or Punes. The Phoenicians were certainly not the first to ply North African waters; despite the dangers of this section of the Mediterranean coast, there is evidence for commercial and cultural contact across the sea from the fourth millennium BC. Iberian pottery and imitations of it are found in Morocco, and obsidian from the Lipari islands off Sicily is found in Northern Tunisia (Brett and Fentress 1996: 15), demonstrating early contact across the straits of Gibraltar and the Sicilian channel. Further to the east, pottery from Cyprus and the Aegean, as well as from Egypt and the Levant, at the fourteenth-century island site of Marsa Matruh off the coast of Cyrenaica (D. White 2002: 1–45) points to local involvement at least temporarily in the larger eastern Mediterranean Bronze Age trading circuits (cf. B. Shaw 2003: 102–3).

But these early and intermittent contacts would have involved only short hops across the sea, with land always in sight. Long-distance exploration and colonization, by contrast, began around the ninth century BC, and led to the foundation of a series of colonies throughout the Mediterranean by Phoenician Tyre, linking that city with the Atlantic metal-trading network which operated from Ireland to Southern Spain in the late Bronze Age. Phoenician ships working this route channeled the metal resources of the far West to the Levant, where they were used for trade, the production of luxury items, and the payment of tribute to the great inland kingdom of Assyria (Aubet 2001); it now seems that Greeks too were exploring the Maghrib at an early date (Boardman 2006).

Some of these early Phoenician colonies were in North Africa, including Carthage and Utica in Tunisia and Lixus in Morocco. Undoubtedly the best known is Carthage, where the latest information from the city provides striking new evidence for its origins. The traditional foundation date of 813 (D.H. *Ant. Rom.* 1.74.1) was long thought too early due to the lack of archaeological evidence of such antiquity, but a late ninth-century date for the first settlement may now be supported by the carbon dating of bone samples from a newly discovered archaic cemetery (Docter et al. 2004). Excavations of the last few years also show that the early settlement at Carthage was not merely a rest and repair stop for ships on their way back east; already walled and densely built up in the eighth century, it developed a large metal-working area in the seventh (Docter et al. 2003: 44–45), perhaps for the initial processing of the metals from the Spanish mines, as well as industrial facilities for pottery and murex (purple dye) production (Aubet 2001: 219), presumably for export. Eighth and early seventh-century pottery from the Levant, Aegean, mainland Greece, and southern Spain illustrates the widespread connections of the new African city (Docter et al. 2003: 47).

But in addition to long-distance east–west trade, the north–south Mediterranean "zones" of the pre-colonial period reappear, albeit on a larger scale, in the archaeology of the Phoenician colonies. Maria Eugenia Aubet has explored at length the economic and cultural connections between, on the one hand, Morocco and Iberia in this period, and on the other, Carthage and the islands of the central Mediterranean (Aubet 2001). The two zones exhibit different patterns of material culture and settlement, as well as separate trading circuits. While Phoenician sites in the west tend to be smaller, with commercial rather than civic buildings, those in the central Mediterranean are characterized by early signs of permanence and established civil society. Cities have substantial territories, defensive systems, industrial facilities and civic sanctuaries, including tophets, or cemeteries for sacrificed children, which have been found neither west of Sardinia nor in Phoenicia itself. And north–south connections extend beyond the Phoenician world; Carthage's commercial and cultural relations with Etruria in this period, for instance, are illustrated not only by the sudden abundance of Etruscan *bucchero nero* pottery in Carthaginian graves in the later seventh century, but also by the beautiful gold bilingual Punic-Etruscan dedication found at the Etruscan port of Pyrgi in 1963, made by an Etruscan ruler to the Phoenico-Punic goddess Astarte. The world of Cyrenaica also fits into this pattern, colonized by Greeks in the seventh and sixth centuries, and for several generations very much part of an Eastern Mediterranean world, with no apparent connections to the Maghrib and the West.

From the later seventh century, the shape and nature of coastal connectivity changed. As Tyre weakened, control of the Phoenician trading network shifted definitively to the new cities of the West, and in particular to Carthage and Cadiz (Gadir, Gades). Carthage's political and imperial domination of the region increased alongside closer cultural unification among Punic communities of the central and western Mediterranean (Aubet 2001: 212–13), and in Africa the density of coastal settlement also changed. Early Phoenician colonies had been few and often far between, far-flung stops on long-distance routes, but settlements (whether indigenous or colonial in origin) multiplied in the sixth to fourth centuries, leaving the coastal belt speckled with small towns and ports about a day's sailing from each other. These smaller towns on the coast rarely seem to be involved in international trade; while this might be due to poor reporting and publication of excavations, the combination of increase in number of sites and decrease in range of trade may point to the development of a more local form of cabotage, or port-to-port trade, in addition to the long-distance, high-seas trade that had characterized the archaic period and was still bringing a large quantity of Attic pottery to Carthage itself.

From the fourth century the coastal towns experienced an economic boom. At Carthage the volume of trade with the western Mediterranean, including Italy, increases (Lancel 1995: 407–8), and seems to peak between the second and third Punic wars with Rome, with a huge importation of Campanian A black-glaze pottery from Italy (Chelbi 1992), as well as amphorae from as far away as Rhodes (Marasco 1987: 227). As often, trade and warfare are not mutually exclusive, and along with increased trading connectivity come cultural imports. Although domestic architecture in Carthage remained basically Phoenician, motifs co-opted from the Greek East (perhaps via Sicily) began to appear in public art and buildings, with the port acquiring Ionic columns, and akroteria ubiquitous on the late stelae from the tophet (Quinn 2003).

Economic growth and cultural connectivity on the Punic coast in the Hellenistic period was not limited to Carthage. On the island of Jerba in western Tripolitania, there were high levels of economic activity from the late third century, with substantial rural villas producing olive oil and wine for export (Fentress 2001). Even smaller settlements outside the Mediterranean proper had long-range connections in this period: a few miles inland of the Atlantic coast of Mauretania the site of Thamusida has yielded amphorae and black-glaze pottery from Italy (Papi 2003).

Dramatic new evidence for coastal connectivity within and without Africa in this period has come from recent excavations at the Greek colony of Euesperides in the far west of Cyrenaica (c.600 to c.250) which demonstrate the significance and range of sea-trading networks in this period. More than 90 percent of the fineware at Euesperides is imported, mostly from Attica and, later, Italy (A. Wilson 2003: 1665). Even more interestingly, a third of the coarseware (the cooking-pots and everyday crockery) is imported, along with substantial quantities of oil and wine. Innovative studies of the coarseware and amphorae at Euesperides also demonstrate connections between Greek Cyrenaica and Punic North Africa, which have often been denied because of the lack of evidence for the exchange of finewares and amphorae (B. Shaw 2003: 99). From the fourth century on, almost half the imported coarseware at Euesperides is from the Punic world (A. Wilson et al. 2005: 165), and a large number of Punic amphorae were found at the site (A. Wilson et al. 2002); conversely amphorae from Cyrenaica have now likely been recognized at Punic Sabratha (A. Wilson et al. 2005: 170). And there seems to be technological transfer between these zones as well, including the Cyrenaican adoption of the Punic technique of using tesserae rather than pebbles in mosaics (A. Wilson 2003: 1660).

So the Punic coast of North Africa participates in a set of long-distance overlapping networks of trade and culture which fluctuate in size, scope and density over time. By the Hellenistic period in particular there is a high level of seaborne exchange of goods, technologies and ideas over medium to long distances, including between North African regions, with opportunities for profit presumably setting the parameters of acceptable risk.

3   Connections Across the Sand

On maps the Sahara looks like a dangerously empty space, a gap between places. But
the world's largest hot desert is in fact a place of transit, from nomadic pastoralism
through cigarette smuggling to oil transportation; the latest example is Colonel Gha-
daffi's "Great Man-Made River," an underground pipeline delivering – so far – three
million cubic meters of water a day 1,200 km from the desert aquifers in southern
Libya to the thirsty coastal belt in the north. This is nothing new: travel and contact
across the desert between the Maghrib and Egypt goes back at least as far as the thirteenth century BC, when "Libyans" appear in tomb frescoes at Amarna, and Libyan
tribes are reported to attack settlements in the Nile Delta (Brett and Fentress 1996:
22). Like the sea, the desert has always been a gateway between North Africa and the
rest of the world rather than a barrier between them (Liverani 2000a).

As on the coast, organized networks for the exchange of trade and technology
across the Sahara seem to date from the early first millennium BC, and they coincide
with the beginnings of urbanism and agriculture in the desert. As David Abulafia has
noted "[d]eserts, like seas, have their islands, or oases" (Abulafia 2005: 65), and one
of the best examples of this is the Fazzan region of southern Libya, inhabited in
antiquity by people known to the Greeks and Romans as Garamantes. Far from the
picture painted of these people in sources such as Herodotus, who sees them as so
perverse, uncivilized and unlike "us" that even their cows graze backwards (4.183),
a major recent archaeological project there has revealed a powerful Saharan state
based on cities, settled agriculture and long-distance trade (Mattingly 2003). It has
often been thought that the evidence for intensive ancient use and occupation of the
desert means that the region must have been wetter then, but new research on climate
change has made it clear that the move to urbanism, agriculture and trade in the
Fazzan coincides instead with the final desertification of the region. It seems that the
change in lifestyle from pastoralism to sedentary agriculture was due not to a kinder
climate, but precisely to the need to respond to an increasingly hostile one (Liverani
2000a: 19). This creative response made good use of contacts through and beyond
the desert.

The first permanent settlements in the Fazzan date from the ninth century BC.
These are easily defended hillforts overlooking the valley of the Wadi al Ajal, later
the heart of the Garamantian state. Although there were probably still springs in the
valley at this time (Brooks et al. in Mattingly 2003: 67, 73), wells helped to water
new winter crops (wheat and barley) characteristic of the Near East. Paleobotanical
investigation now suggests these were imported as a package from the Nile Valley
(R. Pelling 2005: 401).

This link with the Nile Valley was not limited to imports of agricultural technology; commerce quickly became a crucial component of the local economy. The
Fazzan has the largest group of oases in the desert and has long been recognized as
a crucial crossroads in medieval and early-modern Saharan trade routes, but it now
seems likely that this role started much earlier. In the fifth century BC Herodotus

described the peoples of inland Africa, including the Garamantes, as living at ten days distance from each other in places with palm trees, springs and salt mines, along a ridge of sand stretching from Thebes in the Nile Valley to the Pillars of Hercules (4.181–85). Notwithstanding the ethnographic fantasies which decorate the account, Mario Liverani has recently forcefully re-put the case that this is a schematic description of a contemporary caravan trading route leading south-west from the Nile valley. Rejecting earlier assumptions that the later stages were fictional, he has traced Herodotus's oases at least as far as the Niger Bend (Liverani 2000b). This was doubtless not the only caravan route in operation: Herodotus also mentioned connections between southern oases and the Mediterranean coast, specifically between the Garamantes and the "Lotus Eaters" of Tripolitania (4.183), a 20–30-day caravan ride to the north (Mattingly 2003: 7).

What was being traded along this route? Liverani suggests that (as in the medieval period) the basic exchange to the south was salt for gold and slaves from the sub-Saharan kingdoms such as Ghana which were developing at much the same time. These were in turn were exchanged to the north for olive oil and luxury items from the Mediterranean (Liverani 2000a: 26, 2000b: 507–8). Although this model is not universally accepted, Herodotus's account certainly emphasizes the importance of salt mining in the oases, and he mentions Garamantian slave-hunts among the Ethiopians to the south (4.183). Garamantian links to Tripolitania also point to a slave trade: Lepcis Magna was later heavily associated with slaving (di Vita 1982: 588–95, Braconi 2005), and there is a hint in Homer that such trade began early on the coast, with the tale of a Phoenician attempt to sell Odysseus as a slave in Libya (*Od.* 14.287–300). Trade in gold is also likely: Herodotus does discuss Phoenicians trading for gold somewhere on the Atlantic sea-coast of Africa (4.196), and gold artifacts have been found in Garama (Mattingly 2003: 360). The gold mines of ancient Ghana were certainly exploited by the fourth century AD, when the amount of gold in African coinage increases dramatically and the Romans begin to demand taxes in gold (Garrard 1982, A. Wilson 2007), but the small-scale export of gold may have started long beforehand.

Whatever the exact nature of trans-Saharan trade, the Garamantes did well out of it: they moved their settlements down into the valleys in the fourth century, suggesting that they no longer needed to fear attacks from elsewhere, and founded the impressive oasis city of Garama, which remained their capital until the final decline of their civilization c.500 AD. Punic and some Italian pottery of the last centuries BC is found at Garamantian sites, and soon Mediterranean goods including glass and faience are very common in the Fazzan, as well as amphorae which would have carried oil and wine; amphorae from Tripolitania are found as far south as the oasis of Ghat (Mattingly 2003, Liverani 2000b).

Technological innovation as well as trade continued to travel along the east–west caravan route: the foggara, a complex irrigation technology originally developed in Persia which reached the Fazzan via Egypt in the fourth or third centuries BC (Wilson in Mattingly 2003: 261–65), and new summer crops from sub-Saharan Africa including sorghum and pearl millet were introduced in the late first millennium, both enabling an intensification of the agricultural regime. It seems that the Fazzan was not simply a consumer of technology: Andrew Wilson has suggested that Roman-period foggaras in southern Tunisia, the Aurès mountains, and the Touat region of Algeria are the result of technological diffusion northwards and westwards from the Fazzan (Wilson 2005, 2006). Similarly, pearl millet did not reach the Nile valley until the early first century AD (R. Pelling 2005), perhaps via the same route.

As we have seen above, trade and technology are not all that travel across seas and deserts; networks of culture and religion often map the same routes (Abulafia 2004). Zeus Ammon, for instance, was worshipped at Thebes in Egypt, and by the mid-sixth century he had a famous shrine at the oasis of Siwa, one step along the caravan route (Hdt. 2.55 for the traditional explanation). A step further again the cult of Ammon persisted in Augila until the time of Justinian (Procop. *Aed.* 6.2.16), and in the first centuries BC/AD. Roman sources firmly associate him with the Garamantes as well (Verg. *Aen.* 4.198, Sil. *Pun.* 2.58, Luc. 9.511–12, with Mattingly 2003: 89). Beyond religion, the eclectic architecture of the temples and tombs of the Garamantes, with Ionic and Corinthian columns and engaged pilasters (Mattingly 2003: 20, 189–92), recalls that of the Hellenistic Mediterranean as well as that of Carthage of the same period.

Overall, the new excavations among the Garamantes highlight the extent to which this region, apparently beyond the ken of classical ethnographers, was, like the Punic coast, a booming center in intensifying long-range networks along which people were exchanging not only commercial but also technological and cultural capital.

4   Inland Connectivity

What of Africa between the coast and the desert? According to Pliny the Elder, in the first century AD there were 463 separate *nationes* in Numidia and Africa (Pliny, *HN* 5.29), but they seem for most of the previous millennium to have kept themselves to themselves. On the minimal evidence so far available, there were for a long time few cities and little evidence of trade and exchange beyond the very local. This is not surprising: land can be much harder to cross than sea and desert, and mountains can be a more formidable barrier than water or sand. Local economic growth, agriculture and urbanization inland seem to have begun in the fourth century (Camps 1961: 59–91, Brett and Fentress 1996: 32–34, de Vos 2000: 59), at the same time as political networks of tribes began to emerge. Particularly important were the "Numidian" confederations of the Massyli and Massaesyli who played important roles in the Hannibalic war as Carthage and Rome vied for the support of the famous Numidian cavalry. After the war Massinissa, the leader of the Massyli, was crowned as king by the Romans (Livy 30.15.11–12, 17.12). State and network formation inland thus coincided neatly with intensive growth in the sea and desert networks to the north and south as well as with the Punic wars, and the Numidians consolidated their networks of power as mercenaries, just as the Garamantes and Carthaginians had done as merchants. This seems to be a classic case of a "secondary" empire, one which grew up as a result of Carthaginian and Roman imperialism, and whose emergence was prompted at least in part by new levels of connectivity within and beyond its borders.

Finds of Campanian A pottery and Italian amphorae at Bulla Regia (Broise and Thébert 1993, 217–18), and Italian and Rhodian amphorae in the mausoleum at El Khroub (Rüger 1979), confirm that the Numidians were trading with Italy and the eastern Mediterranean by the second century BC. It is striking, however, that Numidian political and commercial involvement with Rome did not translate into other kinds of networks between the two powers. Instead, Massinissa linked his kingdom into broader international diplomatic and cultural networks, sending gifts of wheat all over the Mediterranean, cultivating relationships with Hellenistic monarchs and cities in the East as well as with the Romans, sending offerings to the temple of Apollo at Delos and erecting a statue there, and sending his son to take part in the Panathenaic games (Brett and Fentress 1996: 27).

As well as asserting their involvement in the Hellenistic Mediterranean, the kings and elites of Numidia were naturally also interested in exploiting more local connections and associations in Africa, and their coins illustrate the flamboyant cultural mélange that resulted (fig. 24.1). Usually inscribed in Punic, they often feature on one side portraits of the kings with diadems (an attribute of Hellenistic kingship), and on the other galloping horses with or without riders. These latter recall not only the cavalry strength on which the kingdom depended but also the series of small stelae of the same period, mostly from the Kabylie region of Algeria, which

A   B

24.1 A bronze coin issued by the Numidian king Syphax, inscribed in Punic, featuring the king wearing a diadem (obv.), and a galloping horse and rider (rev.). Twice actual size. (Copyright Trustees of the British Museum.)

24.2 A "chieftain stele" from the Kabylie, Hellenistic period

feature local chiefs on horseback (fig. 24.2; Laporte 1992 for the dating). In sum, the Numidian kings were reaching in every direction to reinforce their local power by creating networks of local and international identity.

Such networks of identity offer an extra dimension in which to think through the connectivity of North Africa. Although we have seen in the Fazzan that cultural mobility often maps onto trading contacts, we have also seen in Numidia that networks of power and culture can extend in quite different geographical directions. A final example from inland North Africa, this time from an urban rather than a royal context, may show that networks of cultural identity could extend in different directions from political networks in time as well as space. An inscription from Dougga dated to 139 BC, i.e. after the destruction of Carthage, shows us that the local magistracies had Libyan titles at this time (*RIL* 2). But by the first century AD, they are Punic: the town's chief magistrates are suffetes (*CIL* VIII.26517 with Khanoussi and Maurin 2000: 137–42). And Dougga is by no means a unique case: the evidence for the widespread use of Punic titles for magistracies in inland African cities (by no means all of Punic origin) derives from the first century BC at the earliest (Belkahia and Di Vita-Évrard 1995). The perceptible shift at Dougga suggests that this was in fact a development of the Roman period, not that we simply lack earlier evidence (cf. Ferchiou 1987: 66). While there were of course still Punic towns after the destruction of Carthage, Punic domination was long gone, and Carthage has arguably become a virtual node in a network of (false) memory. These cities turn to an older source of power and authority in the region in the face of the new threat of Rome. This is also a nice example of socio-political localization, even archaizing, in the face of increasing and perhaps enforced economic globalization.

So it is possible to see the people and places of North Africa in the first millennium BC in a perspective very different from that of Mela, as centers of fluctuating economic, political, technological and cultural networks, extending in different directions, but all intensifying in the Hellenistic period. A network approach to North Africa also reveals the similarities and interconnections between very different African peoples. But just because there was connectivity does not mean that it applied to all peoples at all social levels in the same way (Morris 2003). Levels of trade and cultural networks don't tell us about social or economic organization. We know little about the power structures of the commercial networks of the coast and desert, for instance: Who ran them? How were the benefits of prosperity distributed? The Garamantes are particularly mysterious, since they are so little discussed in ancient literary sources: we do not know to what extent the trans-Saharan trade was in the hands of one or more states, and to what extent in the hands of individuals, we do not know who paid the cost of the geographical expansion of the Garamantian state in this period (Liverani 2000b: 511), or how Garamantian society was structured – though given the difficult and dangerous nature of foggara construction, and the rewards of trade, slavery is very likely to have been common (Wilson in Mattingly 2003: 276–77).

So to come back to my initial question, can a connectivity approach make sense of ancient North Africa? It does seem that a "Mediterranean" paradigm of simultaneous fragmentation and connectivity makes increasing sense in the region during the first millennium BC, although this pattern presents a paradox for the Mediterranean model in that it relies on the desert as well as on the sea. But "North Africa" itself may not make much sense at all as an independent unit of analysis, not only because it is in some ways so fragmented and isolated, but because it is at other times and in other ways so connected to the rest of the world (cf. B. Shaw 2003: 94–95). The same might be said of the sea, and indeed of the desert: environmentally coherent spaces are not always historically coherent subjects.

FURTHER READING

Decret and Fantar 1998 is a general textbook on ancient North Africa; there is unfortunately nothing comparable in English. For more details on the Punic world, Aubet 2001 and Lancel

1995 take the story as far as the destruction of Carthage in 146. A catalog from an exhibition in Paris celebrating "the Tunisian season," *Carthage, l'histoire, sa trace et son echo* (1995), has useful essays and beautiful images, as does *Hannibal ad portas* (2004) from a more recent show in Karlsruhe. The Fazzan archaeological project is being published in several volumes, of which Mattingly 2003 and 2007 are the first; we still await a full modern study of the Garamantes. The Numidians are better served, not least by Brett and Fentress 1996, Roller 2003, and most recently, with much bibliography and a refreshing lack of emphasis on the kings, by Fentress 2006. Horn and Rüger 1979, the catalog accompanying the *Die Numider* exhibition in Bonn that reignited interest in these kingdoms, publishes much of the relevant archaeological material, including the tombs and altars; a catalog from a 2003 exhibition to commemorate the "Year of Algeria" updates the story: *L'Algérie au temps des royaumes numides* (Sennequier and Colonna 2003). Mattingly 1995 on Tripolitania is also essential reading, on an area not considered in any detail in this chapter.

Roman North Africa is another vast topic not covered here, but exhaustively discussed elsewhere. On the early stages of Roman domination, see Whittaker 1996; for reviews of archaeological developments, Mattingly and Hitchner 1995 and Bullo 2002. Two books of essays by Brent Shaw (1995a, b) illuminate a huge variety of relevant topics, as does *ANRW* II.10.2 (1982). The proceedings of the bi-annual *L'Africa romana* conferences provide the most up-to-date information and ideas. Finally, Benabou 1976 is a fascinating post-colonial analysis of Roman–African interactions, and Mattingly 1996 puts the history of scholarship on Roman North Africa into its broader colonial perspective.

CHAPTER TWENTY-FIVE

The Iberian Peninsula in the Roman Period

A. T. Fear

1 The Cultural Background

The Iberian peninsula presented Rome, as it does moderns today, with a wide variety of people living within its confines. The Mediterranean coast and its hinterland were inhabited by the Iberians, a sophisticated, town-dwelling race speaking an as yet undeciphered group of non-Indo-European languages with their own distinctive script. The Iberians were capable of spectacular works of plastic art, the best known being the funerary statue, the *Dama de Eleche*. In addition to this people, the area had been heavily settled by colonists from Phoenicia and Carthage, particularly in the period after the first Punic War (264–241 BC) when the Barcids established a Carthaginian empire in the region. The most notable and oldest of these Phoenician settlements was Gades, the modern Cadiz, a foundation which predated Carthage herself. The depth of Punic settlement along the southern coast led Agrippa when compiling his map of the world in the Augustan period to come to the opinion that "this entire coast was inhabited by Phoenicians" (Pliny *HN* 3.1.8).

The central areas of Spain were occupied by the Celtiberians. Held in antiquity to be a racial blend of Celts and Iberians, modern scholarship prefers to see this group as Celts who adopted many features of Iberian civilization, including the Iberians' script in which they wrote their own Indo-European language (Fernández Castro 1995). While a more pastoral people than the Iberians, they too possessed urban centers of some sophistication, such as the fortified site at Numantia, near modern Soria. The north and west of the peninsula were the preserve of Celtic tribes, dwelling in characteristic round-house settlements known as *castros*, such as that found at Citania de Briteiros in northern Portugal (for Celtiberians, Witt, THE "CELTS," section 2d).

2 The Beginnings of an Empire

Rome's decision to establish a permanent presence in the Iberian peninsula is in itself highly significant, and could be said to mark the beginning of Rome's imperial ambitions. She had become involved in the peninsula only by accident, her hand being forced by Hannibal's use of Spain as a base to attack Italy. After a series of successful campaigns in the region during the Second Punic War led by Scipio Africanus (211–206 BC), Rome decided at the end of the conflict not to evacuate the area, something which would have been perfectly strategically sound, but rather to create two provinces in the peninsula: Hispania Ulterior, initially comprising what is now Andalusia with its capital at Cordoba, and Hispania Citerior, embracing the coastal areas of Catalonia and Valencia with its capital at Tarragona, Rome's earliest base in the peninsula. These two provinces, established in 197 BC, were the first to be founded beyond the immediate ambit of Italy and show a wish at Rome to become a Mediterranean rather than merely a regional power.

Unsurprisingly, having just become free of Carthaginian rule, the local inhabitants were less than happy with this new dispensation, and rose up in "rebellion." These uprisings among the Iberian peoples of the Mediterranean coast were suppressed with ease in the south, and with a little more difficulty in Hispania Citerior. However, this swift consolidation was not a harbinger of future success: Roman expansion across the peninsula met with far greater opposition among the Celtiberians and Celts, forcing Rome to engage in a protracted struggle which was only finally brought to close when the Asturias and Cantabria were incorporated into the empire in 19 BC. By this time, the peninsula had been divided into three by the emperor Augustus. Hispania Ulterior was divided into two new provinces: Hispania Ulterior Baetica, essentially the area of the original province, and Hispania Ulterior Lusitania, roughly modern Portugal, with its capital established at the Spanish border-town of Merida (Augusta Emerita), which was initially a colony for veterans of the Cantabrian campaign. The remainder of the peninsula, along with some areas of mineral wealth previously found in Ulterior, remained as the province of Hispania Citerior, often referred to as Hispania Tarraconensis after its capital. This arrangement was to last until a further subdivision into five provinces in c. AD 293 by the emperor Diocletian. This was done by creating new provinces from the north-west (Gallaecia) and south-east (Hispania Carthaginiensis) sections of the old Hispania Citerior.

3 The Spanish Ulcer?

The peninsula had proved a hard nut to crack in terms of both time and losses of men. The 178 years for its conquest is in striking contrast to the decade required by Caesar to subjugate Gaul, an area of equivalent land-mass.

Spain is famously a country where "large armies starve and small armies are swallowed up," and the terrain and climate of the peninsula certainly hampered Roman military efforts at conquest, which were also often hamstrung by a political system which rewarded short-term opportunism and encouraged self-seeking rather than any long-term strategy. Roman setbacks included eleven years of war fighting Viriathus (150–139 BC), a Lusitanian leader who was finally only defeated by treachery (Pastor 2004), a ten-year-long, and initially disastrous, war against the Celtiberians of Numantia (143–133 BC), and another ten-year war (82–72 BC) against the Roman renegade Sertorius (Spann 1987 and García Morá 1991), who, after rallying many natives to his cause, used them to continue in Spain his own private political war against the establishment in Rome. The conquest of Cantabria and the Asturias, which Augustus had hoped would give a swift boost to his weak military reputation, also went badly wrong. The emperor was forced to retreat in frustration and with severe ill health in 24 BC, leaving the campaigns to be finished off by his subordinates. This was eventually done by Agrippa in 19 BC, but not without severe difficulties. *Legio I Augusta* was stripped of its titles after mutinying, and the area experienced several further uprisings. After the conquest of Cantabria, three legions were stationed in the peninsula until the civil wars of AD 69–70, which began with a coup launched by Galba, the governor of Hispania Citerior. But after these wars, only one legion, the *VII Gemina* which had been raised by Galba for his coup, was retained, being stationed at León. Acts of low-level violence were ever present, Lucius Calpurnius Piso, the governor of Hispania Citerior, was murdered by bandits in AD 25 (Tac. *Ann.* 4.45), and a major raid from Mauretania in the mid-second century caused disruption in the south of the peninsula, but the peaceful state of the region can be seen in a comparison with the province of Britain, which was only one quarter of Iberia's size, but required a permanent garrison of three legions.

This extended fighting produced important repercussions at Rome. In 153 BC, the official beginning of the year was changed from March to January in order to allow the new consul, Quintus Fulvius Nobilior, to take up his post immediately. This change remained permanent. The Roman army, too, was changed by the prolonged fighting. Several Roman weapons, including the *gladius* (sword) and the *pilum* (javelin), appear to have been derived from weapons encountered in the Iberian campaigns, and the transition from the maniple to the cohort as the basic division of the legion may also have begun here.

4   Cultural Change

Agrippa, as part of his pacification program, forced his enemies to abandon their traditional dwelling places and resettled them on flat land where they were easier to police; the town of Juliobriga in Cantabria was a product of this policy (Flor. 2.33.59). Rome also intervened to prevent the growth of large native political groupings. This was an early part of her policy, as can be seen from the way that in 189 BC she "liberated" the minor settlement of the *Turris Lascutana* from its mother town (*ILS* 15), and it was this suppression of native synoecism which sparked off the Numantine War in 143 BC.

In general, however, Rome appears to have pursued a *laissez-faire* approach to cultural change. Agrippa's comments of the Punic nature of the southern coast of

Spain were not merely provoked by the race of those he found there. Punic culture also flourished. Towns such as Malaga and Adra coined in neo-Punic well into the Julio-Claudian period – some two hundred years after Roman occupation had begun in the region. This was also true of Cadiz, where the great Semitic-style temple dedicated to Melkart, syncretized to Hercules, remained a major feature of the peninsula and a focus of pilgrimage until the end of the Roman period (García y Bellido 1963, Fear 2005). At Carmona in the Guadalquivir valley, Punic shaft burials continued well into the imperial period. Such an easy-going attitude also prevailed in the north. A striking example is that the thoroughly Celtic, and fortified, *castro* of Viladonga was allowed to exist alongside the Roman town of Lugo in Galicia. Language also persisted – Calpurnius Piso's murderers spoke only Celtiberian.

Many in the peninsula, however, embraced the Roman way of life, and while change was slow in the republican period, the imperial period saw the growth of towns with many typical and at times luxurious Roman features; the amphitheaters at Cordoba and Italica were among the largest in the Roman world, and the spectacular aqueduct at Segovia constructed by the local town council and standing 90 feet high is perhaps emblematic of the peninsula in this period. This enthusiasm for Roman cultural *mores* may have been stimulated by Vespasian's grant of the Latin right, *ius Latii*, to the peninsula (Gonzalez 1986; for the Latin right, Lintott, CITIZENSHIP, sections 4 and 5). In the countryside, too, villas are found, such as that at Olmeda in Palencia or La Milreu in the Algarve, which could rival those to be found in any other part of the empire.

5   Mineral Wealth

Strabo (3.2.8) when writing his world *Geography* comments that "The whole of Iberia is full of metals" and that "neither gold, silver, copper, nor iron has been found anywhere else in the world in such quantities or of such quality" – sentiments which are echoed by his near-contemporary Diodorus (5.35), and later by the Elder Pliny (*HN* 3.3.30). It was these mineral resources that led to Rome's initial decision to occupy the peninsula. Indeed, in terms of the variety and volume of metal ores to be found there, the Iberian provinces proved to be the wealthiest in the entire empire. In the long run the region's conquest certainly proved financial value for money.

Iberia had long been famous for its minerals. Herodotus (1.163) speaks of the wealth of Arganthonius, "the man on the silver mountain," the ruler of Tartessos, a native kingdom located in southern Spain; and Ptolemy (3.10.11) asserts that another Iberian, Aletes, was deified after his discovery of mines near Cartagena.

These native mine-workings were what attracted the Carthaginians to Spain. Indeed, the center of the Carthaginians' Spanish province, Cartagena (Carthago Nova), lay in one of the main mining areas. The Punic mine at Baebulo, near modern Linares, where adits over a mile long were to be found, yielded 210 pounds of silver daily for Hannibal (Pliny *HN* 33.31.96). Diodorus's comment that silver was so plentiful it was casually used for ships' anchors is likely to be fanciful, but captures the sense of wealth to be found in the region (5.35), as does the myth, credulously retold by the philosopher Poseidonios, that the Pyrenees literally ran with rivers of silver after extensive forest fires there (Strabo 3.2.9). In the decade prior to the formal creation of her provinces, Rome had received over 4,000 pounds of gold and almost 220,000 pounds of silver (this is excluding large amounts of lead, a natural by-product of silver mining) from mines captured from the Carthaginians. While silver was the main attraction, other minerals such as gold, copper, tin, and cinnabar were also to be found in abundance

After the foundation of the two *provinciae*, there was a "gold rush" of Italian prospectors eager to work the Spanish mines, and by the middle of the second century BC 40,000 men were already working the mines round Cartagena, producing a daily amount of silver equivalent to the value of 25,000 *drachmae* (Diod. 5.36, Polyb. 34.9.8). It was from the middle of this century that production of the standard Roman silver coin, the *denarius*, rose sharply, no doubt with the aid of this major influx of wealth. Roman mining was undertaken on a massive scale. At Mazarrón in the province of Murcia, galleries were again driven over a mile into the hillside.

Other areas further to the south were equally heavily exploited. The Sierra Morena range, which seals the northern side of the Guadalquivir valley in Andalusia, held rich resources of gold and silver and, above all, highly prized (Pliny *HN* 34.2.4) copper ore. The mining of these resources was again undertaken on a colossal scale. At the El Centenillo mine, near Baños de La Encina, galleries running into the hillside for three-quarters of a mile and reaching a depth of over 600 feet have been found. The range's name, Mons Marianus in antiquity (Ptolemy 2.4.15), is derived from the mine owner Sextus Marius, the wealthiest man in the Iberian provinces according to Tacitus (*Ann.* 6.19), who was executed in AD 33 on trumped-up charges to allow the state to sequestrate his mines.

Further south again were mines producing silver, copper, and tin, such as those at Rio Tinto near Huelva, where there are 20 million tons of ancient spoil attesting to the intensity of the working. Here, as at other sites in Spain, deep mining was practiced, the levels being drained by a series of enormous waterwheels.

Alamdén in central Spain was the empire's main source of mercuric sulfide, or cinnabar, which was used for red lettering on inscriptions and books. The mine was strictly guarded, and the raw ore was taken to Rome for smelting (Pliny *HN* 33.40.118). The end-product was used across the empire: a representative of the Almadén company is attested in Capua (*ILS* 1875), Pausanias (8.39.6) mentions the use of Spanish cinnabar in Greece, and it was available in Carthage in the fifth century AD (August. *Ep.* 30).

An even more profound financial impact on the empire came after the final incorporation of the Asturias into the empire in 19 BC. This allowed the exploitation of this region's gold reserves. According to Pliny (*HN* 33.21.78), Asturia, Gallaecia, and Lusitania yielded 14,000 pounds of gold to the Roman exchequer annually. This amount was sufficient to pay enough legionary soldiers for seventeen legions – over half of Rome's entire contingent of these troops. Casual data give some idea of the volume of production involved– Hispania Tarraconenis was able to send the emperor Claudius a gold triumphal crown weighing almost 5,000 pounds to celebrate his conquest of Britain (Pliny *HN* 33.16.54). Mining in the north-west was practiced through a form of "hushing," accurately called by the Elder Pliny, who for a period was stationed in this region, the "destruction of mountains," or *ruina montium* (*HN* 33.21.70–78); the extent of this technique's effects can be seen most clearly at Las Medulas in León. For Pliny the scale of these mining operations dwarfed the activities of the giants of mythology (*HN* 33.21.70). Tunnels were excavated into the hill to be mined, and water was then introduced from specially constructed aqueducts, exploding the hill from within by hydraulic pressure.

Gold mining was kept strictly under state control, and the only legionary base in the peninsula in the imperial period was to be found at León, close to the richest auriferous regions. Other mineral resources were often allowed to remain in private hands (Strabo 3.2.10), but many over time became imperial property. Such mines were normally franchised out to private contractors under the supervision of an imperial procurator. Details of such arrangements have survived for the mining community at Vipasca, modern Aljustrel, in southern Portugal (*ILS* 6891, discussion in Domergue 1983). These show the thoroughgoing nature of this practice – even the posts of schoolmaster and barber are state-franchised monopolies. The labor force involved in the mines varied. Slaves and convicts undoubtedly played a part (Diod. 5.38), but the Vipasca inscription and evidence from the Asturias show that the bulk of the labor force often appears to have been composed of free men.

Mineral wealth is a finite resource, and it appears that the reserves in the peninsula began to diminish after the second century AD. The *Expositio Totius Mundi* (59), an anonymous overview of the known world written in the mid-fourth century, while fulsome in its praise of Spain's wealth, significantly fails to mention minerals as forming part of it.

6   Agricultural Wealth

The *Expositio* does, however, mention the peninsula's agricultural wealth, underlining in particular the production of olive oil and fish sauces. Along with its mineral wealth, Iberia's agricultural output formed a major contribution to the empire. While much of the peninsula is arid, the province of Hispania Ulterior from its very beginning incorporated the extremely productive Guadalquivir (the ancient Baetis) valley. Pliny believed that the valley had a unique degree of fertility (*HN* 3.1.7).

In Roman hands, this area was to become the center of a major olive oil industry, being planted with over five million olive trees. Spanish oil was rated among the finest produced in the empire (Pliny *HN* 15.8), and Rome's appetite for it was seemingly insatiable. The volume of this trade is attested to not only by the *Expositio Totius Mundi*, but also physically by the Monte Testaccio (fig. 22.1). Found at the foot of the Aventine Hill in Rome, this artificial hill, over 100 feet high and with a diameter of over 260 feet, is composed almost entirely of olive oil amphorae from Baetica, discarded when the oil was transhipped into skins for sale in the city. Forty million amphorae probably contributed to the hill's composition, representing the importation into Rome of around 550 billion gallons of Spanish olive oil.

While the bulk of this olive oil trade was with Rome, the distinctive amphorae (the Dressel 20) in which the oil was exported have been found at other sites in Italy such as Pompeii, and also as far east as Alexandria and Antioch. A more important market, however, was the northern provinces. Oil was shipped to Britain and the German frontier by sea and via the Rhône–Rhine river corridor. Amphorae carrying the name of C. Antonius Quietus, which are found all along this corridor and throughout Britain, extending as far as the fort at Newstead in lowland Scotland beyond the line of Hadrian's Wall, give an idea of the scope of this northern trade.

The organization of the industry, which reached its zenith in the second century AD, is not perfectly understood. The olive estates appear to have been medium-sized holdings rather than enormous estates. After being decanted into amphorae, the oil was then shipped down the river Guadalquivir to Seville, where it was transferred onto sea-going freighters and hence taken to its final destination. The figure of the lustful Spanish sea captain is already found in Horace (*Odes* 3.6). The traders in oil, the *negotiatores*, were sufficiently numerous and well organized to have a permanent collegiate organization in Rome itself (*ILS* 1340, 7490).

The state was more than aware of the importance of this traffic, and though it was left in private hands, a specific official, the *curator ad ripam Baetis* (*CIL* 2.1180), was appointed to ensure the Guadalquivir, along whose banks are possible signs of canalization, remained fully navigable.

Iberia was also the main producer in the empire of *garum*, or fermented fish sauces. The manufacture of these somewhat disgusting-sounding Roman delicacies, whose precise recipes are unknown, was undertaken in fermenting vats around the Mediterranean and southern Atlantic coasts of the peninsula. Like mining, the industry was a Roman development of previous endeavors – Spanish fish sauce is mentioned by the comic poet Eupolis in fifth century BC Athens, and, like Iberian olive oil, the end-product was widely distributed: a company of *garum* traders from Malaga is attested in Rome (*ILS* 7278), high-quality *garum* has been found in Pompeii (*CIL* 4.2648, 5659), Aelian (*NA* 13.6) asserts that a group of Spanish sauce traders had their stock stolen by a sewer-dwelling octopus at Puteoli, while Libanius (*Or.* 32.28), based in Antioch in the fourth century AD, sang the praises of fish sauce from Cadiz for being both good and cheap. Like olive oil, fish sauce was also transported to the north: sauce amphorae have been found at London and Chester, and *garum* is listed on the Vindolanda tablets. High-quality sauce could be very expensive – "director's *garum*" cost 166 *sestertii* a pint, the equivalent of over two months' wages for a legionary soldier (Pliny *HN* 31.43.94).

Wine, though of indifferent quality (Pliny *HN* 14.4.41), produced both in Baetica and the Ebro valley, was another significant Iberian export in the early empire, while Cartagena had a high reputation for esparto rope, even gaining the epithet, esparto town, "Spartaria" (Pliny *HN* 31.43.94). In the late Roman period clothing appears to have become an important export (*Expositio Totius Mundi* 59).

The volume of the export trade and hence shipping passing through the straits of Gibraltar undoubted helped the prosperity of Cadiz, which possessed some 500 citizens of equestrian status in the imperial period, a number higher than any Italy town save Padua (Strabo 3.5.3). The disruption of inter-provincial trade left Cadiz a ghost town in the fourth century, though the temple of Hercules/Melkart continued to flourish (Avienus, *Ora Maritima* 265–70).

A final export from Iberia that should not be overlooked is that of man (and woman) power. The peninsula was a major military recruiting ground. This is true not just of the substantial number of auxiliary units which were raised in the peninsula, but also of legionary troops. A good example is the *optio* Caecilius Avitus from Merida, who was only one of several legionaries serving at Chester with *Legio XX Valeria Victrix* (*RIB* 492). Dancing girls from Cadiz were also in much demand, as we can see from Martial's enthusiasm (14.203) and the younger Pliny's rather priggish surprise that his friend Septicius Clarus preferred to attend a party in Rome where they were the main attraction rather than his own literary soirée (Pliny *Ep.* 1.15)

7   Political Contributions

According to Orosius (5.23.16), "Hispania, ever loyal and mighty . . . has given excellent, invincible kings to the republic." The historian's pride stems mainly from two emperors who hailed from Spain – Trajan and Theodosius the Great. However, the earliest native of the peninsula to make a significant contribution to Roman politics was Balbus, a wealthy Phoenician banker from Cadiz who obtained his citizenship from Pompey, becoming Lucius Cornelius Balbus in 72 BC. He became Caesar's close confidant, managing his affairs in Rome during the Gallic Wars. His reward was to become Rome's first foreign-born consul in 40 BC. His nephew, also named Balbus, also achieved consular rank, and was the last individual outside the imperial family to be awarded a full military triumph (Rodríguez Neila 1992).

Of Orosius's two emperors, the more intriguing figure is Trajan, who became the Roman world's archetypal "good emperor" (Eutrop. 8.5). Trajan was born in one of the first Roman settlements in the peninsula, Italica, the modern Santiponce lying just outside Seville, and is normally believed to have been part of the *Hispaniensis* population, i.e. those descended from Roman settlers. However, Dio (68.4) firmly describes the emperor as a "man of a different race," opening up the possibility that an Iberian was the first non-Roman ruler at Rome (Canto 2003). Apart from his Hispanic roots, Trajan had little do with the peninsula, apart from showing some preference for *Hispanienses* senators who came to form an important part of his inner circle, the most prominent being the three times *consuls* Lucius Licinius Sura and Lucius Iulius Ursus Servianus. It is unsurprising, therefore, that his successor was another *Hispanienis*, Hadrian, who also hailed from Italica. Unlike Trajan, Hadrian built extensively in his home town, adding an additional quarter to the town which included a massive amphitheater and a major temple in honor of his deified predecessor. Marcus Aurelius may be a third emperor from the peninsula. His grandfather, Annius Verus, who was consul three times and prefect of Rome, was a native of Ucubi, modern Espejo, in Baetica.

In the high empire, it was Baetica that made the main contribution to wider Roman politics. However, the most important political figure to emerge from the peninsula was born further to the north. This was the emperor Theodosius (ruled AD 379–95) who was born in c. AD 346 in Coca, modern Cauca, to an influential family. His father, the Count Theodosius, was a leading general responsible for the recovery of Britain after it had been overwhelmed by barbarians in AD 367, but who fell from favor and was executed in AD 376. His son followed in his father's footsteps in the army, but was forced into retirement after his father's demise. However, in the year after the death of the emperor Valens in the disastrous Roman defeat by the Goths at Adrianople in AD 378, he was appointed joint *Augustus* by the emperor Gratian. Theodosius was instrumental in stabilizing the Roman East after this major defeat, but made the fateful decision to allow the Goths to settle within the Roman empire – a move which some would argue eventually sealed the empire's fate. He became involved in the politics of the Western empire, suppressing Gratian's murderer, a fellow Spaniard, Magnus Maximus. Theodosius's enthusiastic embrace of the principle of nepotism led to an even greater influx of Iberians to the imperial court than there had been under Trajan (*Epitome de Caesaribus* 48.18). The most important of these men was Maternus Cynegius, Praetorian Prefect of the East and an enthusiastic suppressor of paganism.

Theodosius shared Cynegius's robust faith, and ensured that Rome, and by extension, Europe, was to have a Christian and Trinitarian future. In AD 380 he issued an edict outlawing paganism and non-Niceaean forms of Christianity (*Cod. Theod.* 16.1.2), and a further edict outlawing pagan sacrifice followed in AD 391 (*Cod. Theod.* 16.10.10). While not openly promoting the destruction of pagan temples, he turned a blind eye to the practice. This legal attack on paganism was followed three years later by the defeat in arms of the usurper Eugenius, who led the last serious attempt to return Rome to its pagan past.

Theodosius set the seal on what another Spaniard, Bishop Ossius of Cordoba, probably began. Ossius was a close confident of Constantine, and may well have had a hand in his conversion. He was to preside over the Council of Nicaea, and remained a leading light in the newly established Church until his death in the mid-fourth century. Although full of devout Christians, the peninsula produced no theologians of note. The controversial ascetic Priscillian, to whom belongs the dubious honor of being the first Christian to be executed by a Christian ruler (his fellow Spaniard Magnus Maximus in AD 385) as a heretic, appears to have had little influence outside the peninsula, although here his followers were to persist for centuries.

8   Cultural Contributions

Latin letters had an early, if undistinguished, start in the peninsula – Cicero sees fit to sneer at the "dull" poetasters of Cordoba (*Arch.* 10, 26). But perhaps Cicero underestimated the vibrancy of cultural life in the peninsula, as one of the leading orators of Augustan Rome was the *Hispaniensis*, Marcus Porcius Latro (Sen. *Con.* I, *praef.* 16).

The most well-known literary group are the Seneca family who formed part of *Hispaniensis* population of Cordoba. However, only the Elder Seneca, an author of works on a rhetorical theory and a lost history of Rome, spent any amount of time in his home town (Griffin 1972). Both his son, the Younger Seneca, poet, essayist, philosopher, and sometime confident of Nero, and his nephew, the epic poet Lucan, left Cordoba in their early youth, never, as far as can be ascertained, to return. Another notable *Hispaniensis* was the rhetorical theorist Quintilian of Calatayud, who was given the first imperial endowed chair of rhetoric at Rome by the emperor Vespasian. Other literary figures from the peninsula included the agricultural writer Columella, a native of Cadiz, and the geographer Pomponius Mela from Tingentera near Gibraltar.

Mela was proud of his Iberian background (2.6.86), and this pride was shared by the poet Martial, a *Hispanus*, i.e. native Iberian born in Calatayud. He was happy to boast about the ferocious reputation of his people and their local toponyms which the elder Pliny had complained were unpronounceable (Mart. 1.49, 10.65, 12.18; Pliny *HN* 3.1.8). A favorite of the emperor Domitian, Martial was happy to retire to Calatayud after leaving Rome, perhaps under a cloud, on the accession of Trajan.

Iberia also provided important literary figures in the late empire. Most produced devotional writing, reflecting the peninsula's enthusiastic embrace of Christianity. Juvencus composed a verse version of the gospels in the mid-fourth century, while the retired civil servant Prudentius produced an output of Christian apologia in sophisticated verse. Egeria, perhaps a nun, wrote an account of her travels in the Holy Land, and the priest Paulus Orosius, probably a native of Corunna, wrote the first Christian secular history, his *Seven Books of History against Pagans*, which was destined to become a major historical text in the middle ages. Secular writing was not entirely absent: the *De Re Militari* of Vegetius was to remain influential until the early modern period.

9   The Collapse

Roman Hispania's demise, like that of Roman Britain was a product of the British usurper Constantine III. His armies overwhelmed the peninsula in AD 407, and in the chaos that ensued they were followed by large numbers of Sueves, Vandals, and Alans. Constantine then quarreled with his *magister militum* Gerontius, who set up a puppet emperor, Maximus, at Tarragona. On the collapse of Constantine's coup, Rome used an alliance with the Visigoths to remove Maximus and reassert her control over the peninsula. But the relationship between the allies was always strained, and Roman writ can only be said to have extended to the province of Tarraconensis. Euric's Visigoths, by now fully independent of Rome, took Tarragona in the mid-470s, bringing almost seven centuries of Roman rule in the region to an end.

FURTHER READING

Sadly, there are very few ancient sources which give a continuous narrative of the peninsula. The most extensive is Appian's *Iberike* (edited with notes and an English translation by

J. Richardson as *Appian: wars of the Romans in Iberia*, 2000), which covers the period from the Second Punic War to the death of Sertorius. Plutarch's *Life of Sertorius* (edited and annotated by C. F. Konrad, 1994) also contains much of interest. The longest extended description of the peninsula is found in book three of Strabo's *Geography*.

Fernández Cruz 1995 provides a detailed account of the peninsula's prehistory, including the Phoenician settlements. The Punic temple at Cadiz is discussed *in extenso* in Spanish in García y Bellido 1963, and more briefly in English by Fear 2005. The best general works on the Roman period are J. Richardson 1996 and Keay 1998, while de Alarcão 1988's study of Roman Portugal is a useful survey of this neglected area. An overview in Spanish, including useful physical data, is provided by Cabo and Vigil 1973.

González 1986 examines the grant of the *ius Latii* to the peninsula and provides an annotated translation of the most important evidence in his study of the *Lex Irnitana*. Viriatus is discussed by Pastor 2004 and Sertorius by García Morá 1991 and Spann 1987. Mining is Spain is dealt with by Domergue 1990, who has also written an detailed account of the regulations found at Vipasca in Domergue 1983. Two English articles on the subject are Lewis and G. Jones 1970 and R. Jones and Bird 1972. Edmondson 1987 gives detailed examination of garum and oil production in Lusitania. Haley 2003 looks at the wealth produced in Baetica. Rodríguez Almeida 1984 examines the remains forming the Monte Testaccio and his *La annona militaris y la exportacion de aceite bético a Germania* (1986) provides a stimulating hypothesis about possible state intervention in this area. The Balbi are discussed by Rodríguez Neila, 1992. The Seneca family are discussed by Griffin 1972 and Griffin 1976. Canto 2003 makes a forceful case for Trajan's Iberian roots, though Bennett's biography of Trajan (2001) is inclined to see the emperor as an *Hispaniensis*. For a more optimistic view of the end of Roman Spain than presented here, see Kulikowski 2004.

CHAPTER TWENTY-SIX

The "Celts"

Constanze Witt

All of the Gauls, who are called both Galli and Galatai, are absolutely mad about war. They are high spirited and quickly seek out a fight, but on the other hand, they are sincere and not at all malicious. [. . .] They also possess a lack of seriousness and a love of boasting along with a great affection for ornaments. They wear golden jewelry such as necklaces and bracelets around their arms and wrists, while the upper classes wear dyed clothing decorated with gold. Because of their lightness in character, they are both unbearable to be around when they are victorious, and panic-stricken when things go against them. (Strabo 4.4.2, 5, relying on Poseidonios, trans. Freeman)

Some of the most compelling and colorful players on the stage of ancient history are peoples variously known to the Mediterranean cultures as Keltoi, Celtae, Galli, Galatai, Galatae. Non-literate, their pre-Roman Iron Age cultures are known only through the emerging archaeological record and the spotty Mediterranean sources. Much received wisdom and traditional views of the "Celts" are currently being reconsidered. It is an exciting time indeed in "Celtic" studies.

1 Were There Ancient Celts?

"The Celts were the first European people north of the Alps to emerge into recorded history. At one time they dominated the ancient world from Ireland in the west to Turkey in the east, and from Belgium in the north, south to Spain and Italy" (P. Ellis 1990: i). But contrast this with the following: "the Celts are, and always were, a creation of the human mind" (Morse 2005: 185). The former statement is typical of traditional introductions to the ancient Celts as the "first Europeans." The latter reflects a current trend in Celtic studies to revisit the entire question of "Celtic" identity.

The ancient "Celtic" world is divided roughly into continental and insular, the latter encompassing Ireland and the British Isles. The word "Celtic" itself has too many meanings and associations to be used without qualification. There are many ancient "Celts": the popular Celts; linguistic Celts; ethnic and "cultural" Celts; archaeological Celts; and historical and literary Celts.

1   *Popular Celts.* In art, music, neo-paganism, Druidism and other new age philosophies, and fictional treatments of antiquity, the ancient Celts form a complete and instantly recognizable picture. Scholars may wonder about ancient Celtic identity; the general public have no such doubts. The ancient Celts of popular culture have little in common with the picture of the Iron Age Europeans that is emerging from study of the archaeological evidence.

2   *Linguistic Celts.* Ancient continental Gallic/Gaulish, Celtiberian, and bilingual inscriptions in Etruscan, Greek, Latin, or indigenous scripts amount to several hundred, mostly very short, related texts (conveniently in *RIG* and *Études Celtiques*). Modern Breton, Welsh, Irish, Scots Gaelic, Manx and Cornish belong to a single Indo-European language group. The revival and preservation of the Celtic languages play a central role in the self-identification of modern Celtic populations.

3   *Ethnic and "cultural" Celts.* The modern "invention" of the Celts began in the seventeenth century (Collis 2003, Morse 2005). An awareness that preserved names of places and people mentioned in the classical sources bear similarities to modern Gaelic forged a link between ancient and modern. The Celtic language group was early associated with the notion of a common "Celtic culture" and "spirit." Language was understood as an inextricable component of ethnic and even racial identity, which was to be uncovered through craniology and the like. The seductions of the idea that science can answer questions of identity have not lost their allure. Today, mtDNA and Y-chromosome studies are being performed to discover genetic affinity between ancient and modern, insular and continental "Celtic" populations. These studies usually use exclusively modern DNA samples taken from areas designated by linguistic historians as having been Celtic at some time (McEvoy et al. 2004; caveat, see Sims-Williams 1998). There are grave scientific and statistical, as well as theoretical and ideological, concerns attendant on such research models. On the other hand, very valuable work is being done on well-selected ancient genetic samples by Stefan Burmeister, Jan Kiesslich, and others, addressing specific questions of kinship within cemeteries and grave groups. Today it is clear that language is only one variable component of cultural identity; multilingualism was probably not uncommon in Iron Age Europe (Sims-Williams 2006: 2). "Race" is a construct that is continually being redefined, and exists, if at all, on a completely different plane from language.

4   *Archaeological Celts.* Since the early eighteenth century archaeology has been exercised to identify the material culture of "Celts" defined as such on linguistic and literary grounds. The typologies thus established were then used to identify "Celtic culture" in turn. However, we now know that "[t]here is no *a priori* reason to assume that 'archaeological cultures' correlate with socio-political or ethnic groupings; they are effectively modern constructs" (Herring, ETHNICITY AND CULTURE, p. 125).

5   *Historical and literary Celts.* Written sources for the ancient "Celts" fall into three
    main categories: ancient inscriptions, classical Greek and Latin texts, and insular
    early medieval literary and legal texts such as those from Ireland.
        Pre-Roman Gaulish inscriptions on stone are rare and fall mainly into the cate-
    gory of simple tomb inscriptions, dedications or religious stelae in various scripts.
    Smaller inscriptions such as possessives on weapons, workshop marks, winsome or
    erotic notes on spindle whorls, *tesserae hospitalis* and bilinguals are more common.
    A potter's accounting on a plate at La Graufesenque gives us a set of numbers. A
    magical text or *defixio*, enchanting or binding its victims, is recorded on a frag-
    mentary lead tablet from a woman's tomb at L'Hospitalet-du-Larzac; mentioned
    are the underworld names of a list of "women of magic," or sorceresses. A lead
    tablet deposited in an important spring sanctuary at Chamalières may be a curse
    or incantation, invoking the god Maponus, the gods of the underworld, and appar-
    ently the pan-Celtic deity Lugus/Lugh. (Meid 1994, Delamarre 2003).
        Classical Mediterranean authors play an integral part in forming our picture of
    the "Celts." They can tell us only about those "Celts" with whom they came in
    contact, or heard tell about, and only from their own cultural and personal per-
    spectives. The labels "Keltoi," "Celtae," "Galatai," etc. had to come from locals
    in the contact zones, speaking either of themselves or others. They may be indig-
    enous names of what the Romans called *pagi* or *civitates* (sing. *civitas*), mistrans-
    lated as "tribes," or some other communal, political or ethnic designation. Often
    all that is preserved are ancient place or personal names (Sims-Williams 2006).
    We might expect those authors who were actually in contact with the "Celts" to
    provide the most accurate and "objective" information. Even in our own sophis-
    ticated time, however, proximity or military contact does not necessarily produce
    the most historically "objective" of writings. A Greek or Latin author is dealing,
    often at second or third hand, with the barbarian "other," inherently inscrutable.
    The conventions of literary genre, and such tropes as environmental determinism,
    play their parts. Often the "Celts" are spoken of in the same formulaic terms as
    other northern barbarians, or any other foes. A single author may portray conflict-
    ing versions. For example, Cicero vilifies the Gauls in his defense of Fonteius or
    his address *On the Consular Provinces*, but he relies on the Gallic Allobroges to
    betray the Catilinarian conspiracy (*Cat.* 3) and speaks respectfully of Caesar's
    friend, the Druid Divitiacus (*Div.* 1.41.90), and his acquaintance, the Galatian
    tetrarch Deiotarus (*Deiot.*).
        The early Irish literature is based on an oral tradition that goes back as far as
    the first century but was first written down as late as the eighth to tenth centuries
    AD by Christians with strong biases, by no means flattering to the outrageously
    sinful pagan tales. A great deal of exaggeration and distortion is inevitable. The
    early Irish laws, Fénechas or "Brehon Laws," were codified sometime after the
    early sixth century AD and were already influenced by Christian doctrine. The early
    insular texts are often used to reconstruct pre-Roman continental conditions (Karl
    2006); their context should be kept in mind (McCone 1990).

    We may expect continued lively debate on the issue of Celticity. It is very much
in the eye of the beholder. This is of course because it is a construct, imposed by

outside observers on groups of ancient people who may or may not have perceived themselves as having anything in common, let alone associated themselves with any form of the term "Celtic."

2   When and Where Were the "Celts"?

A picture of continental "Celticity" is emerging, not as a clear-cut, uniform entity, but rather as a very mobile, permeable and constantly changing network or cline, fluid over time, and characterized by great internal local variability. If we can agree that there were European peoples producing related material cultures and associated with groups the Mediterranean authors called "Celts," it remains to localize them in space and time. Herodotus reports that the Danube rises in the land of the Keltoi (2.33). To the west, he finds them outside the Pillars of Herakles on the Atlantic coast of Iberia (4.49). The Phokaian colony of Massalia (Marseille) was founded near the Rhône delta around 600 BC in Ligurian/"Celtic" territory. The Galli are attested in western Europe and northern Italy, the Celtiberi/Hispano-Celts in Iberia, and the Galatai in Anatolia. The northern boundary of the early Keltike is shrouded in mist. "Celtic"-style material is found as far north as Scandinavia. Caesar and Tacitus describe the "Celts" in contrast to the more savage north/eastern "Germans," although some of their Germani are "Celtic" and vice versa (cf. Strabo 4.4.2). The very existence of "Germans" as a meaningful pre-Roman category is not clear (Lund 1998).

2a   Hallstatt and La Tène

The earliest Iron Age period is conventionally called Hallstatt D, after an important salt-mining site and Bronze- to Iron-Age cemetery in Austria. The continent is traditionally subdivided into western and eastern zones. The western Hallstatt zone ranges from central France and Germany southward into the Swiss Alps; the eastern zone extends from eastern Austria and Hungary and includes scattered sites in eastern Europe, primarily cemeteries and hillforts, that are distinguished by the type-find, the socketed axe, instead of the western sword. The term "Hallstatt" is used to designate, in addition to the site itself, (a) the period of the seventh to mid-fifth century BC, (b) the artistic style, and (c) the archaeological and social or ethnic "cultures." In any one context, it can be unclear how exactly the term is being used. The same is true of "La Tène," the designation for the Iron Age after c.450 BC, named after a submerged site on Lake Neuchâtel in Switzerland, but also the common designation for (a) the style of art, (b) the "culture," etc.

   Stamped belt plates, torcs, flagons, daggers, bronze fibula types, and ornamentation in a geometric style in metal and pottery are characteristic of the sixth to early fifth-century BC Hallstatt D 2–3 assemblages found in the western Hallstatt zone. The style varies locally but is based on lines, dots and geometric shapes, except in the case of human and animal figurines, which are plastic and flowing. Hallstatt-style finds turn up in many contexts throughout west-central Europe, indicating a lively flow of information and goods. The great centers such as Bragny-sur-Saône are often strategically sited on rivers or at points of trans-shipping. The hillfort at the Heuneburg on the Danube was fortified multiple times during the Hallstatt period, including a short-lived experiment with Mediterranean-style plastered mud-brick in the sixth century. Hallstatt itself derived its wealth from salt mining and export. Preserved in the salt are baskets, colorful textiles, leather shoes, wooden tools that give insight into the day-to-day backbreaking work in the mines and the varied craft production of the town (Bichler et al. 2005). Wood-clad chamber burials under great tumuli dot the landscape in southern Germany, France and Switzerland. The conspicuous mound in the landscape is a work of considerable planning, communal cooperation and expenditure of energy. There are often secondary burials in the mound as well as remains of feasting. Associated with the mound may be a life-sized sculpture more or less anthropomorphic in style.

Around the mid-fifth century BC a new artistic style developed. It is based on individual curvilinear shapes, additively arranged. The short Hallstatt dagger grows into an ever-longer sword, and in tombs the four-wheeled wagon is replaced by a two-wheeled chariot. This period is dubbed La Tène A, or Early La Tène (LT). Scholars divide the succeeding developments into subcategories of LT, until the Roman conquests and the "Gallo-Roman" era. In the core Hallstatt zone, several hillforts were abandoned, and a general decrease in burials is seen as areas to the north and east came to the fore. Excavations, particularly in the Champagne, the Moselle–Rhine, and Bohemian areas, reveal intensification of wealth, concentrations of craft activity and elite burial, and interregional exchange of goods in the new LT style. Tumuli also gave way to flat inhumation cemeteries. Coinage, introduced in the third century, quickly caught on and was minted locally in distinctive deconstructive styles. Production of iron objects and wheel-made pottery took on industrial dimensions. *Oppida*, extensive fortified settlements, usually on hilltops, began to take on urban characteristics, with their own artisans' quarters, military installations, religious facilities, perhaps coin production. They could accommodate large concentrations of population at times; suburbia and road networks could be extensive (Guichard et al. 2002).

In the second century BC the Romans expanded their territory from Massalia far up the Rhône and into Gaul. They perfected their tactics of setting the "king" of one *civitas* against another and exacerbating and exploiting internal rivalries by bribery and deception. The *provincia* of Transalpine Gaul was organized in 121 BC. A series of governors institutionalized the ruthless exploitation of the natives. The enigmatic northern Cimbri cut loose in the late second century and, gathering up several groups of *Galli*, cut a bloody swath through western Europe. They were finally crushed by the Roman general Gaius Marius in 101. Violence and upheaval touched much of the Keltike. In the later LT inhumation burial was largely superseded by cremation, leaving fewer artifacts to study. Mass production reduced the flow of innovation in forms, and Romanization made itself felt in anthropomorphism in sculpture and the introduction of stone architecture.

Caesar's invasion in the middle of the first century BC was devastating. From 58 to 54 his legions were relatively free to hone their skills against the native forces, sell the vanquished into slavery, and plunder the sacred deposits. An unexpected revolt in 52 brought harsh vengeance down on Gaul. Numerous *civitates*, normally at odds, were driven to form an alliance, and the leaders met at Bibracte (Mont Beuvray) in a council of war. Under the leadership of Vercingetorix of the Arverni they withdrew to the oppidum of Alesia, where after a siege Vercingetorix surrendered to Caesar. The revolt was effectively over; the vanquished were either killed or sold into slavery, and Vercingetorix himself was paraded through the streets of Rome as part of Caesar's triumph and then executed. The Rhine became the north-eastern boundary of Gaul and was fortified and staunchly defended. Roman occupation permeated every aspect of life, affecting settlements and material culture, extending even to the *interpretatio Romana* of the gods. Study of the final century BC in Gaul and thereafter is generally devoted to the provincial Romans and, at best, to the process of "Romanization" (Woolf 1998; P. Wells 1999).

2b Italy

Hallstatt and in much greater numbers LT-style imports from north of the Alps, and local imitations, are found in north Italian tombs and settlements. The finds suggest a long history of settlement and gradually increasing immigration. Excavations of cemeteries such as that at Monte Bibele reveal stable local "Celtic" communities consistently burying men with LT iron weapons, helmets and fibulae (Vitali 1992). On a second-century terracotta frieze from Civit'Alba, Gallic warriors with a chariot leave the site of a raid, strewing plunder as they go. The "Celts" had become part of the local landscape. Clashes with Etruscans and Romans were inevitable.

In 390/389, or 387/386, a group of Gauls led by a Brennus defeated the Roman army at the Allia river and took the unwalled city of Rome, occupying it for several months (for delightfully imaginative accounts, Livy 5.36ff., Plut. *Cam.*, Dio 7.25ff.). How the sack of Rome is rendered in the literary accounts reveals something of the terror with which the "Celtic" *tumultus* was regarded. These Gauls stand outside the order created by civilized law, custom and systems of honor. They are superstitious and sacrilegious; above all, they are invincible warriors. The vulnerability of the Romans so glaringly exposed, their radically changed self-perception and resulting new developments in military organization and internal and foreign policy are among the repercussions of the Gallic sack. The Gauls withdrew to the north, but many remained to dwell in Cisalpine Gaul. Continued clashes with the Romans punctuated the next two centuries, as the "Celts" occasionally challenged the Romans directly from the north, or in league with Italians, and as mercenaries in turn to Dionysios of Syracuse and to the Carthaginians in the course of the Punic Wars. The late third century was particularly bloody, culminating in the crushing Roman victory at Telamon in 225 (Polyb. 2.27–31). Although the north Italian Gauls attained Roman citizenship in 49 BC, the Romans continued to be harried by "Celtic" incursions into the Augustan era.

2c The Balkans and Galatia

In 279 BC a large group of "Celts" moved southward into Greece (Paus. 1.4; 10.19–23; Diod. 22.92ff.). They fought their way to Delphi via Thermopylae,

committing all manner of atrocities along the way. Although they found the anthropomorphic sculptures in wood and stone risible (Diod. 22.97), they plundered the
sanctuary before being driven off; some of the loot ended up dedicated in watery
deposits near Toulouse, France (Strabo 4.1.13; Just. 3.3.36; Nachtergael 1977). The
remaining army was driven northward; some crossed the Hellespont into Asia Minor,
where they became the "Galatians." The brutal attack on Delphi was a shattering
blow to the Greeks, no less potent a threat than the Persian invasions, and so it would
enter into cultural memory and panhellenic mythology. In the Greek spin on the
event, the Delphic god Apollo averted the destruction of the sanctuary with a spectacular display encompassing lightning, earthquake, snowstorm, hailstorm, rock fall,
and ghostly apparitions, throwing the invaders into confusion and panic. Their departure was subsequently commemorated in the *Soteria* festival. The attack epitomized
to the Greeks the "Celtic" threat of total, unthinkably, horrifically barbaric annihilation. It would be referred to again and again in hymns to Apollo.

During the third and second centuries, various groups of "Celts" served
nearly every major power as mercenaries. When the Galatians, who had originally
crossed into Asia at the invitation of the Bithynian king Nikomedes, were not fighting
for the Seleukids or Ptolemies, they were raiding cities and extorting outrageous
amounts of protection money. Campaigns against the Galatians are celebrated in the
victory iconography of Pergamene monuments, notably the sculptures of Attalos I
Soter, such as the large "Dying Gaul" and "Gallic Chieftain Kills Wife and Self,"
both of which exhibit an unexpected, humanizing pathos and even dignity (fig. 26.1).
Anyone wishing to attain the status of a *soter* (savior) need only win a battle against
the Galatians (Mitchell 2003: 283–87). Strabo reports that in Asia Minor the Galatians organized themselves into "tetrarchies," with their own leaders, judges, and
generals, and that a representative council of 300 met annually (12.5.1). The main
Galatian strongholds were concentrated in Phrygia and central Anatolia. These
included a wide network of hillforts, built in the local style. Widely scattered finds of
weapons, torcs and other adornments are tantalizing but inconclusive. Recent excavations at Gordion suggest that a portion of the Lower Town was effectively a Galatian
quarter during the Hellenistic period. The excavators believe they have found not
only "Galatian" architecture and minor arts, but also evidence of human sacrifice,
head taking and unusual burial practices (Dandov et al. 2002). Aside from these
sensational finds, little concentrated LT material culture has been uncovered. Without
the Greek inscriptions and the references in ancient and early Christian texts, we
would have little evidence that a large population of "Celts" invaded Greece and
inhabited Asia Minor, retaining their customs and language for many centuries
(Mitchell 2003).

2d   Iberia

Theories abound as to the origins, locales and movements of the Iberian "Celts" and
Celtiberians. A popular theory in antiquity was that they were descendants of indigenous Iberians and immigrant Celts; for example, the Latin poet Martial claimed

26.1 Ludovisi Gaul Group (Gaul killing his wife and himself) in the Museo Nazionale delle Terme, Palazzo Altemps, Rome. Roman copy, found in the former Gardens of Sallust, after Hellenistic original from the Acropolis at Pergamon, c.220 BC. (Photo: Marie-Lan Nguyen/ Wikimedia Commons)

descent from both Celts and Iberians (4.55, 12.18; cf. Lucan 4.10; App. *Hisp.* 2; Diod. 5.33ff.). Groups with names beginning in Celt- or Gall- (Celti, Celtici, Gallaeci, etc.) are attested throughout the peninsula, particularly in the north-western portion. Archaeologically, there is no evidence of incursions of "Celts" into Iberia. The few true Hallstatt and LT finds, typical *oppidum*-style hillforts and inscriptions, are concentrated generally in the central Meseta. The local versions of swords, torcs, fibulae, and pottery vary substantially from their counterparts in Gaul.

Hoards contain fabulously detailed gold torcs. Horses and horsemen are popular motifs on fibulae and in sculpture. These are occasionally shown with severed heads pendant from the harness. Beginning in the fourth century BC, zoomorphic stone sculptures of cattle and pigs, called *verracos*, mark cemeteries and urban centers. We must rely on rare settlement and survey finds because of the dearth of inhumation burials.

The "Castro culture" of the far north-west area of the Gallaeci (Galicia into northern Portugal) persisted well into the Roman period. A lively Celtic revival movement plays a large part in modern Galician identity, whether expressed in the political or the musical/artisanal cultural arenas. Ancient "castros," or very well-fortified hilltop settlements, preserve Atlantic roundhouse types. Life-sized freestanding stone warriors guard the entrances of hillforts; bearded and helmeted, they wear a thick buffer-ended torc and carry a small, round shield and a dagger. Decapitated heads and abstract, geometrical motifs are part of the sculptural repertoire. The inhabitants are called "Keltoi" by Herodotus and "Galli" by Pliny (*HN* 3.3.1; 3.20), for what that is worth. Further south lies Lusitania; the few inscriptions are in a language with Celtic and non-Celtic elements. The entire coastal area may be more closely associated with an Atlantic cultural zone than with Gaul (Cunliffe 2001).

2e Britain and Ireland

Very few Hallstatt but more numerous LT artifacts are found in the British Isles and Ireland. The LT style of art was quickly adopted and developed further in distinctive local idioms on weapons, feasting items and jewelry. However, many local traditions continued from the Bronze Age, and developed independently of the continent. The insular roundhouse types and fortified settlements became more elaborate, in places growing into brochs and hillforts, and often accruing multiple concentric fortifications or earthworks. Burial evidence, particularly of the "Arras culture" of east Yorkshire, reveals that the two-wheeled chariot did not go out of use, as it did on much of the continent (Cunliffe 2004; Caes. *BG* 4.33.1–3; Dio 39.51.3). Imported pottery and wine are not found until the second century BC. The insular LT style was applied to the local stone uprights, resulting in enigmatic relief sculptures such as the Turoe stone.

The ancient authors never refer to the populations of the British Isles or Ireland as "Celts." Proto- or pre-Irish place names of "Ierne" are first recorded in Ptolemy's *Geography* of the second century AD (II.1). Caesar and Tacitus describe similarities between Britons and Gauls, including parallel names of *civitates* (Caes. *BG* 5.12ff.; Tac. *Agr.* 11). The early Irish literature is often thought to reflect values, ideas and practices of the Iron Age in the islands and possibly on the continent (Karl 2006; but see McCone 1990). Until recently, great waves of "Celtic" migrations from the continent have been assumed. However, few people need actually be involved in the transmission of goods, ideas, styles and motifs. It is safe to think of the Channel and the Atlantic as facilitating interchange and traffic in both directions from earliest times (Cunliffe 2001; cf. Raftery 1998; Morse 2005).

3 Economy and Social Structure

Archaeology reveals habitations at the levels of farmsteads, villages, trading centers or entrepôts, mining complexes, hillforts and hilltop towns, and in the later LT periods extensive flatland towns and huge, urban "oppida." In addition to agriculture and pastoralism, the "Celts" favored direct acquisition of goods. They raided for livestock and plundered sanctuaries, homes, and entire cities rich in gold. Goods acquired through invasion and exploitation of newly settled territory entered into circulation. Mediterranean bronze vessels and pottery, Tyrrhenian coral, Baltic amber, African ivory, rare stones and shells, Near Eastern dyes, Scythian and Thracian finds, and possibly east-Asian textiles hint at the breadth of "Celtic" exchange networks. What the "Celts" gave in long-distance exchange remains archaeologically invisible; tin from the British isles is likely, as are other ores, salt and salted meats, furs, hides, live animals, textiles, timber, honey, other perishable products, and slaves (Nash Briggs 2003). A good living could always be made by might of arms, directly by raiding, pillaging and conquest of new lands, indirectly by extortion of protection money and ransom, or for hire as mercenary soldiers.

Early "Celtic" societies have been interpreted as "chiefdoms" headed by the equivalent of Homeric *basileis*, or as "princely" societies on the analogy of medieval feudalism (Karl 2006). Post-capitalist world-systems theory of center and periphery as well as peer polity, central place, and various state-formation models have more recently been applied (Arnold and Gibson 1995). That these were ranked societies is indisputable; our evidence suggests great local variability and change over time. Mediterranean, particularly Greek imports found in "Celtic" contexts, have long inspired a prestige-goods economy model. This and similar diffusionist reconstructions rest on the assumption that Greek goods were privileged over all others. To the "Celts" is attributed a consciousness of peripherality and a desire to ape their betters. This is not demonstrable archaeologically. It is rather more likely that the "Celts" did not indulge in romantic philhellenism.

Much was directly or indirectly disrupted through Roman occupation. The ancients interpreted the indigenous structures they observed in their own familiar political language; thus, Latin terms such as *reges*, *principes*, *equites*, are opaque labels that reveal little about internal Gaulish dynamics. We are told of three groups of "Celts" that were particularly influential: the bards, vates and druids (Strabo 4.4.4, citing Poseidonios). The task of the bard was to perpetuate a leader's immortality by praising his or her genealogy, generosity and deeds, or conversely, damning his enemies with biting satire (Diod. 5.31; Athen. 4.152; 6.246). Vates were natural philosophers and interpreters of sacrifices. Druids were keepers of the knowledge of natural sciences and moral philosophy as well as presiders at rituals (section 6 below).

4 Warfare

At Ciumeşti in Romania, a burial of the third century BC contained greaves, chain mail, and a helmet consisting of a cap of iron crowned with the bronze figure of a bird of prey. The wings are movable so that, as the warrior rode or ran at the enemy, his helmet produced a frightening cacophony and motion (Zirra 1991). That this helmet type was also used in the western LT zone to make "the wearer look even taller and more fearsome" is suggested by Poseidonios (Diod. 5.30). Mounted warriors, worked in repoussé on the controversial Gundestrup cauldron, wear similar helmets. The innovative mail shirt is only one of several types of "Celtic" body armour found in burial and depositional contexts, depicted in art and described in the literature. The "Celtic" warrior of the third to first centuries was armed with a sword suspended on a chain, at least one spear with a wicked head, and an ovoid shield of wood and leather with a central boss or umbo. The terrifying appearance of "Celtic" warriors did not depend on their armour, however; some warriors such as the Gaesatae at the battle of Telamon in 225 BC famously rushed into battle naked save for their sword belts and jewelry (Polyb. 2.28). The Gaesatae were not a *civitas*, but rather a sort of shock troop of specialized itinerant mercenaries. The armies of the north Italian *civitates* wore trousers and light cloaks; the northern Gauls also wore shirts. The expert use of the chariot to transport the warrior into the midst of battle continued in Britain after it was superseded on the continent by the cavalry (Caes. *BG* 4.33; Diod. 5.29.1). Both the Gauls and the Celtiberi were revered and feared as horsemen. The Romans paid them the highest compliment in learning and imitating their exercises (Arr. *Tact.* 33–34). "Celtic" contingents formed the most effective of the Roman cavalry (Strabo 4.4.2).

The most potent weapon of the "Celtic" military was the headlong, furious charge. What made it the more terrifying was its cacophony, a combination of shouting and war-cries, horns and trumpets (Polyb. 2.29, cf. Diod. 5.30). As an alternative to the headlong charge, a Celtic army might assemble before the enemy. One warrior would challenge a champion from the other side to single combat (Diod. 5.29.2). In Livy's colorful tale of the single combat of T. Manlius Torquatus, the gigantic Gaul prances about, sticks his tongue out and taunts the ranked Roman army. Manlius, the embodiment of republican Roman virtue, evoking his ancestor who had expelled the Gauls from Rome, slips his Spanish sword under the blundering Gaul's shield and guts the brute. He then dons the dead Gaul's bloodied torc in triumph (7.9–10, Gell. 9.13.4–19, cf. Dio 7.35). This tale illustrates neatly the popular Roman trope that the Gauls are frightening, over-life-size and hubristic, but easily defeated by the smaller, cleverer, better-armed and better-strategizing Romans.

5 Feasting

The Celts were famously prodigious drinkers (Diod. 5.26.3). Remains of beer, mead and wine have been found in preserved vessels; tomb assemblages include all manner of metal and pottery beverage containers as well as plates, knives, butchery and cooking equipment, and foodstuffs, including whole or butchered pigs. Food was consumed "cleanly, but with a lion-like appetite" (Poseidonios in Athen. 4.151). The colorful accounts of mustachioed "Celts" at banquet suggest that Mediterranean foreigners were able to interact with them in the context of the banquet setting. The convivial feast was an important venue for the formation and establishment of an individual's identity in relation to his/her society, as well as that of the social unit itself (Dietler 1999).

An essential part of the feast is the narrative that it weaves. In the process of agonistic boasting and insults, and the recitation and singing of ancestral and more recent deeds, the identities and relationships of those present are recreated. The feast itself enters into the biography and mythology of the participants. It is tragic that we have no records of their songs and tales. On the other hand, this highly oral society would have been fundamentally altered with the introduction of writing. Our authors are impressed with the influential status and even military function of bards (Strabo 5.31, 4.197; cf. Lucian 5.1–6). It is only in early Irish texts like the Ulster cycle that we get a taste of the fabulous histories, deeds, genealogies, and interwoven epics whereby generations of heroes' lives were shaped and immortalized.

Diodorus (5.28.4) likens the "Celtic" distribution of the hero's portion to the situation in Homer (*Il.* 7.321): "Brave warriors they honor with the choicest portion of the meat, just as the poet says that the chieftains honored Ajax when he returned having defeated Hektor in single combat." The assignment of the champion's portion, consisting not only of food and drink but also of great treasure, is one of the great themes in early Irish literature. The implication is that the heroes' respective standings can change from feast to feast, even boast to boast. Unlike the Iliadic episode above, where it is King Agamemnon who actually distributes the spoils, in the epic feasts the distribution is the result and instrument of agonistic exertions, verbal and physical. Outrageous boasting and sparring escalates into armed combat and real bloodshed (Poseidonios via Athen. 4.154, Diod. 5.28.5).

Women are prominent at the feasts in the early Irish tales, engaging in competitions of their own. In the foundation legends of Massalia, the leader of the Phokaian traders is invited to the wedding banquet of the local princess, Gyptis, or Petta. She selects him to be her husband by giving him the drinking cup, and thereby a form of legitimation (Just. 43.3.4; Athen. 13.576). The rich late Hallstatt and early LT female burials containing feasting vessels inspire a vision of hard-drinking female leaders hosting or receiving agonal feasts, which may sit uneasily with our entrenched stereotype of testosterone-driven "Celtic" booze-ups. The funerary assemblages may not only reproduce aspects of the deceased's identity and defining activities in the here and now, but also give her something practical to take into the afterlife.

6 Religion

Of the three non-military classes generally named by the ancients, two, the Druids and vates, were responsible for the spiritual and ritual life of the Gauls (Strabo 4.4.4, Diod. 5.31.5). The course of study to become a Druid could last up to twenty years, and consisted mainly of memorizing an enormous corpus of verses and teachings that was never written down. The Druids thus incorporated the accumulated wisdom of their people. Caesar tells us that they also practiced divination, preached transmigration of the soul, dispensed justice, and studied the natural sciences such as astronomy

(Caes. *BG* 6.14–16). A fragmentary bronze inscription found at Coligny, France, outlines winter and summer holy days on a combined 62-month lunar and solar calendar (fig. 3.1). Female practitioners included the black-clad furies (Druidesses?) of Mona (Anglesey) (Tac. *Ann.* 14.30), the maenads living on an island at the mouth of the Loire (Strabo 4.4.6), and the sorceresses named in the lead tablets from Larzac. Human sacrifice was apparently performed under all manner of circumstances, even divination (Diod. 5.31). Prisoners of war were routinely offered up. The sacrifice of criminals was propitious for the prosperity of the land (Diod. 5.32; Strabo 4.4.4). Many well-preserved bodies of tortured and killed victims have been discovered in the peat bogs of northern Europe, Britain, and Ireland – recently the well-preserved fourth- to third-century BC finds at Clonycavan and Old Croghan near Dublin. However, their relationship *vis-à-vis* the "Celts" is unclear.

Many of our weapons finds are from watery contexts such as rivers, streams, springs, or lakes. In the case of lakeside dwellings, some accidental or incidental loss may be expected, but some deposits are clearly deliberate, such as the hundreds of weapons and wagon fittings found at La Tène in Switzerland, or those at Llyn Cerrig Bach in Anglesey, which include such horrific items as slave-gang chains. Many weapons found in ritual deposits have been "killed," bent completely out of shape and rendered useless. Inscribed tablets, jewelry, textiles, coins, and anthropoid sculptures are other common watery deposits.

At a sanctuary at the center of the oppidum of Gournay-sur-Aronde, a sequence from the fourth century BC through to the Roman period has been excavated. Thousands of "killed" weapons were exposed to rust away in a ditch outside a square enclosure surrounding sacrificial pits, together with thousands of animal bones and the remains of decapitated humans. Fifty kilometers away at Ribemont-sur-Ancre hundreds of disarticulated human long-bones were stacked in a square formation, while other skeletons were merely halved and left in place. A roofed structure over a ditch displayed the bodies of dozens of fully armed warriors, decapitated and propped upright. The building, bodies and all, was left to deteriorate and collapse into the ditch below (Brunaux 1999). Ribemont is usually interpreted as a victory monument displaying the vanquished foe. Alternatively, it may have commemorated fallen comrades. An enormous amount of cooperative effort went into the configuration of these sites. We can only imagine the social and psychological dimensions.

The find contexts of "Celtic" arms and armour suggest that there was a profoundly religious aspect to the practice of warfare. Coupled with evidence from burials, these deposits suggest beliefs in chthonic powers as well as a lively afterlife filled with fighting and feasting, analogous to scenes in early Celtic poetry. Freestanding sculptures of men in armour sitting cross-legged at Roquepertuse and Entremont have been interpreted as warrior deities. Decapitated heads form part of the iconography. According to Poseidonios the "Celts" "hang the heads of their slain enemies from the necks of their horses when they leave a battlefield and then hang them up on a peg when they get home" (Strabo 4.4.5, cf. Diod. 5.29). Livy's account of the death of Postumius explicitly makes the religious connection: "the Boii took his severed head in a procession to the holiest of their temples. There it was cleaned and the bare skull was adorned with gold, as is their custom. It was used thereafter as a sacred vessel on special occasions and as a ritual drinking-cup by their priests and temple officials" (23.24). No gilded skulls have been found in the Keltike, but there is ample archaeological evidence of decapitation, defleshing, dismemberment and manipulation of the corpses of warriors. Conspicuous display of decapitated heads is attested at various sites in France and Iberia.

Since Aristotle, the "Celts' " lack of fear of injury or death seemed to the Greeks to border on the insane (e.g. *Eth. Nic.* 3.7). This incomprehensible trait contributed to their characterization as utterly strange and barbarian. An enemy who has no thought for bodily harm is highly motivated to perform reckless feats of daring and to fight to the death (Diod. 5.29). Complete freedom from any fear of death is often attributed to a belief in quasi-Pythagorean reincarnation (Caes. *BG* 6.13, 6.14.5; Diod. 5.28). We are left again with a conceptual divide which the Greeks and Romans attempted to bridge in their own familiar terms.

7   Who Were the Ancient "Celts"?

Ancient attitudes toward the "Celts" were ambivalent, or rather situational. On the one hand, the irrational brutes were to be resisted at any cost; on the other, they made fine mercenaries and slaves. Some authors such as the Stoic Poseidonios occasionally counted the "Celts" among those barbarians who were untouched by the evils of contemporary civilization. Their view of the "Celts" was inevitably tinged by the topos of the northern barbarian – the unbridgeable gap between the civilized and the wild, inscrutable other who at base remains unreliable, unpredictable, untamed.

Thus, the ancient authors give us many fragmentary but vivid, often stereotyped, often propagandistic, sometimes contradictory, always constructed glimpses. Archaeology shows us an artistically innovative, lavish, stubbornly abstracting, colorful, and gorgeous craft production. In the preserved material culture, in burials, deposits, and settlements, we find unique and powerful expressions of local identities. Burials, bones, pots, coins, weapons, minor arts, tools, textiles, metals, plant and animal remains, traces of architecture, inscriptions, and above all their contexts and relationships help to flesh out our picture of the Iron Age Europeans. Whether, in any single case, they are among peoples who would have called themselves "Celts" is a question we cannot answer, and which is probably irrelevant.[1]

FURTHER READING

A good introduction is Cunliffe 2003. Excellent are Biel et al. 2002, Collis 2003, Cunliffe 1997, Megaw and Megaw 2001, Rieckhoff and Biel 2001. The protean Birkhan 1997–2000 covers the early medieval period as well. M. Green's collection *The Celtic World* (1995) is devoted primarily to the insular Celts. Moscati et al. 1991, the catalog of the *I Celti* exhibit

---

[1] This offering is dedicated to the indelible memory of Mark Southern.

in Venice, covers the entire spectrum of the Celtic world, but sadly provides almost no bibliography. Karl and Stifter 2007 is admirably documented and brings together four volumes' worth, primarily new translations of articles previously published elsewhere.

On "Celtic" drinking and identity, as well as further-ranging work on the anthropology of feasting, see Dietler 1999. Essential reading on gender issues is a series of articles by Arnold (e.g. 1995). On social structure, most useful in English is still the spectrum of contributions in Arnold and Gibson 1995. Brunaux 2000 describes several important excavations in France and synthesizes much of the information available on "Celtic" ritual.

Cunliffe 2001 offers a unique perspective on the "Celtic" and neighboring populations on the Atlantic coasts. Morse 2005 presents a fascinating investigation into the origins and progress of Celtic studies in Britain; much is also applicable to the continent. On the propagandistic and military roles of the Galatians: Mitchell 2003; for the Gauls of north Italy, J. Williams 2001; for Caesar in Gaul, Riggsby 2006.

McEvoy et al. 2004 is only one example of the kind of studies of "Celtic DNA" appearing steadily in scientific journals. Collis 2003 is especially relevant to the question of Celtic identity, cf. also Dietler 1994 on the role of Celtic identity in Europe and in particular France; laudably comprehensible on material culture, agency and identity is P. Wells 2001.

Websites to watch are:
Mont Beuvray (Bibracte) and the state-of-the-art European Research Center, publisher of the "Les Celtes et les Gaulois" series, among others: www.bibracte.fr

A Landscape of Ancestors: The Heuneburg Archaeological Project with excavation updates: www.uwm.edu/~barnold/arch

The French Ministry of Culture: The Gauls in Provence: the oppidum of Entremont (includes finds from Roquepertuse): www.entremont.culture.gouv.fr

e-Keltoi: peer-reviewed on-line Journal of Interdisciplinary Celtic Studies, particularly Vol. 6: The Celts in the Iberian Peninsula:
www.uwm.edu/Dept/celtic/ekeltoi/volumes/vol6/index.html

Most of the translations appearing in the chapter are from P. Freeman, *War, Women and Druids. Eyewitness Reports and Early Accounts of the Ancient Celts* (Austin 2002).

PART IV

Encountering the Divine

CHAPTER TWENTY-SEVEN

Religion

Mark Humphries

1 The Problem of Ancient Religion

In AD 341 (or thereabouts) the Christian Roman emperor Constans (337–50) issued a law against traditional forms of religion that we call paganism: "Superstition shall cease; the madness of sacrifices shall be abolished" (*Cod. Theod.* 16.10.2; T. Barnes 1993: 102). The law, like others of its ilk, failed to suppress paganism (E. Hunt 1993), but it remains striking for its strident language: it derided the centuries-old pagan cults as "superstition" (*superstitio*), and their central ritual acts as "madness" (*insania*). Such language was not unique to Christian condemnations of paganism; it had been used by pagans of Christians (Humphries 2006: 196–202), as well as by pagan authority figures about certain pagan cult practices of which they did not approve (Grodzynski 1974). Even so, the law epitomizes the Christian view of ancient pagan religion as essentially a form of error. Indeed, around the time that it was enacted, Firmicus Maternus, a pagan convert to Christianity, wrote an angry denunciation of ancient religion, the title of which, *De Errore Profanarum Religionum* (*Concerning the Error of Pagan Worship*), emphasizes the same point.

This chapter is concerned with the religions that Constans and Firmicus Maternus were condemning. It may seem strange to begin with details drawn from paganism's twilight years, but such vignettes serve to underline the crucial point that ancient religion is often interpreted from unsympathetic (or even hostile) perspectives. The Judeo-Christian cultural background against which modern scholars have worked has influenced attitudes towards paganism, either implicitly or explicitly. In practice, this means that certain characteristics of Judaism and Christianity are regarded as normative, and that ancient religion is often assessed in terms of how it measures up to such norms. For example, it has been stated that the worship of Roman emperors "never involved its spectators in the intense mental participation of the congregation of a Jewish or Christian service" (Liebeschuetz 1979: 82). More recent analyses of ancient religion, however, have sought to distance themselves from what are now generally termed "Christianizing assumptions" (Beard and Crawford 1985: 26–27; S. Price 1984: 11–19).

The traditional approach has also, more insidiously, tended to regard pagan religious practice as somehow insincere or invalid, since it lacked much that is considered as normal in modern religions. Unlike Judaism, Christianity, or Islam, Greco-Roman religions apparently laid much less emphasis on notions of dogma, salvation and the afterlife, priestly vocation, morality (but cf. McDonald 1998: 191–93), and revealed texts; similarly, ancient temples were houses for images of the gods, not places of congregation like synagogues, churches, or mosques; above all, the myriad divinities of ancient polytheism stand in stark contrast to religious systems that stress the uniqueness of Yahweh, God, or Allah (Finley 1985). We must be constantly on guard against succumbing to assumptions that denigrate the importance of ancient religions. Such prejudices inform even the basic terminology used. The very word pagan (and so its derivative paganism) is a case in point: it is itself a Christian coinage, derived from the word *pagus*, meaning a country district, and was meant to emphasize the boorish backwardness that Christians associated with adherents of ancient cults (O'Donnell 1977). In recent times, there has been considerable debate about the validity of the term "paganism," and alternatives (such as polytheism, traditional cult, and so on) have been suggested (Lee 2006: 164–65). None yet has succeeded in commanding universal assent; hence I use here the terms "pagan" and "paganism" because they are familiar, but with the caveat that they must not be allowed to cloud our analyses by suggesting that there was something inherently wrong with ancient religion.

Christianizing assumptions have prompted various misunderstandings in the study of ancient religion. For instance, to talk of paganism as an identifiable phenomenon (like Judaism, Christianity, or Islam) gives the wholly wrong impression that it was a unified religious system. It was not. While there certainly were broadly comparable features that characterized religious practice throughout the classical world, it must always be borne in mind that its most distinguishing feature was its great diversity and adaptability (as we will see later in this chapter). Paganism's lack of certain characteristics of, say, Christianity has been used also as a form of historical explanation. If the differences between paganism and Christianity could be construed in such a way as to present pagan religion as "empty" of central religious value, then that could help to explain why Christianity ultimately "triumphed" over it: by its very nature, so the story would go, paganism failed to provide spiritual sustenance, leaving the worshipers of the old gods hungry for something more satisfying, and this they found in Christianity. More recent work, in contrast, has emphasized the continuing vigor of traditional cults in the early Christian period (see esp. Lane Fox 1986).

Indeed, Christianizing assumptions have influenced the evaluative framework within which scholars investigate Greco-Roman religions. A well-known example is provided by what are often termed "mystery cults," such as the worship of Isis and Mithras. Since such cults involved rituals of initiation, the divulging of esoteric divine knowledge, and speculations about the afterlife – aspects that resemble Christian baptism, catechism, and soteriology – they have sometimes been regarded as more genuine in terms of how they appealed to the religious needs of individuals, and thus could be regarded in almost evolutionary terms as occupying a middle ground between paganism and Christianity (cf. Humphries 2004). This idea has been particularly influential on studies of the cult of Mithras in the Roman empire. Belgian scholar Franz Cumont (1868–1947), while sure to point out that the two religions were different, nevertheless stressed certain parallels between them and talked of them being engaged in a long and bitter struggle (Cumont 1956: 188–208); but the most forceful statement was made by the French philosopher of religion Ernest Renan (1823–92), who notoriously remarked that if Christianity had failed, then Mithraism might well have become the religion of the Roman world in its place (M. Clauss 2000: 168). Such notions still have some currency today, but critically astute scholars are apt to observe that they are thoroughly misconceived, and reflect the unfortunate repercussions of the Christianizing perspectives that have bedeviled the study of ancient religion generally (M. Clauss 2000: 168–69).

In addition to falling prey to assumptions brought in from modern religious traditions, ancient paganism has also suffered from the secularizing or rationalizing tendencies that have colored approaches to religions of all varieties in Western intellectual discourses since the nineteenth century (O. Chadwick 1975). Karl Marx's famous dictum that religion "is the opium of the people" (Marx 1844/1978: 54) is particularly pertinent here, given the links between religion and politics in Greco-Roman culture (section 3 below). Hence religion could be regarded as something that was cynically manipulated by social elites to achieve control over their inferiors (criticism in Beard and Crawford 1985: 27–30; Bowden 2005: 1–11), or as something so self-evidently irrational that no serious-minded individual would have taken it seriously (criticism in Gould 1985). Such views might seem to have support in ancient evidence. The descriptions of the gods as capricious participants in human affairs in the Homeric epics prompted Xenophanes in the sixth century BC to complain that poetry presented the gods as behaving in ways that would be regarded as shameful for humans (S. Price 1999: 127). Hence we might reasonably argue that such presentations of the gods amount to little more than "a romantic, trivial, and not very edifying mythology" (G. Murray 1935: 1). But this evidence needs to be interpreted sensitively: the portrayal of the gods in myth was only one way of thinking about the gods and their roles in human affairs, and others existed (Buxton 1994: 145–65).

Rationalizing assumptions, like Christianizing ones, impose modern western ideas on the evidence for ancient religion. Indeed, the very term "religion," signifying a belief system, is a modern, Western category, not strictly paralleled in antiquity (Vernant 1980: 88), although it remains useful as a collective term to describe the nature of a society's relationship with its gods. When investigating the nature of ancient religion, we need to be wary of imposing alien frameworks on ancient experiences, while at the same time endeavoring to be as sympathetic as possible in our readings. Recent studies have sought to arrive at such understandings of Greco-Roman religious practice by appealing to anthropological studies of religion, which aim to make sense of it by regarding it as a manifestation of particular cultural systems (e.g. Geertz 1973: 87–125). Thus the seemingly irrational nature of Greek oracles has been fruitfully examined through the prism of similar practices observed among the Azande tribe of the Sudan in the 1920s (Evans-Pritchard 1976; Bowden 2005: 28–33), while the peculiarities of Roman cult have been rendered less strange through comparison with Japanese Shintoism (Feeney 1998: 13).

It is not only the modernizing assumptions of modern scholars that have caused problems for the study of ancient religion, however. The character of the surviving evidence presents another difficulty. Since historians traditionally have prioritized written sources, whether literary texts or inscriptions, and have interpreted archaeology within a framework provided by them, there has been a tendency to regard the religion of those societies that have left most written documentation as paradigmatic. Thus, for classical Greece, religion is often seen through the lens of Athenian sources (McKesson 2005: xi; S. Price 1999: 9), while in the Roman world, the experience of Rome itself dominates the discourse (e.g. Beard, North, and Price 1998; Scheid 2003). It is only fair to warn readers that Athenian and Roman evidence will loom large in much of my account. In spite of this limitation, the chief aim of this chapter is to highlight ways in which the study of ancient religion can overcome the pitfalls of modernizing assumptions. It will focus on paired discussions on the role of religion in society broadly and the nature of the relationships between individuals and their gods, and will finish by highlighting the perils of seeking to squeeze the evidence for ancient religion into overly neat or systematic categories that take no account of its basic diversity. But before launching into these topics it will be worth meditating briefly on the physical presence of religion in the ancient world, since that provides the context against which all other topics must be seen.

2 Between Heaven and Earth: a World Full of Gods

Anyone who travels through the lands once occupied by the civilizations of Greece and Rome will be struck by the profusion of temples that dot the landscape. Such edifices may be grand, like the Doric temples of Athens or of Paestum in southern Italy, or the sanctuary of Jupiter Heliopolitanus at Baalbek in Lebanon; equally they may be humble, like the tiny temple of Mithras near the fortress of Carrawburgh on Hadrian's wall in the north of England. There were other sorts of religious places in addition to temples. Some might comprise little more than an altar, such as that in honor of Zeus on Mount Lykaion in Arcadia (Paus. 8.38.7), or the wayside shrines of the Lares Compitales (neighborhood spirits) in Rome. Private space too had its sacred spots, ranging from the hearth, a focus of rituals in Greek households, to the elaborate domestic shrines found, for instance, at Pompeii.

The ubiquity of temple buildings and shrines can sometimes obscure the particular significance that many of them possessed. The curious building on the Athenian acropolis called the Erechthion provides an eccentric, but telling, example (Hurwitt 1999: 200–209). Its unusual plan was designed to encompass a number of sites of religious significance, such as the primeval olive tree planted by Athena, a salt-water spring created by a blow from Poseidon's trident, and a fissure left by a thunderbolt hurled by Zeus. Moreover, the building linked the world of the gods with that of humankind, since within its precincts lay tombs of the mythical Athenian kings

Erechtheus and Kekrops. The Roman world provides similar examples. When town planners established new colonial settlements in territories brought under the Rome's control, they sought out for the temple of Jupiter, Juno, and Minerva (the patron deities of the Roman state) a high vantage point that mirrored the location of the gods' temple at Rome itself (Vitr. 1.7.1). The gods themselves could exercise choice in the matter. When the cult of Asclepius was brought to Rome from Epidauros in Greece in 291 BC, it was thought that the god, in the form of a snake, slithered ashore on the island in the River Tiber near the middle of the city, and there a sanctuary was built for him (Livy, *Per.* 11). Certain gods had temples located where they could oversee activities with which they were particularly associated. Thus Hephaistos, the god associated with metal working, had a temple overlooking the blacksmiths' workshops in the Athenian agora (Camp 2001: 102–3). Elsewhere in Attica, at Cape Sounion, a large sanctuary rose in honor of the sea god Poseidon: its location on a promontory made it an important landmark for sailors, whose activities were under Poseidon's care (Mikalson 2005: 3–5).

Like Poseidon at Sounion, many gods had sanctuaries in the countryside. Among the most spectacular of ancient religious sites are the temple of Apollo at Bassae, in the rugged terrain of the western Peloponnese, and the sanctuary to the same god located at Delphi, on the flanks of Mount Parnassus in central Greece. Neither site was too far from local settlements, but the choice of mountains in both cases reminds us that it was not just urban centers that were associated with the gods, but also the landscape in general (Buxton 1994; Jost 1994). Indeed, the whole ancient conception of the world was influenced by religious ideas: while Greeks and Romans often regarded their immediate neighbors as barbarians, they also held that at the remote edges of the inhabited world there existed fortunate peoples who still enjoyed an intimate relationship with the gods of a kind that had otherwise departed from humankind after the prehistoric Golden Age (Romm 1992).

The omnipresence of the gods in physical terms reflected their omnipotence in all aspects of life. However much we might be impressed by the scientific advances made by the Greeks and Romans, it is important to remember that they knew little about such everyday perils as the incidence of disease or changes in the weather. These were regarded as unpredictable, and power over them was held by the gods, whose goodwill might be sought out through prayer, sacrifice, and votive offerings. It is little wonder, then, that religious rituals punctuated the life cycles of ordinary men and women, whether in their participation in public ceremonies at major sanctuaries, or through the assiduous observance of rituals of the gods who oversaw the well-being of individual households.

3   Religion and the State

In this world suffused with divine presences, where gods had the power to control even the unpredictable forces of nature, any human success was regarded as being influenced by the gods (cf. Cic. *Nat. D.* 2.60). Nowhere is the evidence on this point more explicit than in terms of the good fortunes of the state; but here we confront an aspect of ancient religion that apparently supports the view that it was cynically manipulated by political elites. How else are we to interpret evidence, such as a letter from Brutus to Cicero in which the latter is canvassed for his support for the candidature of one of Brutus's friends in an election to a college of priests (Cic. *Ad Brut.* 1.7)? The point seems to be underscored by the later concentration at Rome of supreme political power together with the chief priesthood of the state (*pontifex maximus*) in the hands of emperors from Augustus onwards. But to regard such phenomena as the crude manipulation of religion by elites represents an inability to engage sympathetically with the character of ancient religion.

It is clear, for instance, that at classical Athens elite domination of religion was impracticable. Not only did the Athenian citizenry (*demos*) play a key role via the assembly (*ekklesia*) in financing religious activities, but also it would have been difficult for the elite to exercise influence over the diffuse conglomeration of priesthoods and other religious personnel (Garland 1990). At Rome, the situation was rather different. There was certainly often an overlap between the holding of priesthoods and magistracies, but the Romans themselves did not regard this as problematic. Rather, they saw divine support for (elite) politicians, and the consequent involvement of such politicians in religious life, as wholly natural. As Cicero put it:

> Among the many things that our ancestors created and established under divine inspiration, nothing is more renowned than their decision to entrust the worship of the gods and the highest interests of the state to the same men. In this way, the most eminent and illustrious citizens might ensure the maintenance of the state by the prudent interpretation of religion. (*Dom.* 1.1)

If we regard the situation as anomalous, then that represents our failure to penetrate Roman *mentalités* (Beard 1990).

Religion punctuated the life of the state in other ways. In cities throughout the Greco-Roman world, official calendars calibrated what time was to be given over to the festivals in honor of the gods, when all other public business would cease. Such festivals were important not only for venerating the gods, but also for articulating community identities, which in many cases were associated with a particular god. At classical Athens, for instance, detailed arrangements were set out in law for the celebration of the Pananthenaia, the main festival in honor of Athena, in such a way as to emphasize "the inseparability of festivals from the very definition of Greek civic life" (Bruit Zaidmann and Schmitt Pantel 1992: 110). A second-century AD decree from Ephesos in Asia Minor makes the point emphatically. It describes how, for an entire month, public business would cease for the festival in honor of the city's patron goddess Artemis: "in this way," the decree concluded, "with the god honored more highly, our city will remain from time to time more famous and more blessed" (*SIG*[3] 867; S. Price 1999: 181).

Religious ritual also attended political action. Formal business at the Athenian assembly began with sacrifices, offerings, and prayers to purify the Pnyx where the citizens met (Hansen 1987: 90–91). Meetings of similar bodies in the Roman world, such as the senate at Rome or town councils throughout the empire, also began with prayers and the swearing of oaths (Ando 2000: 359–62; Talbert 1984: 224–25). Military action, given its risky nature, also involved religious rituals performed by generals on campaign. Xenophon's celebrated account of the retreat of the 10,000 Greek mercenaries through Persian territory in 402 BC contains frequent references to sacrifices and the interpretation of dreams and omens. The Romans were no less assiduous. Before he captured the Etruscan city of Veii in 396 BC, the Roman commander Camillus performed the ceremony of *evocatio*, calling out the city's tutelary deity Juno Regina and promising her a new temple in Rome, all in order to avert her wrath (Livy 5.21; cf. Macrob. *Sat.* 3.9). Other generals vowed temples to gods in return for success on the battlefield (Orlin 1997). Indeed, the traditional Roman procedure for declaring war was bound up with religious rituals performed by a priest, the *fetialis*, who also served as an envoy (Livy 1.32). If such rites were followed scrupulously, then the Romans could be sure of waging a just war, blessed by the gods (Brunt 1978).

Such intersections between religion and politics reached their most apparently eccentric manifestation in the divine honors awarded to individuals, particularly Hellenistic kings and Roman emperors. Such cults have traditionally been dismissed, either as the most egregious example of the cynical manipulation of religion for political ends, or as examples of the degenerate character of traditional paganism under pernicious "oriental" influences (S. Price 1984: 17–19). There can be little doubt that ruler-cult helped to articulate power relationships between rulers and their subjects: an early, and spectacular, example is provided by the extraordinary festivities for the Macedonian king Demetrios Poliorketes at Athens in the late fourth century BC (A. Bell 2004: 99–107). Such honors, however, were often the willing reactions of subjects to their rulers, rather than impositions from above. The old model that portrays Roman emperor worship as an import from the East, for instance, is confounded by evidence from as early as the reigns of Augustus (27 BC to AD 14) and Tiberius (AD 14–37) for spontaneous cults in their honor in Italy and Spain (Suet. *Aug.* 59; Tac. *Ann.* 4.37–8). Furthermore, recent scholarship has suggested that ruler-worship may have been a straightforwardly organic development from within Greek and Roman religious systems. In the Greek world, the sharp distinctions between humans and gods were blurred by the existence of quasi-divine heroes, many of whom received cult honors: this included not only those, such as Herakles, who are known from mythology, but also those who founded communities such as the demes of Attica or the various colonial cities (Polignac 1995: 128–49; cf. Lefkowitz 2003: 30–41 on gods as ancestors). Meanwhile at Rome, the established tradition of worshipping the *genius* (divine essence) of the *paterfamilias* (head of the household) could easily be transferred to the potent figure of the emperor (Gradel 2002).

4   Religion and "Belief"

The perception of generals, kings, and emperors as divine prompts further questions about the wider nature of individuals' engagement with their gods. Such questions are sometimes articulated in terms of whether or not the Greeks and Romans believed in their gods, and here the influence of Christianizing and rationalizing assumptions has often led to a negative answer. In particular, since the evidence for ancient religion focuses on external acts, such as sacrifice, it has been doubted that it involved the intense psychological engagement of modern faiths. Attention has been drawn to statements of skepticism about gods and rituals found in the sources, such as Lucretius's apparent denial that they had any efficacy at all (Lucr. 5.1197–1201). Much ancient skepticism about the gods and rituals, however, hinged primarily on the *correct* interpretation of religious signs. A famous example is provided by the story told by Herodotus (1.53–5) of King Croesus of Lydia (c.560–546 BC) who, before attacking the Persian empire, asked the oracle of Apollo at Delphi about the likely outcome of his venture. The response was that if Croesus embarked on his campaign, he would destroy a great empire, which he did – his own. Modern scholars have sometimes argued that this provides support for the notion that the ancients could not have believed in such a seemingly capricious religious system. However, as Herodotus explains, Croesus, having initially criticized the oracle for giving him bad advice, ultimately concluded that the fault lay not with the god, but with himself, because he had misinterpreted Apollo's response (Hdt. 1.90–91).

Debate over such episodes is often influenced by rationalizing assumptions, particularly those that take an evolutionary view of human development. According to this view, belief in the gods can be regarded as somehow infantile, to be associated with the early stages of ancient society; later, as that society became more sophisticated, such belief must have fallen away, leaving only a shell of rituals cynically manipulated by social elites. According to such an interpretation, Croesus was simply naive, or foolishly over-confident. But this rationalizing view is unsatisfactory, above all because it imposes an explicitly modern way of thinking on ancient experiences. Moreover, Croesus's credulity cannot simply be dismissed as primitive ignorance: Galen and Pausanias, writing under the Roman empire, could accept certain myths as true, even while being skeptical of others (Veyne 1988: 54–56, 95–102).

Moreover, consultation of the gods sometimes produced responses that could not be easily manipulated by political or military elites. Such examples show that the gods could not be easily hoodwinked: they possessed real power, and that power demanded respect through scrupulous ritual observance. We have already seen how the retreat of Xenophon and the 10,000 from Persia involved regular sacrifices and consultations with diviners; on occasion, these rituals yielded divine advice that defied military logic, as when the Greeks were compelled to delay their march if the omens were not propitious (e.g. Xen. *Anab.* 6.4). Sometimes the consequences could be serious: the fatal delay of the Athenian forces in Sicily in 413 BC was caused by superstitious horror at a lunar eclipse (Thuc. 7.50.4). Similarly at Rome, the establishment of the cult of Asclepius in 291 BC only occurred after the Romans failed to follow divine advice to the letter. Two years earlier, when the city was afflicted by bad weather and plague, the Romans had consulted the Sibylline oracles, which had recommended that Asclepius be brought to Rome; but, since the chief magistrates of Rome were busy fighting a war, they did not do this, but only offered public prayers to the god (Livy 10.47; Parke 1988: 194). Asclepius was not appeased, and the misfortunes afflicting the city only ceased when the Roman authorities complied with the recommendation of the oracle. Clearly messages from the gods had to be taken seriously.

Another objection sometimes raised against the possibility of belief in ancient religions is the astonishing diversity that they presented, not least in terms of contradictory stories told about the gods themselves in mythology. Here again, however, scholarship has fallen victim to modernizing assumptions about religion. Unlike Judaism, Christianity, or Islam, there was no orthodoxy, no strictly defined set of true beliefs in Greco-Roman religion. This contrast, however, may be quite misleading, not least because questions of orthodoxy in modern monotheistic faiths have been hotly contested. Furthermore, it is quite possible for people to hold contradictory beliefs or to be both superstitious and rational at the same time (I like to think I am fairly reasonable, but I regard the magpies in my garden with paranoid suspicion . . .). The notion of believing contradictory stories has been explored by Paul Veyne in a study of the credence the Greeks gave to their myths (Veyne 1988), and his insights have been applied successfully to Roman evidence (Feeney 1998). Put simply, this approach emphasizes the importance of reading Greco-Roman accounts of the gods in ways that are sensitive to the contexts in which such narratives were produced. Furthermore, it stresses that the monolithic conception of belief that moderns often apply to the ancient world is itself a product of a particular cultural milieu, in that it regards Judeo-Christian notions of belief as normative.

In broader terms, any effort to understand the nature of ancient beliefs needs to construct notions of belief that fit the evidence that survives. As has been noted, that evidence focuses above all on the performance of rituals. It might be observed, therefore, that the range of evidence for ancient rituals – ranging from magic spells and votive offerings, to incubation at healing shrines, to the wealth invested in public rites and the embellishment of temples – suggests not that they were empty, but that they were an honest acknowledgement of the great power that the gods possessed (Gould 1985: 14–24). As such, they are of themselves important evidence for belief in the gods.

5   The Variety of Ancient Religion

The preceding discussion of the specific contexts of religious experience in antiquity leads me to my final topic: the diversity of ancient religions. Indeed, some modern scholars choose to speak in terms of a plurality of Greek and Roman religions, thus emphasizing their difference from the organized unity that the singular noun religion implies. Compared with the unified systems found in Judaism, Christianity, and Islam, ancient paganism presents a variety that borders on the anarchic. This is most obvious in the case of myth, where very different stories could be told – even about apparently central myths, such as the destruction of Troy (Erskine 2001: 2–6) – in a way that flies in the face of Judeo-Christian notions of canonicity. Moreover, gods could have specific areas of responsibility at certain sites that did not wholly align with their more general representation. While Poseidon was generally associated with seafaring, he could have responsibility for other areas of life: at Athens he appears in the form of Poseidon Hippios, and was specifically associated with horses; at Delos he appears as Poseidon Asphaleios, and was regarded as keeping the island safe from earthquakes (Mikalson 2005: 33–34).

Such diversity increases when we turn to look at the world of the Roman empire, which encompassed an astonishing variety of cultures and, with them, a range of different religious traditions (Mellor 1992). This provoked various reactions. On the one hand, Roman public religion displayed, from the earliest times, an inexhaustible capacity to absorb new cults: we have already seen the example of Asclepius, but there were many others (Beard, North, and Price 1998: 1.64–98). At the same time, through a process of syncretism, deities with broadly similar characteristics could be regarded as diverse forms of the same divine power. The second-century AD novelist Apuleius provides a striking account of how the Egyptian goddess Isis was identified by different names in different places:

> My sole divine power is adored throughout the world in manifold guise, with varied rites, and by varied names. Hence the Phrygians, first born of humankind, call me the Mother of the Gods at Pessinus; the autochthonous Athenians call me Cecropian Minerva; the sea-girt Cyprians call me Paphian Venus; the arrow-bearing Cretans call me Dictynnian Diana; the trilingual Sicilians call me Stygian Proserpina; the Eleusinians call me their ancient goddess Ceres; some call me Juno, others Bellona, others Hecate, others Rhamnusia. (Apul. *Met.* 11.5)

Syncretism, although it is especially pronounced in the Hellenistic world and Roman empire, was a feature of ancient religions from very early times. Archaeological evidence from Rome suggests that Romans were identifying their gods Vulcan and Minerva with the Greeks' Hephaistos and Athena already by the sixth century (Cornell 1995: 147–48, 162). Shortly afterwards, we find Herodotus trying to draw equivalences between the religious systems of Greece and Egypt (2.42–50; T. Harrison 2000b: 182–89). These instances indicate how ancient religion was diverse not only across space, but also through time. New cults arose as the Greeks and Romans encountered the deities of other peoples; the system was endlessly dynamic.

This astonishing adaptability was not, at first, dented by paganism's encounter with more intractable monotheistic systems like Judaism and Christianity (North 1992). An astonishing series of inscriptions from the Eastern Roman empire records the presence in Jewish synagogues of "god-worshipers" (*theosebeis*), apparently pagans with a sympathy for, or perhaps just a lively curiosity in, Jewish cult (Levinskaya 1996: 51–126). Elsewhere in the East, there is evidence for a pagan cult of the Most High God (*Theos Hypsistos*) with clear monotheistic tendencies (Mitchell 1999). This evidence points not only to the diversity of ancient religion, but also to how it does not always fit into the neat categories that we would wish to impose upon it: if polytheism is thought to be an essential characteristic of paganism, then what are we to make of the worship of Theos Hypsistos?

Another example, with which I will finish, similarly shows how the evidence for ancient religion cannot be as easily pigeonholed as modern scholars might wish. At

Mamre in Palestine stood an oak tree where, according to Jewish scriptures (the Christian Old Testament), the Hebrew patriarch Abraham met with three angels. (Genesis 18:1–8). In the fifth century AD, we know of a festival celebrated here that attracted Jews, because they claimed descent from Abraham, and Christians, because they regarded the three angels as a biblical sign of the Holy Trinity. Such Jewish and Christian attendance hardly occasions surprise, but our late antique report also notes that the festival was frequented by many pagans also, attracted by the story of the angelic apparition (Soz. *HE* 2.4.2–3). The festival at Mamre clearly had different meanings for different groups, and cannot simply be described as *either* Jewish *or* Christian *or* pagan: it was all three of these at once. In this blurring of the boundaries of religious identity at the very end of antiquity, we gain a particularly dizzying insight into the potential, and problems, presented by the study of ancient religion, in which simplistic interpretations derived from modern religious assumptions should have no place.

FURTHER READING

Several excellent accounts of ancient religion have appeared recently. On the Greek side, see especially S. Price 1999 and Mikalson 2005, but older handbooks such as Bremmer 1994, Bruit Zaidmann and Schmitt Pantel 1992, and Burkert 1985 remain useful; Parker 1996 and 2005 are invaluable on Athens. For Roman religion, volume 1 of Beard, North, and Price 1998 is outstanding; for briefer accounts, see Scheid 2003 and Warrior 2006; Feeney 1998 is a suggestive essay; Liebeschuetz 1979 is still worth reading. Useful essay collections include Easterling and Muir 1985, Buxton 2000, Bispham and Smith 2000, and Ando 2003. Roman religion is better served by source books: the collection of material, both texts and artifacts, in volume 2 of Beard, North, and Price 1998 is excellent; see also Klauck 2000 and Warrior 2002. For basic themes, see: on priests, Beard and North 1990; on temples, Alcock and Osborne 1994, Orlin 1997, and Spawforth 2006; on concepts of divinity, A. Lloyd 1997, Lefkowitz 2003, and Athanassiadi and Frede 1999; on the vexed question of religion and politics, including ruler-cult, Bowden 2005, Chaniotis 2003, S. Price 1984, D. Potter 1994, and Gradel 2002. For religious diversity, see Parker 1989 (contrasting Athens and Sparta), Sourvinou-Inwood 1978, Mellor 1992, and Turcan 1996; regional histories (e.g. Mitchell 1993) should be consulted, and there are case studies on the Roman period, such as Henig 1984, Rives 1995, and Schowalter and Friesen 2005. On "mystery" cults, see Burkert 1987, Takács 1995, and M. Clauss 2000. For the end of paganism, see Chuvin 1990. On methodological questions, see J. Z. Smith 1990 and Humphreys 2004. Finally, the studies of Lane Fox 1986 and Hopkins 1999 provide riveting accounts of religion in practice that no student or scholar should ignore.

CHAPTER TWENTY-EIGHT

The Emergence of Christianity

John Curran

1 Introduction

Jesus of Nazareth did not call his disciples "Christians"; his grieving followers in Jerusalem did not use the word to describe themselves; the term was coined by observers in the city of Antioch some time in the 30s or 40s AD who witnessed Greek-speaking followers of Jesus passionately affirming his unique status as the *christos* (anointed) Jewish "Son of God" who had risen from the dead (Acts 11:26). The neologism illustrates a point of exceptional importance in tracing the emergence of Christianity: that it was a process based upon the physical *movement* of ideas into a world beyond Galilee and Roman Judaea. And as the ideas traveled, they found themselves in cultural surroundings significantly different from the world that Jesus had known. This in turn stimulated an astonishingly extensive and diverse series of responses to Jesus and his teachings as reported. And the emergence of Christianity is the history of the relationship between those ideas and their origins in the ancient Near East.

2 Jesus of Nazareth

At the time of Jesus's birth (4 BC), the Jews were an ancient people who had endured recent upheavals. Greek desecration of the Temple of Yahweh (167 BC) had been followed by a dynamic war of liberation led by the vigorous and idealistic Maccabees. As Jewish independence became more assured, the succeeding Hasmonaeans had taken for themselves not only the kingship of the Jews but also the High Priesthood of the Temple itself. But innovation and discourse on institutions and beliefs were historic features of Palestinian Judaism (Bohak, THE JEWS). Distinct and varied perspectives on the focus of Jewish life emerged (Grabbe 1996; Sanders 1992): "Pharisees" pursued the study and development of the Law; "Sadducees," about whom little is known, were apparently of high standing and enjoyed some connection to the High Priesthood (Jos. *AJ* 18. 17; Acts 4:1; 5:17). Others, called by Josephus a "fourth philosophy" for the benefit of his Greek readers, seem to have possessed an uncompromising devotion to national, ethnic, and religious liberty, leading some scholars to identify them with the "Zealots" prominent in the later revolt against Rome (Jos. *AJ* 18. 9–10; Hengel 1989). At the same time, living at Qumran on the shores of the Dead Sea was a small group which had repudiated those in charge of the Temple during the second century BC to found a deeply pious community devoted to preparing for a divinely inspired returning of the Temple to "true" Jewish piety (Vermes 2004; Davies et al. 2002). This group may well have been the "Essenes" known later to Pliny the Elder (*HN* 5.73). At the same time, however, and fundamental to Jewish discourse, was the place occupied by the charismatic individual, whether priest, rabbi, "holy man," or all three together. Jesus of Nazareth thus takes his place in the fluid and variegated world of Second Temple Judaism (Nickelsburg 2003). More specifically, he and his followers would seem to have enjoyed some early connection with the life and work of John the Baptizer, an eschatological figure who preached powerfully on the need for repentance and baptism in the face of a coming intervention on the part of the Jewish god (Jos. *AJ* 18. 116–19; John 1:35–37).

At the core of human memory of Jesus seem to have been a number of arresting parables and phrases, themselves characteristic of his remarkable gift for preaching. Like John the Baptist, he suggested that a new intervention by the Jewish God in human affairs was imminent (Matthew 25:1–13; Jos. *AJ* 18.116–19). In anticipation, he denounced the many laxities visible in the lives of the rich, the powerful, the learned, and those conducting cult in the Temple in Jerusalem (Matthew 21:12–17; Mark 11:15–19). By contrast, he exalted the simple goodness of the poor and the pure of heart, and leading the symbolically significant number of twelve disciples he called for a sense of renewal in Jewish piety (Jos. *AJ* 18. 63–64; 20. 200; the former passage shows signs of Christian interpolation). His enthusiasm for Gentiles was on occasion strikingly subordinate to his interest in his fellow Jews (Matthew 15:24; Mark 7:25–30). The popularity of the message and the messianic overtones of some of his behavior brought him to the attention of both sacred and secular authority in Judaea. A perception that he was a threat to the life of the Temple and the convenience of Roman government secured his execution on the orders of Pontius Pilate on a date recently reconstructed as Friday April 7th AD 30 (Vermes 2005).

The death of Jesus, far from extinguishing the enthusiasm of his followers, came to be seen as merely the prelude to his resurrection and persisting fellowship with them. In Jerusalem, a small group of supporters came to cluster around his disciples and surviving family members, with Peter and James the brother of Jesus prominent (Galat. 1:16–19). A communal mystical experience shortly after the death of Jesus transformed the confidence, size, and sense of mission of this group (Acts 2:8–11; 41). It began to attract new followers among both Judaean and Diaspora Jews, leading to some early tensions. While Peter and John continued to attend prayers at the Temple (Acts 3:1) other members of the community thought that it was no longer acceptable. One prominent and vociferously Greek-speaking member of the group, Stephen, was stoned to death following his perceived blasphemy in attacking

28.1 Debris from the Roman destruction of the Temple in Jerusalem (AD 70), for many Christians an apparent fulfilment of one of the prophecies of Jesus (Mark 13: 1–4). (Photo: author)

the Temple and its priests (Acts 7:55–8:1). Among those looking on was a dedicated and gifted Pharisee called Paul, from the diaspora community of Tarsos.

3 Paul of Tarsos

The dramatic miracle experience of Paul of Tarsos on the road to Damascus (Acts 9:1–19) should not distract from the astonishing human energy exhibited by the "converted" Paul in his career subsequently. Paul's vision of the risen Jesus prompted him first to make contact with those whom he had been determined to arrest, but just as significantly led him to withdraw for a period from Jewish society to reflect (Galat. 1:16–18). Returning to the world, he made tentative contact with Jesus's surviving disciples. Like Peter and James, Paul retained a powerful sense of the proximity of Jesus's teaching to Jewish ideas and institutions, but he came to believe that the message of Jesus should be brought to those beyond the synagogue. Though Paul's "mission" in the 40s and 50s enjoyed the formal support of the disciples in

Jerusalem, there was an inherent tension between his vision of a vast and diverse community of believers, which included Gentiles, and their understanding of a post-messianic Judaism. Some followers of Jesus in Jerusalem were dismayed to learn that Paul was not requiring his followers of the risen Jesus to be circumcised, prompting a meeting between Paul, his associate Barnabas, and Peter and James, at which the absolute necessity of avoiding sacrificial meat and fornication were agreed (Galat. 2; Acts 15). But Paul's teachings continued to unsettle those leading the Jerusalem community, and James subsequently sought reassurance with regard to Paul's devotion to the Temple (Acts 21:20–27).

Away from Jerusalem by contrast, Paul was a traveler and preacher of indefatigable commitment and self-possession. He visited numerous communities in Asia Minor and Greece, including Athens, where he declaimed before the Areopagus council (Acts 17:16–33). He communicated also with a group of Christ-followers whom he found in Rome (Romans 1:13–15). Paul's challenge above all was to bring his message both to those seeking to uphold Jewish practices (Galat. 2:12; Titus 1:10–15; Romans 2:7–3:31) and also to those who were resolutely Gentile (Galat. 5:2–12), leading him to reflect upon himself as "all things to all men" (1 Cor. 9:19–22). To the Christians of Corinth he declared that the Law had been superseded by Jesus (1 Cor. 9:21), an idea that stimulated followers there to abandon conventional sexual morality, provoking an exasperated rebuke from Paul (1 Cor. 5). But in other respects he upheld the core values of the Greek city in terms of obedience to authority and acceptance of the institution of slavery (Titus 2:1–9).

On one of his periodic return visits to colleagues in Jerusalem he was arrested and famously invoked his Roman citizen status, prompting his dispatch to the court of the emperor (Acts 22:22–29). Characteristically, while awaiting trial, he preached openly and enthusiastically in the empire's capital, where he seemingly met his death (Acts 28:30–31).

Paul's contribution to the emergence of Christianity is of the profoundest historical significance. He was the ablest of those who took knowledge of Jesus to the world beyond Judaea. Many Jewish communities in the Diaspora already offered an honorable role to "god-fearing" Gentiles, and the latter are likely to have been an important avenue for the message of Paul into the wider world. To the weak, the sick and the disheartened came the powerful idea of a special relationship with a god who understood and had shared in human suffering. More than this, death itself had been overcome, bearers of the "good news" were reported to possess extraordinary powers (Acts 9:36–42; 16:25–40), and believers could look forward to a blissful eternity in the company of their living god. A new beginning was possible, not through expensive and elaborate rituals controlled by a civic elite, but in individual baptism, communal ritual dining and the acceptance of Jesus of Nazareth as redeemer of all mankind.

4   The Status of Converts (Who *Were* the "Christianoi"?)

Calculating numbers and assessing the velocity of "Christianization" is highly problematic. There are few secure figures, although statistical extrapolation has been deployed by some, suggesting that up to 10,000 people in the empire might have been Christians by the early second century, and perhaps 200,000 by the third (Stark 1996; Hopkins 1998). Identifying the social status of "Christianoi" in the first two centuries AD is also fraught, as details are so sketchy. According to Paul's First Letter to the Corinthians (1:26): "Not many of you were wise by human standards, not many were powerful, not many were of noble birth." The literature of the Christians had a special place for those whose turning towards Jesus was a dramatic and sudden affair, but these affecting stories should not obscure the evidence that for many conversion was a *process* rather than an event (S. Hall 2005). Early Christian sources show clearly the concept of stages of entry into the Christian community. Following basic induction, the status of *auditor* (hearer) followed, after which the candidate became a "catechumen" for up to three years, a process culminating in exorcism, anointing, and the laying-on of hands, after which the candidate was permitted to "hear the Gospel" (Hippolytus, *Apostolic Tradition* 20).

5   Polemic and Persecution

Initially, the worship of Christians was invisible to the authorities of the empire. But the violence and vituperation of their disputes presently attracted attention (Acts 17:6; 1 Thessalonians 2:14–16). Sometime in the 40s vigorous police action was required at Rome, where Jews were expelled from the city on account of riots which had been occurring at the instigation of "Chrestus" (Suet. *Claud.* 25.4). By the time that Nero needed to fix upon convenient scapegoats to deflect rumors that he had himself destroyed part of the city by fire, the "Christianoi" of Rome were a group to whom the authorities could attribute "outrages" (*flagitia*) and degeneracy without arousing the sympathy of the pagan population (Tac. *Ann.* 15.44.2–8). Henceforth, citizens of Rome minded to take action against Christians had a powerful legal precedent for doing so, the mere name of "Christian" (*nomen christianum*) becoming a crime in itself (de Ste. Croix 1963). There was no enthusiasm for state-sponsored persecution, however (Pliny *Ep.* 10. 97). The number of victims was small, and it is likely that most "Christianoi" threatened with judicial power complied promptly with *ad hoc* pagan sacrifice tests demanded as part of proceedings. The emperors were anxious, moreover, that due process should be observed. Pliny was rebuked by Trajan (c.112 AD) for admitting anonymous accusations in his court, and Hadrian (AD 117–138) insisted that proper trials should be the only means of addressing the problem of Christians (Pliny *Ep.* 10. 96–97; Euseb. *HE* 4. 9.1–3). Nevertheless, Christians were periodically victims of popular and spontaneous violence sprung from the perception that their beliefs were those of a degenerate and anti-social cult (*superstitio*) practiced by "godless people" (*atheoi*) whose presence in a community might even prompt the gods to send natural disasters (Cyprian, *Letters* 75.10.1). Prudent governors and civic authorities in places as diverse as Smyrna (the martyrdom of Polycarp, AD 156) or Lyons (AD 177) could acquiesce legally to such promptings of public outrage.

Most Christians, however, never became martyrs; they sought an accommodation between their piety and the world around them. The author of *1 Peter* exhorted his readers: "For the Lord's sake, accept the authority of every human institution, whether of the emperor as supreme, or of the governors, as sent by him to punish those who do wrong and to praise those who do right" (2:13–14). Tertullian (c.160–post-220 AD) was at pains to reassure the readers of his *Apology* that Christians prayed for the emperors, their agents, and government itself (*Apology* 39; cf. 24; 27; 30). The Athenian philosopher and convert Aristides wrote to the second-century emperor Antoninus Pius to suggest that only Christians possessed true understanding, the goal of every philosopher (Euseb. *HE* 4.3.3). And the great physician Galen made the connection explicitly: "they [the Christians] include . . . individuals who, in self-discipline and self-control, have attained a pitch not inferior to that of genuine philosophers" (*Plato Arabus* 1.99).

But other pagan commentators were strongly critical (Wilken 2003). The idea that a convicted criminal might be the object of veneration was a shocking challenge to the values of Jews, Greeks, and Romans (Deut. 21:23; Galat. 3:13; 1 Cor. 1:23). In his second-century work *True Doctrine*, the philosopher Celsus ridiculed the idea that a savior of humankind could be unveiled in so wretched a location as the land of the Jews; and asked what kind of savior would tolerate the daily suffering of millions (Origen, *C. Cels.* 6.78). Christians, Celsus further noted, were ferocious in their disputes with each other: "since they have expanded to become a multitude, they are divided and rent asunder, and each wants to lead his own party" (3.10). Their disdain for the imperial cult showed how alienated they were from the values of civilized life (8.62).

The early years of the third century witnessed unparalleled challenges to the authority of emperors in the form of invasions, economic disruption, usurpation, and widespread disease. The most successful emperors of the period continued to see in Roman *religio* both a means of expressing the aspirations of government and a way of protecting the ancient values of Roman society. Thus Decius (AD 250–51) heralded his own accession as a new age in which all Romans were encouraged to return to the altars of the ancient gods (Euseb. *HE* 4.41.9–13; Knipfing 1923; Rives 1999b). The policy caused upheaval in the Christian community. Many followers of Jesus, including bishops, promptly complied with orders to sacrifice (Cyprian *Letters* 10.4; 11.1; 14.1). Others illicitly bought the certificates (*libelli*) being distributed to those who had sacrificed, drawing upon themselves contemptuous denunciations as "libellatici" from those who had suffered for their faith (*confessores*). Only great resolution and leadership upheld the standing of episcopal office (Cyprian *Letters* 27.3; 68.1–2, see below).

By then, however, the empire itself had been overtaken by ecological and military disaster (including widespread plague and the capture of the emperor Valerian by the Persians in AD 260). Valerian's co- and successor-emperor Gallienus brought official government action against the Christians to an end, allowing them possession again of their cemeteries and cult buildings, and ushering in a period of steady growth for the Christian community (Euseb. *HE* 7.13). At Antioch c. AD 271 a dispute between Christian rivals was even referred to the emperor Aurelian's court, prompting a resolution upholding the special authority of bishops in Italy and Rome (Euseb. *HE* 7.30.9). But later Christian writers reflected that the "great" persecution of

Diocletian (emperor AD 284–305, see below) was a fitting punishment for a community that had grown complacent and self-indulgent (Origen, *Comm. Matt.* 13.24; Euseb., *Martyrs of Palestine* 12; *HE* 8.1.7).

6   Discerning the Message: Authority, Discourse, and Text

In the very earliest years of the Christian movement, it is clear that devotion to Jesus could be the result of any one of a number of experiences: miracle, vision, possession by "the spirit", or compelling instruction. Powerful ethical and theological ideas could be conveyed by brief stories and phrases (Ephesians 4:5; 1 Clement 54; *Shepherd of Hermas* Vision 1.1). Between communities (*ekklesiai*) of believers traveled individuals professing various claims to authority. Within communities, Paul's letters referred to people identified as *episkopoi* (overseers) and *diakonoi* (servitors), the latter possibly including women (Philippians 1:1; Romans 16:1; 1 Timothy 1:15; 3:11. Eisen 2000). Acts 21:18 reported the followers of Jesus in Jerusalem led by a group of *presbuteroi* (elders), although the standing and duties of none of these groups are clear precisely.

As the imminence of Christ's return receded, however, the question of protracted leadership engaged believers. By the beginning of the second century *episkopoi* were to be found alongside *presbuteroi*, no longer interchangeable with them. The former were charged with appointing the latter, according to the Letter of Paul to Titus 1:5. Ongoing trouble in Corinth led to the expulsion of *episkopoi* there, a development that unsettled prominent figures in the Roman community (1 Clement 44). Ignatius of Antioch, on his way to execution in Rome in the early second century, urged acceptance of "the deacons as Jesus Christ, just as the bishop (*episkopos*) is also a type of the Father and the presbyters are like the council (*sunhedrion*) of God" (*Letter to the Trallians* 3.1). Elsewhere, he applied the significant adjective "*katholikos*" to the Christian community, an entity that was "whole" and over which Christ presided, like a bishop over his congregation (*Letter to the Smyrneans* 8.2).

Victor, the bishop of Rome, unilaterally declared c. AD 190 that the date of Easter determined in the West ought to be observed by Asiatics in Rome who had clearly been commemorating one of several Eastern alternatives. The order prompted the first attested dissonance between Eastern and Western Christendom, and was an innovation that alarmed the Greek Christian Irenaeus (Euseb. *HE* 5.24.9–13). The confidence of the bishops of Rome continued to increase, however, with Callistus (AD 217–222) reportedly offering reconciliation to penitent murderers, apostates, and adulterers, to the dismay of the presbyter Hippolytus, who established himself consequently as a rival bishop (*Refutation of all heresies* 9.7).

Cyprian of Carthage, presiding over a church ravaged by persecution in the middle of the third century, upheld episcopal authority in the face of the inspirational example offered by the "confessors" and martyrs who had suffered and died for their faith. He emphasized what he saw as the divine foundations of the office ("One Christ, one church, one chair": *Letters*, 43.5). And despite his own difficulties with the bishop of Rome, he specifically identified the Petrine tradition of the latter as an institution of the highest importance ("it is the womb and root of the catholic church": *Letters* 48.3). Cyprian went further in summoning *councils* of bishops by which much more extensive analysis could be brought to bear on problems, and enemies could be authoritatively repudiated (*Letters* 55; 64; 72).

As the generation of eye-witnesses to Jesus passed away and the hazards of charismatic individuals became more manifest, the orality of early Christian culture began to be supplemented by the composition of texts (Young et al. 2004; Stanton 2004; Metzger 1987; Campenhausen 1972). A number of "Gospels" appeared, some seemingly drawing upon earlier and now lost material. These Gospels recorded both details of the life and "sayings" (*agrapha*) of Jesus. Letters attributed to Paul were preserved and copied. Documents setting down beliefs and practice within individual Christian communities were also produced (*The Shepherd of Hermas* [Rome]; *Didache* [Syria]). The threat to orality disturbed some. Papias of Hierapolis (c.130 AD), who had known followers of the Apostles, lamented: "to me writings seem of less value than what began and remains as living speech" (Euseb. *HE* 3.39).

By the middle of the second century Christians began to discriminate between authoritative and inferior documents. Marcion of Pontus, living at Rome c.140 AD, drew up formally the first "canon" of acceptable writings, but found himself unable to accept the validity of ancient Jewish literature. Paul's letters too were drastically edited to expunge any "Judaizing" sentiments. And of the Gospels, only a pared-down version of *Luke* survived his scrutiny. Justin Martyr (died c.165 AD) by contrast saw rather more in Jewish literature, and conceded the inspired authority of the Jewish Torah, although with significant reservations (*Dialogue with Trypho* 118.3; Boyarin 2004).

Following his return from study in Rome c.172 AD, the Syrian churchman Tatian produced the *Diatessaron*, a sophisticated publication in parallel columns of at least five "Gospels." And perhaps by the end of the second century, the Christian community in Rome was beginning to think in terms of a list of authentic and approved writings. The so-called "Muratorian Fragment" included alongside the four Gospels works like *The Apocalypse of Peter*, but not Peter's first and second letters (Hahneman 1992). The annexation of Jewish scriptures meanwhile proceeded apace. Alexandrian exegetes in the third century subjected the Hebrew Bible to unprecedented Christian scholarly inquiry. Origen (c.185–254 AD) in his *Hexapla* was able to compare Hebrew and multiple Greek versions of texts in use among Christians, marking a high-point of analysis in the historic process of forming the "Old" as well as the "New" Testament of God.

Theological divergences and disputes between followers of Jesus were a feature of the movement from its earliest times (R. Williams 1989). When Ignatius of Antioch surveyed the many problems posed by those with differing views, he deployed naturally the language of the Greek *gymnasion*. He observed people promoting "heresies," like public philosophers disputing and disagreeing; and, just as with the pagans, some of the ideas he heard struck him as "strange" or "other" ("heterodox"). But the range and complexity of the discourse was much more than an "orthodox" versus "heterodox" struggle, and the description of the development of

Christian doctrine in those terms is in fact an echo of the polemic of the triumphant parties.

The theological identification of "son," "father," and the continuing and mysterious presence of "spirit" inevitably stimulated reflection upon the precise relationship of the entities to each other. But in a world where Christians were seeking to uphold the superiority of their beliefs over polytheism, theological speculation about these entities was fraught with complexity and danger. Justin had thought of the divine "Logos" as "other" than the Father (*Apology* 2.13) while Irenaeus understood that the implication of Jesus as "the anointed" (*christos*) presupposed a separate anointer in the Father (*Apology* 2.13). But to those who suggested that Jesus had not been fully human, possessing merely the "appearance" (*dokesis*) of a man, Irenaeus declared robustly that any part of human nature which Jesus had not shared was not saved; "the glory of God is a living human being" (*Against Heresies* 4.20.7). Tertullian introduced the concept of divine "persons," distinguishing "one substance in three persons" (*Against Praxeas* 2.3–4), a position that was to prove enduringly influential among Christians living in the Latin-speaking West of the empire. In the great intellectual center of Alexandria towards the end of the second century, thinkers deeply influenced by the philosophy of both Plato and the Jewish writer Philo (c.20 BC to AD 50) brought new sophistication to the question (Kelly 1977). Clement conceived of the Father as transcendent and the Son as the embodiment of the Logos, the Father's will, putting the Son in a distinctly subordinate position relative to the Father (*Stromateis* 7.2.3). But the most influential exponent of Alexandrian thinking was Origen who brought highly skilled and allegorical exegesis to the texts of Christian belief. On the Son, Origen stated that He was no mere creature. Adopting the language of neo-Platonist philosophy, Origen conceived of the Son as a *hypostasis* (essence) of the Father and an agent of the Father's will. Father and Son were not identical, however, and while suggesting that there was never a time when the Son had not existed (*Commentary on Romans* 1.5), he stated that the Son's position relative to the Father was undeniably subsequent. Origen was working in a world which had not yet witnessed Christian councils of bishops issuing statements of faith. His contribution to the discourse on the nature of the Christian God was highly influential in his own day, but he was to fall victim to the politics surrounding later definitions of "orthodoxy."

By contrast, other followers of Jesus believed that the world was contaminated by evil in many forms, and only a divinely transmitted knowledge (*gnosis*) could redeem the individual (K. King 2003; Rudolph 1987). For Valentinus, a "Gnostic" teacher in Rome in the second century, creation was the work of a powerful but inferior demiurge. Only an elite group, the *electi*, would escape it through Jesus and enjoy the company of God (Irenaeus, *Against Heresies* 1.1.1–3). Other groups looked to Simon Magus, while the "Ophites" detected in the knowing serpent (*ophis*) of *Genesis* the emissary of a higher God, unmasking the inferior creation of a lower (Origen, *C. Cels.* 6. 31).

Individual charismatic figures continued to declare and explore direct contact with the Christian God. In the middle years of the second century one Montanus, allegedly an ex-priest of Cybele, argued that the world had reached its "last days" and that spiritual or "pneumatic" graces, unmediated by clerics, would shower down upon those present at the Second Coming, in Pepuza in Phrygia (C. Trevett 1996). The African Christian writer Tertullian (c.160 to post-220 AD), after a generation of courageous apologetic service on behalf of clerical friends, abandoned his loyalties and became a devoted follower, claiming defiantly that he sought "a church of the spirit, not of bishops" (*On Modesty*, 21).

"Gnosticism" was eventually overshadowed by the teachings of Mani (died c.276 AD) whose ideas gave a place both to Jesus and the Spirit. Like Christianity, Manicheism was strongly missionary and came to enjoy great success in the lands of both Roman and especially Persian emperors (Lieu 1994). For Mani, the material world was a cosmic battleground between the forces of light and darkness. Individuals might enhance the light within themselves through strict asceticism and dietary control. They developed a hierarchy, a sophisticated set of rituals and a distinctive literature, all focused on reuniting the pious believer with the True God. The intellectual and spiritual credibility of Manicheism detained no less a mind than that of the young Augustine of Hippo for many years (*Conf.* 3.6.10).

7 Asceticism

The proximity of the Judaean wilderness had historically and periodically drawn pious Jews into it: the sectaries at Qumran had established a community devoted to prayer and study in the second century BC (Davies et al. 2002). Individually, the piety of John the Baptist and Jesus of Nazareth included periods of withdrawal and seclusion in isolated places. The latter was reported to have urged followers to abandon the familial and familiar (Luke 14:26, cf. 9:60). Consequently, among the earliest expressions of Christianity was a readiness to renounce some of the most fundamental social institutions of the ancient world. Paul found followers of Jesus at Corinth who within a generation of the latter's death had forsaken marriage, and he was compelled to suggest delicately that celibacy was a special vocation not issued to all (1 Cor. 7). These ideas took their place among the many Greco-Roman meditations on the world of the senses and the pursuit of the moral life (Goehring 1992; Meredith 1976). Epictetus considered the philosopher's struggle to master the senses and emotions to be like an athlete's training regime (*askesis*), but so demanding that a student might find himself crying out *kyrie eleison* (Lord, have mercy) to his loving divine protector (2.7.12).

In Egypt in the third century the great Origen knew of the impulse for "flight" (*anachoresis*) from the world, but observed that one could not flee one's mind; his own struggles culminated in self-emasculation (Euseb. *HE* 6 8.1–3). Around AD 270 in Egypt, however, a charismatic 18-year-old Antony renounced worldly wealth and family connections to pursue a spiritual path in the limen between Egyptian desert and city (Athanasius, *Life of Antony*). The generation which followed witnessed the appearance of significant numbers of ascetic individuals throughout the Christian Near East (P. Brown 1971a; 1988; T. Shaw 1998). The monk Pachomius (AD 292–346) led both men and women to seek "a life in common" (*koinobion*) in Egypt under close supervision and guidance, establishing a pattern of community life that was to exert a powerful influence on Christian culture.

8   The Age of Diocletian and Constantine

With the accession of Diocletian (AD 284) government of the empire came into the hands of a man of energy, vision and *pietas*. His college of four emperors associated itself explicitly with Jupiter and his able helpmate Hercules (S. Williams 1985; T. Barnes 1981; 1982; Corcoran 2000). This "tetrarchy" spent its early years restoring security and order to an empire and an economy that had seemed on the verge of anarchy. In due course Diocletian turned his attention to the condition of Roman religion. The emperor's court had long hosted a formidable critic of Christianity in Porphyry of Tyre (died c.305 AD) whose fifteen books *Against the Christians* subjected the latter's literature, philosophy and morality to unprecedentedly rigorous criticism. Porphyry conceded that Jesus had been a man of unusually fine character who was elevated to special companionship with the divine but was not divine himself (Euseb. *Dem. Evang.* 3.7; August. *De civ. D.* 19.23). He could not, however, comprehend the humiliation to which Jesus had allowed himself to be subject (*Against the Christians* frg. 63). Porphyry's Christian enemies were sufficiently impressed to imagine him an embittered apostate (Socrates *HE* 3.23.38).

In 296/7 Diocletian issued a stern edict against Manicheism, denouncing as "the height of criminality" challenges to ancient Roman religious beliefs (*Lex Dei sive Mosaicarum et Romanorum Legum Collatio* XV. iii). Hostile Christian authors suggested that Diocletian's virulently anti-Christian co-emperor Galerius urged the old emperor to attack Christianity (Lactant. *De mort.* 11), but the momentum of Diocletian's own outlook brought him into collision with the followers of Jesus, now numbering perhaps 200,000 people (Stark 1996). Following consultation with Apollo himself, a purge of Christians in the senior ranks of the army was carried out (Lactant. *De mort.* 11.7–8; Euseb. *HE* 8.4.2–4) and preparations were completed for a final and "Great" persecution of Christians in the Roman empire (de Ste. Croix 1954; Lane Fox 1986). Beginning in February 303, a series of edicts was published which aimed to destroy places of worship, seize and destroy holy books, and deny Christian citizens some of the fundamental privileges offered by Roman law (Lactant. *De mort.* 11–13). Prominent Christians were targeted, including the bishop of the imperial capital Nikomedia, and the cruelest devices of torture were deployed against believers elsewhere (Euseb., *The Martyrs of Palestine*, 2). As before, however, the processes of persecution were cumbersome and frequently evadable (*P.Oxy.* 31.2601). Additionally, the enthusiasm of Diocletian's colleagues did not always match his own. In Britain and Gaul the emperor Constantius (father of Constantine) reportedly contented himself with gentler repression (Euseb. *VC* 1.16; 2.49).

When Constantius died in Britain in 306, his legions declared his son Constantine emperor, and the latter embarked upon a long struggle for supremacy (T. Barnes 1981; MacMullen 1969). Alongside his gifts for power-politics, however, Constantine possessed a remarkable sense of destiny. A pagan panegyrist speaking before Constantine in Gaul in AD 310 shrewdly assessed the emperor's character and reported flatteringly that the god Apollo had manifested himself to the emperor to aid his enterprises and promise many years of power (*Panegyrici Latini* 6 (7). 21. 3–6; Rodgers 1980).

In May 311 the senior emperor of the East, Galerius, issued a dramatic edict of toleration from his sick-bed, imploring Christians to pray to their God for his own and the empire's good health (Lactant. *De mort.* 33–34; Euseb. *HE* 8.17). Galerius's junior colleague Maximin Daia's response was to intensify persecution in his own domains, where he also attempted to reinvigorate and organize civic religion (Euseb. *HE* 8.14.9; 9.4.2–5.2). Pious polytheistic towns like Arykanda in Lykia appealed to the emperors to liquidate Christians in the community (*CIL* 3.12132).

In the West, Constantine's maneuverings brought the city of Rome within range of his ambitions. The Christian writers Lactantius and Eusebius of Caesarea (the latter citing the testimony of Constantine himself) affirm that the God of the Christians now intervened to persuade him to include Christian symbols among the military standards carried by his soldiers against vastly superior enemy forces in the battle for Rome (Lactant. *De mort.* 44.3–6; Euseb. *VC* 1.26–29; P. Weiss 2003). On October 28th 312, he overcame his rival Maxentius at the battle of the Milvian Bridge and entered the city. The "prompting of the divinity" was duly acknowledged on Constantine's arch of victory in Rome (*ILS* 694), even if the precise identity of the deity eluded many. Initially he continued to see the value and utility of pagan institutions, remaining *Pontifex Maximus* of the Roman state, and receiving reports from the *haruspices* of prodigious events in nature (*Cod. Theod* 16.10.1, AD 321) and at least tolerating the juxtaposition of his own and pagan images on the coinage until the 320s (P. Bruun 1954). By the 330s, however, giving permission for a temple to be erected in honor of his family, Constantine stipulated that the structure should never be "defiled by the evils of any contagious *superstitio*" (*ILS* 705).

Constantine's interest in Christian affairs by contrast intensified dramatically following his capture of Rome. He began to place large amounts of formerly imperial property at the disposal of the Christian community in the city, including the *fundus Lateranus*, which was to become the site of the bishop of Rome's own church (Curran 2000; Krautheimer 1980).

At Milan early in 313 Constantine and his co-emperor Licinius issued an historic statement extending to Christianity the same legality as that enjoyed by the *religio* of the Roman state (Lactant. *De mort.* 48.2–12). But the *rapprochement* between the emperors could not survive their mutual suspicions, and at Chrysopolis on the eastern Bosporus in September 324 a decisive battle was fought which brought the Eastern Roman empire into the power of Constantine. His governmental and theological ambitions burgeoned. A magnificent city was laid out on the site of old Byzantium, self-consciously to be a "new Rome" (Socrates *HE* 1.16. Mango 2002; Dagron 1974). The treasures of pagan antiquity were uprooted and transferred to the new capital, where Constantine's magisterial image, a remodeling of a statue of Apollo the Sun-god, took its place in a landscape dominated by magnificent new churches to Peace and Holy Wisdom (*Hagia Sophia*) (Euseb. *VC* 3.54–58). To the East, Jerusalem was adorned with a new church on the site of Golgotha commemorating the Resurrection (*Anastasis*), while at Bethlehem a grand basilica was built over the reported site of Jesus's birth (Krautheimer 1986). The emperor himself began to dream of being baptized in the Jordan (Euseb. *VC* 4.62.2). To Eusebius, the career of Constantine looked like another intervention by the Christian God in the affairs of men (*VC* 2.24–27), inspiring him to conceive of a new type of history, a history of the church itself (*historia ecclesiastica*).

But new challenges for the earthly governor of a Christian empire now appeared (Kelly 1977; R. Hanson 1988; R. Williams 2001). Christian scholars and theologians had long sought to comprehend the precise character of the relationship between Jesus Christ the Son and God the Father (section 6 above). At Alexandria in the early years of the fourth century, bishop Alexander denounced and excommunicated one of his own presbyters, Arius, on the grounds that the latter seemed in his theology to have subordinated the Son excessively to the Father (Socrates *HE* 1.5; Soz. *HE* 1.15.1–6). Specifically, in upholding the idea that the Son's existence was dependent upon the Father's will, Arius is reported to have stated "there was when the Son was not" (Socrates *HE* 1.6.4–13). Arius's own exposition does not survive, and the meticulousness of his thought was disregarded by his enemies, who began to accuse him of making of Christ an inferior and subordinate figure. Both sides possessed powerful church allies: Alexander enjoyed the support of the bishop of Rome while Arius had the ear of Eusebius, Bishop of Nikomedia. The virulence of the dispute shocked Constantine deeply. He wrote a letter imploring the parties to lay aside their differences (*VC* 2. 64–72). Unsatisfied, however, with the churchmen's attempts to resolve their disagreements, Constantine decided to summon a great council of bishops which would represent the whole world (*oikoumene*) and could decisively address the various issues besetting the church. Designed to coincide with the twentieth anniversary (*vicennalia*) of Constantine's own accession, the "Council of Nicaea" convened in May/June of AD 325.

According to Eusebius of Caesarea, the emperor joined more than two hundred bishops in conclave, and participated in the discussions. Later historians suggested that he intervened at a critical point to suggest the term "*homoousios*" (of one being) as a satisfactory description of the shared essence of Father and Son (Euseb. *VC* 3.13–14; Socrates *HE* 1.8; Theod. *HE* 1.12). But it was a word long problematic in the East as admitting the seemingly heretical possibility that the Father might have suffered a humiliating death along with the Son ("patripassionism"). Nevertheless, probably through a combination of a desire to be rid of Arius and to impress Constantine, all but two bishops endorsed the Nicene "creed" and canons. And while the deliberations of Nicaea did not end the controversy of Arianism, they did demonstrate the unprecedented degree to which the institutions of government could now be placed at the disposal of theological imperatives (R. Hanson 1988).

In May 337 the dying Constantine was baptized by Eusebius, Bishop of Nikomedia. Following his death, his remains were interred at Constantinople in a specially designed *martyrion* alongside twelve sarcophagi symbolizing the apostles of Jesus and illustrating the dead emperor's self-perceived companionship with the most exalted Christians (*VC* 4.70; Mango 1990).

9 Conclusions

One of the most enduring ideas held by Christians ancient and modern about the emergence of Christianity is that the message of a marginal Jewish prophet repudiated by his own people came to subdue the most powerful empire in history. Careful study of the evidence suggests a significantly more complex reality. The teachings and reported teachings of Jesus and his followers took their place in a matrix of ideas, languages, beliefs and locations around the Mediterranean and beyond. They engaged with non-believers on a range of issues long studied by the ancients: what constituted an ethical life in the world; how the widespread sense of divine presence might best be explored and honored; how suffering and death might be understood and endured. Leaders of the highest caliber emerged from among the followers of Jesus using charisma, courage, persistence, and learning to bring his sayings to those experiencing the many sorrows of life. Alongside the leaders there developed a literature capable of conveying not only inspiring stories about Jesus and redemption, but also offering moral and theological speculation of great sophistication. "Christians," like others, were initially perceived by many to offer a threat to Roman *religio*, and the violence they suffered became an important means of inspiring believers. But the ordinary inhabitants of the empire seem to have had little stamina for widespread persecution, and over time the demeanor of the persecuted, whether apostate or *confessor*, drained credibility from the process. The torch-bearers of paganism long remained the upper-class elite, but once Christian writing had become sufficiently engaging to detain them, and the Christian God had claimed the devotion of an emperor of Constantine's energy and conviction, they too began to see a future that was "Christian." Christianity thus came to offer an extraordinarily varied range of responses to human experience, enabling it to subsume and transcend many of the institutions of Rome and allowing the words of Jesus to take flight in ways utterly unforeseen by many of those who had known him.

FURTHER READING

General studies include: Beard, North, and Price 1998, H. Chadwick 2001, G. Clark 2004, Frend 1984, Hopkins 1999, Humphries 2006, Rousseau 2002. For a useful collection of translated sources which includes texts mentioned in this chapter such as the *Shepherd of Hermas*, see Ehrman 2003. For bibliography on Judaism, see chapter 19 above.

For Jesus of Nazareth read: Crossan 1991, Davies and Sanders 1999, Fredriksen 2000, Freyne 2004, J. Meier 1991–2001, Sanders 1987 and 1993, Vermes 2001, 2005, and 2008; and for Paul of Tarsos: Barnett 2005, W. Davies 1999, Meeks 2003, Sanders 1977.

Boyarin 1999, Bowersock 1995, Frend 1965 should be consulted for polemic and persecution; and for discerning the message – authority, discourse and text, see: Bauer 1972, Burtchaell 1992, R. Campbell 1994, Kee 1996.

PART V

Living and Dying

CHAPTER TWENTY-NINE

The Family

Mary Harlow and Tim Parkin

1   Meeting the Family

In a schoolbook, plausibly assigned by its editor to fourth century AD Gaul, we are given, in Greek and in Latin, the textbook description of a Roman freeborn son greeting the members of his *familia* (Dionisotti 1982):

> I go and greet my parents, my father and mother and grandfather and grandmother, my brother and sister and all my relations, my uncle and aunt, my nurse and my carer, the major domo, all the freedmen, the doorkeeper, the housekeeper, the neighbors, all our friends, the other residents and those who live in the apartment block, and the eunuch.

The order of events preceding this passage is a little bizarre (the boy gets up twice, for example, and goes out to greet his friends before returning home to greet his family); part of the reason must be that, as with our passage, any opportunity of reciting vocabulary is not missed. It is highly unlikely that a Greek or Roman child typically greeted all these individuals as part of his or her morning ritual. On the other hand, we should not think of the ancient family as a static or unchanging institution. The family not only evolved in the course of history, but changed on a generational basis as family members came and went. At the same time, the family in both Greek and Roman societies was deemed absolutely fundamental and a reflection of the wider society, in effect a microcosm of the state, as both Aristotle (*Pol.* 1.2) and Cicero (*Off.* 1.54) declared.

It is impossible to give a narrative chronological survey of the ancient family over a period of more than a millennium and across vast geographical space, especially in a brief introductory chapter such as this. Instead, in order to introduce diverse realities, attitudes, and ideals, we shall offer two particular case studies, one Greek, one Roman, and develop a number of themes from there. Plutarch, in writing of illustrious Greeks and Romans, composed his biographies as "parallel lives," one Greek, one Roman: Demosthenes and Cicero were to him an obvious pairing (Plut. *Dem.* 3); it is also a useful point of comparison for our purposes.

First a few words about the nature of the topic. The study of the history of the family in the Greek and Roman worlds has had a profound effect on all other areas of ancient history. It has moved historians away from solely political and military arenas which tended to dominate until the last decades of the twentieth century; this has shifted most historical analyses to include the private and domestic realm; from an area of an arguably segregated male world to one also inhabited by women and children. The change of focus has also brought about a sharpening of methodological approaches and a more sophisticated interpretation and analysis of our sources – written, visual, and material. In order to find "individuals" (or at any rate, "types") other than politicians and generals (who tend to be the main writers of history in the ancient world) it has been necessary to learn how to approach the evidence in new ways; to look at groups who do not write their own history (women, children, slaves, non-citizens and perceived outsiders) but who appear, more often than not, as bit-part players in the writings of elite citizen males.

Finding the family is not a simple business. Early studies concentrated on the evidence of law-codes and court cases (often purely rhetorical) associated with marriage and inheritance, with smatterings of supporting evidence from, say, Greek drama and writers such as Cicero and Pliny the Younger, and inscriptions. The critical interpretation of such material has become increasingly rigorous. The understanding and deconstruction of genre, style, and author and audience expectation are key when trying to extrapolate information about the "family." The relationship between social ideals (literary, male, and elite) and social reality, especially for those who do not themselves have a voice, has to be carefully interpreted (Joshel 1992). More recently historians of the family have embraced a more diverse range of evidence from looking at the layout of domestic space (see Nevett, HOUSING) and the cultural appearance of family groupings in art, to the role of patronage and particular social relationships within the family.

It is also very important to admit from the outset that the reality of the family would have been vastly divergent over time and space. To generalize about the ancient family, as if there were no difference between the Greek and the Roman, would be patently absurd; indeed differences probably outweigh similarities. As we proceed we shall seek to highlight significant divergence as well as overlap.

The societies of Athens and Rome were patriarchal: power was vested in men and perceived masculine roles in society. Citizenship implied masculinity which in itself bestowed upon certain individuals superior social power: men were ostensibly the decision makers in ancient society. They might make jokes about the ability of wives, children, and slaves to undermine their power, such as we see, for example, in the anecdote several times recorded by Plutarch in the second century AD about the fifth century BC Athenian statesman Themistokles:

> Themistokles once said jokingly of his son, who was spoilt by his mother and, through her, by his father, that he was the most powerful person in Greece: "For the Athenians

command the rest of Greece, I command the Athenians, your mother commands me, and you command your mother." (Plut. *Them.* 18, *Cato Mai.* 8, *Mor.* 185d)

But such stories were only funny because they apparently represented a transgressive form of behavior that could patently not be true. Women were perceived through a culturally constructed idea of biology and physiology as "failed men," as not having the physical or mental capacity to run a city-state, and only with training to run a household (Xenophon, *Oikonomikos* or *On Household Management*; Plutarch, *Coniugalia Praecepta* or *Advice to the Bride and Groom*). We should not be completely taken in by the male view, however, as it tends to be the image that husbands and fathers wish to present to the outside world. Instead we need to unpick the evidence to get glimpses of life inside the family grouping. Here we are looking primarily at the elite, since they are the group for whom most evidence has survived. Assumptions can be made, however, about the lives of other social groups using a wider range of evidence and anthropological comparata. We have to assume that many of the ideals that surround the upper classes are a result of having status and property to pass on to the next generation – without these controlling parameters social behavior is not so essential to the public image of an individual. Another crucial factor to remember in analyzing the testimony that we have is that it describes families that are atypical or at atypical times; we tend to meet families when they are at critical moments – of formation or, even more often, of fragmentation and dissolution.

For most individuals in the ancient world, we know very little of their personal family life, but sometimes a few words can tell us a great deal. Consider, for example, the tombstone of Veturia, the wife of a centurion, from Aquincum, Pannonia Inferior:

> "Here do I lie at rest, a married woman, Veturia by name and descent, the wife of Fortunatus, the daughter of Veturius. I lived for thrice nine years, poor me, and I was married for twice eight. I slept with one man, I was married to one man. After having borne six children, one of whom survives me, I died. Titus Julius Fortunatus, centurion of the Second Legion Adiutrix Pia Fidelis, set this up for his wife: she was incomparable and notably respectful to him" (*CIL* 3.3572).

A relatively short but eventful life.

2 Demosthenes and Cicero

Our two more detailed case studies, while highlighting critical moments, will also focus diverse and complex material and illuminate features both shared between societies and those that are quite disparate. One case study comes from fourth-century BC Athens, the other from first-century BC Rome. It is inevitable, in an introductory survey such as this, that our attention is drawn towards classical Athens and Rome, simply because the vast majority of our material dates from these periods. Recent scholarship, however, is increasingly becoming aware of the danger of periodization, and in the reading list at the end of this chapter we highlight some of the most recent material.

Demosthenes and Cicero are relevant because they wrote about themselves and their families; they are not alone in this, but they are rare. Their political lives are of interest here only insofar as they influenced the choices each made in terms of his marriage, and his behavior to his wife, children, friends and family.

Demosthenes, the great Athenian orator and politician (384–322 BC), was born to a well-off family. We are able to reconstruct, from biographies and legal speeches, Demosthenes' family tree, even though, as is common in the Athenian context, most of the females in the tree remain unnamed (S. Pomeroy 1997: 165); it was the social convention that respectable women should not be named in public. His father, also named Demosthenes, had married Kleoboule early in the 380s (when she was probably in her early or mid teens; he would have been twice her age). Demosthenes senior died when his son was only seven years old. The father had made provision for an untimely death: in his will he had betrothed his wife to his sister's son, Aphobos (he was probably about the same age as his intended bride, highly unusually), and his daughter (5 years old at the time) to his brother's son, Demophon – a typically endogamous arrangement (i.e. within the wider family group), and also a very clear sign that women should not be left unattached, especially where property was concerned. Both had large dowries included. Demosthenes junior being so young, the family estate – a sizeable one – was left to the management of Aphobos and Demophon, along with a friend, Therippides, as guardians (*kurioi*). They did not manage the estate well (if we believe Demosthenes, they were more than just careless, they were positively evil), nor did the intended marriages to Demosthenes' mother and sister take place as planned; indeed Demosthenes' young sister would not be married for another decade, to her mother's nephew. Demosthenes meanwhile grew up under his mother's care. At the age of 18, when he was able to assert his financial independence, Demosthenes found himself in serious straits. On claiming his patrimony from his guardians, long and difficult negotiations ensued. Finally, at the age of 21, Demosthenes succeeded in the action he brought against his guardians; it would be another two years, however, before he received what little was left of the property. In all this it is revealing to see the way the family grouping effectively and publicly disintegrated into litigious squabbling, and on occasions even into physical violence. At least his experiences gave Demosthenes real grounding in the law, and his career would blossom thereafter.

He married at least once: we do not know the name of any wife, nor the name of a daughter he had. The latter died before her father, in 336 BC, and too young to have married. Allegedly, and much to the disgust of his enemy Aeschines, Demosthenes' grief was assuaged by the assassination of Alexander the Great's father a week later (Plut. *Dem.* 22). Demosthenes himself committed suicide in 322, and left a rich estate to his sister and her kin.

Cicero (106–43 BC) was a "new man" and not particularly wealthy, so he needed to make the right choice in his marriage partner. In c.79 BC he married Terentia, a wealthy heiress, at a point where his legal career had had a good start but his political career needed a boost – in financial and social terms. Cicero would have been aged 26 or 27, and as this was Terentia's first marriage, we can assume that she was in her mid- to late-teens. This age gap between husband and wife in a first marriage was normal practice. Without the evidence of personal letters this marriage could have the appearance of a business and political alliance, but the partnership demonstrated in correspondence, particularly at times of stress, suggests that Terentia and Cicero managed a semblance, and perhaps a reality, of *concordia* for a large part of their thirty years together. They had two children, Tullia (born in the first years of the marriage) and Marcus (born over a decade later, in 65 BC), and again Cicero's correspondence reflects a personal affection and concern. Cicero, very much the traditionalist in some ways, arranged for Tullia's first marriage to take place when she was aged 13–15 to an aspiring politician aged 25. While Roman ideals and laws suggest that a father should have complete control over his children (*potestas* – see section 3 below), Cicero's relationship with his offspring suggests that the reality might sometimes be rather problematic. Young Marcus caused his father angst while he was away studying in Athens, and Tullia demonstrated a strong independence of mind, supported by her mother, in the choice of her third, and last, husband. Finding suitable partners was considered a key parental duty, as was the provision of dowry for daughters. The reality, as the letters of Cicero show, was that the womenfolk of a family were often closely involved in both the process of choice and the provision of dowry.

Alongside the immediate family, Cicero's letters also allow us glimpses into wider family relations – particularly that with his brother Quintus and close friend Atticus. The families were joined by the marriage of Atticus's sister, Pomponia, to Quintus Cicero. This marriage was not a happy one, and the seemingly accepted interference of brother and brother-in-law in the relationship of the troubled couple is quite revealing, as is Cicero's concern for his nephew and the effect that his parent's divorce might have on him. The marriage of Quintus and Pomponia is atypical in that they appear to be very close in age – this might suggest that this was not Pomponia's first marriage. Cicero's own marriage was not always rosy; it is not irrelevant that Terentia was independently wealthy (and it should be noted that Roman husbands and wives could not normally make each other gifts of money or property). Cicero disagreed with the choice of Tullia's third husband – a selection made by the two women while he was out of the country – and his long marriage finally ended in divorce in 46 BC. In the same year Cicero married a young heiress, Publilia, when he was 60 and she was at the age of first marriage and younger than his daughter. The marriage did not last, and it allegedly attracted the ridicule of Terentia (Plut. *Cic.* 41), and was defended by Tiro (Cicero's secretary and freedman) on the more traditionally accepted grounds that the marriage was for financial and political reasons. Unlike the representation of Demosthenes' grief at the death of his young daughter, the grief Cicero felt at the death of Tullia was overpowering – it preoccupied him for many months in 45 – to the extent that his friends began to worry about the very public nature of his grief. The information we have on Cicero's family and friends is not unproblematic in terms of its provenance but it does expose emotive reasoning and moments of affection that are lacking in many of our sources, and serves as a reminder that social interaction, particularly in the close confines of family living, is not all about ideals and rules (for a fuller discussion, K. Bradley 1991, chap. 8, and Treggiari 2007).

3   What Does "Family" Mean?

While we might feel that we understand the tribulations and motivations at work in Demosthenes' and Cicero's family lives, we should be careful not to read twenty-first-century Western mores into ancient family structures. It is only in early modern times that the sense of the English word "family," namely of the traditional and stereotypical triad of father, mother and children, which we dub the nuclear family, has emerged. The English term "family" derives from the Latin *familia*, but the Latin word actually means something else: not only parents and children (and in fact legally it might not even include the mother, as we shall see shortly) but also other kin, family retainers and even property (in the last category might be put slaves). *Familia* is best translated into English as "household," as in the Roman emperor's vast *familia*, including his freedmen and slaves. *Familia* in the Roman context meant all those people and things in the father's power (*potestas*); the Romans – or at least the fathers among them, including Cicero – saw the institution of *patria potestas*, the total power of the oldest living male ascendant over all those in his *familia*, as fundamental to their way of life and as an object of considerable pride and satisfaction (Gai. *Inst.* 1.55; it is still being talked about in the sixth century: Justinian, *Institutes* 1.9.2). The Roman term *domus* (which can also refer to the physical abode) better conveys the modern idea of the nuclear triad, at least to the extent that it more regularly included the conjugal couple. The Greek word *oikos* also conveys the sense of a wider grouping, and like Latin *familia* is based around the male line (in Roman law the agnates). Our sense of the Greek household is based much more on a patrilineal line (a reflection of its endogamous basis), and the Athenian family appears much more patriarchal than the Roman, despite the fact that the Athenians did not have an institution which equates with *patria potestas*. This Athenian male dominance is a reflection of the gendered nature of the society and the sources, with less evidence (than in the Roman context) that illustrates women's ability as a group to act outside the patriarchal arena (though sometimes circumstances might dictate otherwise: Kleoboule was unusual, Terentia was less so). In Aristophanic comedy, for instance, women *are* depicted as acting independently, but this is not meant to be viewed as a typical scene from daily life: it is comic precisely because it is (to a male audience at least) extraordinary.

4   Mum, Dad, and the Kids

Ideally Athenian upper-class women would lead a segregated lifestyle, only meeting males at family occasions. The reality for the lower classes was necessarily different, but that was simply an illustration of failing to meet the ideal, for economic reasons. The contrast with Roman society is patent, as the Latin writer Cornelius Nepos notes, from the time of Augustus, in the preface to his *Lives of Great Generals of Foreign Nations* (on the theme of segregation see now also Nevett, HOUSING):

Many things which we Romans think seemly are thought shameful by the Greeks. For example, what Roman would be embarrassed to take his wife to a dinner party with him? What *materfamilias* does not hold first place in the house and take part in its social life? But things are very different in Greece. There no woman is present at a dinner party unless it is one held by her relatives, and she sits only in the inner part of the house, the so-called women's quarters, which no one enters unless he is a close relative.

As we have already noted, our use of the word "family" to convey the idea of the father-mother-children triad is relatively recent. It has become very evident to historians in recent decades that the institution of the nuclear family type in the Western world stretches far further back in time (even though the Greeks and Romans had no word for nuclear family). The classic article illustrating this in the Roman context, by means of the statistical scrutiny of epitaphs (tombstones being afforded by not just the very wealthy but also those of more moderate means), is Saller and Shaw (1984), which remains essential reading. Key to Saller and Shaw's method is the analysis of the commemorator's relationship to the deceased. Epitaphs, unless they were set up by the person himself or herself while still alive (*se vivo*), typically refer to commemorations between husband and wife, parents and children, brothers and sisters; much less often are there mentioned relationships between extended kin (grandparents, uncles, etc.). Indeed in civilian populations (as compared with populations of soldiers) friends, patrons, freedmen, masters, and slaves – that is, individuals unrelated by blood – feature more frequently than extended kin.

This sort of evidence suggests very strongly that the focus of obligations, where possible, was usually between close family members – what we would now call the nuclear family group, rather than the extended kin grouping. In a society where the *paterfamilias* in theory maintained complete control over the family, the pattern displayed by the tombstones is very surprising, and telling. This focus of obligations in civilian populations confirms what Cicero tells us:

If there should be a debate about and comparison of those to whom we ought to offer the greatest duty (*officium*), then in the first rank are one's country and one's parents, to whose good services we have the deepest obligations; next come our children and the entire *domus*, which looks to us alone and can have no other refuge; then come relatives, with whom we get on well and with whom even our fortunes are generally held in common. (Cic. *Off.* 1.58)

So the father-mother-children triad in Roman times (and, our literary and legal sources imply, in classical Athens as well) was the primary focus of family obligations: feelings of affection, duty of commemoration, and transmission of property, as well as maintenance of the family cult.

In this context it is easy and tempting to focus on the evident similarities between now and then. But note the transitory nature of Greek and Roman father-mother-children triads. Awareness of the differences is vital: much higher mortality levels at younger ages then than now, meaning that fertility levels need to be correspondingly higher and that the chances of your parents being alive when you yourself came to marry are relatively small. Very few Greeks or Romans knew their grandparents.

Other factors must be taken into account when considering the structure of the ancient family, allowing for its life course, as its members age, leave home, marry, have children, lose a spouse (through death or divorce), move back to the family home (with or without children), and at some point, sooner or later, die. In short, nuclear does not mean simple: we can glimpse a complex network of connections within family marriage patterns. Aristocratic families, with political ties at the forefront, undergo many changes, with divorce and remarriage leading to step-parents and stepchildren (K. Bradley 1991).

5   Families from Egypt

Lower down the social scale, the provincial census returns from Greco-Roman Egypt (first–third centuries AD) provide unparalleled evidence for variety in household structures (Bagnall and Frier 1994). The diversity is astounding, ranging from the most simple (one person living alone) to highly complex multiple family and extended family groups. Shorter returns have a greater chance of being preserved, but even so 36 percent of households in the sample can be classified as complex rather than simple. Fewer than 23 percent of the sample of 167 are made up of a father, mother and children – and, interestingly enough, such couples are on average much older than one might expect. When one considers the village/metropolis split between simple and complex, there is clearly a marked difference: metropolite households have a greater tendency towards simple; village households also tend to be slightly bigger (complex does not necessarily mean big), though lodgers and slaves boost the metropolite numbers. The urban/rural divide is revealing; these census returns reinforce the suspicion that outside urbanized sectors in the West and lower down the social ladder, at least at some points in the family life cycle more complex family groupings were much more common than many may have assumed.

It is easy to forget that we are dealing not with numbers but with people. Fascinating examples of households abound within the census returns. For example, in *P.Berl.Leihg.* III.52B, AD 147, there are at least five co-resident siblings, all declared as *apatores* (i.e. illegitimate), ranging in age from 14 to 30 years, two married to each other, and the oldest married to an outsider. In *P.Berl.Leihg.* I.17, AD 161, three brothers and two sisters live in a house that they rent from two wards of one of the brothers; all five siblings are (or have been) married, two of them to each other (but now divorced), and two of the brothers to two sisters. All have children; a divorced or widowed sister also lives in the house with her child. The ex-wife of one of the brothers also lives there, with a child. Finally there are two slaves (mother and son) of that child. Compare *P.Ryl.* II.111, AD 161, for a similarly complex situation, where a man's former wife (his sister) and their children co-reside with the man's new wife and their children; in total 27 individuals are in the household. At the extreme is *BGU* I.115 i, AD 189, where a 50-year-old male lives with his wife (who is also his sister and who is 54); they have eight children, five boys and three girls, the youngest 7, the oldest 29. The 29-year-old son has married his sister, and their two

1-year-old sons live in the house; another brother, aged 26 years, has married, this time outside the family, and also has two sons, the older 13 years old (which means this brother became a father at the age of 13). In this household 27 people reside (at least five of them named Heron!), including some lodgers who are also related by blood.

Quite apart from such fascinating examples, the evidence in total makes for at least one inevitable conclusion: on the basis of these returns, newly married Egyptian couples did not regularly leave their parents' homes and form new households. The complexities of the households are further emphasized when one remembers that the returns give us a snapshot of an ever-changing scene, in which as the life course of each member of the household evolves, the household structure continually changes, even from simple to complex and vice versa.

6 Marriage

In terms of the life course of the ancient family, the birth of the family was marriage. In both classical Athens and imperial Rome patriarchy and paternalism are reflected in marriage ideals and practices. The aim of marriage was the joining of a couple in order to produce legitimate offspring for the greater good of the state – to maintain the citizen body and provide soldiers for the army, to maintain and hopefully expand the patrimony, to continue the family name, as well as to provide security in the parents' old age. Remaining unmarried was not really an option for the vast majority of citizens in either Athens or Rome – for women outside the "working classes" it was essentially the only available career option. At many points through history legislators insisted that people should marry and produce children: the Augustan marriage legislation (18 BC and AD 9) is perhaps the best known example, but both Greek and Roman legislators had already been concerned about falling birth rates, particularly among the upper classes, and sought to reverse the perceived trend either with inducements or penalties. Marriage and motherhood gave women status in the Greek and Roman worlds. It can be argued that Perikles' citizenship law of 451 BC, and in a different way Augustus's social legislation on marriage and childbearing, increased the public status of the citizen mother. To be unmarried and/or infertile as a woman was unfortunate, in several senses; indeed it was felt to be detrimental to a woman's health not to fulfill her biological role as a mother. In both societies the lack of children was easy grounds for divorce. It was not uncommon to resort to the adoption of adults into the family line in order to resolve the disaster of a lack of heirs.

Marriages were arranged at an early stage in children's lives, by fathers and mothers, together with other interested parties. In classical Greek the verb "to marry" was *sunoikein*, literally "to live together," and in both Athenian and Roman contexts it was the intent of being married that most mattered. Ceremony was secondary. Marriage thus at first glance looks like a semi-business arrangement between groups of men, especially in the case of Athens and *epikleroi*, where an orphaned unmarried daughter with no siblings had the absolute right to inherit the estate from her father.

In this case Athenian legislation ensured the *oikos* lived on: the girl would be immediately "attached" to a close male relative.

In Athens the wife moved household and took her dowry with her; she became a member of a different *oikos*. Athenian marriage was typically endogamous, at least among the upper classes. Romans tended more towards exogamy (i.e. marriage outside the wider family grouping), as far as our evidence suggests. In early Roman times the situation was similar to the Athenian in terms of the wife's place in the household: she entered the *manus* or control of her husband (or his father if he was still in *patria potestas*) and so she was in effect in the position of a daughter, just as in Athens. But over the course of the later Roman republic there was a significant, albeit gradual, change in marriage structure, and most wives did not fall into the *manus* of their husbands: they remained within the property and inheritance network of their natal family, even though they lived in their husbands' household. One of the legal consequences of this was that the mother was not in the same *familia* as her children. Again, this legal viewpoint must not be read as a straight description of affective family relationships, but it did have significant implications for family structures and inheritance patterns.

While it is difficult and sometimes impossible to track affective relationships in the past, this should not lead us to assume that arranged marriages precluded affection. Even Aristotle allowed for this, stating that marriage is not just for procreation but also for companionship (*Eth. Nic.* 8.12). In Athens and in Rome it was expected that marital harmony (*homonoia, concordia*) developed *within* marriage, not in advance of it. Traditionally, in Athenian society, men of about 30 would marry brides at the age of puberty. In Roman society too there was a smaller but still notable disparity between the ages of husband and wife at first marriage (on age of marriage, Scheidel, POPULATION AND DEMOGRAPHY, section 4). Almost inevitably, marriages of this nature took on an air of paternalism, at least at the outset: a bride's status in her husband's household would increase as she aged and (hopefully) became a mother. Xenophon in his *Oikonomikos*, for example, encouraged the subordinate position of women. Yet there is material to suggest that even Athenian wives did not internalize this ideal of secondary status (see Richlin, WRITING WOMEN INTO HISTORY). In both Athenian and Roman society it was accepted and expected that the wife and mother would in practical terms run the household.

7 Children

Whatever the degree of affection between the couple, it was certainly true that the primary aim of marriage was to produce children and to raise them in a way that would not only reflect well upon their parents but also inculcate traditional social mores. In effect, the family, as a fundamentally conservative unit, served as an arena for socialization. The experience of children in ancient times is difficult to ascertain, as they leave no direct literary record of their lives and what we see of them is viewed through the prism of adult fathers. As children grew they would come into contact with a number of adult carers; they might stay with their own parents, or through the death or divorce of a parent they might find themselves with a number of step-parents and step-siblings. Within an upper-class household a child would certainly have experienced a number of slave carers, some of whom assumed duties we might today consider the proper role of parents. In some cases the relationship between child and carer could become a close one, and this potential for closeness caused anxiety among some male commentators.

Children were generally considered a desirable asset in the ancient world, but the care they received depended on their status, rank, and economic position, and, ultimately, on the whim of their parents and carers. Children whose parents had sufficient economic resources could expect a reasonable period of childhood when they could be admired and indulged for their childish behavior and exploits (B. Rawson 2003). Those in less-well-off families could expect to work in some form or other from an early age; they no doubt helped in family businesses or on farms as soon as they were capable.

Within the family a child would learn from an early age how to negotiate the power dynamics of society: between husband and wife, parents and children, master and slave, men and women. In Roman society in particular, where the evidence exists, familial bonds appear strong among all social groups, even those who could not form legal unions. Among ex-slaves, who could legally marry, the desire to emulate the family life of patrons is striking. As well as influencing social behavior, ideals also mask some of the less palatable realities of life. Some marriages were doubtless made entirely for the convenience of male alliances. Some were unhappy; wives, husbands and children could suffer abuse, as did many slaves.

8   Death, Divorce, and Inheritance

Much family law is concerned with inheritance and the transfer of the family property from one generation to the next. In Athens inheritance was partible, among sons. Daughters were entitled to only a dowry, itself often a sizeable portion. In Rome the dowry, however, was not considered the daughter's sole claim to the patrimony. The figure of the *epikleros* did not exist in Roman society, where by the second century AD women were legally allowed to dispose of property themselves; the law here was clearly following social practices established much earlier.

The difference in the status of Athenian and Roman wives is illustrated by what happens at the end of a marriage, whether through death or divorce. Demosthenes' father had made arrangements for his widow's remarriage. The wealthy Roman widow or divorcee might choose to remarry, and under the Augustan laws was actively encouraged to do so, but she might be independently wealthy if her father had already died. Cicero's daughter Tullia married three times, presumably returning to her father's house between husbands; Terentia, on the other hand, remained a widow (although there developed an intriguing rumor that she married the historian Sallust after her divorce). On the death of the father children in Athens would be in the care of a guardian (*kurios*) who would usually be a male relative. In the case of Demosthenes, as we have seen, this was not a successful arrangement, but it highlights the strong sense of power and family control lying in the male line. At Rome guardianship was also common in the sense that those under age could not engage in financial dealings, and the sense of the dominance of the paternal line in the legal construction of the *familia* meant that children were supposed to stay with close paternal relatives, rather than with their mother. Again, demographic realities not infrequently subverted this idea and there are many instances of widowed mothers raising their children.

Fundamental as the family was to ancient societies, at its heart it was also a fragile institution. Both Demosthenes and Cicero experienced the vagaries of life in both the public and the private spheres. The unpredictable nature not only of human emotions but also of high mortality levels meant that the Greeks and Romans lived with the notion of instability ever present. Familiar as so many aspects of the ancient family may appear to us in modern Western societies, we should always be aware that the ancient framework for envisaging the family was fundamentally alien to our own.

FURTHER READING

The modern study of the ancient family in socio-historical terms can be said to have begun with three innovative and influential works: Lacey 1968 on the Greek family, B. Rawson 1966 on lower-class Roman families, and Crook 1967 on Roman law and social realities. Since then the field has flourished, though separately and at somewhat uneven pace.

On the Greek (or, more precisely, Athenian) side, there is less to mention, despite Lacey's lead, but some significant landmarks since Lacey include works by S. Pomeroy 1997, Cox 1998, C. Patterson 1998 and Nevett 1999 (on archaeological aspects). For a useful overview of the life course, Garland 1990. On children: M. Golden 1990, and articles in Neils and Oakley 2003 for visual and material culture, and, in general terms: Humphreys 1983.

Dixon 1992 offers a comprehensive introduction to the Roman family, as do the volumes from the Roman family conferences first organized by Beryl Rawson: Rawson 1986 and 1991, Rawson and Weaver 1997, M. George 2005. Excellent papers on a range of topics are also provided in Kertzer and Saller 1991. Further awareness of social practices that affect family life is provided by K. Bradley 1991 and Saller 1994 – to cite only two works by these scholars – and Gardner 1986 and 1998. On marriage see the magisterial volume by Treggiari 1991. For roles of parents and children see Dixon 1988, Wiedemann 1989, Rawson 2003, Huskinson 1996 (for iconography), and papers in Dixon 2001. For a life-course approach see Harlow and Laurence 2002; Parkin 2003 on old age.

On the predominance of the nuclear family see Saller and Shaw 1984 (critiqued in D. Martin 1996). For an introduction to the demographic aspects: Parkin 1992 and Scheidel 2007; Bagnall and Frier 1994 for Roman Egypt, along with Edmondson in M. George 2005. For the family and domestic space see Wallace-Hadrill 1994 and 1996 and Hales 2003. For continuity and change in late antiquity see Rousselle 1988, Evans Grubbs 1995, Arjava 1996, Nathan 2000, Moxnes 1997, Balch and Osiek 2003.

Sourcebooks for primary material: on the Roman side Gardner and Wiedemann 1991; for women see especially Evans Grubbs 2002, and for Greco-Roman Egypt Rowlandson 1998;

for Roman society in general consult Shelton 1998, and Parkin and A. Pomeroy 2007. Again the Greek side is less well covered, though worthy of note are S. Pomeroy 1994 and 1997. V. Vuolanto maintains a useful online bibliography of the history of childhood from the eighth century BC to the eighth century AD:

www.uta.fi/laitokset/historia/sivut/BIBChild.pdf

CHAPTER THIRTY

Food

John Wilkins

1 Introduction

Eating food is a natural function (Galen, *Natural Faculties* 1.1), which, like growth to adulthood, is shared with plants and animals. Food provides essential nutriment, without which the body dies. This key need accompanies others which all human beings face, such as the need for clothes and shelter. These needs interact with social and psychological forces to shape human cultures. Mediterranean cultures, for example the Jews, Greeks and Romans, imagined their mythical origins at the point where human beings were separated from the gods and recognized their need for nourishment that would henceforth be met by agriculture. The myths of Eden and Prometheus accounted for what went before (unlimited food and no women) and for the hierarchy newly established in those ancient cultures between gods (at the top), human beings in the middle, and animals at the bottom (Detienne and Vernant 1989). These (and other) distinctions between gods, human beings, and animals were fundamental to ancient thought. Fire (for cooking, sacrifice, and technology) and the hard labor of agriculture were at the heart of the new order. Ancient texts from Hesiod to Galen stress the deficit between food production and consumption. Adequate provision, always a key concern for city authorities, more often failed in rural areas, particularly in the spring. This is a constant refrain in Galen's review of nutrition (Garnsey 1999, Sallares 1991, Gallant 1991).

Many cultures of the ancient Mediterranean shared myths and technologies of food production, but social practice and religious belief distinguished one from another. Eating customs distinguished neighboring peoples in ancient ethnography. Herodotus says that the Persians celebrated birthdays and liked cakes, while the Egyptians kneaded bread with their feet. Poseidonios identifies the Celts as eaters of meat, who drank wine (if they belonged to the elite) and disliked olive oil (Athen. 4.151e–2d, cf. chap. 26.5 above). Timaios reports naked slave-girls at Etruscan feasts and Nicolaos of Damascus armed warriors at Roman meals (Athen. 4.153d–4a).

These cultural snapshots taken from outside intrigue, but give a very partial picture of the society under scrutiny. Much remains unsaid. This chapter faces the same problem. What assumptions does a modern reader bring to the topic? How do we interrogate the ancient sources? How do we fill in the gaps? Some are enormous. Galen in the late second century AD wrote a treatise on nutrition, *On the Powers of Foods*, which provides an invaluable social commentary ranging (unusually) over all classes of free citizen. But he says almost nothing about the female half of the population, even though he insists that the property of any given food must be considered alongside the particular constitution of the individual (and women in Hippocratic thought had very different natures from men). Athenaeus, another major commentator of the same period on ancient foods and eating practices, has more to say about women, but almost all of it about entertainers at men's drinking parties. Sources driven by political ideology are more anxious to tell us that women in the Roman republic and in Miletos did not drink wine, than how they cooked their food, organized food preparation by their slaves (if they had any), and fed their families.

Modern studies raise important questions about women. There are many more such questions. Once a modern reader has established what the Greeks and Romans ate (see Garnsey 1999, Dalby 1996, 2003), how the centers of population were supplied (see Garnsey 1988), and whether the rich really did exist on dormice and exotic birds, as testified in the pages of Petronius and the *Historia Augusta* (some did), big differences between ancient and modern emerge. The eating of the elite captures the headlines and sets the pace for change and innovation, but it is the eating culture of all classes that shapes the society. In the modern West, the majority of the population is separated from the point of agricultural production. This was much less the case in antiquity, with consequent implications for the slaughtering of animals and possible abstinence from the premier food, meat. Massive provision of food by supermarkets has led to looser ties with the seasons of the year, and with local and regional foods. Again, the ancient experience was different. Human beings were more subject to regional and seasonal influences, particularly if they belonged to the majority who lacked the resources of the elites and did not live in the major cities.

Peasants, Galen tells us, sent their best produce to town, reserving for themselves the lesser cereals and pulses. Food shortages were less likely in cities, but were always a potential threat to order if supplies were threatened. (Thucydides notes the danger to order once war removes the ready supply of daily needs, 3.82.2.) Meanwhile, for the minority who controlled the resources of courts and cities, a different threat loomed, namely the danger of excess, of the luxurious indulging of desire. It is this aspect which dominates much ancient literature on the subject, and to which we shall return. It might seem, in what follows, that the elites enjoyed all good things at their tables, while the food supply of the rural peasant was precarious and can only be viewed in negative terms. Such a conclusion is probably misleading, for small farmers enjoyed good harvests as well as bad. Furthermore, small farmers often diversified their crops as a strategy against crop failure. This increased the range of foods available, as did the storage of surplus. Milk was stored as cheese, pork as ham, and grapes as wine. Such preservation of surpluses to meet future shortages was a survival strategy, which, as a by-product, produced strong and desirable tastes that might be enjoyed or sold. Wine and preserved fish were important traded items. Food was also built into their social and religious life. Special foods (sometimes meat) were eaten to mark feast days and key points in the life cycle, and food was shared through family networks. Hospitality (*xenia*) extended to strangers is attested in all periods and classes: the first element was to offer food. Food, in short, marked a person's identity, however rich or poor.

Cities, particularly those on the coast, enjoyed access to outside influence through trade and international networks. These generated strong ideological debate over the neglect of traditional values and the inflated enthusiasm for foreign imports on the one hand, and celebration of the variety available on the other. Appeals to simple ways now abandoned characterize Greco-Roman literature and history: see Juvenal *Satire* 11 and Purcell (2005b) for Rome. In Athens, the *Acharnians* of Aristophanes ambivalently portrays both the virtues of traditional farming and the desirability of imports. Food played an important role within this debate about town-based luxury. Two important aspects require discussion. The first is the desire among the powerful to express their competitive success through display to peers and the patronage of dependents. This led to fine tableware, increased meat consumption, and a taste for new and exotic foods. The second is the continual arrival of new foods over millennia, usually from Asia (birds, fruits, vegetables, and spices), but also from Africa (birds) and western Europe (rabbits). Asian influences on the ancient Mediterranean were enormous. In the prehistoric period, it is likely that new varieties and techniques came into the Mediterranean from the fertile crescent in Mesopotamia. The cultivated vine and olive, for example, seem to have been introduced westwards by the Greeks and Phoenicians (see e.g. Luce 2000). New animals arrived, including the chicken and the pheasant. The style of dining changed radically with the introduction of reclining rather than sitting at table, a practice apparently imported from the Assyrians and Persians. The Persians showed how a centralized court could harness innovation and draw in new resources. The march of Alexander to India opened opportunities to expand existing trade routes for spices and precious goods (on armies and their dissemination of food in general see Davies 1971). The Hellenistic kingdoms, particularly those based in Alexandria and Pergamon, brought new forms of courtly life, which, together with Macedon itself, provided models for imperial dining in Rome. This process helped to transform the courtly dining of the Persian king in the sixth and fifth centuries BC (see Herakleides of Cumae in Athen. 4.145a–6a) into a format that was acceptable to Rome. The Roman emperor could now project grandeur on certain occasions if he wished – Asian birds on gold and silver plate; he could import special non-luxurious foods, such as Tiberius's German parsnips; or he could snack alone, as Suetonius reports of Augustus. The emperor, like his richer subjects, had access to all the varieties of the known world. These imports could be exotic imports like cloves and pepper; specialties from imperial lands such as French ham and cheese, or fine regional products such as the olive oil of Venafrum in Campania.

Some of these influences affected only the rich, though others were diffused to much of the population. They generated not only new items in the diet but also food-oriented literary and historical works, accounts of exotic travels (*periploi*), and technical treatises in medicine, pharmacology (by Dioscorides and Galen), and the preparation of recipes (by Archestratos of Gela). Many of these commentaries were not merely descriptive, but also brought moral and cultural evaluation of change, often, as we shall see, with a strong emphasis on simplicity and tradition.

2   The Main Foods in the Diet

First, I summarize the foods available to the Greeks and Romans (for details, Dalby 1996 and 2003). The cereal base of the diet was broadly barley in Greece and wheat in Italy, with local variations according to climate and altitude. For example, millets were grown in Italy, as well as in parts of the Black Sea, rye in the western Black Sea. In Asia Minor, and elsewhere, various primitive wheats were grown. Wheat was the cereal of choice, for its bread-making properties, but often primitive wheats and barley provided a more reliable crop. Varieties of bread wheat became more common, and over time bread became commercially available. There is evidence in Athens from the fourth century BC, in Rome from the second. Bread was normally made at home. Cereals were often made into flat-breads, cakes and porridges, with even wheat being boiled in water and served as a porridge. In a key passage (*On the Powers of Foods* 1.7), Galen notes peasants eating indigestible wheat porridge when their bread (made by the women) had run out. Manual workers could not necessarily wait for more of the preferred bread, even when wheat was available. Rich people, meanwhile, might prefer Cappadocian bread, according to Athenaeus 3.112c, 4.129e, or even certain barley breads (Archestratos fr. 5 Olson and Sens). The porridge-like mixtures of cereal with water (or milk) might be eaten immediately they were cooked, or dried in the sun and stored for later use in rehydrated form. Beans and pulses offered a valuable and necessary addition to cereals. Country people might go without cereals altogether, as occurred in Europe in later periods (Wilkins and Hill 2006). Staples were complemented with vegetables (such as gourds, beets, cabbage, lettuce, wild leaves, celery, onions, and garlic), fruits (such as pears, apples, figs, and later peaches), walnuts and other nuts, and numerous cakes for those who could afford the necessary cereals and honey. The majority of the population ate meat in small quantities and infrequently. All parts of the animal were eaten, with a particular liking for head, vital organs and feet, the parts which offered contrasting textures and strong flavors.

Taste is important here, since the characteristic flavors of Greek and Roman food were not those of the modern "Mediterranean" diet, such as tomatoes, peppers ("Columbian" foods from the Americas), and lemons (like rice, not widely introduced until later centuries), but the ranker flavors of sulphur and garlic found in the highly favored plant silphium and its cousin asafetida, and the fermented fish sauce *garum* (for which see p. 279 above) – flavors comparable to those of south-east Asia. These powerful flavors were used with salt, olive oil, herbs such as thyme and rosemary, and, for the rich, imported spices such as pepper and ginger.

3   Meals and Social Occasions

The consumption of meat was limited, and normally linked to sacrifice. The most commonly sacrificed animal was the pig, the most prestigious, cattle. Goats and sheep were also eaten. The rich ate larger animals and more often, with particular emphasis on hunted animals such as wild boar. They also ate a wide range of birds, the chicken one among many. Poorer people ate smaller birds and animals. Of fish, shoaling fish such as sardines and anchovies went to the poorer citizens, more solitary fish that were difficult to catch, such as turbot, bream, and sea bass, to the richer. In other words, differences in class and wealth were marked by bigger, better, and tastier versions of what the majority ate, served on vessels made of precious metals rather than wood and ceramics. The rich table offered vintage and imported wines, the poor homemade, the rich imported salt fish, the poor consumed their own produce.

Food was normally eaten within the family group, for which we have some limited evidence. Most descriptions are of special occasions such as weddings, with other brief references to breakfasts and lunches taken with family or friends. We know much more about the formal meals, the Greek *deipnon* and symposium and the Roman *cena* or *convivium*, of which many descriptions survive. On the Greek occasion, emphasis was given to the wine-drinking by taking out the small tables on which the reclining diners had eaten, and by invoking the gods and starting the drinking again. The dessert course was eaten during the symposium, and there had been some drinking during the *deipnon*, but a clear division was established by ritual toasts. With the symposium came a series of cultural events and entertainments, music and recitation (O. Murray 1990b, Lissarrague 1990). This was the creative time of the evening, with elaborate rituals surrounding the mixing of wine with water. It was a time devoted to Dionysos and set apart from normal family life in other ways through the exclusion of women of status (but not female "companions" or hetaerae) and through a rule of equality between all male participants who drank equally and were in theory of equal status. At the Roman *cena*, food and drink were less strictly separated, women of status were present (though often in fewer numbers than the men), and a hierarchy was visibly displayed through the seating order and sometimes through tableware and the foods served. These differences are important and often rehearsed, as they were in antiquity, but we should emphasize the wide variety of occasions on which people ate together and the vast numbers of cities and communities in which these occasions took place in Italy, the Greek mainland, and throughout the Mediterranean world. Many variations of standard practice are likely once the Roman rule of the Greek east was well established, and local practices are also factored in. To take a very literary example, the diners in Athenaeus's *Deipnosophistae* (*The Philosophers at Dinner*) are Greeks and Romans dining in Rome. They speak Greek and have Greek entertainments, but they drink wine from the start, they appear to be equal under the guidance of a symposiarch, and no women (of status or as entertainers) are present. Similarly, at feasts offered by Roman officials in Asia Minor, we should not expect strict Roman practice on every occasion.

These occasions were formal meals, which the most wealthy citizens enjoyed regularly, others perhaps only on major occasions such as weddings, and poorer citizens rarely, if at all. There were other forms of communal dining, which took place in local groups organized according to political, religious, commercial, and other affiliations. These are widely attested in Greek and Latin inscriptions, which set out the regulations and show how dining associations were part of the social infrastructure (Schmitt-Pantel 1992, Donahue 2005). Dining with peers and associates often took place at local level, as did some civic festivals, which complemented major religious occasions.

Food consumption was closely linked to systems of state control, private patronage, and a combination of the two. In most cities, state festivals were organized by the city authorities to honor the city's gods and integrate the citizens. At the Athenian Panathenaia and Dionysia festivals, alongside processions and rituals for Athena and Dionysos, dances, contests and military displays, cattle were slaughtered in large numbers and distributed to the participating officials and all the participating citizens. For many, this was an opportunity (a relatively infrequent opportunity) to eat beef at the city's expense (a vast expense). Honoring the god in sacrifice, the affirmation of identity, and the pleasure of drinking wine and eating chewy beef were all enjoyed together. The festivals in a democratic city had a different political emphasis from festivals in cities such as Sparta, Ephesos, or Rome. But the communal eating with the god after a procession to express political identity is comparable. These examples may be compared with the procession of Ptolemy Philadelphos, as reported by Kallixenos of Rhodes (Athen. 5.196–203e). The vast procession wound its way through Alexandria, honoring Dionysos and the Ptolemies. Clear divisions for eating were imposed between royal guests and others (soldiers, visitors, and artisans). The Ptolemaic procession, focusing on the royal couple and their parents, had clearly adapted the elements from the city-state to a new purpose. It is not clear whether all citizens will benefit from the royal largesse of meat. This is patronage writ large. On a smaller scale, festivals and meals were available in many cities of Greece and Asia Minor in Hellenistic and Roman times, sponsored by eminent citizens who wanted to commemorate themselves as benefactors with a sacrifice, a feast, or a free drink (Schmitt-Pantel 1992).

Such patronage was not greatly different from the practice of the Roman emperors, who gave games to the people and also gifts of food according to rank. The emperors were working within the Roman patronage system in which powerful senators and the wealthy supported their clients with meals and other benefits. This hierarchical system was reflected in the organization of Roman mealtimes, as mentioned above. It should not be thought, however, that the support of the poor by the rich was absent in Greek cities. In addition to individual benefactions to the populace (such as Kimon's opening his orchards), rich citizens from the *Odyssey* onwards supported retainers in return for entertainment. Athenaeus 6 provides rich comic and historical evidence, which includes a generic description of a poor diner in Syracuse (from a comedy of Epicharmos, early fifth century BC), the rich patron Kallias in Athens (fifth century BC), and the relationship in the fourth century between Greek politicians and Philip II of Macedon. Patronage through gifts of meals (alongside other gifts) existed widely in the Greek world, albeit more ambivalently than in the Roman. Greek equality at table was sometimes extremely theoretical.

If we want to know the full variety of opportunities for dining and eating (for men but also for women in numerous designated festivals), we should factor in many different levels of wealth. Between the extremes of the emperor and the peasant whose food might run out in the spring there were many strata of society, with different abilities to control their resources. The inns, bars, and shops selling hot and cold foods in Greek and Italian towns (Athens, Pompeii, and Herculaneum offer many examples) are frequently dismissed as lower-class places by authors such as Juvenal, but for the majority of the population they offered a regular or occasional venue for eating. They sold takeaway food and drink for town dwellers, the majority of whom lacked dedicated kitchens. Only the largest homes had dedicated dining space, though some of those had numerous dining rooms. Much dining, and indeed cooking, took place outside (Fisher 2000, Wilkins and Hill 2006). Interior space for most was dedicated to food storage.

4   Change and Development

We can detect trends in the adoption of new developments. A new food or practice was often taken up by a court or small group of wealthy citizens, and then diffused more widely in the population over time. Take reclining at the symposium. Reclining appears to have been introduced into the Greek and Italian cities in the archaic period, and is attested on vase paintings and in literature. The major change from sitting at table spread from city to city until the practice was apparently standard for formal dining and symposia. It is widely attested in iconography and literature, and underpinned the aristocratic ideology of the archaic period in Greece. The oligarchs expressed their solidarity and opposition to lower-class politics through the camaraderie of the symposium. The poetry of Theognis of Megara offers a good example. It can be seen too in Athens, in the oligarchic parodying of the Mysteries in 415 BC (O. Murray 1990a) and in Aristophanes' *Wasps*, in which the son with oligarchic sympathies initiates his father (of democratic leanings) into the polite society of the symposium. But the rituals of the symposium were much more widely diffused at this period, and poets writing for the popular genre of comedy took it for granted that their mass audiences would accept symposia as their own (Wilkins 2000, Fisher 2000). Davidson (1997) contrasts the aristocratic symposium and its elaborate rituals with the commercial bars to which the majority of the male population resorted for communal drinking. This is misleading. The elite may have enjoyed more symposia more often in private homes and with more expensive wines, furniture, and drinking vessels. But the majority of the population almost certainly attended symposia at weddings, when holding some political offices, and at some public festivals. If they could not afford finely crafted couches, they made informal couches and reclined on the ground. But they followed essentially the same practice, and continued to do so in later centuries.

The second example concerns the royal court. The King of Persia had all good things brought to him, including new foods that had been discovered. In the hierarchical Persian world, everything came from all points of the empire to the king, who redistributed much to his courtiers, and thence more widely through Persian society. Some unsympathetic Greek commentators noted the enormous meals and interpreted them as expressions of gluttony rather than hierarchical redistribution. Others such as Ktesias and Herakleides of Cumae give much more nuanced accounts of the mechanisms at work, and noted the Persians' own account of their simple beginnings and characteristic foods (Sancisi-Weerdenburg 1995, Briant 1996). Kings and tyrants in the Greek world have something in common with the Persian king, though on a much more limited scale. The courts of the Sicilian tyrants seem to have nurtured a thriving culture of innovation (Wilkins 2000 chap. 7) which produced cookery books and new styles of cooking (Olson and Sens 2000). Later, the Hellenistic monarchs provided a focus for books on plants, foods, and medicines, partly through their fears of poisoning. This mechanism probably brought cherries, damsons, and peaches to a wider clientele.

Many texts imagine a progress from an early society based on gathering wild foods, or on cannibalism and savagery, moving thence through sacrifice and other religious and legal regulations to the "civilized life," where human beings ate the foods of culture. These are agricultural products, parts of which must be offered as first-fruits or thank-offerings to the gods in the smoke of sacrifice. Human beings generally ate food that had been processed, though more wild plants were eaten than is common in western Europe now. Doctors looked on wild plants with some concern, since the raw juices they contained might overpower the heat of the body and impair digestion, thereby causing disease. What was normally looked for was food properly prepared and cooked, though Galen conceded that it was possible to survive on uncooked food, and even a vegetarian diet, as a young acquaintance of his once demonstrated over a four-year period (*On the Powers of Foods* 1.25). Balance was needed, however, since food cooked by professional chefs was often considered to be damaging. The cook represented culture that had gone too far towards pleasure and excess (ibid. 2.51).

Culture brings its anxieties, and in particular in the field of luxury and desire. Pleasure is closely allied to the consumption of food. It is a basic mechanism of the body that bad-tasting food should be rejected and good-tasting food ingested. With Galen it is axiomatic that food that has a good taste (*chulos*) will have a similar beneficial effect internally on fluids of the body (*chuloi*), including the balance of the humors (*chumoi*). The problem with good-tasting food, however, is that enjoyment of it (as with all objects of desire) may lead to the desire for more (Davidson 1997). This area of concern dominates many ancient discussions of food (e.g. Athenaeus 12). While a poor citizen may derive the greatest pleasure from the taste of sacrificial meat eaten occasionally at city festivals, such a person is not the principal concern of the moralist. Rather, it is the rich young man who may be tempted to spend ancestral resources in gratifying his desire for pleasure.

Such fears ran deep. Plato and the Stoics reflected on the need for control of desire. Epicureans offered an alternative (much maligned) solution. Some authors took this to considerable lengths. Musonius Rufus, the Stoic philosopher, refused to eat cooked food, which removed him in effect from Olympian religion and Hippocratic medicine. This is an extreme formulation, which meets strict philosophical requirements to curb desire. Another Stoic philosopher, Seneca, became a vegetarian, for a time. Interesting arguments for the vegetarian life are offered in Plutarch; in Ovid's representation of Pythagoras in *Metamorphoses* 15.60–142, and in Porphyry and Iamblichus, who comment on Pythagoreanism. Porphyry declares the vegetarian life suitable only for the ascetic philosopher. Not eating meat (or fish) seems to have been part of the Pythagorean life from the sixth century BC, though most details come from a later period. The belief in kinship with animals and the transmigration of souls was part of Pythagorean mysticism, which represented a very different conception of animals from the mainstream of Greco-Roman religion. (Burkert 1987, Detienne 1994).

Few followed these ideas about animals. Most authors ignored vegetarianism and were much more concerned with understanding the success of Rome as an empire and cosmopolis. The mapping of food and drink onto these developments is the objective of Athenaeus in the *Deipnosophistae*. The semi-fictional host, Larensis, recognizes that Rome was once a simpler city with few slaves and leaders who ate frugally, while now tables such as his reflect wealth and employ many slaves. Athenaeus offers an overarching perspective of history, in which pristine simplicity and self-control is (curiously) policed by Homer. He is the unfailing guide for correct conduct at table, and between the time of Homer and the present (about 200 AD) many manifestations of luxury have been seen, most, like the Sybarites of southern Italy, the Persians, and the Macedonians, following a trajectory of rise and fall. There is no model for constant progress and development, such that what is now enjoyed is more advanced than it was in classical or Hellenistic times. Rather, what is enjoyed now is keyed into the past. Within this timeframe Athenaeus and his characters review thousands of Greek and other communities in all their array and difference. They focus on the details, such as dining customs at Naukratis town hall, fish sacrifice in Attica, and the bread of Lesbos. These are the identifying features of communities across the Mediterranean. It is encyclopedic in its scale, and covers the variety of eating in the empire in a less nationalistic spirit than does Pliny in his similarly encyclopedic *Natural History*. Athenaeus mixes civic and private eating, and although he focuses on kings and the privileged few, his greatest contribution is the sheer variety of eating and drinking customs he attests within the known world, in hundreds of cities. Through his special interests, he alerts his readers to the preoccupations of texts with eating and drinking. In his account, this applies both to canonical authors such as Herodotus and Polybius, and to otherwise poorly attested local and regional histories.

Galen has a wider focus. He follows Hippocratic and Hellenistic doctors in addressing the medical needs of the human animal, examining different classes of people and the different stresses on their bodies. Hence his review of food shortages among the peasants and their enforced eating further down the food chain than they would choose. He considers too the effect of manual work and athletics on the body's food requirements. Though doctor to the emperor, much of his evidence is taken from his native Mysia in Asia Minor, and, like Athenaeus, he provides a valuable corrective to those who focus on the Greek and Italian peninsulas. He strikes other chords, too. He castigates cooks, as Plato had done in *Gorgias*, for encouraging pleasure over health, but is not above writing a cookery book himself, even though for many this was on the way to luxury. He shares other prejudices of the ruling class, against inns, where he reports human flesh being served (*On the Powers of Foods* 3.1), and against the pollution of Rome, where his evidence coincides with the vitriolic Juvenal (Wilkins 2005).

Galen and Athenaeus each express the prejudices of their class. They also adduce extensive detail over the widest geographical area and a long historical perspective, underpinning in detail the general claims made in this chapter. They show that many foods differ not in raw materials but in preparation and cooking. Barley, honey, and water were the ingredients for many breads, biscuits, and cakes. These had hundreds of names, according to shape, cooking method, and place of origin. Like cheeses, they may be the mainstay of a particular village. But when collected by Roman merchants or listed by Athenaeus and Pliny, they represent the imperial cornucopia (as well as expanding the Greek and Latin lexicon). The poor villager, meanwhile, may have one type of cheese and one barley bread.

FURTHER READING

Garnsey 1999 gives an excellent short overview of the topic. There are wide-ranging collected studies in Wilkins et al. 1995, Longo and Scarpi 1989, W. Slater 1991 and Luce 2000. Hordern and Purcell's study of the Mediterranean (2000) offers a rich context, while Wilkins and Hill 2006 provide a cultural overview. On foods, dates, and provenances Dalby (1996) and (2003) is excellent. On drinking and the symposium, see O. Murray 1990b, Murray and Tecusan 1995, Davidson 1997, with Lissarrague 1990 on the iconography. Schmitt-Pantel 1992 presents Greek communal dining, Donahue 2005 its Roman counterpart. On many aspects of Athenaeus see the essays in Braund and Wilkins 2000, on Galen's food treatises Grant 2000 and Powell 2003. Food in Roman literature is discussed in Gowers 1993, in Greek literature (mainly comedy) in Wilkins 2000. On plants, see Sallares 1991, Dalby 2003 and Renfrew 1973, on meat and animals Detienne and Vernant 1989 and Jameson 1988. On kitchens see Sparkes 1962, on bars Davidson 1997 and (with other eating spaces) Laurence 1994, and on mosaics and dining space Dunbabin 2003.

CHAPTER THIRTY-ONE

Eros: Love and Sexuality

James Davidson

Courtesans, pederasts, Sappho, Venus, phalluses, Catullus, Pompeian pornography, Armies of Lovers, vulvas on amulets and love-curses on lead, the sexiness of ancient culture seems to be one of its key characteristics, what distinguishes it most strikingly from our post-pagan civilization: "the Romans, like the Greeks, drew the boundary between the erotic and the everyday and between the private and the public, somewhere other than where we put it, or might like it to be put" (Hopkins 1996). Certainly no one comes to the topic of ancient sexuality expecting to find nothing to talk about. Recently, such talk has burgeoned beyond brief summary, so I will focus on highlights and controversies.

1 Vocabularies

There were two common verbs for loving in Greek, *philein* and *eran*. *Philein* takes a direct, *eran* an indirect (genitive) object, leading Apollonius Dyscolus to suppose that the former was an activity like looking, the latter a quasi-passivity like smelling: 'Everyone knows that being in love means being *affected by* the beloved (*eromenos*)' (*Syntax* 2.418–19). Nowadays *eran*'s genitive is viewed as a "genitive of goal," targeting someone across a distance, an expeditionary love, which is why Eros has wings and a bow or driving goad, an important figure for Socratic questing after knowledge (Pl. *Symp.* 200e–4c). *Eros* is highly subjective and one-sided – "carrying a torch for someone"; reciprocal *eros* is as paradoxical as "two people carrying a torch for each other." The goal is *philia*, the "intimacy" of friends, lovers, family; so Stoics glossed *eros* as "intimates-making impulse," *epibole philopoiias* (Schofield 1991: 28–31). In magic, *eros*-spells resemble curses, driving someone to distraction, while *philia* spells are remedies designed to *restore* fond feeling (Faraone 1999). Latin equivalents *amare/diligere*, which govern no syntactical difference, or English "be in love with"/ "love," are not quite so extremely polarized.

2 Homosexual Eros

A certain kind of morally anxious and prurient philology has long attempted sexually to pin down love-words such as *erastes* "of old . . . taken for *a flagitious love of Boys*" (Bentley 1697: 53 *contra* Boyle 1698: 65–66), culminating in a recently popular theory that the ancient (and modern) Mediterranean had a quite different kind of sexuality, obsessed with sexual acts and otherwise mostly oblivious of the sex of sexual objects, seeing sexual (penetrator – penetrated) not amatory (admirer – beloved) polarity in the paired terms *erastes – eromenos/ – mene*, even assimilating all "penetrateds" to women (Foucault 1985: 187–225). Translating *eros* as "sexual lust," *erastes* as "penetrator," and *eromenos* as "penetrated," however, makes nonsense of Plato and almost any other Greek text on love. Moreover, Greeks rarely discussed actual practices, and no evidence indicates that sex between the thighs ("*diamerion*" cf. BA 306425), the commonest position in images from the reign of Peisistratos, was "more just" than "true penetration" (*pace* Dover 1978: 106). *Eros*, a particularly supercharged construction of what modern psychologists call "Romantic Love," is not defined by the presence of lustfulness, nor *philia* by its absence. An *erastes* is someone in love, a demonstrative admirer, a passionate devotee, not *necessarily* one's "lover" or "sexual partner." Hence we hear of men "pretending" to be *erastai* or pretending not to be (Aeschin. 1.171, Pl. *Lysis* 222a, *Phdr.* 237b). *Philia* is "love-at-close-quarters," not "just-good-friendship." Sex might or might not be a feature of both types of relationship. Courtesans know "how to be intimate (*philein*)" or "refuse to be intimate" (Xen. *Mem.* 3.11,10, Athen. 13.581f), while Plato (*Symp.*183c) glosses "amatory favoring" (*charizesthai*) as "becoming intimates (*philoi*)" (*pace* Konstan 1997). Plato's speakers in *Symposium* and *Phaedrus* think hard about the difference between earthy fleshly attraction towards the beloved's flesh (*soma*) and unearthly, more enduring love for his invisible personality (*psyche*), but no one suggests that *eros* without lust is nonsensical, nor is it redundant in Latin to talk of "lustful loves", *amores lubidinosos* (Cic. *Tusc.*4.71). In fact, Aristotle twice uses *eros* and *epithumia* (lust) as examples of how logically to prove a difference between similar things, concluding that "the end of *eros* is to be loved" (*phileisthai*), and sexual favors are sought only to the degree that they are part of being loved (A. Price 1989: 238–39).

Athenian same-sex love comes in two forms: (a) strongly patterned practices of distant admiring, especially "following," and rigidly formulaic acclaiming – "beautiful (*kalos*) is Leagros" – on the part of multiple admirers (N. Slater 1998; Lissarrague 1999), with vase-workshops, for instance, actually organized, it seems, as quasi-fan-clubs, "The Leagros Group," etc. (cf. Neer 2002), or (b) a publicly recognized one-to-one relationship. A similar distinction explains contradictory accounts of the phenomenon in Crete and Sparta, sometimes assuming a pack of admirers, sometimes a one-to-one (Cartledge 2001). Moreover, Greek *poleis* were "age–class polities" in which "those who had reached the age of citizenship," which in Athens, for instance, meant those deemed 18, were put in year sets, which gradually rose through the age grades (Davidson 2006b; 2007: ch. 3). The object of amatory obsession is a "boy" (*pais*): either *formally* someone in the Athenian "grade of Boys," under-18 *not yet a citizen*, represented as under-height, or *informally* someone under-20 *not yet a man*, a group which includes new citizens (called "*meirakia*," or "*neaniskoi*"), represented fully developed but still not fully bearded (puberty came about four years later before c.1800 AD; Moller 1987); hence ephebic Apollo is "always a boy" (Lucian *On Sacrifices* 11). Confusion about Greek "boy-admiring" *paiderastia* derives not only from confusion about which kind of love, but which kind of "boy," we are talking about, with sources shifting between the general and the narrow sense in one sentence. So Pausanias in Plato's *Symposium* (181c–e) identifies the exalted Heavenly Aphrodite with "love of boys (= not fully bearded yet)" and then suggests "there should be a law against falling in love with Boys (= under 18, here capitalized for clarity)."

Numerous fourth-century BC texts insist that while distant admiring and acclaiming of under-18 Boys was not a problem, even "providing a guard of their honor," unchaperoned intimacy broke the rules (Aeschin. 1.139). Only *neaniskoi* and old men were allowed in the gymnasium when boys were exercising, and even they were only allowed to "mingle" or "chat" during festivals of Hermes (Pl. *Lysis* 203ab, 206d). Wealthy families even had slaves (*paidagogoi*), employed exclusively to escort Boys. Even the lover of a slave/prostitute feels the need to repeat that he was of age, a *meirakion*, 16 times, a *neaniskos*, three times, in what is a very short speech (Lysias 3). A few frequently reproduced fifth-century images seem to contradict the texts, showing Boys being molested by men and *neaniskoi*. They are probably intended vividly to represent Boys resisting chastely (*BA* 200977), itself *to kalon* (beautiful), or illustrations of *to aischron* (ugly, shameful), how *not* to behave, rather than to reflect daily realities (cf. Beazley 1947: 220–21). Certainly they are flimsy evidence for a revolution in attitudes between the fifth and fourth centuries BC. Moreover, where we have evidence for those "in a relationship" they are often quite close in age, in stark contrast to the large gaps between wives, who were married as young as 13 (younger in Crete) to men in their (late) 30s or above. Same-sex *eros* was consistently presented as a young man's game (e.g. Mimnermus fr. 3, Pl. *Phdr.* 227cd). Archidamos was probably about 22 at the time of his relationship with Kleonymos, "just out of Boys," and men over 40 were assumed no longer to present a threat (Xen. *Hell.* 5.4.25 Aeschin. 1.11). It is quite bizarre that students of Greek homosexuality are regularly asked to steel themselves to face up to realities of child abuse, whereas students of ancient marriage or of pre-modern heterosexuality, e.g. of *Romeo and Juliet* aged 14, never are (Vattuone 2004: 11–42). Greek Boys were probably better protected from premature sexual relations than any under-18s right up to the twentieth century. It was always their little sisters we should have been more concerned for (Davidson 2007: 76–9).

There is good evidence in images and texts for sex and passion between coevals. This is perhaps especially noticeable in Thessaly and Macedonia in the relationships between Alexander and Hephaistion, for instance, or among the Macedonian 'Royal boys' (in fact *meirakia*). But even in Athens we hear that on Mt Lykabettos "utter *meirakia* gratify their age-mates" (Theopompos Com. fr. 30, Davidson 2006b: 49–51, Hupperts 1988), but it is clear that it was outrageous for a precocious *meirakion* to court a bearded man, undermining the age–class order (Xen. *Anab*. 2.6.28, *Symp*. 4.28), though it was even more outrageous for an under-18 to take a courtesan (Lysias 14.25). On the other hand, there is evidence for the ideal of lifelong relationships, continuing even after death (e.g. Aeschin. 1.146, Pl. *Symp*. 181d, *Phdr*. 256ae, Theocr. *Id*. 12). There is evidence too for formal troth plighting. The idea of a single special brother-like "dear companion" (*hetairos*) is already present in Homer (W. Clarke 1978) and Hesiod (*Works* 707–13), and Ephoros described the very public way such attachments were made in Crete, culminating in a sacrificial feast in honor of Zeus, and formal acceptance of the association (*homilia*) (*FGrHist* 70 F 149 in Strabo 10.4.21). In Boiotia the pair "associate together (*homilousi*), having been yokemated (*suzugentes*)" (Xen. *LP* 2.12); Theban pairs exchanged pledges at the tomb of Iolaos (Plut. *Pel*. 18.5). Something similar, "a genuinely matrimonial type of relationship," is implied by Sappho's use of the term "yokemate" (Gentili 1988: 76, cf. Koch-Harnack 1989: 119, 138–43). Such a conspicuous institution probably explains Anacreon's jibe: "she is from Lesbos . . . and is gagging for another girl" (fr. 358, Marcovich 1983).

In Rome the government of sexual morality normally belonged to the *paterfamilias*, but public laws on *stuprum* (illicit sex), particularly the *Lex Sca(n)tinia*, may have gone further in maintaining the integrity of free-born males than Greek laws. Most alleged crimes involve (a) violence or (b) corruption, *normally* of (c) under-age boys, and if the *Lex Scantinia* prohibited in theory or practice "homosexual sex between consenting adults," we would probably know of it. Nevertheless it is clear same-sex love for elite young men was not as central, as public, or as exalted as in Greece (C. Williams 1999).

Rome provides more straightforward evidence for penetration as domination and humiliation, anticipating the modern "Fuck You" culture (a culture in which the act of penetrative sex is viewed as intrinsically aggressive and humiliating: "Up yours," "They shafted us," "He well and truly screwed me," etc.) (M. Skinner 2005: 197; Hubbard 2003: 344–45). But we should be careful of our interpretation of the evidence here. Catullus 16's famous "I will fuck you two in the mouth and asshole" is a sophisticated joke about the risks of reading a text as *embodying* its author. Romans also emphasized status, rather than age, which leads, paradoxically, to greater prominence in Roman homoerotic discourse and imagery on unde-rage (slave) boys, understood as sex-slaves far more often in Plautus, for instance, than in his (fragmentary) Greek models (Hubbard 2003: 309). Related is the distinctively Roman (Plut. *Ant*. 59, 8) phenomenon of keeping decorative children, *deliciae*, *glabri* (smooth boys), as ostentatious symbols of wealth and power. But we should not assume the Romans were less subtle than the Greeks in distinguishing admiring from abusing. References to Tiberius's genital-nibbling "minnows" – "even greater and more disgusting indecency scarcely proper to mention or hear mentioned, let alone believed" – to toy-boys in Petronius or to monstrous Commodus's boy sharing his bed hardly proves otherwise (Suet. *Tib*. 44, Herodian 1.17.3, A. Pomeroy 1992). Allegations that a 17-year-old was seen at the symposia of Maximus, governor of Egypt, sometimes *monos* (unchaperoned), are clearly expected to cause as much outrage in Roman Egypt as they would have in classical Greece (Musurillo 1954: 7.49–59).

There are references to Roman same-sex marriages (C. Williams 1999: 245–52), and Petronius often calls boyfriends "brothers," indicating a formal arrangement of shared ownership – "If that is how you want it, tomorrow I'll go and find myself another lodging and another brother" – with rancorous divorce – "This is not the way to divide things up with your brother" (*Sat.* 9, 79–80, 127, etc.). Loving quasi-marital relationships of "adoptive (*adscitus*) brother" were central to the propaganda of the Tetrarchs (Rees 2002: 63), who were shown as two same-sex couples embracing Greek-style, bearded Augusti, unbearded Caesars, on the monument of "Brotherly love" (*Philadelphion*) in Constantinople, linking Greek love to the Byzantine institution of amatory brotherhood, *adelphopoiesis* (Boswell 1994, B. Shaw 1997, Rapp 1997).

Anacreon's joke about the girl from Lesbos certainly implies acknowledgment of the possibility of a sexual orientation, and Aeschines' sexual characterization of Misgolas and Xenophon's of Ariaeus are used to imply things about the necessarily sexual nature of their interest in Timarchos and Meno respectively (Aeschin. 1.41–2, Xen. *Anab.* 2.6.28). But the clearest statement of the existence of born homosexuals and born heterosexuals, men and women, each searching for their other half *either* among members of the same *or* from among the opposite sex comes in Aristophanes' speech in *Symposium* (191d–192b). The gender-bending *kinaidos* (lewd fellow), an aggressive seducer and molester of males, not passively submissive (Davidson 2001: 95 *pace* Younger 2004: sv "*cinaedi*") is often identified with his close cousin the *moichos* (seducer of women); sometimes they are amalgamated as "moechocinaedi" (Lucil. 1058 Marx cf. Plut. *Mor.*126a, 705e). What differentiates them, it seems, is whether they are more interested in corrupting females or males (including, on one vase, a male donkey! Younger 2004: 196 no. 190), i.e. by their sexual orientation (Phylarchus *FGrHist* 81 F 45 in Athen. 12.521b). Demosthenes' *kinaidia* is linked to his seduction of vulnerable young men (Aeschin. 1.131, Fisher 2001: 271–3); likewise Juvenal's effeminate moralist should fear the *Lex Scantinia* because it targeted seducers, not sexually passive men (Juv. 2.43–4, C. Williams 1999: 120 *pace* 122).

In the third century Sotades invented a new genre of obscene, political, satirical, parodic, and palindromic "cinaedic poetry," "Kinaidoi," with its own *loose* meter used by literary cinaedi in, for example, Petronius's Satyricon and perhaps by real-life "professional" *kinaidoi* (R. Hunter 1996: 78–79; Petron. *Sat.* 21; section 3 below). The effeminate *character* quickly came to be seen as a *type* with a specific nature produced by astrology or malicious magic – close contact with a stone from the "cinaedus fish" –, a nature which might be hidden on the outside by e.g. hard agricultural labor, requiring a skilled human scientist to discover it in an unguarded sneeze (D.L. 7.173, Richlin 1993; Gleason 1990: 395; T. Barton 2002: 117). In the early fourth century AD Eusebius argued against such essentializing theories: the homosexuality revealed in Celtic men marrying each other was surely caused by *nomos* (convention) rather than birth (*Praep. Evang.* 6.10.27, cf. B. Shaw 1997: 335).

3   Adulterers, Prostitutes, Escorts, Entertainers

Late marriage meant not only that Greece was full of young brides with old husbands, but that there were also plenty of unattached young men around to stimulate suspicion and paranoia. One husband, cuckolded by a *neaniskos*, expertly exploits this paranoia in order to win the elderly jury's sympathy: "I asked why the doors made a noise in the night, she said the baby's lamp had gone out . . . But it seemed to me she had powdered her face . . ." (Lysias 1.14). Greek women were generally kept apart from men not members of their family; the crime of *moicheia*, the seduction of a free woman married or unmarried, therefore, resembles sexual burglary. Under Athens' "Draconian legislation" such a burglar could be killed with impunity, whereas an adulteress was merely divorced. Hence it was dangerous even to enter a house when the householder was not there (Todd 1993: 276–79). The Gortyn law-code has different fines depending on the relative status of the miscreants, halved if the woman was in "another's house" at the time (Arnaoutoglou 1998: no. 20).

Roman women were not nearly as invisible: ". . . many things which are quite proper according to our conventions are among Greeks considered shameful. For what Roman shrinks from taking his wife to a dinner-party? Or whose *materfamilias* does not occupy a prime position in the home and go to and fro in public?" (Nep. *Praef.* 6–7). With greater social promiscuity went tougher laws. Punishment of the seduced woman, not excluding death, was left to the *paterfamilias*, probably in consultation with the girl's family. Augustus's *Lex Julia on repressing adulteries* (18 BC) made adultery an actionable offence. The right to execute adulterous wives and daughters with impunity was confirmed under certain circumstances, but the normal punishment was banishment to separate islands, "normal," at least, for those members of the elite whose adulteries drew the attention of historians. Husbands and fathers had exclusive right to bring charges for 60 days, after which anyone could initiate a prosecution, and, if successful, receive a share of the confiscated property, giving everyone an interest in others' immorality, which was the main point of the legislation (Treggiari 1991: chap. 9). Whether this was an attempt to restore traditional morality after late republican sexual disorder, exemplified by Clodia Metelli, who is probably Catullus's "Lesbia," and paramour of Cicero's client Caelius, or to revolutionize sexual morality under the flag of traditionalism, or simply a response to "moral panic" about Rome degenerating, is debated – probably all three were factors – but there was certainly a political aspect to the legislation, both as part of the Augustan ideology of "restoring the republic," and as a new weapon in *politically* motivated attacks (C. Edwards 1993: chap. 1, M. Skinner 1983, Richlin 1981).

Provided men left citizen-women and underage boys alone, there were no legal restrictions on their extramarital activities and a multifaceted sex industry to cater to their needs (Herter 2003). A critical, though slippery, distinction is between (a) explicit "commoditized" transactions, "sex for sale," associated either with "whores" (*pornai, scorta*) in brothels (*porneion, lupanar*) offering a "range" of women or with women or boys stationed in solitary cubicles (*oikemata, cellae meretriciae*) and (b) the deliberately imprecise exchanges of "gift and favor" (*charis, gratia*) associated with courtesans (*hetairai, meretrices*), mistresses (*puellae*) or boyfriends. Between these two poles we find women and boys under contract for an extended period (Davidson 1997: chaps 3–4) and *mousourgoi* (hired sympotic entertainers): oboe-girls (players of the double-reeded *aulos*), female "pluckers" (i.e. harpists), *cithara*-boys (the *cithara* is the most elaborate type of lyre), exploding after 300 BC into a vast array of sometimes wildly popular "cabaret artistes" (*mimae, pantomimi,* etc.), including professional *kinaidoi* (Montserrat 1996: 117, Davidson 2000a, 2006a).

Sometimes *mousourgoi* composed their own material, which will have included lyrics, scenarios, and roles, probably to be identified with the licentious mimes Plutarch calls *paignia* (plays). Aristophanes (*Frogs* 1301, 1325–28) claimed Euripides was influenced by "whore-songs," particularly those of Cyrene, to whom Agathon is also compared (M. West 1994: 353–54), and his "Hag scene" towards the end of *Ecclesiazusae* draws on or directly parodies adulterous love-mimes, explicitly contrasting the scenario presented with the old-fashioned "world of Charixene," "an *aulos*-girl" and/or *melopoios* (composer of songs or *erotika,* "love stuff") (Hesych. E5413, Phot. *Lex.* E1797). Ubiquitous, short, and simple, the popular entertainments of the *mousourgoi* probably made a much greater contribution to ancient culture than has been hitherto recognized (Davidson 2000a).

Mousourgoi constituted an enormous, highly evolved, service industry, though one neglected by economic historians. It could take years to learn an instrument, and although, doubtless, many *mousourgoi* were bought and trained by other *mousourgoi,* we hear of "schools" to which slaves could be sent for skills – and value-enhancement; vase-images indicate they were already operating in the early fifth century (Isoc. 4.287, Plaut. *Rud.* 43, *BA* 204827, 206436, 214766). A contract of 13 BC between Philios and Eros for a year's-worth of *aulos*-training for one Narcissus, all distinctly homo-amatory names, lists exactly which *auloi* are to be taught, with an examination at the end to guarantee Philios has not wasted his investment. Teaching a boy to sing while playing the *cithara* will have taken far longer. The types of *auloi* listed indicate Narcissus would be expected to play in a wide range of contexts, not merely at symposia (Delattre 1995). Likewise the harpist Habrotonon in Menander's *Arbitration* seems almost indistinguishable from a *hetaira,* but she had also accompanied a maiden chorus at a religious festival (476–78). Given the investment, it is only to be expected that *mousourgoi* would work wherever, whenever. For the same reason, although *mousourgoi* are often assumed to be readily or ultimately "available," it seems most unlikely that sex with the musicians was *automatically* assumed to be included in the fee (Davidson 2006a: 39–40).

The same construction of *mousourgoi* as performing prostitutes is found, unsurprisingly, in Greek-inspired Roman comedies, but Rome lacked the exalted tradition of tragic actors, *aulos*-players and citizen performers, to whom *mousourgoi* were structurally opposed, another cultural difference noted by Nepos (1) and ignored by Nero (C. Edwards 1994). Hence, in contrast to Greece, these entertainers were classified with (sometimes quite respectable) actors, rather than prostitutes, but all performers were legally classified alongside prostitutes as *infames.* Mime-actresses were traditionally encouraged by the audience to strip off at the festival of Flora (Val. Max. 2.10.8).

Horace (*Sat.* 1.2.58) lumps them with courtesans, and Tiberius expelled actors from Italy for spreading "foulness in private houses" (Tac. *Ann.* 4.14, C. Edwards 1993: 119–31).

Antiquarian philologists identified a distinct group of superior courtesans, sometimes referred to ironically as "Big-Fee Hetaeras," "trained" or "molded" by their owners in arts of beauty and manners (Alexis fr. 103 *PCG*) rather than musicianship. They were later perceived to belong to a bygone era, to have had a heyday in the classical/early Hellenistic period, first in Athens, then as royal mistresses, mostly because that was when they were most conspicuous in representation (oratory, comedy, art, anecdote), the antiquarians' main interest (Ogden 1999: 223–6). The best, though very negative, source, Apollodoros's "Against Neaira" ([Dem.] 59), describes the Corinth-based operation of Nikarete, a freedwoman. Apollodoros lists seven girls, "daughters," trained by Nikarete in the first quarter of the fourth century, of whom no fewer than six are referred to elsewhere, as if well known. The speech reveals a very small-scale operation with only a couple of girls under Nikarete's "care" at any one time, by no means a "brothel" as the term is commonly understood (*pace* Hamel 2003: 3). They would visit certain cities at festival time, e.g. Athens at the Panathenaia, and attend *symposia* in private houses. They mixed with a Panhellenic elite, Lysias, Simos of Thessaly, Hipponikos the famous actor, one or more of whom might establish an exclusive arrangement, eventually perhaps purchasing a girl outright from Nikarete for enormous sums – 3,000 drachmas in the case of Neaira. On marriage these lover-masters might be persuaded to free the girls for a fee, in which case they might cohabit with men who had contributed to the freedom fund, accompanying them to elite gatherings. They might be installed on a property, even to run it. They might set up "their own" establishment, where they entertained, or hostel. They were believed to be able to read and write, and some acquired a reputation for witty, even erudite, spontaneous jokes, which were recorded, supposedly, by anecdotal writers. They were believed to live a life of luxury, expensively subsidized by admirers or rich in their own right (Davidson 2006a: 42–45, 1997 chap. 4).

This extraordinary phenomenon of haughty (*semnai*) (ex-)slaves monopolizing elite heteroerotic intercourse is explained by the principle of "approximation" or "erotic circulation," i.e. that you did not want to associate with a woman who associated with vulgar tradesmen or runaway slaves, a principle which underpins a series of jokes about or ascribed to courtesans (Athen. 13.580ab, 581cf, 585bc, 588f). By (discreetly) paying huge sums, or negotiating exclusive access, men ensured their women would mix only with men like them. If courtesans seemed to dissemble the brutal facts of prostitution and slavery with a discourse of *charis* and refinement, it was a very serious game, in which their lovers were complicit. Courtesans were tokens in international elite homosocial exchange, endowed by their lovers with symbolic capital (Davidson 2004).

The same principle explains the shame attached to visiting brothels, where you might mix with women who mixed with slaves. Aristophanes vividly imagines the taint Ariphrades' mouth picked up at the brothel circulating among his acquaintances and *their* acquaintances by drinking out of the same cup (*Eq.* 1285–89). Stratonikos was ashamed to be seen leaving the city of Herakleia "as if exiting a brothel" (Athen. 8.351d). The only brothel identified in Athens, "Building Z" in the "red-light" district of Kerameikos, opened discreetly onto an alleyway (Davidson 1997: 72). Brothels in Pompeii, whose divine patron was Venus, may not have been so "zoned," but do seem generally to have kept their entrances off thoroughfares (Laurence 1994: 73, Wallace-Hadrill 1995, *contra* McGinn 2004 chap. 3). There are, however, serious problems in identifying Pompeian brothels (masonry bed? rude pictures? rude graffiti? Wallace-Hadrill 1995: 52), the latest study reckoning 13 *cellae*, minimum, plus 26 brothels for a population of c.10,000, compared to c.45–46 officially listed in Rome (pop. c.1 million) (McGinn 2004: 167, 289).

4 Religion

One of the keys to the importance of love in antiquity is its central place in religion. The sexual was a feature of many cults. The phalluses carried in honor of Dionysos (also mentioned in cults for Roman Father Liber) were construed by myths told by later writers as images of frustrated homosexual desire for the god's body: "He went among them in the form of a beautiful boy and made them quite mad with impulse for sex . . ." (Lowe 1998: 168–69). One of the most explicit of the Peisistratid scenes of intercrural sex was dedicated to the goddess Aphaia on Aigina (*BA* 14701, Ohly-Dumm 1985). Images of genitals and obscene banter alternated with symbolic practices of extreme asexualness in Demeter's festivals of Thesmophoria and Eleusis (Parker 2005: 270–89). In her temple at Priene bizarre belly-faced figurines were identified with Baubo, who made the mournful goddess smile by lifting her skirts and flashing (Olender 1990). Images of penises and vulvas "averted evil" (Johns 1982: 61–75).

Love was a crucial element in myth, often reflecting cult. The love between Herakles and Iolaos, model for Theban same-sex couples, was configured in shared altars and shrines (Paus. 1.19.3, Plut. *Mor.* 492c). Thessalians offered something to Patroklos whenever they made offerings to Achilles at Troy (Philostr. *Her.* 53.8–13). Apollo's throne sat on top of his beloved Hyakinthos at Amyklai, where on summer evenings his other lover, the katabatic evening wind Zephyros, would sweep down dramatically from Mt Taygetus (*LIMC* sv Hyakinthos). Aphrodite and Hermes were celebrated as the perfect happy couple, sharing shrines and a month-day (Day Four), a harmonious heterosexuality embodied in their son Hermaphroditos, who blended a female top and a male bottom, celebrated above all at Halicarnassus as having "first bound the marriage bed with law" (Isager 1998; Sourvinou-Inwood 2004). But the central figure of love between heaven and earth was Ganymede, a Trojan prince abducted by Zeus to serve immortals with ambrosia. He is sometimes represented at an altar (*BA* 16200), linking sacrifice to gods' nourishment. The myth was especially resonant at Achaean Aigion, where "a boy who won a beauty contest" served as Zeus's priest until puberty, and around Zeus's altar at Olympia, site of three Ganymede sculptures (Paus. 5.24.5; 26.2; 7.24.4). At Tiberius's cave at Sperlonga and Nero's Golden House, spectacular Ganymedes recalled the unique relationship between Zeus and the Trojan lineage and provided a model for imperial apotheosis (Beard and Henderson 2001: 81).

Aphrodite was an important goddess with widespread cults in many Greek cities. She was especially associated with magistrates and "*Pandemos*" ("the body politic"): "a striking illustration of the power of Greek gods to span the division between private and public, because of her capacity to bring citizens together no less than lovers" (Parker 2005: 408). The Theban Polemarchs celebrated a festival of Aphrodite in midwinter at the end of their term of office. Aphrodite/Astarte was the tutelary goddess of Cyprus. From here around 500 BC she inspired the ruler of Etruscan Caere to build an important sanctuary on the coast at Pyrgi, guaranteeing the length of his reign, as the golden Cypriot-Phoenician foundation document records (P. Schmitz 1995). Such promiscuous cosmopolitanism seems characteristic of love-gods and their cults, properly *Mediterranean* divinities, bringing strangers together no less than members of a community (Scholtz 2002/3, Bonnet and Pirenne-Delforge 1999).

It was specifically Roman magistrates, consuls and praetors, who were obliged to honor Venus of Eryx in Sicily: "they take part in frolics (*paidias*) and intercourses (*homilias*) with women with great merriment, believing this is the only way they will make their presence pleasing to the goddess," "repaying her who was the cause of their aggrandizement" (Diod. 4.83). Temples to Erycian Venus, one on the Capitol, one outside the Colline gate, were built in 215 and 181 respectively (Livy 23.30.13, 40.34). Venus's importance in founding myths of Rome, especially for "Trojan lineages" like the Iulii and Memmii, which claimed descent from her son Aeneas, explains Lucretius's celebratory overture to the goddess as *Aeneadum genetrix* (1.1–2), her central and benign role in Vergil's national epic, and the special relationship, revealed in a series of privileges and exemptions, between Rome and the city of Aphrodisas in Turkey. Venus was patron successively of Sulla, Pompey, and Caesar, and in AD 121 Hadrian dedicated to Venus and Roma the biggest temple Rome had ever seen, climax of a long association between Sex and City.

If his mother was the embodiment of feminine charm, Eros was closer to males. He was honored with sacrifices before war in Crete and Sparta (Sosicrates *FGrHist* 461 F7 in Athen. 13.561ef). His main cult in Athens was founded in the Academy gymnasium by Charmos, said to have been the beloved of the Tyrant Peisistratos, Polemarch under the Tyranny and *erastes* of Peisistratos's son Hippias. The presence of Eros here must go some way to explaining the extraordinary honors paid to Eros in Plato's philosophy (*Symposium, Phaedrus*). Here naked ephebes lit their torches for night races into the city, perhaps to the apparently more ancient altar of Eros-Anteros below the Erechtheum (Athen. 13.609d, Paus. 1.30.1; Musti and Beschi 1982: 379, Scanlon 2002: 255–56). Eros's most important cult, at Thespiai, probably goes back at least to the time of Hesiod, who made fourth-born Eros more ancient than the Olympians. Here Plutarch came, he says, after his marriage, so that his wife could ask the god's help in reconciling their parents (*Mor.* 748e–771e, esp. 749b). The statue was removed to Rome, by Caligula and again by Nero, where it perished in the great fire. Eros punished them for their crimes (Paus. 9.27.3). Hadrian made amends when he came to honor the god with his own dedicatory composition in

AD 124, ". . . you who dwell in Heliconian Thespiai beside Narcissus's flowering garden, be merciful" (*IG* 7.1828 cf. Robert 1978: esp. 441, n.29).

Courtesans and prostitutes supported sanctuaries of love-gods and advertised there, as Nossis of Lokroi makes clear: "Kallo had her portrait painted exactly like herself and hung it in the house of fair-haired Aphrodite . . . Hail to her, for there is no cause for censure in her life" (*Anth. Pal.* 9.605 cf. M. Skinner 2005: 187–90). More explicit is a woman's dedication from Vari in Attica: "for many straddlings" (*SEG* 18.93), while Ovid describes Erycian Venus outside Rome's Colline gate as "richly furnished with the earnings of licensed ladies" (Ovid *Fasti* 4.866). Some temples actually owned "sacred prostitutes" (*pace* Budin 2006, Beard and Henderson 1998). Strabo talks of "sacred bodies" at Eryx, though reduced in number from its heyday (6.2.6) and a thousand "sacred prostitutes" (*hierodouloi, hetairai*) in pre-Roman Corinth (8.2); it is the numbers, not the practice, he finds remarkable. Pindar (fr. 107) celebrates the epinician dedication of a number of girls there in 464 (Kurke 1999b). Aristophanes calls Aphrodite's shrine "near Hymettos" a *porneion* (brothel) (283 *PCG*). So too, archaeologists suggest, was the newly discovered Markopoulou temple in central Attica (*AR* 50, 2004: 8). Similar Venereal complexes are known from notorious Lokroi and seaside Pyrgi with its "Pyrgensian whores" (Lucil. 1271 Marx); Plautus thinks prostituting daughters for dowries was "Etruscan custom" (*Cist.* 562–63). Justin says "the Cypriots send their daughters to the seashore" for the same purpose (18.5). Evidence for "sacred prostitution" was recently discovered in the Samnite temple of Erycina (?) in Pompeii, thus partly anticipating the distinctive sexualness of "Venus's city" in comparison with Ostia and Rome (E. Curti, *The Washington Post*, 28/7/2004, p. A11). The evidence is patchy – we know almost nothing about cults of (Aphrodite) Hetaira apart from the fact that they were "ubiquitous" (Philet. fr. 5)! – but enough of it is solid enough to indicate it is not the phenomenon of "sacred prostitution" which is patchy so much as talk about it.

5 Conclusion

We often take the publicity of ancient eros for granted, as if it were data "given" for our information. And we often blithely compare these noisy and showy materials with the quite different kinds of data that are available from other societies, such as early modern Italy, nineteenth-century Britain or Papua New Guinea in the 1960s: inquisitorial records, coded diaries, information about secret rites wheedled out of informants by ethnographers. But the very existence of intimate data, the effortful publication of privacies, is antiquity's most peculiar characteristic, leaving us torn between excessive naiveness and excessive skepticism: "Leagros was so charming that many potters fell in love with him," "Hadrian/Alexander must have been besotted with Antinous/Hephaistion to react like that after his death," "Antony fell hopelessly in love with Cleopatra," "Cleopatra put her political alliance with Antony under the sign of Eros, when she first came to meet him in Cilicia," "Sappho's woman-loving songs are just ritualistic," "Latin love-poetry is formulaic, not sincere."

The comments Plato ascribes to Pausanias in *Symposium* concerning Athenian homosexuality really apply to the whole field: "intricate . . . not easy to grasp" (182ad). There are, however, some principles: (a) It does not seem useful to think of different societies simply drawing the private–public boundary at different points along a universal sexual to non-sexual continuum, some cultures buttoned-up, others letting it all hang out. The ancients were not "more open" or "less embarrassed about sex." They simply organized things differently. (b) Material, including images, needs to be *read*, meanings decoded, voices placed, registers distinguished, intensities gauged. Then a society's cultural topography must be mapped, its closets and attics identified, its front rooms and facades. Finally we can try to put the data on the map: what is said/shown to whom about whom, using what voice in what style, how noisily, when and where. Immediately we will notice that contexts make a great deal of difference, i.e. love and sex manifest differently in different cities and at different periods. What's appropriate in one place on one day of a festival might be quite inappropriate in another place on a different day. What's appropriate for Archilochos or Martial may be inappropriate for Euripides or Statius. It might be quite scandalous for a woman or a boy to be seen unchaperoned with a man he or she is not related to, while to commission a portrait of yourself to be placed on a herm with a big erection is a very appropriate monument to your honor and dignity.

BIBLIOGRAPHIC ESSAY

Serenely summarizing recent work on Greco-Roman sexuality is impossible. Indeed the disputatiousness (e.g. Boswell 1990a, Hindley 1991, D. Cohen 1991b, Paglia 1991, Eribon 1994: 56) can startle those new to the field and has become an issue in itself (Vattuone 2004: 7–10, Karras 2000, M. Skinner 1996). Fortunately two recent synoptic works, Younger 2004's encyclopedic *A to Z* and M. Skinner 2005's judicious history, survey the field at book length. Snapshots of "the state of the debate" can also be found in the introductions to some recent collections of articles, old and new (e.g. McClure 2002, Golden and Toohey 2003, Nussbaum and Sihvola 2002; on prostitution, Faraone and McClure 2006; on relationships between women, Rabinowitz and Auanger 2002), and sourcebooks on sexuality in general (Johnson and Ryan 2005), and homosexuality in particular (Hubbard 2003). This chapter has to some extent been in dialogue with them, complementing them. I have put my own views on recent work down on paper in several critiques at greater length.

If peaceful consensuses are lacking, one can at least survey some of the battlefields and battle history; it's a convoluted story, but one full of surprises and ironies. The main arguments seem to concern the agency of courtesans and the degree to which they are (truly) represented in texts and artifacts (Kurke 2002, S. Lewis 2002, Ferrari 2002: chap. 2, Dalby 2002, Davidson 2006a), or are largely figments of the ancient and modern male *imaginaire* (Keuls 1985: 160–86), the existence, or not, of "sacred prostitution" (in Greece: McClure 2003: 126–65, in Italy: Glinister 2000; even in the Near East: M. Roth 2006, Bird 2006), what that might mean in the first place (Pirenne-Delforge 1994: 100–127), whether it's just a hostile projection onto the Other; the nature of "homosexuality," whether we can even talk of any "nature" (Halperin 1990: 15–53), or whether it is a question of contingent roles in sex (Veyne 1978: 50–53, J. Winkler 1990: 17–70, Halperin 1990: 88–112 cf. Davidson 2007: 23–32, 101–34), or if, on the other hand, it is just a question of "initiation" (itself a controversial topic, Dodd and Faraone 2003), a kind of sacred duty performed by adults for young boys, as in Papua New Guinea and nothing to do with homosexuality in the modern West (Patzer 1982, cf. Halperin 1990: 54–61, Davidson 2007: 504–8), if in fact the boys involved in sex were indeed "young" (Hupperts 1988, Davidson 2007: 68–98), whether it's just an elite and elitist practice (Hubbard 1998, Davidson 2007: 459–63). The now rather venerable suggestion that the Greeks practiced something equivalent to same-sex marriage (Bethe 1907: 450, Gentili 1988, cf. Koch-Harnack 1989: 119, 138–43, Davidson 2007: 300–315, 475–77, 514–16) has provoked new controversy (Rapp 1997, B. Shaw 1997, Bray 2000).

The weapons of choice in such battles are accusations of "naiveness" or credulity, on the one hand, and of excessive skepticism, "cynicism," and "denial" on the other, with students of ancient homosexuality often worried that others are representing "it" as merely "ritualistic" or "gestural" or in some other way not "properly homosexual," and students of women worried that others are taking representations at face value; an odd kind of identity-politics adds fuel to the flame, gay-identifying scholars arguing that ancient homosexuality has nothing to do with them, feminist historians engaged in a kind of "unhistorying" of women, arguing that male scholars are seduced by imaginary courtesans and sacred prostitutes created by and ventriloquized by men. Much of it comes down to the notion of "construction," which comes in several varieties. Feminism, inspired by critiques of racial stereotyping, has long been concerned with the way artifacts make pictures and draw up taxonomies at odds with a real world (real women) they affect to describe: "constructions of." It comes in soft (not the same as reality) and hard (nothing to do with reality) forms, which we might label "imagism" (e.g. *Images of Women in Antiquity*) and "inventionism" (as in *Inventing the Barbarian*) respectively. Students of sexuality are more concerned with the way a culture actually affects its world through images and taxonomies etc. – "social construction," "constructions as" – with "soft constructionists" allowing that it modifies that world to a degree (being a lesbian in antiquity was different from being a lesbian today), and "hard constructionists" (or "creationists") arguing that it creates a radically different world (there were no lesbians in antiquity; they had "neither the concept nor the experience" Foucault 1994: iv 286).

Most problematic is a "double-hard" position, which argues that a culture radically misrepresents the radically other world it creates for itself, a courtesan, for instance, in reality nothing like "the courtesan" created for her by her culture (Davidson 2006a: 34), a homosexual subject in a world for which homosexuals don't exist (Richlin 1993). In the first place there is a problem of knowledge, of getting access to the world a culture constructs for itself when its "constructions of it" in artifacts are utterly false. More seriously, since constructions of a world (its taxonomies, representations, etc.) are an important part of the "apparatus" (Foucault's *dispositif*), which constructs (/creates) that world in the first place, a "double-hard" position might seem oxymoronic. Some try to get around these paradoxes by positing radical fissures between the speaking subject, master of a culture's discourse, and its "Others" (between men and women, free and slave) so that quite separate worlds or bubbles are constructed within the same population (Davidson 2000b) or within the *dispositif*: a homosexual in her own world happily cocooned from the fact she does not exist in the (male/sexuality-oblivious) ancient world, or the question-begging notion of radical resistance of a sub-culture to a culture's constructions of it, a courtesan resolutely refusing to conform to the witty, literate, or manipulative type, or subverting the hierarchy with her jokes (McClure 2003: 79–105 cf. J. Winkler 1990: 188–209). The softer kinds of constructionism, on the other hand, which view representations as differing mostly in angle, omission and emphasis ("spinning" facts, half-lying), and which view social constructions as molding and shaping rather than creating, seem unexceptionable. In battle context they may seem a bit limply moderate, but beyond the putative battlefields they do allow a messier and less tyrannical view of cultures and of the relationship between the world and its representations.

All this disputatiousness has had some odd consequences. Some good scholarship often goes missing from bibliographies, while some not-so-good stuff has become a permanent fixture. Hoary old (pre-1980) articles and old-fashioned translations often turn out to be improvements on their updated replacements. One example: Aristotle (*Pol.* 1311b) says that Hellanokrates of Larisa killed Archelaos, king of Macedonia, because Archelaos's subsequent duplicity made it clear that their relationship had been one of *hubris* (abuse) rather than *erotike epithumia* (love-inspired desire); in other words Hellanokrates realized he had been used. Sinclair got it exactly right in his 1962 Penguin translation: Hellanokrates grasped that Archelaos had felt no "passionate love" for him; even Jowett's lack of "affection" got the tepid gist of it in 1885. But Jowett has been revised. Modern readers are told that Hellanokrates murdered Archelaos because Hellanokrates later realized Archelaos had not had "sexual desire" for him (J. Barnes 1984: 2082), which rather misses Aristotle's (and doubtless Hellanokrates') point.

Some of the most important contributions have come from those outside the field, or indeed outside the Academy entirely. It took a medievalist, for instance, to notice the straightforward truth that Ephoros's Cretan "little custom" was an initiation into a publicly recognized same-sex relationship (Boswell 1994: 89–94), not a rite of passage into adulthood (Graf 2003) "deeply rooted in ape prehistory" (Burkert 1979: 29).

Above all there are some important works which meticulously gather a lot of information, but in the service of a shaky premise. Sergent (1986) is by far the fullest collection of material on homosexuality in Greek myth, and in many ways a superb piece of scholarship, but not even Dumézil who wrote the preface was, it seems, wholly convinced by the author's insistent interpretations of these myths as echoes of prehistoric Indo-European rites of passage. Dover 1988 offers the most lucid critique of Sergent's initiation theory, but his own work (1978) was based on the premise that *eran* and its compounds refer to a sexual "desire to penetrate" and that all the contradictions in the sources can be resolved with reference to double standards regarding the sexually active dominant *erastes* and the sexually subordinate and vanquished *eromenos*. If one rejects that premise, as, I think, one must (on vocabulary cf. Calame 1999: 13–48), Dover's analysis and the work of the now countless scholars who depend on him and that premise, is vitiated (or somewhat vitiated, depending on one's point of view), a hard thing, inevitably, to acknowledge.

Such disputes go all the way back to the beginnings of modern philology in the argument between Bentley and Boyle over whether *erastes* necessarily referred to a flagitious love of boys – one of the few issues on which Boyle was right (Bentley 1697: 53; Boyle 1698: 65–66). As that example demonstrates, part of the problem is the very nature of the topic, the "immorality" or not, of the revered Greeks and less revered Romans. By contrast, the first classic of the field (M. Meier, 1837), still considered by some of us (e.g. Demand 1980, Davidson 2007: 105–7) the most reliable overview of Greek homosexuality, followed a Rankean methodology of "empiricism," i.e. prioritizing "primary" documentary "sources" and eschewing judgment ("amoralism"). Meier's Rankean approach for the first time elevated Aeschines' speech at the trial *Against Timarchos* (1) to the central position it enjoys today. Commentaries on that (Fisher 2001) and, for female prostitution, on Apollodoros's *Against Neaira* [Dem. 59] (Carey 1992, Kapparis 1999) often provide the most soundly based and relatively peaceful introductions to the topic. More recently, images too have been prioritized as primary documents, "showing" what texts don't tell (DeVries 1997, Hupperts 1988). The evidence of the most "primary" source on Spartan homosexuality, however, Xenophon, is routinely dismissed out of hand (cf. Hindley 1994, 1999, Davidson 2007: 326–31), while images are no less

complicated than texts to read, and although Aeschines 1 provides a lot of interesting information on homosexuality in Athens, its main concern is the peace with Macedonia, which he was
in favor of and which Timarchos vociferously opposed, and corrupt "whorish" relationships
between politicians; it remains a distinct possibility that Timarchos was not only not a prostitute
in any ordinary understanding of that term but that neither Aeschines nor the jurors who
convicted him ever believed he was.

Moreover, "amoralism" can itself become a problem, as scholars have competed to prove
themselves steelily determined to face up to "nasty truths" which older scholars like Jowett,
or indeed the ancients themselves, might have been tempted to veil. So that it is precisely what
sources don't mention that becomes the most important thing: hence *semnotatai* (classy) jet-
setting, Homer-parodying, coin-eschewing "courtesans" are just euphemistic "whores" (cf.
Davidson 2004b), and all the heavily romantic idealization in the materials on same-sex Eros
is designed to disguise relationships based on penetration and humiliation, "a sign not of tolerance but embarrassment" (Foucault 1994: iv 286–87 cf. Davidson 2004a 107–14).

"Constructionist" theories generally take their inspiration from twentieth-century battles
against racial (especially Nazi) theory, with anthropologists led by the Boasian school postulat-
ing a super-strong culture, hard-wired like a language (a cultural "idiom") and/or with language itself playing a central role in how that culture remakes the world, its people, and things
(like a "tool-kit" or a "prison"), to oppose to nature and biology (itself founded on historical
linguistics, "Semitic," "Aryan"). At its most extreme it resulted in the "Whorfian hypothesis"
(Barnard and Spencer 1996): no homosexuality without the word "homosexuality" (Halperin
1990: 15–18 cf. Davidson 2007: 135–39). Two other students of Boas meanwhile are ultimately responsible for the slightly different idea that different cultural "configurations" produce
different "misfits," and that it is the experience of misfitting that makes homosexuals neurotic
in a way they were not in Plato's time (the soft constructionism of Benedict 1934: 188–89,
191), or indeed is largely responsible for producing them (whatever that might mean) in the
first place (Mead 1943: 178, cf. Davidson 2007: 140–151). Mead was the most important
influence on West, who argued that Western societies should adopt a more casual "Samoan"
approach to sex, a kind of "mental hygiene" which might substantially reduce the number of
homosexuals in society (1960: 177–78). West in his turn was an important influence on
Dover's view (1978: vii–viii, 2, 202–3) that Greek homosexuality was a cultural product; more
precisely it was a pseudo-sexuality, "behavioral" rather than "psychological," an idea he took
from the "ethnopsychoanalyst" George Devereux (1967; 1970).

The second wave of anthropo-linguistic superstrong culture theories was no less concerned
with racist biological theories, determined to prove that homosexuals were a contingent category which did not constitute a Jewish-style "people," no more than Jews did, or "Aryans"
(Veyne 1979: 17–18, cf. Davidson 2007: 152–66). It took inspiration from the "structuralism"
of the linguist Saussure through the mediation of the "structural anthropologist" Lévi-Strauss.
Saussure viewed signifying systems such as language as nothing more than an abstract structure
of differences (between e.g. voiced syllables) at any one time. Michel Foucault, considered by
far the most important recent influence on the study of ancient sexuality, applied the same
approach to systems of knowledge (*epistemes*), especially knowledge of humans viewing each
discipline not so much as (or not at all as) an empirical response to the world but as merely
another structure existing in one time and place but not in another, "games of truth." Latterly
he turned his attention to structures of knowledge of sexuality, focusing especially on sexual
self-knowledge, sexual autobiographies, confessions, psychoanalytic sessions (1978). Foucault
himself posthumously published two books on sexuality in the ancient world (1985 and 1986).
The first was really two books rolled into one, one about citizen ethics of self-mastery (*enkra-
teia*), one about sex, but he brought the two concepts together with the metaphor of "being

penetrated by desires," self-control assimilated to the active position in homosexual sex, and so made sodomy the centerpiece of the problematization of the Self. Timarchos managed to retain his starring role, no longer as a primary documentary Rankean witness but as a perfect combination of politician, wastrel and (supposedly) pathic. Foucault's last book (1986) argued for a more severe and more private approach to pleasure in the first centuries AD, practices of abstinence, idealization of marriage as a loving couple, and the decline in status of same-sex relationships which did not seem to compare well. Despite all the complexity of his work on the ancient world, and frequent statements as to his enormous influence, much of what he said about antiquity has been ignored. Foucault's followers have been content to use the strangeness of ancient sexuality more straightforwardly as proof of his earlier claim that there was no "homosexuality" as such before it was invented by psychologists in the nineteenth century. Rather the ancients had a typically macho Mediterranean "ethos of penetration and domination," which Foucault famously claimed to consider "disgusting" (1984: 346).

Focusing on the disputes and arguments is the only way to make sense of the volumes of disagreeing work on ancient sexuality, but it does mean that some useful work which is tangential to those disputes or bypassed by them tends to get overlooked. The disputes are interesting central and important in their own right. Few other fields of ancient study have been as thoroughly engaged with other disciplines and methodologies and few have had as much influence on other disciplines or have been as directly relevant to the lives of modern people. But there has been a downside to being at the center of attention as the business of contributing to the debate has sometimes got in the way of contributing to knowledge. Ancient sexuality may be an especially difficult field, with especially slippery kinds of data, but that does not mean truth is here, uniquely, merely a matter of subjective opinion or there is no truth: either Theban magistrates made love to courtesans at the end of their term of office or they didn't, either temples of Venus Erycina owned prostitutes or they didn't, either Timarchos was a common prostitute or he wasn't. Perhaps it might be better if it was not considered a separate field at all, for there are few areas of the ancient world where love and sexuality does not encroach, and that includes the kinds of things mainstream historians of politics, states, and dates are interested in, Tyrants and Tyrannicides, Perikles's Funeral Speech, relationships between Meno of Pharsalus with Tharypas the Molossian and the Persian Ariaeus, Theognis, Alkaios, and archaic aristocratic factions, Demosthenes and his pupils, the rise of Thebes, politics at the court of Alexander. Experts in other fields outsource the job of understanding ancient sexuality to the disputatious sexperts at their peril.

CHAPTER THIRTY-TWO

Housing

Lisa C. Nevett

Since the early 1990s our knowledge of ancient housing and our understanding of its significance in social terms have transformed rapidly. Research in this field has proceeded along a separate path from work on Greek and Roman families (discussed in Harlow and Parkin, THE FAMILY). Historically, attention focused on relatively straightforward questions: what did houses look like, and how were their interior spaces used at different times and in different places? Recently, however, there has been a shift in emphasis as scholars have realized that studying housing offers a new means to explore a variety of broader, more complex social and cultural issues which are largely inaccessible through traditional research methods. It has become clear that although ancient houses may seem familiar to us because they provided space for some of the same activities as modern, Western homes, there are also significant conceptual differences. For example, the distinction between "public" and "private" which is now so central was not drawn in the same way in antiquity, when a house could also be important for storing agricultural produce, for craft production and for trade. At the same time, in addition to the basic nuclear family, ancient households often incorporated a variety of slaves and other dependents. The central role played by houses and households in ancient life means they can shed light on a range of wider questions. This chapter reviews some major directions taken by research since the late nineteenth century and explores the surviving evidence for ancient housing, highlighting similarities and differences between the approaches to Greek and to Roman material and looking at the relative emphasis placed on texts, archaeological and iconographic sources.

1 Evidence and Approaches

A key role has been played by references to domestic buildings and their patterns of use in surviving ancient texts. The numbers and genres of such accounts vary depending on the period in question, but for any given location and century there are rarely more than a handful of relevant passages. Among them, detailed descriptions of individual dwellings are relatively uncommon compared with isolated details about the form or use of a domestic building. Most Greek references date to the fifth and fourth centuries BC and are by Athenian authors. Roman writers offer a larger number of detailed descriptions, although they cover a wider geographical and chronological span, and while many key passages were produced in early imperial Italy, relevant material is also found in provincial works. Such accounts are obviously useful in providing first-hand observations about various aspects of ancient housing, but they do not represent a large number of examples and so are likely to be unrepresentative. As with any text the context also needs to be assessed: each work was composed with a particular purpose in mind, and each author articulates only a limited viewpoint – that of the elite, male population.

Since the nineteenth century the importance of archaeological data has gradually increased as more domestic structures have been discovered and excavated, although written texts have continued to play a central role in their interpretation. Excavators' aims have generally been relatively straightforward. Key questions have been the date of construction and any subsequent phases of rebuilding, details of the plan, decoration and superstructure, and in some cases also the uses of individual rooms. Attention centered on the architectural remains. If collected at all, small finds (such as fragments of pottery, or coins and other metal objects) were either used only very selectively to date the architecture, or were cataloged and published in separate lists according to the materials of which they were made, with little or no indication of the precise location in which they were found or of the other objects found with them. The terminology of ancient authors, particularly Vitruvius, has customarily been used to label different spaces, and assumptions about the uses of rooms have often tended to be influenced as much by the ancient texts as by the architecture and the items found there. In the late nineteenth century the popularity of evolutionary theories, combined with contemporary ideas about the close relationship between Greek and Roman cultures, led to a conflation of data from different dates and locations. The result was a model which embraced all known excavated residential structures and traced a single, continuous path of development from the Late Bronze Age palatial buildings at Greek sites like Mycenae, through the Hellenistic to early Roman houses on the Cycladic island of Delos, down to the Roman mansions of Pompeii and Herculaneum preserved by the eruption of Vesuvius in AD 79. A gap in the material evidence for the classical period in the Greek world was filled partly by concentrating on texts of that period and partly by using earlier and later archaeological sites, notably Pompeii (for example Rider 1916: chap. 16).

As more areas of housing were uncovered during the earlier twentieth century, the diversity of building forms became clearer and a distinction developed between work on Greek and on Roman housing. In the Greek context publication of relatively large residential areas in the cities of Delos, Priene (western Turkey) and Olynthos (Greek Macedonia) facilitated formulation of an architectural typology based on Vitruvius's description of Greek houses (see section 2 below). This typological approach has continued to be followed as a means of contextualizing structures found at a single site within a wider body of evidence. For Roman material a broader variety of approaches was followed. In part this was due to the greater number and better preservation of many sites, together with the large size and lavish decoration of some of the dwellings themselves (see section 3 below). Nevertheless the vast area encompassed by the Roman empire has also played a role, since in some provinces (for example, Britain) Roman housing has been viewed more in the context of the long-term cultural development of the region, rather than being compared with contemporary structures elsewhere in the empire. Thus, in Italy questions about decorative styles were often prominent (for example Mau 1899), while elsewhere the aim was frequently more basic, focusing, for instance, on identifying "Greek" or "Roman" architectural features (for example Gsell 1901: 15).

Recently, the emphasis of some archaeological work has shifted: advances made in other disciplines such as prehistoric archaeology and ethnography have suggested new ways of looking at the evidence. These place more emphasis on identifying complete functional groups of objects and understanding how different activities were arranged in relation to the architecture. Cross-cultural work shows wide variation in the way housing is conceptualized and activities separated and combined, stressing the importance of setting aside modern assumptions about how a house is defined, how its space is organized, who is permitted to enter, and how they are expected to behave. It is now clear that the domestic sphere is shaped by the social customs and cultural attitudes of the wider community, and investigation of ancient housing has therefore come to be understood as a route to explore a variety of much broader questions. Some of the insights stimulated by this new view of ancient housing are touched on below.

2 Housing in the Greek World

Athenian texts from the fifth and fourth centuries suggest that land and property of Athenian citizens, including houses, were regarded as important symbols of the continuity of a family across generations. One of the worst punishments that could be inflicted was to have such property confiscated and sold. At the same time, however, inscriptions from Attica and from elsewhere in the Greek world show that houses were used as security and were bought and sold. At fourth-century Olynthos, values of similar-size houses seem to have varied considerably depending on their location within the town, those close to the market (*agora*) being most sought after. By today's standards Olynthos was small: no house would have been more than 500 m from the *agora*, so that distances and travel times would have been relatively quick even from the furthest properties. The price difference is therefore likely to be explained by the fact that those houses close to the *agora* were more prominent, conferring economic and perhaps also social and political advantage on their owners (Nevett 2000).

Between the tenth and sixth centuries BC there was considerable variation in the size, layout and construction techniques used for houses in different areas of the Greek world. Some of the smallest were composed of only two or three rooms and an open courtyard. By the late fifth century a new type, the single-entrance courtyard house, had spread across the Greek world (fig. 32.1). Its form suggests the emergence of specific ideas about how domestic activities should be organized and about the way a household should interact with the wider community. In particular there is a gradual trend towards increasingly elaborate decoration, suggesting that houses took on a role as symbols through which their owners asserted wealth and status. Today the excavated evidence of these structures can look disappointingly unimpressive: often all that remains are low stone wall-bases (socles) standing two or three courses high, of dressed masonry or undressed field stones. The superstructures were originally of sun dried mud bricks (a building material used in vernacular architecture in Greece until the twentieth century, and still visible in some older buildings). While mud bricks are easy to obtain and insulate well from summer heat and winter cold, they are vulnerable to decay if in contact with moisture. The stone socle raised the bricks above the ground surface, protecting them from puddles. The walls were probably also faced with plaster, which has been found on the exteriors of houses in Hellenistic Morgantina (a Greek community in Sicily) and Delos. The facades of these structures, and probably earlier ones too, were enhanced by the addition of painted decoration and molded plaster designs, which would have drawn the eyes of passers-by and echoed the lively and colorful decoration of public buildings (Nevett 2009). These walls would generally have abutted directly, without any intervening garden space.

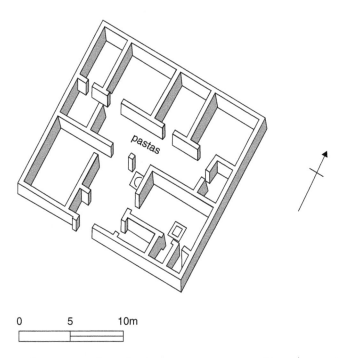

32.1 Axonometric reconstruction of a single-entrance courtyard house: a *pastas* house from Olynthos. (Nevett 1999, fig. 2)

The interior of such a house was normally reached through a single street door which led into a central courtyard around which the individual rooms were arranged. In most cases a portico ran along at least one side, usually the north. Modern scholars have distinguished several different forms following terminology used by Vitruvius. The *prostas*, which sheltered the entrance to the major living room, is more common in Greek cities in Asia Minor. The *pastas*, which is longer and gave access to several different rooms, is more characteristic of mainland Greece. In the peristyle, a widespread form more commonly found at a slightly later date, a colonnade ran around three or all four sides of the court. Courtyard and portico would have been functional spaces used for daily activities. For example there was no piped water, and supplies had to be drawn from a well or cistern in the court, or carried from a public fountain in the street. The courtyard was also the means of access to the individual rooms and, together with interior windows, their main source of daylight. Any openings in the street façade of the house were probably small and high, providing ventilation rather than light. Additional rooms in an upper story were accessed via a wooden staircase and a gallery looking out over the courtyard. Above, a pitched roof of terracotta tiles had deep eaves to keep the rain off the mud brick walls. Such properties could be quite spacious: those at Olynthos generally covered a ground area of around 290 m^2 and comprised eight or more rooms. At the same time smaller houses continued to be built, and textual evidence suggests that some of the poorest families might have lived in shared accommodation or apartments, although these were poorly constructed and their remains are therefore difficult to detect archaeologically (Ault 2005). Some of the population also lived for all or part of the year on isolated rural farms. Excavated examples of these tend to retain the basic plan of the single entrance courtyard house, but with a considerably larger courtyard.

Alongside the architectural remains, fragments of furniture and small objects are also an important source of information. While organic materials such as wood rarely survive, a variety of other items were often left behind by the occupants, depending on the circumstances under which a house was abandoned. These give an indication of the kinds of activities carried out, which include small-scale manufacturing, as well as production of textiles for domestic use, food preparation, and bathing (in a terracotta hip bath). Inscriptions listing items from houses belonging to prominent Athenians, auctioned off in 415–414 BC, show that furnishings were quite sparse in comparison with today's houses (Pritchett 1956: 210–11), and it is sometimes difficult to find sufficient evidence to know how a specific room was used. Nevertheless, decorative and luxurious elements were increasingly included during the fourth and third centuries. Painted wall plaster and mosaic pavements, at first limited to one per house, were soon sometimes found in suites. Fragments of molded terracotta plaques show that ornaments were sometimes displayed on interior walls. Painted scenes on Athenian vases also hint at a rich array of patterned textiles which may have been covered cushions and couches. In the courtyard and portico the tops of columns (capitals) echoed the architectural styles (orders) of contemporary public architecture, and further mosaic and painted plaster added color and variety. All of these elements may have served to emphasize to visitors the wealth and status of the owner of the house, as well as providing a comfortable living environment for members of the household.

Both domestic architecture and references in surviving Athenian texts suggest that strict protocol determined who could enter and leave a house, and perhaps also who could use particular rooms inside. The single street entrance was often screened from the rest of the interior so that even when the front door was open it would not have been possible to see into (or out of) the house. But this did not mean that visitors were not welcome: texts and iconography demonstrate the importance of entertaining guests. From the late fifth century onwards many houses incorporated a room with an off-center doorway and raised platform around the walls which was designed to accommodate couches. Such rooms were the best decorated in the house and provided an intimate setting for the symposium, at which the male householder would have entertained small groups of male guests who reclined on couches and were provided with wine, conversation, and music.

A central idea of the most detailed ancient discussions of Greek housing surviving today is a conceptual distinction between two different areas that are referred to as the *andron* or *andronitis* (usually translated as men's quarters) and *gunaikon* or *gunaikonitis* (usually translated as women's quarters). For this reason, many scholars have interpreted the Greek domestic environment as one dominated by a physical separation between men and women. But while the room with couches can probably be identified as the *andron*, a corresponding female part of the house is difficult to find. In fact the layout normally defies any kind of binary division, since individual rooms radiate from the central courtyard. On analogy with more recent cultures, such as areas of Islamic North Africa, it seems likely that the distinction underlying the ancient texts is between female members of the household and male outsiders (Nevett 1994). Thus, rather than a divided house, what would have been necessary would have been a way to separate male visitors from residents. This was the role of the *andron*, which formed a distinct, enclosed space with a closable door and often also had a small anteroom, a further barrier between its occupants and those in other rooms.

By the third and second centuries, while some houses continued to be built along similar lines to those described above, in others there was also a gradual increase in the maximum size and the amount and complexity of decoration. Mosaic floors, initially of black and white pebbles, were now composed of cut stone cubes (tesserae) forming intricate, often representational, images. Painted wall plaster, which originally consisted of large colored panels and dados, came to be used in combination with molded plaster features, and figured friezes were sometimes also included. The largest structures now regularly had a variety of decorated rooms of different sizes, and occasionally also two different courtyards, a peristyle giving access to reception rooms, and a plainer court with a simple portico leading to cooking, washing and storage areas. The increasing differentiation between properties suggests that among one sector of society the house was becoming increasingly important as a target for expenditure, with greater resources being invested and the structure itself viewed as a status symbol. Although on a much larger scale, the Macedonian palace at Vergina can be seen as belonging to this trend, as it served many of the same functions as an elite house and exhibits many similar features. A large peristyle was surrounded by a variety of reception suites, and in its later phase a separate service courtyard was constructed to the west. The palace's monumental scale (the ground area was over 4,000 m²) and prominent hillside location overlooking the town and plain below may have given symbolic expression to the monarch's political power. It is debatable whether this idea of using domestic architecture as a means of personal display was adopted by Greek communities from the civilizations of the Near East (Nielsen 1996). Nevertheless, the monarchical system placed an emphasis on personal power and wealth, and on social and political hierarchy and inequality, and domestic architecture provided an ideal medium for expressing such distinctions, as can be seen clearly at sites like Macedonian Pella and Pergamon in Asia Minor.

The story of domestic architecture in Greek communities continues into the period of Roman domination, from the mid-second century BC onwards, when the layout and decoration of elite housing remained distinctively different from that in other Roman provinces. At this point, however, the Greek world must be set in context as one of a number of different architectural traditions coexisting within the much larger and more diverse area now governed by Rome.

3   Housing in the Roman World

The popular image of housing from Roman Italy is of a large "*atrium* house" (fig. 32.2). This was constructed of ashlar masonry with a terracotta-tiled roof. The main entrance was through a narrow passage (*fauces*) leading into a large interior space (*atrium*). A central rectangular pool (*impluvium*) in the floor caught any rain entering through an opening (*compluvium*) in the roof. Around the *atrium* were a number of small, decorated rooms (*cubicula*) each accommodating a single couch. At the far

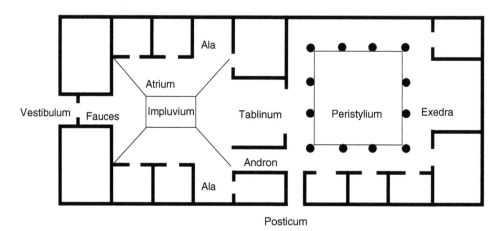

32.2   Generalized plan of a Pompeian *atrium* house. (Mau 1899, fig. 115)

end of the *atrium* an intermediate area, the *tablinum*, opened into a colonnaded peristyle beyond. The center of the peristyle was enhanced by sculpture, fountains and ornamental plantings, and formal dining rooms opened onto this space, some (known as *triclinia*) through narrow doorways, others (*exedrae*) through wide entrances which seem designed to give their occupants the maximum possible view. As in Greek symposia, the occupants of these dining rooms reclined on couches, but texts and wall paintings depicting such occasions suggest that they were rather different affairs: the focus was on food, as well as wine, and respectable women could appear alongside their husbands. The arrangement of diners was a means of mapping out social hierarchies, with strict etiquette governing the positions of the host and his guests of different statuses. These dining rooms, along with the *atrium* and *cubicula*, often had mosaic floors with black and white or colored (polychrome) mosaics, sometimes featuring figural designs. The walls were normally also painted using one of a distinctive set of styles which depicted fantasy interior or exterior architectural features, landscapes or gardens, or figured scenes. Viewed from the entrance or in plan there was an emphasis on symmetry and axiality, with an open vista down the *fauces*, across the *atrium*, through the *tablinum* and into the garden beyond.

This familiar stereotype of a Roman house is partly based on Vitruvius's description of an urban property suitable for a member of the Roman elite holding public office, and on comments by other Roman authors of republican and early imperial date: many of the terms used to label the different spaces are borrowed from their descriptions. But the model owes its form to the larger houses uncovered from the eighteenth century onwards during excavation at Pompeii and Herculaneum. As with Greek housing, the ancient writers' terminology has been applied in great detail in order to differentiate between various architectural designs (distinguishing, for example, between *atria* whose roofs were supported in contrasting ways). Recent study has sought to develop the connection between texts and architecture a stage further, exploring how domestic space may have been used to map social difference, the *atrium* and *tablinum* serving for reception of social inferiors (*clientes*) while social equals may have been entertained in the peristyle and *triclinia* (Wallace-Hadrill 1994: 3–64; but disputed by Dickmann 1999). In-depth analysis of decorative motifs and schemes has also suggested that these may have been used to enhance the image and status of house owners, highlighting their business interests, alluding to their benefactions to public causes, or hinting at their erudition in matters of elite literary and philosophical culture (*paideia*) (for example, Leach 2004).

This image of the *atrium* house has been useful in providing generations of scholars and students of Latin with a basic tool for characterizing elite housing in Roman Italy and for contextualizing discussions of urban domestic arrangements in Latin texts. But it also has certain limitations: like the texts themselves, the model has tended to focus attention on the role of elite, male householders while ignoring the presence of women and the activities of slaves, children, and other household members. Study of objects found in houses at Pompeii reveals equipment used for a range of activities, such as preparation of food and manufacture of textiles. These occur in many areas of the house, including in major rooms such as the *atrium* (Allison 2004), and are important reminders of the presence here at certain times of the women, servants, and slaves who would have used them. Approaching the archaeological material with an eye to exploring the roles played by these less visible individuals also encourages fuller consideration of the plainer, more functional areas. It becomes clear that private bath suites, shops and workshops, stables, service courts, and storage facilities were all important facilities for large households, and were frequently planned at the time of construction. In order to accommodate them alongside decorated reception rooms there was much more variation in layout than the normative *atrium* house model might suggest: for example, many properties did not incorporate a full peristyle, substituting instead a small garden or light-well. At the same time many large *atrium* houses incorporated additional forms of dwelling occupied by members of other social groups. The shops, frequently built into façades, often featured living accommodation on a mezzanine above. Careful examination of doors and staircases also reveals the important role played by rented rooms and apartments on the upper floors of *atrium* houses (Pirson 1999). The architectural and social make-up of housing and households at Pompeii and neighboring towns were thus more varied and complex than appears at first glance.

The excellent preservation and early and large-scale excavation of the Campanian sites has meant that they have tended to dominate, but recent study of other, less-well-preserved urban sites in central and northern Italy suggests that in these regions *atrium* houses were much less common (M. George 1997). At Ostia, the port of Rome, scattered evidence of early imperial *atrium* houses has been found, but the most complete elite houses date between the second and fourth centuries AD. Axial views are still in evidence, but *atrium* houses have disappeared. Instead, space is organized around a single courtyard, which is sometimes surrounded by a portico supported on columns or on brick piers (fig. 32.3). Decorative elements include colored marbles used for panels (revetments) and cut into shapes to make patterned floors (opus sectile), along with mosaic and sculpture. Purpose-built apartment blocks are an especially prominent feature and cater for a range of requirements (DeLaine 2004). While some offer only a single rented room, in others accommodation is more spacious and comfortable, consisting of interconnected suites with painted walls and large windows overlooking formal gardens. As well as providing evidence about a different period in history from what we see in Campania, the Ostian material there-fore also hints at a population with a different social make-up, featuring more house-holds of middle or lower income.

Ostia provides extensive evidence for housing due to its gradual abandonment, which left buildings relatively well preserved. In contrast, the continuous history of occupation at Rome makes complete plans of ancient houses difficult to uncover. Examples of *atrium* houses have been found along with later forms of elite residence, but here, too, these were only one element of the urban fabric, with mixed neighborhoods, including apartment blocks, being the norm (Wallace-Hadrill 2003a). At the top end of the city's socio-economic scale the remains of the palaces of successive emperors reveal how these acted as symbols, occupying large areas of the city center and incorporating elaborate state apartments which catered for a range

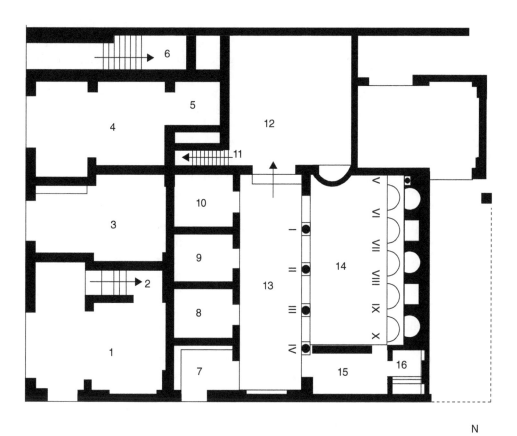

Key:

1, 3, 4, 5	independent shops
6	staircase to an upper storey apartment
7	main entrance with vestibule
8, 9, 10	living rooms
12	principal reception room
13	portico
14	garden with fountains along east wall
16	latrine

32.3 Plan of a house from Ostia: the *domus* of Cupid and Psyche, fourth century AD. (Packer 1967, fig. 2)

of official functions (for example Nero's "Golden House," the *Domus Aurea*: Ball 2003).

The Italian countryside is also an important source of evidence. Here again our picture is based both on descriptions from ancient textual sources and on the remains of buildings traced through surface remains during archaeological field survey, or investigated through excavation. Major towns such as Pompeii were ringed by spacious suburban villas which took advantage of their setting by incorporating terraces and walkways with views across the countryside. A similar phenomenon is found on the coast, where maritime villas strung along the cliff-tops had belvederes looking out to sea. Villas adopted some of the architectural principles found in large town houses, with axial plans and symmetrical vistas, and also featured dining and reception rooms furnished with elaborate mosaics and wall-paintings (Frazer 1998). Among the most magnificent is Hadrian's villa at Tivoli, with its monumental water features and sculpture collections (MacDonald and Pinto 1995). In some cases a large country villa also appears to have been the center of a working agricultural estate, and alongside living apartments the buildings also included facilities for processing and storing agricultural goods such as grain, wine, and olive oil. A range of smaller farms have also been excavated, some with a few comfortable living rooms for a caretaker or less wealthy owner, while others seem to have been purely utilitarian.

The size of Rome's empire and the diversity of its indigenous societies and building traditions makes generalization about housing throughout the provinces impossible. The amount of information available varies according to the previous settlement history of different regions. Southern Britain, for example, saw the development of a dense network of villas constructed on rectangular plan, with stone construction and mosaic floors. These first appeared under Roman influence and contrasted with indigenous patterns of construction. While relatively large settlements also grew up, it seems to have been the rural villas which were the homes of the elite. By contrast, the provinces of North Africa had a long tradition of masonry construction and urban living, and had been influenced by the presence of Greek and Phoenician traders and settlers before the advent of Rome. Here, high-status housing seems to have been primarily an urban phenomenon, with a variety of different construction techniques being adopted, including the use of terracotta tubes to provide lightweight vaulted roofs, and the hollowing out of rock-cut chambers to form cool basement areas, as at Bulla Regia (northern Tunisia). Outside the major urban centers the elites seem to have been limited to a string of maritime villas, although the fertile land of north-western Libya and northern Tunisia was occupied by working farms producing large quantities of grain and olive oil for shipment to Rome.

In the east of the empire the communities which were formerly part of the Greek world retained many aspects of their previous architectural traditions: the canonical *atrium* is rare, and elite houses tend to ignore the principles of axiality and symmetry which are so prominent in Roman Italy. Fashions did not remain unchanged, however: by the first century BC restrictions on movement into and out of the house seem to have relaxed, and multiple entrances were common, suggesting a change in social attitudes (Nevett 2002). At the same time, many of the individual features of domestic architecture would have looked familiar to travelers from Roman Italy: decorated reception rooms included mosaic floors and wall paintings, and peristyle courtyards were common. In fact scholars have debated how far the wall paintings and peristyles of Campanian *atrium* houses consciously echoed Greek models (Zanker 1998), raising the larger issue of cultural interaction during the late republic and early empire. Questions like these give an indication of some of the problems that are beginning to be tackled using ancient housing. Although the structures are interesting in their own right, they have therefore also come to be seen as vital sources of information about some of the most difficult and complex aspects of ancient society. Future research promises to continue this trend: households must have been profoundly affected by the social transformations accompanying changes like the formation of the Greek city-state or the spread of Christianity; they offer a key context for investigating relationships between different social groups such as men and women or inhabitants and visitors; and they provide detailed evidence for studying microeconomic strategies. As the material remains of households, housing will therefore continue to be a rich source of new insights into ancient society.

FURTHER READING

The most detailed surviving ancient discussions of Greek domestic arrangements are Xenophon's *Oikonomikos* (commentary: S. Pomeroy 1994) and Lysias I (discussion of the domestic arrangements: G. Morgan 1982). The Roman architect Vitruvius's description of a Greek house (*De arch.* 6.7.1–7) has also frequently been used, although its relevance to fifth- and fourth-century Greece is unclear, given that he was writing in first-century Italy (introduction, translation and commentary: Rowland 1999). Of Latin texts providing information about Roman housing some of the most detailed are *De arch.* 6.3–5 (on the design of *atrium* houses) and 6.6 (on farms). Others include Younger Pliny's description of his villa at Laurentum (Pliny *Ep.* 23) and Cicero's description of his brother Quintus's villas in Arpinum (Cic. *Q. Fr.* 14).

Modern scholarship focuses on archaeological evidence, and falls into four main categories: excavation reports, synthetic studies of a single site, syntheses of a whole region or regions, and interpretative works. Many of the most important are published in French, German, Italian, or Greek, but listed below are some of the major English-language publications of the latter three types, covering topics discussed in this chapter.

Early Iron Age Greek housing is catalogued by Fagerström 1998. Classical Greek evidence is summarized in Nevett 1999. Symbolic use of Greek housing is discussed in Walter-Karydi 1998, while Nielsen 1994 catalogs Hellenistic palaces. Ault and Nevett 2005 offers a taste of some wider questions.

Literature on Roman housing is vast. While new material is constantly being published, older syntheses remain valuable. Overviews include McKay 1975, I. Barton 1996, S. Ellis 2000 and Gros 2001 (the latter in French, but the most up-to-date and comprehensive account, with numerous illustrations and extensive bibliography). Percival 1976 sets out evidence for villas, while J. T. Smith 1997 offers a more idiosyncratic perspective. Of numerous works on Campania, J. Clarke 1991 provides a well-illustrated, scholarly treatment of selected houses. For a recent study of a single Pompeian insula, see Ling 1997. Gazda 1991 and Laurence and Wallace-Hadrill 1997 include examples of more problem-oriented studies. Evidence from North African cities is summarized and interpreted by Thébert 1987, while housing from Britain is treated comprehensively by Perring 2002.

Useful material on both Greek and Roman housing, including preliminary information on houses in the Athenian Agora, and material from the excellent monographs by Cahill 2002 and Allison 2004 can be found on the website www.stoa.org/ (under Highlights, "Pompeian Households" and "Olynthus"). www.ostia-antica.org/index.html contains a wealth of information and references on Ostia.

CHAPTER THIRTY-THREE

Entertainment

David Potter

1 Introduction

In the early years of the second century AD, the satirist Juvenal lamented that the Roman people, once concerned with weighty issues of war and peace, were now devoted solely to bread and circuses (Juv. 10. 78–81). The line is often quoted as summary of the impact of the imperial system on the city of Rome, of the effective disenfranchisement of the Roman people by the increasingly autocratic monarchy. A few years later an advisor to Marcus Aurelius remarked that the emperor had to do what the people wanted at the games, while legislation from this period sought to check the tendency of the crowd to demand the release of the guilty, the condemnation of the innocent, and the freedom of slaves belonging to the emperor (Fronto *Aur.* 1.8; *Dig.* 4.9.17; *Cod. Iust.* 7.11.3). In point of fact Juvenal's comment is wholly misleading. Centuries earlier, in the last generation of formally democratic government at Rome, Cicero listed the theater and games as the best places to discern the true feelings of the Roman people, and reasonably so (*Pro Sestio* 106). Far more people could be accommodated for chariot races than in the voting pens of the Campus Martius.

From the earliest to the last years of the classical city-state, public entertainment played a crucial role in defining the political order. The fact that sport and entertainment occupy a very similar position in early twenty-first century society is one of the genuine debts that the modern world owes to the ancient. For it was the admittedly bogus image of the amateur athlete in classical Greece that inspired the modern Olympic movement, and the inclusion of competitive sport in elite Anglo-American educational curricula (Young 2004: 138–57; Karabel 2005: 42–44; Guttmann 2004: 89). In both cases, although sport was intended to reinforce hierarchical relationships, the result was the development of vast networks of professional athletics that encouraged social mobility and restricted elite domination of society.

To suggest that ancient civic society, based upon rigid hierarchical structures that were ostensibly reinforced by monarchical governments throughout most of its history, could possibly support structures that allowed members of the lower classes an opportunity to improve their status simply on the basis of talent might seem to be a blatantly false statement. My point will be to demonstrate that this is not so. Power in the ancient world was ultimately dependent upon the possession of wealth, and recent work on the economics of professional entertainers have revealed that quite staggering amounts of money were there to be made by extremely successful performers, both on the stage and in the arena (Lebek 1996; D. Potter 2006: 399). More importantly, even average performers had the ability to change the conditions of their lives. Then, as now, careers in entertainment involved a great deal of risk, but they still offered paths to advancement that were not completely controlled by the interests of those who held power in the aristocratically dominated states of the Greco-Roman world. Successful entertainers developed fan bases that could not be ignored, and often required respect.

2   Sport in Archaic Greece

Competitive sport appears to play two important roles in the world of the Homeric poems, one connected with personal self-definition, the other, arising from the former, is as a marker for significant moments of transition. The most obvious point of transition is the funeral: the *Iliad* ends with the funeral games for Hektor, and the twenty-third book is largely taken up with the games that Achilles offers in memory of Patroklos. For Homer, the placement of these games appears to be deeply meaningful, as they mark not only the conclusion of his own work, but also the beginning of the process by which Achilles will come to recognize the humanity he shares with others, and grow into the person who will be able to return Hektor's body to Priam. In book eight of the *Odyssey*, the games celebrated by the Phaeacians appear to be connected with general joy for life, but, in a thematic sense, they too indicate an important point of transition (S. Miller 2004: 27–30). It is through his participation in the games that Odysseus refutes the charge that he is a disreputable person (in this case that he is not a merchant), which makes it possible for him to claim his own identity at the beginning of book nine. Within the narrative of book twenty-three, two characters use participation in the games to assert high status vis-à-vis their foes. One of these characters is old Nestor, who says that the fact that he cannot now compete should not obscure his great achievements as a multi-sport competitor in the distant past, at the funeral games of Amarykeus; the other is Epeios, whom audience-members would immediately think of in a different context – he designed the Trojan horse – from that of boxing (*Il* 23. 624–50; 664–75). Yet it is as a boxer that Epeios claims that he has standing with other heroes.

In both the *Iliad* and the *Odyssey*, sport is the province of the aristocrat. Commoners are excluded, and it is implied the superior aristocrat can compete in events as radically different as a foot-race and a wrestling match. To what extent does this reflect the situation in the real world inhabited by members of Homer's audience? This is very hard to know, though the admittedly sketchy evidence that we do have for athletic dedications in the course of the seventh century suggests that participation was for those who could afford expensive cauldrons as memorials of victory. Dedications by the wealthy do not prove that members of less elite groups were not competing as well, but it is suggestive in light of the tenor of Homeric discourse. Also suggestive is the absence of a calendar: in sport as in democracy, open participation is facilitated if events run according to a set schedule. The Homeric vision of athletic organization is notably ad hoc: either a famous person has died or a monarch has decided that the elite youth of his town should have a contest. In the world of the city-state linkage between games and the festival calendar was absolutely crucial, and this seems something yet to come in the early seventh century BC.

When did Greeks begin to celebrate games on a regular cycle? We cannot know for certain. Although later Greek tradition put the foundation of the Olympic games in 776 BC, and later athletic record keeping was extremely precise, there is no reason to believe that the Olympic victor list is accurate in the earlier years. The only event in the early years of the Olympic list is the stadion race, and this simply does not accord with the evidence for competition that we have from Homer, any more than does the notion that there should be a four-year cycle squares with what appears to be the practice of the heroes. Homer himself, of course, did not intend his poem to be read as a history of sport, but he does provide some important clues. The games that Achilles sponsors include events such as spear fighting and stone throwing that have no place in the classical repertoire, and are at odds with two other lists, those of the games for Amarykeus and those offered by the Phaeacians, which look very much like later Greek festivals. The games for Amarykeus include boxing, wrestling, a foot-race, and a chariot race, while the Phaeacians contest a foot-race, wrestling, jumping, the discus, and a boxing match. In all probability these two lists reflect practices that are contemporary with Homer, while the more warlike events reflect the practice of an earlier age (S. Miller 2004: 23).

In all probability the standard form of Greek athletic contests only became set around the end of the seventh and the beginning of the sixth century BC, and, while the Olympics may be older than the other three festivals that formed the cycle of regularly scheduled contests that came to be known as the "periodic" cycle of great games, they are unlikely to be two hundred years older, as the tradition suggests. The other three festivals – the Pythian games at Delphi, the Isthmian games and the Nemean games – were founded in 582, 581 and 573 respectively. The Pythian games were celebrated quadrennially in August of the third year of an Olympiad, the Nemean games were held every second and fourth year of an Olympiad in July (ending just before the Olympics opened in August), while the Isthmian games took place on the same schedule in April or May. The schedule thus concentrated competition into the twelve months at the end of each Olympiad. In order to win the *periodos*, an athlete would have to have four very good festivals within a year, but would only have to keep himself in first-rate competitive condition during that period. That said, the fact that Isthmian and Nemean games occurred on a more frequent cycle made it more possible to claim the glory of being a *periodos nikês*, or winner at all the festivals that made up the *periodos*, even in the event of a defeat during the decisive twelve-month span. It was indeed possible to claim this title with victories in festivals that fell in different cycles, if an athlete was able to maintain peak competitive condition over a number of years.

Within the periodic cycle, athletic events included four foot-races, the pentathlon, boxing, wrestling and pancration. The foot races were the *stadion*, the *diaulos* (a double *stadion*), the *dolichos* (a distance event defined as twelve laps of the Olympic stadium), and a race in armour. The pentathlon included the long jump, discus, javelin, a *stadion* and a wrestling match. Victory went, on a formula that is still not fully understood, to the victor in three events. Victory in wrestling required being the first in a match to win two out of three falls, while *pancration* and boxing were contested until one or the other contestant surrendered (or, as sometimes happened, died). The equestrian events included races for colts and grown horses, for two-horse and four-horse chariots (S. Miller 2004: 31–83). The latter seems to have been both especially prestigious and – at least at Olympia, where as many as 48 teams could run on a very restricted track – an extremely dangerous event (Humphrey 1986: 7–9). Otherwise, with many events held on one day, and, at major festivals, in three categories – boys, young men, and men – the number of contestants had to be severely restricted (Crowther 1993). Evidence for restriction in the number of contestants is also offered by the nature of the contests themselves: there were no heats for the foot-races, and room in the starting gates for only 20 contestants, the pentathlon appears to have been unworkable with more than five to ten competitors, and the "heavy events" seem to have been limited to somewhere between four and twelve contestants (I suspect that eight was the ideal number, allowing for two rounds before the final, and sufficient chance for serious injury to explain frequent reference to byes in our sources). It would appear that the period before each festival, when athletes were required to train on site, may have provided an opportunity for the judges to determine who they should allow in – athletes had to pass an inspection of credentials on the day of their event before they could compete.

The connection between aristocratic status and athletic success, hallowed by Homer, had the important and unusual result that certain forms of Greek entertainment would remain part of a contest where victory conferred high social status upon the competitor. Although figures in the Near Eastern tradition like Gilgamesh or the biblical Jacob are described as great wrestlers (or, at least, capable of wrestling all night with a representative of the Almighty), there is no evidence to suggest, post Bronze Age, that Near Eastern athletes were other than entertainers whose existence was predicated upon their ability to please those more important than themselves. The same view held good in Italy, where free men might dance as apotropaic performers in religious rites that benefited the community as a whole, but they could never be seen as performers for public pleasure.

One result of the Greek linkage between performance and competition for status was wholly unpredictable. This was the rise of competitive drama. Contests of bards were evidently a feature of Bronze and Dark Age funeral rites, and selected choral and solo performances were later included as part of major festivals, chiefly the Pythian and Isthmian, sanctifying some artistic competition as being appropriate for high-status individuals (S. Miller 2004: 83–86). But it was later, at Athens in the course of the sixth and fifth centuries, that new forms of drama – tragedy and comedy – emerged in civic contests dedicated to Dionysos during the winter months. The Great Dionysia, established by the tyrant Peisistratos in the course of the sixth century, and held in March, became the principal venue for competitions in tragedy in the mid-sixth century (534 BC), and for comedy in the early part of the fifth (486 BC). Further competitions in both forms were added to the Lenaia, held in January, as well as in lesser Dionysia held in rural areas during December. Although the contests were technically between *choregoi*, members of the elite who undertook the provision of plays as a form of civic service, the result of these contests was to elevate talented actors and successful playwrights to superstar status throughout the Greek world, ensuring as well that comedy and tragedy would become set parts of the school curriculum.

3   The Civic Role of Entertainment

In the summer of 400 BC, a band of Greek mercenaries that had fought its way free of a seemingly impossible trap in the heart of the Persia empire reached the Black Sea. They celebrated their arrival by holding games (Xen. *Anab.* 4.8.25). Some decades earlier the historian Herodotus had stressed exercise in the nude as a defining feature of Greek, as opposed to barbarian, culture. It is not known when Greeks began to exercise this way – the practice is certainly post-Homeric, though prior to the end of the sixth century (McDonnell 1991) – but the ideological significance attached to athletic training and competition by the end of the fifth century is undeniable. The fact that the Spartans, dominant in Greece by the end of the fifth century, had instituted state-supported athletic training for all citizens centuries earlier, inspired other states to do likewise for their young men. Well before Alexander of Macedon transformed the geopolitical balance of power between Mesopotamia and the Mediterranean at the end of the fourth century, exercise in the nude in state-supported gymnasia had become a fundamental feature of urban life for all Greeks. As Alexander and his successors spread Greek-style urbanism throughout the former territory of the Persian empire (not without moments of opposition, most notably among the Jews of Palestine during the second century), athletic contests achieved new significance. Festivals were created throughout the new Greek kingdoms, and the sponsors of these festivals competed to have the best athletes from around the world compete at them. These new celebrations only served to elevate the status of the traditional festivals of the mainland as cities offered their own versions of "Olympic"- or "Pythian"-style competition (Robert 1982: 37). At the same time, the fact that Alexander, and his father, Philip II, had enjoyed the theater gave new impetus to the spread of dramatic entertainment. To be a Greek city was to be equipped with a theater and a gymnasium (often more than one). The further consequence of the spread of Greek culture in the East, and cultural unification of the cities of western Asia with those of the mainland, was an upsurge in demand for dramatic performers. Good actors could receive significant civic honors from cities to which they traveled to perform, and, perhaps in response to the demand, actors began to organize into professional associations or synods before the end of the fourth century BC. These synods, of which the most successful would be the artisans of Dionysos, set the terms under which their members would perform at a civic festival, and guaranteed that these members would actually appear (Lightfoot 2002).

The tale of the agonistic performer, that is to say the performer who was entitled to compete in a crowned festival, or *agôn* – usually a citizen and thus a person of relatively high status – is easier to trace than that of the mass of others who provided pleasure (of many sorts) on the fringes of the great festivals (Robert 1982: 36). Flute girls were plainly regarded as an essential component of many expensive private parties, while what we might now classify as "circus" performers – e.g. tightrope walkers – operated wherever large groups of people gathered for entertainment. Additionally, it seems, the years after Alexander saw an increase in the importance of two forms of drama that were not included in the competitive festivals – mime (a stylized situation comedy involving a troupe of actors) and pantomime, or "rhythmic tragic dance," in which a single dancer performed scenes from myth to musical accompaniment, originally, it seems, while also singing. By the end of the first century BC, however, while the dancer remained the star of the show, a soloist or chorus took over the singing (there was evidently no uniform practice at this point), while the music came (or continued) to be provided by a group with a heavy percussion base. With the passing of time, pantomimes and mimes, whose acts were more popular than those of agonistic thespians, began to be able to command very large fees for their appearance. The great transformation of Greek athletics from what appears to have been an "aristocrats only" system in the archaic period to one involving all male citizens did not evolve towards an even more open system of entertainment so long as the cultural politics of the Greek city-state, which equated status with the ability to perform, was supported by the tastes of Greek rulers. With the rise of Rome to dominance in the Greek world, the cultural politics of public entertainment would be altered to accommodate the eclectic tastes of the new rulers of the Mediterranean. The result was that there would be greater opportunities for people whose skills fell outside the traditional range of agonistic performance, and whose origins were often humble. This was not, however, a development that can simply be attributed to greater open-mindedness on the part of Roman aristocrats. Prior to the conquest of the eastern Mediterranean, they appear to have been well satisfied with traditions in which public performers were regarded as simple appendages to their own contests for dominance. It was the Greek sense that the skilled performer was entitled to profit that injected a significant new element into Roman practice.

4   Rome and Greece

Pantomime appealed greatly to the Romans. It was at Rome in the first century BC that the "developed" form of the art was fully established, and it was Rome that was riven by partisans of two great performers, Bathyllus and Pylades, who attracted the attention (and admiration) of Augustus himself. The arrival of pantomime in Augustan Rome was merely the latest in a long series of adaptations of foreign forms of entertainment to the Roman stage. Indeed, perhaps the only form of entertainment familiar from the late republican and imperial periods that may have developed at Rome itself was circus chariot racing.

The valley of the Circus Maximus gave shape, quite literally, to Roman chariot racing. It was here that chariot races were held, evidently from the earliest times, and it was here that the outlines of a professional track began to take shape in the course of the fourth century BC. At the same time it would appear that the domination of the sport by four factions, the Reds, Greens, Whites, and Blues, was established. The factions ran the stables that provided the competitors for the races, and their support staff. These competitors were always provided in groups of four (one from each faction) to a maximum of twelve. The charioteers themselves, once we get direct evidence for them (only after Augustus) appear to have come from relatively humble backgrounds, and, if they survived, to have become fabulously wealthy. It may also be a sign of the very early development of circus factions that they were administered by corporations consisting of members of the elite equestrian order who were otherwise engaged in commerce and contracting for public service when not seeking admission to magistracies or serving in the cavalry force that gave their order its name. This is an anomaly in the Roman system, where the training and management of performers was left in the hands of lower-status individuals. It may be, though the point is impossible of proof, that the equestrian corporations were relicts of some sort of early choragic system at Rome connected with the administration of *ludi* (*ludus* sing.), or public festivals, for it was at these *ludi* that the chariots were run.

Ludi, being festivals of the gods, seem to have been relatively conservative in the sorts of entertainment that they would admit – it was only in the third century BC that we find that they would include Greek-style drama (in Latin) along with the chariot races and some forms of traditional dance. Romans who wanted to experiment were inclined to do so in festivals that they offered for the people in their own name, *munera* (*munus* sing.). *Munera*, as the name suggests – they were literally "gifts" to the people – were vehicles of aristocratic self-display, often being offered in the context of funerals, triumphs, and office holding, prospectively when men were seeking office in the late republican period, retrospectively under the empire, when magistrates were charged with offering *munera* to "thank" the people for their term in office. As theoretically "one-off" events, early *munera* were held in specially constructed wooden theaters, a stark contrast with chariot races, for which permanent starting gates had been erected in the fourth century BC, and, quite possibly, some permanent seats erected to honor prominent individuals at an equally early date.

It was at a *munus* held in 264 BC that what would prove, according to later tradition, to be a momentous event took place. The *munus* was the funeral of Lucius Junius Brutus Pera, and it was here, allegedly for the first time, that pairs of gladiators fought at Rome (Ville 1981: 42). Gladiatorial combat had its origins in central Italy, and our earliest evidence (tomb paintings at Paestum), suggests that they featured, as they would in their first appearance at Rome, in funeral games. The inclusion of gladiators in this context does not mean, however, that they were intrinsically linked with death. Rather it means that they were intrinsically linked with the martial virtues of the warlike governing class of the region, and it was this that seems to have accounted for their immediate appeal to the Romans, once central Italy had been brought firmly under the control of the republic. Our most important early reading of the meaning of these games comes from a festival held at Daphne in 166 BC by the Seleukid king Antiochos IV, who had been a hostage at Rome. He included gladiators in a display of royal power to inspire the young men of his time with thoughts of martial virtue (Polyb. 30.25–26; D. Potter 1999b: 306).

The royal processions of the post-Alexandrine Greek world – the best known is a fabulous procession staged by Ptolemy II in 271/270 – were meant to illustrate the power of the king, and they could include elaborate mythological tableaus as well as displays of military might and theatrical events (Rice 1983). As Roman power expanded into the eastern Mediterranean during the second century BC, we begin to see efforts on the part of Roman magistrates to imitate these events, both to impress their new subjects, and to impress the people of Rome (Edmondson 1999; Kuttner 1999). In the course of the second century BC, the scale of their *munera* also increased, as dominant men at Rome, whose wealth increased dramatically, sought to equate themselves with rulers of the Greek world. One significant new element in these events at Rome was the beast hunt, or *venatio*, possibly inspired by a Carthaginian example (North African animals seem to have been at a premium in the earliest of these events). Like gladiatorial combat, hunting displays enabled the Roman people some vicarious enjoyment of the pleasure of the aristocracy (many of whom seem to have had a passion for hunting). So too did theatrical events increase in number, with the second century BC standing as the heyday of original dramatic production at Rome, initially in the form of comedy and tragedy written in Latin, as well as mime, and, ultimately, as we have seen, pantomime. As befitted a class that was itself becoming highly Hellenized in its cultural tastes, the entertainments with which they displayed their magnificence likewise changed into an amalgam of events adapted from around the empire.

5   Imperial Entertainments

The expansion of the Roman entertainment industry was not without the occasional hiccup. In the late seventies BC, a gladiator named Spartacus, assisted by a band of companions who had been oppressed by their owner, led a serious revolt in rural Italy, and in the course of the sixties the increasing connection between *munera* and political corruption led to efforts to restrict their scope. The chief offender in this regard was Julius Caesar, who accumulated a large band of gladiators, whom he was ultimately, if not already in the sixties, to keep near Capua. It is likely that Caesar, as did other aristocrats, would hire his gladiators out for shows by his peers, possibly also restricting the damage that could be done to them in the process. Certainly his political rivals thought that Caesar's troupe was a potential pro-Caesarian fifth column when the civil war broke out in 49 (*BC* 1.14.4), which is unlikely to have been the case if he treated them with the brutality of Spartacus's owner. In the fifties Gnaeus Pompey broke with tradition by constructing a massive theater at Rome, attached to a temple to avoid what had become a ban on the building of a permanent theater, while various political rivals continued to display their munificence by ignoring his building to construct their own theaters. The grandest of these was a wooden building erected by Gaius Curio on rollers so that the two halves could be joined to form an amphitheater or separated to make two theaters (Pliny, *HN* 36.116 with D. Potter 2006: 400). In the same period we also begin to gain some impression of the profits that could be made by actors of all sorts. Cicero provides a picture of a Greek poet named Archias, who seems to have obtained virtual rock-star status, and of a comic actor named Roscius who commanded vast fees to train actors for others and gave elocution lessons to members of the upper class. It is in the same period that we learn of a mime-actress whose fees reached 200,000 HS a performance, a sum greater than the annual income of a typical member of the Roman senate (Lebek 1996: 36–44).

Late republican aristocrats depended upon the good will of performers to further their political designs, opening new paths of advancement to people who might have begun life in relative obscurity or slavery. Very little changed after Augustus's victory at Actium. The first *princeps* had a well-known affection for pantomimes (so well known that pantomimes were featured in the games that were founded to honor him after his death), and took steps to limit the brutality of gladiatorial shows by requiring that anyone wishing to stage an exhibition in which gladiators were required to fight to a determined conclusion (a *munus sine missione*) needed imperial dispensation (D. Potter 1999b: 307). Thus, while fights to the death between gladiators, which seem to have developed in the republican period, might still be offered, the average bout became less perilous, and possibly ever more lucrative (the figure of 100,000 HS as appearance money for champion fighters is attested under Augustus). The increase in costs, which could have a serious impact on men required to offer *munera* as a consequence of holding municipal office, led to ever more elaborate efforts at price control – best attested for us in a decree of the senate passed in AD 177 which sets the prices for slave gladiators and restricts fees that free men could charge (Oliver and Palmer 1955) – and even the introduction of fights between men armed with wooden weapons. Gladiators themselves begin to commemorate their lives with monuments that mirrored the monuments that members of the aristocracy erected to commemorate moments of munificence, and appear to have led active lives outside the arena.

Gladiators and actors were not the only ones to profit from the alliance between government and the entertainment industry. In the first half of the first century BC, we get our first evidence for synods of professional athletes, and a great deal of evidence for what seems a virtual explosion in the number of opportunities for them to ply their trade. Augustus himself commemorated the battle of Actium by founding quadrennial games at Nikopolis on the site of his victory, and cities competed for imperial attention by sponsoring new festivals. At the same time, wealthy individuals commemorated themselves by funding civic festivals, often called *themides* to contrast their entirely monetary prizes with the crowns (albeit often now accompanied by monetary prizes) offered at traditional *agones* (Klose 2005: 126). Athletes who were able to contend victoriously in major festivals could gain a series of freedoms from compulsory public services if they were admitted to what would become an international synod of victors at crowned games. This association appears to have been largely self-governing from a headquarters at Rome, and to have been able to negotiate the privileges of its members with the emperors themselves.

Perhaps the most significant feature of the imperial period was the breakdown in geographical distinction between the locus of entertainments. Greek athletes performed regularly in Italy, especially after the Augustan foundation of games at Naples and the foundation (first by Nero, later by Domitian) of the Capitoline games at Rome. There is also evidence for the spread of Greek style games in the warmer regions of the western Mediterranean (especially North Africa), while gladiatorial combat spread throughout the eastern provinces. Initially the impulse for the spread of gladiatorial combat to the East seems to have come in the context of the imperial cult, where the courage of gladiators was seen to be emblematic of the martial virtues of the empire as a whole. It may indeed be a sign of the greater integration of Greeks into the imperial system that several civic festivals that were established in the course of the third century bypassed athletic events in favor of gladiators (Nollé 1992/1993).

The tale of the imperial entertainment industry had darker sides as well. One is that it proved impossible to restrain public desire for more dangerous exhibitions of gladiators. Several texts from Beroia, all dating to the third century AD, record imperial dispensation for bouts to the death, and the record of an exhibition in Pontos suggests even more extensive bloodshed (*AE* 1971 n. 431; *SEG* 1999 n. 815; 817). Deaths among gladiators were, however, by no means the most prevalent form of slaughter. Even before the reign of Augustus public executions began to be included in the programs of public spectacles. These took two forms: exposure to the beasts (*damnatio ad bestias*), and bouts between individuals condemned to a gladiatorial *ludus* (*damnatio ad ludum*), who fought with little training or equipment. Apuleius suggests that prospective *munerarii* would purchase people condemned to the beasts (*Met.* 4.13), and the contemporary decree of the senate on the prices for public combatants reveals that the cost per condemned was set at a minimum of six *aurei*. By the end of the third century, if not well before, *damnatio ad ludum* seems to have dropped out of the regular penalties employed by governors, perhaps because it was too easily survived if the condemned excited the favor of the crowd. Burning at the stake, conversely, became a much more common amphitheatric penalty. We can only estimate how many people were killed for the entertainment of others as a result of the judicial system, but it would appear that, across the empire, many thousands suffered this fate every year. The theory behind this form of punishment was that the population at large should share in the vengeance extracted from miscreants, and this seems indeed to have been a popular theory. That said, the imperial justice system was sufficiently lacking in protections for the innocent or simply unpopular that popular participation in this aspect of government unquestionably involved horrific injustices.

6   From the Ancient World to the Modern

The vast entertainment industry that spread across the Roman empire in the second century was a function of the wealth of a society that was largely at peace. By the end of the third century AD, the civic resources that had supported this industry were rapidly becoming exhausted through fiscal and political crises. It was fiscal exhaustion rather than the progressive Christianization of government that spelled the end of traditions that had existed since the emergence of the classical city-state. For, while the fifteenth book of the *Theodosian Code* preserves ample evidence for the continuation of theatrical events, the wealth of individual entertainers, and local athletic festivals during the fourth century, the basic trend was towards the concentration of all events, except those involving gladiators, into the context of chariot racing. While Roman-style circuses were built in increasing numbers throughout the major cities of the empire from the second century onwards, these remained very much a feature of only the largest urban areas, often those where there was also an imperial palace (new circus construction tended to be linked to the construction of imperial palaces). As the power of the imperial government declined in the West, the system of public entertainment largely disappeared before the end of the fifth century. In the East, while chariot racing remained important at Constantinople, especially as a venue for communication between the emperors and their people, into the tenth century, it seems to have been limited to the capital after the Arab conquests of the seventh century. The result was a return to a social situation not unlike that of the archaic period, where lower-class entertainers were limited in their opportunities, and aristocrats, especially in the West, evolved new, martial forms of entertainment that served solely to enhance their own status. It was only with the rise of the modern film industry in the twentieth century, and a new linkage between education and athleticism at the end of the nineteenth, that careers in popular entertainment began to rival, or exceed, those that has been available in the heyday of the Roman empire.

FURTHER READING

S. Miller 2004 is a splendid introduction to sport in classical Greece, combining a thorough command of ancient and modern literature with a deep knowledge of the sites themselves. Moretti 1953 is still a useful collection of the primary evidence for athletes. Poliakoff 1987 offers a far-ranging study of combat sports in the Near East and the Greek world, as well as to their modern descendants, while Guttmann 2004 is useful survey of the history of sport in the Western tradition as a whole. For Roman entertainments, there is still a great deal to be learned from Friedlander 1922, while Alan Cameron 1976 and Humphrey 1986 are crucial for the history of chariot racing. The fundamental works on gladiatorial combat remain Ville 1981 and Robert 1940, though more recent work on all aspects of Roman spectacle is accessible through Köhne, and Ewigleben 2001. Our greatest debt, on virtually all these topics, is owed to the work of Louis Robert, whose impeccable command of the epigraphic record of the ancient world is combined with a sharp eye for the human interactions that lie behind each text.

CHAPTER THIRTY-FOUR

Education

Jason König

1 Education: Ancient and Modern

European education has been marked throughout its many centuries by engagement with Greek and Roman culture. Greek and Latin language and literature have dominated higher-education syllabuses – in some times and places to the exclusion of nearly all else: Aristotelian logic and the ancient *trivium* and *quadrivium* in the medieval curriculum (Cobban 1975; 1999; Knowles 1988); revived attention to classical literature in Italian Renaissance humanism, with its focus on rhetorical style and moral education (Grendler 1989); and the central (but always disputed) place of classical learning within the universities and elite society of nineteenth- and twentieth-century Europe (Stray 1998). Moreover, many educational theorists have invoked in general terms the ideals of ancient Greek learning as models for their own cultures, usually with some acknowledgement about how those ideals must be adapted (e.g. Castle 1961; Nussbaum 1997); and many of the key principles of the European educational tradition are themselves derived from the ancient world, for example commitment to particular visions of how the sum of human knowledge ought to be divided (see O. Pedersen 1997 on conceptual continuities between classical and medieval education). However, it is also striking that we rarely see in modern writing on education any more concrete ideal of close adherence to ancient institutions and techniques of learning. In that sense, ancient education is both a close ancestor and at the same time a very unfamiliar counterpart to our own – although that has not stopped modern scholarship from imposing the language of modern educational institutions on their ancient equivalents, in ways which sometimes mean that their distance from us is lost to view.

2 Where?

My starting-point, for that reason, is with the question of where ancient education can be found. What are the institutions of ancient education? How useful, for example, are the terms "school" and "university" for describing ancient education? And how far can answering those questions help to shed light on what is really distinctive in ancient education (as far as we can generalize about such a massive subject at all)?

It is striking, for one thing, that we have relatively little archaeological evidence for dedicated school buildings. Organized teaching, especially in classical Greek society, must often have happened in spaces not designed exclusively for that purpose (Cribiore 2001: 21–24). For many, the proper place for learning was not within a school context at all, but rather within other institutions. The symposium, for example, could be represented as a place of learning, a place for young men to take their place in elite society. Festival participation and even spectatorship allowed a more civic-minded inculcation of adult responsibilities and local traditions: for instance, the foundation of the rich benefactor Vibius Salutaris in Ephesos in the second century AD involved the "ephebes" of the city (young men going through a formal period of physical and military education – on which more below) in processions which wove their way through the iconic centers of the city, initiating them into a sense of their own historical and mythical inheritance (Rogers 1991). Plato's appropriation of the educational spaces and genres of the city of Athens for his own ideals of philosophical speech is an influential adaptation of those assumptions about learning as something which should arise from within the landscape of civic life (Nightingale 1995). Libanius, in the fourth century AD, describes himself at one point teaching in the public baths in the city of Nikomedia: "the whole city had become a *mouseion*" (*Autobiography* 55) (with reference to the scholarly institution of the Mouseion attached to the Library of Hellenistic Alexandria). Moreover the family was often presented as the very first starting-point for education. It is no accident that Ps-Plutarch *On the Education of Children* (placed by editors at the head of Plutarch's work, despite its doubtful authenticity, as a programmatic starting-point to the massive project of philosophical education and exploration which Plutarch's *Moralia* represents) focuses almost exclusively on the child's ethical education at home, almost entirely ignoring institutionalized schooling (cf. Bremmer 1995 on religious education in the family).

Another factor in the difficulty of tracking the physical space of schools is the fact that teaching was so often organized around individual teachers rather than specific institutions. That pattern is common across Greek and Roman culture from the most basic levels of primary education – for example, elementary schools in Egyptian papyri are often named after specific teachers (Cribiore 2001: 18–19) – through to the ideals of succession from master to teacher which structured disciplines like oratory, philosophy, and medicine, and which Philostratus and Diogenes Laertius regularly refer to in their biographical writing (*Lives of the Sophists* and *Lives and Opinions of the Eminent Philosophers* respectively). It is in the late-antique world that we come closest to seeing higher education which resembles modern university education (and indeed the word "university" has sometimes been applied to these systems: e.g. Walden 1912), but even here the obsession with individual teachers is remarkable. For Libanius, for example, writing in the fourth century AD, education lies at the very heart of his autobiographical self-presentation – from his account of attendance at grammar classes as a young child through to his experiences as a renowned teacher of rhetoric in Antioch. Involvement in the world of *paideia* (a Greek word which like the English "learning" can refer to both the processes and the socially empowering accomplishments of education) is for him the defining feature of his Hellenism, and it is a fascinating exercise to chart the changing contours of that involvement across his life's work. Like many of his contemporaries, he also gives us vivid glimpses of his own higher education in Athens. We might imagine cities like Athens and Antioch as university towns, full of young men who have left home to gain the best education. But one of the most striking differences is the prominence of individual rhetoricians and philosophers as objects of student allegiance, operating, on Libanius's account, without visible signs of the constraints of any formal institution (although there are some counter-examples of deliberately founded and formally regulated institutions, perhaps most obviously in the higher education institutions of Constantinople, founded in AD 425: M. Clarke 1971: 130–32). Libanius is kidnapped, for example, on arrival, until he agrees to assign himself to one particular teacher (not the one he has come to study with) (*Autobiography* 16), and he repeats horror stories of lecturers being mocked and abused by the students of their rivals (e.g. 85). That is not to say that Libanius's account is a straightforward reflection of a situation which was unthinkingly accepted. Instead, a full reading of Libanius's evidence for late-antique education needs to take account of the nuanced texture of the works in which it is embedded. At times in the *Autobiography*, for example, he even seems ambivalent about the prominence of individual lecturers. He stands apart from most of this factional squabbling as a student in Athens, even when he suffers an unprovoked attack from a partisan student (21), and for much of this section of the work he gives the impression that he views educational factionalism as a distraction from the pursuit of true learning (in much the same way as the Galen advertises his own lack of interest in adhering to any single medical sect, standing apart from their bickering [Boudon 1994: 1436–41]). Later, however, we are forced to reassess that impression when we see Libanius establishing himself as a teacher and boasting about how he has poached the pupils of his rivals (90). It seems that the only reason for his dislike of the individual-centered system is his scorn for the quality of the schoolteachers and professors who attract such devotion (e.g. 8, 17), or for those who use it against himself (e.g. those who accuse him of magic in *Autobiography* 98). In that sense his work is after all a celebration of the culture of individual educators, even if it flirts with a more negative portrayal of that culture. Mechanisms for examination of students are relatively recent inventions within the modern university, and the prioritization of attendance at the classes of particular lecturers ahead of assessment and accreditation would have seemed much more familiar to one educated within the European universities of the eighteenth century. But the lack of any strong central regulation in most ancient centers of higher education is remarkable even by those standards (although of course the prestige of linking oneself with big names may in some cases have led the details of educational administration to be lost from view within our sources, dominated as they are by the priorities of self-promotion).

None of this means, of course, that the idea of the school as a defined institution was non-existent or even unfamiliar within the ancient world. The earliest attested schools are from the fifth century BC: Thucydides 7.29, for example, mentions a massacre of children by Thracian soldiers in a school (*didaskaleion*) in Mykalessos; Herodotus 6.27 describes the fall of a roof in Chios in 494 BC, which killed 119 boys who were "learning letters." The lack of any word for school in the latter example is typical of ancient vagueness about school buildings, but the number of pupils suggests a substantial institution. Moreover, there are signs of an increase in the uniformity of education in the Hellenistic world, and in some cases also of an increasing interest on behalf of cities to control educational activities – although such control was always very partial by modern standards, and regional variations are always apparent when we look closely (Marrou 1956: 147–64; T. Morgan 1998: 21–33). Here, however, we come up against one of the most conspicuous divergences between ancient and modern education, that is the institution of the *gymnasion* (and its smaller equivalent the *palaistra*), an institution far removed from its English-language namesake the gymnasium. If rhetorical and philosophical apprenticeship forms one side of the higher education of the ancient world, then the ephebic education of the *gymnasion* forms the other (see Marrou 1956: 161–80; Kleijwegt 1991: 91–101; Kah and Scholz 2004; König 2005: 47–63). It is sometimes hard to catch the nuances of the relationship between these two very different types of learning, but it seems clear that they would standardly have been viewed as having very different functions: the one aimed at individual, cosmopolitan intellectual aspirations; the other aimed at training young men to play their part in the life of their city and local elite. Moreover, the precise content of *gymnasion* education is much debated, and must anyway have varied across its long history. It did always have a strongly physical side, linked with military training, but the applicability of that training must have been increasingly open to doubt in the east of the Roman empire, when Greek cities no longer had responsibility for organizing their own defense. Increasingly in the Hellenistic world that physical aspect seems to have been supplemented by literate education (e.g. Delorme 1960: 316–36). For example, visiting lecturers are attested in many cities teaching in the *gymnasion*. There is very little sign, however, of the development of full-scale curricula of literate education in the *gymnasion* at any point (Cribiore 2001: 34–36). The famous *gymnasion* law of Beroia in Macedonia (*SEG* 27.261 = Austin 118), dating from the early second century BC, give us a remarkable glimpse inside the walls of these institutions, revealing a regime of fierce discipline, focused almost exclusively on athletic and military education. That training is not confined to the institution of the *ephebeia*, with its recruits ("ephebes") between the ages of 17 and 19, but it applies to other age groups too, both older and younger: formal association with the *gymnasion* continued in many cities well into adulthood (see Forbes 1933 on the category of *neoi*). Here, too, however, we have to deal with local particularity: it may well be the case that the militarized *gymnasia* of Hellenistic Macedonia were themselves very untypical of that institution more widely, given the military priorities of Macedonian society (Gauthier and Hatzopoulos 1993: 173–76).

3 Who?

Who were the teachers and pupils involved in ancient education? How can we map the contours of that involvement across the many centuries of Greek and Roman culture? Clearly, those who came from wealthy backgrounds were more likely to receive a thorough education, especially at the higher level. However, we do also see signs of excessive education being viewed as incompatible with elite status: Pindar is careful to downplay the involvement of athletic trainers in the education of his subjects, in order to keep intact aristocratic ideals of inherited virtue (Nicholson 2005); Tacitus praises Agricola for resisting the temptations of immoderate and un-Roman devotion to philosophical education in Massilia (modern Marseille) (*Agr.* 4). The *gymnasion* maintained an elitist bias right through its long history: the Beroia law is careful to exclude men involved in trade (along with other categories like drunkards and madmen), presumably on the grounds that they will not be able to guarantee the regular attendance that military training requires; and before that the classical Athenian *gymnasion* seems to have drawn its membership mainly from the wealthiest levels of society (although see Fisher 1998 and Pritchard 2003 for debate about the possibility that it may have become more egalitarian over time). In addition to military and athletic prowess, rhetorical skill was a standard badge of elite status. Rhetorical skills were exercised in both Greek and Roman culture in a great range of practical applications. Maud Gleason has shown how elite oratorical training relied on physical habits of bearing, gesture, and "manly" performance as much as erudition, habits learned through painstaking processes of practice (Gleason 1995; cf. Hawhee 2004 on the physicality of rhetorical education within classical Athens). Admittedly only a few attained the heights of oratorical prowess: the sophists of Philostratus, who have standardly been taken as emblematic of the educational priorities of the "Second Sophistic," were in fact highly exceptional figures. But on one level these iconic figures acted as symbolic representatives of elite superiority, removing the need for their counterparts to train themselves to anything like the same level (T. Schmitz 1997: esp. 63–66). In that sense, *paideia* upheld social order. And yet at the same time it was often viewed as precarious and hard to guarantee, always open to challenge, always in need of restatement and reperformance (Gleason 1995); and as a transformative power, offering access to high status and cultural prestige even to outsiders, in a way which always the potential to disturb comfortable social and cultural hierarchies (Whitmarsh 2001: 90–130). Rhetorical learning could also in some cases offer a resource for subverting political hierarchies as much as upholding them. For example, there are recurring images within Latin and (especially) Greek literature of philosophers giving advice to their political masters (and related to that, a much broader interest in the question of how rulers should be educated; one particularly influential example of that is Xenophon's *Cyropaedia*, with its portrait of the education of the young Persian king, Cyrus). These recurring images in some cases conjure up an impression of harmony between the philosophical and political spheres; but at other times the exercise of offering advice to a political ruler can be an opportunity for hiding more subversive connotations beneath a cooperative surface, connotations which often rely on erudite allusions and require close familiarity with rhetorical tradition (e.g. see Whitmarsh 1998 on the philosopher-orator Dio Chrysostom and his *Kingship Orations*, which may have been delivered to the emperor Trajan).

Of course there were many ancient students whose educational achievements did not even come close to guaranteeing them access to the higher levels of social, let alone political empowerment. Ancient educational theorists like Plutarch and Quintilian tend to provide idealized reading programs and idealized pictures of the progression from elementary learning to rhetorical prowess and philosophical maturity. In many ways the extensive surviving papyrus evidence from Hellenistic and Roman Egypt is remarkably consistent with our literary sources for educational practice (T. Morgan 1998: esp. 50). But it also reminds us, in a way which Quintilian and others do not, of the painstaking graft and the highly variable levels of attainment which were the norm within day-to-day education. It hints at the way in which even elementary schooling could contribute to the quest for social advancement – not least by the way it gave access to membership of a wider Greek community – but it also shows us that this kind of membership could be attained on many different levels, and for many only minimally. Teresa Morgan (1998: 74–89) argues for a core-periphery model of ancient education: familiarity with canonical texts like Homer and with basic grammar as essential and widely attained starting-points; but also countless other opportunities for educational attainment, by which individuals could raise themselves to much higher levels of erudition. In that sense a basic education might not be straightforwardly empowering: "it is typically those who have invested a certain amount in education who are most inclined to respect those with more" (T. Morgan 1998: 78). Levels of literacy in the Greek and Roman world are much disputed (see W. Harris 1989, who estimates a maximum of 20–30 percent in some Hellenistic cities; Bowman and Woolf 1994). But whatever the precise figure, the papyri reveal to us vividly the enormous gulf between elementary training (which is the category into which most of the surviving papyrus evidence seems to fall) and the higher reaches of rhetorical accomplishment.

The masculine, free-born bias of ancient education is impossible to ignore. It is clear that young women and slaves tended not to receive education in the same numbers, or with the same degree of systematization. Ps.-Plutarch, *On the Education of Children*, makes that bias clear even in its opening lines, which specify the education of "free children," where "free" has connotations of philosophical independent-mindedness as well as legal status. The work is addressed to a notional father, and assumes throughout a masculine subject. And yet if we look closely we do find a considerable volume of evidence relating to women's education, even if it is generally more scattered and less prominent (Cribiore 2001: 74–101; Hemelrijk 1999 on the education of upper-class Roman women). The Hellenistic school in Teos where we see provisions for appointment of schoolteachers to teach "the boys and the girls" ("free" children are again specified) (*SIG*[3] 578 = Austin 120) may not be quite such an anomaly as is usually assumed.

Equally intriguing in a way is the question of what kind of status we should envisage for Greek and Roman teachers. Not surprisingly, the gap between the highest and lowest social levels of the teaching profession seems to have been very wide.

Moreover, we often see signs of a degree of ambiguity in the position of teachers, who have authority over the children under their care, but are also themselves subject to the authority of parents and city (Cribiore 2001: 45–73), and who must often have been heavily dependent on patronage (e.g. Kaster 1988: 201–30 on grammarians). Certainly the instructors in the Beroia gymnasium decree discussed above are subject to punishments, in some cases equivalent to those prescribed for the ephebes and *paides*, if they fail to fulfill their duties. The school in Teos mentioned above gives us some fascinating glimpses of the teachers of the Greek world, as does a very similar inscription from the same period from Miletos (*SIG*³ 577 = Austin 119). In both, we hear of carefully regulated election procedures, careful state control over the money given by private benefaction for the running of the school, including guarantees of salary payment to teachers, and details of variations in salary for teachers according to specialty. In Miletos, for example, appointments are made annually, via an elaborate system of public election: here, the teachers are themselves subject to precisely the kind of ritualized public competition and public scrutiny they require from their charges in the regular school competitions which were the nearest ancient education ever gets to examination. Four schoolteachers are to be appointed annually (at a salary of 40 drachmas per month) and four gymnastic trainers (at a salary of 30 drachmas), with sanctions available to them if their salary is not paid – assurances which must have been a welcome defense against the kind of financial insecurity which Libanius complains about on behalf of his own teaching assistants in Antioch (Cribiore 2001: 63–64, with reference to Libanius, *Or.* 31 and 43). In Roman education, too, there are some signs of attempts to put pedagogical income on a firmer footing – for example, Vespasian granted tax exemptions to teachers and founded chairs of Greek and Latin rhetoric in Rome (see Kaster 1988: 216–30 on these state interventions and the way in which they were extended in the centuries following, albeit rather patchily) – but for many the luxury of a guaranteed salary must have been beyond them.

4   What?

Inevitably we have had glimpses of some of the answers to this question already. I have left it till last because it is in a sense the most difficult of all of these questions to answer. A summary answer is easy enough – it *is* possible to generalize, especially from the Hellenistic period onwards, about some of the standard contents of school and higher education. But a full answer needs to capture something of the way in which education was itself always contested within the ancient world; and something of the way in which ancient texts are so often performing and testing education even as they talk about it.

One of the recurring principles of ancient education is that of *enkyklios paideia* ("circular," or "complete" learning) – the ideal of a balanced combination of core subjects which might include literature, rhetoric, grammar, astronomy, music, geometry, and logic, sometimes also philosophy, but most often not (Morgan 1998: 33–39; and for one of the fullest ancient discussions of this concept, Quint. *Inst.* 1.10.1).

Another important recurring structure is the idea of a progression from elementary skills of reading and writing, through to study of grammar, and finally rhetoric (a progression perhaps too easily equated by modern writers with the movement between primary, secondary, and higher education). After elementary schooling, the second level would be the school of the grammarian, both in the East and later (from the late second century BC onwards) in the West. Grammarians typically taught correct Latin or Greek language, line-by-line analysis of canonical poetic texts, and preliminary skills of composition (Bonner 1977: 189–249); some also published their own scholarly writings (e.g. Kaster 1988, with a focus on the late-antique *grammaticus*; E. Rawson 1985: 66–76). From there, the most obvious next step (although not an inevitable step, given the alternative option of advanced philosophical training) would be the school of the rhetor, who would offer training in different types of speech-making through repeated practice (T. Morgan 1998: 190–239; Bonner 1977: 250–327) – although it should be stressed that the boundaries between elementary schoolteacher/grammarian/rhetor were often far from clear in practice (Cribiore 2001: 36–44). The homogenization of Greek education seems to have progressed rapidly after the conquests of Alexander. Conventionally Greek education is viewed as a bond for uniting diverse populations (T. Morgan 1998: 21–25; Bowman 1996: 125–26 on *gymnasion* membership as a badge of Greek identity in Hellenistic Egypt). But though we do see increasing signs of state intervention in educational provision (exemplified by the texts from Miletos and Teos discussed above), it is striking that we rarely find state attempts to control the content of education; and the prevalence of a shared structure should not lead us to underestimate the degree of local variation. The iconic variations between Athenian and Spartan education are an obvious example; but it is the less conspicuous variations, as revealed to us again through papyrus evidence, which have recently been the subject of the most exciting new scholarship (see esp. Cribiore 2001).

In that sense the educational theory of the Greek and Roman world sometimes looks like an attempt to impose coherence on an inherently incoherent set of practices. Moreover, it is crucial to take account of the processes of debate and dispute which so often surround the subject of ancient education. To take one example, it is clear that the work of classical Athenian writers like Isocrates (on whom see Poulakos and Depew 2004) and Plato was highly influential on much which came after them. We repeatedly find writers and educators at least paying lip-service to Plato's ideals of balance between musical and physical education; so much so that it is tempting to view this as one of the few places where we can see a general consensus within educational theory and practice. Not surprisingly, however, the precise significance of the educational theory of these authors is constantly debated and reshaped for self-serving ends. The role of physical education is once again a case in point: Plato is regularly used both to praise and to criticize the role of athletic education (e.g. see König 2005: 315–25 on the dispute between Galen and Philostratus over the precise significance of Plato's portrayal of physical education). More generally speaking, we need to take account of the fact that many writers who express opinions on what education should involve are engaged in a struggle against alternative viewpoints: Galen's arguments for medical training as coextensive with philosophical education (e.g. *Protrepticus* 38–39) – aimed in part against professional rivals who offered different versions of medical expertise – are only the most vehement example of the process by which controversial educational ideals can be presented as if they are self-evident and indisputable. Another area where the impression of ancient consensus on proper education breaks down is in the area of cross-cultural influence. Greek education in the Roman republic, for example, was controversial, and treated with great ambivalence: Roman education was increasingly influenced by Greek practices; Greek *paideia* was also, however, an object of suspicion (note, for example, the relatively small number of Greek rhetors operating in Rome in the late republic, and the atmosphere of distrust in which they had to operate: E. Rawson 1985: 76–9). Similarly the question of how and how far to reshape Greco-Roman *paideia* within Christian education was a major and controversial preoccupation of early Christian scholars (Rappe 2001; W. Jaeger 1962; Marrou 1956: 419–51).

In some cases we even find ancient educational writers drawing attention to the difficulty of pinning down what exactly a proper education should involve. It is not just that it is hard for us to see what ancient education was, but also that the difficulty of seeing the answer to that question is itself one of the defining interests of ancient writing on this subject. The second-century AD satirist Lucian exemplifies perhaps better than any other ancient author the self-reflexive quality which ancient writing on education so often has. He is often quoted for the glimpses he gives us into scenes of ancient schooling; but too often these quotations ignore his wider satirical purpose of disturbing any attempt whatever to identify and pin down a reliable version of what *paideia* is, and his love of exposing the inconsistencies and absurdities inherent within received educational traditions (Branham 1989). We have seen already Maud Gleason's arguments for the importance of rhetorical education in marking elite identity, and for the insight that those marks of education are often precarious, in danger of slipping out of the speaker's control, or open to rival interpretations. No doubt many sophistic orators were not self-consciously aware of the unstable nature of their own claims to erudition. Lucian, however, certainly is, in his untiring mockery (and sometimes self-mockery) of figures whose claims to *paideia* on close inspection do not stand up to scrutiny.

His longest work, the *Hermotimos,* is a brilliant example of that (M. Edwards 1993; Mollendorf 2000; cf. Lucian's *Anacharsis* for satire of traditional *gymnasion* education, discussed by Branham 1989: 82–104; König 2005: 80–96). It takes the form of a dialogue between two speakers, Lykinos and Hermotimos. Hermotimos is hurrying to a philosophy lecture; Lykinos interrupts him, and quizzes him on the content of the education to which he is so devoted, ironically drawing out the absurdities of the metaphors Hermotimos relies on to describe his ascent to philosophical virtue. In the deceptively simple, conversational opening of the dialogue he gives his attention to Hermotimos's appearance: "To judge by your book and by your hasty walk, you look like someone hurrying to his teacher . . . waving your hand around this way and that like someone composing a speech to himself or putting together some difficult question or solving some sophistical inquiry" (Lucian, *Hermotimos* 1).

Here, indeed, we have a tantalizing glimpse of the trappings of learning, but it is also a scene which mocks the sophistic ideals of the physicality of *paideia* (the figure of the philosopher, whose conspicuous philosophical uniform of pale face and long beard hides only hypocrisy is a common one throughout Lucian's work). Lykinos questions his interlocutor relentlessly, destabilizing Hermotimos's cherished assumptions about his progress towards philosophical accomplishment – insisting, for example, on knowing exactly how far up the metaphorical steep path of learning he is and when he is scheduled to arrive; or revealing the absurdity of Hermotimos's claim to know for certain that his own (Stoic) sect is the true one. Lykinos's own questioning, of course, uses the techniques of philosophical education through its reliance on the structure of question and answer so familiar to ancient readers from Plato's Socratic dialogues. Ironically, that quasi-philosophical method leads Hermotimos, finally converted to his interlocutor's viewpoint, to renounce all devotion to philosophy at the end of the dialogue.

In a sense Lucian's dialogue brings us full circle to the question I started with, the question of where education is to be located: Lykinos characteristically phrases his search for education in spatial, locational terms – in the school of Hermotimos's teacher, or at the top of the metaphorical path of virtue. In the end Lucian leaves us with nowhere to stand – he turns his mockery against us as readers if we read him with too straight a face in the search for evidence of ancient education, and in our search for what education should mean in our own lives, exposing the absurdity of seeking a simple definition of such an intangible and contested entity. But he also shows his readers the difficulty of thinking beyond and outside their own involvement with the conventions of *paideia*: Lykinos, like Lucian's readers, is unable to escape from deeply ingrained habits of philosophical thought. Lucian may be highly atypical in the relish with which he dismantles easy assumptions and unthinking convention. But he is typical in the sense that ancient writing about education is so often not just *about* education; it also challenges and destabilizes our view of what education is as we read, keeping us always on our guard.

FURTHER READING

Ancient education is a subject which has attracted a large number of surveys, many of which I have drawn on in the main text of this chapter. The most comprehensive of those is Marrou 1956, still a highly influential account, ranging all the way from archaic Greece to the late-antique world. Other surveys, many of them focused on smaller parts of that history, include W. Jaeger 1939–45 and Beck 1964 on classical Greece (see also Beck 1975 for a collection of visual representations of education from the same period); Bonner 1977 on Rome; M. Clarke 1971 on higher education. More recently, a number of studies have opened up new approaches. T. Morgan 1998 and Cribiore 2001 both exploit the very rich Egyptian papyrus material. Pailler 2004, Too 2001 and Too and Livingstone 1998 contain many thought-provoking essays. Many important works have focused on particular levels of educational activity in depth. W. Harris 1989 discusses elementary education at length in the course of his study of literacy. Kaster 1988 on the figure of the grammarian in the late-antique world is a masterful in-depth study of one of the most important areas of educational activity in the ancient world. Kaster's work supplements already established scholarship on the sphere of rhetorical education, which was standardly thought to follow the school of the grammarian: for an introduction, see M. Clarke 1996 and the many works of George Kennedy (e.g. 1994) and Donald Russell (e.g. 1983). For translations of rhetorical exercises and sample speeches see Kennedy 2003, Russell and Wilson 1981. For a challenging interpretation of the ways in which these texts engage with Roman ideals and anxieties, Gunderson 2003; and on rhetorical training as a vehicle for (always precarious) displays of masculinity: Gleason 1995, Gunderson 2000; cf. Whitmarsh 1998 and 2001 on the contested role of *paideia* within imperial Greek literature and identity. Connected with that growth in interest in the physicality of rhetorical education, there has also been an expansion of interest in *gymnasion* training. Delorme 1960 is still important; for more recent work, see e.g. Kah and Scholz 2004, König 2005, the former dealing especially with the institution of the *gymnasion*, the latter with literary representations of athletic training in the context of wider debates over education and cultural value. Kennell 1995 analyses the intensely physical practices of Spartan education, especially its archaizing manifestation within the Roman empire. Finally, on classical influences over modern education, see Stray 1998, who charts the changing social and educational role of Classics within the nineteenth and twentieth centuries.

CHAPTER THIRTY-FIVE

Medicine

Helen King

The study of the history of medicine – of theories of how the body works, what causes disease, how best to cure it, and who is best qualified to try – poses in a particularly clear way the difficulties of understanding the past. On the one hand, we would seem to share with the people of the ancient world the experiences of being born, living as a body, suffering and dying: but, on the other hand, it is hard to know how much is really "shared," when our interpretations of the body can be so different. How far can those who believe in the circulation of the blood understand others who thought of their bodies in terms of various fluids, produced in the liver from their food and then pulled to the parts of the body where they were most needed? Can someone who regards the pulse as a numerical indication of heart rate make sense of someone who thought of it not so much as quantitative, but rather as a qualitative clue to emotion? Believing in fever as a symptom of various types of infection, how do we react to cultures in which the fever itself is instead seen as the disease?

The many surviving medical texts from the Greek and Roman worlds have always been of interest to scholars, but until the last century they were studied more by medical doctors and philologists than by ancient historians. Because the theories of the workings of the human body discussed by the writers of the Hippocratic corpus in the fifth century BC onwards, and then developed by Galen (129 until after 210 AD) in the Roman empire, formed the basis of medicine during the middle ages and the Renaissance and beyond, medical doctors valued the ancient texts as a useful resource; when Emile Littré translated the Hippocratic medical texts from Greek to French in the middle of the nineteenth century, he did so because he thought they were relevant to the medicine of his own day. An often complex manuscript tradition, with some works of Galen having been translated from Greek into Arabic before being translated into Latin, meant that the original technical terms for parts of the body and for the materials used in remedies could be difficult for philologists to reconstruct. However, medical texts provided a useful source of alternative meanings for the words they studied. In the third century BC in particular, expressions for newly discovered parts of the body and its processes were coined by variation on the everyday vocabulary; for example, "retina" is based on the word for "net."

The legacy of many centuries of practical medical interest in these texts leads to the temptation to read back modern theories and discoveries into the past, ranking ancient medicine according to how closely its practitioners came to the truth as we now perceive it. For example, third-century BC accounts of the blood vessels have tempted some writers to suggest that the circulation of the blood was "nearly" discovered in the third century BC. There are still medical attempts to "diagnose" the plague affecting Athens from around 430 to 426 as smallpox, anthrax, measles, typhus, ergotism, toxic shock syndrome, or a host of other possibilities. However, the symptoms of diseases change over time as the causative organism alters, and the population affected adapts, and so perhaps the condition no longer exists today in any form that we could recognize. Some modern readers of our only literary source for the plague, Thucydides (2.47–55), still argue that his description reveals knowledge of transmission by contagion, and of acquired immunity; but, even if we accept that Thucydides noted these features, it remains the case that he had no theoretical framework in which they could have made sense.

As the rise of modern medicine has made the theories of disease and recommended remedies of Greek and Roman medicine increasingly irrelevant, so ancient history has come to find the same texts of ever greater interest. They are now seen as providing valuable insights into a range of areas, including the history of ideas, social history, and gender history. In dialogue with those studying the medicine of other historical periods, historians of ancient medicine now focus more on making sense of ancient medicine in the philosophical, social, and cultural context of its own time.

1   Accidents of Survival

The problems raised by the sources for ancient medicine represent an extreme version of those found in other fields of Greek and Roman history; to put it simply, how is our picture of the past formed by what happens to have survived, and does the nature of the evidence mean that we must close off some avenues of inquiry? There are two peaks in the quantity of evidence: the survival of the Hippocratic corpus, although the texts in it appear to date from a long time-period covering several centuries, and the still-expanding body of work by Galen, active in the second century and the beginning of the third century AD.

Between the survival of the works of Hippocrates and Galen, a less-well-documented peak occurred with the work of Herophilos (fl. c.280 BC) and Erasistratos (fl. 250 BC) in third-century BC Alexandria where, for a brief generation, human dissection was practiced. It is still not clear why this became possible, or why it stopped; suggestions for its introduction include changing Greek notions of the soul, a powerful monarchy which could permit anything it pleased, Greek presence in a culture in which the dead body had been treated very differently from funerary practices on mainland Greece, and the availability of an Egyptian subject population on whom to experiment (Flemming 2003). In the heady intellectual climate of Alexandria, Herophilos and Erasistratos not only opened bodies to explore parts such as the heart and the brain, but also used images taken from other fields of study, such as geometry, music (to explain the rhythm of the pulse), and mechanics (to explain how fluids were processed in the body). But their discoveries had surprisingly little lasting influence; while they made numerous anatomical observations, they were not able to understand physiology. Of the many treatises they are known to have written, none now survives in full.

It was, above all, their methods that later writers criticized. Some claimed that they had performed not merely dissection, but human vivisection; following Aristotle, animals and humans were seen as part of a single continuum, making it possible to extrapolate from animal dissection to the human body, and the roots of much early Greek knowledge of the body in sacrificial practice are clear. As animal vivisection was thought valid – Galen, in particular, seems to have performed this not only in private but also in public, to admiring audiences (Rocca 2003) – it is feasible that human vivisection would have been considered acceptable in Alexandria, particularly if its objects were non-Greek, low status or condemned criminals; Mithridates VI of Pontus (132–63 BC) was later alleged to have experimented on criminals in order to increase his (preventative) knowledge of poisons. Another reason why vivisection may have been carried out was that some critics of medical claims regarded knowledge gained from the dead body alone as irrelevant when it came to understanding how living bodies function.

The continued existence, or loss, of all these texts relates to their supposed authors and how subsequent historians have chosen to assess them. Already in the work of Seneca Hippocrates was seen as "the greatest physician and the founder of medicine" (*Ep.* 95.20), and by the Renaissance he had become the "Father of Medicine." Works that could be attributed to Hippocrates were clearly highly valued. Only a few centuries after his death, he was attributed with a genealogy going back to the god of medicine, Asclepius, himself; he was seen as a culture-bringer, bringing medicine to humans just as Prometheus had brought fire and Triptolemos the gift of grain. The group of over 60 treatises that have come down to us as the Hippocratic corpus was put together in Alexandria, perhaps as early as the third century BC (W. Smith 1979: 204–46). But the historical Hippocrates remains a figure known to us only in two brief passages of Plato which may themselves be constructions for literary effect more than simple statements (*Prt.* 311b; *Phdr.* 270c–d). As for Galen, his wide-ranging synthesis of the ideas of some Hippocratic texts – in particular, *On the Nature of Man*, in which the theory of the four humors is described – with those of Aristotle and Plato quickly became the foundation of Western medicine.

Galen's work was written in Greek but subsequently translated into many other languages including Arabic, Syriac, and Latin; where Greek originals are now lost, these texts can to some extent be reconstructed by working on surviving translations. While the Galenic corpus still continues to grow, the contents of the Hippocratic corpus are now being challenged afresh. For past generations, the "Hippocratic question" consisted of the attempt to identify a genuine work of the historical Hippocrates within the heterogeneous group of texts that goes under his name: today, most would accept that there is not a single one of those texts which can with certainty be attributed to Hippocrates. The date and context of the most famous one, the "Hippocratic Oath," are still unclear, but there is in fact nothing to connect even this to Hippocrates. But some scholars are now going even further, questioning the value of the term "Hippocratic corpus" itself, with its inbuilt suggestions that the texts within the collection somehow represent the best of ancient Greek medicine, and that other medical texts dating from the same period must be inferior.

So what do we know of medicine outside the Hippocratic corpus and Galen? The *Anonymus Londinensis* papyrus, dating from the second century AD but discovered only at the end of the nineteenth century, is thought to have been written by a pupil of Aristotle. It names many early medical writers who would otherwise be unknown. Galen too identifies a large number of lost medical writers, from classical Greece up to the generation of his own teachers (W. Jones 1947). The work of some can be reconstructed, if only at a very basic level, from the fragments preserved by Galen himself and by the encyclopedic writers of late antiquity, such as the fourth-century compiler Oribasius and his successors Aetius of Amida and Paul of Aegina. However, here as in other fields of ancient history, the use of fragments is far from straightforward (Hanson 1996). It is not always easy to distinguish between a direct quotation and a summary and, just as quotations can be taken out of their original context, summaries may be skewed in order to present an inaccurate view of the writer being quoted. In the past few decades, very valuable collections of the fragments of some of the lost medical writers have been produced: for example, Diokles (van der Eijk 2000), Herophilos (von Staden 1989), Erasistratos (Garofalo 1988), and the Methodists, followers of one of the ancient medical "sects" (Tecusan 2004).

2   Individuals and Groups

While the need to read much of ancient medicine through fragments twists the evidence in its own way, the mere existence of Galen, the most prolific prose writer of antiquity, doctor to emperors and the Roman elite, distorts our picture of ancient medicine. The son of a wealthy architect, no other doctor had his privileged upbringing (in the Roman empire, many practicing medicine were Greek slaves) or his extensive education. Born in Pergamon, where he was doctor to the gladiators, he spent much of his career in Rome, a city offering unparalleled opportunities for the ambitious man. His particular context within the lively debates between medical authorities in the city of Rome meant that his views on other individuals or medical groups were heavily biased. Bizarrely, this means that we sometimes know more about those of whose theories and practices he most disapproved; because he disagreed with the role of bloodletting in the medicine of the third-century Alexandrian writer, Erasistratos, we learn a good deal about work that would otherwise have been lost from Galen's *On Bloodletting, Against Erasistratos* (Brain 1986).

But while much of what we know of ancient medicine concerns named individuals, far more is anonymous, although hints of its authorship may remain. Within the Hippocratic corpus, some texts draw heavily on others; for example, in the field of women's medicine, the two volumes on *Diseases of Women* share material with *Nature of Woman* and also with the general treatise, *Aphorisms*. The relationship between them is not yet clear, nor is the explanation for the repetitions of case histories between some of the seven volumes of *Epidemics*. What is, however, obvious is that many Hippocratic texts are the work of several hands, over a period of time.

The "Hippocratic Oath," already mentioned, gives us one possibility for how different doctors worked together, showing a group within which relationships are modeled on those of the family; the one swearing the oath promises, for example, to look after his medical teacher if he is in need, and to treat his teacher's children like his own brothers (von Staden 1996). From evidence including inscriptions, we know of medical guilds in some ancient cities, with regular processions and sacrifices. While the image of the ancient doctor found in the Hippocratic texts is one of isolation, traveling between towns and villages in search of patients, in larger centers of population a group presence was possible.

It used to be thought that ancient medicine was organized into larger groupings, or "schools." This is an unfortunate term, as there is no evidence for such units in training, which was instead carried out within the family or on an apprenticeship basis, although it was always possible merely to assert your identity as a doctor, and then hope that the results justified the claim. It used to be thought that Hippocratic medicine was divided into the doctors of Kos and those of Knidos, with different theories and therapies being favored in each "school"; because the historical Hippocrates was associated with Kos, treatises which seemed to represent more effective medicine (read from a modern perspective) were assigned to the school of Kos (Thivel 1981). A third grouping was linked to Sicily. By the early Roman empire, three "sects" are named by some sources, such as Celsus; these are the rationalists, empiricists, and methodists. The rationalists (or dogmatic sect) emphasized the role of theory, while the empiricists (who went back to Philinos, a student of Herophilos) argued that theories were the wrong place to start, and direct observation of the patient was more important. The methodists – particularly successful in the Roman world – believed that all diseases in all patients could be divided into those characterized by relaxation/looseness, those featuring constriction/tightness, and those which have features of both. Whether these labels would have made sense to those to whom they were applied remains far from clear.

3   Medicine as Literature

One aspect of the historical remains of ancient medicine that is the subject of much recent work concerns the status of the sources as literature. Some of the sections of the Hippocratic corpus represent the earliest sustained examples of prose surviving, while Galen was the most prolific prose writer of antiquity. Why was writing so important to ancient medicine? In some cases, it could have been about gaining a wider audience, or demonstrating one's authority.

The Hippocratic corpus contains examples of texts demonstrating the features of literacy in its very earliest stages (Lonie 1983; Langholf 1990). In particular, some treatises are in the form of lists, reminiscent of inventories of treasure from the palace societies of early Greece. Once a list has been composed, it is relatively easy for its writer, or another user, to draw out shared features, which become more obvious once there is a written text to be read and reread; so, for example, in a list of aphorisms recording "A nosebleed is a good thing if the menstrual period is suppressed" and "Vomiting blood ceases if the menstrual period begins," the next stage would be to group these together, as indeed has happened in the text of the fifth part of the *Aphorisms.* This suggests that the current form of *Aphorisms* represents the second stage, and that there was once an earlier medical text from which it derives. The third stage would occur when somebody not only noted the similarities exposed by grouping similar points together, but went on to develop a theory to explain them.

For the ancient historian, one of the most seductive aspects of medical writing is its sense of immediacy and reality; a case history, such as those in the Hippocratic corpus that give the progress of a disease from day to day, or Galen's description of the woman sick with love for Pylades whose pulse changes when merely his name is mentioned (*Prog.* 6; Nutton 1979), seems to provide us with privileged, even unmediated access to the people of the classical world. This is, of course, an illusion. The case histories of the *Epidemics* are not like a modern hospital case history; we are not even sure of the audience or purpose for which they were written, or whether we have them in close to their original form, or only after several rewritings. Comments such as "Is this the rule in an abscess?" (*Epid.* 6.3.21) or "Does such excrement suggest a crisis, as in that of Antigenes?" (*Epid.* 2.3.11) suggest that they could be "notes to self" rather than something written for other people to read, meaning that even the unspoken assumptions behind them may need to be reconstructed. When the writer noted the season in which the illness began, this may be because he believed that the body was affected by the temperature and humidity of the time of year, or may be a reference to jog his memory when going back over his records.

Galen's case histories were rather different, being written in order to publicize his talents and enhance his reputation; their focus is therefore more on the doctor and the reactions of his audience than on the patient. His work *On Prognosis* opens with the comment that it is "impossible for most doctors to predict the things that will happen in each disease suffered by their patients." Instead of acquiring an accurate knowledge of medicine, most doctors spend their time pleasing their patrons, "going with them as they go home, and amusing them at dinner." But Galen's point is that he differs from "most doctors," and so, when he makes an accurate prediction of what will happen next in the course of a disease, to those ignorant of his methods he appears to be a "wonder-worker" (*Prog.* 1 and 8). This is represented by Galen as a dangerous reputation to have; he claims that Quintus, "the best doctor of his generation," was framed for murder by those envious of his talents and expelled from the city. This is very much a picture of medicine in the city of Rome, where several doctors can be assembled at the bedside of a sick person and engage in debate, and where considerable rivalry exists for the patronage of the wealthiest men.

Such rivalry was not only found between doctors, but extended to others caring for the sick. When the wife of Boethus was affected by a gynaecological complaint, she was too embarrassed to speak to the doctors, and instead consulted her midwives – who, Galen reckoned, "were the best in Rome." When their treatments were unsuccessful, Boethus called together the doctors and they agreed to follow Hippocratic methods, which they interpreted as being to administer drugs to dry out not only the womb, but the whole body (*Prog.* 8). This course also proved unsuccessful, but neither "reasoning" nor "experience" offered any alternatives. When the woman's nurse – also praised by Galen – was bathing her, she suddenly suffered severe pain and lost a considerable amount of watery fluid. Galen described her attendants "screaming and shouting," and he rushed in to rub her stomach and warm her extremities, telling the women to "stop standing uselessly about." The cure took place once Galen reflected on the feeling of the woman's stomach muscles and concluded that the warming and drying treatments – which included laying the woman on warm sand – should be altered. Instead, he rubbed her body with honey and tried to remove excess fluid through the skin rather than just from the bladder, before going on to treat her with dietary changes, purgatives, and more honey massages. His treatment regime lasted for 17 days – unthinkable except with an elite patient such as this – and Galen's reward for success was 400 *aurei*. When first-century AD Roman writers such as Pliny the Elder attacked Greek doctors, it was partly in terms of the enormous sums they demanded from their patients.

4 Culture Contact

A further theme addressed by the study of ancient medicine is how we tie together the stories of Greece and Rome. Pliny, enemy of over-priced, over-complicated, and over-talkative Greek doctors, also preserves a fragment of the historian Cassius Hemina that represents our only source for Archagathos, a Greek doctor who arrived in Rome to practice medicine in 219 BC (*HN* 29. 6.12–7.15). Why did he come? Could the Romans make any sense of him (Nijhuis 1995)? According to the story, he was welcomed with open arms and given privileges by the state, but was subsequently denounced as a "butcher."

Writers such as Cato and Pliny presented medicine as something that happened within the context of the family, under the *paterfamilias*; they praised their own traditional medicine based on a few household ingredients: wool, cabbage, milk. But although they claimed that these were traditional remedies, they may in turn have owed a good deal to the Greek; for example, the Greek Chrysippos wrote a book on the healing powers of cabbage. Would this picture of idealized self-sufficiency be duplicated for the Greeks, if only similar types of source material survived? Medical options would be greater for both Greeks and Romans in the big city, where a wider range of drugs would be sold in the market, as well as a wider range of types of healer being available. Because the focus on Rome is undoubtedly misleading, one of the main themes of recent work on Roman medicine looks at the different types of medicine practiced within the area influenced by Rome (Nutton 1993: Baker and Carr 2002); but in order to tell this story, we need to move away from the literary sources and concentrate instead on epigraphy and archaeology. Even in Italy, the range of medical activities was very different from what happened in the metropolis. For example, in the hills of central Italy lived the Marsi, Roman allies from the fourth century BC, whose skill in healing through snake venom and other remedies impressed even Galen: yet in southern Italy, where Greek influence had long been felt, doctors were part of a wider Greek medical forum, and both their theories and their professional groupings looked Greek. Nor was movement all one way, from Greece to Rome: by the early Roman empire, many drugs used in Greek pharmacopoeias used substances from Italy.

5 Women

Galen's references to nurses and midwives remind us that some of the alternatives to a doctor using Greek medicine were female (Demand 1994). While no writings by women survive in this field, Galen attributes some recipes to women, and Pliny refers to other named women healers (Flemming 2007). For example, Galen gives us "Spendousa's remedy for pus in the ears"; using pig bile and Attic honey, this does not seem any different from the remedies used by Greek men (*Comp. Med. Loc* 3.1, 12.631 Kühn; Flemming 2000).

The sheer amount of recipes in the Hippocratic treatises on women's diseases has sometimes been seen as evidence for a female origin for this material (von Staden 1992a; Dean-Jones 1994; H. King 1998). However, other than in its quantity, the material is very similar to what is found elsewhere in the corpus. Women are also described as the source for some of the more esoteric claims of the Hippocratic texts, for example the comment that prostitutes know when they have conceived and can make the conceptus fall out at will (*On Flesh* 19); this recalls the claim of the anonymous writer of *History of Animals* 10 that women emit "seed" after erotic dreams (*HA* 634b29–31; 635a34–36). But rather than real women, these may be imaginary women made up to impress one's fellow doctors (H. King 1995).

In response to any suggestion that women in the ancient world had their own, separate, medical knowledge handed down from mother to daughter, we may consider the story of the slave entertainer who finds she is pregnant and tells her owner, given in the Hippocratic *On Generation/Nature of the Child*. Far from having access to "women's lore," here the (female) owner of the girl does not know how to solve the problem and goes to her kinsman, the Hippocratic writer of the text. As in the idealized medicine of Rome, medicine functions within the family, and the owner has no hesitation in giving her relative, the doctor, access to this unrelated patient. This recalls the "Hippocratic Oath" and its quasi-familial structure, with each doctor enjoined to treat his teachers' family as his kin. The "Oath" also reveals considerable unease at giving non-family members access to the women of the family, described elsewhere as "possessions very precious indeed" (*The Doctor* 1); it seems that this is of less concern where the woman is a slave.

6 Ancient Patients

The thoughts of one, atypical, ancient patient survive in the work of Aelius Aristides, whose chronic ill health led him to spend long periods of time at another source of ancient medicine, the temple of Asclepius (Perkins 1995; H. King 1998: 126–30). Where older studies saw temple medicine as existing in opposition to the work of doctors, it is now clear that temples had resident doctors, and that, in Edelstein's memorable words, the god learned medicine from the doctors (Edelstein 1945, vol. 2: 144 and n.13; based on the words of Johannes Ilberg); in other words, that what was offered at the temples varied in relation to what was happening in medicine.

But other patients' stories survive in the Hippocratic *Epidemics*. In the seventeenth century, when detailed reports based on observation were regarded as particularly important, the *Epidemics* were rated very highly, because they provided day-by-day accounts of the progress of diseases in individual patients, but they still give us a range of insights into ancient medicine. A cobbler stabbed himself in the thigh with a needle when sowing the sole of a shoe, and died three days after, when the swelling in his leg had extended above his groin (*Epid.* 5.45). Other patients in this section of *Epidemics* are injured playing with their friends or running on rough roads; they fall off cliffs, are accidentally hit with a door, or are run over by a loaded cart. These case histories include many examples where the patients are self-medicating, indicating clearly that the doctor was not the first port of call. A young man drinks a medicine made of the root of the squirting cucumber – used as a purgative – but dies four days later (*Epid.* 5.34), while a woman drinks a purgative drug "for the sake of conception," but becomes very ill; she lives, but the only treatment that helps her is to pour large amounts of cold water over her body (*Epid.* 5.42). A man with a leg wound uses *attikon* – possibly Attic honey, as used by Spendousa – and comes out in a large red rash (*Epid.* 4.47). In the case of a boy injured in the head by a potsherd wielded by another child, the ensuing fever appears to be blamed on "the woman who washed the wound"; once the doctor is called, he performs trepanning (cutting a small hole in the skull), but this does not work, and the boy dies (*Epid.* 4.11). In these cases, the descriptions make sense even across the millennia. Others are far harder for us to understand; for example, a man in Abdera passes "things like lizards" (*Epid.* 4.56), while when the womb moves to touch the hip joints, there is "something like balls" in the stomach (*Places in Man* 47).

As we have seen with the pregnant slave entertainer, patients included slaves and servants too. In one passage, the Hippocratic doctor comments on examining a "newly purchased household servant-girl"; perhaps the purchaser, noticing her abdominal swelling, was worried that he had made a bad buy (*Epid.* 4.38). But we do not know if, for those accustomed to use doctors, such "medicals" were a normal part of household management.

7 Efficacy

The many centuries of use of ancient medical texts, in which different Hippocratic treatises have gone in and out of fashion, raises the issue of how we should assess the effectiveness of ancient medicine for its patients. Traditionally, efficacy was judged by setting ancient medicine alongside existing knowledge. If we no longer believe in the disease described – a classic example would be the "wandering womb" – then to what extent can we judge how effective the remedies given to cure it would have been?

One approach is to re-evaluate ancient drug treatments in the light of modern scientific study, investigating how the different ingredients would have affected the bodies of those on whom they were used. This is not easy, as the identification of plants used in ancient medicine is not always straightforward, and, furthermore, the amount of volatile oils they contained would depend on factors such as the soil in which they were grown, and the time of year at which they were harvested. One group of healers in the ancient world were the "root-cutters," who may have based their authority on precisely this kind of knowledge; drugs were also sold in the markets of large cities. The main problem in assessing ancient drugs by modern standards is that ancient medicine used "polypharmacy"; in other words, in most remedies several different ingredients were combined. Modern studies to date do not replicate this, but acknowledge that the combination would have had different effects than the use of ingredients in isolation. Another approach is to consider the plants and animals used in drugs as having value because their users made culturally specific connections between them and myths or rituals (Totelin 2007). Two examples from the gynaecological texts can illustrate this. Animal excrement was used in women's disorders, perhaps to remove "bad" substances by sympathy, perhaps as fertilizer for the womb, widely compared to a field in Greek literature (von Staden 1992a). The *vitex agnus castus*, or "chaste tree," used in gynaecological remedies, was also employed in the Thesmophoria, where it was placed under the couches of the women taking part in the ritual, to ensure their chastity during the three days in which they took part in the ceremonies, and/or their subsequent fertility on returning to normal life (von Staden 1992b).

Comparative work in anthropology suggests a third alternative. This is to think outside the context of drug treatments, and instead to concentrate on the explanations for ill health and for the remedies used given by doctors. According to this approach, illness means a breach in the patient's ability to make sense of existence; the patient's "story" is broken and the role of the doctor is to help fix it (Brody 1987) by creating a narrative, telling "the Good Story" (French 2003). We can see evidence of this in the Hippocratic *Epidemics*. The statement that the fever suffered by the wife of Euxenos "seemed to come from the steam bath" (*Epid.* 7.50) suggests an attempt to find a cause by looking into the recent past for anything unusual, as do the comments that the man from Baloia "had been very careless in his way of life" (*Epid.* 7.17), or that pain in the chest and ribs affected the wife of Simos, "shaken in childbirth" (*Epid.* 7.49). However, shaking was an established remedy to speed up a difficult birth, so this could be seen as a condition caused by previous medical treatment. The Hippocratic *Prognostics* also suggests that the doctor can tell the patient their past, present and future, again suggesting the creation of a story to explain the symptoms, and also to give the hope of a successful outcome. This story, on its own, was not always sufficient; the wife of Euxenos died. However, the focus on the story supports the suggestion that ancient medicine grew out of common beliefs. Just as medical language was based on everyday vocabulary, so medical theories may well have been only a little more developed than what people already believed; if the public did not believe in the importance of keeping their fluids in balance, it is hard to see how the Hippocratics, or even Galen, could have persuaded them.

FURTHER READING

H. King 2001 provides a short introduction to the subject; while Nutton 2003 is a detailed and comprehensive work, it is daunting for the beginner and despite its appearance as a text-book it contains much that remains controversial. Van der Eijk et al. 1995 is a very useful collection of essays on a range of topics, demonstrating different approaches to ancient medicine. Those interested in women's diseases will find useful for Greek material Dean-Jones 1994, Demand 1994 and H. King 1998; for Roman material, much less studied in this field, Flemming 2003. Roman medicine is covered by Jackson 1988 and now also by Cruse 2003; both make considerable use of archaeological materials, but the most innovative work on this front is that of Baker (e.g. 2004). Lloyd 1979 and 1983 set the agenda in terms of locating ancient medicine within a wider social and cultural context; Lloyd 2004 is recommended as a set of essays on key themes which also gives the most important primary sources. Medicine from the patient's point of view was a topic that developed in the 1980s but took some time to find its place in studies of the ancient world. Perkins 1995 looked at why the sources allow us to look at this topic more effectively for the second century AD, and H. King 1998 includes an attempt to link this theme to the wider sociological literature of chronic pain. For those interested in the subsequent fortunes of the ancient medical texts, W. Smith 1979 remains a very important study of the way in which Galen's own views have influenced the history of medicine, online at www.bium.univ-paris5.fr/amn/Hippo2.pdf, while Cunningham 1997 and French 2003 set the ancient materials within a wider context of the history of medicine. English translations of the main Hippocratic writings can be found in the Loeb Classical Library.

Useful websites:
Medicina Antiqua which includes articles on a range of medical topics:
    www.ucl.ac.uk/~ucgajpd/medicina%20antiqua
The Asclepion, created for teaching by Nancy Demand:
    www.indiana.edu/~ancmed/into.HTM
"Greek Medicine," National Library of Medicine, originally part of an exhibition, with links to rare printed editions of the ancient texts:
    www.nlm.nih.gov/hmd/greek/index.html

CHAPTER THIRTY-SIX

Death

David Noy

1 Dying Well

No death in the ancient world had more of an impact than that of Socrates. Plato's account ensured that it had a literary circulation not matched until the development of Christian literature on the crucifixion of Jesus and martyrs' deaths. Far from being depicted as the execution of a convicted criminal, it came to be seen as the archetypal good death: a suicide freely chosen with divine approval by someone who talked meaningfully to his friends as he slipped painlessly into oblivion. The image may owe more to Plato's literary skill than to the realities of death by hemlock poisoning in a state prison (although his much-doubted accuracy is defended by Bloch in Brickhouse and Smith 2002), but its influence was felt among the Roman elite even into the Christian period; Greeks and Romans died at their own hands with the *Phaedo* next to them.

The nature of a "good death" varied according to time, place, and context. Suetonius (*Aug.* 99) describes how the emperor Augustus died peacefully and painlessly as he had wished: "For almost every time he heard that someone had died swiftly or with no pain, he used to pray for a similar *euthanasia* – for he used this word too – for himself and his family." A cultural difference is highlighted in the fact that Augustus said his last words to his wife, while Socrates' wife was not with him when he died – the women and children were dismissed to avoid a display of emotion. Augustus's death, although "good," was hardly in the heroic tradition of glorious death in battle, achieving honor for self and country, typified by the supposed regulation at Sparta (Plut. *Lyc.* 27) that the only people who could have their names on tombs were men who died in battle and women who died in childbirth. At Athens, death in battle was "rewarded" by a place in an annual state funeral and collective tomb, with a funeral oration spoken by a leading citizen. The Romans, however, did not normally provide honors at home for their war dead.

Death could also be represented as a test which had to be passed; hence the admiration for courage and resolution shown by gladiators in the face of death, which could be seen as an example to everyone. Philosophical advice on how to approach death could concentrate on the rational argument that there was nothing to fear and death could be a positive good in some circumstances. The Epicurean view of death as an instant return to the same state of nothingness as before one was born is paralleled in the Roman epitaphs which read: "I didn't exist, I existed, I don't exist, I don't care."

Suicide raised some ethical questions. In general, attitudes were favorable to it, especially among the Roman elite for whom it was an acceptable solution to loss of quality of life, and sometimes a dignified and legally advantageous way out of a difficult position. The story of Lucretia's suicide after she was raped (Livy 1.57–58) was a foundation myth for the Roman republic, even if some of the issues it raised (e.g. her defiance of male authority when she killed herself) were not fully explored. A brave suicide, such as those of Cleopatra and the emperor Otho, could help to repair a damaged reputation. There are, however, hints of a different viewpoint: special places for suicides in some versions of the underworld; a cemetery from which those who hanged themselves were excluded (*CIL* I.2123). Method also made a difference: stabbing was particularly admired for women; opening the veins tended to be the method preferred by aristocratic Romans; hanging was disapproved for men. At Athens in the Roman period, the bodies of people who hanged themselves were thrown into a pit along with the executed. Some philosophical movements, including Platonism, rejected suicide because it meant opting out of the lifespan allotted by the gods.

For those who did not die in battle, the best end was like Augustus's, at home, surrounded by family or friends, in possession of one's faculties and in full control of events until the last. In 115 BC Q. Caecilius Metellus Macedonicus "died at a very advanced age, and by a kind form of death, amid the kisses and embraces of his dearest children" (Val. Max. 7.1.1), happy in his own and his children's good fortune. The idealized deathbed provided, among other things, the opportunity to produce some memorable last words, such as Vespasian's "Oh dear, I think I'm becoming a god" (Suet. *Vesp.* 23). Practical arrangements could be made, and dependents committed to someone's care. The reverse, dying alone and away from home, was always to be feared, both at the time of death (when there would be no one to perform the required rituals) and afterwards, when the funeral and tomb would be neglected. Rites such as closing the dying person's eyes and mouth or catching their last breath do not seem to have been given particular significance in terms of the soul's destiny, but were a comfort through symbolizing companionship and care (fig. 36.1). Deathbed repentance was largely a Christian innovation; pagans who believed in an afterlife did not think that it depended on one's state of mind at the point of death.

Executions should have been the opposite of dying well, but hemlock poisoning at Athens and enforced suicide at Rome gave people the opportunity to imitate a good death. Rome reserved a deliberately bad death for those who were crucified or thrown to the wild beasts – slaves and non-citizens until the late empire. Such deaths were intended as a deterrent and an act of revenge: crucifixion of rebels led to roads lined with crosses, and executions in the arena enabled the audience to unite in a collective Roman identity from which the victims had been excluded. The traditional

36.1 Sarcophagus, c.160/170 AD, with the death of Meleager. This mythological scene shows some of the ideals of real deathbeds, with the hero in a sleep-like pose surrounded by attendants; the mourning Atalanta is depicted on the right. (Dep. des Antiquités Grecques et Romaines, Musée du Louvre, Paris, Ma 654.) (Photo: akg-images/Erich Lessing)

punishment for parricide (to be sewn in a sack with a snake, cock, dog and monkey and drowned in the Tiber) was supposed to be so extreme that it would never be enforced. The execution of unchaste Vestal Virgins through burial alive in a special underground chamber was intended to combine maximum publicity and horror (through a public parade) with a superstitious avoidance of directly killing someone consecrated to divine service. The first case of a dramatized execution was in the time of Augustus when the Sicilian bandit Selurus was killed by beasts on a collapsing model of Etna (Strabo 6.273); after this, real deaths in mythological re-enactments became commonplace.

Desecration of the body after death, something regularly practiced on enemies during Rome's civil strife of the first century BC, was an exacerbation of (or substitute for) execution, and denial of burial at home (or burial of any sort) could be a punishment in itself; its tragic consequences are explored in Sophocles' *Antigone*. The executed might be thrown into the Tiber, and this also happened to the corpse of the emperor Vitellius – and would have happened to Tiberius too if an element in the crowd had had its way. But if the authorities went too far and allowed the audience to sympathize with the victim of execution, as in the cases of some Christian martyrs, dying bravely earned admiration and sympathy.

2 Funerals

Greek funerals, particularly Athenian ones, are illustrated by vase-paintings as well as being described in literature. In the works of Homer, a hero's funeral involves games, extravagant gestures of mourning by men, large-scale animal and even human sacrifice, and cremation on a massive pyre. Some of these elements were replicated in reality, but Athens (through Solon in 594 BC) and other Greek states tried to control the scale of funerals because of the disruption which could be caused when they were used for political purposes. The body was washed, dressed, and laid out for the *prothesis*. This was presumably the point at which a coin was placed in the mouth for Charon's fare, but this custom is attested archaeologically only from the Hellenistic period, and its frequency varied very much according to time and place (Morris 1992: 106). Mourners around the body (particularly female ones; the Homeric acceptance of emotional displays by men later declined) are characterized in art by disheveled clothing and torn hair and cheeks. The opportunity for lamentation, and presumably appeasement of the deceased's soul, seems to have been the main purpose of the *prothesis*, rather than the need to ensure that death really had occurred (Pl. *Laws* 12.959a).

The funeral procession itself had to take place before sunrise under Solon's legislation, and took the body with musical accompaniment to the place of cremation or burial. In classical Greece, cremation and inhumation were both practiced, but inhumation became commoner in the Hellenistic period. Where cremation was used, a pyre was specially built for one individual, and it was one of the horrors of the Athenian plague that corpses were cremated on pyres meant for others (Thuc. 52.4). The body or cremated remains were placed in a tomb along with grave-goods, and this is the reason for the preservation of the bulk of surviving Greek vases. Relatives took part in a banquet at the end of the funeral, at which the deceased was present symbolically. Meals for the deceased alone were prepared at the tomb on the third and ninth days (counting from the day of death or burial). A ritual on the thirtieth day after the death marked the end of strict mourning, at least at Athens. Some temples banned (for a variable length of time) people who were polluted through contact with a corpse, and there were social expectations of what those in mourning should not do.

There is very little artistic evidence for Roman funerals: just one relief from Amiternum (probably from the late first century BC) depicting a procession with mourners, musicians, and pall bearers (fig. 36.2); and a scene on the tomb of the Haterii at Rome (late first/early second century AD) showing a woman's laid-out body with assembled mourners and musicians. The classic description of a Roman funeral by Polybius (6.53–54) can only ever have applied to a limited number of elite families, and only to their adult members, as children's funerals were held at night and with limited rites; women began to receive large-scale funerals in the first century BC, after Polybius's time. The model he describes for the second century BC was adopted for emperors' funerals; until Vespasian, the emperors came from families which would have had this sort of funeral anyway. The body was carried to the Rostra in the

36.2 Relief from Amiternum showing a funeral procession (probably late first century BC). The widow and children are shown to the left of the deceased, while the musicians and mourning women to the right lead the procession. (L'Aquila, Museo d'Arte Nazionale d'Abruzzo.) (Photo: akg-images/Nimatallah)

Forum, where the son or other relative delivered a eulogy to the assembled people. In the procession, chariots carried actors who wore the masks (*imagines*) of deceased ancestors. The masks were normally kept in wooden "shrines" in the atrium of the family home. They were made of wax, and were evidently expected to be a recognizable likeness, but they were not death-masks since they represented people in the prime of life. According to Polybius, "It would be hard to imagine a more impressive scene for a young man who aspires to win fame and to practice virtue."

For Polybius, the important part of the funeral took place in the Forum, and he barely mentions what happened before or afterwards. Professional undertakers were available, and at Puteoli an inscription (*AE* 1971.88; Hinard and Dumont 2003) shows that a contractor had a monopoly on funerals (and also on carrying out the city's corporal punishments and punishing and executing slaves). Between death and the funeral, the corpse was laid out in the atrium of the home, and mourners, including hired women, performed *conclamatio*, the ritual calling of the deceased's name, around it. Cremation was the normal rite for the people Polybius was interested in, although the Cornelii practiced inhumation until the death of L. Cornelius Sulla in 78 BC; Sulla's cremation after (apparently) Rome's first state funeral was intended to prevent his remains being desecrated.

Roman cremation, as described in literary sources and depicted very rarely in art, usually involved the body being placed on top of a box-shaped pyre, which was lit by a torch. Only the close family would be expected to stay to the end of the cremation, which might last up to eight hours, after which the pyre was ritually quenched (often with wine) and the remains of the bones were gathered for burial. Julius Caesar's cremation lasted through the night, and large crowds remained at the pyre; Livia stayed for five days by Augustus's. Cremated remains, placed in a special container (*cinerarium*), could be transported long distances, as when Agrippina brought the remains of Germanicus from Syria to Rome. After the remains were placed in the tomb, there was a meal there for the remaining mourners (*silicernium*), and another on the ninth day (*cena novendialis*). From 264 BC, an aristocratic funeral might be followed, and effectively prolonged, by gladiatorial games, but these were controlled by Augustus and apparently stopped under Tiberius; gladiators became an imperial monopoly and lost their original funerary function.

Archaeology has allowed something of the funerary rites of provincial Romans to be recovered. There must have been substantial variations according to time and place, but recurring finds include burnt food from offerings which were thrown on the pyre; crockery which was ritually broken; bones from animal sacrifices; objects placed in the tomb with the deceased's remains, including crockery, food, drink, jewelry, clothing, tools (the best finds of medical instruments come from tombs), utensils, perfumes, lamps, coins, and gaming-counters. In the *Iliad* (23.50–51), Achilles asks Agamemnon to provide the dead Patroklos with "all that is fitting for the dead man to have when he goes down under the gloom and darkness," but it is not clear even there, let alone in the Roman world, that the objects were thought to be transferred directly for use in the underworld, and archaeology shows that some pottery was faulty and could not have been in normal use. Food and drink played a bigger part than would be expected from the literary texts. Lucian (*Luct.*15) says that the real motive for all the show of funerals is "the impression it will make on the other mourners." The cremated remains might be carefully separated from the pyre debris or left mixed with it. The remains were most often placed in a ceramic container, but it might be made of glass, metal, stone, or something perishable: wood, cloth or leather.

3 Tombs

Tombs normally had to be outside cities, and even Augustus's Mausoleum in the Campus Martius was outside Rome's religious boundary (*pomerium*). This regulation seems to have been understood as deriving from death-pollution, but may really have involved hygienic or practical considerations. Burial within a city was usually reserved for a founder or someone equivalent, such as Alexander the Great at Alexandria. The provision of a tomb at public expense was an exceptional honor, e.g. to the Athenian war dead, or individual members of civic elites. Normally the building of tombs was a matter of private enterprise, and some tomb builders (particularly in Roman Asia Minor) went to considerable lengths to protect their tomb, formally cursing anyone who violated it or imposing a fine payable to a public body such as a city council, which was thus given a vested interest in watching for violation. In practice, the reuse and destruction of tombs were clearly common.

Archaic Greek tombs were sometimes marked by mounds, statues or stelai, and heroic imagery could link the deceased to the world of myth. Tall vases (*lekythoi*) were popular tomb markers at Athens in the fifth century BC, perhaps because more elaborate ones were forbidden – a law probably from the sixth century limited tombs to the work which ten men could do in three days, and restraint was normal throughout Greece in the fifth century. Elaborate tomb markers developed at Athens in the late 5th century BC, possibly as a result of the skilled sculptors who had worked on the Parthenon needing to create new commissions, or (Morris 1992: 129) through a desire to imitate the honors which the state gave to the war dead. In the fourth century BC, the wealthy established family plots (*periboloi*), particularly well attested in the Kerameikos and at Rhamnous, but in 317 BC Demetrios of Phaleron banned elaborate tomb markers, and there was a return to restraint.

Early Greek epitaphs were in verse. They could address the passer-by in the voice of the tomb or of the deceased. Prose epitaphs might consist of no more than the deceased's name, perhaps with a patronymic (and further details such as a name and ethnic or demotic). Sometimes details of the commemorator are given, but this is more a Roman phenomenon. Information about the deceased included achievements and, more usually, virtues. Apart from the obvious function of identifying who was in the tomb beyond the period of living memory, epitaphs were also intended to preserve the memory of the deceased indefinitely, if only by making a literate passer-by read the name and share in the grief (particularly if the death was a "bad" one through youth or circumstances), effectively continuing the lamentation of the funeral. A later development (from the fourth century BC; Sourvinou-Inwood 1995: 181) was the use of the epitaph to greet the deceased personally with the expression *chaire*, and other reflections of belief in the afterlife for the ordinary dead also begin to be found.

Visiting the tomb of a relative was a significant ritual at Athens. Legal texts make it important for men in proving genuine kinship, while vase-paintings depict women carrying offerings to tombs decorated with ribbons. It would have been one of the few acceptable reasons for a respectable Athenian woman to leave home without her husband. Apart from individual anniversaries, the day of mourning called Genesia was fixed by Solon on 5th Boedromion, and there was also a nocturnal festival for the dead called Nemeseia. In the Hellenistic period, wealthy people began to set up trusts which would produce an income to ensure that the tomb was maintained and the deceased honored, rather than relying on the family.

The best example of the mindset of a Roman who commissioned a tomb is provided by the fictional wealthy freedman Trimalchio in the *Satyricon*. His creator Petronius clearly intended him as a humorous caricature of the *nouveaux riches* of the Neronian period. Trimalchio insists on reading out his will at dinner. Wealthy Romans paid much more attention in their wills to their tombs than their funerals, for reasons which Trimalchio makes clear. The tomb which Trimalchio commissioned during his lifetime has many resemblances to the more elaborate surviving tombs. It was to include a statue of the deceased (so that "I'll be able to live on after I'm dead"), along with scenes from his life and depictions of his wife, dog, and favorite slave-boy and gladiator. There would be an orchard and vineyard around the tomb, a freedman to protect it, and an elaborate epitaph. The area of 200 × 100 feet was very large, although exceeded by real examples, e.g. one of 375 × 300 feet (Narbonne, *CIL* XII 4449). There would also be a sundial so that anyone who looked at the time would have to read Trimalchio's name, "like it or not." Trimalchio refers to the tomb as a house where he will live after death, but it is not clear if he means this literally or if he is thinking of the immortality in people's memories which the tomb will give him.

Eye-catching tombs could be on a very large scale: the cylindrical tomb of Caecilia Metella and the pyramid of Gaius Cestius are still well-known landmarks in Rome. However, Augustus's Mausoleum dwarfed all potential competition around the city, and seems to have led to ostentatious monuments becoming largely the preserve of freedmen and municipal elites rather than the Roman aristocracy. Trimalchio's tomb may have been something like that of the Iulii at Glanum (and various similar ones), where a podium decorated with mythological battle scenes was surmounted by a four-way arch and then a circular *tholos* containing statues of the deceased.

Tombs were meant to be seen, hence their proliferation near the roads leading out of cities, as can now be seen clearly at Ostia, Pompeii, and on the Via Appia at Rome. Landes (2002) has shown the great variety of elaborate tombs in Gaul, difficult to sort into a typology, and with no trend towards uniformity or direct imitation. At Rome, some of the most enthusiastic participants in tomb building were ex-slaves, who in the late first century BC tended to have themselves portrayed in marital or family groups with archetypal Roman dress and features, to match their Roman names and disguise their non-Roman origins. Family tombs often specified that they were for the founder's ex-slaves as well as (or even instead of) direct descendants. This device increased the number of people with an interest in caring for the tomb, and ensured that it would be used by those who shared the founder's family name.

For those who could not afford a recognizable tomb, archaeological evidence shows that individual burial might take place in an amphora or a grave lined with tiles. An area which appears to contain *puticuli* (pits for mass burial) was discovered at Rome on the Esquiline in the nineteenth century. It seems only to have been used until the first century BC, and it is likely that mass cremation was used in the city after that. Abandoned corpses were a recurrent problem for other municipal authorities. Respectable burial was made available to a broader social spectrum through the development of high-density tombs (with capacity in the hundreds or even thousands), often partly below ground level, whose walls were lined with niches for *cineraria*. The modern name for such a tomb is columbarium, the Latin word for dovecote. It was a development brought about by a specific set of circumstances at Rome: the practice of cremation; the existence of large numbers of people who desired permanent individual commemoration but could not afford (or find space for) traditional family tombs; the development of societies with funerary and religious functions which received state acceptance if not outright approval, and which took over the family's role of protecting and maintaining the tomb; the availability of sites around the edge of the city, mainly provided by wealthy benefactors.

When the custom changed from cremation to inhumation, the catacomb took over the role of the columbarium, something which would probably have happened even if Christianity had not become the dominant religion. A catacomb is a high-density burial area in which the walls of underground galleries and chambers are lined with body-sized recesses (usually slots running parallel to the gallery, known as *loculi*). The development of the catacombs involved various factors, including the existence around Rome of large areas of tufa, a volcanic stone which was relatively easy to cut but stable enough not to collapse; the cooperation and ultimately control of the Church; the desire to be buried among coreligionists and near the remains of saints. Christian principles meant that burial in catacombs was available to the poor, unlike the columbaria. Catacombs are a more widespread phenomenon across the Roman empire than columbaria, and they have some resemblance to more traditional forms of burial from the Eastern provinces. Recent studies have suggested putting back the date of the catacombs' origins at Rome to the first century AD, but the incorporation of clearly pagan tombs in some of them shows that they were generally a late development in areas which already had a funerary use.

During the second and third centuries AD, in Italy and the Western provinces, there was a general change from cremation to inhumation, where the whole body was buried, normally in some sort of container: archaeology suggests that wooden coffins were often used, but sarcophagi are the most spectacular and enduring form, and lead coffins also came into use in the third century. The change was on a scale not repeated again until the reverse change in some of western Europe in the late twentieth century, yet it has left no real trace in surviving literature; it is known only from archaeological evidence, and its motivation is still debated. Those at the top (emperors, although there is some doubt about which rites were used for which emperors) and on the fringes (rural Gaul, Britain) were among the last to change, but most people made the change within a few decades, to the extent that tombs built for cremation burials were hastily adapted to take inhumations. It is too early to be connected to Christian influence, although it may represent a mindset which subsequently proved susceptible to Christianity. There is no evidence that it was connected to any altered belief about the afterlife. Nero's decision to have Poppaea "not cremated in the Roman fashion, but stuffed with spices and embalmed in the manner of foreign potentates" was not an encouraging precedent, and struck Tacitus (*Ann.*16.6), writing half a century later, as odd. Contributory factors were probably the influence of people and cults from the Greek-speaking provinces where inhumation had remained the norm; the availability of mass-produced sarcophagi; the trend setting of members of the elite at Rome; the expense of cremation in the city of Rome. None of these is sufficient in itself to provide an explanation, and it seems that to some extent the change built up its own momentum, helped by cultural homogenization across the provinces (Morris 1992: 31–69). The Romans themselves believed that inhumation was the traditional rite, and this was one of the justifications used by Christians for their rejection of cremation; cremation was, however, already practiced in the West before the Roman takeover.

4   The Afterlife

Belief in an underworld with regions, landmarks and a fully functioning governmental system was not as widespread as might be imagined. It is not how Homer depicts the world of the dead, and some of its fullest descriptions come from texts of the Roman empire (particularly Lucian, *Luct.*) and epitaphs which deny its existence.

Hypereides (6.43), in the funeral oration for the Athenian war dead of 322 BC, expressed considerable ambiguity: "But if in Hades we are conscious still and cared for by some god, as we are led to think . . ." Plutarch regarded disbelief in the afterlife as normal, whereas Lucian thought that most people still believed in the underworld.

Greek writers including Aristophanes and Euripides refer to aspects of the afterlife from which a picture of the conventional literary view can be reconstructed; many of the details were borrowed by Romans such as Vergil and Ovid – and also, in order to deny their veracity, by Cicero. It involved the soul (*psyche*) of the deceased being led by Hermes the *psychopompos* (or, in vase-painting, the brothers Death and Sleep) to the edge of the underworld, where Charon ferried it across a stretch of water, usually understood as the River Acheron. It was then judged and went to eternal reward (in the Elysian Fields), punishment, or something in between. Cerberus the multi-headed dog prevented the dead from leaving. The underworld was ruled by Hades (also called Pluto), whose name was used for the realm itself too. However, the variations are more numerous than the consistencies, e.g. in Plato's and Vergil's versions the souls are waiting for reincarnation. Herakles in Aristophanes' *Frogs* mentions the happy afterlife of initiates of the Eleusinian Mysteries, and privileges in the afterlife were one of the benefits offered by mystery cults. Texts on gold leaves found in tombs, traditionally called Orphic, but more probably Pythagorean, give very detailed instructions to their bearers about where to go in the underworld. Eternal punishment tended to be imagined as the fate of epic sinners like Sisyphos and Ixion rather than ordinary people, and they are sometimes depicted on Roman sarcophagi. However, Plato makes Socrates (*Grg.*523a–524a) describe how Kronos ordained that the righteous should go to the Isles of the Blessed and the wicked to Tartaros, and Zeus established that his sons Minos, Rhadamanthys and Aiakos should judge the souls only after death so as not to be misled by beauty or status.

Ovid (*Met.* 4.439–45) is among those who conceived the underworld as a continuation of people's earthly existence ("some crowd the Forum . . . some pursue various trades, imitations of their former life"), a view which was presumably attractive to the leisured and wealthy but not to those who had to work hard for a living. Greek and Roman tomb reliefs often depict banquets, suggesting a popular view of the afterlife as a long feast. Some tombs contain a libation tube through which offerings could be made. This implies a belief that the deceased in the tomb needed to be "fed," something which Lucian mentions as a popular idea. A variation is found in the tombs which contain a dining-room where relatives could share a meal with the deceased. People who asked for their tombs to be decorated, e.g. with roses at the Rosalia festival, may also have thought that they would somehow benefit in their post-death existence, rather than just wanting their memory prolonged. The very common formula in Latin epitaphs "may the earth be light for you" may also indicate, or at least refer back to, a belief in continued existence within the tomb.

Roman epitaphs around the second century AD regularly began with the formula *Dis Manibus,* which was so common that it was often inscribed (as the abbreviation D.M.) on blank stones before a specific epitaph had been commissioned. Despite this, it is unclear exactly what was understood by it. In literature, the *Manes* are the souls of the deceased, originally referred to collectively but gradually given individual identity. *Di Manes* should therefore be the deified deceased, but people clearly did not believe that every mortal became a god, and how could one person have plural *Di Manes*? It seems more likely that they represent the inhabitants of the underworld in general, now including the deceased of the epitaph.

Many people apparently considered that burial of some sort was necessary to lay the deceased to rest. Several ghost stories involve the discovery of unburied or inadequately buried remains whose interment ends the haunting; Caligula was a notable example (Suet. *Calig.* 59). Murder could also lead to the perpetrator being pursued by a ghost, or (as in the mythological case of Orestes, consciously recalled by Nero) by the Furies on the victim's behalf. The annual Roman ceremonies of the Parentalia and Lemuria could lead to general hauntings if not properly performed; it was also believed that a pit called the *mundus* gave access from the underworld three times a year. The possibility of calling up the dead deliberately through necromancy is first mentioned by Homer, but Odysseus has to travel to the world of the dead to do it. There are occasional literary references to necromancy from the upper world, often performed by witches, and legal regulations against rituals in cemeteries may indicate that it was a real practice too.

The spread of Christianity led to some changed attitudes and practices concerning death, without entirely replacing the pagan traditions. Cremation had already gone out of fashion before Christianity became the dominant religion in the fourth century AD; Christians claimed that their use of inhumation was Rome's true ancient tradition, but it also reflected Jewish custom. Christianity gave great importance to the spiritual state of a dying person, introducing practices such as deathbed baptism and extreme unction; suicide ceased to be acceptable. It should also have given the dying a feeling of certainty about what awaited them, since belief in a specific sort of afterlife became a religious requirement rather than a matter for the individual. The Church gradually took control of funerals and burials, which had previously been a secular matter. In some other respects there was considerable continuity: Fourth- and fifth-century Christian literature is full of deathbed scenes in which the dying person's orchestration of events and the mourners' displays of emotion show little difference from the pagan past, much to the displeasure of the writers who recorded them.

FURTHER READING

For the Greek world, the most helpful general survey is Garland 2001. For tombs, Kurtz and Boardman 1971 remains a good general guide. More sophisticated approaches, respectively based on texts, archaeology and anthropology, are offered by Sourvinou-Inwood 1995, Morris 1987 and Humphreys 1983. Alexiou 2002 studies funerary rituals and lament; Loraux 1998 deals with mourning by women. The sources for Socrates' death, along with discussion, are in Brickhouse and Smith 2002. Philosophical views of death are discussed by Warren 2004.

For the Roman world, J. Toynbee 1971 provides a very wide-ranging introduction; Walker 1985 is much briefer and copiously illustrated. Carroll 2006 covers western Europe. Aristocratic funerals are dealt with by Flower 1996, and there are some important papers on the treatment of the dead in Hope and Marshall 2000. The fullest discussion of the inscription from Puteoli is now Hinard and Dumont 2003. Executions and death in the arena are discussed by Kyle 1998, and Coleman 1990 is an important study of theatrical executions. Hopkins 1983 pioneered a sociological approach to Roman death. Champlin 1991 is a thorough study of Roman wills.

P. Davies 2000 studies emperors' tombs. There are monographs on sarcophagi by Koortbojian 1995 and Huskinson 1996; the German series *Die antiken Sarkophagreliefs* provides a large number of catalogs and discussions of sarcophagi with specific themes. Stevenson 1978 is a good introduction to the catacombs, although much evidence has come to light more recently. Greek and Roman archaeological evidence is analyzed by Morris 1992; numerous collections of papers on Roman funerary archaeology include Reece 1977, Pearce et al. 2000 and Landes 2002. Various aspects of Greek and Roman funerary epigraphy are covered by Oliver 2000.

The afterlife throughout antiquity (including the Near East) is studied by J. Davies 1999; the most influential work on this topic is Cumont 1922, and other interpretations of some aspects can be found in Bremmer 2002. See also Felton 1999 on ghosts and Ogden 2001 on necromancy. Van Hooff 1990 looks at suicide throughout antiquity; Hill 2004 concentrates on Roman literary evidence.

PART VI

Economy

CHAPTER THIRTY-SEVEN

The Mediterranean and the History of Antiquity

R. Bruce Hitchner

1 Introduction

The Mediterranean as a thematic historic framework was first posited by Fernand Braudel (Braudel 1949: 1972). He ambitiously extended the powerful French geographical concept of the *paysage* to the world's largest inland sea (c.2.5 million square miles), its coasts and islands. Braudel envisioned a Mediterranean world that was broadly homogeneous both ecologically and culturally. Despite its breathtaking force and enormous appeal, Braudel's vision did not achieve broad interdisciplinary acceptance. Nevertheless, the allure of the Mediterranean as a concept has not deterred those drawn to it from asserting its vitality or at least its relative competitive strength in the heated modern market of ideas on the relationship between human history, space, and time (Abulafia 2003). The appeal of a distinctively Mediterranean history has recently attracted anew the interest of students of antiquity, and particularly of Greco-Roman culture, not only because of the congruence between the latter and the sea, but also because of its perceived potential as a mega-model capable of absorbing and sorting the enormous richness and diversity of the human history of antiquity. Indeed that interest has crystallized around the emergence of a new vision of the unity of Mediterranean history that contends that it is a function of the region's ecological diversity, i.e. a space comprised, *contra* Braudel, of multiple, diverse *paysages* or regions, which compelled repeated and ever more complex forms of human connectivity and interaction (Horden and Purcell 2000). Such a vision privileges space and environment over time and human institutions as primordial forces in the shaping of the history of the Mediterranean prior to the modern period. In its favor, this is perhaps the most all-embracing approach to that past. However, as this chapter will argue, time, the evolution of human institutions, and even the great land masses on which those institutions rested, must share the stage with the vast seascape of the Mediterranean if we are to understand the place of the latter in the shaping of the history of antiquity.

2 Defining the Mediterranean

That we know the Mediterranean as the world's largest inland sea is a consequence of the Age of Discovery. And in conceptualizing it as a single large sea, we have attempted to comprehend its geography and ecology within that framework. So, in structural terms, the sea is understood to be compartmentalized into eastern and western basins separated by the Italian peninsula and Sicily. And within each basin, the northern coasts are distinguished from those along North Africa and the Levant by long indented coastlines providing numerous opportunities for secure harborage.

One of the problems of viewing the whole of the Mediterranean as a space unto itself is that it is often decontextualized from the spaces surrounding it and the influences they exerted upon it. This is most notable with respect to the Sahara. The Mediterranean is more profoundly affected by its proximity to the world's largest desert than the temperate climatic forces of Europe to its north. Were it not for the climatic effects emanating northward from the desert, the famed "Mediterranean" climate of hot, dry summers and mild, intermittently rainy winters (sub-regional variations notwithstanding) would not exist. Indeed the great inland sea and the Sahara share much in common in "operat[ing] as bridges as well as barriers, as contact and exchange zones, places of work, habitation and transit" (Quinn, NORTH AFRICA).

It is also possible to conceptualize a specific Mediterranean ecology shaped by a combination of climate, the sea and a predominantly limestone landscape combining mountains, tablelands, wetland, desert, and islands that together foster a characteristic vegetation that includes various types of conifers, the Holm Oak, pistachio, carob, fig, maquis (the latter also a product of fire), and, most famously, the cultivation of the so-called Mediterranean triad of cereals, vines, and olives (Blake and Knapp 2006; Sallares, ENVIRONMENTAL HISTORY).

Thus there is much that lends itself to the modern idea of the Mediterranean as a definable physical space within the larger world of south-west Eurasia and northern Africa. But, apart from Braudel and those who have held to a mytho-romantic view of the Mediterranean, this unitary framework has not achieved universal acceptance among historians, social scientists, and even modern policy makers (Horden and Purcell 2000; Morris 2003). The reasons for this are many, but in essence all aggregate around two opposing poles: the first, that it is too large a space, however defined, to be held together by a single idea across time, and the second, that it is not in the end a sufficiently validated space on which to frame human history.

3   The Evolution of the Mediterranean as an Idea in Antiquity

The ancients were never cognizant of the true place of the Mediterranean in the world's geography, but their knowledge and understanding of it evolved and expanded considerably over the long period extending from the Bronze Age to the end of antiquity. In second millennium Egypt and the Levant, the Mediterranean was referred to simply as the "the Great Sea," and was still so identified as late as the sixth century by the Greek logographer Hekataios (*FGrH* 1 F26). Phoenician and Greek exploration and colonization of the western Mediterranean beginning in the tenth century increased awareness of the existence of the Atlantic Ocean and a consequent shift in Greek identification of the sea as "our sea," "the inner sea," or the "sea in our part of the world (*oikoumene*)" (W. Harris 2005). Pliny the Elder took this more nuanced conceptualization one step further and asserted that the Mediterranean was essentially a creation of the ocean having pushed its way through the straits of Gibraltar (*HN* 3.1.5). Indeed, as the few surviving ancient maps demonstrate, the sea was not entirely distinguishable in ancient thinking from other smaller bodies of water such as rivers and gulfs.

It should hardly be surprising, therefore, that both the Atlantic and Mediterranean competed in geographic importance with the continents in the estimation of Greek and Roman geographers. Strabo in particular makes plain, that it is on the great landmasses where men, governments and resources are to be found (2.5.26), though interestingly, as a Greek geographer writing in the early Roman principate, he accords the Mediterranean shores of Europe terrestrial pre-eminence as the place where "tradition places more deeds of action, political constitutions, arts, and everything else that contributes to practical wisdom" (2.5.18).

Despite its carefully circumscribed place in ancient thought the importance of the Mediterranean lay in its capacity to promote interregional connectivity. This is first evident on a significant scale in the Bronze Age with the emergence of highly centralized states in the eastern Mediterranean – in particular Anatolia, the Levant, Crete, and Egypt (Van de Mieroop 2005; Horden and Purcell 2000: 143, 400; Bresson 2005; Kristiansen and Larsson 2005: 249–50). The nature of trade and exchange in this period, as illuminated in the archival and archaeological record, does not point inexorably to any sort of essential[ist] economic interdependence in the eastern Mediterranean, but rather to a world in which sufficient surpluses were being generated to promote a healthy seaborne commerce, despite its risks. As one scholar has observed, "there was, perhaps, an inexorable expansionist logic in this Bronze Age social formation [which] given time . . . might have spread around the entire Mediterranean" (Morris 2003: 44).

The destruction of the eastern Mediterranean state system around 1200 BC put an end to this cycle. However, a new and sustained period of state-driven interregional connectivity materialized in the tenth century with the appearance of the highly militaristic and tribute-based Assyrian empire in the Near East and the emergence of dynamic city-states in Phoenicia and the Greek Aegean. Assyrian tribute, as well as a growing elite demand in the Eastern Mediterranean for raw materials, especially metals, fuelled first Phoenician and then Greek commercial expansion into Europe and the western Mediterranean. This was followed in the early eighth century, thanks in part to growing population pressures, by the establishment of both Phoenician and Greek colonies and emporia along the coasts of Italy, Sicily, North Africa, France, and Spain, a very notable extension and intensification of the connections between the eastern and western Mediterranean. The growth of the Greek *polis* system and the extension of the Persian empire into Anatolia in the archaic and classical period led to an increasingly competitive political and economic environment within the Aegean and Black Seas. Naval military activity and expeditions were commonplace. Trade also intensified though often within the constraints imposed by imperial systems such as the Persian, Athenian, and Spartan empires.

These developments were paralleled in the western Mediterranean by the appearance of institutionally sophisticated and territorially large city-states such as Carthage and Syracuse, as well as indigenous proto-states in Spain, the Maghrib, and along the riverine and land routes to central and western Europe, first exploited by Marseille (Massalia) and the Etruscan city-states, well beyond the Mediterranean. Their emergence was no doubt stimulated in part by their long and deep connections, in some instances as colonial foundations themselves, with older city-states in the eastern Mediterranean, as well as the Greek and Punic communities in south Italy, Sicily, and Sardinia.

Alexander's conquest of the Persian empire and the Greco-Macedonian successor states the Levant and Egypt that were established upon his death introduced the large kingdom/empire as a new political form into the eastern Mediterranean. These states promoted the intensification of connections across the region, leading to greater complexity in governmental institutions and enhanced exchanges of technologies and ideas. Within the domain of ideology this included the introduction of an overarching Hellenic cultural veneer, as evidenced in the spread of Greek as the language of urban-elite interaction, as well as hybridized forms of Greek social and political institutions, and material culture.

In sum, the period from the Bronze Age to the Hellenistic period may be characterized as one of increasing levels of regional interconnectivity across the Mediterranean, driven largely by ancient forms of state imperialism. Cabotage or small-scale coastal trade continued unabated throughout this period, but it was states that proved to be the crucial force in the creation of a Mediterranean increasingly defined by common institutions and social formations. Indeed, any privileging of the role of the Mediterranean in shaping and defining interconnectivity in antiquity must be set against the equally important and no less complex evolution of land-based communications and interaction in the period.

Despite the increasing complexity of the Mediterranean down to the Hellenistic period, the ancient world remained deeply fragmented politically and highly compartmentalized economically. However, it is clear that the potential for the creation of just such a space was emerging much in the way that it occurred in Europe on the eve of the Age of Exploration: i.e. through the emergence of large, populous states, first in the eastern Mediterranean, but ultimately in the west, with the emergence of the powerful Roman republic on the Italian peninsula.

4 Rome and the Mediterranean

On the eve of its transmarine and transalpine expansion in the third century BC, the Roman republic had succeeded in building what amounted to the only proximate model of a nation state to emerge from the ancient world. The cultural and linguistic diversity of Italy notwithstanding, the republic claimed sovereignty over most of the peninsula and a large citizen (c.150,000) and non-citizen population numbered in the millions and ruled by a government – the city-state institutions of Rome – which could legitimately be defined as unitary (the social war of 90–88 BC may be seen in this regard as but the final violent step in the institutionalization of Roman sovereignty). The combination of stable state and large citizen-allied armies placed the republic in a position to win most of the wars in which it was engaged. The Italian peninsula's location at the center of the Mediterranean also afforded Rome a particular strategic advantage to its imperial designs by providing equal access to both the eastern and western Mediterranean basins, an advantage which all previous and subsequent hegemons lacked in their visions of uniting the Mediterranean under their authority.

In a world, both within and beyond the Mediterranean, where wars of national liberation were unknown and where campaigns were frequently decided by a single decisive battle or the capture of an enemy's capital, Rome's repeated and often rapid victories created an aura of Roman invincibility and imperial destiny. Over the space of some two centuries this transformed an unparalleled military hegemony over the eastern and western Mediterranean into an empire whose power and influence extended over what the ancients believed to be both the inhabited and known world well beyond the narrow confines of the Mediterranean (K. Clarke 1999).

The central historic achievement of the Roman conquest was to cause numerous societies across the Mediterranean and Europe to be lifted out of their relative isolation and dependency on locality as the primary or sole driving force in defining their culture, institutions, and sense of identity. In effect, Rome destroyed the highly fragmented system of ancient states and replaced it with a new interdependent system of dependent territorial entities known as provinces. In so doing, it swept away the ancient Mediterranean system of states for ever, and with the latter, in one sense, the ancient political world as well. In stating this I am not suggesting that the affected societies were in any way genuinely isolated from the outside world prior to contact with the Romans; rather that the impact of the Roman conquest process introduced enhanced connectivity with the larger world in more places than at any previous time in antiquity. This transformation took place via the mechanism of increased exposure to various external "phenomena," such as distant wars, economic fluctuations, and other historic events. Put in other words, the establishment of the empire fundamentally transformed the relationship between locality and local culture and thus established the only sustained globalization in antiquity (Hitchner 2008).

This reality is especially evident in way in which the Romans understood and interacted what they called "our sea" (*mare nostrum*). From a strategic and administrative standpoint they divided their empire into two broad categories: transmarine and transalpine provinces and possessions. Much like the Alps, the Mediterranean was perceived both as a physical barrier to be feared and therefore dealt with cautiously, not least because of its enormous destructive potential for commercial and military shipping, and as a natural frontier that stood between Rome and its overseas territories; this is perhaps most clearly evidenced, for example, in its decision to secure

Spain by moving legions overland rather than transporting them by sea. The Mediterranean therefore required securing, something which the Romans achieved by establishing naval bases which guarded the critical sea lanes of Gibraltar, the Gulf of Lyon, the Tyrrhenian Sea, the Adriatic, Egypt, the Levant, and Asia Minor. Similar naval arrangements were also deployed in the Atlantic, the great temperate European rivers, and the Black Sea.

On the other hand, the Romans also envisioned the Mediterranean much like the land, as a space dominated by lines of communication through which vital provincial revenues, commodities, resources, ideas, news, technologies, and labor reached and nourished the capital as well as other centers around its shores. Significant state and private resources were therefore invested in building and sustaining trade and supply systems well beyond the customary cabotage levels as early as the second century BC, not only in foodstuffs but mass-produced commodities, including quarried and worked stone, pottery, metals, wood, slaves, etc. (A. Wilson 2008). Shipwreck information, however quantitatively inadequate (and potentially misleading, particularly for the second century AD), demonstrates the fundamental role played by the Mediterranean in facilitating this unparalleled level of economic activity driven by empire.

The high volume of sea-based trade and communications in the Roman period also facilitated the movement of ideas, tastes, institutions, and beliefs in all directions. Perhaps the most obvious manifestation of this is the seaborne migration of Christianity from the eastern Mediterranean westward, but it is also evident in the way in which highly localized cultural identities along the shores of the Roman Mediterranean were informed and redefined by the import of broadly standardized images, monuments, state ideologies, laws, forms of governance, goods emanating from Rome and other dominant or emerging cultural centers as the empire matured. The impact of the Mediterranean as a carrying force for trade was greatest along its coasts, and could be easily diminished just a few miles inland away from rivers and large coastal towns, as the trade in pottery reveals, or even more starkly in the more limited connectiveness between Atlantic Mauretania just beyond Gibraltar (B. Shaw 2006).

All that being said, dilating on the important role of the Mediterranean in the shaping of the ancient world especially in the Roman period must be balanced against the recognition that similar processes were occurring along the great land routes of Europe, Asia, and Africa, producing often significantly different patterns of exchange and identity formation which together constituted the rich global matrix of the Roman world. The impact of the Roman state on its European provinces is clear. In the late republic and throughout the first century AD, Mediterranean goods were imported into the European hinterland on a considerable scale. Over time, however, the imperial system stimulated economic and political developments in the region that were environmentally distinctive from the Mediterranean. The Mediterranean, therefore, was but one part of a larger global reality created by the empire, a reality clearly manifested in the Romans' reference to the sea as *mare nostrum*.

Finally, the drop-off in both the extensity and intensity of Mediterranean connectiveness following the break-up of the Western half of the Roman empire in the fifth century is a clear demonstration of the centrality of the state in the shaping of Mediterranean history in antiquity (Wickham 2005, Ward-Perkins 2005, McCormick

2001). Indeed, any argument in favor of the Mediterranean as a fundamental framework for understanding the history of south-west Eurasia and North Africa must contend with the fact that its political and cultural unity as a region has only been achieved once in its history, and that under a land-based state in its center, not on either its eastern, northern and western shores.

5 Conclusion

As this chapter has attempted to demonstrate, a history of the Mediterranean as an overarching paradigm for understanding the history of antiquity has both great merit and significant limitations. On the positive side, there can be no doubt that the Mediterranean was the fundamental defining force behind the ancient human experience in western Eurasia and North Africa, and recent scholarship has gone further than ever before in explicating that role (W. Harris 2005). That being said, it is difficult to arrive at an adequate definition of the Mediterranean, as an historical concept, that will hold across time, space, and the modern disciplinary domains of knowledge. In the end, any attempt to privilege an historic perspective that places its emphasis on a seascape must contend with the fact that it is ultimately the former's interaction with terrestrially bound human communities that matters. Both have been studied, but rarely together. Fortunately, the prospects for a more integrated vision of land and sea in the ancient world are greater now than they have ever been.

FURTHER READING

The literature on the Mediterranean in history is ever expanding, but all research on the sea and its impact in antiquity must now take as its starting point *The Corrupting Sea* by Horden and Purcell (2000), in tandem with B. Shaw 2001, Morris 2003, Manning and Morris 2005, the rich collection of articles in the *Mediterranean Historical Review* (2003, vol. 18, 2 = Malkin 2005) and W. Harris 2005 (which includes a response to reviews of *The Corrupting Sea* by Purcell), and of course the groundbreaking work of Braudel 1972. For the late prehistoric Mediterranean see now Guillane 1994 and the papers in Blake and Knapp 2005. Although there is no systematic treatment of the Mediterranean in the late antique, early medieval and Islamic periods, the reader is directed to Wickham 2005, Ward-Perkins 2005 and McCormick 2001, all of which offer many useful insights on the role of the Mediterranean in shaping the human history of these periods. On Mediterranean history in general see Abulafia 2003. There are now a number of social science journals and monographic series dedicated specifically to the Mediterranean, most notably in English the *Mediterranean Historical Review*, already cited above, the *Journal of Mediterranean Archaeology*, and *Monographs in Mediterranean Archaeology*. Finally, this chapter also draws on a book now in preparation by the author on the Roman empire as an early globalization for Oxford University Press, but see also now Hitchner 2008.

CHAPTER THIRTY-EIGHT

Ancient Economies

John Davies

The economic historian of the ancient world faces two major problems. The first is the extent of that world. "Ancient history" nowadays encompasses a period of at least 1,500 years, from the new starts in the eastern Mediterranean after c.1000 BC to the break-up of the Roman empire in the West by c.500 AD. True, there is debate whether the latter epoch was economically as significant in the Mediterranean zone as were the realignments of production, exchange, and consumption which were generated by the Islamic conquests, but the pace of change over Europe as a whole by the late fifth century makes AD 500 an acceptable rough terminus. The choice of 1000 BC, also debatable, is determined mainly by the new patterns of control, demand, and outreach which, following a long period of military and social disruption, can be detected within the societies of Mesopotamia (i.e. Babylonia and the Assyrian empire) and the eastern Mediterranean (Anatolia, the Levant, Egypt, and marginally Greece). Strictly speaking, "new" is a misnomer, for they largely comprised the resumption of forms of behavior and routes of outreach that were already present in the Bronze Age, but what came to be "new," and to define our period, was their intensification and their long-term political and military consequences.

The second problem is that of linking description with "theory." Ever since debate about the nature of ancient economies began in the 1860s, scholars have attempted to devise a theory which could both accommodate and explain visible behavior in antiquity, in terms which addressed both its long-term stabilities and its gradual changes. Intrinsic to the problem throughout this period has been an awareness both of the development of economics as a discipline and of stark differences between ancient and modern economies. No expedient, whether that of adopting modern economic theory wholeheartedly, or that of relaxing its assumptions, or that of devising a wholly different analytical language, has yet met with any kind of general acceptance. As an interim solution, therefore, this chapter will broach wider questions only towards the end, largely confining itself to sketching the three main modes of behavior which can be observed. Of course the same region, the same polity, and even the same person will show more than one mode of behavior simultaneously, but to distinguish them analytically is one way of rendering their inter-relationships comprehensible.

1 The Subsistence Mode

The first and fundamental mode was that of "the subsistence economy." By the start of the first millennium BC, this, the most basic way in which men and women could wrest a living from a tract of cultivable land with the tools and techniques available, had probably been the predominant productive mode for centuries, if not millennia, across the Euromediterranean zone and beyond. It is already visible in stable established form in our earliest extant European literary texts, Homer's *Odyssey* and especially Hesiod's *Works and Days* (late eighth century BC), as also in the Old Testament and in texts from Mesopotamia and Egypt, for its prevalence did not depend on whether the work was done by a family of cultivators on land which they owned, or by the various forms of dependent labor sketched below. Though the endless variations dictated by geology and rainfall render all generalizations precarious, a simplistic expansion of the phrase "subsistence economy" is that it denotes the sum of all agrarian activity by sedentary populations practicing dry (i.e. non-irrigated) farming within self-sufficient productive units, the primary product, grain, being supplemented by stock rearing, vine and olive cultivation where practicable, legumes, pulses, herbs, and perhaps the produce of hunting and fishing (on farming and the countryside, see also Witcher, THE COUNTRYSIDE).

Each component of this description needs comment. "Sedentary" itself requires two qualifications. First, there were always nomadic communities, living especially in the desert margins of North Africa, Syria and Saudi Arabia, who were productive in a small way as stock rearers, living in complex symbiosis with adjacent agrarian regimes, but were important as the masters of the long-distance desert transit routes across the Sahara, between the coastal cities of the eastern Mediterranean and Mesopotamia, or between the Nile valley and the Red Sea (cf. Quinn, NORTH AFRICA). Secondly, though prehistorians nowadays downplay the importance of migration as an explanation of cultural change, large-scale migration into or within the Euromediterranean zone had an enormous impact. Within the zone, the continuous trickle of Phoenicians and Greeks colonizing substantial tracts of the Mediterranean and Black Sea coasts in the archaic and classical periods, or the military settlements and land-grabs perpetrated by Alexander of Macedon and his successors or by the Roman state, both transformed ethnic and linguistic distributions and generated new patterns of production, distribution, and consumption. Equally, irruptions from outside the zone, including that of the Kimmerioi from south Russia into Anatolia and Mesopotamia in the seventh century BC, the Gallic invasions of Italy in 390 and of Greece in 279, the Germanic invasions of Italy in the late second century BC, and above all those of the various peoples who became Visigoths, Vandals, Franks, Huns, and Lombards from the mid-third century AD onwards, did not simply replace one land-owning class by another, whether violently or not, but also disrupted exchange patterns to a very substantial degree.

"Dry farming" also needs qualification, for small-scale irrigation, tapping seasonal streams on the scale of the single farm, came to be common enough, especially in those areas of the Aegean where precipitation might fall short of the minimum annual level of 300 mm necessary for cereal cultivation. Large-scale irrigation, however, is attested only in the Nile valley and Mesopotamia, where already well before 3000 BC the opportunities offered by large permanently flowing rivers in zones of very low rainfall had generated systems of water distribution large enough to require central management. Whatever the water source, the principal agrarian product throughout our entire zone and period, providing some 75% of nutrition, was grain, the choice of species (mainly wheat or barley, millet and oats being of marginal importance) depending on soil and rainfall. Though grain was supplemented everywhere by vegetables, pulses, and forest products such as herbs and honey, and by olives, grapes, and wine up to their northern limit of cultivation, subsistence farming on its own will have provided most people with a very monotonous and often inadequate diet, for even if the productive unit was at or above the size (c.5 ha) reckoned to be the minimum to maintain a nuclear family, grain yields may well not have normally reached 10 : 1, with high interannual variation, while animals were kept for traction and for their hides, bones, wool, and milk as much as for their meat: the latter might be eaten only on religious feast days.

The "self-sufficient productive unit" therefore had its limits. Certainly, both at the level of the individual "farm" and by extension at that of the individual community, it formed a cultural ideal, reflected both in literary texts and in the sizes of land-allotments which were made to colonists in conquered or confiscated territories by regimes throughout antiquity. However, reality differed in four salient respects. Firstly, few such individual productive units had internal access to essentials such as salt or metals, perhaps not even to the products of all four ecological zones (arable land, forest, mountain, sea). Such needs required a surplus of produce over and above what was necessary for hand-to-mouth subsistence, such that it could be stored and exchanged for whatever goods or services were needed and available: space and equipment for storage were therefore essential. By the same token those same needs had brought into existence non-agrarian occupations such as the potters, carpenters, bards, and smiths cited by Hesiod, and with them workable means of payment: at least in its primary sense, to be discussed further below, a "market" for such products and services has to be postulated even when evidence other than the occasional surviving artifact is absent.

Secondly, even by the time of our earliest European texts, land had come to be a good which could be held in private ownership. Apart from conquest by invaders, the processes by which this came to be the case are opaque and much debated, not least because other forms of "ownership," e.g. by rulers, by divinities through temples and sanctuaries, or by communities collectively, are also well attested and generated various forms of the "command mode" (section 2 below). Nor can we follow the ways in which, or the extent to which, initially non-arable land could be taken in for cultivation, or fully understand how and when customary inheritance procedures had to be codified. All the same, major consequences follow. No matter how hard a community might try to ensure that access to arable land was evenly spread among its members (eldest sons had no privileges), and even if the presence of subordinated populations (as in archaic and classical Thessaly, Lakonia, and Crete, or the Carthaginian hinterland) is left out of account, nevertheless differences in human fertility and survival rates, coupled with various mutually inconsistent customs of dowry and bride-price, inevitably made some lineages better off than others. Though the social consequences of the deprivation therefore experienced by others less fortunate were of fundamental importance, not least in helping to fuel political pressures or to force formal or informal emigration, they cannot be traced here in detail. What matters is that since some lineages or individuals came to possess tracts of land which were too large to be worked by one family, the use of subordinated labor was essential. The patterns of dependency which were thus generated varied greatly. At the extreme of brutality, a workforce tied to the landowner as chattel slaves could be exploited mercilessly, though some of our texts make allowance for manumission as an incentive or at least for rational management (Cato, *On agriculture* 5). A workforce tied to the land as serfs, such as the Helots of Lakonia and Messenia or the *coloni* on estates in Roman North Africa, was more likely to function as sharecroppers, but freemen did so too (Cato, *Agric.* 136–37). Only in the case of formal rental agreements made with tenants who were legally free (e.g. Lysias 7.9–10, or the short-term tenancies documented in Egyptian papyri) can one speak of a price-setting market for land and labor.

It is quite impossible to estimate what proportion of arable and other land was worked under each regime in each region or period, but for present purposes the common thread is what matters, namely that the ultimate landowner stood to gain, whether directly or through bailiffs or contractors, a net revenue from the surplus labor of others which in theory was his to use as he pleased. This is the third, and much the most significant, difference between "self-sufficiency" and reality, for such revenues, supplemented by rents from urban landlordism, became one of the three prime motors of economies throughout antiquity. Among the many tangible conversions of such revenues came to be the elegant houses and landscaped villas with their mosaics, plate and statuary, fine furniture and jewelry, which generations of archaeological work have helped to reveal, as well as the elegant clothes and textiles which we know only from written sources or from miserable excavated scraps. If one adds what is known only from literary sources, e.g. the ostentatious expenditure on sexual services which Athenian New Comedy reflects, or the shameless gastronomy of Trimalchio in Petronius's *Satyricon*, one gains the clear impression of the enormous scale of such consumption as a tiny wealthy minority came to be able to indulge in. Yet, visible though it is in our texts and our museum displays, and reflected though it is in the picture of moral disapproval presented in Aristotle's *Nicomachean Ethics* or Seneca's *Dialogues* or St John Chrysostom's *Easter Sermons*, such clarity is less helpful than it seems, for what we see are the final stages of an endless set of processes of production and distribution. While the archaeologist or the art historian will seek to assign dates and evaluate techniques of production or artistic qualities, and the cultural historian will seek to read the meanings cached in iconography or ritualized customs, the economic historian's needs are firstly to trace the changing institutions and mechanisms of market or patronage which underlay those processes at various dates and, secondly and ideally, to assign at least an order of magnitude to the proportion of GNP which the production and provision of such goods and services for a wealthy elite generated through the centuries. Realistically, while much progress has been made in the last fifty years in tackling the first of these, especially for the better-documented periods of Athenian and Roman imperial history, the kind of quantification needed for the second remains wholly out of reach: and yet without it we have little hope of being able to assess whether wealth in the Achaemenid Persian empire, say, or in Periklean Attica or in Egypt, Italy, or North Africa in the second century AD was heavily concentrated within a small echelon of super-rich or was rather more evenly spread through the population.

In any case there was a countervailing fourth aspect. The wealthier a rentier landowner was, the more pressing, in most societies of antiquity, became the social obligations incumbent upon him. Those which were legal or quasi-formal are reviewed below, but informal ones, though wholly unsystematic, could be equally peremptory: while earlier centuries had expected that objects of value acquired by violence or exchange should be buried with the owner, or thereafter, and consistently throughout antiquity, that the achievement of some personal distinction should be marked by a visible thank-offering to the gods, later centuries could expect public benefactions, such as the gardens created by Kimon, Sallust, and Maecenas for public amenity, or contributions towards the costs of public works, or the allocation of land or money for cultic or educational purposes. However, such behavior was not "charity" in any selfless sense so much as an investment in public goodwill, reaching its extremes in the enormous sums spent by Roman public men on games, contests, and spectacles in theaters or amphitheaters. The return on such investment could be so politically profitable that Roman emperors took care to retain a monopoly on their provision.

2 Command Mode

The term "command mode" is inexact, but serves well enough to encompass all transfers of goods, property, or money from one "owner" (whether a person or a collective entity) to another, which derived from the exercise of power and took place under the threat of violence or legal sanctions. Though, of course, alien to conventional economic analysis, which largely confines itself to transactions within established polities or theoretically free markets, such transfers cannot be left out of account, for they formed a very large component of the sum of all transfers throughout antiquity. Some, of course, would always have been seen as illegitimate, such as the low-level haemorrhage of goods due to theft. Towards others, however, attitudes changed: the cattle-raiding forays of Nestor's youth, which Homer makes him recount with pride, would have ceased to be seen as admirable exploits in most Greek communities by 500 BC at the latest, and Hesiod's "bribe-eating kings" might have met legal sanctions in a later generation. However, it is hard to be confident that the practice of acquiring women by violence which underlies the myths of the Lemnian women or the Sabine women survived only in the ritualized form known in Sparta. Yet even brigandage by land and piracy by sea, powerfully disruptive of economic life and movement though they intermittently were until Pompey's naval campaigns of the early 60s BC, took root within a world where any person who was not of one's own community, or was not protected by some treaty or grant of immunity, was (with his goods) fair game, to be seized with impunity as an object of value, for ransom or sale into slavery: it took centuries for piratical activity to be checked by a network of treaties and by the emergence of polities such as classical Athens or Hellenistic Rhodes which had both the resources and the will to cripple the perpetrators.

In any case, the acquisition of resources by violence on the part of polities and their agents was always seen as legitimate, at least in certain circumstances. War, especially if formally declared, was held to allow not simply death and destruction but also the seizure of movables (goods, animals, and humans) as booty which then became the rightful property of the victor: just as Roman generals vowed temples as commemorations of successful campaigns, so too booty captured from the Persians helped to give imperial Athens temples and gardens. Even more telling is the lovingly obsessive way in which the Roman annalistic tradition records the booty paraded in triumphs. Thus, in 194 BC,

> the triumph lasted three days. On the first day there was a procession bearing the armour, weapons, and the statues of bronze and marble, more of which had been taken from Philip [V of Macedon] than had been received from the cities of Greece. On the second day the gold and silver, wrought, unwrought, and minted, was displayed. Of unwrought silver there were 18,270 pounds; of wrought silver there were many vessels of all kinds, many of them embossed and some of outstanding craftsmanship; there were also many of bronze manufacture, and in addition ten silver shields. Of coined silver there were 84,000 pieces of Attic money . . . There was 3,714 pounds' weight of gold, one shield entirely of gold, and 14,514 gold coins bearing Philip's likeness. On the third day 114 gold crowns, gifts from the Greek states, were borne in procession . . . [and so on]. (Livy 34.52)

Roman generals were not alone in exhibiting such predatory behavior, but they especially took it to remorseless extremes, denuding region after region of all movable items of value.

Besides movable items, all regimes at all times saw land as a legitimate objective. Again, convention would remove such activity from the sphere of economic description: wrongly, not just because in the event the benefits accruing to the invader were economic as well as military or political, but also because, time after time, behind the casuistry of justification there lurks the inference that some, perhaps many, such acquisitions were deliberately made for economic reasons, at least in part. Just as Achaemenid Persia targeted for conquest and annexation regions which would yield significant sums of tribute in bullion or in kind, while leaving poor mountain areas largely to their own devices, or as classical Athens sought for over a century to control and exploit the silver-mining areas of Thrace and kept relentless hold on the fertile volcanic soil of Lemnos, so too Ptolemaic Egypt annexed Cyprus in 310 as much for its copper mines as for its role as a military base. In the same way, behind Rome's decision to make Sicily her first overseas province in 227 lay not just the threat of a resurgent Carthage but also the need to assure a supply of grain for Rome herself as a rapidly growing urban agglomeration, while her decision in or by 198 to retain a presence in Spain had at least as much to do with protecting her annexation of land in the Guadalquivir valley and securing exclusive access to the silver mines of the Sierra Nevada as with preventing a Carthaginian revanche. Three centuries later, the same logic saw the final Roman defeat of King Decebalus of Dacia, followed by the annexation and exploitation of the gold and iron mines of western Transylvania.

Implicit in the foregoing paragraph is the assumption that communities and regimes could tax the persons, animals, lands, and activities within their territories and power. Systems varied widely. Communities which saw themselves as corporate bodies, with citizens as members, developed transaction taxes of considerable sophistication, but also levied obligations and privileges, graded by property, of military service, political participation, and financial payments as needed. Service as captain-cum-financier of a warship, or as angel of a play's production, or as guarantor of a tax-yield was among the most conspicuous in the Greek and Ptolemaic contexts. Monarchies, led in our period by Darius's reorganization of the Persian empire after 521 BC, likewise created systematic tribute-collecting mechanisms which were imitated by imperial Athens, briefly by Sparta, and subsequently by the Hellenistic regimes and by Rome.

However, "tax" did not necessarily mean "payment in coin." Though recognizable coinage systems based on gold, silver, and bronze gradually came into use from the sixth century BC, not all states issued coinage, continually or at all, while areas which generated few urban centers or were more remote from sea-routes showed little evidence throughout antiquity of the everyday use of coin. True, some regimes did demand payments in coin, notably the Hellenistic monarchies of the eastern Mediterranean in order to pay their armies, but others stuck willy-nilly to older systems of exacting "tax" in the form of personal service (usually military), or of contributions in kind, like the hides which the Romans demanded from the Frisii (Tac. *Ann.* 4.72), or of "gifts" to the powerful. The largest such tax in antiquity, by bulk and value, was undoubtedly the exactions of grain from Sicily, Egypt, and North Africa which went to feed the population of Rome, just as other flows had earlier gone to Athens and Alexandria, and later to Antioch and to Byzantium after its refoundation as Constantinople. Indeed, tithes of agrarian or animal produce not only went on being a regular way of supporting the activity of temples and sanctuaries but came back into mainstream use as part of the reforms of the emperor Diocletian, after the great monetary inflation of the mid-third century AD had disrupted the yield of coin-based tribute systems.

Behind that inflation lay a final aspect of the "command mode." Throughout antiquity, the ownership of mines and quarries was claimed and exercised by rulers and communities. Contractors normally did the work, and might get a cut of production, but most regimes saw yields as a major source of bullion, and consequentially of power. Of course, most of the major bullion-producing areas, such as Spain (Sierra Nevada and Galicia), Laurion in Attica, Thrace, and Dacia, have long been identified from extant workings and written sources, but only now, with chemical and spectrographic analysis of cores from as far away as Sweden and Greenland, is the enormous scale of extraction being revealed. The two peaks of the graphs of pollutant residues in our period seem to correspond to the late fifth century BC (presumably from Laurion), and above all to the first two centuries AD. It becomes ever clearer that the apparent collapse of extraction in Spain after c.190 AD, for unknown reasons, and the abandonment of Dacia after the 260s AD, had far-reaching effects on Mediterranean economies.

3 Market Mode

There remains "market mode." It may seem strange to assign it third place only, for in a primary sense it denotes all effective demand, whether overall or for a single commodity. It exists universally, without specific institutions of exchange, or coinage, or "merchants," and can be theorized satisfactorily even within a single household, within the subsistence mode, or within craftsman–patron relations. Moreover, if intangible but socially real returns such as "honor" and "protection" are factored into an exchange function, even transactions located within the command mode, such as bribes or gifts to social superiors, can be incorporated within a wider market mode as relationships of "negative reciprocity." All the same, in practical terms it is useful to be able to distinguish transactions which are currently analyzed, for the more archaic societies of antiquity, as being "embedded" within the same social orbit from those where distance precludes the exercise of power or direct producer–consumer contact. It is this latter category which has generated the long-running debate, for given the prevalence throughout antiquity of the subsistence and command modes as sketched above, the scope of application of a genuine price-setting market might seem to have been limited.

Not so, it appears, though its growth was spasmodic. True, from the eighth century BC onwards in Greece, festivals and sanctuaries had been providing safe passage for long-range, low-frequency gatherings which offered opportunities for exchange, while Herodotus's sketch of Carthaginian "silent trade" on the west African coast (4.197) portrays a mode of ritualized but undeniably commercial exchange which had a long future and probably a long past. However, it was the emergence of identifiable "towns," many of whose inhabitants did not work directly on the land, which drove the development of high-frequency (e.g. monthly or weekly), short-range markets: detectable in Athens by 500, gradually elsewhere, and in Rome by the late third century BC, such markets eventually spread widely, reaching central Anatolia and lowland Britain by the second century AD and changing the meaning of the words *agora* and *forum* on the way. Coined money helped (though Mesopotamia had used market-based exchange systems for centuries without benefit of coin), but the effective driving force was the purchasing power wielded by town- and especially capital city-based elites. Their appetite for elegance and display fuelled a network of supply which lasted for many centuries, already Mediterranean-wide for certain commodities by the eighth century BC, and extending far into the Indian Ocean and beyond by AD 100. It was assisted by the later development of the transport and support systems by land and sea, ranging from harbors and lighthouses to Roman roads, which the (largely military) needs of the command mode had stimulated, for they allowed transaction costs to fall substantially. Correspondingly, to judge from the vertiginous drop in the number of Mediterranean shipwrecks after c.200 AD, use of the network seems to have fallen back drastically once the supply of silver could no longer provide sufficient lubrication, and once immigrant landlords with different tastes had taken over much of the Roman empire in the West, but its skeleton survived for use by pilgrims and diplomats and by a core of long-distance trade.

4   Envoi

For nearly fifty years scholars have been weighing the respective merits of two models of the economies of classical antiquity – the substantivist and the formalist. The latter model assumes that since the members of all societies past or present have needs, experience scarcities, make choices, and exchange goods and services, if only within the household, their behavior can be analyzed via the normal laws and vocabulary of "formal" economics. The former model challenges their appropriateness, on the grounds that much, if not most, behavior was not profit-oriented but "embedded" within relationships of patronage, reciprocity, and redistribution, price-setting markets not appearing until the fourth century BC. Neither model convinces, the formalist because it underestimates the political and social dimensions of exchange and because the temptation to use language appropriate only to modern commercial firms has not always been resisted, the substantivist because it is over-influenced by Homeric language, fails to distinguish the various senses of "market," and unduly marginalizes risk taking and profit seeking: the mosaic inscriptions of Pompeii which proudly proclaim *Lucrum gaudium* (profit [is] happiness) and *Salve lucrum* (Hail profit!) send a different message. The alternative model sketched above, which identifies three separable but interlocking "modes" of economic activity, suggests instead that no single analytic formulation can adequately characterize the economies of the 1,500 years of classical antiquity: any area at any time will have shown a complex blend of all three modes, in ratios which underwent perpetual slow change.

Also unhelpful in its effects has been the quest to identify "growth" within ancient economies. Expansion and development as such are palpable, if only from the still visible signs of investment in infrastructure and from the artifacts which fill our museums. However, the objection has been that expansion was purely predatory, using violence and repression in order to suck resources of men, money, and materials out of a periphery towards a prosperous exploitative center, whether imperial Athens or Ptolemaic Alexandria or imperial Rome or Constantinople, and was not accompanied by planned or sustainable technological transformations. The objection has some force (though it seriously underrates the degree of continual technological advance), for while, for example, states and regimes gradually adopted the new technology of coinage, such credit systems as can be detected remained marginal: money supply therefore never progressed beyond M1 (the amount of coin in circulation at any one time), so that any interruption to the flow of new silver could threaten the viability of any state that needed to pay coin reliably to its principal employees, the armed forces. However, other objections have less force. Status-boundaries, for example, did indeed discourage the employment of free men by free men, and thereby to some degree impeded the flexibility of labor, but neither freedmen nor monarchs and their employees had such inhibitions, while the widespread recourse to chattel slavery both enhanced the availability of labor, by moving slaves across long distances to where it was needed, and allowed the creation of effective command structures, however brutal they may have been.

The economic life of classical antiquity did not unfold on a distant planet. The industrial and technological revolutions of the last 250 years have interposed a barrier to understanding, but the many long-established rural and craftsman technologies which have been observable till recently (some still are) are as much a window onto the past as are the seascapes and landscapes of Europe and the Mediterranean: when in 1990 H. W. Pleket likened the economy of the second-century Roman empire to that of western Europe in the eighteenth century, it was a just and useful comparison.

FURTHER READING

The most detailed overview is now the *Cambridge Economic History of the Greco-Roman World* (Scheidel et al. 2007), supplemented by Scheidel and von Reden 2002. Besides full descriptive chapters, it takes further the theoretical debate initiated by Finley 1973 (3rd edn 1999) and pursued in Duncan and Tandy 1994, Morris 1994, Silver 1995, Cartledge 1998, Aubet 2001 (chap. 4), Landmesser 2002, Christesen 2003, K. Greene 2005, Nafissi 2005, and Eich 2006. Agrarian conditions, extensively studied in the last thirty years, are described by K. White 1970, Foxhall and Forbes 1982, Whittaker 1988, Garnsey 1988 and 1998, Gallant 1991, Burford 1993, and Flint-Hamilton 1999. For production in general, especially non-agrarian, see Burford 1972, K. Greene 1986, and Cartledge et al. 2002, and for the role and context of trade and exchange see Garnsey et al. 1983, Aubet 2001, von Reden 1995, and Bresson 2000, with Meadows and Shipton 2001, von Reden 2002, and Schaps 2004 for processes of monetization and K. Greene 2000 for technological progress. Specific periods are reviewed by Snodgrass 1980 (archaic Greece), E. Burke 1992 and Morris 1994 (classical Greece, especially

Athens), Archibald et al. 2001 and 2005 (Hellenistic period), and K. Greene 1986 (Roman empire), while aspects of Egypt's well-documented economy are presented in Bowman and Rogan 1999, Manning 2003, Rathbone 1991, and Rowlandson 1996. Postgate 1992 and Aubet 2001 provide pre-classical contexts, with McCormick 2001 and Wickham 2005 for the early medieval period.

AFTERWORD (2012)

The final paragraph of Section 1 (p. 440 above) understates both the extent to which charitable and altruistic acts gained in economic importance during the centuries reviewed in this *Companion* and the distance which separates such acts from modern economists' rational choice models. A supplementary note may therefore be useful. The descriptive task is straightforward enough, for even if "strangers and beggars are from Zeus" (*Odyssey* 6. 207–8), republican Greek and Roman practice was to direct assistance, or distributions of land or food, in terms of status (above all that of being a citizen or his dependants), not of need. Though Polybios' acerbic comment "Absolutely no-one [in Rome] ever gives away anything to anyone if he can help it" (31. 26. 9) was overstated, though Hellenistic Greek kings sponsored public benefit foundations, and though a system of poor-relief in Italy (the *alimenta*) was formalized by Trajan, it is hard to detect much institutionalized approach to altruism within Graeco-Roman societies until well into the Imperial period: benefits might indeed be conferred, but the transaction was social, legitimating social position and conferring status as benefactor (though there is no precise Latin equivalent for the Greek *euergetes*). It was rather the Jewish and Egyptian traditions of giving alms and of supporting the destitute and the marginalized that offered an alternative model, whether directly via their diasporas or indirectly via their influence on Christianity: and even there, hugely important though Christian charity became in supplementing or replacing civic provision, bishops had still to be on their guard against pressure from their wealthy to memorialize their donations.

We are therefore looking at a pattern of behavior that was in turn communal, euergetistic, and charitable. That pattern fits none of the three modes described above, and is best characterized as a fourth, redistributive mode. Insofar as it was driven by emotions – of pity, of civic solidarity, of ambition, or of piety – it can readily be theorized within the frameworks which economic sociologists are now developing.

Further reading for this note may start with the entries "*alimenta*" and "Euergetism" in the *Oxford Classical Dictionary*, 4th ed. The older books of Bolkestein 1939 and Hands 1968 are still useful.

Bolkestein, H. (1939), *Wohltätigkeit und Armenpflege im vorchristlichen Altertum*. Utrecht: A. Oosthoek Verlag A.G.

Hands, A.R. (1968), *Charities and social aid in Greece and Rome*. London: Thames and Hudson.

CHAPTER THIRTY-NINE

Labor: Free and Unfree

Peter Fibiger Bang

Then came the various arts and crafts. Labor conquered everything, relentless and unbecoming labor, pressed by need and hardship. Ceres first instructed mortals to turn the earth with the iron share.

Vergil, *Georgics*, I, 145–48

1   Opening Pandora's Box

"To open Pandora's Box" has entered our language as a proverbial expression; it signifies an ominous act which will unleash a host of insoluble problems. Pandora is a female character of Greek mythology and makes her appearance at the very beginning of Greek and therefore of European literature and civilization. In the epic poem *Works and Days*, believed to date from the seventh or perhaps even eighth century BC, the bard Hesiod describes her as a girl of intense beauty, a divine creation (lines 46–105). She was Zeus's revenge on human society because it had furtively acquired the use of fire through the cunning trickery of Prometheus, the rebellious Titan. Meaning "the gift of all," the name Pandora carries a certain ambiguity. That was intended. She was sent with all the appearance of an attractive present, but with her she carried a jar, the proverbial box, which had been filled with all sorts of plagues and evils. That was the real "gift of all" – a curse to "bread-eating man" from *all* of the Olympian gods; and when Pandora was handed over, she immediately removed the lid to unleash a torrent of trials and tribulations on human kind, leaving only hope inside the jar. From then on, as Hesiod explains, the human condition had been one of misery and illness, of ceaseless toil and unending labor.

This Greek version of *The Fall of Man* is only one of a series of striking and powerful images of labor produced by classical culture and passed on to us. The sturdy peasant Cincinnatus of Roman political legend who was said to have been called to save the state while diligently plowing his small plot of land, has been held out to generations of Europeans and Americans as a model of self-sacrificing service and patriotism (Col. I, pr. 13–14). An entire genre of poetry, the pastoral, was predicated on the life of ancient shepherds. Spartacus, the famous leader of a serious slave rebellion in Roman Italy of the 70s BC, has served as a symbol of the struggle for social justice, celebrated alike by the labor movement and Hollywood. The Athenian sculptor and stone mason Pheidias has ranked as an emblem of unsurpassable artistic perfection for later ages.

Yet, in spite of the prominence of such cultural icons, the world of ancient labor is only vaguely known to us. Of course, the remains of its products lie scattered all around the Mediterranean and are stored as objects in museums all over the world. Impressive ruins and exquisite products of art all testify to the attainment of high levels of craftsmanship. But few practitioners speak to us directly. They emerge from the vast majority, which remains voiceless. The carriers of Greco-Roman culture, as the author of a Latin handbook of agriculture Columella remarked, were "called away and occupied" elsewhere, mainly by the aristocratic pursuits of civilization, politics interlaced with literature and philosophy (1.1.19). Indeed, Hesiod, being probably of peasant stock, is one of the few authors centrally placed within Greco-Roman civilization to express the world view of working people, albeit of the more well-to-do kind. But the veneration due to his poems as some of the oldest of Greek literature never came close to that enjoyed by the roughly contemporary, equally old, Homeric poems which depicted a world of proud aristocratic warriors high above the lot of the common working people. When the Romans set about to create a literature in their own language to match that of the Greeks, it was not a modest yeoman farmer, but the aspiring poet laureate of the Augustan aristocratic court, Vergil, who took it upon himself to produce a Latin counterpart to the old poem describing the labors of agricultural life. The result was the *Georgics*, a piece of refined and delicate poetry. Few things could be further from the robust and simple style of Hesiod than the verbal virtuosity and exquisite polish of Vergil's art. This was an art intended for the sensibilities and connoisseurship of a leisured elite with enough time on its hands to cultivate an ability to appreciate the subtle modulations of urbane poetry.

The poem addressed the concerns, doubts and anxieties, not of the peasantry, but of the Roman governing class. The aristocracy had been torn apart in a string of bloody civil wars which ended in the imposition of monarchy by Augustus, Caesar's heir. The *Georgics* was written in the spirit of restoration and peace. Agriculture received glowing praise as a quintessential force of civilization, and the Italian countryside was celebrated no less as the basis of Roman society. For all its attention to the struggle with a shifting nature – sometimes generous, sometimes cruel – and inspired descriptions of the hardship of drought and disease, Vergil's portrait of agriculture is romantic and highly idealized; it pictures a world inhabited by independent peasants, frugal, diligent and pious. We hear nothing of slaves, nor does he speak of landlords and tenants, as Heitland noticed long ago (1921: 233–40), even though such exploitative relations of labor were widespread in his day. At the end of the poem, however, Vergil narrates the myth of Orpheus, the singer who by his art gained access to the underworld to fetch back his beloved Eurydice and almost managed to conquer death. This is an image of the power of poetry and civilization.

By alluding to the myth of Orpheus, Vergil stakes out a claim to have mastered the countryside with his art (cf. Schiesaro 1997: 80). The world of agricultural production was domesticated and subjected to the hegemony of the values of lettered, aristocratic life.

Agriculture was valued above all other forms of income and investment by Greek and Roman aristocrats. This was not because they saw it as a source of character-building work, but because it was the most important wealth-producing sector of society. It created the riches which provided the underpinnings of civilization. True, civilization was only won at a high price, endless toil or, as Vergil put it in the epigraph to this chapter "*labor improbus*," relentless and unbecoming work. That was better performed by others. Civilization and inequality were self-evidently tied together for ancient people (Arist. *Pol.* 2.3.3). The secret, if that is indeed the right word, was to accumulate an amount of landed property sufficient to generate an income which would render the owner independent and free from the need to work. Roman high society liked to refer to their landed estates as a source of leisure and quiet, *otium* and *quies*, a world free from cares as the poet Horace charmingly pointed out to his benefactor Maecenas by telling the parable of the country mouse and the town mouse (*Satires* 2.6). Labor for others, in this view, was demeaning – a stamp of domination – and was performed by dependents, frequently of slave status. Agriculture to the aristocracy meant supervising and commanding the labor of others; it was a matter of husbandry such as it was described by Xenophon in the short, but influential dialogue *Oikonomikos*.

In the eyes of the dominant classes in Greco-Roman society labor was ideologically tainted; it was a symbol of insufficient independence and deficient liberty. Trade and manufacture, in this scheme, were frequently criticized because, so it was claimed, they were sordid and made their practitioners dependent on serving the needs of others. The Greeks simply applied the derogatory label "banausic" to such occupations; and Xenophon complained that they damaged and corrupted the physique and mental attitude of their members (*Oik.* 4.2). All sorts of tasks which, in one way or other, impaired the bodily integrity of those who performed them were judged unworthy of a free man or woman. Hard manual labor was problematic for the same reasons. The Romans even used condemnation to the dangerous work in the mines as one of the harshest forms of legal punishment. Labor, in short, was conceived of in hierarchical terms, demeaning and dishonorable by degrees: the greater the dependency and the smaller the income, the worse, as can be seen from a famous and much cited passage in Cicero (*Off.* 1.150–51):

> Now regarding the trades, which ones are worthy for a free man and which ones sordid . . . Illiberal and sordid, however, are the pursuits of all the hired workers whom we pay merely for the sake of their labor rather than their skills. For in their case, it is the very wage which is the instrument of their slavery. Sordid, too, we should consider the people who buy from merchants only to sell immediately, because they cannot make a profit without lying grossly; and nothing is worse than pretence. All craftsmen are occupied in sordid trades. There is nothing freeborn about the workshop. Least worthy of approval are the arts which cater to our sensual pleasures: fishmongers, butchers,

cooks, poulterers, fishermen, as Terentius says; add to these, if you like, ointment makers, dancers, and the whole gang of musicians. But those professions which require a higher degree of wisdom or yield a not mediocre benefit – like medicine or architecture or instruction in the honorable way of life – these should be considered honorable for those whose social station they are becoming . . . But of all the ways in which an outcome is secured, none is better than agriculture, none more abundantly yielding, none sweeter, none more suitable to a free man.

These observations, however, should not be taken to imply that the great majority of people, those outside the circles of aristocratic landownership, necessarily thought with disdain of their lot. An aristocratic lifestyle was, at any rate, beyond their reach; they had to cultivate other goals. The basic claim of hierarchy is that men are, in essence, different. People from different walks of life are not judged according to the same standards (Arist. *Pol.* 1.5.5). Indeed, from an aristocratic perspective there is no one more suspect than the man who attempts to rise above his station. On the other hand, playing the game of your social superiors could be a dangerous pursuit, not easily afforded by most. As Hesiod admonished the peasant: "work is not dishonorable, but idleness is" (*Works* 311). Occasionally, we find artisans and laborers displaying pride in their skills or achievements. Some Athenian vase-painters of the fifth century BC playfully included their own portraits in their depictions of aristocratic symposiasts (Neer 2002). Just outside the city-wall of Rome the master baker Eurysaces had himself buried in a loud and humorous monument with the shape of a breadbasket. From the city of Mactar in the Roman province of Africa, a harvester proudly proclaimed his success in rising from modest conditions to a position in the local governing class (*CIL* VIII, 11824).

None of this, however, developed into a fortified conception of labor able to rival and challenge the hegemony of the aristocratic view. Of the numerous inscriptions put up around the Greco-Roman world, the numbers mentioning the professional occupation of the persons commemorated are trifling in most regions and always a minority. Even in the Athens of the Peloponnesian War, where egalitarian notions were as prominent as they would ever become in antiquity, it was still possible for the playwright Aristophanes to score some easy points off the political leadership of Kleon by throwing a few gibes at his connection with the "banausic" tanning business (*Pax* 266–74; 645–90). Set in a world of rural villages and humble fishermen and carpenters, the Christian Gospels might be thought to have provided the basis for a radical challenge to the established hierarchy of values. But that never materialized (De Ste. Croix 1981: 418–41). In fact, the Church served as an ideological prop for the rigid hierarchy of the late antique world. The famous Benedictine formula, "pray and work/*ora et labora*," was a prescription for life in the monastery, a world which acquired its status precisely because it had put itself outside the norms of regular life. Only during the Renaissance and Reformation period did such values emerge from the calm of the cloister to penetrate society, as Max Weber noted in his famous work on "the Protestant ethic and the spirit of Capitalism."

2   Peasant and Slave Economies

The hegemony enjoyed by the values of the land-holding aristocracy is nothing peculiar to Greek and Roman culture. Similar notions were dominant in most pre-industrial societies. Think, for instance, of the medieval metaphor of society as composed by *the plough, the sword and the book,* in other words, the peasantry, the knights and the clergy. Peasants in all such societies constituted the bulk of the working population. This is an important fact to keep in mind when we try to understand agrarian economies. The basic unit of such economies is the household; it is within the family unit that most production is organized, frequently along gender lines (Saller 2007), and afterwards consumed. But peasant producers never exist in isolation. They are spun, often forced into a web of relationships with the surrounding world, the hegemonic aristocratic and urban civilization.

Nevertheless, to many commentators Greek and Roman antiquity is primarily associated with another type of labor: slavery. In classical Marxist theory, antiquity was simply treated as the basic expression of the so-called slave-mode of production. But ancient slavery cannot be understood outside the context of a peasant economy. Even in antiquity, chattel slavery dominated labor relations only in a very restricted set of areas and periods: in the Greek world, particularly the Attica of Athens in the fifth and fourth centuries BC, together with an unknowable, but far from all-encompassing number of other *poleis* like the island of Chios; in the Roman world, the Tyrrhenian coast of Italy, and the province of Sicily between approximately 200 BC and AD 200. The slave economies of these regions emerged as enclaves in a vast sea of peasants (Finley 1980).

The basic production logic of the peasant household is satisficing (Wolf 1966, Garnsey 1980, Gallant 1991, Cartledge 2002b). Labor is organized not with a view to the largest possible profit, but with the goal of *satisfying* the basic wants of the family members. When these have been met, peasant families have frequently been inclined to stop working. Against the prospect of further drudgery, they have tended to prefer the enjoyment of immediate leisure. The ability of the peasant household to reach its goals, however, is determined by a range of external factors. Most important is the availability and quality of land or, stated differently, the man : land ratio. In a ground-breaking work of agricultural economics, Boserup (1965) was able to show that population growth drove peasants to intensify production by increasing their work effort. When more people had to be fed from the same land, peasants had to put in longer hours in order to increase production. Population growth, in short, forced peasant families to exploit their means of production more efficiently and with greater intensity. In practice, that might, for instance, entail shortening the fallow period or taking in new land which had previously served as a resource for grazing or firewood. The small irrigated plots of Chinese rice-peasants, cultivated with minute care and back-breaking intensity, are a prime example of such a process. But there are also several likely candidates in antiquity such as the terracing of land in classical Attica or the expansion of olive cultivation into very marginal zones of late antique North Africa and Syria (Mattingly 1997; Decker 2001). The rise of extensive pottery production for export in some rural districts of southern France during the first and early second centuries AD would be a further example. The proto-industrial production of so-called *terra sigillata*, red-slipped table ware, in the villages of Lesoux and La Graufesenque benefited from a combination of plentiful firewood and the seasonal availability of rural surplus labor (Whittaker 2003).

By arguing for a positive relationship between population growth and agricultural productivity, Boserup attempted to stand the basic demographic insight of Thomas Malthus on its head. Malthus had made a seminal contribution to the early development of economics as a discipline by pointing out that population growth tended to outstrip increases in production. The prominence of this principle earned early economics the nickname of "the dismal science." Any attempt by man to improve his economic condition was, in this view, bound to prove futile in the long run. Expanding production would not translate into growth in per capita income, but rather result in more mouths to feed. One cannot say that Boserup has disproved Malthus. Indeed, his basic assumption is still built into her interpretation as *the* underlying premise. Population growth produces a downward pressure on per capita income. Peasants, however, may respond and try to alleviate this situation by increasing their work-load and thus expand production. Agricultural production and population size remain locked into an uneasy competition. In a pre-industrial agricultural economy, however, Malthusian pressures are bound ultimately to prevail. Based on organic technology (muscle power and animal manure) without access to chemical fertilizer or industrial machines, there are very set limits to how much a peasant can continue to boost his productivity (Scheidel 2007).

One implication of this condition is that the working population in the ancient world is unlikely ever to have achieved a standard of living much above basic subsistence (Hopkins 1995/6, Garnsey 1999: 12–61, Scheidel and Friesen 2008). In medieval Europe the dramatic drop in population caused by the Black Death actually improved living standards for the survivors. With fewer hands available, aggregate production in society plummeted. But with the smaller number of persons to share the land, peasants experienced rising per capita incomes. Generally not enough information has been transmitted on prices and wages from the Greco-Roman past to enable the historian to document such processes. But just enough evidence survives from Roman Egypt to suggest the probable unfolding of a similar scenario in the wake of the arrival of the so-called Antonine Plague which hit the empire in AD 165. A fall in the Egyptian population seems to have been followed by a rise in real wages (Scheidel 2002). Similarly one might hypothesize that living standards of the broad population were generally higher in the north-western part of the Roman empire than in the eastern. Though more prosperous and more intensively cultivated, the eastern regions were also much more densely populated. Hence peasants would have had to compete harder for land, work more and subsist on a diet containing less meat because grazing was scarcer.

But demographic pressures are not the only external influence on the production of the peasant household. Equally important are political pressures (Finley 1976b,

Foxhall 1990). Sometimes authorities mobilized peasant resources for their own purposes in a very direct manner. Forced requisitions by state personnel of transport animals, wagons, or lodging would be one type, corvée labor, for instance to facilitate road building or maintenance of irrigation canals, another (e.g. *Cod. Theod.* XI, xvi, 15, 18; *P.-Oxy.* 1409; Mitchell 1976). But much of the time, the peasant producers were simply made to pay for the frequently ambitious construction projects of the political elites, a process which culminated under the Roman emperors. The famed highways which came to span the length and breadth of the empire like a vast cobweb were to a large extent the work of the legions – the professional body of soldiers paid for out of the imperial tribute whose main contributors were the population of the countryside. Peasants have historically had to hand over a substantial part of their produce to others, the lords, the land-owning aristocracy. This imposes a need on the *oikos* to increase and intensify production to satisfy external demands also. In practice, the process of surplus appropriation has been organized in a whole range of ways. Most of these were also present within the orbit of the Greco-Roman world (De Ste. Croix 1981: 133–74). Serfdom, for instance, has often been discussed as exclusive to medieval feudalism. Certainly, the practice by which peasants cultivate for their own subsistence on their own plots of land for some days of the week and then work on the estate of the lord for the remainder, does not seem to have been in general use in antiquity. But there are many examples of serf-like relationships where peasants seem to be under some sort of control by the landlords either through ties of patronage or from legal obligation. During the wars of the late Roman republic, the nobleman Domitius Ahenobarbus is famously reported to have manned several ships with "his freedmen, slaves and peasants" (Caes. *BC* 1.34.3). An edict issued by the Roman emperor Caracalla commanded Egyptian peasants to be expelled from the Greek city of Alexandria and returned to their villages to cultivate the land (*P.Giss.* 40 II 16–29). Similarly, the Seleukid king Antiochos II is on record selling a village with its lands, people (*laoi*), and households to his former queen Laodike (Welles 1934: no. 18).

We can rarely study in detail such serf-like relations. Our information is simply too scanty. But several groups are on record. Most famous are the Helots of Sparta, an agrarian majority population subjected to a kind of state-serfdom where they had to supply auxiliaries to the army and provide their Spartan citizen-masters with agricultural rents (Alcock 2002; Luraghi and Alcock 2003). Other groups would include the Thessalian *penestai*, the *laoi* and temple peasants of Anatolia and various crown peasants or tenants, enjoying a mixture of special privileges and particular obligations to the monarch (Rowlandson 1985; Kehoe 1988). Another candidate for inclusion in this group is the so-called late Roman colonate. It was formerly believed that the late Roman state had tied all peasants in the empire to the land. That belief is now in need of serious modification. The state simply did not control the countryside to the extent that it could impose such a measure uniformly across its vast realm. The regulations issued by the emperors only form part of a complex of factors which increasingly strengthened the position of the landowners in relation to the peasantry (*Cod.Iust.* XI, 51; Wickham 2005: 520–27; Carrié 1997; Grey 2007).

At any rate, landlords did not necessarily need special legal privileges to tap the resources of the peasant population. Tenancies were used in many areas to organize the relationship between the elite and the free peasantry. The latter was granted the right to cultivate the land in return for a stipulated rent, the specific contents of which varied from region to region. With this often came relations of debt. It seems that most peasant farms were small and therefore walked a tightrope (Brunt 1971, chap. 19; D. Crawford 1971, chap. 8). Harvest failure, a recurrent curse of pre-industrial agriculture, might leave the peasant unable to pay his rent or feed his family and thus force him to approach the bigger landholders to obtain a loan to see him through till next harvest or provide him with seed grain. But that was a risky strategy. Further complications might see the peasant family descend down a slippery slope of rising debts, growing obligations and increasing dependency. Listen to how a peasantry reduced to submission might have to grovel: "To Flavius Apion, the all-honored and most magnificent . . . from the council of the chief men of the village of Takona . . . which village is dependent upon your honor's house . . . We acknowledge that we have received from your honor on loan . . . as seed for the crops . . . two hundred artabas of uncleansed corn . . . We will pay back without fail to your honor the same amount of corn, new and sifted . . . without delay and on the security of all our property which is thereto pledged" (*P.Oxy.* 133, editor's trans.).

This is where the much-disputed concept of autarky enters the picture. It has frequently been objected against the emphasis on peasant household production that these units were not self-sufficient, not autarkic (e.g. Horden and Purcell 2000). But that is beside the point. Autarky does not describe economic reality. No peasant household could be completely self-sufficient and therefore they had to band into villages and city-states, as Aristotle remarked in the *Politics* (1.4–8). Autarky was an economic strategy. By attempting to produce most, but not all, of what they needed at home, householders sought to retain a measure of control in relation to the outside world in order to safeguard their independence or at least keep the level of dependency to a minimum, as Horace's charming description of the unfortunate peasant Ofellus makes clear (*Sat.* 2.2). The condition of the peasants was shaped by the combined pressures of population and aristocratic power and the ability of peasant households to resist. All these factors varied locally, and results would have been equally diverse, as our evidence indicates. But high rents in Egypt (Rowlandson 1996: 249) and the short-term period of lease envisaged by classical Roman law (*Dig.* 19.2.13.11; 19.2.24.4) both indicate that the balance was frequently tilted against the peasantry.

In some city-states, however, particularly Athens and Rome, the peasantry succeeded in tilting the balance somewhat their way for a while (Finley 1980, chaps 2, 4). Following the legal abolition of debt bondage, the peasant populations managed to strengthen their position within the state. The reason behind this success was that they were needed as soldiers. This improved their bargaining strength and enabled them, or at least a sizeable portion of them, to assert their independence from the landlords. The latter, in turn, accepted this because they were able to find a substitute – slaves. Slavery as a dominant form of surplus appropriation seems to be the exception in world history. Based on brute force, it has normally only been employed when labor was otherwise unavailable. This, for instance, was the case with the New World plantation economies of the early modern period. Black slaves were imported because the indigenous populations, suffering heavily from the introduction of lethal epidemic deceases hitherto unknown to the region, were unable to shoulder the task. Slavery, in other words, made it possible to intensify agricultural production in the absence of a capable or willing peasantry (Wallerstein 1974, chap. 2). There was no shortage of hands either in classical Attica or in the Italy of the Roman republic. This is a major difference from New World slavery. But based on military service and political participation, a sizeable portion of the peasant populations had been able to assert a degree of independence for themselves. As a result, the aristocracies had to resort to the exploitation of slaves, the quintessentially dependent and disenfranchised form of labor.

In Italy the effects were dramatic. Following in the wake of the ceaseless Roman military triumphs, won by armies manned by peasant soldiers from the third to the first century BC, a slave economy emerged centered on the Tyrrhenian coastal regions of central and southern Italy and Sicily (Scheidel 2004, 2005, 2008b; Schiavone 2000; Hopkins 1978b). Plentiful supplies of slaves captured by Roman arms enabled the aristocracy to man a system of intensively farmed middle-sized estates existing in symbiosis with small independent peasant farms. Frequently needing to supplement their meager earnings in order to subsist, the peasants constituted a ready source of casual labor to be hired onto the slave-operated estates during periods of peak activity such as harvest time (Foxhall 1990). At the end of antiquity, on the other hand, one can see the opposite process taking place. There we find landowners resisting the recruitment of peasants into the imperial army; they needed them to cultivate their lands even to the extent that they were willing to pay a tax, the *aurum tironicum*, to avoid having to supply recruits for the draft. In consequence, the Roman state had increasingly to resort to the recruitment of foreign mercenaries, in other words Germanic federate troops (Amm. Marc. 31.4, 31.11; B. Shaw 1999).

3 Aristocratic Retinues and Urban Bazaars

Pre-industrial agriculture was relatively low yielding. This means that by far the biggest part of the working population had to be employed in agriculture. As a rough rule of thumb (precision cannot be hoped for), it took four peasant families to maintain one occupied in another trade. But if the non-agricultural sector was smaller, it was all the more diversified. The concentrated expenditure of aristocratic rent and tax-incomes in urban locations created a basis for the development of an impressive range of specialized urban trades. More than 200 different occupations are attested for Rome, as many as 90 crafts estimated for the Egyptian town of Oxyrhynchus (Hopkins 1978a: 71–72; Alston 2002: 275). The extant ruins of Pompeii may provide us with a good impression of the pattern prevailing in the most densely settled and therefore richest regions of the Greco-Roman world (Laurence 1994, chaps 4,

6; Wallace-Hadrill 1994, chaps 4–6). Two characteristic features of the townscape are the existence of some very large households and the numerous small shops lining many of the streets, the former the abodes of the aristocracy, the latter best described in terms of the bazaar.

Behind the walls of the great houses, the luxurious lifestyle of the urban landowning elite unfolded in ostentatious grandeur. Such people surrounded themselves with a sizeable retinue or staff of slaves, freedmen, and the occasional freeborn person to cater for their every wish and whim, ranging from recitation of literature to sexual gratification (Lucian, *Dom.*; Treggiari 1975; K. Bradley 1994: 61–65). Dresser, masseuse, cook, doorkeeper, bedchamber servant, secretary, house teacher, the list of occupations in domestic service is almost endless, the potential for exotic, refined or simply quaint specialization without limits. "*Silentiarius*" (silence maker), "*a speculum*" (caretaker of mirrors), "*a corinthis*" (caretaker of Corinthian ware), even "*alipilus*" (plucker of body hair), titles such as these taken from real life give resonance to the caricature, offered by the Neronian writer Petronius in the literary fragment known as *Trimalchio's Dinner Party*, of the extreme, indeed decadent, sophistication of functions within the largest and richest households (Joshel 1992, appendix 2). Not all urban landowners could go to such lengths, to be sure. It was normally courts and the upper reaches of the aristocracy which set the pace. But to judge from Pompeii, emulation, as far as people were able, reached deep down into the urban gentry (Wallace-Hadrill 1994, chap. 7).

Ownership of slave servants was the established rule within the propertied classes (K. Bradley 1994). Urban slavery, therefore, was prominent, even in regions where slave labor played a less significant role in the countryside. Slaves cannot merely be forced to work hard, they carry the added advantage that they have been divested of any independent social identity; they have no legitimate existence outside their master's control. In an almost perverse way, this has made slaves, together with eunuchs, a useful source of trusted and dependable servants for rulers and aristocratic elites across the spectrum of agrarian civilizations, not least in Muslim societies (Gellner 1983, chap. 2). Cicero's confidential secretary and literary executor, Tiro, is the model for such a relationship (Cic. *Fam.* 16.17, 16.19, 16.22), while the slaves owned by the emperors who rose to high and influential positions in the imperial administration reveal the underlying rationale (Weaver 1972). Greek and Roman masters managed their slaves by holding out the promise of rewards and privileges: high positions within the household, permission to find a wife/husband among the other slaves, and, the greatest prize, freedom (Hopkins 1978a, chaps 2, 3).

Many urban slaves seem to have won manumission after years of service, to judge from the great quantity of inscriptions commemorating freedmen. But selection of some implies rejection of others. Not everyone was able or willing to do what was required to secure the goodwill of their master or mistress, at least not all the time. For them, there were hard words and the whip, or more draconian measures. Most suffered beatings and humiliations quietly. They had to, or suffer the risk of losing whatever little privilege they had already been granted. On the quiet, they might try to get back by acts of sabotage and passive resistance (K. Bradley 1994, chap. 6). Driven to desperation some would try to run away to a life among outlaws, but occasionally one or more would snap. The senator Pliny relates with a shudder how a group of slaves, who had finally had enough, one morning assaulted their cruel master in the bath and ended by throwing him on a steaming hot floor to make sure he was dead (*Ep.* 3.14). Such incidents, however, were surprisingly rare, to say nothing of full-scale rebellion, probably because retaliation was ruthless. Roman law did not shy away from savage torture and summary execution of many or all the slaves in the household (*Dig.* 29.5.1 (Ulpian); Tac. *Ann.* 13.32.1, 14.42–46). Terror and collective punishment served to hold dissatisfied individuals at bay.

Most of the time, however, the combination of carrot and stick managed to do the trick for the masters. Numerous slaves were even employed outside or in connection with the household as a form of investment (Wallace-Hadrill 1991; Garnsey 1976). They served as shopkeepers, craftsmen, and business representatives to earn back profits to their masters and, frequently, money with which to buy their own freedom. A famous example of such investment practices is the establishment (*ergasterion*) belonging to the Athenian metic family of the speechwriter Lysias and his brother, which may have employed 100–120 slaves in shield making (Lysias 12.8, 12.19). But that scale of operation was unusual. A small business archive found just outside Pompeii is more indicative of the normal standard (Camodeca 1999). Stemming from the banking operations of the freedmen Sulpicii in Puteoli under the Julio-Claudian emperors, the documents reveal a world of businesses manned by perhaps up to a handful of persons. Roman law developed an elaborate set of provisions to deal with such slaves and freedmen engaged in business for their masters and patrons (*Dig.* 14; 15; Gai. *Inst.* 4. 69–74). The most successful of these would eventually obtain control of their shops or set up new businesses to become masters in their own right, with all that entailed of a household and perhaps ownership of a few slaves.

In the great majority of cases, the workshops and businesses of slaves and freedmen were organized no differently from those of their freeborn colleagues with whom they coexisted. The concentration of capital would generally have been low, in relative terms. The division of labor and specialization of functions, therefore, tended to be less impressive within the workshop than between workshops. As Xenophon explained: "In large cities, however, because many make demands on each trade, one is enough to support a man, and often even less than one: for instance, one man makes shoes for men, another for women, there are places even where one man earns a living just by mending shoes, another by cutting them out, another just by sewing the uppers together, while there is another who performs none of these operations but assembles the parts" (*Cyr.* 8.2.5). The predominance of small workshops and horizontal division of labor (E. Harris 2002; van Minnen 1987: 43–48) resembles, most of all, a bazaar with its mixture of many small traders and artisans (Geertz 1963; 1979; cf. DeLaine 2005 on the physical layout of Ostia). This was formerly pronounced a terminal illness of the ancient economy (Rostovtzeff 1957: 172–77). But the decentralized organization of labor and business represents a rational response to the low degree of mechanization and the many uncertainties and irregularities which characterized trade and manufacture in the ancient world. The many small establishments made the bazaar a flexible and adaptable environment. A couple of traders might band briefly together to take advantage of a sudden opportunity in the market. Traveling craftsmen, possessing rare skills, might travel from place to place to find employment. For instance, stonemasons capable of carving the most refined sculpture and relief work might have had to move from job to job. Many cities in the Greek and Roman world would not have been big enough to offer permanent occupation to such people (Burford 1969: 145–58; further Fülle 1997: 143; C. Smith 1998). In richer areas, horizontal specialization facilitated the emergence of local styles and schools. The visitor to Pompeii and Herculaneum is immediately struck by the subtle but distinct difference in flavor exhibited by the style of wall-painting in each of the two contemporary Vesuvian cities (Ling 1991: 215; in general, Burford 1972: 111).

Important trades in the bazaar were, among others, metal working, the preparation and selling of all kinds of food and spices, and cloth (weaving, dyeing, fulling, and selling). Other important urban sectors included building, carpentry, and pottery. The small scale of business operations in the bazaar seems to combine two features. At the lower end of the scale, products reveal a great degree of uniformity. Individual businessmen frequently simply copied what their neighbors did (but with huge variations in quality). However, at the higher end of the scale, extreme specialization enabled the achievement of very high levels of delicate craftsmanship and the selling of rare, luxurious goods to urban connoisseurs (Burford 1972: 93–96, 107–14). The attraction of such products was more than mere beauty and rarity. They were not meant for generalized consumption in a mass-market such as our present-day designer labels (Bayly 2002). These products were held to be invested with unique and almost esoteric qualities that reflected the splendor of their owners and served to elevate them above the common run. As was repeatedly asserted by elite prejudice, persons of lower standing who obtained possession of such goods would immediately stand revealed as deficient, vulgar upstarts. Ownership was not enough, a whole civilizational code had to be mastered (Hor. *Sat.* 2.8).

Students of bazaar economies have frequently commented on their relative lack of collective organization. To be true, they seem to have lacked the strong regulatory merchant and artisan guilds governing some cities in medieval Europe. But traders and craftsmen certainly joined together in societies and associations for the various purposes of burial, cult and business (Alston 2002: 207–12; van Nijf 1997; Patterson 1994; Rauh 1993; van Minnen 1987). Such clubs helped carve out a position for the members within the symbolic and ritual order of the ancient cities while giving shape to the social environment and culture of business in the bazaar. The collective experience of dinners, festivities, and rituals promoted a sense of community and reinforced common values, and a shared ethic among participants. It also constituted a basis for collective action, at times. Groups of practitioners of a trade are occasionally attested in Pompeian graffiti as declaring their support for particular candidates to public office (*CIL* IV, 183; 336; 609; 710). In the *Acts of the Apostles*, the silversmiths of Ephesos are reported to have taken to the streets to protest against Christian proselytizing which they felt threatened their lucrative trade of producing small silver replicas of the city's famous temple of Artemis (*Acts* 19, 23–40). In Tarsos, the linen-weavers lacked the franchise. Nevertheless, they were still sufficiently obtrusive to

39.1 Products manufactured in the bazaar: The products of ancient craftsmen spanned a wide spectrum, from the most exquisite art works to the relatively coarse and stereotyped products. The illustration shows a sample of such objects in the collection of the Danish National Museum. In the center: a terracotta figurine of Venus, from Thapsos, Tunisia, first to second century AD; a bronze statuette of Mercury, from Saguntum, Spain, first to second century AD; and a terracotta lamp with a representation of two gladiators, acquired in Rome, first century AD. Flanking these objects is the brilliant pair of silver cups found in an aristocratic Iron Age tomb at Hoby on the Danish island of Lolland. The cups were made about or shortly before the early first century AD in the Roman empire by a Greek silversmith, proudly declaring in Greek, but using Latin letters, "Chirisophos epoi/Chirisophos made this." On the cups are depicted scenes from the *Iliad*: left, Philoktetes having his foot washed after being bitten by a snake; right, Priam humbling himself in front of Achilles to ask for the return of his dead son Hektor. (National Museum of Denmark, inv. no. 10115, Chr. VIII 708, 3839, 920 and 1020)

attract the attention of Dio Chrysostom, who referred to their grievances in a speech urging civic concord on the inhabitants (34.21–23). But such action never gained for urban trades collective control of city governments. Successful individuals were sometimes able to improve their situation and claim membership of urban governing bodies. But that did not represent a serious challenge to the hegemony enjoyed by the land-owning elite.

In this, urban associations resembled the village councils which, in more or less formal fashion, would have organized peasant cultivators across the entire

Greco-Roman world. Occasionally peasant collectives crop up in the inscriptional evidence as having successfully challenged the claims of their more powerful landlords (*CIL* VIII, 10570; *OGIS* 519; Hauken 1998). On rare occasions we even see them rebel against their lords. Augustine tells with indignation how Donatist insurgents had reduced some of their former masters to a condition of slavery: "tied to a mill-stone and forced by a whip to drive it round and round, like contemptible mules" (*Ep.* 185). But that was as far as it went: a reversal of roles. Dissatisfaction among peasants, urban workers, or slaves did not offer a fundamentally different alternative to the reigning order; these groups were, as Michael Mann has observed, "organiza-tionally outflanked" by the aristocratic elite, and were unable to substitute a different set of social institutions for those already in place (1986: 7). Resistance, therefore, was thrown back on (ultimately futile) hopes of millenarian justice, of which we catch a glimpse in the fevered *Book of Revelations*. Most of the time, however, that kind of aspiration was channeled into the safe ceremonial space of public festivals. Discontent and frustration found an outlet in the performance of carnivalesque rituals, like the Roman Saturnalia. On such festive occasions, conventional rules were allowed to lapse; established hierarchies were momentarily suspended and masters would pretend to become slaves and the serfs masters. The carnivalesque festivals re-enacted the golden age, the era of Saturn (Bachtin 1968); they offered a brief respite from the drudgery and anxieties of daily life. Here people would come together in celebration of their common humanity and to laugh at misery, the curse of Pandora. It was a blissful state, as we learn from the inspired portrayal in Aristophanic comedy, a return of abundance where even Zeus, the instigator of human misery, would eventually be brought to heel, abandon his heaven, and seek the company of men (Aristoph. *Plut.* 1171–96).

FURTHER READING

The starting point for the student of labor in antiquity remains the relevant chapters of Finley 1999 and Austin and Vidal Naquet 1977; for economic history in general see the bibliographies of chapters 11 and 38 above. De Ste. Croix 1981 is a classic, if cumbersome, Marxist work with much to say about labor in the ancient world. Burford 1972 still offers a valuable synthesis of craftsmen in antiquity; K. Greene 1986 and Oleson 2008 contain much relevant information on production processes. MacMahon and Price 2005, Cartledge, Cohen and Foxhall 2002 and Mattingly and Salmon 2001 are recent collections of papers on labor and processes of work in the ancient world. DeLaine 1997 is an attempt to quantify the sources of labor for great monumental building projects. Easily the most closely studied craftsmen from antiquity are the celebrated individual Greek sculptors and potters from the classical fifth and fourth centuries BC, on whom see Boardman 2001. During the last decades, the study of labor in antiquity has focused on three areas: the cultural and social standing of labor, slavery and slave-economies, and peasants and non-slave labor.

The status of labor and particularly traders became a hotly debated topic after the publica-tion in 1973 of Finley's *The Ancient Economy* (for 3rd edn Finley 1999). Much of the reaction was ill guided. D'Arms 1981 questioned the basic interpretation, but it can hardly be doubted that agriculture enjoyed the higher status. More fruitful were Garnsey 1976, Wallace-Hadrill 1991, and Joshel 1992, the latter examining inscriptions put up by slaves and freedmen. Cuomo 2007, chap. 3 treats the representation of ancient craftsmen in funeral monuments while van Nijf 1997 and Patterson 1994 draw attention to the inclusion of some professional associations in the public ceremonies, processions and symbolic order of urban communities. Lucian's *The Dream* is a charming parable asserting the hegemony and pre-eminence of lettered civilization over manual occupations.

Wiedemann 1987 and K. Bradley 1994 provide an excellent introduction to ancient slavery. Wiedemann 1981 contains a useful collection of sources. Hopkins 1978b, chaps. 1–3, remains important on the rise of a slave society in Roman Italy and the organization of slave labor. Finley 1980 with its comparative perspective revolutionized the field; for a new comparative collection of papers, Dal Lago and Katsari 2008; Scheidel 1997, 2004–5 and 2008b are now fundamental on the sources, supply and position of slaves in the Romano-Italian economy. The slave-population could only be maintained by considerable home-breeding; Schiavone 2000 for an example of the Italian view of the Roman slave economy. Garnsey 1996 treats the ideological aspects while Hopkins 1993 drew attention to the fears and concerns of a slave-holding society. In the Plautine comedy, *Pseudolus*, we see Roman society laughing at its fears of the crafty servant.

No study of ancient labor is really possible without drawing on the comparative experience of other pre-industrial economies. Wolf 1966 is still the best short introduction to peasant societies; Braudel 1972 (vol. 1) and 1981 are indispensable. Livi-Bacci 1997 provides a useful introduction to demography, while Geertz (1963 and 1979) offers a valuable approach to the bazaar economy on which see also Bang 2008. Within ancient history, the study of the peasantry in the setting of pre-industrial society as a whole was pioneered by Finley 1976b. Some important contributions are Garnsey 1980, de Neeve 1984, Rowlandson 1985 and 1998, Foxhall 1990, Gallant 1991, Sallares 1991, Horden and Purcell 2000 and Wickham 2005 (pt III). With the increased interest in the ecology of the peasant household, questions of demography have moved to the center. Scheidel 2007 now synthesizes this research, and Saller 2007 is an instructive discussion of the gendered division of labor within the household. U. Roth 2007 draws attention to the significance of female labor and family units also in the slave work-force.

CHAPTER FORTY

The Countryside

Robert Witcher

1 Introduction

The ancient countryside is a paradox: rural life was rarely represented in art and literature, yet every aspect of the ancient world was dependent upon the control and exploitation of rural landscapes. In effect, the very basis of society was systematically repressed in self-representation (Osborne 1987). Today's society demonstrates its own paradox: as global urbanization accelerates, we are showered with ever more images of idyllic rural lifestyles. But while the focus of anthropology and geography has shifted from rural to urban matters, reflecting the changing modern world, studies of antiquity have moved in precisely the opposite direction (W. Harris 2005: 1–42). In fact, over the past 25 years, studies of the ancient Mediterranean have been thoroughly "ruralized." The reasons are not hard to find. Agricultural innovation, urbanization, and tourism have transformed the physical and social landscape of the Mediterranean. A perceived timeless way of peasant life has vanished during living memory. Simultaneously, these processes have revealed a wealth of archaeological evidence which has stimulated further interest. This rural fascination may occasionally betray nostalgia: Hanson's *The Other Greeks* (1995) laments a world where small farms are replaced by agribusiness, and scholars of Greek agriculture have no first-hand experience of farming. But this fascination does not mean that ancient historians have shunned the modern world: Horden and Purcell's (2000) profoundly rural approach to Mediterranean history is a clear response to globalization (Manning and Morris 2005: 1–44). As all these paradoxes and the responses to them suggest, the ancient countryside is a subject of lively debate. A short chapter such as this cannot cover the full range of primary and secondary literature, but aims instead to discuss a varied sample as an introduction to the subject.

It is a simplification to suggest that scholars have only recently become aware of a world "beyond the acropolis." Nevertheless, until a generation ago, rural matters were of marginal interest. Even during the 1980s, publications might invoke an evangelical tone about the need and means of studying rural landscapes (Snodgrass 1987). Today, no assessment of the Greek *polis* or the Roman economy is complete without consideration of the countryside; it is a central component of a "paradigm shift" in classical archaeology (Snodgrass 2002). However, though its importance is not in doubt, there is no consensus about how the evidence should be interpreted.

Understanding of the countryside is closely connected with debate about the ancient economy; a brief sketch of economic history is therefore a necessary starting-point (see Morley, ECONOMIC AND SOCIAL HISTORY). During the twentieth century, attention focused on two key debates: (a) primitivism (or minimalism) versus modernism, and (b) substantivism versus formalism. Respectively and simplistically, these contested the scale of economic activity and whether or not the "economy" was socially embedded. The key text was Finley's *The Ancient Economy* (1973; 3rd edn 1999). However, during the 1990s studies developed along two parallel courses. The first concerns the ideology of economy, considering texts and material culture as fields of representation, negotiation, and meaning. For example, Roman elite self-representation stressed the importance of land and agriculture as the proper sources of wealth. But why was this particular aspect of elite identity emphasized – and what was omitted? Sources do not therefore provide direct access to the ancient economy because they were produced by individuals representing themselves and others in particular socio-political settings. The second approach concentrates on model building and quantification, supplementing texts with comparative and archaeological data (Cartledge 1998).

These two approaches developed from distinct backgrounds and proclaim different objectives. The former draws on the humanities, searching for specific meanings through the particular. The latter, drawing on the social sciences, aims to generalize and explain (Manning and Morris 2005: 1–44). There are few attempts to reconcile these approaches, though the need for a *rapprochement* is clear: methods based purely on representation lose touch with the brute realities of life; conversely, comparative approaches may underestimate the socially embedded nature of the economy and the specific contexts in which texts were generated (Morris 1994). These brute realities and ideological representations intersect nowhere more powerfully than in the ancient countryside.

2 Evidence and Approaches

Explanations for the inconspicuousness of the countryside in ancient literature include the banality of rural life and elite disdain of physical labor (though there is also a tension here with the idea of work as morally improving). However, it is easy to exaggerate the scarcity of references. Even though there are few sustained descriptions, the "persistent if brief obtrusions" (Snodgrass 1987) of the countryside into plays, comedies, satires, and histories provide much source material. Arguably, modern scholarly prioritization of certain discourses and texts forms an important, if partial, explanation of the apparently limited visibility of the countryside.

In reality, these textual glimpses of rural life are no more or less problematical than those for any other aspect of antiquity. The key question is how much of this incidental detail can be taken as useful evidence. This requires consideration of writers' motivations and intentions: in other words, how and why individuals and groups represented themselves and others. Different conclusions can be found. For example, despite the moralizing tone of Hesiod's *Work and Days* and Apuleius's satirical aims in *The Golden Ass*, both have been seen as valuable evidence for agricultural practices (Hanson 1995; Isager and Skydsgaard 1992; Millar 1981b). In contrast, others have questioned normative readings of uncouth rustics in Greek plays, noble peasant-farmers in Vergil's *Georgics* and Juvenal's idyllic countryside as antidote to urban immorality (Braund 1989; N. Jones 2004). The Roman agricultural writers appear to tackle the countryside more directly, but these texts are no less problematical. Are they descriptive or prescriptive? Though they draw on Greek and Carthaginian literature, do they pertain to practice beyond Central Italy? Can Columella's (3.3.3–4) claims about cereal yields be accepted if his interest is the promotion of viticulture (cf. Varro *RR* 1.44.1–2; Frank 1940)? Finally, legal texts provide another category of evidence: for example, the *Digest* summarizes legal cases including lease disputes. But does this text illuminate practices of the early empire or were cases recast in light of sixth-century AD concerns? How far was the *Digest* an elite self-representation of attitudes towards, for example, investment and profit (Kehoe 1997)? Hence, there is no consensus on the value of source material for the study of the ancient countryside.

Though written sources are more plentiful than sometimes claimed, their number is finite. In contrast, archaeological data, inscriptions, and papyri continue to provide fresh evidence (N. Jones 2004; Rathbone 1991). Archaeology has been central to recent studies of the ancient countryside, in particular through field survey or landscape archaeology. The South Etruria survey in Italy and the Minnesota–Messenia survey in Greece pioneered the collection of artifacts from ploughed fields as a method for identifying sites and mapping settlement patterns (T. Potter 1979; McDonald and Rupp 1972). Subsequent surveys have refined methodologies and extended coverage to many other regions. Without doubt, the key contribution of archaeological survey has been the identification of numerous small, dispersed, rural sites around the Mediterranean.

Historical and archaeological evidence can be superbly complementary. For example, the former emphasizes the cultivation and exchange of grain, while the latter brings wine and oil production to the fore through studies of press technology and amphorae distributions. However, the interpretation of the archaeological record is no less disputed than the reading of historical texts. How many sherds of pottery constitute a site? Was it a habitation site, and, if so, was it permanently or seasonally occupied? Is the low-density scatter of sherds between sites the result of modern agricultural erosion or of ancient agricultural practices such as manuring? Nevertheless, archaeology may add nuance to specific texts. The archaeological evidence for intensive, settled agriculture and "proto-urban" centers refutes representations of the Samnites as pastoralists (Livy 9.13.7; Barker 1995; Dench 1995). In contrast, despite the anachronistic language used by Livy (1–10) to describe the fifth-century BC Italian landscape, survey confirms the existence of dispersed settlement and intensive agriculture (Attema 2000). However, even if both archaeological and historical evidence is in apparent agreement, care is still needed. For example, the decline of rural site numbers in Roman Greece appears to correspond with the *oliganthropia* (depopulation) described by Polybius (36.17.5–9) and others. However, *oliganthropia* is a *topos* associated with moral and political weakness in both Greek and Roman literature, and may not therefore reflect actual demographic trends. Further, a number of different processes may explain the abandonment of rural sites, for example the migration of rural populations to cities. In the case of Roman Greece, it seems difficult to deny some demographic decline (Alcock 1993). However, Strabo's (5.3.1–2) list of the towns around Rome that had been reduced to villages or even abandoned altogether must be read against the background of marked contemporary growth of rural populations (Morley 1996; T. Potter 1979).

As well as illuminating the historical sources at a localized level, field survey has significant implications for wider models of the ancient countryside. For example, clear regional diversity questions the validity of any single model of the ancient economy and the rural distribution of centrally manufactured goods indicates a less exploitative town–country relationship than suggested by the parasitic consumer city model (Finley 1973; Lloyd 1991). Generally, therefore, archaeologists have been more eager than ancient historians to move on from Finley. The scale of population, specialized surplus production, and long-distance exchange all seem incompatible with Finley's vision of unintegrated and minimal economic activity. However, while the quantity of evidence for surplus production and long-distance exchange undermines the idea of primitivism, Finley's supporters argue that scale of production and exchange alone does not disprove the argument that economic activity remained socially embedded (i.e. substantivism, Cartledge 1998; Mattingly and Salmon 2001). Hence, a key polarity of economic debate remains unresolved.

3   Ecology and Risk

The physical environment of the Mediterranean has only recently entered considerations of the ancient countryside. Palaeo-environmental and ecological studies have transformed this situation. In particular, studies of recent peasant societies in Greece and Italy (ethnoarchaeology) have generated data and theories which have deepened appreciation of the complexity of past socio-economic practices, especially agricultural regimes (H. Forbes 1992).

The climate and physical landscape of the Mediterranean are highly distinctive. Two key characteristics include: (a) highly fragmented topography and (b) low, seasonally and annually variable rainfall (there is no evidence of significant difference from modern climate and environment, Grove and Rackham 2001). Ethnoarchaeological studies identify a range of general cultural responses to this ecosystem. In particular, risk-avoidance strategies were of central importance and have had a profound impact on studies of the ancient countryside. All agricultural societies are vulnerable to unexpected variation in their ecosystem, but a defining characteristic of the Mediterranean is the variability of its landscape and climate. To mitigate the associated risks, societies developed strategies to ensure their survival. For example, specialization in any single crop was hazardous; a dry winter or a late frost could destroy an entire harvest. As a result, farmers spread the risk by diversifying production, including the Mediterranean "triad" of cereals, olives, and vines, but also legumes, figs, and other crops. Another strategy was the fragmentation of landholdings, facilitating access to varied ecological niches and minimizing the risk of losing whole harvests to localized hazards. In turn, the diversification of crops and the fragmentation of landholding had implications for broader social and economic organization.

Such ecological approaches have been criticized as environmentally deterministic, historically insensitive and for the implication that societies applied rational thinking to agricultural regimes and even social structures (Isager and Skydsgaard 1992). However, environment did not limit human agency absolutely, and strategies and technologies were developed to exceed these limits – for example, extending agriculture into the Libyan pre-desert (Barker 1996). Generally, responses to environment were historically contingent and drew upon tradition rather than rational planning (Garnsey 2002). A more pressing criticism concerns the relevance of models derived from studies of nineteenth- and twentieth-century societies. Is it valid to assume basic continuities over three millennia, especially if recent peasantries have been enmeshed in modern global economies? Similarly, though environment and technology remained broadly similar throughout antiquity, labor is an important variable. For example, ethnoarchaeological evidence for low seed:yield ratios, which correspond well with Columella's figures, may significantly underestimate the productivity of ancient agriculture because of the higher yields possible through labor-intensive "gardening" (Osborne 1987). Such issues do not invalidate ecological insights, but suggest caution in their application (further on ecology, Sallares, ENVIRONMENTAL HISTORY).

4   The Corrupting Sea

Historical, archaeological, and ethnoarchaeological approaches to the ancient countryside are brought together in Horden and Purcell's sweeping account of long-term history of the Mediterranean, *The Corrupting Sea* (2000). Using an ecological premise, a range of misconceptions is systematically refuted. For example, three common stereotypes of Mediterranean peasantries are subsistence (autarky), self-determination (social independence), and immemorial stability (successful resistance to change); in other words, self-sufficient citizen-farmers, morally uncorrupted by urban vice or social dependency. Horden and Purcell dismiss each aspect of this interpretation, arguing it derives from romantic notions of peasant societies and normative readings of texts. In reality, self-sufficiency in the Mediterranean was suicidal; farmers had to produce a good surplus to allow for the inevitable famine. These strategies involved not simply producing more, but also the storage and redistribution of the surplus, whether through markets or social networks. Inevitably, this surplus and the insurance it offered were appropriated by the powerful, leading to dependency and socio-economic reorganization. Fragmented topography did not impede the exchange of this surplus, as Finley (1973) argued, in fact it demanded the greater mobility of people and goods between regions of glut and famine. Hence, from an ecological perspective, no individual or community was truly isolated, and connectivity ensured that no society could successfully resist change (further on the Mediterranean, Hitchner, THE MEDITERRANEAN AND THE HISTORY OF ANTIQUITY).

These misconceptions of the Mediterranean peasant have been critical to an understanding of the ancient countryside, so their rejection has broader implications. For example, the assumption that farms were socially and economically autarkic has led to specific readings of the evidence. Discussing Campania, Jongman (1988) argues that an ox requires 10–12 hectares of fodder per annum. As this is more land than the average peasant owned, agriculture must have been based on human labor, with low returns and poor integration of arable and pastoral strategies. However, this ignores the possibility of pooling resources such as draft animals as part of horizontal or vertical relationships, and the importance of common land (Evans 1980; Lirb 1993).

Horden and Purcell's ecological approach is part of their broader aim to "ruralize" history. By this, they do not simply intend to view the ancient world through a rural lens, but a more radical effort to eliminate the category of "town" altogether. Instead they envisage a spectrum, from peasant farm through to imperial capital, based on the same ecological strategies of diversification, storage and redistribution. In other words, they argue for a purely quantitative rather than qualitative difference between town and country. However, towns are only an extraneous category because of their irrelevance to Horden and Purcell's purely ecological argument (Fentress and Fentress 2001; W. Harris 2005: 1–42). In this sense, *The Corrupting Sea* does not help us to understand the distinctive qualities of either urban or rural life.

5   Towns and Hinterlands

In contrast to Horden and Purcell, the ancient sources have no difficulty distinguishing town and country. For a variety of ideological reasons, these categories are almost universally defined as distinct and opposed: civilization versus boorishness, consumption versus production (MacMullen 1974). Historians have often perceived the relationship as antagonistic and exploitative, for example the consumer city model. More recently, the distinction has been blurred through considerations such as the cultivation of crops in urban areas and the mobility of populations. However, it should be no surprise that, just as ancient towns were highly variable, relations with their hinterlands were equally diverse. For example, the emergence of urbanization in archaic Greece and Etruria was frequently associated with the dispersal of dense rural settlement. This may reflect the need to claim territory and to increase agricultural surplus. However, the development of towns in Samnium during the first centuries BC/AD was associated with a reduction in the number of rural sites. This may reflect an elite strategy to monopolize resources and to direct them at urban munificence, with the aim of prestige and entry into the Roman senate (Patterson 2006). These contrasting rural developments may be explained by the differing motives for urbanization. The rise of the *polis* was internally-driven in the context of competing peer-polities, while towns in Samnium were promoted by local elites in response to asymmetrical imperial relations with Rome. Rural landscapes are therefore a useful indicator of diverse urban histories and functions.

Whether the majority of people lived in cities or dispersed in the countryside is still debated. The issue is complicated by the interpretation of field surveys: were sites in contemporary occupation? how many individuals lived on a site? Demographical models usually assign five persons to each small site, but rural families were probably larger than their better-documented wealthy urban counterparts (Bagnall and Frier 1994; Osborne 2004). In reality, the situation was geographically and chronologically variable. Another issue concerns whether the populations of town and country were in harmony or competition. In other words, did urban and rural populations rise and fall in tandem or one at the expense of the other? Again, there is conflicting evidence and opinion, but a diversity of relationships is to be expected.

The type of settlement in which people live is closely connected with their agricultural strategies and social organization. In the context of archaic and classical Greece, two competing interpretations have emerged. The traditional model argues that peasants lived in "agro-towns" and commuted daily to surrounding fields. Landholding was fragmented, lessening the risk of losing an entire harvest. However, fragmentation meant livestock were few and poorly integrated. Deprived of animal manure, fields required fallowing. Therefore, the system spread risk at the cost of productivity. The overall system is similar to medieval and early modern regimes in which, notably, elites controlled land and monopolized agricultural surplus. In the alternative model, "agro-towns" were supplemented with dispersed rural settlement. Farmers lived and worked on consolidated landholdings and may even have owned them. Time previously lost commuting was spent on agricultural activities, and the integration of livestock meant that soil fertility could be maintained without fallowing. As a result, the alternative model was more productive. However, it also entailed more risk: land was consolidated, and so harvests were vulnerable to one-off events; dispersed residence also diminished community cohesion and hence support.

These ideas are the subject of much debate. Opponents of the alternative model note the lack of historical evidence and question interpretations of the archaeology. Nonetheless, opinion is moving away from the traditional model because the absence of detailed descriptions of agriculture in historical texts may relate to the broader repression of rural representations. Ethnoarchaeological comparison has also found more favor. Meanwhile, the archaeological evidence demonstrates ever more clearly the density of dispersed settlement and the restricted size of many urban centers. Yet again, there was much variation across the ancient world, but dispersed rural settlement and the associated socio-economic structures were widespread.

6 People in the Landscape

Orthodoxy populates the ancient countryside with free citizens, farming their own land and participating in hoplite warfare and political duties as the agricultural calendar allowed (Hanson 1995). The ecological limitations of such social and economic autonomy have already been outlined; frequently survival meant the sacrifice of independence. The literary emphasis on equality and moral rectitude of citizen-soldier-farmers is strongly ideological. In practice, landownership was unequal and was concentrated into fewer hands over the course of antiquity. The apparent egalitarianism of colonial land-division schemes is deceptive; Roman land assignment could be explicitly engineered to reproduce existing inequalities (at Aquileia in 181 BC, infantry received 50 *iugera*, centurions 100 *iugera* and cavalry 140 *iugera*, Livy 40.34.2). More generally, regular plots take no account of land quality (or labor inputs) and hence potential productivity. Some families may therefore have quickly accumulated greater wealth and social power than their neighbors. Hence, even if the original division were equitable, it may have quickly lapsed and dependent relationships emerged.

Where the evidence permits detailed insight into dependent relationships such as tenancy and sharecropping, the diversity of arrangements is impressive. Examples include the Younger Pliny's Italian properties, the Roman imperial estates in Africa and the third-century AD Appianus estate in Egypt (de Neeve 1990; Kehoe 1988; Rathbone 1991). Land was leased by individuals, cities, and temple-estates on varied terms, which indicate regional differences in the balance of power between landowners and lessees and differing expectations about financial returns. It is impossible to generalize such isolated examples; however, archaeology can begin to map broad socio-economic categories on a wider scale than possible through individual inscriptions or the archives of a single estate (Helots, Alcock 2002; *perioikoi*, Cavanagh et al. 1996; tenants, Foxhall 1990).

The recognition of debt-bondage and slavery is far more contentious. Slaves appear in some of the earliest representations of the Greek countryside (e.g. *Od.* 24.205–12), but have been marginalized by the ancient and modern focus on citizen-farmers. Archaeologists have also struggled to identify slavery. However, a recent review of the stone towers of classical Greece concludes that they were used to confine slaves and were associated with profit-motivated activities, especially wine production and metal extraction (Morris and Papadopoulos 2005). Discussion of slavery in Roman Italy has long focused on the late republican slave-estate (Carandini 1988). However, this phenomenon was less ubiquitous than the sources might suggest, geographically concentrating on the narrow western coastal plain. It also increasingly appears to have been a particularly short-lived development, focusing on the first century BC. Further, demographic modeling and comparative data suggest a significant reduction in the number of slaves involved (Scheidel 2005). Hence, as recognition of rural slavery in Greece expands, the dominance of slave-labor in studies of Roman Italy has receded.

7   Late Republican Italy

Roman history is punctuated by agrarian crises and their associated political effects. However, new research challenges conventional interpretations of these rural developments and their broader significance. Late republican Italy is a good case study, being the subject of two well-known models, one general and one specific. The first argues that changing military conditions led to the breakdown of the seasonal integration of farming and warfare. As wars shifted further from Rome, it was impossible for soldiers to return to their farms to plough and harvest. Deprived of their principal source of labor, rural families fell into debt and were forced from their land, leading to a reduction in the number of free citizen-farmers over the last two centuries BC (Sall. *Iug.* 41.7–8; Plut. *TG* 8.3; Brunt 1971). The Gracchan agrarian reforms were a partial response to this situation. A more specific issue concerns the long-term impact of the Hannibalic war on southern Italy: Toynbee's famous thesis argues that the population and economy never recovered from the devastation, with repercussions extending to the modern era (App. *BC* 1.7; Cornell 1996; Toynbee 1965).

Various aspects of these narratives are now disputed. Close re-reading of texts suggests that soldiers were not seasonally discharged in time to return to their farms from as early as the fourth century BC; in other words, another means of reconciling war and agriculture already existed long before c.200 BC. The supposed incompatibility of military and agricultural duties after this date had therefore already been resolved and cannot explain the decline of small farmers. However, this raises the question of how war and agriculture were integrated if not seasonally. To answer this, Rosenstein (2004) creates hypothetical families of different sizes and age profiles and compares their calorific needs, their potential labor and the amount of land needed to sustain them. These families are then subject to various scenarios to assess their resilience in the face of military recruiting. The approach requires disparate data and questionable assumptions, and consequently the results should not be confused with reality. However, they place informative parameters on the claims of ancient and modern authors alike. The results suggest that small farms and warfare could indeed be compatible, and a "typical" family of five could spare the labor of a son. However, the critical factor was not when during the year his labor was removed, but when during the family cycle. By delaying marriage until the age of 30, men were recruited before they took over farms and started their own dependent families (on age of marriage, Scheidel, POPULATION AND DEMOGRAPHY, section 4).

If war and agriculture were compatible, how do we account for the decline of small farmers during the late republic? Several scholars not only argue there was no decline to explain, but there might even have been substantial *expansion*. Without doubt, the Hannibalic war led to considerable short-term depopulation. But for surviving farmers, conditions improved: for example, there was automatically more land available; for surviving soldiers, marriage prospects also improved. Such conditions favor demographic growth (Erdkamp 1999). In fact, the census figures, though problematical, do indeed indicate growth. A key historical debate is whether this growth represents free farmers or the descendants of manumitted slaves. The latter has been the dominant view (Brunt 1971), though this is now disputed on several grounds. For example, the downward revision of slave numbers makes it impossible that their reproduction could account for the growth suggested by the census figures (Scheidel 2005). Although the late republic was a period of high population mobility (Scheidel 2004), immigration on the necessary scale seems unlikely. The best explanation is therefore the substantial growth of free rural populations. In turn, this radically different view of late republican rural demography requires reconsideration of wider issues such as colonization and the Gracchan crisis.

Such models are generalized across Italy. However, both historical and archaeological evidence indicate regional variation. In Etruria, post-war conditions promoted strong economic development. Largely untouched by Hannibal, the area experienced high demand for urban and military supplies, leading to inflated grain prices. Combined with immigration from the war-torn south, the local elite had incentive to intensify agricultural production and the labor and capital with which to achieve it (Erdkamp 1999). Archaeological evidence adds another level of detail. Close to Rome, there was a marked increase in site numbers, from the mid-second century BC through to a peak in the early imperial period. This area is notable for its density of settlement, including wealthy rural villas, and associated large population. In contrast, across inland Etruria the expansion of dispersed rural settlement peaked during the second century BC before a slight decline by the early imperial period. In this area, the density of settlement and population was much lower, and villas both fewer and less opulent (Witcher 2006). These contrasting patterns of settlement, agriculture, and demography suggest distinct late republican trajectories. The key difference was proximity to Rome, its growing market, and its wealthy elite (Morley 1996).

In Campania, military action devastated agriculture and population alike. But once Hannibal was expelled, Rome needed Campania to supply its armies. Migration and recruiting meant that labor was in short supply and survivors lacked the seed and capital with which to revive farming. This situation favored the use of slave-labor by external landowners with capital to invest (Erdkamp 1999). Again, archaeological evidence adds some detail. Military supply quickly gave way to specialized viticulture on large estates along the coast owned by Roman senators. Bulk wine was exported during the late republic, but declined due to provincial competition in the early imperial period. In contrast, inland areas experienced limited economic growth, but greater long-term stability (Arthur 1991). Again, external elite involvement and proximity to markets were critical to economic developments.

In southern Italy, the focus of Toynbee's thesis, military action continued for longer, causing widespread devastation and depopulation. After the war, capital and labor were scarce, but by then falling grain prices meant there was little profit to be made through intensive agriculture in the short term. Investment and recovery were therefore limited and delayed (Erdkamp 1999). Archaeological evidence indicates significant settlement dislocation during the third century BC, some of it, perhaps, predating Hannibal (Lo Cascio and Storchi Marino 2001). However, though the dramatic and permanent decline of settlement around Metaponto fits Toynbee's model well, it is exceptional (Carter 2005). Elsewhere the evidence points to slow revival, though there was much local variation. Particular trends include extensive colonization and villa building by absentee landlords developing slave-based viticulture on the coasts and sheep rearing and textile production across inland areas (Fentress 2005). Hannibal's legacy was not permanent economic and demographic stagnation, but the alienation of landownership and subsequent vulnerability to external developments. In summary, the nature of the late republican countryside of Italy is still hotly debated; insights from comparative and archaeological studies mean new narratives are less "tidy" but more realistic.

8   Summary

Recent approaches to the ancient countryside have integrated texts with archaeological surveys, ecological studies, comparative data, inscriptions, and papyri. The results have revolutionized understanding of the centrality of the countryside to key political, social, and economic developments, from urbanization and demography to warfare. Intense debate continues about the value of the written sources, the significance of archaeological data, and the insights provided by ecological approaches. Accordingly, there is no consensus, even on such key issues as where the majority of the population lived. However, some general trends include new emphasis on social dependency, the mobility of people and goods, the role of profit-motivated agriculture, and the scale of agricultural surplus. Other recent research themes not discussed here include the scale of rural manufacturing (e.g. pottery and tile production), quarrying and extraction, and zooarchaeological studies of animal husbandry.

Ecological approaches provide a framework for assessment of subsistence strategies and cultural responses; however, there is need to integrate detailed analysis of literary representations and ideologies. Moreover, no single model can encompass the full diversity of the ancient countryside and, as more surveys are published, Mediterranean regionality becomes ever more obvious. A key challenge is to articulate the connections between these distant landscapes. How did incorporation into political structures such as the Roman empire or a Hellenistic kingdom transform local economies and agricultural strategies? It is impossible to understand the transformation of individual landscapes without consideration of their wider contexts. The Greek world's demand for agricultural surplus transformed *chorai* from Sicily and Cyrenaica to the Crimea, while the needs of the city of Rome dramatically remodeled the economies of Baetica and North Africa. The study of such connectivity through detailed historical analysis and comparative survey will be one of the major trends in future studies of the ancient countryside.

FURTHER READING

There are few syntheses of either the Greek or the Roman countryside, and no over-arching volume. For the Greek world, key texts include Osborne 1987 on the archaic and classical periods and Alcock 1993 on the Roman period. Studies of Attica include Osborne 1985, N.

Jones 2004 and Lohmann 1993. On Greek agriculture, see Halstead 1987 (traditional/ alternative strategies), Isager and Skydsgaard 1992, and collected papers in Wells 1992. For Greek labor arrangements, see Burford 1993, Hanson 1983, Jameson 1992, Morris and Papadopoulos 2005, and Wood 1988. Hanson 1995 uses a lifetime's farming experience to interpret the ancient sources in a provocative and engaging argument for the centrality of Greek farmers to the rise of the *polis*. For land division at Greek colonial sites, see Carter 2005 and Carter et al. 2000. On Pausanias as a guide to the rural landscapes of Greece, see Alcock et al. 2001 and Hutton 2005.

For agriculture in the Roman world, see Marcone 1997, Sirago 1995–96, and papers in Carlsen 1994. For Italy, see Dyson 1992 and 2003, Jongman 1988, and papers in *Misurare la terra* (1988). On Roman agriculture, see de Neeve 1984, Frayn 1979, Jongman 1988, Spurr 1986, and K. White 1970. For olive oil and wine production, Amouretti and Brun 1993, Mattingly 1988, Tchernia 1986 and Foxhall 2007. For Roman labor arrangements, Carandini 1988, Scheidel 2005, U. Roth 2007 (slavery); Kehoe 1988 and Rathbone 1991 (tenancy); Evans 1980 and de Ligt 1990 and 1991 (peasantry). For the Roman villa, Marzano 2007. On Roman land division, see Choquer et al. 1987 and Choquer and Favory 1991; for a translation and commentary on the *agrimensores* (land surveyors), see B. Campbell 2000.

Ecological contributions include Gallant 1991, Garnsey 1988 and 1998, Horden and Purcell 2000, and Sallares 1991. On the physical environment, Braudel 1972 is an invaluable introduction; also see Grove and Rackham 2001. For zooarchaeological studies of Greece and Italy, see Kotjabopoulou et al. 2003 and Mackinnon 2004 respectively; for a natural history of Pompeii, see Jashemski and Meyer 2001. Key archaeological surveys include South Etruria (T. Potter 1979), Biferno valley (Barker 1995), *ager Cosanus* (Carandini et al. 2002), Messenia (McDonald and Rupp 1972), northern Keos (Cherry et al. 1991), southern Argolid (Jameson et al. 1994), Metaponto (Carter 2005), Dalmatia (Chapman et al. 1996), and the Libyan valleys (Barker 1996). For a range of other surveys, see Barker and Lloyd 1991. For a series of survey issues, especially methodology, see the POPULUS volumes (Barker and Mattingly 1999–2000). Other survey issues of particular relevance are addressed by Alcock et al. 1994, Ault 1999, Osborne 1992, and Pettegrew 2001.

For an impression of the geographical diversity of the ancient countryside, see relevant sections of regional syntheses, such as Anatolia (Mitchell 1993), North Africa (Mattingly and Hitchner 1995), Spain (Keay 2003), and Syria (Butcher 2003). For comparative regional studies see papers in Alcock and Cherry 2004. Finally, there are also useful papers on various aspects of the countryside in volumes by Cartledge et al. 2002, Mattingly and Salmon 2001, Rich and Wallace-Hadrill 1991, Salmon and Shipley 1996, Vera 1999, and Rosen and Sluiter 2006.

CHAPTER FORTY-ONE

Finance and Resources: Public, Private, and Personal

Paul Millett

1 Public Goods

Towards the beginning of his history, Thucydides argues by analogy that Agamemnon's Mycenae, though physically unimpressive, might have been as powerful as Homer implies:

> Suppose, for example, that the city of Sparta were to become deserted and that only the temples and the foundations of buildings remained, I think that future generations would find it very difficult to believe that the place had really been as powerful as it was represented to be . . . Since, however, the city is not regularly planned and contains no temples or monuments of great magnificence, but is simply a collection of villages in the ancient Greek way, its appearance would not come up to expectation. If, on the other hand, the same thing were to happen to Athens, one would conjecture from what met the eye that the city had been twice as powerful as in fact it is. (1.10, trans. R. Warner)

Thucydides' striking prediction of the fate of Sparta has often been noted; less so his observation about Athens, presumably made shortly after the defeat of 404 and loss of empire. The double paradox of power and appearances reflects different choices made about the exaction and deployment of resources. Thucydides later reminds the reader (1.19) that, whereas the Spartans did not demand tribute from their allies, the Athenians certainly did.

This chapter is about changing patterns in the provision of "public goods" – that is, collective goods and services: those aspects of communal life that cannot be divided into units susceptible of support by individual beneficiaries or consumers. Such monolithic wants (the Parthenon with its priests, or Hadrian's Wall and its garrison) have to be satisfied by public or quasi-public provision. Taxation is therefore at the heart of the process, though in the broadest sense of compulsory (occasionally voluntary) transfer of resources and services of all types to satisfy collective wants: implicit in Thucydides' contrast of Athenian and Spartan practices is the military manpower required of Sparta's allies. It is the notorious inevitability of "death and taxes" that makes both potentially valuable to the ancient historian. We are increasingly aware of the significance of "mortuary evidence" as an indicator of socio-cultural change. Public goods also have their story to tell. Their provision is intimately connected with the prevailing political system: members of the Athenian *demos* being paid for public office; the plebs of Rome receiving free handouts of grain.

Not least informative is changing emphasis on provision through time. From two thousand years of antiquity, a consolidated list of public goods would be formidable. But Thucydides on Athens and Sparta hints at two major and enduring strands in the collective mobilizing of resources: cities and warfare. Both are deeply embedded in the Classicist's psyche. The heroic materialism of city-building might seem to stand as proxy for the achievement of antiquity; urban decline being conventionally (if controversially) associated with the ending of the classical world (Liebeschuetz 2001). The waging of war was at the heart of the ancient writing of history and arguably of ancient history itself. It is a commonplace that the ability of states to realize policy goals depends on adequate resources. "War needs money," as Roosevelt warned the joint Congress in January 1942, before introducing the biggest war budget in history ($56 billion); effectively implementing Cicero's observation that "infinite money is the sinews of war" (*Philippics* 5.2.5; cf. Thuc. 1.83). Caesar supposedly put it more pragmatically, reflecting the political realities of the late republic: "Money and soldiers: if you are without one, you will at once be without the other" (Dio 42.49).

The redistributive function of public goods serves as a second historical indicator: who benefits and loses from reallocation of resources; critical in the absence of appreciable economic growth (P. Millett 2001: esp. 35–37). This is in turn tied in with power relations: a material manifestation of Lenin's "Who – Whom?" Plunder won by generals in the later Roman republic was effectively their property to do with as they pleased; under the principate, it was routinely rendered to the emperor. Any Athenian commander thought to have appropriated what was considered the property of the *demos* would find himself in court facing a capital charge. Several did so (Lysias 28).

2   The Discipline of Public Economy

Scope, provision, and allocation of public goods have always been at the heart of the part of political economy traditionally labeled "public finance," though "public economics" (after the German *Staatswirtschaft*) is marginally more accurate. It is probably the oldest branch of formal economic thought, as exemplified from the earlier fourth century BC by Xenophon's essay *Poroi*, or "Resources" (Gauthier 1976). The modern literature is intermittently useful to the ancient historian, more for prompting questions than providing answers. The *locus classicus* for taxation theory consists of "four maxims" from Adam Smith's *Wealth of Nations* of 1776 (bk 5, chap. 2, pt

2): (a) Taxpayers should contribute "as nearly as possible in proportion to their respective abilities; that is, in proportion to the revenue which they respectively enjoy under the protection of the state." (b) Taxation should be "certain not arbitrary," with clear agreement as to timing, manner, and quantity of payment; otherwise, warns Smith, taxpayers will be at the mercy of tax-gatherers, "encouraging their insolence and favoring their corruption." (c) Taxes should be levied at the time and in the manner convenient for the payer. (d) Every tax should be so contrived as to have the lowest possible administrative costs.

Smith intended these reflections to be prescriptive: they supposedly influenced the fiscal policy of Pitt the Younger. For the historian of antiquity, the maxims indicate possible pressure points in ancient regimes of taxation. High on the list were the corruption and waste traditionally associated with tax farming, the regular mechanism for collecting revenues throughout the ancient world. Caesar's displacing of tax farmers in Asia may have reduced the burden on payers by as much as one-third (Dio 42.6.3; Appian 5.4). Payments in cash rather than kind (or *vice versa*) might be imposed on those with no effective power to negotiate (von Reden 2007: 296–302; Manning 2008). Conscription and corvée labor might be inflicted alongside other more-or-less unpredictable exactions: requisition of fodder and draught animals, forced billeting, *angariae* (compulsory transport) and the like (N. Lewis 1983: 172–76 for Egypt). At the extreme of Smith's arbitrariness-index stood the right of Roman soldiers to insist that passing locals carry their packs. Its appearance in the Sermon on the Mount ("going the extra mile"), alongside turning the other cheek, indicates the likely degree of resentment (Matthew 5:38–41; cf. de Ste. Croix 1981: 14–15).

Subsequent thinking by classical economists focused on the ambiguity of Smith's first maxim, distinguishing taxation of the individual according to extent of benefits received (those with most property gained most from its security) from ability to pay. Conservative theorists favored the former, going hand in hand with "small government": national defense, protection of property, and little else. In the debate over the so-called "allocation function" (public vs. private), Smith had allowed expenditure on defense, justice, education, and limited public works "for facilitating the commerce of society" (bk 5, chap. 1). Ricardo in his *Political Economy and the Theory of Taxation* (1817) quoted with approval the maxim of his French contemporary John Baptiste Say: "The very best of all plans of finance is to spend little, and the best of all taxes is that which is least in amount" (chap. 16).

More liberal theorists came to support the principle of the ability to pay, as exemplified by John Stuart Mill's concept of "equality of sacrifice" (1848): surrender of one-tenth of one's income meant much more to a poor than to a rich man (*Principles of Political Economy*, bk 5, chap. 2). "Sacrifice theory" seemed to lead logically not only to progressive taxation (equal absolute sacrifice), but even the equalizing of incomes (equal marginal sacrifice) (Dalton 1964: 59–60). Neo-classical economists performed a similar service for the provision of public goods (the "distribution function"), determining the theoretical conditions of optimal want-satisfaction. *Economics of Welfare* was the title chosen by A. C. Pigou for his formal account of public economy from 1920.

It will be appreciated how distant much of this theorizing seems from the perspectives of the ancient world, where equality of sacrifice, maximization of benefit, and optimizing public welfare through "social spending" were alien concepts. (Their direct applicability even to modern capitalist economies has been forcefully questioned: Musgrave 1968: 156–59.) Hellenistic benefactors routinely stipulated that better-off beneficiaries of their generosity should receive more than poorer citizens – means-testing in reverse. Three linked inscriptions from Sillyium in Pamphylia (second century AD) detail gifts of *denarii* according to status: councilors (85), elders (80), assemblymen (77), citizens (9), non-citizens (3), freedmen (3), wives of the first three grades (3) (*IGRR* 3 800–802; Hands 1968: D41). The *alimenta* (family allowances) paid in Italy under Trajan and his successors, apparently intended to boost manpower, seem to have benefited established families rather than targeting the destitute (Hands 1968: D16–22). Status was a key factor regulating exaction and allocation right through antiquity.

Even more remote from ancient experience is the so-called "stabilization function" of post-Second World War fiscal policy, effectively the creation of Keynes's *General Theory of Employment, Money and Interest* (1936), concerned with managing aggregate demand so as to promote full employment and economic growth. Vespasian's reported rejection of improved technology for column shifting in favor of traditional muscle-power ("I have to feed my plebs") is better read as benign Luddism rather than visionary demand management (Suet. *Vesp.* 18.2). The timing of expenditure on fourth-century building-works for the sanctuary of Demeter at Eleusis suggests that significant operations were feasible only when casual labor (and oxen for haulage) were not needed on the land (Osborne 1987: 14–16). It is therefore ironic to find Harold Macmillan speaking in Parliament in July, 1935, supporting a reflationary program of public works by invoking Perikles' expenditure on the Parthenon (Macmillan 1966: 303).

Two major discrepancies further compromise the direct mapping of ancient practices onto modern theory of public finance. Taxation of income (preferably progressive), generally regarded as the "fairest" type of tax, and the mainstay of modern fiscal practice, is essentially a twentieth-century phenomenon (though considerably earlier in Britain), and virtually unknown in the ancient world. Tithes on produce (not always 10 percent) came closest (Isager and Skydsgaard 1992: 135–44). Athenian farmers producing a minimum of 100 measures offered a *dekate* (1/600th barley, 1/1200th wheat) to Demeter at Eleusis (ML 73 = Fornara 140); the Roman *decuma* is attested in republican Sicily, Asia, and Syria, with a *vicensuma* (one-twentieth) in Spain. Payment of a fixed proportion of the crop (effectively regressive) hit hardest when harvests were poor. The staple revenue raisers in antiquity were taxes on property and persons, and, in particular, customs, excise, harbor, and transit duties (normally 2–5 percent).

These ubiquitous "taxes on mobility" were a response to the high connectivity of the Mediterranean region, generating a "dizzying variety of ways of exacting value from those moving and their goods" (Purcell 2005c: 205–6; cf. de Laet 1949). Pliny explains how the best-quality frankincense imported from Arabia costs six *denarii* a pound (*HN* 11.32.63–65), the consequence of accumulated tithes, taxes, and *octrois*.

An inscription from Kaunos in south-western Anatolia reveals the regime of harbor taxation typical of a medium-sized port in the Roman empire: two local benefactors temporarily took on the payment of dues (Bean 1954; Pleket 1958). A tax law from Palmyra (AD 137) details in both Greek and Aramaic duties on donkey- and camel-loads of commodities crossing over its land frontiers (*OGIS* 269 = Sherk 1988 no. 158; cf. Matthews 1984; Zahrnt 1986). Taxes on movement were uniformly concerned with generating income, never controlling imports or exports.

There is a part-parallel with tax regimes characteristic of so-called developing countries, where a high proportion of primary producers (many aiming at subsistence), coupled with a rudimentary administrative infrastructure, have compromised effective taxation of income (Prest 1985: 30–40). The usual sources of revenue overlap those of antiquity – import duties, sales and land taxes, and death duties. Taxes of this type are vulnerable to recession and also relatively inflexible, responding slowly and often inadequately to sudden demands for revenue.

The identical problem afflicted all ancient states to a greater or lesser degree; as a general rule, the smaller the community, the greater the rigidity of public revenue and therefore expenditure. Significant resources were rarely held in reserve, save by the largest states. Even the Athenians regarded, and resorted to, the gold adorning the statue of Athena in the Parthenon as a legitimate reserve (Thuc. 2.14). In the modern Third World, public borrowing has been a frequent if problematic way forward; likewise throughout antiquity (Migeotte 1992). *Polis*-states faced with financial crises (typically resulting from war or food-shortage) responded with a range of *ad hoc* measures, including privatization, monopolies, forced loans, fiscal sleights of hand, fiduciary coinages, and barely disguised confiscation. All this, and more, is anecdotally recounted in Book 2 of the Aristotelian *Oikonomika* (van Groningen 1933). The title reflects the origin of *polis*-economics in the regulation of the *oikos* or household: the connection is made explicit by Xenophon's Socrates (*Mem.* 3.4.12). Xenophon also tells of a longer-term solution devised by fourth-century Pharsalos in Thessaly (*Hell.* 6.2–3). The Pharsalians placed their financial affairs in the hands of Polydamas, their leading citizen, who then collected and disbursed the annual revenues. "He gave a yearly account and, whenever there was a deficit, made it good out of his own fortune, paying himself back whenever there was a surplus of revenue."

The case of Polydamas was presumably recorded as remarkable: the feuding Pharsalians trusted him to the extent of making their acropolis over to him. But Polydamas serves to introduce the second feature – distinguishing ancient from more modern public economy. This is the existence of what might loosely be labeled "intermediaries," wealthy individuals whose resources bridged public and private, the "Personal" element of my title. They might be relatively modest civic benefactors, *euergetai* (do-gooders), who, in return for recognition, expended their resources in the cities of the Hellenistic and Roman worlds. Underpinning euergetism was a complex fiscal psychology, as yet incompletely understood (Veyne 1976; Gauthier 1985; Garnsey 1991).

The Younger Pliny's record-breaking benefactions to his home-town of Comum in northern Italy, approximately 4,000,000 sesterces for baths, school, banquets, and *alimenta*, were memorialized by inscription (*CIL* 5 5262 = Sherk 1988 no. 200), and in a carefully published letter (4.13) addressed to Tacitus, no less (Duncan-Jones 1974). On a correspondingly larger scale were the kings and emperors who blurred the boundary between the state and their estates. *Euergetes* (the giver) was the honorary title adopted by Antigonos Doson and by Ptolemies III and VIII (Bringmann 1993). It is clear from the monies mentioned in *Res Gestae* (15–24) that the resources deployed by Augustus (over a thousand million sesterces) were a substantial proportion of overall "public" expenditure (Millar 1981a: 191–92).

3   Public Economy and Historians

Modern writers on public finance typically refer in asides to the high profile of taxation at crucial moments in history: the English Civil War (Charles I and Ship Money), the American Revolution (taxation without representation), the French Revolution (summoning the Estates General to raise taxes), the Napoleonic Wars (income tax as "the tax that beat Napoleon"), the dominance of the House of Commons over the Lords (the "People's Budget" of 1909), and, of course, "the fall of the Roman empire" through "tax bankruptcy": the phrase is Hicks's (1968: 8). Recent decades have seen the emergence of more systematic "fiscal history" as a recognized subdiscipline of modern European history (Bonney 1999). Exponents build on the work of the radical economic theorist Joseph Schumpeter (briefly Austrian Minister of Finance after the Great War), who in 1918 made public his concerns over "the crisis of the tax state."

This piece of "fiscal sociology" (Schumpeter's own label) was first to stake out, if somewhat extravagantly, the claim of public finance on historians (7): "The spirit of a people, its cultural level, its social structure, the deeds its policy may prepare – all this and more is written in its fiscal history, stripped of all phrases. He who knows how to listen to its message here discerns the thunder of world history more clearly than anywhere else." Essentially, Schumpeter was concerned with the long-term shift from what he termed the "demesne state" characteristic of the middle ages, where resources derived substantially from rulers' estates and dependents, to the "tax state" of early modern Europe, then (as he argued) in crisis owing to the massive demands on resources made by the Great War. Recent scholars (associated with the European Science Foundation's project, "The Origins of the Modern State in Europe, 13th–18th centuries") have built on Schumpeter's broad distinction to construct a developmental model of state-formation in modern Europe.

Bonney and Ormrod (1999) identify four stages in their "conceptual model of change" in European fiscal history, moving from tribute state, through domain (demesne) state and tax state, to fiscal state. Their twenty or so indicators (useful for classicists at least to think with) include contemporary financial theory, forms of government and administration, status of office holders, methods of finance, nature of expenditure, credit structures, public enterprises, and causes of instability and chance within the system. For each stage, they seek to determine the dynamic interaction between expenditure, revenue, and credit, and to identify the fiscal crises and resultant fiscal revolutions which mark shifts between stages (18). Although their remit is early modern and modern Europe, they push back their analysis into the Roman empire (11), where they identify elements of tribute, domain and taxation states (cf. Bonney 1999: 7–9).

Historians of the ancient economy will recognize in the ambivalence of their labeling the heuristic possibilities and epistemological problems of "stage theories" of development (Bücher's "Household," "City," and "National Economy"). Bonney and Ormrod are alert to these limitations, prompting their subdivision of domain states into "primitive," "less primitive," "entrepreneurial," and "colonial" (14–15); favoring the concept of a "financial constitution" – a snapshot of a fiscal system at a particular point in time (Bonney: 1999: 5), and acknowledging that before 1815 there was no guarantee of linear development in taxation regimes.

Their emphasis on fiscal pluralism and flux echoes the experience of antiquity; more clearly still when analyzing the interplay of warfare with taxation. Behind what Bonney terms the "predatory principle," dominating the European scene down to 1945, the power of the state to coerce depended ultimately on the fiscal strength to underwrite its armed forces; successively, Castile, the Dutch republic, France, Britain, and Prussia (1999: iv). Warfare repeatedly emerges as the fiscal imperative driving taxation and expenditure: chronic insufficiency of revenues to fund warfare precipitated crises in taxation and the forced remodeling of financial regimes, with conspicuous success in Britain 1793–1815, and again 1914–18. From antiquity, it is sufficient to point to the extensive restructuring of finance undertaken by the Athenians in the course of the Peloponnesian War, by Augustus in the aftermath of the Civil Wars, and by Diocletian, consequent on the military upheaval of the third century. But differences again prove illuminating: "the world we have gained" in the modern fiscal state, with its integration of progressive income tax, central banking, planned budgeting and public borrowing, to promote sustained economic growth and even social justice.

A crucial element in modern fiscal stability is the notion of "fiscal compliance." Although people habitually grumble about taxation and strive legitimately to avoid payment, relatively few practice outright evasion. Behind this observance are key components of the modern fiscal constitution. In *Trusting Leviathan* (2001), Martin Daunton has detailed the role of the Commons and local government in providing "avenues of appeal and mediation" serving to legitimate the fiscal system in the eyes of nineteenth-century British taxpayers (4–22): "Consent, trust, and legitimacy are crucial to the history of taxation" (7). Leading considerations include confidence in the compliance of other taxpayers: absence of "free riding" through either evasion or glaring grants of exemption; conviction that revenue is not wasted either through inefficient or corrupt collection, or by being diverted to unworthy recipients; and, conversely, trust by the state that the majority of taxpayers honestly make payments, avoiding the need for draconian regimes of collection and deterrence. All these factors constitute more-or-less contested areas within antiquity. The theme of exemption from taxation for individuals and even whole communities runs right through the fiscal history of Rome.

Within the fiscal state can be discerned a complex fiscal psychology; far more subtle than the elemental conflict between the revenue-maximizing state and the tax-minimizing public, envisaged by the Virginia school of public economics (Daunton 2001: 8–9). From the ancient world it is difficult to penetrate beyond inevitable (though not necessarily unjustified) complaints about the burden of taxation (N. Lewis 1983: 161–65). But there are occasional hints of a more complex fiscal mentality, as indicated by the "voluntary contributions" (*epidoseis*) from the wealthy that were, alongside liturgies, such a feature of Athenian public economy. When Theophrastus from later fourth-century Athens wishes to caricature an "over-zealous man," he has him stand up in the assembly and pledge more money than he can afford; his "illiberal man," when donations are being solicited, quietly gets up and leaves (*Characters* 13.2, 22.3; cf. Migeotte 1983; 1992).

Implicit here and elsewhere is the manipulation of taxation in the construction of identity: the rhetoric of resource allocation. This is most apparent where individuals are involved and historical reality is not at a premium, as in anecdotes preserved by Suetonius. Nero was devastatingly pilloried during a food shortage for having ordered that a grain ship from Alexandria be loaded with sand for the arena (*Nero* 45.1). Gaius supposedly levied extraordinary taxes on the sale of food, on legal transactions, porters, prostitutes, and pimps, perversely posting the new regulations where no one could read them (*Calig.* 40). When Vespasian was allegedly challenged by his son for levying a tax on public urinals, his response was, "the money does not stink" (*Vesp.* 23.3). Hardly at stake here is whether such a tax was levied (le Gall 1979: 121–26); more pertinent is the moral dimension represented by the son's ethical orthodoxy, countered by the earthy pragmatism of Vespasian, disassociating ends from means.

The *Historia Augusta*, even more remote from (f)actual accuracy, routinely characterizes emperors through their fiscal activities. The "good" emperor Marcus Aurelius encourages the compliance of other payers by his careful public expenditure (11), especially over superfluous handouts (23); but he spends freely to relieve flood, famine (8), and plague (13). The needs of the imperial treasury never influence his judgment in lawsuits (12). After emptying the Treasury through successful wars, he makes up the deficit by a two-month sale of personal possessions (17). By contrast, his son Commodus "squandered the resources of empire" by drinking till dawn (3), murdered for personal profit (5), embezzled funds provided for a faked African journey (9), was ludicrously generous to the plebs and, "having drained the Treasury," excessively tightfisted to those more deserving (16). He performed hardly any public works, falsely claiming others' efforts as his own (17). It was left to his successor Pertinax to set things straight (7–9).

4 Ancient Public Economies Through Time

The creation of any community generates social wants; at the most basic level, the *soteria* (security) identified by Aristotle as fundamental to the good life (*Pol.* 1252a24–35). Resources available to satisfy such wants are limited by "taxable capacity" – that which remains after what is needed for individual subsistence (food, clothes, housing) has been deducted. The concept is necessarily flexible. Societies deploying rudimentary technology will dispose of a minimal taxable surplus. This may help explain the Bronze Age systems of Minoans and Mycenaeans (c.1900–1200 BC), unique from the Greek world in the degree of their centralized control over resources. Testimony of the Linear B tablets (enumerating everything down to broken chariot wheels) combines with extensive storage facilities of the palace-complexes to suggest a "redistributive" system of goods and services: "mobilization" so as to support and maintain the ruling elite (Scheidel et al. 2007: 175–210, esp. 188–90). Without any formal idea of private property, taxation as such cannot exist. Totalitarian control made feasible (at least, in theory) appropriation of the maximum surplus beyond subsistence.

The supposed "Dark Age" that followed on from the Myceneans (c.1100 BC) was conceivably brightened for peasants and other producers by destruction of the apparently all-encompassing palaces. The well-stocked storeroom of Odysseus (*Od.* 2.337–46) may faintly echo the Bronze Age palace economy, but redistribution was replaced in the world of Homer by reciprocity between aristocratic *oikoi* (Finley 1978; Scheidel et al. 2007: 212–13, 295–97). "When Agamemnon . . . offers to Achilles for his friendship the sovereignty of seven Greek cities, the sole advantage which he mentions as likely to be derived from it, was, that the people would honour him with presents." Adam Smith cites Homer (*Il.* 9.291–98) as a commentary on "nations of husbandmen who are but just come out of the shepherd state" (bk 5, chap. 1, pt 2). Competitive gift giving encouraged donors to temper the impulse to impress with a realistic "self-assessment." Alcinous planned to recoup the gifts he and his fellow-aristocrats offered to Odysseus by collecting from the people, "since it would be hard on us singly to show such generosity with no return" (*Od.* 8.385–405; 13.13–15). As *their* return, the people received protection, as the warrior Sarpedon reminded Glaucon (*Il.* 12.310–21).

In the course of the archaic period emerged, unevenly and incompletely, the sets of fiscal structures familiar from the remainder of antiquity, corresponding, however imperfectly, to popular conceptions of "public finance." Fiscal systems were socially embedded, reflecting local economic conditions along with shifting political preferences and imperatives. It is possible here only to hint at the range of developments. Essentially, individual communities were concerned with two sets of relations: the reallocation of internal resources, which would regularly be augmented or diminished through control either over or by other communities.

Early Athens conformed to the *polis* pattern of small government. As late as the 480s, it was proposed that a windfall gain of 100 talents from the silver mines at Laurion be divided among the citizens, ten drachmas per head ([Arist.] *Ath. Pol.* 22.7; Hdt. 8.144). The decision to build a navy instead had far-reaching consequences. Athenian finances were transformed by the acquisition of a tribute-paying empire, policed by the fleet. Some 250 states contributed in cash or kind, from 100 drachmas up to 30 talents, according to the estimated extent of their resources (Plut., *Aristides* 24.1; cf. Nixon and Price 1990). Figures from the eve of the Peloponnesian War give an impression of scale. From a total annual revenue of approximately 1,000 talents (Xen. *Anab.* 7.1.27), some 600 derived from the empire (Thuc. 2.13), equivalent to the annual wage-bill for a workforce of c.12,000 men. This made possible the simultaneous maintenance of a massive navy of c.300 triremes (Thuc.2.24), provision of public payment for some 20,000 citizens ([Arist.] *Ath. Pol.* 24.3), accumulation on the Acropolis of a strategic reserve of close on 10,000 talents (Thuc. 2.13), and an extended program of public building – the origin of Thucydides' Athenian paradox, with which this chapter began.

The Athenian experiment in democratic fiscality (exceptional before the nineteenth century in that poorer citizens had effective control over the allocation of resources) was ended in 322 by the Macedonian takeover. Athens under the Macedonians provides the template for fiscal constitutions through the remainder of antiquity. Although city-states continued to survive with their financial systems more or less intact, these were overlaid and distorted by the demands of imperial powers (Migeotte 1995; Corbier 1991): briefly and unevenly by Philip and Alexander; more systematically by the successor monarchies; finally and emphatically under the Romans. The themes already identified hold good: crucially, the interaction of warfare and redistribution. But concepts of status, intermediaries, incidence, and compliance combine to present a set of fiscal constitutions very different from the Athenian experience.

From the brief reign of Alexander (336–23), two figures may be highlighted. From Philip, Alexander inherited debts amounting to 200 talents (Plut. *Alex.* 15); but, shortly before his death, as a hospitable gesture, he was able to settle the debts of 9,000 dining-guests, totaling 9,870 talents (ibid. 70). The figures need not be taken at face value: Arrian (7.5) mentions 20,000 talents. But Alexander plainly turned warfare into a uniquely profitable enterprise, which others emulated with mixed success. For the Hellenistic world, testimony is patchy (exceptionally rich from Ptolemaic and Roman Egypt); but warfare and its fiscal consequences loom large as Alexander's successors sought repeatedly and violently to redivide their inheritance (Rostovtzeff 1941: 137–40; Austin 1986). Basically, monarchs combined specific taxes with block tribute levied on the cities in their territories, inflicting on local taxpayers a double indemnity (A. Jones 1974: 159–60). The process of reallocation was complicated by the phenomenon of royal euergetism: some five hundred recorded donations (surely the tip of an iceberg) were made over to Greek cities and sanctuaries by Hellenistic kings; motives extended from anticipated honor to more material support (Bringmann 1993: esp. 10–11).

The First Book of *Maccabees* (10.29–30) discloses that by 152 BC the Jews of Judaea were paying to the Seleukid treasury, in addition to the regular taxes, a "tithe" of one-third of the grain and half the fruit harvest. This massive impost is plausibly explained as the response of later Seleukids to the arrears of war damages imposed by the Romans on Antiochos III after his defeat at Magnesia in 190: 12,000 talents, of which 1,000 were to be paid annually (Baesens 2006).

The episode is indicative of the fiscal consequences of Roman engagement in the East. To an unparalleled extent, Rome's imperialism drove the collective redeployment of resources throughout the Mediterranean, and beyond. Roman taxation grew organically, consequent on conquest, with tax inequalities crudely representing winners and losers, the latter subdividing into those initially resisting or submitting. According to Livy's testimony, the total of uncoined silver carried in triumphs between 200 and 174, representing only a fraction of total spoils, easily exceeded

100 tons (*CAH*[2] V.ii 128). Plunder and reparations were transformed into regular taxes. Citizens appreciated that their fiscal privileges depended on maintaining their grip over external resources. After 167 and the annexation of Macedonia (yielding some 2,400,000 sesterces per year), Roman citizens in Italy were exempted from the *tributum* or property tax (Cic. *Off.* 2.76). Henceforth, *tributum* designated the basic tax levied on the provincials. Each of the major republican laws inaugurating and extending the *annona* or corn dole may plausibly be associated with some significant addition to provincial revenue: the *Lex Sempronia* from 123 (Asia), *Lex Terentia Cassia* from 73 (Cyrenaica), *Lex Claudia* from 58 (Cyprus) (Badian 1968: 36, 76). Cicero's speeches (in particular *Verrines* and *de lege Manilia*) bear witness to communal concern over the financial side of empire. His letters as proconsul of Cilicia (51–50) offer an insider's view of everyday problems (and temptations) facing a late-republican governor. (Pliny's correspondence with Trajan as governor of Bithynia-Pontus provides an imperial counterpart.) The prevailing set of fiscal relations was later to be reconfigured according to sides taken in the Civil Wars: Appian and Cassius Dio together testify to the desperate scramble to raise resources and their direct influence on the outcomes of the struggle.

Only after Actium was Augustus able to assert fiscal discipline. *Res Gestae* bear witness to his personal role restoring financial stability to Rome: "Four times I helped the state treasury with my money." The total of 150,000,000 sesterces established Augustus as super-patron-cum-liturgist (*CAH*[2] X 130–31), providing the model for combining fiscal restraint with personal generosity, from which later emperors anecdotally deviated (section 3 above). The tax system remained relatively unchanged until the third century, arguably serving economically to link outlying provinces to the center and even to stimulate local growth, as people had to work harder (Hopkins 1980, 1995/6; but cf. Duncan-Jones 1990 and 1994).

Whatever the extent of the so-called "third-century crisis," the regime of taxation proved "unfit for purpose." Successive emperors (or their agents) had proved unable to resist the apparently easy option of raising revenue, specifically for army pay, through debasement, with disastrous consequences. By 260, "silver" coinage contained only 5 percent silver. The detail of the radical regeneration of the system by Diocletian and its subsequent development is still imperfectly understood: "gratuitously complicated" is Jones's summing-up of the public finances of the later Roman empire (1964: 411–68; cf. *CAH*[2] XI 360–61). In essence, money taxes were consistently replaced by increased personal services and inflation-proof payments in kind.

The anonymous *de Rebus Bellicis* ("On Military Matters") (E. Thompson 1952) provides a glimpse from the later fourth century of perceived financial difficulties facing the empire and one man's remarkable set of remedies. The emperors, the author argues, need to cut back on *largitiones* (imperial handouts), so reducing taxes by up to a half. Corruption in the imperial mint, resulting in widespread debasement, is to be eradicated by relocating all the minting operations to a desert island. The cost of the army is identified as the single factor endangering the whole tax system. Increased productivity in warfare, in part ensured through an ingenious set of military inventions, will double imperial revenues. The author blames current fiscal problems on the extravagance of previous emperors, specifically Constantine, who raided pagan temples for precious metals which he lavished on the rich (cf. Amm. Marc. 15.8.12). The poor, increasingly oppressed and exploited, ceased paying taxes and turned instead to brigandage. Although the overall accuracy of the analysis is open to question, the author seems to anticipate the principle underlying the "Laffer curve": a theoretical exposition of the common-sense notion that, beyond a certain point, increased rates of taxation bring diminishing and even negative returns.

In any event, the taxable surplus ultimately proved inadequate to provide for the Western empire the security highlighted by Aristotle as the essential public good.

FURTHER READING

Ancient public economy remains relatively unexplored, as indicated by Purcell 2005, itself a significant contribution. This is also an area where new and important material continues to come to light; see Stroud 1998 for a previously unsuspected grain tax law from Athens. A. H. M. Jones 1974 remains the best overview of ancient taxation. Recent work for Greece is briefly surveyed by Migeotte 1995, including his own important contributions; B. D. Shaw 1988 provides a brilliant reading of the Roman material. Entries in the *Oxford Classical Dictionary* (4th edn forthcoming) supply basic information on key aspects of public finance, with bibliography and plenty of cross-referencing: "Finance, Greek and Hellenistic" and "Finance, Roman" offer promising points of departure. The crucial relationship between warfare and resources may be explored in Sabin et al. 2007. Chapters in Scheidel et al. 2007 supply up-to-date syntheses (and far more) from the Bronze Age Mediterranean to late antiquity. Otherwise, individual volumes of the *Cambridge Ancient History* (2nd edn) provide helpful orientation, particularly for the Roman world. Specifically on the Greek side, Andreades 1933, though dated, continues to be useful. Key aspects of Athenian public economy are covered by de Ste. Croix 1953, Gabrielsen 1994, and P. Wilson 2000. It is to be hoped that the important work by Fawcett 2006 on Athenian taxation will become more widely available. For the Hellenistic world, Rostovtzeff 1941 continues to be essential, now supplemented by Oliver 2007 on Athens and Aperghis 2004 on the Seleukid economy. Von Reden 2007 and N. Lewis 1983 offer introductions to the particular cases of Ptolemaic and Roman Egypt. For the Roman world, Brunt 1990 contains several relevant chapters, including a helpful review of Neesen 1980. Nicolet 1980 supplies a convenient summary of his important, earlier work on Roman republican taxation. Republican tax-farmers find a supportive advocate in Badian 1972. Cerati 1975, Corbier 1974, and de Laet 1949 cover in detail central areas of taxation under the empire. Public finance under the later empire was a particular concern of A. H. M. Jones 1964.

CHAPTER FORTY-TWO

Ancient Technology

Tracey Rihll

1 Hidden Technology

Although largely unnoticed today, technology was an integral part of ancient life. Some of it is obvious when one stops to think about it, other technologies were well hidden (often by design), and still others pass by undetected partly because people do not think of them *as* technologies that were invented and developed by the people who used them. For instance, in the obvious category, almost every classical house contained wool-working equipment and loom, to make the clothes on people's backs, and oven and hearth, to cook every grain they consumed. In addition, the typical house contained things that were the result of a variety of different technologies, such as furniture, baskets and mats, pots and pans, jewelry, and metalwork, such as weapons, plate, and coin. An example of technology in the hidden category occurs in the story of the emperor Hadrian's design for a temple of Venus and Roma, which incorporated machines of an unspecified type. Apollodoros, an architect and engineer who had bridged the Danube and superintended the construction of Trajan's column, criticized the plans because he thought that the machines could have been accommodated unseen in a basement, had Hadrian included one (Dio 69.4.4). The professional architect Apollodoros would have rendered the machines invisible – perhaps to enhance the wonder of visitors, who thereby would have seen the result achieved by them, without seeing the means by which it was achieved. What exactly the machines were or were for remains an open question. Another case of a hidden technology is metal plating, whereby a variety of techniques were used to produce a thin coat of a precious metal over an object made of base metal, e.g. coins in the later Roman empire (Vlachou-Mogire 2006). An example of a technology that does not normally leap to mind as a technology is writing (Teffeteller 2006). It is debatable what proportion of the population at any particular time and place in antiquity could and did read and write on a regular basis, but a number of institutions and practices worked on the assumption that people could do it, e.g. the Athenian legal system, writing rude words on slingshot, and inscribing gravestones.

2   Specialization

Specialists who made a particular technology or family of technologies their principal occupation and source of income, such as cobblers, or teachers, or doctors, tended to live in urban areas where there was enough demand to sustain them. Some ancient technologies were specialized, but many were not. People living in rural areas were of necessity largely self-reliant and, like Odysseus, probably made almost everything they needed with the labor and materials available within their own *oikos* or household. Nevertheless, even in one of the busiest and most cosmopolitan places (Olympia at festival time) during the zenith of classical Greek culture (late fifth/early fourth century BC) an educated man could boast that he himself made everything on his person, including his metal ring (Plato, *Hippias minor*).

The ability of most people to make or procure for themselves most of the material goods that they needed to survive resulted in a limited market for ready-made goods, which in turn restricted the numbers of specialists making such goods. The Cynics – "Dogs," so named because they lived like them – notoriously limited their requirements to the biological necessities, rejecting even the most basic comfort goods: they satisfied themselves with just food, water, and shelter. Normal ancient living conditions included comforts that were not strictly necessary to survival as an animal, but were considered necessary to survival as a civilized person, such as clothing, a house, a mattress of straw if not a timber-frame rope-strung bed, a dish from which to eat, and so on. All of these are technological products. Most luxury goods were expensive versions of the same, made by someone who specialized in making the said goods, who therefore knew where to source rare and unusual materials, and who made the item to a higher standard than could the average householder engaging in a bit of occasional DIY carpentry, basketry, engraving, or whatever. But no one would have given up the practice of food production or procurement in order to spend their time practicing a particular technology unless they were confident of two things. Firstly, that they would make enough sales on a regular basis to cover their necessary expenses, and secondly, that there would be enough food for sale, on a sufficiently regular basis, to buy with the money that they earned as a technologist. The centrality of that issue is well illustrated in a fragment of a lost comedy, wherein the poet has a soon-to-be manumitted slave plan to open a food stall in the market, because he sees that as his best assurance of having something to eat when he is free and entirely responsible for his own survival (Menander, *The Cut-locks*). A professional craftsman or service provider would have had even less secure access to food than a food-stall holder, and so if he or she wanted to minimize his risk, he or she would have moved to practice the trade in a place that he or she thought most likely to have food for sale, every day (in general on food in antiquity, see Wilkins, FOOD AND DRINK).

Large urban centers therefore became the habitats in which full-time practitioners of technology could develop and specialize. As specialization encouraged higher standards of production and better quality goods, so such goods in turn encouraged demand for specialist-made products, and over time raised the baseline of acceptability within the urban environment. This led to perceived distinctions in lifestyle

and attitude between townies and rustics that are revealed in, for example, the Aeso-
pian fable of "Town mouse and country mouse." "Rustic" and "old-fashioned" can
be used as positive or negative descriptors, of course, some seeing the words as synonymous with notions such as "wholesome" or "traditional," while others might
associate them with "backwardness" or "simplicity." The comic dramatist Aristophanes depicts the country bumpkin as someone who's a bit smelly (*Clouds* 49–50),
while for Aesop the acknowledged delights of town life come at the too-high cost
of increased personal anxiety and danger. The honest simplicity of the self-sufficient
farmer could be contrasted with the pretentious and even suspicious products for sale
in the urban market – for example, the medical writer Galen warned patients and
doctors alike about buying drugs in the market, when they had to take on trust any
information offered about what ingredients went into them. Technology, like its gods
and heroes Hephaistos, Prometheus, and Daidalos, is not an unalloyed good, but has
defects. Perceptions played a role in the reception of technology, then as now: it
could be challenging and frightening as well as liberating and exciting. War machines
terrified, and automata entertained, in literature *and* in reality.

3   Technical Development

An old view, that there was little technological development in antiquity, asserted
more often than assessed, was based on a rather simplistic notion of technology and,
frankly, a wholly inadequate and superficial knowledge of the relevant material.
Failure to appreciate just how limited was the technological base inherited by the
Greeks from their Mycenaean, Near Eastern, and Egyptian predecessors led to gross
foreshortening of the story. This was particularly noticeable in the oversight of many
fundamental inventions and discoveries that were made by the Greeks, such as the
winch, the compound pulley and the ratchet, which three devices come together in
the crane, which was also a Greek invention. It is all too easy to miss the depth here.
Every technological area is replete with devices and techniques nesting inside one
another like Russian dolls. For example, as pointed out above, writing is a technology. Now there was writing before the Greeks, but the Greeks invented the alphabet,
which is probably one of the most important technologies ever devised. They invented
the wax tablet and stylus, of which the modern electronic notebook is just the latest
version, and which, incidentally, has reverted to the approximate size of the original.
Meanwhile the Romans invented shorthand, and the book, *qua* a codex of parchment
sheets bound together at the spine. From humble and low beginnings, a world
without the alphabet and the winch and much else besides, the ancient Greeks and
Romans went very far indeed.

By the first century BC, if not before, there were people capable of making machines
that could show the changing positions in the sky of the sun, moon, Saturn, Jupiter,
Mars, Venus, and Mercury (the five planets that are visible with the naked eye). For
this, you need not only to be handy with a metal file to cut a lot of gear wheels of
the right size and number of teeth, you need also to have a reasonably accurate theory
of planetary motion, and an ability to translate that theory into a hands-on working

model. This ancient device, which is known as the Antikythera Mechanism (after the find-spot), and was (probably) once composed of more than 70 gear wheels, allowed the user via a single knob to wind the appearance of the night sky backwards or forwards to see where these celestial bodies were on any particular date, past, present, or future (Wright 2006). It should be noted that this device, fished up from deep water by sponge divers over a century ago, and scandalously neglected for most of the time since, is far more complex than any surviving Greek or Roman treatise on mechanical topics. The old idea that those texts were flights of fancy describing machines that couldn't be built was a reflection of the intellectual limitations of the moderns who said it, rather than of the mechanical abilities of the ancients who wrote them.

4 Technical Stagnation

Another old idea about ancient technology that is superannuated is that of technological stagnation. The driving force behind this idea was perhaps the need to explain why the overall technological level of society reached a plateau and then declined in late Roman times, why post-Roman settlements look more like pre-Roman settlements than Roman ones, why the story was not just one of progress, onwards and upwards, but of decline and fall too. Now we know that a raft of factors were involved in that decline, factors which varied over the huge space of the Roman empire, and most of them had little or nothing to do with the technology as such. Ancient technology didn't "stagnate" – it was lost where and when the conditions in which it flourished ceased to exist. The particular conditions that specialized technologists require are stable, secure, populous centers with regular and adequate food supplies. If these failed, technological practitioners were forced to give up their trades and become food producers (in the case of chronic crises), or to move in search of food (in the case of acute crises), or they would have died of starvation. Sometimes recovery, partial or total, was possible; sometimes the loss of technological know-how was permanent. There is, for example, good reason to think that the Athenian silver mines at Laurion never really recovered from the loss of skilled slave-workers who ran away when the Spartans occupied Dekeleia in 413 BC, during the Peloponnesian War (Rihll 2009). The most specialized and complex technologies were most susceptible to habitat decline or destruction, while the most general and robust technologies were likely to survive changing and new circumstances. Thus pottery was made from one end of antiquity to another, and from one frontier to another, but glass production was always confined to relatively few areas, and was only in widespread use during the heyday of the Roman empire. While relatively simple ships sailed the Mediterranean and Euxine throughout the ancient period, super-freighters and floating pleasure palaces were confined to a few monarchies of Hellenistic and imperial times. And archers and slingers campaigned on the battlefield and in siege throughout the length and breadth of the ancient world, but catapults and sophisticated siege towers were largely confined to the period between the third century BC and the third AD.

Social, economic, political, and military conditions formed the context in which technologies existed, and as they varied over time and space in the ancient world, so too did the technologies that were developed and could be supported within it. Metal production, for example, requires not only the presence of ore, but also of people who are willing and able to risk their time and resources in an attempt to extract that ore, and who have the know-how to turn that extracted rock into metal. The history of the discovery and exploitation of ore bodies over the course of world history reflects the patchy and changing nature of that knowledge and investment. Metal production also requires the existence or development of whatever tools and plant may be required for the extraction and processing of the ore; it requires security so that thieves or thugs, official or freelance, cannot rob of their due rewards those who have had the luck and the skill to achieve their goal. It requires infrastructure such as roads and support services, so that, at the very least, necessary materials can be moved into and out of the working area, and food and water is available for the miners and others involved in the metallurgical production processes. Thus a whole concatenation of conditions must be "right" for a particular technology to be exploited at a particular place and time. Consider the modern situation with regard to power generation, for example; nuclear power stations and even wind farms are built in certain places at certain times for reasons that have little to do with their technologies and much to do with local and national politics. Rarely were the constraints in antiquity purely technological, though it did of course happen. An example is cast iron, which when made accidentally was discarded as waste, because the ancients lacked any means by which they could work it and render it useful in their world; cast iron is hard but brittle. Steel, on the other hand, strong and flexible, they could make from wrought iron, so called because it was wrung out of a spongy mass of fused metal and rock that emerged from an ancient iron furnace, by prolonged hammering and reheating – unless, of course, the temperature had been allowed to rise too high and cast iron resulted.

Then as now, "big" technologies were sponsored, economically and politically, by government action. The cost of an aqueduct, for example, was beyond the reach of almost everyone except tyrants, kings, and emperors, relatively few of whom could and were prepared to spend the funds of the nation on what would now be considered prestige projects or long-term investments in infrastructure. There were no compulsory purchase orders, so an aqueduct's routing required political if not military domination too (Livy 40. 51). Roman roads announce Rome's domination, as they march across the empire, almost as loudly as, and much more persistently than, the armies that used them to get from A to B (Witcher 1998). Rome controlled and ordered the countryside through technology, as it cut tunnels through mountains, bridged valleys, stabilized bogs, drained marshes, dammed gorges, and by-passed rapids with canals.

War machines were another state-sponsored domain, whose development reflected very closely the foreign policies of the states concerned (Rihll 2007). Those with ambition to rule needed to invest in the material and immaterial technologies of war: weaponry, other military equipment such as mines, pontoon bridges, and siege devices, and tactics and training for all conceivable situations, offensive and defensive.

Those with ambitions for autonomy needed to invest heavily in the latest fortifications, if not also military hardware, when the shadow of an imperialistic power began to fall near their border, or if they were threatened with involvement as allies in larger wars between superpowers. Those communities with no such pretensions to independence, which includes those places whose acquisition had been consolidated, territories pacified, and provinces disarmed, had no such need to spend time and money on the production and maintenance of the accoutrements of war. Of course, when conditions deteriorated, such places often found themselves at the mercy of other people who by force of arms attempted to take whatever those people had spent their surpluses on. It is in such conditions that we find hastily and poorly built city walls, constructed of stone plundered from old buildings in the vicinity and rubble. Again, economic, social, and political conditions could be such that disputes were settled without recourse to arms, and the relevant war technology held by both sides was rendered redundant, for the moment or in perpetuity. Philip II of Macedon, famous for his radical development of Macedonian arms and military organization, when told that a proposed target was unassailable, astutely observed that he had yet to find a city that was impregnable to a donkey laden with gold (Cic. *Att.* 1.16.12). A single traitor can circumvent the best military technology in the world. And Rome long bought off assorted barbarians with tribute, or "foreign aid" (the term is Peter Heather's, 2005).

Other technologies were widely if erratically distributed across space and time for similar reasons of need and use. The diving-bell, for example, would only have been of interest to sponge-, pearl-, and other divers, and so, although it was in existence from at least the fourth century BC ([Aristotle] *Problems* 32. 5), it probably had a very limited distribution. Likewise, the construction and use of a scallop dredger (Aristotle *History of Animals* 8.20) was probably of interest to a very limited proportion of the populace that walked the streets with Aristotle, as it is among us, though no doubt a larger proportion then, as now, had an interest in the supply of the scallops. People are usually more interested in the products of a technology than in the technology itself; most of us watch television or use computers with little (if any) interest in how they work, for example, and we enjoy central heating without giving the thermodynamic principles of the boiler and radiator a second thought – unlike the Byzantine artist who apparently depicted them in a miniature (Fountas 2006).

Methods of preserving common agricultural foodstuffs, meanwhile, would have been common knowledge to all involved in growing them, as the technologies of basic textile production would have been common knowledge among women. As a result, our sources usually take such knowledge for granted, and so, ironically, we lack specific and detailed accounts of the most common technologies. On the other hand, when errors are recorded in the surviving literature, for example the notion that asbestos came from a plant rather than a rock (Pliny *HN* 19.19), they are pretty good indications that the author's knowledge of the relevant technology of production was at best partial, and suggests that such products were known to that author only in their finished or semi-finished state. But ignorance of a material's true nature or properties did not prevent its use in a rational way. Asbestos was used to protect the legs of those working with molten metals and glass from splashes of liquid that would cut unprotected flesh to the bone in seconds (Dioscorides 5.138). Indigo, imported from India, was used as a pigment instead of a dye, since it is insoluble in water and the ancients apparently never discovered a method to dissolve it.

5   Mass Production

Mass production existed where supply or demand was concentrated and heavy, or where it was uneconomic to produce small quantities. Many natural resources, such as ore bodies, particular plants, and particular minerals, occur densely in limited localities, while the great cities of antiquity, or an army on the move, constituted heavy localized demand that could only be met by production levels raised significantly above subsistence levels, if only temporarily. Papyrus and glass are both examples of the raw materials occurring in limited localities. Papyrus (N. Lewis 1974) was an Egyptian monopoly because it only grew in the Nile, and papyrus making was therefore confined to Egypt; when the Ptolemies forbade the export of papyrus, apparently as a political manoeuvre to annoy if not harm the Seleukids, parchment was invented in Anatolia to satisfy local demand for something to write on. Most Roman glass was mass produced in large blocks at a few sites in the empire (e.g. Apollonia, Israel), because a particularly suitable sand was found there, whence it was distributed across the empire. Once made, the blocks of basic glass were broken up into chunks, and the chunks were transported as required, and remelted at the destination (and sometimes colored during this reprocessing phase) to make a variety of finished glass products, such as beakers and bottles, in the provinces (Freestone 2003). Leather and metals were mass produced for slightly different reasons. Tanning, though it requires no rare and unusual ingredients, does require a series of vats containing increasingly strong solutions of preservative (tannins) (Waterer 1976). This intrinsically encourages mass production, because one must start with the weakest solution, which is the oldest, and end with the strongest, which is the most recently made brew, which would be a hugely wasteful process were it not employed on a series of hides, so that hides begin their journey in the leftovers from prior production, so to speak. Metal production, meanwhile, is an example of production where economies of scale are critical, over and above the fact that the raw materials are normally concentrated in a very limited number of localities. Those who sought and paid for a license to extract the very rich ore in Laurion, for example, needed to mine and process 16 kilograms of ore (on average) to make each 4-gram silver drachma; a process like this was only economic when conducted on a large scale (Rihll 2000).

Scaling-up production from the domestic to the commercial, for those industries that could do it, sometimes entailed scaling-up of equipment, with or without multiplication of units, and that in turn sometimes encouraged mechanization, which over time developed in both quantitative and qualitative terms. The most easily demonstrable example of these developments is in bread production. A concentration of consumers was the *sine qua non* for the mass production of goods such as bread. The eruption of Mount Vesuvius in AD 79 captured, as it destroyed, the city of

Pompeii in the Bay of Naples. Excavation of this city has so far revealed a number of bakeries. Each of these were equipped with several flourmills of a type now named "Pompeian" after them, with an hour-glass-shaped upper mill rotating around a conical, static, base stone. Some were also furnished with dough machines, to knead large quantities of dough mechanically. Both allowed the simultaneous processing of much larger quantities of material than would have been possible by hand. The rotating mill has been described as "one of the greatest discoveries of the human race" (Jasny 1950: 238). Those set to work on them might have begged to differ. Apuleius has left us a graphic account of the misery he imagines a mill worker to suffer (*Met.* 9.12) – far worse than, but in key respects similar to, that endured by the free bakers in eighteenth-century Paris and described so well by Kaplan (1996). It was a horrible job – physically hard, mind-numbingly boring, and the flour dust made the eyes sore, the lungs choke, and the skin itch. However, the same design of machines might be powered by human muscle, by animal muscle, or by water power. Several centuries later Ostia was abandoned, as its harbor silted up, leaving the city to fall into a neglect that preserved it almost as well as Vesuvius preserved Pompeii. And from it we can see that the design of mill and dough machine was largely unchanged through these centuries, but the scale of production had increased significantly: the bakeries of Ostia contain, on average, nine millstones, rather than the three or four more commonly found elsewhere (Bakker 2001). Elsewhere, water power, supplied typically by aqueduct, was sometimes utilized to drive the millstones. The water might come direct to the mill, as at Barbegal near Arles in France, where 16 wheels were powered by one purpose-built aqueduct which divided into two races (Leveau 1996), or second hand, after passing through some other facility such as a fountain house or bath, as in the basement of the Baths of Caracalla (Schiøler and Wikander 1983). Part of a similar multi-wheel facility has recently been found on a steep slope of the Ianiculum in Rome – not the main sets of mills mentioned in the literary sources, but an outlier group (M. Bell 1994) – and more are known in Israel and Tunisia and suspected elsewhere, e.g. Kolossai in Phrygia (M. Lewis 1997: 71).

The earliest evidence that we currently have for the water mill is literary, and dates to the end of the first century BC or thereabouts. Antipater of Thessalonica, a contemporary of Vitruvius (who mentions the water mill at 10.5.2), celebrated the new technology and the new Utopia it promised – machines to take the workers' places, machines to perform the chores, while those who used to perform them could enjoy a lie-in in bed and the fruit without the toil:

> Hold back the hand that works the mill; sleep long
> You grinding-women, though cocks announce the day
> Demeter has put your work out to the nymphs
> Who jump onto the very top of the wheel
> And spin the axle which with twisting cogs
> Revolves the Nisyrus millstones' hollow weights.
> A golden age has come again, we learn
> To feast on Demeter's produce without work.
> (*Anth. Pal* 9.418, trans. A. Elliot, modified).

The number of water mills attested archaeologically, ranging in date from the first to the fourth centuries AD, is 62 and counting (Wikander 2000; Wilson 2002), and there is possibly quite some way to go. And it wasn't just the food supply that could have been transformed by technology. Recent discoveries of water-powered saws that cut a block of stone simultaneously into several sheets of thin veneer show us that Roman politicians could transform cities of brick and concrete into cities of marble economically, using mass-produced cladding (Colloque international, "Force hydraulique et machines à eau dans l'Antiquité romaine," le Pont du Gard, September, 2006, papers by Grewe, Mangartz, and Seigne).

6   Epilogue

Hodge pointed out that the Barbegal mill (which is now dated to the second century AD, not the fourth) was ignored until the 1930s, despite the fact that it did not need excavating, it is located in a densely populated area of a modern, developed country, and it is a large, obvious ruin on a hillside (1991: 260–61). He rightly asked, if a site as imposing as Barbegal can go unrecognized for so long, how many more Barbegals await discovery in less populated, more remote, and less studied regions of the Roman empire. How many, indeed? Perhaps the real reason for the neglect is that, from its inception until very recently, classical archaeology has attracted those who are interested in art and architecture, while those who are interested in industrial archaeology choose to study more recent periods, where they expect to find grist for their mill, and not antiquity, where they do not. Changing perceptions of ancient technology will no doubt help transform the situation, and provide new data, and new challenges, in an area that is as yet barely touched.

FURTHER READING

Primary sources are almost limitless. I have yet to read a surviving classical source that has nothing to contribute to the subject of ancient technology, for even the punctuation is a technological artifact. There is an excellent selection of sources on all of the more obvious *and* some of the less obvious technologies of antiquity in Humphrey et al. 1998, which should be the first port of call for anyone interested in the subject. Obviously, with such a large and diverse field, there are few syntheses in existence, and most works concentrate on one particular area, or a few, e.g. K. White 1984, K. Greene 1986, Lucas 2006. Oleson's handbook of engineering and technology (2008) gives sound overviews of most topics (though there are omissions, e.g. color production), which will help those new to the field navigate the landscape (published after this chapter was completed but see my review, *Aestimatio* 2008). Some modern works on ancient technology are rather old-fashioned in their approach, their interpretation, or their analysis, but at the same time they may present a valuable or significant collection of evidence that is ignored at one's peril. Cuomo 2007 offers a very different sort of history of ancient technology, that focuses more on attitudes to technology than to the products themselves, more on the knowledge required to make or do something than on how it was made or operated.

Modern scientific techniques are transforming our understanding of both production and distribution of ancient manufactured goods. Here the literature overlaps with works on trade in antiquity. New analytical tools developed in pursuit of modern political goals, such as the principle that the polluter should pay for the clean-up, can have spin-offs for ancient historians trying to estimate output from particular ancient mining areas, for example (Rihll 2009). Such tools are also being applied to the scores of newly discovered fragments of the Antikythera Mechanism, discussion and color photographs of some of which can be found in the *Proceedings of the Second International Conference on Ancient Greek Technology* (Athens 2006, 820–32); see also the Antikythera Mechanism Research Project at http://antikythera-mechanism.gr

The recent educational principle of life-long learning, together with the long-standing tradition of retired or leisured professionals pursuing the ancient roots of their profession, both contribute significantly to studies in ancient technology. Classicists are not, after all, by that training equipped to understand mechanics, or pharmacology, or thermodynamics, or a host of other physical processes that lie at the heart of ancient technologies. For example, retired naval engineers contribute to debates over ancient ship design (Tilley 2004); civil engineers study Roman bridges (O'Connor 1993); mechanical engineers explain the operation of ancient vehicles and mills (Lawton 2004). There is, in short, no end to the literature on ancient technology, and this guide can barely scratch its surface.

There is a significant amount of relevant material, with references and links to other websites, on my website on Greek and Roman science and technology: www.swan.ac.uk/grst/ Home%20Page%20G&RS&T.htm. For specialist book reviews, see *Aestimatio: Critical Reviews in the History of Science* (http://www.ircps.org/publications/aestimatio/aestimatio.htm).

PART VII

Politics and Power

CHAPTER FORTY-THREE

Structures

Hans Beck

1 Introduction

The term *structure* is used in many academic and non-academic contexts, yet it is rarely conceptualized. Social scientists collect and analyze structural data; a starship's hull has a structural integrity, as have atoms, high-rise buildings and rituals; epics such as the *Odyssey* or *The Lord of the Rings* follow a narrative superstructure; many ethnic groups are exposed to structural violence; linguistic approaches towards language include attempts to explore its logical structure, while structuralism in anthropology, as pioneered by Claude Lévi-Strauss, investigates the modes by which meaning is produced within a culture. The common implication underlying these examples is that something – material elements, a political organization, an academic discipline – consists of multiple parts that relate to each other, their structure being both the multiplicity of parts and their mutual relation. This meaning is already inherent in the Latin word *structura*, from which the modern term derives.

Historians have a difficult relation with structure. Ever since Herodotus of Halicarnassus presented his *historias apodeixis* ("Display of Inquiry," though "Histories" is the more common translation), historians have sought to uncover the past. History, as a discipline, investigates systematically collected sources rather than deterministic structural forces. The study of the latter was extremely popular in the 1960s and 1970s, when the followers of structuralism claimed to offer a "scientific" approach to history through the meticulous calculation of, for instance, unemployment rates, GNPs and poverty lines. The refinement of sociologically inspired methodologies and anthropological concepts added to the discovery of structural patterns which are specific to human society. This approach was tremendously fruitful and continues to be influential, but it also faces criticism. The main objection is that structuralism, while rightly emphasizing the *longue durée* of historical processes (Braudel 1972), overstretches the concept of synchronicity. It oftentimes leaves too little space for diachronic change and development through time (cf. Renfrew/Cherry 1986: 18).

Although more recent trends in history writing emphasize various and at times competing concepts, it is fair to assert that the notion of culture, and the way it is transmitted and transformed, is at the core of today's research. Current approaches, which are greatly inspired by the cultural studies turn, include a renewed interest in the processes and practices of generating, perpetuating and communicating power (political, religious, sexual, etc.). At the same time, human agency – that is, the capacity of individuals to shape the process of history – has regained its deserved scholarly attention.

But processes such as the communication of power require a viable structure. Human action is embedded in a set of norms, patterns and sentiments that give meaning to that action and "structure" it. This set embraces both the horizontal distribution of structures as well as vertical patterns of hierarchy. Niklas Luhmann's œuvre on system theory (cf. Luhmann 1995) is built on the assumption that those features are shared by bureaucracies, chains of command, or family bonds alike. Hence, when social scientists and scholars in the humanities speak of political or social structures, they refer to entities, institutions, and/or groups as they exist in definite relation to each other, and to their horizontal and vertical interaction within their respective systems. The dense network of this interaction constitutes a landscape that prefigures human action and contextualizes its behavior. Despite the historian's concern with process and change, history is therefore inexorably driven by structure.

Yet structures are never static. They have their own history. Take the unfolding of political institutions or, in the economic domain, the interaction between trade and cultural transmission. Even though this interaction is shaped by patterns of continuity, it is susceptible to human action and oftentimes moments of contingency that punctuate episodes of structural change. In the Aegean, always a highway for the exchange of ideas and goods, the structures of trade and cultural communication changed so dramatically towards the end of the Bronze Age that it is virtually impossible to forge a structural account that covers the time span of any two generations. Similarly, a static approach to the Roman republic has become increasingly difficult. Current research on the interaction between the senatorial elite and the *populus Romanus* stresses the exposure of this relation to constant change and adaptation. While the formal arrangement of politics, that is the organization of magistracies and assemblies, in principle remained the same throughout the republic, modern scholarship detects a great fluidity and in some periods even a dramatically accelerated change in the actual mechanics of republican government. It has been argued that when the republic fell, this was due to a perpetuated crisis, in fact a "crisis without alternative" (C. Meier 1982), which implies a structural deficit of Roman politics that would not allow for adaptability – and hence had to be replaced in an act of revolution (see section 3 below). This view has been challenged by Erich Gruen, who forcefully denied the necessity of such a development: "Civil war caused the fall of the republic – not vice versa" (Gruen 1974: 504). What caused the fall of the Roman republic, then, a structural deficit of politics, a series of more or less contingent wars, or the human agency of men like Sulla, Pompey, and Caesar? It is the historian's task to disclose the underlying structural principles of human action. At the same time, the historian must present an account that is open enough to reflect the dynamics of continuity and change. History writing juggles process, structure, and event.

2 Political Structures and Institutional Power

The problem is not new, nor is the attempt to compose a narrative that balances the outlined principles. Some time in the third quarter of the fourth century BC, one of Aristotle's pupils wrote an account on the "Constitution of the Athenians" (*Athenion politeia*). Classical Athens was the flagship of democracy in a world in which hundreds of city-states (*poleis*, sing. *polis*) lived under different degrees of popular participation. Although by then the glory days of democracy had already been shattered, the work was a forceful homage to Athenian achievements. Since the first paragraphs of the papyrus have not survived, it is uncertain whether it included an opinionated introduction such as the one found in Cicero's *De officiis* ("On Duties"), which in some ways seems to have been inspired by Aristotle's approach. Notwithstanding this gap, the main body of the text may very well provide a telling clue as to what the author wanted to portray. It presents a history of Athenian political institutions showing how the "classical" form of democracy had been brought about and how it determined the "present form of the constitution" ([Arist.], *Ath. Pol.* 42).

The idea of composing a study of Athenian institutions was ground breaking. It seems to have triggered the collection of information on other Greek constitutions. The corpus of Aristotle's works included at least 158 such treatises on the governments of tribes and city-states, only a few lines of which have been preserved through dispersed excerpts found in medieval and Renaissance literature. A generation before Aristotle, Xenophon, an exiled Athenian who had close relations with Sparta, published an account entitled *Lakedaimonion politeia* ("Constitution of the Lakedaimonians," i.e. Spartans) that did survive in full. Xenophon's approach to Sparta's "constitution" can be considered more comprehensive, in the sense that it deals with cultural traditions, social practices and religious beliefs. Despite the differences in style and scope, both works present a remarkable attempt to conceptualize, and systematize, the mechanics of government through the study of political structures. Their underlying assumption is manifold: that the *polis* community recognizes the authority of institutionalized power, that citizens obey laws and institutions that exercise that power, and that citizens participate in the vexed interplay of institutional checks and balances so that they are allowed an equal share in the institutions of state power.

Greek city-states possessed similar political structures. The common distinction between democracies and oligarchies related mainly to differences in the distribution of power, eligibility for office, or the concept of citizenship. *Polis* institutions included a body of annually elected magistrates (*archai*), a primary assembly (*ekklesia*), mostly for legislature, and some sort of council (*boule*) that served as a more permanent administration than the assembly. While popular law courts often supplemented the system, in smaller city-states the assembly also served as juristic body, resulting in an even more rudimentary arrangement. In many ways, this matrix – magistrates, assembly, council – resembles the organization of other Mediterranean city-state cultures.

In Athens, institutions had been significantly refined toward the end of the sixth century BC. Under the archonship of Kleisthenes, the citizen body was reorganized in such a way that citizens were to be members of one of over 100 local units called *demes*. These *demes* were grouped to form 30 new *trittyes* (thirdings) from three regions of Attica, which were distributed among ten *phylai* (tribes). The *phylai* were arranged so that each of them included *trittyes* from three different zones – coast, city, and inland. In the future, the *phylai* served as constituencies for the election of magistrates, the selection of members of the city's council and law courts, and also as brigading units for the army. At the same time, they had their own corporate life, with their own magistrates, sanctuaries, and hero cults. The Kleisthenic system provided a grand mixture of political, social, and spatial structures that integrated the citizen body in multiple ways. Even though this appears to have been only one goal of the many envisioned by Kleisthenes, the system gave Athenians an effective internal articulation. Athens' political stability throughout long periods of the fifth and fourth centuries BC was also due to this structural arrangement.

In other city-states similar systems seem to have been in place. Yet, on a more general level, it is striking to see how rudimentary the institutional apparatus for governing domestic affairs and conducting foreign policy was. The cohesion of citizenries in the classical and the Hellenistic *polis* can never be fully understood through the study of its political structures. Institutions such as a council or primary assembly were based on, and practically geared toward, the belief that only the citizen body as a whole was the representative of the state. This thought was already prominent in the seventh century BC, as is well attested by an inscription from the city of Dreros on Crete that uses the term *polis* both for the institutionalized assembly and in the more general sense of city (Fornara no. 11). The city and the legislative body of Dreros were thus perceived as one. It was this strong sense – or ideology – of a common civic identity rather than the structural arrangement of politics that was at the heart of the Greek city-state.

The habit of falling into the "constitutional-law trap" (Finley 1983: 56) is probably more common among Roman historians, thanks to the great corpus of Roman juristic tradition from the Twelve Tables to Gaius's *Institutiones* and Justinian's Code, and thanks even more to Theodor Mommsen's towering *Römisches Staatsrecht* (three volumes, 1871–88). Mommsen's approach was that of a full-fledged systematization of Roman constitutional law. The keystone of his reconstruction was the term *imperium*, a magistrate's power, that was regarded as a common point of reference for the hierarchy of public offices and for the administration of empire. Yet Mommsen was certainly aware that Rome's ruling elite had always been reluctant to govern subject territories by means of carefully planned administrative action, let alone integrate those subjects into a formalized administrative superstructure. While overseas conquest and territorial expansion accelerated, the senate refused to respond to that development.

Only a few years before the Hannibalic war (218–201 BC) the senate started to dispatch two newly established praetors to Sicily and Sardinia on an annual basis. Both islands became the first two Roman provinces, yet neither had a uniform administration. A province was often a mosaic of territories with varying statuses and the administration of justice, and local constitutions differed considerably from one province to another (in light of this it is not surprising that the early meaning of the word *provincia* was not "province," but rather "area of magisterial command"). The reason for the senate's indifference vis-à-vis a tighter structure was that any such measure might have had severe implications for the domestic equilibrium. In light of persistent aristocratic competition for public offices, the creation of new offices *cum imperio* (with the power of *imperium*) might have easily distorted that competition. Consequently, towards the end of the republic, Rome ruled the Mediterranean world with a political infrastructure that was hardly larger than that of a Greek city-state's.

It is not exactly true that "the Roman empire had no government" (Millar 1981a: 52), but it is nearly so. The essential feature of Rome's administration of the provinces under the emperors was that, while the republican structures remained largely intact, a diversified pattern of new posts and institutions answering to the extended activities of the state and the interests of the emperor had grown around them. Senatorial magistrates, called proconsuls, were appointed by lot to some of the provinces, serving there for their year of office. In other provinces, mainly the ones in which the legions were stationed, the emperor appointed governors who were called *legati Augusti* and served until they were recalled by the emperor. The distinction between imperial and senatorial provinces has often been perceived as a structural characteristic of the empire's administration, with the emperor ruling one half of the provinces and the senate the other. However, it seems now that, from the beginning, proconsuls and *legati* alike received their instructions from the emperor. The dichotomous structure of imperial and senatorial provinces is more apparent than real.

In Edward Gibbon's famous account on *The History of the Decline and Fall of the Roman Empire* (three volumes, 1776–88), it is argued that Rome succumbed to barbarian invasions because of a dramatic disintegration of social codes and civic virtues among its citizens. This view remains influential in more modern explanations, although a re-examination of anthropological records and of material culture invites a more complex interpretation. It is striking to note how little the political structure-paradigm has to offer in this regard. To be sure, towards the later period of the Roman empire notable attempts were made to respond to the demands of the day. For instance, the emperor Diocletian decentralized the structures of government in AD 293 by reducing the city of Rome's role as operational capital, replacing it with four capitals that formed the so-called tetrarchy, a term meaning a leadership of four. Yet even efforts such as this could not provide an institutional framework that was capable of channeling the wholesale transformation of the social stratum in and around the empire.

3 The Social Stratum: Micro- and Macro-Structures

Classical antiquity is not an age notorious for social revolutions (despite de Ste. Croix 1981). The Greek world was probably more susceptible to social unrest and turmoil than Rome. Internal strife (*stasis*) was endemic in many *poleis*, and rivalries between competing factions would often result in violent civil wars. But, rather than being initiated by social agendas, *stasis* only fuelled them. Domestic warfare was determined by a deadly ethos of revenge that required the disadvantaged faction to retaliate more forcefully, resulting in a vicious circle of violence and counter-violence. The competing factions hardly ever envisioned a thorough change of the social arrangement.

At Rome, the social equilibrium was more stable. Once the so-called struggle of the orders between patricians and plebeians had been settled in the early decades of the third century BC, the social stratification that distinguished the ruling aristocracy from the common people was frozen. It remained largely intact until it was annihilated in a series of civil wars in the later decades of the first century BC. The final death blow came during what Ronald Syme famously called the "The Roman Revolution." In this masterly analysis (published in 1939), Syme was able to trace the transformation of the aristocratic elite of the republic into a new ruling class that was exclusively focused on, and perpetuated by, the imperial power of the *princeps* (the first citizen). This radical social restructuring of the Roman aristocracy was carefully orchestrated by Augustus to secure his monarchical position. Hence, in this revolution – if one wants to adopt Syme's terminology – Augustus was the main revolutionary.

The other end of the social order is marked by the family, the nucleus of any society. Both the concept's underlying connotations and familial structures have changed significantly during their long history. Family in antiquity hardly resembles modern, let alone Western understandings. The Greeks did not even have a word for family. The closest is *oikos* ("house" or "household"), which embraces a wider range of political, social and economic meanings. While parents and children formed the biological core of the *oikos*, Greek households also included grandparents; a number of other extended family members, especially unmarried female relatives; as well as non-kin members, such as freedmen and slaves. Women never relinquished membership of their native household, which means that whereas men lived only in one *oikos*, women usually lived in two (S. Pomeroy 1975: 62). By comparison, the Roman *familia* was actually more exclusive and also more structured than the Greek *oikos*. The Roman family had strict hierarchies: the male was the head of the household (the *paterfamilias*), dominating over his wife and children, who were under his legal power (even though this power was less straightforward than the Roman tradition would have us believe). The strongest familial ties were blood relations between *cognati*, normally parents and their children. Children from another wife or a father's siblings were *agnati*, a secondary relationship that was detailed already in the Twelve Tables (M. Crawford 1996: II: 634–51). In short, the Roman family was tightly structured and defined through laws and customs that privileged blood relations over remoter relations such as marriage or adoption.

The familial structures into which a person was born in Greece and Rome differed remarkably. But when one looks at the wider stratum of social differentiation, those differences seem to diminish in importance. Throughout the Greco-Roman world, societies were based on a dichotomy between the privileged few and the not-so-privileged many. In Rome, whereas the ruling class of the senatorial aristocracy – and, in particular, its leading inner circle, the so-called nobility – was the political, social, and, for the most part, economic *classe dirigeante*, the vast majority of citizens were considered ordinary people, the *populus*. This dichotomy occurred in Greece as well, even though in less obvious terms. As indicated above, the assembly of people was considered to be the *polis*'s ultimate decision-making body, an arrangement that triggered a strong sense of popular power. But this shared impression of power did not rule out the existence of other mechanisms of social polarization and exclusion. The most common feature of social polarization was the division of citizens into property classes. In Athens, the citizenry consisted of four classes with only the (rich) members of the higher classes eligible for certain magistracies. The Roman voting assemblies operated along the lines of a similar, yet once again more tightly structured scheme. The most prominent assembly, the *comitia centuriata*, comprised 193 voting units. These were divided among five property classes in such a way that the higher census classes contained the highest number of centuries, while the proletarians (*proletarii*), who fell below the minimum property qualification for membership of the fifth class, were enrolled in a single century and were effectively disfranchised (Taylor 1966).

Other features of social polarization included the distinction between males and females, exemplified, for example, in the exclusion of women from politics; the differentiation between citizens and aliens, often accompanied by, and expressed through, a perception of self- and otherness; the divide between free people and slaves; and, ultimately, the distinction between mortals and gods, each occupying separate, but related realms. The social position of a person was hence defined by various dichotomies. It was shaped by "polarized oppositions" (Cartledge 2002a: 13) that signaled someone's status in negative terms, that is, it determined a person's social standing by the dual structure of what someone was understood to be only in opposition to what he or she was not. This pattern of bipolarity and mutual exclusion is among the most salient legacies of antiquity. One might add that it is also among the most burdensome.

It is worth looking more closely at the structuring forces behind the social stratification of Rome. As mentioned above, Rome's social order was characterized by a *longue durée* of political and social institutions. This order was not enforced by ruling bodies or laws, but rather by tradition. The *mos maiorum* (ways of the ancestors) provided the Romans with a tight network of collective codes of political, social and cultural practices. These codes were based on the assumption that the achievements of the Roman people were mostly due to time-honored principles and traditions. In the early second century BC, the poet Quintus Ennius coined a formula which famously encapsulates this idea: "On ancient customs stands the Roman state as well as on men" (*Moribus antiquis res stat Romana virisque*) (*Annales* 5.156 Skutsch). Later traditions offered countless examples of the glory, honor, and piety of such men who had made Rome great, from the founding fathers of the republic to Appius Claudius Caecus, Fabius Maximus, the elder Cato and many more. Livy's monumental Roman history *ab urbe condita* (Books from the Foundation of the City) projects a "written Rome" (M. Jaeger 1997), a narrative that is full of references to the exemplary deeds that constituted the ways of these men. Tradition, and the past in general, thus became obligatory points of reference that gave both meaning and stability to the present. They not only encouraged the current generation to surpass its ancestors in their achievements for the *res publica*, but also demanded obedience to traditional political procedures and social norms.

One of the landmarks of ancestral traditions was the overall consensus on social hierarchies. The senatorial elite was regarded as a leading status group, which, in turn, respected, often ostentatiously, the integrity of the common people. This mutual consensus included the conduct of politics itself. While the assemblies of the Roman people acted as decision-making bodies, they would never reach a decision without prior consultation of the senate. This principle was never put into question before the Gracchi. Mutual consensus provided an underlying, deeply rooted structure to Roman political behavior. When Tiberius Gracchus and his brother Gaius did challenge this procedure in the 130s and 120s BC, it marked the beginning of a century of civil wars. Despite the lively discourse on tradition and its structuring forces that came to light during this conflict, the clock of tradition was never set back.

4　Structuring Space – Spatial Structures

The Greek term *polis* has a twofold meaning. On the one hand, *polis* is used to designate the city-state as political entity, with a strong emphasis on the political organization of the city body. On the other hand, *polis* simply means city, a settlement with a town center and a certain degree of urban infrastructure (Hansen/Nielsen 2004). This double meaning is already omnipresent in Homer's poetry: Odysseus not only visits many cities, but living in a city is portrayed as characteristic of an advanced society. "Who are you among men, from whence? Where is your *polis*, your parents?" (*Odyssey* 1.170) was a standard address to a stranger. In this formulaic salutation, the city is juxtaposed to a person's descent and cultural identity.

What exactly constitutes a city in an ancient Mediterranean context, and how were cities structured? Archaeological indications of city development in Greece such as fortification walls, temples and public works appear in several sites dating as early as the eighth century BC. Survey archaeology suggests that smaller settlement units in the countryside were abandoned at this time, their populations migrating to nearby urban centers. Recent scholarship has extrapolated the emergence of different, yet closely interrelated structural paradigms that accompanied these processes. The first is the conceptual development of space and spatiality as underlying presumptions of urbanization. The rise of the *polis* was determined by various separations of space, especially of urban centers and sub- or extra-urban countrysides (de Polignac 1995); of spaces for the living and the dead; and also of private spheres and public spaces. In the course of this new spatial conceptualization, the Greek city became a realm defined by various internal bipolarities, while its boundaries separated its "civilized" space from the outside world. The transformation of Athens from an ancient citadel to a vibrant city with a stratified urban topography might in many ways have been exceptional. But the structural integration of the countryside and the city center under Kleisthenes (see section 2 above) also highlights the outlined principle of perceiving spaces that were separate, yet complementary parts of a *polis*.

Spatial stratification is also the key to the second paradigm. When the Greeks started to found new cities throughout the Mediterranean in the course of the eighth and seventh centuries BC, this process was not distinct from the process of urbanization. On the contrary, it was a part of it. Town planning from scratch in colonies such as Selinous in western Sicily (c.650 BC) or Metapontion required architectural expertise, and a successful outcome reassured town planners that their methods were on the whole applicable. The urban structure of Selinous was characterized by the centrality of reserved areas of profane and religious public spaces with a central axis between them. A so-called Hippodamic grid (named after Hippodamos of Miletos, antiquity's most famous town planner) was applied, which means that the city was covered by orthogonal cross-roads: streets ran from east to west, crossing the main north–south road at a right angle. In other words, Selinous's urban structure was thus shaped by an elaborate spatial stratification embedded in a grid of roads and *insulae*, a pattern that has been copied in many North American cities.

The third aspect that added to the momentum marking the rise of the Greek city was monumentalization. Once the dichotomy of urban center and hinterland had been conceptualized, and once the space within the city's boundaries reflected the internal separation of private and public space, it was only a small step toward the refinement of infrastructures. Religious buildings already stood out among the structures of the earliest *poleis*. Temples soon spread, multiplied and increased greatly in size and sophistication. The profane followed. The market place (*agora*) became the focus of the city's economic and political life. Firmly located in the center of the *polis*'s spatial framework, the *agora* symbolized the heart of the citizen community. Monuments such as honorary statues or *stelai* (stone slabs) with public inscriptions (treaties, laws, decrees, and other important writings stipulated by the people's assembly) were set up in the *agora*, which placed them, quite literally, before the eyes of the citizenry. In addition, office buildings for annually elected magistrates and meeting places for the city council were located on, or around, the *agora* to display the institutions of governmental action to the community. Just as the city, as such, expressed the civilized order of the citizenry, its central market place symbolized the internal order of this community. Hence, the *agora* not only fulfilled the primary function of providing a public space for the conduct of business and political affairs, but it also assumed the function of a 'symbolic structuring of the community' (Hölkeskamp 2004: 30).

Antiquity's most famous market place, the *forum Romanum*, in many ways fits into this picture. The city of Rome resembles the principle of a diversely structured urban space, but the complexity of the spatial arrangement in the fateful triangle between Capitol, Forum and Palatine beats that of any other Mediterranean city. The Capitol – according to a Roman tradition the *caput mundi*, or the center of the world – was regarded as the religious center of the *res publica*, while the Palatine became a distinct space occupied by the republican elite, and then, as the long process of monumentalization went on, a location reserved for the imperial household.

Between Capitol and Palatine, the Forum became the center of Rome's commercial, communal and ceremonial life. It was surrounded by monumental buildings, such as basilicas, temples and, in the earlier period, shops that soon gave way to the growing demand for public space. Assemblies of the common people were held in the adjacent Comitium, which was neighbored by the senate-house, the Curia. The close vicinity of Comitium and Curia symbolized the unity of the people and the ruling aristocracy, a unity that the Romans clothed in the famous formula *SPQR* (*senatus populusque Romanus*). But the spatial organization of the Forum also generated social meaning in more subtle ways. Many *lieux de mémoire* ("realms of memory," as coined by the French historian Pierre Nora) were situated in its square. The *lacus Curtius* and the *ficus Ruminalis*, a sacred fig tree on the spot where tradition said the trough containing Romulus and Remus landed on the banks of the Tiber, were but two. The heart of the republic was hence characterized by a highly charged, dense urban network that combined administrative, religious, public, and commemorative functions. Enriched with monuments and memorials, this setting provided a public space that not only reflected the order of society, but also gave meaning to this order and its inherent structure (for Rome, see further Bruun, ROME).

Places of memory generate a collective matrix of memorialization. They serve as points of reference to oral and written traditions. In turn, they structure, and verify, those traditions by providing additional evidence that "proves" their case. Some time in the second half of the second century AD, a Greek by the name of Pausanias composed a *Description of Greece* in ten books that became the world's first Baedeker. Pausanias's *Periegesis* was a skillful account of the geography of Roman Greece that covered the natural environment, archaeological remains, and the topography of mythical traditions as well as its *lieux de mémoire*. The text was organized along the lines of a long journey, its narrative loaded with living remainders of an enchanted past. It took the reader on a vicarious journey in Pausanias's own footsteps, recapitulating his impressions and insights. Doing so, the *Periegesis* projected an imaginary picture of Greece with a landscape that was translated from geography into text. From Hekataios to Strabo, forerunners to Pausanias had produced accounts that were written at the crossroads of culture, geography, and history. Yet, only in the *Periegesis* does a truly transdisciplinary approach emerge. Pausanias was the only one who managed to describe the geographic and topographic particularities of Greece, while evoking a picture that embodied distinct sets of historic and cultural achievements that were of immediate value to his reader. His writing thus reflects the ongoing process of "wrestling with a transcription" (Elsner 2001: 20) that faces every historian. It attests to the historian's eternal quest for a formula that translates human action into narrative, and it discloses how much our reading of history depends on the structure of that narrative.

FURTHER READING

The works of the French pioneers Claude Lévi-Strauss and Fernand Braudel have been translated into English, which makes them accessible to the Anglophone reader. This is also true for Pierre Nora's *Les lieux de mémoire* (1984–92), which has inspired a fascinating volume on realms of memory in antiquity: Hölkeskamp and Stein-Hölkeskamp 2006. Luhmann 1995 is but one monograph of a truly exhausting œuvre. His notorious self-references have provoked a pile of Luhmann companions to further the understanding of his work. The political structures of Greece and Rome are covered in most introductions to the ancient world. The debate on the fall of the republic has been reopened in the course of the current debate on Roman political culture (cf. Morstein-Marx, POLITICAL HISTORY). Hansen/Nielsen 2004 have produced an inventory of Greek city-states that comprises not fewer than 1,035 entries. The approach of de Polignac 1995 puts less emphasis on completeness, but it has greatly improved existing perceptions of the origins of the early Greek city. This can also be said of the inspiring essay of Cartledge 2002a, which projects a dazzling picture of ancient Greek world views free from classical nostalgia. De Ste. Croix 1981 is an unparalleled attempt to establish the validity of a Marxist analysis of the ancient world. His most vocal opponent is Finley, a famous advocate of Weberian societal analysis (1983 is again but one example). Studies in gender issues and sexual asymmetries profit immensely from McClure 2002, who assembles a team of eminent scholars to comment on select sources. Greco-Roman family structures are covered in the standard work of reference, Pomeroy 1975, that deals mainly with the social roles of women in classical antiquity, and see Harlow and Parkin, THE FAMILY. Current trends and approaches towards space and spatiality are summarized in the extremely thoughtful article by Hölkeskamp 2004. The interplay of texts and imaginary pictures of places, cities, or landscapes has been disclosed by M. Jaeger 1997 and Elsner 2001. The most extensive treatment of historical narratives and their characteristic structures is that of H. White 1987. Morley 1999 (chap. 3) is a bit more easy-going on this.

CHAPTER FORTY-FOUR

Citizenship

Andrew Lintott

1 The Theory of Citizenship

In the practical politics of the ancient world there was no concept of human rights to defend the individual against the powerful forces around him. The only protection both within a person's own community and to some extent outside was membership of a citizen body. Citizenship was not, however, only a defense: it was a source of opportunity for the individual to acquire greater significance by acting in conjunction with his fellow citizens. The concept of citizenship arises and changes in accordance with the history of the city. In what follows I trace the development of Greek notions and then show how they were overtaken and modified by the domination of Rome to the extent that a new concept arose that would have been as alien to the early Romans as to the Greeks of the Archaic Age.

For Aristotle citizenship was essentially active participation in the political life of the community:

> Who is the citizen and what is the meaning of the term? For here again there may be a difference of opinion. He who is a citizen in a democracy will often not be a citizen in an oligarchy . . . We may say, first, that a citizen is not a citizen because he lives in a certain place, for resident aliens and citizens share in the place; nor is he a citizen who has legal rights to the extent of suing and being sued; for this right may be enjoyed under the provisions of a treaty. Resident aliens . . . we call citizens only in a qualified sense as we might apply the term to children who are too young to be on the register, or to old men who have been relieved from state duties . . . But the citizen whom we are seeking to define is a citizen in the strictest sense, against which no such exception can be taken, and his special characteristic is that he shares in the administration of justice, and in offices. (*Politics* 3.1274a 1–23, adapted [trans. Everson])

It is immediately apparent that citizenship is activity and that it involves duties as well as privileges. Mere social and economic association is not enough. As Aristotle says later:

Again, if men dwelt at a distance from one another, but not so far off as to have no intercourse, and there were laws among them that they should not wrong one another in their exchanges, neither would this be a state. Let us suppose that one man is a carpenter, another a shoemaker, and so on, and that their number is 10,000: nevertheless, if they have nothing in common but exchange, alliance (in war), and the like, that would not constitute a state. (*Pol.* 3.1280b 17–23)

Aristotle of course is putting forward his own concept of the city-state (*polis*), deriving from his belief that the *polis* is a natural organization and that man is a "political animal." Moreover, for him the aim of the city is not merely life (i.e. physical survival) but good living (*Pol.* 1.1252b27–53a4). This is why its legislators concern themselves not only with avoiding injustice but with *eunomia*, good behavior in general (3.1280 5–6). However, Aristotle is both idealist and empiricist. His *Ethics* and the *Politics*, which is a pendant to it, take men's opinions about what is good and just as a basis for inquiry, and the greater part of the *Politics* is not the construction of an ideal community, like Plato's *Republic*, but a consultant's advice to statesmen in differing sorts of existing community. His concept of the citizen reflects the rules of the city-states he investigated.

2   The Origin of the Concept

The vast majority of city-states that existed in the Greek world c.700 BC would not have matched Aristotle's vision of the city. You would have sought in vain for any concept of citizenship, because power was in the hands of one or a few men, and neither law-codes nor the ideal of *eunomia* yet existed. Sparta was renowned for the development of its monarchy into a constitutional government by the mid-seventh century. With this came laws and a social system designed to ensure the community's survival, and indeed superiority over its rivals on the battlefield, which they termed *eunomia*. Definition of citizenship was fundamental to the system. This status belonged to the heavily armed soldiers who formed its hoplite phalanx who, as a counterpart to their duty to defend the community, received both political rights as voters in the assembly of the Spartans and economic rights through the assignation of land. Sparta was in many ways an exceptional city-state, but its concept of citizenship was archetypal. As cities developed hoplite armies, it is clear that the members of these armies came to claim an enhanced political status. How soon it was defined, and what rights, if any, were granted to those members of the community who did not serve as hoplites, varied from city to city and depended on the activity of lawgivers.

The origin of some of Aristotle's principles is apparent. The unwarlike – women, children, and slaves – could not be full citizens, though old men, formerly warriors, did not lose their status: in fact the latter were on occasion called up in an emergency. Resident aliens might acquire some of the rights and duties of citizens, but they remained members of a different community. The city was of course an aggregate of families – the starting-point of Aristotle's *Politics* (1.1252b) – and membership of the citizen-body was accordingly normally acquired through birth, though not fully at birth. It follows that questions of citizen-status were raised most acutely when colonies, new communities, were founded. This is neatly illustrated in an early (c.500 BC) document from a small, recently settled community in the Lokrian territory on the Corinthian Gulf:

> This covenant about the land shall be valid in accordance with the division of the plain of Hyla and Liskara, both for the divided lots and the public ones. Pasturage rights shall belong to parents and son; if no son exists, to an unmarried daughter; if no unmarried daughter exists, to a brother; if no brother exists, by degree of family connection, let a man pasture according to what is just . . . Unless under compulsion of war it is resolved by a majority of the one hundred and one men, chosen according to birth, that two hundred fighting men, at the least, are to be brought in as additional settlers, whoever proposes a division (of the land) or puts it to the vote in the Council of the Elders, or in the Select Council or who creates civil discord relating to the distribution of land, that man shall be accursed and all his posterity, and his property shall be confiscated and his house leveled to the ground in accordance with the homicide law. This covenant shall be sacred to Pythian Apollo . . . (ML 13, trans. Fornara 33)

We can see how land is expected to remain within the kinship group, how loss of citizenship on account of a criminal offence strikes at the whole family and deprives them of property, how the right to land is bound up with military service and the defense of the community. On the same principle, when the Greek colonists of Cyrene needed to expand their citizen body, they invited men in with the offer of a redivision of the land (Hdt. 4.159). It is also clear from other documents about early colonization that, when a man left his mother-city for a colony, he might be granted a right to return under certain circumstances, but he was essentially losing one citizenship in favor of another (ML 5 = Fornara 18, 34ff.; ML 20 = Fornara 47).

3   The Classical and Hellenistic Greek World

At Athens some definition of citizenship must have been implicit in Solon's legislation of 594–593 BC, but a major development took place later through the reforms of Kleisthenes in 507. Citizen-registration was put in the hands of the *demoi*, local districts, and in addition, according to Aristotle (*Pol.* 3.1275b 34ff.; cf. *Ath. Pol.* 13.5), slaves and aliens were enfranchised. Thus at this moment an infringement was made of the kinship principle, even if for the future citizenship was to be chiefly dependent on birth. In fact, as more people came to settle at Athens and share its prosperity, the community grew more jealous of its citizenship. Perikles passed a law in 451–450 limiting citizenship to those, both whose parents were *astoi*, of Athenian birth (*Ath. Pol.* 26.4) – this concept being distinguished from that of the *politai*, the adult males with full political rights. Previously we hear of Athenian aristocrats, e.g. the younger Miltiades, being married to foreign women, but it would be wrong to suppose that this practice was necessarily confined to the rich and powerful. Even after the overthrow of the Athenian democracy in 404 and its reinstatement the following year with the help of non-citizens, Perikles' law was reimposed (*Ath. Pol.* 40.2; cf. Tod II.100 = Harding 3), and it remained the rule. Other Greek cities were as restrictive, and more so if they were oligarchic, since a financial qualification would be required for the exercise of full political rights. At Sparta, for example, there was a variety of classifications of those who for one reason or another failed to qualify for membership of the "Equals," the full citizens of Sparta.

Citizenship was, however, awarded to foreigners both as an honor and because of its practical value by Athens and by other Greek cities. So Thrasyboulos of Kalydon, one of the assassins of the oligarch Phrynichos, was granted Athenian citizenship in 409 (ML 85 = Fornara 155), and the Samians as a whole were given the same in 405 (ML 94 = Fornara 166). The fundamental formula in the Athenian decrees is stark and revealing: "It has been resolved by the *boule* and the People that the Samians shall be Athenians." The Samians are, as it were, being relocated in political space. For the integration of an individual a more precise location was also required: Thrasyboulos was to be placed in whatever tribe and phratry he preferred, that is, in whatever political subdivision of the city and kinship group. The Akarnanians Phormion and Karphinas, when the Athenian citizenship acquired through their grandfather was confirmed in 337, were to choose their tribe, phratry, and deme (Tod II.178 = Harding 100, 20ff.). It was also possible to give foreigners privileges normally associated with citizenship without granting the status. So Eudemos of Plataea received in return for his financial support of Athens "the privilege of possession of land and a house and he shall go out on campaigns and pay the capital levies of the Athenians" (Tod II.198 = Harding 118, 29ff.). The right to own land within a city was the most valued privilege short of citizenship that it could give, but, as we have seen, it was closely associated with the duty to defend the city's territory as a whole, either in person or through financial contributions – a condition that was compendiously described in other documents as *isoteleia*. For Eudemos it meant that he would be treated the same as an Athenian, where ordinary resident aliens would also be required to pay taxes and perform some military service, but as people of inferior status.

The in principle self-sufficient and unique citizenship of a member of an ancient Greek city might be modified in other ways. A group of cities might form a federation. By the end of the fifth century the Boiotians had an elaborate federal constitution (*Hellenica Oxyrhynchia* 16.2); the Aitolians and (briefly) the Arcadians followed this example in the fourth century, and in the third century the Achaean league, whose establishment was described by its later citizen Polybius (2.41), became one of the major powers in Greece. On a smaller scale a group of cities, for example those on one island or neighboring islands, might unite their citizenships in a *sympoliteia* or *homopoliteia*, for example the cities of Keos in the fourth century (Tod II.142 = Harding 55), or Kos and Kalymnos about 200 BC (Austin 133). This did not entail that the original communities lost their civic identity, as happened in earlier "*synoikismoi*," such as those of Athens or Argos, where the dominant city eclipsed its inferiors.

The age of Alexander and his successors was one of founding and refounding cities, thus creating new citizen-bodies. Associated with this was the need to find homes for demobilized members of the armies of these kings. These might of course simply be sent back home, which caused problems when the soldiers and their families had been exiled from their former communities. We find elaborate measures documented, resulting from an edict of Alexander, reinserting these men in their citizen body:

> To the exiles that have returned their paternal property shall be restored, which they possessed when they went into exile and (to the women) their maternal property, to all those who were unmarried and held possession of the property and happened not to have brothers . . . As regards the houses, each man shall have one according to the edict. If a house has a cultivated plot beside it, another plot may not be taken. But if there is not a cultivated plot beside the house but nearby there is within a *plethron*, let him take the plot. (Tod II.202, trans. Harding 122, 4–14; cf. Tod II.201 = Harding 113, 2–12)

Soldiers were also settled in units as garrisons attached to cities, and might receive from the cities in question citizenship or some form of citizen-rights. This sort of arrangement is revealed in a later treaty between Smyrna and Magnesia by Mt Sipylus in the time of Seleukos II. The garrison of the fort near Magnesia surrendered to Smyrna, which was acting in Seleukos's interest, and Smyrna decreed "that they are to be citizens and to have all the same things the other citizens have, and they are to have, free from the tithe their allotments, the two which the god and savior Antiochos granted them and the one about which Alexander has written, . . . as many of them as are without allotments, (resolved) for a cavalryman's allotment to be given them from the (lands) located by the place" (*OGIS* 229, trans. BD 29 [= Austin 182], lines 99–103).

Our best evidence for the arrangements in one of the new or reconstituted cities is the constitution granted by Ptolemy I to Cyrene, oligarchic like that which preceded it. This draws a distinction between citizens – who may include children of former citizens of Cyrene, of members of Cyrene's own colonies, and of unions between Cyrenean men and Libyan women from Cyrenaica – and the body politic (*politeuma*): "The body politic is to be the Ten Thousand. There shall belong to it the exiles, the ones who have fled to Egypt, whomever Ptolemy receives, and who have an assessment of possessions (that are) permanently secure, together with those of the wife, worth twenty Alexander minas, (an assessment) that the assessors rate as unencumbered' (*SEG* IX.1 & XVIII.726 = Harding 126, 6ff.). The text goes on to describe the selection from this body of sixty assessors, a council of Elders, and a Council of 500 appointed by lot.

The wars of Alexander and his successors led to a greater mobility among Greeks and Macedonians and more manipulation of cities to suit the interests of the ruling kings. Nevertheless, there remained the same concept of citizenship as an exclusive privilege, which one either acquired by birth or was awarded for services rendered, and this concept continued to be associated with the cities themselves, even if they were subject to a Hellenistic king, not with their ultimate rulers.

4 The World of Rome

This situation was to change, though far from completely, through the subjection of the Mediterranean world to Rome. In a famous letter of 214 BC, King Philip V of Macedon, who had recently concluded an alliance with Hannibal against Rome, wrote as follows to the city of Larisa in Thessaly:

> I learn that those who were enrolled as citizens in accordance with my letter and your decree and who were inscribed on the stelai have been struck out. If indeed this has happened, those who advised you have missed the mark regarding what is of benefit for (your) fatherland and regarding my decision. For that it is the fairest thing of all for the city to grow strong, with as many as possible having a part in the state, and for the land to be worked not badly, as is now the case, I believe not one of you would disagree, and it is also possible to look at the others who make use of similar enrolments of citizens, among whom are the Romans, who receive into their state even slaves, when they have freed them, giving them a share in the magistracies, and in such a way not only have they augmented their own fatherland but they have also sent out colonies to almost 70 places. (*SIG*³ 54, trans. BD 32 [= Austin 60], lines 27–34)

Philip made Roman practice seem more extreme than it was. Former slaves could not normally become magistrates, though their later descendants might. He also exaggerated the number of Roman colonies, though the impression was not false, given the Roman practice of settling their citizens also in individual allotments, with no city as a focus. In general he had appreciated an important difference between Roman and Greek attitudes.

Roman writers maintained that their city was formed by a confluence of diverse immigrants, who had left their former communities, including people from outside Latium. An area between the two saddles of the Capitoline hill was called the Asylum, and Romulus was said to have used the area to receive new citizens (Livy 1.8.5–6). The tradition was reinforced by the myth of the rape of the Sabine women (Livy 1.9–13) and the fact that kings of Rome had foreign origin – the Sabine Numa and the Etruscan Tarquinii. One of the most distinguished families in the Roman aristocracy, the Claudii Pulchri, was of Sabine origin, and was said to have arrived in Rome with its clients as late as c.500 BC (Livy 2.16.4–5). However, Rome by geography and language belonged to the wider community of the Latins, which meant that from the start the city had the experience of belonging to a fairly loose federation, which joined in religious cults and military expeditions.

We have no secure evidence for the early period, but, if we extrapolate from the later "Latin right" (*ius Latii*), it seems that the cities freely granted citizenship to immigrants from their Latin neighbors, while at the same time affording asylum to those who had gone into exile when faced with criminal penalties. Legitimate marriages could be concluded between a man and a woman of different cities, and associated with this was the right to own land in another Latin community, which would be the likely consequence of the receipt of a dowry, and to make a Roman will. The cities developed systems of justice that were probably similar but not identical. Access to the courts in another city would have been facilitated by the common language. Rome gradually absorbed neighboring Latin communities, such as Gabii and Tusculum, into her own citizenship, and became the dominant city in the League.

In 338 BC as a result of a successful war against the Campanians and dissident Latin cities, Rome dissolved the old Latin league, absorbed some of its members into full citizenship, and left others with a diminished form of the former Latin right. At the same time she created a new category of "citizenship without the vote" – that is, the rights of a Roman private citizen without political rights – for communities outside Latium, such as Capua, Fundi, and Formiae (Livy 8.14). All this gave her access to the manpower for a formidable army, which in turn was augmented by the acquisition of allies outside the community of Romans and Latins. The settlement of Romans in colonies and elsewhere and the extension of forms of Roman citizenship or Latin right brought it about that by the time of Philip's letter to Larisa a large area of Italy was either Roman or Latin. Adult male Romans numbered some 270,000. In the Hannibalic war, despite the defection of many of Rome's Italian allies and the half-citizens of Capua, the Latins remained loyal.

There was a comparative lull in the expansion of Roman citizenship after the Hannibalic war, though some communities with citizenship without the vote were upgraded to full citizenship. The right of the Latins to acquire citizenship by migration to Rome and registration there was removed in the early second century BC in response to complaints by the Latins themselves that their cities were becoming depopulated. Towards the end of the century this privilege was reinstated for those who had held magistracies in Latin communities. It was only with the outbreak of the War of the Allies (the "social war") in 90 BC that the Romans were forced to limit the rebellion by the offer of full Roman citizenship to her Italian allies. The close of the social and subsequent civil wars through Sulla's victory and dictatorship was in theory the point when Italy south of the river Po became unified in citizenship. However, some time elapsed before the new citizens could be properly registered and the status of the former independent communities in relation to Rome could be regulated. By the time of Caesar's dictatorship the process seems to have been completed, and Italy had in effect become a territorial state with Rome as its capital.

The citizen body of Rome had in the meantime been increased by a growing number of manumitted slaves. Manumission was attractive to owners in that slaves by buying their freedom could repay their owner for some of his expenditure on them, while the expansion of the empire had created a large and therefore cheap supply of fresh slaves. Moreover, the practice of "informal" manumission, without the traditional legal ceremonies, made the process simpler and quicker. The number of liberated slaves cannot be even conjecturally calculated before the late republic (when we may suppose some 150,000–200,000), but some indication of its earlier significance can be found in the repeated controversy over the allocation of the freedmen to voting districts (tribes). Traditionally a freed slave was placed in one of the four urban tribes, where his voting significance would be dwarfed by the members of the 31 rural tribes. However, from the late fourth century onwards persistent efforts were made to redistribute at least some of them in the rural tribes.

Like the Greek cities, Rome granted its citizenship as a reward to individuals or groups. Gaius Marius enfranchised two whole cohorts of Umbrian infantry on the battlefield for their services against the Cimbri in 101 (Cic. *Balb.* 46). We possess a bronze tablet recording the grant of citizenship to a squadron of Spanish cavalry by Gnaeus Pompeius Strabo at Asculum in 89 (*FIRA* I.17 = *ROL* IV.272–5). The privilege was also granted to non-Romans if they had conducted a successful prosecution in the "extortion court." This commenced with the legislation of Gaius Gracchus in 122:

> If any of those who shall not be a Roman citizen shall have prosecuted someone else according to this statute . . . and if the other person shall have been condemned in that trial under this statute, then . . . he (the claimant) is to be a lawful Roman citizen and the sons born to him, when he shall become a Roman citizen according to this statute, and his grandsons provided they are born to that son, are to be lawful Roman citizens, [and] are to cast [their vote in the tribe of the person, who shall have been condemned according to this statute,] and they are to register them in that tribe, and they are to have exemption from military service, and their periods of military service and campaigns [are all to be credited to them.] (*RS* 1,76–7)

Important general points about the acquisition of Roman citizenship by individuals in this period arise from this text. As Cicero remarked in his speech for Balbus (28), "no citizen of ours can belong to two citizenships according to the civil law." The man rewarded was being in fact plucked out of his previous community and inserted into the Roman citizen body. This meant that he would have to take a Roman (or Latin) wife if he wished to have children legitimate under Roman law. His past family were expected to remain in their former community. As a Roman citizen, he would be normally liable to the duties imposed on Roman citizens. They were no longer subject to direct taxation but they were to military service. So, as an exceptional privilege, this man was to be exempted from such duties. The separation of individuals given Roman citizenship from their former community is illustrated by one of those rewarded by Pompeius Strabo, P. Otacilius Arranes, who appears later as a magistrate of the Italian town of Casinum, and indeed by Cicero's client, the millionaire from Gades, L. Cornelius Balbus, whose prosecution stemmed from the people of Gades themselves, who wished to retain him as their citizen.

As an alternative form of reward, non-Romans could be given a bundle of privileges, such as they would have received from citizenship, exercisable in their own home city. In the "extortion law" those who did not want citizenship were offered *provocatio*, the right of appeal against Roman magistrates, and freedom from military service and civic obligations in their own communities (*RS* 1, 78–79). An elaborate decree of the senate in 78 BC rewarded three Greek sea-captains who had loyally served Rome. The senate decided that inter alia:

> they, their children, and their descendants are to be immune in their own cities from all liturgies and financial contributions . . . whatever lawsuits they, their children, their descendants, and their wives may bring against another person, and if other persons bring lawsuits against them, their children etc., the men, their children, etc. are to have

the right and the choice of having the case decided in their own cities by their own laws, if they wish, or before our magistrates by Italian judges, or in a free city, which has remained constantly in the friendship of the people of the Romans . . . (*FIRA* I.35, trans. Sherk 1984 no. 66, 11–30)

5   A New Concept of Citizenship

It seems, however, that about the time of Julius Caesar's dictatorship the belief in the incompatibility of two citizenships was abandoned. We find that in the triumviral period his adopted son, later Augustus, grants to a Syrian sea-captain citizen-privileges that are clearly meant to be used in his own home, even though he is to be registered in a Roman tribe: citizenship is extended to his parents, wife, sons, and grandsons without qualification; they are to be free from Roman taxation and other burdens, while the Syrian captain is to possess a similar recourse to Roman magis-trates, when bringing or defending a lawsuit, as the captains in 78 BC (*FIRA* I.55 = trans. Sherk 1984 no. 86). The converse of this development can be seen in Augus-tus's third Cyrene edict of 7–6 BC, where he orders those honored with Roman citi-zenship to perform their local civic obligations as Greeks, unless they have been specifically granted immunity from them with their Roman citizenship (*FIRA* I.68 = Sherk 1984 no. 102, III). The emphasis is now on not separating those rewarded with Roman citizenship from their local communities.

Julius Caesar had extended Roman citizenship over the rest of Cisalpine Gaul from the Po to the Alps. He also planned to give Latin rights to Sicily, a project abandoned after his death. However, there were no mass extensions of citizenship beyond what is now Italy either then or in the first two centuries of the principate. What we find is a few grants to cities – Gades, Utica, Tingi, and Volubilis – and a considerable, though ultimately unquantifiable, number of grants to individuals. Of course, the settlement of Roman citizens in colonies overseas spread the citizenship geographi-cally. Furthermore, the creation of *municipia* with Latin rights provided an automatic route for local elites to achieve citizenship through the tenure of a local magistracy (this was extended to the whole local senate by Hadrian). Vespasian granted Latin rights to the cities of Spain, and the survival on bronze of most of the local constitu-tion given to the small town of Irni under Domitian now provides us with an illustra-tion of how this worked (Gonzalez 1986, Fear, THE IBERIAN PENINSULA, section 4). The ex-magistrates in these towns were not exempted from local duties and burdens through their citizenship, nor were either the acquisition of citizenship nor the general subjection of Latin communities to Roman law allowed to infringe the rights possessed earlier under local law.

Roman citizenship remained a privilege in the early empire. Its value as a means of political activity under the principate was at a discount even to the population of Rome, as the Roman assemblies became more ceremonial than the source of effective decisions. It did, however, give the wealthier potential access to political careers and membership of the senate, and in time the latter came to contain a good representa-tion of provincials. At a lower level it allowed men to be recruited into the Roman legions – better paid and affording greater prospects of military and civil promotion than the non-Roman auxiliaries. It also retained one important feature of the citizenship of the republic – *provocatio*, the right of appeal that entailed protection against arbitrary action by Roman magistrates and their subordinates, including official brutality. This was now associated with the invocation of the name of the emperor, as illustrated in the story of St Paul.

The privilege remained a privilege by virtue of being limited. This was also enforced in the realm of manumission under Augustus by legislation that put precise limits on the number of manumissions that might be made and on the age of manumitters and manumitted. It also stigmatized informal manumission by relegating those so liberated to the degraded category of Junian Latins, which they could only escape through a marriage to someone of equal or superior status and the production of a 1-year-old child. Nevertheless, in Rome and the cities of Italy the evidence of funerary inscriptions makes it clear that the vast majority of the poor could trace their descent back to a slave.

The situation in the Roman empire was changed radically in AD 212: "The emperor Caesar Marcus Aurelius Severus Antoninus Augustus [Caracalla] declares: . . . I may show my gratitude to the immortal gods for preserving me . . . if I can incorporate whoever joins my people into the worship of the gods. Accordingly, I grant Roman citizenship to all aliens throughout the world, with every form of citizen body remaining, except the *dediticii* [those in the condition of surrendered enemies with no rights] . . ." (*FIRA* I.88). The contemporary historian Cassius Dio (77.9.5) saw this as an emergency measure to make up for a deficit in imperial revenue. However, it had the long-term consequence of extending the principle of double citizenship – of Rome and of one's own community – to all free people in the empire. The resulting citizen body would have seemed totally anomalous to Aristotle, but has more in common with those of certain super-states of today, the United States of America and the European Union.

FURTHER READING

I have worked from the translation of Aristotle's *Politics* by Stephen Everson (Cambridge, 1988). The issue of citizenship in the *Politics* is briefly explained by Mulgan 1977, but see also Mulgan 1990 and Mossé 1967. On some related questions concerning Aristotle see Keyt and Miller 1991. The notion of citizenship is treated in most books on the ancient city. Most helpful in my view is Ehrenberg 1969, which has a special section on the Hellenistic world. On Athens see Hansen 1991, chap. 4. For the Roman world there are two important special studies, Nicolet 1980 and Sherwin White 1975. We owe to E. Rawson 1987 the demonstration of the point in time when the notion of double citizenship was accepted at Rome. For further on ancient law and related bibliography, see Meyer, LAW.

CHAPTER FORTY-FIVE

Law

Elizabeth A. Meyer

In the ancient world, law was one of the most valued achievements of a city or a people. Laws were the instrument and embodiment of the polity as well as a form of civic definition and civic identity. In seeking to regulate aristocratic competition, Greek and Roman law have the same origin. But Greek law, the rivalrous product of rivalrous states, never achieved the unity that Roman law, which developed from a single tradition, did; unlike Roman law, Greek law also never became the object of serious intellectual study in itself. "Greek" law consequently has also never had Roman law's historical impact. Yet it was less world empire, and more the different Roman dynamic of legal development (which encouraged interpretation of law that then became codified as new law) that kept Roman law one tradition and accounts for its influence.

1 The Greeks

In archaic Greece, the development of law is closely indexed to the development and emerging visibility of the political form of the *polis*, the ancient Greek city-state. Iron Age settlements no doubt had some sense of community and a strong sense of appropriate behavior, as well as punishments for violating such norms, but laws that actually set (some of) these out as principles for the community to live by are first attested only between 650 and 600 BC, and are the first incontrovertible evidence of the existence of independent Greek-speaking political communities in Crete, mainland Greece, southern Italy, and Sicily. The strong association of law, political independence, and individual civic identity will continue to characterize the experience of the Greek *poleis* through the Roman conquest: for much of the archaic and classical periods a Greek city-state defined itself through its laws, thought of these laws as expressions of its own unique character and exclusivity, and competed with other city-states in the excellence of its laws (and the consequent excellence of the citizens shaped by them) for as long as independence or the illusion of it permitted this way of thinking. So, at least, surviving evidence, with its heavy bias towards the city-states of Crete, Sparta, and Athens, would suggest. Religious "laws" regulating behavior in sanctuaries, including the definitions of, and punishments for, athletic misdemeanors, also survive (and some of these are very early indeed). But the world of lawmaking is, *par excellence*, the world of the self-conscious and independent city-state.

Often, in *poleis*, there is the implication of a unified system of law in place from the very start, no matter the historical reality: hence one lawmaker or one inscribed "code" (which was never comprehensive enough, incidentally, to meet a modern definition of a "code," just as no system of ancient laws ever covered as many activities as a modern legal system does). There is also a marked emphasis on classification and procedure (which types of murder are justifiable, who was to hear what kind of case, what the penalties should be) in the earliest phases of law-giving. Belief in a unified system underpinned the self-characterization of each city-state as possessed of a unique constitution and shaped by a set of coherent, unique, and preferably early laws. The focus on classification and process reveals the basis of legal conflict in intense competition: such laws, in life as in athletics, map the arena of behavior subject to official community ruling and penalty, and are a way of regulating (rather than preventing) competition, for they make clear who could compete with whom, and over what; how the competition was to take place; and how winning was to be defined (and by whom).

Despite these similarities, the two characteristics display themselves differently in different places. Crete, an island crowded with *poleis*, preserves the earliest surviving law in Greek, from Dreros, and also the greatest number of inscribed laws, and the only one that, because of its great length (more than 600 lines long), has been called a law "code," from the city of Gortyn. This was inscribed in the middle of the fifth century BC on the walls of a building, and later incorporated into a Roman-period odeion; scholars date its core provisions to the sixth and fifth centuries BC. It was obviously an object of pride to Gortynians living centuries after its provisions' promulgation: laws were part of their definition of who they were, which included who they had been. Like the law from Dreros, it sets out how Gortynians are to exercise their privileges, whether those privileges are those of standing for office, passing on property, copulating by force, or judging a case – with differential penalties depending on the status of those involved. Although the implication of carefully laid-out inscription in a central public place is that "the law" was complete and unchanging, this is the nostalgic immutability of (certainly by the Roman period) impressively changed political circumstances, and within the inscribed "code" it has been possible to trace chronological levels and clear amendments. Codification, monumentalization, and self-identification contributed to the survival of the "code," but not necessarily as a living body of law.

Spartans, on the other hand, deemed that their law-giver Lycurgus had left them laws as a living monument. He (tradition held) rid the city of its internal instability by imposing (Crete-derived and Delphi-approved) laws on an unruly populace, requiring an oath that they would not be changed until he returned, and then leaving the city and killing himself. Unlike at Gortyn, or Athens, Lycurgus's laws were unwritten, "rhetras," or "utterances." They are more prescriptive than those of Gortyn ("houses should have their roofs fashioned by an axe, their doors by a saw," Plut. *Lyc.* 13.3) and created, and lived on through, Sparta's institutions, particularly the educational system of the young, "for education performs the office of law-giver for every one of them" (Plut. *Lyc.* 13). All aspects of life in classical Sparta were intertwined, and all of them were governed by the laws of Lycurgus, famously severe, famously unchanging, and famously, as far as the Spartans were concerned and as they asserted to the world, "the best": Sparta was a place of *eunomia*, a "well-lawed" place, where, as one of the consequences, there were no lawsuits.

The Spartans thought Lycurgus a real and very early figure. It is much more likely that he never existed at all, and that the laws associated with his name started to accumulate in the seventh century BC and were added to thereafter. Yet the Spartans thought it important to create a law-giver and compress, freeze, and retroject the story of the development of their own city-state. Had Lycurgus existed in the late seventh century he would have been in good company, however, for this was the century of law-givers, the century in which a number of men were said to have given laws to newly founded or desperately disordered Greek communities of south Italy and Sicily – many laws, all at once, reorganizing the life of the city and its constitution together. In Athens this role was played by the indisputably historical Solon, the man elected sole archon in 594/593 BC to avert either civil war or tyranny. He was not the first named law-giver there – Draco was (621 BC) – but he had an impact far greater than Draco's, not least because he repealed almost all of Draco's laws. In Solon's case there survives some of his poetry, which describes his understanding of what he was accomplishing: "I stood with a mighty shield in front of both" – the *demos*, people, and "those with power and wealth" – "and allowed neither to be victorious unjustly" (frag. 5, quoted in Plut. *Sol.* 18.5). Solon acted like a referee in a contest; he claimed his solutions – which he ordered left unaltered for one hundred years – made Athens a city of *eunomia*: Athens was also "well lawed." This must be in competition with the Spartans' assertions, for 170 years later Perikles was still comparing the laws of Sparta and the laws of Athens, and finding the laws – and citizens – of Athens superior (Thuc. 2.37.1,3). No fewer than 152 laws or law-fragments are later attributed to Solon, many unreliably cited by fourth-century BC orators who thereby demonstrate, yet again, that their audience believed that a set of core laws must have shaped Athens, and Athenians, from early times.

Yet at Athens lawmaking does not stop with Solon's law-giving, does not freeze, even hypothetically or in rhetoric, in the *eunomia* stage, but moves on, and indeed despite an attempt in the late fifth century BC at codification, is more open to change, discussion, and extension than any other Greek legal system we can see. This is because at Athens, as in every other Greek *polis*, laws help to create the polity, but in Athens also that polity changed quite dramatically over time, probably through law but also with clear consequences for the role of law in the city. As Solon sought to reshape Athens through law, so too did his successors, and it is from later Athens that we have the best examples of laws that are clearly and directly the result of the political activity of the city itself. These laws, which were passed on specific occasions to confront specific problems, were called *psephismata* or "things voted on". In the fifth century all laws were called *nomoi* (laws); in the fourth, Athenians distinguished between these *psephismata* and *nomoi* (now defined as laws that laid down permanent rules for all Athenians). With the two Athens had democratic rule through law, rare in the Greek world.

In Athens in the second half of the fifth century, and in the century that followed, civic culture was also legal culture: classical Athenians were famous for being restless, argumentative, and litigious. "That's Athens down there," says a student to Strepsiades in Aristophanes' *Clouds* (206–7); "I don't believe you," says Strepisiades, "I don't see any jurors sitting!" Court cases were called "contests" (*agones*) and were the chief arena of dispute settlement and competition (for winning, for fame as the best speaker, for prestige), rivaling violence and murder as ways of getting even. Rhetoric is an art that thrives when the audience has the power to make a decision, and the fact that Athens had, by this time, transformed itself from an aristocratic city into a democratic one helped to ensure that the old connection between law, a city-state's "constitution," and that city's competitive self-image would survive to bloom in this new form.

The Athenians were the most conspicuously law- and courts-oriented of the classical Greeks, yet even so the equally important activity of enforcement was not a civic task, but the responsibility of the private citizen. Individuals, not public prosecutors, brought cases and hauled defendants in front of the appropriate city officials; individuals saw to it that the assessed penalties were paid, by using force or prosecuting again when they were not; individuals and community exacted much more conformity to civic ideals through the various tools of social control (like gossip, shaming, and close scrutiny of neighbors) than they did even through the courts. And if so for Athens, then that much more for Sparta (where such tools of social control were extremely powerful, even extending to not picking cowards for ball games and refusing to marry their sisters, as Xenophon relates, *LP* 9.5) and probably so for Gortyn as well, about which we otherwise know virtually nothing. At Athens so much law and so much process (the Athenians in the fourth century had numerous different magistrates who supervised numerous city courts, and numerous offences could be prosecuted in a variety of different ways) led to constant legal strategizing and constant discussion about law. These served to reaffirm law's central place in the Athenians' self-definition without always making clear what, exactly, that place was. They had called their city, since the time of Kleisthenes, a city of *isonomia* – an "equal-lawed" city – which, although usually interpreted as "equality under the law," can also mean, on analogy with the *eunomia* that it replaced, "a city with equal participation in law": the best people in the archaic period made a well-lawed city, while the citizens in classical Athens made Athens an "equal-lawed" one. For Athenians, the process mattered as much as the result.

Each classical city-state had its own laws and took pride in them. Yet even so, proudly idiosyncratic processes produced laws that could resemble the laws of other city-states as well, leading some scholars to posit the existence of a panhellenic or quasi-universal "Greek law." In the law of inheritance, adoption, commerce, and contract there are indeed similarities. But such similarities can be created through both competition and contact, and indeed even through imitation (although there is less direct evidence for this). Athens in the fifth century required allies to try their cases in Athenian courts, which contemporary Athenians claimed was actually a boon (the allies thought otherwise); Athens' widespread trading contacts, and the vast maritime traffic moving through its harbor, led Athenians in the fourth century to adjust court procedures to allow disputes over that trade to be speedily settled, and to create law that foreigners could use. Types of "Greek" law with a more international reach and common flavor could have their origins here – or could be even older, rooted in interactions between cities in the archaic period, when intermarriage between the great of different cities was more common than it was later.

The sense that there was a common "Greek" law was more a product of the historical circumstances of the Hellenistic period than it had been a reality in the classical. Alexander took a mostly Macedonian army over most of the eastern Mediterranean world, and further east than most Greeks had ever known. He and his warring successors founded cities, usually populated by army veterans and settlers from Greece, and if these cities flourished they usually came to look like the cities left behind in Greece, with gymnasia, agoras, and laws. The principles of self-definition and self-governance survived, in these cases with mild limitations (since an absent king also ruled most cities), and the common Greco-Macedonian elites of these cities, and their sense of constituting an oasis of power and culture in a world of non-Greek barbarians, no doubt contributed to the writing of laws that looked similar from city to city, just as the same forces reduced dialectal differences into *koine* Greek in the Hellenistic world.

There is not, however, enough evidence to prove extensive similarity early in the Hellenistic period. Later law – as late as law from the Roman period – written in Greek, or explicitly said to apply to Greek populations, does provide evidence of similarity and, thus, of probable continuity. The best evidence comes from Egypt, seized and settled by Ptolemy and leaving a rich source of papyrus documentation that makes clear the separation of the Greek population from the native Egyptian in matters of law. When this kingdom, like so many other cities and kingdoms, came under Roman domination, the contrast with the law of the conquerors again makes the differences between the laws of the various Greek populations in the eastern Mediterranean seem even smaller. Even so, in every place the Romans attempted to govern they found a pre-existing set of laws in place for their Greek populations by which members of that population could or had to be judged, the legacy of hundreds of years of self-governance and civic definition, as well as of competition between cities (which continued unabated), expressed (among other ways) through law.

2   The Romans

Had sixth- and fifth-century Spartans come to enjoy world empire, or been required in some other rewarding way to come to grips with the concept of change, they might well have chosen to accommodate the new world in their laws as the Romans did – by keeping the laws of the past untouched, but adding to them or commenting on them in such a way as to make those laws applicable to newer situations. Spartans found legislation in their assembly unappealing and its results in general disastrous; Romans too generated much less law through legislation in their assemblies than they did through interpretation of what they already had. For the Romans had a very ancient law-code, the XII Tables, supposedly written by a Committee of Ten in 451–450 BC and Greek in inspiration, but three hundred years later its provisions were not reliably relevant and the equally ancient five formal ways of initiating legal actions were inflexible. From this conundrum developed a quintessentially Roman institution, interpretative commentary – by priests, expert private citizens (jurisconsults), and (indirectly) magistrates – that all in one way or another took the laws of the past and suggested ways in which they actually did apply to the present. The law of the Romans' past lived in their present too, and was recited by the young even in Cicero's boyhood; but it also lived in the ways in which Romans carefully built around and on it.

The linked institutions of promulgated law and commentary thereon, itself capable of achieving the status of accepted law over time, were unknown in the Greek world. Gortyn emended even before inscribing; Sparta let inconvenient laws "sleep"; Athens repealed laws by vote of the majority of citizens, even if the enthusiasm of would-be proposers could be restrained by the threat of prosecution "for proposing something against the laws." Romans, by contrast, would invalidate laws passed in their assemblies only because of religious fault, but otherwise preferred to keep even unsatisfactory laws, voting repeated exceptions to them rather than repealing them. This pattern of retentiveness shows itself even in language. In Athens, laws were written in unexceptional everyday Greek, whereas the language of Roman law retained archaisms for over eight hundred years. This deep-seated desire not to lose the past while nevertheless making it useful in the present demonstrates that the Romans too saw law as a significant component of their city-state's self-definition, one element of the *mos maiorum* (custom of the ancestors) that was at the heart of their Romanness – and also of their greatness, since they too were ferociously competitive with, and so often victorious over, outsiders.

This pattern of accepting a "code" of law, passing (some) other laws (which would add to, rather than openly correct, what already existed), and commenting on laws repeated itself more than once in Rome's long legal history. Commentary on the XII Tables built up directly (in jurists' written studies) and indirectly (in "additional" legislation and in the form of the praetor's edict, the annual law decreed by the urban praetor every year in which he laid out the legal actions that could be brought). For once "additional" laws made the initiation of actions through a flexible formula possible, the praetor could expand the types of cases he would allow, thereby also expanding the types of case for which the XII Tables were relevant, even if only by a bit of stretching. Jurisconsult friends would help him; some of these also wrote actual commentary on the Tables, or on other laws that Rome's assemblies had been persuaded to pass. Each praetor's edict then became the basis of the next. After a very developed form of the praetor's edict was "frozen" in AD 131, commentary on the edict itself intensified, repeating the pattern and creating yet another body of juristic commentary. And so on: even after Justinian's great codification of Roman law in the sixth century AD – which among other sources also excerpted, collated, and endorsed as law the juristic commentary of the preceding eight centuries in one of its parts – commentary did not cease.

The desire to keep the ancient law alive was one factor that created this characteristic structure of law, interpretation, and interpretation accepted as law in Rome. The other was Rome's steeply hierarchical and deferential society, which accepted the making of law by high-status experts. Magistrates promulgated edicts or proposed laws for the people to approve, but usually with the help of their knowledgeable friends; emperors too would call on expert advice, eventually finding it useful to keep some of the greatest jurists of the day on government retainer, or, in late antiquity, as actual officials or drafters in government bureaus. Like the Spartans, the Romans were always in the *eunomia* phase, accepting that law given to them by the best people made theirs a "well-lawed" state. Certainly theirs was not a city of *isonomia*, for although the Roman people could and did vote for laws, they approved only 800 of these (that we know of) in the approximately six hundred years in which law-making assemblies were active, and were not allowed to discuss them, but only listen to the experts, when they did. The flurry of law-making activity in the last century of the republic was a sign of unsettled times and of a fatally competitive aristocracy jockeying for dominance by appealing to the people; although *leges* (passed by the centuriate and tribal assemblies) and *plebiscita* (passed by the *concilium plebis*) were accepted as legitimate sources of law, the generation of so many laws in the openly hostile context of the late republic rather than in the quietly but firmly hierarchical context of the centuries that preceded and followed was always a matter for unease, not celebration.

The final sources of law in the Roman world – after the XII Tables, magisterial edicts, *leges, plebiscita,* and juristic commentary on all of the above – were the edicts, *decreta* (decisions in court), rulings (in letters and rescripts), and even utterances of the emperor, as well as *senatusconsulta* (consultations of the senate), which were treated as law by the time of the first emperor's death. When Octavian Augustus became the undisputed master of the Roman world after the Battle of Actium in 31 BC, the structures and institutions of that hierarchical Roman world, including law-making, began to reorient around him, a process that he did not in every case initiate, but which he and his successors did not discourage. In his third decade of sole rule, opinions of the senate (which had enjoyed only advisory force in the republic) were accepted and classified as law, although we do not know how this transformation was achieved. In theory *senatusconsulta* should have been a source of law independent of the emperor; in practice, the senate seemed eager to follow the emperor's lead or anticipate his wishes when no such lead was apparent. It is over the next two hundred years that the emperor's very words would be accepted as law: his verdicts and impromptu interpretations, initially intended for one-time use, were in turn collected and codified. The emperor as the source of law is a firmly established figure by the time of Diocletian (AD 284–305), and celebrated as such in panegyric and art.

To the time of Diocletian belong the first attempts to collect together and organize in coherent form imperial "constitutions" (the varied types of emperor's "law" noted above) from the many times he had given his opinion. These collections, called the Gregorian and Hermogenian Codes, do not survive, but the next two do, the

Theodosian Code, promulgated in AD 438, and the *Codex Justinianus*, promulgated (in a second edition) in AD 534. Justinian himself, in commissioning the general legal codification of which the latter was a part, was striving to order a disordered subject and bring a kind of perfect completeness and renewal to the state of Roman law, all the while saving what was best and most important from the past. The result was an impressive three-part effort: the mild editing of a second-century textbook, Gaius's *Institutes*, into Justinian's *Institutes* (533); the *Codex Justinianus* (534); and the fifty books of the *Digest* (533), the result of weeding and (some) rewriting of juristic opinions of the preceding centuries. And yet, despite the perfection and monumental achievement of these three works, there was one last collection of material that would become the fourth part of what is called the *Corpus Iuris Civilis*: Justinian's *Novellae*, the new laws he felt obliged to pass between AD 535 and his death in AD 565. No matter how perfect a collection, there is always a need for more interpretation, and thus more law.

This body of Roman law, as it survives, shows a strong emphasis on the law of property, the law of procedure, and law of status. This itself is unlikely to be distortion, given the way in which law was made and who made it. The XII Tables showed a strong interest in classification and procedure, like the early Greek laws that survive, but as Roman law developed through commentary and edict some parts of the law received more attention, others less. It is a true but uninteresting generalization that the law favors the powerful; it is more challenging to identify which parties lawmakers saw as antagonists or competition, and which activities they found most in need of classification or control. The standard assumption in the class- and law-obsessed modern world is that the lower classes are the most important enemy of those in whose power it is to make law – or that law is the only weapon that will dislodge the wealthy from their unfairly acquired and unjustly exercised positions of power and influence. In antiquity, however, neither view is likely to be true. In an archaic city-state in the process of self-formation, those who are making the law are likely to see as the most dangerous threat unregulated competition for leadership or wealth that will constantly redefine the rules and, by allowing some then to "win" unfairly, break a community apart into irreconcilable factions, making the city incapable of achieving anything great as a unit that is greater than the sum of its parts. Thus early laws, by classifying and defining, sought not to unseat an aristocracy or oppress a people, but to restrain the consequences of unbridled competition by making everyone agree on, or at least admit the existence of, a set of rules; in this way an aristocracy and a city could remain united and survive. One of Sparta's chief competitions was in obedience to the laws, which meant that participants in Sparta's other manifold competitions – in courage, in hunting, in laconic speaking, in submission to age, and in ruling over inferiors – were strictly rule-bound as well, since a competitor who trespassed against the laws would automatically lose. Even Athens' laws and Athens' juries, solidly democratic as they were in the fourth century, preferred putting aristocrats through their paces as public speakers (Athens allowed speech-writers but not pleaders) to destroying them and seizing their assets. In practice, also, the Athenian legal system saw a substantial amount of repeat business – antagonists meeting for the second or fifth time – which meant that it must have been more important to keep the dispute in the courts than it was to build a system that would deliver a decisive triumph over one's foes, class enemies or not.

In Rome it was hardly different, despite the obvious dissimilarities. *Leges* were, for example, passed to regulate political competition – to create an order in which magistracies were to be held, for example, or to lay out a necessary interlude of ten years between consulships – but exceptions were allowed when the people voted for ineligible favorites. Such laws were to assist the cohesion of the nobility, and with them (they would have said) the cohesion of the state: they were aimed at each other, their class equals, not at inferiors or superiors. Laws passed against election bribery in the late republic were, similarly, aimed at those who could afford to bribe (probably the wealthy from new families), not those who could not. So too much of the body of private law that developed pertains especially to issues of concern to the lawmaking group and its peers – a nobility of achievement, descent, wealth, and imperial favor – in its conflicts with each other, not with its inferiors. There are exceptions, like the body of landlord–tenant law, where the outcome solidly favors the landlord (of course), but the issues first arose because landlords and tenants associated only on the (weak) basis of contract rather than on the (strong) basis of an acknowledged social relationship. But class relations otherwise took care of themselves in long-established and traditional ways deriving from the claims of superiors to deference, obedience, and clientage, and from their monopoly of physical force and benefaction; legal tools were hardly necessary. Thus Roman law and legal practice reveal an endless fascination with disputes over property and inheritance, which all involved people of the same social level, usually related to each other; a close attention to the rules of the game, which combined their respect for ancient forms and concepts with a desire to allow no one else an unfair advantage; a tendency for only people of the same social level to meet each other in court; and a firm hand on issues of status, where the question was really one of deciding where one belonged on a complex and sliding scale.

Status itself was breathtakingly varied, with every component itself an element of Roman society's process of ranking. Free, freed, or slave; freed in a formal or an informal way; citizen, part citizen, non-citizen; soldier or civilian; town-councilor, senator, or equestrian; provincial, Italian, or inhabitant of Rome; "more honorable" or "more humble": all mattered, and virtually all were defined, over time, in law. Not because Romans were unclear on any of the concepts, but because movement between statuses could happen and was allowed, and therefore all had to know, and agree on, when such a change had occurred. No Greek city-state had anything approaching this range of legally defined statuses, for no Greek city-state had Rome's hierarchies, or welcomed this kind of social mobility, or incorporated outsiders (in the persons of former slaves or citizens of other *poleis*) into the city to the extent that Romans did. This too was an element of Rome's definition of itself as a different kind of city-state from its earliest days, when its king-founder Romulus offered asylum to others in Latium. The eventual legal definitions and classifications of status were to order the competition by making the benchmarks clear, not to prevent even the lowliest, like slaves, from improving their position – albeit only with the master's support and requiring repayment in the form of deference, gratitude, and service.

The law of the Romans was the law of Roman citizens, a distinctive privilege they carried with them wherever they went, and which they asserted even when far from the city of Rome. The experience of ruling rather than conquering an empire broadened their acquaintance with legal systems other than their own, however; and although most Roman magistrates, who also served as chief judges in their own provinces, were no students of comparative law and ruled by common sense and tenets of gentlemanly appropriateness rather than by knowledge of local law, the spread of Roman rule was also accompanied by, first, the development of informal Roman-law acts in which non-citizens could participate, and then also by a growth in the level of abstract thinking in the Roman legal tradition. The greatest of the "classical" Roman jurists to tackle questions of legal definition and legal essence behind the confining specificity of the XII Tables or the praetor's edict, or behind the confusion of detail in legal consultations and in the hypothetical cases they so loved, were all Roman citizens of provincial origin. Although little is known about them personally, the trajectories of the lives of three, Paulus, Ulpian, and Papinian (trajectories that brought all three to Rome, the latter two to the position of praetorian prefect), might also have granted to them a perspective on Roman law not enjoyed by others. Their use of abstractions, intellectual rigor, and clear enunciation of juridical principles were not specifically intended to make Roman law a pragmatically universal law for all of Rome's new citizens after AD 212 (many of whom preferred to be judged by the local laws that had governed their lives before Caracalla's grant of citizenship anyway), but these jurists' increasingly universal language is part of the striking achievement of Roman law, and part of its enormous appeal, in subsequent centuries, to those who rediscovered Justinian's *Corpus*.

The law of the Greek city-states and the law of Rome thus began by playing a similar role in their evolving societies – classifying behavior, regulating competition, embodying what was best and most characteristic of each city – but ended by making a very different contribution indeed. There never was one "Greek" law, although each Greek city-state had laws that it considered best; but there assuredly was one "Roman" law, and the complex dynamic of its development that led to its last and greatest compilation made possible an influence far beyond its specific time and place, and a kind of exemplary influence Athenians could only grandiosely assert. The Athenians' great contribution was a concept, the rule of law; the Romans', a tradition of legal interpretation and codification that showed how even the most ancient of laws, and the most conservative of societies, could maintain both their unique character and their relevance, making their law to this day a well that has never run dry.

FURTHER READING

For Greek law in general, see the essays in Gagarin and Cohen 2005, esp. J. Davies on the Gortyn Code (305–27); for Sparta, MacDowell 1986; for Athens, three books are the basis of modern study, A. Harrison 1968–71, MacDowell 1978, and Todd 1993. New evaluations of Solon can be found in Blok and Lardinois 2006, especially part II, and a listing of references to his laws in E. Ruschenbusch 1966. Collections of the texts of Greek laws can be found in Arnaoutoglou 1998 and, for the earliest laws, van Effenterre 1994–95. Roman law and society are even vaster subjects. Fundamental and helpful – and two very different ways of thinking about Roman law – are Jolowicz and Nicholas 1972 and Crook 1967. The growth of the Roman juristic movement is discussed in Frier 1985 and, for landlord–tenant law, Frier 1980. The thought and style of the great "classical" jurists have been the focus of T. Honoré's careful attention: (1962 on Gaius and 2002 on Ulpian). Honoré is also the pre-eminent scholar of late-antique imperial law, for which see his *Emperors and Lawyers* (1994), *Tribonian* (1978), and *Law in the Crisis of Empire, AD 379–455* (1998). An essential collection of Roman legal documents in the original language is S. Riccobono et al. *Fontes Iuris Romani Anteiustiniani* (*FIRA*). Texts and translations of Roman laws are found in M. Crawford 1996; of the *Digest*, Watson 1985; of Justinian's *Institutes*, trans. P. Birks and G. McLeod (1987); no accurate and up-to-date translations of Justinian's *Codex* or his *Novellae* exist.

On-line Roman law texts can be found at the Project Volterra website which provides (among much else useful) many of these (Latin) texts, and also gives web links to other sites where such texts can be found: www.ucl.ac.uk/history/volterra

CHAPTER FORTY-SIX

Warfare

Louis Rawlings

"War is the father of all." (Herakleitos frg. 53)

1 War and History

Historical writing was born a child of war. It was so that "the great and marvelous deeds of Greeks and barbarians would not be without their glory and to show why the two peoples fought against each other" that Herodotus (1.1), the Father of History, undertook his "inquiry." While his sprawling history related much information that did not have an obviously military flavor, nevertheless his account, at its core, explored the causes and course of the great Persian expedition to conquer Greece in 480–479 BC. Herodotus, along with his near-contemporary, Thucydides, who wrote (but did not complete) an account of the Peloponnesian War (431–404 BC), firmly established the central concern of historical narrative writing to be warfare. Herodotus was a great traveler, but no soldier; on the other hand, despite an indifferent spell as an Athenian general in 424 BC, the military eye of Thucydides ultimately gave him a particular perspective on the events of the conflict he chose to write about. Thucydides was not unique in using his own experience of war to inform his narrative (Whitby 2007). Writers such as Xenophon (who had helped to lead the Ten Thousand out of the middle of the hostile Persian empire, 401–400 BC), Polybius and Josephus (both of whose military careers were curtailed by Roman victory and who both found themselves in the hands of the conquerors) gave the benefit of their own military training and experience to their accounts.

It could be argued that an important stimulus in the development of Roman history writing was the Second Punic War (218–202 BC); the earliest historians, Fabius Pictor, Cincius Alimentus, and Cato the Elder had all played a part in the conflict and had written about it. Their Carthaginian enemy, Hannibal, had brought with him men such as Sosylos and Silenos, who composed accounts of his campaign.

The Punic commander was, himself, following in the footsteps of Alexander the Great, who had been accompanied on his campaigns in the Persian empire (334–323 BC) by the historian Kallisthenes, while several of his officers – Ptolemy, Nearchos and Aristoboulos – wrote their own narratives of the Macedonian conquest. Alexander's successors, Hellenistic kings such as Pyrrhos, had composed memoirs of their own campaigns, and Romans too came to describe their campaigns; the commentaries of Caesar, detailing his conquest of Gaul and subsequent civil war, are only the most complete to survive. War, then, was an important facet of the literary and historical output of politicians and generals. Inevitably it was also a concern of academics like Diodorus and Livy, whose histories were constructed, at least in part, from the military events of the past. Even under the *pax Romana* of the emperors, a writer like Tacitus included accounts of Roman military campaigns in his *Annals* (covering the period AD 14–68), while the surviving third of his *Histories* describe the civil wars that erupted at the end of Nero's reign in AD 69.

2 Memory and Militarism

The centrality of war to historical inquiry was natural in a world where warfare was common and loomed large in the collective experiences of peoples. War played a significant part in the construction of memory and group identity. The annual records compiled by the college of pontiffs in Rome included among the lists of portents, magistrates, and domestic events, the wars waged by the state by land and sea (Serv. *Aen.* 1.373). The Roman calendar included the *dies Alliensis*, a defeat of the Romans by the Gauls at the River Allia (18 July). Among the Greek states, some victories were commemorated with annual festivals where common prayers of thanksgiving, sacrifices and competitive athletic events were staged (Pritchett 1979: 157–86). From the fifth century the Greeks raised battlefield trophies to mark their victories. These could persist in the landscape for many years. At Koroneia, a trophy commemorating the defeat of the Athenians in 447 BC could still be observed by those who fought a later battle in the vicinity in 394 BC (Plut. *Ages.* 19). Writers of the classical period such as Thucydides and Xenophon almost obsessively recorded the erection of such monuments (Pritchett 1979: 263–71), indicating their importance as cultural artifacts. Battlefield burials, such as the mass grave of Athenian dead at Marathon, were also landmarks that aided in the construction of memory; an annual procession of the ephebes (youths) to the site ended in the offering of sacrifices to "those who died on behalf of freedom" (*IG* II^2 1006). Herodotus himself had visited the site of the battle of Thermopylae, read the grave-markers and memorized the names of the Spartans who had fallen; he chose to recite their epitaphs in his history (7.224, 228).

The importance of commemorating its war dead led the Athenian state to organize public funerals (Thuc. 2.34) and annually set up stone-cut casualty lists placed prominently on display in the *Demosion Sema* (Bradeen 1964). The funeral speeches made by prominent politicians at state funerals lauded the military commitment of the citizen body and its past successes, while the burial rites and longer-term commemoration of the fallen was of great significance in the construction of collective citizen identity (Loraux 1986). The celebration of the martial prowess and related civic virtues of the war dead served as a militarizing factor in this construction of identity, as the living were encouraged to attempt to aspire to these ideals and remember the context of death, while the fallen (or at least their stone-cut names listed by tribe) became part of the fabric of the city itself. Orphans whose fathers had been killed in war were raised at state expense and during the festival of the City Dionysia, those who had come of age were presented with a hoplite panoply (Aeschin. 3.154). Such displays served to promote the martial ideology of the democracy (Goldhill 1987: 60–68). By contrast, it appears that the Roman state did not publicly bury or even commemorate its citizen war dead (Gilliver 1999: 123). Such rites were left in private hands; nevertheless, Polybius (6.53–54) describes how funerals of members of the senatorial elite were open to the general populace to attend, and not only celebrated the lives and glorious deeds of the deceased, but also all of his ancestors, whose death masks were displayed in the forum and their achievements related. Polybius noted, with evident approval, how such funerals encouraged emulation of glorious deeds, not just from the younger members of the family but all those who witnessed them.

While warriors could be remembered for their military activities, their careers reflected the militarism of contemporary society. As early as the Homeric poems, there are indications that war was integral to the identity and social standing of some men. The son of Kastor, one of the alternative personas assumed by Odysseus, claimed that "labor in the field was never to my liking, nor the care of a household, which rears goodly children, but oar-swept ships and wars, and pitching spears with treated hafts and arrows, dismal things that are shuddering and bitter to other men, to me were sweet; a god put them in my heart; for different men take joy in different works" (Hom. *Od.* 14.223–28). It was his martial talents that enabled the son of Kastor to rise in his community, claiming that "I gained a wife from men with many land-holdings, since I had martial excellence" (*Od.* 14.211–12; van Wees 1992: 207–14). On numerous occasions, when men were attempting to persuade their fellows during political debates in Rome, they displayed their wounds or recounted their military careers (e.g. Livy 45.39). According to Sallust (*Iug.* 85.29–30; cf. Plut. *Mar.* 9.2), Marius once argued:

> I am unable to claim your confidence by producing death masks or the triumphs and consulships of my ancestors; but if necessary, I can present spears and standards, medals and other military prizes, as well as the scars on my chest. These are my masks, my proof of nobility, not inherited . . . but won through many personal toils and dangers.

Another notable example is that of Spurius Ligustinus, who, despite his extremely humble origins, rose through the ranks to *primus pilus*, chief centurion, because of his bravery on campaign (in his speech, he claimed that he was decorated 34 times, and awarded the *corona civica* six times for saving fellow citizens in combat, Livy 42.34). Spurius's career serves an exemplary purpose in Livy's account (Cadiou 2002, Hoyos 2007: 63–64) and reveals the importance of martial prowess in the construction of masculine identity in Roman society. Such committed warriors may have been exceptional – after all, the son of Kastor acknowledged the less martial callings of other men for whom weapons were "dismal things" – but military achievement was evidently perceived as deserving of a good deal of respect. One poet of archaic Sparta, Tyrtaeus (frg. 12. 35–43), argued that any veteran who was "victorious and famous for the work of his spear" would be "honored by young and old alike . . . Aging, he is conspicuous among the citizens. No one tries to cheat him of honors or all he deserves; all men withdraw before his presence, and yield their seats to him." Members of the Roman elite who proved to be able fighters and commanders found that political influence and power was within their reach (W. Harris 1979: 30–34). Valerius Corvus (348 BC, Livy 7.26) and Claudius Marcellus (in 222 BC, in his late forties, Plut. *Marc.* 7) both overcame enemies in single combat and subsequently enjoyed multiple consulships (Oakley 1985). The spectacular successes of Scipio Africanus against the Carthaginian armies in Spain and Africa earned him early high office. He was even given the great privilege and accolade of being *Princeps Senatus* (first in the Senate) at 36, an age when few senators were even regarded as eligible for the higher military and political positions (Scullard 1970: 173–75).

Successful generals like Scipio Africanus and Marius enjoyed popularity among the citizens of Rome, but it must not be forgotten that this was a group who not only voted for such men in elections, but who also regularly undertook military service under their command. Many of these men were drawn from small farmsteads that studded much of the hinterland of city-states, and, in the eyes of elite Greek and Roman writers, it was such men who made the best soldiers (V. Hanson 1995: 221). The citizen-farmer-warrior was an ideal type based on the perception that "agriculture contributes greatly to the construction of manliness; because, unlike the banausic crafts, it does not make bodies unfit, but it accustoms them to living outdoors and to toil and gives them the energy to undertake the hazards of war. For only the farmer's possessions, unlike those of other men, are outside the city-defenses" ([Arist.] *Oec.* 1343b 2–6; cf. Xen. *Oec.* 5.4–5; 6.6–7, 9–10; Veg. 1.3). They were, conveniently, the largest proportion of the manpower of most settled communities, since agricultural production was the primary mode of sustenance and of economic activity for much of the ancient world. Of course, few such men could be full-time soldiers; even Spurius Ligustinus claimed to have worked a very small landholding (Livy 42.34). For the most part, Greek and Italian city-states raised militias from their populations on an ad hoc and short-term basis, at the end of brief campaigns the men returned to their peacetime occupations. Consequently, the abilities of militia armies to undertake complex manoeuvre on campaign and in combat were limited. Although some communities attempted to introduce military training or state-supported elite units (such as the Theban Sacred Band), few states could emulate Sparta, where the citizens lived substantially off the labor of their servile Helot population, and seemingly devoted themselves to the arts of war (Lazenby 1985; van Wees 2004, 87–93). Elsewhere, a high degree of specialization was only possible for states with complex and well-developed economic structures capable of maintaining men in the relatively unproductive pursuits of the military.

Pay was often considered a compensation for time away from regular occupations (and often calculated by the day) rather than a wage in itself (Rawlings 2007a: 170–

71), although it allowed states to keep armies in the field for longer (if it could be afforded: sometimes pay had to be obtained from plunder, or deferred so that arrears might mount up). The introduction of pay (*stipendium*, traditionally c.406 BC, Livy 4.59–60) for service in the Roman army gave it the capacity to wage protracted wars, although in the difficult years of the Second Punic War the state was forced to obtain loans from syndicates of wealthy citizens (Livy 23.49). While some legions were in the field for many years during the wars of the middle republic, nevertheless they were, theoretically, still temporary forces raised for specific campaigns and disbanded at the end of them (Hoyos 2007: 63–66). Permanent standing armies were found only generally among the rich and powerful Hellenistic kingdoms or in the Roman and Persian empires. Similarly, large naval forces required massive amounts of resources in materials, supplies and pay and, in turn, forced states to develop financial and logistical structures to provide them (Rawlings 2007a: 112–17, 161–67). So it is unsurprising that the richest and most economically advanced states tended to have the most effective and powerful navies: the Athenians, Carthaginians, Rhodians and, despite their landlubberly image, the Romans.

States might resort to hiring mercenaries to make up for skill shortages (Rhodian and Balearic slingers and Cretan archers were, for a time, sought-after commodities), or to bolster their military strength and army sizes (as in the case of the Phokians during the 350s BC). Such specialists were expensive and posed an ideological problem for most advocates of a farmer-militia ideal (Trundle 2004). Their employment was potentially subversive to such an ideology since their loyalty could be bought, or they might choose to seize power for themselves (as when the Mamertines took control of Messana, c.289 BC: Diod. 21.18; 22.7.4, 13; Polyb. 1.7–8; cf. Plut. *Pyrrh.* 23–24). It was often the case that tyrants had seized or maintained their power in Greek communities by relying on mercenary outsiders. The army of Carthage was characterized, by Polybius (1.81, with much prejudice) as a primarily mercenary force that drew on the worst sorts of outsiders: barbarians such as Spaniards, Gauls and Libyans whose own customs and upbringing, no less than the brutalizing treatment of their Punic superiors, gave them the potential for savage and bestial actions (exemplified by the horrific atrocities of the "Truceless War," a four-year revolt, initially over arrears of pay, waged by such employees against Carthage, 241–237 BC).

A less expensive and ideologically more appealing option (since it could enhance the "security, honor, and self-interest" of the dominant party, Thuc. 1.76) was to acquire subject communities and allies. These could be required to provide troops, as the commitment by the men of Erxadieis c.426/425 BC, to "go by land and by sea wherever the Spartans might lead" (Peek 1974; Baltrusch 1994: 21–24; van Wees 2004: 14). Indeed the Roman republic's military might derived, in part, from the effective exploitation of the manpower of its allies, as many commentators from Polybius onwards have recognized (A. Toynbee 1965: 1.502–5, 2.128–35; Brunt 1971: 669–86; W. Harris 1984; Rawlings 2007b: 51–53).

Throughout the republic, frequent campaigning served to militarize much of the population of both Rome and its Italian allies. While not every legionary was a brave and committed careerist like Spurius Ligustinus, Harris's analysis of the belligerency of the Roman republic rightly emphasized the warlike ethos of the Roman community as a whole, in which aristocratic glory seeking and popular, religious and moral support for warfare were only the most notable manifestations (1979). Of course, the successful outcomes of wars, along with their economic pay-offs of booty, tribute and territory, undoubtedly helped to reinforce this ethos: on only one occasion did the Roman assembly (*comitia centuriata*) reject a proposal to declare war – this at the end of the exhausting 16-year conflict with Hannibal, and then only for a few weeks (200 BC, Livy 31.6). Yet Rome was not operating in a vacuum; nor was it as exceptional in its militarism and aggressive foreign policy as has sometimes been imagined (Eckstein 2006). The Roman state flourished in a world where many communities, from the smallest to the largest, were often engaged in military activities. Each had their own internal pressures (economic, demographic, institutional, ideological), encouraging them to act aggressively, and many were as bellicose, if not as militarily effective, as Rome. At times, war was so frequent that it seemed to have an almost annual rhythm. In the period 510–338 BC the Athenians found themselves fighting, on average, seven years in every decade. The Roman republic was at war approximately nine in every ten years, and the Hellenistic kingdoms had similar levels of military involvement (Lévêque 1968: 279; Garlan 1975: 15; Eckstein 2006: 215–16). Even during the principate, when the obligations placed on citizens were diminishing as Rome's frontiers solidified and those living in Italy rarely saw military units, the *pax Romana* was not entirely tranquil. Warfare on the frontiers was frequent and civil conflict was sometimes severe, as in AD 69, when the Capitol at Rome itself appears to have been burned (Tac. *Hist.* 3.70–72).

Mechanisms existed to promote peaceful relations, and were sometimes effective, at least locally or regionally. Heralds were considered inviolable, truces could be organized to enable negotiations between warring parties to take place, treaties guaranteeing peace for specified periods of time or "for ever" could be made, and third-party arbitration might be available in the cases of disputes (van Wees 2004: 14–15; Raaflaub 2007). There was also a general recognition of the dangers of war. Even Homer's ultimate warrior, Achilles, recognized that "Men can raid cattle and sturdy sheep, and men can win tripods and bay horses by the head; but there is no raiding or winning a man's life back again, when once it has passed the guard of his teeth" (*Il.* 9.406–9), while Euripides' *Suppliant Women* (949–54) exhorted "mortals to live quietly and to cease from the toils of battle, since life is so short." Xenophon suggested that although "it is fated by the gods that wars should exist, man should be cautious about beginning them and anxious to end them as soon as possible" (Xen. *Hell.* 6.3.6). Nevertheless, despite such sentiments and despite diplomatic attempts to maintain peaceful relations, states were often ready to go to war, their citizens persuaded to support such ventures because of perceptions such as those offered by Perikles: "It must be thoroughly understood that war is a necessity; but that the more readily we accept it, the less will be the ardor of our opponents, and that out of the greatest dangers communities and individuals acquire the greatest glory" (Thuc. 1.144.3). A combination of aggressive deterrence and ideological pay-off (glory) could be combined with a commonly expressed view that war was a "necessity" or "fated to exist," to reflect what, for most communities, must have been a common attitude to an ever-present reality (or potentiality). That is not to say that decisions were taken lightly, and disagreements within communities over the correctness of some decisions could be sharp, but in a world of aggressive neighbors, fear and mistrust of foreign motives, combined with the attractions of victory, glory, respect, and enrichment, war was often a seductively simplifying response to difficult diplomatic (and domestic) situations.

3   Patterns of Violence

Ancient combat was shaped by practical and ideological factors. The nature of ancient technology forced men to fight close-up with stabbing, slicing, and smashing weapons propelled by little more than their own physical strength. There were exceptions: from the fifth century BC, siege engines were developed that harnessed the principles of torsion and traction, while navies often represented the cutting edge of technological sophistication, combining oar power with hydrodynamic efficiency born from effective construction using fabrics such as timber and bitumen. For the most part, however, the majority of individuals who came to engage their enemy could see their faces and feel the impact of blows upon bodies. Archers, slingers, and javelin throwers also witnessed their effect on opponents, and while rowers rarely saw their adversaries, their bodies still shuddered at the kinetic power of their ramming and oar shearing. Inevitably, this intimate experience had its psychological effects, although whether the recent attempts to psychoanalyze participants from modern perspectives reveals more about ancient or modern war-trauma has yet to be resolved (Shay 1994, Tritle 2000). The study of the practicalities of violence has drawn inspiration from Keegan's landmark study, *The Face of Battle*, and his methods have been productively applied to both Greek and Roman warfare (e.g. V. Hanson 1989, Goldsworthy 1996, Daly 2002). Battlefield dynamics and the visceral experience of combat have thus received much attention and debate.

The recognition that the battlefield was a brutal and terrible place, requiring great personal courage and collective commitment to close with enemies and kill or be killed, raises the question of why pitched battle was ever undertaken. It seems clear that the desire to engage in massed combat sprang from a combination of ideological and practical impulses (V. Hanson 2000). Battle could be a brutally efficient form of warfare: in practical "body-count" terms, it could show which side had suffered the most casualties or, psychologically, by inflicting more casualties than the enemy were willing to take, it could break their resistance in a single day. Battles tended to be fought on open plains where manoeuvre was relatively straightforward; such landscape was familiar and ideologically appealing to the farmer-militias of Greece and Italy (and equally appealing to the cavalries of the Persians, Parthians, Scythians, and Huns). Battle was a crucible for "manliness" (Greek *andreia*, Latin *virtus*): it was a place where men showed that they were brave and good citizens, and could display their prowess (Lendon 2005). Battle was also where collective identity and communal solidarity was displayed and tested, where memories were forged that could loom large over a community, as in the case of the Athenian victory at Marathon, celebrated in an annual festival (Pritchett 1979: 183–84), monumentalized by a battlefield tomb and a painting in the Stoa Poikile (Paus. 1.32.3, 1.15.3–4), evoked in patriotic speeches (Loraux 1986: 155–71), and recalled by the Marathonomachai, the veterans of the battle, to add luster to their daily pursuits and claims for respect and consideration (Aristoph. *Eq.* 780–84, *Ach.* 692–701, *Vesp.* 706–12). Battles were "headline" events for communities to remember, since they connected the largest number of people to particular shared and often traumatic, but temporally circumscribed, experiences. They even presented exciting and dramatic set-pieces for history writers (both ancient and modern) to display their talents.

However, concentrating on pitched battle could give us a somewhat distorted view of warfare if it comes at the expense of a consideration of the broader canvas of violence and military activity. It has been noted that the Peloponnesian war involved only a handful of major battles, but many more sieges, raids, and skirmishes in its 27-year course (Krentz 1997: 56–57). Most states and armies undertook far more of these sorts of activities than battles. Many Roman campaigns involved much low-level raiding and violence, both before and after pitched battles, and the nature of Roman conquest and of the suppression of uprisings in the republican and imperial periods required Roman forces often to disperse to operate against a variety of small enemy groups and objectives (Goldsworthy 1996: 114–15). Caesar's campaigns in Gaul, despite a number of major engagements with tribal and confederate armies, were, for the most part, characterized by the deployment of individual legions and their constituent elements of cavalry *alae* and infantry cohorts in the raiding and suppression of specific communities.

> Well, I, for my part, comrades, am tired of packing up and walking and running and carrying my arms and being in line and standing guard and fighting. What I now long for is to be rid of these toils. (Xen. *Anab.* 5.1.2)

These words were spoken by Leon of Thurii as he and over ten thousand fellow mercenaries struggled to travel back to their homelands from the heart of the Persian empire after their employer, Cyrus, a pretender to the Persian crown, had fallen in battle at Cunaxa (401 BC). His words are a useful reminder that warfare was not just about the experience of pitched battle. Ancient campaigning was mostly marching and foraging, with some maneuvering to obtain objectives (sometimes, but not always, including locating enemy forces). The expedition of the Ten Thousand benefited from one of the most interesting and informative descriptions of an army on the move: that of the eyewitness and commander in the force, Xenophon. Despite his aristocratic background, Xenophon often presents a soldier's-eye view of warfare in his account. For him, the main concerns of the soldiers, revealing much about their individual and collective psychological states, revolved around the everyday realities of campaigning: the walking, camping, search for supplies, and combat in its many forms.

By contrast, Caesar's account of his campaigns in Gaul (59–51 BC), while addressing the issues of logistics and the motivation of troops, reveals a far more managerial perspective of the general, befitting a powerful politician writing dispatches (*commentarii*) for consumption by allies, supporters and political rivals at home. The difference in tone is evident in Caesar's description of the siege of Avaricum:

> For several days they (the Romans) had no grain and preserved themselves from starvation only by collecting cattle from outlying villages. Yet not a word were they heard to utter that was unworthy of successful and experienced Roman soldiers. Indeed, when Caesar addressed the legions as they worked, telling them he would abandon the siege if their conditions proved unbearable, with one voice they begged him not to do so . . . (Caes. *BG* 7.17)

Both types of account, because they lack specific details of calorie consumption, rates of attrition, and so forth, are frustrating for those scholars interested in analyzing the practicalities of supplying men and animals on campaign, forcing them to rely on modern comparative data (Engels 1978). However, it is clear from such accounts that logistical factors had a major impact on the success of specific campaigns, while the methods employed by communities to ensure that their armies were sufficiently provisioned reveal some of the structural and cultural aspects of their war making (Erdkamp 1998, J. Roth 1999). Imperial powers such as the Persians, Macedonians, Carthaginians, and Romans developed systems to maintain their armies in the field for many months, or even years, at a time, and to project their power over great distances. By contrast, much warfare conducted by Greek city-states, western European tribes, and many of republican Rome's Italian adversaries was rather less sustained, partly because of the lack of adequate logistical structures and partly because of the expectations that warfare might consist of raiding or brief demonstrations of prowess on the field of battle that would allow militia-farmers to return to their fields.

Thucydides, an urbane and sophisticated inhabitant of Athens, writing at a time when his city ruled a naval empire that embraced as many as two hundred communities spread in and around the Aegean Sea, could look at the inhabitants of other regions of Greece and see the difference. Thucydides (1.5) imagined that the earliest Greeks had waged predatory warfare, chieftains had led piratical expeditions that plundered all and sundry, and everyone carried weapons in daily life. The Athenians, followed by most other Greeks, he observed (1.6), eventually abandoned the wearing of arms in public, and apparently gave up predation for more civilized pursuits. Nevertheless he noted that

> Even today some of the inhabitants of the mainland regard successful sea-piracy as something to be proud of . . . The same practice of raiding by land used also to prevail; indeed much of Greece still follows the old way of life especially among the Ozolian Lokrians, and the Aitolians and the Akarnanians and the others who live on the mainland in that area. (Thuc. 1.5)

Thucydides (1.49) could also comment on the manner in which the relatively advanced and well-organized communities of Corinth and Corcyra had fought the recent naval battle of Sybota (434/433 BC) as "old fashioned" and "more akin to a land battle than a naval one." At the time, Athens was the most sophisticated and well-organized proponent of naval warfare in the Mediterranean, while most of its rivals had yet to develop the same skills and tactics. Contemporary discourse in Athens had, in fact, reached the stage where different forms of empire and military power could be juxtaposed and subjected to philosophical and political analysis. Both

Thucydides and the Old Oligarch, among others, considered the nature of thalassocracy and compared it with land power (Momigliano 1944). They recognized that the Athenians were capable of waging protracted wars overseas because of their imperial structures and economic sophistication, whereas the hoplite states of the Peloponnese were limited in what they could achieve by marching overland, and had political, social, and economic structures that restricted the duration of their campaigns and appetite for protracted war (Rawlings 2007a: 111–12, 161). That is not to say that the Athenians, or, indeed, the Romans, Carthaginians, or Macedonians, were averse to short conflicts of limited objectives or intensity, to smash-and-grab raids on neighboring territories or acts of reprisal and revenge. Nor was it the case that the Peloponnesians were incapable of prosecuting long wars; after all, they eventually defeated the Athenians after 27 years of (sporadic) warfare and had adapted to the nature of the conflict by attacking Athens' allies in northern Greece (by land) and later the eastern Aegean (by sea). States, although often shaped by their cultural expectation of what war should be about and constrained by their political, social and economic structures, nevertheless might adapt (not always successfully) to different modes of war. Writers of the Augustan era, looking back on the rise of the Roman state to dominance, held a dual perspective. They imagined that early Romans possessed a similar sophistication and appreciation of warfare and empire that they themselves possessed, while at the same time imagining that Roman warfare had been periodically improved by learning the military formations and technologies of their adversaries. An ability to adapt to enemy ways, to master the skills the enemy possessed and to overcome them, was something that the Romans celebrated about their war making (Cornell 1995: 170). Such a two-fold view masked a rather more gradual and complex process of interchange and assimilation, however (Rawlings 2007b: 53–55). The great variety of forms of violence that the Romans (and others) encountered and employed, which slowly shaped their military, also shaped their society and their outlook on war.

4   Conclusion

Warfare was a common experience for many communities, and the frequent demands of war on society led to the development of a variety of elements: weapons and other technologies for war, specialists (military elites, mercenaries), institutions (financial and logistical, armies, navies, officers, and magistrates with military powers), physical structures (defensive systems, armories, ship-sheds, etc.). These are susceptible to study in their own right, for what they reveal about the types of warfare that could be conducted and for the consequent demands on society. They can also help to reveal the cultural processes at play, the expectations of what war involved, and beliefs about how it should be conducted. Of course, the study of the conduct of warfare itself can also reveal such values and conceptions.

The study of warfare in antiquity, therefore, not only includes the development of fighting techniques, equipment, and the study of the campaigns of the great commanders, but also the role war plays in shaping society and how it in turn is shaped by cultural processes, structures, and values. By investigating the warfare waged by communities and states in antiquity, we reveal a fundamental element in their identity, organization and historical development. Furthermore, it is clear that warfare is the product both of structural internal impulses and of international dynamics. The chances are high that these broader patterns and interactions influenced specific states' actions and historical development (Eckstein 2006: 186–88). A case can be made for needing to appreciate both the internal dynamics and the external pressures caused by war. Furthermore, it is important to investigate how war was shaped by the culture and society of the protagonists and also to understand war's militarizing effects upon their culture, identity and memory.

FURTHER READING

There is a huge array of serious studies of almost all aspects of ancient warfare. Excellent starting points for further investigation are the two-volume *Cambridge History of Greek and Roman Warfare* (Sabin et al. 2007) and the *Oxford Handbook of Classical Warfare* (Campbell and Tritle, forthcoming). These can be augmented by the useful bibliographical essays of V. Hanson 1999 and Lendon 2005: 393–440. Whitby 2007 is a solid and critical discussion of the nature of the ancient evidence. On Greek warfare, the work of Pritchett (1971–91) underpins much new scholarship. The monographs of J. K. Anderson 1970, Ducrey 1985, V. Hanson 1989 and 1995, van Wees 1992 and 2004, and Rawlings 2007a should be consulted, while there are many valuable discussions of Greek (and Roman) warfare in collections such as those of Vernant 1968, Rich and Shipley 1993a and 1993b, A. Lloyd 1996, van Wees 2000 and Raaflaub 2007. Chaniotis 2005 considers non-operational aspects of Hellenistic warfare; chapters by Lévêque 1968, Baker 2003 and Bugh 2006 touch on a variety of issues. On Roman warfare, *A Companion to the Roman Army* (ed. Erdkamp, 2007) covers a wide range of topics. Goldsworthy 1996 and Gilliver 1999 provide discussions of operational aspects of the late republican and early imperial periods, while H. Elton 1996 and Lee 2007 discuss the later Roman army and warfare. On the bellicosity of Rome, see W. Harris 1979, with important modifications by North 1981 and Rich 1993; on the aggressive impulses of ancient states in general, Eckstein 2006, and on militarism see Garlan 1975 and, particularly, Dawson 1996.

PART VIII

Repercussions

CHAPTER FORTY-SEVEN

The Impact of Antiquity

Rosamond McKitterick

1 Introduction

The impact of antiquity reverberates even now. That modern Western culture is based ultimately upon Greco-Roman civilization can be understood first of all in terms of direct inheritance and continuity. Greek and Roman ruins scatter the landscape from Hadrian's Wall to eastern Anatolia, and are still visited by awed tourists. Classicizing buildings of the Renaissance and modern period continue or echo the styles, decorative features, and monumental characteristics of classical architecture; major cities around the world – Washington, Pretoria, Paris, London, Berlin, and many more – evoke imperial architecture in many of their state buildings and triumphal arches, though the choice of such a classicizing imperial style was sometimes fiercely contested (Mordaunt Crook 1972; Onians 1988; J. Ziolkowski 1988). Greek and Roman buildings in form and scale, as well as in their function as symbols of technological progress and feats of engineering, even inspired many of the grand railway stations of Britain, the United States, and continental Europe, such as the former Euston in London, the Stazione Leopoldo in Florence or Pennsylvania Station in New York (DeLaine 1999). Our use of Roman capital script and an alphabet derived from the Roman script system is taken completely for granted (Bischoff 1990). Many modern place names and urban sites have an unbroken history from antiquity, or, like the Greek and Roman place names in new countries, such as Ithaca and Syracuse in upstate New York, link the new world with the old. Modern highways, such as the British A1 or A6, still follow the old Roman road network. Further debts are the basic geometry, astronomy, algebra, mathematics, medicine, and Aristotelian methods of reasoning which underlie modern science. Greek theories of music played a strong role in the Western musical tradition, and extensive linguistic and literary debts have vastly enriched European language and literature (E. Butler 1935; Bolgar 1956, 1971, 1976, 1979; Ziolkowski and Putnam 2008). The influence of classical culture on seventeenth- and eighteenth-century European art, literature, and music was particularly remarkable, and remains, through display and performance in many media, part of our own culture now. Themes and stories from classical mythology and literature, for example, were popular from the middle ages to modern times, though operas on historical subjects, primarily from Roman history and most usually performed to celebrate political marriage alliances and coronations, had their heyday in the seventeenth and eighteenth centuries between Monteverdi's *L'Incoronazione di Poppea* in 1642 and Mozart's *La Clemenza di Tito* of 1791 (P. Smith 1971; Loewenberg 1978; McKitterick 1997). Less visible inheritances from antiquity might also be mentioned, such as political organization, the notion of democracy, and the authority of civil law, our social and ethical expectations, and civic values. Then there are the curious recreations or adaptations inspired by original events such as marathon runners and the Olympic Games (Biddiss 1999). Because of the global influence of Western culture, moreover, the legacy of antiquity plays a role in non-Western cultures throughout the world.

Yet "antiquity" was not passively received and did not survive by accident. Much of the impact of antiquity is due, on the contrary, to forceful and dedicated preservation on the one hand, and imitation, emulation, modification, adaptation, and even distortion as a constituent element of new and independent cultures on the other. Much of all this is expressed, among others, by John Keats in his sonnet *On first looking into Chapman's Homer* (Keats 1817; Finley 1981b; Jenkyns 1992; Parrinder 1999). In the schools from antiquity until the twentieth century, the ancient classics constituted a part of the educational curriculum in the West, and Latin remained an indispensable language of communication (Curtius 1953; M. Clarke 1959). After all, Isaac Newton published his *Principia mathematica* in 1687 in Latin. While Latin persisted as an important element of law and of the Christian liturgy, a large section of the population of the world would have had some exposure to the Latin language.

The contexts in which such preservation, adaptation, and education were conceived, and the purposes to which ancient learning and culture were put, changed constantly. In the space of this chapter only the merest impression of these can be given. By means of a few examples I shall chart, therefore, the range of imaginative and learned responses to antiquity that ensured its continuing impact. I shall try to trace the awareness of ancient history and processes of reception, as well as the motives and decision making in relation to the preservation or conservation of antique knowledge and culture. My particular examples will be from the crucially formative period of the early middle ages. I shall discuss the western European reception of Roman culture and, via the Latin translations and borrowings of the Romans, some of Greek learning as well. Further, by focusing on the idea of Rome in the early middle ages as a case study, I shall indicate how one central symbol and physical remnant of antiquity could be interpreted in many different ways simultaneously. In this respect we see the impact of antiquity within the context of a Christian culture. Certainly the Christian middle ages chose to sideline elements of classical culture, despite the fact that the Christian tradition itself was deeply indebted to classical civilization. Even though scholars in the Renaissance re-emphasized other aspects of antiquity not promoted in the middle ages, we owe the survival of the Latin classics largely to the scribes of the Christian early middle ages. By far the greater proportion of the earliest extant manuscripts of all surviving Roman texts is the work of Frankish scribes in Carolingian monasteries in the ninth century (Reynolds 1983; Reynolds and Wilson 1991).

2 Antiquity Displayed

For many in the modern world, direct confrontation with the antique past is not so much in the landscape, education, or literature, as in museums. A visitor to the Kunst-historisches Museum in Vienna, for instance, will find a major remounting of their collection of Greek and Roman antiquities, deploying all the resources of a modern museum in terms of dramatic lighting, huge projections of film sequences to show off details of a section of the Greek vases and Roman cameos, and precise information about context and provenance. Much of this fine collection was assembled by the Hapsburg rulers of the Austro-Hungarian empire from the Kunst and Wunderkammer of Archduke Ferdinand and the emperor Rudof II onward. It was put on general display with the opening in 1891 of the massive Renaissance-style building in which it is still housed. Yet the collection reflects more than Hapsburg patronage. It mirrors both local history and an international scholarly interest in antiquity which combine in modern Austria to form an essential element of local and even national identity. Many of Vienna's Roman artifacts, for example, come from the Roman city of Car-nuntum, near Vienna, as well as from various sites in the Roman Danube *limes* and the Roman provinces of Pannonia and Noricum. Examples among many possible are the Greco-Roman Apollo from the first century BC found in Romania, the fourth-century mosaic from the so-called Roman villa on the *Loigerfelder* near Salzburg found in 1815, with its depiction of Theseus killing the Minotaur at the center of the Labyrinth, and the memorial to Titus Calcidius Severus, centurion of the 15th legion stationed at Carnuntum, who died when he was 58 after 34 years of service. His stone depicted his military equipment – cuirass, greaves, helmet, and staff – and a small bas-relief sculpture of a stable boy with Titus's horse. Other artifacts reached Austria at different stages, such as the Greek marble sarcophagus from the second half of the fourth century BC, with its striking relief sculpture of a Greek defending himself with his shield against the Amazons. It was found in a burial chamber in Cyprus in the sixteenth century and brought to Vienna via the Fuggers, the famous Augsburg merchants. Greek vases, Roman cameos, Greek and Roman coins, sculpture, jewelry, silver table-ware, and the beautiful series of mummy portraits from Roman Egypt came into the imperial collection partly piecemeal as a consequence of royal family interest, and partly more systematically in direct relation to the increasing amount of scholarly investigation and amateur excavation in the Mediterranean region, the Balkans, and Asia Minor in the eighteenth and nineteenth centuries. The love scene on the first-century AD mosaic from Centocelle near Rome was found in 1865 as a result of such scholarly research, and was brought thereafter to Vienna.

Vienna is but one of many European cities within the former Roman empire full of mementoes of its history within a Roman province. Budapest's National Museum, founded between 1832 and 1856, also proudly displays in its lapidarium the artifacts from Aquincum (both the civilian and the military towns of Obuda) excavated in 1787. Similarly, Bavaria has many surviving artifacts from the former Roman provinces of Raetia and Noricum, not least a set of memorial stones from Regina Castra in Regensburg Museum and the mosaic pavement from Westerhoven near Ingolstadt, the large Roman dinner service from the noble necropolis at Wehringen, and the silver tableware from Manching now in the Glyptothek in Munich. Ludwig I of Bavaria, in particular, revered Greek and antique culture. With the help of his architect Leo von Kleuze, he created his "Athens on the Isar" between 1806 and 1830, to house the remarkable collection of antique sculpture he had put together with the help of agents. It was Ludwig I, moreover, who, inspired by the excavations at Pompeii, commissioned Friedrich von Gärtner to build between 1843 and 1850 a completely equipped and decorated replica of the "Castor and Pollux house" at Aschaffenburg. Incidentally, the Pompeii excavations inspired a host of responses, ranging from Giovanni Pacini's opera *L'Ultimo Giorno di Pompei*, first performed in Naples in 1825, translated into German and also performed in Mexico in 1838, to Bulwer Lytton's novel *The Last Days of Pompeii* published in 1838.

In Paris, London, Mainz, and Cologne local artifacts from the antique past join materials brought from Asia Minor and the Mediterranean by scholars and collectors. The temple of Artemis at Ephesos, one of the Seven Wonders of the Ancient World, was excavated by J. T Wood between 1863 and 1874. Charles Townley's collection of Roman sculpture in the British Museum was mostly bought in Rome in the later part of the eighteenth century and excited enormous public interest in England. It formed the subject of a famous painting by Johann Zoffany (1782), now in the Townley Hall Art Gallery and Museum, Burnley, Lancs. The Vindolanda tablets with samples of letters from Roman soldiers stationed on Hadrian's Wall (cf. fig. 4.1), the Hinton St Mary mosaic, and the Water Newton treasure of Roman silver tableware, on the other hand, are precious remnants of the Roman occupation of Britain.

The wider dissemination of a taste for antiquity among the elites (Haskell and Penny 1981) and the formation of collections of antique art were also a cause and consequence of the growing popularity of the Grand Tour in eighteenth- and nineteenth-century Europe (Elek and Johnston 1967; Gill 1990; Babel and Paravicini 2005). Thomas Coke of Holkham Hall in Norfolk, for example, first learned to appreciate classical art as a young man during his Grand Tour of Europe between 1712 and 1718; the entrance hall of his new house, designed by William Kent, is reminiscent of the Pantheon in Rome, and Coke filled his new statue gallery with antique sculptures procured on his travels. Many aspiring collectors had to settle for copies, such as the plaster Laocoon made in 1810 for Louis Napoleon, briefly king of Holland, and now in the Stedelijk Museum De Lakenhal in Leiden.

Even beyond the frontiers of the former Roman empire, it was a standard demonstration of princely culture and patronage to accumulate a collection of ancient artifacts. Berlin's Alter Museum and Pergamon Museum, for example, originated in the activities of the Brandenburg princes, at the heart of which was the purchase in 1698 of the collection formed by the archaeologist Giovanni Pietro Bellori (1613–96). Berlin's Alter Museum opened its doors to the public in 1830, and the Pergamon

Museum was formed a century later to house the Pergamon Altar and the Market Gate of Miletos.

These museums do not simply display antiquity to the public. They represent an appropriation of antique culture as part of a dynamic process of the formation of each national culture. These collections are presented not just as knowledge of the human past but as knowledge of an integral element of each country's or city's own past and cultural inheritance. Although the great national museums are notably rich in the spoils of conquest and of eager collectors, they are nevertheless implicated in the self-image of nations or, on occasion, of its rulers. The Spinario sculpture (of a boy extracting a thorn from his foot) from the Capitoline, for example, formed part of Napoleon's triumphal procession in 1798 of great works of art he had sequestrated for his grand new museum in Paris; it was returned to Rome in 1815. Similarly, another symbolic monument stolen by Napoleon was the tomb of Charlemagne; it was returned to Aachen in 1815 (Schmidt 1999). Charlemagne's tomb, however, indicates that the symbolic resonance of antique artifacts could be just as powerful in the ninth as in the nineteenth century: it is a massive and beautiful third-century Italian Carrara marble sarcophagus depicting the Rape of Proserpina. It is worth considering the possible contexts for the reuse of a Roman monument in this way in rather more detail, for such reuse raises at once the question of knowledge of antiquity, how antiquity was understood and what had survived. These issues need to be considered first of all in terms of the physical remains, and secondly in terms of texts.

3 Knowledge of Antiquity: the Buildings and the City of Rome

The buildings of the Roman empire, especially those of the third, fourth, and fifth centuries, were only as distant from the peoples of Europe and the Mediterranean littoral as those of the sixteenth or seventeenth century are in many towns in Britain. A vast number was still visible, especially in cities such as Reims, Trier, Lyon, Arles, Paris, Tours, Verona, Jerusalem, Carthage and Constantinople/Istanbul, let alone Rome itself (Greenhalgh 1989). Yet the perception of the Roman remains was necessarily affected by the transformation of function of many of the remaining buildings. Constantine's great aula at Trier, for example, had been converted into a Christian basilica, but the most dramatic shift of focus was in Rome itself. After the foundation of Constantinople, Rome developed as the capital of the Bishop of Rome and as a Christian city (Pfeil 1929; Krautheimer 1980, 1983; J. Smith 2000). These changes are evident even in the physical orientation of the city. In the third and fourth centuries Rome was still focused on the forum but, for political reasons, Constantine tried to locate the Pope some little distance away at the Lateran, Rome's official cathedral. St Peter's basilica, also built by Constantine, however, was established on the site of his shrine and became the center of pilgrimage and the *de facto* cathedral. Traders, stall holders, inn keepers and the like began to congregate in Trastevere and the area now known as the Old City in order to serve and benefit from the pilgrim traffic. In consequence the Lateran became increasingly isolated and the Forum also less used, though archaeological evidence indicates that the latter remained unaltered and unencroached upon until the end of the eighth century. Recent excavations as part of the papal Millennium Project have unearthed a very fine Carolingian villa built in the forum c.800 alongside a street of similar date, though the grandee for whom it might have been built is a matter of conjecture. The Forum, therefore, despite the consecration and Christianization of many of the great buildings, and the rich decoration of such churches as Santa Maria Antiqua and SS Cosmo e Damiano, would nevertheless have retained much of the character and majesty it had possessed in late antiquity. Knowledge of the buildings of Rome and the emperors who had had them erected was entwined with Christian traditions. There were, for example, hosts of martyrs associated with the excesses of Nero in AD 64 and possibly Domitian AD 81–96, and persecutions under Decius 249–51 and Diocletian c.303. Many obscure members of Roman families from the period of the principate were elevated as martyrs and saints. As well as the shift in the concentration of the population of Rome there is the extraordinary building activity in the city, with an impressive number of new basilicas erected between 380 and 440. Building styles incorporated many classical reminiscences (especially in the use of Ionic and Corinthian columns). Classical antiquity, therefore, was reshaped within a new Christian context, which in its turn inspired architecture in the early middle ages and beyond.

Some indication of how early medieval visitors and pilgrims reacted to Rome is to be found in the itineraries and syllogai. These are collections of recorded inscriptions from monuments, especially in Rome, which resemble in some respects the "walking routes" provided in modern tourist guides. They are arranged in a sequence following the route of pedestrians and are the consequence of pilgrims, visitors, or tourists noting and copying down the inscriptions they saw. The Einsiedeln sylloge from the early ninth century is one of the best known of these texts. It walks readers from St Peter's and the Tiburtine bridge into the city, taking them to Trajan's column and the baths of Diocletian, the Palatine Forum and then over many bridges and under many arches, including the triumphal arches of Constantine and Severus. It records the inscriptions concerning the warmaking and imperial expansion under Hadrian, Trajan, and Marcus Aurelius. The ninth-century visitor also visited the Capitoline hill and the theater of Pompey, and recorded the Christian inscriptions of such major Roman churches as St Peter's, S. Paolo fuori le mura, Sta Sabina, S. Pancrazio, S. Sebastiano (Rossi 1857–1888; Walser 1987). These accounts, of course, also served as possible guides for what to see in Rome for other visitors in the future.

The combination of interests in classical and secular antiquity, in the military successes of the imperial past and in the saints of the early Christian city in these syllogai and itineraries represents a tradition on which the twelfth-century author of *The Marvels of Rome* clearly drew. He, too, combined the accounts of Roman churches and Roman martyrs and saints with ancient classical and secular monuments on which there is laconic detail (Gregorius Magister trans. Osborne 1987). *The Marvels of Rome* provides a guide to the devout pilgrim as well as to the monuments of Roman civic life, therefore, and it incorporates a certain amount about the city of Rome itself. Certainly the Christian basilicas and the subsequent elaborate building programs of many popes reoriented the religious places and created many new locations of religious devotion. Recent research on medieval church buildings in Rome has revealed a history of transformation and new building work as well as places that simply ceased to be used and were replaced by others. Rome, despite having been treated over the past sixteen hundred years as a giant quarry, with many fine buildings despoiled (though some were converted for alternative use), the marble burnt for lime for further building work, and the metal stripped off, has continued to impress all who see it and to inspire those wealthy enough to adorn it further in a constant process of renewal. Yet even the Christian sacred topography was anchored in the pagan Roman past, for Livy described a topography of religious devotion supporting the political life of the city. Livy's expression of Rome's religious centrality may well have exerted some influence in Francia and Italy, for his work was known and copied with, for example, ninth- and tenth-century witnesses to the text in two main families from Corbie, Fulda, the Loire region, and elsewhere. A host of other texts from classical antiquity, all widely disseminated throughout Europe from the Carolingian period onwards, moreover, offered similarly vivid reflections on Rome's physical structures, its religious cults, its history, and its role as a symbol of power. The importance of place and the physical and symbolic resonance of Rome as a political and religious center are thus as crucial for the Christian middle ages as they were in the pagan ancient world

4 Knowledge of Ancient History: the Texts

The reactions to Rome, and the information about what to see, rested on knowledge of Rome and the Roman past, and this awareness was conveyed into the middle ages from two major categories of written source in addition to the physical remains. The first of these is the ancient histories written by Livy, Tacitus, Caesar, Justinus, Sallust, Velleius Paterculus, Ammianus Marcellinus, and many more. Monasteries under strong royal patronage in the Carolingian period appear to have cultivated an interest in Roman history, for it was in such centers as Lorsch, St Amand, and Corbie that late antique codices were copied and studied. Indeed, the initial promotion and distribution of Roman history books can be traced to the Carolingian court itself. Further, selections from Roman history were often incorporated into Frankish history books as prefatory sections to the narratives of Frankish history. A tenth-century codex in St Omer, for example, starts with Eutropius's *Roman history*, a summary of the simple facts of Roman history written at the request of the emperor Valens (AD 364–378), in which he condensed the history of Rome from Romulus to his own time. It adds the Chronicle of Count Marcellinus and the *Notitia galliarum* primarily for the fifth century, an abbreviated version of the *Histories* of Gregory of Tours relating the deeds of the early Merovingian Frankish kings to the end of the sixth century, and Frankish chronicles and annals covering the seventh, eighth, and ninth centuries. Such a collection of texts is a remarkable witness to the consistency and longevity of the association of Roman and Frankish history in Carolingian perceptions of the past. The Roman past became part of successive dynastic projections of their origins by ruling families in medieval and early modern Europe (Morrissey 2003; McKitterick 2004).

Count Marcellinus, whose work was included in the Frankish codex just mentioned, presents the Roman empire as part of universal history (Croke 2001). In doing so the author followed the model offered by the Chronicle of Eusebius and Jerome, in which local and national history, including the history of Greece and Rome, was placed in the context of God's time. Eusebius's text was translated into Latin and continued by Jerome to 378 (Helm 1956; Fotheringham 1905, 1923). The Chronicle presents Roman and Christian history on a world stage and in succession to the empires of the Assyrians, Medes, Persians, Hebrews, and Greeks, set out in parallel columns whose numbers wax and wane until finally only Rome is left. It was hugely influential (McKitterick 2006). Rome is portrayed primarily as the locus of old imperial power. Subsequent world chronicles written during the middle ages Christianize the portrait of Rome still further. The ninth-century writer Ado of Vienne, for example, stretched the chronology of the bishops of Vienne, to make the first bishop a disciple of St Paul and arrive from Rome in order to establish Vienne as virtually of Apostolic origin. In the tenth century too, Flodoard of Rheims traced the history of the bishops of Rheims from Sixtus, the first bishop of Rheims, allegedly sent by St Peter. Flodoard also augmented the city's secular Roman associations with the suggestion that Rheims might have been founded by members of Remus's military retinue.

What these authors stressed above all is Christian Rome, from the arrival of Saints Peter and Paul onwards. Rome emerges particularly strongly in the tenth-century Chronicle by Regino of Prüm. He offered a long list of the Roman martyrs in the persecutions of Nero, which was then echoed in the catalog of martyrs under nearly every section of the narrative during the reigns of the emperors Domitian, Nerva, Trajan, Decius, Galienus, Aurelian, and, above all, Diocletian. In the last-mentioned reign, men and women received the martyr's crown throughout the Roman empire – Africa, Antioch, Aquileia, Augsburg, Bithynia, Britain, Cologne, Gaul, Illyria, Naples, Nicaea, Palestine, Raetia, Scythia, Sicily, Sirmium, Smyrna, Soissons, Spain, and Spoleto – as well as Rome itself. Thus in texts as well as physical structures the Christian past of Rome, city of the martyrs and the city of St Peter and his successors, is intertwined with that of the Roman empire. The medieval perception of the Roman past was one in which the sacred and the secular history of Rome and of the Roman empire were integrated. It rested on knowledge of the Roman past communicated in Roman histories carefully copied and preserved for the succeeding generations. It was ninth-century copies of Tacitus and Ammianus Marcellinus, for example, which were used by the humanists of the Renaissance and the sixteenth century in preparing their editions for the new printing-presses.

5 Knowledge of Ancient Learning

The early medieval scribes and scholars knew not only Roman historians. They also copied and stored in their libraries the works of Roman philosophers, grammarians, poets, rhetors and encyclopedists, dramatists, astronomers, surveyors, and architects. Early medieval scholars in the West rarely knew Greek. But this does not mean that they were ignorant of Greek thinking, at least in so far as it was transmitted in Latin translation and passed on to the West simply as a consequence of so much of Greek learning and culture having been absorbed by the Romans. The spates of translation of Greek texts in the fourth and sixth centuries in Italy, and in the ninth century in Carolingian Francia and Italy, are well documented (Siegmund 1949; Berschin 1988; Kascynski 1988). Particular categories of text are better represented than others. There was, of course, Greek mythology (Nees 1991), geometry, mathematics, medicine, and astronomy mediated through Latin versions or translations made in antiquity, as well as such texts as the *Physiologus*, a translation of Dioscorides, the *Ilias Latina*, and natural science transmitted via such authors as Pliny and Aratus. Little Greek philosophy survived, apart from the *Timaeus* of Plato in the partial translation by Cicero and full translation with commentary by Chalcidius, though the latter was well known and studied as early as the ninth century in Carolingian Francia (Gersh 1986; McKitterick 1992). Some Aristotelian thought was channeled through Boethius's works, and particularly in the text known as *On the ten categories* (Marenbon 1981). Late Latin and early Christian writers, moreover, incorporated a great deal of Greek teaching into their own work. A prime example is Theodore, Archbishop of Canterbury from 668 to 690, a monk of Greek origin, whose learning survives in a small corpus of his own writings as well as biblical commentaries and glosses made by his pupils to record his oral teaching at Canterbury (Bischoff and Lapidge 1994; Lapidge 1995). Thus we should not underestimate the indirect transmission of Greek thought and knowledge to the West in the earlier middle ages, together with a certain knowledge of who the great Greek thinkers were. The further interest in, and knowledge of, Greek thought in the twelfth and thirteenth centuries in western Europe is also well attested. Arabic or Hebrew translations of Greek texts had been made from the ninth century AD onwards (Carmody 1956; Gutas 1998). These in their turn were translated into Latin (Pines 1986). More Greek learning began to filter to the West during the Crusading period, especially after the sack of Constantinople in 1204, so that most of the major classical Greek writings had reached Europe by the middle of the fifteenth century (N. Wilson 1983). Many scholars then set to work to provide translations, with a particularly remarkable contribution made as a result of the enterprise of Pope Nicholas V (1397–1455), who commissioned a series of translations of Greek historical and philosophical books.

Why were all these texts translated or copies made and further disseminated? One impulse was undoubtedly admiration and a wish to preserve and communicate the learning and understanding of the ancient scholars in both the technical sciences (though these were superseded or modified in due course) and in humane learning (philosophy, religion, poetry, drama, and history). Just as the Romans had absorbed, transmitted, and added creatively to Greek culture, so the heirs of Rome emulated antique culture and built on it in their turn. Texts transmitted on papyrus and parchment, preserved in monastic, cathedral, and royal libraries, and recopied in the current scripts of the day, represented authority and provided secure, tangible links with the past. Texts were not only symbols of power and authority but also the means of exercising power and authority (McKitterick 1989; Nelson 1992). Written transmission lent special authority and status to the ideas they contained, and ensured their place in the Western intellectual tradition.

The impact of antiquity is not to be regarded, therefore, only as the reaction to a curious and exotic culture of the past, of interest to those generally interested in the development of world civilizations. Greek and Roman antiquity and ancient history are also essential elements of the culture and identity of the peoples of Europe, in the regions once within the Greco-Roman world and, by the extension of Greco-Roman culture as part of Christianity, to the peoples of northern and eastern Europe conquered and converted in the period between the fifth and fourteenth centuries. This inheritance is undoubtedly a complex one. As the fate of the Trojan treasure, excavated by Schliemann, displayed in Berlin until the Second World War, and now in the Pushkin Museum in Moscow (Pushkin Museum 1996), or that of the Parthenon friezes known as the Elgin marbles (Beard 1995b; St Clair 1998) reminds us, the tension between national or local history and universal cultural legacy has sometimes led to bitter disputes about ownership and the duties of conservation for subsequent generations. However much its relevance has been challenged or championed (Lowenthal 1985; Beard and Henderson 1995; Stray 1998; Goldhill 2002; Donahue and Fullerton 2003), the culture of antiquity retains a place at many levels in our contemporary world.

FURTHER READING

Several excellent surveys of the legacy of antiquity exist. Livingstone 1921 has historical interest, and Bolgar 1954 still has value, but should be augmented by Finley 1981b and Jenkyns 1992. One of the most influential books concerning the reception of antiquity and its impact on a national culture was E. Butler 1935, but within the educational tradition of particular cultures M. Clarke 1959 and Stray 1998, both with reference to Britain, are illuminating. An understanding of the enduring strength of the classical inspiration in architecture can be gained from Onians 1988, and a thought-provoking essay on the layers of symbolism in the use of *spolia* is in Esch 2005. Grafton 1983 provides an excellent case study of a humanist and classical scholar in early modern Europe, and Beard 2000 an engaging discussion of Jane Harrison in the early twentieth century, though Sandys 1908 remains useful on the general context. The influence exerted, in Britain at least, by Edward Gibbon's (in)famous interpretation of *The Decline and Fall of the Roman Empire* (London, 1776–78) could not be treated in this chapter, but it looms in the background of many modern expositions nevertheless: McKitterick and Quinault 1997 provide guidance and further reading. On art, Haskell and Penny 1981 are indispensable. Those interested in the post-classical history of Rome should start with Krautheimer 1980 and 1983. The significance of the deployment of classical themes in opera has not been assessed fully, but P. Smith 1971 and Loewenberg 1978 together provide the essential basis for such a study. Biddiss and Wyke 1999 offer a lively set of essays on the uses and abuses of antiquity, primarily in the nineteenth and twentieth centuries, and Wyke 1997 provides a further dimension by examining the representation of Rome in modern cinema.

CHAPTER FORTY-EIGHT

Ancient History and National Identity

Andrew Erskine

In January 2002 the international media announced the death of the world's oldest currency: the drachma had been replaced by the euro. In this we see the power of national mythologies. There is no denying that the drachma had been the currency of the Greeks of antiquity, but the story implies that it had been continuously in use since then. It overlooks the succession of empires that had ruled over Greece and the various coins of these occupying powers, the Roman denarius, the Byzantine solidus, the Ottoman akçe. The drachma had long been out of circulation when in 1832 the recently created Greek state decided to invoke its memory by naming their new currency after it. By asserting continuity with the classical past, the Greeks claimed that past for their new nation and effectively erased the intervening centuries.

The Greek and Roman past has played and continues to play an important part in modern national identity, not only in Greece and Italy, where it might seem to have a particular relevance, but also in other European countries such as Germany, France, and most controversially the former Yugoslavian republic of Macedonia. It is not, however, limited to Europe and the Mediterranean, as the example of the United States of America with its senate and senators demonstrates. At various times the classical past has turned out to be a very real and potent presence in the formation and development of nations. In the 1990s it was a central feature in the often bitter diplomatic dispute between Greece and its neighbor the Republic of Macedonia, while earlier in the twentieth century ancient Rome was firmly worked into the ideology of Mussolini's Fascist regime. This chapter explores some of the ways in which the ancient past has been appropriated by nations of modern times, and also considers why this should be so.

1 Creating a National Past

The eighteenth and nineteenth centuries saw major changes in the political structures of Europe, notably the formation of nation-states, which gradually came to replace the shifting alliances of ruling aristocracies so common in the West, or the sprawling Ottoman, Tsarist and Austro-Hungarian empires further East. These emerging states often looked back to the ancient world as part of the process of establishing their identity in the present. By highlighting ancient roots they were able to show that the nation, new as it might appear, was not the creation of the moment but something that had, in spirit at least, existed all along, and had a right to exist now. At the same time this could allow the divisions of more recent times to be by-passed in the interests of promoting unity. The ancient past was of relevance to two of these states in particular, neither of which existed at the beginning of the nineteenth century – Greece and Italy.

Greece came into existence in a somewhat piecemeal fashion during the course of the nineteenth and early twentieth century, progressively adding parts of the Ottoman empire. In the early 1830s its territory for the most part covered the Peloponnese and central Greece, in 1881 Thessaly was added, and in 1913 the state was extended southward to include Crete and northward into Epirus and Macedonia. It is in this northern area that territorial battles were at their most intense as Greece competed with other new states such as Serbia and Bulgaria for the spoils of the failing Ottoman empire. Italy's situation was rather different. Whereas Greece had been under the single rule of the Ottoman empire for centuries, Italy had been politically divided since the end of antiquity, a mix of independent kingdoms and principalities, papal states and foreign powers, only coming together as a unified state between 1859 and 1871. Nevertheless, in both cases local, regional, and other identities would generally have been stronger than any identity as Greeks or Italians.

These new states had to create an identity, not only for their own citizens but also for the outside world. Both Greece and Italy had the classical past to look back to, and they drew on it as they defined themselves in their new status, Greece rather more so than Italy, at least until Mussolini took power (section 2 below). It is evident in the choice of capitals, Athens and Rome, cities that recalled former greatness and, more disturbingly perhaps, imperial power. When these cities became capitals of their respective modern states, however, neither was an obvious powerhouse of national change; Athens was a modest town, although with impressive ancient remains, while the papal state still occupied part of Rome, as it does to this day (for the debate about whether Rome should be designated capital, Giardina and Vauchez 2000: 185–89). But Athens and Rome had tremendous symbolic value. Greece and Italy's desire to possess their classical past is nowhere clearer than in the laws each state produced early in their development to control the practice of archaeology. Already in 1834 Greece passed a law that all antiquities were "national heritage" and "state property" (Hamilakis and Yalouri 1996: 119), while the Italian government shortly after unification instituted a ban on foreign excavations in Italy or its territories and established its own archaeological service (Dyson 2006: 98–101). This might seem only to be expected, but the point is that to legislate was to make an explicit claim to the past. As Kyriakos Pittakis, ephor of antiquities in the new Greek state, said of archaeological discoveries, this was "material to be used to demonstrate that the inhabitants of Greece are descendants of the ancient Greeks" (quoted in Dyson 2006: 75). Similarly the names of the various administrative regions of the state were deliberately modeled on ancient Greece. As a government directive at the time said, this was in order "to resurrect, through this measure, antiquity, to connect the present of Hellas with its illustrious past, to give birth to noble competition among the Hellenes through old memories, to present a picture of classical Hellas abroad, and, finally, to enrich the neo-Hellenic language with names both Hellenic and melodious" (quoted in Alexandri 2002: 192).

Beyond Greece and Italy the relation with the classical past was more complex. France, for example, was shaping a new post-revolutionary national identity, while a German nation-state was progressively being formed out of several hundred principalities and free cities until a German empire was established in 1871. In nations such as these we see two distinct approaches at work. Their existence as a separate people is affirmed by emphasizing their resistance to Roman rule, and consequently heroes of that resistance are celebrated (Schulze 1996: 95–97), while at the same time a Roman heritage is claimed through their having been part of the Roman empire.

France's Napoleon III encapsulates this very neatly. In the 1860s he was an active promoter of the idea of France as a Gallic nation, something which had gained force since the revolution of 1789, whereas the toppled aristocrats were associated with the Frankish invaders of late antiquity. This Gallic/Celtic character is still a major element in French identity today (cf. Dietler 1994 on its use from Napoleon I and Mitterand to Asterix and Gauloises cigarettes). In particular Napoleon III sponsored archaeological excavations at the site of Alesia, where Vercingetorix, the leader of the Gallic rebellion against Rome in 52 BC, made his last stand against Caesar (cf. Witt, THE "CELTS," section 2a). The conclusion of the excavations was marked by the erection of a large statue of Vercingetorix, the features of which were said to resemble Napoleon III. Nor was this assertion of France's Celtic past to have mere local significance; the 6.6-meter-high bronze statue was first displayed in Paris and then carried upright on a wagon through the French countryside to Alesia, where it was placed on a 7-meter-high plinth. The equation between the French people and the ancient Gauls was made explicit in the two inscriptions in French, one reading "Napoleon III, Emperor of the French people, to the memory of Vercingetorix," the other "Gaul united, forming a single nation, animated by the same spirit, can defy the world" (Dietler 1998: 72–76). Significantly, however, the second is loosely based on words attributed to Vercingetorix by Caesar in his account of the war (*BG* 7.29); thus the site, the hero, and even his words are all determined by the Roman Caesar. Napoleon's debt to Caesar and his preoccupation with him was such that he wrote a two-volume study of the Roman general in which Rome's place in the development of the French nation was treated as fundamental:

> In honoring the memory of Vercingetorix, we must not lament his defeat. Let us admire the ardent and sincere love of this Gallic chief for the independence of his country, but let us not forget that it is due to the triumph of the Roman armies that we owe our civilization; our institutions, our customs, our language, all of this comes to us from the conquest. (quoted and translated in Dietler 1998: 76)

Two German monuments convey something of this dual heritage not long after the establishment of the German state. In 1875 Kaiser Wilhelm I, his title evocative of

Rome, dedicated the Hermann Monument near Detmold, which honored Arminius, chieftain of the Cherusci, whose most famous achievement had been the annihilation of three Roman legions in the Teutoburg Forest in AD 9 (on the battle, P. Wells 2003); this massive bronze statue on a pedestal towers up over 50 meters and holds a sword on which is inscribed "German unity is my strength, my strength is Germany's power" (*Deutsche Einigkeit, meine Stärke, meine Stärke, Deutschlands Macht*). Here then Arminius stands as a precursor to the German nation of the nineteenth century, an image larger and more triumphant than the meditative statue of Vercingetorix to be found across the border in France; the sword for example is raised aloft rather than at his side. Near Bad Homburg in Hessen, however, it is the Roman heritage that is recalled; a visitor will find the Saalburg, a full-scale reconstruction of a Roman legionary fort that was part of the *limes* frontier defense system that linked the Danube with the Rhine. The building of the Saalburg took place between 1898 and 1907 on the basis of earlier excavations, and was a project encouraged by Kaiser Wilhelm II, who was there to lay the cornerstone in 1900 (Schallmayer 1997). Together these monuments root Germany in the ancient past, but at the same time their military tone carries a powerful message for the present and for their neighbors in particular.

2   Past and Future Glory

The classical past could provide a new state with traditions and identity, but that identity itself would also be shaped by present goals and ambitions. Former glories might be seen to serve the present well. Several nations sought to legitimize imperial and expansionist ambitions by reference to the achievements of their ancestors.

In Greece, for example, there was the Great Idea (*Megale Idea*), that all Greeks should be unified in one state (Greene 2000). Given the scattered nature of the Greek community, this was problematic from the beginning, but it did act as one of the driving forces for the extension of the Greek state. This justification was put very clearly by Ioannis Kolettis, Greek prime minister from 1844 until his death in 1847:

> The Kingdom of Greece is not Greece. [Greece] constitutes only one part, the smallest and poorest. A Greek is not only a man who lives within this kingdom, but also one who lives in Jannina, in Salonica, in Serres, in Adrianople, in Constantinople, in Smyrna, in Trebizond, in Crete, in Samos and in any land associated with Greek history or the Greek race . . . There are two main centers of Hellenism: Athens, the capital of the Greek kingdom, [and] "The City" [Constantinople], the dream and hope of all Greeks. (quoted and translated in Clogg 1979: 76)

This also reveals an early tension in the concept of Greek national identity, on the one hand looking back to Athens and a classical past, on the other to Constantinople and an Orthodox Christian identity. The Great Idea came to an abrupt halt in 1922 with the failure of Greek forces to occupy the region of Asia Minor around Smyrna.

The resulting débâcle led to massive population transfers: some one million Greeks moved from Asia Minor to Greece, and almost 400,000 Turks went the other way, both defined by religion (Orthodox Christian or Muslim), not language. These new Greeks also helped to bolster the Greek presence in the parts of Macedonia that had been acquired in 1913 (Clogg 1979: 120–23).

The great imperial power of antiquity, of course, was Rome, and the new Italian state looked backed to it for inspiration. Thus parallels were drawn between Italy's intervention in North Africa in 1911–12 and Scipio Africanus's assault on Carthage at the end of the Second Punic War, the latter recaptured in one of most spectacular films of early Italian cinema, the 1914 *Cabiria* (Wyke 1999, Llewellyn-Jones, HOL-LYWOOD'S ANCIENT WORLD, section 1). But it was Mussolini's Fascist movement in the wake of the First World War that really took hold of Rome's ancient past. For a country that was still very much in the process of unifying and becoming a nation-state (cf. M. Clark 1996: 177), Rome offered a national story, one that the Fascists embraced and made their own. The appeal to the past also made it easier for the Fascist regime to inaugurate radical change (cf. Quentin Skinner 1974: 294–95 on the need for every revolutionary "to march backward into battle"); it was merely the revival of the Roman empire, a return to Rome's greatness.

The Fascist party modeled first itself and then the state after Rome. One of the most prominent symbols of Fascism and later the Italian state was the *fasci*, the bundle of rods (*fasces* in Latin) that the lictors in ancient Rome carried in front of a magistrate to represent his authority. The *fasci* were a very visible presence on public buildings throughout Italy. Mussolini's sobriquet, *Il Duce*, harked back, sometimes explicitly so, to the Latin *dux*, leader (cf. fig. 48.1; Giardina and Vauchez 2000: 220–24). As the regime came to be identified with the state, so there also came into force a new system of dating, which marked the Fascist era as beginning in 1922. This was the year Mussolini, in imitation of Sulla and Caesar, came to power with his "march on Rome," but the new calendar also defined this as the year that the *fasces* were restored – in other words Fascist Italy was the true successor of the Roman: 1940, for example, was the eighteenth year since the restoration of the *Fasces* (*Anno XVIII Fascibus Restitutis*). Rome becomes not merely the past but also a means of looking forward. In 1937 there was a great exhibition to celebrate two thousand years since the birth of the emperor Augustus, the *Mostra Augustea della Romanità* (The Augustan Exhibition of Romanness). As the many visitors from all over Italy entered the exhibition, they would have passed through an entrance above which were written the words of Mussolini: "Italians, you must ensure the glories of Rome's past are surpassed by the glories of the future" (Cannistraro 1972: 127).

Fascist Italy saw the re-emergence of imperial Rome, not only in exhibitions and symbols but also as a physical reality. Much of it had long disappeared beneath medieval and later structures. Mussolini stripped these away to expose the true Rome beneath, and in the process created the ancient city that tourists see today, just as the Greeks in the nineteenth century had cleared the Acropolis of post-classical buildings. This was archaeology as propaganda (Dyson 2006: 76–77, 177–79; for similar treatment of more recent monuments in nineteenth-century Paris, Colin Jones 2007). The focus of this activity was the imperial fora and the area around the Mausoleum

48.1 Mosaics from the Foro Italico, Rome, formerly the Foro Mussolini in the manner of an imperial forum. An old Roman art form, but twentieth-century Fascist themes. Note the rifles and the repeated salutation of Mussolini as *Il Duce*. (Photo: author)

of Augustus. Through the middle of the newly excavated imperial fora Mussolini built a huge road, essentially a parade route for military display. It ran from his headquarters in Palazzo Venezia to the Colosseum, linking the new Rome with old, and its name, Via dell' Impero (Empire Road), captured both the achievements of the past and the aspirations of the present, although those of the present would remain largely unfulfilled (Hyde Minor 1999). They do, however, reveal the continuing vitality of the ancient world in the construction of modern national identity.

3   Contested Symbols: Macedon and Greece

The turbulent and violent break-up of Yugoslavia's federal structure in the early 1990s led to the formation of a series of independent republics, one of which was the Republic of Macedonia, previously a constituent part of Yugoslavia as the People's Republic of Macedonia created at the end of the Second World War. Now, as an emerging nation-state it sought to shape its identity in the modern world by appropriating symbols associated with the ancient kingdom of Macedon. This rapidly brought it into conflict with Greece, which claimed sole ownership of the ancient Macedonian past.

48.2 The gold casket (*larnax*) from Vergina; on its lid is the symbol of the star/sun adopted for the short-lived Macedonian flag. (Drawn by Dora Kemp, first published in *Antiquity* 1994)

New states need an identity, and symbols help to define and affirm that identity. The republic of Macedonia not only had a name that recalled ancient Macedon, it also chose to make that connection explicit on its flag. Here was displayed a golden-yellow 16-pointed sun against a red background. This symbol of the sun was derived from the decoration of a gold casket (*larnax*) found during Manolis Andronikos's excavations of the royal Macedonian tombs at Vergina in Greece in the late 1970s; that motif was variously known as the Sun or Star of Vergina (fig. 48.2). Since the flag of the former Socialist republic had been a five-pointed star outlined in gold or yellow on a red background, the new flag in its design expressed a degree of continuity with the recent past, but the use of the Vergina imagery also suggested that, however new the state might seem, it had in some sense always existed. Nor was this any old Macedonian symbol: Andronikos believed that the casket had contained the bones of Philip II and that the symbol was "the emblem of the Macedonian dynasty" (Andronikos 1981, esp. 212–13, and 1984; contrast Borza 1990: 253–66).

A symbol that transcended the recent past had a particular value in this new Republic of Macedon, a nation inhabited by a multitude of ethnic groups, each with its own traditions. In the 1994 census there were questionnaires in six languages – Macedonian, Albanian, Turkish, Rom, Serbo-Croat and Vlach, the largely Orthodox Christian Macedonian group making up two-thirds of responses, with almost a quarter coming from the mostly Muslim Albanian-speakers (K. Brown 2000: 127). This diversity is in part a consequence of centuries of Ottoman rule, though shaken up somewhat by the radical population transfers that affected the Balkans and western Turkey in the early twentieth century. Unlike, for example, Christian symbols, those rooted in the Macedon of Philip and Alexander had the potential to unify. By their remote, essentially mythical character they did not exclude; instead they could bring together the peoples of this complex nation at a time when ethnic conflict was rife among its neighbors, most notably in Bosnia-Herzegovina (K. Brown 1994, 2000).

Greece, however, felt threatened by a state on its borders laying claim to any kind of Macedonian heritage, especially when its own northern region, acquired in 1913, was also known as Macedonia. From the Greek perspective it was especially provocative to take the imagery for the flag from an archaeological site within Greek territory. Greece, therefore, campaigned vigorously against the pretensions of this new state, partly by seeking to prevent the use of the name "Macedonia" and associated symbols in international fora, partly by promoting itself as the true heir of ancient Macedon. When the Macedonian republic was accepted into the United Nations in April 1993, it was as a state with no name. Whereas the republics of Serbia, Bosnia and Herzegovina, Slovenia, Croatia, and Montenegro have all now been recognized by the United Nations under those names, the Republic of Macedonia at the time of writing still appears in the United Nations membership lists under the provisional title of "the former Yugoslav Republic of Macedonia" (www.un.org/members/list.shtml listed under "T" for "The," a compromise between M and F). Nor would Greece allow the Macedonian flag to be hoisted at the United Nations (on the complex diplomatic maneuver that allowed FYR Macedonia, as it is often known, into the UN, see M. Wood 1998). Only in 1995, after a year-long economic blockade on its Greek border, did the Macedonian government finally agree to abandon its use of the Vergina sun/star symbol. The new flag did not, however, break all links with its predecessor; it consisted of a golden sun dramatically splashed across a red backdrop.

At the same time, ancient history became heavily politicized and pervasive. In 1992 Kavala airport in northern Greece was renamed Alexander the Great Airport, while two years later Alexander the Great appeared on the Greek 100-drachma coin with the Vergina Star on the reverse. Greece was making absolutely clear that this was her heritage. Arguments and counter-arguments flowed: the Skopje republic (so called by the Greeks, after its capital) was not where the kingdom of Macedon had been, and the population anyway were Slavs who only arrived in the sixth century AD; on the other side it was argued that the ancient Macedonians were not Greeks, and that had been said by no other than Demosthenes (Danforth 2000: 349–52). The debate was waged not only between Greece and the new Macedonian republic, but among their respective diaspora communities as far away as Canada and Australia (Danforth 1995). The dispute between the two states may have become less vocal since the mid-90s, but Macedonia remains without a name at the United Nations and there is no sign that it has abandoned its claim to an ancient past; in 2007 the Skopje International Airport was renamed Skopje Alexander the Great Airport.

Both Greece and the Republic of Macedonia have been providing themselves with a past where no national past existed, due to their earlier incorporation within larger political structures. Ancient history is one route to such a past, one that because of its very remoteness has the flexibility to be inclusive and so allows for the possibility of a unified identity. It can be the subject of conflict, however, because by having a past a nation also has a future. But the relationship between ancient history and national identity is a two-way process. Just as ancient history may shape a nation's conception of itself and its past, so that conception in turn may feed into the way the ancient past is studied, taught, and understood. The ancient historian today, so practiced at analyzing the historical context of the sources, needs also to think about more recent interpretations of antiquity and the context in which they too have evolved.

FURTHER READING

There is much written on nationalism and national identity and much disagreement. Starting points would Gellner 1983, Hobsbawm 1990, Hobsbawm and Ranger 1983 and B. Anderson 1991, who in various ways stress the constructed, invented, or imagined character of national identity. A good overview of the varying interpretations is provided by A. D. Smith 2001, whose own position highlights the ethnic background of nations (e.g. A. D. Smith 1986). For the development of the modern European nation, note Schulze 1996.

The diplomatic conflict between Greece and Macedonia has generated a large body of literature, particularly from anthropologists, see the papers in Cowan 2000. The dispute over ancient symbols is best treated by K. Brown 1994, with an update in 2000. The *Journal of Modern Greek Studies* devoted a special issue to essays on the conflict and its background (vol. 14.2, 1996). Danforth 1995 is an illuminating and full study of the diaspora reaction. Agnew 2007 helps to place the dispute within its broader context.

Clogg 2002 provides a succinct history of modern Greece. A number of topics on modern Greek history are addressed in Graham Speake's *Encyclopedia of Greece and the Hellenic Tradition* (2000). Alexandri 2002 looks at the way Greek communities in the late nineteenth and early twentieth century looked to antiquity when renaming themselves, and the emblems they chose. For the reinvention of the Olympics, see Biddiss 1999.

There is considerable literature on Italian fascism and ancient Rome. The best introduction is probably Giardina and Vauchez 2000 (in Italian), which sets the subject in context and explores the myth of Rome from Charlemagne through the French Revolution to Mussolini. A useful review of bibliography since 1970 can be found in Nelis 2007. Note also the papers by Cannistraro 1972, Quartermaine 1995, M. Stone 1993 and 1999, Visser 1992, Hyde Minor 1999. For a eulogistic contemporary account of Mussolini as the new Augustus, see K. Scott 1932.

For the role of Celts in modern French national identity, note Dietler 1994 and 1998; for the tension between modernity and antiquity in nineteenth-century Paris see Colin Jones 2007's fascinating account of Theodore Vacquer and the archaeology of Paris; and on Napoleon I as a new Augustus, Huet 1999. The role of antiquity in the development of British national identities has not been covered here. Where the Scots, Welsh, and Irish may have been happy with a Celtic past, English national identity has tended to prefer the Anglo-Saxons (with a slight nod to Boudicca), cf. Hingley 2000 and 2008 and C. D. Williams 1999.

CHAPTER FORTY-NINE

Hollywood's Ancient World

Lloyd Llewellyn-Jones

In the beginning there was silent cinema and black-and-white pictures, and they brought forth *The Ten Commandments* and *Ben-Hur*, and so successful were these films that they went forth and multiplied and begat, in glorious Technicolor and CinemaScope, *The Ten Commandments* and *Ben-Hur*. And they found favor and were called epics. But with the good also came *Cleopatra*; and so costly was this film that Hollywood spurned it and the epic cinema died. But in the latter days it rose again and *Gladiator* triumphed at box office and DVD store.

From its earliest inception, Hollywood cinema has been fascinated with the ancient world. Antiquity offered a natural vehicle to film makers, perhaps because the stories of larger-than-life characters and events were generally familiar to cinemagoers. But Hollywood epics were not overly reverential towards the antique past, and directors ploughed the history books with abandon, often shattering the fragments of factual information in favor of spectacle, eroticism, sensuality, weighty morality, or pure fantasy.

The interaction between cinema (and popular culture generally) and historical representation is a growing field of scholarship. Scholars now question how historical films reflect the societies in which they were made, and speculate on how attitudes towards the past have been molded in the popular imagination by its depiction in movies. This chapter aims to give an introduction to the subject of cinema and ancient history by offering a brief chronological outline of how epic films developed as a distinct Hollywood genre, before moving on to explore how we can identify the genre *per se*, in terms of narrative, visualization, marketing, and spectatorship. While epic movies are products of film studios across the globe (and particularly strong traditions exist in eastern Europe, Italy, Britain, Japan, China, and India), nothing has come close to the American Hollywood studios' identification of the epic movie as the quintessential spectacular experience. This chapter will concentrate, therefore, on the Hollywood genre alone, although in using that term I mean to convey a conceptual framework, rather than a strict geographical one. Derek Elley in *The Epic*

Film (1984) focuses on epics beginning with biblical history and ending with the early medieval period, defining the historical epic by the historical distance of its temporal content from the present. Because of the limitations of the timescale established by the remit of this volume, I will concentrate on the same period, although I would emphasize that the Hollywood epic genre also encompasses epics set in historical periods post AD 1000 (like *El Cid*, dir. Mann, 1961; and *Marie Antoinette*, dir. van Dyke, 1938), epics of the American West and Civil War (like *Gone With The Wind*, dir. Fleming, 1939; and *Dances With Wolves*, dir. Costner, 1990), and more contemporary historical events (like *The Last Emperor*, dir. Bertolucci, 1987; and *Titanic*, dir. Cameron, 1997).

1   History of the Genre

The two great ancient-world epic cycles in American films occurred during the silent period (1915–27) and throughout the 1950s and early 1960s, periods in which epics were produced as self-conscious demonstrations of film's capabilities in cinematic virtuosity. D. W. Griffith's *Intolerance* (1916) proved that, in terms of the treatment of space, time, and spectacle, the cinema was capable of producing grander subject matter than the physical limitations of the theater. It is no coincidence that the first full-length motion picture in the American repertoire was *Judith of Bethulia* (dir. Griffith, 1913), which thrust the actress Blanche Sweet into the limelight and made her one of Hollywood's first superstars, and established the movies as a new art form. Elaborate as it was, Griffith's movie was overshadowed by a 12-reel Italian screen adaptation of the popular novel *Quo Vadis* (dir. Guazoni, 1912), released in America at the same time that Griffith was filming *Judith*.

These early epics exploited the nineteenth-century vogue for theatrical spectacle (Flanders 2006: 292–342) and drew heavily on the established norms of gesture and iconography familiar to audiences of theatrical melodrama, giving silent films a timeless quality not attained by sound films. DeMille's *King of Kings* (1927), for instance, draws on the symbolic force of heroic gestures to give his Christ a suitably mystic aura unrealized in any Christ-film of the sound era.

In 1914 the Italians topped their production of *Quo Vadis* with *Cabiria*, directed by Giovanni Pastrone and written by Gabriele D'Annunzio. *Cabiria* is often regarded as the pinnacle of the early Italian spectacle, and the film helped push cinema into the age of feature-length pictures. It cost some $210,000 to make and was a financial success, although due to the Great War it was not as successful as *Quo Vadis* of 1912. Set in Carthage in North Africa, *Cabiria* established the visual vocabulary of the epic film. The film contains generous amounts of spectacle: Hannibal's elephant army crossing the Alps in the snow, Scipio's battle against the Carthaginians, an erupting volcano, and, most influentially, the temple of Moloch where little children are sacrificed to a hungry god. The camera shots are somewhat static, opting in the battle sequence, for instance, for one high-angle long shot, but the set designs contain real imagination, especially the hell-mouth entrance to the temple of Moloch and the elephant columns of the royal place. *Cabiria* had a direct influence on D. W. Griffith's production of *Intolerance*, and according to Griffith's biographer Richard Schickel, Griffith insisted on including huge elephant statues in the Temple of Ishtar set (even though his researchers could find no evidence that pachyderms were ever a significant part of Babylonian iconography) simply because Pastrone had used them in *Cabiria* (Schickel 1996: 310).

In fact Griffith attempted to outdo the Italian film-makers in all respects. With *Intolerance* in 1916, Griffith set a standard for screen spectacle that has seldom been equaled. The film tells four stories simultaneously, and its Fall of Babylon sequence hit a new high in cinematic opulence. Griffith's experiments with film techniques, such as cross-cutting, close-ups, masking, and movement quickly developed film's potential for narrating epic themes, and for all its romantic clichés and moralizing *Intolerance* has a visual energy that rooted the epic at the bedrock of early cinema (Drew 2001).

However, at the time of its release, at the height of the atrocities of the Great War, *Intolerance* proved unpopular with audiences and resulted in a financial disaster for Griffith. His career would never fully recover from this blow, although his problems did not deter other directors from making their contributions to the epic genre. The following decade brought such notable productions as *The Queen of Sheba* (dir. J. Gordon Edwards, 1921; see Llewellyn-Jones 2002a: 19–21), another imported *Quo Vadis* (dir. D'Annunzio, 1925) and MGM's enormously successful and influential *Ben-Hur* (dir. Niblo, 1925).

But it was Cecil B. DeMille who best realized the potential of the epic, with his productions of *The Ten Commandments* (1923) and *The King of Kings* (1927); for DeMille had hit on the perfect epic formula with his mixtures of sex, splendor, and sanctity. With these two films he became the undisputed "King of the Spectacle," a title he would retain throughout his long career up to the time of his death in 1959, shortly after the release of his rework of *The Ten Commandments* (Birchard 2004: 363–64; Orrison 1999).

Michael Curtiz's mammoth retelling of *Noah's Ark* (1929) was the last of the great silent spectaculars, but by the time it was released to theaters the advent of sound had already destroyed any chances for box-office success. The last-minute addition of some sound sequences did little to improve the situation, and the days of the silent movies and of Latin lovers (like Valentino) and kohl-eyed vamps (like Theda Bara) were over (E. Golden 1996).

During the 1930s, DeMille almost singlehandedly kept the ancient-world epic alive, with his films *The Sign of the Cross* (1932) and *Cleopatra* (1934). It was unusual for a director to return time and again to this particular type of film. Most of the major Hollywood directors were tempted to tackle the epic at least once in their careers, but only DeMille built his entire reputation on filming spectaculars. The one film which might have threatened DeMille's eminence was RKO's *The Last Days of Pompeii* (dir. Schoedsack, 1935), which certainly helped satisfy the Great Depression's taste for spectacle. The film fancifully rearranges history by linking Christ to the apocalyptic eruption of Vesuvius as it weaves together the tale of a gruff pagan who converts to Christianity in a morality drama closely modeled on the types of films made successful by DeMille.

The emergence of *film noir* in the 1940s heralded an especially lean period for epics, and even DeMille temporarily abandoned ancient history for Americana. The Second World War had audiences much more interested in the present than the past, although *The Sign of the Cross* was reissued during this time, with a modern prologue linking ancient Rome to fascist Europe, and an epilogue showing American bombers flying over Rome while an army chaplain compares Mussolini to Nero.

Late in the decade, in 1949, DeMille returned to the Bible for inspiration, and the result was *Samson and Delilah,* the biggest film of his career up to that time. It also turned out to be one of the most successful movies of the 1940s, and upon its release, *Samson and Delilah* broke all box office records for Paramount studios. Lavish and vacuous, *Samson and Delilah* was the precursor to the Golden Age of the Hollywood epic; for during the early 1950s the epic film flourished as never before, as extravagance increased with each new production (Forshey 1992). In 1953, as Hollywood began to realize that large-scale historical spectaculars might be the way to lure audiences away from their television sets, Twentieth Century-Fox added further inducement by introducing the CinemaScope widescreen process in the Roman epic *The Robe* (dir. Koster). CinemaScope turned out to be the perfect medium for this type of film, and most of the major studios quickly adopted Cinema-Scope for their new films, and those who didn't invented their own widescreen processes. Eventually, DeMille outdid them all with his Vista Vision and Technicolor remake of *The Ten Commandments* (1956).

The popularity of *The Robe* quickly prompted Fox to release a sequel, *Demetrius and the Gladiators* (dir. Daves, 1954), a crude epic potboiler which nevertheless convinced the studio to release an epic cycle, beginning with an adaptation of Mika Waltari's best-selling novel *The Egyptian* (dir. Curtiz, 1954), and concluding, by the end of the decade, with threadbare films like *The Story of Ruth* (dir. Koster, 1960) and the dismal *Esther and the King* (dir. Walsh and Bava, 1960; see Llewellyn-Jones 2002a: 19–20).

Following the lead set by Fox, other studios plummeted cinemagoers into the ancient world: Metro-Goldwyn-Mayer produced *The Prodigal* (dir. Thorpe, 1955), *Ben Hur* (dir. Wyler, 1959) and *King of Kings* (dir. Ray, 1961); Warner Brothers produced *The Silver Chalice* (dir. Saville, 1954), *Land of the Pharaohs* (dir. Hawks, 1955), and *Helen of Troy* (dir. Wise, 1956); Paramount offered *The Ten Commandments* (dir. DeMille 1956); Columbia produced *Salome* (dir. Dieterle, 1953) and *Barabbas* (dir. Fleischer, 1962); Universal, *Spartacus* (dir. Kubrick, 1960); even Walt Disney entered into the spirit of the age with a production of *The Big Fisherman* (dir. Borzage, 1959).

Screenplays set in ancient Greece, Rome, Egypt, and the Near East, subjects taken from the Bible or adapted from best-selling novels, became hot commercial properties throughout the 1950s. Christ-films were especially popular, and any film that touched in some way on the life of Christ (*Ben Hur, The Robe, Barabbas*) was almost guaranteed a box-office success (Babington and Evans 1993: 91–139; Kinnard and Davis 1992). Each major studio had its own contender in the epic sweepstake, and epic movies were manufactured as vehicles for major movie stars such as Richard Burton, Charlton Heston, and Victor Mature. Even screen goddesses were utilized in the genre, hence the inappropriate displays of Rita Hayworth as Salome and Lana Turner as the pagan high priestess of Astarte. The stars, as well as the directors, wanted to prove themselves in the epic revival.

In 1963 the notorious production problems and $40 million cost of *Cleopatra* (dir. Mankiewitz) nearly destroyed Twentieth Century-Fox studios and the epic genre. Escalating production costs indicated that the heyday of this type of film was drawing to a close. Big-budget box-office failures like *The Fall of the Roman Empire* (dir. Mann, 1964), *The Greatest Story Ever Told* (dir. Stevens, 1965), and *The Bible . . . In the Beginning* (dir. Huston 1966) dealt the final blows. The few theatrical releases in the ensuing years, such as *King David* (dir. Beresford, 1985), seemed anachronistic and met with slim success both critically and financially.

During the past two decades the epic film has flourished on television. It is ironic that the type of film once used to combat the growing threat of television has been kept alive by that same medium. In the 1990s two companies emerged as leaders in the production of epic TV films: the Italian company Lube/Lux Vide produced a series of made-for-television biblical films ranging from *Genesis* to *Jesus*; Hallmark Entertainment contributed new versions of such classic tales as *The Odyssey* and *Jason and the Argonauts*, in addition to a remake of *Cleopatra*.

The new millennium saw the triumphant return of the epic genre to the big screen with the release of Ridley Scott's *Gladiator* (2000). This mega-budgeted Roman spectacle was no doubt a gamble, but it paid off handsomely for everyone involved. In addition to being a tremendous winner at the box office, *Gladiator* also won the Academy Award for Best Picture (M. Winkler 2004; Landau 2000). The film established a trend for the return of the epic in cinemas: in 2004 Wolfgang Petersen's *Troy* opened to popular, if not critical, success (M. Winkler 2007a); in the same year Oliver Stone's biopic *Alexander* attracted less critical and popular acclaim than had been supposed (Lane Fox 2004; Nisbet 2006).

The renaissance of the epic genre has yet to take hold of early twenty-first-century cinema, but forays into the field continue, although stylistically the newest "epic" is a far cry from the glitz of a DeMille movie. Zack Snyder's *300*, based on Frank Miller's graphic novel about the Battle of Thermopylae in 480 BC, takes epic film conventions firmly into the digital age (Nisbet 2006). The commercial success of *300* possibly bodes well for the future production of more "ancient world" movies.

2   Defining the Genre

An epic can qualify as being a work of elevated, if lengthy, character, describing the exploits of heroes and composed in a lofty narrative style. As a literary genre, epics like *Iliad*, *Odyssey*, *Aeneid*, and, it has been claimed, even certain books of the Old Testament, center on a hero and involve him in an event or series of events – a battle, journey, or quest – connected to a bigger theme, such as the destiny of a people or a nation. Epics are action-filled historical or legendary stories which enforce fundamental moral, religious, cultural, or political norms, and as such, epics are among the oldest narrative forms in world history. Epics are the national ballads that publicly celebrate the heroic aspects of a historic society; the protagonists of these exhilarating sagas have little time (or use) for tormented inner lives of self-doubt and inertia, which is why Aeneas and not Hamlet represents the quintessential epic hero.

With its broad movements through time and locale and its emphasis on action and external characterization, the epic is ideally suited for film. Whether produced on a shoestring budget like *The Silver Chalice* (dir. Saville, 1954), or at a cost of millions, like the 1963 version of *Cleopatra* (dir. Mankiewitz), all movie epics are concerned with momentous events and larger-than-life characters. The ancient world has always held a strong fascination for both filmmakers and moviegoers, since they permit modern audiences a glimpse – whether accurate or not – into the historic or historico-mythic past. The vastness and scale that define the epic literary genre are directly realized in the medium of epic film. The vastness of the length of the average literary epic is also inherited by its cinematic successor, which is not necessarily considered a good thing; take as an example this review of *Quo Vadis*: "The colour is magnificent, the crowd scenes stupendous, the taste poor and the length appalling" (*The Spectator*, 1951).

The advertising rhetoric that sells the Hollywood ancient-world epic to its American middle class, Caucasian, consumer audience provides the most blatant and compressed invocation of the genre's self-centered significance (figs 49.1 and 2). Consider, then, the following litany: "An Epic Film that Sweeps Across the Horizon of Ancient Times!" (*Sodom and Gomorrah*; dir. Aldrich, 1962); "The Mightiest Story of Tyranny and Temptation Ever Written – Ever Lived – Ever Produced!" (*The Silver Chalice*; dir. Saville, 1954); "The Glory that was Egypt! The Grandeur that was Rome!" (*Cleopatra*; dir. DeMille, 1934); or just "The Power, the Passion, the Greatness, the Glory!!" (*King of Kings*; dir. DeMille, 1927). Other slices of marketing rhetoric condense the epic nature of both film spectacle and narrative plot into bite-size chunks: "Buried Alive! The Cruel Pharaoh's Decree . . . for his Wives . . . his Slaves . . . his Court!" (*Land of the Pharaohs*; dir. Hawks, 1955). This kind of exclamation, generalization, and hyperbole is not necessarily dead; consider the marketing of *Gladiator* throughout 1999 and 2000: "A general who became a slave. A slave who became a gladiator. A gladiator who defied an emperor," or else the popular poster slogan: "A hero will rise."

Gladiator's use of the term "hero" in the publicity campaign (as well as the film's other marketing tag, "What we do in Life echoes through Eternity") reminds us that the "mythic" elements of history are as important an aspect of the filmic take on the past as "conventional" history, and that Hollywood's ancient world is a temporal space in which mythology and history converge, unite, and interweave. This is certainly true of Hollywood's treatment of Homeric epic as history in *Helen of Troy* (dir. Wise, 1956) and *Troy* (dir. Petersen, 2003; see M. Winkler 2007a), and to the validity accredited to biblical stories such as the plagues on Egypt and the Hebrew Exodus in *The Ten Commandments* (dir. DeMille, 1923 and 1956), or the destruction of the (first) Jewish temple in *Solomon and Sheba* (dir. Vidor, 1959). Hollywood's conception of ancient history has a distinctly Herodotean flavor to it, since it can encompass Helen, Moses, and the Queen of Sheba alongside the building of the pyramids, the Golden Age of Athens and the spread of Greek civilization, the reign of Cleopatra

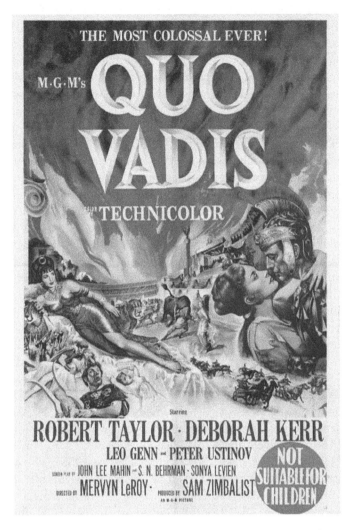

49.1   Poster for Mervyn LeRoy's *Quo Vadis* (1951). (Author's private collection)

VII, the rise and fall of the Roman empire, and the birth of Christianity. Hollywood has reflected all of this directly in, for example, *Land of the Pharaohs* (dir. Hawks, 1955), *300 Spartans* (dir. Maté, 1962), *Alexander* (dir. Stone, 2004), *The Serpent of the Nile* (dir. Castle 1953), *Julius Caesar* (dir. Mankiewitz, 1953), *The Fall of the Roman Empire* (dir. Mann, 1964), and *Quo Vadis* (dir. LeRoy, 1951, fig. 49.1). Hollywood's Herodotean form of history as a blurring of legend, myth, and fact is even reflected in the tag lines of the movie posters themselves. Thus for *Helen of Troy* we have: "Its towering wonders span the age of Titans," while *Alexander*'s publicity depended on a direct quotation from Vergil's epic poem *Aeneid* ("Fortune Favors the Bold"), and enticed cinemagoers into the theaters with the assurance that "The Greatest Legend Of All Was Real."

3 Engaging with History

Yet despite its close association with oral epic, as a film genre the epic movie has not enjoyed the same high cultural *kudos* bestowed on its literary cousin. Epic movies are customarily dismissed as vulgar and garish burlesque spectacles which trade on a crude sensationalism that is usually masked beneath turgid religious morality, a facet of the genre self-consciously explored by the undisputed master of the ancient-world epic, Cecil B. DeMille. Biblical sex and biblical spectacle were DeMille's trademarks, and when it came to filming equal loads of moralizing and debauchery, he was the master showman, and audiences, safe in their understanding that they were going to see a film of high religious morality, actually flocked to his epics specifically for the sex and violence: "I am sometimes accused," he said, "of gingering up the Bible with lavish infusions of sex and violence but I wish my accusers would read their Bible more closely, for in those pages are more violence and sex than I could ever portray on the screen" (DeMille 1960: 366). He apologized, however, for rewriting the Book of Judges in his *Samson and Delilah* (1949), but for Paul Rotha the film was merely "manna for illiterates," while John Steinbeck recorded: "Saw the picture. Loved the book" (Tanitch 2000: 50). At the release of Robert Aldrich's *Sodom and Gomorrah* (1962) the satirist Dougald B. MacEachen mocked the pseudo-morality of the biblical epic in his poem *The Hollywood Bible*, which begins "The Bible's one huge girlie show, / As now all moviegoers know."

The derogatory way in which the epic movie has traditionally been regarded still persists. The cultural historian Robert Rosenstone, for example, has argued that, "film is a disturbing symbol of an increasingly post-literate world in which people can read but won't" (Rosenstone 1995: 46), and for many film critics and film historians (and many movie audiences too) the epic film lays at the nadir of the cinematic experience, condemned for its overtly elaborate décor and impoverished imagination, and its presentation of history in a mode that is both contemporary and provincial. Hollywood's history films are often regarded are perverting history to the point that it becomes unrecognizable, a concern that has led Rosenstone to complain that, "the Hollywood historical drama . . . like all genres . . . locks both filmmaker and audience into a series of conventions whose demands – for a love interest, physical action, personal confrontation, movement towards a climax, and denouement – are almost guaranteed to leave the historian of the period crying foul" (Rosenstone 1995: 29, cf. Cooper 1991: 19 on *Spartacus*).

But does Hollywood have a responsibility, a duty, to educate? "There is nothing duller on the screen than being accurate but not dramatic," argues Stephen Ambrose (1996: 239). Certainly film changes the rules for approaching history, insisting on its own sort of "truths" which arise from a visual and aural realm that is difficult to capture adequately in the written word. This engagement with the past on film is potentially much more complex and hazardous than it is via any written text: on the screen many "historical" things can occur simultaneously – images, sound, speech, even text – fundamentals that support or contradict each other to create a realm of engagement and understanding as different from written history as written history is from oral history. So different and so complete is our engagement with history on film that it forces us to acknowledge that cinema constitutes a seismic shift in consciousness about how we think about, and reinterpret, our past.

More immediately, some critics have suggested that, "Hollywood, by providing splendid entertainment, has sent people to the history shelves in their millions" (McDonald Fraser 1988: 19), a comment which can be endorsed not only by the meteoric rise of reception studies as a significant academic focus among historians, but also by the number of students regularly enrolled on cinema-and-history courses in universities worldwide. For Oliver Stone, "[There's] only [one] answer to people who say that movies brainwash young minds: Movies are just the first draft. They raise questions and inspire students to find out more" (Stone cited in Carnes 1996: 306). Perhaps the most temperate approach to the thorny problem of film's relationship to academic history is that offered by the film director Federico Fellini, himself no stranger to the historical movie, who notes that, "The essential question must be: 'What is the director trying to do, and is he succeeding?' If historical authenticity is part of what he is trying to achieve, then it must be brought into question; if not, then in all fairness dramatic criteria alone must be used" (Fellini cited in Solomon 2001: 23).

Certainly in general reviews of the epic genre historical veracity is of little consequence, and while one occasionally finds praise for historical accuracy, most of the enthusiasm is reserved for the epics' extravagant generality and excess – in terms of sets, costumes, extras, stars, and spectacle, as well as the millions of dollars spent on making such lavish entertainment. Take for example a review of a video release of *Quo Vadis*: "Colossal is just one of the many superlatives trumpeting the size and scope of this mammoth drama about Romans, Christians, lions, pagan rites, rituals, and Nero. Roman soldier Robert Taylor loves and pursues Christian maiden Deborah Kerr. It's Christians versus Nero and the lions in the eternal fight between good and evil. The sets, scenery, and crowd scenes are nearly overwhelming. Peter Ustinov as Nero is priceless" (Martin and Porter 1987: 674).

However, the epic film has traditionally been dismissed by auteur theorists as submerging the director's voice beneath the rich panoply of the films' visual needs (although some directors have managed to preserve something of their auteur voice in the mêlée: think of Ridley Scott and *Gladiator* or the *Alexander* of Oliver Stone; Cecil B. DeMille even represents the personification of the epic movie in the public perception). Unlike other popular Hollywood movie genres – the western, the gangster film, and the musical – the epic has proved to be less than congenial in its attitude towards directorial idiosyncrasy, mainly due to the size and cost of mounting such a vast project. While most movie genres have proved elastic enough to accommodate the off-beat styles of even the most subversive directors, the epic's need to reach a wide audience so that it can reap in some profit over the huge production budget calls for restraint on originality. As a result, the epic is the most conservative of all Hollywood genres, and the flavorless high tone of lofty nobility that often classifies the epic in terms of storyline, characterization, dialogue, and design spurns novelty and innovation, and positively encourages self-referencing and repetition. Thus, Gore Vidal, the one-time script-writer on *Ben Hur*, noted that, "William Wyler studied not Roman history but other Roman movies in preparation for *Ben Hur*" (Vidal 1992: 84). When Ridley Scott regenerated the epic with *Gladiator* in 2000, he acknowledged its success being dependent on the winning format created by the big-budget Roman epics of the 1950s (Landau 2000: 22, 64–66). Likewise, Oliver Stone explained to the production team of *Alexander* that he had been deeply influenced by films such as *Ben Hur* and *Intolerance*, and that *Alexander* was to be part of the long epic film legacy (Lane Fox 2004: 124).

The self-reflection inherent in the epic genre has had a major cultural impact on how people envisage the past. Many Western audiences receive their principal contact with the ancient world through popular culture, so much so that "the Romes created in popular culture are so pervasive and entrenched in the contemporary imagination that television programs purporting to present the real Rome use clips from Hollywood's historical epics to bring ancient Rome to life" (Joshel et al. 2001: 1). Visions of antiquity are frequently generated from scenes in Hollywood movies (Toplin 2002: 198 and 203).

Ridley Scott and Oliver Stone devotedly modeled their twenty-first-century epics on 1950s patterns because they understood that the epics of the 1950s had major box-office appeal for the reason that they employed all the tricks of the Hollywood trade – big stars, thrilling spectacle, cohesive narrative – and that for the epic to survive in the more cynical 2000s, the exact same formula should to be applied (albeit with a slight contemporary angle in the theme of the movie). After all, the epic film, like the epic poem, must be immediately accessible to a broad popular audience.

Recent work on the Hollywood "History Films" of the 1950s has revealed that ancient history received notable attention from the film makers throughout the decade, and that between 1950 and 1959 some 16 films were set in the BC period, with another 11 set in the era AD 1–500, and a further 16 set between AD 500 and 1000 (Eldridge 2006: 12–13). When compared with only 29 movies set between 1865 and 1890 (the American Civil War and Reconstruction era), the 43 films set in antiquity (if we extend the term to encompass the very early middle ages) was a testimony to the mass appeal of the ancient world during the Cold War period. While the much-anticipated post-*Gladiator* appeal of ancient-history films has not materialized in any concrete form, the epic is far from defunct; new styles of film making, respectful of, but not dependent on, the 1950s models, are reinventing the genre for twenty-first-century audience demands. Zack Snyder's film *300* (2007) has certainly moved the epic into a new realm and reinvigorated the mass appeal which *Troy* and *Alexander* mysteriously lacked.

The tyranny of the Hollywood studio system may have discouraged any radical approach to epic subject matter, yet it is important not to classify all epic films together; there have been many honorable, popularly conceived Hollywood epics which stand head and shoulders over the commonly perceived detritus of many epic movies: *Intolerance*, *Spartacus*, and even, arguably, *Alexander* have attained a dignity and magnitude worthy of the literary epic, and should not be dismissed merely because they inhabit the same genre-space as, say, the weak *Esther and the King* (dir. Walsh and Bava, 1960), *The Prodigal* (dir. Thorpe, 1955) or, more recently, *Troy*.

4   Sound and Vision

The standard Hollywood ancient-world epic often displays visual amplitude and a well-designed *mise-en-scène*, but even the most well respected of epics have problems with the on-screen dialogue. Howard Hawks criticized his own film, *Land of the Pharaohs* (1955), because, he said, he didn't know how ancient Egyptians really talked. Discovering a truly convincing voice for ancient characters is always a challenge for the film maker, since the poetry of the ancient epics is too difficult for on-screen dialogue which is meant to be heard rather than read, and contains an affectation of vocabulary at odds with the physical reality that the film is trying to establish. Nevertheless, many epic movie directors have been lured into creating a pseudo Egypto-Biblo-Classical voice for the screen recreations of antiquity, resulting in a weighty, turgid dialogue which is an over-reverent conception of how people spoke in the past, whereby "Whither goest thou?" is preferable to the plain-speaking "Where are you going?" To add to this, in many epic movie prologues the authoritative voice of history was represented by the sonorous – and patriarchal – "Voice of God" narration. In *The Ten Commandments* (1956) the divine voice was that of Cecil B. DeMille himself.

At the same time, however, on-screen dialogue often cuts through the ancient-world clichés with a contemporary approach to language at odds with the intended verisimilitude of the *mise-en-scène*. Thus in *The Ten Commandments* (1956) we have queen Nefretiri's passionate *cri de coeur* to Charlton Heston's Hebrew Lawgiver: "Oh Moses, Moses – you stubborn, splendid, adorable fool!" or Samson's catchy invective against Delilah: "You sweet-talking she-cat of hell!" (*Samson and Delilah*, 1950). These pseudo-historical forms of speech, more at home in fast-talking dialogues of *film noir* or gangster flicks, are at odds with the full-blown stuffiness of the epic script, and frequently throw the audience into a state of bewilderment (if not outright hilarity).

The Hollywood epic also defines history as occurring to music – large-scale symphonic scores underlying every dramatic on-screen moment. With their reliance on music, and their difficulty with finding appropriate "historical" dialogue, it is not surprising that epic films enjoyed their greatest critical acclaim in the silent period. The talking historical blockbusters of the 1950s and 1960s never managed to find the balance of on-screen sound, their dialogue remaining a stiff compromise between pseudo-classical and contemporary rhythms. Even the latest forays into the epic tradition, from *Gladiator* to *Alexander*, have succumbed to the same problem, and while Mel Gibson attempted to give voice to the ancient world by employing the languages of antiquity in *The Passion of the Christ* (2004), his subtitled translations of Aramaic and High-Church Latin had the same cumbersome turn of phrase as any DeMille movie of the 1950s. The epic film still has to learn to speak.

Therefore epic cinema looks to the *visuals* to convince its audience that history is a vital subject, and an entertaining one too. Thus, when the film critic George Mac-Donald Frasier reflects on what history means to him, he immediately remembers the many lumbering prologues of the epic genre; for McDonald Fraser, History is therefore written in pretentious calligraphy, in gilt, and with a capital H, with the words "In the Year of Our Lord," followed by "a concise summary of the War of the Spanish Succession, or the condition of the English peasantry in the twelfth century, or the progress of Christianity under Nero" (McDonald Fraser 1988: ix). Maps often accompanied the prologues, promising the viewer epic scope, empire building, and adventure – and at the same time signaling the remoteness of the past and its safe history-book distance from the present. As McDonald Fraser puts it, "In the heyday of the historicals there were few things more exciting, yet at the same time more tranquilizing in their effect on the front stalls on a Saturday afternoon than a good map, Olde Worlde for choice" (McDonald Fraser 1988: 80). As recently as 2004, Oliver Stone resorted to the tried and tested formula of the map to bring to life his version of the world of *Alexander* (although not without some critical embarrassment; Lane Fox 2004).

The importance of the visual design of the epic is endorsed by the tags used on movie posters and in theater trailers where audiences are customarily invited to SEE! SEE! SEE! the spectacle of the past. *Salome* (dir. Dieterle, 1953), the New Testament story of the Jewish princess and her infamous Dance of the Seven Veils, provides an appropriate example: with the sex goddess Rita Hayworth in the starring role and shedding the gossamer scarves, the film promised "Pomp, Pageantry, Spectacle Unsurpassed! The Glory and Excitement of Rome . . . in all its Greatness and Badness!" and confirmed that "Your Eyes Will See The Glory!" The spectacular extravagance and excess of Hollywood's conception of the past is emphasized time after time in studio publicity: "The All Time Spectacle" (*Solomon and Sheba*; dir. Vidor, 1959); "History's Most Seductive Woman! The Screen's Magnificent Spectacle! A Love Affair That Shook The World Set In A Spectacle Of Thrilling Magnificence!" (*Cleopatra*; dir. DeMille, 1934; fig. 49.2). *The Robe* (dir. Koster, 1953), the

49.2   Poster for Cecil B. DeMille's *Cleopatra* (1935). (Author's private collection)

first film ever to be released in CinemaScope (and the perfect blend of technology and genre) was marketed with the tag-line, "No Special Glasses Needed!" The wide-screen epics of the 1950s and 1960s also promised the audience an involvement with the action unimagined with earlier movies. With its curved screen, CinemaScope thrust the audience into the midst of the action, and *The Robe* could thus imitate the physical recreation of ancient Rome in a way that a tourist visiting the ruins of the city could never experience. Audiences were encouraged to feel as if they were conceivably one of the "cast of thousands" in the battle scenes or pageants. Ancient history on film therefore needed to be spectacular for that belief to be sustained, and any depiction of private or intimate moments in history would risk disrupting this by reminding audiences that they were "voyeurs" *of* history and not participants *in* history. It is important to note, then, that by the early 1950s technological advances in film manufacture and projection dictated how the epic should conduct itself.

The spectacle of the epic movie is created in the *mis-en-scène*'s extravagance of action and locale: chariot races, slave markets, temples and their extravagant rituals, land and sea battles, gladiators in the arena, Christians crucified in their hundreds at the roadside. There is also the vastness of deserts, oceans, and cities; the monumentality of Rome under the Caesars, the pyramids of the Pharaohs, the Jewish temple in Jerusalem, or Babylon under Persian rule. Epic movies regularly produce historical monuments, derived from Victorian painted visions or fascist-designed aspirations, which capture film makers' imperialist or orientalist fantasies of the ancient world.

The epic also evokes spectacular, fantastic costumes – gold lamé ones, with push-up underwire bras (Llewellyn-Jones 2002c and 2005). The Hollywood epic insists that people of the ancient world – and women in particular – almost always wore extravagant clothes and spent a good deal of time changing them (Llewellyn-Jones 2005). In the pressbooks we are told, typically, that *The Prodigal* (dir. Thorpe, 1955), starring Lana Turner, "had more than 4,000 costumes . . . with 292 costumes for the principals alone"; one for Lana Turner was created "entirely of seed pearls, thousands of which were handsewn." The result of this glamorous take on the past is not so much "realist history" as "designer history," in which "Historical references become secondary to design, although they are never totally absent . . . Designer history . . . combines the apolitical focus of costume melodrama with the impersonal affect of the traditional History Film. The past becomes a movement of empty forms and exquisite objects" (Tashiro 1998: 95–96).

The Art Direction of an epic must be particularly aware of creating historical "authenticity" which also appeals to contemporary taste (Llewellyn-Jones 2002c and 2005). As Tashiro suggests, make-up, hairstyles, and costumes of the typical epic are often adjusted to the period of filming, becoming the primary focus of Designer History. It is no surprise, therefore, to see Cleopatra in high heels. Epic movies are major vehicles for influential and important stars, and the Hollywood star system allows major stars' (especially A-list actresses) input into the look of their film wardrobes. Consequently there is an undeniable contemporary emphasis in the ancient-world costumes of Hollywood's major movie stars: Elizabeth Taylor notoriously demanded personal approval of all her costumes for *Cleopatra*, and even designed her own make-up (Llewellyn-Jones 2002c), while Angelina Jolie rejected the original set of authentic Macedonian-type costumes created for her for *Alexander*, and forced the costume designer to come up with something more fitted, "contemporary," and decidedly more Hollywood (Llewellyn-Jones 2004: 2).

Part of the visual appeal of the epic is seeing Hollywood's most glamorous movie stars disport themselves in these elaborate costume, often exposing more leg, more midriff, more chest than is normally afforded in a contemporary picture. Unfortunately, famous stars tend to be more themselves than the people they play, and consequently there is a big risk of confusing historic figures with modern actors and actresses. In the epic tradition we find familiar faces and figures – Elizabeth Taylor, Victor Mature, Richard Burton, Charlton Heston, Jean Simmons – rigged up again and again in strange costumes, as if to attend an endless fancy-dress party. Yet stars themselves add weight to the figures they represent. As Vivian Sobchack puts it, "the very presence of stars in the historical epic mimetically represents not real historical figures but rather the real significance of historical figures. Stars literally lend magnitude to the representation" (Sobchack 1990: 36).

But as recent scholarship has pointed out, there is more to the epic than glitz, glamour, and movie stars' on- and off-screen personas: the epic movie is a deeply socio-political expression (Wyke 1997). Hollywood's epic films overlay questions of faith and paganism with the theme of freedom versus tyranny, although admittedly this is often done with sledgehammer subtlety: *The Ten Commandments* is explicit in this respect, pitting the noble proto-Christian Moses against the evil dictator Ramesses who enslaves God's chosen people while worshipping pagan idols. In 1956 Ramesses' catch phrase – "So let it be written, so let it be done" – came to stand, in the public imagination, for all that was perceived to be oppressive in the atheist Soviet state under Stalin and Khruschev. This basic conflict-narrative is repeated in numerous New Testament movies – such as *Quo Vadis*, *The Robe* (dir. Koster, 1953), *Demetrius and the Gladiators* (dir. Daves, 1954), and *Androcles and the Lion* (dir. Erskine, 1952) – in which early Christians are persecuted by despotic Roman emperors (usually Caligula or Nero) who see themselves as living gods.

The influence of this conception of polarization extends well beyond the biblical films. *The Egyptian* (dir. Curtiz, 1955), set c.1300 BC, takes as its source the Egyptian Middle Kingdom literary classic *Tale of Sinuhe*, and interweaves it with the historical evidence for the reign of the New Kingdom "heretic" pharaoh Akhenaten. The film presents the monotheistic beliefs of Akhenaten as "a pre-vision of a Christian-like God" (Montserrat 2000). Horemheb, the army general who overthrows Akhenaten and massacres his disciples, becomes associated with the ungodly beliefs of the pagan priests who fear that Akhenaten's new religion of all-embracing love and tolerance will overthrow the old order and their hold over the populace. Even Robert Rossen's *Alexander the Great* (1956) holds onto this mindset, playing up Alexander's insistence that his Greek and Persian subjects worship him as a god. When, late in the film, Alexander's attitude changes to a realization that "We are all alike under God, the Father of all," his expansionist policy of conquest is tempered and his tyrannical rule over his subjects ceases.

There have, of course, been attempts to present a different perspective. The two Hollywood takes on the life of Alexander of Macedon (*Alexander the Great*, dir.

Rossen, 1956 and *Alexander*, dir. Stone, 2004), for instance, look for a psychological interpretation of the protagonist, influenced by the 1950s preoccupation with troubled and alienated youth (à la *Rebel Without a Cause*, dir. Ray, 1955), or the early twenty-first century's quest for the sensitive "new man" (a major theme of Scott's *Gladiator*, too). Interestingly, both accounts of Alexander's life opt to depict the king as the scion of a highly dysfunctional family, in which the young ruler is determined to override the pressures of being a son of a great man, Philip II, while attempting to establish himself as an individual out of the shadow of his power-mad mother, Olympias.

William Wyler and Stanley Kubrick also sought out new ground with *Ben Hur* (1959) and *Spartacus* (1960), both of which can be classified as "the thinking man's epic," and both of which reacted against the camp melodramatics of Cecil B. DeMille's films. Audiences were not short-changed of spectacle, however, in *Ben Hur*'s chariot race and great sea skirmish, or in *Spartacus*'s gladiatorial fights and battle scenes. In these two films the theme is not really the struggle between faith and paganism, but in the political differences between Judah Ben Hur and Massala and between Spartacus and General Crassus. Both protagonists challenge the power of Rome, not for spiritual ends, but for a personal vision of social equality and freedom; in doing so they asked cinema audiences of McCarthy-era America to question their own accessibility to free speech and free action at a time of national and international crisis (M. Winkler 2007b).

How far are movie audiences convinced that they are seeing the past as it was lived? And how far are they aware of political subtexts and social comments within the epic films they are watching? These questions are impossible to answer definitively, but it is my belief that film makers and audiences of the epic genre are always conscious that the notion of "experiencing the past" through film is a deception, albeit one that can be indulged. The presence of stars like Colin Farrell, Russell Crowe, Charlton Heston, and Elizabeth Taylor, the burnished marble of the palaces and Forum sets, or the gold lamé push-up bras and glittery eye-shadow are factors which render epic films compelling, but simultaneously stop audiences from fully believing in the highly stylized images projected on the screen. In the same way, film makers know what to include in the production of an ancient-world history film, and they understand the compromises they have to make with the historical truth; all film makers, whether they choose to publicly acknowledge it or not, are aware that their historical filmic representation is merely one construction of many possible pasts. Most directors are also conscious that their intentions in making a historical film differ from that of an academic historian. Hollywood directors make history films to make money at the box office and in tie-in merchandise, and to make an impact upon contemporary popular culture. The academic historian has a different agenda (it is presumed): to reflect accurately on the past and to enter into and open up debate with peers. There can be no debate in a Hollywood film; there is only one take on history as it is projected onto the screen, and while the projected picture may be sharp, the focus between historical fiction and historical reality will always be blurred.

FURTHER READING

There are many good books which tackle cinema's response to ancient history. A starting point must be Jon Solomon's excellent study *The Ancient World in the Cinema* (2nd edn, 2001) which contains a comprehensive account of the epic genre with plenty of photographs. Bruce Babington and Peter Evans have provided an excellent critique of the Old and New Testament movies in *Biblical Epics* (1993), while Maria Wyke's *Projecting the Past* looks at Roman history in the movies. Gideon Nisbet's *Ancient Greece in Film and Popular Culture* (2006) provides a much-needed overview of the cinematic response to Greek history and culture. Martin Winkler's edited volumes on *Gladiator* (2004), *Troy* (2007), *Spartacus* (2007) and *The Fall of the Roman Empire* (2009) are valuable and detailed readings of the movies. Diana Landau's *Gladiator: the Making of the Ridley Scott Epic* (2000) and Robin Lane Fox's *The Making of Alexander* (2004) provide lively and lavishly illustrated guides to the creation of two epic films. See also the stimulating set of essays in the special cinema volume of *Arethusa* (41.1, 2008).

Bibliography

Abbott, J. and Valastro, S. 1995. The Holocene Alluvial Records of the *chorai* of Metapontum, Basilicata, and Croton, Calabria, Italy. In Lewin et al. 1995: 195–205.

Abdy, R. A. 2002. *Romano-British Coin Hoards*. Princes Risborough.

Abulafia, D. (ed.) 2003. *The Mediterranean in History*. Los Angeles.

Abulafia, D. 2005. Mediterraneans. In W. Harris 2005: 64–93.

Adams, J. N., Janse, M., and Swain, S. 2002. *Bilingualism in Ancient Society: Language Contact and the Written Text*. Oxford.

Adams, J. N. 2003. *Bilingualism and the Latin Language*. Cambridge.

Adams, W. 1977. *Nubia: Corridor to Africa*. London.

Ado of Vienne, *Chronicon*, reprint of Paris 1561 edition, *Patrologia Latina* 123.

Agnew, J. 2007. No Borders, No Nations: Making Greece in Macedonia. *Annals of the American Association of Geographers* 97: 398–422.

Agostiniani, L. and Nicosia, F. 2000. *Tabula Cortonensis*. Rome.

Ahl, F. 1984. The Art of Safe Criticism in Greece and Rome. *AJP* 105: 174–208.

Aicher, P. 1995. *Guide to the Aqueducts of Ancient Rome*. Wauconda, IL.

Alcock, S. 1993. *Graecia Capta: The Landscapes of Roman Greece*. Cambridge.

Alcock, S. 2002. A Simple Case of Exploitation? The helots of Messenia. In Cartledge, Cohen and Foxhall 2002: 185–99.

Alcock, S. and Osborne, R. (eds) 1994. *Placing the Gods: Sanctuaries and Sacred Space in Ancient Greece*. Oxford.

Alcock, S., Cherry, J., and Davis, J. 1994. Intensive Survey, Agricultural Practice and the Classical Landscape of Greece. In I. Morris (ed.) *Classical Greece: Ancient Histories and Modern Archaeologies*. Cambridge. 137–70.

Alcock, S., Cherry, J. and Elsner, J. (eds) 2001. *Pausanias: Travel and Memory in Roman Greece*. Oxford.

Alcock, S. and Cherry, J. (eds) 2004. *Side-by-Side Survey. Comparative Regional Studies in the Mediterranean World*. Oxford.

Aldrete, G. 1999. *Gestures and Acclamations in Ancient Rome*. Baltimore.

Aldrete, G. 2007. *Floods of the Tiber in Ancient Rome*. Baltimore.

Alexandri, A. 2002. Names and Emblems: Greek Archaeology, Regional Identities and National Narratives at the Turn of the 20th Century. *Antiquity* 76: 191–99.

Alexiou, M. 2002. *The Ritual Lament in Greek Tradition*. 2nd edn. Lanham.

Allen, J. P. 2000. *Middle Egyptian: An Introduction to the Language and Culture of Hieroglyphs*. Cambridge.

Allison, P. 2004. *Pompeian Households*. Los Angeles.

Almond, G. and Verba, S. 1963. *The Civic Culture: Political Attitudes and Democracy in Five Nations*. Princeton.

Alston, R. 2002. *The City in Roman and Byzantine Egypt*. London.

Amandry, M., Carradice, I., and Burnett, A. M. 1999. *Roman Provincial Coinage*. Vol. 2: *From Vespasian to Domitian (AD 69–96)*. London.

Ambrose, S. 1996. The Longest Day. In Carnes 1996: 236–41.

Amouretti, M. and Brun, J.-P. (eds) 1993. *La production du vin et de l'huile en Méditerranée*. Athens.

Anderson, B. 1991. *Imagined Communities: Reflections on the Origins and Spread of Nationalism*. 2nd edn. London.

Anderson, J. C. 2003. Emperor and Architect: Trajan and Apollodorus and their Predecessors. In P. Defosse (ed.), *Hommages à Carl Deroux* III. Bruxelles. 3–10.

Anderson, J. K. 1970. *Military Theory and Practice in the Age of Xenophon*. Berkeley.

Ando, C. 2000. *Imperial Ideology and Provincial Loyalty in the Roman Empire*. Berkeley.

Ando, C. (ed.) 2003. *Roman Religion*. Edinburgh.

Andreades, A. 1933. *A History of Greek Public Finance*. Vol. I. Cambridge, MA.

Andrieu-Ponel, V., Ponel, P., Bruneton, H., Leveau, P., and de Beaulieu, J.-L. 2000. Palaeoenvironments and Cultural Landscapes of the Last 2000 Years Reconstructed from Pollen and Coleopteran Records in the Lower Rhône Valley, Southern France. *The Holocene* 10: 341–55.

Andronicos, M. [Andronikos] 1981. The Royal Tombs at Aigai (Vergina). In M. Hatzopoulos and L. Loukopoulos (eds), *Philip of Macedon*. London. 188–223.

Andronicos, M. [Andronikos] 1984. *Vergina: the Royal Tombs and Ancient City*. Athens.

Aperghis, G. 2004. *The Seleukid Royal Economy: The Finances and Financial Administration of the Seleukid Empire*. Cambridge.

Archibald, Z., Davies, J. K., Gabrielsen, G., and Oliver, G. (eds) 2001. *Hellenistic Economies*. London.

Archibald, Z., Davies, J. K., and Gabrielsen, G. 2005. *Making, Moving, and Managing: The New World of Ancient Economies, 323–31 BC*. Oxford.

Arjava, A. 1996. *Women and Law in Late Antiquity*. Oxford.

Arjava, A. 2005. The Mystery Cloud of 536 CE in the Mediterranean Sources. *Dumbarton Oaks Papers* 59: 73–94.

Arnaoutoglou, I. 1998. *Ancient Greek Laws: A Sourcebook*. London.

Arnold, B. 1995. Honorary Males or Women of Substance? Gender, Status and Power in Iron Age Europe. *Journal of European Archaeology* 3.2: 153–68.

Arnold, B. and Gibson, D. (eds) 1995. *Celtic Chiefdom and Celtic State*. Cambridge.

Aronoff, M. J. 2001. Political Culture. In N. J. Smelser and P. B. Baltes (eds), *International Encyclopedia of the Social and Behavorial Sciences* 17: 11640–44.

Arthur, P. 1991. *The Romans in Northern Campania: Settlement and Land Use around the Massico and the Garigliano Basin*. London.

Athanassiadi, P. and Frede, M. (eds) 1999. *Pagan Monotheism in Late Antiquity*. Oxford.

Attema, P. 2000. Landscape Archaeology and Livy: Warfare, Colonial Expansion and Town and Country in Central Italy of the 7th to 4th c. BC. *Bulletin Antieke Beschaving* 75: 115–26.

Aubet, M. 2001. *The Phoenicians and the West: Politics, Colonies and Trade*. Trans. M. Turton. 2nd edn. Cambridge.

Ault, B. 1999. Koprones and Oil Presses at Halieis: Interactions of Town and Country and the Integration of Domestic and Regional Economies. *Hesperia* 68: 549–73.

Ault, B. 2005. Housing the Poor and Homeless in Ancient Greece. In Ault and Nevett 2005: 140–59.

Ault, B. and Nevett, L. (eds) 2005. *Ancient Greek Houses and Households: Chronological, Regional, and Social Diversity.* Pennsylvania.

Austin, M. M. 1986. Hellenistic Kings, War, and the Economy. *CQ* 36: 450–66.

Austin, M. M. 2006. *The Hellenistic World from Alexander to the Roman Conquest: a Selection of Ancient Sources in Translation.* 2nd edn. Cambridge (1st edn 1981).

Austin, M. M. and Vidal-Naquet, P. 1977. *Economic and Social History of Ancient Greece: An Introduction.* London.

Avenarius, G. 1956. *Lukians Schrift zur Geschichtsschreibung.* Meisenheim am Glan.

Avigad, N. 1983. *Discovering Jerusalem.* Jerusalem.

Babel, R. and Paravicini, W. 2005. *Grand Tour: adeliges Reisen und Europäische Kultur von 14. bis zum 18. Jahrhundert.* Stuttgart.

Babington, B. and Evans, P. 1993. *Biblical Epics. Sacred Narrative in the Hollywood Cinema.* Manchester.

Bachtin, M. 1968. *Rabelais and His World.* Cambridge, MA.

Badian, E. 1968. *Roman Imperialism in the Late Republic.* 2nd edn. Oxford.

Badian, E. 1972. *Publicans and Sinners. Private Enterprise in the Service of the Roman Empire.* Ithaca, NY.

Baesens, V. 2006. Royal Taxation and Religious Tribute in Hellenistic Palestine. In Bang et al. 2006: 179–99.

Bagnall, R. 1993. *Egypt in Late Antiquity.* Princeton.

Bagnall, R. 1995. *Reading Papyri, Writing Ancient History.* London.

Bagnall, R. (ed.) (forthcoming.) *Oxford Handbook of Papyrology.* Oxford.

Bagnall, R. and Frier, B. 1994. *The Demography of Roman Egypt.* Cambridge.

Bagnall, R. and Derow, P. 2004. *The Hellenistic Period: Historical Sources in Translation.* Oxford (earlier edn published as *Greek Historical Documents: the Hellenistic Period,* 1981).

Bagnall, R. and Rathbone, D. 2004. *Egypt from Alexander to the Copts: an Archaeological and Historical Guide.* London.

Bagnall, R. and Cribiore, R. 2005. *Women's Letters from Ancient Egypt 300 BC–AD 800.* Ann Arbor.

Baines, J. and Malek, J. 2000. *Cultural Atlas of Ancient Egypt.* London.

Baker, P. 2003. Warfare. In Erskine 2003: 373–88.

Baker, P. 2004. Roman Medical Instruments: Archaeological Interpretations of their Possible "Non-Functional" Uses. *Social History of Medicine* 17: 3–21.

Baker, P. and Carr, G. 2002. *Practitioners, Practices and Patients: New Approaches to Medical Archaeology and Anthropology: Conference Proceedings.* Oxford.

Bakker, J. T. 2001. Les boulangeries à moulin et les distributions de blé gratuites. In J.-P. Descoeudres (ed.), *Ostia: Port et porte de la Rome antique.* Geneva. 179–85.

Bakker, J. T., van Dalen, J. H., Heres, Th. L., Meijlink, B., and Sirks, A. J. B. 1999. *The Mill-Bakeries of Ostia: Description and Interpretation.* Amsterdam.

Balch, D. and Osiek, C. (eds) 2003. *Early Christian Families in Context: an Interdisciplinary Dialogue.* Grand Rapids, MI.

Balista, C. and Ruta Serafini, A. 1992. Este preromana. Nuovi dati sulle necropoli. In G. Tosi (ed.), *Este Antica*: 111–23.

Balista, C., Gambacurta, G. and Ruta Serafini, A. 2002. Sviluppi di urbanistica Atestina. In A. Ruta Serafini (ed.) *Este preromana: una città e i suoi santuari.* Treviso. 104–21.

Ball, L. 2003. *The Domus Aurea and the Roman Architectural Revolution*. Cambridge.

Baltrusch, E. 1994. *Symmachie und Spondai: Untersuchungen zum griechischen Völkerrecht der archaischen und klassischen Zeit (8.-5. Jahrhundert v. Chr.)*. Berlin.

Banaji, J. 2001. *Agrarian Change in Late Antiquity. Gold, Labour and Aristocratic Dominance*. Oxford.

Bang, P. F. et al. (eds), *Ancient Economies, Modern Methodologies*. Bari.

Bang, P. F. 2008. *The Roman Bazaar*. Cambridge.

Barbanera, M. 1998. *L'archeologia degli italiani*. Rome.

Barclay, J. 1996. *Jews in the Mediterranean Diaspora, from Alexander to Trajan (323 BCE–117 CE)*. Edinburgh.

Barker, G. (ed.) 1995. *A Mediterranean Valley. Landscape Archaeology and* Annales *History in the Biferno Valley*. London.

Barker, G. (ed.) 1996. *Farming the Desert. The UNESCO Libyan Valleys Archaeological Survey*. Vol. 1: *Synthesis*. Paris.

Barker, G. and Lloyd, J. A. (eds) 1991. *Roman Landscapes. Archaeological Survey in the Mediterranean Region*. London.

Barker, G. and Hunt, C. 1995. Quaternary Valley Floor Erosion and Alluviation in the Biferno Valley, Molise, Italy: the Role of Tectonics, Climate, Sea Level Change, and Human Activity. In Lewin et al. 1995: 145–57.

Barker, G. and Rasmussen, T. 1998. *The Etruscans*. Oxford.

Barker, G. and Mattingly, D. J. (eds) (1999–2000). *The Archaeology of Mediterranean Landscapes*. Vols 1–5. Oxford.

Barnard, A. and Spencer, J. (eds) 1996. Sapir-Whorf hypothesis. In *Encyclopedia of Social and Cultural Anthropology*. London. 499–501.

Barnes, J. (ed.) 1984. *Complete Works of Aristotle. Revised Oxford Translation*. Princeton.

Barnes, T. D. 1981. *Constantine and Eusebius*. Cambridge, MA.

Barnes, T. D. 1982. *The New Empire of Diocletian and Constantine*. Cambridge, MA.

Barnes, T. D. 1993. *Athanasius and Constantius: Theology and Politics in the Constantinian Empire*. Cambridge, MA.

Barnett, P. 2005. *The Birth of Christianity: The First Twenty Years*. Grand Rapids, Michigan.

Barrett, J. C. 1997. Romanization: a Critical Comment. In D. Mattingly (ed.) *Dialogues in Roman Imperialism: Power, Discourse and Discrepant Experience in the Roman Empire*, 51–64. Portsmouth, RI.

Barthes, R. 1972. *Mythologies*. New York.

Barton, I. (ed.) 1996. *Roman Domestic Buildings*. Exeter.

Barton, T. 2002. *Power and Knowledge*. Ann Arbor.

Bartsch, S. 1994. *Actors in the Audience: Theatricality and Double-Speak from Nero to Hadrian*. Cambridge, MA.

Baudy, G. 1991. *Die Brände Roms. Ein apokalyptisches Motiv in der antiken Historiographie*. Hildesheim.

Bauer, W. 1972. *Orthodoxy and Heresy in Earliest Christianity*. London.

Baumgarten, A. I. 1997. *The Flourishing of Jewish Sects in the Maccabean Era: An Interpretation*. Journal for the Study of Judaism Suppl. 55. Leiden.

Baumgarten, J. M. 1999. Art in the Synagogue: Some Talmudic views. In S. Fine (ed.), *Jews, Christians and Polytheists in the Ancient Synagogue*. London. 71–86.

Bayly, C. A. 2002. "Archaic" and "Modern" Globalization of History? In A. Hopkins (ed.), *Globalization in World History*. London. 47–73.

Beal, R. 1992. *The Organisation of the Hittite Military*. Heidelberg.

Bean, G. E. 1954. Notes and Inscriptions from Caunus. *JHS* 74: 86–110.

Beard, M. 1980. The Sexual Status of Vestal Virgins. *JRS* 70: 12–27.

Beard, M. 1990. Priesthood in the Roman Republic. In Beard and North 1990: 19–48.

Beard, M. 1995a. Re-reading (Vestal) Virginity. In R. Hawley and B. Levick (eds), *Women in Antiquity: New Assessments*. New York. 166–77.

Beard, M. 1995b. *The Parthenon*. London.

Beard, M. 2000. *The Invention of Jane Harrison*. Cambridge, MA.

Beard, M. and Crawford, M. 1985. *Rome in the Late Republic*. London.

Beard, M., and North, J. (eds) 1990. *Pagan Priests: Religion and Power in the Ancient World*. London.

Beard, M. and Henderson, J. 1995. *Classics. A Very Short Introduction*. Oxford.

Beard, M. and Henderson, J. 1998. With this Body I Thee Worship: Sacred Prostitution in Antiquity. In M. Wyke (ed.), *Gender and the Body*. Oxford. 56–79.

Beard, M., North, J., and Price, S. (eds) 1998. *Religions of Rome*. 2 vols. Cambridge.

Beard, M. and Henderson, J. 2001. *Classical Art. From Greece to Rome*. Oxford.

Beazley, J. D. 1947. Some Attic Vases in the Cyprus Museum. *Proceedings of the British Academy* 33: 195–242.

Beck, F. 1964. *Greek Education, 450–350 BC*. London.

Beck, F. 1975. *Album of Greek Education. The Greeks at School and at Play*. Sydney.

Behar, D. M. et al. 2006. The Matrilineal Ancestry of Ashkenazi Jewry: portrait of a recent founder event. *AJHG* 79 (3): 487–97.

Belkahia, S. and Di Vita-Évrard, G. 1995. Magistratures autochtones dans les cités pérégrines de l'Afrique proconsulaire. In P. Trousset (ed.), *Monuments funéraires. Institutions autochtones*. Paris. 255–74.

Bell, A. 2004. *Spectacular Power in the Greek and Roman City*. Oxford.

Bell, M. 1994. An Imperial Flour Mill on the Janiculum. In *Le ravitaillement en blé de Rome et des centres urbains des débuts de la république jusqu'au Haut Empire*. Naples and Rome. 73–89.

Belle, E. et al. 2006. Serial Coalescent Simulations Suggest a Weak Genealogical Relationship between Etruscans and Modern Tuscans. *Proceedings of the National Academy of Sciences* 103: 8012–17.

Bellotti, P., Milli, S., Tortora, P. and Valeri, P. 1995. Physical Stratigraphy and Sedimentology of the Late Pleistocene-Holocene Tiber Delta Depositional Sequence. *Sedimentology* 42: 617–34.

Beloch, J. 1886. *Die Bevölkerung der griechisch-römischen Welt*. Leipzig.

Beltrán Lloris, F., Hoz, J. de., Untermann, J. 1996. *El tercer bronce de Botorrita (Contrebia Belaisca)*. Zaragoza.

Bénabou, M. 1976. *La résistance africaine à la romanisation*. Paris.

Benda-Weber, I. 2005. *Lykier und Karer. Zwei autochthone Ethnien Kleinasiens zwischen Orient und Okzident*. Bonn.

Benedict, R. 1934. *Patterns of Culture*. New York.

Benner, H. 1987. *Die Politik des P. Clodius Pulcher. Untersuchungen zur Denaturierung des Clientelwesens in der ausgehenden römischen Republik*. Stuttgart.

Bennett, J. 2001. *Trajan, Optimus Princeps*. London.

Bentley, R. 1697. *A Dissertation upon the Epistles of Phalaris*. London.

Benvenuti, M., Mariotti-Lippi, M., Pallecchi, P. and Sagri, M. 2006. Late-Holocene Catastrophic Floods in the Terminal Arno River (Pisa, Central Italy) from the Story of a Roman Riverine Harbour. *The Holocene* 16: 863–76.

Bérard, F., et al. 2000. *Guide de l'épigraphiste: bibliographie choisie des épigraphies antiques et médiévales*. 3rd edn. Paris.

Bergmann, B. and Kondoleon, C. (eds) 1999. *The Art of Ancient Spectacle*. New Haven.

Bernal, M. 1987–91. *Black Athena: the Afroasiatic Roots of Classical civilization.* 2 vols. New Brunswick, NJ.

Bers, V. 2003. *Demosthenes, Speeches 50–59.* Austin.

Berschin, W. 1988. *Greek Letters and the Latin Middle Ages from Jerome to Nicholas of Cusa* (trans J. Frakes). Washington, DC.

Bethe, E. 1907. Die Dorische Knabenliebe. *Rheinisches Museum fur Philologie* 62: 438–75.

Bianchi, R. et al. 1996. Egypt, Ancient. In J. Turner (ed.), *The Dictionary of Art.* London. IX: 769–X: 94.

Bichler, P. et al. 2005. *Hallstatt Textiles. Technical Analysis, Scientific Investigation and Experiment on Iron Age Textiles.* Oxford.

Bickerman, E. J. 1952. *Origines Gentium. CP* 47: 65–81.

Biddiss, M. 1999. The Invention of Modern Olympic Tradition. In Biddiss and Wyke 1999: 12544.

Biddiss, M. and Wyke, M. (eds) 1999. *The Uses and Abuses of Antiquity.* Bern.

Biel, J., et al. (eds) 2002. *Das Rätsel der Kelten vom Glauberg. Glaube–Mythos–Wirklichkeit.* Stuttgart.

Bintliff, J. (ed.) 1991. *The Annales School and Archaeology.* New York.

Birchard, R. 2004. *Cecil B. DeMille's Hollywood.* Lexington.

Bird, P. A. 2006. Prostitution in the Social World and Religious Rhetoric of Ancient Israel. In Faraone and McClure 2006: 40–58.

Birkhan, H. 1997–2000. *Kelten. Versuch einer Gesamtdarstellung ihrer Kultur.* 2 vols. Vienna.

Bischoff, B. 1990. *Latin Palaeography and the Middle Ages* (trans. D. Ó Cróinin and D. Ganz). Cambridge.

Bischoff, B. and Lapidge, M. (eds) 1994. *Biblical commentaries from the Canterbury school of Theodore and Hadrian.* Cambridge.

Bispham, E., and Smith, C. (eds) 2000. *Religion in Archaic and Republican Rome and Italy: Evidence and Experience.* Edinburgh.

Blake, E. and Knapp, B. 2005. *The Archaeology of Mediterranean Prehistory.* Oxford.

Blanchard, A. (ed.) 1989. *Les débuts du codex* (Bibliologia 9). Turnhout.

Blok, J. and Lardinois, A. (eds) 2006. *Solon of Athens. New Historical and Philological Approaches.* Leiden.

Blondel, J. and Aronson, J. 1999. *Biology and Wildlife of the Mediterranean Region.* Oxford.

Blondell, R., Gamel, M., Rabinowitz, N. and Zweig, B. (eds and trans) 1999. *Women on the Edge: Four Plays by Euripides.* New York.

Blümel, W., Frei, P., and Marek, C. 1998. Colloquium Caricum. Akten der Internationalen Tagung über die karisch-griechisch Bilingue von Kaunos 31.10.–1.11.1997 in Feusisberg bei Zürich. *Kadmos* 37.

Blundell, S. 2005. Gender: The Virtues and Vices of the Mainstream. In M. Skinner (ed.), Gender and Diversity in Place: Proceedings of the Fourth Conference on Feminism and Classics. www.stoa.org/diotima/essays/fc04/Blundell.html.

Boardman, J. 2001. *The History of Greek Vases: Potters, Painters, and Pictures.* London.

Boardman, J. 2006. Early Euboean Settlements in the Carthage Area. *Oxford Journal of Archaeology* 25: 195–200.

Bodel, J. P. 2001. *Epigraphic Evidence: Ancient History from Inscriptions,* London.

Boedeker, D. and Raaflaub, K. A. (eds) 1998. *Democracy, Empire, and the Arts in Fifth-Century Athens.* Cambridge, MA.

Bohak, G. 1999. Theopolis: A Single-Temple Policy and Its Singular Ramifications. *Journal of Jewish Studies* 50: 3–16.

Bohak, G. 2000. The Impact of Jewish Monotheism on the Greco-Roman World. *Jewish Studies Quarterly* 7: 1–21.

Bohak, G. 2002a. The Hellenization of Biblical History in Rabbinic Literature. In P. Schäfer (ed.), *The Talmud Yerushalmi and Graeco-Roman Culture III*. Texts and Studies in Ancient Judaism 93. Tübingen. 3–16.

Bohak, G. 2002b. Ethnic Continuity in the Jewish Diaspora in Antiquity. In J. R. Bartlett (ed.) *Jews in the Hellenistic and Roman Cities*. London. 175–192.

Bolgar, R. R. 1954. *The Classical Heritage and its Beneficiaries*. Cambridge.

Bolgar, R. R. (ed.) 1971. *Classical Influences on European Culture 500–1500*. Cambridge.

Bolgar, R. R. (ed.) 1976. *Classical Influences on European Culture 1500–1700*. Cambridge.

Bolgar, R. R. (ed.) 1979. *Classical Influences on Western Thought, AD 1650–1870*. Cambridge.

Bolgar, R. R. 1981. The Greek Legacy. In Finley 1981b: 429–72.

Bonfante, G. and Bonfante, L. 2002. *The Etruscan Language: An Introduction*. 2nd edn. Manchester.

Bonnell, V. and Hunt, L. (eds) 1999. *Beyond the Cultural Turn: New Directions in the Study of Society and Culture*. Berkeley.

Bonner, S. 1977. *Education in Ancient Rome, From the Elder Cato to the Younger Pliny*. London.

Bonnet, C. and Pirenne-Delforge, V. 1999. Deux déesses en interaction: Astarté et Aphrodite dans le monde égéen. In C. Bonnet and A. Motte (eds), *Les syncrétismes religieux dans le monde méditerranéen antique*. 249–73.

Bonney, R. (ed.) 1999. *The Rise of the Fiscal State in Europe, c.1200–1815*. Oxford.

Bonney, R. and Ormrod, W. 1999. Introduction. In W. Ormrod, M. Bonney, and R. Bonney (eds), *Crises, Revolutions and Self-Sustained Growth. Essays in European Fiscal History, 1130–1830*. Stamford. 1–21.

Borza, E. 1990. *In the Shadow of Olympus: the Emergence of Macedon*. Princeton.

Boserup, E. 1965. *Conditions of Agricultural Growth: the Economics of Agrarian Change Under Population Pressure*. Chicago.

Boswell, J. 1990a. Concepts, Experience and Sexuality. *Differences: A Journal of Feminist Cultural Studies* 2.1: 67–87.

Boswell, J. 1990b. *The Kindness of Strangers: The Abandonment of Children in Western Europe from Late Antiquity to the Renaissance*. New York.

Boswell, J. 1994. *The Marriage Of Likeness. Same-Sex Unions In Premodern Europe*. London.

Bottéro, J. 1998. *La plus vieille religion: en Mésopotamie*. Paris.

Bottéro, J. 2001. *Everyday Life in Ancient Mesopotamia*. Edinburgh (first published in French, 1992).

Boudon, V. 1994. Les oeuvres de Galien pour les débutants ("De sectis", "De pulsibus ad tirones", "De ossibus ad tirones", "Ad Glauconem de methodo medendi" et "Ars medica"): médecine et pédagogie au IIe s. ap. J.-C. *ANRW* 2.37.2: 1421–67.

Bowden, H. 2005. *Classical Athens and the Delphic Oracle: Divination and Democracy*. Cambridge.

Bowersock, G. 1965. *Augustus and the Greek World*. Oxford.

Bowersock, G. 1995. *Martyrdom and Rome*. Cambridge.

Bowman, A. K. 1970. A Letter of Avidius Cassius? *JRS* 60: 20–26.

Bowman, A. K. 1996. *Egypt after the Pharaohs*. 2nd pb. edn. London.

Bowman, A. K. 2000. Urbanization in Roman Egypt. In E. Fentress (ed.), *Romanization and the city. Creation, Transformations and Failures (JRA Suppl. 38)*: 173–87.

Bowman, A. K. 2001. Some Romans in Augustan Alexandria. *Bulletin de la Société d'Archéologie d'Alexandrie* 46 (Festschrift for Prof. Mostafa el-Abbadi): 13–24.

Bowman, A. K. 2003. *Life and Letters on the Roman Frontier: Vindolanda and its People.* 2nd edn. London.

Bowman, A. K. 2007. Roman Oxyrhynchus: City and People. In Bowman, Coles et al. 2007: chap. 13.

Bowman, A. K. and Thomas, J. 1983. *Vindolanda: the Latin Writing-tablets.* London.

Bowman, A. K. and Thomas, J. 1994. *The Vindolanda Writing-tablets (Tabulae Vindolandenses II).* London.

Bowman, A. K and Woolf, G. (eds) 1994. *Literacy and Power in the Ancient World.* Cambridge.

Bowman, A. K. and Deegan, M. (eds) 1997. *The Use of Computers in the Study of Ancient Documents,* special issue of *Literary and Linguistic Computing* Vol. XII, no. 3.

Bowman, A. K. and Rogan, E. (eds) 1999. *Agriculture in Egypt from Pharaonic to Modern Times.* Oxford.

Bowman, A. K. and Thomas, J. 2003. *The Vindolanda Writing-tablets (Tabulae Vindolandenses III).* London.

Bowman, A. K and Brady, J. (eds) 2005. *Images and Artefacts of the Ancient World.* London.

Bowman, A. K. and Tomlin, R. 2005. Wooden Stilus Tablets from Roman Britain. In Bowman and Brady 2005: 7–14.

Bowman, A. K., Coles, R., Gonis, N., Obbink, D., and Parsons, P. (eds) 2007. *Oxyrhynchus: a City and its Texts.* London.

Boyarin, D. 1993. *Carnal Israel: Reading Sex in Talmudic Culture.* Berkeley.

Boyarin, D. 1999. *Dying for God: Martyrdom and the Making of Christianity and Judaism.* Stanford.

Boyarin, D. 2004. *Borderlines: The Partition of Judaeo-Christianity.* Philadelphia.

Boyle, C. 1698. *Dr. Bentley's Dissertations on the Epistles of Phalaris, and the Fables of Æsop, Examin'd.* London.

Braconi, P. 2005. Il "Calcidico" di Lepcis Magna era un mercato di schiavi? *JRA* 18: 213–19.

Bradeen, D. W. 1964. The Athenian Casualty Lists. *Hesperia* 33: 16–62.

Bradley, G. 1997. Iguvines, Umbrians and Romans: Ethnic Identity in Central Italy. In Cornell and Lomas 1997: 53–68.

Bradley, G. 2000. *Ancient Umbria. State, Culture and Identity in Central Italy from the Iron Age to the Augustan Era.* Oxford.

Bradley, G., Isayev, E., and Riva, C. (eds) 2007. *Ancient Italy: Regions Without Boundaries.* Exeter.

Bradley, K. 1991. *Discovering the Roman Family.* New York and Oxford.

Bradley, K. 1994. *Slavery and Society at Rome.* Cambridge.

Brain, P. 1986. *Galen on Bloodletting.* Cambridge.

Branham, R. 1989. *Unruly Eloquence. Lucian and the Comedy of Traditions.* Cambridge, MA.

Brashear, W. 1996. An Alexandrian Marriage Contract. In R. Katzoff, Y. Petroff, and D. Schaps (eds), *Classical Studies in Honor of David Sohlberg.* Ramat Gan. 367–84.

Braudel, F. 1972. *The Mediterranean and the Mediterranean World in the Age of Philip II* (tr. S. Reynolds,1st French edn 1949, 2nd 1966). London.

Braudel, F. 1980. *On History.* Chicago.

Braudel, F. 1981. *Civilization and Capitalism, 15th–18th century.* Vol. 1: *The Structures of Everyday Life. The Limits of the Possible.* London.

Braudel, F. 1982. *Civilization and Capitalism, 15th-18th century.* Vol. 2: *The Wheels of Commerce.* London.

Braudel, F. 2001. *Memory and the Mediterranean*. New York.

Braund, D. and Wilkins, J. 2000. *Athenaeus and his World*. Exeter.

Braund, D. and Gill, C. (eds) 2003. *Myth, History, and Culture: Studies in Honour of T. P. Wiseman*. Exeter.

Braund, S. M. 1996. *Juvenal Satires Book I*. Cambridge.

Braund, S. 1989. City and Country in Roman Satire. In S. Braund (ed.), *Satire and Society in Ancient Rome*. Exeter. 23–47.

Bray, A. 2000. Friendship, the Family and Liturgy: A Rite for Blessing Friendship in Traditional Christianity. *Theology and Sexuality* 13: 15–33.

Bremmer, J. 1994. *Greek Religion*. Oxford.

Bremmer, J. 1995. The Family and Other Centres of Religious Learning in Antiquity. In Drijvers, J. and MacDonald, A. (eds), *Centres of Learning. Learning and Location in Pre-Modern Europe and the Near East*. Leiden: 29–38.

Bremmer, J. 2002. *The Rise and Fall of the Afterlife*. London.

Bremmer, J. and Horsfall, N. 1987. *Roman Myth and Mythography*. London.

Brent, A. 1995. *Hippolytus and the Roman Church in the Third Century: Communities in Tension before the Emergence of a Monarch-Bishop*. Leiden.

Bresson, A. 2000. *La cité marchande*. Bordeaux.

Bresson, A. 2005. Ecology and Beyond: the Mediterranean Paradigm. In W. Harris 2005: 94–116.

Brett, M. and Fentress, E. 1996. *The Berbers*. Oxford.

Briant, P. 1996. *Histoire de l'Empire perse*. Paris.

Brickhouse, T. and Smith, N. D. 2002. *The Trial and Execution of Socrates. Sources and Controversies*. New York.

Bridenthal, R. and Koonz, C. (eds) 1977. *Becoming Visible: Women in European History*. Boston.

Brillante, C. 1990. Myth and History. In L. Edmunds (ed.), *Approaches to Greek Myth*. Baltimore. 91–138.

Bringmann, K. 1993. The King as Benefactor: Some Remarks on Ideal Kingship in the Age of Hellenism. In A. Bulloch et al. (eds), *Images and Ideologies. Self-Definition in the Hellenistic World*. Berkeley. 7–24.

Brixhe, C. 1997. Le Phrygien. In F. Bader (ed.), *Langue indo-européennes*. Paris. 167–80.

Brixhe, C. 2004a. Nouvelle chronologie anatolienne et date d'élaboration des alphabets grec et phrygien. *Comptes rendus des Séances de l'Académie des Inscriptions et Belles-Lettres.* 271–89.

Brixhe, C. 2004b. Corpus des inscriptions paléo-phrygiennes: Supplément II. *Kadmos* 43: 1–130.

Brixhe, C. and Waelkens, M. 1981. Un nouveau document néo-Phrygien au Musée d'Afyon. *Kadmos* 20: 68–75.

Brock, R. and Hodkinson, S. 2000. *Alternatives to Athens. Varieties of Political Organization and Community in Ancient Greece*. Oxford.

Brody, H. 1987. *Stories of Sickness*. New Haven and London.

Broise, H. and Thébert, Y. 1993. *Récherches archéologiques franco-tunisiennes à Bulla Regia. II. Les Architectures. 1. Les thermes Memmiens*. Rome.

Brooten, B. 1996. *Love Between Women: Early Christian Responses to Female Homoeroticism*. Chicago.

Brosius, M. 2000. *From Cyrus II to Artaxerxes I*. London.

Brosius, M. 2006. *The Persians. An Introduction*. London.

Broughton, T. R. S. 1929. *The Romanization of Africa Proconsularis*. Baltimore.

Broughton, T. R. S. 1951–86. *The Magistrates of the Roman Republic.* 3 vols. New York.

Brown, A. 2004. Political Culture. In A. Kuper and J. Kuper (eds), *The Social Science Encyclopedia* (3rd edn) 2: 743–45.

Brown, A., Meadows, I., Turner, S., and Mattingly, D. 2001. Roman Vineyards in Britain: Stratigraphic and Palynological Data from Wollaston in the Nene Valley, England. *Antiquity* 75: 745–57.

Brown, K. S. 1994. Seeing Stars: Character and Identity in the Landscapes of modern Macedonia. *Antiquity* 68: 784–96.

Brown, K. S. 2000. In the Realm of the Double-Headed Eagle: Parapolitics in Macedonia 1994–9. In Cowan 2000: 122–39.

Brown, P. R. L. 1971a. The Rise and Function of the Holy Man in Late Antiquity. *JRS* 61: 80–101.

Brown, P. R. L. 1971b. *The World of Late Antiquity.* London.

Brown, P. R. L. 1988. *The Body and Society: Men, Women and Sexual Renunciation in Early Christianity.* New York.

Browning, R. 2002. Greeks and Others: from Antiquity to the Renaissance. In T. Harrison (ed.), *Greeks and Barbarians.* Edinburgh. 257–77. (Article first published in 1989 in R. Browning, *History. Language and Literacy in the Byzantine World,* chap. 2).

Bruhns, H. 1978. *Caesar und die römische Oberschicht in den Jahren 49–44 v. Chr. Untersuchungen zur Herrschaftsetablierung im Bürgerkrieg.* Göttingen.

Bruit Zaidmann, L. and Schmitt Pantel, P. 1992. *Religion in the Ancient Greek City.* Cambridge.

Brulé, P. 1992. Infanticide et abandon d'enfants: Prâtiques grecques et comparaisons anthropologiques. *Dialogues d'Histoire Ancienne* 18: 53–90.

Brunaux, J.-L. 1999. Ribemont-sur-Ancre (Somme). Bilan préliminaire et nouvelles hypotheses. *Gallia* 56: 177–283.

Brunaux, J.-L. 2000. *Les religions gauloises, Ve-Ier siècles av. J-C.* rev. edn. Paris.

Brunt, P. A. 1971. *Italian Manpower.* Oxford.

Brunt, P. A. 1978. Laus Imperii. In Garnsey and Whittaker 1978: 159–91.

Brunt, P. A. 1980a. Cicero and Historiography. In *Philias Charin. Miscellanea . . . Eugenio Manni.* Rome. I.311–40. Repr. in Brunt 1993: 181–209.

Brunt, P. A. 1980b. Free Labour and Public Works at Rome. *JRS* 70: 81–100.

Brunt, P. A. 1986. Cicero's *Officium* in the Civil War. *JRS* 76: 12–32.

Brunt, P. A. 1988. *The Fall of the Roman Republic and Related Essays.* Oxford.

Brunt, P. A. 1990. *Roman Imperial Themes.* Oxford. 134–62.

Brunt, P. A. 1993. *Studies in Greek History and Thought.* Oxford.

Bruun, C. 1989. The Roman *Minucia* Business – Ideological Concepts, Grain Distribution and Severan Policy. *Opuscula Instituti Romani Finlandiae* 4: 107–21.

Bruun, C. 1991. *The Water Supply of Ancient Rome. A Study of Roman Imperial Administration.* Helsinki.

Bruun, C. 2000. Senatorial Owners of What? *JRA* 13: 498–506.

Bruun, C. 2003. Velia, Quirinale, Pincio: note su proprietari di *domus* e su *plumbarii*. *Arctos* 37: 27–48.

Bruun, C. (ed.) 2005. *Interpretare i bolli laterizi di Roma e della Valle del Tevere: produzione, storia economica e topografia.* Rome.

Bruun, C. 2006. Der Kaiser und die stadtrömischen *curae*: Geschichte und Bedeutung. In A. Kolb (ed.), *Herrschaftsstrukturen und Herrschaftspraxis. Konzepte, Prinzipien und Strategien der Administration im römischen Kaiserreich.* Berlin. 89–114.

Bruun, P. 1954. The Consecration Coins of Constantine the Great. *Arctos* 1: 19–31.

Bryce, T. 2005. *The Kingdom of the Hittites.* rev. edn (first edn 1998). Oxford.

Bryer, A. and Winfield, D. 1985. *The Byzantine Monuments and Topography of the Pontos.* Washington, DC.

Bucher, G. 1987 [1995]. The *Annales Maximi* in the Light of Roman Methods of Keeping Records. *AJAH* 12: 2–61.

Buchner, G. and Ridgway, D. 1993. *Pithekoussai I. La necropoli: tombe 1–723 scavate dal 1953 al 1961.* Rome.

Budelmann, F. 2004. Greek Tragedies in West African Adaptations. *PCPS* 50: 1–28; repr. in Goff 2005: 118–46.

Budin, S. L. 2006. Sacred Prostitution in the First Person. In Faraone and McClure 2006: 77–92.

Bugh, G. 2006. Hellenistic Military Developments. In G. Bugh (ed.), *The Cambridge Companion to the Hellenistic World.* Cambridge. 265–94.

Bullo, S. 2002. *Provincia Africa: Le città e il territorio dalla caduta di Cartagine a Nerone.* Rome.

Burford, A. 1969. *The Greek Temple Builders at Epidauros.* Liverpool.

Burford, A. 1972. *Craftsmen in Greek and Roman Society.* London.

Burford, A. 1993. *Land and Labor in the Greek World.* Baltimore, MD.

Burke, E. 1992. The Economy of Athens in the Classical Era: Some Adjustments to the Primitivist Model. *TAPA* 122: 199–226.

Burke, P. 1990. *The French Historical Revolution: the Annales School 1929–89.* Cambridge.

Burke, P. 2005. *History and Social Theory.* Cambridge.

Burkert, W. 1979. *Structure and History in Greek Mythology and Ritual.* Berkeley.

Burkert, W. 1987. *Ancient Mystery Cults.* Cambridge, MA.

Burkert, W. 2004. *Babylon, Memphis, Persepolis: Eastern Contexts of Greek Culture.* Cambridge, MA.

Burnett, A. M. 1987. *Coinage in the Roman World.* London.

Burnett, A. M. 2005. The Roman West and the Roman East. In Howgego et al. 2005: 171–80.

Burnett, A. M., Amandry M. and Ripollès, P. P. 1992. *Roman Provincial Coinage.* Vol. 1: *From the Death of Caesar to the Death of Vitellius (44 BC–AD 69).* London.

Burrell, B. 2005. Iphigeneia in Philadelphia. *Classical Antiquity* 24: 223–56.

Burstein, S. M. 1985. *The Hellenistic Age from the Battle of Ipsos to the Death of Kleopatra VII.* Translated Documents of Greece and Rome 3. Cambridge.

Burtchaell, J. T. 1992. *From Synagogue to Church: Public Services and Offices in the Earliest Communities.* Cambridge.

Butcher, K. 1988. *Roman Provincial Coins.* London.

Butcher, K. 2003. *Roman Syria and the Near East.* London.

Butler, E. M. 1935. *The Tyranny of Greece over Germany. A Study of the Influence Exercised by Greek Art and Poetry over the Great German Writers of the 18th to the 20th Centuries.* Cambridge.

Butler, S. 2002. *The Hand of Cicero.* London.

Buxton, R. 1994. *Imaginary Greece: The Contexts of Mythology.* Cambridge.

Buxton, R. (ed.) 2000. *Oxford Readings in Greek Religion.* Oxford.

Cabo, A. and Vigil, M. 1973. *Historia de España Alfaguara I.* Madrid.

Cadiou, F. 2002. À propos du service militaire dans l'armée romaine au IIe siècle avant J.-C.: le cas de Spurius Ligustinus (Tite-Live 42, 34). In P. Defosse (ed.), *Hommages à Carl Deroux,* vol. 2. Brussels. 76–90.

Cagnat, R. 1914. *Cours d'épigraphie latine.* 4th edn. Paris.

Cahill, N. 2002. *Household and City Organization at Olynthus.* New Haven.

Calame, C. 1999. *The Poetics of Eros in Ancient Greece.* Princeton.

Calderini, A. 1935–2003. *Dizionario dei nomi geografici e topografici dell'Egitto greco-romano.* Cairo.

Caldwell J. 2004. Fertility Control in the Classical World: Was there an Ancient Fertility Transition? *Journal of Population Research* 21: 1–17.

Cameron, Alan. 1976. *Circus Factions: Blues and Greens at Rome and Constantinople.* Oxford.

Cameron, Alan. 1995. *Callimachus and his Critics.* Princeton.

Cameron, Averil, and Kuhrt, A. (eds) 1983. *Images of Women in Antiquity.* Detroit.

Caminos, R. A. 1954. *Late-Egyptian Miscellanies.* Oxford.

Camodeca, G. 1999. *Tabulae Pompeianae Sulpiciorum, Editione critica dell'archivo puteolano dei Sulpicii.* Rome.

Camp, J. M. 2001. *The Archaeology of Athens.* New Haven.

Campbell, B. 2000. *The Writings of the Roman Land Surveyors. Introduction, Text, Translation and Commentary.* London.

Campbell, B. and Tritle, L. (forthcoming.) *The Oxford Handbook of Classical Warfare.* Oxford.

Campbell, R. A. 1994. *The Elders: Seniority Within Earliest Christianity.* Edinburgh.

Campenhausen, H. von. 1972. *The Formation of the Christian Bible* London.

Camporeale, G. 2001. *The Etruscans Outside Etruria.* Los Angeles.

Camps, G. 1961. *Aux origines de la Berbérie. Massinissa ou les débuts de l'histoire.* Alger.

Canali de Rossi, F. 2004. *Iscrizioni dello Estremo Oriente Greco. Un reportorio.* Inschriften griechischer Städte aus Kleinasien 65. Bonn.

Cannadine, D. (ed.) 2002. *What is History Now?* Houndmills and New York.

Cannistraro, P. 1972. Mussolini's Cultural Revolution: Fascist or Nationalist? *Journal of Contemporary History* 7: 115–39.

Canto, A. 2003. *Las raíces béticas de Trajano: los Traii de la Itálica turdetana, y otras novedades sobre su familia.* Seville.

Capasso, L. 1999. Brucellosis at Herculaneum (79 AD). *International Journal of Osteoarchaeology* 9: 277–88.

Capasso, L. 2000. Indoor Pollution and Respiratory Diseases in Ancient Rome. *Lancet* 356: 1774.

Capogrossi Colognesi, L. 1995. The Limits of the Ancient City and the Evolution of the Medieval City in the Thought of Max Weber. In Cornell and Lomas 1995: 27–38.

Carandini, A. 1988. *Schiavi in Italia: gli strumenti peasanti dei romani fra tarda repubblica e medio impero.* Rome.

Carandini, A. 1997. *La nascità di Roma.* Turin (2nd edn 2003).

Carandini, A. 2004. *Palatino, Velia, Sacra Via. Paesaggi urbani attraverso il tempo.* Rome.

Carandini, A. and Cappelli, R. (eds) 2000. *Roma. Romolo, Remo e la fondazione della città* (exhibition catalog, Rome).

Carandini, A., Cambi, F., Celuzza, M. G. and Fentress, E. (eds) 2002. *Paesaggi d'Etruria. Valle dell'Albegna, Valle d'Oro, Valle del Chiarone, Valle del Tafone.* Rome.

Carey, C. 1992. *Apollodoros against Neaira: (Demosthenes) 59.* Warminster.

Carey, C. and Reid, R. 1985. *Demosthenes: Selected Private Speeches.* Cambridge.

Carlsen, J. (ed.) 1994. *Land Use in the Roman Empire.* Rome.

Carmody, F. 1956. *Arabic Astronomical and Astrological Sciences in Latin Translation: a Critical Bibliography.* Berkeley.

Carnes, M. (ed.) 1996. *Past Imperfect. History According to the Movies.* New York.

Carr, E. H. 1961. *What is History?* London (republished with a new introduction by Richard J. Evans. London 2001).

Carradice, I. and Price, M. 1988. *Coinage in the Greek World.* London.

Carrié, J.-M. 1997. "Colonato del Basso Impero": la resistenza del mito. In E. Lo Cascio (ed.) *Terre, proprietari e contadini dell' impero romano.* Urbino.

Carroll, M. 2006. *Spirits of the Dead: Roman Funerary Commemoration in Western Europe.* Oxford.

Carson, R. A. G. 1990. *Coins of the Roman Empire.* London.

Carter, J. C. 2005. *Discovering the Greek Countryside at Metaponto.* Ann Arbor.

Carter, J. C., Crawford, M., Lehman, P., Nikolaenko, G., and Trelogan, J. 2000. The Chora of Chersonesos in Crimea, Ukraine. *AJA* 104: 707–41.

Carthage, l'histoire, sa trace et son echo. 1995. Editions des les Musees de Villes de Paris. Paris.

Cartledge, P. 1998. The Economy (Economies) of Ancient Greece. *Dialogos* 5: 4–24 (= Scheidel and von Reden 2002: 11–32).

Cartledge, P. 2001. The Politics of Spartan Pederasty. In P. Cartledge (ed.) *Spartan Reflections.* London. 91–105 (= *PCPS* 27 (1981), 17–36).

Cartledge, P. 2002a. *The Greeks. A Portrait of Self and Others.* 2nd edn. Oxford (1st edn 1993).

Cartledge, P. 2002b. *The Political Economy of Greek Slavery.* In Cartledge et al. 2002: 156–66.

Cartledge, P., Cohen, E. E., and Foxhall, L. (eds) 2002. *Money, Labour and Land: New Approaches to the Economies of Ancient Greece.* London.

Cary, M. 1949. *The Geographic Background of Greek and Roman History.* Oxford.

Casabonne, O. 2004. *La Cilicie à l'époque achéménide.* Paris.

Castle, E. 1961. *Ancient Education and Today.* Harmondsworth.

Catalano, P. and Siniscalco, P. 1983–86 (eds) *Da Roma alla Terza Roma* I–III. Naples.

Cavalli-Sforza, L., Menozzi, P., and Piazza, A. 1994. *The History and Geography of Human Genes.* Princeton.

Cavanagh, W., Crouwel, J., Catling, R. W. V., and Shipley, G. 1996. *The Laconia Survey: Continuity and Change in a Greek Rural Landscape. Methodology and Interpretation.* London.

Cerati, A. 1975. *Caractère annonaire et assiette de l'impôt foncier au bas-empire.* Paris.

Černý, J. 1973. *A Community of Workmen at Thebes in the Ramesside Period.* Cairo.

Chadwick, H. 2001. *The Church in Ancient Society: From Galilee to Gregory the Great.* Oxford.

Chadwick, O. 1975. *The Secularization of the European Mind in the Nineteenth Century.* Cambridge.

Champion, C. 2004. *Cultural Politics in Polybius'* Histories. Berkeley.

Champlin, E. 1982. The Suburbium of Rome. *AJAH* 7: 97–117.

Champlin, E. 1991. *Final Judgments.* Berkeley.

Chandezon, Chr. 2003. Les campagnes de l'Ouest d'Asie Mineure à l'époque hellénistique. In F. Prost (ed.), *L'Orient méditerranéen de la mort d'Alexandre aux campagnes de Pompée.* Rennes. 193–217.

Chaniotis, A. 1988. *Historie und Historiker in den griechischen Inschriften: epigraphische Beiträge zur griechischen Historiographie.* Stuttgart.

Chaniotis, A. 2003. The Divinity of Hellenistic Rulers. In Erskine 2003: 431–45.

Chaniotis, A. 2005. *War in the Hellenistic World: A Social and Cultural History.* Oxford.

Chapman, J., Sheil, R., and Batovic, S. 1996. *The Changing Face of Dalmatia. Archaeological and Ecological Studies in a Mediterranean Landscape,* London.

Charlesworth, J. (ed.) 1983–85. *The Old Testament Pseudepigrapha,* 2 vols. Garden City, NY.

Chastagnol, A. 1981. L'inscription constantinienne d'Orcistus. *Mélanges d'archéologie et d'histoire de l'École française de Rome* 93/1: 381–416.

Chelbi, F. 1992. *Ceramique à vernis noir de Carthage.* Tunis.

Cherry, J., Davis, J., and Mantzourani, E. 1991. *Landscape Archaeology as Long-Term History. Northern Keos in the Cycladic Islands from Earliest Settlement until Modern Times.* Los Angeles.

Choquer, G., Clavel-Lévêque, M., Favory, F. and Vallat, J.-P. 1987. *Structures agraires en Italie centro-méridionale cadastres et paysage ruraux.* Rome.

Choquer, G. and Favory, F. 1991. *Les paysages de l'Antiquité. Terres et cadastres de l'Occident romain (IVe s. avant J.-C. / IIIe s. après J.-C.).* Paris.

Chorfi, C. 2006. DeRacinating Drama: Post-Orientalism and Ancient Literatures in Tawfiq al-Hakim's Al-Malik Udib and Izis. Unpublished MA diss., University of Exeter.

Christesen, P. 2003. Economic Rationalism in Fourth-Century BCE Athens. *Greece and Rome* 50: 31–56.

Chuvin, P. 1990. *A Chronicle of the Last Pagans.* Cambridge, MA.

Cima, M. and La Rocca, E. (eds) 1995. *Horti Romani.* Rome.

Claridge, A. 1998. *Rome* (Oxford Archaeological Guides). Oxford (2nd edn, 2010).

Clark, E. A. 2004. *History, Theory, Text: Historians and the Linguistic Turn.* Cambridge, MA.

Clark, G. 1993. *Women in Late Antiquity: Pagan and Christian Lifestyles.* Oxford.

Clark, G. 2004. *Christianity and Roman Society.* Cambridge.

Clark, M. 1996. *Modern Italy 1871–1995.* 2nd edn. London.

Clark, P. 1998. Women, Slaves, and the Hierarchies of Domestic Violence: The Family of St Augustine. In Joshel and Murnaghan 1998: 109–29.

Clark, S. 1985. The *Annales* Historians. In Q. Skinner (ed.), *The Return of Grand Theory in the Social Sciences.* Cambridge. 177–98.

Clarke, J. R. 1991. *The Houses of Roman Italy, 100 BC–AD 250: Ritual, Space and Decoration.* Berkeley.

Clarke, K. 1999. *Between Geography and History: Hellenistic Constructions of the Roman World.* Oxford.

Clarke, M. 1959. *Classical Education in Britain 1500–1900.* Cambridge.

Clarke, M. 1971. *Higher Education in the Ancient World.* London.

Clarke, M. 1996. *Rhetoric at Rome.* 2nd edn, rev. D. Berry. London.

Clarke, W. 1978. Achilles and Patroclus in Love. *Hermes* 106: 381–96.

Clarysse, W. 1983. Literary Papyri in Documentary "Archives". In *Egypt and the Hellenistic World* (Studia Hellenistica 27): 43–61.

Clauss, J. 1997. *Domestici Hostes*: The Nausicaa in Medea, the Catiline in Hannibal. *Materiali e discussione* 39: 165–85.

Clauss, M. 2000. *The Roman Cult of Mithras: The God and His Mysteries.* Edinburgh.

Clay, D. 2004. *Archilochos Heros: the Cult of Poets in the Greek Polis.* Washington, DC.

Clayton, P. and Price, M. (eds) 1988. *The Seven Wonders of the Ancient World.* London.

Cline, E. H. 2000. *The Battles of Armageddon.* Ann Arbor.

Clogg, R. 1979. *A Short History of Modern Greece.* Cambridge.

Clogg, R. 2002. *A Concise History of Greece.* 2nd edn. Cambridge.

Coale, A. and Demeny, P. 1983. *Regional Model Life Tables and Stable Populations.* 2nd edn. New York and London.

Coarelli, F. 1983–85. *Il Foro Romano* I–II. Rome.

Coarelli, F. 1997a. *Il Campo Marzio* I. *Dalle origini alla fine della repubblica.* Rome.

Coarelli, F. 1997b. La consistenza della città nel periodo imperiale: *pomerium, vici, insulae.* In *La Rome impériale.* 89–109.

Coarelli, F. and La Regina, A. 1984. *Abruzzo Molise* (*Guide archeologiche Laterza* 9). Bari.

Cobban, A. 1975. *The Medieval Universities: Their Development and Organization*. London.

Cobban, A. 1999. *English University Life in the Middle Ages*. London.

Cohen, D. 1991a. *Law, Sexuality, and Society*. Cambridge.

Cohen, D. 1991b. Reply to Hindley 1991. *Past and Present* 133: 184–94.

Cohen, G. M. 1995. *The Hellenistic Settlements in Europe, the Islands, and Asia Minor*. Berkeley.

Cohen, S. J. D. 1999. *The Beginnings of Jewishness: Boundaries, Varieties, Uncertainties*. Berkeley.

Cohen, S. J. D. 2005. *Why Aren't Jewish Women Circumcised?: Gender and Covenant in Judaism*. Berkeley.

Cohen, S. J. D. 2006. *From the Maccabees to the Mishnah*. 2nd edn (1st edn 1987). London.

Cole, S. G. 2004. *Landscapes, Gender, and Ritual Space: The Ancient Greek Experience*. Berkeley.

Coleman, K. M. 1990. Fatal Charades: Roman Executions Staged as Mythological Enactments. *JRS* 80: 44–73.

Coleman, K. M. 1993. Launching into History: Aquatic Displays in the Early Empire. *JRS* 83: 48–74.

Collins, J. J. 1983. *Between Athens and Jerusalem: Jewish Identity in the Hellenistic Diaspora*. New York. (2nd edn, Grand Rapids, MI, 2000.)

Collis, J. 2003. *The Celts. Origins, Myths and Inventions*. Stroud.

Conkey, M. and Hastorf, C. (eds) 1990. *The Uses of Style in Archaeology*. Cambridge.

Connor, W. R. 1987. Tribes, Festivals and Processions: Civic Ceremonial and Political Manipulation in Archaic Greece. *JHS* 107: 20–50.

Conte, G. B. 1994. *Latin Literature: a History*, trans. J. B. Solodow, rev. by D. Fowler and G. W. Most. Baltimore.

Cooper. D. 1991. Who Killed Spartacus? *CINEASTE* 18. 18–27.

Cooper, J. S. 1986. *Sumerian and Akkadian royal inscriptions*, vol. 1: *Presargonic inscriptions*. New Haven.

Corbier, M. 1974. *L'Aerarium Saturni et l'Aerarium Militare. Administration et prosopographie sénatoriale*. Rome.

Corbier, M. 1991. City, Territory and Taxation. In Rich and Wallace-Hadrill 1991: 211–39.

Corcoran, S. 2000. *The Empire of the Tetrarchs: Imperial Pronouncements and Government A. D. 284–324*. rev. edn. Oxford.

Cornell, T. 1986. The Formation of the Historical Tradition of Early Rome. In I. Moxon, J. Smart and A. Woodman (eds), *Past Perspectives: Studies in Greek and Roman Historical Writing*. Cambridge. 67–86.

Cornell, T. 1995. *The Beginnings of Rome: Italy and Rome from the Bronze Age to the Punic Wars (c.1000–264 BC)*. London.

Cornell, T. 1996. Hannibal's Legacy: The Effects of the Hannibalic War on Italy. In T. Cornell, B. Rankov, and P. Sabin (eds), *The Second Punic War. A Reappraisal*. London. 97–117.

Cornell, T. and Lomas, K. (eds) 1995. *Urban Society in Roman Italy*. London.

Cornell, T. and Lomas, K. (eds) 1997. *Gender and Ethnicity in Ancient Italy*. London.

Corvisier, J.-N. and Suder, W. 1996. *Polyanthropia – Oliganthropia: Bibliographie de la démographie du monde grec*. Wroclaw.

Corvisier, J.-N. and Suder, W. 2000. *La population de l'antiquité classique*. Paris.

Côte, M. (ed.) 2002. *Le Sahara, cette "autre Méditerranée"*. Aix-en-Provence (= *Méditerranée* 99.3–4).

Cottier, M. et al. 2008. *The Customs Law of Asia*. Oxford.

Cotton, H. M. 1995. The Archive of Salome Komaise, Daughter of Levi: Another Archive from the "Cave of Letters". *ZPE* 105: 171–208.

Cotton, H., Cockle, W. and Millar, F. 1995. The Papyrology of the Roman Near East: a Survey. *JRS* 85: 214–35.

Courtois, C., Leschi, L., Perrat, C., and Saumagne, C. 1952. *Tablettes Albertini, Actes privés de l'époque Vandale*. Paris.

Cowan, J. K. (ed.) 2000. *Macedonia: the Politics of Identity and Difference*. London.

Cox, C. 1998. *Household Interests: Property, Marriage Strategies, and Family Dynamics in Ancient Athens*. Princeton.

Crawford, D. J. 1971. *Kerkeosiris. An Egyptian Village in the Ptolemaic Period*. Cambridge.

Crawford, M. H. 1969. *Roman Republican Coin Hoards*. London.

Crawford, M. H. 1970. Money and Exchange in the Roman World. *JRS* 60: 40–48.

Crawford, M. H. 1974. *Roman Republican Coinage*. Cambridge.

Crawford, M. H. 1985. *Coinage and Money Under the Roman Republic: Italy and the Mediterranean Economy*. London.

Crawford, M. H. (ed.). 1996. *Roman Statutes*. 2 vols. London.

Crawford, M. H. and Whitehead, D. 1983. *Archaic and Classical Greece: a Selection of Ancient Sources in Translation*. Cambridge.

Cribiore, R. 1996. *Writing, Teachers and Students in Graeco-Roman Egypt*. Atlanta.

Cribiore, R. 2001. *Gymnastics of the Mind. Greek Education in Hellenistic and Roman Egypt*. Princeton.

Cristofani, M. (ed.) 1990. *La grande Roma dei Tarquinii* (exhibition catalog Rome).

Croke, B. 2001. *Count Marcellinus and his Chronicle*. Oxford.

Crook, J. 1967. *Law and Life of Rome*. Ithaca, NY.

Crossan, J. 1991. *The Historical Jesus. The Life of a Mediterranean Jewish Peasant*. Edinburgh.

Crowther, N. 1993. Numbers of Contestants in Greek Athletic Contests. *Nikephoros* 6: 39–52.

Cruse, A. 2003. *Roman Medicine*. Stroud.

Csapo, E. 2005. *Theories of Mythology*. Malden, MA.

Culham, P. 1990. Decentering the Text: The Case of Ovid. *Helios* 17: 161–70.

Culham, P. 1997. Did Roman Women Have an Empire? In M. Golden and P. Toohey (eds), *Inventing Ancient Culture: Historicism, Periodization, and the Ancient World*. London. 192–204.

Culler, J. 1975. *Structuralist Poetics: Structuralism, Linguistics and the Study of Literature*. London.

Culler, J. 1997. *Literary Criticism: a Very Short Introduction*. Oxford.

Cumont, F. 1922. *After Life in Roman Paganism*. New Haven.

Cumont, F. 1956. *The Mysteries of Mithra*. New York.

Cunliffe, B. 1997. *The Ancient Celts*. London.

Cunliffe, B. 2001. *Facing the Ocean: The Atlantic and Its Peoples, 8000 BC–AD 1500*. Oxford.

Cunliffe, B. 2004. *Iron Age Communities in Britain: An Account of England, Scotland and Wales from the 7th Century BC until the Roman Conquest*. 4th edn. London.

Cunliffe, B. *The Celts: a Very Short Introduction*. Oxford.

Cunningham, A. 1997. *The Anatomical Renaissance: The Resurrection of the Anatomical Projects of the Ancients*. Aldershot.

Cuomo, S. 2007. *Technology and Culture in Greek and Roman Antiquity*. Cambridge.

Curran, J. 2000. *Pagan City and Christian Capital: Aspects of Rome in the Fourth Century*. Oxford.

Curtius, E. 1953. *European Literature in the Latin Middle Ages*. Princeton.

D'Arms, J. 1981. *Commerce and Social Standing in Ancient Rome*. Cambridge, MA.

Dagron, G. 1974. *Naissance d'une capitale: Constantinople et ses institutions de 330 à 451*. Paris.

Dal Lago, E. and Katsari, K. 2008. *Slave Systems. Ancient and Modern*. Cambridge.

Dalby, A. 1996. *Siren Feasts*. London.

Dalby, A. 2002. Levels of Concealment: the Dress of *Hetairai* and *Pornai* in Greek Texts. In Llewellyn-Jones 2002d: 111–24.

Dalby, A. 2003. *Food in the Ancient World from A to Z*. London.

Dalton, H. 1964. *Principles of Public Finance*. 4th edn. London.

Daly, G. 2002. *Cannae: the Experience of Battle in the Second Punic War*. London.

Dandov, J., Selinsky, P., and Voigt, M. 2002. Celtic Sacrifice. *Archaeology* 55(1): 44–49.

Danforth, L. 1995. *The Macedonian Conflict: Ethnic Nationalism in a Transnational World*. Princeton.

Danforth, L. 2000. Alexander the Great and the Macedonian Conflict. In J. Roisman (ed.), *Brill's Companion to Alexander the Great*. Leiden.

Daniels, P. T. and Bright, W. 1996. *The World's Writing Systems*. New York.

Darbyshire, G., Mitchell, S., and Vardar, L. 2000. The Galatian Settlement in Asia Minor. *Anatolian Studies* 50: 75–97.

Daremberg, C. and Saglio, E. 1877–1919. *Dictionnaire des Antiquités Grecques et Romaines*. Paris.

Daris, S. 1968. *Spoglio lessicale papirologico*. Milan.

Daunton, M. 2001. *Trusting Leviathan. The Politics of Taxation in Britain, 1799–1914*. Cambridge.

David, J. 1996. *The Roman Conquest of Italy*. Oxford.

Davidson, J. 1997. *Courtesans and Fishcakes*. London.

Davidson, J. 2000a. Gnesippus Paigniagraphos. The Comic Poets and the Erotic Mime. In J. Wilkins and D. Harvey (eds), *The Rivals of Aristophanes*. London. 41–64.

Davidson, J. 2000b. Review article. *Classical Review* 50: 532–36.

Davidson, J. 2001. Dover, Foucault and Greek Homosexuality. Penetration and the Truth of Sex. *Past and Present* 170: 3–51 (= Osborne 2004a: 78–118).

Davidson, J. 2004b. *Liaisons Dangereuses*. Aphrodite and the Hetaera. *JHS* 124: 169–73.

Davidson, J. 2006a. Making a Spectacle of Her(self): The Greek Courtesan and the Art of the Present. In M. Feldman and B. Gordon (eds), *The Courtesan's Arts: Cross-cultural Perspectives*. Oxford. 29–51.

Davidson, J. 2006b. Revolutions in Human Time. In S. Goldhill and S. Osborne (eds), *Rethinking Revolutions Through Ancient Greece*. Cambridge. 29–67.

Davidson, J. 2007. *The Greeks and Greek Love*. London.

Davies, J. 1999. *Death, Burial and Rebirth in the Religions of Antiquity*. London.

Davies, J. K. 1993. *Democracy and Classical Greece*. 2nd edn. London.

Davies, P. J. E. 2000. *Death and the Emperor*. Cambridge.

Davies, P. R., Brooke, G. J. and Callaway, P. R. (eds) 2002. *The Complete World of the Dead Sea Scrolls*. London.

Davies, R. 1971. The Roman Military Diet. *Britannia* 2: 122–42.

Davies, W. D. 1999. Paul: From the Jewish Point of View. In Horbury et al. 1999: 678–730.

Davies, W. D. and Sanders, E. P. 1999. Jesus: From the Jewish Point of View. In Horbury et al. 1999: 618–77.

Dawson, D. 1996. *The Origins of Western Warfare*. Boulder, CO.

de Alarcão, J. 1988. *Roman Portugal*. Warminster.

de Callataÿ, F. 1995. Calculating Ancient Coin Production: Seeking a Balance. *Numismatic Chronicle* 155: 289–311.

de Callataÿ, F. 1997. *Recueil quantitatif des emissions monétaires hellénistiques*. Wetteren.

de Callataÿ, F. 2003. *Recueil quantitatif des emissions monétaires archaïques et classiques*. Wetteren.

de Certeau, M. 1988. *The Writing of History*. New York.

de Laet, S. J. 1949. *Portorium. Étude sur l'organisation douanière chez les Romaines, surtout à l'époque du haut empire*. Bruges.

de Ligt, L. 1990. Demand, Supply, Distribution: The Roman Peasantry between Town and Countryside: Rural Monetization and Peasant Demand. *Münstersche Beiträge zur Antiken Handelsgeschichte* 9: 24–56.

de Ligt, L. 1991. Demand, Supply, Distribution: The Roman Peasantry between Town and Countryside II: Supply, Distribution and a Comparative Perspective. *Münstersche Beiträge zur Antiken Handelsgeschichte* 10: 33–77.

de Ligt, L. and Northwood, S. (eds) 2008. *People, land and politics: demographic developments and the transformation of Roman Italy 300 BC–AD 14*. Leiden.

De Maria, S. 1988. *Gli archi onorari di Roma e dell'Italia romana*. Rome.

de Neeve, P. W. 1990. A Roman Landowner and His Estates: Pliny the Younger. *Athenaeum* 78: 363–42.

de Neeve, P. W. 1984. *Colonus. Private Farm-tenancy during the Republic and the Early Empire*. Amsterdam.

de Polignac, F. 1995. *Cults, Territory, and the Origins of the Greek City-State*. Chicago (published in French 1984).

de Romilly, J. 1977. *The Rise and Fall of States according to Greek Authors*. Ann Arbor.

de Souza, P. 1999. *Piracy in the Graeco-Roman World*. Cambridge.

de Ste. Croix, G. E. M. 1953. Demosthenes' TIMHMA and the Athenian *Eisphora* in the Fourth Century. *Classica et Mediaevalia* 14: 30–70.

de Ste. Croix, G. E. M. 1954. Aspects of the "Great" Persecution. *Harvard Theological Review* 47: 73–113.

de Ste. Croix, G. E. M. 1963. Why were the Early Christians Persecuted? *Past and Present* 26: 6–38.

de Ste. Croix, G. E. M. 1981. *The Class Struggle in the Ancient Greek World from the Archaic Age to the Arab Conquests*. London.

de Vos, M. 2000. *Rus Africum. Terra Acqua Olio nell'Africa settentrionale*. Trento.

Dean-Jones, L. 1994. *Women's Bodies in Classical Greek Science*. New York.

Decker, M. 2001. Food for an Empire: Wine and Oil Production in North Syria. In S. Kingley and M. Decker (eds), *Economy and Exchange in the East Mediterranean during Late Antiquity*. Oxford. 69–86.

Decret, F. and Fantar, M. 1998. *L'Afrique du nord dans l'antiquite*. Paris.

Degrassi, A. 1965. *Inscriptiones Latinae liberae rei publicae, imagines*. Berlin.

Del Tutto Palma, L. (ed.) 1996. *La tavola di Agnone nel contesto italico: Convegno di studi: Agnone 13–15 aprile 1994*. Florence.

DeLaine, J. 1997. *The Baths of Caracalla. A Study in the Design, Construction, and Economics of Large-Scale Building Projects in Imperial Rome*. JRA Suppl. 25. Portsmouth, RI.

DeLaine, J. 1999. The Romanitas of the Railway Station. In Biddis and Wyke 1999: 145–60.

DeLaine, J. 2004. Designing for a Market: "Medianum" Apartments at Ostia. *JRA* 17: 146–76.

DeLaine, J. 2005. The Commercial Landscape of Ostia. In MacMahon and Price 2005: 29–47.

Delamarre, X. 2003. *Dictionnaire de la langue gauloise*. 2nd edn. Paris.

Delattre, D. 1995. Contrat d'apprentissage d'un joueur d'*auloi*. In A. Muller (ed.), *Instruments, musiques et musiciens de l'antiquité classique*. Lille. 55–69.

Delorme, J. 1960. *Gymnasion. Etude sur les monuments consacrés à l'éducation en Grèce*. Paris.

Demand, N. 1980. Review of Dover 1978. *AJP* 101: 121–24.

Demand, N. 1994. *Birth, Death, and Motherhood in Classical Greece*. Baltimore, MD.

DeMille, C. B. 1960. *Cecil B. DeMille. Autobiography*. London.

Dench, E. 1995. *From Barbarians to New Men: Greek, Roman and Modern Perceptions of Peoples from the Central Apennines*. Oxford.

Dench, E. 1997. From Sacred Springs to the Social War: Myths of Origins and Questions of Identity in the Central Apennines. In Cornell and Lomas 1997: 43–52.

Dench, E. 2005. *Romulus' Asylum: Roman Identities from the Age of Alexander to the Age of Hadrian*. Oxford.

Depauw, M. 1997. *A Companion to Demotic Studies*. Brussels.

Désy, P. 1993. *Recherches sur l'économie apulienne au IIe et au Ier siècle avant notre ère*. Brussels.

Detienne, M. 1986. *The Creation of Mythology*. Chicago.

Detienne, M. 1994. *The Gardens of Adonis*. Princeton.

Detienne, M. and Vernant J-P. 1989. *The Cuisine of Sacrifice Among the Greeks*. Chicago.

Devereux, G. 1967. Greek Pseudo-Homosexuality. *Symbolae Osloenses* 42: 69–92.

Devereux, G. 1970. The Nature of Sappho's Seizure. *CQ* 20: 17–31.

DeVries, K. 1997. The "Frigid Eromenoi" and Their Wooers Revisited: A Closer Look at Greek Homosexuality in Vase Painting. In M. Duberman (ed.), *Queer Representations: Reading Lives, Reading Cultures*. New York. 14–24.

Di Vita, A. 1982. Gli *emporia* di Tripolitania dall'età di Massinissa a Diocleziano: un profilo storico-istituzionale. *ANRW* II.10.2: 515–95.

Dickmann, J. 1999. *Domus Frequentata*. Munich.

Dietler, M. 1994. "Our Ancestors the Gauls": Archaeology, Ethnic Nationalism, and the Manipulation of Celtic Identity in Modern Europe. *American Anthropologist* 96: 584–605.

Dietler, M. 1998. A Tale of Three Sites: The Monumentalization of Celtic Oppida and the Politics of Collective Memory and Identity. *World Archaeology* 30.1: 72–89.

Dietler, M. 1999. Rituals of Commensality and the Politics of State Formation in the "Princely" Societies of Early Iron Age Europe. In P. Ruby (ed.), *Les princes de la protohistoire et l'émergence de l'état*. Naples: 135–52.

Dionisotti, A. 1982. From Ausonius' Schooldays? A Schoolbook and its Relatives. *JRS* 72: 83–125.

Dixon, S. 1988. *The Roman Mother*. Norman, OK.

Dixon, S. 1992. *The Roman Family*. Baltimore.

Dixon, S. (ed.) 2001. *Childhood, Class and Kin in the Roman World*. London.

Docter, R., Chelbi, F., and Telmini, B. 2003. Carthage Bir Massouda. Preliminary Report on the First Bilateral Excavations of Ghent University and the Institut National du Patrimoine (2002–2003). *Bulletin Antieke Beschaving* 78: 43–70.

Docter, R., Niemeyer, H., Nijboer, A., and van der Plicht, J. 2004 [2005]. Radiocarbon Dates of Animal Bones in the Earliest Levels of Carthage. *Mediterranea* 1: 557–73.

Dodd, D. and Faraone, C. (eds) 2003. *Initiation in Ancient Greek Rituals and Narratives: New Critical Perspectives*. London.

Domergue, C. 1983. *La Mine Antique d'Aljustrel (Portugal) et les Tables de Bronze de Vipasca.* Paris.

Domergue, C. 1990. *Les mines de la péninsule ibérique dans l'Antiquité romaine.* Rome.

Donadoni, S. (ed.) 1997. *The Egyptians.* Chicago.

Donahue, A. and Fullerton, M. (eds) 2003. *Ancient Art and its Historiography.* Cambridge.

Donahue, J. 2005. *The Roman Community at Table During the Principate.* Ann Arbor.

Dougherty, C. 1993. *The Poetics of Colonization: From City to Text in Archaic Greece.* New York.

Dougherty, C. 2001. *The Raft of Odysseus: The Ethnographic Imagination of Homer's Odyssey.* New York.

Dover, K. 1978. Greek Homosexuality. London.

Dover, K. 1988. Greek Homosexuality and Initiation. In K. Dover, *The Greeks and Their Legacy, Collected Papers, ii.* Oxford. 115–34.

Drew, W. M. 2001. *D. W. Griffith's "Intolerance" – Its Genesis and Its Vision.* Jefferson.

Drew-Bear, T., Thomas, C. M., and Yıldızturan, M. 1999. *Phrygian Votive Steles.* Ankara.

Drews, R. 1993. *The End of the Bronze Age. Changes in Warfare and the Catastrophe ca.1200 BC.* Princeton.

Drijvers, H. and Healey, J. 1998. *The Old Syriac Inscriptions of Edessa and Osrhoene.* Leiden.

Drioton, E. and Vandier, J. 1962. *Les peuples de l'Orient méditerranéen II: L'Egypte.* 4th edn. Paris.

Droysen, J. G. 1877–78. *Geschichte des Hellenismus.* Gotha (repr. Basel 1952).

duBois, P. 1982. *Centaurs and Amazons: Women and the Prehistory of the Great Chain of Being.* Ann Arbor.

duBois, P. 1988. *Sowing the Body: Psychoanalysis and Ancient Representations of Women.* Chicago.

Ducrey, P. 1985. *Warfare in Ancient Greece.* New York.

Dudley, D. 1967. *Urbs Roma. A Source Book of Classical Texts on the City and Its Monuments.* New York.

Dunbabin, K. 2003. *The Roman Banquet: Images of Conviviality.* Cambridge.

Duncan, C. and Tandy, D. (eds) 1994. *From Political Economy to Anthropology: Situating Economic Life in Past Societies.* Montreal.

Duncan-Jones, R. 1974. The Finances of the Younger Pliny. In R. Duncan-Jones, *The Economy of the Roman Empire: Quantitative Studies.* Cambridge. 17–32.

Duncan-Jones, R. 1978. Review of Huttunen 1974. *JRS* 68: 195–97.

Duncan-Jones, R. 1990. *Structure and Scale in the Roman Economy.* Cambridge.

Duncan-Jones, R. 1994. *Money and Government in the Roman Empire.* Cambridge.

Duncan-Jones, R. 1996. The Impact of the Antonine Plague. *JRA* 9: 108–36.

Duval, P. M. 1985. *Recueil des inscriptions gauloises.* Paris.

Dyson, S. 1992. *Community and Society in Roman Italy.* Baltimore.

Dyson, S. 2003. *The Roman Countryside.* London.

Dyson, S. 2006. *In Pursuit of Ancient Pasts: A History of Classical Archaeology in the Nineteenth and Twentieth Centuries.* New Haven.

Eagleton, T. 1991. *An Introduction to Ideology.* New York.

Earl, D. 1961. *The Political Thought of Sallust.* Cambridge.

Easterling, P. and Knox, B. (eds) 1985. *The Cambridge History of Classical Literature*, vol. 1: *Greek literature.* Cambridge.

Easterling, P., and Muir, J. (eds) 1985. *Greek Religion and Society.* Cambridge.

Eck, W. 1986. Augustus' administrative Reformen: Pragmatismus oder systematisches Handeln? *Acta Classica* 29: 105–20 = idem. *Die Verwaltung des Römischen Reiches in der Hohen Kaiserzeit. Ausgewählte und erweiterte Beiträge* I. Basel, 1995. 83–102.

Eck, W. 1989. Inschriften und Grabbauten in der Nekropole unter St. Peter. In *Vom frühen Griechentum bis zur römischen Kaiserzeit*. Wiesbaden. 55–90.

Eck, W. 1995–. *Die Verwaltung des Römischen Reiches in der hohen Kaiserzeit: ausgewählte und erweiterte Beiträge*. Basel.

Eck, W. 1996. *Tra epigrafia, prosopografia e archeologia: scritti scelti, rielaborati ed aggiornati*. Rome.

Eck, W., Caballos, A., and Fernández Gómez, F. 1996. *Das Senatus consultum de Cn. Pisone patre*. Munich.

Eckhel, J. H. 1792–8. *Doctrina Numorum Veterum*. Leipizg.

Eckstein, A. 2006. *Mediterranean Anarchy, Interstate War, and the Rise of Rome*. Berkeley.

Edelstein, E. and L. 1945. *Asclepius: a Collection and Interpretation of the Testimonies*. 2 vols. Baltimore.

Edmondson, J. 1987. *Two Industries in Roman Lusitania: Mining and Garum Production*. Oxford.

Edmondson, J. 1999. The Cultural Politics of Spectacle in the Greek East, 167–66 BCE. In Bergmann and Kondoleon 1999: 77–96.

Edwards, C. 1993. *The Politics of Immorality*. Cambridge.

Edwards, C. 1994. Beware of Imitations: Theatre and Subversion of Imperial Identity. In J. Elsner and J. Masters (eds), *Reflections of Nero*. London. 83–97.

Edwards, C. 1996. *Writing Rome: Textual Approaches to the City*. Cambridge.

Edwards, C. (ed.) 1999. *Roman Presences: Receptions of Rome in European Culture 1789–1945*. London.

Edwards, C. and Woolf, G. (eds) 2003. *Rome the Cosmopolis*. Cambridge.

Edwards, M. 1993. Lucian and the Rhetoric of Philosophy. *Acta Classica* 62: 195–202.

Edwards, M. 1994. *The Attic Orators*. Bristol.

Eginitis, D. 1908. Le climat de l'Attique. *Annales de Géographie* 17: 413–32.

Ehling, K., Pohl, D., and Sayar, M. 2004. *Kulturbegegnung in einem Brückenland. Gottheiten und Kulte als Indikatoren von Akkulturationsprozessen im Ebenen Kilikien*. Bonn.

Ehrenberg, V. 1969. *The Greek State*. London.

Ehrman, B. 2003. *The New Testament and Other Early Christian Writings: A Reader*, 2nd edn. Oxford.

Eich, A. 2006. *Die politische Ökonomie des antiken Griechenland (6.–3. Jahrhundert v. Chr.)*. Köln.

Eilberg-Schwartz, H. and Doniger, W. (eds) 1995. *Off with her Head! The Denial of Women's Identity in Myth, Religion, and Culture*. Berkeley.

Eisen, U. 2000. *Women Office-Holders in Early Christianity: Epigraphical and literary studies*. Collegeville.

Eldridge, D. 2006. *Hollywood's History Films*. London.

Elek, P. and E., and Johnston, M. 1967. *The Age of the Grand Tour*. London.

Elias, A. et al. 2007. Active Thrusting Offshore Mount Lebanon: Source of the Tsunamigenic AD 551 Beirut-Tripoli earthquake. *Geology* 35: 755–58.

Elley, D. 1984. *The Epic Film*. London and New York.

Ellis, P. B. 1990. *The Celtic Empire: The First Millennium of Celtic History, 1000 BC–AD 51*. London.

Ellis, S. 2000. *Roman Housing*. London.

Elsner, J. 2001. Structuring Greece. In Alcock et al. 2001: 1–20.

Elton, G. R. 2002. *The Practice of History*. London.

Elton, H. 1996. *Warfare in Roman Europe, AD 350–425*. Oxford.

Engels, D. 1978. *Alexander the Great and the Logistics of the Macedonian Army*. Berkeley.

Erdkamp, P. 1999. *Hunger and the Sword. Warfare and Food Supply in Roman Republican Wars (264–30 BC)*. Amsterdam.

Erdkamp, P. 2001. Beyond the Limits of the "Consumer City": A Model of the Urban and Rural Economy in the Roman World. *Historia* 50: 332–56.

Erdkamp, P. (ed.) 2007. *Companion to the Roman Army*. Oxford.

Eribon, D. 1994. *Foucault et ses contemporains*. Paris.

Errington, R. M. 2008. *A History of the Hellenistic World 323–30 BC*. Oxford.

Erskine, A. 2001. *Troy between Greece and Rome: Local Tradition and Imperial Power*. Oxford.

Erskine, A. (ed.) 2003. *A Companion to the Hellenistic World*. Oxford.

Erskine, A. 2005. Unity and Identity: Shaping the Past in the Greek Mediterranean. In E. Gruen (ed.), *Cultural Borrowings and Ethnic Appropriations in Antiquity*. Stuttgart. 121–36.

Esch, A. 2005. *Wiederverwendung von Antike im Mittelalter*. Berlin.

Evans Grubbs, J. 1995. *Law and Family in Late Antiquity: the Emperor Constantine's Marriage Legislation*. Oxford.

Evans Grubbs, J. 2002. *Women and the Law in the Roman Empire: a Sourcebook on Marriage, Divorce and Widowhood*. London.

Evans, J. K. 1980. *Plebs rustica*. The Peasantry of Classical Italy. *AJAH* 5: 19–47 and 134–73.

Evans-Pritchard, E. E. 1976. *Magic, Witchcraft, and Oracles among the Azande*. Oxford.

Eyben, E. 1980/81. Family Planning in Graeco-Roman Antiquity. *Ancient Society* 11/12: 5–82.

Fagerström, K. 1988. *Greek Iron Age Architecture*. Göteborg.

Fantham, E., Foley, H., Kampen, N., Pomeroy, S. and Shapiro, H. 1994. *Women in the Classical World*. New York.

Faraone, C. 1999. *Ancient Greek Love Magic*. Cambridge, MA.

Faraone, C. and McClure. L. (eds) 2006. *Prostitutes and Courtesans in the Ancient World*. Madison.

Farber, W. 1983. Die Vergöttlichung Naram-Sins. *Orientalia* 52: 67–72.

Faulkner, R. O. 1969. *The Ancient Egyptian Pyramid Texts*. Oxford.

Faulks, K. 2000. *Political Sociology: A Critical Introduction*. New York.

Fawcett, P. 2006. Athenian Taxation from the Pisistratids to Lycurgus 550–325 BC. Unpublished PhD dissertation, Durham.

Fear, A. 2005. A Journey to the End of the World. In J. Elsner and I. Rutherford (eds), *Pilgrimage in Graeco-Roman and Early Christian Antiquity*. Oxford. 319–32.

Feeney, D. 1998. *Literature and Religion at Rome: Cultures, Contexts, and Beliefs*. Cambridge.

Feldman, L. H. 1993. *Jew and Gentile in the Ancient World: Attitudes and Interactions from Alexander to Justinian*. Princeton.

Felton, D. 1999. *Haunted Greece and Rome*. Austin.

Fentress, E. 2001. Villas, Wine and Kilns: the Landscape of Jerba in the Late Hellenistic Period. *JRA* 14: 249–68.

Fentress, E. 2005. Toynbee's Legacy: Southern Italy after Hannibal. *JRA* 18: 482–88.

Fentress, E. 2006. Romanizing the Berbers. *Past and Present* 190: 3–33.

Fentress, E. and J. 2001. The Hole in the Donut. *Past and Present* 173: 203–19.

Ferchiou, N. 1987. Le paysage funéraire pré-romain dans deux régions céréalières de Tunisie antique. *Antiquités africaines* 23: 13–70.

Fernández Cruz, M. C. 1995. *Iberia in Prehistory*. Oxford.

Ferrari, G. 2002. *Figures of Speech: Men and Maidens in Ancient Greece.* Chicago.

Figueira, T. 1998. *The Power of Money: Coinage and Politics in the Athenian Empire.* Philadelphia.

Finley, M. I. 1971. *The Ancestral Constitution.* Cambridge.

Finley, M. I. 1973. *The Ancient Economy.* 1st edn (3rd edn 1999). London.

Finley, M. I. 1975. *The Use and Abuse of History.* New York.

Finley, M. I. (ed.) 1976a. *Studies in Roman Property.* Cambridge.

Finley, M. I. 1976b. Private Farm Tenancy in Italy Before Diocletian. In Finley 1976a: 103–22.

Finley, M. I. 1978. *The World of Odysseus.* 2nd rev. edn. London.

Finley, M. I. 1980. *Ancient Slavery and Modern Ideology.* London.

Finley, M. I. 1981a. The Ancient City from Fustel de Coulanges to Max Weber and Beyond. In M. I. Finley, *Economy and Society in Ancient Greece.* London: 3–23.

Finley, M. I. 1981b. *The Legacy of Greece. A New Appraisal.* Oxford.

Finley, M. I. 1983. *Politics in the Ancient World.* Cambridge.

Finley, M. I. 1985. Foreword. In Easterling and Muir 1985: xiii–xx.

Finley, M. I. 1999. *The Ancient Economy.* 3rd edn. Berkeley (1st edn 1973).

Fisher, N. 1998. Gymnasia and the Democratic Values of Leisure. In P. Cartledge, P. Millett, and S. von Reden (eds), *Kosmos: Essays in Order, Conflict and Community in Classical Athens.* Cambridge. 84–104.

Fisher, N. 2000. Symposiasts, Fish-Eaters and Flatterers: Social Mobility and Moral Concerns. In D. Harvey and J. Wilkins (eds), *The Rivals of Aristophanes.* London. 355–96.

Fisher, N. 2001. *Aeschines* Against Timarchos, *Translated with Introduction and Commentary.* Oxford.

Flaig, E. 1992. *Den Kaiser herausfordern. Die Usurpationen im Römischen Reich.* Frankfurt.

Flanders, J. 2006. *Consuming Passions. Leisure and Pleasure in Victorian Britain.* London.

Fleming, D. 2004. *Democracy's Ancient Ancestors.* Cambridge.

Flemming, R. 2000. *Medicine and the Making of Roman Women. Gender, Nature, and Authority from Celsus to Galen.* Oxford.

Flemming, R. 2003. Empires of Knowledge: Medicine and Health in the Hellenistic World. In Erskine 2003: 449–63.

Flemming, R. 2007. Women, Writing and Medicine in the Classical World. *CQ* 57: 257–79.

Flint-Hamilton, K. B. 1999. Legumes in Ancient Greece and Rome: Food, Medicine, or Poison? *Hesperia* 68: 371–85.

Flodoard, *Historia remensis ecclesiae,* ed. M. Stratmann, 1998. *Flodoard von Reims. Die Geschichte der Reimser Kirche, MGH Scriptores* 36. Hannover.

Flower, H. 1996. *Ancestor Masks and Aristocratic Power in Roman Culture.* Oxford.

Foley, H. P. (ed.) 1999. *The Homeric Hymn to Demeter: Translation, Commentary, and Interpretive Essays.* Princeton.

Foraboschi, D. 1967. *Onomasticon alterum papyrologicum. Supplemento al Namenbuch di F. Preisigke.* Milan.

Forbes, C. 1933. *Neoi. A Contribution to the Study of Greek Associations.* Middletown, CT.

Forbes, H. 1992. The Ethnoarchaeological Approach to Ancient Greek Agriculture. Olive Cultivation as a Case Study. In B. Wells (ed.) *Agriculture in Ancient Greece.* Stockholm. 87–104.

Fornara, C. 1971. *Herodotus. An Interpretative Essay.* Oxford.

Fornara, C. 1983a. *Archaic Times to the End of the Peloponnesian War.* Translated Documents of Greece and Rome, vol. 1. 2nd edn. Cambridge.

Fornara, C. 1983b. *The Nature of History in Ancient Greece and Rome.* Berkeley.

Forshey, G. 1992. *American Religious and Biblical Spectaculars.* Westport.

Fotheringham, J. (ed.) 1905. *The Bodleian Manuscript (Auct.T.II) of Jerome's Version of the Chronicle of Eusebius.* Oxford.

Fotheringham, J. (ed.) 1923. *Eusebii Pamphili Chronici canones latini vertiti adauxit ad sua tempora produxit S. Eusebius Hieronymus.* London.

Foucault, M. 1978. *The History of Sexuality: Volume I: An Introduction.* New York.

Foucault, M. 1984. *The Foucault Reader* (ed. P. Rabinow). New York.

Foucault, M. 1985. *The Use of Pleasure.* New York.

Foucault, M. 1986. *The Care of the Self.* New York.

Foucault, M. 1994. *Dits et Écrits.* 4 vols. Paris.

Fountas, P. G. 2006. To Buzantino anaktoriko puriathrio. In *Proceedings of the Second International Conference on Ancient Greek Technology.* Athens. 527–34.

Fowler, D. 1997. On the Shoulders of Giants: Intertextuality and Classical Studies. *Materiali e Discussioni* 39: 13–34; repr. in D. Fowler, *Roman Constructions: Readings in Postmodern Latin.* Oxford, 2000. 115–37.

Fox, M. V. 1985. *The Song of Songs and the Ancient Egyptian Love Songs.* Madison.

Foxhall, L. 1990. The Dependent Tenant: Land Leasing and Labour in Italy and Greece. *JRS* 80: 97–114.

Foxhall, L. 2007. *Olive Cultivation in Ancient Greece: Seeking the Ancient Economy.* Oxford.

Foxhall, L., and Forbes, H. 1982. Sitometreia. The Role of Grain as a Staple Food in Classical Antiquity. *Chiron* 12: 41–90.

Frank, T. 1916. Race Mixture in the Roman Empire. *AHR* 21: 689–708.

Frank, T. 1924. Roman Census Statistics from 225 to 28 BC. *CP* 19: 329–41.

Frank, T. 1940. *An Economic Survey of Ancient Rome V. Rome and Italy of the Empire.* Baltimore.

Frayn, J. 1979. *Subsistence Farming in Roman Italy,* London.

Frayn, J. 1984. *Sheep-Rearing and the Wool Trade in Italy During the Roman Period.* London.

Frazer, A. (ed.) 1998. *The Roman Villa: Villa Urbana.* Philadelphia.

Frederiksen, M. W. 1984. *Campania* (ed. N. Purcell). London.

Fredriksen, P. 2000. *From Jesus to Christ: The Origins of the New Testament Image of Jesus.* rev. edn. New Haven.

Freeman, P. 2007. *The Best Training Ground for Archaeologists: Francis Haverfield and the Invention of Romano-British Archaeology.* Oxford.

Freestone, I. 2003. Primary Glass Sources in the Mid-First Millennium A. D. *Annales du 15e Congres de l'Association Internationale pour l'Histoire du Verre,* 111–15.

French, R. 2003. *Medicine Before Science. The Business of Medicine from the Middle Ages to the Enlightenment.* Cambridge.

Frend, W. H .C. 1965. *Martyrdom and Persecution in the Early Church.* Oxford.

Frend, W. H. C. 1984. *The Rise of Christianity.* London.

Freyne, S. 2004. *Jesus. A Jewish Galilean.* London.

Frézouls, E. 1987. Rome ville ouverte. Réflexions sur les problèmes de l'expansion urbaine d'Auguste à Aurelien. In *L'Urbs. Espace urbain et histoire Iᵉʳ siècle av. J.-C. – IIIᵉ siècle ap. J.-C.* Rome. 373–92.

Friedländer, L. 1922. *Darstellungen aus der Sittengeschichte Roms,* 4 vols. Leipzig, 10th edn. (Translation as Friedländer, L. 1908–13. *Roman Life and Manners under the Early Empire,* 4 vols [tr. J. H. Freese, A. B. Gough, and L. A. Magnus]. New York.)

Frier, B. 1980. *Landlords and Tenants in Imperial Rome.* Princeton.

Frier, B. 1985. *The Rise of the Roman Jurists. Studies in Cicero's* Pro Caecina. Princeton.

Frier, B. 1994. Natural Fertility and Family Limitation in Roman Marriage. *CP* 90: 318–33.

Frier, B. 2000. The Demography of the Early Roman Empire. In *CAH*² 11: 787–816.

Fülle, G. 1997. The Internal Organization of the Arretine *Terra Sigillata* Industry: Problems of Evidence and Interpretation. *JRS* 87: 111–55.

Gaballa, G. A. 1977. *The Memphite Tomb-Chapel of Mose*. Warminster.

Gabrielsen, V. 1994. *Financing the Athenian Fleet. Public Taxation and Social Relations*. Baltimore.

Gaca, K. L. 2003. *The Making of Fornication: Eros, Ethics, and Political Reform in Greek Philosophy and Early Christianity*. Berkeley.

Gagarin, M. and Cohen, D. (eds) 2005. *Cambridge Companion to Ancient Greek Law*. Cambridge.

Galinsky, K. 1994. Roman Poetry in the 1990s. *Classical Journal* 89: 297–309.

Galinsky, K. 1996. *Augustan Culture: an Interpretive Introduction*. Princeton.

Galinksy, K. (ed.) 2005. *Cambridge Companion to the Age of Augustus*. Cambridge.

Gallant, T. W. 1991. *Risk and Survival in Ancient Greece. Reconstructing the Rural Domestic Economy*. Cambridge.

Gammie, J. G. 1986. Herodotus on Kings and Tyrants: Objective Historiography or Conventional Portraiture? *Journal of Near Eastern Studies* 45: 171–85.

Gantz, T. 1993. *Early Greek Myth: A Guide to Literary and Artistic Sources*. Baltimore.

García Morá, F. 1991. *Quinto Sertorio. Roma*. Granada.

García y Bellido, A. 1963. Hercules Gaditanus. *Archivo Español de Arqueologia* 36: 70–153.

Gardiner-Garden, J. 1987. Dareios' Scythian Expedition and its Aftermath. *Klio* 69: 326–50.

Gardner, J. F. 1986. *Women in Roman Law and Society*. Bloomington.

Gardner, J. F. 1998. *Family and Familia in Roman Law and Life*. Oxford.

Gardner, J. F. and Wiedemann, T. 1991. *The Roman Household: A Sourcebook*. London.

Garlan, Y. 1975. *War in the Ancient World: A Social History* (trans. J. Lloyd). London.

Garland, R. 1990. Priests and Power in Classical Athens. In Beard and North 1990: 75–91.

Garland, R. 1990. *The Greek Way of Life: from Conception to Old Age*. Ithaca, NY.

Garland, R. 2001. *The Greek Way of Death*. 2nd edn. Bristol.

Garlick, B., Dixon, S., and Allen, P. (eds) 1992. *Stereotypes of Women in Power: Historical Perspectives and Revisionist Views*. New York.

Garnsey, P. 1976. Urban Property Investment. In Finley 1976a: 123–36.

Garnsey, P. (ed.) 1980. *Non-Slave Labour in the Greco-Roman World*. Cambridge.

Garnsey, P. 1988, *Famine and Food Supply in the Graeco-Roman World: Responses to risk and crisis*. Cambridge.

Garnsey, P. 1991. The Generosity of Veyne. (review of Veyne 1976) *JHS* 81: 164–8.

Garnsey, P. 1996. *Ideas of Slavery from Aristotle to Augustine*. Cambridge.

Garnsey, P. 1998. *Cities, Peasants and Food in Classical Antiquity* (ed. W. Scheidel). Cambridge.

Garnsey, P. 1999. *Food and Society in Classical Antiquity*. Cambridge.

Garnsey, P. 2002. The Land. In *CAH*² 11: 679–709.

Garnsey, P. and Whittaker, C. (eds) 1978. *Imperialism in the Ancient World*. Cambridge.

Garnsey, P., Hopkins, K., and. Whittaker, C. (eds) 1983. *Trade in the Ancient Economy*. London.

Garnsey, P. and Whittaker, C. (eds) 1983. *Trade and Famine in Classical Antiquity*. Cambridge.

Garnsey, P. and Saller, R. 1987. *The Roman Empire: Economy, Society, Culture*. London.

Garofalo, I. 1988. *Erasistrati Fragmenta*. Pisa.

Garrard, T. F. 1982. Myth and Metrology: the Early Trans-Saharan Gold Trade. *Journal of African History* 23: 443–61.

Gauthier, P. 1976. *Un commentaire historique des "Poroi" de Xénophon*. Geneva.

Gauthier, P. 1985. *Les cités grecques et leurs bienfaiteurs.* Paris.

Gauthier, P. and Hatzopoulos, M. 1993. *La loi gymnasiarque de Beroia.* Athens.

Gazda, E. (ed.) 1991. *Roman Art in the Private Sphere.* Ann Arbor.

Geertz, C. 1963. *Peddlers and Princes, Social Development and Economic Change in Two Indonesian Towns.* Chicago.

Geertz, C. 1973. *The Interpretation of Cultures.* New York.

Geertz, C. 1979. Suq: The Bazaar Economy in Sefrou. In C. Geertz, H. Geertz and L. Roan, *Meaning and Order in Moroccan Society.* Cambridge.

Gellner, E. 1983. *Nations and Nationalism.* Oxford.

Gentili, B. 1988. The Ways of Love in the Poetry of *Thiasos* and Symposium. In B. Gentili, *Poetry and its Public.* Baltimore. 72–104.

Gentili, B. and Cerra, G. 1975. *Le teorie del discorso storico nel pensiero greco e la storiografia romana arcaica.* Urbino.

George, A. R. 1999. *The Epic of Gilgamesh. The Babylonian Epic Poem and Other Texts in Akkadian and Sumerian.* London.

George, M. 1997. *The Roman Domestic Architecture of Northern Italy.* Oxford.

George, M. (ed.) 2005. *The Roman Family in the Empire: Rome, Italy, and Beyond.* Oxford.

Georges, P. 1987 [1995]. Darius in Scythia: The Formation of Herodotus' Sources and the Nature of the Campaign. *AJAH* 12: 97–147.

Gersh, S. 1986. *Middle Platonism and Neo-Platonism: the Latin Tradition.* Notre Dame.

Giardina, A. (ed.) 2000. *Storia di Roma dall'antichità a oggi. Roma antica.* Rome.

Giardina, A. and Vauchez, A. 2000. *Il Mito di Romada Carlo Magno a Mussolini.* Rome.

Gibbon, E. 1776–88. *The History of the Decline and Fall of the Roman Empire.* London (modern edition with introduction by D. Womersley, Harmondsworth, 1994).

Gill, D. W. J. 1990. *Antiquities of the Grand Tour.* Cambridge.

Gilliver, K. 1999. *The Roman Art of War.* Stroud.

Giovannini, A. 1982. La clause territoriale de la paix d'Apamée. *Athenaeum* 60: 224–36.

Gjerstad, E. 1953–63. *Early Rome* I–VI. Lund.

Glassner, J. J. 2003. *Writing in Sumer. The Invention of Cuneiform,* ed. and transl. by Z. Bahrani and M. Van De Mieroop. Baltimore.

Gleason, M. 1990. Semiotics of Gender. In F. Zeitlin, J. Winkler, D. Halperin (eds), *Before Sexuality.* Princeton. 389–415.

Gleason, M. 1995. *Making Men. Sophists and Self-Presentation in Ancient Rome.* Princeton.

Glinister, F. 2000. The Rapino Bronze, the Touta Marouca, and Sacred Prostitution in Early Central Italy. In A. Cooley (ed.), *The Epigraphic Landscape of Roman Italy.* London. 19–38.

Goedicke, H. 1967. *Königliche Dokumente aus dem Alten Reich.* Wiesbaden.

Goerhing, J. 1992. The Origins of Monasticism. In H. Attridge and G. Hata (eds), *Eusebius, Christianity and Judaism.* Leiden. 235–55.

Goff, B. (ed.) 2005. *Classics and Colonialism.* London.

Gold, B. and Donahue, J. 2005. *Roman Dining.* Baltimore.

Golden, E. 1996. *Vamp. The Rise and Fall of Theda Bara.* New York.

Golden, M. 1990. *Children and Childhood in Classical Athens.* Baltimore.

Golden, M. and Toohey, P. 2003. *Sex and Difference in Ancient Greece and Rome.* Edinburgh.

Goldhill, S. 1987. The Great Dionysia and Civic Ideology. *JHS* 107: 58–76.

Goldhill, S. 2000. Civic Ideology and the Problem of Difference: The Politics of Aeschylean Tragedy, Once Again. *JHS* 120: 34–56.

Goldhill, S. 2002. *Who needs Greek? Contests in the Cultural History of Hellenism.* Cambridge.

Goldsworthy, A. 1996. *The Roman Army at War, 100 BC–AD 200*. Oxford.

Gonzalez, J. 1986. The *Lex Irnitana*: a New Copy of the Flavian Municipal Law. *JRS* 76: 147–243.

Goodman, M. (ed.) 2002. *Oxford Handbook of Jewish Studies*. Oxford.

Goodman, M. 2007. *Rome and Jerusalem: The Clash of Ancient Civilisations*. London.

Gordon, A. E. 1958–1965. *Album of Dated Latin Inscriptions*. Berkeley.

Gordon, A. E. 1983. *Illustrated Introduction to Latin Epigraphy*. Berkeley.

Gould, J. 1985. On Making Sense of Greek Religion. In Easterling and Muir 1985: 1–33.

Gould, J. 1994. Herodotus and Religion. In S. Hornblower (ed.) *Greek Historiography*. Oxford. 91–106.

Gourevitch, D. 2001. *I giovani pazienti di Galeno: per una patocenosi dell'impero romano*. Rome.

Gowers, E. 1993. *The Loaded Table*. Oxford.

Grabbe, L. 1996. *An Introduction to First Century Judaism. Jewish Religion and History in the Second Temple Period*. London.

Grabbe, L. 2000. *Judaic Religion in the Second Temple Period: Belief and Practice from the Exile to Yavneh*. London.

Gradel, I. 2002. *Emperor Worship and Roman Religion*. Oxford.

Graf, A. 1882–83. *Roma nella memoria e nelle immaginazioni del medio evo* I–II. Torino.

Graf, F. 2003. Initiation: a Concept with a Troubled Past. In Dodd and Faraone 2003: 3–24.

Grafton, A. 1983. *Joseph Scaliger: a Study in the History of Classical Scholarship*. Oxford.

Gran-Aymerich, E. 1998. *Naissance de l'archeogie moderne*. Paris.

Grandet, P. 1994. *Le papyrus Harris I (BM 9999)*. 2 vols. Cairo.

Grant, M. 2000. *Galen on Food and Diet*. London.

Grayson, A. K. 1975a. *Assyrian and Babylonian Chronicles*. Locust Valley, NY.

Grayson, A. K. 1975b. *Babylonian Historical-Literary Texts*. Toronto.

Green, M. (ed.) 1995. *The Celtic World*. London.

Green, P. (trans). 1987. *Herodotus. The History*. Chicago.

Greene, E. (ed.) 1996. *Reading Sappho: Contemporary Approaches*. Berkeley.

Greene, K. 1986. *The Archaeology of the Roman Economy*. Berkeley.

Greene, K. 2000. Technical Innovation and Economic Progress in the Ancient World: M. I. Finley reconsidered. *Economic History Review* 53: 29–59.

Greene, K. 2005. Roman Pottery: Models, Proxies and Economic Interpretation. *JRA* 18: 34–56.

Greene, M. 2000. Great Idea. In Speake 2000: 688–90.

Greenhalgh, M. 1989. *The Survival of Roman Antiquities in the Middle Ages*. London.

Gregorius, Magister, 1987. *Narracio de mirabilibus urbis Romae*. Translated with introduction and commentary in J. L. Osborne, *The Marvels of Rome*. Toronto.

Grelot, P. 1972. *Documents araméens d'Egypte*. Paris.

Grendler, P. 1989. *Schooling in Renaissance Italy. Literacy and Learning, 1300–1600*. Baltimore.

Grey, C. 2007. Contextualizing *Colonatus*: The *Origo* of the Late Roman Empire. *JRS* 97: 155–75.

Griffin, M. 1972. The Elder Seneca and Spain. *JRS* 62: 1–19.

Griffin, M. 1976. *Seneca: a Philosopher in Politics*. Oxford.

Griffiths, J. G. 1970. *Plutarch's De Iside et Osiride*. Wales.

Grimal, N. 1992. *A History of Ancient Egypt*. Trans. I. Shaw. Oxford.

Grmek, M. 1989. *Diseases in the Ancient Greek World*. Baltimore.

Grodzynski, D. 1974. Superstitio. *REA* 76: 36–60.

Gros, P. 2001. *L'architecture romaine*, vol. 2: *Maisons, villas, palais et tombeaux*. Paris.

Grove, A. and Rackham, O. 2001. *The Nature of Mediterranean Europe: An Ecological History*. New Haven.

Gruen, E. 1974. *The Last Generation of the Roman Republic*. London.

Gruen, E. 2002. *Diaspora: Jews Amidst Greeks and Romans*. Cambridge, MA.

Gsell, S. 1901. *Les monuments antiques de l'Algérie*, vol. 2. Paris.

Guarducci, M. 1967–78. *Epigrafia greca*. Rome.

Guarducci, M. 1987. *L'epigrafia greca dalle origini al tardo impero*. Rome.

Guichard, V., Sievers, S., and Urban, O.-H. (eds) 2002. *Les processus d'urbanisation à l'âge du Fer. Eisenzeitliche Urbanisationsprozesse*. Glux-en-Glenne.

Guilaine, J. 1994. *La mer partagée: la Méditerranée avant l'écriture, 7000–2000 avant Jésus-Christ*. Paris.

Guilhembet, J.-P. 2001. Les résidences aristocratiques de Rome, du milieu du Ier siècle av. n.è. à la fin des Antonins. *Pallas* 55: 215–41.

Gunderson, E. 2000. *Staging Masculinity. The Rhetoric of Performance in the Roman World*. Ann Arbor.

Gunderson, E. 2003. *Declamation, Paternity, and Roman Identity. Authority and the Rhetorical Self*. Cambridge.

Gutas, D. 1998. *Greek Thought. Arabic Culture: the Graeco-Arabic Translation Movement in Baghdad and early Abbasid Society* (2nd–4th/8th–10th centuries). London.

Guttmann, A. 2004. *Sports: the First Five Millennia*. Amherst, MA.

Habermann, W. 1998. Zur chronologischen Verteilung der papyrologischen Zeugnisse. *ZPE* 122: 144–60.

Habermann, W. 2000. *Zur Wasserversorgung einer Metropole in kaiserzeitlichen Ägypten*. Munich.

Habicht, C. 1997. *Athens from Alexander to Antony*. Cambridge, MA.

Habinek, T. 1998. *The Politics of Latin Literature: Writing, Identity, and Empire in Ancient Rome*. Princeton.

Haensch, R. 1997. *Capita Provinciarum. Statthaltersitze und Provinzialverwaltung in der römischen Kaiserzeit*. Mainz.

Hagen, F. 2005. The Prohibitions: a New Kingdom Didactic Text. *JEA* 91: 125–64.

Hahneman, G. 1992. *The Muratorian Fragment and the Development of the Canon*. Oxford.

Hales, S. 2003. *The Roman House and Social Identity*. Cambridge.

Haley, E. W. 2003. *Baetica Felix*. Austin.

Hall, E. 1989. *Inventing the Barbarian: Greek Self-Definition Through Tragedy*. Oxford.

Hall, E. 1996. When is a Myth Not a Myth? Bernal's "Ancient Model". In Lefkowitz and Rogers 1996: 333–48. Reprinted in Harrison 2002b: 133–52.

Hall, J. M. 1997. *Ethnic Identity in Greek Antiquity*. Cambridge.

Hall, J. M. 2002. *Hellenicity: Between Ethnicity and Culture*. Chicago.

Hall, J. M. 2006. *A History of the Archaic Greek World. ca.1200–479 BCE*. Oxford.

Hall, S. G. 2005. *Doctrine and Practice in the Early Church*. 2nd edn. London.

Hallett, J. P. 1984. *Fathers and Daughters in Roman Society: Women and the Elite Family*. Princeton.

Hallett, J. P. 1989. Women as *Same* and *Other* in the Classical Roman Elite. *Helios* 16: 59–78.

Hallett, J. P. 1993. Feminist Theory, Historical Periods, Literary Canons, and the Study of Greco-Roman Antiquity. In Rabinowitz and Richlin 1993: 44–72.

Halliwell, S. 1990. The Sounds of the Voice in Old Comedy. In E. M. Craik (ed.), *"Owls to Athens"*. Oxford. 69–79.

Halperin, D. 1990. *One Hundred Years of Homosexuality*. London.

Halstead, P. 1987. Traditional and Ancient Rural Economies in Mediterranean Europe: Plus Ça Change? *JHS* 107: 77–87.

Hamel, D. 2003. *Trying Neaira. The True Story of a Courtesan's Scandalous Life*. New Haven.

Hamilakis, Y. and Yalouri, E. 1996. Antiquities as Symbolic Capital in Modern Greek Society. *Antiquity* 70: 117–329.

Hands, A. R. 1968. *Charities and Social Aid in Greece and Rome*. London.

Hannibal ad portas: Macht und Reichtum Karthagos. 2004. Edited by Badischen Landesmuseum Karlsruhe. Stuttgart.

Hansen, M. 1985. *Demography and Democracy: The Number of Athenian Citizens in the Fourth Century BC*. Herning.

Hansen, M. 1987. *The Athenian Assembly in the Age of Demosthenes*. Oxford.

Hansen, M. 1989. On the Importance of Institutions in an Analysis of Athenian Democracy. *Classica et Mediaevalia* 40: 107–13.

Hansen, M. 2003. 95 Theses About the Greek Polis in the Archaic and Classical Periods. A Report on the Results Obtained by the Copenhagen Polis Project 1993–2003. *Historia* 52: 257–82.

Hansen, M. 2006a. *The Shotgun Method: The Demography of the Ancient Greek City-State Culture*. Columbia, MO.

Hansen, M. 2006b. *Polis. An Introduction to the Ancient Greek City-State*. Oxford.

Hansen, M. and Nielsen, T. 2004. *An Inventory of Archaic and Classical Poleis*. Oxford.

Hanson, A. E. 1979. Documents from Philadelphia Drawn from the Census Register. *Actes du Xve congrès international de papyrologie* (Papyrologica Bruxellensia 16). Brussels: 60–74.

Hanson, A. E. 1984. Caligulan Month-Names at Philadelphia and Related Matters. *Atti del XVII congresso internazionale di papirologia* III. Naples. 1108–18.

Hanson, A. E. 1990. P. Princeton I 13: Text and Context Revised. In M. Capasso, G. M. Savorelli, and R. Pintaudi (eds), *Miscellanea Papyrologica* (Papyrologica Florentina 19): 259–83.

Hanson, A. E. 1996. Fragmentation and the Greek Medical Writers. In G. Most (ed.), *Collecting Fragments*. Göttingen. 289–314.

Hanson, R. P. C. 1988. *The Search for the Christian Doctrine of God: the Arian Controversy 318–81*. Edinburgh.

Hanson, V. 1983. *Warfare and Agriculture in Ancient Greece*. Pisa.

Hanson, V. 1989. The Western Way of War. Oxford (2nd edn 2000).

Hanson, V. 1995. *The Other Greeks: The Family Farm and the Agrarian Roots of Western Civilization*. New York (2nd edn 1999).

Hanson, V. 1999. The Status of Ancient Military History: Traditional Work, Recent Research and On-Going Controversies. *Journal of Military History* 63: 379–414.

Hanson, V. 2000. Hoplite Battle as Ancient Greek Warfare: When, Where and Why? In van Wees 2000: 201–32.

Harding, P. 1985. *From the End of the Peloponnesian War to the Battle of Ipsus*. Translated Documents of Greece and Rome 2. Cambridge.

Hardwick, L. 2000. *Translating Words, Translating Cultures*. London.

Hardwick, L. 2003. *Reception Studies*. Oxford.

Harlow, M. and Laurence, R. 2002. *Growing Up and Growing Old in Ancient Rome: a Life Course Approach*. London.

Harris, E. M. 2002. Workshop, Marketplace and Household: the Nature of Technical Specialization in Classical Athens and its Influence on Economy and Society. In Cartledge, Cohen and Foxhall 2002: 67–99.

Harris, W. 1971. *Rome in Etruria and Umbria*. Oxford.

Harris, W. 1979. *War and Imperialism in Republican Rome, 327–70 BC*. Oxford.

Harris, W. 1984. The Italians and the Empire. In W. Harris (ed.), *The Imperialism of Mid-Republican Rome*. Rome. 89–113.

Harris, W. 1989. *Ancient Literacy*. Cambridge, MA.

Harris, W. 1994. Child-Exposure in the Roman Empire. *JRS* 84: 1–22.

Harris, W. (ed.) 1999. *The Transformation of "Urbs Roma" in Late Antiquity*. JRA Suppl. 33. Portsmouth, RI.

Harris. W. (ed.) 2005. *Rethinking the Mediterranean*. Oxford.

Harrison, A. R. W. 1968–71. *The Law of Classical Athens*. 2 vols. Oxford.

Harrison, S. (ed.) 2005. *A Companion to Latin Literature*. Oxford.

Harrison, T. 2000a. *The Emptiness of Asia: Aeschylus' Persians and the History of the Fifth Century*. London.

Harrison, T. 2000b. *Divinity and History. The Religion of Herodotus*. Oxford.

Harrison, T. 2002a. The Persian Invasions. in E. Bakker, I. de Jong, and H. van Wees (eds), *Brill's Companion to Herodotus*. Leiden. 551–78.

Harrison, T. (ed.) 2002b. *Greeks and Barbarians*. Edinburgh.

Hartog, F. 1988. *The Mirror of Herodotus: The Representation of the Other in the Writing of History*, tr. J. Lloyd. Berkeley.

Haselberger, L. 2007. *Urbem adornare. Rome's urban metamorphosis under Augustus*. Portsmouth, RI.

Haskell, F. and Penny, N. 1981. *Taste and the Antique. The Lure of Classical Sculpture 1500–1900*. New Haven.

Hatzopoulos, M. V. 2000–03. Νέο ἀπότμημα ἀπὸ τὴν ῎Αφυτι τοῦ ἀττικοῦ. ψηφίσματος περὶ νομίσματος, σταθμῶν καὶ μέτρων. *Horos* 14–16: 31–43.

Hauken, T. 1998. *Petition and Response*. Bergen.

Häussler, R. 2002. Writing Latin – From Resistance to Assimilation: Language, Culture and Society in N. Italy and S. Gaul. In A. Cooley (ed.), *Becoming Roman, Writing Latin. Literacy and Epigraphy in the Roman West*. Portsmouth, RI. 61–75.

Hawass, Z. (ed.) 2002. *Egyptology at the Dawn of the Twenty-first Century*. 2 vols. Cairo.

Hawhee, D. 2004. *Bodily Arts. Rhetoric and Athletics in Ancient Greece*. Austin, TX.

Hayes, W. C. 1953–59. *The Scepter of Egypt*. 2 vols. New York.

Head, B. V. 1911. *Historia Numorum*. 2nd edn. Oxford.

Heather, P. 2005. *The Fall of the Roman Empire*. London.

Heitland, W. 1921. *Agricola. A Study of Agriculture and Rustic Life in the Greco-Roman World From the Point of View of Labour*. Cambridge.

Helck, W. et al. 1975–92. *Lexikon der Ägyptologie*. 7 vols plus indexes and supplements, Wiesbaden.

Helm, R. (ed.) 1956. Eusebius-Jerome, *Chronicon*. In *Eusebius Werke 7. Die griechischen christlichen Schriftsteller der ersten Jahrhundert 7*. 2nd edn. Berlin.

Hemelrijk, E. 1999. *Matrona docta: Educated Women in the Roman Elite from Cornelia to Julia Domna*. London.

Hengel, M. 1989. *The Zealots: Investigations into the Jewish Freedom Movement in the Period from Herod I until AD 70*. Edinburgh.

Henig, M. 1984. *Religion in Roman Britain*. London.

Henneberg, M., Henneberg, R., and Carter, J. 1992. Health in Colonial Metaponto. *National Geographic Research and Exploration* 8: 446–59.

Henrichs, A. 1968. Vespasian's visit to Alexandria. *ZPE* 3: 51–80.

Henry, M. M. 1995. *Prisoner of History: Aspasia of Miletus and her Biographical Tradition.* New York.

Herring, E. 1995. Emblems of Identity. An Examination of the Use of Matt-Painted Pottery in the Native Tombs of the Salento Peninsula in the 5th and 4th Centuries BC. In N. Christie (ed.), *Papers of the Fifth Conference of Italian Archaeology, Settlement and Economy, 1500 BC–AD 1500.* Oxford. 135–42.

Herring, E. 2000. "To see oursels as others see us!" The Construction of Native Identities in Southern Italy. In Herring and Lomas 2000: 45–78.

Herring, E. and Lomas, K. (eds) 2000. *The Emergence of State Identities in Italy in the 1st Millennium BC.* London.

Herter, H. 2003. The Sociology of Prostitution in Antiquity in the Context of Pagan and Christian Writings. In Golden and Toohey 2003: 57–113.

Hicks, U. K. 1968. *Public Finance.* 3rd edn. Cambridge.

Hill, T. D. 2004. *Ambitiosa Mors.* London.

Hin, S. 2008. Counting Romans. In de Ligt and Northwood 2008: 187–238.

Hinard, F. and Dumont, J. C. 2003. *Libitina. Pompes funèbres et supplices en Campanie à l'époque d'Auguste.* Paris.

Hindley, C. 1991. Debate: Law, Society, and Homosexuality in Classical Athens. *Past and Present* 133: 167–83.

Hindley, C. 1994. Eros and Military Command in Xenophon. *CQ* 44: 347–66.

Hindley, C. 1999. Xenophon on Male Love. *CQ* 49: 74–99.

Hingley, R. 2000. *Roman Officers and English Gentlemen: the Imperial Origins of Roman Archaeology.* London.

Hingley, R. 2005. *Globalizing Roman Culture: Unity, Diversity and Empire.* London.

Hingley, R. 2008. *The Recovery of Roman Britain 1586–1906.* Oxford.

Hirschfeld, Y. 2004. A Climatic Change in the Early Byzantine Period? Some Archaeological Evidence. *Palestine Exploration Quarterly* 136.2: 133–49.

Hitchner, R. B. 2008. Globalization *avant la lettre*: Globalization and the History of the Roman Empire. *New Global Studies* 2 (http://www.bepress.com/ngs/vol2/iss2/art2).

Hobsbawm, E. 1990. *Nations and Nationalism since 1780.* Cambridge.

Hobsbawm, E. and Ranger, T. (eds) 1983. *The Invention of Tradition.* Cambridge.

Hoch, J. E. 1994. *Semitic Words in Egyptian Texts of the New Kingdom and Third Intermediate Period.* Princeton.

Hodder, I. 1991. *Reading the Past.* Cambridge.

Hodge, A. T. 1991. *Roman Aqueducts and Water Supply.* London.

Hohti, P., 1975. Aulus Caecina the Volaterran: Romanization of an Etruscan. In P. Bruun (ed.), *Studies in the Romanization of Etruria.* Rome.

Hölkeskamp, K.-J. 2000. The Roman Republic: Government of the People, by the People, for the People? *Scripta Classica Israelica* 19: 203–23.

Hölkeskamp, K.-J. 2001a. Fact(ions) or Fiction? Friedrich Münzer and the Aristocracy of the Roman Republic – Then and now. *International Journal of the Classical Tradition* 8: 92–105.

Hölkeskamp, K.-J. 2001b. Capitol, Comitium und Forum. Öffentliche Räume, sakrale Topographie und Erinnerungslandschaften der römischen Republik. In S. Faller (ed.), *Studien zu antiken Identitäten.* Würzburg. 97–132.

Hölkeskamp, K.-J. 2004. The Polis and its Spaces – the Politics of Spatiality. *Ordia Prima* 3: 25–40.

Hölkeskamp, K.-J. 2006. History and Collective Memory in the Middle Republic. In Rosenstein and Morstein-Marx 2006: 478–95.

Hölkeskamp, K.-J. and Stein-Hölkeskamp, E. (eds) 2006. *Erinnerungsorte der Antike. Die römische Welt.* Munich.

Holloway, R. R. 1994. *The Archaeology of Early Rome and Latium.* London.

Holum, K. G. 1982. *Theodosian Empresses: Women and Imperial Dominion in Late Antiquity.* Berkeley.

Homeyer, H. 1965. *Lukian: wie man Geschichte schreiben soll.* Munich.

Hong, S., Candelone, J.-P., Patterson, C. and Boutron, C. 1994. Greenland Evidence of Hemispheric Lead Pollution Two Millennia Ago by Greek and Roman Civilizations. *Science* 265: 1841–43.

Hong, S., Candelone, J.-P., Patterson, C., and Boutron, C. 1996. History of Ancient Copper Smelting Pollution During Roman and Medieval Times Recorded in Greenland Ice. *Science* 272: 246–49.

Honoré, T. 1962. *Gaius.* Oxford.

Honoré, T. 1978. *Tribonian.* London.

Honoré, T. 1994. *Emperors and Lawyers.* 2nd edn. Oxford.

Honoré, T. 1998. *Law in the Crisis of Empire, 379–455 AD.* Oxford.

Honoré, T. 2002. *Ulpian.* 2nd edn. Oxford.

Hooker, J. T. 1990. *Reading the Past: Ancient Writing from Cuneiform to the Alphabet.* Berkeley.

Hope, V. and Marshall, E. (eds) 2000. *Death and Disease in the Ancient City.* London.

Hopkins, K. 1966. On the Probable Age Structure of the Roman Population. *Population Studies* 20: 245–64.

Hopkins, K. 1978a. Economic Growth and Towns in Classical Antiquity. In P. Abrams and E. A. Wrigley (eds), *Towns in Societies.* Cambridge. 35–77.

Hopkins, K. 1978b. *Conquerors and Slaves: Sociological Studies in Roman History 1.* Cambridge.

Hopkins, K. 1980. Taxes and Trade in the Roman Empire (200 BC–AD 400). *JRS* 70: 101–25.

Hopkins, K. 1983. *Death and Renewal.* Cambridge.

Hopkins, K. 1993. Novel Evidence for Roman Slavery. *Past and Present* 138: 3–27.

Hopkins, K. 1995/6. Rome, Taxes, Rents and Trade. *Kodai* 6/7: 41–75 (repr. in Scheidel and von Reden 2002: 190–230).

Hopkins, K. 1996. Review of Luciana Jacobelli, *Le Pitture Erotiche delle Terme Suburbane di Pompei. TLS* (18.10.1996).

Hopkins, K. 1998. Christian Number and its Implications. *Journal of Early Christian Studies* 6: 185–226.

Hopkins, K. 1999. *A World Full of Gods: Pagans, Jews, and Christians in the Roman Empire.* London.

Hoppa, R. and Vaupel, J. (eds) 2002. *Paleodemography: Age Distributions from Skeletal Samples.* Cambridge.

Horbury, W., Davies, W., and Sturdy, J. (eds) 1999. *The Cambridge History of Judaism III: The Early Roman Period.* Cambridge.

Horden, P. and Purcell, N. 2000. *The Corrupting Sea. A study of Mediterranean History.* Oxford.

Horden, P. and Purcell, N. 2006. The Mediterranean and "the New Thalassology". *AHR* 111: 722–40.

Horn, R. and Rüger, C. (eds) 1979. *Die Numider: Reiter und Könige nördlich der Sahara.* Bonn.

Hornblower, S. 1980. *Mausolus*. Oxford.

Horsfall, N. 2003. *The Culture of the Roman* Plebs. London.

How, W. W. and Wells, J. 1912. *A Commentary on Herodotus in Two Volumes. vol. II (bks V–IX)*. Oxford.

Howgego, C. J. 1990. Why Did Ancient States Strike Coins? *Numismatic Chronicle* 150: 1–25.

Howgego, C. J. 1995. *Ancient History from Coins*. London.

Howgego, C. J. 2005. Coinage and Identity in the Roman Provinces. In Howgego et al. 2005: 1–17.

Howgego, C. J., Heuchert, V., and Burnett, A. M. 2005. *Coinage and Identity in the Roman Provinces*. Oxford.

Hoyos, D. 2007. The Age of Overseas Expansion (264–146 BC). In Erdkamp 2007: 63–79.

Hubbard, T. 1998. Popular Perceptions of Elite Homosexuality in Classical Athens. *Arion* ns 6: 48–78.

Hubbard, T. 2003. *Homosexuality in Greece and Rome: A Sourcebook of Basic Documents*. Berkeley.

Huet, V. 1999. Napoleon: a New Augustus? In C. Edwards 1999: 53–69.

Hughes, J. 1994. *Pan's Travail: Environmental Problems of the Ancient Greeks and Romans*. Baltimore.

Hughes, J. 2005. *The Mediterranean: an Environmental History*. Santa Barbara, CA.

Humbert, J. 1925. *Les Plaidoyers écrits et les plaidoiries réelles de Cicéron*. Paris.

Hume, D. 1998. Of the Populousness of Ancient Nations (1752). In S. Copley and A. Edgar (eds), *Selected Essays*. Oxford. 223–74.

Humphrey, J., Oleson, J., and Sherwood, A. 1998. *Greek and Roman Technology: a Sourcebook*. London.

Humphrey. J. H. 1986. *Roman Circuses: Arenas for Chariot Racing*. Berkeley.

Humphreys, S. 1983. *The Family, Women and Death: Comparative Studies*. London.

Humphreys, S. 2004. *The Strangeness of Gods. Historical Perspectives on the Interpretation of Athenian Religion*. Oxford.

Humphries, M. 2004. Review of Klauck 2000. *Irish Theological Quarterly* 69: 316–17.

Humphries, M. 2006. *Early Christianity*. Abingdon.

Hunt, E. D. 1993. Christianising the Roman Empire: The Evidence of the Code. In J. Harries and I. Wood (eds), *The Theodosian Code*. London. 143–58.

Hunt, P. 1998. *Slaves, Warfare and Ideology in the Greek Historians*. Cambridge.

Hunter, R. 1996. *Theocritus and the Archaeology of Greek Poetry*. Cambridge.

Hunter, V. 1982. *Past and Process in Herodotus and Thucydides*. Princeton.

Hunter, V. 1994. *Policing Athens: Social Control in the Attic Lawsuits, 420–320 BC*. Princeton.

Huntington, E. 1910. The Burial of Olympia: a Study in Climate and History. *Geographical Journal* 36: 657–86.

Hupperts, C. 1988. Greek Love: Homosexuality or Paederasty? Greek Love in Black Figure Vase-Painting. In J. Christiansen and T. Melander (eds), *Proceedings of the 3rd Symposium on Ancient Greek and Related Pottery*. Copenhagen. 255–68.

Hurwitt, J. 1999. *The Athenian Acropolis: History, Mythology, and Archaeology from the Neolithic Era to the Present*. Cambridge.

Huskinson, J. 1996. *Roman Children's Sarcophagi: Their Decoration and Social Significance*. Oxford.

Hutchinson, J. and Smith, A. 1996. *Ethnicity*. Oxford.

Hutton, W. 2005. *Describing Greece: Landscape and Literature in the Periegesis of Pausanias*. Cambridge.

Huttunen, P. 1974. *The Social Strata in the Imperial City of Rome.* Oulu.

Hyde Minor, H. 1999. Mapping Mussolini: Ritual and Cartography in Public Art during the Second Roman Empire. *Imago Mundi* 51: 147–62.

Imhausen, A. 2003. *Ägyptische Algorithmen.* Wiesbaden.

Immerwahr, H. 1966. *Form and Thought in Herodotus.* Cleveland.

Institut Fernand-Courby. 1971. *Nouveau choix d'inscriptions grecques; textes, traductions, commentaires.* Paris.

Isaac, B. 2004. *The Invention of Racism in Classical Antiquity.* Princeton.

Isager, S. 1998. The Pride of Halikarnassos. *ZPE* 123: 1–23.

Isager, S. and Skydsgaard, J. E. 1992. *Ancient Greek Agriculture. An Introduction.* London.

Issar, A. and Zohar, M. 2007. *Climate Change: Environment and History of the Near East.* Berlin.

Jackson, R. 1988. *Doctors and Diseases in the Roman Empire.* London.

Jaeger, M. 1997. *Livy's Written Rome.* Ann Arbor.

Jaeger, W. 1939–45. *Paideia. The Ideals of Greek Culture.* 3 vols. Oxford.

Jaeger, W. 1962. *Early Christianity and Greek Paideia.* Cambridge, MA.

Jal, P. 1963. *La guerre civile à Rome: Étude littéraire et morale.* Paris.

James, T. G. H. 1991. Egypt: The Twenty-fifth and Twenty-sixth Dynasties. In *CAH*² 3.2: 677–750.

Jameson, M. 1988. Sacrifice and Animal Husbandry in Classical Greece. In Whittaker 1988: 87–119.

Jameson, M. 1992. Agricultural Labor in Ancient Greece. In Wells 1992: 135–46.

Jameson, M., Runnels, C., and van Andel, T. 1994. *A Greek Countryside: The Southern Argolid from Prehistory to the Present Day.* Stanford.

Janssen, J. 1975. *Commodity Prices from the Ramessid Period.* Leiden.

Jashemski, W. and Meyer, F. (eds) 2001. *The Natural History of Pompeii.* Cambridge.

Jasny, N. 1950. The Daily Bread of the Ancient Greeks and Romans. *Osiris* 9: 227–53.

Jeffery, L. and Johnston, A. 1990. *The Local Scripts of Archaic Greece: a Study of the Origin of the Greek Alphabet and its Development from the Eighth to the Fifth Centuries BC.* Rev. edn. Oxford.

Jehne, M. 2006. Methods, Models and Historiography. In Rosenstein and Morstein-Marx 2006: 3–28.

Jenkyns, R. (ed.) 1992. *The Legacy of Rome: a New Appraisal.* Oxford.

Joannès, F. 2004. *The age of Empires. Mesopotamia in the First Millennium BC.* Edinburgh.

Johns, C. 1982. *Sex or Symbol: Erotic Images of Greece and Rome.* London.

Johnson, J. H. 1974. The Demotic Chronicle as a Historical Source. *Enchoria* 4: 1–17.

Johnson, J. H. (ed.) 1992. *Life in a Multi-Cultural Society: Egypt from Cambyses to Constantine and Beyond.* Chicago.

Johnson, J. H. 1994. Ancient Egyptian Linguistics. In G. Lepschy (ed.), *History of Linguistics. Volume I: Eastern Traditions of Linguistics.* London. 63–76.

Johnson, M. and Ryan, T. 2005. *Sexuality in Greek and Roman Society and Literature. A Sourcebook.* London.

Johnston, A. 1983. Die Sharing in Asia Minor: the View from Sardis. *Israel Numismatic Journal* 6–7: 59–78.

Jolowicz, H. M. and Nicholas, B. 1972. *Historical Introduction to the Study of Roman Law.* Oxford.

Jones, A. H. M. 1964. *The Later Roman Empire, 284–602: a Social, Economic and Administrative History.* Oxford.

Jones, A. H. M. 1974. Taxation in Antiquity. In *The Roman Economy. Studies in Ancient Economic and Administrative History*. P. A. Brunt (ed.). Oxford: 150–85.

Jones, C. P. 1986. *Culture and Society in Lucian*. Cambridge, MA.

Jones, C. P. 1996. The Panhellenion. *Chiron* 26: 29–56.

Jones, C. P. 1999. *Kinship Diplomacy in the Ancient World*. Cambridge, MA.

Jones, Colin. 2007. Theodore Vacquer and the Archaeology of Modernity in Haussmann's Paris. *Transactions of the Royal Historical Society* 17: 157–83.

Jones, N. F. 2004. *Rural Athens under the Democracy*. Philadelphia.

Jones, R. and Bird, D. 1972. Roman Gold-Mining in North West Spain: Workings on the Rio Duerna. *JRS* 62: 59–74.

Jones, S. 1997. *The Archaeology of Ethnicity*. London.

Jones, W. H. S. 1947. *The Medical Writings of Anonymus Londinensis*. Cambridge.

Jongman, W. 1988. *The Economy and Society of Pompeii*. Amsterdam.

Jongman, W. 2003. Slavery and the Growth of Rome. The Transformation of Italy in the Second and First Centuries BCE. In Edwards and Woolf 2003: 100–22.

Jongman, W. 2007. The Early Roman Empire: Consumption. In Scheidel, Morris and Saller 2007: chap. 22.

Joshel, S. 1992. *Work, Identity, and Legal Status at Rome: A Study of the Occupational Inscriptions*. Norman, OK.

Joshel, S. 1993. The Body Female and the Body Politic: Livy's Lucretia and Verginia. In A. Richlin (ed.), *Pornography and Representation in Greece and Rome*. New York. 112–30.

Joshel, S. 1997. Female Desire and the Discourse of Empire: Tacitus's Messalina. In J. P. Hallett and M. B. Skinner (eds), *Roman Sexualities*. Princeton. 221–54.

Joshel, S. and Murnaghan, S. (eds) 1998. *Women and Slaves in Greco-Roman Culture*. London.

Joshel, S., Malamud, M. and McGuire, D. (eds) 2001. *Imperial Projections. Ancient Rome in Modern Popular Culture*. Baltimore.

Jost, M. 1994. The Distribution of Sanctuaries in Civic Space in Arkadia. In Alcock and Osborne 1994: 217–30.

Jouffroy, H. 1986. *La construction publique en Italie et dans l'Afrique romaine*. Strasbourg.

Judson, S. 1968. Erosion Rates near Rome, Italy. *Science* 160: 1444–46.

Just, R. 1989. *Women in Athenian Law and Life*. London.

Kaczynski, B. 1988. *Greek in the Carolingian Age. The St Gall Manuscripts*. Cambridge, MA.

Kah, D. and Scholz, P. (eds) 2004. *Das hellenistische Gymnasion*. Berlin.

Kampen, N. 1982. Social Status and Gender in Roman Art: The Case of the Saleswoman. In N. Broude and M. Garrard (eds), *Feminism and Art History: Questioning the Litany*. New York. 62–77.

Kampen, N. (ed.) 1996. *Sexuality in Ancient Art*. Cambridge.

Kaplan, S. L. 1996. *The Bakers of Paris and the Bread Question 1700–1775*. London.

Kapparis, K. 1999. *Apollodoros' Against Neaira*. Berlin.

Karabel, J. 2005. *The Chosen: the Hidden History of Admission and Exclusion at Harvard, Yale and Princeton*. New York.

Karl, R. 2006. *Altkeltische Sozialstrukturen*. Budapest.

Karl, R. and Stifter, D. (eds) 2007. *The Celtic World. Critical Concepts in Historical Studies*. 4 vols. London.

Karras, R. 2000. Active/Passive, Acts/Passions: Greek and Roman Sexualities. *AHR* 105: 1250–65.

Kastelic, J. 1966. *Situla Art. Ceremonial Bronzes of Ancient Europe*. London.

Kaster, R. 1988. *Guardians of Language*. Berkeley.

Kayan, I. 1999. Holocene Stratigraphy and Geomorphological Evolution of the Aegean Coastal Plains of Anatolia. *Quaternary Science Reviews* 18: 541–48.

Keats, J. 1817. *On First Looking into Chapman's Homer*. In A. Quiller Couch (ed.), *The Oxford Book of English Verse, 1250–1900*, Oxford (1919), No. 634.

Keay, S. 1998. *Roman Spain*. London.

Keay, S. 2003. Recent Archaeological Work in Roman Iberia (1990–2002). *JRS* 93: 146–211.

Keay, S. and Terrenato, N. (eds) 2001. *Italy and the West: Comparative Issues in Romanization*. Oxford.

Kee, H. C. 1996. *Who Are the People of God? Early Christian Models of Community*. New Haven.

Keegan, J. 1976. *The Face of Battle*. London.

Keenan, J. (ed.) 2005. *The Sahara: Past, Present and Future*. London.

Kees, H. 1961. *Ancient Egypt: A Cultural Topography*. London.

Kehoe, D. 1988. *The Economics of Agriculture on Roman Imperial Estates in North Africa*. Göttingen.

Kehoe, D. 1997. *Investment, Profit and Tenancy: The Jurists and the Roman Agrarian Economy*. Ann Arbor.

Kelly, J. N. D. 1977. *Early Christian Doctrines*. 5th edn. London.

Kemp, B. J. 1978. Imperialism and Empire in New Kingdom Egypt. In Garnsey and Whittaker 1978: 7–58.

Kemp, B. J. 1989. *Ancient Egypt: Anatomy of a Civilization*. London (rev. 2006).

Kennedy, D. 1992. "Augustan" and "anti-Augustan": Reflections on Terms of Reference. In A. Powell (ed.), *Roman Poetry and Propaganda in the Age of Augustus*. Bristol. 26–58.

Kennedy, G. 1994. *A New History of Classical Rhetoric*. Princeton.

Kennedy, G. (ed.) 2003. *Progymnasmata. Greek Textbooks of Prose Composition and Rhetoric* (translated with introductions and notes). Leiden.

Kennell, N. 1995. *The Gymnasium of Virtue. Education and Culture in Ancient Sparta*. Chapel Hill.

Kenney, E. (ed.) 1982. *The Cambridge History of Classical Literature, vol. 2: Latin Literature*. Cambridge.

Kertzer, D. and Saller, R. (eds) 1991. *The Family in Italy: from Antiquity to the Present*. New Haven.

Keuls, E. 1985. *The Reign of the Phallus*. New York.

Keynes, J. M. 1936. *The General Theory of Employment, Interest and Money*. London.

Khanoussi, M. and Maurin L. 2000. *Dougga, Fragments d'histoire. Choix d'inscriptions latines éditées, traduites et commentées de Dougga (Ier–IVe siècles)*. Bordeaux.

Kienitz, F. 1953. *Die politische Geschichte Ägyptens vom 7. bis zum 4. Jahrhundert vor der Zeitwende*. Berlin.

King, H. 1995. Medical Texts as a Source for Women's History. In A. Powell (ed.), *The Greek World*. London. 199–218.

King, H. 1998. *Hippocrates' Woman: Reading the Female Body in Ancient Greece*. London.

King, H. 2001. *Greek and Roman Medicine*. Bristol.

King, K. (ed.) 1988. *Images of the Feminine in Gnosticism*. Philadelphia.

King, K. (ed.) 1997. *Women and Goddess Traditions*. Minneapolis.

King, K. 2003. *What is Gnosticism?* London.

Kinnard, R. and Davis, T. 1992. *Divine Images. A History of Jesus on the Screen*. New York.

Kinzl, K. 2006. *A Companion to the Classical Greek World*. Oxford.

Kitchen, K. A. 1995. *The Third Intermediate Period in Egypt.* Warminster.

Klauck, H.-J. 2000. *The Religious Context of Early Christianity. A Guide to Graeco-Roman Religions.* London.

Kleijwegt, M. 1991. *Ancient Youth. The Ambiguity of Youth and the Absence of Adolescence in Greco-Roman Society.* Amsterdam.

Klose, D. 2005. Festivals and Games in the Cities of the East during the Roman Empire. In Howgego et al. 2005: 125–34.

Knipfing, J. 1923. The *libelli* of the Decian Persecution. *Harvard Theological Review* 16: 345–90.

Knowles, D. 1988. *The Evolution of Medieval Thought.* 2nd edn. London.

Koch-Harnack, G. 1989. *Erotische Symbole. Lotosblüte und gemeinsamer Mantel auf antiken Vasen.* Berlin.

Koepke, N. and Baten, J. 2005. The Biological Standard of Living in Europe during the Last Two Millennia. *European Review of Economic History* 9: 61–95.

Köhne, E. and Ewigleben C. (eds) 2001. *Gladiators and Caesars: The Power of Spectacle in Ancient Rome* (Trans. R. Jackson). Berkeley.

Kolb, F. 2002. *Rom. Die Geschichte der Stadt in der Antike.* München (1st edn 1995).

Kolb, F. and Thomsen, A. 2004. Forschungen zu Zentralorten und Chora auf dem Gebiet von Kyaneai (Zentrallykien): Methoden, Ergebnisse, Probleme. In F. Kolb (ed.), *Chora und Polis.* Munich. 1–42.

König, J. 2005. *Athletics and Literature in the Roman Empire.* Cambridge.

Konstan, D. 1997. *Friendship in the Classical World.* Cambridge.

Koortbojian, M. 1995. *Myth, Meaning, and Memory on Roman Sarcophagi.* Berkeley.

Kotjabopoulou, E., Hamilakis, Y., Halstead, P., Gamble, C., and Elefanti, V. (eds) 2003. *Zooarchaeology in Greece. Recent Advances.* London.

Kraay, C. M. 1976. *Archaic and Classical Greek Coinage.* London.

Kraemer, R. S. 1992. *Her Share of the Blessings.* New York.

Kraemer, R. S. (ed.) 2004. *Women's Religions in the Greco-Roman World: A Sourcebook.* New York. (Revised edn of *Maenads, Martyrs, Matrons, Monastics*, Minneapolis, 1988).

Kraft, K. 1972. *Das System der kaiserzeitlichen Münzprägung in Kleinasien.* Berlin.

Krause, J.-U. 1994–95. *Witwen und Waisen im römischen Reich*, vols 1–4, Stuttgart.

Krautheimer, R. 1980. *Rome, Profile of a City 312–1208.* Princeton.

Krautheimer, R. 1983. *Three Christian Capitals: Topography and Politics.* Berkeley.

Krautheimer, R. 1986. *Early Christian and Byzantine Architecture.* 4th edn. Harmondsworth.

Krawiec, R. 2002. *Shenoute and the Women of the White Monastery: Egyptian Monasticism in Late Antiquity.* New York.

Krentz, P. 1997. The Strategic Culture of Periclean Athens. In C. Hamilton and P. Krentz (eds), *Polis and Polemos: Essays on Politics, War, and History in Ancient Greece in Honour of Donald Kagan.* Claremont. 55–72.

Kristiansen, K. and Larsson, T. 2005. *The Rise of Bronze Age Society: Travels, Transmissions, and Transformations.* Cambridge.

Kron, G. 2005a. Anthropometry, Physical Anthropology, and the Reconstruction of Ancient Health, Nutrition, and Living Standards. *Historia* 54: 68–83.

Kron, G. 2005b. The Augustan Census Figures and the Population of Italy. *Athenaeum* 93: 441–95.

Kuhrt, A. 1995. *The Ancient Near East c.3000–330 BC.* 2 vols. London.

Kulikowski, M. 2004. *Late Roman Spain and its Cities.* Baltimore.

Kurke, L. 1991. *The Traffic in Praise: Pindar and the Poetics of Social Economy.* Ithaca, London.

Kurke, L. 1999a. *Coins, Bodies, Games, and Gold: the Politics of Meaning in Archaic Greece.* Princeton.

Kurke, L. 1999b. Pindar and the Prostitutes, or Reading Ancient "Pornography". In J. I. Porter (ed.), *Constructions of the Classical Body.* Ann Arbor. 101–25.

Kurke, L. 2002. Gender, Politics and Subversion in the Chreiai of Machon. *PCPS* 48: 20–26.

Kurtz, D. and Boardman, J. 1971. *Greek Burial Customs.* London.

Kuttner, A. 1999. Hellenistic Images of Spectacle, Alexander to Augustus. In Bergmann and Kondoleon 1999: 97–124.

Kyle, D. 1998. *Spectacles of Death in Ancient Rome.* London.

La Regina, A. 1999. *Roma: L'archeologia del novecento e le nuove prospettive degli studi* (preface by K. Zaboklicki, introduction by C. Nylander). Rome.

La Rocca, E. 2004. Templum Traiani et columna cochlis. *RM* 111: 193–238.

La Rome impériale = La Rome impériale démographie et logistique (Coll. ÉFR 230). Rome 1997.

Lacey, W. K. 1968. *The Family in Classical Greece,* London.

Lamboley, J. L. 1996. *Recherches sur les Messapiens: IVe-IIe siècle avant J.-C.* Paris.

Lampe, P. 1989. *Die stadtrömischen Christen in den ersten beiden Jahrhunderten. Untersuchungen zur Sozialgeschichte.* 2nd edn. Tübingen.

Lancel, S. 1995. *Carthage: a History.* (trans. A. Nevill). Oxford.

Lanciani, R. 1988. *Notes from Rome* (ed. A. Cubberley). Rome.

Lanciani, R. 1989–2002. *Storia degli scavi di Roma e notizie intorno le collezioni romane di antichità* I–VII. Rome.

Landau, D. 2000. *Gladiator: the Making of the Ridley Scott Epic.* New York.

Landes, C. 2002. *La Mort des Notables en Gaule Romaine.* Lattes.

Landmesser, D. 2002. *Wirtschaftsstil und wirtschafliche Entwicklung im klassischen Athen.* Frankfurt-am-Main.

Lane Fox, R. 1986. *Pagans and Christians.* Harmondsworth.

Lane Fox, R. 2004. *The Making of Alexander.* Oxford.

Langholf, V. 1990. *Medical Theories in Hippocrates. Early texts and the "Epidemics".* Berlin and New York.

Langlands, R. 2006. *Sexual Morality in Ancient Rome.* Cambridge.

Lapidge, M., 1995. *Archbishop Theodore,* Cambridge.

Laporte, J.-P. 1992. Datation des stèles libyques figurées de Grande Kabylie. *L'Africa romana* 9: 389–423.

Larsen, M. T. 1996. *The Conquest of Assyria. Excavations in an Antique Land.* London.

Lassère, J.-M. 2005. *Manuel d'épigraphie romaine.* Paris.

Laurence, R. 1994. *Roman Pompeii: Space and Society.* London.

Laurence, R. and Wallace-Hadrill, A. (eds) 1997. *Domestic Space in the Roman World: Pompeii and Beyond.* Providence.

Lawton, B. 2004. *Various and Ingenious Machines.* Leiden.

Lazenby, J. F. 1985. *The Spartan Army.* Warminster.

Lazzarini, M. L. and Poccetti, P. 2001. *L'iscrizione paleoitalica di Tortora, in: Il mondo Enotrio tra VI e V secolo a.C., Atti dei seminari napoletani (1996–1998), Quaderni di Ostraka 1, 2.* Naples.

Le Gall, J. 1979. Les habitants de Rome et la fiscalité sous le Haut-Empire. In H. van Effenterre (ed.), *Points de vue sur la fiscalité antique.* Paris. 113–26.

Le Glay, M. 1987. Sur l'implantation des sanctuaires orientaux à Rome. In *L'Urbs. Espace urbain et histoire Ier siècle av. J.-C. – IIIe siècle ap. J.-C.* (Coll. ÈFR 98). Rome. 545–62.

Le Roy Ladurie, E. 1980. *Montaillou: Cathars and Catholics in a French village, 1294–1324.* Harmondsworth.

Leach, E. 2004. *The Social Life of Painting in Ancient Rome and on the Bay of Naples.* Cambridge.

Leahy, M. 1988. The Earliest Dated Monument of Amasis and the End of the Reign of Apries. *JEA* 74: 183–99.

Lebek, W. D. 1996. Moneymaking on the Roman Stage. In W. J. Slater (ed.), *Roman theater and society.* Ann Arbor. 29–48.

Leclant, J. 2005. *Dictionnaire de l'Antiquité*, Paris.

Lecoq, P. 1997. *Les inscriptions de la Perse achéménide.* Paris.

Lee, A. D. 2006. Traditional Religions. In N. Lenski (ed.), *The Cambridge Companion to the Age of Constantine.* Cambridge. 159–79.

Lee, A. D. 2007. *War in Late Antiquity: A Social History.* Oxford.

Lefkowitz, M. 2003. *Greek Gods, Human Lives.* New Haven.

Lefkowitz, M. and Fant, M. (eds) 1992. *Women's Life in Greece and Rome.* 2nd edn. Baltimore. Now in 3rd edn 2005.

Lefkowitz M. and Rogers, G. (eds) 1996. *Black Athena Revisited.* Chapel Hill.

Lehner, M. 1997. *The Complete Pyramids.* London.

Lelis, A., Percy, W., and Verstraete, B. 2003. *The Age of Marriage in Ancient Rome.* Lewiston.

Lendon, J. 2005. *Soldiers and Ghosts: A History of Battle in Classical Antiquity.* New Haven.

Lenski, N. 1999. Basil and the Isaurian Uprising of A. D. 375. *Phoenix* 53: 308–29.

Leone, A., Palombi, D. and Walker, S. (eds) 2007. *Res bene gestae. Ricerche di storia urbana su Roma antica in onore di Eva Margareta Steinby.* Rome.

Leveau, P. 1996. The Barbegal Water Mill in its Environment. *JRA* 9: 137–53.

Lévêque, P. 1968. La Guerre à l'époque hellénistique. In Vernant 1968: 261–87.

Levi, A. C. 1952. *Barbarians on Roman Imperial Coins and Statues.* New York.

Levine, L. I. 1998. *Judaism and Hellenism in Antiquity: Conflict or Confluence?* Seattle.

Levine, L. I. 2000. *The Ancient Synagogue: The First Thousand Years.* New Haven.

Levinskaya, I. 1996. *The Book of Acts in its Diaspora Setting.* Grand Rapids.

Lewin, J., Macklin, M., and Woodward, J. (eds) *Mediterranean Quaternary River Environments.* Rotterdam.

Lewis, M. J. T. 1997. *Millstone and Hammer.* Hull.

Lewis, N. 1974. *Papyrus in Classical Antiquity.* 2nd edn. Oxford.

Lewis, N. 1983. *Life in Egypt under Roman Rule.* Oxford.

Lewis, N. 1993. The Demise of the Demotic Document: When and Why? *JEA* 79: 276–81 = Id. *On Government and Law in the Roman Empire* (1995): 351–56.

Lewis, P. and Jones, G. 1970. Roman Gold-Mining in North West Spain, *JRS* 60: 169–85.

Lewis, S. 2002. *The Athenian Woman: An Iconographic Handbook.* London.

Lianeri, A. and Zajko, V. (eds) 2008. *Translation and the Classic: Identity as Change in the History of Culture.* Oxford.

Lichtheim, M. 1973–80. *Ancient Egyptian Literature: A Book of Readings.* 3 vols. Berkeley.

Lieberman, S. 1942. *Greek in Jewish Palestine*, New York (2nd edn 1965).

Lieberman, S. 1950. *Hellenism in Jewish Palestine*, New York (2nd edn 1962).

Liebeschuetz, J. 1979. *Continuity and Change in Roman Religion.* Oxford.

Liebeschuetz, J. 2001. *The Decline and Fall of the Roman City.* Oxford.

Lieu, S. 2004. Libanius and higher education at Antioch. In I. Sandwell and J. Huskinson (eds), *Culture and Society in Later Roman Antioch.* Oxford. 13–23.

Lieu, S. N. C. 1994. *Manichaeism in Mesopotamia and the Roman East.* Leiden.

Lightfoot, J. 2002. Nothing to do with the *Technitai* of Dionysus. In P. Easterling and E. Hall (eds), *Greek and Romans Actors: Aspects of an Ancient Profession.* Cambridge. 209–24.

Lightfoot, J. 2008. *The Sibylline Oracles.* Oxford.

Lincoln, B. 1999. *Theorizing Myth.* Chicago.

Linder, A. 1987. *The Jews in the Roman Imperial Legislation.* Detroit and Jerusalem.

Linderski, J. 1990. Mommsen and Syme: Law and Power in the Principate of Augustus. In K. A. Raaflaub and M. Toher (eds), *Between Republic and Empire: Interpretations of Augustus and his Principate.* Berkeley, Los Angeles, and London. 42–53.

Ling, R. 1991. *Roman Painting.* Cambridge.

Ling, R. 1997. *The Insula of the Menander at Pompeii.* vol. 1: *The Structures.* Oxford.

Linke, B. and Stemmler, M. (eds) 2000. *Mos Maiorum: Untersuchungen zu den Formen der Identitätsstiftung und Stabilisierung in der römischen Republik.* Stuttgart.

Lintott, A. W. 1972. Imperial Expansion and Moral Decline in the Roman Republic. *Historia* 21: 626–638.

Lipiński, E. 2000. *The Aramaeans: their Ancient History, Culture, Religion.* Leiden.

Lippi, M., Bellini, C., Trinci, C., Benvenuti, M., Pallecchi, P., and Sagri, M. 2007. Pollen Analysis of the Ship Site of Pisa San Rossore, Tuscany, Italy: the Implications for Catastrophic Hydrological Events and Climatic Change during the Late Holocene. *Vegetation History and Archaeobotany* 16: 453–65.

Lirb, H. 1993. Partners in Agriculture. The Pooling of Resources in Rural *societates* in Roman Italy. In H. Sancisi-Weerdenburg, R. Van der Spek, H. Teitler and H. Wallinga (eds), *De Agricultura.* Amsterdam. 263–95.

Lissarrague, F. 1990. *The Aesthetics of the Greek Banquet.* Princeton.

Lissarrague, F. 1999. Publicity and Performance: Kalos Inscriptions in Attic Vase-Painting. In S. Goldhill and R. Osborne (eds), *Performance Culture and Athenian Democracy.* Cambridge. 359–73.

Littré, É. 1839–61. *Œuvres complètes d'Hippocrate.* Paris.

Liverani, M. 1988. *Antico Oriente. Storia, societa, economia.* Rome.

Liverani, M. (ed.). 1993. *Akkad. The First World Empire.* Padua.

Liverani, M. 1998. *Uruk. La prima città.* Rome.

Liverani, M. 2000a. The Garamantes: a Fresh Approach. *Libyan Studies* 31: 17–28.

Liverani, M. 2000b. The Libyan Caravan Road In Herodotus IV.181–185. *Journal of the Economic and Social History of the Orient* 43: 496–520.

Livi-Bacci, M. 1997. *A Concise History of World Population.* 2nd edn (tr. Carl Ipsen). Oxford.

Livingstone, R. 1921. *The Legacy of Greece.* Oxford.

Llewellyn-Jones, L. 2002a. Eunuchs and the Royal Harem in Achaemenid Persia (559–331 BC). In S. Tougher (ed.), *Eunuchs in Antiquity and Beyond.* London. 19–49.

Llewellyn-Jones, L. 2002b. The Queen of Sheba in Western Popular Culture 1850–2000. In St. J. Simpson (ed.), *Queen of Sheba. Treasures from Ancient Yemen.* London. 12–30.

Llewellyn-Jones, L. 2002c. Celluloid Cleopatras or Did the Greeks Ever Get to Egypt? In D. Ogden (ed.), *The Hellenistic World. New Perspectives.* London. 275–304.

Llewellyn-Jones, L. (ed.) 2002d. *Women's Dress in the Ancient Greek World.* London.

Llewellyn-Jones, L. 2003. *Aphrodite's Tortoise. The Veiled Woman of Ancient Greece.* Swansea.

Llewellyn-Jones, L. 2004. The King and I. Costumes and the Making of *Alexander. Classical Association News* no. 18. December. 1–2.

Llewellyn-Jones, L. 2005. The Fashioning of Delilah. Costume Design, Historicism and Fantasy in Cecil B. DeMille's *Samson and Delilah* (1949). In L. Cleland, M. Harlow and L. Llewellyn-Jones (eds), *The Clothed Body in the Ancient World*. Oxford. 14–29.

Lloyd, A. B. 1975–88. *Herodotus Book II: Introduction and Commentary*. 3 vols. Leiden.

Lloyd, A. B. 1994. Egypt, 404–332 BC. In *CAH*² 6: 337–60.

Lloyd, A. B. (ed.) 1996. *Battle in Antiquity*. London.

Lloyd, A. B. (ed.) 1997. *What is a God? Studies in the Nature of Greek Divinity*. London.

Lloyd, G. E. R. 1979. *Magic, Reason and Experience: Studies in the Origin and Development of Greek Science*. Cambridge.

Lloyd, G. E. R. 1983. *Science, Folklore and Ideology: Studies in the Life Sciences in Ancient Greece*. Cambridge.

Lloyd, G. E. R. 2004. *In the Grip of Disease: Studies in the Greek Imagination*. Oxford.

Lloyd, J. 1991. Conclusion: Archaeological Survey and the Roman Landscape. Forms of Rural Settlement in the Early Roman Landscape. In Barker and Lloyd 1991: 233–40.

Lloyd, J. 1995. Pentri, Frentani and the Beginnings of Urbanisation (c.500–80 BC). In Barker 1995: 181–212.

Lo Cascio, E. 1994. The Size of the Roman Population: Beloch and the Meaning of the Republican Census Figures. *JRS* 84: 23–40.

Lo Cascio, E. 1997. Le procedure di recensus dalla tarda repubblica al tardo antico e il calcolo della popolazione di Roma. In *La Rome impériale: démographie et logistique*. Rome. 3–76.

Lo Cascio, E. 1999. The Population of Roman Italy in Town and Country. In J. Bintliff and K. Sbonias (eds), *Reconstructing Past Population Trends in Mediterranean Europe (3000 BC–AD 1800)*. Oxford. 161–71.

Lo Cascio, E. (ed.) 2000. *Roma imperiale. Una metropoli antica*. Rome.

Lo Cascio, E. 2001. Recruitment and the Size of the Roman Population from the Third to the First Century BCE. In Scheidel 2001d: 111–37.

Lo Cascio, E. and Storchi Marino, A. (eds) 2001. *Modalità insediative e strutture agrarie nell'Italia meridionale in età romana*. Bari.

Lo Cascio, E. and Malanima, P. 2005. Cycles and Stability: Italian Population before the Demographic Transition (225 BC–AD 1900). *Rivista di Storia Economica* 21: 197–232.

Loewenberg, A. 1978. *Annals of Opera 1597–1940*. London.

Lohmann, H. 1993. *Atene: Forschungen zu Siedlungs- und Wirtschaftstruktur des klassischen Attika*. Cologne.

Lohmann, H. 1994. Ein "alter Schafstall" in neuem Licht: die Ruinen von Palaia Kopraisia bei Legrena (Attika). In P. Doukellis and L. Mendoni (eds), *Structures rurales et sociétés antiques*. Paris. 81–132.

Lomas, K. 1993. The City in South-East Italy. Ancient Topography and the Evolution of Urban Settlement, 600–300 BC. *Accordia Research Papers* 4: 63–77.

Lomas, K. 1996. *Roman Italy, 338 BC–AD 200. A Sourcebook*. London.

Lomas, K. 1997. The Idea of a City. Elite Ideology and the Evolution of Urban Form in Italy, 200 BC–AD 200. In H. Parkins (ed.), *Roman Urbanism: Beyond the Consumer City*. London. 21–41.

Lomas, K. 2000. Cities, States and Ethnic Identity in Southeast Italy. In Herring and Lomas 2000: 79–90.

Longo, O. and Scarpi, P. 1989. *Homo Edens*. Verona.

Lonie, I. M. 1983. Literacy and the Development of Hippocratic Medicine. In F. Lasserre and P. Mudry (eds), *Formes de pensée dans la Collection hippocratique: Actes du Colloque hippocratique de Lausanne 1981*. Geneva, 145–61.

Loraux, N. 1986. *The Invention of Athens: The Funeral Oration in the Classical City* (trans. A. Sheridan). Cambridge, MA.

Loraux, N. 1993. *The Children of Athena: Athenian Ideas about Citizenship and the Division between the Sexes.* Trans. C. Levine. Princeton.

Loraux, N. 1998. *Mothers in Mourning* (trans. C. Pache). Ithaca.

Lott, J. B. 2004. *The Neighbourhoods of Augustan Rome.* Cambridge.

Lowe, N. J. 1998. Thesmophoria and Haloa: Myth, Physics, and Mysteries. In S. Blundell and M. Williamson (eds), *The Sacred and the Feminine in Ancient Greece.* London. 149–73.

Lowenthal, D. 1985. *The Past is a Foreign Country.* Cambridge.

Lucas, A. 2006. *Wind, Water, Work.* Leiden.

Luce, C. (ed.) 2000. *Paysage et alimentation dans le monde grec.* Toulouse.

Luce, T. J. 1989. Ancient Views on the Causes of Bias in Ancient Historiography. *CP* 84: 16–31.

Luckenbill, D. 1926–27. *Ancient Records of Assyria and Babylon II.* 2 vols. Chicago.

Lugli, G. et al. 1952–60. *Fontes ad topographiam veteris urbis Romae pertinentes* I–VIII. Rome.

Luhmann, N. 1995. *Social Systems.* Stanford (published in German 1984).

Lund, A. A. 1998. *Die ersten Germanen. Ethnizität und Ethnogenese.* Heidelberg.

Luraghi, N. and Alcock, S. (eds) 2003. *Helots and their Masters in Laconia and Messenia: Histories, Ideologies, Structures.* Cambridge, MA.

Lyne, R. O. A. M. 1987. *Further Voices in Virgil's* Aeneid. Oxford.

Ma, J. 1999. *Antiochus III and the Cities of Western Asia Minor.* London.

Ma, J. 2000. The epigraphy of Hellenistic Asia Minor: A Survey of Recent Research (1992–1999). *AJA* 104: 95–121.

MacDonald, W. and Pinto, J. 1995. *Hadrian's Villa and its Legacy.* New Haven.

MacDowell, D. M. 1978. *The Law in Classical Athens.* London.

MacDowell, D. M. 1986. *Spartan Law.* Edinburgh.

Mackil, E. 2004. Wandering Cities: Alternatives to Catastrophe in the Greek Polis. *AJA* 108: 493–516.

MacKinnon, M. 2004. *Production and Consumption of Animals in Roman Italy: Integrating the Zooarchaeological and Textual Evidence.* Portsmouth, RI.

MacMahon, A. and Price, J. (eds) 2005. *Roman Working Lives and Urban Living.* Oxford.

Macmillan, H. 1966. *Winds of Change.* London.

MacMullen, R. 1969. *Constantine.* New York.

MacMullen, R. 1974. *Roman Social Relations, 50 BC–AD 284.* New Haven.

Magie, D. 1950. *Roman Rule in Asia Minor.* Princeton.

Maischberger, M. 1997. *Marmor in Rom. Anlieferung, Lager- und Werkplätze in der Kaiserzeit.* Wiesbaden.

Malkin, I. 1994. *Myth and Territory in the Spartan Mediterranean.* New York.

Malkin, I. 1998. *The Returns of Odysseus: Colonization and Ethnicity.* Berkeley.

Malkin, I. (ed.) 2001. *Ancient Perceptions of Greek Ethnicity.* Washington.

Malkin. I. 2003. Networks and the Emergence of Greek Identity. *Mediterranean Historical Review* 18: 56–74 (= Malkin 2005: 56–74).

Malkin, I. (ed.) 2005. *Mediterranean Paradigms and Classical Antiquity.* London (= *Mediterranean Historical Review* 18 [2003]).

Mango, C. 1990. Constantine's Mausoleum and the Translation of Relics. *Byzantinische Zeitschrift* 83: 51–61.

Mango, C. (ed.) 2002. *The Oxford History of Byzantium.* Oxford.

Mann, M. 1986. *The Sources of Social Power.* vol. 1. Cambridge.

Manning, J. G. 2003. *Land and Power in Ptolemaic Egypt: the Structure of Land Tenure.* Cambridge.

Manning, J. G. 2008. Coinage as "Code" in Ptolemaic Egypt. In W. V. Harris (ed.), *The Monetary Systems of the Greeks and Romans.* Oxford. 84–112.

Manning, J. G. and Morris, I. (eds) 2005. *The Ancient Economy: Evidence and Models.* Stanford.

Mansouri, M. (ed.) 2000. *Le Maghreb et la Mer à travers l'histoire, Mesogeios 7.* Paris.

Marasco, G. 1987. Aspetti dell' economia cartaginese fra la seconda e la terza guerra punica. *L'Africa romana* 5: 223–28.

Marcone, A. 1997. *Storia dell'agricoltura romana. Dal mondo arcaico all età imperiale.* Rome.

Marcovich, M. 1983. Anacreon, 358 PMG. *AJP* 104: 372–83.

Marek, C. 2003. *Pontus et Bithynia. Die römischen Provinzen im Norden Kleinasiens.* Mainz.

Marenbon, J. 1981. *From the Circle of Alcuin to the School of Auxerre.* Cambridge.

Marincola, J. 1997. *Authority and Tradition in Ancient Historiography.* Cambridge.

Marincola, J. (ed.) 2007. *A Companion to Greek and Roman Historiography.* 2 vols. Oxford.

Marincola, J. (forthcoming.) "Alliance" and "Alienation": The Historian's Attitude.

Marinetti, A. M. 2003. Il "signore del cavallo" e i riflessi istituzionali dei dati di lingua. Venetica *ekupetaris.* In G. Cresci Marrone and M. Tirelli (eds), *Produzioni, merci e commerci in Altino preromana e romana.* Rome. 143–160.

Marrou, H. 1956. *A History of Education in Antiquity.* 3rd edn. New York.

Martin, A. 2007. Papyruskartell: The Papyri and the Movement of Antiquities. In Bowman, Coles et al. 2007: chap. 4.

Martin, D. B. 1996. The Construction of the Ancient Family: Methodological Considerations. *JRS* 86: 40–60.

Martin, G. T. 1991. *A Bibliography of the Amarna Period and its Aftermath: The Reigns of Akhenaten, Smenkhkare, Tutankhamun and Ay.* London.

Martin, M. and Porter, M. 1987. *Video Movie Guide 1988.* New York.

Martin, R. 1981. *Tacitus.* London and Berkeley.

Martin, R. 2003. *The Myths of the Ancient Greeks.* New York.

Martin, R. and Woodman, A. J. 1989. *Tacitus: Annals IV.* Cambridge.

Martin, T. R. 1985. *Sovereignty and Coinage in Classical Greece.* Princeton.

Martin, T. R. 1996. Why did the Greek Polis Originally Need Coins? *Historia* 45: 257–83.

Martindale, C. 1992. *Redeeming the Text: Latin Literature and the Hermeneutics of Reception.* Cambridge.

Martindale, C. 1993. Descent into Hell: Reading Ambiguity, or Virgil and the Critics. *Papers of the Virgil Society* 21: 111–50.

Martindale, C. and Thomas, R. (eds) 2006. *Classics and the Uses of Reception.* Oxford.

Martínez-Cortizas, A. et al. 1999. Mercury in a Spanish Peat Bog: Archive of Climate Change and Atmospheric Metal Deposition. *Science* 284: 939–42.

Marx, K. 1844/1978. Contribution to the Critique of Hegel's *Philosophy of Right*: Introduction. (Originally published in 1844.) In R. C. Tucker (ed.), *The Marx-Engels Reader.*[2] New York. 53–65.

Marzano, A. 2007. *Roman Villas in Central Italy. A Social and Economic History.* Leiden.

Matthews, J. 1984. The Tax Law of Palmyra: Evidence for Economic History in a City of the Roman East. *JRS* 74: 157–80.

Matthews, R. (ed.) 1998. *Ancient Anatolia. Fifty Years' Work by the British Institute of Archaeology at Ankara.* Ankara.

Mattingly, D. 1988. Oil for Export? A Comparative Study of Olive-oil Production in Libya, Spain, and Tunisia. *JRA* 1: 33–56.

Mattingly, D. 1995. *Tripolitania*. London.

Mattingly, D. 1996. From One Colonialism to Another: Imperialism and the Maghreb. In J. Webster and N. Cooper (eds), *Roman Imperialism: post-colonial perspectives*. Leicester. 49–69.

Mattingly, D. 1997. Africa: a Landscape of Resistance? In D. Mattingly (ed.), *Dialogues in Roman Imperialism*. JRA Suppl. 23. Portsmouth RI.

Mattingly, D. 2002. Vulgar and Weak "Romanization", or Time for a Paradigm Shift? *JRA* 15, 536–540.

Mattingly, D. (ed.) 2003. *The Archaeology of Fazzan: Volume 1*. London.

Mattingly, D. (ed.) 2007. *The Archaeology of Fazzan. Volume 2*. London.

Mattingly, D. and Hitchner, R. 1995. Roman Africa: An Archaeological Review. *JRS* 85: 165–213.

Mattingly, D. and Salmon, J. 2001. *Economies Beyond Agriculture in the Classical World*. London.

Mau, A. 1899. *Pompeii: its Life and Art*. New York.

Mazza, R. 2001. *L'archivio degli Apioni. Terra, lavoro e proprietà senatoria nell'Egitto tardoantico*. Bari.

McClure, L. (ed.). 2002. *Sexuality and Gender in the Classical World. Readings and Sources*. Oxford.

McClure, L. 2003. *Courtesans at Table: Gender and Literary Culture in Athenaeus*. London.

McCone, K. R. 1990: *Pagan Past and Christian Present in Early Irish Literature*. Maynooth.

McCormick, M. 2001. *Origins of the European economy: Communications and Commerce*, AD *300–900*. Cambridge.

McDonald Fraser, G. 1988. *The Hollywood History of the World*. London.

McDonald, J. I. H. 1998. *The Crucible of Christian Morality*. London.

McDonald, W. and Rupp, G. (eds) 1972. *The Minnesota Messenia Expedition: Reconstructing a Bronze Age Regional Environment*. Minneapolis.

McDonnell, M. 1991. The Introduction of Athletic Nudity. *JHS* 111: 182–93.

McDowell, A. 1990. *Village Life in Ancient Egypt: Laundry Lists and Love Songs*. Oxford.

McEvoy, B., Richards, M., Forster, P., and Bradley, D. 2004. The *longue durée* of Genetic Ancestry: Multiple Genetic Marker Systems and Celtic Origins on the Atlantic Façade of Europe. *AJHG* 75.4: 693–702.

McGing B. 2002. Population and Proselytism: How Many Jews Were There in the Ancient World? In J. R. Bartlett (ed.), *Jews in the Hellenistic and Roman Cities*, London and New York: 88–106.

McGinn, T. 1998. *Prostitution, Sexuality, and the Law in Ancient Rome*. Oxford.

McGinn, T. 2004. *The Economy of Prostitution in the Roman World: A Study of Social History and the Brothel*. Ann Arbor.

McKay, A. G. 1975. *Houses, Villas and Palaces in the Roman World*. London.

McKitterick, R. 1989. *The Carolingians and the Written Word*. Cambridge.

McKitterick, R. 1992. Knowledge of Plato's *Timaeus* in the Ninth Century and the Implications of Valenciennes, Bibliothèque Municipale MS 293. In H. Westra (ed.), *From Athens to Chartres. Neoplatonism and Medieval Thought. Studies in Honour of Edouard Jeauneau*. Leiden, 85–95. Reprinted in R. McKitterick, *Books, Scribes and Learning in the Frankish Kingdoms, Sixth to Ninth Centuries* (Aldershot, 1994), Chapter X.

McKitterick, R. 1997. Gibbon and the Early Middle Ages in Eighteenth-Century Europe. In McKitterick and Quinault 1997: 162–89.

McKitterick, R. 2004. *History and Memory in the Carolingian World*. Cambridge.

McKitterick, R. 2006. *Perceptions of the Past in the Early Middle Ages*. Notre Dame.

McKitterick, R. and Quinault, R. (eds) 1997. *Edward Gibbon and Empire*. Cambridge.

McLean, B. H. 2002. *An Introduction to Greek Epigraphy of the Hellenistic and Roman Periods from Alexander the Great down to the Reign of Constantine (323 BC–AD 337)*. Ann Arbor.

McManus, B. F. 1997. *Classics and Feminism: Gendering the Classics*. New York.

McNeill, J. R. 1992. *The Mountains of the Mediterranean World*. Cambridge.

McNicoll, A. W. 1997. *Hellenistic Fortifications from the Aegean to the Euphrates*. Oxford.

Mead, M. 1943. *Coming of Age in Samoa*. Harmondsworth.

Meadows, A. R. 2001. Money, Freedom and Empire in the Hellenistic World. In Meadows and Shipton 2001: 53–64.

Meadows, A. R. and Shipton, K. (eds) 2001. *Money and its Uses in the Ancient Greek World*. Oxford.

Meadows, A. R. and Williams, J. H. C. 2001. Moneta and the Monuments: Coinage and Politics in Republican Rome. *JRS* 91: 27–49.

Meeks, W. A. 2003. *The First Urban Christians: The Social World of the Apostle Paul*, 2nd edn. New Haven.

Megaw, M. R. and Megaw, J. V. 2001. *Celtic Art From its Beginnings to the Book of Kells*. rev. edn. London.

Meid, W. 1994. *Gaulish Inscriptions*. Budapest.

Meier, C. 1982. *Caesar*. Berlin (translated into English, 1995).

Meier, J. P. 1991–2001. *A Marginal Jew. Rethinking the Historical Jesus*. 3 vols. New York.

Meier, M. 1837. Päderastie. *Allgemeine Encyclopädie und Kunsten*. Leipzig, 1837. vol. 4: 149–88.

Meiggs, R. 1982. *Trees and Timber in the Ancient Mediterranean World*. Oxford.

Meiggs, R. and Lewis, D. M. 1988. *A Selection of Greek Historical Inscriptions*. rev. edn. Oxford.

Meijer, F. and van Nijf, O. 1992. *Trade, Transport and Society in the Ancient World*. London.

Melchert, H. C. (ed.) 2003. *The Luwians*. Leiden.

Mélèze Modrzejewski, J. 1995. *The Jews of Egypt: From Rameses II to Emperor Hadrian* (trans. R. Cornman). Edinburgh.

Mellor, R. 1992. The Local Character of Roman Imperial Religion. *Athenaeum* 80: 385–400.

Mercer, S. A. B. 1939. *The Tell El-Amarna Tablets*. 2 vols. Toronto.

Meredith, A. 1976. Asceticism – Christian and Greek. *Journal of Theological Studies* 27: 313–32.

Merkelbach, R. and Stauber, J. 1998. *Steinepigramme aus dem griechischen Osten. Band I: Die Westküste Kleinasiens von Knidos bis Ilion*. Stuttgart.

Meshorer, Y. 1997. *A Treasury of Jewish Coins From the Persian Period to Bar Kochba*. Jerusalem.

Meskell, L. 2002. *Private Life in New Kingdom Egypt*. Princeton.

Metzger, B. 1987. *The Canon of the New Testament: Its Origin, Development, and Significance*. Oxford.

Metzger, H. et al. 1979. *Fouilles de Xanthos*. Paris.

Meyer, E. A. 2004. *Legitimacy and Law in the Roman World: Tabulae in Roman Belief and Practice*. Cambridge.

Meyers, C., Craven, T., and Kraemer, R. (eds) 2000. *Women in Scripture*. Grand Rapids, MI.

Meyers, E. M. 1997. *The Oxford Encyclopaedia of Archaeology in the Near East.* 5 vols. New York.

Michels, R. 1915. *Political Parties; a Sociological Study of the Oligarchical Tendencies of Modern Democracy.* Trans. E. and C. Paul. New York.

Midant-Reynes, B. 2000. *The Prehistory of Egypt.* Trans. I. Shaw. Oxford.

Migeotte, L. 1983. Souscriptions athéniennes de la période Classique. *Historia* 32: 129–48.

Migeotte, L. 1984. *L'emprunt public dans les cites grecques.* Quebec.

Migeotte, L. 1992. *Les souscriptions publiques dans les cites grecques.* Geneva.

Migeotte, L. 1993. De la liturgie à la contribution obligatoire: le financement des Dionysies et des travaux du théâtre à Iasos au IIe siècle avant J.-C. *Chiron* 23: 267–94.

Migeotte, L. 1995. Les finances publiques des cités grecques: bilan et perspectives de recherché. *Topoi* 5: 7–32.

Mikalson, J. D. 2005. *Ancient Greek Religion.* Oxford.

Mikesell, M. 1969. The Deforestation of Mount Lebanon. *Geographical Review* 59: 1–28.

Miles, G. B. 1995. *Livy: Reconstructing Early Rome.* Ithaca.

Mill, J. S. 1848. *Principles of Political Economy.* London.

Millar, F. 1977. *The Emperor in the Roman World (31 BC–AD 337).* London.

Millar, F. 1981a. *The Roman Empire and its Neighbours.* London.

Millar, F. 1981b. The World of the Golden Ass. *JRS* 71: 63–75.

Millar, F. 1983. Epigraphy. In M. Crawford (ed.), *Sources for Ancient History.* Cambridge. 80–136, reprinted in Millar 2002.

Millar, F. 1984. The Mediterranean and the Roman Revolution: Politics, War and the Economy. *Past and Present* 102: 3–24.

Millar, F. 1992. The Jews of the Graeco-Roman Diaspora between Paganism and Christianity, AD 314–438. In J. Lieu, J. North, and T. Rajak (eds), *The Jews among Pagans and Christians in the Roman Empire.* London: 97–123.

Millar, F. 1998. *The Crowd in Rome in the Late Republic.* Ann Arbor.

Millar, F. 2002. *Rome, the Greek World, and the East.* Edited by H. Cotton and G. Rogers. Chapel Hill.

Millar F. 2004. Christian Emperors, Christian Church and the Jews of the Diaspora in the Greek East, CE 379–450. *Journal of Jewish Studies* 55: 1–24.

Miller, M. C. 1997. *Athens and Persia in the Fifth Century BC: A Study in Cultural Reciprocity.* Cambridge.

Miller, S. 2004. *Ancient Greek Athletics.* New Haven.

Millett, M. 1990. *The Romanization of Britain.* Cambridge.

Millett, P. C. 2001. Productive to Some Purpose? The Problem of Ancient Economic Growth. In Mattingly and Salmon 2001: 17–48.

Mills, S. 1997. *Theseus, Tragedy and the Athenian Empire.* Oxford.

Misurare la terra: Centuriazione e coloni nel mondo romano. Città, agricoltura, commercio: materiali da Roma e dal suburbio. 1988. Rome.

Mitchell, S. 1976. Requisitioned Transport in the Roman Empire. A New Inscription from Pisidia. *JRS* 66: 106–31.

Mitchell, S. 1990. Festivals, Games, and Civic Life in Roman Asia Minor. *JRS* 80: 183–93.

Mitchell, S. 1993. *Anatolia. Land, Men and Gods in Asia Minor.* 2 vols. Oxford.

Mitchell, S. 1995. *Cremna in Pisidia. An Ancient City in Peace and War.* Swansea.

Mitchell, S. 1999. The Cult of Theos Hypsistos between Pagans, Jews, and Christians. In Athanassiadi and Frede 1999: 81–148.

Mitchell, S. 2003. The Galatians: Representation and Reality. In Erskine 2003: 280–93.

Mitchell, S. 2005. Olive Cultivation in the Economy of Roman Asia Minor. In S. Mitchell and C. Katsari (eds), *Patterns in the Economy of Roman Asia Minor*. Swansea. 83–113.

Mitchell, S. and Greatrex, G. (eds) 2000. *Ethnicity and Culture in Late Antiquity*. Swansea.

Mitteis, L. and Wilcken, U. 1912. *Grundzüge und Chrestomathie der Papyruskunde*. Leipzig-Berlin.

Moles J. 1990. The *Kingship Orations* of Dio Chrysostom. *Papers of the Leeds Latin Seminar* 6: 297–375.

Moles, J. 1993. Truth and Untruth in Herodotus and Thucydides. In C. Gill and T. P. Wiseman (eds), *Lies and Fiction in the Ancient World*. Exeter. 88–121.

Moles, J. 1996. Herodotus Warns the Athenians. *Papers of the Leeds International Latin Seminar* 9: 259–84.

Möllendorf, P. von. 2000. *Lukian*, Hermotimus, *oder* Lohnt es sich Philosophie zu Studieren?. Darmstadt.

Moller, H. 1987. The Accelerated Development of Youth: Beard Growth as a Biological Marker. *Comparative Studies in History and Society* 29: 748–62.

Momigliano, A. 1944. Sea Power in Greek Thought. *Classical Review* 58: 1–7 (repr. in *Secondo contributo alla storia degli studi classici*. 1960. Rome. 57–67).

Momigliano, A. 1950. Ancient History and the Antiquarian. *Journal of the Warburg and Courtauld Institute* 13: 285–315.

Momigliano, A. 1966. Time in Ancient Historiography. *History and Theory*. 6: 1–23.

Momigliano, A. 1972. Tradition and the Classical Historian. *History and Theory* 11: 279–93 (reprinted in *id.*, *Essays in Ancient and Modern Historiography* 1977. Oxford. 161–75).

Momigliano, A. 1994. *Studies in Modern Scholarship*. Berkeley.

Mommsen, T. 1881–86. *Römische Geschichte*. 7th edn. 5 vols. Berlin (repr. Munich 1976; translated as *The History of Rome* by W. P. Dickson, 1894).

Mommsen, T. 1887–88. *Römisches Staatsrecht*. 3rd edn. 3 vols. Leipzig (rpr. Graz 1965).

Montevecchi, O. 1973–88. *La Papirologia*. Milan.

Montserrat, D. 1996. *Sex and Society in Graeco-Roman Egypt*. London.

Montserrat, D. 2000. *Akhenaten: History, Fantasy and Ancient Egypt*. London.

Moran, W. L. (ed.) 1992. *The Amarna Letters*. Baltimore.

Morandi, A. 1982. *Epigrafia italica*. Rome.

Mordaunt Crook, J. 1972. *The British Museum. A Case Study in Architectural Politics*. Harmondsworth.

Morel, J. P. 1989. The Transformation of Italy, 300–133 BC: The Evidence of Archaeology. In *CAH*² 8: 477–516.

Morello, R. 2002. Livy's Alexander Digression (9.17–19): Counterfactuals and Apologetics. *JRS* 92: 62–85.

Moreno, P. 1981. Modelli lisippei nell'arte decorativa di età repubblicana ed augustea. In *L'art décoratif à Rome à la fin de la République et au début du Principat*. Rome. 173–206.

Moretti, L. 1953. *Iscrizioni agonistiche greche*. Rome.

Morgan, G. 1982. Euphiletos' House: Lysias I. *TAPA* 112: 115–23.

Morgan, T. 1998. *Literate Education in the Hellenistic and Roman Worlds*. Cambridge.

Mørkholm, O. 1991. *Early Hellenistic Coinage from the Accession of Alexander to the Peace of Apamea*. Cambridge.

Morley, N. 1996. *Metropolis and Hinterland: the City of Rome and the Italian Economy*. Cambridge.

Morley, N. 1998. Political Economy and Classical Antiquity. *Journal of the History of Ideas* 26: 95–114.

Morley, N. 1999. *Writing Ancient History*. Ithaca.

Morley, N. 2001. The Transformation of Italy, 225–28 BC. *JRS* 91: 50–62.

Morley, N. 2004. *Theories, Models and Concepts in Ancient History*. London.

Morley, N. 2007. *Trade in Classical Antiquity*. Cambridge.

Morpurgo Davies, A. 1987. The Greek Notion of Dialect. *Verbum* 10: 7–27. Reprinted in Harrison 2002b: 153–71.

Morris, I. 1987. *Burial and Ancient Society*. Cambridge.

Morris, I. 1992. *Death Ritual and Social Structure in Classical Antiquity*. Cambridge.

Morris, I. 1994. The Athenian Economy Twenty Years after *The ancient Economy*. *CP* 89: 351–66.

Morris, I. 2002. Hard Surfaces. In Cartledge et al. 2002: 8–43.

Morris, I. 2003. Mediterraneanization. In *Mediterranean Historical Review* 18: 30–55. (= Malkin 2005: 30–55).

Morris, I. 2004. Economic Growth in Ancient Greece. *Journal of Institutional and Theoretical Economics* 160: 709–42.

Morris, I. and Raaflaub K. (eds) 1998. *Democracy 2500? Questions and Challenges*. Dubuque.

Morris, I. and Powell, B. 2006. *The Greeks. History, Culture, and Society*. Upper Saddle River.

Morris, S. and Papadopoulos, J. 2005. Greek Towers and Slaves: An Archaeology of Exploitation. *AJA* 109: 155–225.

Morrissey, R. 2003. *Charlemagne and France. A Thousand Years of Mythology*. Notre Dame.

Morse, M. A. 2005. *How the Celts Came to Britain. Druids, Ancient Skulls, and the Birth of Archaeology*. Stroud.

Morstein-Marx, R. 2004. *Mass Oratory and Political Power in the Late Roman Republic*. Cambridge.

Morstein-Marx, R. (forthcoming.) *Dignitas* and *res publica:* Caesar and Republican legitimacy. In K.-J. Hölkeskamp (ed.), *Eine politische Kultur (in) der Krise? Die "letzte Generation" der römischen Republik*. Munich.

Morton Braund, S. 2002. *Latin Literature*. London.

Moscati, S. et al. (eds) 1991. *I Celti. Catalogo della mostra, Venezia*. Milan.

Mossé, C. 1967. La conception du citoyen dans la Politique d'Aristote. *Eirene* 6: 17–21. Keyt, D. and Miller, F. D. (eds) 1991. *A Companion to Aristotle's* Politics. Oxford.

Mouritsen, H. 2001. *Plebs and Politics in the Late Roman Republic*. Cambridge.

Moxnes, H. (ed.) 1997. *Constructing Early Christian Families: Family as Social Reality and Metaphor*. London.

Mudry, P. 2007. Vivre à Rome ou le mal d'être citadin: réflexions sur la ville antique comme espace pathogène. In *Medicina, soror Philosophiae*. Lausanne. 231–42.

Mulgan, R. G. 1977. *Aristotle's Political Theory*. Oxford.

Mulgan, R. G. 1990. Aristotle and the Value of Political Participation. *Political Theory* 18: 195–215.

Müller, K. E. 1972. *Geschichte der antiken Ethnographie und ethnologischen Theorienbildung*. vol. 1. Wiesbaden.

Muñoz, A. 1932. *Via dei Monti e Via del Mare*. 2nd edn. Rome.

Münzer, F. 1920. *Römische Adelsparteien und Adelsfamilien*. Stuttgart (translated as *Roman Aristocratic Parties and Families*, Baltimore. 1999).

Mura Sommella, A. 2000. "La grande roma dei Tarquini". Alterne vicende di una felice intuizione. *Bullettino della Commissione Archeologica comunale di Roma* 101: 7–26.

Murnane, W. J. 1990. *The Road to Kadesh: A Historical Interpretation of the Battle Reliefs of King Sety I at Karnak*. Chicago.

Murnane, W. J. 1977. *Ancient Egyptian Coregencies*. Chicago.

Murnane, W. J. 1995. *Texts from the Amarna Period in Egypt*. Atlanta.

Murray, G. 1935. *Five Stages of Greek Religion*. London.

Murray, G. W. 1935. *Sons of Ishmael: A Study of the Egyptian Bedouin*. London.

Murray, O. 1990a. The Affair of the Mysteries: Democracy and the Drinking Group. In Murray 1990b: 149–61.

Murray, O. (ed.) 1990b. *Sympotica*. Oxford.

Murray, O. 1993. *Early Greece*. 2nd edn. London.

Murray, O. and Price, S. (eds) 1990. *The Greek City from Homer to Alexander*. Oxford.

Murray, O. and Tecusan, M. (eds) 1995. *In Vino Veritas*. Rome.

Musgrave, R. 1968. Public expenditure. In *International Encyclopaedia of the Social Sciences*. 18 vols. London.

Musti, D. 1981. *L'economia in Grecia*. Bari.

Musti, D. and Beschi, L. (eds) 1982. *Pausania. Guida della Grecia 1. L'Attica*. Rome/Milan.

Musurillo, H. 1954. *Acts of the Pagan Martyrs*. Oxford.

Myres, J. L. 1944. *Mediterranean Culture* [The Frazer Lecture, 1943]. Cambridge.

Nachtergael, G. 1977. *Les Galates en Grèce et les Soteria de Delphes: recherches d'histoire et d'epigraphie hellenistiques*. Bruxelles.

Nafissi, M. 2005. *Ancient Athens and Modern Ideology. Value, Theory and Evidence in Historical Sciences: Max Weber, Karl Polanyi and Moses Finley*. London.

Najbjerg, T. and Trimble, J. 2004. Review of Rodriguez-Almeida 2002. *JRA* 17: 577–83.

Namier, L. 1957. *The Structure of Politics at the Accession of George III*. 2nd edn. London.

Nash Briggs, D. 2003. Metals, Salt and Slaves: Economic Links between Gaul and Italy from the Eighth to the Late Sixth Centuries BC. *Oxford Journal of Archaeology* 22.3: 243–59.

Naso, A. 2000. I Piceni: storia e archeologia delle Marche in epoca preromana. Milan.

Nathan, G. 2000. *The Family in Late Antiquity: the Rise Of Christianity and the Endurance of Tradition*. London.

Neer, R. T. 2002. *Style and Politics in Athenian Vase-Painting: The Craft of Democracy, ca. 530–460 BCE*. Cambridge.

Nees, L. 1991. *A Tainted Mantle. Hercules and the Classical Tradition at the Carolingian Court*. Philadelphia.

Neesen, L. 1980. *Untersuchungen zu den direkten Staatsabgaben der römischen Kaiserzeit*. Bonn.

Neils, J. and Oakley, J. 2003. *Coming of Age in Ancient Greece: Images of Children in the Classical Past*. New Haven.

Nelis, J. 2007. La romanité ("romanità") fasciste. Bilan des recherches et propositions pour le future. *Latomus* 66: 987–1006.

Nelson, J. L. 1992. Translating Images of Authority: the Christian Roman Emperors in the Carolingian World. In M. Mackenzie and C. Roueché (eds), *Images of authority. Papers Presented to Joyce Reynolds on the Occasion of her 70th Birthday*. Cambridge. 194–205.

Neumann, G. 1993. Zu den epichorischen Sprachen Kleinasiens. In G. Rehrenböck, G. Dobesch (eds), *Die epigraphische und altertumskundliche Erforschung Kleinasiens: hundert Jahre Kleinasiatische Kommission der Österreichischen Akademie der Wissenschaften: Akten des Symposiums von 23. bis 25. Oktober 1990*. Vienna.

Neumeister, C. 1993. *Das antike Rom: ein literarischer Stadtführer*. 2nd edn. München.

Nevett, L. 1994. Separation or Seclusion? Towards an Archaeological Approach to Investigating Women in the Greek Household in the Fifth to Third Centuries BC. In C. Richards and M. Parker Pearson (eds), *Architecture and Order: Approaches to Social Space*. London. 98–112.

Nevett, L. 1999. *House and Society in the Ancient Greek World*. Cambridge.

Nevett, L. 2000. A "Real Estate Market" in Classical Greece? the Example of Town Housing. *Annual of the British School at Athens* 95: 329–43.

Nevett, L. 2002. Continuity and Change in Greek Households under Roman Rule: the Role of Women in the Domestic Context. In E. Ostenfeld (ed.), *Greek Romans or Roman Greeks*. Aarhus. 81–97.

Nevett, L. 2009. Domestic Façades: a Feature of the Greek "Urban" Landscape? In L. Preston and S. Owens (eds), *Inside the City in the Greek World*. Oxford. 118–30.

Newlands, C. 2002. *Statius' Silvae and the Poetics of Empire*. Oxford.

Nicholson, N. 2005. *Aristocracy and Athletics in Archaic and Classical Greece*.

Nickelsburg, G. 1981. *Jewish Literature Between the Bible and the Mishnah*. Philadelphia.

Nickelsburg, G. 2003. *Ancient Judaism and Christian Origins: Diversity, Continuity and Transformation*. Minneapolis.

Nicolet, C. 1980. *The World of the Citizen In Republican Rome*. London (French edn 1976).

Nielsen, I. 1994. *Hellenistic Palaces*. Aarhus.

Nielsen, I. 1996. *Oriental Models for Hellenistic Palaces*. In G. Brands and W. Hoepfner (eds), *Basileia: die paläste der hellenistischen Könige*. Mainz. 209–12.

Niemeier, B. and Niemeier, W.-D. 1997. Milet 1994–1995. *Archäologischer Anzeiger*. 189–248.

Nightingale, A. 1995. *Genres in Dialogue. Plato and the Construct of Philosophy*. Cambridge.

Nijhuis, K. 1995. Greek Doctors and Roman Patients: a Medical Anthropological Approach. In van der Eijk et al. 1995: 49–67.

Nippel, W. 1995. *Public Order in Ancient Rome*. Cambridge.

Nisbet, G. 2006. *Ancient Greece in Film and Popular Culture*. Bristol.

Nissen, H. J. 1988. *The Early History of the Ancient Near East: 9000–2000 BC*. London.

Nissen, H. J., Damerov, P. and Englund, R. 1993. *Archaic Bookkeeping. Writing and Techniques of Economic Administration in the Ancient Near East*. Chicago.

Nixon L. and Price, S. 1990. The Size and Resources of Greek Cities. In Murray and Price 1990: 137–70.

Nollé, J. 1992/93. Kaiserliche Privilegien für Gladiatorenmunera und Tierhetzen. Unbekannte und ungedeute Zeugnisse auf städtischen Münzen des griechischen Ostens. *Jahrbuch für Numismatik und Geldgeschichte* 42/43: 49–82.

Nollé, J. 2005a. Boars, Bears and Bugs. Farming in Asia Minor and the Protection of Men, Animals, and Crops. In S. Mitchell and C. Katsari (eds), *Patterns in the Economy of Roman Asia Minor*. Swansea. 53–82.

Nollé, J. 2005b. Beiträge zur kleinasiatischen Münzkunde und Geschichte 1–3. *Gephyra* 2: 73–94.

North, J. 1981. The Development of Roman Imperialism. *JRS* 71: 1–9.

North, J. 1990. Democratic Politics in Republican Rome. *Past and Present* 126: 3–21. (= Osborne 2004a: 140–58)

North, J. 1992. The Development of Religious Pluralism. In J. Lieu, J. North, and T. Rajak (eds), *The Jews Among Pagans and Christians in the Roman Empire*. London. 174–93.

Noy, D. 2000. *Foreigners at Rome. Citizens and Strangers*. London.

Nunn, J. F. 1996. *Ancient Egyptian Medicine*. London.

Nussbaum, M. 1997. *Cultivating Humanity. A Classical Defence of Reform in Liberal Education*. Cambridge, MA.

Nussbaum, M. and Sihvola, J. (eds) 2002. *The Sleep of Reason: Erotic Experience and Sexual Ethics in Ancient Greece and Rome*. Chicago.

Nutton, V. 1979. *Galen, On Prognosis*, CMG V.8.1, Berlin.

Nutton, V. 1993. Roman Medicine: Tradition, Confrontation, Assimilation. *ANRW* II 37.1: 49–78.

Nutton, V. 2000. Medical Thoughts on Urban Pollution. In Hope and Marshall 2000: 65–73.

Nutton, V. 2003. *Ancient Medicine*. London.

O'Connor, C. 1993. *Roman Bridges*. Cambridge.

O'Donnell, J. J. 1977. Paganus. *Classical Folia* 31: 163–69. http://ccat.sas.upenn.edu/jod/texts/paganus.html.

Oakley, S. P. 1985. Single Combat in the Roman Republic. *CQ* 35: 392–410.

Oates, J. F. et al. 2001. *Checklist of Editions of Greek, Latin, Demotic and Coptic Papyri, Ostraca and Tablets*. 5th edn. Bulletin of the American Society of Papyrologists, Supp. 9, Oakville, Conn. Also available and regularly updated at http://scriptorium.lib.duke.edu/papyrus/texts/clist.html.

Ober, J. 1989a. *Mass and Elite in Democratic Athens*. Princeton.

Ober, J. 1989b. The Athenians and Their Democracy. *CP* 84: 322–34.

Ober, J. 2005. *Athenian Legacies: Essays on the Politics of Going on Together*. Princeton.

Ogden, D. 1999. *Polygamy, Prostitutes and Death, the Hellenistic Dynasties*. London.

Ogden, D. 2001. *Greek and Roman Necromancy*. Princeton.

Ogden, D. 2002. Controlling Women's Dress: *gynaikonomoi*. In Llewellyn-Jones 2002d: 203–26.

Ohly-Dumm, M. 1985. Tripod-Pyxis from the Sanctuary of Aphaia in Aegina. In D. von Bothmer, *The Amasis Painter and His World*. London. Appx 4, 236–38.

Olender, M. 1990. Aspects of Baubo. In F. Zeitlin, J. Winkler, and D. Halperin (eds), *Before Sexuality*. Princeton. 83–113.

Oleson, J. (ed.) 2008. *The Oxford Handbook of Engineering and Technology in the Classical World*. Oxford.

Oliver, G. (ed.) 2000. *The Epigraphy of Death*. Liverpool.

Oliver, G. 2007. *War, Food and Politics in Early Hellenistic Athens*. Oxford.

Oliver, J. H. and Palmer, R. 1955. Minutes of an Act of the Roman Senate. *Hesperia* 24: 320–49.

Olmsted, G. 1992. *The Gaulish Calendar: a Reconstruction from the Bronze Fragments from Coligny, with an Analysis of its Function as a Highly Accurate Lunar-Solar Predictor, as well as an Explanation of its Terminology and Development*. Bonn.

Olson, D. and Sens, A. 2000. *Archestratos of Gela*. Oxford.

Onians, J. 1988. *Bearers of Meaning: the Classical Orders in Antiquity, the Middle Ages and the Renaissance*. Cambridge.

Orlin, E. M. 1997. *Temples, Religion, and Politics in the Roman Republic*. Leiden.

Orrieux, B. 1983. *Les papyrus de Zénon: l'horizon d'un grec en Egypte au III siècle avant J.-C.* Paris.

Orrison, K. 1999. *Written in Stone. Making Cecil B. DeMille's Epic "The Ten Commandments"*. Lanhan.

Osborne, R. 1985. *Demos: The Discovery of Classical Attika*, Cambridge.

Osborne, R. 1987. *Classical Landscapes with Figures. The Ancient Greek City and its Countryside*, London.

Osborne, R. 1992. "Is It a Farm?" The Definition of Agricultural Sites and Settlements in Ancient Greece. In B. Wells 1992: 21–27.

Osborne, R. 1998. Early Greek colonisation? The nature of Greek Settlement in the West. In N. Fisher and H. van Wees (eds), *Archaic Greece. New Evidence and New Approaches*. London. 251–70.

Osborne, R. 2000. *Classical Greece 500–323 BC*. London.

Osborne, R. (ed.) 2004a. *Studies in Ancient Greek and Roman Society*. Cambridge.

Osborne, R. 2004b. Demography and Survey. In Alcock and Cherry 2004: 163–72.

Packer, J. 1967. The Domus of Cupid and Psyche in ancient Ostia. *AJA* 71: 121–31.

Packer, J. 1968–69. La casa di Via Giulio Romano. *Bullettino della Commissione Archeologica comunale di Roma* 81: 127–48.

Packer, J. 1971. *The Insulae of Imperial Ostia* (MAAR 31). Rome.

Packer, J. 1997. *The Forum of Trajan in Rome. A Study of the Monuments*. Berkeley.

Packer, J. 2001. *The Forum of Trajan in Rome. A Study of the Monuments in Brief*. Berkeley.

Packer, J. 2003. TEMPLVM DIVI TRAIANI PARTHICI ET PLOTINAE: a debate with R. Meneghini. *JRA* 16: 109–36.

Paglia, C. 1991. Junk Bonds and Corporate Raiders: Academe in the Hour of the Wolf. *Arion* 3rd ser. 1.2: 139–212.

Pailler, J.-M. (ed.) 2004. *Que reste-t-il de l'éducation classique? Relire le "Marrou", Histoire de l'éducation dans l'antiquité*. Toulouse.

Pallottino, M. 1991. *A History of Earliest Italy*. London.

Panciera, S. 2000. Nettezza urbana a Roma organizzazione e responsabili. In X. Dupré Raventós and J.-A. Remolà (eds), *"Sordes urbis". La elimination de residuos en la ciudad romana*. Rome. 95–103.

Panciera, S. 2003. Domus a Roma. Altri contributi alla loro inventariazione. In M. G. Angeli Bertinelli and A. Donati (eds), *Usi e abusi epigrafici*. Rome. 355–74.

Papagrigorakis, M. J. et al. 2006. DNA Examination of Ancient Dental Pulp Incriminates Typhoid Fever as a Probable Cause of the Plague of Athens. *International Journal of Infectious Diseases*.

Papi, E. 2003. Benvenuti a Thamusida. *Archeo* 19.2: 74–95.

Parke, H. W. 1988. *Sibyls and Sibylline Prophecy in Classical Antiquity*. London.

Parker, R. 1989. Spartan Religion. In A. Powell (ed.) *Classical Sparta: Techniques behind her Success*. London. 142–72.

Parker, R. 1996. *Athenian Religion. A History*. Oxford.

Parker, R. 2006. *Polytheism and Society at Athens*. Oxford.

Parkin, T. 1992. *Demography and Roman Society*. Baltimore and London.

Parkin, T. 2003. *Old Age in the Roman World: a Cultural and Social History*. Baltimore.

Parkin, T. and Pomeroy, A. 2007. *Roman Social History: a Sourcebook*. London.

Parkins, H. (ed.) 1997. *Roman Urbanism: Beyond the Consumer City*. London.

Parkinson, R. B. 1991. *Voices from Ancient Egypt: An Anthology of Middle Kingdom Writings*. London.

Parkinson, R. B. 1997. *The Tale of Sinuhe and Other Ancient Egyptian Poems 1940–1640 BC*. Oxford.

Parkinson, R. B. 1999. *Cracking Codes: The Rosetta Stone and Decipherment*. London.

Parrinder, P. 1999. Ancients and Moderns: Literature and the "Western Canon". In Biddiss and Wyke 1999: 263–78.

Parrish, D. (ed.) 2001. *Urbanism in Western Asia Minor*. Portsmouth.

Parsons, P. J. 1980. The Papyrus Letter. *Didactica Classica Gandensia* 20: 3–19.

Pastor, M. 2004. *Viriato: el primer guerrillero*. Barcelona.

Patterson, C. 1998. *The Family In Greek History*. Cambridge, MA.

Patterson, J. 1994. The *collegia* and the transformation of the towns of Italy in the second century AD. In *L'Italie d'Auguste à Dioclétien*. Collection de l'École Francaise de Rome 198. Rome 1994. 227–38.

Patterson, J. 2000. *Political Life in the City of Rome*. London.

Patterson, J. 2006. *Landscapes and Cities: Rural Settlement and Civic Transformation in the Early Imperial Italy*. Oxford.

Patzer, H. 1982. *Die Griechische Knabenliebe*. Wiesbaden.

Pearce, J., Millett, M., and Struck, M. 2000. *Burial, Society and Context in the Roman World*. Oxford.

Pedersen, O. 1997. *The First Universities*. Studium Generale *and the Origins of University Education in Europe*. Cambridge.

Pedersen, S. 2002. What is Political History Now? In Cannadine 2002: 36–56.

Pedley, J. G. 1990. *Paestum: Greeks and Romans in Southern Italy*. London.

Peek, W. 1974. Ein neuer spartanischer Staatsvertrag. *Abhandlungen der sachsischen Akademie der Wissenschaft* 65: 3–15.

Pelgrom, J. (forthcoming.) Archaeology and Demography: A Re-Appraisal of the Evidence, PhD thesis. University of Leiden.

Pelling, C. (ed.) 1997. *Greek Tragedy and the Historian*. Oxford.

Pelling, C. 2000. *Literary Texts and the Greek Historian*. London and New York.

Pelling, R. 2005. Garamantian Agriculture and its Significance in a Wider North African Context: The Evidence of the Plant Remains from the Fazzan Project. In J. Keenan (ed.), *The Sahara: Past, Present and Future*. London. 397–412.

Pensabene, P. 1997. *Le vie del marmo. I blochi di cava di Roma e di Ostia*. Rome.

Percival, J. 1976. *The Roman Villa: an Historical Introduction*. London.

Peremans, W. and Van't Dack, E. 1950–. *Prosopographia Ptolemaica*. Louvain.

Pergola, P. et al. (eds) 2003. *Suburbium. Il suburbio di Roma dalla crisi del sistema delle ville a Gregorio Magno*. Rome.

Perkins, J. 1995. *The Suffering Self: Pain and Narrative Representation in the Early Christian Era*. London.

Perlman, S. 1976. Panhellenism, the Polis and Imperialism. *Historia* 25: 1–30.

Pernot, L. 2005. *Rhetoric in Antiquity*. Washington DC.

Perring, D. 2002. *The Roman House in Britain*. London.

Peruzzi, E. 1992. Cultura greca a Gabii nel secolo VIII. *Parola del Passato* 47: 459–68.

Pestman, P. W. 1990. *The New Papyrological Primer*. Leiden.

Pettegrew, D. 2001. Chasing the Classical Farmstead: Assessing the Formation and Signature of Rural Settlement in Greek Landscape Archaeology. *Journal of Mediterranean Archaeology* 14: 189–209.

Pfeil, E. 1929. *Die fränkische und deutsche Romidee des frühen Mittelalters*. Munich.

Pietilä-Castrén, L. 1987. *Munificentia publica. The Victory Monuments of the Roman Generals in the Era of the Punic Wars*. Helsinki.

Pietri, C. 1976. *Roma Christiana. Recherches sur l'Eglise de Rome, son organisation, sa politique, son idéologie de Miltiade à Sixte III (311–440)* I–II. Rome.

Pigou, A. C. 1920. *The Economics of Public Warfare*. London.

Pines, S. 1986. *Studies in Arabic Versions of Greek Texts and in Medieval Science*. Jerusalem.

Pirenne-Delforge, V. 1994. *L'Aphrodite Grecque. Contribution à l'étude de ses cultes et de sa personnalité dans le panthéon archaique et classique*. Liège.

Pirson, F. 1999. *Mietwohnungen in Pompeji und Herkulaneum*. Munich.

Pleket, H. 1958. Note on a Customs-Law from Caunus. *Mnemosyne* 11: 128–35.

Pleket, H. 1990. Wirtschaft und Gesellschaft des Imperium Romanum: Wirtschaft. In W. Fischer et al. (eds), *Handbuch der europäischen Wirtschafts – und Sozialgeschichte*, I. Stuttgart. 25–160.

Poccetti, P. 1979. *Nuove documenti Italici*. Pisa.

Podes, S. 1991. Polybios' Anakyklosis-Lehre, diskrete Zustandssysteme und das Problem der Mischverfassung. *Klio* 2: 382–90.

Poliakoff, M. 1987. *Combat Sports in the Ancient World: Competition, Violence and Culture*. New Haven.

Polignac, F. de 1995. *Cults, Territory, and the Origins of the Greek City-state.* Chicago.

Pollock, S. 1999. *Ancient Mesopotamia. The Eden that Never Was.* Cambridge.

Pomeroy, A. 1992. Trimalchio as Deliciae. *Phoenix* 46: 45–53.

Pomeroy, S. 1975. *Goddesses, Whores, Wives, and Slaves. Women in Classical Antiquity.* New York.

Pomeroy, S. 1977. *Technikai kai Mousikai*: The Education of Women in the Fourth Century and in the Hellenistic Period. *AJAH* 2: 51–68.

Pomeroy, S. 1983. Infanticide in Hellenistic Greece. In Cameron and Kuhrt 1983: 207–22.

Pomeroy, S. 1994. *Xenophon*, Oeconomicus: *a Social and Historical Commentary.* Oxford.

Pomeroy, S. 1997. *Families in Classical and Hellenistic Greece: Representations and Realities.* Oxford.

Pomeroy, S. 1999. *Plutarch's Advice to the Bride and Groom and A Consolation to his Wife.* New York.

Pontrandolfo Greco, A. 1982. *I Lucani: etnografia e archeologia di una regione antica.* Milan.

Porten, B. and Yardeni, A. 1986. *Textbook of Aramaic Documents from Ancient Egypt.* Jerusalem.

Posener, G. 1957. *Littérature et politique dans l'Egypte de la XIIe dynastie.* Paris.

Posener-Kriéger, P. 1976. *Les archives du temple funéraire de Néferirkarê-Kakaï (les papyrus d'Abousir).* 2 vols. Cairo.

Postgate, J. 1992. *Early Mesopotamia. Society and Economy at the Dawn of History.* London.

Potter, D. 1994. *Prophets and Emperors: Human and Divine Authority from Augustus to Theodosius.* Cambridge, MA.

Potter, D. 1999a. *Literary Texts and the Roman Historian.* London.

Potter, D. 1999b. Entertainers in the Roman Empire. In D. Potter and D. Mattingly (eds), *Life, death and entertainment in the Roman Empire.* Ann Arbor. 256–325.

Potter, D. 2006. Spectacle. In D. Potter (ed.), *A Companion to the Roman Empire.* Oxford. 385–408.

Potter, T. 1979. *The Changing Landscape of South Etruria.* New York.

Potts, D. T. 1999. *The Archaeology of Elam.* Cambridge.

Pouilloux, J. 1960. *Choix d'inscriptions grecques; textes, traductions et notes.* Paris.

Poulakos, T. and Depew, D. (eds) 2004. *Isocrates and Civic Education.* Austin, TX.

Powell., J. and Paterson, J. (eds) 2004. *Cicero the Advocate.* Oxford.

Powell, O. 2003. *Galen on the Properties of Foodstuffs.* Cambridge.

Pratesi, F. and Tassi, F. 1977. *Guida alla natura del Lazio e Abruzzo.* 2nd. edn. Milan.

Preisigke, F. 1915–. *Sammelbuch griechischer Urkunden aus Ägypten.* Strasburg.

Preisigke, F. 1922. *Namenbuch enthaltend alle . . . Menschnamen, soweit sie in griechischen Urkunden . . . Ägyptens sich vorfinden.* Heidelberg.

Preisigke, F. 1925–. *Wörterbuch der griechischen Papyrusurkunden.* Berlin.

Preisigke, F. and Bilabel, F. 1922–. *Berichtigungsliste der griechischen Papyrusurkunden aus Ägypten.* Berlin-Leipzig.

Prest, A. R. 1985. *Public Finance in Developing Countries.* 3rd edn. London.

Price, A. W. 1989. *Love and Friendship in Plato and Aristotle.* Oxford.

Price, S. R. F. 1984. *Rituals and Power: The Roman Imperial Cult in Asia Minor.* Cambridge.

Price, S. R. F. 1996. The Place of Religion: Rome in the early Empire. In *CAH*² 10. 812–47.

Price, S. R. F. 1999. *Religions of the Ancient Greeks.* Cambridge.

Priester, S. 2002. *Ad summas tegulas: Untersuchungen zu vielgeschossigen Gebäudeblöcken mit Wohneinheiten und Insulae im kaiserzeitlichen Rom.* Rome.

Pritchard, D. 2003. Athletics, Education and Participation in Classical Athens. In D. Phillips and D. Pritchard (eds), *Sport and Festival in the Ancient Greek World.* Swansea. 293–349.

Pritchard, J. B. 1955. *Ancient Near Eastern Texts Relating to the Old Testament.* 2nd edn. Princeton.

Pritchett, W. K. 1956. The Attic Stelai: Part II. *Hesperia* 25: 178–328.

Pritchett, W. K. 1971–91. *The Greek State at War.* Berkeley (1979 = Part 3).

Prosdocimi, A. 1984. *Le tavole iguvine.* Florence.

Purcell, N. 1994. The City of Rome and the *Plebs Urbana* in the Late Republic. In *CAH*² 9: 644–88.

Purcell, N. 1995. Forum Romanum (the Republican Period), (the Imperial Period). In Steinby 1993–2000, vol. II: 325–42.

Purcell, N. 1996. Rome and its Development under Augustus and his Successors. In *CAH*² 10: 782–811.

Purcell, N. 2000. Rome and Italy. In *CAH*² 11: 405–43.

Purcell, N. 2005a. Colonization and Mediterranean History. In H. Hurst and S. Owen (eds), *Ancient Colonizations. Analogy, Similarity and Difference.* London. 115–39.

Purcell, N. 2005b. The Way We Used to Eat: Diet, Community and History at Rome. In Gold and Donahue 2005: 1–30.

Purcell, N. 2005c. The Ancient Mediterranean: the View from the Customs House. In W. Harris 2005: 201–32.

Pushkin Museum 1996. *The Treasure of Troy. Heinrich Schliemann's Excavations.* Moscow.

Pyatt, F., Amos, D., Grattan, J., Pyatt, A., and Terrell-Nield, C. 2002. Invertebrates of Ancient Heavy Metal Spoil and Smelting Tip Sites in Southern Jordan: their Distribution and Use as Bioindicators of Metalliferous Pollution Derived from Ancient Sources. *Journal of Arid Environments* 52: 53–62.

Quartermaine, L. 1995. "Slouching towards Rome": Mussolini's Imperial Vision. In Cornell and Lomas 1995: 203–16.

Quinn, J. C. 2003. Roman Africa? In J. Prag and A. Merryweather (eds) *Romanization?, Digressus* Supplement 1 (www.digressus.org/articles/romanization.pdf): 7–34.

Quirke, S. 1991. *Middle Kingdom Studies.* New Malden.

Quirke, S. 2004. *Egyptian Literature 1800 BC: Questions and Readings.* London.

Raaflaub, K. (ed.) 2007. *War and Peace in the Ancient World.* Oxford.

Rabinowitz, N. 1993. *Anxiety Veiled: Euripides' Traffic in Women.* Ithaca.

Rabinowitz, N. and Richlin, A. (eds) 1993. *Feminist Theory and the Classics.* New York.

Rabinowitz, N. and Auanger, L. (eds) 2002. *Among Women: From the Homosocial to the Homoerotic in the Ancient World.* Austin.

Radt, W. (ed.) 2006. *Stadtgrabungen und Stadtforschung im westlichen Kleinasien.* Istanbul.

Raftery, B. 1998. *Pagan Celtic Ireland. The Enigma of the Irish Iron Age.* rev. edn. London.

Raia, A., Luschnig, C., and Sebesta, J. (eds) 2005. *The Worlds of Roman Women.* Newburyport, MA.

Rapp, C. 1997. Ritual Brotherhood in Byzantium. *Traditio* 52: 285–326.

Rappe, S. 2001. The New Math: How to Add and Subtract Pagan Elements in Christian Education. In Too 2001: 405–32.

Rathbone, D. W. 1991. *Economic Rationalism and Rural Society in Third-Century AD Egypt: The Heroninos Archive and the Appianus Estate.* Cambridge.

Rathbone, D. W. 2001. The Muziris Papyrus (SB XVIII 13167): Financing Roman Trade with India. *Bulletin de la Société d'Archéologie d'Alexandrie* 46 (Festschrift for Prof. Mostafa el-Abbadi): 39–50.

Rathje, A. 1979. Oriental Imports in Etruria. In D. Ridgway and F. Ridgway (eds), *Italy before the Romans.* London. 145–83.

Ratté, C. 2001. New Research on the Urban Development of Aphrodisias in Late Antiquity. In Parrish 2001: 116–147.

Rauh, N. 1993. *The Sacred Bonds of Commerce. Religion, Economy and Trade Society at Hellenistic and Roman Delos, 166–87 BC.* Amsterdam.

Rawlings, L. 2007a. *The Ancient Greeks at War.* Manchester.

Rawlings, L. 2007b. Army and Battle during the Conquest of Italy (350–264 BC). In Erdkamp 2007: 45–62.

Rawson, B. 1966. Family Life Amongst the Lower Classes at Rome in the First Two Centuries. *CP* 61: 71–83.

Rawson, B. (ed.) 1986. *The Family in Ancient Rome: New Perspectives.* Ithaca.

Rawson, B. (ed.) 1991. *Marriage, Divorce and Children in Ancient Rome.* Oxford.

Rawson, B. 2003. *Children and Childhood in Roman Italy.* Oxford.

Rawson, B. and Weaver, P. (eds) 1997. *The Roman Family in Italy: Status, Sentiment, and Space.* Canberra and Oxford.

Rawson, E. 1985. *Intellectual Life in the Late Roman Republic.* London.

Rawson, E. 1987. Cicero and the Areopagus. *Athenaeum* 63: 44–66 (= E. Rawson 1991: 444–67).

Rawson, E. 1990. The Antiquarian Tradition: Spoils and Representations of Foreign Armour. In W. Eder (ed.), *Staat und Staatlichkeit in der frühen römischen Republik.* Stuttgart. 157–73 (= E. Rawson 1991: 582–98).

Rawson, E. 1991. *Roman Culture and Society: Collected Papers.* Oxford.

Ray, J. D. 1976. *The Archive of Hor.* London.

Ray, J. D. 1987. Egypt: 525–404 BC. In *CAH²* 4.1: 254–86.

Ray, J. D. 2001. *Reflections of Osiris: Lives from Ancient Egypt.* London.

Reale, O. and Dirmeyer, P. 2000. Modeling the Effects of Vegetation on Mediterranean Climate during the Roman Classical Period. Part I: Climate History and Model Sensitivity. *Global and Planetary Change* 25: 163–84.

Reale, O. and Shukla, J. 2000. Modeling the Effects of Vegetation on Mediterranean Climate during the Roman Classical Period. Part II: Model Simulation. *Global and Planetary Change* 25: 185–214.

Redfield, J. 1985. Herodotus the Tourist. *CP* 80: 97–118 (= Harrison 2002b: 24–49).

Redford, D. B. 1967. *History and Chronology of the Eighteenth Dynasty of Egypt: Seven Studies.* Toronto.

Redford, D. B. (ed.) 2001. *The Oxford Encyclopedia of Ancient Egypt.* 3 vols. New York.

Reece, R. (ed.) 1977. *Burial in the Roman World.* London.

Reece, R. 2002. *The Coinage of Roman Britain.* Stroud.

Reece, R. 2003. *Roman Coins and Archaeology: Collected Papers.* Wetteren.

Rees, R. 2002. *Layers of Loyalty in Latin Panegyric: AD 289–307.* Oxford.

Regino of Prüm, *Chronicon,* ed. F. Kurze, 1890. *Reginonis abbatis Prumiensis Chronicon cum continuatione treverensi, MGH Scriptores rerum germanicarum* 50. Hannover.

Renberg, I., Persson, M., and Enteryd, O. 1994. Pre-Industrial Atmospheric Lead Contamination Detected in Swedish Lake Sediments. *Nature* 368: 323–62.

Renfrew, C. and Cherry, J. F. (eds) 1986. *Peer Polity Interaction and Socio-Political Change.* Cambridge.

Renfrew, J. 1973. *Palaeoethnobotany.* New York.

Reynolds, L. (ed.) 1983. *Texts and Transmission. A Survey of the Latin Classics.* Oxford.

Reynolds, L. and Wilson, N. 1991. *Scribes and Scholars: a Guide to the Transmission of Greek and Latin Literature.* 3rd edn. Oxford.

Rheidt, K. 1997. Römischer Luxus – anatolisches Erbe: Aizanoi in Phrygien – Entdeckung, Ausgrabung und neue Forschungsergebnisse. *Antike Welt* 28: 479–500.

Rheidt, K. 1999. Ländlicher Kult und städtische Siedlung: Aizanoi in Phrygien. In E.-L. Schwandner and K. Rheidt (eds), *Stadt und Umland. Neue Ergebnisse der archäologischen Bau- und Siedlungsforschung.* Mainz. 237–53.

Rhodes, P. J. 1981. *A commentary on the Aristotelian* Athenaion Politeia. Oxford.

Rhodes, P. J. 2003a. *Ancient Democracy and Modern Ideology.* London.

Rhodes, P. J. 2003b. Nothing to Do with Democracy: Athenian Drama and the *Polis. JHS* 123: 104–19.

Rhodes, P. J. 2005. *History of the Classical Greek World, 478–323 BC.* Oxford.

Rhodes, P. J. and Lewis, D. M. 1997. *The Decrees of the Greek States.* Oxford.

Rhodes, P. J. and Osborne, R. 2003. *Greek Historical Inscriptions: 404–323 BC.* Oxford.

Ricardo, D. 1817. *Principles of Political Economy and Taxation.* London.

Ricci, C. 2005. *"Orbis in urbe". Fenomeni migratori nella Roma imperiale.* Rome.

Ricci, C. 2006. *Stranieri illustri e comunità immigrate a Roma. "Vox diversa populorum".* Rome.

Riccobono, S. et al. 1943–68. *Fontes Iuris Romani Anteiustiniani.* 3 vols. Florence.

Rice, E. E. 1983. *The Grand Procession of Ptolemy Philadelphus.* Oxford.

Rich, J. 1993. Fear, Greed and Glory: the Causes of Roman War-Making in the Middle Republic. In Rich and Shipley 1993b: 38–68.

Rich, J. and Wallace-Hadrill, A. (eds) 1991. *City and Country in the Ancient World.* London.

Rich, J. and Shipley, G. (eds) 1993a. *War and Society in the Greek World.* London.

Rich, J. and Shipley, G. (eds) 1993b. *War and Society in the Roman World.* London.

Richardson J. 1983. The Tabula Contrebiensis. Roman Law in Spain in the Early First Century BC. *JRS* 73: 32–41.

Richardson, J. 1996. *The Romans in Spain.* Oxford.

Richardson, L. R. 1992. *A New Topographical Lexicon of Ancient Rome.* Baltimore.

Richlin, A. 1981. Approaches to the Sources on Adultery at Rome. In H. Foley (ed.), *Reflections of Women in Antiquity.* London. 379–404.

Richlin, A. 1993. Not Before Homosexuality: The Materiality of the *Cinaedus* and the Roman Law Against Love Between Men. *Journal of the History of Sexuality* 3.4: 523–73.

Richlin, A. 1997a. Carrying Water in a Sieve: Class and the Body in Roman Women's Religion. In King 1997: 330–74.

Richlin, A. 1997b. Pliny's Brassiere. In J. Hallett and M. Skinner (eds), *Roman Sexualities.* Princeton. 197–220.

Rickman, G. 1980. *The Corn Supply of Ancient Rome.* Oxford.

Riddle, J. M. 1992. *Contraception and Abortion from the Ancient World to the Renaissance.* Cambridge, MA.

Riddle, J. M. 1997. *Eve's Herbs: A History of Contraception and Abortion in the West.* Cambridge, MA.

Rider, B. 1916. *The Greek House: its History and Development from the Neolithic Period to the Hellenistic Age.* Cambridge.

Ridgway, D. 1986. The Etruscans. In *CAH*² 6: 634–75.

Rieckhoff, S. and Biel. J. 2001. *Die Kelten in Deutschland.* Stuttgart.

Riggsby, A. 2006. *Caesar in Gaul and Rome. A War in Words.* Austin.

Rihll, T. 1999. *Greek Science.* Greece and Rome, New Surveys 29. Oxford.

Rihll, T. 2000. Making Money in Classical Athens. In Mattingly and Salmon 2000: 115–42.

Rihll, T. 2007. *The Catapult: A History.* Yardley, PA.

Rihll, T. 2009. Skilled Slaves and the Economy: the Silver Mines of Laurion. In A. Binsfeld, J. Deissler, and H. Heinen (eds), *Beiträge zur antiken Sklaverei im Spiegel der*

Forschungsgeschichte und der archäologischen Zeugnisse. Forschungen zur antiken Sklaverei. Stuttgart.

Rijkels, D. 2005. *Agnosis en Diagnosis: over pestilentiën in het Romeinse Keizerrijk*. University of Leiden.

Rives, J. 1995. *Religion and Authority in Roman Carthage from Augustus to Constantine*. Oxford.

Rives, J. 1999a. *Tacitus: Germania*. Oxford.

Rives, J. 1999b. The Decree of Decius and the Religion of Empire. *JRS* 89: 135–54.

Roaf, M. 1990. *Cultural Atlas of Mesopotamia and the Ancient Near East*. Oxford.

Robert, L. 1939. L'épigraphie grecque au Collège de France, Leçon d'ouverture donnée le 25 Avril 1939. In *Opera Minora Selecta* III (1969), Amsterdam. Also in Robert 2007.

Robert, L. 1940. *Les gladiateurs dans l'Oriente grec*. Paris.

Robert, L. 1952. Communication inaugurale. Actes IIe Congrès Int. Epigr. Paris 1952. In *Opera Minora Selecta* III (1969), Amsterdam. Also in Robert 2007.

Robert, L. 1955. *Hellenica. Recueil d'épigraphie, de numismatique et d'antiquités grecques*. vol. X. Paris.

Robert, L. 1961. "Épigraphie". *Encyclopédie de la Pléaide*. Paris. 453–97. Reprinted in *Opera Minora Selecta* V (1989), Amsterdam: 65–109. Also in Robert 2007.

Robert, L. 1969–90. *Opera Minora Selecta*. 7 vols. Amsterdam.

Robert, L. 1977. La titulature de Nicée et de Nicomédie: la gloire et la haine. *HSCP* 81: 1–39.

Robert, L. 1978. Documents d'Asie Mineure. *Bulletin de Correspondance Hellénique* 102: 395–543.

Robert, L. 1980. *A travers l'Asie Mineure. Poètes et prosateurs, monnaies grecques, voyageurs et géographie*. Athens and Paris.

Robert, L. 1982. Discours d'ouverture du VIIIe Congrès international d'épigraphie grecque et latine à Athènes, 1982. *Actes du VIIIe Congrès international d'épigraphie grecque et latine* vol. 1. Athens. 31–42. Reprinted in Robert, Opera Minora Selecta V (1989), Amsterdam. 709–19.

Robert, L. 1987. *Documents d'Asie Mineure*. Athens and Paris.

Robert, L. 1990. *Opera Minora Selecta: épigraphie et antiquités grecques. Tome VII*. Amsterdam.

Robert, L. 1994. *Le martyre de Pionios, prêtre de Smyrne*. Washington, DC.

Robert, L. 2007. *Choix d'écrits*. Edited by D. Rousset. Paris.

Robert, L. and Robert, J. 1954. *La Carie: histoire et géographie antique. II: Le plateau de Tabai et ses environs*. Paris.

Robert, L. and Robert, J. 1983. *Fouilles d'Amyzon en Carie. Tome I: Exploration, histoire, monnaies et inscriptions*. Paris.

Roberts, C. H. and Skeat, T. C. 1983. *The Birth of the Codex*. London.

Robertson, A. 2000. *An Inventory of Romano-British Coin Hoards*. London.

Robins, G. 1993. *Women in Ancient Egypt*. Cambridge, MA.

Rocca, J. 2003. *Galen on the Brain: Anatomical Knowledge and Physiological Speculation in the Second Century AD*. Leiden.

Roccati, A. 1982. *La littérature historique sous l'Ancien Empire égyptien*. Paris.

Rodd, C. S. 2001. Psalms. In J. Barton and J. Muddiman (eds), *The Oxford Bible Commentary*. Oxford. 355–405.

Rodgers, B. S. 1980. Constantine's Pagan Vision. *Byzantion* 50: 259–78.

Rodríguez Almeida, E. 1984. *Il Monte Testaccio: ambiente, storia, materiali*. Rome.

Rodríguez Almeida, E. 1986. *La annona militaris y la exportacion de aceite bético a Germania*. Madrid.

Rodriguez Almeida, E. 2002. *Formae Urbis Antiquae. Le mappe marmoree di Roma tra la repubblica e Settimio Severo.* Rome.

Rodriguez Almeida, E. 2003. *Terrarum dea gentiarumque: Marziale a Roma: un poeta e la sua città.* Rome.

Rodríguez Neila, J. F. 1992. *Confidentes de César: Los Balbos de Cádiz.* Madrid.

Rogers, G. M. 1991. *The Sacred Identity of Ephesos: Foundation Myths of a Roman City.* London.

Roller, D. W. 2003. *The World of Juba II and Kleopatra Selene. Royal Scholarship on Rome's African Frontier.* London.

Romm, J. S. 1992. *Edges of the Earth in Ancient Thought.* Princeton.

Rood, T. 1999. Thucydides' Persian Wars. In C. S. Kraus (ed.), *The Limits of Historiography: Genre and Narrative in Ancient Historical Texts.* Leiden. 141–68.

Rosen, R. and Sluiter, I. (eds) 2006. *City, Countryside and the Spatial Organization of Value in Classical Antiquity.* Leiden.

Rosenstein, N. 2004. *Rome at War: Farms, Families and Death in the Middle Republic.* Chapel Hill.

Rosenstein, N. and Morstein-Marx, R. (eds) 2006. *A Companion to the Roman Republic.* Oxford.

Rosenstone, R. (ed.) 1995. *Revisioning History: Film and the Construction of a New Past.* Princeton.

Rosivach, V. 1987. Autochthony and the Athenians. *CQ* 37: 294–306.

Rossi, G. B. de (ed.) 1857–88. *Inscriptiones Christianae urbis Romae septimo saeculo antiquiores.* 2 vols. Rome.

Rostovtzeff, M. 1922. *A Large Estate in Egypt in the Third Century* BC. Madison.

Rostovtzeff, M. 1941. *The Social and Economic History of the Hellenistic World.* Oxford (corrected reprint, 1953).

Rostovtzeff, M. 1957. *The Social and Economic History of the Roman World.* 2nd edn. Oxford (1st edn 1926).

Roth, J. P. 1999. *The Logistics of the Roman Army at War (264* BC–AD *235).* Leiden.

Roth, M. 2006. Marriage, Divorce and the Prostitute in Ancient Mesopotamia. In Faraone and McClure 2006: 21–39.

Roth, R. and Keller, J. (eds) 2007. *Roman by Integration: Dimensions of Group Identity in Material Culture and Text.* Portsmouth RI.

Roth, U. 2007. *Thinking Tools: Agricultural Slavery between Evidence and Models.* London.

Röthlisberger, F. 1986. *10,000 Jahre Gletschergeschichte der Erde.* Aarau.

Rousseau, P. 2002. *The Early Christian Centuries.* London.

Rousselle, A. 1988. *Porneia: On Desire and the Body in Antiquity.* Translated by F. Pheasant. Oxford.

Rowland, I. 1999. *Vitruvius: Ten Books on Architecture.* Cambridge.

Rowlandson, J. 1985. Freedom and Subordination in Ancient Agriculture: the Case of the *Basilikoi Geórgoi* of Ptolemaic Egypt. In P. Cartledge and F. Harvey (eds), *Crux.* London. 327–47.

Rowlandson, J. 1996. *Landowners and Tenants in Roman Egypt. The Social Relations of Agriculture in the Oxyrhyncite Nome.* Oxford.

Rowlandson, J. (ed.) 1998. *Women and Society in Greek and Roman Egypt, a Sourcebook.* Cambridge.

Rowlandson, J. 1999. Agricultural Tenancy and Village Society in Roman Egypt. In Bowman and Rogan 1999: 139–58.

Royo, M. 1999. *Domus imperatoriae. Topographie, formation et imaginaire des palais impériaux du Palatin.* Rome.

Rudhardt, J. 1992. Les attitudes des Grecs a l'égard des religions étrangères. *Revue de l'Histoire des Religions* 209: 219–38, translated as "The Greek Attitude to Foreign Religions" in Harrison 2002b: 172–85.

Rudolph, K. 1987. *Gnosis: The Nature and History of Gnosticism.* San Francisco.

Rüger, C. 1979. Die Keramik des Grabes von Es Soumâa bei El Khroub. In R. Horn and C. Rüger (eds), *Die Numider: Reiter und Könige nördlich der Sahara.* Bonn. 339–44.

Ruschenbusch, E. 1966. *SOLONOS NOMOI. Die Fragmente des Solonischen Gesetzeswerkes mit einer Text- und Überlieferungsgeschichte.* Historia Einzelschrift 9. Wiesbaden.

Russell, D. 1983. *Greek Declamation.* Cambridge.

Russell, D. and Wilson, N. (eds) 1981. *Menander Rhetor.* Oxford.

Rutherford, R. 2004. *Classical Literature: a Concise History.* Oxford.

Rutter, N. K. 2000. Coin Types and Identity: Greek Cities in Sicily. In C. Smith and J. Serrati (eds), *Sicily from Aeneas to Augustus.* Edinburgh. 73–83.

Rutter, N. K. et al. (eds) 2001. *Historia Numorum. Part 1. Italy.* London.

Sabin, P., van Wees, H., and Whitby, M. (eds) 2007. *The Cambridge History of Greek and Roman Warfare.* 2 vols. Cambridge.

Sadori, L. and Narcisi, B. 2001. The Postglacial Record of Environmental History from Lago di Pergusa, Sicily. *The Holocene* 11: 655–71.

Sadurska, A. and Bounni, A. 1994. *Les sculptures funéraires de Palmyre.* Rome.

Säflund, G. 1932. *Le mura di Roma repubblicana. Saggio di archeologia romana.* Lund.

Said, E. W. 1978. *Orientalism: Western Conceptions of the Orient.* London.

Saïd, S. 1984. Grecs et barbares dans les tragédies d'Euripide: le fin des différences. *Ktema* 9, 27–53. Translated as "Greeks and Barbarians in Euripides' Tragedies: the End of Differences?", in Harrison 2002b: 62–100.

Saïd, S. and Trédé, M. 1999. *A Short History of Greek Literature.* London.

Sallares, R. 1991. *The Ecology of the Ancient Greek World.* London.

Sallares, R. 2002. *Malaria and Rome: A History of Malaria in Ancient Italy.* Oxford.

Sallares, R. 2005. Pathocoenoses Ancient and Modern. *History and Philosophy of the Life Sciences.* 27: 221–40.

Sallares, R. 2007. Ecology, Evolution, and Epidemiology of Plague. In L. Little (ed.), *Plague and the End of Antiquity: The Pandemic of 541–750.* Cambridge. 231–289.

Sallares. R., Bouwman, A. and Anderung, C. 2004. The Spread of Malaria to Southern Europe in Antiquity: New Approaches to Old Problems. *Medical History* 48: 311–28.

Saller, R. 1994. *Patriarchy, Property and Death in the Roman Family,* Cambridge.

Saller, R. 2007. Household and Gender. In Scheidel et al. 2007: chap. 4.

Saller, R. and Shaw, B. D. 1984. Tombstones and Roman Family Relations in the Principate: Civilians, Soldiers and Slaves. *JRS* 74: 124–56.

Salmon, E. T. 1965. *Samnium and the Samnites.* Cambridge.

Salmon, E. T. 1982. *The Making of Roman Italy.* London.

Salmon, J. and Shipley, G. (eds) 1996. *Human Landscapes of Classical Antiquity: Environment and Culture.* London.

Sancisi-Weerdenburg, H. 1995. Persian Food. In Wilkins et al. 1995: 286–302.

Sanders, E. P. 1977. *Paul and Palestinian Judaism.* Philadelphia.

Sanders, E. P. 1987. *Jesus and Judaism.* 2nd edn. London.

Sanders, E. P. 1992. *Judaism: Practice and Belief, 63 BCE–66 CE.* London.

Sanders, E. P. 1993. *The Historical Figure of Jesus.* London.

Sandys, J. E. 1908. *A History of Classical Scholarship.* 3 vols. Cambridge.

Sapelli, M. (ed.) 1999. *Provinciae fideles. Il fregio del Tempio di Adriano in Campo Marzio.* Rome.

Sasson, J. M. (ed.) 1995. *Civilizations of the Ancient Near East.* New York.

Satlow, M. L. 1995. *Tasting the Dish: Rabbinic Rhetorics of Sexuality.* Atlanta.

Sauneron, S. et al. 1972. *Textes et langages de l'Egypte pharaonique: Hommage à Jean-François Champollion.* 3 vols. Cairo.

Scagliarini Corlaità, D. 1993. Per un catalogo delle opere di Apollodoro di Damasco, architetto di Traiano. *Ocnus* 1: 185–93.

Scanlon, T. 2002. *Eros and Greek Athletics.* Oxford.

Schäfer, P. 1995. *The History of the Jews in Antiquity,* Luxembourg (repr. London 2003).

Schallmayer, E. (ed.) 1997. *Hundert Jahre Saalburg: vom römische Grenzposten zum europäischen Museum.* Mainz.

Schaps, D. M. 1979. *Economic Rights of Women in Ancient Greece.* Edinburgh.

Schaps, D. M. 2004. *The Invention of Coinage and the Monetization of Ancient Greece.* Ann Arbor.

Scheid, J. 2003. *An Introduction to Roman Religion.* Edinburgh.

Scheidel, W. 1996. *Measuring Sex, Age and Death in the Roman Empire: Explorations in Ancient Demography,* Ann Arbor.

Scheidel, W. 1997. Quantifying the Sources of Slaves in the Early Roman Empire. *JRS* 87: 156–69.

Scheidel, W. 1999. Emperors, Aristocrats and the Grim Reaper: Towards a Demographic Profile of the Roman Elite. *CQ* 49: 254–81.

Scheidel, W. 2001a. *Death on the Nile: Disease and the Demography of Roman Egypt.* Leiden.

Scheidel, W. 2001b. Progress and Problems in Roman Demography. In Scheidel 2001d: 1–81.

Scheidel, W. 2001c. Roman Age Structure: Evidence and Models. *JRS* 91: 1–26.

Scheidel, W. (ed.) 2001d. *Debating Roman Demography,* Leiden.

Scheidel, W. 2002. A Model of Demographic and Economic Change in Roman Egypt after the Antonine Plague. *JRA* 15: 97–114.

Scheidel, W. 2003a. Germs for Rome. In Edwards and Woolf 2003: 158–76.

Scheidel, W. 2003b. The Greek Demographic Expansion: Models and Comparisons. *JHS* 123: 120–40.

Scheidel, W. 2004. Human Mobility in Roman Italy I: The Free Population. In *JRS* 94: 1–26.

Scheidel, W. 2005. Human Mobility in Roman Italy II: The Slaves. *JRS* 95: 64–79.

Scheidel, W. 2007a. Demography. In Scheidel et al. 2007: chap. 3.

Scheidel, W. 2007b. Roman Funerary Commemoration and the Age at First Marriage. *Classical Philology* 102: 389–402.

Scheidel, W. 2008a. Roman population size: the logic of the debate. In L. de Ligt and S. Northwood (eds), *People, land and politics: demographic developments and the transformation of Roman Italy 300 BC–AD 14.* Leiden. 15–70.

Scheidel, W. 2008b. The Comparative Economics of Slavery in the Greco-Roman World. In Dal Lago and Katsari 2008: 105–26.

Scheidel, W. 2009. Sex and Empire: A Darwinian Perspective. In I. Morris and W. Scheidel (eds), *The Dynamics of Ancient Empires.* New York. 255–324.

Scheidel, W. (forthcoming.) Sex Ratios and Femicide in the Ancient Mediterranean World.

Scheidel, W. and Friesen, S. 2008. The size of the economy and the distribution of income in the Roman Empire. *Princeton Stanford Working Papers in Classics* (http://www.princeton. edu/~pswpc/papers/authorMZ/scheidel/scheidel.html)

Scheidel, W. and von Reden, S. (eds) 2002. *The Ancient Economy.* Edinburgh.

Scheidel, W., Morris, I. and Saller, R. (eds) 2007. *The Cambridge Economic History of the Greco-Roman World*. Cambridge.

Schiavone, A. 2000. *The End of the Past. Ancient Rome and the Modern West*. Cambridge, MA.

Schickel, E. 1996. *D. W. Griffith. An American Life*. New York.

Schiesaro, A. 1997. The Boundaries of Knowledge in Virgil's *Georgics*, *The Roman Cultural Revolution*. Cambridge. 63–89.

Schiffman, L. H. 1991. *From Text to Tradition: A History of Second Temple and Rabbinic Judaism*. Hoboken, NJ.

Schiøler, T. and Wikander, O. 1983. A Roman Water-Mill in the Baths of Caracalla. *Opuscula Romana* 14: 47–64.

Schmandt-Besserat, D. 1992. *Before Writing*. 2 vols. Austin, TX.

Schmidt, T.-M. 1999. Proserpina-Sarkophag. In C. Stiegemann and M. Wemhoff (eds), *799 Kunst und Kultur der Karolingerzeit. Karl der Grosse und Papst Leo III in Paderborn*. Mainz. vol. 2: 758–63.

Schmitt, R. 1991. *The Bisitun Inscriptions of Darius the Great*. Old Persian Text, London.

Schmitt-Pantel, P. 1992. *La cité au banquet*. Paris.

Schmitz, P. 1995. The Phoenician Text from the Etruscan Sanctuary at Pyrgi. *Journal of the American Oriental Society* 115: 559–75.

Schmitz, T. 1997. *Bildung und Macht. Zur sozialen und politischen Funktion der zweiten Sophistik in der griechischen Welt der Kaiserzeit*. Munich.

Schmitz, T. 2002. *Moderne Literaturtheorie und antike Texte: eine Einführung*. Darmstadt.

Schneider, R. 1986. *Bunte Barbaren. Orientalenstatuen aus farbigem Marmor in der römischen Repräsentationskunst*. Worms.

Schofield, M. 1991. *The Stoic Idea of the City*. Cambridge.

Scholtz, A. 2002/03. Aphrodite Pandemos at Naukratis. *GRBS* 43: 231–42.

Schow, N. 1787. *Charta papyracea graece scripta Musei Borgiani Velitris . . . edita a Nicolao Schow*. Rome.

Schowalter, D. N. and Friesen, S. J. (eds) 2005. *Urban Religion in Roman Corinth: Interdisciplinary Approaches*. Cambridge MA.

Schubart, W. 1913. Alexandrinische Urkunden aus der Zeit des Augustus. *Archiv für Papyrusforschung* 5: 35–131.

Schulze, H. 1996. *States, Nations and Nationalism from the Middle Ages to the Present*. Oxford (first pub. in German 1994).

Schumacher, L. 1988. *Römische Inschriften: Lateinisch, Deutsch*. Stuttgart.

Schumpeter, J. A. 1918. The Crisis of the Tax State. In *International Economic Papers* No. 4, A. T. Peacock et al. (eds), London. 5–38. (First published as Die Krise des Steuerstaats. *Zeitfragen aus dem Gebiete der Soziologie*. Graz and Leipzig, 1918.)

Schürer, E. 1973–87. *The History of the Jewish People in the Time of Jesus Christ*, revised by G. Vermes et al., 3 vols. Edinburgh.

Schwarcz, H. 2002. Tracing Human Migration with Stable Isotopes. In K. Aoki and T. Akazawa (eds), *Human Mate Choice and Prehistoric Marital Networks*. Kyoto. 183–201.

Schwartz, S. 2002. *Imperialism and Jewish Society, 200 BCE to 640 CE*. Princeton.

Scott, J. 2002. Feminist Reverberations. *Differences* 13.3: 1–23.

Scott, K. 1932. Mussolini and the Roman Empire. *Classical Journal*. 27: 645–57.

Scullard, H. H. 1970. *Scipio Africanus: Soldier and Politician*. London.

Seaford, R. 2004. *Money and the Early Greek Mind: Homer, Philosophy, Tragedy*. Cambridge.

Semino O. et al. 2004. Origin, Diffusion, and Differentiation of Y-Chromosome Haplogroups E and J: Inferences on the Neolithization of Europe and Later Migratory Events in the Mediterranean Area. *AJHG* 74: 1023–34.

Semple, E. C. 1932. *The Geography of the Mediterranean Region: Its Relation to Ancient History.* London.

Sennequier, G. and Colonna, C. 2003. *L'Algérie au temps des royaumes numides.* Paris.

Sergent, B. 1986. *Homosexuality in Greek Myth.* London.

Sevcenko, I. and Sevcenko, N. 1984. *The Life of Saint Nicholas of Sion.* Brookline, MA.

Shaw, B. D. 1982. Fear and Loathing: the Nomad Menace and Roman Africa. In C. M. Wells (ed.), *L'Afrique Romaine/Roman Africa.* Ottowa. 29–50.

Shaw, B. D. 1987. The Age of Roman Girls at Marriage: Some Reconsiderations. *JRS* 77: 30–46.

Shaw, B. D. 1988. Roman Taxation. In M. Grant and R. Kitzinger (eds), *Civilization of the Ancient Mediterranean.* New York. vol. II, 809–27.

Shaw, B. D. 1995a. *Environment and Society in Roman North Africa.* Aldershot, Hampshire.

Shaw, B. D. 1995b. *Rulers, Nomads, and Christians in Roman North Africa.* Aldershot, Hampshire.

Shaw, B. D. 1996. Seasons of Death: Aspects of Mortality in Imperial Rome. *JRS* 86: 100–38.

Shaw, B. D. 1997. Ritual Brotherhood in Roman and Post-Roman Societies. *Traditio* 52: 327–55.

Shaw, B. D. 1999. War and Violence. In G. Bowersock, P. Brown, and O. Grabar (eds), *Late Antiquity. A Guide to the Postclassical World.* Cambridge, MA. 130–69.

Shaw, B. D. 2001. Challenging Braudel: a New Vision of the Mediterranean. *JRA* 14: 419–53.

Shaw, B. D. 2003. A Peculiar Island: Maghrib and Mediterranean. *Mediterranean Historical Review* 18: 93–125 (= Malkin 2005: 93–125).

Shaw, B. D. 2006. *At the Edge of the Corrupting Sea: the Twenty-Third J. L. Myres Memorial Lecture.* Oxford.

Shaw, I. (ed.) 2000. *The Oxford History of Ancient Egypt.* Oxford.

Shaw, I. and Nicholson, P. 1995. *British Museum Dictionary of Ancient Egypt.* London.

Shaw, T. 1998. *The Burden of the Flesh: Fasting and Sexuality in Early Christianity.* Minneapolis.

Shay, J. 1994. *Achilles in Vietnam.* New York.

Shelton, J. 1998. *As the Romans Did: a Sourcebook in Roman Social History.* 2nd edn. New York.

Sherk, R. K. 1969. *Roman Documents from the Greek East: Senatus Consulta and Epistulae to the Age of Augustus.* Baltimore.

Sherk, R. K. 1984. *Rome and the Greek East to the Age of Augustus.* Translated Documents of Greece and Rome 4. Cambridge.

Sherk, R. K. 1988. *The Roman Empire: Augustus to Hadrian.* Translated Documents of Greece and Rome 6. Cambridge.

Sherwin-White, A. N. 1973. The *Tabula* of Banasa and the *Constitutio Antoniniana. JRS* 73: 86–98.

Sherwin-White, A. N. 1975. *The Roman Citizenship.* 2nd edn. Oxford.

Shipley, G. 2000. *The Greek World after Alexander 323–30 BC.* London.

Shotyk, W. et al. 1998. History of Atmospheric Lead Deposition since 12,370 ^{14}C yr BP from a Peat Bog, Jura Mountains, Switzerland. *Science* 281: 1635–40.

Shrimpton, G. 1997. *History and Memory in Ancient Greece.* Montreal.

Shupak, N. 1993. *Where Can Wisdom be Found? The Sage's Language in the Bible and in Ancient Egyptian Literature.* Fribourg.

Sickinger, J. 1999. *Public Records and Archives in Classical Athens.* Chapel Hill.

Siegmund, A. 1949. *Die Überlieferung der griechischen christlichen Literatur in der lateinischen Kirche bis zum zwölften Jahrhundert.* Munich.

Silver, M. 1995. *Economic Structures of Antiquity*. Westport, CT and London.

Simpson, W. 1963. Studies in the Twelfth Egyptian Dynasty I–II. *Journal of the American Research Center in Egypt* 2: 53–63.

Sims-Williams, P. 1998. Genetics, Linguistics, and Prehistory: Thinking Big and Thinking Straight. *Antiquity* 72: 505–27.

Sims-Williams, P. 2006. *Celtic Place-Names in Europe and Asia Minor*. Oxford.

Sirago, V. 1995–96. *Storia agraria romana*. 2 vols. Naples.

Sissa, G. 1990. *Greek Virginity*. Trans. A. Goldhammer. Cambridge, MA.

Skinner, J. (forthcoming.) Fish Heads and Mussel-Shells: Visualizing Greek Identity. In L. Foxhall and H-J. Gehrke (eds), *Intentionale Geschichte: Spinning History*. Stuttgart.

Skinner, Q. 1974. Some Problems in the Analysis of Political Thought and Action. *Political Theory* 2: 277–303.

Skinner, M. B. 1983. Clodia Metelli. *TAPA* 113: 273–87.

Skinner, M. B. 1989. Sapphic Nossis. *Arethusa* 22: 5–18.

Skinner, M. B. 1996. Zeus and Leda: The Sexuality Wars in Contemporary Classical Scholarship. *Thamyris* 3.1: 103–23.

Skinner, M. B. 2005. *Sexuality in Greek and Roman Culture*. Oxford.

Slater, N. 1998. The Vase as Ventriloquist: *Kalos*-Inscriptions and the Culture of Fame. In E. Mackay (ed.), *Signs of Orality: The Oral Tradition and its Influence in the Greek and Roman World*. Leiden. 143–61.

Slater, W. (ed.) 1991. *Dining in a Classical Context*. Ann Arbor.

Smith, A. 1776. *An Inquiry into the Nature and Causes of the Wealth of Nations*. London.

Smith, A. D. 1986. *The Ethnic Origins of Nations*. Oxford.

Smith, A. D. 2001. *Nationalism: Theory, Ideology, History*. Cambridge.

Smith, C. J. 1996. *Early Rome and Latium*. Oxford.

Smith, C. J. 1998. Traders and Artisans in Archaic Central Italy. In H. Parkins and C. J. Smith (eds), *Trade, Traders and the Ancient City*. London. 31–51.

Smith, J. M. H. (ed.) 2000. *Early Medieval Rome and the Christian West. Essays in Honour of Donald Bullough*. Leiden.

Smith, J. T. 1997. *Roman Villas: a Study in Social Structure*. London.

Smith, J. Z. 1990. *Drudgery Divine: On the Comparison of Early Christianities and the Religions of Late Antiquity*. Chicago.

Smith, P. 1971. *The Tenth Muse. A Historical Study of the Opera Libretto*. London.

Smith, R. R. R. 1998. Cultural Choice and Political Identity in Honorific Portrait Statues in the Greek East in the Second Century AD. *JRS* 88: 56–93.

Smith, W. 1979. *The Hippocratic Tradition*. Ithaca.

Snell, D. 2005. *A Companion to the Ancient Near East*. Oxford.

Snodgrass, A. 1980. *Archaic Greece: The Age of Experiment*. London.

Snodgrass, A. 1987. *An Archaeology of Greece. The Present State and Future Scope of a Discipline*, Berkeley.

Snodgrass, A. 2002. A Paradigm Shift in Classical Archaeology? *Cambridge Archaeological Journal* 12: 179–94.

Snowden, F. 1983. *Before Color Prejudice. The Ancient View of Blacks*. Cambridge, MA.

Snyder, J. 1989. *The Woman and the Lyre: Women Writers in Classical Greece and Rome*. Carbondale, IL.

Sobchack, V. 1990. Surge and Splendour. A Phenomenology of the Hollywood Historical Epic. *Representations* 29. 24–49.

Solin, H. 1971. *Beiträge zur Kenntnis der griechischen Personnenamen in Rom* I. Helsinki.

Solomon, J. 2001. *The Ancient World in Cinema*. 2nd edn. New Haven.

Sourvinou-Inwood, C. 1978. Persephone and Aphrodite at Locri: a Model for Personality Definitions in Greek religion. *JHS* 98: 101–21.

Sourvinou-Inwood, C. 1990. What is Polis-Religion? In Murray and Price 1990: 295–332.

Sourvinou-Inwood, C. 1995. *"Reading" Greek Death*. Oxford.

Sourvinou-Inwood, C. 2003. Herodotus (and Others) on Pelasgians: Some Perceptions of Ethnicity. In P. S. Derow and R. Parker (eds) *Herodotus and his World*. Oxford. 103–44.

Sourvinou-Inwood, C. 2004. Hermaphroditos and Salmakis: The Voice of Halikarnassos. In S. Isager and P. Pedersen (eds), *The Salmakis Inscription and Hellenistic Halikarnassos*. Odense. 59–84.

Spann, P. O. 1987. *Quintus Sertorius and the Legacy of Sulla*. University of Arkansas.

Spannagel, M. 1999. *Exemplaria principis. Untersuchungen zu Entstehung und Ausstattung des Augustusforums*. Heidelberg.

Sparkes, B. 1962. The Greek Kitchen. *JHS* 82: 121–37.

Spawforth, A. 1999. The Panhellenion Again. *Chiron* 29: 339–52.

Spawforth, A. 2006. *The Complete Greek Temples*. London.

Speake, G. (ed.) 2000. *Encyclopedia of Greece and the Hellenic Tradition*. London.

Speidel, M. 1996. *Die römischen Schreibtafeln von Vindonissa (Veröffentlichungen der Gesellschaft pro Vindonissa* 12). Brugg.

Speranza, A., van Geel, B., and van der Plicht, J. 2002. Evidence for Solar Forcing of Climate Change at ca. 850 cal. BC from a Czech Peat Sequence. *Global and Planetary Change* 35: 51–65.

Spivey, N. and Stoddart, S. 1990. *Etruscan Italy: an Archaeological History*. London.

Spoerri, W. 1959. *Späthellenistische Berichte über Welt, Kultur und Götter: Untersuchungen zu Diodor von Sizilien*. Basel.

Spurr, M. S. 1986. *Arable Cultivation in Roman Italy c.200 BC–AD 100*. London.

St Clair, W. 1998. *Lord Elgin and the Marbles*. 3rd rev. edn. Oxford.

Stadter, P. 1992. Herodotus and the Athenian *arche*. *ASNP* 22.3–4: 781–809.

Stambaugh, J. E. 1988. *The Ancient Roman City*. Baltimore.

Stanton, G. 2004. *Jesus and Gospel*. Cambridge.

Stark, R. 1996. *The Rise of Christianity: A Sociologist Reconsiders History*. Princeton.

Starr, C. G. 1966. Historical and Philosophical Time. *History and Theory*. 6: 24–35.

Steel, C. 2005. *Reading Cicero*. London.

Stefani, G. 2003. *Menander: la casa del Menandro di Pompei*. Milan.

Steinby, E. M. (ed.) 1993–2000. *Lexicon Topographicum Urbis Roma* I–VI. Rome.

Stemberger, G. 1996. *Introduction to the Talmud and Midrash*. Translated and edited by M. Bockmuehl. 2nd edn. Edinburgh (1st edn 1991).

Stern, M. 1976–84. *Greek and Latin Authors on Jews and Judaism*. 3 vols. Jerusalem.

Stern, S. 1994. *Jewish Identity in Early Rabbinic Writings*. Leiden.

Stevenson, J. 1978. *The Catacombs*. London.

Stone, A. 1980. *Pro Milone*: Cicero's second thoughts. *Antichthon* 14: 88–111.

Stone, L. 1971. Prosopography. *Daedalus* 100: 46–79.

Stone, M. 1993. Staging Fascism: the Exhibition of the Fascist Revolution. *Journal of Contemporary History* 28: 215–43.

Stone, M. 1999. A Flexible Rome. Fascism and the Cult of *romanità*. In C. Edwards 1999: 205–220.

Storey, G. R. 1997. The Population of Ancient Rome. *Antiquity* 71: 966–78.

Stothers, R. and Rampino, M. 1983. Volcanic Eruptions in the Mediterranean before 630 AD from Written and Archaeological Sources. *Journal of Geophysical Research* 88: 6357–71.

Strasburger, H. 1972. *Homer und die Geschichtsschreibung.* Heidelberg.

Stray, C. 1998. *Classics Transformed: Schools, Universities and Society in England 1830–1960.* Oxford.

Strobel, K. 1994. Keltensieg und Galatersieger. Die Funktionalisierung eines historischen Phänomens als politischer Mythos der hellenistischen Welt. In E. Schwertheim (ed.), *Forschungen in Galatien.* Bonn. 67–96.

Stroh, W. 1975. *Taxis und Taktik: die advokatische Dispositionskunst in Ciceros Gerichtsreden.* Stuttgart.

Stroud, R. S. 1998. *The Athenian Grain Tax Law of 374–373 BC. Hesperia* Supplement 29. Princeton.

Strubbe, J. 1984–86. Gründer kleinasiatischer Städte. Fiktion und Realität. *Ancient Society* 15–17: 253–304.

Suder, W. 1988. *Census Populi: Bibliographie de la démographie de l'antiquité romaine.* Bonn.

Sünskes-Thompson, J. 1993. *Demonstrative Legitimation der Kaiserherrschaft im Epochenvergleich. Zur politischen Macht des stadtrömischen Volkes.* Stuttgart.

Suny, R. G. 2002. Back and Beyond: Reversing the Cultural Turn? *AHR* 107: 1–56.

Susini, G. 1973. *The Roman Stonecutter: an Introduction to Latin Epigraphy.* Totowa, NJ.

Syme, R. 1939. *The Roman Revolution.* Oxford.

Syme, R. 1958a. *Tacitus.* Oxford.

Syme, R. 1958b. The Senator as Historian. In *Histoire et historiens dans l'Antiquité classique.* Vandoevres-Genève. 187–201 (= Syme 1970: 1–10).

Syme, R. 1970. *Ten Studies in Tacitus.* Oxford.

Tacoma, L. 2006. *Fragile Hierarchies: The Urban Elites of Third-Century Roman Egypt.* Leiden.

Takács, S. A. 1995. *Isis and Sarapis in the Roman World.* Leiden.

Talbert, R. J. A. 1984. *The Senate of Imperial Rome.* Princeton.

Tanitch, R. 2000. *Blockbusters! 70 Years of Best-Selling Movies.* London.

Taplin, O. (ed.) 2000. *Literature in the Greek and Roman Worlds.* Oxford.

Tashiro, C. 1998. *Pretty Pictures. Production Design and the History Film.* Austin.

Tatum, W. J. 1999. *The Patrician Tribune Publius Clodius Pulcher.* Chapel Hill.

Taylor, L. R. 1961. Freedmen and Freeborn in the Epitaphs of Imperial Rome. *AJP* 82: 113–32.

Taylor, L. R. 1966. *Roman Voting Assemblies. From the Hannibalic War to the Dictatorship of Caesar.* Ann Arbor.

Tchernia, A. 1983. Italian Wine in Gaul at the End of the Republic. In Garnsey et al. 1983: 87–104.

Tchernia, A. 1986. *Le vin de l'Italie romaine.* Rome.

Tecusan, M. 2004. *The Fragments of the Methodists. Volume 1: Methodism outside Soranus.* Leiden.

Teffeteller, A. 2006. Script Technology and Political Identity. In Technical Chamber of Greece (ed.), *Proceedings of the Second International Conference on Ancient Greek Technology.* Athens. 726–31.

Terrenato, N. 1997. The Romanisation of Italy: Global Acculturation or Cultural *bricolage*? In C. Forcey, J. Hawthorne, and R. Witcher (eds), *TRAC 97: Proceedings of the 7th Theoretical Roman Archaeology Conference.* Oxford. 20–27.

Thébert, Y. 1987. Private Life and Domestic Architecture in Roman Africa. In P. Veyne (ed.), *A History of Private Life: from Pagan Rome to Byzantium.* Cambridge, MA. 313–409.

Thivel, A. 1981. *Cnide et Cos?* Paris.

Thomas, R. 2000. *Herodotus in Context. Ethnography, Science and the Art of Persuasion.* Cambridge.

Thomas, R. 2001. *Virgil and the Augustan Reception.* Cambridge.

Thompson, D. J. 1988. *Memphis under the Ptolemies.* Princeton.

Thompson, D. J. 1992a. Literacy in Early Ptolemaic Egypt. *Proc. XIX International Congress of Papyrologists.* Cairo: 77–90.

Thompson, D. J. 1992b. Literacy and the Administration in Early Ptolemaic Egypt. In J. H. Johnson (ed.), *Life in a Multi-Cultural Society. Egypt from Cambyses to Constantine and Beyond* (Studies in Oriental Civilization 51, Chicago): 323–26.

Thompson, D. J. 2003. The Ptolemies and Egypt. In Erskine 2003. 105–20.

Thompson, E. A. 1952. *A Roman Reformer and Inventor.* Oxford.

Thompson, M., Mørkholm, O., and Kraay, C. 1973. *Inventory of Greek Coin Hoards.* New York.

Tilley, A. 2004. *Seafaring on the Ancient Mediterranean.* Oxford.

Tod, M. 1948. *Greek Historical Inscriptions.* vol. 2. Oxford.

Todd, S. C. 1993. *The Shape of Athenian Law.* Oxford.

Toepel, L. R. 1973. Studies in the Administrative and Economic History of Tebtunis in the First Century AD. Diss. Duke University.

Tomlin, R. S. O. 1998. Roman Manuscripts from Carlisle: the Ink-Written Tablets. *Britannia* 29: 31–84.

Too, Y. L. (ed.) 2001. *Education in Greek and Roman Antiquity.* Leiden.

Too, Y. L. and Livingstone, N. (eds) 1998. *Pedagogy and Power. Rhetorics of Classical Learning.* Cambridge.

Toplin, R. 2002. *Reel History. In Defence of Hollywood.* Kansas.

Torelli, M. 1982. *Etruria* (*Guide Archeologiche Laterza* 3). Bari.

Torelli, M. (ed.) 2001. *The Etruscans.* Rome/London.

Torjesen, K. J. 1993. *When Women Were Priests: Women's Leadership in the Early Church and the Scandal of their Subordination in the Rise of Christianity.* San Francisco.

Tosh, J. 2002. *The Pursuit of History.* London.

Totelin, L. 2007. Sex and Vegetables in the Hippocratic Corpus. *Studies in History and Philosophy of Biological and Biomedical Sciences* 38: 531–40.

Toynbee, A. J. 1965. *Hannibal's Legacy: The Hannibalic War's Effects on Roman Life.* 2 vols. London.

Toynbee, J. M. C. 1971. *Death and Burial in the Roman World.* London.

Toynbee, J. M. C. 1978. *Roman Historical Portraits.* London.

Treggiari, S. 1975. Jobs in the Household of Livia. *PBSR* 43: 48–77.

Treggiari, S. 1976. Jobs for Women. *AJAH* 1: 76–104.

Treggiari, S. 1980. Urban Labour in Rome: Mercenarii and Tabernarii. In Garnsey 1980: 48–64.

Treggiari, S. 1991. *Roman Marriage*: Iusti Coniuges *from the Time of Cicero to the Time of Ulpian.* Oxford.

Treggiari, S. 2007. *Terentia, Tullia and Publilia: The Women of Cicero's Family.* London.

Trevett, C. 1996. *Montanism. Gender, Authority and the New Prophecy.* Cambridge.

Trevett, J. 1996. Did Demosthenes Publish his Deliberative Speeches? *Hermes* 124: 425–41.

Trigger, B., Kemp, B. J., and O'Connor, D. 1983. *Ancient Egypt: A Social History.* Cambridge.

Trigger, B. G. 1989. *A History of Archaeological Thought.* Cambridge.

Tritle, L. 2000. *From Melos to My Lai: War and Survival.* London.

Trüdinger, K. 1918. *Studien zur Geschichte der griechisch-römischen Ethnographie.* Basel.

Trundle, M. 2004. *Greek Mercenaries from the Late Archaic Period to Alexander.* London.

Turcan, R. 1996. *The Cults of the Roman Empire*. Oxford.

Turner, E. G. 1973. *The Papyrologist at Work*. Durham, NC.

Turner, E. G. 1978. *The Terms Recto and Verso, the Anatomy of the Papyrus Roll*. In J. Bingen, and G. Nachtergael (eds), *Actes du XVe congrès international de papyrologie* (Papyrologica Bruxellensia 16), Brussels: 1ᵉ partie.

Turner, E. G. 1979. Oxyrhynchus and Rome. *HSCP* 79: 1–24.

Turner, E. G. 1980. *Greek Papyri, an Introduction*. 2nd edn. Oxford.

Turner, E. G. 1987. *Greek Manuscripts of the Ancient World*. 2nd rev. edn. (P. J. Parsons). Bulletin of the Institute of Classical Studies, Suppl. 46. London.

Turner, G. 1990. *British Cultural Studies: An Introduction*. 2nd edn. London.

Untermann, J. 1975–. *Monumenta linguarum Hispanicarum*. Wiesbaden.

Urbach, E. E. 1975. *The Sages: Their Concepts and Beliefs* (trans. I. Abrahams). 2 vols. Jerusalem.

Van de Mieroop, M. 1999. *The Ancient Mesopotamian City*. Oxford.

Van de Mieroop, M. 2004. *A History of the Ancient Near East ca.3000–323 BC*. Oxford.

Van de Mieroop, M. 2005. The Eastern Mediterranean in Early Antiquity. In W. Harris 2005: 117–37.

van der Eijk, P. 2000. *Diocles of Carystus: a Collection of the Fragments with Translation and Commentary*. 2 vols. Leiden.

van der Eijk, P., Horstmanshoff, H., and Schrijversm P. (eds) 1995. *Ancient Medicine in its Socio-Cultural Context*. 2 vols. Amsterdam.

van Dommelen, P. and Terrenato, N. (eds) 2007. *Articulating Local Cultures: Power and Identity under the Expanding Roman Republic*. Portsmouth, RI.

van Effenterre, H. 1994–95. *Nomima. Recueil d'inscriptions politiques et juridiques de l'archaïsme grec*. 2 vols. Rome.

Van Groningen, B. A. (ed.) 1933. *Aristote, le second livre de l'Economique*. Leiden.

van Hooff, A. J. L. 1990. *From Autothanasia to Suicide: Self-Killing in Classical Antiquity*. London.

Van Minnen, P. 1987. Urban Craftsmen in Roman Egypt. *Münstersche Beiträge zur antiken Handelsgeschichte* 6.1: 31–88.

Van Minnen, P. 1993. The Century of Papyrology (1892–1992). *Bulletin of the American Society of Papyrologists* 30: 5–18.

Van Minnen, P. 1994. House-to-House Enquiries: an Interdisciplinary Approach to Roman Karanis. *ZPE* 100: 227–51.

Van Minnen, P. 1998. Boorish or Bookish? Literature in Egyptian Villages in the Fayum in the Graeco-Roman Period. *Journal of Juristic Papyrology* 28: 99–184.

Van Minnen, P. 2000. An Official Act of Cleopatra (with a Subscription in her Own Hand). *Ancient Society* 30: 29–34.

Van Minnen, P. 2001. Further Thoughts on the Cleopatra Papyrus. *Archiv für Papyrusforschung* 47: 74–80.

Van Minnen, P. 2002. Hermopolis in the Crisis of the Roman Empire. In W. Jongman and M. Kleiwegt (eds), *After the Past: Essays in Ancient History in Honour of H. W. Pleket*. Leiden. 285–304.

Van Minnen, P. 2003. A Royal Ordinance of Cleopatra and Related Documents. In S. Walker and S.-A. Ashton (eds), *Cleopatra Reassessed*. London: 35–44.

Van Minnen, P. 2007. The Millennium of Papyrology (2001–?). In B. Palme (ed.), *Akten des 23 internationalen Papyrologenkongresses*. Vienna. 703–14.

van Nijf, O. M. 1997. *The Civic World of Professional Associations in the Roman East*. Amsterdam.

van Nijf, O. M. 2001. Local Heroes: Athletics, Festivals and Elite Self-Fashioning in the Roman East. In S. Goldhill (ed.), *Being Greek under Rome: Cultural Identity, the Second Sophistic and the Development of Empire*. Cambridge: 306–34.

van Wees, H. 1992. *Status Warriors: War, Violence and Society in Homer and History*. Amsterdam.

van Wees, H. (ed.) 2000. *War and Violence in Ancient Greece*. London.

van Wees, H. 2004. *Greek Warfare: Myths and Realities*. London.

Vanderbroeck, P. 1987. *Popular Leadership and Collective Behaviour in the Late Roman Republic (ca.80–50 BC)*. Amsterdam.

Vandersleyen, P. 1995. *L'Egypte et la vallée du Nil, II: De la fin de l'Ancien Empire à la fin du Nouvel Empire*. Paris.

Vandorpe, K. 1994. Museum Archaeology or How to Reconstruct Pathyris Archives. In *Acta Demotica. Acts of the Fifth International Conference for Demotists, Pisa 4–8 September 1993. Egitto e Vicino Oriente* 17: 289–300.

Vattuone, R. 2004. *Il mostro e il sapiente. Studi sull'erotica greca*. Bologna.

Veenhof, K. R. 1972. *Aspects of Old Assyrian Trade and its Terminology*. Leiden.

Vera, D. (ed.) 1999. *Demografia, sistemi agrari, regimi alimentari nel mondo antico*. Bari.

Vermes, G. 2001. *Jesus the Jew: a Historian's Reading of the Gospels*. new edn. London.

Vermes, G. 2004. *The Complete Dead Sea Scrolls in English*. rev. edn. London.

Vermes, G. 2005. *The Passion*. London.

Vermes, G. 2008. *The Resurrection. History and Myth*. London.

Vernant, J.-P. (ed.) 1968. *Problèmes de la guerre en Grèce ancienne*. Paris.

Vernant, J.-P. 1980. *Myth and Society in Ancient Greece*. Brighton (first published in French 1974).

Verner, M. 2001. *The Pyramids: Their Archaeology and History*. New York.

Vernet, J.-L. 1997. *L'homme et la forêt méditerranéenne de la préhistoire à nos jours*. Paris.

Vetter, E. 1953. *Handbuch der italischen Dialekte*. Heidelberg.

Veyne, P. 1976. *Le Pain et le Cirque: Sociologie historique d'un pluralisme politique*. Paris. (Abridged as *Bread and Circuses: Historical Sociology and Political Pluralism*. Introduction by O. Murray; translated by B. Pearce. London, 1990.)

Veyne, P. 1978. La famille et l'amour sous le haut-empire romain. *Annales ESC* 33: 35–63.

Veyne, P. 1979. Témoignage hétérosexuelle d'un historien sur l'homosexualité. *Actes du Congrès International: Le regard des autres*. Paris. 17–24.

Veyne, P. 1988. *Did the Greeks Believe in their Myths? An Essay on the Constitutive Imagination*. Chicago.

Vidal, G. 1992. *Screening History*. Cambridge, MA.

Vidal-Naquet, P. 1986. *The Black Hunter: Forms of Thought and Forms of Society in the Greek World*. Baltimore.

Ville, G. 1981. *La gladiature en Occident des origenes à la mort de Domitien*. Paris.

Virlouvet, C. 1985. *Famines et émeutes à Rome des origines à la mort de Néron* (Coll. ÉFR 87). Rome.

Visser, R. 1992. Fascist Doctrine and the Cult of the *Romanità*. *Journal of Contemporary History* 27: 5–22.

Vita-Finzi, C. 1969. *The Mediterranean Valleys*. Cambridge.

Vitali, D. (ed.) 1992. *Tombe e necropoli galliche di Bologna e territorio*. Bologna.

Vlachou-Mogire, C. 2006. Silver Amalgam Plating and its Application in Roman Coin Production. In Technical Chamber of Greece (ed.), *Proceedings of the Second International Conference on Ancient Greek Technology*. Athens. 128–34.

von Fritz, K. 1954. *The Theory of the Mixed Constitution in Antiquity*. New York.

von Hesberg, H. 2005. Die Häuser der Senatoren in Rom; gesellschaftliche und politische Funktion. In W. Eck and M. Heil (eds), *Senatores populi Romani. Realität und mediale Präsentation einer Führungsschicht.* Stuttgart. 19–52.

von Kaenel, F. 1980. Les mésaventures du conjurateur de Serket Onnophris et de son tombeau. *BSFE* 87–8: 31–45.

von Reden, S. 1995. *Exchange in Ancient Greece.* London.

von Reden, S. 2002. Money in the Ancient Economy: a Survey of Recent Research. *Klio* 84: 141–174.

von Reden, S. 2006. The Ancient Economy and Ptolemaic Egypt. In Bang et al. 2006: 161–77.

von Reden, S. 2007. *Money in Ptolemaic Egypt. From the Macedonian Conquest to the End of the Third Century BC.* Cambridge.

von Staden, H. 1989. *Herophilus. The Art of Medicine in Early Alexandria,* Cambridge.

von Staden, H. 1992a. Women and Dirt. *Helios* 19: 7–30.

von Staden, H. 1992b. Spiderwoman and the Chaste Tree: the Semantics of Matter. *Configurations* 1: 23–56.

von Staden, H. 1994. Anatomy as Rhetoric: Galen on Dissection and Persuasion. *Journal of the History of Medicine and Allied Sciences* 50: 47–66.

von Staden, H. 1996. "In a Pure and Holy Way": Personal and Professional Conduct in the Hippocratic Oath? *Journal of the History of Medicine and Allied Sciences* 51: 404–37.

Vout, C. 2003. Embracing Egypt. In Edwards and Woolf 2003: 177–202.

Waddell, W. G. 1940. *Manetho* (Loeb Classical Library). Cambridge, MA.

Waelkens, M. 2002. Romanization in the East. A case study: Sagalassos and Pisidia (SW Turkey). *Istanbuler Mitteilungen* 52: 311–68.

Waelkens, M. et al. 1999. Man and Environment in the Territory of Sagalassos, a Classical City in SW Turkey. *Quaternary Science Reviews* 18: 697–709.

Waelkens, M. et al. 2006. The Late Antique to Early Byzantine City in Southwest Anatolia. Sagalassos and its Territory: A Case Study. In J.-U. Krause and C. Witschel (eds), *Die Stadt in der Spätantike – Niedergang oder Wandel?* Stuttgart. 199–255.

Walbank, F. W. 1951. The Problem of Greek Nationality. *Phoenix* 5: 41–60 (= *Selected Papers,* Cambridge 1985, 1–19).

Walbank, F. W. 1957. *A Historical Commentary on Polybius I.* Oxford.

Walbank, F. W. 1965. *Speeches in Greek Historians.* Oxford.

Walbank, F. W. 1972. *Polybius.* Berkeley.

Walbank, F. W. 1984. Monarchies and Monarchic Ideas. *CAH²* 7: 63–100.

Walbank, F. W. 1992. *The Hellenistic World.* rev. edn. London.

Walbank, F. W. 1993. Polybius and the Past. In H. D. Jocelyn (ed.), *Tria Lustra: Essays and Notes presented to John Pinsent.* Liverpool. 15–23; repr. in Walbank 2002: 178–92.

Walbank, F. W. 2002. *Polybius, Rome and the Hellenistic World: Essays and Reflections.* Cambridge.

Walden, J. 1912. *The Universities of Ancient Greece.* London.

Walker, S. 1985. *Memorials to the Roman Dead.* London.

Wallace-Hadrill, A. 1991. Elites and Trade in the Roman Town. In Rich and Wallace-Hadrill 1991: 241–72.

Wallace-Hadrill, A. 1994. *Houses and Society in Pompeii and Herculaneum.* Princeton.

Wallace-Hadrill, A. 1995. Public Honour and Private Shame: The Urban Texture in Pompeii. In K. Lomas (ed.), *Urban Society in Roman Italy.* London. 39–63.

Wallace-Hadrill, A. 1996. "Engendering the Roman House" in D. Kleiner and S. Matheson (eds), *I Claudia: Women in Ancient Rome.* New Haven. 104–15.

Wallace-Hadrill, A. 2003a. Domus and Insulae in Rome: Families and Housefuls. In D. Balch and C. Osiek (eds), *Early Christian Families in Context*. Grand Rapids. 3–18.

Wallace-Hadrill, A. 2003b. The Streets of Rome as a Representation of Imperial Power. In L. De Blois et al. (eds), *The Representations and Perception of Roman Imperial Power* (Impact of Empire 3). Amsterdam. 189–206.

Wallace-Hadrill, A. 2008. *Rome's Cultural Revolution*. Cambridge.

Wallerstein, I. 1974. *The Modern World-System I. Capitalist Agriculture and the Origins of the European World-Economy in the Sixteenth Century*. San Diego.

Walser, G. (ed.) 1987. *Die Einsiedler Inschriftensammlung und der Pilgerführer durch Rom (Codex Einsidlensis 326)*. Stuttgart.

Walter-Karydi, E. 1998. *The Greek House: the Rise of Noble Houses in Late Classical Times*. Athens.

Ward-Perkins, B. 2005. *The Fall of Rome and the End of Civilization*. Oxford.

Warren, J. 2004. *Facing Death. Epicurus and His Critics*. Oxford.

Warrior, V. M. 2002. *Roman Religion: A Sourcebook*. Newburyport, MA.

Warrior, V. M. 2006. *Roman Religion*. Cambridge.

Wasserstein, A. 1996. The Number and Provenance of Jews in Graeco-Roman Antiquity: A Note on Population Statistics. In R. Katzoff (ed.), *Classical Studies in Honor of David Sohlberg*. Ramat Gan. 307–17.

Waterer, J. 1976. Leatherwork. In D. Strong and D. Brown (eds), *Roman Crafts*. London. 179–193.

Watson, A. (ed.) 1985. *The Digest of Justinian*. 4 vols. Philadelphia.

Weaver, P. R. C. 1972. *Familia Caesaris. A Social Study of the Emperor's Freedmen and Slaves*. Cambridge.

Weber, M. 2001. *The Protestant Ethic and the Spirit of Capitalism* (tr. Talcott Parsons) with an introduction by A. Giddens, New York.

Wegner, J. R. 1988. *Chattel or Person? The Status of Women in the Mishnah*. Oxford.

Weiss, P. 2000. Eumeneia und das Panhellenion. *Chiron* 30: 617–39.

Weiss, P. 2003. The Vision of Constantine. *JRA* 16: 237–59.

Weiss, P. 2005. The Cities and their Money. In Howgego et al. 2005: 57–68.

Weiss, Z. 2005. *The Sepphoris Synagogue: Deciphering an Ancient Message through Its Archaeological and Socio-Historical Contexts*. Jerusalem.

Wells, B. (ed.) 1992. *Agriculture in Ancient Greece*. Stockholm.

Wells, P. S. 1999. *The Barbarians Speak*. Princeton.

Wells, P. S. 2001. *Beyond Celts, Germans and Scythians*. London.

Wells, P. S. 2003. *The Battle that Stopped Rome*. New York.

Welsby, D. 1996. *The Kingdom of Kush: The Napatan and Meroitic Empires*. London.

West, D. J. 1960. *Homosexuality*. Harmondsworth.

West, M. L. 1994. *Ancient Greek Music*. Oxford.

Whitby, M. 2007. Reconstructing Ancient Warfare. In Sabin et al. 2007: 54–81.

White, D. 2002. *Marsa Matruh*. Philadephia.

White, H. 1973. *Metahistory: The Historical Imagination in Nineteenth-Century Europe*. Baltimore.

White, H. 1978. *Tropics of Discourse. Essays in Cultural Criticism*. Baltimore/London.

White, H. 1987. *The Content of Form: Narrative Discourse and Historical Representation*. Baltimore.

White, K. D. 1970. *Roman Farming*. London.

White, K. D. 1984. *Greek and Roman Technology*. London.

Whitmarsh, T. 1998. Reading Power in Roman Greece: the *Paideia* of Dio Chrysostom. In Too and Livingstone 1998: 192–213.

Whitmarsh, T. 2001. *Greek Literature and the Roman Empire: the Politics of Imitation.* Oxford.

Whitmarsh, T. 2004. *Ancient Greek Literature.* Cambridge.

Whitmarsh, T. 2006. True histories: Lucian, Bakhtin, and the Pragmatics of Reception. In Martindale and Thomas 2006: 104–15.

Whittaker, C. 1964. The Revolt of Papirius Dionysius AD 190. *Historia* 12: 348–69.

Whittaker, C. 1980. Rural Labour in Three Roman Provinces. In Garnsey 1980: 73–99.

Whittaker, C. (ed.) 1988. *Pastoral Economies in Classical Antiquity.* Cambridge.

Whittaker, C. 1995. Do Theories of the Ancient City Matter?. In Cornell and Lomas 1995: 9–26.

Whittaker, C. 1996. Roman Africa: Augustus to Vespasian. In *CAH*² 10: 586–618.

Whittaker, C. 2003. Roman Proto-Industry in Southern France. In P. F. Bang and C. A. Bayly (eds), *Tributary Empires in History: Comparative Perspectives from Antiquity to the Late Medieval.* Medieval History Journal 6.2 (special issue). 293–301.

Whittow, M. 2001. Recent research on the Late-Antique City in Asia Minor: the Second Half of the 6th c. Revisited. In L. Lavan (ed.), *Recent Research in Late-Antique Urbanism.* Portsmouth. 137–53.

Wickham, C. 2005. *Framing the Early Middle Ages. Europe and the Mediterranean, 400–800.* Oxford.

Wiedemann, T. 1981. *Greek and Roman Slavery.* London.

Wiedemann, T. 1987. *Slavery.* Greece and Rome. New Surveys in the Classics 19. Oxford.

Wiedemann, T. 1989. *Adults and Children in the Roman Empire.* London.

Wiedemann, T. 1992. *Emperors and Gladiators.* London.

Wiesehöfer, J. 2002. *Ancient Persia.* 2nd edn. London.

Wiessner, P. 1990. Is There a Unity to Style? In Conkey and Hastorf 1990: 105–12.

Wikander, O. (ed.) 2000. *Handbook of Ancient Water Technology.* Leiden.

Wilhelm, G. 1989. *The Hurrians.* Warminster.

Wilken, R. 2003. *The Christians as the Romans Saw Them.* rev. edn. New Haven.

Wilkins. J. 2000. *The Boastful Chef: The Discourse of Food in Ancient Greek Comedy.* Oxford.

Wilkins, J. 2005. Land and Sea: Italy and the Mediterranean in the Roman Discourse of Dining. In Gold and Donahue 2005: 31–48.

Wilkins J., Harvey D. and Dobson M. (eds) 1995. *Food in Antiquity.* Exeter.

Wilkins, J. and Hill, S. 2006. *Food in the Ancient World.* Oxford.

Wilkinson, T. A. H. 1999. *Early Dynastic Egypt.* London.

Williams, C. 1999. *Roman Homosexuality.* Chicago.

Williams, C. D. 1999. "This Frantic Woman": Boadicea and English Neoclassical Embarrassment. In Biddiss and Wyke 1999: 19–35.

Williams, J. H. C. 2001. *Beyond the Rubicon: Romans and Gauls in Republican Italy.* Oxford.

Williams, R. D. 1989. Does it Make Sense to Speak of a pre-Nicene Orthodoxy? In Williams, R. D. (ed.), *The Making of Orthodoxy.* Cambridge. 1–23.

Williams, R. D. 2001. *Arius: Heresy and Tradition.* 2nd edn. London.

Williams, S. 1985. *Diocletian and the Roman Recovery.* London.

Wilson, A. I. 2002. Machines, Power and the Ancient Economy. *JRS* 92: 1–32.

Wilson, A. I. 2003 [2005]. Une cité grecque de Libye: fouilles d'Euhésperidès (Benghazi). *Comptes rendus de l'Académie des Inscriptions et Belles-Lettres.* 1648–75.

Wilson, A. I. 2005. Foggara irrigation, early state formation and Saharan trade: the Garamantes of Fazzan. In Schriftenreihe der Frontinus Gesellschaft 26, Internationales Frontinus-Symposium, Wasserversorgung aus Qanaten – Qanate als Vorbilder im Tunnelbau, 2.–5. Oktober 2003, Walferdange, Luxemburg. 223–34.

Wilson, A. I. 2006. The Spread of Foggara-Based Irrigation in the Ancient Sahara. In D. Mattingly et al. (eds), *Natural Resources and Cultural Heritage of the Libyan Desert*. London. 205–16.

Wilson, A. I. 2007. The Metal Supply of the Roman Empire. In E. Papi (ed.), *Supplying Rome and the Empire*. JRA Suppl. 69. Portsmouth, RI.

Wilson, A. I. 2008. Large-Scale Manufacturing, Standardization, and Trade. In Oleson 2008: 393–417.

Wilson, A. I. et al. 2002. Euesperides (Benghazi): Preliminary Report on the Spring 2002 Season. *Libyan Studies* 33: 85–123.

Wilson, A. I. et al. 2005. Euesperides (Benghazi): Preliminary Report on the Spring 2005 Season. *Libyan Studies* 36: 135–82.

Wilson, N. G. 1983. *Scholars of Byzantium*. London.

Wilson, P. 2000. *The Athenian Institution of the Khoregia: the Chorus, the City and the Stage*. Cambridge.

Wilson, P. 2003. *Hieroglyphs: A Very Short Introduction*. Oxford.

Winkler, J. 1990. *The Constraints of Desire*. London.

Winkler, M. (ed.) 2004. *Gladiator. Film and History*. Oxford.

Winkler, M. (ed.) 2007a. *Troy: From Homer's "Iliad" to Hollywood Epic*. Oxford.

Winkler, M. (ed.) 2007b. *Spartacus. Film and History*. Oxford.

Winkler, M. (ed.) 2009. *The Fall of the Roman Empire*. Oxford.

Winlock, H. E. 1947. *The Rise and Fall of the Middle Kingdom at Thebes*. New York.

Wiseman, T. P. 1979a. *Clio's Cosmetics: Three Studies in Greco-Roman Literature*. Leicester.

Wiseman, T. P. 1979b. Topography and Rhetoric: the Trial of Manlius. *Historia* 28: 32–50, reprinted in *Roman Studies Literary and Historical*, Liverpool 1987, 225–43, 382.

Wiseman, T. P. 1986. Monuments and the Annalists. In I. S. Moxon, J. D. Smart, and A. J. Woodman (eds), *Past Perspectives: Studies in Greek and Roman Historical Writing*. Cambridge. 87–100; repr. in Wiseman 1994: 37–48.

Wiseman, T. P. 1994. *Historiography and Imagination: Eight Essays on Roman Culture*. Exeter.

Wiseman, T. P. 1995. *Remus: A Roman Myth*. New York.

Wiseman, T. P. 2000. Review of Carandini 1997. *JRS* 90: 210–12.

Witcher, R. 1998. Roman Roads: Phenomenological Perspectives on Roads in the Landscape. In C. Forcey, J. Hawthorne, and R. Witcher (eds), *TRAC 97: Proceedings of the 7th Theoretical Roman Archaeology Conference*. Oxford. 60–70.

Witcher, R. 2000. Globalisation and Roman Imperialism: Perspectives on Identities in Roman Italy. In Herring and Lomas 2000: 213–26.

Witcher, R. 2005. The Extended Metropolis: *Urbs, Suburbium* and Population. *JRA* 18: 120–38.

Witcher, R. 2006. Settlement and Society in Early Imperial Etruria. *JRS* 96: 88–123.

Wolf, E. 1966. *Peasants*. Eaglewood Cliffs.

Wood, E. M. 1988. *Peasant-Citizen and Slave: the Foundations of Athenian Democracy*. London.

Wood, M. C. 1998. Participation of Former Yugoslav States in the United Nations and in Multilateral Treaties. In J. Frowein and R. Wolfrum (eds), *Max Planck Yearbook of United Nations Law 1997*, vol 1. London. 231–59.

Woodard, R. D. 1997. *Greek Writing from Knossos to Homer: a Linguistic Interpretation of the Origin of the Greek Alphabet and the Continuity of Ancient Greek Literacy*. New York.

Woodard, R. D. 2004. *The Cambridge Encyclopedia of the World's Ancient Languages*. Cambridge.

Woodhead, A. G. 1959. *The Study of Greek Inscriptions*. Cambridge.

Woodman, A. J. 1988. *Rhetoric in Classical Historiography. Four Studies*. London.

Woods, R. 2007. Ancient and Early Modern Mortality: Experience and Understanding. *Economic History Review* 60: 373–99.

Woolf, G. 1992. The Unity and Diversity of Romanization. *JRA* 5, 349–352.

Woolf, G. 1998. *Becoming Roman. The Origins of Provincial Civilization in Gaul*. Cambridge.

Woolf, V. 1929. *A Room of One's Own*. London.

Wörrle, M. 1975. Antiochos I., Achaios der Ältere und die Galater. *Chiron* 5: 59–87.

Wörrle, M. 1988. *Stadt und Fest im kaiserzeitlichen Kleinasien: Studien zu einer agonistischen Stiftung aus Oinoanda*. Munich.

Wright, M. 2006. Understanding the Antikythera Mechanism. In Technical Chamber of Greece (ed.), *Proceedings of the Second International Conference on Ancient Greek Technology*. Athens. 49–60.

Wyke, M. 1997. *Projecting the Past: Ancient Rome, Cinema and History*. New York.

Wyke, M. 1999. Screening Ancient Rome in the New Italy. In C. Edwards 1999: 188–204.

Yavetz, Z. 1969. Plebs *and* Princeps. Oxford.

Young, D. C . 2004. *A Brief History of the Olympic Games*. Oxford.

Young, F., Ayres, L., and Louth, A. (eds) 2004. *The Cambridge History of Early Christian Literature*. Cambridge.

Younger, J. 2004. *Sex in the Ancient World From A to Z*. London.

Youtie, H. C. 1973a. The Papyrologist: Artificer of Fact. *GRBS* 4: 19–32 = Id. *Scriptiunculae* I: 9–23, Amsterdam.

Youtie, H. C. 1973b. Text and Context in Transcribing Papyri. *GRBS* 7: 251–8 = Id. *Scriptiunculae* I: 1973: 25–33. Amsterdam.

Youtie, H. C. 1974. *The Textual Criticism of Documentary Papyri. Prolegomena*. 2nd ed. *Bulletin of the Institute of Classical Studies*, Suppl. 33, London.

Yunis, H. 1996. *Taming Democracy: Models of Political Rhetoric in Democratic Athens*. Ithaca.

Zahrnt, M. 1986. Zum Fiskalgesetz von Palmyra und zur Geschichte de Stadt in hadrianischer Zeit. *ZPE* 62: 279–94.

Zanker, P. 1988. *The Power of Images in the Age of Augustus*. Ann Arbor.

Zanker, P. 1998. *Pompeii: Public and Private Life*. Cambridge, MA.

Zeitlin, F. I. 1984. The Dynamics of Misogyny: Myth and Mythmaking in the *Oresteia*. In J. Peradotto and J. P. Sullivan (eds), *Women in the Ancient World: The* Arethusa *Papers*. Albany. 159–94.

Zelener, Y. 2003. Smallpox and the Disintegration of the Roman Economy after 165 AD. PhD thesis, Columbia University.

Zimmerman, K. 2002. Eine Steuerbefreiung für Q. Cascellius adressiert an Kaisarion. *ZPE* 138: 133–39.

Ziolkowski, A. 1992. *The Temples of Mid-Republican Rome and Their Historical and Topographical Context*. Rome.

Ziolkowski, A. 2004. *Sacra Via Twenty Years After*. Warsaw.

Ziolkowski, J. 1988. *Classical Influence on the Public Architecture of Washington and Paris: A Comparison of Two Capital Cities*. New York.

Ziolkowski, J. and Putnam, M. 2008. *The Virgilian Tradition*. New Haven.

Zirra, V. 1991. La necropoli e la tomba del capo di Ciumesti. In Moscati et al. 1991: 382–83.

Index

Greek names and places have generally been transliterated in the text except in the cases of authors whose works survive and especially well-known names that would not otherwise be easy to identify. So items which in the latinized form begin with "C" should be found under "K", for example Kadmos rather than Cadmus, Kaunos rather than Caunus.

Lightning Source UK Ltd.
Milton Keynes UK
UKHW031241061119
352990UK00001B/2/P